HEBREWS

VOLUME 36

THE ANCHOR BIBLE is a fresh approach to the world's greatest classic. Its object is to make the Bible accessible to the modern reader; its method is to arrive at the meaning of biblical literature through exact translation and extended exposition, and to reconstruct the ancient setting of the biblical story, as well as the circumstances of its transcription and the characteristics of its transcribers.

THE ANCHOR BIBLE is a project of international and interfaith scope: Protestant, Catholic, and Jewish scholars from many countries contribute individual volumes. The project is not sponsored by any ecclesiastical organization and is not intended to reflect any particular theological doctrine. Prepared under our joint supervision, THE ANCHOR BIBLE is an effort to make available all the significant historical and linguistic knowledge which bears on the interpretation of the biblical record.

THE ANCHOR BIBLE is aimed at the general reader with no special formal training in biblical studies; yet it is written with the most exacting standards of scholarship, reflecting the highest technical accomplishment.

This project marks the beginning of a new era of cooperation among scholars in biblical research, thus forming a common body of knowledge to be shared by all.

William Foxwell Albright
David Noel Freedman
GENERAL EDITORS

THE ANCHOR BIBLE

HEBREWS

◆

A New Translation
with Introduction and Commentary

CRAIG R. KOESTER

THE ANCHOR BIBLE
Doubleday
New York London Toronto Sydney Auckland

THE ANCHOR BIBLE
PUBLISHED BY DOUBLEDAY
a division of Random House, Inc.
1540 Broadway, New York, New York 10036

Library of Congress Cataloging-in-Publication Data
Bible. N.T. Hebrews. English. Koester. 2001.
Hebrews : a new translation with introduction and commentary / by Craig R. Koester. — 1st ed.
p. cm. — (The Anchor Bible; v. 36)
Includes bibliographical references and indexes.
ISBN 0–385–46893–8 (alk. paper)
1. Bible. Hebrews—Commentaries. I. Koester, Craig R. II. Title. III. Bible. English. Anchor Bible. 1964; v. 36.
BS192.2.A1 1964.G3 vol. 36
[BS2725.3]
220.7′7 s—dc21
[227′.81077] 00-021363
CIP

ISBN 0–385–46893–8

Printed in the United States of America
2001

First Edition

10 9 8 7 6 5 4 3 2 1

For

Raymond E. Brown†

and

J. Louis Martyn

Contents

◆

TRANSLATION, NOTES, AND COMMENTS

PREFACE

◆

This commentary invites readers into the intriguing world that emerges in the pages of Hebrews. The opening section on the history of interpretation and influence considers how given sets of questions and perspectives shape one's reading. The modern penchant for calling Hebrews a "riddle," which was not shared by readers of previous centuries, says as much about the interpreter's viewpoint as it does about the text. Assessing the ways in which readers have previously approached Hebrews puts our own views in a larger perspective, while opening up new ways of reading the text.

A promising approach that emerges from this study of previous interpretations shifts attention from questions about Hebrews' relationship to datable events, like the destruction of the Temple, to the dynamics within the community for which Hebrews was written. By considering the author's references to three phases of his community's history in light of his creatively anachronistic retellings of biblical narratives in Heb 11, the text offers valuable glimpses into the life of the community addressed by this book (pp. 64–72).

The rhetorical qualities of Hebrews, which have been noted for generations, invite a fresh development of the outline of the work. The section Formal and Rhetorical Aspects (pp. 79–96), offers a rather simple proposal about the flow of the argument, as well as observations about the role of emotion and character in the author's communication strategy. Theologically, a number of recent studies have noted how the question of God's intentions for humanity pervades Hebrews. This issue, which is formulated in Heb 2:5–9 and culminates in the vision of the heavenly Jerusalem in 12:22–24, offers a way to integrate other themes, including cosmology, eschatology, promise, covenant, priesthood, sacrifice, completion, and faith.

The commentary is designed for a variety of audiences. Written in a nontechnical style, the COMMENT section offers a sustained reading of Hebrews and gives attention to major interpretive and theological questions. Readers who want a sense of the whole passage should read the COMMENT sections first. The NOTES provide the kind of detailed information that underlies the interpretations given in the COMMENT. Readers should consult the NOTES for help on particular verses and when engaged in more specialized study of a passage. One of my hopes is that scholars who bring technical questions to their study of Hebrews will find that this volume makes a contribution to current research. Another hope is that those who are drawn to Hebrews because of its subject matter—God, Christ, and the life of faith—will find these pages to be helpful in their reflections about the meaning of Hebrews for contemporary Christian life.

This volume is dedicated to the late Raymond E. Brown and to J. Louis Martyn, my teachers at Union Theological Seminary in New York, both of whom have contributed to the Anchor Bible Commentary series. I have deeply appreciated their attention to historical and theological questions and their patient sifting of issues pertaining to biblical texts. Their scholarship, encouragement, and friendship have been true gifts. I want to express my appreciation to Luther Seminary and Lutheran Brotherhood for their support during the sabbatical leave in which I began this project and to the Center of Theological Inquiry for their support and hospitality during that year. Thanks are due to Todd Nichol for reading sections of the manuscript, to Alice Loddigs for technical assistance, and to my student assistants Stephan Turnbull, Julie Smith, and Kathleen McCallum. I also want to thank the library staffs at Luther Seminary and Princeton Theological Seminary for their help at many points. Finally, I want to acknowledge my gratitude to David Noel Freedman for his careful editing and to Andrew Corbin and the staff at Doubleday for bringing the project to completion.

LIST OF FIGURES

◆

ABBREVIATIONS

◆

PRINCIPAL ABBREVIATIONS

AB — Anchor Bible
ABD — *Anchor Bible Dictionary*. Edited by D. N. Freedman. 6 vols. New York: Doubleday, 1992
ACNT — Augsburg Commentaries on the New Testament
AJBI — *Annual of the Japanese Biblical Institute*
AnBib — Analecta biblica
ANF — *Ante-Nicene Fathers*
ANRW — *Aufstieg und Niedergang der römischen Welt: Geschichte und Kultur Roms im Spiegel der neuren Forschung*. Edited by H. Temporini and W. Haase. Berlin: de Gruyter, 1972–
ANTC — Abingdon New Testament Commentaries
ARG — *Archiv für Reformationsgeschichte*
AThR — *Anglican Theological Review*
ATJ — *Ashland Theological Journal*
AUSS — *Andrews University Seminary Studies*
BAGD — Bauer, W., W. F. Arndt, F. W. Gingrich, and F. W. Danker. *Greek-English Lexicon of the New Testament and Other Early Christian Literature*. 2nd ed. Chicago: University of Chicago, 1979
BBB — Bonner F. biblische Beiträge
BC — *The Book of Concord*. Edited by T. Tappert. Philadelphia: Fortress, 1959
BDF — Blass, F., A. Debrunner, and R. W. Funk. A *Greek Grammar of the New Testament and Other Early Christian Literature*. Chicago: University of Chicago Press, 1961
BETL — Biblotheca ephemeridum theologicarum lovaniensium
Bib — *Biblica*
BibLeb — *Bibel und Leben*
BiPa — Biblia Patristica: Index des citations et allusions bibliques dans la littérature patristique. Paris: Éditions du Centre national de la recherche scientifique, 1975–
BNTC — Black's New Testament Commentaries
BR — *Biblical Research*
BSac — *Bibliotheca Sacra*
BT — *The Bible Translator*
BTB — *Biblical Theology Bulletin*
BU — Biblische Untersuchungen

BWANT Beiträge zur Wissenschaft vom Alten und Neuen Testament
BZNW Beihefte zur Zeitschrift für die neutestamentliche Wissenschaft
CAM *Civilization of the Ancient Mediterranean*. Edited by M. Grant and R. Kitzinger. 3 vols. New York: Scribner's, 1988
CB *Cultura bíblica*
CBQ *Catholic Biblical Quarterly*
CBQMS Catholic Biblical Quarterly Monograph Series
CCCM Corpus Christianorum: Continuatio mediaevalis. Turnhout: Brepols, 1969–
CCSL Corpus Christianorum: Series latina. Turnhout: Brepols, 1953–
CIG *Corpus inscriptionum graecarum*. Edited by A. Boeckh. 4 vols. Berlin: Reimer, 1828–77
CisF Cistercian Fathers
ConBNT Coniectanea biblica: New Testament Series
CSEL Corpus scriptorum ecclesiasticorum latinorum
CTM *Concordia Theological Monthly*
CWS Classics of Western Spirituality. New York: Paulist, 1978–
DACL *Dictionnaire d'archéologie chrétienne et de liturgie*. Edited by F. Cabrol. 15 vols. Paris: Letouzey et Ané, 1907–53
DivThom *Divus Thomas*
EBib *Etudes bibliques*
EDNT *Exegetical Dictionary of the New Testament*. Edited by H. Balz and G. Schneider. ET. Grand Rapids: Eerdmans, 1990–93
EKK Evangelisch-katholischer Kommentar zum Neuen Testament
Epigr. Graec. *Epigrammata Graeca ex lapidibus conlecta*. Edited by G. Kaibel. Berlin: Reimer, 1878
ErFor Erträge der Forschung
ERT *Evangelical Review of Theology*
EstBib *Estudios bíblicos*
ETR *Etudes théologiques et religieuses*
EvQ *Evangelical Quarterly*
EvT *Evangelische Theologie*
ExpTim *Expository Times*
FB Forschung zur Bibel
FC Fathers of the Church. Washington, D.C.: Catholic University of America, 1947–
FRLANT Forschungen zur Religion und Literatur des Alten und Neuen Testaments
GCS Die griechische christliche Schriftsteller der ersten Jahrhunderte
GLAJJ *Greek and Latin Authors on Jews and Judaism*. Edited by M. Stern. Jerusalem: Israel Academy of Sciences and Humanities, 1974–84
GTJ *Grace Theological Journal*
HKNT Handkommentar zum Neuen Testament
HNT Handbuch zum Neuen Testament
HSS Harvard Semitic Studies
HTR *Harvard Theological Review*
HUCA *Hebrew Union College Annual*
IBS *Irish Biblical Studies*

ICC	International Critical Commentary
IDB	*Interpreter's Dictionary of the Bible*. Edited by G. A. Buttrick. 4 vols. Nashville: Abingdon, 1962
Int	*Interpretation*
ISBE	*International Standard Bible Encyclopedia*. Edited by G. W. Bromiley. 4 vols. Grand Rapids: Eerdmans, 1979–88
JBL	*Journal of Biblical Literature*
JETS	*Journal of the Evangelical Theological Society*
JJS	*Journal of Jewish Studies*
JPFC	*The Jewish People in the First Century*. Edited by S. Safrai and M. Stern. Philadelphia: Fortress, 1974–87
JSJ	*Journal for the Study of Judaism in the Persian, Hellenistic, and Roman Periods*
JSNT	*Journal for the Study of the New Testament*
JSNTSup	Journal for the Study of the New Testament: Supplement Series
JSOTSup	Journal for the Study of the Old Testament: Supplement Series
KD	*Kerygma und Dogma*
KEK	Kritisch-exegetischer Kommentar über das Neue Testament (Meyer-Kommentar)
KJV	King James Version
LCC	Library of Christian Classics. Philadelphia: Westminster, 1953–
LCL	Loeb Classical Library
LJ	*Liturgisches Jahrbuch*
LSJ	Liddell, H. G., R. Scott, H. S. Jones. *A Greek-English Lexicon*. 9th ed. with supplement. Oxford: Clarendon, 1968
LuthW	*Luther's Works*. Edited by J. Pelikan and H. Lehman. 55 vols. Philadelphia: Fortress, 1958–86
MelT	*Melita theologica*
MHT	Moulton, J. H., W. F. Howard, and N. Turner. *A Grammar of New Testament Greek*. Edinburgh: Clark, 1906–63
MM	Moulton, J. H., and G. Milligan. *The Vocabulary of the Greek New Testament*. London, 1930. Reprint, Grand Rapids: Eerdmans, 1980
MTS	Marburger theologische Studien
MTZ	*Münchener theologische Zeitschrift*
NA^{27}	Nestle, E., B. Aland, et al. *Novum Testamentum Graece*. 27th ed. Stuttgart: Deutsche Bibelgesellschaft, 1993
NAB^{2}	New American Bible. 2nd ed.
NASB	New American Standard Bible
NCBC	New Century Bible Commentary
NCE	*New Catholic Encyclopedia*. Edited by W. J. McDonald et al. 15 vols. New York: McGraw-Hill, 1967
NedTT	*Nederlands theologisch tijdschrift*
Neot	*Neotestamentica*
NIBCNT	New International Biblical Commentary on the New Testament

NICNT New International Commentary on the New Testament
NIGTC New International Greek Testament Commentary
NIV New International Version
NJB New Jerusalem Bible
NJBC *The New Jerome Biblical Commentary*. Edited by R. E. Brown et al. London, 1995
NovT *Novum Testamentum*
NovTSup Novum Testamentum Supplements
NPNF[1] Nicene and Post-Nicene Fathers, Series 1
NPNF[2] Nicene and Post-Nicene Fathers, Series 2
NRSV New Revised Standard Version
NRTh *La nouvelle revue théologique*
NTAbh Neutestamentliche Abhandlungen
NTD Das Neue Testament Deutsch
NTS *New Testament Studies*
NZSTh *Neue Zeitschrift für systematische Theologie*
OCD *Oxford Classical Dictionary*. Edited by S. Hornblower and A. Spawforth. 3rd ed. Oxford: Oxford University, 1996
OED *Oxford English Dictionary*
OGIS *Orientis graeci inscriptiones selectae*. Edited by W. Dittenberger. 2 vols. Leipzig: Hirzel, 1903–5
OLZ *Orientalistische Literaturzeitung*
OPTT *Occasional Papers in Translation and Textlinguistics*
OTP *Old Testament Pseudepigrapha*. Edited by J. H. Charlesworth. 2 vols. New York: Doubleday, 1983
PG Patrologia graeca. Edited by J.-P. Migne. 162 vols. Paris: Migne, 1857–86
PL Patrologia latina. Edited by J.-P. Migne. 217 vols. Paris: Migne, 1844–64
RAC *Reallexikon für Antike und Christentum*. Edited by T. Klauser et al. Stuttgart: Hiersmann, 1950–
RB *Revue biblique*
RBén *Revue bénédictine*
REAug *Revue des études augustiniennes*
REB Revised English Bible
ResQ *Restoration Quarterly*
RevExp *Review and Expositor*
RevistB *Revista bíblica*
RevQ *Revue de Qumran*
RevScRel *Revue des sciences religieuses*
RivB *Rivista biblica italiana*
RivBSup Rivista biblica italiana supplement
RomCiv *Roman Civilization*. Edited by N. Lewis and M. Reinhold. 2 vols. 3rd ed. New York: Columbia University, 1990
RSPT *Revue des sciences philosophiques et théologiques*
RSR *Recherches de science religieuse*
RTR *Reformed Theological Review*
SBFLA *Studii biblici Franciscani liber annuus*
SBLDS Society of Biblical Literature Dissertation Series

SBLMS	Society of Biblical Literature Monograph Series
SBLSBS	Society of Biblical Literature Sources for Biblical Study
SC	Sources chrétiennes. Paris: Cerf, 1943–
SE	*Studia evangelica*
SNTSMS	Society for New Testament Studies Monograph Series
SNTSU	Studien zum Neuen Testament und seiner Umwelt
SR	*Studies in Religion*
ST	*Studia theologica*
STJ	*Southwestern Journal of Theology*
Str-B	Strack, H. L., and P. Billerbeck. *Kommentar zum Neuen Testament aus Talmud und Midrasch.* 6 vols. Munich: Beck, 1922–61
SUNT	Studien zur Umwelt des Neuen Testaments
TBl	*Theologische Blätter*
TCGNT	Metzger, B. M., A *Textual Commentary on the Greek New Testament.* New York: United Bible Societies, 1971
TDNT	*Theological Dictionary of the New Testament.* Edited by G. Kittel and G. Friedrich. Translated by G. W. Bromiley. 10 vols. Grand Rapids: Eerdmans, 1964–76
TDOT	*Theological Dictionary of the Old Testament.* Edited by G. J. Botterweck and H. Ringgren. Translated by J. T. Willis, G. W. Bromiley, and D. E. Green. Grand Rapids: Eerdmans, 1974–
TGl	*Theologie und Glaube*
THKNT	Theologischer Handkommentar zum Neuen Testament
ThWAT	*Theologisches Wörterbuch zum Alten Testament.* Edited by G. J. Botterweck and H. Ringgren. Stuttgart: Kohlhammer, 1970–
TJ	*Trinity Journal*
TLI	*Talmud of the Land of Israel.* Edited by J. Neusner. Chicago: University of Chicago, 1982–
TLNT	*Theological Lexicon of the New Testament.* C. Spicq. Translated and edited by J. D. Ernest. 3 vols. Peabody, Mass.: Hendrickson, 1994
TLZ	*Theologische Literaturzeitung*
TNTC	Tyndale New Testament Commentaries
TRE	*Theologische Realenzyklopädie.* Edited by G. Krause and G. Müller. Berlin: de Gruyter, 1977–
TTZ	*Trierer theologische Zeitschrift*
TU	Texte und Untersuchungen
TynBul	*Tyndale Bulletin*
TZ	*Theologische Zeitschrift*
USQR	*Union Seminary Quarterly Review*
WA	Luther, M., Weimar Ausgabe (Kritische Gesamtausgabe)
WBC	Word Biblical Commentary
WMANT	Wissenschaftliche Monographien zum Alten und Neuen Testament

WTJ	*Westminster Theological Journal*
WUNT	Wissenschaftliche Untersuchungen zum Neuen Testament
ZNW	*Zeitschrift für die neutestamentliche Wissenschaft und die Kunde der älteren Kirche*
ZST	*Zeitschrift für systematische Theologie*
ZTK	*Zeitschrift für Theologie und Kirche*

DEAD SEA SCROLLS

1QapGen	*Genesis Apocryphon*
1QH[a]	*Thanksgiving Hymns[a]*
1QpHab	*Commentary ("Pesher") on Habakkuk*
1QS	*Rule of the Community*
1QSa	*Rule of the Congregation,* appendix A to 1QS
1QSb	*Rule of the Blessings,* appendix B to 1QS
4Q400	*Songs of the Sabbath Sacrifice[a] (fragment)*
4QDeut	Cave 4, text of Deuteronomy (4Q28–4Q46)
4QFlor	*Florilegium* (4Q174)
4QPBless	*Patriarchal Blessings* (4Q252)
4QTest	*Testimonia* (4Q175)
8ḤevXIIgr	Greek Scroll of the Minor Prophets
11QMelch	*Melchizedek*
11QT[a]	*Temple Scroll*
CD	*Damascus Document*

RABBINIC TEXTS

'Abot R. Nat.	*'Abot de Rabbi Nathan*
b.	*Babylonian Talmud* (tractate named)
B. Bat.	*Baba Batra*
Ber.	*Berakot*
Exod. Rab.	*Exodus Rabbah*
Gen. Rab.	*Genesis Rabbah*
Lev. Rab.	*Leviticus Rabbah*
m.	*Mishnah* (tractate named)
Meg.	*Megillah*
Mek.	*Mekilta*
Menaḥ.	*Menaḥot*
Midr. Ps.	*Midrash on Psalms*
Ned.	*Nedarim*
Pesaḥ.	*Pesaḥim*
Pesiq. Rab.	*Pesiqta Rabbati*
Qidd.	*Qiddushin*
Rosh Hash.	*Rosh Hashana*
Sanh.	*Sanhedrin*
Shabb.	*Shabbat*
Shek.	*Shekalim*
t.	*Tosephta* (tractate named)
Ta'an.	*Ta'anit*
y.	*Jerusalem Talmud* (tractate named)
Yebam.	*Yebamot*
Zebaḥ.	*Zebaḥim*

OTHER ABBREVIATIONS

Ag. Ap.	Josephus, *Against Apion*
Alleg. Interp.	Philo, *Allegorical Interpretation*
Ant.	Josephus, *Jewish Antiquities*
Apoc. Ab.	*Apocalypse of Abraham*
Apos. Con.	*Apostolic Constitutions and Canons*
2 Bar.	*2 Baruch*
Barn.	*Barnabas*
Bib. Ant.	Ps.-Philo, *Biblical Antiquities*
1 Clem.	*1 Clement*
2 Clem.	*2 Clement*
Did.	*Didache*
Diogn.	*Diognetus*
Disc.	*Discourse*
Eccl. Hist.	Eusebius, *Ecclesiastical History*

Ench.	Epictetus, *Encheiridion*
Ep.	*Epistle*
Ep. Arist.	*Epistle of Aristeas*
frg.	fragment
Frg. Tg.	*Fragment Targum*
Gk. Apoc. Ezra	*Greek Apocalypse of Ezra*
Herm. *Mand.*	Shepherd of Hermas, *Mandate*
Herm. *Sim.*	Shepherd of Hermas, *Similitude*
Herm. *Vis.*	Shepherd of Hermas, *Vision*
Ign.	Ignatius of Antioch
Ign. *Eph.*	Ignatius, *To the Ephesians*
Ign. *Magn.*	Ignatius, *To the Magnesians*
Ign. *Phld.*	Ignatius, *To the Philadelphians*
Ign. *Pol.*	Ignatius, *To Polycarp*
Ign. *Rom.*	Ignatius, *To the Romans*
Ign. *Smyrn.*	Ignatius, *To the Smyrnians*
Ign. *Trall.*	Ignatius, *To the Trallians*
Inst.	Quintilian, *Institutio Oratoria*
Jos. Asen.	*Joseph and Aseneth*
J.W.	Josephus, *Jewish War*
Jub.	*Jubilees*
L. A. E.	*Life of Adam and Eve*
Liv. Pro.	*Lives of the Prophets*
LXX	Septuagint
Mart. Ascen. Isa.	*Martyrdom and Ascension of Isaiah*
Mart. Pol.	*Martyrdom of Polycarp*
MS(S)	manuscript(s)
MT	Masoretic Text
NHC	Nag Hammadi Codex
Nic. Ethics	*Nicomachean Ethics*
NT	New Testament
OT	Old Testament
par.	parallel passages
Par. Jer.	*Paraleipomena Jeremiou*
P. Mich.	*Michigan Papyrus*
Pol. *Phil.*	Polycarp, *To the Philippians*
P. Oxy.	*Oxyrhynchus Papyrus*
P. Ryl.	*Rylands Papyrus*
Ps.-	pseudo
Pss. Sol.	*Psalms of Solomon*
QE	Philo, *Questions and Answers on Exodus*
QG	Philo, *Questions and Answers on Genesis*
Rhet. ad Alex.	*Rhetorica ad Alexandrum*
Rhet. ad Her.	*Rhetorica ad Herennium*
Sib. Or.	*Sibylline Oracles*
T.	*Testament*
T. Benj.	*Testament of Benjamin*
T. Jos.	*Testament of Joseph*
T. Jud.	*Testament of Judah*
T. Mos.	*Testament of Moses*
T. Reub.	*Testament of Reuben*
Tgs.	Targums
Tg. Neof.	*Targum Neofiti*
Tg. Onq.	*Targum Onqelos*
Tg. Ps.-J.	*Targum Pseudo-Jonathan*
Tusc. Disp.	*Tusculan Disputations*

HEBREWS: A TRANSLATION

I. Exordium

1 1God, having spoken on many occasions and in many forms to the forebears
of old by the prophets, 2has in these final days spoken to us by a Son, whom he
made heir of all things, through whom he also created the universe; 3who, after
having made purification for sins, sat down at the right hand of the Majesty on
high as the radiance of his glory and the impress of his substance, bearing all
things by his word of power, 4having become as superior to the angels as the
name he has inherited is more excellent than they.

5For to which of the angels did he ever say, *You are my Son, I have begotten*
you today? And again, *I will be his Father and he will be my Son?* 6And when,
again, he brings the firstborn into the world, he says, *And let all the angels of God*
bow down before him. 7And to the angels he says, *He is the one who makes his an-*
gels spirits and his ministers a flame of fire. 8But to the Son, *Your throne, O God,*
is forever and ever, and the upright staff is the staff of your kingdom. 9*You have*
loved righteousness and hated lawlessness; therefore, O God, your God has anoint-
ed you with oil of gladness beyond your companions. 10And, *You, O Lord, found-*
ed the earth at the beginning, and the heavens are the works of your hands. 11*They*
will perish, but you remain; they will all become old like a garment, 12*and you will*
roll them up like a cloak; as a garment, indeed, they will be changed, but you are
the same, and your years will never cease. 13But to which of the angels has he ever
said, *Sit at my right hand until I make your enemies a footstool for your feet?* 14Are
they not all ministering spirits, sent for service for the sake of those who are to inherit salvation?

2 1Therefore, we must keep holding fast to what we have heard so that we do
not drift away. 2For if the word spoken through angels was valid, and every transgression and act of disobedience received a just reward, 3how will we escape if
we neglect such a great salvation, which was first spoken through the Lord and
validated for us by those who heard, 4while God corroborated the testimony by
signs and wonders and various powerful deeds and distributions of the Holy Spirit according to his will?

II. Proposition

5Now, it was not to angels that he subjected the world to come, about which
we are speaking, 6but there is a passage that testifies: *What is man that you re-*
member him, or son of man that you watch over him? 7*You made him for a little*
while lower than the angels, you crowned him with glory and honor, 8*you placed*
all things in subjection under his feet.

Now in *placing all things in subjection,* he left nothing that is not subject to
him. At present we do not yet see *all things subjected to him;* 9but we do see that
Jesus, who was *for a little while made lower than the angels,* is *crowned with glory*
and honor because of the suffering of death, in order that by the grace of God he
might taste death for everyone.

III. Arguments

A. First Series

Argument

10Now it was fitting for him, for whom all things and through whom all things
exist, in bringing many sons [and daughters] to glory, to make the pioneer of
their salvation complete through sufferings, 11for the one who sanctifies and
those who are sanctified are all of one. This is the reason he is not ashamed to
call them brethren, 12saying, *I will declare your name to my brethren, in the mid-*
dle of the assembly I will praise you. 13And again, *I will trust in him*, and again,
Here am I, and the children whom God gave me. 14Since, therefore, the children
share in blood and flesh, he also shared in the same way with them, in order
that through death he might destroy the one who has the power of death, that
is, the devil, 15and deliver those who, in fear of death, were subject to a lifetime
of slavery. 16Now [in doing this] he surely does not take hold of the angels but
takes hold of the descendants of Abraham. 17Moreover, this is why he had to become like his brethren in all things, that he might become a merciful and faithful high priest in matters pertaining to God, to make atonement for the sins of
the people. 18Because he suffered when he was tested, he is able to help those
who are being tested.
3 1Because of this, holy brethren who share a heavenly calling, consider that
Jesus, the apostle and high priest of our confession, 2was faithful to the one who
appointed him as Moses was in his house. 3For he has been deemed worthy of
more glory than Moses to the extent that the builder of a house has more honor
than the house. 4For every house is built by someone, and the builder of all things
is God. 5Indeed, *Moses was faithful in his whole house* as a *servant*, to bear witness
to what was to be spoken, 6but Christ [was faithful] as a Son over his house. And
we are his house, if we hold fast to our boldness and the pride of our hope.

7Therefore, just as the Holy Spirit says, *Today, if you hear his voice,* 8*do not*
harden your hearts as in the rebellion, on the day of testing in the desert, 9*where*
your forebears tested and tried [*me*], *and they saw my works* 10*for forty years. There-*
fore, I was angered at this generation and said, "They always go astray in their
heart and they have not known my ways"; 11*so I swore in my wrath, "They shall*
never enter my rest."

12Brethren, see that there is not in any one of you an evil, unbelieving heart,
prone to abandon the living God, 13but exhort one another each day, as long as
it is called *today*, that none of you become hardened by the deceptiveness of sin.
14For we have become partners with Christ, if we hold fast the assurance that
was ours at first, firm to the end. 15When it says, *Today, if you hear his voice, do*
not harden your hearts as in the rebellion, 16who then heard and rebelled? Was
it not all who came out of Egypt through Moses? 17With whom was he angered
for forty years? Was it not those who sinned, whose corpses fell in the desert?
18To whom did he swear that they would not enter his rest if not to those who

were faithless? [19]Indeed, we see that they were not able to enter because of unbelief.
4 [1]Therefore, let us fear that, while a promise of entering his rest remains, any
of you think to fall back. [2]For the good news indeed has been spoken to us, just
as it was to them, but the word that was heard did not benefit them, since they
were not joined in faith with those who actually listened. [3]For it is we who believe who are entering his rest, as he has said, *So I swore in my wrath, "They shall*
never enter my rest," even though the works were accomplished from the foundation of the world. [4]For there is a passage that has spoken about the seventh day
in this way, *And God rested on the seventh day from all his works,* [5]while in our
text it says, *they shall never enter my rest.*

[6]Therefore, since it is still possible for some to enter it, and those to whom the
good news was spoken in former times failed to enter because of unbelief, [7]he
again ordains a certain day, namely, *today*, speaking through David a long time
later, as it has been said, *Today if you hear his voice, do not harden your hearts.*
[8]For if Joshua had given them rest, he would not have spoken afterward of another day. [9]Therefore, a Sabbath remains for the people of God. [10]For the one
who has entered his rest, he indeed rests from his works just as God did from his.

[11]Let us strive, therefore, to enter that rest, in order that no one fall by the
same example of unbelief. [12]For the word of God is living and active, more cutting than any two-edged sword, penetrating to the division of soul and spirit, of
joints and marrow, and able to scrutinize the thoughts and intentions of the
heart, [13]and nothing created is concealed before him, but all are naked and defenseless before the eyes of him to whom we must render an account.

[14]Therefore, since we have a great high priest who has passed through the
heavens, Jesus the Son of God, let us hold fast the confession. [15]For we do not
have a high priest who is unable to sympathize with our weaknesses, but one who
has been tested in every respect, in these same ways, without sin. [16]Therefore, let
us with boldness approach the throne of grace, in order that we might receive
mercy and find grace for help at the right time.
5 [1]Now every high priest taken from human beings is appointed for human beings with respect to matters pertaining to God, in order to offer both gifts and sacrifices for sins. [2]He is able to curb his emotions toward the ignorant and erring
since he himself is also clothed with weakness, [3]and because of this he is obliged
to make an offering for sins: as for the people, so also for himself. [4]And one does
not take the honor for himself, but is called by God, just as Aaron was.

[5]So also Christ did not glorify himself so as to become high priest; rather it was
he who said to him, *You are my Son, I have begotten you today,* [6]just as in another place he says, *You are a priest forever according to the type of Melchizedek.*
[7][This is the one] who, in the days of his flesh, offered both prayers and supplications with loud cries and tears to the one who was able to save him from death,
and he was heard because of [his] reverence. [8]Although he was a Son, he learned
obedience by what he suffered, [9]and having been made complete, he became for
all who obey him the source of eternal salvation, [10]having been designated by
God high *priest according to the type of Melchizedek.*

Transitional Digression

11We have much to say about this, and it is difficult to explain since you have
become sluggish in listening. 12For though by this time you ought to be teachers, you again need someone to teach you the most elementary matters of the oracles of God and have come to need milk rather than solid food. 13Now everyone who partakes of milk is not proficient in reasoning about righteousness since
he is a child. 14But solid food is for the complete, who, because of this state, have
their faculties trained to discern both good and evil. **6** 1Therefore, granting the
basic message of Christ, let us go on to completeness, not again laying a foundation of repentance from dead works and of faith in God, 2of instruction about
baptisms and laying on of hands, of resurrection of the dead and eternal judgment. 3And this we will do, God willing.

4For it is impossible to restore to repentance those who have once been enlightened, who have tasted the heavenly gift and become partakers of the Holy
Spirit, 5who have tasted the good word of God and the powers of the age to
come, 6but who then fall away, since they crucify the Son of God to themselves
and make a spectacle of him. 7For earth, which drinks the rain that repeatedly
comes upon it and produces vegetation beneficial to those for whom it is cultivated, receives blessing from God. 8But if it bears thorns and thistles, it is useless
and near to being cursed, so that its end is to be burned.

9But concerning you, beloved, we remain confident of the superior things that
belong to salvation, even though we speak this way. 10For God is not unjust, so
that he would forget your work and the love that you showed for his name when
you served and continue to serve the saints. 11But we want each of you to show
the same striving for the full assurance of hope until the end 12in order that you
not be sluggish, but imitators of those who through faith and perseverance inherit what was promised.

13Now, when God made a promise to Abraham, since he had no one greater
by whom to swear, he swore by himself, 14saying, *I will surely bless you and give*
you many descendants. 15And thus, after persevering, he obtained what was
promised. 16Now, people swear by someone greater [than themselves], and the
oath for validation brings all argument to an end. 17Accordingly, when God intended to demonstrate as clearly as possible to the heirs of the promise the unchangeable nature of his intention, he guaranteed it with an oath, 18so that
through two unchangeable things, in which it is impossible that God should lie,
we refugees have strong encouragement to hold fast the hope that lies ahead,
19which we have as a sure and steadfast anchor for the soul, [a hope] that enters
the inner region behind the curtain, 20where Jesus has gone as a forerunner on
our behalf, having become a high *priest forever according to the type of*
Melchizedek.

B. Second Series

Argument

7 1Now this *Melchizedek—king of Salem, priest of God Most High, who met*
Abraham when he returned from the defeat of the kings and blessed him, 2*the one*
to whom Abraham apportioned a tithe of everything—is first interpreted as "king
of righteousness" and then also as king of Salem, which is "king of peace"; 3with-
out father, without mother, without genealogy, having no beginning of days nor
end of life, but being made to resemble the Son of God, he remains a priest for
all time.

4See how great is *this one to whom Abraham* the patriarch *gave a tithe* of the
spoils! 5Those of the descendants of Levi who receive the priestly office have, according to the Law, a command to receive tithes from the people, that is, from
their brethren, even though they have come from the loins of Abraham, 6but the
one who does not have their genealogy received a tithe from Abraham and
blessed the one who had the promises. 7Now, without any dispute the lesser is
blessed by the superior; 8indeed, in the one case people who die receive tithes,
but in the other it is someone about whom it is attested that he lives. 9One might
even venture to say that Levi, who receives tithes, actually paid a tithe through
Abraham, 10for he was still in the loins of his forebear when Melchizedek met
him.

11Now, if there had been completion through the Levitical priesthood—for
the people had been given Law about it—what need would there still be for a
different priest to be raised up *according to the type of Melchizedek* instead of
speaking about one "according to the type of Aaron"? 12For when there is a
change of the priesthood there is also, of necessity, a change of Law. 13For the
one about whom these things are spoken belongs to a different tribe, from which
no one has served at the altar. 14For it is clear that our Lord has sprung from
Judah, a tribe to which Moses said nothing about priests.

15And this is even more abundantly clear when a different priest arises in the
likeness of Melchizedek, 16who has not become [a priest] according to a Law of
fleshly command, but according to the power of an indestructible life. 17For it is
attested that *you are a priest forever according to the type of Melchizedek.* 18There
is, then, an abrogation of a previous command because of its weakness and uselessness—19for the Law made nothing complete—and the introduction of a superior hope, through which we draw near to God.

20And to the extent that it was not without swearing an oath—for they have become priests without the swearing of an oath, 21but he through the swearing of
an oath, through the one who says to him, *The Lord has sworn and will not*
change his mind, "You are a priest forever"—22to that extent Jesus has become the
surety of a superior covenant.

23Those who have become priests are numerous because death prevents them
from continuing to serve, 24but he holds the priesthood inviolate, because he
continues forever. 25Because of this he is indeed able to save completely those

who approach God through him, since he always lives to intercede on their behalf.

26Now, such a high priest was indeed fitting for us: holy, blameless, undefiled,
separated from sinners, exalted above the heavens, 27one who has no need, as do
the high priests, to offer sacrifices each day first for their own sins and then for
those of the people, because he did this once for all when he offered himself.
28For the Law establishes as high priests men who have weaknesses, but the word
sworn on oath, which came after the Law, establishes a Son who has been made
complete forever.

8 1Now, the point of what we are saying is that we have such a high priest, who
sat down at the right hand of the throne of the Majesty in the heavens, 2a minister of the sanctuary, that is, of the true tent which the Lord, not a human being,
set up. 3For every high priest is appointed to offer gifts and sacrifices; therefore
this one also must have something to offer. 4So if he were on earth he would not
be a priest, because there are those who offer gifts in accordance with Law, 5who
serve in a representation and a shadow of the heavenly [sanctuary], just as Moses
was divinely admonished when he was about to construct the tent; for [God]
said, *See that you make everything according to the pattern that was shown to you*
on the mountain. 6But now [Jesus] has received a ministry that is superior to the
same extent that he is also mediator of a superior covenant, which has been lawfully established upon superior promises.

7Now if that first [covenant] were faultless, no place would be sought for a second. 8For finding fault with them, he says, *Behold, days are coming, says the*
Lord, when I will complete with the house of Israel and with the house of Judah a
new covenant, 9*not like the covenant that I made with their forebears in the day*
when I took hold of their hand to bring them out of the land of Egypt, because they
did not remain in my covenant, and I paid no attention to them, says the Lord.
10*For this is the covenant that I will establish with the house of Israel after those*
days, says the Lord: Putting my laws into their mind, I will even write them on their
hearts, and I will be their God and they shall be my people, 11*and no one shall*
teach his fellow citizen and no one his brother, saying, "Know the Lord," because
they shall all know me, from the least to the greatest of them, 12*for I will be merci-*
ful toward their unrighteous deeds and I will not remember their sins anymore. 13In
speaking of a new covenant, he has made the first one obsolete. And what is becoming obsolete is also old and near obliteration.

9 1Now, the first [covenant] indeed had regulations for service and the earthly sanctuary. 2For the first tent was prepared, in which were the lampstand and
the table and the presentation of the loaves, and it is called a "sanctuary." 3Be-
hind the second curtain was the tent called the "holiest sanctuary," 4containing
a golden incense altar and the ark of the covenant covered all over with gold,
in which were a golden jar containing the manna, the staff of Aaron that blossomed, and the tablets of the covenant; 5and above it were the cherubim of
glory overshadowing the place of atonement—concerning these things we cannot now speak in detail.

6With these things prepared in this way, the priests continually go into the first
tent to conduct their services, 7but into the second the high priest alone goes
once a year, not without blood, which he offers for himself and for the people's
sins of ignorance. 8By this the Holy Spirit indicates that the way into the sanctuary has not yet been manifested while the first tent still has standing, 9and this is
a symbol for the present time, according to which gifts and sacrifices are offered
that are not able to make complete the conscience of the one who serves,
10[since they] only concern foods and drinks and various ablutions—regulations
of the flesh imposed until a time of correction.

11–12But Christ, having arrived as high priest of the good things that have occurred, entered once for all into the sanctuary, securing an eternal redemption
through the greater and more perfect tent, which was not made by hand—that
is, [it is] not of this creation—and not through the blood of goats and calves, but
through his own blood. 13For if the blood of goats and bulls and the sprinkled
ashes of a heifer sanctify those who have been defiled so as to purify the flesh,
14how much more will the blood of Christ, who through the eternal Spirit offered himself without blemish to God, cleanse our conscience from dead works
to serve a living God.

15And for this reason he is mediator of a new covenant, so that after a death
took place to bring redemption from transgressions incurred on the basis of the
first covenant, those who are called might receive the promised eternal inheritance. 16For where there is a testament, it is necessary that the death of the testator be presented. 17For a testament becomes valid upon death, since it has no
force as long as the testator lives.

18Accordingly, not even the first [covenant] was dedicated without blood.
19For after every commandment had, in accordance with the Law, been spoken
by Moses to all the people and after he had taken calves' blood with water and
scarlet wool and hyssop, he sprinkled the book itself and all the people, 20saying,
This is the blood of the covenant that God commanded you. 21And the tent and
all the utensils for the service he sprinkled with blood in a similar way. 22Indeed,
according to the Law almost everything is cleansed with blood, and without an
outpouring of blood forgiveness does not occur. 23Therefore, it is necessary that
the representations of the heavenly things be cleansed by these things, but the
heavenly things themselves with sacrifices superior to these.

24For Christ did not enter a sanctuary made with hands, an antitype of the true
one, but into heaven itself, now to appear before the face of God on our behalf.
25And he did not do this in order to offer himself many times, as the high priest
enters the sanctuary year after year with the blood of another; 26in that case he
would have had to suffer many times from the foundation of the world. But now
he has appeared, once, at the consummation of the ages, for the abolition of sin
by his sacrifice. 27And just as it is ordained for human beings to die once, and afterward comes the judgment, 28so also Christ, having been offered once to bear
the sins of many, will appear a second time, not to deal with sin, but for the salvation of those who eagerly wait for him.

10 1Now since the Law contains a shadow of the good things to come and not
the actual manifestation of these events, it cannot make complete those who
draw near year after year with the same sacrifices, which they are constantly offering. 2Otherwise would they not have ceased to be offered, since the worshipers who were once cleansed would have no consciousness of sin? 3Yet in
them there is actually a reminder of sin year after year. 4For it is impossible for
the blood of bulls and goats to take away sins.

5Therefore, upon coming into the world he says, *Sacrifice and offering you did*
not want, but you fashioned a body for me; 6*whole burnt offerings and sin offerings*
you did not find pleasing. 7*Then I said, "Behold, I have come (it has been written*
about me in the book) to do your will, O God." 8His first point was that *sacrifices*
and offerings, whole burnt offerings and sin offerings are not what you wanted or
what pleased you. These are offered according to the Law. 9His next point was,
Behold, I have come to do your will. He abolishes the first in order to establish the
second. 10And by that *will* we have been sanctified through the offering of the
body of Jesus Christ once and for all.

11Indeed, every priest has stood ministering each day and offering repeatedly
the same sacrifices, which can never remove sins, 12but this one, after offering
for all time a single sacrifice for sins, sat down at the right hand of God, 13from
now on waiting until his enemies are made a footstool for his feet. 14For by a single offering he has made complete for all time those who are sanctified.

15And the Holy Spirit also testifies to us, for after saying, 16*This is the covenant*
that I will make with them after those days, says the Lord: Putting my laws upon
their hearts, I will even write them on their mind, [he also says,] 17*and I will not*
remember their sins and their lawless deeds anymore. 18Where there is forgiveness
of these, there is no longer any offering for sin.

19Therefore, brethren, since we have boldness for an entryway into the sanctuary by the blood of Jesus, 20a new and living way that he dedicated for us
through the curtain, that is, [by means] of his flesh, 21and a great priest over the
house of God, 22let us approach with a true heart, with full assurance of faith,
with our hearts sprinkled clean from an evil conscience and our body washed
with pure water. 23Let us hold fast the confession of hope without wavering, for
he who has promised is faithful, 24and let us consider how to provoke one another to love and good works, 25not abandoning our gathering, as is the custom
of some, but exhorting [one another], and this all the more as you see the Day
drawing near.

Transitional Digression

26For if we persist in sinning willfully after receiving knowledge of the truth,
there no longer remains a sacrifice for sins, 27but, shall we say, a terrifying
prospect of judgment and fiery zeal that is coming to consume those who stand
in opposition. 28Anyone who abrogates the Law of Moses dies without pity on the
basis of two or three witnesses. 29How much more severe a punishment do you
suppose a person deserves who trampled upon the Son of God and considered

profane the blood of the covenant by which he was sanctified, and was insolent
toward the Spirit of grace? 30For we know the one who said, *Mine is the
vengeance, I will repay*. And again, *The Lord will judge his people*. 31It is terrifying to fall into the hands of the living God.

32But remember the former days in which, after you were enlightened, you
endured a great contest with sufferings, 33in part by being made a public spectacle through denunciations and afflictions, and in part by showing solidarity with
those who were treated that way. 34For you showed compassion for the prisoners
and accepted the seizure of your possessions with joy, knowing that you yourselves have a superior and abiding possession.

35Therefore, do not cast away your boldness, which has a great reward. 36For
you need endurance, so that having done the will of God you may receive what
was promised. 37For *yet a little while and the one who is coming will arrive, and
he will not delay*. 38*But my righteous one will live by faith, and if he shrinks back,
my soul will not be favorable to him*. 39Now, we are not characterized by shrinking back to destruction, but by faith for the preservation of the soul.

C. Third Series

Argument

11 1Now, faith is the assurance of things hoped for, the proof of things not
seen, 2for by this the elders were attested. 3By faith we understand that the universe was fashioned by the word of God, so that from what cannot be seen that
which is seen has come into being. 4By faith Abel offered to God a more acceptable sacrifice than Cain did, through which it was attested that he was righteous, since God himself testified concerning the gifts, and through it he, although dead, is still speaking. 5By faith Enoch was taken so that he did not see
death, and *he was not found because God had taken him*. For it is attested that before being taken *he had pleased God*. 6Without faith it is impossible to please
[him], for it is necessary for one who draws near to God to believe that he exists
and rewards those who seek him. 7By faith Noah, after being divinely warned
about things that could not yet be seen, in reverence prepared an ark for the salvation of his household, through which he condemned the world and became
an heir of the righteousness that is based on faith.

8By faith Abraham, when he was called, obeyed and set out for a place that he
was to receive for an inheritance, and he set out not knowing where he was
going. 9By faith he resided as an alien in a land of promise as if it belonged to another, dwelling in tents with Isaac and Jacob, who were joint heirs of the same
promise; 10for he awaited the city with foundations, whose builder and maker is
God. 11By faith, even though Sarah herself was barren, he received power to father children even beyond the usual time, since he considered the one who
promised to be faithful. 12Therefore, from one person, indeed from one who was
"dead," were begotten [descendants] as numerous as the stars of the heaven and
the countless grains of sand by the shore of the sea.

13These all died in faith, without having received the things that were promised, but having seen them and greeted them from afar and having confessed that
they were foreigners and transients on the earth. 14Now, those who say such
things make clear that they are seeking a homeland. 15And if they had in mind
that [land] from which they had gone out, they would have had opportunity to
return. 16But in fact they desire a better one, that is, a heavenly one. Therefore,
God is not ashamed to be called their God, for he prepared for them a city.

17By faith Abraham, when he was tested, offered Isaac; indeed, the one who
was offering his only son had received the promises; 18he was the one to whom
it was said, *through Isaac shall your descendants be called.* 19[He did so] since he
considered that God was able to raise even from the dead, so that he received
him back as a symbol. 20By faith Isaac blessed Jacob and Esau, also [speaking]
about things to come. 21By faith Jacob, when he was dying, blessed each of the
sons of Joseph and *bowed over the end of his staff.* 22By faith Joseph, when he was
dying, remembered the exodus of the children of Israel and gave instructions
concerning his bones.

23By faith Moses, after his birth, was hidden for three months by his parents,
since they saw the child's good character and were not afraid of the king's edict.
24By faith Moses, when he had grown up, refused to be called a son of Pharaoh's
daughter, 25choosing to be maltreated with the people of God rather than to
have the fleeting pleasure of sin, 26since he considered the denunciation of
Christ to be wealth greater than the storehouses of Egypt, for he looked ahead to
his reward. 27By faith he left Egypt without fearing the king's rage, for he persevered as if he saw the One who cannot be seen.

28By faith he kept the Passover and spread the blood in order that the one sent
to destroy the firstborn might not touch them. 29By faith they crossed the Red
Sea as if it were dry land, but when the Egyptians attempted it, they were
drowned. 30By faith the walls of Jericho fell after they had been encircled for
seven days. 31By faith Rahab the prostitute did not perish with the unbelievers,
since she received the spies in peace.

32And what more shall I say? For time does not allow me to tell of Gideon,
Barak, Samson, Jephthah, David and Samuel, and the prophets, 33who through
faith overcame kingdoms, worked righteousness, obtained things that were promised, shut the mouths of lions, 34quenched the power of fire, escaped the edges of
the sword, were made powerful out of weakness, became mighty in war, routed
the camps of foreigners. 35Women received their dead back by resurrection.

But others were tortured, after refusing release, in order that they might obtain
a superior resurrection. 36And others experienced ridicule and scourging, and
even chains and imprisonment. 37They were stoned, sawn in two, murdered by
the sword; they went about in sheepskins and goatskins, deprived, afflicted, maltreated—38of whom the world was not worthy—while they wandered over
deserts and mountains and in caves and holes in the earth.

39And all these, although attested through faith, did not receive what was
promised, 40since God provided something superior for us, so that without us
they would not be made complete.

12 1Therefore, since we indeed have such a great cloud of witnesses surrounding us, and laying aside every weight and the sin that readily besets us, let us run
with endurance the contest that is set before us, 2looking to Jesus, the pioneer
and completer of faith, who for the joy that was set before him endured a cross,
disdaining its shame, and is seated at the right hand of the throne of God. 3So
consider the one who has endured from sinners such opposition against himself,
in order that you may not give up and grow weary in your souls. 4You have not
yet resisted to the point of bloodshed in your contest with sin.

5And you have forgotten the exhortation that addresses you as sons: *My son, do
not neglect the instruction of the Lord, and do not give up when reproved by him,*
6*for the Lord instructs the one whom he loves and chastises every son whom he receives.* 7Endure for the sake of instruction; God is treating you as sons. For what
son does a father not instruct? 8But if you are without the instruction in which
all have shared, then you are illegitimate children and not sons. 9Furthermore,
we had human fathers who instructed us, and we showed respect. Shall we not
to a greater extent be subject to the Father of spirits, and live? 10For they instructed for a few days as seemed good to them, but he does so on the basis of
what is beneficial, in order that we might share his holiness. 11All instruction
seems grievous rather than joyful at the time, but later it yields peaceful fruit of
righteousness to those who have been trained through it.

12Therefore, stretch out the drooping hands and weak knees, 13and set your feet
on straight paths, in order that what is lame might not be twisted, but might heal
instead. 14Pursue peace with all and the holiness without which no one will see
the Lord, 15remaining watchful so that no one falls back from the grace of God; *so
that no root of bitterness puts forth a shoot and causes trouble* and that through it
many become defiled; 16so that no one becomes immoral or profane like Esau,
who for a single serving of food gave up his rights as firstborn. 17For you know that
later on, when he wanted to inherit the blessing, he was rejected, for he found no
opportunity for repentance, even though he sought [the blessing] with tears.

18For you have not approached something palpable, and a blazing fire and
darkness and gloom and a tempest, 19and a trumpet blast and a voice with words,
whose hearers refused that any further message be given to them, 20for they
could not bear the command: *If even an animal touches the mountain, it shall be
stoned;* 21indeed, so fearsome was the phenomenon that Moses said, *I am terrified and trembling.* 22Instead, you have approached Mount Zion and the city of
the living God, heavenly Jerusalem, and myriads of angels in festival gathering
23and the assembly of the firstborn, who are registered in heaven, and a judge,
who is God of all, and the spirits of the righteous, who have been made complete, 24and the mediator of the new covenant, Jesus, and the sprinkled blood
that speaks in a manner superior to that of Abel.

Transitional Digression

25See that you do not refuse the one who is speaking! For if they did not escape when they refused the one who admonished them on earth, how much less

will we who turn away from the one who admonishes from the heavens, 26whose voice then shook the earth, but who now has promised, saying, *Yet once more I will shake not only the earth but also the heaven*? 27The *once more* portends removal of the things that are shaken, as things that have been made, in order that what is not shaken might abide.

IV. Peroration

28Therefore, since we are receiving an unshakable kingdom, let us be grateful and thereby offer pleasing service to God with reverence and awe, 29for indeed, our *God is a consuming fire.* 13 1Let care for the brethren abide. 2Do not neglect caring for strangers, for through this some have cared for angels without knowing it. 3Remember the prisoners as though imprisoned with them, and those who are mistreated as though you yourselves were in [their] body. 4Let marriage be honored among all and let the marriage bed be undefiled, for God will judge the immoral and adulterers. 5Let your conduct be without care for money and be content with what you have. For he himself has said, *I will never abandon you or forsake you*, 6so that we can take courage and say, *The Lord is my helper and I shall not fear; what can a human being do to me?* 7Remember your leaders, who spoke the word of God to you; consider the outcome of their conduct and imitate their faithfulness. 8Jesus Christ is yesterday and today the same—and forever. 9Do not be carried away by all sorts of strange teachings, for it is good for the heart to be made firm by grace and not by foods that have not benefited those who walk in them.

10We have an altar from which those who serve in the tent have no authority to eat. 11For the bodies of the animals, whose blood is brought into the sanctuary by the high priest as a sacrifice for sin, are burned outside the camp. 12So too Jesus, in order to sanctify the people by means of his own blood, suffered outside the gate. 13Therefore, let us go out to him outside the camp, bearing denunciation for him, 14for we have here no abiding city, but seek the one that is to come.

15Through him, therefore, let us continually offer to God a sacrifice of praise, that is, the fruit of lips that confess his name. 16Do not neglect acts of kindness and fellowship, for such sacrifices are pleasing to God. 17Heed your leaders and yield to them, for they are keeping watch for the sake of your souls as those who must give an account for them, so that they might do this with joy and not with groaning, for this would be unprofitable for you. 18Keep praying for us, for we are persuaded that we have a good conscience, desiring to act rightly in all things. 19I especially urge you to do this in order that I might be restored to you sooner.

20And may the God of peace, who by the blood of the eternal covenant brought up from the dead the great shepherd of the sheep, our Lord Jesus, 21provide you with everything good that you might accomplish his will, accomplishing in us that which is pleasing in his sight through Jesus Christ, to whom be glory forever. Amen.

V. Epistolary Postscript

22I urge you, brethren, bear with my word of exhortation, for I have written to
you briefly. 23Know that our brother Timothy has been released. If he comes
soon, I shall see you with him. 24Greet all your leaders and all the saints. Those
from Italy send you greetings. 25Grace be with you all.

INTRODUCTION

I. History of Interpretation and Influence

◆

Biblical interpretation is the art of asking questions of texts. The way questions are posed reflects the assumptions and concerns of the interpreter and shapes the answers that are given. An account of the major questions asked of Hebrews and the controversies in which the book has played a part can be a valuable prolegomenon for our own reading, helping us assess the questions and assumptions that we bring to the interpretive task. There have been three major shifts in the study of Hebrews. First, theological controversies in the fourth and fifth centuries concluded several centuries of uncertainty about the status of Hebrews and led to the broad acceptance of Hebrews as canonical Scripture. Second, disputes in the sixteenth century reopened questions concerning the status of Hebrews and led to differences between Catholic and Protestant readers of Hebrews, especially concerning matters of priesthood and sacrifice. Third, the late eighteenth century witnessed the emergence of historical critical readings of Hebrews that led to ongoing controversy about the book's authorship, context of composition, and Hebrews' place in the history of Christianity and history of religion. Vestiges of older debates continue to shape the contemporary study of Hebrews, sometimes in subtle ways.[1]

A. The Early Church to A.D. 600

Hebrews was originally sent to one of the small groups of Christians that gathered in the towns and cities of the Roman Empire in the last half of the first century A.D. Three centuries later, Christianity was the dominant religion of the empire, and Hebrews was included among its canonical Scriptures. This development did not occur smoothly, and until the fourth century Christians in the eastern and western parts of the Mediterranean world differed sharply in their estimation of Hebrews. Those in the east, whose perspective was informed by a concern for the soul's pilgrimage to God, valued the book and considered it to have authoritative status. Those in the west, who grappled with questions of church discipline, largely ignored or rejected the book. The Trinitarian controversies of the fourth century led to a more positive evaluation of Hebrews throughout the church. As a consensus formed about its authorship, Hebrews

[1]See Lindars, *Theology*, 135–42; Ellingworth, *Epistle*, viii–ix.

was connected more directly to the church's liturgy and its understanding of priesthood, forming the context in which medieval interpreters would work.

1. THE EAST TO A.D. 300

Alexandrian interpreters made three assumptions about Scripture that are closely related to Hebrews. First, they used the concept of old and new "covenant" to identify the unity and diversity within the Bible. Christians used Scriptures inherited from Judaism together with a number of Christian texts. The contrast between old and new "covenants," or "testaments," that appears in 2 Cor 3:6, 14 and in Heb 8–10 was eventually applied to the collection of sacred writings. Using the same word, "covenant," for both parts pointed to their unity, while the modifiers "old" and "new" identified the differences between them.[2] Second, the relationship between the two testaments was said to be one of "shadow" and "reality," drawing on Heb 8:5 and 10:1. If the New Testament conveyed divine reality, the Old Testament foreshadowed it, so that interpreters could read the Old Testament spiritually in light of the New Testament.[3] Third, they understood Christianity to be congruent with Greek philosophy. When Heb 1:1 declared that God had "spoken in many forms and many ways," Clement of Alexandria (d. 214) took this to mean that God had spoken through Israel's prophets and through philosophy—especially Platonism—although Scripture was finally the criterion for truth (*Stromata* 1.5, 9; 6.7, 8, 11; 7.16). Origen (d. 254) had a similar view (*On First Principles* 4.2.4, 9).

The interpretive framework used by Clement and Origen centered on the believer's pilgrimage to true knowledge. Christians were to "train" their senses (Heb 5:14) in order to move toward perfection, so that by faith they could apprehend "things unseen" (11:1; Clement, *Stromata* 1.6, 11; 2.2, 4; 7.1). Origen understood that Christ is the "radiance" of God's glory (Heb 1:3), who manifests transcendent reality to mortals, drawing their souls to God. Because of his mediating role, Christ is the "high priest" who leads the way to God's heavenly dwelling.[4]

A disturbing issue for many readers is Hebrews' statement that apostates cannot be restored to repentance (Heb 6:4–6; 10:26–31; 12:17). Clement and Origen did not find these warnings especially troublesome, but understood them to give Christians incentive to persevere on their spiritual journey, not to cause them to despair (Clement, *Stromata* 2.13; 4.20). Clement said that a person's first repentance involved turning away from sins committed prior to faith. There was a second repentance for believers who fell into transgression, but those who willingly persisted in sin could not rely on Christ's sacrifice (Heb 10:26–27). Origen observed that the rigor of Hebrews was comparable to Jesus' warning about the sin against the Holy Spirit that could not be forgiven (Matt 12:31–32).[5]

---

[2]See von Campenhausen, *Formation*, 262–68; Lehne, *New Covenant*, 88–89; McKane, "Old," 227–35.

[3]Origen, *On First Principles* 4.2.4, 6. On Heb 8:5 and 10:1 in Origen see BiPa 3.453–55.

[4]*On First Principles* 2.11.6–7. Cf. Greer, *Captain*, 42–64; Bright, "Epistle."

[5]Origen, FC 89.319; GCS 38.238–390. Cf. Theognostos in *ANF* 6.156; Greer, *Captain*, 37–39.

Those who committed apostasy (Heb 6:4–6; 10:29) were like those who put their hand to the plow and turned back (Luke 9:62). Therefore, Christ warned them in order to prevent them from meeting the fate of Lot's wife, who turned back to Sodom (Luke 17:32; Gen 19:26), and in order to encourage them to flee to Jesus Christ, who is the place of salvation (SC 238.58–63).

Christians in the east, as early as the second century, believed that Paul was the author of Hebrews. The oldest extant manuscript of Hebrews (P^{46}), an Egyptian text from about A.D. 200, placed Hebrews after Paul's letter to the Romans, perhaps because of its length and the mention of Italy in Heb 13:24. Christians in the east probably based their understanding of authorship on inferences from Hebrews, rather than on traditions about the author's identity (§1 COMMENT). Assuming the unity of Scripture and the congruence of Scripture with philosophy, they sought to make Pauline authorship plausible by overcoming several objections:

(a) Paul's name is never mentioned in Hebrews. The Alexandrians related the anonymity to virtue. Pantaenus (d. ca. 190) argued that Paul did not identify himself because he showed modesty. Calling himself an "apostle" would have been presumptuous since *apostolos* was used for Jesus in Heb 3:1. Moreover, Paul was an apostle to the Gentiles, but he was not an apostle to Hebrews (Eusebius, *Eccl. Hist.* 6.14.4). Clement added that Paul acted prudently—another virtue—when he omitted his name, since Jewish readers were suspicious of him (ibid., 6.14.3).

(b) Hebrews' style differs from the Pauline letters. Clement accounted for the differences by proposing that Paul wrote the letter in Hebrew and that Luke translated it into Greek (ibid., 6.14.2). Origen suggested that "the style and composition belong to one who called to mind the apostle's teachings and, as it were, made short notes of what his master said." Some thought that Hebrews was written down by Clement of Rome and others by Luke. Origen remarked that "who wrote the epistle, God truly knows," but he commonly referred to Paul as the author.[6]

(c) Hebrews alludes to nonbiblical traditions, like the story that Isaiah was sawn in two (NOTE on Heb 11:37). Some thought Paul would not have done this, but Origen found this to be consistent with what Jesus (Matt 23:29–38), Paul (1 Thess 2:14–15), and Stephen (Acts 7:52) said about the persecution of the prophets. Therefore, he argued that the allusion to Isaiah's martyrdom could not be invoked against Pauline authorship (*ANF* 4.388).

2. THE WEST TO A.D. 300

Western Christians differed sharply from eastern Christians in their assessment of Hebrews, largely because they worked within a different interpretive framework. Rather than dealing with the soul's pilgrimage to God, western writers tended to focus on patterns of church order, which affected their views of the authorship and authority of the book. The earliest evidence for the use of Hebrews in the west is *1 Clement*, which was written in Rome about A.D. 96 and addressed to the

[6]The quotations of Origen are from Eusebius, *Eccl. Hist.* 6.25.11–14. For examples of ascriptions of Pauline authorship see, *On First Principles* 1.1; *Commentary on John* 2.72 (FC 80.113).

church at Corinth. The author does not explicitly refer to Hebrews, but there are striking similarities between Hebrews (1:1–14; 2:17–18; 4:14–16) and *1 Clement* 36:1–5, which reads as follows, with the similarities to Hebrews in italics[7]:

> Beloved, this is the way in which we found our salvation, *Jesus Christ, the high priest* of our offerings, the guardian and *helper of our weakness . . . who, being the radiance of his majesty is greater than angels to the extent that he has inherited a more excellent name.* For it is written, "*Who makes his angels spirits and his ministers a flame of fire.*" But of his Son the Master says, "*You are my Son. Today I have begotten you.* Ask of me and I will give you the nations for your inheritance, and the ends of the earth for your possession." And again he says to him, "*Sit at my right hand until I make your enemies a footstool for your feet.*"

A few scholars have argued that *1 Clement* and Hebrews relied on a common liturgical source,[8] but most think that *1 Clement* drew elements from several parts of Hebrews. The wording often follows Hebrews, even where Hebrews differs from the LXX and from *1 Clement*'s own style. Although many think that the language in Heb 1:3 was used liturgically, there is little evidence that the catena of biblical quotations in Heb 1:5–13 was used in that way. The author of Hebrews appears to have selected these quotations himself for use in his opening argument (§4 COMMENT). Moreover, it is highly unlikely that Hebrews drew on a source that already acclaimed Jesus as high priest, because the author would not have to argue at length for a priestly Christology if his listeners were already familiar with it. It is the distinctive *combination* of elements that so strongly suggests that *1 Clement* depended on Hebrews.[9]

1 Clement weaves material from Hebrews into a plea for discipline within the church. The exalted portrait of Christ, which was quoted above, is followed by a comparison of church life to military order (*1 Clem.* 37:1). The high-priestly Christology is connected to an appreciative treatment of Levitical priestly service (40:2, 5), which in turn is compared to the orders of ministry that the apostles established when they appointed bishops and deacons. Although Clement does not fully develop the correspondence between Levitical and Christian min-

---

[7]The most important similarities are as follows: Jesus is one "who, being the reflection of [God's] majesty is greater than angels to the extent that he has inherited a more excellent name" (*1 Clem.* 36:2 / Heb 1:2–4). Jesus is "the high priest of our sufferings" and "helper in our weakness" (*1 Clem.* 36:1 / Heb 2:18; 4:14–16). There are quotations of Pss 2:7–8; 104:4; 110:1 in *1 Clem.* 36 and Heb 1:5–13. Both authors list examples of Enoch, Noah, Abraham, Rahab, and those who went about "in the skins of sheep and goats" (*1 Clem.* 9:3–10:1; 12:1–3; 17:1 / Heb 11). Both exhort listeners to hasten toward their goal with eyes fixed upon God (*1 Clem.* 19:2 / Heb 12:1), caution that God searches people (*1 Clem.* 21:9 / Heb 4:12), say that it is impossible for God to lie (*1 Clem.* 27:2 / Heb 6:18), recall that Moses was faithful in God's house (*1 Clem.* 43:1 / Heb 3:5), quote Prov 3:12 (*1 Clem.* 56:4 / Heb 12:6), and identify God as the master or father of spirits (*1 Clem.* 64:1 / Heb 12:9).

[8]Theissen, *Untersuchungen*, 35–37; Mees, "Hohepriester-Theologie," 115–24.

[9]For detailed arguments for the idea that *1 Clement* is dependent upon Hebrews see Hagner, *Use*, 179–95; Ellingworth, "Hebrews," 262–69; Cockerill, "Heb 1:1–14," 437–40; Attridge, *Epistle*, 6–7.

istries, he reflects a tendency that in later centuries will result in Hebrews being read in terms of an emerging Christian priesthood and a doctrine of eucharistic sacrifice (Brown and Meier, *Antioch,* 171).

If *1 Clement* correlated Hebrews with church life in a positive way, others found the relationship much more problematic. The disturbing issue concerned the possibility of repentance after apostasy (Heb 6:4–6; 10:26–31; 12:17). In the Shepherd of Hermas (ca. A.D. 120–140), Hermas said that he had heard that there is no second repentance beyond that made at the time of baptism. This question probably reflects knowledge of Hebrews since Hebrews is apparently the only text prior to the Shepherd of Hermas that formulated the issue of second repentance in this way. A heavenly messenger told Hermas that what he heard was correct, but because of human weakness, the Lord allowed one repentance after baptism, although those who persistently sinned would perish (Herm. *Mand.* 4.3.1–7). Later, this rigorism was modified when Hermas learned that people could repent of sins committed prior to this revelation, but those who sinned in the future would not obtain salvation (Herm. *Vis.* 2.2.4–5). A final statement seems to modify the rigor even further by saying that people may repent until the end of the age, for only after that time will repentance become impossible (Herm. *Sim.* 9.26.5–6; Osiek, *Shepherd,* 28–30).

The interpretation of the warnings against apostasy became a volatile issue in the third century. Tertullian (d. ca. 225), arguing as a Montanist, criticized ecclesiastical laxity and insisted—contrary to Hermas, the "apocryphal 'Shepherd' of adulterers"—that no second repentance was allowed for serious sins committed after baptism, including sins of adultery and apostasy (*On Modesty* §20; cf. Heb 6:4–8). After the Decian persecution of A.D. 249–250, the church debated whether to reinstate those who had apostatized, and the Novatians cited Hebrews when insisting that apostates could not be forgiven.[10] Against them, however, Cyprian (d. 258) declared that lapsed Christians would be allowed to repent and to be restored to communion with the church (*Ep.* 51 of A.D. 252).

Western readers disputed the Pauline authorship of Hebrews and its authoritative status more vigorously than those in the east. Tertullian observed that Hebrews was not written in a Pauline style, although it preserved apostolic teaching. He proposed that it was written by Barnabas, who followed Paul by practicing abstinence (cf. 1 Cor 9:6), and he considered it authoritative because it preserved apostolic teaching.[11] Other western leaders disagreed. The presbyter Gaius (early third century), when defending the Catholic position against Montanism, explicitly rejected the idea that Hebrews could be counted among the epistles of Paul (Eusebius, *Eccl. Hist.* 6.20.3). Irenaeus's (d. ca. 200) view of Hebrews is unclear, but Hippolytus (d. 236) is said to have rejected Pauline authorship.[12] The

---

[10]On the Novatians see Filastrius (PL 12.1200–1202); Epiphanius, *Panarion* 59.1.1–59.3.5 (GCS 31.363–66).

[11]Gregory of Elvira (d. after 392) also ascribed Hebrews to Paul (Battifol, "De l'attribution").

[12]Hippolytus's rejection of Hebrews is noted by Photius in the ninth century (PG 103.404A; 103.1104D). Irenaeus apparently knew of Hebrews but did not cite it in his extant theological writings. His attitude is unclear (Eusebius, *Eccl. Hist.* 6.20.3).

Muratorian canon (ca. 170–190) accepts the thirteen letters that bear Paul's name, but makes no mention of Hebrews. In none of his extant writings does Cyprian cite Hebrews.

3. CONTROVERSY AND CONSENSUS: A.D. 300–600

The Trinitarian controversies in the fourth and fifth centuries led to the formulation of positions that shaped the reading of Hebrews for centuries. The Arians argued that God's Son was a created being, pointing out that Heb 1:4 said that the Son "became" greater than the angels and that 3:1–2 said that the Son was faithful to God who "made" him. Athanasius and his followers countered that God's Son was divine, for he shared God's being (1:3) and was immutable (13:8). When Athanasius's view prevailed, readers came to consider the high Christology in 1:1–4 as a major bastion against Arianism's lower Christology (cf. Hilary, NPNF2 9.74), although questions about Christ's humanity and divinity continued to occupy orthodox interpreters for generations. Alexandrian scholars emphasized Christ's divinity and the unity of his two natures, while Antiochene scholars like John Chrysostom (d. 407), Theodore of Mopsuestia (d. 428), and Theodoret (d. 466) more clearly distinguished the two natures and emphasized Christ's humanity.[13] Interpreters often tried to determine whether a given statement referred to Jesus' humanity or his divinity. For example, to say that Christ is "without father" (7:3) applies to his humanity, since he was born of the virgin Mary and had no earthly father, but to say that he is "without mother" (7:3) applies to his divinity, which was eternally begotten of the Father.[14]

The exalted statements about Melchizedek in 7:3 led some in the second century to think that Melchizedek was superior to Christ, for Melchizedek had no parents whereas Christ had a mother, and Melchizedek interceded for angels whereas Christ interceded for human beings.[15] Origen was more reserved, taking Melchizedek to be an angel, but others argued that Melchizedek had a divine nature and could be identified with the Holy Spirit, the Logos, or God the Father.[16] Orthodox theologians countered that 7:3 did not say that the Son of God was like Melchizedek but that Melchizedek was "like the Son of God." In other words, Christ is the truly divine figure and Melchizedek foreshadows Christ (see §17 COMMENT *a*). Some Gnostic texts (second–fourth cent.) also depict Melchizedek as a heavenly figure. The Nag Hammadi text *Melchizedek* (NHC IX,1) identifies Melchizedek, who receives revelations, with Jesus Christ. Because the text is fragmentary, however, it is not clear whether Jesus is

---

[13]Young, "Christological," 155; Greer, *Captain*, 262–63, 305–6, 353–55; Gonnet, "L'utilisation."

[14]For example, Theodore of Mopsuestia in Greer, *Captain*, 238, 259; Theodoret (PG 723D–726A).

[15]Hippolytus, *Against All Heresies* 7.35–36; 10.23–24; Ps.-Tertullian (PL 2.91B–92A); Epiphanius, *Panarion* 55.1.1–5. See the discussion in Horton, *Melchizedek*, 90–101.

[16]Origen's view is noted by Jerome (PL 22.677). On Melchizedek as the Holy Spirit see Ps.-Augustine (CSEL 50.257–68); as the Logos see Mark the Hermit (PG 65.1117–40); as God the Father see Epiphanius, *Panarion* 55.9.11. See Horton, *Melchizedek*, 105–13.

Melchizedek redivivus or whether Melchizedek is the earthly counterpart of the risen Christ.[17] Other Gnostic texts move completely outside the biblical tradition, referring to Melchizedek as a heavenly figure who helps to free the light fragments in human souls from their material prison, gathering them into the Treasury of Light.[18]

The orthodox recognition of Hebrews' theological importance was accompanied by a widely accepted interpretation of the passages concerning apostasy. Ambrose (d. 397) maintained that Heb 6:4–6 did not prohibit restoring lapsed Christians to communion with the church but only forbade rebaptizing them: **(a)** He argued that Hebrews moves readers beyond the idea of multiple "baptisms" (Heb 6:2), since there is only "one baptism" (Eph 4:5). **(b)** Christians participate in the death of Christ through baptism. Therefore, when Heb 6:6 warns against "recrucifying" the Son of God, it means that they should not seek to participate in his death again by being rebaptized. **(c)** Warnings against apostasy are accompanied by assurances that what is impossible with men is possible with God. Therefore, no one should hesitate to turn to God in repentance. This argument, which was rarely challenged for the next thousand years, removed the main obstacle to the acceptance of Hebrews in the west.[19]

A further development that affected interpretation was the practice of calling Christian ministers "priests." The origin of this practice cannot be attributed primarily to exegesis of Hebrews, but as the priestly understanding of Christian ministry evolved, exegesis and ecclesiastical practice were mutually reinforcing. Although Cyprian was reticent about Hebrews, he identified Melchizedek as a priest and a type of Christ who offered bread and wine. Since Jesus is the high priest, a Christian priest who offers a similar sacrifice of bread and wine in the Mass discharges Christ's office (*ANF* 5.359). In the east, Theodore of Mopsuestia and the liturgy of St. Basil reflect similar views.[20] The late-fourth-century *Apostolic Constitutions* insisted that no layperson could take upon himself the duties of a priest, since Heb 5:4–5 said of priests that "no one takes the honor upon himself" (*ANF* 7.410, 429). When explaining the service for consecrating priests, Ps.-

---

[17]Probably the earliest Gnostic treatment of Melchizedek is a brief text from Bala'izah that clearly echoes Heb 7:3. The text is so fragmentary that the author's own understanding of Melchizedek is not clear (Pearson, *Gnosticism*, 108–23; Schenke, "Die jüdische"; Heldermann, "Melchizedeks"). On Melchizedek and Jesus in NHC IX,1 see Franzmann, *Jesus*, 148–49. On Gnostic interpretations see also Pagels, *Gnostic Paul*, 141–56.

[18]The principal texts are from 2 *Jeu* and the *Pistis Sophia*. On these sources see Horton, *Melchizedek*, 131–51; Pearson, *Gnosticism*, 114–21.

[19]See Ambrose, *De paenitentia* 2.2. His contemporary, Filastrius, connected the argument with Ezek 33:16, which assured forgiveness to the penitent (PL 12.1200B–1202A). Pelagius follows the same argument as Ambrose (de Bruyne, *Pelagius's*, 97–98). Eastern writers who follow this same argument include Chrysostom, *Homilies*, NPNF[2] 14.410–11; Ephraem, *Epistolas*, 214–15. Cf. Epiphanius, *Panarion* 59.2.1–5 (GCS 31.365). An alternative view followed by Theodore of Mopsuestia was that after the resurrection there would be no further chances to repent (Greer, *Captain*, 234–35). The baptismal interpretation was questioned by Severian of Gabala (Staab, *Pauluskommentare*, 349).

[20]On Theodore see Tonneau, *Les homélies*, 497; Greer, *Captain*, 188. On Basil see Nairne, *Epistle*, 138.

Dionysius (ca. 500) recalled that Jesus "did not exalt himself" to the priesthood (Heb 5:5–6), warning that no monk should attempt to overrule a priest.[21]

The Mass was understood to be the sacrifice offered by Christian priests. Roman Christians had linked the bread and wine offered by Melchizedek with the Eucharist by the third century, and Melchizedek's offering was later included in eucharistic prayers and artwork as a type of the Mass.[22] Eastern Christians also connected Hebrews with the eucharistic meal by the third century. Later, the liturgy of St. James included a prayer for the unveiling of the bread and wine that paraphrases Hebrews: the priest gives thanks for confident access into the holy place through the new and living way Christ opened through the veil of his flesh (cf. Heb 10:20), he acknowledges the fear and trembling that accompany the offering of a bloodless sacrifice for his own sins and those of the people (cf. 5:1–3), and he prays that they might with a pure conscience offer the sacrifice of praise (cf. 9:14; 13:15–16).[23] Although Hebrews insists that Christ's sacrifice precludes further sacrifices, presumably including the sacrifice of the Mass, Chrysostom explains that we "offer, indeed, but making a remembrance of his death," so that the sacrifice of the Mass is "a figure and remembrance of Christ's sacrifice" (NPNF[1] 14.449). This became a standard interpretation during the Middle Ages.

Christians in the east continued placing Hebrews among the Pauline epistles as they had done since the second century.[24] In the west, the writers who used Hebrews to combat Arianism helped popularize the idea that it was a letter of Paul.[25] Rufinus (d. 410) spoke of fourteen Pauline letters, which would include Hebrews (NPNF[2] 3.557–58), and Ambrose said that "Paul" or "the apostle" wrote Hebrews, introducing quotations from it with the formula "it is written."[26]

---

[21]Ps.-Dionysius, *Ecclesiastical Hierarchy* 5, §512c (CWS, 241); *Letter* 8, §1096A–C (CWS, 277). The use of Hebrews in these texts was taken by some to show Pauline authorship, since Dionysius was assumed to have known Paul and would therefore have known Paul's work. See Aquinas, *Ad Heb.* §5 and the references in Hagen, *Hebrews*, 36, 45, 52 n. 106, 54, 56 n. 115, 73.

[22]Melchizedek's bread and wine are connected with the Eucharist by Cyprian (*ANF* 5.359). Cf. Ambrose (NPNF[2] 10.323). Melchizedek was included in the eucharistic prayer (Jungmann, *Mass*, 1.51–52, 2.229–30) and artwork (*DACL* 11,1.230–40).

[23]Melchizedek's offering of bread and wine was considered a type of the Eucharist by Clement of Alexandria in *Stromata* 4.25; Eusebius, *Proof of the Gospel* 5.3, §223; Jerome, *Hebrew Questions*, 47. On the liturgy of St. James see *ANF* 7.543; Lindars, *Theology*, 138–42.

[24]For citations of Hebrews as a letter of Paul see Peter of Alexandria (PG 18.485A); Alexander of Alexandria (PG 18.557A, 576B); Didymus (PG 39.317B, 393C); Cyril of Alexandria (PG 75.40A, 49D, 212A); Severian of Gabala (Staab, *Pauluskommentare*, 345); Theodoret (PG 82.673–78); Ephraem, *Epistolas*, 200–203; Theodore of Mopsuestia (Staab, *Pauluskommentare*, 200–201); Chrysostom *Homilies* (NPNF[1] 14.363–65). Cf. Eusebius, *Eccl. Hist.* 3.3.4; Athanasius (NPNF[2] 4.552); Cyril of Jerusalem, *Catechesis* 4.36 (PG 33.499C).

[25]On the Arian use of Hebrews see Hilary (NPNF[2] 9.74). On Pauline authorship see Hilary (PL 9.302); Caius Marius Victorinus (PL 1085B, 1091D, 1138C); Lucifer of Cagliari (PL 13.782–83); and his disciple Faustinus (PL 13.61, 67–68). Theodoret (PG 82.673C) reported that the Arians rejected Hebrews, apparently because of its importance for orthodox Christology.

[26]Ambrose uses "Paul" in *De fide* 5.13, §161 (PL 16.680B). Cf. "the apostle" (PL 14.711–12) and "it is written" (PL 14.694). A commentary that circulated under the name of Ambrose—later dubbed "Ambrosiaster"—ascribed only thirteen letters to Paul, although it does quote Hebrews in the same way that it quotes other NT books (PL 17.485D).

A canonical list of the Third Council of Carthage in 397 referred to "the thirteen Epistles of the Apostle Paul" and "of the same [author] one [Epistle] to the Hebrews."[27] Most important were the comments of Jerome (d. 420), who said, "We must admit that the epistle written to the Hebrews is regarded as Paul's, not only by the churches of the east, but by all church writers who have from the beginning written in Greek." At the same time, he acknowledged the western church's doubts about this position, noting that some ascribed it to Barnabas or Clement (*Ep.* 129.7).[28] Augustine's earlier writings simply identified Paul as the author, and he used Hebrews extensively when demonstrating his understanding of human sin in contrast to the Pelagians.[29] Later Augustine, perhaps influenced by Jerome, refrained from identifying Paul as the author, although he included it among the church's authoritative Scriptures. This view was followed by others.[30]

The position of Hebrews among the NT writings varied, reflecting in some measure its peculiar history of acceptance into the canon. Some in the east placed Hebrews after Romans or after 1 and 2 Corinthians, the longest Pauline letters, or occasionally at other points among Paul's letters to churches. Alexandrian texts often follow an alternative arrangement: The letters to churches are first (Romans through 2 Thessalonians), followed by Hebrews, which was written to a group, and last come the letters written to individuals (1 and 2 Timothy, Titus, and Philemon). The most common arrangement in the west, which was also followed by some eastern Christians, was to place Hebrews after Philemon, at the very end of the Pauline corpus. This reflects the idea that Hebrews belongs in the outer ring of the Pauline writings, and the arrangement remained dominant until Pauline authorship was challenged in the sixteenth century (Hatch, "Position").

B. HEBREWS FROM A.D. 600 TO A.D. 1500

The Middle Ages began with challenges for the Christian popes and emperors in the form of tribal invasions from the north and west and in the rise of Islam in

---

[27]Text in Theron, *Evidence*, 126–27. The authority of Hebrews was also acknowledged by the Council of Hippo in 393. The Council of Carthage in 409 no longer distinguished Hebrews from the other Pauline letters but simply referred to the fourteen letters of Paul. See Leipoldt, *Geschichte*, 1.230.

[28]On doubts about Paul's authorship see Jerome (CCSL 73, pp. 86, 118; 76A, p. 807; 77 p. 247). On arguments for Pauline authorship see NPNF² 3.363. Jerome sometimes quotes Hebrews along with other letters of Paul, implying Pauline authorship (NPNF² 6.389).

[29]See Augustine in NPNF¹ 5.34; cf. generally Bonnardière, "L'épître"; Quinot, "L'influence"; Rottmanner, "Saint Augustin." On the Pelagian use of Hebrews see NPNF¹ 5.60; Souter, *Pelagius's*, 171; de Bruyne, "Étude," 372; Spicq, *L'Épître*, 1.182–83.

[30]For an early reference to Pauline authorship see Augustine's *Ep. ad Rom. inchoata*, 11.3–4 (PL 35.2095). On criteria for accepting Hebrews and other books see *On Christian Doctrine* 2.8.12–13. Later texts that refrain from identifying Paul as the author include *De peccatorum meritis et remissione* 1.50 (PL 44.137) and *The City of God* 10.5 (CCSL 47.278). Although Pelagius apparently did not write a commentary on Hebrews, he did speak of Paul as the author. See the comments and citations in de Bruyne, *Pelagius's*, 11, 97, 106, 111, 139. Isidore of Seville includes fourteen letters of Paul in his *De ecclesiasticis officiis* 1.11.6 (CCCM 113.10–11).

the east. When instability and hardship gave way to a more stable society in the ninth century, biblical scholarship was renewed within the framework forged by earlier generations. Theologically, interpreters followed the formulations developed in the fourth and fifth centuries. Exegetically, commentators noted the ancient debates concerning the authorship of Hebrews, but agreed that Paul must have written the book. This gave Hebrews a prominence it almost certainly would not have had otherwise, since the Pauline epistles were widely studied during the Middle Ages because of their doctrinal content.[31]

1. MONASTIC AND DEVOTIONAL WRITINGS

The monastic *Rule of St. Benedict of Nursia* (ca. 540) allowed two to three hours a day for the reading of Scripture to foster greater devotion to God and moral rigor. The interpretive framework was the soul's pilgrimage to God. Echoing Heb 11:13–16, the *Rule* called Scripture "the truest of guides for human life," a text that was indispensable for those "hastening toward [their] heavenly home" (48.1; 73.3, 7). Monastic readers treated the biblical text as a mystery to be encountered, and commentators often spoke in the first person. When Herveus of Bourgdieu (d. 1150) read that Christ "had to become like his brethren in all things" (Heb 2:17), he responded that the Son of God "had to become *like us*," so that he "might be stung in his heart by *our* miseries and infirmities—just as the gospels tell how frequently he groaned and wept *for us*—that he might be truly compassionate *toward us* and sympathetic with *our* miseries" (PL 181.1540D–41A).

Warnings were also part of the monastic reader's encounter with the text. Where academic writers explained the warnings against apostasy as prohibitions against rebaptism, monastic writers sought to let the warnings move readers to self-examination and repentance. When William of St. Thierry (d. 1148) read the warning about those who spurn the Son of God (Heb 10:26–31), his response was not explanation but confession: "Lord, truly I have sinned," but "have I spurned you also, Son of God?" He prays, "No, no, most merciful!" But grant that "I may repent" with "a faith devout and pure," so that you say even to me, "Go, for your faith has made you whole."[32]

Patristic writers held that the Scriptures had both literal and spiritual levels of meaning. Hebrews seemed to invite spiritual interpretation, since the author said that the institutions of the old covenant represented transcendent realities (Heb 8:5; 9:9; 10:1). Commentators developed interpretations of each item in the Tabernacle, drawing inspiration from earlier writers. The table was the Scriptures, and the bread upon it was the body of Christ. The lampstand referred to preaching or to the gifts of the Spirit, and the censer was Christ. The ark was the incarnate Lord, while the urn was the flesh that encompassed the "manna" of his

---

[31]For lists of early medieval commentaries on biblical books see Riché and Lobrichon, *Le Moyen*, 154–57. On the theme of the preeminence of Christ see Hagen, *Theology*, 31–33, 43–51. On themes of shadow and reality, and old and new covenants in medieval exegesis see Lubac, *Medieval*, 1.237, 243–44.

[32]*Meditation* 5.6–7 (CisF 3.121–22, 124). Cf. Herveus (PL 181.1636D).

divinity. Aaron's rod signified Christ's priesthood, and the tablets of the Law stood for the two covenants.[33] For Hugh of St. Cher (d. 1263) the earthly Tabernacle symbolized the church militant, while the heavenly Tabernacle was the church triumphant. For Bonaventure (d. 1274) the priest's journey through the courts of the Tabernacle provided a way to speak of the soul's journey into mystical communion with God (CWS, 94).

As the faithful journeyed to their heavenly destination, they remained pilgrims and strangers upon earth (Heb 11:13). The call to renounce earthly security was issued by Jesus, who said, "If you would be perfect, go, sell what you possess and give to the poor . . . and come, follow me" (Matt 19:21). In a similar fashion the devotional classic *The Imitation of Christ,* ascribed to Thomas à Kempis, used the language of Heb 11:13 and 13:14 to define the situation of the Christian: "Keep yourself a stranger and pilgrim upon earth, to whom the affairs of the world are of no concern. Keep your heart free and lifted up to God, for you have here no abiding city" (1.23). Remember that "wherever you may be, you are a stranger and a pilgrim; you will never enjoy peace until you become inwardly united to Christ" (2.1).[34]

2. SCHOOL AND UNIVERSITY

Schools in the early Middle Ages were connected with monasteries, and their purpose was training people for service in the church and government. The first flowering of biblical scholarship occurred in the reign of Charlemagne (d. 814), and its principal architect was Alcuin (d. 804), who produced commentaries that synthesized resources from the patristic period. Using the Latin translation of Chrysostom's homilies, Alcuin correlated elements from Hebrews with the Catholic tradition.[35] When Heb 1:3 declares that the Son is "the radiance of God's glory," Alcuin echoes the creed, calling the Son "light from light and God from God" (PL 100.1033D). When Heb 4:14 exhorts listeners to hold fast to "the confession," Alcuin in effect identifies the confession with the second article of the creed, which describes the person and work of Christ (PL 100.1050D). He restates the idea that apostates can be restored to communion with the church, but not rebaptized[36]; and he regularly recalls that Melchizedek offered bread

[33]Augustine said that the ark—which contains the Law, Aaron's rod signifying its power, and the manna, which signifies grace—is the mystery of God (PL 34.633–34). Bede identified the table with the Scriptures, the twelve loaves with the twelve apostles and their teachings, the seven lamps on the lampstand with the gifts of the Spirit, and Aaron's rod with Christ's priesthood (CCCM 119A; *De tabernaculo* book 1, lines 470–74, 771–84, 850–83, 1226–30). Of the medieval scholars, Sedulius Scotus follows Augustine, but Alcuin and others are closer to Bede.

[34]Thomas à Kempis, *Imitation of Christ* 1.17; 3.48. Cf. William of St. Thierry, "The Golden Epistle" (CisF 12.60–63).

[35]Chrysostom's homilies were translated into Latin in the mid-sixth century (Cassiodorus, *Institutiones* 1.8.3). Much of Alcuin's commentary is from Chrysostom, though the explanations of Psalm citations draw on Augustine and Cassiodorus (Riggenbach, *Die ältesten,* 24).

[36]A few thought that the passage warned against the possibility of repenting after this life, and Nicolaus of Lyra proposed that repentance was not "impossible" but merely "difficult." See Hagen, *Hebrews,* 12.

and wine as a type of the offerings made by priests in the church (PL 100.1053D–54B; 1062C–63B; 1077C).

The universities that were established in the twelfth and thirteenth centuries consisted of assemblies of noted scholars and their students. One question that arose concerned the goal of exegesis. Most scholastic commentators began by summarizing Chrysostom's view that Hebrews showed the superiority of Christ (*eminentia Christi*) over the institutions of the old covenant, but soon their commentaries ranged widely over other topics.[37] The early scholastic writer Lanfranc (d. 1089) followed a simple dialectic method that attempted to reconstruct the logic of a passage like Heb 7:4–10, which describes Abraham's encounter with Melchizedek (PL 150.375A). Later scholastic writers, however, often debated issues concerning original sin and the sinlessness of Christ on the basis of the remark "One might even venture to say that Levi, who receives tithes, actually paid a tithe through Abraham, for he was still in the loins of his father when Melchizedek met him" (Heb 7:9–10). When Hebrews says that Levi shared in the action of his ancestor, Abraham, this implies that people might also participate in other actions performed by their ancestors. Scholars agreed that people partake in the original sin of their ancestor Adam, yet they did not want to conclude that Christ also shared in the original sin, even though as a man, Christ descended from Adam and Abraham. They concluded that Christ was exempted from original sin because he was not conceived through human carnality but through the Holy Spirit and because he was born of the virgin Mary.[38]

A second question concerned the relationship between the literal and spiritual senses of Scripture. Scholars agreed that Scripture had multiple senses, but problems arose when allegorical interpretations proliferated and seemed removed from the plain sense of the text.[39] Moreover, the literal sense was not always easy to identify. A test case was God's promise concerning David's heir, "I will be his father and he will be my son" (2 Sam 7:14; 1 Chron 17:13). Aquinas observed that in one sense the text refers to David's son Solomon (cf. 1 Chron 22:10), but Heb 1:5 could use the text for Christ because Christ is *prefigured* in Solomon (*Ad Heb.* §§50–51). Nicolaus of Lyra (d. 1340) in time developed the idea of a double literal sense, since the OT applied 2 Sam 7:14 literally to Solomon and Hebrews applied it literally to Christ.

A third and related question was what made an interpretation of Scripture authoritative. On one side, Henry Totting (d. 1396) argued that the christological interpretation in Heb 1 was valid because an apostle presented it. Jean Gerson

---

[37]Alcuin, PL 100.1032D; Sedulius Scotus, PL 103.251C; Robert of Melun, *Questiones*, 284–85; Ps.-Hugh of St. Victor, PL 175.607D; Aquinas, *Ad Heb.* §§1–5. Cf. Colish, *Peter Lombard*, 197–99.

[38]This interpretation follows Augustine, *The Literal Meaning of Genesis* 10.19–21. See the extended discussion of this matter in the marginal notes in Anselm of Laon, *Glossa ordinaria* on 7:9–10; Peter Lombard (PL 192.450D–451C); Robert of Melun (*Questiones*, 303); Ps.–Hugh of St. Victor, *Quaestiones in Epistolas Pauli*, which circulated around 1180–1230 (PL 175.624D–625B); Thomas Aquinas (*Ad Heb.* §346); Martin Luther (*LuthW* 29.189–90).

[39]Aquinas paraphrases Heb 7:14 as biblical warrant for allegorical interpretation in his *Summa theologiae* 1a.I,10. See Lubac, *Medieval*, 1.15–75.

(d. 1429) developed this line of thinking, declaring that valid interpretation finally depended upon the authority of the church's magisterium. On the other side, Lyra emphasized the authority of the text. He had assumed that Hebrews' use of the OT was valid because Paul followed the rule that legitimate arguments had to be based on the literal sense of the OT text. Paul of Burgos (d. 1435) went further, insisting that the OT texts themselves pointed to a literal christological sense. For example, in Ps 2:7 God said, "You are my son, today I have begotten you." The text speaks of a singular son, which can only apply to Jesus, and Jesus was uniquely "begotten" by God, rather than created.[40] This issue of the authority of the text versus the authority of the interpreter would become explosive during the sixteenth century.

3. ECCLESIASTICAL PRACTICE

Hebrews had gained acceptance in the western church during the Trinitarian disputes of the fourth and fifth centuries, when the high Christology of Heb 1:3 was commonly used against Arianism. As the medieval church established lectionaries, Heb 1 was regularly identified as a Christmas text so that it would help disclose the mystery of the incarnation: What happened at Bethlehem was not simply the birth of a man, but an act of divine condescension in which God the Son took on human flesh to redeem humanity. Hebrews 1 was read alongside Isaiah's promises that a virgin would conceive and bear a son (Isa 7:14), who would be called Mighty God and Prince of Peace (Isa 9:1–7). Thus what was spoken in various ways by the prophets (Heb 1:1) was fulfilled in Christ (*DACL* 5,1.335).

One controversy in which Hebrews played a role concerned predestination. Augustine had taught that a person's salvation depended wholly upon divine grace and that people were saved by God's decision to include them among the elect. The monk Gottschalk (d. 868) found comfort in the idea that eternal life came from God's unchangeable decision rather than the church's penitential system, but his teaching that God also predestined some to damnation outraged many. A letter written in his defense by the church of Lyons pointed out that God's oath was irrevocable (Heb 6:13–18) and that God not only promised grace but also swore in his wrath that some would not enter his rest (3:7–4:13), which meant that he could predestine either to salvation or to punishment. Gottschalk's opponent Rabanus Maurus (d. 856) and later Haimo commented that even though some took the statement that Christ tasted death "for everyone" (2:9) to mean "for the elect who are predestined to eternal life," most recognized that Christ died "for everyone, faithful and unfaithful" and that the reason that all are not saved is that not all believe.[41]

A second issue concerned the nature of the Lord's Supper. The consensus was that the Mass could be considered a sacrifice even though Hebrews said that

---

[40]See Preus, *Shadow*, 89. On the literal sense and ecclesiastical authority see pp. 46–101.

[41]For the letter from Lyons see LCC 9.159–60. For Rabanus Maurus's comments on 2:10 see PL 112.724D–725A and on 3:7–4:12 see PL 112.730A–736D. Haimo's comments are in PL 117.836D; cf. Herveus, PL 181.1535D; Aquinas, *Ad Heb.* §125; Ps.-Bruno, PL 153.499C. For discussion of the controversy, see Seeberg, *Text-Book*, 2.30–33.

Christ's death precluded other sacrifices, since Chrysostom had said that the sacrifice of the Mass is a figure and remembrance of Christ's singular sacrifice.[42] Yet controversy arose over the *manner* of Christ's presence in this sacrifice. On one side, Ratramnus of Corbie (d. 868) insisted that the physical bread and wine could not be equated with the spiritual realities they signified. According to Heb 11:1, faith receives that which is unseen, and if Christ's body were physically and visibly present, there would be nothing for faith to receive (LCC 9.121, 129). On the other side, Paschasius Radbertus (d. 865) insisted that Christ's body was indeed physically present in the sacrament. This view became dominant in the Middle Ages and is reflected in Haimo's comments on Heb 10:2–3, in which he argues that Christ's body was singular and a unity; therefore, the body physically born of Mary is the same body present in the sacrament (PL 117.836D).

A third area of conflict was the relationship of secular and spiritual authority. Pope Gelasius I (492–496) distinguished secular from spiritual authority. He noted that prior to Christ there were figures like Melchizedek who were both kings and priests, but after Christ, "who was true King and true priest, the emperor no longer assumed the title of priest, nor did the priest claim royal dignity." Spiritual and secular authority were to remain separate (Rahner, *Church*, 177–78). In the seventh century, however, the emperor Constans II tried to settle a theological controversy by imperial edict. When Maximus the Confessor (d. 662) objected, his opponents cited Melchizedek as a precedent for a king performing priestly functions. Maximus replied that a figure like Melchizedek had to be without father or mother, living for days without end (Heb 7:3). No mortal, including the emperor, met these requirements; they applied to Christ alone (Rahner, *Church*, 261). Later, Pope Innocent III (d. 1216) found in Melchizedek a precedent for expanding papal power. Melchizedek foreshadowed the fusion of kingly and priestly power that was realized in Christ. Since the pope was the vicar of Christ, the pope also possessed both spiritual and secular authority. In 1214, Innocent declared, "The King of kings and Lord of lords, Jesus, Christ, a priest forever after the order of Melchizedek," has set over all people the "one whom He has appointed as His Vicar on earth, so that, as every knee is bowed to Jesus, of things in heaven and things in earth, and things under the earth, so all men should obey his Vicar."[43] Innocent's successor, Gregory IX (d. 1241), advanced the pope's legislative authority by issuing a new collection of decretals that superseded previous collections, declaring that "when there is a change in the priesthood there must be a change in the law as well" (Heb 7:12). What was said of Christ's priesthood was applied to the pope, who defined the shape of the new law (*Luth*W 36.137–38).

Hebrews was also used by critics of church practice. John Wyclif (d. 1384) observed that according to Heb 13:14, "we have here no lasting city." He cited this text against papal establishments and property-owning monasteries. Although for a time he viewed the mendicant orders favorably, he became disillusioned with them, even raising the possibility that they might be the apostates mentioned in

---

[42]Chrysostom, *Homilies*, NPNF1 14.449. For discussion see Clark, *Eucharistic Sacrifice*, 75–77.

[43]See Cheney and Semple, *Selected Letters*, 177–78. Cf. J. M. Powell, *Innocent III*, 77, 173–77.

Heb 6:4–6.[44] Similarly, Jan Hus (d. 1415) turned the warnings about apostasy (Heb 10:28–29 and 6:6) against priests he deemed guilty of simony.[45] He used statements about Christ's priesthood, which had often been cited to support the idea that the church's priests represented Christ's priesthood, to argue that the priestly office was fulfilled in Christ alone.[46] Similarly, many had used the idea that no one should seek the honor of priesthood for himself (5:4–5) to protect ecclesiastical order by warning those in the lower ranks not to usurp the priesthood. Hus, however, directed the text at church leaders, insisting that bishops were not to seek honors for themselves.[47] For both Wyclif and Hus, Christians lived by what is unseen, which meant that the true church was not the visible institution, but a community that could only be perceived through faith (11:1).[48]

C. HEBREWS FROM A.D. 1500 TO A.D. 1750

Theological and social changes in the sixteenth century decisively altered the context in which Hebrews was read. Humanist scholars reconsidered the biblical and patristic sources of the Christian tradition, reopening questions concerning the authorship and authority of Hebrews that had not been seriously debated since the fifth century. Lutheran and Reformed interpreters developed new patterns of theological thought—which we will consider under the theme of testament or covenant in the Lutheran Tradition and Reformed Tradition sections below—and they rejected the traditional correlation of Christ's priesthood and sacrifice with the church's priesthood and the sacrifice of the Mass. The doctrines of the priesthood and the Mass were reaffirmed by the Roman Catholic Church at the Council of Trent using language from Hebrews.

During this period the textual basis for debate shifted from the Latin Vulgate to the Greek text, and as scholars explored the meaning of Greek terms they began to ask questions about the relationship of Hebrews to the broader cultural and religious environment of antiquity—questions that would dominate the historical-critical study of Hebrews in the nineteenth and twentieth centuries.

1. HUMANIST TRADITION

The early humanist Lorenzo Valla (d. 1457) regarded Hebrews as a Pauline epistle.[49] Jacques Lefèvre d'Etaples (Faber Stapulensis, d. 1536) accepted the

---

[44]The page numbers refer to *Wyclif's Latin Works*. *De officio Regis*, pp. 62–63; *De potestate Pope* §§7–8, p. 163; *Dialogus sive speculum ecclesie militantis* §21, p. 42; "Die paupertate Christi" §32, in *Opera minora*, p. 7; "De quattuor sectis novellis" §§2 and 8, in *Polemical Works* vol. 1, pp. 245, 273. On 6:4–6 see *Opus evangelicum* part 1, chap. 60, p. 223.

[45]Hus, *De Ecclesia* 11.116.

[46]Ibid., 12.122.

[47]*On Simony* 4 and 5 (LCC 14.215, 222).

[48]Wyclif, *De fide catholica* 1 (*Wyclif's Latin Works*, 100); Hus, *The Church*, 5.

[49]See Valla's comments on Heb 13:22 (*Collatio*, 250) and on Heb 10 (*Adnotationes*, 1.887).

traditional view that Paul wrote Hebrews, but was not persuaded by the ancient claim that Paul omitted his name out of modesty or prudence. He thought it more likely that Paul's name had been lost due to manuscript transmission (Hagen, *Theology*, 23). Thus, instead of attributing Hebrews' anonymity to the virtue of the apostle as the ancients had done, Lefèvre ascribes it to the accidents of history—a rather modern argument. In a series of *Adnotationes* written in 1516, Desiderius Erasmus (d. 1536) rejected the idea that Paul wrote Hebrews, given the book's anonymity, distinctive style, and the objections mentioned by Jerome (see p. 27). Erasmus argued that Paul would not have applied Ps 8 to Christ since the psalm refers to humanity, and he could not believe that Paul would deny repentance to apostates (6:4–6), since Paul hoped for salvation even of a man who slept with his father's wife (1 Cor 5:1–2). In his *Paraphrase* of 1521, however, Erasmus simply attributed Hebrews to Paul. When questioned about his views by the theological faculty at Paris in 1527, Erasmus said that he found Pauline authorship implausible, but he accepted the church's judgment concerning the book's canonical status (*Opera* 9.863F–865A). Those who continued the humanist tradition, including the Arminian Hugo Grotius (d. 1645) and the Socinian Jonas Schlichting (d. 1661), followed Erasmus in denying Paul's authorship of Hebrews while accepting its canonical status.[50]

Erasmus made a basic distinction between lower and higher forms of religion. The institutions of the old covenant represented a lower form of religious life, while the new covenant in Christ pointed to a higher spiritual and moral order. "The Law was crude, the reward crude, but care was taken in this way to make the crude minds of humans gradually become accustomed to move from the things of the senses to the things of the mind" (*Paraphrase*, 231). Although Erasmus's earlier work cited the apparent denial of repentance after apostasy in 6:4–6 as a reason to reject Pauline authorship of Hebrews, his *Paraphrase* transformed the text into an exhortation to a more fervent striving in the moral life. Since Christ rose, we too "must rise again with him into a new state of life in such a way that we do not relapse into the death of the life left once and for all behind"; rather, we "must make our industry match God's kindness to us" (*Paraphrase*, 227–28).

Early humanists worked within a Trinitarian framework, with textual discoveries providing new impetus for christological debate. Study of Greek and Hebrew showed that Hebrews often followed the LXX, which sometimes differed from the MT. The LXX of Ps 8 said the Son of Man was made lower than the angels, but the MT said he was made lower than God; the LXX also said he was lower for a little while, but the MT said he was a little lower in degree (Heb 2:6–8). Erasmus accepted the LXX alternatives, stressing how intensely Christ suffered, but Lefèvre d'Étaples thought the emphasis on humiliation detracted from the deity of Christ, and he insisted that even in his humanity Christ was lit-

[50]On Arminian views of authorship see Grotius, *Annotations* (Leipoldt, *Geschichte*, 2.153–54 n. 3). On Socinian views see idem, 2.31, and Schlichting's prolegomenon, 8. On the authority of Hebrews see Grotius, *Truth*, 144–45; Socinus, et al., *Racovian Catechism*, 1–6.

tle less than God (Feld, "Humanisten," 5–35). Later, the Socinians broke with Trinitarian formulations. They argued that calling the Son "the radiance of God's glory" (Heb 1:3) meant only that he manifested God's glory on earth, and declaring that the Son was "begotten" by God (1:5) simply meant that the Holy Spirit dwelt within him.[51] The Socinians also gained notoriety for arguing on the basis of Heb 7–10 that Jesus' death was not a perfect sacrifice, but only the preparation for his entry into heaven, where his sacrifice was offered.[52] Rejecting the Socinian position, Grotius insisted that the crucifixion was indeed the sacrifice that moved God to forgive sins (*Defence*, 207–49).

2. LUTHERAN TRADITION

Martin Luther (d. 1546) evinced both high regard for and deep misgivings toward Hebrews. His early writings follow the medieval consensus that Paul wrote the book, although his lectures on Hebrews of 1517–18 note that the discrepancies between the depiction of the Tabernacle in the OT and Heb 9 might make some question whether Paul was the author (Hagen, *Theology*, 26–28). Luther's break with the theory of Pauline authorship appears in the preface to his translation of Hebrews (1522). Luther noted the patristic disputes over the authorship of Hebrews and pointed out that Hebrews was written by someone who received the gospel secondhand (Heb 2:3), which was not true of Paul (Gal 1:11–12). Like Erasmus, he thought that passages barring sinners from repentance ran counter to Paul's teaching (Heb 6:4–6; 10:26–31; 12:17). In the preface Luther said only that Hebrews was "the work of an able and learned man, a disciple of the apostles." Later, he speculated that Apollos may have written Hebrews (Acts 18:24), but the preface continued to treat the author as an anonymous figure.[53]

Luther, together with the English reformer William Tyndale (d. 1536), moved Hebrews from its usual place after the Pauline epistles and put it after 3 John, so that it became one of the last four books in the NT. He called it "a marvelously fine epistle," while insisting that "we cannot put it on the same level with the apostolic epistles" (*LuthW* 35.395). For years Lutheran scholars debated whether Hebrews should be considered apocryphal or fully canonical.[54] Printed editions

---

[51]See Socinus, et al., *Racovian Catechism*, 72, 90–100, 106–10, 124–25, 139–41.

[52]See Socinus, et al., *Racovian Catechism*, 349–59.

[53]Quotations from Luther's preface to Hebrews are from *LuthW* 35.394–95. The preface of 1522 was reprinted almost without change in the edition of 1546. His proposal that Apollos was the author appeared in a sermon on Heb 1:1–4 which was published in 1522 (*Sermons*, 7.167) and in some later works. See Feld, *Martin Luthers*, 31–34. The theory of Apollos's authorship was noted by Georg Major (d. 1574; see Hagen, *Hebrews*, 86). Philip Melanchthon (d. 1560) and Johann Bugenhagen (d. 1558) commonly introduced quotations from Hebrews with formulas that left the author's identity vague. The German text of the *Formula of Concord* (1577) introduces texts from Hebrews without identifying the author, but the Latin version of the same text ascribes them to "the apostle" (part II, "Solid Declaration," art. 1 §43 and art. 4 §30 [*BC* 516, 555]).

[54]In 1520 Andreas Bodenstein von Karlstadt proposed dividing the NT into three categories: (1) Gospels and Acts; (2) thirteen Pauline letters, 1 John, 1 Peter; and (3) James, 2 Peter, 2 and 3 John, Jude, Hebrews, Revelation. See Leipoldt, *Geschichte*, 2.108, 116–17.

of the Luther Bible numbered the first twenty-three books of the NT, but not the last four (Hebrews, James, Jude, Revelation).[55] Martin Chemnitz (d. 1586) argued that these four books—as well as 2 Peter, and 2 and 3 John—were apocryphal writings of the NT, comparable to the apocryphal writings of the OT (*Examination* 1.134). Matthias Flacius Illyricus (d. 1575), however, argued for the authority of Hebrews, because the book was an important source of doctrine (Hagen, *Hebrews*, 83–85). Eventually, Johann Gerhard (d. 1637) concluded that Hebrews was among the *antilegomena*, or "disputed" writings, since its status had been disputed in the early church, but he insisted that it was not "apocryphal" or theologically suspect. Gerhard himself held that the principal cause of Hebrews was the Holy Spirit, while the efficient cause was the apostle Paul.[56]

Luther's prefatory remarks to his lectures of 1517–18 state that Hebrews "exalts grace as opposed to the arrogance of legal and human righteousness" (WA 57,3.5). In his preface of 1522, Luther called the passages dealing with apostasy "a hard knot" (*Luth*W 35.394), but elsewhere he interpreted these passages in terms of faith and works. He charged that those who taught that people could satisfy the righteousness of God through their own efforts and not through the work of Christ trampled Jesus' blood underfoot (Heb 10:29). Thus Hebrews spoke of the impossibility of repentance *outside of Christ*, since one would then be relying on one's own merits.[57] Hebrews also contributed to a revolution in Luther's understanding of the Lord's Supper. When Jesus took the cup at the last supper, he called it a new *diathēkē* (Luke 22:20; 1 Cor 11:25), which in Heb 9:16–17 (cf. Gal 3:15) means a "testament," a promise of a gift to one's heirs (*Luth*W 36.38). The Mass, therefore, is not a sacrifice that people offer to God, but a testament or promise that Christ offers to people. Since faith receives the promise, "faith alone is the true priestly office. It permits no one else to take its place" (*Luth*W 35.101). In polemical writing, Luther would argue that Christ was sacrificed once and for all (cf. Heb 7:27; 9:25–26) and warned that those who presumed to sacrifice him again in the Mass were therefore holding him up to contempt (6:6).[58]

Faith remained a central point in the Lutheran interpretation of Hebrews. Lutheran scholastics closely associated faith with doctrine. Chemnitz thought that Hebrews was written to those who were "drifting away" from true doctrine (Heb 2:1) and who faced the prospect of being "carried away by all sorts of strange teachings" (13:9). He valued Hebrews because it correctly defined the

---

[55]The practice of not numbering the last four books in the NT persisted until 1689. In 1596 an edition of the Bible called these books the "apocrypha" (Leipoldt, *Geschichte*, 2.95).

[56]See Bleek, *Brief*, 1.259. Lutherans who argued for Pauline authorship from a scholastic perspective included Calov (*Biblia*, 2.1095) and Carpzov (*Sacrae*, 62–67). Arndt often referred to Hebrews without attributing it to Paul in his *True Christianity*, but Bengel ascribed Hebrews to Paul ("Epistle," 4.333–34).

[57]*Luth*W 52.282. Similar views were held by Bugenhagen (Hagen, *Hebrews*, 12) and Calov (*Biblia*, 2.1236). On the importance of faith (Heb 11) in Lutheran theological writing see the *Loci communes theologici* of Melanchthon (LCC 19.97–102).

[58]See his treatise *The Misuse of the Mass* of 1521 (*Luth*W 36.147). Melanchthon commented that Hebrews teaches that "we do not have a priesthood like the Levitical" (*Apology of the Augsburg Confession*, art. 13, [*BC* 212]).

doctrine of the gospel. Devotional writing understood faith as "living faith," which included the apprehension of religious truth in one's heart and its expression in one's life. Johann Arndt (d. 1621) understood that Hebrews sought to move readers to repentance and to the living faith that is the Christian's true "substance" (Heb 11:1; *True Christianity* 1.21.9). Accordingly, Arndt recognized that the warnings about those who "crucify the Son of God to themselves" (6:6) and trample his blood underfoot (10:29) are designed to unsettle readers, yet he could also affirm that where there is repentance and faith, forgiveness follows (*True Christianity*, 1.7.8; 1.8.9; 1.9.1; 1.16.11).

3. REFORMED TRADITION

Reformed scholars accepted the canonical status of Hebrews without the ambivalence found among Lutherans, but their views of authorship varied. Pauline authorship was simply affirmed by Ulrich Zwingli (d. 1531; Leipoldt, *Geschichte*, 2.140–41). Johannes Oecolompadius (d. 1531) and Heinrich Bullinger (d. 1575) repeated traditional arguments for this position, adding that 2:3 did not mean that the author received the gospel secondhand, but only that he received it after the other apostles (1 Cor 15:3–8).[59] Moreover, 2 Pet 3:15 says "our beloved brother Paul wrote to you." If 2 Peter was written to Jewish Christians, this pasage could refer to Hebrews, thereby strengthening the case for Pauline authorship.[60]

Anonymous authorship was favored by some interpreters. William Tyndale declined to say who wrote Hebrews, but his preface to Hebrews argues that the book clearly has authoritative status because of the quality of its contents. Passages that appear to deny repentance to the lapsed are no more severe than what the gospels say about the unforgivable sin or what 2 Pet 2 and 2 Tim 3 say about divine judgment. He concluded that the author was a member of the Pauline circle who knew Timothy (Heb 13:23). John Calvin (d. 1564) cited common objections to Pauline authorship, adding that the differences from Paul's other letters cannot be explained by claiming that Hebrews was written in Hebrew and translated into Greek. Hebrews had to have been composed in Greek, since the argument in 9:16–17 cannot be based on the Hebrew word *berît*, which means only "covenant," but must be based on the Greek *diathēkē*, which means both "covenant" and "testament." Nevertheless, Calvin said, "I class it without hesitation among the apostolical writings." The reason seems to have been doctrinal: Hebrews presents the priesthood of Christ and the meaning of his sacrifice more clearly than any other book of the Bible.[61]

---

[59]The primary sources for Oecolompadius and Bullinger, as well as Konrad Pellikan (d. 1556), are found in Hagen, *Hebrews*, 27–35, 42–46.

[60]The Catholic scholar Claude Guilliaud (d. 1551) cited 2 Pet 3:15 as evidence supporting Pauline authorship in a commentary published in 1543 (Hagen, *Hebrews*, 56). This argument was also used by Reformed writers Theodore Beza (ibid., 93), Pool (*Annotations*, 3.808), and Henry (*Commentary*, 6.1240).

[61]See Calvin, *Epistle*, 1–2. In his comments on 13:23 Calvin speculates that Luke or Clement may have authored Hebrews after the death of Paul.

Finally, inspired authorship has been widely affirmed among the Reformed. According to this view, the question is not the identity of the author but whether the author was inspired by the Holy Spirit. The Spirit's influence was discerned by the quality of Hebrews' doctrinal content and its consistency with the whole of Scripture.[62] Some who considered the book to have been inspired thought it fruitless to speculate about the author's identity,[63] but others remained convinced that Paul wrote Hebrews, even though the book's authority did not depend upon the identity of its "penman."[64] Reformed confessional statements listed Hebrews among the canonical Scriptures, although most refrained from taking a position on the author's identity.[65]

Reformed theologians understood the old and new covenants to be different expressions of God's sovereign will for salvation and the ordering of human life. In form, the old covenant was provisional and the new covenant was final, but there was continuity between them. The opening lines of Hebrews affirm that one and the same God spoke through the prophets and in Christ, thereby establishing "the agreement between the Law and the Gospel" (Calvin, *Epistle*, 5). If for Luther the gospel marked the end of the Law, for Calvin the gospel perfected the Law.

People enter a covenant relationship with God by divine election, and the doctrine of election shaped Reformed interpretations of the passages concerning apostasy. The major issue was not whether God could deny salvation to someone—clearly God could do so if he wished—but whether it was possible for someone whom God had elected to fall away. Calvin concluded that the reprobate could exhibit the gifts of the Spirit (6:4–5) and later fall away, whereas the elect would persevere.[66] The interest in election and perseverance is evident at a popular level in the works of John Bunyan (d. 1688), who was troubled by the idea that Esau was not permitted to repent (12:16–17). Bunyan overcame his despair by connecting these texts with other passages that spoke of divine mercy toward sinners. His enormously popular *Pilgrim's Progress* depicts life as an earthly pilgrimage toward the city of God (cf. Heb 11:13–16).[67]

Reformed theologians cited Hebrews when arguing against Roman Catholic practices. Zwingli and Calvin insisted that since Christ was sacrificed once and

---

[62]See Henry, *Commentary*, 6.1240; cf. Beza (Hagen, *Hebrews*, 91) and Gouge, *Commentary*, 1.3–4.

[63]See the Geneva Bible of 1560 and Beza's introduction of 1565 (Hagen, *Hebrews*, 78, 91).

[64]See Beza's preface of 1588 (Hagen, *Hebrews*, 92–93). Those who ask first about the divine authority of Hebrews and only later about the author or "penman" include J. Owen (*Exposition*, 1.25–92) and Henry (*Commentary*, 6.1240).

[65]Page numbers in parentheses refer to Schaff, *Creeds*, vol. 3. In article 3 of the French Confession of 1559 (p. 361), in section 2 of the Irish Articles of Religion of 1615 (p. 527), and in section 2 of the Westminster Confession of 1647 Hebrews is identified as canonical but not listed as a Pauline letter. Article 4 of the Belgic Confession of 1561 includes it among the letters of Paul (p. 386). The Thirty-nine Articles, adopted by the Church of England in 1562, affirms the canonical status of all the commonly accepted NT books in its article 6, but it does not list them (p. 491).

[66]See Calvin, *Epistle*, 76; idem, *Institutes* 3.2.11; 3.3.21; 3.3.23; Jonathan Edwards (d. 1758) in his *Ethical Writings*, 162–65, 751–59; "Notes," 1.808–9.

[67]See Stranahan, "Bunyan"; "Bunyan's Special Talent." Note also Perkins, *Commentary*.

for all, the Mass cannot be a sacrifice. A true sacrifice entails death, so to say that Christ is sacrificed in the Mass means that he is struck down and killed every time the Mass is celebrated, which is absurd since a man dies only once (Heb 9:27). Although some Catholic theologians considered the Mass to be a bloodless sacrifice, Calvin and Zwingli argued that any true sacrifice had to involve the shedding of blood (Heb 9:22), so that to say that a sacrifice is bloodless denies the essential character of sacrifice.[68] On the other hand, Socinian theology prompted Reformed scholars to reaffirm the priestly office of Christ and the necessity of his death as a blood sacrifice made to God in order to satisfy the demands of divine justice.[69]

4. ROMAN CATHOLIC TRADITION

Medieval arguments for Pauline authorship formed the dominant view of Hebrews among Catholic scholars in the early sixteenth century.[70] The consensus was shaken by Cardinal Cajetan (Thomas de Vio, d. 1534), who insisted that Hebrews could not have been written in Hebrew, since the author explained the meaning of the Hebrew name *Melchizedek*, which would have been unnecessary for those who knew the language, and since the argument of 9:16–17 only works on the basis of the Greek word *diathēkē*, which means both "covenant" and "testament." Cajetan listed the doubts of Jerome and other Latin writers concerning Pauline authorship and noted that the author received the gospel secondhand (2:3). Unlike Erasmus, Cajetan challenged the authority as well as the authorship of Hebrews, declaring that "it is not canonical if it is not Paul's" (Hagen, *Hebrews*, 18–20).

Other Roman Catholic scholars vigorously restated the traditional arguments for Pauline authorship, citing Jerome, Theophylact, and others to support their position. The faculty at Paris had condemned Erasmus's position, insisting that the denial of Pauline authorship of Hebrews was "arrogantly and schismatically asserted contrary to the use and determination of the church in many councils."[71] Cajetan's views were similarly condemned at Paris in 1544. The fourth session of the Council of Trent (April 8, 1546) unequivocally included Hebrews among the fourteen letters of Paul.[72]

---

[68]Zwingli, *Defense*, art. 18 (1.92–127); Calvin, *Institutes*, 4.18. Cf. Clark, *Eucharistic Sacrifice*, 395, 400.

[69]J. Owen, *Exposition*, 2.108–24, 139–40, 194–96; 6.301–2.

[70]For example, Steinbach (Feld, *Martin Luthers*, 22–25).

[71]Quoted by Guilliaud; the text is in Hagen, *Hebrews*, 54. Other Catholic rejoinders to Cajetan include Nicholas Le Grand (d. 1560), Gasparo Contarini (d. 1542), and Jean de Gagny (d. 1549) in Hagen, *Hebrews*, 36–39, 46–47, and 48–49 respectively.

[72]On the condemnation of Cajetan see Spicq, *L'Épître*, 1.191, and Tanner, *Decrees*, 2.663–64. After the council, Sixtus of Siena (d. 1599) and Robert Bellarmine (d. 1621) dubbed the books about which there had been no dispute "protocanonical" and those which had been disputed "deuterocanonical." Books in both categories were authoritative (Leipoldt, *Geschichte*, 2.52–54). Note the similar development among Lutherans.

Roman Catholic theologians maintained that the priestly institutions of the old covenant foreshadowed the new covenant, which was instituted by Christ and practiced through his priests who performed the Mass. Kaspar Shatzgeyer (d. 1527) argued that the Mass was a representation of the timeless sacrifice of the cross, since Jesus Christ is "yesterday and today the same—and forever" (Heb 13:8).[73] Although the Protestant reformers attacked the sacrificial understanding of the Mass, Roman Catholic writers responded that Christ was a priest forever after the order of Melchizedek, and since Melchizedek offered bread and wine, the continuance of Christ's priesthood requires the continuance of this offering in the Mass.[74]

The twenty-second session of the Council of Trent (1562) reaffirmed that the Mass was a sacrifice, drawing heavily on Hebrews. There "was no perfection under the former Covenant because of the insufficiency of the Levitical priesthood (Heb 7:11)" so that it was necessary that "another priest arise after the order of Melchizedek (7:15)" who could "make perfect all who were sanctified (10:14)." Christ offered himself once and for all upon the altar of the cross to accomplish this everlasting redemption, but since "his priesthood was not to end with his death (7:24)," he left the church a visible sacrifice. Declaring himself "a priest forever after the order of Melchizedek," Christ "offered his body under the species of bread and wine to God the Father" and gave them "to the disciples (whom He then established as priests of the New Covenant), and ordered them and their successors in the priesthood to offer, saying: 'Do this as a memorial of Me.' " In this "divine sacrifice which is celebrated in the Mass, the same Christ who offered Himself once in a bloody manner (9:14, 26) on the altar of the cross is contained and is offered in an unbloody manner." Therefore, the Mass is truly propitiatory, and those who draw near with true faith and repentance "receive mercy and find grace to help in time of need" (4:16; Neuner and Dupuis, *Christian Faith*, 424–25).

The impact of the council on exegesis can be seen in the commentary by Cornelius à Lapide (d. 1637), which is based on the Latin text, but also uses Greek and Hebrew. His preface affirms the canonical status and Pauline authorship of Hebrews. He repeats the medieval view that 6:4–6 does not deny penance but only prohibits rebaptism. The earthly tent symbolizes the church militant, while the heavenly tent is the church triumphant. There are extensive correlations of the priesthood and sacrifice in Hebrews with the Catholic priesthood and the sacrifice of the Mass, and arguments against the positions of the Socinians and the Reformed.[75]

---

[73]Clark, *Eucharistic Sacrifice*, 84–86, 266, 326; Spicq, *TLNT* 1.244 n. 30.

[74]Johann Eck (d. 1543) held that the Mass was not a bloody sacrifice but a mystical and representative one (Clark, *Eucharistic Sacrifice*, 338). Jerome Emser (d. 1527) argued that Christ by a single sacrifice perfected for all time those who are to be sanctified (Heb 10:14), yet the mystery of the sacrifice is repeated in the Mass (ibid., 391–92).

[75]See also the discussion of the Mass in Lapide, *Commentarius*, on Melchizedek (Heb 7:3, 17), the Levitical sacrifices (8:5; 9:23), the Christian altar and sacrifice (13:10, 15), and the blood of the eternal covenant (13:20).

D. HEBREWS FROM A.D. 1750 TO THE PRESENT[76]

The Reformation and Counter Reformation established theological traditions that shaped the interpretation of Hebrews for centuries. Roman Catholic scholars often gave special emphasis to Christ's priesthood and sacrifice, which provided the basis for worship and ministry within the Catholic Church.[77] Protestants from the Lutheran and Reformed traditions accented Hebrews' emphasis on the Word of God that strengthens faith, and noted the centrality of exhortations to hold fast to the confession (3:1; 4:14–16; 10:23).[78] Liberal scholars followed the humanist idea that Hebrews moves people from lower to higher forms of religious life. They took Christ to be the subject of the most perfect personal religion, which is uniquely able to bring people nearer to God, because his obedient self-offering affects people internally, satisfying the underlying religious need associated with sacrifice.[79]

1. HISTORICAL SETTING

Historical criticism emerged alongside theological interpretation after religious warfare between Protestants and Catholics in Europe formally ended in 1648. Historical study of the Bible is based on the assumption that the texts were shaped by the circumstances in which they were composed. Therefore, scholars could apply to the Bible the same critical questions that would be asked of any piece of ancient literature. The idea was that the interpreter, under the guidance of reason, could stand critically over against tradition. Historical inquiry was not entirely new, for even in antiquity interpreters assumed that information about the context in which Hebrews was written could explain why the author addressed certain topics. What changed was the use of an ever widening range of ancient sources to interpret the biblical text and the formation of new paradigms that sought to locate Hebrews and other early Christian texts within developing streams of early Christian thought.

---

[76]For surveys of research see Buchanan, "Present State"; Carlston, "Commentaries"; Feld, "Hebräerbrief"; idem, *Hebräerbrief*; Grässer, *Aufbruch*, 1–99; P. E. Hughes, "Hebrews"; idem, "Epistle"; C. R. Koester, "Epistle"; McCullough, "Hebrews."

[77]The Second Vatican Council used language from Heb 5:1 in connection with the appointment of priests (W. M. Abbott, *Documents of Vatican II* [New York: Herder and Association, 1966], 536). Cody centers on the heavenly sanctuary and liturgy (*Heavenly*). Swetnam interprets portions of Hebrews in relation to the Eucharist (e.g., "Christology"). Vanhoye's outline of Hebrews gives central place both structurally and theologically to the priestly section of Hebrews (*La structure*, 237–47), and he explores the implications of Hebrews' priestly Christology for patterns of church life (*Old Testament*).

[78]Käsemann's emphasis on the promises that motivate Jesus' followers in their journey of faith was done with special attention to the needs of the embattled Confessing Church in Germany (*Wandering*, 13, 22–48). Bornkamm pointed to the importance of holding fast to the confession in his 1942 essay, "Bekenntnis." Later, the centrality of the Word of God was accented by Grässer (e.g., "Das Heil als Wort" in *Aufbruch*, 129–42).

[79]See Ritschl, *Christian Doctrine*, 472–84; von Harnack, *What Is Christianity?*, 156–58.

Hebrews had traditionally been read as a letter that was written by Paul to Jewish Christians, who were thought to live in or near Jerusalem prior to the destruction of the Temple in A.D. 70. By the end of the twentieth century, however, all of this had changed, as many came to think that Hebrews might be an unknown author's homily to Christians of an indeterminate ethnic background, who may have resided in Italy rather than in Palestine. No consensus emerged on the date of writing. As a result of historical study, Hebrews came to be called the riddle of the New Testament.[80]

Authorship and Authority

Hebrews does not mention the name of its author. The ancient church interpreted the silence in terms of philosophy (see pp. 20–21). Some second-century writers in the east ascribed Hebrews to Paul (p. 21), and medieval interpreters followed church tradition (p. 28). Although the issue was reopened in the sixteenth century (pp. 34–35), the tradition of Pauline authorship remained common until intensive historical investigation overturned it in the nineteenth century. Possible names for the author that had previously been raised were reconsidered, and new theories of authorship were developed. Although the number of candidates is remarkable, there are, with few exceptions, three main options[81]:

(1) Paul.[82] Formally, the personal greetings and warnings in Heb 13:16–25 are similar to those found at the end of Paul's letters. Stylistically, there are similarities in vocabulary, style, and imagery.[83] Theologically, Paul and Hebrews speak of Christ as the one through whom all things were created (Heb 1:1–4; 1 Cor 8:6; 2 Cor 4:4), who was humiliated by his suffering and death, yet exalted to God's right hand (Heb 2:9; Rom 8:3, 34; Phil 2:5–11), thereby abolishing the old Mosaic order and instituting a new covenant (Heb 7:19; 8:6–13; 2 Cor 3:1–18). Historically, Paul was a close associate of Timothy (Heb 13:23), and the hypoth-

---

80For example, E. F. Scott, *Epistle*, 1; Schierse, *Verheissung*, 1; Laub, *Bekenntnis*, 1; Feld, *Hebräerbrief*, 1; Grässer, *Hebräer*, 1.15; Thompson, *Beginnings*, 1; Löhr, "Thronversammlung," 185; idem, "Umriss," 218; Übelacker, *Hebräerbrief*, 11.

81Suggestions that fall outside these categories have met with virtually no acceptance. Peter was proposed by Welch, *Authorship*. The deacon Philip was suggested by Ramsay, *Luke*, 299–328; Kirby, "Authorship," 375–76. Aristion, the elder mentioned by Papias (Eusebius, *Eccl. Hist.* 3.39), was proposed by Chapman, "Aristion," 50–62. Jude was suggested by Dubarle, "Rédacteur." Mary was the author according to Ford, "Mother."

82See especially Storr, *Pauli*, 5–84; Stuart, *Commentary*, 112–49; Lindsay, *Lectures*, 5–18; von Hofmann, *Die heilige*, 5.520–61. Additional nineteenth-century names in Lünnemann, *Critical*, 350–51. In the twentieth century see esp. Leonard, *Authorship*.

83Spicq lists sixty-five words that are found only in Hebrews and the wider Pauline corpus in the NT (*L'Épître*, 1.159). Stylistically, Hebrews and Paul use expressions like *echontes oun* in hortatory sections (Heb 4:14; 10:19; 2 Cor 3:12; 7:1) and *te gar* when making a proposition (Heb 2:11; Rom 1:26; 2 Cor 10:8). Both refer to "the God of peace" (Heb 13:20; Rom 15:33; 16:20; 2 Cor 13:11; Phil 4:9; 1 Thess 5:23). Christians are made to be a spectacle (Heb 10:33; 1 Cor 4:9), and they compete in a spiritual contest (Heb 12:1; Phil 1:20; 1 Thess 2:2; cf. Col 2:1; 1 Tim 6:12; 2 Tim 4:7). On these and other similarities see Spicq, *L'Épître*, 1.155–60.

esis that Paul wrote Hebrews while in prison in Rome would account for the request for prayer and the assertion of a clear conscience (13:18–19), the reference to Timothy's release, the indication that the author was not at liberty to come to his addressees, and the greetings from Italy (13:23–24).

Against direct Pauline authorship, many pointed to the western church's doubts concerning the author's identity (pp. 23, 27) and noted the absence of the usual epistolary introduction.[84] Extensive studies of vocabulary and style demonstrated differences, noted in antiquity, between the Greek used in Hebrews and that used by Paul.[85] Hebrews weaves exposition and exhortation together throughout the epistle rather than placing most of the hortatory material at the end as is common in Paul's letters, and the Scripture citations in Hebrews are introduced with comments indicating that God, his Son, or the Spirit "says" rather than following Paul's pattern of "it is written" or "the Scripture says." Theologically, the view of Christ as high priest plays no role in Paul's letters and Paul's doctrine of justification does not appear in Hebrews. Paul emphasized Jesus' resurrection whereas Hebrews concentrates on his exaltation. Historically, many noted that the author received the gospel secondhand (Heb 2:3) rather than from Christ as Paul did (Gal 1:11–12). By the early twentieth century the theory that Paul wrote Hebrews had few supporters.

Indirect Pauline authorship was advocated by some scholars. Since antiquity, Hebrews was sometimes thought to have been put into its present form by *Luke*, who drew the ideas from Paul, and a few modern scholars have followed this idea.[86] Stylistically, both Luke's gospel and Hebrews begin with intricate sentences that mention the "many" who had spoken previously (Luke 1:1–4; Heb 1:1–4), and like Luke and Acts, Hebrews exhibits a graceful Greek style. Moreover, Luke was not an eyewitness but, like the author of Hebrews, received his information from others (Luke 1:1–4; Heb 2:3). The problem is that nothing in Hebrews points particularly to Luke, and the general similarities in style indicate only that both came from a similar Hellenistic environment. The other ancient

---

[84]See the comments by Schulz and Seyffarth in Stuart, *Commentary*, 150–223.

[85]Hebrews has 154 NT hapax legomena (listed in Spicq, *L'Épître*, 1.157; Ellingworth, *Epistle*, 12–13), which is higher than for the Pauline epistles. Words in Hebrews that are missing from Paul include: *to hagion* ("sanctuary"), *hiereus*, ("priest"), and *archiereus* ("high priest"). Conversely, Hebrews lacks Pauline terms like *apokalypsis, apokalyptein, gnōsis, dikaioun, ethnos, euangelion, katallagē, katallassein, kērygma, kēryssein, kauchesthai, mystērion, nous, oikodomein, oikodomē, parousia, peritomē, plēroun, pneumatikos, sophia, sophos, syn, synergos, tapeinos, tapeinoun, hyparchein, phronein, phronēma, phronimos, physis, charisma,* and *charizesthai*. Paul uses *apostolos* for Christian leaders, but Hebrews uses the term only for Christ (Heb 3:1). Stylistically, Spicq (*L'Épître*, 1.154) notes that the following Pauline expressions are not found in Hebrews: *ei tis, eite, pote, ei de kai, eiper, ektos ei mē, mē pōs, mēketi, men oun*. The same is true of Pauline rhetorical formulas like *tì oun, ti gar, all' erei tis, tí oun eroumen, ereis oun, mē genoito, ouk oidate, touto de phēmi*. Other Pauline formulas are used only once in Hebrews: *ei mē, ei kai, ei ou, hotan, hōste, pōs, pantote*.

[86]A connection between Luke and Hebrews was mentioned by Eusebius (*Eccl. Hist.* 3.38.2; 6.25.14). See p. 21. For sixteenth-century opinion see Calvin's comments on Heb 13:23 (*Epistle*, 216) and Grotius's discussion (Leipoldt, *Geschichte*, 2.153–54 n.3). Nineteenth-century proponents include Delitzsch, *Commentary*, 1.18; Ebrard, *Biblical Commentary*, 615–23, and others. Recently, see D. L. Allen, "Lukan"; D. A. Black, "Pauline."

suggestion was that *Clement of Rome* put Hebrews into its present form. The style and contents of the letter known as *1 Clement* have many similarities to Hebrews, and there was a Clement among Paul's coworkers (Phil 4:3).[87] Yet the relationship of *1 Clement* to Hebrews can best be accounted for by positing a relationship of literary dependance of *1 Clement* upon Hebrews (pp. 22–23).

(2) Companion of Paul. Virtually all the other names proposed for the author of Hebrews are those of Paul's companions. This recognizes that Hebrews' high-priestly Christology does not appear in Paul, and Hebrews' style differs so markedly from the Pauline epistles that Paul himself could not have written Hebrews. Yet Hebrews and Paul's letters do have certain theological affinities, and if the Timothy mentioned in 13:23 is Paul's companion, then the author must have been connected to the Pauline circle[88]:

(a) Barnabas.[89] Barnabas was an early companion of Paul who nevertheless maintained some independence (Acts 13:2; 15:39). He was a Levite (Acts 4:36) who would have been interested in the subject matter of Hebrews. He came from Cyprus and may have been influenced by the kind of Alexandrian thought that seems to have shaped Hebrews.

(b) Apollos.[90] This coworker of Paul (1 Cor 3:5–6; 16:12) was an eloquent Jewish Christian from Alexandria (Acts 18:24). Stylistically, Carpzov's work of 1750 identified many similarities between Hebrews and Philo of Alexandria, especially the idea that earthly things are shadows for eternal heavenly realities. Historically, Apollos was remembered for attempting to show from the Scriptures that Jesus was the Messiah (Acts 18:28), and Hebrews too develops christological arguments on the basis of the OT.

(c) Silas (Silvanus). Historically Silas worked with Timothy, whose name appears in Heb 13:23 (see Acts 17:14–15; 18:5; 2 Cor 1:19; 1 Thess 1:1; 2 Thess 1:1). Stylistically, Hebrews has affinities with 1 Peter (pp. 57–58), and since Silas was said to have written 1 Peter (1 Pet 5:12), he could also have written Hebrews.[91]

---

[87]The theory that Clement of Rome put Hebrews into its present form was noted by Eusebius (*Eccl. Hist.* 3.38.2–3; 6.25.14). In the sixteenth century Erasmus noted it as a good possibility at the end of his *Adnotationes* on Hebrews (*Opera*, 6.1024). In the modern period it was favored mainly by Roman Catholic scholars (see, e.g., Bisping, *Erklärung*; Seisenberger, *Erklärung*, 11–13). On June 24, 1914, the Pontifical Biblical Commission affirmed that Hebrews was genuinely Pauline, but left open the possibility that it was put into its present form by someone else (NJBC, 1172).

[88]In addition, Timothy was suggested by Legg ("Our Brother," 22–23), and Epaphras (Col 1:6–7; 4:12–13) was proposed by C. P. Anderson ("Hebrews"; cf. Jewett, *Letter*, 7–9).

[89]In antiquity, Gregory of Elvire (see Battifol, "De l'attribution"). Modern scholars include B. Weiss, *Brief*, 18–19; Riggenbach, *Brief*, XXXVIII–LXIII. See the extended listing in Spicq, *L'Épître*, 1.199–200.

[90]Apollos was proposed by Luther (p. 35). On nineteenth-century proponents see Bleek, *Brief*, 1.423–30; Tholuck, *Kommentar*, 78–95; Lünnemann, *Critical*, 364–67 (with additional names listed on p. 365). In the twentieth century see Spicq, *L'Épître*, 1.209–19; idem, "Apollos," 365–90; Montefiore, *Commentary*, 9–11.

[91]See Mynster, "Untersuchung," 91–140; Böhme, *Epistola*, preface. See recently Barr, "Structure," 64.

(d) Priscilla and Aquila. Paul's fellow tentmaker Aquila was occasionally proposed as the author of Hebrews, but greater attention focused on Priscilla.[92] Stylistically, the author sometimes uses the plural "we," which suggests that Hebrews was sent from two or more people (e.g., 13:18), yet the occasional use of "I" (e.g., 13:22) indicates that one person was primarily responsible for the work. Historically, Hebrews may have been written to a house church in Rome, and this would be suitable for Aquila and Priscilla, since they hosted a house church in Rome (Rom 16:3–5). They were well acquainted with Timothy and Paul since both men had spent time with them at Corinth and Ephesus (Acts 18–19; Rom 16:3–5, 21; 2 Tim 4:19). The possibility of Priscilla having written it is suggested by the fact that her name is often given before that of her husband. She was a capable teacher who, along with Aquila, had instructed Apollos (Acts 18:26). Von Harnack argued that the name of the author may have been suppressed because ecclesiastical practice opposed the idea that women could serve as teachers. One serious objection to this theory is that the author uses a masculine participle when referring to himself in 11:32.

(3) Unknown Author. Origen commented that the identity of the author of Hebrews is known to God alone, and this view has been widely adopted by scholars.[93] Hebrews does not include the author's name, and all attempts to overcome the anonymity remain speculative. Historically, no firm correlations can be made between Hebrews and known episodes in the life of the first-century church or its leaders (pp. 50–52). Theologically, Hebrews' presentation of Christ's priesthood is unique among early Christian writings, and the elements that are not peculiar to Hebrews are generally found in a number of other sources, making it difficult to connect Hebrews with any one line of NT thought (pp. 54–58).[94] The vocabulary and style of Hebrews have affinities with various writings, including the Lukan writings,[95] 1 Peter,[96] and the letters of Paul (pp. 42–44, 54–56), yet Hebrews is distinctive enough that it cannot be clearly identified with any known writer.

---

[92]The possibility that Aquila wrote Hebrews was seriously considered by Bleek (*Brief*, 1.420–22), but he thought Apollos more likely. Von Harnack argued that Priscilla was the primary author in "Probabilia"; cf. Hoppin, *Priscilla*, 13–116. More recently, Priscilla's authorship has been advocated by Kittredge, "Hebrews," 430–34. Priscilla's authorship is rejected by D'Angelo, "Hebrews," 364–65.

[93]Among the nineteenth-century scholars who acknowledged that the author's identity was unknown were Moll, Ewald, von Soden, Ménégoz, Rendall, Westcott, A. B. Bruce, and Milligan. Among twentieth-century scholars are Attridge, Bénétreau, Ellingworth, Grässer, D. Guthrie, Hagner, Hegermann, Lane, Michel, and H.-F. Weiss.

[94]The high Christology in Heb 1:1–4 bears some resemblance to Col 1:15–20; Phil 2:5–11; 1 Tim 3:16; John 1:1–18. The emphasis on Jesus' divine sonship and the application of Ps 110:1 to Christ are common in early Christian sources. See further §3 COMMENT A.

[95]Among the similarities with Luke and Acts is the idea that Jesus is the Pioneer or Author (*archēgos*) of faith (Heb 2:10; 12:2; Acts 3:15; 5:31) and the use of words like *hilaskesthai*, *hierateia*, *katapausis*, and *lytrōsis* (see Lünnemann, *Critical*, 356–63; Spicq, *L'Épître*, 1.98 n. 3).

[96]Hebrews and 1 Peter share some distinctive vocabulary: *ekousiōs*, *ennoia*, *parepidēmos*, *planōmenoi*, *sympathein-sympathēs*. Jesus is the great or chief shepherd (Heb 13:20; 1 Pet 2:25). The term *antitypos* is also used, but in different senses (Heb 9:24; 1 Pet 3:21).

The authoritative status of Hebrews was reconsidered in light of these historical uncertainties. Johann David Michaelis (d. 1791) said that if Hebrews "was written by the apostle Paul, it is canonical. But if it was not written by an apostle, it is not canonical: for however excellent its contents may be, they alone will not oblige us to receive it as a work inspired by the Deity."[97] The American scholar Moses Stuart (d. 1852) tried to secure the status of Hebrews by demonstrating that Paul wrote it, although ironically the extensive arguments in his commentary show how difficult it is to prove Paul's authorship. Johann Salomo Semler (d. 1791) did not think that Paul wrote Hebrews, but insisted that historical uncertainty did not affect the book's status. The main criterion was Hebrews' usefulness in teaching morality.[98]

Roman Catholics regularly understand the biblical canon to have been developed by the church and continue to include Hebrews within the canon because of church tradition. This tradition also makes it possible to debate the question of authorship on historical grounds without making the book's status dependent upon scholarly consensus. Protestants commonly understand the church to have come into being as a response to the gospel. The church does not so much create the canon, as it recognizes in certain writings the authority of the message upon which the church is based. What is finally important is the intrinsic or self-authenticating quality of a book like Hebrews, not a decision about authorship.[99]

Addressees

Traditionally, the people addressed by Hebrews were understood to have been Jewish Christians. In the nineteenth century, there emerged a line of thought that conceived of them as Gentile Christians, or perhaps a mixed group. Historically, however, little can be said about their background prior to entering the Christian community.

(1) Jewish Christian Readership. The title "To the Hebrews" was affixed to the book by the end of the second century. Although the title could have been given to the book by Christians who possessed a now lost salutation or a reliable tradition, it seems more likely that the title is a second-century inference based on the book's contents. Therefore, the title is of little value for historical reconstruction (§1 COMMENT).

The contents of Hebrews would have been of interest to Jewish Christians.[100] The book is replete with OT quotations and allusions. Its arguments compare

---

[97]Quoted in Kümmel, *New Testament*, 72.

[98]Semler, "Beiträgen," 5, 15–16. Cf. Kümmel, *New Testament*, 62–68.

[99]For a nuanced presentation of a Catholic approach to the canon see R. E. Brown, *NJBC*, 1053. For Protestant discussions see Bleek, *Brief*, 1.470–71; Moll, "Epistle," 2; A. B. Bruce, *Epistle*, 24; Westcott, *Epistle*, lxxix. Metzger maintains that the authority of Hebrews rests on its "intrinsic worth" rather than its authorship (*Canon*, 286).

[100]For example, F. F. Bruce; Buchanan; D. Guthrie; Kistemaker; Lane; Strobel; C. P. Anderson, "Who Are"; Dunnill, *Covenant*, 24–29; Feld, "Hebräerbrief," 3588; Isaacs, *Sacred*, 22–45; Lindars, *Theology*, 4–15; Rissi, *Theologie*, 24; Walker, *Jesus*, 216–21.

and contrast the wilderness generation with the early church, the old covenant with the new, the Levitical high priesthood with Christ's high priesthood, and the sacrifices prescribed by Mosaic Law with Christ's singular sacrifice. The intended recipients are by implication "descendants of Abraham" (2:16) and "sons" of God (2:10)—an expression that could be used for Israel (cf. Deut 14:1; Hos 11:1). In addition to the OT, examples are taken from the stories of the Maccabean martyrs (Heb 11:36–38; 2 Macc 5:27; 6:1–7:42; 10:6), who were remembered for their fidelity to the Mosaic Law. The author expects listeners to recognize the angelic mediation of the Mosaic Law (Heb 2:2–3), to be interested in regulations about food (9:10; 13:9–10), and to follow Jewish exegetical techniques, like the *gezērah šāwāh* and argument from silence (NOTES and COMMENT on 4:4–5 and 7:3). Those who think that Hebrews was addressed to Jewish Christians usually understand the occasion to have been the threat of some Christians reverting to Judaism. In order to keep the intended readers within the Christian community, the author seeks to show Christ's superiority to the institutions of Judaism.

(2) Gentile Christian Readership. Other interpreters find evidence that Hebrews was written for Gentile Christians.[101] Repentance from dead works (6:1) and enlightenment (6:4; 10:32) were ways of speaking about conversion from paganism. Warnings about falling away from the living God (3:12) and avoiding strange teachings (13:9) might mean that listeners were attracted to the strange teachings of Hellenistic syncretism, while the exhortation to honor marriage (13:4) could counter the ascetic tendencies of some Hellenistic groups. Although much of Hebrews' argument is based on material from the OT, the fact that Paul makes extensive use of the OT in his letters to Rome, Corinth, and Galatia shows that an author could use such OT arguments when writing to predominantly Gentile congregations.

Those who think that the addressees were of Gentile background often hold that Hebrews was written rather late, probably in the final decades of the first century. Since Hebrews does not reflect the tensions between Jewish and Gentile Christianity that are evident in Paul's letters, one can argue that the distinction between Jewish and Gentile Christians had become a thing of the past. The author addresses his readers simply as Christians. Those who favor a Gentile Christian readership generally argue that the listeners were not in danger of reverting to Judaism, but of giving way to the fatigue and discouragement that was typical of second-generation Christians.[102]

(3) Indeterminate Ethnic Background. Hebrews does not give us enough information to know whether the addressees were of Jewish or Gentile background, and the group could have been mixed.[103] On the one hand, Jewish

---

[101]The theory was first proposed by Röth, *Epistolam*. See also von Soden, "Hebräerbrief"; Braun, *Hebräer*, 2; Delville, "L'Epître"; Hegermann, *Brief*, 10; H.-F. Weiss, *Brief*, 71. Schmithals thinks they were Gentile God-fearers ("Über Empfänger").

[102]Von Soden, *Brief*, 14–15; Käsemann, *Wandering*, 25; H.-F. Weiss, *Brief*, 70–72.

[103]Ellingworth, *Epistle*, 21–27; Eisenbaum, *Jewish Heroes*, 7–11; Larsson, "How Mighty"; Trotter, *Interpreting*, 28–31.

Christians were most clearly defined by practicing circumcision, keeping kosher, and observing the Sabbath, along with confessing Jesus to be the Messiah, yet Hebrews makes no mention of circumcision and speaks only of an eschatological sabbath rest, not the weekly sabbath (4:1–10). The author relegates food laws to the realm of the flesh and a time that is past (9:9–10; 13:9), but if listeners had been committed to keeping the food laws at the time Hebrews was written, the author would probably have needed more extended arguments concerning their obsolescence. On the other hand, if the listeners were of Gentile background, one might expect a clearer indication of this, as in other NT letters (cf. 1 Thess 1:9; Gal 4:8; Rom 1:5–6; 1 Pet 4:3–4). If listeners were in danger of reverting to Greco-Roman religious beliefs, there would probably have been some clearer mention of threats posed by idolatry (cf. 1 Cor 8:1–13; 10:14–30). Although the texts could apply to those who converted from a Gentile background, they could also apply to converts from Judaism (NOTES on Heb 3:12; 6:1).

A simple distinction between Jewish and Gentile Christians does not help the interpretation of Hebrews. The one first-century Christian named in Hebrews is Timothy (Heb 13:23), who was the son of a Greek father and a Jewish Christian mother (Acts 16:1–3), and who was circumcised yet worked primarily among Gentiles. The author's circle included Italian Christians (Heb 13:24), and by the mid-first century these churches were almost certainly mixed. Some of the Christians in Rome were of Jewish descent, like Aquila and Priscilla (Rom 16:3), but most bear Greek and Latin names (e.g., Rom 16:10–11, 14–15), and Paul considers them Gentiles (Rom 1:5–6). In the 60s of the first century, the Roman populace regarded Christians simply as "Christians" (Tacitus, *Annals* 15.44). Therefore, instead of seeking to identify the listeners' ethnic background, we do well to consider the complex way in which they would have related to the dominant Greco-Roman culture, Jewish subculture, and Christian community (see pp. 73–79).

Destination

Speculation about the location of the addressees has produced many proposals.[104] Jerusalem and Rome are the most common, with Rome currently deemed the most plausible:

(1) Jerusalem. Interpreters since at least the fourth century have thought that Hebrews was sent to Christians in Jerusalem on the assumption that the Tabernacle and Levitical priesthood would have been most significant for those living near the Temple. Since the author extends the greetings of "those from Italy" in

[104]Spain was suggested by Nicolaus of Lyra (d. 1340). For proposals from the eighteenth and early nineteenth centuries see Lünnemann, *Critical*, 367–68. For proposals from the late nineteenth and early twentieth centuries see D. Guthrie, *Introduction*, 711–15; F. F. Bruce, "To the Hebrews," 3513–19; Spicq, *L'Épître*, 231–42. Alexandria was often suggested in the nineteenth century (see the summary in Milligan, *Theology*, 44–45). Among the more recent proposals are Corinth (Montefiore), Colossae (Jewett) and Asia Minor (Dunnill, *Covenant*, 23–24).

13:24, many assumed that Hebrews was sent from Italy to Jerusalem.[105] Objections are that it seems unlikely that the author would have written to people in Jerusalem in an elegant Greek style, basing his arguments on the LXX, even where the LXX differs from the MT. The group addressed by Hebrews apparently did not include any who heard Jesus preach (2:3), and the author chided them for not yet being teachers (5:11–14), neither of which seems apt for the Jerusalem congregation. The entire discussion of Levitical institutions is done with reference to the ancient Tabernacle; *no reference is made to the Jerusalem Temple*. Finally, it is not clear that the persecutions mentioned in 10:32–34 included any deaths, although persecutions in Jerusalem led to the deaths of Stephen and James the apostle (Acts 7:58–8:3; 12:1–2).

(2) Rome. Rome was suggested as the destination of Hebrews in the mid-eighteenth century, and it has found increasing support.[106] Internal evidence includes the remark that "those from Italy send you greetings" (13:24), which probably means that some Italians who were living outside of Italy were sending greetings back home (NOTE on 13:24). The title "leader" (*hēgoumenos*, 13:7, 17, 24) fits a Roman destination, since the similar title *proēgoumenos* was used in literature associated with early Roman Christianity (*1 Clem.* 1:3; 21:6; Herm. *Vis.* 2.2.6; 3.9.7). External evidence also supports a Roman destination. *First Clement*, which was written in Rome near the end of the first century, incorporates material from Hebrews (pp. 22–23). Hebrews is the only NT text to declare that it is impossible to restore to repentance someone who has fallen away (Heb 6:4–8; 10:26; 12:7), and this point is taken up several times in the Shepherd of Hermas, another Roman text. This shows that the issue posed by Hebrews was debated by Christians in Rome in the second century (see p. 23). Affinities with 1 Peter (pp. 57–58) are consistent with a Roman destination, since 1 Peter was probably written from Rome (1 Pet 5:13).

What little is known about early Roman Christianity seems congruent with the character of the audience presupposed by Hebrews. The earliest Christians in the region were probably affiliated with the Jewish communities in Puteoli and Rome (Josephus, *J.W.* 2.104; Philo, *Embassy* 155). In A.D. 49 the emperor Claudius expelled Jews from Rome because of a certain "Chrestus," which probably refers to a dispute over Christ (see p. 51). Hebrews was probably written to one house church within a larger Christian community (pp. 73–74), and by A.D. 60 there were a number of house churches in Rome (Rom 16:3–5, 14, 15) and some Christians in Puteoli (Acts 28:13–15). Timothy, who is mentioned in Heb 13:23, was known to the Roman congregation (Heb 13:23; Rom 16:21). Al-

---

[105]Chrysostom identified Jerusalem as the location, and he was followed by most medieval interpreters. In the nineteenth century see the commentaries by Stuart, Lünnemann, Westcott, A. B. Bruce. In the twentieth century see commentaries by Spicq, Buchanan, and P. E. Hughes; cf. Isaacs, *Sacred*, 45.

[106]Proponents of a Roman destination include Wettstein, *Novum*, 2.386–87; Milligan, *Theology*, 49–50; von Harnack, "Probabilia." More recently see F. F. Bruce, *Epistle*, 13–14; Casalini, *Agli*, 53–55; Ellingworth *Epistle*, 29; Kistemaker, *Hebrews*, 17–18; Lane, *Hebrews*, lviii–lx; H.-F. Weiss, *Brief*, 76; Brown and Meier, *Antioch*, 142–49; Backhaus, "Hebräerbrief," 196–99.

though many members seem to have been of Gentile background (Rom 1:5–6,13–15), Jewish Christians like Prisca and Aquila remained important (Rom 16:3). Paul's letter to the Romans and *1 Clement* suggest that they retained a high level of interest in their Jewish heritage. Many Roman Christians—like much of the city's population—were probably *peregrini* from the provinces, who would understand what it meant to be resident aliens in the earthly city (Heb 11:8, 13–16; 13:14; cf. Lampe, *Die stadtrömischen*, 53–64, 117, 297, 347). At the very least, reading Hebrews with "those from Italy" in mind helps contemporary interpreters consider what the message of Jesus' divine sonship and high priesthood would have meant for those living in an interreligious environment.

Date

Hebrews was probably written between about A.D. 60 and A.D. 90. A more precise date is difficult to determine:

(1) Persons. "Our brother Timothy" (13:23) is the only one of the author's contemporaries to be named in Hebrews. Timothy has apparently been in prison but has now been released and is going to travel to meet those addressed by Hebrews. If this Timothy is the companion of Paul, it means that Hebrews was written in the last half of the first century, after Timothy's conversion and before his death. The dates of Timothy's life can only be approximated. Timothy was old enough to travel with Paul in about A.D. 49 (Acts 16:1–3), and it is conceivable that he was still able to travel toward the end of the first century, although a date beyond A.D. 90 seems unlikely.

Other important persons are the "leaders" of the community, some of whom had apparently died before Hebrews was written (13:7). The author says that the message of salvation was first proclaimed by the Lord, then "validated for us by those who heard" (2:3). The text implies that these evangelists belonged to the first Christian generation, without necessarily indicating that they had personally heard Jesus preach (NOTE on 2:3). Much of the evangelistic work of this generation took place in the 40s and 50s A.D., but nothing more precise can be said about the time that the community was established. The reference to the "outcome" of the leaders' conduct in 13:7 suggests that not just one, but several have died, and probably not by martyrdom (NOTE on 13:7). By speaking in such general terms of the deaths of the community's leaders, the author implies that a generation of leaders has passed. This would mean that Hebrews was probably not written before the 60s A.D.

(2) Events. Hostile actions against the Christian community had taken place prior to the writing of Hebrews (10:32). Since the author asks listeners to "remember" this experience, it would seem that a number of years have elapsed since it occurred (pp. 67–71). Acts and Paul's letters mention various occasions on which Paul and his companions were beaten or imprisoned, but Hebrews refers to hostility against the community itself, not simply against itinerant evangelists.

Events mentioned in Hebrews cannot be connected with known occurrences of Christian martyrdom, such as the deaths of Stephen and James in Jerusalem in the 30s and 40s (Acts 7:58–8:3; 12:1–2) or those of Peter and Paul in Rome under Nero in the 60s (Eusebius, *Eccl. Hist.* 2.25.4–5; 3.1.2–3). No reference is made to Christians being killed during the incident recalled in Heb 10:32–34. The author does exhort listeners to remember past leaders, to "consider the outcome of their conduct and imitate their faithfulness" (13:7), which is sometimes understood in terms of martyrdom. Although this almost certainly refers to the leaders' deaths, "outcome" does not clearly mean martyrdom. Elsewhere the author calls listeners to imitate Abraham and others (6:12), all of whom "died in faith" (11:13), but not by martyrdom (NOTE on 13:7).

The mention of Italy in 13:24 might suggest that the hostilities took place in Rome. The edict of Claudius, which expelled Jews or Jewish Christians from Rome in A.D. 49, is a possible point of contact.[107] Acts 18:2 says that at Corinth Paul "found a Jew named Aquila, a native of Pontus, who had recently come from Italy with his wife Priscilla, because Claudius had ordered all Jews to leave Rome." It seems likely that Aquila and Priscilla left Rome as Jewish Christians, since there is no suggestion that Paul brought them to faith or baptized them, as he did others in Corinth (Acts 18:8). The willingness of Aquila and Priscilla to house and work with a Christian missionary makes it virtually certain that they were Christians prior to meeting Paul. Although they are called Jews, this term can refer to Jewish Christians (Acts 16:1, 20; 21:39; 22:3). The expulsion was apparently not permanent, for by the late 50s Priscilla and Aquila had returned to Rome, where they hosted a house church (Rom 16:3).

Suetonius's record of the event reads: "*Iudaeos impulsore Chresto adsidue tumultuantes Roma expulit*" (*Claudius* 25.4). The text can be translated, "He expelled from Rome the Jews constantly making disturbances at the instigation of Chrestus." The name Chrestus was common among Romans but is not attested to be a Jewish name, and it probably is a variant form of Christos. Such confusion in spelling was not unusual.[108] It therefore seems likely that disorder broke out in one or more synagogues where some Jews claimed that Jesus was the Christ (cf. Acts 6:9–15; 13:45, 50; 14:2, 5, 19; 18:12–17). The edict probably did not expel from Rome the entire Jewish community, which apparently numbered in the thousands, but only those responsible for the disturbance.[109]

---

[107]The date of the edict is disputed. A.D. 49 is given as the year by Orosius (*History* 7.6.15–16). Although this reference is questionable, it fits the evidence from Acts, which says that Aquila and Priscilla had come to Corinth recently, perhaps one to two years before Gallio became proconsul about A.D. 52 (Acts 18:2, 11, 12). See Lampe, *Die stadtrömischen*, 4–9. On the edict and its connections with Hebrews see Lane, *Hebrews*, 1.lxiii–lxvi, with extensive bibliography; F. F. Bruce, *Epistle*, 269–70; Feld, "Hebräerbrief," 3591.

[108]On the frequency of "Chrestos" and the feminine "Chreste" see Lampe, *Die stadtrömischen*, 6; Lane, *Hebrews*, 1.lxv. For texts replacing the *i* in *Christos* and *Christianos* with an *e* see Tacitus, *Annals* 15.44; Tertullian, *Apology* 3; *To the Nations* 1.3; Lactantius, *Divine Institutes* 4.7. In the NT the Greek MS Sinaiticus replaces the *i* with an *ē* in *Christianos* (Acts 11:26; 26:28; 1 Pet 4:16). For arguments that "Chrestos" was not Christ, but the name of one of the disputants see Benko, "Pagan," 1059.

[109]On the size and history of the Jewish community at Rome see Schürer, et al., *History*, 3.73–81. Acts 18:2 says that Claudius expelled "all" Jews from Rome, but this is probably hyperbolic. Acts often uses "all" in a generalizing sense (e.g., 1:8; 3:9, 11; 19:27; 21:27). Suetonius's comment on page

Details of the events that occurred under Claudius are lacking, but it is possible that the disturbance over Chrestos involved the kind of verbal reproach for the sake of Christ that those addressed by Hebrews experienced (Heb 10:32; 11:25–26; 13:13). Those who were expelled from Rome would have suffered the loss of possessions. Although accounts of Claudius's edict do not mention imprisonment, it is possible that some were arrested before being expelled. Hebrews 10:32–34 does not mention expulsion from the city, but the depiction of the people of God as "foreigners and transients" who have no abiding city on earth (11:13–16; 13:14) might suggest that some in the community had experienced the temporary loss of homes. By the time Hebrews was written, however, at least some members of the community had homes from which to extend hospitality (13:2).

Connections with other known persecutions are difficult to make. A few connect Heb 10:32–34 with the persecution that took place under Nero after the fire of A.D. 64 (Windisch; Strathmann; Kistemaker), but this seems improbable. Tacitus says under Nero the Christians "were covered in wild beasts' skins and torn to pieces by dogs; or were fastened to crosses and set on fire in order to serve as torches by night when daylight failed" (*Annals* 15.44.6). The lack of any reference to the deaths of Christians in Heb 10:32–34 makes a connection with Nero's persecution unlikely. Spicq (*L'Épître*, 1.240–41) connected Hebrews to the persecutions in Jerusalem that resulted in the deaths of Stephen and the Apostle James (Acts 7:58–8:3; 12:1–2; 1 Thess 2:14–16), but unless one finds in Heb 13:7 an allusion to the martyrdoms of the church's leaders, a connection with the violence in Jerusalem seems unlikely.

If Hebrews was addressed to Rome, it could have been written about A.D. 60–65 to a community that was able to recall earlier conflict, perhaps the disturbance in A.D. 49 under Claudius.[110] During the 60s, the Christians had not yet "shed blood" (Heb 12:4). The animosity they experienced from the wider society (11:26; 13:13) fits with Tacitus's comment that before Nero's persecution began, Christians were already "hated" by the populace (*Annals* 15.44). If Hebrews was written to Rome in the 70s or 80s, one must assume that in 10:32–34 the author recalls the experience of Christians who did not experience the brunt of Nero's persecution (Attridge, *Epistle*, 8). If Hebrews was addressed to Christians living elsewhere in the Greco-Roman world, however, then no clear correlations can be made with known outbreaks of hostility.

(3) Destruction of the Temple. Hebrews does not mention the Jerusalem Temple. Israel's sanctuary and the Levitical priesthood are discussed solely in terms of the Tabernacle and priestly practices outlined in the Pentateuch. Arguments centering on the Tabernacle would have been suitable either before or after the Temple's destruction in A.D. 70. Before 70, the author might have focused on the Tabernacle because the Mosaic statutes concerning the Tabernacle

---

51 could be translated, "Since the Jews constantly made disturbances at the instigation of Chrestus, he [Claudius] expelled them from Rome." This too would suggest that the entire Jewish community was forced to leave. An incident of this magnitude seems unlikely, however, since Josephus does not mention it. See Lampe, *Die stadrömischen*, 7.

[110]F. F. Bruce, *Epistle*, 20–22; Lane, *Hebrews*, lxvi; Ellingworth, *Epistle*, 33.

constituted the divinely revealed basis for the sanctuary and the priestly practices of subsequent generations. Descriptions of the Tabernacle were available through the Jewish Law, even to those who lived outside of Palestine and who had never seen the Temple. Yet these same factors also obtained after A.D. 70. Although the Temple was destroyed, it was not immediately clear that it would not be rebuilt, and later rabbinic sources include rulings concerning sacrifices. Accordingly, Hebrews' interest in the Law's enduring provisions for a sanctuary could have been designed to move Christians away from hope for a restoration of the old order and toward the new life in Christ.[111] Moreover, Jewish authors interpreted the Tabernacle apologetically, helping to foster a sense of Jewish identity within the Greco-Roman world both before and after A.D. 70 (§22 COMMENT *a*). Therefore, to foster a distinctly Christian sense of identity among his readers, the author of Hebrews might have thought it important to reinterpret the Tabernacle in light of Christ, whether he wrote before or after A.D. 70.

Hebrews often refers to the activity of the Levitical priesthood in the present tense, as if sacrifices were still being offered in the sanctuary (7:27–28; 8:3–5; 9:6–7, 25; 10:1–3, 8; 13:10–11). This could mean that the author wrote before the Temple's destruction, although this is not necessarily the case. Decades after the destruction, Josephus could say that Jews "offer perpetual sacrifices" for the emperor and people of Rome, and "perform these ceremonies daily, at the expense of the whole Jewish community" (*Ag. Ap.* 2.77; cf. 2.193–98).[112] His reasons were apologetic: the present tense emphasizes continuity in the Jewish tradition and its respect for Roman order. In Christian sources, *1 Clem.* 40–41 refers to priestly ministry in the present tense in order to establish a general principle that Christians should not transgress rules of order. In *Diogn.* 3, Jewish sacrificial practices are described in the present tense in order to discredit Judaism, since those who offer sacrifice assume that God needs something (Porter, "Date").

Rhetorically, Hebrews differs somewhat from the writers just mentioned. After insisting that the continual offering of Levitical sacrifices shows their ineffectiveness, the author asks, "Otherwise would they not have ceased to be offered?" (10:2). The question expects that listeners will agree with the author, instead of pointing out that sacrifices have in fact ceased being offered because of the Temple's destruction. This might favor an early date, although the lack of any reference to the Temple makes this argument less than decisive.

(4) Literary Relationships. The earliest text to have made use of Hebrews is *1 Clement* (pp. 22–23), which is often thought to have been written about A.D. 96. This date assumes that "the sudden and repeated misfortunes and calamities which have befallen us" (*1 Clem.* 1) are persecutions under Domitian. The extent to which there was a persecution of Christians under Domitian is disputed, however, and if this connection cannot be made, then dates for *1 Clement* might range from A.D. 70 to 140, or more narrowly, 90 to 120.[113] This means that He-

[111]Dunn, *Partings*, 87; cf. Isaacs, *Sacred*, 67.

[112]Josephus often uses the present tense when discussing the Tabernacle, priestly vestments, and sacrifices (*Ant.* 3.102–87, 224–57), but this could be attributed to narrative style.

[113]Attridge, *Epistle*, 6–8; L. L. Welborn, *ABD* 1.1060.

brews would have been written before the end of the first or perhaps the early second century, but little else can be determined by its relationship to *1 Clement*.

No firm conclusions about the date of composition can be reached on the basis of the evidence noted above. Attempts to date Hebrews by means of its theological development are equally uncertain, since the high Christology of 1:1–4 is comparable to that attested in the Pauline corpus (1 Cor 8:6; Phil 2:6–11; cf. Col 1:15–17). Similarities to 1 Peter might suggest that both come from roughly the same period, yet since the date of 1 Peter is disputed, the similarities do not clarify the date of Hebrews. Many recent scholars find that a pre-70 date best accounts for the reference to persecution (10:32–34) and the absence of any reference to the destruction of the Temple.[114] Others prefer a date in the 80s or 90s, understanding the text to be dealing with the fatigue of second-generation Christians or a sense of loss over the destruction of Jerusalem.[115] Given existing evidence, a date between A.D. 60 and 90 is plausible, but greater specificity is tenuous. Interpretation cannot assume or preclude the existence of the Temple, or rely on connections with persecutions known from other sources.

2. CHRISTIAN ORIGINS

Attempts to ascertain the occasion for the composition of Hebrews have been accompanied by efforts to locate it within the stream of early Christianity. A paradigm that sought to trace developments within NT writings emerged within the nineteenth century, and the paradigm coincided with a changing view of Christianity itself. Interpreters no longer assumed that the NT church was a unified whole, but saw within it groups that exhibited different and sometimes conflicting viewpoints—like the church of their own time. As in the natural sciences, there was interest in creating a taxonomy of early Christian writings. Strong internal connections made it feasible to speak of the developments that took place within the Synoptic tradition, the Pauline tradition, and the Johannine tradition. Many have tried to locate Hebrews within either the Pauline or a Jewish Christian tradition, but Hebrews resists easy placement, calling the adequacy of existing categories into question.

Pauline Christianity

Paul almost certainly did not write Hebrews, but there remain affinities between Hebrews and Pauline Christianity.[116] In content, Hebrews and the Pauline letters proclaim that the preexistent Son of God (Heb 1:2, 3, 6; 1 Cor 8:6; Phil 2:5–6; Col 1:15–17) humbled himself to become human (Heb

---

[114]Bénétreau; F. F. Bruce; Casalini; Ellingworth; D. Guthrie; Hagner; P. E. Hughes; Lane; Lindars, *Theology*, 19–20; idem, "Hebrews"; Strobel; Vanhoye, *TRE* 14.497; cf. Feld, *Hebräerbrief*, 14–18; Walker, *Jesus*, 227–32.

[115]Braun; Grässer; Hegermann; Kistemaker; Smith; H.-F. Weiss; cf. Eisenbaum, *Jewish Heroes*, 7; Isaacs, *Sacred*, 67.

[116]See Backhaus, "Hebräerbrief," 187–90; Hurst, *Epistle*, 107–24.

2:14–17; Rom 8:3; Gal 4:4–5; Phil 2:7). In obedience to God (Heb 5:8; Rom 5:19; Phil 2:8) he offered himself (Heb 9:28; 1 Cor 5:7; Gal 2:20; Eph 5:2) by shedding his blood (Heb 9:11–14; 10:19, 29; 12:24; 13:12, 20; Rom 3:25; 5:9; 1 Cor 10:16; 11:27; Eph 1:7; 2:13; Col 1:20) to provide redemption (Heb 9:12, 15; Rom 3:24; 1 Cor 1:30; Eph 1:7, 14; 4:30; Col 1:14) and atonement (Heb 2:17; Rom 3:25), once for all (Heb 7:27; 9:12, 26; 10:10; Rom 6:9–10). He overcame cosmic powers (Heb 2:14; Col 2:15), was exalted (Heb 1:1–14; Eph 1:20–21; Phil 2:9; Col 2:10), has received a name above all others (Heb 1:4; Phil 2:9), and all shall be subjected to him (Heb 2:8; 1 Cor 15:25–28; Phil 2:10; 3:21). At present, he intercedes with God for others (Heb 7:25; 9:24; Rom 8:34). Christ's work changed or abrogated statutes of the Law (Heb 7:11–19; Gal 3:23–29) and instituted a new covenant (Heb 7:22; 8:6–13; 9:15; 2 Cor 3:6). Christian life is characterized by faith (Heb 11; Rom 4; Gal 2:16–21).

Arguments in Hebrews and Paul's letters rely on Hab 2:4 when discussing faith (Heb 10:38; Rom 1:17; Gal 3:11), connect Ps 110:1 with Ps 8 (Heb 1:3, 13; 2:6–8; 1 Cor 15:24–28), and cite Deut 32:35 when referring to divine vengeance (Heb 10:30; Rom 12:19). Abraham exemplifies one who, by faith, inherits the eschatological promises (Heb 6:13–20; 11:17–19; Rom 4; Gal 3:6–9), and the wilderness generation exemplifies unfaithfulness (Heb 3:7–4:11; 1 Cor 10:1–13). Levels of Christian instruction are compared to milk and solid food (Heb 5:12–14; 1 Cor 3:2), faithful perseverance is likened to running a race (Heb 12:1; 1 Cor 9:24–27), and the Greco-Roman *testament* is used to interpret the biblical *covenant* (Heb 9:15–17; Gal 3:15–17). People walk by faith and not by sight (Heb 11:1; 2 Cor 4:18; 5:7; Rom 8:24).

Formally, Hebrews ends with a peroration and requests for prayer (Heb 13:18–19; Rom 15:30–32; Eph 6:19; 1 Thess 5:25; Phlm 22), a benediction (Heb 13:20–21; Rom 15:13; Phil 4:19–20; 1 Thess 5:23), and an epistolary conclusion that includes greetings and a final benediction that is similar to those in the Pauline letters (Heb 13:22–25; 1 Cor 16:19–24; 2 Cor 13:11–13; Eph 6:21–24; Phil 4:21–23). Especially significant is the mention of "our brother Timothy" (13:23), who is almost certainly to be understood as Paul's coworker. There are several ways to account for these similarities:

(1) Dependence of Hebrews upon Paul. Some have argued that the author of Hebrews drew his ideas from Paul's letters, although the absence of any clear echoes of distinctly Pauline expressions and the general differences in writing style and content make it difficult to prove that Hebrews relied on any of Paul's extant writings.[117] It has been more common to identify Hebrews as a development of Pauline theology without positing literary dependence. F. C. Baur (d. 1860) used the Hegelian framework of thesis, antithesis, and synthesis to argue that if Jewish Christianity (the thesis) met its antithesis in the Gentile Christianity of Paul's churches, then Hebrews marks a step toward a synthesis of

---

[117]For arguments for literary dependence see Witherington, "Influence"; von Soden, "Brief," 3; Wrede, *Das literarische*, 53–55. For criticism see Hurst, *Epistle*, 109; Backhaus, "Hebräerbrief"; Schröger, "Hebräerbrief," 211–22. See also Vanhoye, "L'Epître aux Ephesians."

Jewish and Pauline Christianity. The idea of Christ's priesthood breaks through Jewish particularism, drawing both parties into a higher unity.[118] Alternatively, it might be an application of Paul's thought to the church's critical engagement with Gnosticism.[119] Problems with this approach arise because it emphasizes the similarities between Hebrews and Paul without giving due weight to the differences or to the affinities between Hebrews and other writings, and it relies too heavily on comparisons of ideas without adequately considering the social settings in which those ideas were transmitted (Backhaus, "Hebräerbrief," 189).

(2) Independent Use of Common Tradition.[120] Many similarities between Hebrews and the Pauline writings may result from each writer's reliance on a common pool of early Christian ideas: Christ's preexistence and incarnation (John 1:1–18), his obedience (Matt 26:39; John 5:30); his death as redemption (Matt 20:28; Mark 10:45; Rev 5:9), sacrifice (John 1:29; Rev 5:6), and conflict with the Devil (John 12:31–32); and the use of Ps 110:1 as a principal witness to Christ's exaltation (§4 COMMENT *c*). Comparing levels of education to milk and solid food (Heb 5:12–14), life to a race (12:1), and the biblical covenant to a testament also occurs in other sources (9:15–17). Nevertheless, the reference to Timothy in 13:23 suggests that there was some form of contact between the group addressed by Hebrews and the Pauline churches, calling into question the idea that Hebrews is completely independent from other writings.

(3) Interaction between Christian Groups. Differences in content, style, and outlook do not allow us to think that Hebrews is directly dependent upon Paul's letters, yet the reference to Timothy in 13:23 and the many theological convergences noted above suggest that Hebrews should not be totally separated from the circle of Christians associated with Paul. The early church included individuals and groups whose theological views were somewhat different, but who shaped each other through social interaction. Thus, even though the author of Hebrews did not derive his theological position from Paul, he may have adopted some elements of Paul's teachings from the people and congregations associated with Paul.[121]

Jewish Christianity

Many interpreters have identified Hebrews as an outgrowth of the Jewish Christianity represented by the early apostles.[122] Hebrews focuses on the priest-

---

[118]Baur, *Church*, 114–21; cf. Kümmel, *New Testament*, 133, 140. Augustus Neander said that Hebrews represented a development of Paul's thought by someone who moved from Judaism into Christianity, not by sudden crisis, but by gradual development in which the higher spirit concealed in Judaism was revealed to him. See his *History*, 2.1–15; cf. Pfleiderer, *Primitive Christianity*, 3.296–99.

[119]H. Koester, *Introduction*, 2.275–80.

[120]See Schröger, "Hebräerbrief," 216–17; H.-F. Weiss, *Brief*, 88.

[121]Backhaus, "Hebräerbrief," 204; Erlemann, "Alt"; cf. Hurst, *Epistle*, 130; Vanhoye, *TRE* 14.495–96.

[122]A Jewish Christian context for Hebrews was proposed by D. Schulz in 1818 (*Brief*) and adopted among others by Ritschl, *Entstehung*, 159–71; Westcott, *Epistle*, li–lxi, Rendall, *Epistle*, part 2, 1–10. Cf. Riehm, *Lehrbegriff*, 861–79, who links the early apostles with Paul, as does Acts.

ly and sacrificial aspects of the Law, which were apparently of little interest in Pauline circles, but which would have been important for those centered in Jerusalem. Although Hebrews speaks of the way that Christ's death changed the Law (Heb 7:11–19), the author has a strong sense of the continuity between the history of Israel and the life of the early church (Heb 11). More specific lines of development have been proposed in connection with the Hellenists (Acts 6–7) and with 1 Peter:

(1) **Stephen and the Hellenists.**[123] Although associated with the apostles and the Jerusalem community (Acts 6), Hellenist Christians were more oriented to the Greek-speaking world reflected in Hebrews. The speech ascribed to Stephen in Acts 7 recounts the history of Israel in terms of obedience and disobedience, as does Hebrews. Stephen does not focus on Moses' role as lawgiver, but on his importance as an exemplar of faith in contrast to the unfaithfulness of the wilderness generation and Aaron (Acts 7:17–43; Heb 3:1–19). Stephen finds fault with the Temple that Solomon built, which many take to show that God cannot be confined to any earthly sanctuary (Acts 7:47–50; Heb 9:25). Like Hebrews, Stephen's speech gives God's promise central place (Acts 7:6–7; Heb 6:13–20; 9:15; 10:23; 11:9) and depicts the life of faith as a pilgrimage, recalling how Abraham (Acts 7:2–5; Heb 11:8–19), Joseph (Acts 7:9–10; cf. Heb 11:22), and Moses' generation moved about on earth (Acts 7:36–39; Heb 3:7–4:13). Both the speech and Hebrews also refer to the angelic mediation of the Law (Acts 7:53; Heb 2:2), the "living" word of God (Acts 7:38; Heb 4:12–13), "rest" in the promised land (Acts 7:45, 49; Heb 4:3), and the command in Exod 25:40 (Acts 7:44; Heb 8:5).

Connections between Hellenist Christians and the book of Hebrews are difficult to make, in part because the extant form of Stephen's speech has almost certainly been shaped by Luke. Moreover, there are significant differences between the speech and Hebrews. The speech traces the fulfillment of God's promise to Abraham, culminating with worship in Jerusalem, but Hebrews insists that fulfillment of this promise is still pending (Acts 7:7, 45; Heb 11:13). Stephen's speech assumes that the first covenant is still binding, while Hebrews argues that the Mosaic covenant has become obsolete (Heb 8:13). Most significantly, Stephen criticizes the Temple but views the Tabernacle favorably, because the Tabernacle was designed in accordance with the Mosaic Law, whereas Hebrews points to the limitations of the Tabernacle (Acts 7:44–50; Heb 9:1–14).[124] It is not feasible to call Hebrews an outgrowth of Hellenist theology.

(2) **1 Peter.** Both Hebrews and 1 Peter are exhortations (Heb 13:22; 1 Pet 5:12) that speak of God's "living word" (Heb 4:12–13; 1 Pet 1:23) and give central place to Christ's "once for all" death (Heb 7:27; 9:26; 10:12; 1 Pet 3:18) as a sinless vic-

---

[123]Ritschl, *Entstehung*, 169–70; Riehm, *Lehrbegriff*, 877 n.; Beyschlag, *New Testament*, 2.283–84; E. F. Scott, *Epistle*, 62–65; W. Manson, *Epistle*, 25–46; Dunn, *Partings*, 69–70, 86. Cf. Spicq, *L'Épître*, 1.202 n. 5; Hurst, *Epistle*, 162 n. 3; Thurston, "Midrash." For extended discussion of Manson's proposal see Hurst, *Epistle*, 89–106. For a more recent development of it see Lane, *Hebrews*, 1.cxliv–cl. On issues concerning the origin and character of Stephen's speech see C. R. Koester, *Dwelling*, 76–85.

[124]See further C. R. Koester, *Dwelling*, 76–99; Hurst, *Epistle*, 89–106.

tim (Heb 4:15; 7:26; 1 Pet 1:19; 2:22; 3:18) at the end of the ages (Heb 1:2; 9:26; 1 Pet 1:20). Christ's sprinkled blood (Heb 10:22; 12:24; 1 Pet 1:2) removes sin (Heb 9:11–14, 23–26; 1 Pet 2:24) and sanctifies people (Heb 10:19–20; 1 Pet 1:2), providing access to God (Heb 4:14–16; 10:29; 1 Pet 3:18). Jesus' followers have been called (Heb 3:1; 1 Pet 1:15; 5:10) and enlightened (Heb 6:4; 10:32; 1 Pet 2:9). They belong to the household of God (Heb 3:2–6; 1 Pet 2:5; 4:17), yet live as aliens and sojourners upon earth (Heb 11:8–16; 13:14; 1 Pet 2:11). Christians imitate Christ (Heb 12:3; 1 Pet 2:21) by faithful obedience (Heb 3:18; 4:1–11; 1 Pet 1:2, 14, 22) and offer spiritual sacrifices (Heb 13:15–16; 1 Pet 2:5). They look forward to an eternal inheritance (Heb 1:4, 14; 6:12; 9:15; 1 Pet 1:4–5; 3:9) and wait for the revealing of Christ (Heb 9:28; 1 Pet 1:7, 13), the shepherd of Christians (Heb 13:20; 1 Pet 2:25; 5:4), who is seated at God's right hand, above the angels (Heb 1:1–14; 1 Pet 3:22).[125] In formal terms, the epistolary conclusions of Hebrews and 1 Peter say that the author has written briefly, extend greetings, and refer to a "brother" from the Pauline circle (Heb 13:22–25; 1 Pet 5:12–14).

Similarities between Hebrews and 1 Peter probably stem from several factors, including a common reliance on Christian tradition, the OT, and Greek idioms.[126] References to Paul's companions Timothy and Silas in Heb 13:23 and 1 Pet 5:12 also make it conceivable that Pauline teachings were among the Christian traditions used by each author. Direct dependence of one writer upon the other is unlikely. Hebrews makes no use of 1 Peter's new birth language or household codes, and 1 Peter uses priestly imagery for believers but not for Jesus, as Hebrews does. Shared words are sometimes used in different senses (e.g., *antitypos*, Heb 9:24; 1 Pet 3:21), and ideas that are similar are scattered throughout the texts and are tied together in different ways.

◆

In the history of early Christian theology, Hebrews sometimes is thought to be like Melchizedek: without father, mother, or genealogy (Heb 7:3). The opposite, however, is probably more accurate: Hebrews is not isolated, but has affinities with *a number* of Christian writings. Hebrews presupposes familiarity with common Christian teachings, such as the identification of Jesus as Lord (2:3; 7:14), Christ (3:6, 14), and Son of God (1:2), as well as repentance and faith, baptism and the laying on of hands, resurrection and judgment (6:1–2). Additional similarities to the Pauline letters and 1 Peter suggest that the author of Hebrews had contact with circles associated with Paul, but did not derive his message in any simple way from Paul. Rather than positing trajectories of theological development, Hebrews invites us to think about the complex ways in which Christians with somewhat different points of view related to each other at a given time and place (H.-F. Weiss, *Brief*, 94–95; Backhaus, *Der neue*, 65–70).

---

[125]On the similarities see Spicq, *L'Épître*, 1.139–44; Attridge, *Epistle*, 30–31; Hurst, *Epistle*, 125–30.

[126]Hurst, *Epistle*, 125–30; H.-F. Weiss, *Brief*, 88–89; Achtemeier, *1 Peter*, 20–21; Goppelt, *1 Peter*, 31.

3. HISTORY OF RELIGIONS

Historical critics use non-Christian as well as Christian writings to interpret biblical texts. Early studies found that many of the Greek words and expressions in Hebrews also appeared in works by Philo of Alexandria, a Jewish writer who interpreted biblical texts in light of philosophy; and comparison of the two writers helped to clarify NT word usage.[127] Subsequent studies showed similarities of thought as well as expression, so that by the end of the nineteenth century it was common to speak of the author of Hebrews as a Philonist who had converted to Christianity.[128] Most scholars understood the similarities to mean that the content of Hebrews was the Christian gospel, which the author expressed in the thought forms of his day.[129]

The history-of-religions school challenged this framework of interpretation by taking Christianity and other religions to be the products of cultural forces that shaped and developed the religions over time. Texts were read as expressions of underlying cultural currents, which appeared in different forms in Jewish, Christian, and Greco-Roman sources. By identifying similar ideas, or "parallels," in various writings, one could locate them within the cultural streams of antiquity. For those working within this model, interpretation involves ascertaining the influences that shaped the thought of the biblical writer, and this in turn is associated with judgments concerning the theological direction of the work.

Hebrews and Hellenistic Judaism

Hebrews was written in an elegant Greek style that was suitable for a Greek-speaking audience. The author used the LXX rather than a Hebrew Bible (pp. 115–16) and refers to institutions of the wider Greco-Roman world, such as the stadium (12:1), and to Hellenistic patterns of education (5:11–14). Comparisons between Hebrews and the writings of Philo show many similarities in language and thought forms, especially the distinction between the temporal and eternal worlds.

Interpreters who highlight Hebrews' affinities to Hellenistic Judaism sometimes note that the theologians who defined Christian orthodoxy in the second through the fifth centuries A.D. worked within a framework of Platonic metaphysics. If the author of Hebrews did the same thing, he was simply the first of many who presented the Christian message in a manner appropriate for the Hellenistic world. Ceslaus Spicq identified similarities between Hebrews and Philo,

---

[127]Apparently the first to connect Hebrews with Philo was Grotius, *Ad Hebraeos*, 811. He was followed by Carpzov, *Sacrae*; Wettstein, *Novum*, 2.384.

[128]W. M. L. de Wette (d. 1849) identified Hebrews and John's gospel and epistles as Alexandrian writings, in addition to the Pauline epistles and Jewish Christian writings (Matthew, Mark, Luke, 1 & 2 Peter, James, Jude, Revelation). On the nineteenth-century discussion see Milligan, *Theology*, 203–11; Ménégoz, *La Théologie*, 187–219. For older bibliography see Spicq, *L'Épître*, 1.39–40.

[129]See Milligan, *Theology*, 210–11. Carlston wrote, "In short the unknown author of Hebrews lived in the same 'Platonic' world as Philo . . . but they were citizens of quite different countries" ("Vocabulary," 148).

early Christian catechesis, the gospel of John, and the epistles of Paul and 1 Peter (*L'Épître*, 1.39–166). When commenting, he frequently cites early and medieval Christian writers as well as Philo, developing an interpretation that stands within the Catholic tradition. James Thompson and John Meier noted that the middle Platonism of Hebrews was also the major philosophical milieu in which the ante-Nicene Fathers thought and wrote, and they propose that Hebrews pointed the way into the patristic period.[130]

Critics rightly point out that there is little to suggest that the author of Hebrews knew the writings of Philo, as Spicq proposed, and conclude that the similarities can better be attributed to each author's use of the LXX and common Jewish traditions.[131] At the same time, the similarities between the writers cannot be dismissed; both were familiar with a Hellenistic-Jewish milieu.

Two points should be made. First, the history-of-religions model assumes the existence of general religious ideas that come to expression in particular texts. However, Hebrews can better be understood by reversing that model, going from the specific to the general: observing how a particular event—the crucifixion and exaltation of Jesus—is interpreted through several patterns of imagery, including royal, priestly, and heroic imagery (§8 COMMENT). Second, the cosmology of Hebrews is both similar to and different from Platonic cosmology. The relationship is complex rather than simple. See the detailed discussion on pp. 97–100.

Hebrews and Gnosticism

Possible connections between Hebrews and Gnosticism were noted in the late nineteenth century and considered more intensively after the publication of the Mandaean and Nag Hammadi writings in the twentieth century.[132] Gnostic writings typically work with a sharp metaphysical dualism between earth and heaven, flesh and mind. Some find similar ideas in Hebrews (8:5; 9:9–10, 14). Gnostic thought often assumed that the redeemer was sent to save souls with whom he had a common kinship (*syngeneia*), since they too were of heavenly origin before becoming enmeshed in the physical world. Therefore, the redeemer entered the realm of matter to deliver these souls from hostile powers and take them back to their heavenly abode. Similarly, Heb 2:11–16 says that Jesus and those he came to save were "all of one," that he identified with them by taking on blood and flesh, and that he overcame the power of the devil to deliver them, and to enable them to enter their heavenly rest (4:1–10).

130Meier, "Structure," 181–82; Thompson, *Beginnings*, 158.

131See Williamson, *Philo*; Hurst, *Epistle*, 7–42; Ruina, *Philo*, 74–78; Thurston, "Philo."

132For an early treatment see Pfleiderer, *Primitive Christianity*, 3.279, 286. Windisch was able to make limited use of Gnostic sources in his commentary of 1931. The theory was most fully developed in Käsemann's *Wandering* of 1939. It was adopted to some extent by Theissen, *Untersuchungen*, 121; Grässer, *Hebräer*, 1.135–36; H. Koester, *Introduction*, 2.275–80. More recently, Pearson finds affinities between Hebrews' presentation of Melchizedek and traditions that were developed in Gnostic circles (NOTE on 7:1; cf. Feld, *Hebräerbrief*, 49–51; Attridge, *Epistle*, 193–95). Wray (*Rest*, 141–49) posits a dependence of the *Gospel of Truth* (NHC I,3) on Hebrews.

Critics rightly point out that extant Gnostic sources postdate Hebrews and that there is little first-century evidence for a Gnostic redeemer myth.[133] Moreover, Hebrews does not envision human souls returning to the heavenly spheres from which they have fallen; instead, the faithful journey toward a destination to which they have never been, the heavenly Jerusalem (11:13–16). The similarities between Hebrews and Gnostic texts can better be ascribed to a common Hellenistic Jewish heritage than to Hebrews' reliance upon Gnostic mythology (Attridge, *ABD* 3.103). Significantly, Ernst Käsemann, one of the pioneers of this approach, later acknowledged the problems with the hypothesis and said:

> My religious-historical sketch more or less veiled the theological concern which was important to me. By describing the church as the new people of God on its wandering through the wilderness, following the Pioneer and Perfecter of faith, I of course had in mind that radical Confessing Church which resisted the tyranny in Germany, and which had to be summoned to patience so that it could continue its way through endless wastes. (*Wandering*, 13)

What Käsemann developed in his later work on Hebrews was not the comparison with Gnostic sources, but the idea that the people of God are a pilgrim people who are called to faithfulness (*Jesus*, 101–19). Renewed emphasis on the pilgrimage motif, rather than his history-of-religions hypothesis, is Käsemann's abiding contribution.

Hebrews and Palestinian Jewish Writings

Many scholars trace aspects of Hebrews to traditions attested in intertestamental Jewish texts, the Dead Sea Scrolls, targums, and rabbinic writings. For some, distancing Hebrews from Hellenistic texts helps to place it "in the central stream of early Christian theology, not as somehow off-centre, deflected from the central stream of early Christian thinking by extraneous philosophical doctrines" (Williamson, *Philo*, 580). Two factors enhanced the appeal of Palestinian Jewish texts for the study of Hebrews. One was that some scholars linked Philo's thought world with that of Gnosticism, which, since antiquity, had been viewed as a departure from Christianity. If Philo's philosophical categories placed him on a trajectory leading to Gnosticism, the same would be true of Hebrews. Accordingly, connecting Hebrews with other Jewish writings would seem to help keep it in the mainstream. Another factor was that modern studies of Jesus depicted him as an apocalyptic prophet, whose message concerned the imminent arrival of God's kingdom.[134] If Jesus' message was primarily eschatological, then emphasizing

---

[133]Critiques of the Gnostic hypothesis note that the ideas of heavenly rest and the veil separating heaven from earth have clearer affinities with Jewish writings than with Gnostic texts. See Hofius's two studies, *Katapausis* and *Vorhang*; Hurst, *Epistle*, 67–74; H.-F. Weiss, *Brief*, 103–7; Feld, *Hebräerbrief*, 49–51.

[134]For a survey of recent discussion see Witherington, *Jesus Quest*.

the eschatological elements in Hebrews would help to anchor it in early Christianity.[135]

(1) Apoocalyptic Writings. Hebrews includes apocalyptic elements. The author understands himself to be living "in these final days" (1:2), when God sent his Son to make atonement at "the consummation of the ages" (9:26). He anticipates the return of Christ (9:28) and the coming "Day" of judgment (10:25–31). The listeners look for inheritance in "the world to come" (2:5; 6:5) after God shakes heaven and earth (12:26–27). The temporal distinction between the present age and the age to come is found in various writings from the intertestamental period, as well as in rabbinic sources and targums.[136] Comparison of Hebrews with these Jewish texts allows its eschatological dimension to stand out with greater clarity. What has been most debated is not the presence but the function of the apocalyptic elements in Hebrews. Some have argued that the eschatological, or "horizontal," axis in the book is dominant with the Platonic, or "vertical," axis playing a minor or supporting role in the book.[137] Others insist that the vertical Platonic axis of Hebrews is dominant with the eschatological elements serving a vestigial role, especially in exhortations.[138]

(2) Dead Sea Scrolls. The idea that Hebrews addressed a group of Essenes was proposed by Schulz in 1818, but it received renewed interest after the discovery of the Dead Sea Scrolls in 1947, which enabled scholars to compare Hebrews with the writings of the Qumran community. Early studies noted that the Qumran sect engaged in speculation about angels (cf. Heb 1–2), looked for an Aaronic messiah (cf. Heb 5:1–10) and a prophet like Moses (cf. Heb 1:1–2; 3:1–6), as well as a Davidic messiah, and they understood themselves to be like the people of God sojourning in the wilderness (cf. Heb 3:7–4:10). Accordingly, some proposed that Hebrews was written to former members of the Dead Sea sect who had converted to Christianity but whose understanding of the new faith was obscured by elements from their former way of thought.[139] Further examination, however, showed that there was little evidence that Hebrews was trying to counter sectarian views of angels or hopes for an Aaronic messiah.

---

[135]The emphasis on apocalyptic thinking in NT studies, which was given impetus by Wrede and Schweitzer, was applied in a limited way to Hebrews by Nairne (*Epistle*) and more fully developed by Michel (*Brief*).

[136]See Michel, *Brief*, 58–68; Barrett, "Eschatology"; Strobel, *Brief*, 16.

[137]For example, Michel, *Brief*, 62–65; Barrett, "Eschatology," 363–93; Hurst, *Epistle*, 131–33; Lane, *Hebrews*, 1.cvii–cx.

[138]For example, Thompson, *Beginnings*, 41–52; Dey, *Intermediary*, 123.

[139]In the nineteenth century, connections with the Essenes were proposed by D. Schulz, *Brief*, 67–68; Rendall, *Epistle*, part 2, 86. In the twentieth century see Yadin, "Dead Sea"; Fensham, "Hebrews"; P. E. Hughes, *Commentary*, 10–15; Kistemaker, *Psalm*, 74. Kosmala argued that the addressees were Essenes who had not yet converted to Christianity (*Hebräer*), but this approach found little support, since most recognize that the arguments in Hebrews presuppose that the intended recipients already believe that Jesus is the Messiah and Son of God. For further bibliography see Lane, *Hebrews*, 1.cv; Hurst, *Epistle*, 43–66.

Biblical interpretation was another possible point of contact. Some Dead Sea texts connect OT texts to a community living in "the last days" through devices like conflating texts and making wordplays. Although the author of Hebrews understood himself to be living in the end times (1:1–2), his interpretive devices generally correspond to those known from various Jewish sources, not just those of the Dead Sea sect. Some Dead Sea texts do mention a "new covenant," which is a prominent theme in Hebrews, but the theme is treated in a manner different from Hebrews, making a connection unlikely (see p. 113). Discovery of a Dead Sea text mentioning a "Melchizedek," who is apparently a heavenly being (11QMelch), rekindled interest in the relationship of Hebrews to Qumran, but studies again gave little reason to think that Hebrews had any knowledge of the views of Melchizedek evident in the Scrolls (NOTE on 7:1).

(3) Jewish Mystic Writings. A few authors identify similarities between Hebrews and Jewish writings concerning God's heavenly throne-chariot.[140] These texts are not primarily eschatological, but have some affinities with the cosmology of Hebrews. References to God's heavenly throne (cf. 1:8; 4:16; 8:1; 12:2) and the angelic hosts that worship there (cf. 1:4–14), as well as to God's likeness to fire (cf. Heb 12:29) are common in mystic texts. Mystic worshipers seek to journey through the heavens to the veil (cf. 6:19–20; 10:19–20) that marks the entry into the presence of God. Comparison of Hebrews to these texts is problematic because the pertinent mystic texts may be rather late and most points of comparison can be attributed to a common dependence on the Psalms (Hurst, *Epistle*, 83–84).

◆

History-of-religions approaches to Hebrews have reached an impasse in part because existing categories are inadequate: apocalyptic Jewish texts were composed within the Hellenistic world, Hellenistic thought includes much that is not Gnostic, and Gnostic texts themselves include apocalyptic elements. Another issue is the practice of positing the existence of a basic pattern that underlies particular texts. The pattern is often treated as primary, while the texts that express the pattern are secondary variations on the theme. An alternative is to take Jesus' crucifixion and resurrection or exaltation to be the primary elements that the author of Hebrews elaborates by drawing royal, priestly, and heroic images from various sources. Finally, the history-of-religions approach often gives greater attention to the interplay of ideas than to interactions between human communities and their institutions. Therefore, in the next part of this introduction we will consider some aspects of the complex social world in which Hebrews was composed and first read.

---

[140]See Hofius, *Vorhang*, 95; Schenke, "Erwägungen," 421–37; Williamson, "Background."

II. Social Setting

◆

Social setting has to do with patterns of early Christian life, rather than with questions concerning the author's identity or the specific date and place of composition. Attention shifts to dynamics within the early Christian community and its relationship to other groups. The author's references to the past (2:3–4; 10:32–34) and present situation of the listeners (5:11–12; 6:9–12; 10:25; 12:4) offer starting point for discerning the setting. Some argue that the author wrote of conditions that were typical of the second or third Christian generation but did not address a specific congregation. They also take the personal notes in 13:18–25 to be pseudonymous additions that are designed to make Hebrews resemble a Pauline letter.[141] Nevertheless, this seems unlikely since neither the personal notes nor other features of Hebrews are developed in a manner that suggests pseudonymity (§39 COMMENT). The remarks about the listeners' situation are specific enough to indicate familiarity with a particular circle of Christians, but one whose experiences can be compared to those of other early Christian communities.

There are two useful ways to explore patterns of community life based on the available information. One is to look at developments that occurred over time in the community addressed by Hebrews, seeking to assess how readers were shaped by their past experiences. The author's brief comments offer a few glimpses into the community life of his audience, which can be enhanced by relating them to patterns that are attested in other sources of the period. As a way to understand the community's dynamics, we can interpret these specific comments in light of Hebrews' general interest in the relationship of belief to experience. A second approach is to consider social relations within the community at the time that Hebrews was written. Of special interest are community organization, leadership structures, and ways that the community defined itself with respect to Jewish subculture and the dominant Greco-Roman culture.

A. History of the Community

Hebrews addressed a Christian community that had existed for some time. At several points the author refers to the group's history, allowing us to discern three phases. First, the community was formed when Christian evangelists proclaimed a message of salvation, performing miracles to validate their preaching. Some persons came to faith, experiencing the power of the Holy Spirit and a sense of enlightenment; they received baptism and the laying on of hands. Second, non-

[141]Dibelius, *Botschaft*, 160-63; Grässer, *Hebräer*, 3.30, 57-69; H. Koester, *Introduction*, 2.275-80. For critique see H.-F. Weiss, *Brief*, 72-74.

Christians instigated hostilities against the community by physically accosting Christians and denouncing them before local authorities, who imprisoned them and allowed Christian property to be plundered. During the conflict, Christians maintained their faith commitments and supported each other, attending to the needs of those in prison. Third, overt persecution gave way to a lower level of conflict in which non-Christians continued to verbally harass Christians. Some from the community were in prison, and others felt the effects of being marginalized in society. Although some continued to show faith and compassion, others experienced a malaise that was evident in tendencies to neglect the faith and community gatherings. Hebrews was written during this third phase. We consider each phase in turn. Detailed discussion of particular passages is given in NOTES and COMMENT.

1. PHASE 1: PROCLAMATION AND CONVERSION

Hebrews recalls that the listeners' community was formed when the message that Jesus proclaimed was "validated for us by those who heard, while God corroborated the testimony by signs and wonders and various powerful deeds, and distributions of the Holy Spirit according to his will" (2:3–4). To say that the message of Jesus was conveyed "by those who heard" implies that neither the author nor his audience were eyewitnesses to the ministry of Jesus. Rather, they learned of the message from evangelists who received it from Jesus or his early followers (NOTE on 2:3).[142] Hebrews refers to the evangelists in the plural, which suggests that two or more of them worked together, a common early Christian practice.[143] Those who brought the Christian message could have been missionaries who stayed in a given locale long enough to form a community and then moved on, since miracle-working and spiritual outpourings were often associated with that kind of ministry.[144] Paul used similar language to describe his early work at Corinth when the people received spiritual gifts as the testimony of Christ was "validated" (*bebaioun*) among them (1 Cor 1:6; cf. Heb 2:3).

The message that the evangelists preached focused on "salvation" (2:3), which probably meant deliverance from divine judgment and from the powers of evil and assurance of life in God's kingdom (§5 COMMENT *b*). The evangelists provided visible confirmation of their message by performing "signs and wonders and various powerful deeds" (2:4a). The NT refers to the miracles performed by the

---

[142]Cf. Laub, "Verkündigung," 172. Grässer (*Aufbruch*, 140) finds continuity between Jesus and later generations in terms of the word of God rather than a succession of officeholders. Bénétreau (*L'Epître*, 1.106–7) points out that church tradition makes the word available to later generations.

[143]For example, Acts 13:2–3; 15:30, 39–40; 16:3; 1 Cor 1:1; 2 Cor 1:1; 3 John 6. The pairs sent out by Jesus in Luke 10:1 may correspond to early Christian missionary practice. Some evidence for solitary traveling evangelists appears in Acts 8:4–8, 26–40; *Did.* 11:3–13:7.

[144]Some identify the evangelists of 2:3–4 with the deceased leaders in 13:7, which would mean that the evangelists stayed with the listeners' community (Attridge, *Epistle*, 391; Lane, *Hebrews*, 2.527; H.-F. Weiss, *Brief*, 711–12). It is clear that the work of the initial evangelists and later leaders involved speaking the word, but it is not clear that the evangelists and the leaders are identical (Ellingworth, *Epistle*, 702; Grässer, *Aufbruch*, 220).

apostles (Acts 2:43; 5:12; Rom 15:19; 2 Cor 12:12) and others (Acts 6:8; 8:13), which commonly were healings and exorcisms (Acts 3:1–10; 5:16; 9:32–42; 14:8–18; 16:16–18; 19:11–12). By showing people God's power over illnesses that they could see, the mighty works gave them reason to believe that God could also save them from judgment for life in a kingdom that they could not see.[145]

Listeners understood that God had given them "distributions of the Holy Spirit" (Heb 2:4b), apparently in a perceptible manner. Like other early Christians (Acts 10:44; 1 Cor 2:1–5; Gal 3:1, 5; 1 Thess 1:5), the author of Hebrews considers the Spirit to be a channel of the grace (Heb 6:4–5; 10:29) that comes to expression in a confession of Christian faith (3:1; 4:14; 10:23). Speaking in ecstatic tongues, prophesying, and visions were sometimes included among "distributions of the Holy Spirit" (cf. Acts 10:46; 19:6; 1 Cor 12:10) although Hebrews does not elaborate. Faith and receiving the Holy Spirit were regularly connected to baptism, although the Spirit might be given before baptism (Acts 10:44–48), through baptism (1 Cor 12:13), or through the laying on of hands after baptism (Acts 8:16–17; 19:6). For those addressed by Hebrews, the Spirit's work (Heb 2:3–4; 6:4–5) was apparently understood to have led to repentance and faith (6:1), followed by baptism and the laying on of hands (6:2).

Belief and experience reinforced each other in a positive way according to Hebrews' account of the first phase of the community's life. The evangelists' message awakened hopes for a place in the kingdom of God. Miracles and a vivid sense of the Spirit's activity confirmed the message experientially. The author reflects the positive and palpable character of this coherence between belief and experience by describing conversion in terms of sensory experience. Those who come to faith are those who have been "*enlightened*, who have *tasted the heavenly gift* and become partakers of the Holy Spirit, who have *tasted the good word* of God and the powers of the age to come" (6:4–5).[146] This way of relating faith and experience becomes an issue in subsequent phases of the community's history, when tasting the heavenly gift is accompanied by the loss of earthly goods, when sharing the Spirit means sharing suffering, and when the powers of the age to come seem overwhelmed by the powers of this age.

Socially, the movement from repentance to faith (6:1) involves an interior reorientation and a shift in social relations. One turns from the beliefs of a non-Christian society to the beliefs of a Christian community. In a given locale, a

---

[145]Miracles are common in accounts of early Christian evangelism. Jewish and Greco-Roman sources also attest to a broad interest in miracles as signs of divine power (§5 COMMENT B). Many NT writers recognize that miracles can be misconstrued, since visible manifestations of supernatural power are not unique to Christianity. They interpret miraculous actions by linking them to testimony about Jesus (Dunn, *Unity*, 174–84; C. R. Koester, *Symbolism*, 74–77).

[146]Dunn's survey of the role of the Spirit in the NT concludes that religious experience was of fundamental importance in the beginnings of Christianity. Forms of experience varied, but when understood in explicitly Christian terms, it commonly involved connecting the message of the Christian community with its spiritual experience of the exalted Christ. The ambiguity of such experiences led to varied responses among NT writers, ranging from a generally positive view in Luke-Acts to more qualified treatments in the Pauline and Johannine writings, as well as in Hebrews (*Unity*, 199–202; cf. Kee, *Miracle*, 146–73).

Christian community would include some but certainly not all members of a given ethnic group or social class. The confession of faith (Heb 3:1; 4:14; 10:23) had the dual function of uniting the group, since the confession was what they had in common, while distinguishing the Christian community from groups that did not have the same beliefs. Moreover, for the earliest Christians, baptism was not a rite of passage within an established community, but a boundary marker between the Christian community and non-Christian society. Undergoing baptism meant not only purification from sin but identification with a group of people that was set apart from others (Heb 10:22, 25; Gal 3:28; 1 Cor 12:13; Meeks, *First Urban*, 150–57).

Conversion evidently planted the seeds of conflict between the listeners' community and the wider society. By turning away from certain patterns of belief, the convert makes a negative judgment—either explicitly or implicitly—on beliefs and values that continue to be held by those who do not share the same faith.[147] This can lead to resentment on the part of the group that the convert leaves. Hebrews twice calls conversion "enlightenment" (6:4; 10:32), which implies that the unconverted remain in darkness with its connotations of sin, ignorance, and death (NOTE on 6:4). According to 1 Peter, being called out of darkness into the light means receiving a new identity among the people of God (1 Pet 2:9–11), but it also means being reproached by those whose beliefs the convert no longer shares (1 Pet 2:12; 4:4). Those addressed by Hebrews seem to have experienced something similar, for their "enlightenment" in the Christian faith was followed by hostility from society (Heb 10:32).

2. PHASE 2: PERSECUTION AND SOLIDARITY

The second phase was marked by conflict with those outside the community and solidarity among those inside the community. In a key passage the author tells listeners: "Remember the former days in which, after you were enlightened, you endured a great contest with sufferings, in part by being made a public spectacle through denunciations and afflictions, and in part by showing solidarity with those who were treated that way. For you showed compassion for the prisoners and accepted the seizure of your possessions with joy, knowing that you yourselves have a superior and abiding possession" (10:32–34; see §28 COMMENT *a*).

Officials in local government would have played an important role in the actions taken against Christians. Although physical abuse and loss of property could have resulted from mob action, imprisonment (10:34; 13:3) required the

[147]This idea is reflected in the example of Noah, who embraces the message of salvation and thereby pronounces judgment on the unbelieving world (§30 COMMENT B). Greco-Roman religious tradition assumed that people could move with relative ease from the worship of one deity to another. Since conversion to Judaism or Christianity did not mean venerating a new figure along with other deities, it brought a break with the dominant pattern. The social dimension of conversion is reflected somewhat differently in John's gospel, where professing Jesus to be the Messiah brings expulsion from the synagogue (John 9:22, 34; 12:42).

involvement of a person in authority, such as a governor or magistrate. The extent to which one or more officials participated in the other actions taken against Christians is not clear. To maintain public order, officials had the power of *coercitio*, which allowed them to authorize beatings without following judicial norms when gathering evidence or exacting punishment (Acts 14:5; 16:22–23, 37).[148] The seizure of Christian property was probably not fully legal, but local officials apparently condoned it or at least did not interfere (NOTE on 10:34). What is significant is that the Christians lost property and were subjected to abuse, yet it was they and not the perpetrators of the violence who were imprisoned.

Members of the local populace also would have been involved in the persecution. Their role can best be seen in considering how "denunciation" of Christians led to their imprisonment (10:32–34). In the first century most communities had only a rudimentary police force, and apart from flagrant violations of law, authorities depended upon citizens to bring wrongdoers to their attention. Acts, for example, tells how people verbally and physically accosted Christians before denouncing them to the city magistrates who could choose to imprison (Acts 16:16–24; cf. 21:31–36) or release them (Acts 17:1–9; 18:12–17).[149] The populace might well have participated in the physical violence against the Christians (Acts 14:19; 18:17), and since there is only scant evidence that Christian property could have been seized legally, it seems likely that this was the result of mob action (NOTE on Heb 10:34).

The idea that Hebrews refers to a local outburst rather than to a systematic persecution of Christians and that it involved some of the non-Christian populace attacking Christians and denouncing them to the authorities fits what is known from other sources. In Rome the emperor Claudius in A.D. 49 apparently took action against some Christians in response to disturbances in local synagogues, but he did not initiate any campaign against the church (pp. 51–52). In Asia Minor around A.D. 95 members of local synagogues sometimes denounced Christians, who then faced the prospect of imprisonment and death (Rev 2:9; 3:9), while Christians in other communities were apparently left alone (Rev 3:17). Pliny the Younger in about A.D. 110–12 took action against those who were denounced to him, but neither he nor the emperor Trajan favored any government-sponsored search for Christians (Pliny, *Letters* 10.96–97). Between A.D. 117–38 Hadrian followed the same practice (Eusebius, *Eccl. Hist.* 4.9.1–3). Although Nero did instigate a persecution of Christians in A.D. 64, Hebrews does not suggest that the listeners had been subjected to violence of that magnitude (p. 52). Christians probably fell victim to the reign of terror that

[148]On the use of imprisonment, beatings, and fines in the exercise of *coercitio* see *OCD*, 355; S. A. Arbandt and W. Macheiner, "Gefangenschaft," *RAC* 9.318–45, esp. 322–24. On the magistrates' discretionary powers pertaining to imprisonment see Rapske, *Paul*, 37–70. On the denunciation of Christians and a magistrate's use of *coercitio* see Sherwin-White, *Letters*, 778–81.

[149]On the pattern of citizens denouncing Christians before a magistrate in the first and second centuries see Pliny the Younger, *Ep.* 10.96–97; Eusebius, *Eccl. Hist.* 5.1.7; Sherwin-White, *Letters*, 697, 777.

concluded Domitian's reign (A.D. 81–96), but his campaign was aimed at all perceived enemies of the throne, not only Christians (Eusebius, *Eccl. Hist.* 3.17).[150]

It is not clear whether Gentiles or Jews instigated the persecution described in Heb 10:32–34. Since Christians were sometimes denounced by members of local synagogues (Acts 17:1–9; Rev 2:9; 3:9), this could have been the experience of those addressed by Hebrews. Yet if Hebrews was written for Christians living in Italy (Heb 13:24) or some other location outside of Palestine, it seems likely that those who actually imprisoned the Christians were non-Jews. The magistrates that administered the jails in Greco-Roman cities were commonly Gentiles. In order to imprison Christians, non-Jewish officials had to be persuaded that the Christians posed a threat to Greco-Roman social order (Acts 16:21; 18:12–17).[151] Hebrews reflects a situation in which Christians are not simply estranged from the Jewish community, but from their city and society (Heb 13:14).

Public animosity seems to have been aroused by the distinctive faith commitments of the Christian community. Hebrews reflects this in a creatively anachronistic depiction of Moses as a Christian. First, Hebrews connects the loss of possessions with being denounced for Christ. Moses gave up wealth in Egypt in the hope of a future reward (11:26b) just as the listeners gave up their possessions in the hope of a heavenly inheritance (10:34), and Moses accepted "denunciation for Christ" (11:26a) just as the Christian community must bear "denunciation" for Christ (13:13). Since denunciation was done verbally, Hebrews suggests that the charges leveled at the listeners had specifically to do with their relationship to Christ. Second, Hebrews contrasts belonging to the community of faith with fitting in to the wider society. Moses left the royal household "to be maltreated with the people of God," and by identifying with God's people, he rejected "the fleeting pleasure of sin" (11:25). The implication is that belonging to the people of God sets one apart from sinful society.

A similar pattern is reflected in 1 Peter, which speaks of believers being "reviled for the name of Christ" (1 Pet 4:14, 16). It is not clear that bearing the name of Christ was in itself unlawful, since later sources show that government officials did not have a general policy about the treatment of Christians (Pliny the Younger, *Ep.* 10.96–97). More important is that the denunciation was done by Gentile non-Christians who "are surprised that you no longer join them in the same excesses of dissipation, and so they blaspheme" (1 Pet 4:4). Those whom God calls "out of darkness into his marvelous light" belong to a new peo-

---

[150]Studies of persecutions in the first century recognize that they were generally local and sporadic responses to denunciations of Christians. The hostilities initiated by Nero and Domitian were exceptions rather than the rule. See Lampe and Luz, "Nachpaulinisches," 196–200; Hardy, *Christianity*, 166–67; D. S. Potter, *ABD* 5.231–35; Achtemeier, *1 Peter*, 34–36.

[151]Schmithals proposes that Hebrews addresses former God-fearers who were put out of the synagogue as Jews reorganized themselves in Jamnia after the destruction of Jerusalem ("Über Empfänger"). Hebrews' lack of references to events in Palestine from this period makes the theory unlikely, however.

ple (1 Pet 2:9–10).[152] Enlightenment means social realignment and at least an implicit judgment against the convert's former society.

Some of those known to the author of Hebrews came from Italy (Heb 13:24), where by the mid-first century Christians were considered guilty of "hatred against humankind" (Tacitus, *Annals* 15.44.2). A similar expression was used for Jews: "Toward each other they observe strict fidelity and mercy, but the rest of humankind they hate," for "they separate themselves from others" (Tacitus, *Histories* 5.5; Diodorus Siculus, *Library of History* 34.1.2). Jews did not participate in aspects of civic life that had to do with the honoring of other deities. They were a people "that has made its own life apart and irreconcilable, that cannot share with the rest of humanity in the pleasures of the table nor join in their libations or prayers or sacrifices" (Philostratus, *Life of Apollonius* 3.33). Their distinctiveness was tolerated because it was based on traditions that they had received from their ancestors (Tacitus, *Histories* 5.5). Christians were also perceived as different, but their faith lacked the aura of antiquity. Because they did not honor Greco-Roman religious customs (Acts 16:20–21), they were accused of promoting "a new and mischievous superstition" (Suetonius, *Nero* 16).[153]

The actions taken against Christians presumably were intended to have a twofold effect. One would have been to pressure Christians into relinquishing their beliefs. Public denunciation dishonored people and deprived them of the sense of personal value that most people seek from society. Suffering abuse and the loss of property were physically and emotionally painful. Prison conditions were harsh and degrading. Many people would have preferred to relinquish their beliefs in order to escape such hardship. Second, the actions might have been intended to marginalize those that persisted in their faith and to dissuade others from joining their group. If people learned that belonging to the Christian community jeopardized one's honor, property, and freedom, they would probably be less likely to adopt the Christian faith (§28 COMMENT *a*).

According to Hebrews, however, the actual effect of the persecution was to galvanize solidarity within the Christian community. There are social patterns in which a heightened sense of cooperation within groups results from conflict between groups (e.g., Philo, *Flaccus* 72). Conflict with outsiders helps to establish and reaffirm the group's distinctive identity, while promoting internal cohesion. Attacks by outsiders help to define loyalties and mobilize the energies of people within the group to support one another. Although persecution can weaken affiliation to a religious group, it can also confirm and reinforce the bonds among those who are persecuted, serving to define and deepen religious loyalties (J. H.

---

[152]On the nature of the hostility toward Christians that is mentioned in 1 Peter, see Achtemeier, *1 Peter*, 35–36, 313–14; Goppelt, *Commentary*, 39–41; Lampe and Luz, "Nachpaulinisches," 198–202.

[153]Because of their refusal to worship the usual civic gods, Christians were eventually regarded as atheists (*Mart. Pol.* 3.2; 9.2; Justin, *1 Apol.* 6). Although Christians were sometimes accused of wrongdoing (1 Pet 2:12), disloyalty to the emperor (Acts 17:7), and posing an economic threat (Acts 16:19; 19:24–27), such allegations are not reflected in Hebrews. See generally Sherwin-White, *Letters*, 772–87; Potter, *ABD* 5.231–35; Keresztes, "Imperial," 247–57; Benko, "Pagan Criticism."

Elliott, *Home*, 114–18). This was the case of the community addressed by Hebrews—at least for a time.

3. PHASE 3: FRICTION AND MALAISE

The outburst of hostility that characterized phase 2 gave way to ongoing, but less intense friction between Christians and non-Christians in phase 3. Hebrews assumes that members of the community could expect a continuation of the verbal attacks (13:13), and some members of the community were still in prison (13:3), which burdened morale and material resources. Supporting prisoners over a period of time was discouraging to those who awaited their release, and associating with prisoners brought both a social stigma and the possibility of losing one's own freedom (§37 COMMENT *a*).

Some Christians continued the practice of caring for others in the community (6:10; 13:1), but others showed signs of malaise. The author cautions against "drift," a term that suggests a gradual, perhaps unthinking movement away from the faith (2:1). He points to the danger of "neglecting" the Christian faith and community (2:3; 10:25), and reproves his listeners for their sluggishness (5:11; 6:12). Apostasy could be the culmination of these tendencies, according to the author (3:12; 6:4–6; 10:26; 12:16–17). It seems clear, however, that the listeners had not actually fallen away, since the author can assume that they still affirmed basic Christian beliefs. For example, he does not try to convince the listeners that Jesus died and was exalted to God's right hand, but assumes that they will grant these points as the basis for his argument (1:1–4). Moreover, the exhortations to "hold fast" and not to abandon the Christian hope and confession of faith (3:6; 4:14; 10:23, 35) assume that the listeners have not yet relinquished their beliefs altogether.

Many have thought that the listeners were on the verge of leaving Christianity in order to return to Judaism. Some suggest that the Jewish community was legally protected and would therefore offer Christians shelter from persecution.[154] It seems unlikely that legality was a factor, however. Roman policy toward non-Roman religions was one of broad tolerance as long as there was no threat to the state. There were statutes requiring organized groups, or *collegia*, to be approved, but *collegia* were generally allowed to meet without legal sanction so long as they were deemed harmless.[155] Moreover, 10:25 implies that the

---

[154]Bénétreau, *L'Epître*, 1.28–29; F. F. Bruce, *Epistle*, 382; Ellingworth, *Epistle*, 78–80; Loader, *Sohn*, 258.

[155]*Collegia* were associations that served the interests of their members. Common sorts were professional groups and burial societies. Because some associations were political in nature, the Roman emperors reserved the right to ban them, although groups that had existed for a long period were generally permitted to exist. (Suetonius, *Jul.* 42.3; *Aug.* 32.2; cf. Pliny, *Ep.* 10.92–93). Inscriptional evidence also indicates that many groups existed without official sanction (Hardy, *Christianity*, 172). Jews had a measure of legal protection under the Romans (Josephus, *Ant.* 14.185–267), but were also treated with contempt by many (Daniel, "Anti-Semitism"). Therefore, it is not clear that Christians would have perceived Judaism as a refuge.

Christian gathering was declining not because of suppression, but because of neglect. A variation might be that the Jewish community offered an established identity and clear religious practices, so that the author had to warn listeners against seeking shelter in the "camp" of Judaism and its teachings about food (13:9–13).[156] These warnings are rather general, however, and do not suggest that identifying with a local Jewish community was a significant problem (see §37 COMMENT *c* and §38 COMMENT *a*).

When the author points out the parallels between the wilderness generation and the Christian community, he faults those who do not faithfully adhere to the company of "those who actually listened" (4:2), but he does not warn about joining another community. Similarly, he faults Esau for relinquishing his blessing for the sake of physical gratification, not for changing religious communities. More importantly, the imagery in 13:9–13 moves from speaking of the "camp" to speak about the "city," which is the listeners' situation.

The dispiriting circumstances of this phase of the community's history are reflected in the creatively anachronistic way in which Hebrews weaves the "city" into the story of Abraham. Just as Abraham received promises of an inheritance from God (6:13–14; 11:8–9), the listeners now share in this promise and anticipate an inheritance from God (1:14; 6:12). Just as Abraham is said to have sought a home in *the city,* whose builder and maker is God (11:10, 13–16), the listeners seek a place in *the city* that is to come (13:14). While on earth, Abraham and his family were considered "resident aliens," who were socially and legally inferior to citizens (NOTE on 11:9). Like him the listeners could be regarded as "foreigners" and "transients," who lacked political rights and were regarded with suspicion and contempt by others in society (NOTES on 11:13).

The author of Hebrews recognized that one response to continued reproach would be to "shrink back" (10:39) from the Christian community in the hope of obtaining a more favorable judgment from non-Christian society. If confessing faith in Christ meant losing possessions, one might seek greater economic security by abandoning one's confession. If meeting with Christians meant being treated with contempt, one might hope for more honorable treatment by leaving the Christian community (10:25). As a response, the author places listeners before an alternative court of reputation, one in which God's judgments overturn society's judgments. The world pronounced a negative judgment against Jesus, subjecting him to disgrace and death (12:2), but God overturned the verdict of the lower court by raising Jesus from the dead and exalting him to everlasting glory (1:2–4; 2:8–9). God will do the same for his people, so that listeners are to hope for the glory (2:10) and to fear the judgments that come from God (4:12–13), not from unbelieving society.

---

[156]D. Guthrie, *Hebrews*, 31–38; Lane, *Hebrews*, 2.545–46; Lindars (*Theology*, 4–15) and Dunn (*Partings*, 88) suggest that Judaism was attractive because it offered more tangible means of dealing with a guilty conscience (Heb 9:14; 10:2) . For critique see Backhaus, *Der neue*, 276–82.

B. Profile of the Community and Its Context

Faith in a future that not only is unseen (11:1) but is contradicted by experience needs the support of a community of faith, which is the earthly counterpart to God's divine court. Social contact within a community reinforces the beliefs and hopes that group members hold, allowing them to maintain their convictions in the face of opposition from other groups. "As long as the interaction between Christians remains frequent and vibrant, the alternate court of opinion will remain strong and commitment to the group and its values will remain high." If, however, the community does not "support its members' need for recognition of their worth, and does not provide a strong enough social base for mutual assistance, its members will be tempted increasingly to seek recognition and support from other groups, whether the Jewish communities or the Greco-Roman society."[157] Hebrews seeks to reinvigorate community life by reaffirming and developing the confession of faith and by calling listeners to actions that contribute to the well-being of this community (e.g., 6:10; 13:1–9). Since Christians had affinities with Jewish subculture and the dominant Greco-Roman culture but did not entirely fit either category, Hebrews helps to define their identity by appropriating Jewish and Greco-Roman images, transforming both in ways that reinforce the community's confession.

1. CHRISTIAN COMMUNITY

The "house" or "household" (*oikos*) is one image that Hebrews uses for the Christian community (3:6; 10:21). The author calls his listeners sons and daughters of God (2:10), and addresses them as brethren (3:1; 13:22), implying that they are part of the same family. Referring to fellow believers as family members was common among early Christians, although it was sometimes done in other groups as well (NOTE on 2:11). This practice reinforced the idea that other Christians were to be shown the same kind of loyalty and mutual support that one would show to members of one's family (13:1). An ordinary household might include slaves and other workers along with family members (3:5–6), but those in the Christian community receive the instruction (12:5–11) and the inheritance that are reserved for full members of the family (1:14; 2:10). In response, they owe their gratitude and loyalty to the head of the household namely, to God.

Theologically, the "house" to which the listeners belong differs from other households in that its sons and daughters are identified, not by natural kinship, but by their relation to God. The "children" in the Christian household are the people whom God has given to Jesus (2:13) and who can be considered Jesus' brothers and sisters (2:11b–12). Since they are sanctified, or set apart for God, by

---

157The quotations are from deSilva (*Despising*, 285). He draws on Peter Berger's insights into the way that social structures support "plausibility structures" as well as comments by Julian Pitt-Rivers on the way the perceived "court of reputation" affects thought and behavior.

the death of Christ, these brothers and sisters are holy (3:1) and belong to a household that is headed by one who is both Son and high priest (10:21). They remain in the household by holding firmly to their confession of faith and hope (3:6).

Socially, the Christian "household" included people who did not live under the same roof. Since at least some members were married (13:4), it seems likely that the community included people from various residences. Although some may have lived close enough to exhort each other on a daily basis (3:13), others lived further away. The request to "greet all your leaders and all the saints" (13:24) makes sense only if their Christian network extended beyond their immediate circle. The exhortation to care for strangers (13:2) probably envisions a situation in which Christians traveled and relied on hospitality from Christians in other communities.[158] The author and Timothy were separated from the community, but anticipated rejoining it in the near future (13:23). The "house of God" (10:21) includes this wider Christian community.

The patterns noted above suggest that Hebrews addressed one of several house churches in a given area.[159] Early Christians commonly met in someone's home (e.g., Acts 18:7; 20:8; 1 Cor 16:19; Col 4:15; Phlm 2). Some towns might have had only one house church, whereas there were several house churches in a city like Rome (Rom 16:5, 10–11, 14–16). Limitations of physical space meant that household gatherings would ordinarily not have included more than thirty to forty people. Smaller groups could have gathered in ordinary homes rather frequently, while an assembly of "the whole church" in a more spacious house might have been less common (1 Cor 14:23). The author apparently envisioned his "word of exhortation" (Heb 13:22; cf. Acts 13:15; 1 Tim 4:13) being read to a small "gathering" of Christians (Heb 10:25; cf. 1 Thess 5:27; Col 4:16; Rev 1:3) who would later have occasion to greet "all the saints" in their area (Heb 13:24).

Hebrews calls the local "gathering" of Christians an *episynagogē* (10:25). A principal function of the gathering was the giving of mutual encouragement. Aware that without support people more easily give way to unbelief, the author urged listeners to exhort each other in order to maintain a high level of commitment to the faith (3:12–13). Invitations to approach God are given in the plural, suggesting that listeners might turn to God in prayer together (4:16; 10:22). Since belonging to a community involves a sharing of life as well as a sharing of ideas, the gathering provided opportunities to encourage works of love (10:25),

---

[158]On hospitality among Christians see Acts 21:16; Rom 16:1–2; Phlm 22; 3 John 5–8; *Did.* 11:1–12:5; Meeks, *First Urban*, 109; Osiek and Balch, *Families*, 206–10; John Koenig, *ABD* 3.299–301. Hebrews envisions hospitality being extended to Christians and non-Christians (NOTES and COMMENT on 13:2).

[159]On house churches see Banks, *Paul's Idea*, 26–36; Branick, *House Church*; Meeks, *First Urban*, 75–77; Osiek and Balch, *Families*, 32–35, 207; Klauck, *Hausgemeinde*; cf. Dunnill, *Covenant*, 32–37. Some households converted to Christianity together (Acts 16:15, 31–34; 18:8; 1 Cor 1:16; 16:15–16) while others included both Christians and non-Christians (1 Cor 7:15–16). Those who relate Hebrews to a house church include von Harnack, "Probabilia"; Moffatt, *Critical*, xv; Lane, *Hebrews*, 1.lviii–lx; cf. H.-F. Weiss, *Brief*, 75.

including the kind of moral and material support that builds community (6:10; 10:25; 13:1–3, 16).

The gathering also would have provided an occasion to offer shared praises to God (13:15) and to make "our confession" (3:1; 4:14; 10:23).[160] Early Christian confessions expressed the faith of a group in a brief, memorable form. A confession's meaning might be elaborated in different ways by group members, but all must be able to affirm the confession itself for it to be effective. To "be able to sum up the distinctiveness of one's faith in a single phrase . . . to be able to unite around a single banner; to be able to cling to simply stated conviction in the face of persecution and testing—that is important" (Dunn, *Unity*, 59). The confession of the listeners' community apparently centered on the conviction that "Jesus is the Son of God" (pp. 125–27). Hebrews reaffirms that confession (1:1–14) and elaborates on it by showing how Jesus' sonship can encompass both priesthood (5:5–6) and suffering (5:8). The list of items in 10:22–25 suggests that the confession was connected to baptism and the communal assembly, remaining a rallying point for the group (10:23). On baptism see NOTES and COMMENT on 6:2. On the Lord's Supper see pp. 127–29.

Some members of the Christian community are called "leaders" (13:7, 17, 24). The word *hēgoumenoi* was used for various positions of authority in provinces, cities, communities, and associations.[161] Referring to "your leaders" in the plural indicates that the community was served by a group of leaders rather than by one leading individual (13:7, 17). Hebrews shows no familiarity with the later practice of a single pastor leading a congregation or a single bishop administering a diocese, and it does not differentiate ministries, but uses the same term for all "leaders." When the author says that leaders "keep watch" over the souls of those in the community, he uses the verb *agrypnoun*, which is not the common word for administrative oversight (*episkopein*), but has especially to do with watching in view of God's future judgment (NOTE on 13:17). Leaders speak the word of God (13:7) over against "all sorts of strange teachings" that might erode the listeners' faith (13:9). Leaders were also examples of faith for others, which implies that a leader's life was to be congruent with the word of God that the leader spoke (NOTE on 13:7).

Although the author distinguishes "leaders" from "the saints" generally (13:24), all in the community call each other "brother" (3:1, 12; 10:19; 13:22–23), all must render an account to God (4:12–13), and all are called to approach God (4:14–16). Leaders speak the word of God, yet Hebrews assumes that each person is to develop capacities as a teacher of the faith (5:11–14). Leaders are to give to God an account of the faith of others, yet all have responsibility to help others withstand the deceptiveness of sin (Heb 3:12–13; 12:15–16) and to provoke each other to love and good works with a view to the coming Day of the Lord

---

[160]On the confession see Laub, *Bekenntnis*, 9–50.

[161]On the word *hēgoumenoi* see *TLNT* 3.166–70. On leadership in Hebrews see Dunnill, *Covenant*, 18–20; Grässer, *Aufbruch*, 213–30; Laub, "Verkündigung"; W. D. Meyer, "Obedience"; Willis, "Obey."

(10:25). By requesting that listeners heed and yield to their leaders (13:17a), the author assumes that leaders cannot simply impose their will, but depend upon the respect of the community. Hebrews calls Christ an "apostle" and "high priest" (3:1), but does not use these terms for the community's leaders. No form of priestly sacrifice is uniquely identified with the leaders. Rather, all in the community offer sacrifices of praise and love (13:15).[162]

The relationship of leadership roles in the Hebrews' community to those in other early Christian writings is unclear. Paul uses a general term for leadership when he speaks of those who "labor among you, and have charge of you [*proistamenoi*] in the Lord and admonish you" (1 Thess 5:12). Other NT writings use the terms *presbyteros* ("elder," Acts 14:23; 1 Pet 5:1; 2 John 1), *episkopos* ("overseer," "bishop," Phil 1:1; 1 Tim 3:1; Tit 1:5–7), and *diakonos* ("deacon," Rom 16:1; 1 Tim 3:8). The same persons could be called "elders" and "overseers" or "bishops," and like the leaders in Hebrews, elders and overseers served as a group in a given community (Phil 1:1; Acts 14:23; Tit 1:5). They often had responsibility for preaching and teaching, were to serve as examples for others, and were to attend to the affairs of the community (1 Tim 5:17; Tit 1:5–9). Many of these same things could be said about deacons.[163] Although some have argued that Hebrews shows tendencies toward a hierarchical view of church organization, this seems unlikely. Hebrews evinces respect for leadership but shows little interest in matters of rank and office.[164]

2. CHRISTIAN COMMUNITY AND JEWISH SUBCULTURE

The group addressed by Hebrews had some traits in common with Jewish communities. If Jews gathered as a *synagōgē*, the Christians used the related term *episynagōge* for their own gatherings (NOTE on 10:25). Synagogues provided opportunities for exhortation and prayer (e.g., Acts 13:15), as did the listeners' gathering (Heb 3:13; 10:23–25; 13:22). If Jews used water in ablutions, or baptisms (9:10), Christians also used water in their baptisms (6:2; 10:22). The Scriptures were regularly read in synagogues. Hebrews makes wide use of these same texts, utilizing common Jewish interpretive techniques, such as arguments from the lesser to the greater (2:1–4; 10:28–29), the linking of two texts based on a common word (4:4–5), and the significance of silences in Scripture (7:3). He-

[162]Scholer proposes that Hebrews extends priestly functions to all members of the community (*Proleptic*, 9–10, 112, 149).

[163]Stephen, Philip, and others were set apart to serve (*diakonein*) tables, but were active preachers (Acts 6–8). Timothy, a *diakonos*, was also a teacher (1 Tim 4:6, 11–16).

[164]On presbyters, bishops, and deacons, see R. E. Brown, *Churches*, 31–37. Brown's book shows the variety in early Christian leadership patterns (cf. Dunn, *Unity*, 103–23). Some plot a trajectory moving from the simpler view of leadership in 1 Thess 5:12–13 to the hierarchy reflected in *1 Clem.* 1:3; 21:6; 37:2. They place Hebrews on the hierarchical end of the scale (Zimmermann, *Bekenntnis*, 13; Thurén, *Lobopfer*, 205–6; H.-F. Weiss, *Brief*, 744; T. Schramm, *EDNT* 2.113). For non-hierarchical views see Hegermann, *Brief*, 279–80; Grässer, *Aufbruch*, 228.

brews also draws on postbiblical Jewish traditions, such as the stories of the Maccabean martyrs and apocryphal stories about the prophets (11:35–38).

Nevertheless, the community addressed by Hebrews could not identify itself along the lines of a Jewish community.[165] First, Jewish communities usually had ethnic bonds in which kinship and custom reinforced each other (Barclay, *Jews*, 402–13), but the ethnic background of those addressed by Hebrews is unclear and ethnicity was apparently not a primary bond for Christians from Italy (13:24; cf. pp. 46–48). Second, Jews were known for circumcision, observance of the Sabbath, and distinctive meal practices (Barclay, *Jews*, 434–42). Hebrews does not mention circumcision or the weekly day of rest, using "Sabbath" language only for the everlasting Sabbath in God's kingdom (4:9). More importantly, Hebrews specifically relegates matters of food and drink to a time that is past, implying that Christians who live by the new covenant do not define themselves by adherence to these practices (9:9–10; 13:9).

Hebrews shapes Christian identity by focusing on what might be called "symbolic resources" (Barclay, *Jews*, 413–28). The status of the Law is considered below (pp. 114–15). Here we might note that both before and after the destruction of the Temple, respect for the Levitical priesthood was a mark of Jewish identity (§18 COMMENT). Instead of either accepting the primacy of the Levitical priesthood or dismissing the need for priests altogether, Hebrews argues that Christians have a high priest in Jesus. His priesthood is based on a promise found in Israel's Scriptures (Ps 110:4), but it displaces the Levitical priesthood and establishes a new covenant (§18 COMMENT *a–b*). Similarly, Jews identified with the Jerusalem Temple and its sacrifices, and considered Judea to be their homeland. Rather than either adopting these patterns or dismissing them, Hebrews moves in a third direction by arguing that in Christ the listeners have a heavenly sanctuary (§20 COMMENT *a*), a definitive sacrifice (§25 COMMENT *a–c*), and a heavenly homeland (§31 COMMENT *b*).

Other symbolic resources are created by relating heroes from Israel's history to Christ. Hebrews does not define the Christian community by its relation to Moses and Aaron, but neither does it disparage these venerable figures. Instead, the author affirms that Moses is worthy of honor, since he was God's faithful servant, whereas Jesus is worthy of greater honor since he is God's faithful Son (3:1–6). Moses is important because he bears witness to what God has communicated in Christ (3:5b; §9 COMMENT), and in Moses' suffering people can see the suffering and redemption of Christ foreshadowed (11:26). Similarly, Aaron is worthy of honor, but he also exemplifies a pattern in which one receives the honor of priesthood from God (5:1–4). Since God has now called Jesus to the glory of an eternal priesthood, his glory surpasses that of Aaron (5:5–10; §12 COMMENT *c*).

---

[165]Isaacs, "Hebrews." For a valuable summary of the discussion surrounding the complex topic of Jewish identity in the Greco-Roman world see Barclay, *Jews*, 399–444. Barclay carefully shows the various degrees of assimilation into Greco-Roman culture as well as noting the features that most shaped Jewish identity. On attitudes toward Judaism in Hebrews see Klassen, "To the Hebrews"; Wall and Lane, "Polemic."

3. CHRISTIAN COMMUNITY AND THE DOMINANT GRECO-ROMAN CULTURE

Hebrews' understanding of the Christian community's relationship to its Greco-Roman context is that of a resident alien (11:9). From the perspective of the author, Christians are aliens in that their beliefs set them apart from others in society, evoking the animosity that was evident in phases 2 and 3 of their history (pp. 67–72). Yet Christians do reside in the Greco-Roman world, and not all relations with the wider society are negative. Some Christians known to the listeners may have found Greco-Roman society attractive, tending to ease tensions with it by suppressing their distinctive Christian beliefs and accommodating themselves to the values of non-Christian society. Hebrews does not fully embrace or entirely reject Greco-Roman culture, but appropriates and transforms its imagery in ways that support a distinctly Christian confession.[166]

Hebrews fits the Greco-Roman world in many ways. It was written in Greek for a Greek-speaking audience, and the explanations of Hebrew names suggest that listeners had no knowledge of Semitic languages (7:2). In form, Hebrews' outline and style show a thorough acquaintance with accepted patterns of Greco-Roman rhetoric (pp. 87–96). In content, Hebrews is interlaced with references to Greco-Roman ideas and practices, which are discussed in NOTES. These include the idea that God is the one from whom and for whom all things exist (2:10), that the builder is worthy of more honor than the house (3:3), that people should moderate their feelings (5:2), that one learns by suffering (5:8–9), and that God does not lie (6:18). Stages in the Hellenistic educational process illustrate growth in Christian faith (5:12–14). Common legal practices make it plausible to think that God would confirm his promise by an oath (6:16–17) and appoint Jesus as the surety (7:22). A last will and testament, which becomes effective upon a person's death, helps to show the effect of Christ's death in granting an eternal inheritance to the listeners (9:15–17).[167]

Despite these similarities, Greco-Roman imagery is transformed to reinforce Christian beliefs. Greco-Roman rulers were sometimes said to be sons of a god, bearing divine radiance and directing all things, yet Hebrews ascribes these traits to Christ (§3 COMMENT *a–b*). Heracles was said to have descended to the netherworld in order to battle the lord of the dead before ascending to life and power. Some rulers likened themselves to Heracles, but Hebrews insists that it is Jesus who liberates people from the fear of death (§8 COMMENT *c*). Kings and

---

[166]Attention has often centered on Hebrews' relation to Platonism. Some maintain that the author appropriately drew on Platonic thought forms in an effort to interpret the gospel in a Greco-Roman context. Others assume that affinities with Platonism would erode the integrity of the Christian message. See pp. 59–60. Shifting the focus from philosophy to other aspects of Greco-Roman culture allows for alternative ways to consider how Hebrews appropriates and transforms images taken from its context.

[167]Such use of Greco-Roman imagery was not unique to Hebrews. For example, Hellenistic Jewish authors and Paul also recalled stages in the Hellenistic educational process and used metaphors taken from athletics when speaking of Jewish and Christian life (NOTES on 5:11–14; 10:32).

emperors invited people to approach their thrones in order to find help, but Hebrews invites listeners to approach the throne of grace through Christ (§12 COMMENT *a*). Rulers carried out public works, such as opening new roads or ways, but in Hebrews it is Christ who opens a new way that leads into God's presence (§26 COMMENT *a*).

Religious rites were central to life in most cities. Greco-Roman rulers commonly served as high priests, whereas in Israel's tradition the offices of priest and king were often separated. Hebrews insists that Jesus possesses both kingly power and priestly office, but it makes this claim by appealing to a biblical text (Ps 110:4) rather than to Greco-Roman precedent. The argument that no legitimate high priest takes the honor upon himself also serves as a tacit critique of Greco-Roman practices in which people commonly sought to obtain priestly offices for themselves (§12 COMMENT *b*). Moreover, Hebrews' assumption that there is only one priestly order runs counter to the practice of multiple priesthoods that characterized Greco-Roman life (§18 COMMENT *a*). Sacrifices were offered at many sanctuaries throughout the Roman Empire, but rather than accepting the validity of these sanctuaries or altogether dismissing the need of a sanctuary, Hebrews insists that there is one true sanctuary, which is located in heaven (§20 COMMENT *a*). By directing listeners to this heavenly sanctuary and its high priest, Hebrews gives them a focus for their worship that allows their community to maintain an identity distinct from groups associated with other sanctuaries.

Christians were denounced by non-Christians, yet Hebrews draws on images from the dominant culture in order to support the listeners' identity as outsiders in that culture. Although non-Christians dishonored Christians, the author offers another perspective on the conflict by drawing on honored images from athletics: the followers of Christ endure persecution as one endures the rigors of an athletic contest (NOTE on 10:32), bearing up under society's reproach as runners bear the strain of a footrace (§34 COMMENT *a*). In the eyes of non-Christians, the faithful are dishonored, but in the eyes of God faith is truly valued. The present moment, therefore, calls for perseverance rather than despair.

III. Formal and Rhetorical Aspects

◆

The author of Hebrews gives a human speech that calls listeners to give attention to divine speech. Like the prophets, through whom God spoke "in many forms" (1:1), the author of Hebrews conveys his message in a richly textured way. Writing for a group of listeners rather than a solitary reader, the author consistently addresses his audience in the second person plural. Like others in antiquity, he probably assumed that his text would be read aloud (e.g., 2 Macc 15:39;

1 Thess 5:27; Rev 1:3). Strings of words beginning with *p* help to catch listeners' ears (e.g., 1:1; 11:4–6), and verbal cues such as catchwords, *inclusios*, and repetition help hearers follow the speaker's progression of thought.[168] Classical rhetoric provides useful ways to consider how Hebrews communicates with its audience.[169]

A. Genre of Hebrews

Hebrews was for centuries regarded as a letter that lacked the usual opening salutation.[170] The ancient church's comments about Hebrews' form centered on the question of its authorship. Those who concluded that Paul wrote Hebrews naturally placed it among Paul's other writings, which were letters. This placement reinforced the idea that Hebrews too was a letter (pp. 26–27). Internal evidence for this view comes from the conclusion (13:18–25), which resembles the endings of other NT letters by including a comment on what the author wrote (13:22), together with a request for prayers, benediction, anticipation of a future visit, personal greetings, and final salutation (§39 COMMENT). Despite its refined literary character, most recognize that Hebrews is not a general treatise on Christ's priesthood.[171] Rather, it is a word of exhortation (13:22) that takes account of the situation of the readers (5:11–12; 6:9–10; 10:32–33; 12:4; 13:7, 18–19)—and exhortation was an important feature of early Christian letters (e.g., Rom 12; Acts 15:30–32). A problem with this view is that Hebrews not only lacks an epistolary salutation but is also missing the thanksgiving and prayers or statement of astonishment that introduce other early Christian letters.

The view that Hebrews is a sermon to which an epistolary conclusion (13:22–25) was added has become common during the last two hundred years.[172] One reason is that a "word of exhortation" (13:22) is a way to describe a synagogue

---

[168]Note for example how the words *blepein* ("see") and *apistia* ("unbelief") frame 3:7–19 and how *horkōmosia* ("swearing an oath") frames 7:20–28. The importance of these devices has been demonstrated by Vanhoye, *La structure*, 53–58, 274–303.

[169]The use of rhetorical categories for Hebrews is not new. In antiquity the opening was called an *exordium* (Augustine, PL 44.137) or *prooimion* (Theodoret, PG 82.675A). Aspects of Hebrews' argument were discussed in rhetorical categories by Hemmingson in the sixteenth century (Hagen, *Hebrews*, 80–83) and by Bengel in the eighteenth century (*Epistle*, 335–36). Similar attempts were made in the nineteenth (von Soden, "Brief," 8–11) and early twentieth centuries (Windisch, *Hebräerbrief*, 8; Spicq, *L'Épître*, 1.38).

[170]The lack of a salutation was variously attributed to the author's modesty (p. 21) or historical accident (p. 34). See §1 COMMENT. Recent interpreters who consider Hebrews to be a letter include Ellingworth, *Epistle*, 59–62; Feld, *Hebräerbrief*, 23; Kistemaker, *Exposition*, 3–4; Lindars, *Theology*, 6; Dunnill, *Covenant*, 22.

[171]Hebrews has been variously considered a "treatise" (Ebrard, *Biblical Commentary*, 280), a piece of "artistic literature" (Deissmann, *Light*, 244), a "theological meditation" (Rissi, *Theologie*, 13), and a kind of liturgical text (Dunnill, *Covenant*, 115–23).

[172]This proposal, which was first made in 1797 by J. Berger ("Brief"), has been adopted by many recent scholars. In addition to those surveyed in Grässer, *Aufbruch*, 22–23, note Attridge; Cockerill; Hagner; Lane, Long; Pfitzner; Backhaus, *Der neue*, 42–47; Cahill, "Home"; Cosby, *Rhetorical*, 2;

homily. After the reading of the law and the prophets, the officials of the synagogue at Antioch in Pisidia said to Paul and his companions, "Brothers, if you have any word of exhortation for the people, give it" (Acts 13:15). In the sermon that followed, Paul explicated Jesus' death and resurrection in light of the Jewish Scriptures, which Hebrews also does. The pattern of reading from Scripture and giving exhortation continued in early Christian gatherings. According to 1 Tim 4:13, Timothy was directed to "give attention to the public reading of scripture, to exhorting, to teaching" (cf. Rom 12:6–8). Later Christians also thought of homilies as "words of exhortation" (*Apos. Con.* 8.5). Conceiving of Hebrews as a sermon also seems suitable since the author commonly refers to speaking rather than to writing (2:5; 5:11; 6:9; 8:1; 9:5), is aware of the limits of time available for his address (11:32), and follows patterns of classical rhetoric.[173]

In practice, letters and speeches sometimes shared certain elements. NT letters were usually written to groups of people, rather than to individuals, and would have been read aloud to a number of listeners at one time (Col 4:16; 1 Thess 5:27). Paul dictated his letters, using rhetorical techniques and often referred to speaking rather than to writing (e.g., Rom 6:1; 1 Cor 9:8; Gal 1:9; cf. Rom 16:22). Yet ancient theorists assumed that letter writing and speech making were two different types of activities that could be analyzed using different sets of categories. Letters can be read aloud and speeches can be sent in written form, but in formal terms a composition will correspond more closely to one genre than to the other. If a genre is "a specific way of visualizing a given part of reality," Hebrews envisions communication taking place more in the manner of a speech than a letter.[174]

Hebrews is sometimes called a "homily," which helps modern readers envision a setting in which it would have been read aloud to a group, but does little to clarify our understanding of Hebrews' shape, because so little is known about the contours of Jewish and Christian preaching in the first century. Extant Hellenistic Jewish homilies show little formal similarity to Hebrews, and the difference from rabbinic sermons is even greater.[175] Paul's sermon in Acts 13:16–41 is almost certainly a summary presentation of the Christian message rather than a transcription of his actual sermon, but it indicates how the shape of early Christian preaching was perceived. Studies of Paul's "word of exhortation" and the other speeches in Acts suggest that conventions from Greco-Roman rhetoric helped to shape early Christian preaching.[176] We cannot assume that the author

---

Swetnam, "Literary," 261; Trotter, *Interpreting*, 59–80; Übelacker, *Hebräerbrief*, 22–23; Vanhoye, *Old Testament*, 66; Wray, *Rest*, 52–55.

[173]Michel, *Brief*, 25; Spicq, *L'Épître*, 1.18; Thyen, *Stil*, 16–18; H.-F. Weiss, *Brief*, 35–41.

[174]See J. L. Bailey ("Genre Analysis," 201), who cites work by G. S. Morson and C. Emerson. On the difference between letters and speeches in ancient theory see R. D. Anderson, *Ancient*, 93–109.

[175]On Hellenistic Jewish homilies see Siegert, *Drei*, 1–29; Wills, "Form." On rabbinic preaching see Stegner, "Ancient." Thyen's study of Jewish preaching relied on excerpts from various texts, but concluded that Hebrews was the only completely preserved homily of the period (*Stil*, 106).

[176]See C. C. Black, "Rhetorical Form"; Kennedy, *New Testament*, 124–25; Fitzmyer, *Acts*, 108; H.-F. Weiss, *Brief*, 40.

of Hebrews had received formal training as a speaker, but rhetoric was a basic component of education in the Greco-Roman world, and its conventions were familiar across a broad spectrum of society.[177]

Rhetoric is the art of persuasion, and approaching Hebrews from this perspective allows us to consider how its form, content, and other features might work together to influence its audience. Rhetorical handbooks divide speeches into three main categories.[178] First, judicial rhetoric seeks to elicit a judgment about something that has occurred in the past, commonly through appeals to what is true and just. Most recognize that Hebrews does not fit this category.[179] Second, deliberative rhetoric counsels people to follow a certain course of action in the future, pursuing what is beneficial and avoiding what is harmful. Since Hebrews summons listeners to set a course that will lead to future reward (e.g., 4:11; 6:18; 10:36; 12:1–2), some consider it to be a deliberative speech.[180] Third, epideictic rhetoric seeks to reinforce the present values of the listeners by commending what is praiseworthy and condemning what is shameful. Hebrews does exhort listeners to "hold fast" to the faith they already profess (3:6; 4:14; 10:23) and uses the device of comparison, which was common in epideictic speeches, to show Christ's superiority to persons and institutions from the OT. Therefore, some consider Hebrews to be an epideictic speech.[181]

Categorizing Hebrews as either deliberative or epideictic is finally not helpful, however, since classical handbooks recognized that the two forms of rhetoric were closely related and could occur in the same speech. Thus, when counseling people to adopt a course of action, speakers often urged them to follow what was praiseworthy and to avoid what was shameful. Conversely, praise or blame of someone's conduct helped to motivate listeners to adopt or avoid similar actions (Aristotle, *Rhetoric* 1.9.36; Quintilian, *Inst.* 3.7.28; *Rhet. ad Her.* 3.8 §15). Moreover, assessment of the genre depends in part upon the individual hearer. For listeners who remain committed to God and Christ, Hebrews is epideictic, since it maintains the values they already hold. For those tending to drift away from the faith, Hebrews is deliberative, since it seeks to dissuade them from apostasy and move them toward a clearer faith commitment.[182]

177On education in antiquity see Marrou, *History*; C. W. Wooten, "Roman Education and Rhetoric," *CAM* 2.1109–20; C. Dewald, "Greek Education and Rhetoric," *CAM* 2.1077–1107.

178On the categories see Aristotle, *Rhetoric* 1.3.1–9; *Rhet. ad Her.* 1.2 §2; Quintilian, *Inst.* 3.4.1–16; Lausberg, *Handbook* §61.

179For comparison of Hebrews to judicial rhetoric see von Soden, "Brief," 8–11; Windisch, *Hebräerbrief*, 8.

180Übelacker, *Hebräerbrief*, 214–29; Lindars, "Rhetorical," 386; Backhaus, *Der neue*, 64–65.

181Attridge, *Epistle*, 14; idem, "Paraenesis," 214; Olbricht, "Hebrews," 378; Aune, *New Testament*, 212; Eisenbaum, *Jewish Heroes*, 11–12.

182deSilva, *Despising*, 35; Watson, "Rhetorical," 187; Lane, *Hebrews*, 1.lxxix.

B. Structure of Hebrews

There are numerous suggestions concerning the structure of Hebrews.[183] Most recent discussion, however, has revolved around two types of proposals. One divides Hebrews into five main sections that are framed by an introduction and conclusion (1:1–4; 13:20–21). Albert Vanhoye proposes in *La structure* that the five parts are (I) the name superior to angels (1:5–2:18), (II) Christ's faithfulness and compassion (3:1–5:10), (III) the central exposition on sacrifice (5:11–10:39), (IV) faith and endurance (11:1–12:13), and (V) the peaceful fruit of justice (12:14–13:19). He arranges the five parts concentrically around the theme of Christ's priesthood, which he takes to be the central point of Hebrews (8:1), suggesting that parts I and V have to do with eschatology, that parts II and IV deal with ecclesiology, and that the central section discusses sacrifice (III).

Many interpreters have adopted this carefully argued proposal, sometimes modifying it, but questions remain.[184] Vanhoye's overall conception is one in which the parts of Hebrews fit together in a balanced architectural fashion, so that outlying parts support the center, but much of the imagery in Hebrews moves in a more linear fashion, directing listeners toward the goal of entering God's rest, drawing near to the inner sanctuary, and approaching God's heavenly city. Given the linear movement of these images and the exhortations based on them, it seems unlikely that Hebrews as a whole is structured in a concentric manner. It is not evident that parts I and V deal with eschatology while parts II and IV focus on ecclesiology. The themes are more thoroughly intertwined. Christ's priesthood is one important theme in Hebrews, but it is not clear that it is the central theme, since Christ's priesthood is prominent in Heb 5 and 7–10, but not in other parts of the speech (NOTE on 8:1). Identifying priesthood as the main topic is also problematic because the main arguments were usually not placed in the middle of a speech, but at the beginning and end, where they would have the greatest impact (*Rhet. ad Her.* 3.10 §18). Finally, since Hebrews calls itself a word of exhortation (13:22), one might expect to find clues to the speech's structure in its hortatory sections.

The second approach distinguishes three main sections divided by the calls to hold fast to the community's confession of faith (4:14–16; 10:19–25).[185] The first section is framed by declarations concerning the power of God's word (1:1–4; 4:12–13), the second is framed by comments concerning Christ's priesthood (4:14–16; 10:11–18), and the third calls the listeners to faithfulness (10:19–

---

[183]For surveys of research, see Lane, *Hebrews*, 1.lxxxiv–lxxxix; G. H. Guthrie, *Structure*, 3–41; cf. Garuti, "Alcune strutture"; MacLeod, "Literary Structure"; Stanley, "Structure." See also the proposals by Swetnam in the bibliography.

[184]Those who generally follow Vanhoye include Attridge, Bénétreau, Casalini, Ellingworth, Lane; cf. D. A. Black, "Problem"; F. F. Bruce, "To the Hebrews," 3500; MacLeod, "Literary Structure." For a critique of this approach see Swetnam's two articles on "Form"; idem, "The Structure."

[185]Michel; Hegermann; März; Smith; H.-F. Weiss; cf. Backhaus, *Der neue*, 63. Dussaut also divides Hebrews into three parts on somewhat different formal grounds, arguing that the whole is structured concentrically (*Synopse*, 147–51).

13:25). Giving primary attention to the hortatory sections is consistent with the idea that Hebrews is a word of exhortation (13:22), but this proposal has been less successful in showing the internal logic of the speech. Moreover, the middle section is interrupted by a lengthy digression (5:11–6:20) and is variously said to conclude with 10:18 (H.-F. Weiss), 10:31 (Hegermann), or 10:39 (Michel).

This commentary offers an alternative to these approaches by using classical rhetorical patterns to identify the general structure of Hebrews.[186] Speeches usually include several standard elements, although speakers show considerable freedom in adapting typical patterns to specific situations. An exordium, or introduction, prepares listeners to give proper attention to the speaker. A narration of the facts pertaining to the topic often follows the exordium, but is not essential, and Hebrews omits it.[187] The next main elements are the proposition, which defines the issue to be addressed, and the arguments that support the speaker's position. The final component is a peroration, which brings the speech to a close.

Transitions between sections are created by digressions in which the author appeals for attention and warns about the dangers of neglecting or spurning the word of God (2:1–4; 5:11–6:20; 10:26–39; 12:25–27).[188] Short digressions, which contrast the way that God spoke in the past at Sinai with the way God now addresses the listeners, make the transition from the exordium to the proposition (2:1–4) and from the final series of arguments to the peroration (12:25–27). Longer digressions create transitions between major sections of the argument by warning about apostasy, recalling the listeners' faithfulness, and encouraging perseverance (5:11–6:20; 10:26–39). The main arguments and the transitional sections function somewhat differently, but work together towad the same end, which is that the listeners remain loyal to Christ and the Christian community.

- I. EXORDIUM (1:1–2:4)
- II. PROPOSITION (2:5–9)
- III. ARGUMENTS (2:10–12:27)
  - A. First Series (2:10–6:20)
    1. Argument: Jesus received glory through faithful suffering—a way that others are called to follow (2:10–5:10)
    2. Transitional Digression: Warning and Encouragement (5:11–6:20)

[186]For a summary of attempts to apply classical rhetorical categories to the structure of Hebrews see Watson, "Rhetorical," 182–83. For arguments against the idea that Hebrews follows classical patterns see Garuti, *Alle origini*, 185–315. On Hebrews' approach to persuasion see Lohmann, "Zur Heilsgeschichte"; Matera, "Moral Exhortation"; Walters, "Rhetorical."

[187]On omitting the narration see Quintilian, *Inst.* 4.2.4–5; 5.preface.5. Some propose that Hebrews does contain a narration, but vary widely in identifying the narration as 4:14–6:20 (von Soden, *Brief*, 11), 1:5–4:13 (Backhaus, *Der neue*, 59), 1:5–6:20 (Spicq, *L'Épître*, 1.38), 1:5–2:18 (Nissilä, *Hohepriestermotiv*, 24; Übelacker, *Hebräerbrief*, 185–96).

[188]Using digressions of different lengths was common (Lausberg, *Handbook* §§340–42, 345). Heb 3:7–4:11 has the hortatory features of a digression, but does not interrupt the argument.

- B. Second Series (7:1–10:39)
  1. Argument: Jesus' suffering is the sacrifice that enables others to approach God (7:1–10:25)
  2. Transitional Digression: Warning and Encouragement (10:26–39)
- C. Third Series (11:1–12:27)
  1. Argument: God's people persevere through suffering to glory by faith (11:1–12:24)
  2. Transitional Digression: Warning and Encouragement (12:25–27)

IV. PERORATION (12:28–13:21)

V. EPISTOLARY POSTSCRIPT (13:22–25)

Formally, the exordium (1:1–2:4) is framed by complex sentences, or periods, that deal with God's manner of speaking in the past through prophets and angels, and in the present through his Son (1:1–4; 2:2–4). The first part of the exordium introduces the Son as the heir and creator of all things, who is seated at God's right hand (1:1–4), and the second part provides OT support for these claims (1:5–14). The final paragraph calls for attention by warning about the consequences of neglecting the Christian message (2:1–4). See §2 COMMENT.

The proposition (2:5–9) is a discrete section, consisting of a quotation of Ps 8:4–6, followed by a brief exposition of the text. It is positioned between two other sections of the speech, each of which is neatly framed. In content, the proposition is situated at the juncture where attention turns from the glory of the exalted Christ to the significance of his suffering. With a few brief remarks, the author states the themes that will be developed in the remainder of the speech: Christ's movement from suffering to glory, his suffering on behalf of others, and the idea that one can "see" the fulfillment of God's promises in Christ, despite their apparent nonrealization in human experience. See §6 COMMENT.

The first series of arguments (2:10–5:10) is framed by statements that Christ was made complete through suffering, so that he has become the pioneer or source of salvation for others (2:10; 5:8–10). Before this section the author focused on the glory of the ascended Christ, whereas these arguments emphasize the suffering that preceded Christ's exaltation. Paragraphs comparing Christ's glory to Moses' and Aaron's, together with images from the exodus and wilderness wanderings, help to unify the section.[189] The section concludes with a lengthy period that summarizes Christ's suffering and exaltation (5:5–10). The digression that follows this section interrupts the main argument to reprove the listeners for their lack of learning (5:11–6:20) in contrast to Christ's way of learning through suffering (5:8). The author signals a return to his main argument by

---

[189]Some outlines of Hebrews include Heb 5 with what follows because Christ's priesthood is a topic in 4:14–5:10 and again in 7:1–10:25. Here it is linked with what precedes because 4:14–5:10 emphasizes the theme of glory, which is important in 2:10–5:10, but less so in Heb 7–10. Moreover, 4:14–5:10 emphasizes the similarities between Christ and Aaron, whereas 7:1–10:25 stresses the differences between Christ's priesthood and the Levitical priesthood.

restating the point he made just before the digression, namely, that Christ is a priest forever according to the type of Melchizedek (5:10; 6:20). See §§7 and 13 COMMENT.

The second series of arguments (7:1–10:25) shows that Christ suffered in order to make the sacrifice that allows his followers to enter God's presence. Successive comparisons of the Levitical priesthood and Christ's priesthood, the old and new covenants, animal sacrifices and Christ's self-sacrifice integrate the section. In the previous series of arguments, the author showed the similarities between the priesthood of Aaron and Jesus, but here he stresses the differences between the Levitical priestly service and Christ's priestly service. Formally, this segment concludes with a period that draws together the main themes and invites listeners to draw near to God as the Day of the Lord draws near to them (10:19–25). A digression, which echoes earlier warnings about the dangers of turning from God and encourages listeners to remain faithful, makes the transition into the final series of arguments (10:26–39). The author marks the end of the digression by taking up the matter of faith (10:38–39), which was mentioned at the end of the previous section (10:22–23) and becomes a central topic in the next section. See §§16 and 27 COMMENT.

The third series of arguments (11:1–12:24) begins and ends with comments about the blood of Abel (11:4; 12:24). The section traces the journeys of the righteous who endured conflict, disappointment, and death on earth, culminating with the spirits of the righteous being made complete in God's heavenly city (12:22–24). Abraham lived as a foreigner on earth in the hope of life in God's city (11:10, 16), Moses gave up wealth in Egypt for a future reward (11:26–27), and the martyrs accepted death in the hope of resurrection (11:35). The depiction of the faithful in the heavenly Jerusalem shows that they did not persevere in vain, for God is faithful to his promises (12:22–23). A short digression urging listeners to heed the one who is speaking concludes the section and contributes to the framing effect: the word of God created the world at the beginning (11:3) and will shake the world at the end (12:25–27). See §35 COMMENT.

The peroration (12:28–13:21) refers to service "pleasing" to God in its opening statement (12:28) and final benediction (13:21). The first and last paragraphs of the peroration deal with the importance of offering service or sacrifice to God, serving other people, and remembering one's leaders. The central paragraph, in order to shape and support this view of Christian discipleship, creatively fuses the themes of Christ's priestly sacrifice and the hope of entering the city of God. See §37 COMMENT.

The epistolary postscript (13:22–25) begins after the final benediction and includes many features typical of conclusions on early Christian letters: a comment about what has been written, sharing of personal information and mention of a future visit, an extension of greetings, and a parting wish. See §39 COMMENT.

C. RHETORICAL STRATEGY

Speakers in antiquity understood that persuasion comes from the interplay of three things: the speaker's character, the listeners' disposition, and the content of the speech (Aristotle, *Rhetoric* 1.2.3). People's judgments were affected not only by logic but by the emotions elicited in them by the speaker and by their sense of the speaker's integrity. Hebrews addressed a situation in which listeners were experiencing reproach from those outside the community (13:13) together with some disintegration within the community (5:11; 6:12; 10:25). A compelling summons to a renewed commitment to God, Christ, and the Christian community would affect listeners through logic, emotion, and a sense of the speaker's integrity:

1. LOGIC

Logic (*logos*) is the aspect of persuasive speech that appeals to the mind. Hebrews takes up the question of God's design for humanity. Briefly, the proposition and three main parts of the argument show that:

God's intention is to crown people with glory, but God's people do not "see" God's design fulfilled in their own experience.

a. One must therefore look to Jesus, who was exalted after suffering faithfully, opening the way to glory for others.

b. Through suffering, Jesus offered a complete sacrifice for sins, so that people may draw near to God with confidence.

c. Like previous generations of God's people, who endured disappointment, conflict, and death, the listeners are called to persevere by looking for a future in God's heavenly city and a glory that is not evident to the eye, but that can be perceived by faith in the promises of God.

The exordium introduces the arguments by fixing attention on the exalted Christ, in whom the listeners can see God's promises fulfilled. The peroration relates the service that Christ performed to the ongoing service that his followers perform in their own communities.

The author approaches the main topic indirectly, using the exordium (1:1–2:4) to establish rapport with listeners and to shape a perspective from which the principal issue could be considered (§2 COMMENT). In terms of logic, the exordium stresses that Christ has been exalted to supreme glory at God's right hand. The author assumes that listeners are already familiar with this idea, so that he does not need to argue it as if for the first time. This conviction that Jesus has entered heavenly glory is a presupposition for the arguments that follow.

Defining the issue was a challenge faced by most speakers. The situation of those addressed by Hebrews was probably complex, and the author could not assume that everyone would have understood the causes of decline in community life in the same way. Therefore, before speaking to the problem, he defined it as the apparent contradiction between the glory that God has promised people and the fact that they do not see this promise realized in their own experience (§6 COMMENT). Responding to the problem, the author focuses on the fact that Jesus suffered before he entered the glory that the listeners glimpsed in the exordium. When the author states that Jesus suffered before being glorified (2:9a), he anticipates the first series of arguments, which emphasize that by moving through suffering to glory, Jesus opened the path that the listeners follow (2:10–5:10). When the author states that Jesus suffered death on behalf of everyone (2:9b), he anticipates the second series of arguments, which show how Jesus' death provides atonement and a new covenant relationship for people (7:1–10:25). The third series of arguments returns to the original contradiction between physical sight and God's promises (2:8b), stressing that Jesus' followers walk by faith in a future that cannot be seen with the eye, but is known through God's word (11:1–12:24).

The three series of arguments follow the three ideas introduced in the proposition.

(a) Jesus' movement from suffering to glory involves taking on human flesh and blood, and battling with the devil before assuming his position as heavenly high priest. If Moses is rightly honored for faithfulness, the Son of God receives greater glory for his faithfulness. Moses' contemporaries failed to reach the promised land because of unbelief, showing that Christian listeners, who hope to enter God's rest, must now persevere. Grace for the journey comes from Jesus the high priest, who was exalted because of his suffering.

(b) The second series shows how Jesus suffered and was exalted for others (7:1–10:25). After showing that Jesus can be considered a priest, the author argues that Jesus' death was the definitive sacrifice of atonement that inaugurates a new covenant relationship with God, allowing people to draw near to him with confidence.

(c) The final series turns from the suffering of Christ to the suffering of the faithful. It picks up the theme that the fulfillment of God's designs cannot be seen by the eye, but is only known by faith (11:1–12:24). Accounts of the challenges facing past heroes and heroines of faith lead into a depiction of the listeners' own situation, which can be compared to runners in a race that requires endurance. Like their forebears, the listeners must fix their attention on the joy that awaits them in the future. Present challenges are like the difficulties that toughen athletes in training, but by looking toward the goal of life in God's heavenly city, they can persevere faithfully on earth.

As the arguments progress, Hebrews sends a constant message that faith is a journey that culminates in the fulfillment of God's promises. Initially, listeners are like the wilderness generation, for they have experienced God's act of deliverance but still journey by faith in the hope of entering God's promised rest

(4:1–11). Next they are worshipers in the sanctuary, who stand in the outer court and now have the prospect of entering the inner sanctuary, where God is present (10:19–25). Finally, they are among the generations of Israel who sojourn on earth in the hope of finding a place in Zion, the city of God (12:22–24). Thus different images—the promised land, the sanctuary, Zion—work together to convey the same hope (Dunnill, *Covenant*, 134–48).

The transitional digressions that appear at the end of each major section do not directly advance the main argument but contribute to the persuasive quality of the speech by warnings and words of encouragement (2:1–4; 5:11–6:20; 10:26–39; 12:25–27). Although interpreters who deal with Hebrews in written form might prefer a single sustained argument, speakers in antiquity often digressed to regain the attention of live audiences, who found it difficult to follow a sustained argument without occasional respites. As in other speeches, the digressions in Hebrews seek to secure attention by reproofs, warnings, and appeals to the listeners (§§13 and 27 COMMENT).[190] The two longer digressions contribute to the speech's logic by introducing the hermeneutical keys to the sections that follow. In 6:20 the author recalls how the psalmist said that God would establish a priest forever after the type of Melchizedek (Ps 110:4), and this becomes the lens through which the Genesis story of Melchizedek is read in Heb 7. Similarly, the quotation of Hab 2:3–4 in Heb 10:37–38 gives the principle that the righteous live by faith, which provides the lens through which OT narrative is considered in Heb 11. See §§17 and 30 COMMENT.

The peroration (12:28–13:21) draws Hebrews' arguments into an appeal for service that is pleasing to God. Christ endured suffering to help those who were held captive, and listeners now do the same for the afflicted from their own community (2:11–15; 13:1–3). Christ's self-sacrifice on their behalf enables listeners to offer sacrifices of praise to God and service to other people (9:11–14; 13:15–16). The strength of the peroration comes not from new arguments, but from the application of earlier themes and images to the specific challenges facing the community. See §36 COMMENT.

2. EMOTION

Emotion (*pathos*) is a second element of persuasion. People "decide far more problems by hate or love, or lust or rage, or sorrow or joy, or hope or fear" than by rational argument (Cicero, *De oratore* 2.42 §178). Therefore, it "is in its power over the emotions that the life and soul of oratory is to be found" (Quintilian, *Inst.* 6.2.7).[191] Broadly speaking, "emotions are all those affections which cause men to change their opinion in regard to their judgments, and are accompanied by pleasure and pain" (Aristotle, *Rhetoric* 2.1.8). The dynamics in Hebrews can best be seen through the interplay of positive feelings, such as con-

---

[190]On digressions see Quintilian, *Inst.* 4.3.12–17; Cicero, *De oratore* 3.53 §203; Lausberg, *Handbook* §§340–42.

[191]See Aristotle, *Rhetoric* 1.2.5; Lausberg, *Handbook* §257.2–3; deSilva, *Despising*, 42–46; Eisenbaum, *Jewish Heroes*, 136–37.

fidence and sympathy, which the author uses to draw people to faithfulness, and negative feelings, such as fear and shame, which he uses to create an aversion to unfaithfulness.

Confidence comes from the conviction that "the hope of what is salutary" is near at hand (Aristotle, *Rhetoric* 2.5.16). Hebrews links confident hope to boldness, steadfastness, and an unwavering disposition (Heb 3:6; 6:11, 18; 7:19; 10:23; 11:1). People feel confident when they know that help is available, when they are not guilty of wrongdoing, and when their supporters are numerous (Aristotle, *Rhetoric* 2.5.17). Therefore, Hebrews assures listeners that help is available from God (Heb 4:14–16; 13:6), that Christ cleanses their consciences (9:14), and that they are encircled by a great cloud of faithful witnesses (Heb 12:1).

The opposite of confidence is fear, which is "a painful or troubled feeling caused by the impression of an imminent evil that causes destruction or pain" (Aristotle, *Rhetoric* 2.5.1). Fear of social conflict (10:32–34; 13:13) might lead listeners to abandon their faith in order to feel more secure, but Hebrews warns that it is far more "terrifying to fall into the hands of the living God" (10:31), whose fiery judgment upon the faithless is fearsome (6:4–8; 10:27; 12:29), and whose power is inescapable (2:2–3; 4:12–13; 12:25). Hebrews seeks to move listeners to overcome the fears that come from their social situation (11:23, 27; 13:6) by awakening the fear that comes from the prospect by being judged by God.

Shame "is a kind of pain or uneasiness in respect of misdeeds, past, present, or future, which seem to tend to bring dishonor" (Aristotle, *Rhetoric* 2.6.1). The community addressed by Hebrews had been treated with contempt by nonbelievers, and some Christians may have thought to give up their faith in the hope of regaining respect from others (NOTES and COMMENT on 10:32–34). On the one hand, Hebrews seeks to show that to follow Jesus is to disdain the shame of society (12:2) in the confidence that God and Christ are not ashamed of them (2:11; 11:16). On the other hand, the author seeks to awaken shame by comparing them to children, thereby seeking to provoke them to overcome this disgrace by striving more diligently (5:11–14; 6:12). The account of the listeners' former endurance makes clear that shrinking back at present would be disgraceful (10:32–39). Christ persevered through bloody conflict, and for listeners to falter in face of a lesser struggle would be shameful (12:4). Hebrews presses listeners to discern that true honor and shame must be perceived in relation to God, rather than in relation to society (deSilva, "Despising," 276–313).

Sympathy is a feeling that arises from "the sight of evil, deadly or painful, which befalls one who does not deserve it; an evil which one might expect to come upon himself" (Aristotle, *Rhetoric* 2.7.2). Hebrews makes clear that Christ did not deserve to suffer, since he was without sin (4:15) and he exhibited reverence for God (5:7). Moreover, Jesus suffered because he called mortals his brothers and sisters (2:11–14), felt sympathy for them (4:15), and was "tested in every respect, in the same ways" (4:15). Such reminders of the manner of Jesus' suffering reinforce the listeners' faith by awakening sympathy for one who suffered unjustly as well as by eliciting gratitude for his suffering on their behalf (cf. Mitchell, "Use," 694–98).

The use of logic and appeals to emotion are two aspects of the same persuasive strategy. Logic and emotion function differently, but they serve the same end, which is that listeners persevere in faith. By speaking to the heart as well as to the mind, the author seeks to enlist both in a renewed commitment to Christ and the Christian community.

3. CHARACTER

The character (*ēthos*) of a speaker also contributes to persuasion. Listeners are more likely to be persuaded by a speaker they trust than by a speaker they do not trust.[192] Therefore, one of the functions of an exordium is to make the listeners well disposed toward the speaker. The principal speaker in Hebrews' exordium is God. After hearing that God has spoken through the prophets and through a Son (1:1–2), listeners are confronted with a battery of scriptural quotations in 1:5–13 so that God's words remain the focus of attention. It is a divine voice that lauds the Son (1:5–13), warns of unfaithfulness (3:7–11), and declares the formation of the new covenant (8:8–12). Extended quotations of Scripture function not only as the basis for comment by the author but as direct address to the listeners. Therefore, the author urges them to heed God's voice (4:7; 12:25).[193]

Presenting God as principal speaker in the exordium and elsewhere was helpful because listeners could be expected to recognize the integrity of God's character. Although the listeners' experience of societal reproach did not correspond to God's promise of glory for them, the author could assume that they would agree that God does not lie (6:18) and that God is faithful (10:23; 11:11). Arguments showing how God had been faithful to his promises to bless Abraham (6:15), to raise up a priest like Melchizedek (7:11–28), and to make a new covenant (8:7–13) reinforce the perception of God's integrity. The implication is that those who relinquish their faith in God's promises in effect deny the integrity of God's character.

The character of the anonymous author is also important. References to "brethren" (3:1) and "beloved" (6:9) imply that a positive relationship already existed with the listeners, and the epistolary postscript (13:22–25) promotes a positive reception of the speech by fostering good personal relations (§39 COMMENT). In the speech itself the author frequently identifies himself with the listeners by using the first person plural. Like them, he is addressed by the word of God (1:2; 2:3; 4:2) and shares the confession of faith (3:1; 4:14; 10:23). With them, he must reckon with divine judgment (2:3; 4:13; 10:26), trust in divine mercy (4:15–16; 9:14), and strive in faith (4:11; 10:24; 12:1). The author also demonstrates his familiarity with Scripture by frequent citation of texts, so that before he points out the deficiencies of the old covenant, listeners have been shown that he knows the tradition about which he speaks. Finally, the author is bold in his confession (e.g., 1:1–4) and direct in his exhortations. Therefore, when he urges listeners to be bold in their confession (3:6; 4:16; 10:19, 35) and

---

[192]Aristotle, *Rhetoric* 1.2.3–4; Quintilian, *Inst.* 4.1.7.

[193]See Mitchell, "Use," 691–701; Eisenbaum, *Jewish Heroes*, 90–100.

to exhort one another (3:13; 10:24), his directives have integrity, since he calls listeners to do what he is already doing.

D. Language and Style

Hebrews' style is remarkable for the visual quality of its language. Ideas often find their most powerful expression when "you seem to see what you describe and bring it vividly before the eyes of your audience" so that "attention is drawn from the reasoning to the enthralling effect of the imagination" (Longinus, *On the Sublime* 15.1, 11). Visual language suits the theology and design of Hebrews, which calls listeners to hold fast to what cannot be seen with the physical eye, but must be perceived in the eye of the mind through faith (Heb 11:1). Using speech, the author "takes you along with him . . . and turns hearing into sight" (Longinus, ibid., 26.2).

Christ is presented through several types of imagery. When portraying the situation of the exalted Christ, who is not directly apparent to the senses, the author creates a mosaic of OT citations that gives the impression that listeners have entered the heavenly throne room, where they hear God addressing the Son and the angels in the second person (§4 COMMENT). When speaking about the incarnation, he uses heroic imagery that depicts Christ entering the realm of death in order to battle the devil, thereby liberating the people who were held captive in fear (§8 COMMENT *c*). Christ's atoning work is not treated abstractly. Instead, the author paints a picture of the ancient Tabernacle with its forecourt, inner court, and furnishings. Then he describes Christ's entry into the inner chamber of the sanctuary through the blood that he shed for others (9:1–14). The atoning significance of Christ's death was not empirically visible even to those witnessing the crucifixion; Hebrews makes it visible through language.

Christian discipleship is also depicted through images. The author shows what it means to live by faith by tracing the journeys of Abraham, Sarah, and their descendants; by telling of Moses' conflict with the king of Egypt and of Israel's passage through the sea; and by cataloging the sufferings of the martyrs (Heb 11). The author also casts the listeners in the role of athletes who must run with perseverance in the race that is set before them (12:1–3). These "athletes" cannot look to Jesus or discern the great cloud of witnesses around them on the basis of physical sight, but must do so through a faithful reception of the author's words.

Other matters of style were also important because speakers found that audiences responded most readily to speeches that were stylistically pleasing. When "our audience finds it a pleasure to listen, their attention and their readiness to believe what they hear are both alike increased" (Quintilian, *Inst.* 8.3.5). Rhetorical handbooks favor prose that is rhythmic and varied but not metrical—qualities that are found in Hebrews.[194] They also advise that a proper style is one suitable for

[194]On rhythms in Hebrews see Moffatt, *Critical,* lvi–lix; Spicq, *L'Épître,* 1.359–61; cf. Lausberg, *Handbook* §§977–1054.

the subject matter and the occasion, one in which "neither weighty matters are treated offhand, nor trifling matters with dignity" (Aristotle, *Rhetoric* 3.7.1–2).[195]

The elevated style of Hebrews' exordium suits the grandeur of its subject matter: the exalted Son of God. Features of the grand style in this passage include the use of a complex period rather than a simple sentence (1:1–4), vivid vocabulary ("radiance of his glory and impress of his substance," 1:3), extensive alliteration using the *p* sound (1:1), and paraphrase ("the Majesty on high" for God, 1:4). Such elevated prose can help to gain the favor of the listeners and to inspire their imaginations (Aristotle, *Rhetoric* 3.6.1–7). Elsewhere, however, the author directs a forceful battery of abrupt questions at the listeners, pressing them to consider the grim consequences of unbelief (Heb 3:16–18). Keeping the questions brief increases their intensity. The style resembles that of a diatribe (§10 COMMENT *b*). Similarly, the exhortations in 13:1–9 are stated briefly and directly since they call for obedience, not contemplation(§36 COMMENT).

The periods such as those used in the grand style of 1:1–4 are sentences that draw a number of ideas into an integrated whole. The word *periodos* is based on the roots *hodos* ("a way") and *peri* ("around"), so that it conveys "an image drawn from paths which go round and are in a circle" (Demetrius, *On Style* 10). Thus one period begins by announcing how God's word (*logos*) scrutinizes the human heart, and it ends by recalling that all people must render account (*logos*) to God (4:12–13). Structurally, periods often concluded sections of an argument (*Rhet. ad Her.* 4.19 §27). Hebrews concludes the exordium with an appeal that begins with a reminder of the validity of the word spoken by angels and ends with a reminder of God's validation of the Christian message (2:2–4). The first series of arguments culminates with a period that encircles an account of Christ's suffering with statements about his exaltation to glory (5:5–10). The second series of arguments calls listeners to draw near to God even as they see the Day of the Lord drawing near to them (10:19–25). The third series of arguments ends with a sentence that is less symmetrical, but one that draws themes from the entire speech into a vision of the city of God (12:22–24). On periods see Lausberg, *Handbook* §§941–47.

Examples and enthymemes were two principal ways in which speakers developed their arguments (Aristotle, *Rhetoric* 1.2.8). Examples were typically taken from the past and could relate to the author's point in different ways (Quintilian, *Inst.* 5.11.9; Lausberg, *Handbook* §§410–26). In Hebrews the wilderness generation is a negative example, whose unbelief is to be avoided (Heb 3:7–19), while the figures in chapter 11 are positive examples, whose faith is to be imitated. Good examples demonstrate points by making things so vivid that they can almost "be touched with the hand" (*Rhet. ad Her.* 4.49 §62). The rhetorical function of examples is considered more fully in §29 COMMENT.

An enthymeme is a type of logical deduction that in form is an incomplete syllogism. A syllogism includes two premises and a conclusion. For example, (a) if

---

[195]On style and rhetorical devices in Hebrews see Garuti, *Alle origini*, 33–184; Attridge, *Epistle*, 20–21; Cosby; deSilva, *Despising*, 30–33.

something truly good cannot be put to bad use, (b) and if no one can make bad use of virtue, (c) then virtue is truly good. An enthymeme would make the same point by stating perhaps two of the three parts: "Virtue is a good thing because no one can put it to bad use" (Quintilian, *Inst.* 5.14.24–25; cf. Aristotle, *Rhetoric* 1.2.13; Lausberg, *Handbook*, §371). Among Hebrews' uses of enthymemes are the arguments that neglecting salvation in Christ is worse than disregarding the Law (Heb 2:2–3), that Jesus is worthy of greater honor than Moses (3:3–4), that without faith one cannot please God (11:6), and that Abraham's family sought a new and superior homeland (11:14–16).

Comparison and antithesis sharpen the arguments.[196] Comparison (*synkrisis*) was often used when a speaker praised someone by showing that the person was greater than other illustrious people (Aristotle, *Rhetoric* 1.9.38). Following this practice Hebrews speaks of Christ's superiority to angels (Heb 1:1–14), to Moses (3:1–6), and to the Levitical priesthood (7:1–28). Posing sharp antitheses between one thing and another sharpens the sense that one is better than another. This technique is especially evident in passages like 1:5–14, where the author contrasts what God said to the Son with what God said to angels, and in Heb 8–10, where the author contrasts the practices associated with the old and new covenants.

The way something is said can enhance its effectiveness. Some of the patterns of speech that contribute to Hebrews' argument include:

Anaphora—the repetition of a key word—is most extensive in Heb 11, where the author repeats eighteen times that the people of God must live "by faith," using the dative case *pistei*, and he adds the word *faith* six more times in other constructions. Not merely a matter of style, anaphora reinforces the centrality of faith in the design of Hebrews.

Polysyndeton—the repetition of conjunctions—gives a sense of weight and magnitude. Speaking in a pattern of " . . . and . . . and . . . and . . . " impresses upon listeners the relentlessness of God's word (4:12–13), the oppressive quality of the phenomena at Sinai (12:18–21), and the vastness of the joys in God's heavenly city (12:22–24).

Asyndeton—the juxtaposing a number of items without conjunctions—can create a similar effect. By referring to "Gideon, Barak, Samson, Jephthah, David" and a host of other figures and episodes, the author implies that he could continue listing exemplars of faith indefinitely, thereby suggesting that their number was vast (11:32–38). Using this pattern to list the torments experienced by the faithful creates intensity and helps to ally the listeners' emotions with those who have suffered (11:36–38; cf. 12:18–24; Lausberg, *Handbook* §709).

Assonance—the repetition of sounds in words or syllables—creates a pleasing quality, but it can also reinforce the argument. Linking *apistia* and *apostēnai*

[196]On comparison or *synkrisis* in Hebrews see Aune, *New Testament*, 213; Olbricht, "Hebrews"; Seid, "Rhetorical Form"; Watson, "Rhetorical," 184–87. On antithesis see Attridge, "Uses."

in 3:12 underscores that "unbelief" brings "abandonment"; the use of *emathen* and *epathen* in 5:8 helps listeners recognize how "learning" comes from "suffering"; references to *menousan* and *mellousan* in 13:14 contrast the city that does not "abide" and the city that is "to come."

Alliteration—the repetition of initial sounds—can help foster attentiveness. The author introduces his speech with words that begin with *p*, which calls for attention by its explosive sound: *polymerōs kai polytropōs palai ho theos lalēsas tois patrasin en tois prophētais* ("God, having spoken on many occasions and in many forms to the forebears of old by the prophets," 1:1). When the author calls for attention at the end of the exodium, he again uses words beginning with *p* to catch the listeners' ears: *dei perisoterōs prosechein . . . mēpote pararyōmen* ("we must keep holding fast to what we have heard so that we do not drift away," 2:1).

Figures of speech are often considered to be verbal embellishments that make what is said more appealing. The figures used in Hebrews serve this function, but they also do more by reinforcing theological points (Lausberg, *Handbook* §§552–98). Examples include:

Metaphor entails speaking of one thing in terms appropriate to another, as in calling hope an anchor (6:19). Much of the persuasiveness of a metaphor comes from its power to "set things before the eyes" (Aristotle, *Rhetoric* 3.10.6–7). By referring to basic Christian teaching as milk, in contrast to the solid food taken by adults, Hebrews presses listeners to see their dullness as a mark of immaturity, which they would presumably want to overcome (5:12–14). By calling persecution a contest (10:32) and depicting the life of faith as a footrace (12:1–3), the author seeks to alter the listeners' perceptions so that they see themselves, not as hapless victims, but as athletes engaged in a noble struggle.

Metonymy replaces a word with another term that has some relationship to it. For example, rather than directing listeners to turn to God, the author invites them to approach the throne of grace, thereby assuring them that God will be gracious (4:16). Later the author says that Jesus opened the way to God through his "flesh," a term that points to his death (10:20).

Synecdoche allows a part of something to stand for the whole. When Hebrews says that Christians have an altar (13:10), the term encapsulates the whole process of Christ's self-offering together with its benefits.

Hyperbole is "an elegant straining of the truth" (Quintilian, *Inst.* 8.6.67). The incredible suggestion that Levi paid tithes to Melchizedek while still in Abraham's loins is hyperbole that playfully underscores the superiority of Christ, the priest like Melchizedek, above all other priests (see §17 COMMENT *b*).

Antonomasia means replacing a name with a paraphrase or epithet. Calling God "the Majesty on high" (1:4), the one "for whom all things and through whom all things exist" (2:10), "the one able to save from death" (5:7), and "he who has promised" (10:23; 11:11) reinforces aspects of God's character that are presupposed by Hebrews' theological argument.[197]

Hebrews' vocabulary is rich and varied, including 154 words not found in other NT writings (Ellingworth, *Epistle,* 12–13). New coinages are an especially interesting feature.[198] Speakers occasionally coined new words to add variety to their remarks. To ensure that the meaning was clear, they usually formed new expressions by combining existing parts. After using the existing words *apatēr* ("without father") and *amatēr* ("without mother"), the author introduces the new word by adding an *a* privative on "genealogy" to form *agenealogētos* ("without genealogy," 7:3). Other instances where a new word is formed by combining existing parts to create a clear meaning include *haimatekchysia* ("outpouring of blood," 9:22) and perhaps *synkakoucheisthai* ("be maltreated with," 11:25), *misthapodosia* ("reward," 2:2), and *misthapodotēs* ("rewarder," 11:6). *Proschysis* ("spread," 11:28) is a noun that is created from a verb. An instance where a new coinage creates some confusion is *euperistatos*, which seems to mean "readily beset" (see NOTE on 12:1).

◆

The "many forms" in which Hebrews communicates are designed to foster greater attentiveness to what God communicates through his Son (1:1–2). The varied style and complex rhetorical strategy convey a theological message that aims at strengthening the faith of the listeners. In the next section, therefore, we will consider certain aspects of Hebrews' theology in light of what has been said concerning the speech's style and argument.

IV. Selected Issues in the Theology of Hebrews

◆

God's speech and actions pervade Hebrews from the opening declaration of how God spoke through the prophets and his Son (1:1–2) to the final benediction that summarizes what God has done and continues to do (13:20–21). The

[197]Other tropes are also used. *Litotes* describes something through the negation of its opposite. Thus, "we do not have a high priest who is unable to sympathize with our weaknesses" (4:15) and "God is not unjust" (6:10). *Emphasis* is the device of using an imprecise word to convey a more precise meaning. For example, when the author warns that every transgression receives "a just reward" (2:2), the context demands that listeners take the expression not as "reward" in general, but more specifically as punishment.

[198]Demetrius, *On Style* 96–98; Cicero, *De oratore* 3.38 §154; 3.43 §170; 3.35 §201; Lausberg, *Handbook* §§547–51.

proposition of Hebrews identifies the question of God's intention for humanity as the crux around which the speech is structured (2:5–9). Although the listeners' experience casts doubt on God's faithfulness, Hebrews treats different aspects of the work of God in relation to this basic question, finally bringing the listeners, along with all of God's people, to the heavenly Jerusalem, where God's designs are made complete (12:22–24). An overview of the argument is given on pp. 83–89 while the COMMENT sections on Heb 1–2 serve as an introduction to Hebrews' theology and Christology. Here we take up selected issues in order to explore relationships among ideas that appear at various points in Hebrews.

A. Cosmology and Eschatology

1. COSMOLOGY[199]

Hebrews begins and ends by emphasizing that the world is dependent upon the word of God. The world came into being through divine speech in the past (1:2; 11:3), it is sustained by the word of the Son in the present (1:3), and it will be shaken by the voice of God in the future (12:25–27). God is the one "for whom all things and through whom all things exist" (2:10) and the "builder of all things" (3:4). Hebrews affirms that the world was created and that it will pass away, but God and the Son continue forever (1:10–12). Establishing that the word is primary and the world is secondary is important for Hebrews because faith—like the world—comes into being and is sustained through divine speech (2:1–4; 6:5). Therefore, those who rely on the enduring word can exhibit enduring faith, whereas those who depend on the world embrace what is transient.

The relationship of God's word to the world is connected to questions about the relationship of God's people to the world. The propositional section of Hebrews poses the issue: If God created people for glory and dominion, as Ps 8 says, then why do God's people not see this in their own experience (Heb 2:5–9)? Listeners are vulnerable to fear, weakness, sin, and death (2:14–18). They find that life in the world means labor rather than rest (4:10; 6:10) and that the righteous often suffer (e.g., 10:32–34; 11:4, 23–27, 35–38). In response, Hebrews emphasizes that those who become discouraged by material realities are being moved by what is dependent and transient, whereas faith abides when it is based on the word that abides.

At the same time, creation is the context in which Christ's incarnation is understood. Human blood and flesh are associated with weakness, but since they belong to God's creation, they are not inherently evil. When Christ assumed a human body, he entered fully into the created order, using what God had created to accomplish God's purposes (2:11–15). Blood and flesh connote mortality, yet through blood and flesh (9:12, 14; 10:19–20), that is, through the body that

[199]See Eccles, "Purpose"; Ellingworth, "Jesus"; Rissi, *Theologie*, 35–44; Stewart, "Creation."

God prepared for him (10:5, 10), Christ made definitive atonement for sins, opening the way to life in the presence of God (§8 COMMENT *a–d*). Therefore, things from the created order—blood, flesh, and body—do have a place in the accomplishment of God's purposes.

The outcome of Christ's work and the realization of God's designs are described in terms of rest (4:10), entering a sanctuary (10:19–22), and arriving in the heavenly Jerusalem (12:22–24). Some interpreters have construed this goal in spatial categories, as arrival in a higher realm like that envisioned by Platonic philosophy.[200] Others think of it in temporal categories, as arrival in "the age to come" that is mentioned in apocalyptic sources.[201] The problem is that Hebrews operates with both categories, yet it fits neatly into neither category (pp. 59–63). Rather than focusing on traditions that might lie behind the text, we can compare Hebrews to Platonic and apocalyptic patterns in order to sharpen the way we perceive the constellations of ideas within the text.

HEBREWS			PLATONISM		
True (*alēthinos*)	Pattern (*typos*)	Image (*eikōn*)	Paradigm (*paradeigma*)	Archetype (*archetypos*)	Real (*aleithēs*)
	conscience (*syneidēsis*)			mind (*nous*)	
	(*sarx*) flesh			(*sarx*) flesh	
(*hypodeigma*) Representation	(*antitypos*) Antitype	(*skia*) Shadow	(*mimēma*) Copy	(*skia*) Shadow	(*eikōn*) Image

Hebrews and Platonic writers distinguish what is "true" or "real" from perceptible forms. Plato maintained that people on earth could perceive the visible "shadows" of transcendent realities, but not the realities themselves (*Republic* 514A–515D). Hebrews uses similar expressions when contrasting the "true" heavenly sanctuary in which Christ ministers with its earthly "shadow" (Heb 8:2, 5) and when calling the Law's prescriptions for a priesthood and sacrifices the "shadows" of Christ's ministry (10:1). More complex is Hebrews' contrast of the heavenly sanctuary with its earthly "antitype" (*antitypos*, 9:24), since it is not

[200]On Clement of Alexandria and Origen see pp. 20–21; cf. Eusebius, *Preparation for the Gospel* 12.19. More recent proponents include Spicq, *L'Épître*, 1.72; Laub, *Bekenntnis*, 231; Grässer, *Hebräer*, 2.88; Dunn, *Partings*, 87–88; idem, *Christology*, 52–53; Isaacs, *Sacred*, 52–56; Thompson, *Beginnings*, 152–62. On Platonic cosmology see Dillon, *Middle Platonists*, 45–49, 81–84, 155–78.

[201]For example, Barrett, "Eschatology"; Goppelt, *TDNT* 8.256–59; Williamson, *Philo*, 563–70; Lane, *Hebrews*, 1.72.

clear that *antitypos* had Platonic connotations when Hebrews was written. By the third century, Plotinus used *antitypos* for perceptible reality (*Enneads* 5.3.6.17), but Plato did not do so, and Philo used it for what is "resistant." Moreover in 1 Pet 3:21 the word has a temporal rather than a spatial quality: "prefigurement" (Hurst, *Epistle*, 17–19). Conversely, the terms *paradeigma* and *archetypos*, which Plato and Philo use for heavenly patterns, do not appear in Hebrews. Hebrews uses *hypodeigma*, but for the earthly representation rather than the heavenly archetype (NOTE on 8:5). Moreover, Plato and Philo use "image" (*eikōn*) for perceptible shadows of immaterial archetypes,[202] but Hebrews uses "image" in the opposite sense (NOTE on 10:1).

Hebrews lacks the Platonic term *mimēma* ("copy") and the contrast between the *noēta* ("intelligible") and *aisthēta* ("perceptible") worlds, but some assume that Hebrews alludes to these distinctions when it says that "from what cannot be seen, that which is seen has come into being" (11:3).[203] However, the sentence actually identifies God's word rather than archetypes as the unseen source behind the present universe (NOTE on 11:3).[204] Hebrews does correlate a heavenly sanctuary with its earthly representation (8:1–6), but the author shows remarkable fluidity in developing the imagery, so that the Tabernacle sometimes represents earth and heaven, and sometimes stands for two ages (§22 COMMENT).

Hebrews does not clearly distinguish the created heavens from a transcendent heaven. Some have pointed out that Christ has already passed "through" the visible heavens (4:14) so that he is now exalted "above the heavens" (7:26), having entered a sanctuary that is "not of this creation" but beyond it (9:11). This could suggest that Christ is now in transcendent heaven itself (9:24).[205] Nevertheless, this distinction breaks down as the author refers to those who enjoy eternal life "in the heavens" (12:23), to God's voice speaking "from the heavens" (12:25), and to "heaven" being shaken along with earth (12:26). Moreover, Hebrews associates heaven with what is undefiled (7:26), yet can also suggest that if the lower realm needs purification, then the higher realm does as well—an idea that sits awkwardly with a Platonic worldview (NOTES on 9:23).

Hebrews says that one relates to what is unseen by faith (11:1). In Platonic thought one relates to the unseen through the "mind" (*nous*) and the power of reason; faith belongs to a lower order.[206] Hebrews does not mention the *nous* but

---

[202]Plato, *Timaeus* 29b, 48e–49a; idem, *Republic* 7.515–17; Philo, *Alleg. Interp.* 3.96; idem, *Abraham* 3–4. See Hurst, *Epistle*, 19–20.

[203]The use of the plural for "ages" or "worlds" does not suggest a clear distinction between higher and lower worlds, but seems to be a general way to speak of the universe (NOTES on 1:2; 11:3).

[204]Some have thought that Hebrews works with the idea of creation out of nothing (*ex nihilo*). The extent to which other sources of this period worked with the idea is not clear. See Goldstein, "Creatio"; Winston, "Creation." The doctrine only gradually became common in Christian theology. See P. E. Hughes, *Commentary*, 443–52.

[205]Grässer, *Hebräer*, 3.332–36; deSilva, *Perseverance*, 27–32. On heaven being shaken see Casey, "Christian Assembly."

[206]Plato identified insight (*noēsis*) and understanding (*dianoia*) with truth, and linked faith (*pistis*) and probability (*eikasia*) with appearance (*Republic* 6.511d–e; *Timaeus* 29c). Philo gives a greater place to faith, occasionally saying that faith is superior to reasoning (e.g., *Rewards* 28), but he more

stresses faith in two ways. First, the unseen realities of which the author speaks are made known through divine revelation—including promises, commands, and warnings (e.g., 8:5; 11:7, 8)—and revelation is received by faith.[207] Second, a barrier to the unseen realm comes from a defiled conscience (9:14; 10:29), an idea that has no real counterpart in Platonism. Since the conscience is defiled by human unfaithfulness, cleansing the conscience means evoking faith (§23 COMMENT *b*). A clean conscience fits God's promise to write his laws upon the "mind" (*dianoia*), which is synonymous with the "heart" (8:10; 10:16). Heart and mind do not have so much to do with higher versus lower aspects of human life, or with internal versus external matters, but pertain to obedience that involves the whole self (NOTE on 8:10). Finally, the idea that one must train one's faculties to distinguish between good and evil has counterparts in philosophy, although the criteria for discernment center on faith and on Christ's death and exaltation rather than classic virtues (NOTES and COMMENT on 5:14). "There is no other way from changeableness to unchangeableness than through faith—bound to the Word—which marks the only bridge between the two worlds" (Käsemann, *Wandering*, 41).

2. ESCHATOLOGY[208]

The conviction that the universe is subject to the word of God underlies Hebrews' eschatology. God's word brought heaven and earth into being at the beginning, and his word will shake heaven and earth in the end (11:3; 12:26). Time unfolds in between these two definitive acts of divine speech. God also signaled the onset of what Hebrews calls "these final days" when he "spoke to us by a Son" (1:2). Hebrews understands that God spoke or communicated his will for the world through Christ's life, death, and exaltation to heavenly glory. Interpreting the tradition of Christ's exaltation in light of Ps 110 and other passages, Hebrews offers a glimpse of "the world to come" (Heb 2:5) through a portrayal of the heavenly "world" where the Son now reigns (1:5–6). Seated at the right hand of Majesty, the Son enjoys the glory and rest that the faithful hope to inherit (1:3; 2:7; 4:9–10). Hebrews declares that the created order will come to an end, but the Son's righteous rule will endure (1:10–12). God's designs find their completion when all the righteous join the angelic celebration in God's heavenly city (12:22–24).

---

commonly stresses the centrality of the mind (Sandmel, *Philo*, 99–100). Thompson emphasizes the similarities between the views of faith in Philo and Hebrews (*Beginnings*, 53–80), but Philo lacks Hebrews' emphasis on the future aspect of faith (Heb 11:1) and gives little attention to unbelief as rejection of God's promises (Attridge, *Epistle*, 313; Williamson, *Philo*, 309–85).

[207]The references to the mind (*dianoia*) come from Jer 31:33, where mind is synonymous with "heart" (Heb 8:10; 10:16). The verb *ginōskein* ("to know") appears in OT quotations that emphasize knowing God (8:11) and God's ways (3:10), and in the author's comment about his listeners' knowing that they have an abiding, heavenly possession (10:34).

[208]See Barrett, "Eschatology"; Casey, "Christian Assembly"; Colijn, "Let Us"; deSilva, *Perseverance*, 27–32; Grässer, *Aufbruch*, 240–50; Käsemann, *Wandering*, 17–66; Klappert, "Eschatologie"; Löhr, "Anthroplogie"; MacRae, "Heavenly Temple"; Rissi, *Theologie*, 125–30; Thompson, *Beginnings*, 41–52; Toussaint, "Eschatology"; Vögtle, "Das Neue"; Wider, *Theozentrik*, 88–115.

The issue is that "these final days" are the scene of conflict between the powers of the future and the visible realities of the present. The Son of God reigns, but not all of his enemies have been put under his feet (1:13). He entered the realm of blood and flesh to suffer and die, and through his exaltation to everlasting life he shows that death's power is not final. This act liberates people from the fear of death with which Satan held people captive (2:14–15). Nevertheless, experience teaches that death itself still threatens and that final resurrection has not yet occurred (6:2; 9:27). Through the coming of God's Spirit, listeners have tasted the powers of the age to come (2:3–4; 6:4–5), yet they continue to be subjected to abuse, dispossession, and imprisonment (10:32–34; 13:3, 13). By faith one may claim that in Christ's death and exaltation "the good things to come" have arrived (9:11; 10:1), but experience shows that the faithful have not yet arrived in the blessed city "that is to come" (13:14). According to Hebrews "the visible and invisible do not confront each other in static fashion, but rather as powers contending with each other."[209]

The shift from the old to the new covenant compounds the problem. God's promise of blessing and eternal inheritance states his intentions for people, as we will see below (p. 111). The covenants are means by which God deals with the barriers created by human sin in order to realize his purposes (pp. 112–14). Since the first covenant did not bring God's designs to completion (7:11, 19; 8:7, 13), God declared that he would establish a new covenant in which he would show mercy and put his laws on human minds and hearts. Under the new covenant people would not need to teach each other to know the Lord, for all would know him (Jer 31:31–34; Heb 8:8–12). Hebrews declares that when Christ appeared "at the consummation of the ages," he offered himself as the definitive sacrifice for human sin (9:26). Through Christ's self-offering, God extends the mercy that was promised under the new covenant (10:11–18), yet experience shows that the new covenant is not yet fully in place, since even the faithful are prone to sin and continue to need teaching and exhortation (3:12–13; 5:11–14; cf. 8:10–11; §21 COMMENT *b*).

The conflict between the visible realities of the present time and faith's perception of the reign of Christ will be resolved through Christ's return and related events. If the "final days" begin with Christ's first coming, they culminate with his second coming. Hebrews does not offer a sequential treatment of future events but links Christ's return to resurrection and final judgment.[210] Hebrews acknowledges that people—including faithful ones like Abel, Abraham and his

---

[209]Käsemann, *Wandering*, 44. Studies of Christian eschatology often distinguish what has "already" happened from what has "not yet" occurred (e.g., Dunn, *Theology*, 466–72), but these labels fail to capture the sense of conflict between the future and the present that Käsemann points out. Paul personified sin (Rom 7:8–10), flesh (Gal 5:16–17), Law (Gal 3:23–24), and other elements when describing the battle between the powers of the present evil age (1 Cor 2:6; Gal 1:4) and the reign of God (Martyn, *Galatians*, 97–104). Hebrews does not personify the powers as Paul does, but exhibits a comparable sense of the conflict between future hope and present reality.

[210]On Christ's return see NOTE on 9:28. Resurrection and judgment are connected in 6:2, and judgment is linked to Christ's return in 9:27–28; 10:37–39.

descendants, and the martyrs—die in the world (11:4, 13, 21, 22, 35–37). Christ's exaltation offers the kind of hope that overcomes the fear of death (2:14–15), but death itself will be overcome by life through resurrection (11:19, 35). This will enable all of God's people to experience the completion of God's intentions together (11:39–40). The firstborn in the heavenly city are all whom God raises from the dead, as he raised Jesus, his firstborn (NOTES on 1:6; 12:23).[211]

Resurrection of the dead is connected to the coming Day of the Lord, when the faithful will be rewarded and the faithless punished (6:2; 10:25–31, 36–39). Those addressed by Hebrews embarked on a journey of faith when they received the message of salvation (2:2) and the author assures them that salvation will be made complete when Christ returns (9:28; 10:36–39). Hebrews speaks of this as receiving an inheritance, blessing, and reward (1:14; 6:7; 10:35; 11:26). The underlying conviction is that God is just and will therefore not abandon the faithful, but will grant them the inheritance that he promised to Abraham's heirs (6:10–12, 17; 10:36). Experience shows that the world may condemn the righteous (11:36–38), but Hebrews insists that God will reverse this judgment by bringing the faithful to the glory that he intends for them.

The future also portends judgment upon God's adversaries. Hebrews recognizes that all people fall prey to sin and that all must render an account to God (3:12–13; 4:13). Like other writers, the author speaks of divine judgment in terms of fire and destruction.[212] Hebrews does not make a simple distinction between the people of God who are saved and others who are condemned. The author recalls how Moses' generation perished in the desert and how Esau forfeited his blessing in order to show that God's own people are subject to judgment (3:16–19; 10:30; 12:16–17). Significantly, the warnings of judgment not only deal with the usual sins (13:4), but speak particularly to those who would reject divine grace. Hebrews presupposes that God has provided mercy, cleansing from sin, and the promise of salvation through Christ's death and exaltation, and through the coming of the Spirit. Accordingly, to reject the mercy that God has extended means embracing divine wrath (NOTES and COMMENT on 2:1–4; 6:4–8; 10:26–31).

Conflict between faith's claims concerning the reign of Christ and the contradictory claims that arise from the visible world will end when God or Christ bring the created order to its end. Hebrews envisions the created order being displaced by the kingdom of God, much as the new covenant displaces the old one.

---

[211]On tensions in Hebrews' view of death and afterlife see the NOTE on 6:2.

[212]NOTES on 6:8; 10:27. Final judgment was a common element in Jewish (Dan 12:2; 2 *Bar.* 51:1–6; 4 Ezra 7:33–44) and early Christian eschatology (Matt 13:40–42; 25:31–46; John 5:28–29; Rom 2:5–10; 2 Cor 5:10; Rev 20:11–15). Apart from the common conviction that some would be saved and others condemned, the scenarios varied (survey in Reiser, *Jesus and Judgment*, 19–163). Some referred to the salvation of Israel and judgment against the nations, while others, including Hebrews, anticipate the salvation of the righteous and the judgment of sinners. Some texts expect reward and punishment to be given on at least a provisional basis immediately after death (Wis 3:3; 4:7; *L. A. B.* 23:13; Luke 16:22–23; Rev 6:9). Although Heb 9:27 has sometimes been taken as a reference to a judgment that occurs immediately after death, the author's dominant view concerns judgment at the end of time (cf. 4 Ezra 14:34–35; Reiser, *Jesus and Judgment*, 149).

In 1:10–12 Hebrews applies Ps 102:25–27 to the Son of God, saying that the one who created earth and heaven will eventually roll them up like a cloak. The created order perishes whereas the Son remains. The implication is that faith based on the created order is transient, for the creation is transient. Faith that endures is bound to the Son of God who endures.

Later, a quotation of Hag 2:6 warns that God "will shake not only the earth but also the heaven" (Heb 12:26). The passage distinguishes created things that can be shaken from the unshakable kingdom that will endure (12:27–28). "Heaven" is the place where the redeemed are made complete (12:23) and the place from which God speaks (12:25). Therefore, to say that God's voice shakes heaven as well as earth means that no part of the universe is exempt from the shaking (12:26). As an earthquake leaves only the most secure structures in place, the divine shaking of the universe will leave only God's kingdom with its well-founded city in place (11:10).[213] Although some envision this as the destruction of a lower physical realm and the preservation of a higher spiritual one, the passage has more to do with dominion than with metaphysics: Divine rule endures and whatever impedes divine rule is removed.[214]

The realization of God's designs is portrayed through several types of imagery. One is entry into divine rest. Hebrews recalls that Moses' contemporaries journeyed through the wilderness toward rest in the promised land. Nevertheless, they did not enter the land, and their descendants who entered it did not find true rest there. The realization of God's promises will mean that at the end of time people enter into the condition of rest that God enjoyed at the beginning of time. The faithful glimpse this rest already in the exalted Christ, who is seated at God's right hand (§11 COMMENT *b*). A second image is coming into the presence of God in the sanctuary's inner chamber. Hebrews compares the present time to the sanctuary's forecourt, where people are at some remove from God (9:8–10). By his death and exaltation, Christ passed through the curtain that separates the forecourt from the inner chamber, so that he is now before the face of God (9:24). Listeners can already approach God through prayer (4:14–16), but at the end of this present time they will follow Christ their forerunner completely into God's presence (6:19–20; 10:19). A third image is arrival in the heavenly Jerusalem, the city that God prepared for the heirs of the promises (11:10, 16). The city is described in terms of its inhabitants, for in it the redeemed join in a festival celebration with saints and angels in the presence of God and Jesus (NOTES and COMMENT on 12:22–24).

---

[213]Hebrews speaks of the *metathesis* of things that have been made, which primarily has to do with their removal (NOTE on 12:27). Also see the NOTES on 1:11–12 concerning the end of the created order.

[214]On the preservation of a higher realm see Thompson, *Beginnings*, 41–52; Grässer, *Aufbruch*, 240–50. The description of the city makes this unlikely. Hebrews says that the heavenly city includes not only the spirits of the righteous but the sprinkled blood of Jesus—a remarkably physical detail (12:23–24; Casey, "Christian Assembly," 332). Expectation of a future shaking of the universe appears in a number of places (*Sib. Or.* 3.675–80; 4 Ezra 10:25, 28; 2 *Bar.* 32:1–4). Hebrews uses the shaking as a way to speak about divine judgment (Vögtle, "Das Neue," 253) or divine power (Wider, *Theozentrik*, 108–9) rather than as a basis for speculation about the structure of the universe.

The world and its future depend upon the word of the God "for whom all things and through whom all things exist" (2:10). Therefore, Hebrews calls listeners to live by faith in God's word of promise until the challenges of the current order are overcome and God's purposes are made complete. Hebrews speaks of the future in order to shape the present. The author defines the listeners' future in relationship to God, the Son of God, and the people of God who have a place in the city that is to come. Since these relationships endure, they are central and abiding elements of present life.

B. CHRISTOLOGY

Hebrews' Christology is based on the conviction that Jesus died, rose, and was exalted to heaven.[215] The tradition presupposed by the author also identified Jesus as the Son of God, using language from texts like Ps 2:7 and 2 Sam 7:14 (NOTES on Heb 1:5–6). Because belief in Jesus' divine sonship was part of the listeners' own confession (4:14), the author could cite it in his opening lines and explore its implications later in his speech (pp. 125–27). Calling Jesus the Son of God underscores his lordship, while anticipating the problem facing the listeners: the world that they experience falls short of the kingdom of God (2:5–9). Hebrews reaffirms that Jesus is the royal Son who is seated at God's right hand, using language from Ps 110:1 (Heb 1:13), while enriching this view by depicting Christ as the high priest who has made the consummate sacrifice (2:17–18; 10:12–14) and as the hero or athlete who has persevered faithfully (2:14–16; 12:1–3).[216]

1. PREEXISTENCE AND CONSTANCY[217]

Christ's exaltation is the starting point for consideration of his preexistence. Hebrews first says that in these final days the Son has been designated heir of all things (1:2b) and only then adds that God created the world through the Son (1:2c), implying that the Son existed prior to the creation. Hebrews does not try to demonstrate this point and apparently assumes that it was already part of the listeners' tradition.[218] The logic is that God has "spoken" through a Son, who not only uttered God's word but who *was* God's word, since he communicated God's

[215]Hebrews speaks mainly of Jesus' exaltation to heaven, but Jesus' resurrection is part of the author's tradition (13:20). On the humiliation-to-exaltation schema presupposed by Hebrews see Laub, *Bekenntnis*, 9; Long, *Hebrews*, 22.

[216]See NOTES and COMMENTS on 1:1–4 and 1:5–14. Cf. Loader, *Sohn*, 7–38; Laub, *Bekenntnis*, 14–27; Dunn, *Christology*, 12–64.

[217]See Habermann, *Präexistenzaussagen*, 301–16, 421; Dunn, *Christology*, 206–9; Isaacs, *Sacred*, 186–204; Lindars, *Theology*, 29–35; Pilhofer, "ΚΡΕΙΤΤΟΝΟΣ"; Schenck, "Keeping"; Williamson, "Incarnation."

[218]Cf. Phil 2:6–11; 1 Cor 8:6; Col 1:15–20; John 1:1–18. On the possibility that Heb 1:2–3 depends on an early Christian hymn see NOTE on 1:3.

will through his life, death, and exaltation. Since God created the universe by a word on the first day and spoke by a Son in the final days, Hebrews identifies the Son with the creative word (§3 COMMENT *a*). Although Hebrews may echo traditions concerning divine wisdom (§3 COMMENT *b*), the text that he quotes to support this claim is Ps 102:25–27 (Heb 1:10–12), which is a royal psalm. Hebrews affirms the early Christian conviction that Christ is the Son who is enthroned at God's right hand, then invokes a psalm in which the "anointed" one is called "God" (Ps 45:6–7 = Heb 1:8–9). If the anointed Son is God, then one can ascribe to him the traits of deity, which include creative power and endless existence (Ps 102:25–27 = Heb 1:10–12).

Paradoxically, preexistence underscores both Christ's divinity and his obedience to God—something that characterizes his humanity. Divinity is the principal emphasis in Heb 1, where the exalted Son is called God on the basis of Ps 45:6. The assumption is that if the Scriptures indicate that the Son is God, then preexistence is a fitting trait for him. The same idea is evident later, where endless life points to the deity of the Son, whose image is reflected in the story of Melchizedek (NOTE on 7:3). Note, however, that preexistence also allows Hebrews to speak of the incarnation itself as an act of obedience. The comments about Christ becoming like others by sharing in their blood and flesh (2:10–18) imply this, and Hebrews later makes the obedience theme explicit when Christ enters the world by saying "I have come to do your will, O God" (10:7). Both Jesus' incarnation and his suffering and death are understood to show obedience to God's will.[219]

Tensions in Hebrews' portrayal of Christ have been considered from various perspectives. Some passages speak of continuity in Christ's existence by saying, "You are the same, and your years will never cease" (1:12), for "Jesus Christ is yesterday and today the same—and forever" (13:8). Other statements imply change, for Christ was *made* heir of all things (1:2), he was *made* lower than the angels (2:7), and he *became* high priest (5:5). Those who read Hebrews in terms of historical development often attribute such divergent statements to the merging of two different types of tradition.[220] Those who read Hebrews with questions of Christ's mode of being in mind often relate comments about change to Christ's humanity and comments about changelessness to his divinity (p. 24). An alternative, however, is to shift the question from Christ's being to Christ's faithfulness. To say that Christ is the same means that he is constantly faithful through changing situations. Emphasizing constancy or faithfulness also fits Hebrews' views of God, for the author argues that God's purposes remained unchanging (6:17–18) even while God altered the Law (7:11–19). Similarly, to say that Christ was without sin does not speculate about his mode of being, but emphasizes his constant faithfulness in the face of testing (§12 COMMENT *a*).

---

[219]Dunn finds little sense of personal preexistence in Hebrews (*Christology*, 206–9), but the assumption that the preexistent Son entered the world for the purpose of doing God's will suggests that Hebrews did understand preexistence in personal terms (see Habermann, *Präexistenzaussagen*, 420–21; Loader, *Sohn*, 73–74).

[220]For example, Dunn, *Christology*, 51–56; Attridge, *Epistle*, 25–27.

2. EARTHLY JESUS[221]

Theologically, Jesus' earthly career is important in three ways for Hebrews. First, Jesus must really have suffered for Hebrews' treatment of the atonement to have integrity. The author affirms that without an outpouring of blood there is no forgiveness of sins (9:22), arguing that Jesus' death entailed the effusion of blood that fulfills the need for sacrifice foreshadowed by the OT (9:12, 14). Second, the author assures listeners that Jesus can sympathize with them because he truly suffered (2:18; 4:15). Without real suffering, this assurance has no weight. Third, Jesus' faithfulness through suffering and death offers an example for listeners to follow. If Jesus did not suffer, his example is of no significance (12:3; 13:13).

Hebrews perceives Jesus' earthly life in light of his exaltation and the OT. The author was apparently familiar with some traditions concerning Jesus' life and work, but does not show detailed knowledge of Jesus' ministry. His references to points in Jesus' career are theologically shaped and serve the interests of faith. Concerning Jesus' origins, Hebrews assumes that historically Jesus came from the tribe of Judah (7:14). Nothing is said about Bethlehem or Nazareth, and Jesus' parents are not named. Descent from Judah is noteworthy because it would seem to disqualify Jesus from the priesthood, but Hebrews reverses the argument by insisting that since Jesus *is* a priest, the priesthood based on Levitical descent has been superseded (§18 COMMENT *a*).

Hebrews refers to "sayings" of Jesus in two places. Neither saying comes from an account of Jesus' teachings like those found in the gospels or letters of Paul; both are quotations from the OT. In 2:12–13 Jesus' words come from Ps 22:22 and Isa 8:17–18, and in Heb 10:5–7 Jesus is said to utter Ps 40:6–8. It is true that some ancient writers supplied speeches for historical figures (Thucydides, *Peloponnesian War* 1.21), but the author of Hebrews did not compose speeches for Jesus. Instead, he drew all of Jesus' words from the Scriptures, which he understands to contain a shadow of what is revealed in Christ (10:1). The issue for the author was apparently not whether Jesus actually quoted these OT texts, but whether these texts truly express Christ's mission (G. R. Hughes, *Hebrews*, 62).

Comparison of the OT quotations with sayings of Jesus from other sources suggests that the texts collected in 2:12–13 are generally congruent with statements of Jesus like those the gospels record (§8 COMMENT *b*), but the relation of the quotation criticizing sacrifice (10:5–7) to Jesus' teachings is less clear. Jesus is variously said to have commended sacrifice (Mark 1:40–45), to have assumed its legitimacy (Matt 5:23–24), and to have considered love of God and neighbor to be superior to sacrifice (Mark 12:33–34; Matt 9:13; 12:7). A more negative attitude is evident in his cursing of a fig tree to portend the end of the Temple and its sacrifices (Mark 14:58; 15:29–30; cf. Matt 26:61; 27:40; John 2:19).[222] What is decisive for Hebrews, however, is not the tradition of Jesus'

---

[221]On the earthly or "historical" Jesus in Hebrews see Grässer, *Aufbruch*, 100–28; G. R. Hughes, *Hebrews*, 75–100; Laub, *Bekenntnis*, 51–165; Melbourne, "Examination"; Roloff, "Der mitleidende"; Walter, "Christologie"; H.-F. Weiss, *Brief*, 321–27.

[222]For a summary of interpretations of the Temple cleansing see N. T. Wright, *Jesus*, 405–17.

teachings, but the meaning of his death. By offering himself, Jesus discloses the inadequacy of other sacrifices and makes them unnecessary. Given this understanding of the definitive nature of Jesus' self-offering, the author could cite the critique of sacrifice in Ps 40:6–8 as a summary of Jesus' mission even if he was not familiar with a tradition that ascribed these words to Jesus' own teachings.

The author was familiar with traditions about Jesus' suffering and death by crucifixion. Again, the author interprets Jesus' suffering and death through the lens of Scripture. We consider first the prayer of Jesus in Heb 5:7:

Heb 5:7	*Mark 14:33–36 (cf. Matt 26:37–39)*
with loud cries	distressed and agitated . . . he said to them,
and tears	"I am deeply grieved, even to death . . . "
	And going a little farther,
	he threw himself on the ground and
[he] offered both prayers	prayed that, if it were possible,
and supplications	the hour might pass from him. He said,
to the one who was able	"Abba, Father, for you all things are possible;
to save him from death,	remove this cup from me;
and he was heard	yet, not what I want,
because of [his] reverence.	but what you want."

Listeners familiar with the Gethsemane tradition of Mark and Matthew often hear in Heb 5:7 a reminiscence of Jesus in deep distress, praying for deliverance from death, yet giving assent to the will of God.[223] Unlike 5:7, these gospel accounts do not say that Jesus' prayer was heard, although in other forms of the Gethsemane tradition an answer of sorts was given through angelic help (Luke 22:43–44) or a voice from heaven (John 12:27–28). Connections between these traditions and Heb 5:7 remain tenuous, however, and in none of them is Jesus said to have shed tears.

Crucifixion narratives provide some of the elements missing from the Gethsemane accounts.[224] In Matthew and Mark, "*Jesus cried out with a loud voice*, 'Eloi, Eloi, lema sabachthani?' which means, 'My God, my God, why have you forsaken me?' " Later he "gave a *loud cry* and breathed his last" (Mark 15:34, 37; cf. Matt 27:46, 50). According to Luke, "Jesus, *crying with a loud voice*, said, 'Father, into your hands I commit my spirit' " (Luke 23:46). In these accounts Jesus prays and utters a loud cry, but is not said to have shed tears. Many interpreters rightly note that Heb 5:7 cannot be identified with only one moment in Jesus' passion.[225]

---

[223]For example, Chrysostom; Alcuin; Haimo; F. F. Bruce; P. E. Hughes, *Commentary*, 182; Peterson, *Hebrews*, 87–89; Kistemaker, *Exposition*, 136; Lindars, *Theology*, 63; Bénétreau, *L'Epître*, 1.212; Scholer, *Proleptic*, 87; Dunnill, *Covenant*, 216. See further Zesati Estrada, *Hebreos*, 3.

[224]Nicolaus of Lyra; Luther, WA 57,3.29; Laub, *Bekenntnis*, 127. See further Zesati Estrada, *Hebreos*, 18.

[225]For example, Ephraem; Isho'dad; Sedulius Scotus; Aquinas, *Ad Heb.* §§256–57; Vanhoye, *Old Testament*, 125; R. E. Brown, *Death*, 1.229–33. See Zesati Estrada, *Hebreos*, 21, for further listings and p. 34 for his concurrence with this view.

The form of the passion tradition known to the author of Hebrews is unclear, but his presentation of Jesus' prayer corresponds to portrayals of other righteous sufferers. This probably does not mean that the author relied on an early Christian hymn, but that he drew on biblical and Jewish traditions concerning prayer.[226] This is a less pronounced form of what the author did in 2:12–13 and 10:5–7, where the words ascribed to Jesus are actually taken from the OT. By allowing the Scriptures to shape the way Jesus' passion is presented, the author takes the passion of Jesus, which was a unique event, and helps listeners see in his suffering something of broader significance. One of the best examples is Ps 116[227]:

Heb 5:7	*Ps 116*
in the days of his flesh, offered	*2b* I will call on him as long as I live
both prayers and supplications	*1b* my supplications
to the one who was able to save him	*4b* "O Lord, I pray, save my life!"
	6b he saved me
from death	*8a* you have delivered my soul from death,
with loud cries and tears	*8b* my eyes from tears
and he was heard	*1a* the Lord . . . has heard my voice
because of [his] reverence	*10a* I kept my faith

Other psalm texts speak of the righteous sufferer crying to God for help (22:2; 69:3) with tears (39:12; 42:3) and anguish (42:5–6, 11), and being heard by him (22:24; 31:23). The result is that the presentation in Heb 5:7 relies on the cumulative witness of a number of psalms (Zesati Estrada, *Hebreos*, 39–52), and it both reflects and reshapes tradition. Jesus was heard, but not in the usual sense, since he was not delivered before death, but after death. The favorable answer to prayer came despite suffering, and it did not entail exemption from suffering. Hebrews uses Jesus' example to encourage others in prayer, understanding that God provides help when he considers it to be the right time (Heb 4:16).

The final point in Jesus' career on earth was crucifixion at the hands of his opponents (12:3) outside the city gate (13:12). These passages recall traditions concerning the circumstances of Jesus' death, but give little by way of historical detail. The opponents are never named; there are no references to Pilate or the Jewish authorities. The comment about crucifixion outside the gate corresponds to the gospel passion accounts, though it also fits the common practice (NOTE

[226]Some scholars maintain that Heb 5:7 is based on an early Christian hymn (Brandenburger, "Text"; Friedrich, "Lied"; Lescow, "Jesus"; cf. R. E. Brown, *Death*, 1.228–29). The passage begins with the relative pronoun *hos* ("who") as do other hymnic texts. Parallel expressions like "prayer and supplications" and "loud cries and tears" give the text a poetic quality. Moreover, the phrases just mentioned are unique in Hebrews, which might suggest that the author derived the passage from a source instead of composing it himself. Many of the distinctive literary qualities can, however, be accounted for by the use of language from the psalms. Parallel expressions are found in prose, not just in hymns. While it is possible that a hymnic source informed the author's language here, such hypotheses remain problematic (see Zesati Estrada, *Hebreos*, 61–75; Attridge, *Epistle*, 147–48; Lane, *Hebrews*, 1.112–13).

[227]On Heb 5:7 and Ps 116 see Theophylact (PG 125.244A); Strobel, "Psalmengrundlage."

on 13:12). In both cases, the reminiscence of Jesus' passion is consistent with what appears in other sources, although the author's main interest in the tradition is its value for encouraging people. If listeners find it difficult to be faithful, they may recall how Jesus remained faithful in the face of more severe opposition (12:2–4). If they are reproached by unbelievers, they must recognize that faith sets one apart from others in society. Just as atoning sacrifices were completed outside Israel's camp, Jesus made his self-sacrifice outside the city, exemplifying the way that the faithful may expect to be separated from others in their city (13:12–13).

3. PRIESTHOOD AND EXALTATION

The presentation of Christ's high priesthood is one of Hebrews' most significant contributions to Christology. The way the author seeks to demonstrate that Christ can be considered a priest indicates that this idea was new to the listeners, but the underlying logic is fairly simple. Once the "lord" from Ps 110:1 is identified with Christ—as was common in early Christianity (NOTE on Heb 1:13)—it is but a small step to identify Christ as the priest like Melchizedek mentioned in Ps 110:4. Most questions concerning Christ's priestly work are taken up in the commentary,[228] but an additional topic concerns the moment at which Christ became high priest.

Some passages suggest that Jesus became high priest through his exaltation. If the essential trait of a priest after the type of Melchizedek is that he can serve forever (6:20), Jesus became such a priest when he obtained an indestructible life through his resurrection and exaltation (7:16). Jesus did not glorify himself so as to become high priest, but was given the honor of priesthood through his exaltation (5:5–6). On earth Jesus would not have been a priest, for he did not have the descent (7:13–14) or the type of ministry required by the Law (8:4). Therefore, one might conclude that Jesus became a priest when he was made "complete," a term that encompasses both glorification and priesthood (pp. 122–25).

Other passages suggest that Jesus' priesthood began on earth, since his death was an offering, which implies that at the time of his death he was already a priest (9:11–14). He appeared on the world's scene to remove sin by sacrificing himself (9:25–26), making purification for sins before being exalted to God's right hand (1:3). On the Day of Atonement the high priest sacrificed the victims outside the sanctuary, then brought their blood into the inner chamber. By analogy, Christ's self-offering on earth and his entry into heaven's inner sanctuary would both be priestly acts. Moreover, the prayers that he offered prior to his death are parallel to what priests offered (5:1, 7).

Some, who give priority to the earthly aspects of Jesus' priesthood, insist that he was a priest during his life and that he was a priest from the time of his incarnation (Chrysostom, *Homilies* 13.2; Cody, *Heavenly*, 97; Spicq, *L'Épître*, 2.111). Others, who emphasize the heavenly aspects of Jesus' priesthood, argue

---

[228]See esp. NOTES and COMMENTS on 2:17–18; 4:14–5:10; 7:1–10; 9:11–14; 10:1–18.

that he was not a priest on earth and that his death was not a sacrifice, since atonement is made in heaven.[229] The most realistic view, however, is that the author gives no clear answer to the question of when Jesus became high priest. If the author "did take seriously the notion that Christ became high priest at some particular point, it would have to be the complex 'moment' in which death and exaltation are combined."[230]

The ministry of the heavenly high priest consists of making intercession, which brings help to those in need as well as forgiveness of sins (NOTE on 7:25). Although Christ's appointment to high priesthood involves his exaltation, and his entry into heaven is compared to the high priest entering the inner sanctuary to offer blood, Hebrews does not claim that the ascended Christ offers a continual sacrifice, as some have suggested.[231] Hebrews insists that Christ offered for all time a single sacrifice for sins and is now seated at God's right hand, which indicates that no further sacrifices are being made (10:12–14). The effects of Christ's self-offering continue to be appropriated by human beings, so that the author can speak of atonement in the present tense (2:17), but his offering of sacrifice is depicted in the aorist tense to indicate that it is a singular act, in contrast to sacrifices offered by other priests (7:27; 8:3; 9:14, 28; 10:12).

C. Promises, Covenants, and Law

Promises, covenants, and Law are interrelated ideas in Hebrews. The promises made to Abraham establish the *goal* of God's design for people. The Sinai covenant or Law provided limited *means* for dealing with sin, but did not bring God's purposes to completion. Therefore, God made a new covenant through the death of Christ, displacing the Sinai covenant and providing the definitive *means* of atonement for sin, so that people might come into full and final relationship with God.

1. PROMISES[232]

Hebrews uses words for "promise" to express God's commitments to people.[233] Making a promise means pledging to give a gift or perform an action, usually of

---

[229]The issue was argued sharply in the sixteenth century by Socinus (p. 35), who said, "Christ did not offer himself to God on the cross but only in heaven itself. This is amply supported by the fact that Christ was not properly inaugurated by priesthood until after his death, indeed, until after his ascension into heaven . . . .Thus we understand that Christ was not truly a priest before he had attained to the glorification of his body and to immortality" (quoted by Demarest, *History*, 22). Westcott proposed in his *Epistle* that Jesus fulfilled the type of Aaron while on earth (5:1–10) and the type of Melchizedek when he entered into heaven (7:1–28). This seems unlikely (Peterson, *Hebrews*, 192–93).

[230]Attridge, *Epistle*, 147; cf. Peterson, *Hebrews*, 191–95; Loader, *Sohn*, 245–46; Daly, *Christian*, 267–75. See also Hegermann, "Christologie"; D. L. Powell, "Christ"; J. R. Schäfer, "Relationship."

[231]See pp. 34–35 on the Socinians; cf. Brooks, "Perpetuity." See the critique by P. E. Hughes, *Commentary*, 337–54. See also MacLeod, "Present Work."

[232]Käsemann, *Wandering*, 17–37; G. R. Hughes, *Hebrews*, 36–47; Rose, "Verheissung."

[233]Hebrews uses both the noun *epangelia* and the verb *epangelizein*. The promises most often

a positive sort. In Hebrews the term "promise" is used for the word or pledge that people initially receive from God as well as for the substance they receive when God fulfills his commitment (NOTES on 6:15; 11:33). Because God's promises involve an initial statement of divine intent followed by the giving of a gift at a later time, Hebrews likens them to a pledge of inheritance (6:12, 17; 9:15; 11:8–9). Those who receive God's word of promise are those who hope to "inherit salvation" in the future (1:14). In Hebrews "promise" is synonymous with "good news" or "gospel" (*euangelizein*), a term often used for the Christian message (NOTES on 4:1–2).

The fundamental promises are those made to Abraham, and Hebrews assumes that these promises express commitments that remain in force for all of Abraham's heirs, including the followers of Jesus. God promised to bless Abraham and to give him land and descendants (6:14; 11:9, 12), confirming his promises by an unalterable oath (6:17). Abraham received the fulfillment of the promises in a limited sense through the blessing given to him by Melchizedek (7:1, 6), by the birth of Isaac (6:15; 11:11), and by temporary residence in the promised land (11:8–9). Yet neither Abraham nor the generations that followed him received fulfillment of the promises in the full and final sense (4:1; 11:13, 39). This did not mean that God had proven false to his word (6:18), but that the promises pointed to fulfillment that is future rather than past, and transcendent rather than earthly. God promised to bless Abraham and Abraham received a blessing from Melchizedek, but his heirs can look for God's blessing to be mediated through Christ, the eternal priest foreshadowed by Melchizedek. God promised Abraham a place, yet this place is not finally the land of Canaan, but God's own heavenly city (4:8; 11:10, 16). God promised Abraham many descendants, but through the birth of a son from "one who was 'dead' " (11:12) and through the binding and release of Isaac, God symbolically pointed toward the resurrection of all his people from the dead (11:17–19).

Faith is the corollary to the promises. Giving a promise awakens a sense of expectancy, drawing attention to its fulfillment. Since God expressed his commitments in the form of promises, God's people journey by faith and hope in a future that is as yet unseen (11:1; Käsemann, *Wandering*, 19). Confidence that God would fulfill his promises was vital to the listeners' perseverance, since their faith was awakened by the promise of an eternal inheritance (9:15), and they endured the plundering of their property in the conviction that they had a superior, abiding possession (10:34, 36). Without the conviction that God would give them their promised inheritance as Abraham's descendants (2:16; 6:12, 17), there would be no incentive to continue. Therefore, the author punctuates his arguments with assurances that God issued both a promise and an oath to show "the unchangeable nature of his intention" (6:17). Abraham believed that the

---

pertain to the promises made to Abraham. Exceptions include a more general reference to the promises received by various OT figures (NOTE on 11:33) and the promise that God will shake the universe in the future (NOTE on 12:26). On the promises that underlie the covenants (8:6) see below.

God who promised would be faithful (11:11) and the listeners must do the same (10:23). God's faithfulness is the basis for human faith.

2. OLD AND NEW COVENANTS[234]

Hebrews uses the term "covenant" (*diathēkē*) for the Sinai covenant (Exod 24:3–8) and for the new covenant promised in Jer 31:31–34. God made the "first" or "old" covenant (Heb 8:7, 13; 9:1, 15) after he brought Israel out of Egypt (8:9). It was inaugurated by a blood sacrifice that was offered by Moses (9:18–20), and it included a Law that was written on the tablets that were kept in the ark of the covenant (9:4). Under the new covenant, however, God promised to write his laws on human hearts and minds. This is the covenant that Hebrews declares to have been inaugurated by Christ's self-sacrifice (see NOTES and COMMENT on 7:22; 8:6–13; 9:15–17; 10:12–18).

If the promises made to Abraham establish the goal of God's action, the covenants provide the means through which God achieves the goal. Hebrews regularly relates the old and new covenants to human sin, which God must overcome in order to achieve his purposes. The first covenant prescribed sacrifices, a priesthood, and a sanctuary by which atonement could be made, but the sacrifices cleansed only the flesh, the priests were subject to sin and death, and the sanctuary was earthly (7:23, 27; 8:5; 9:1–7, 13; 10:1–4). Therefore, God appointed Jesus, the sinless priest who now serves in a heavenly sanctuary (7:24, 27; 8:1–2), to be the "mediator of a new covenant, so that . . . those who are called might receive the promised eternal inheritance," for by Christ's death God redeems them "from transgressions incurred on the basis of the first covenant" and cleanses the conscience (9:14–15). There is constancy in God's promises of inheritance, while there is change in the covenants by which God overcomes the problem of human sin in order to bring his promises to their fulfillment. The old covenant was instituted for a time that is now past, but the new covenant is everlasting (8:13; 13:20: cf. §21 COMMENT *b*; Lehne, *New Covenant*, 98–99).

God's promises form the basis of the old and new covenants, according to 8:6. Although the Mosaic covenant was commonly associated with the Law (see below), it was also linked to the promise that Israel would be God's people (Exod 6:7; 29:45; Lev 26:12) and that God would forgive iniquities (Exod 34:7). The promises that underlie the new covenant (Jer 31:31–34; Heb 8:10–12) include the hope that people will belong to God and receive mercy (8:10, 12), and Hebrews argues that the mercy promised under the new covenant has become available through Christ's self-sacrifice (10:11–18). The new covenant also promises that God will inscribe his laws on human hearts and that God's people will know him so completely that no further instruction will be necessary. By offering instruction and exhortation to the listeners, however, Hebrews shows that these aspects of the new covenant still await complete fulfillment.

---

[234]See Backhaus, *Der neue*; Dunnill, *Covenant*, 123–34; Frey, "Die alte"; Grässer; *Der Alte*, 1–134; Isaacs, *Sacred*, 115–26; Lehne, *New Covenant*; Levin, *Verheissung*; Luz, "Der alte"; Penna, "Appunti"; Peterson, "Prophecy"; Swetnam, "Why"; Theobald, "Zwei Bünde."

Jewish sources say virtually nothing about the new covenant. Texts that speak of God giving his people an obedient heart and an everlasting covenant envision the restoration of an existing relationship rather than the formation of a new covenant (Bar 2:30–35; *Jub.* 1:15–28). The new covenant mentioned in the Dead Sea Scrolls (CD VI, 18–19; VIII, 20–21; XIX, 33–34; XX, 11–13; cf. lQpHab II, 3) is essentially the Mosaic covenant, not the covenant mentioned in Jer 31:31–34. Elements in the Dead Sea texts are eschatological and refer to those who have received insight into God's work through the Teacher of Righteousness, but this newness is not correlated with Jer 31 (Wolff, *Jeremia*, 124; Lehne, *New Covenant*, 58–59).

Hebrews probably does not derive the new covenant idea from Jesus' words at the Last Supper, although it does deal with similar themes. Luke and Paul relate that Jesus said, "This cup is the new covenant in my blood" (1 Cor 11:25: Luke 22:20), probably echoing Jer 31:31–34, even though they do not mention forgiveness. Matthew and Mark identify Jesus' blood as a covenant,[235] but do not call it new, although Matt 26:28 does mention "forgiveness."[236] A principal OT text underlying the Last Supper accounts is Exod 24:3–8, which recounts the establishment of the covenant at Mount Sinai. Hebrews explicitly connects the Sinai covenant with the new covenant by quoting both Exod 24:8 and Jer 31:31–34. Hebrews makes the connection to show that just as the Sinai covenant was established by a sacrifice, the new covenant is established by Jesus' sacrificial death (§16 COMMENT). Moreover, the saying of Jesus refers to his blood or the cup being poured out "for you" (Luke 22:20) or "for many" (Mark 14:24; Matt 26:28), which suggests that it would bring redemption from sin. What is implicit in Jesus' saying is explicit in Hebrews: Jesus' death is a sacrifice of atonement (Lehne, *New Covenant*, 80–88).

Hebrews shares aspects of the new covenant theme with Paul, who explicitly contrasts the old and new covenants in 2 Cor 3:1–18, echoing Jer 31.[237] Paul says that the old covenant possesses a merely transient glory, whereas the new covenant in Christ is the work of the Spirit, who writes on human hearts and brings people to everlasting glory. Paul's argument and principal OT text (Exod 34:29–35) differ from Hebrews, but like Hebrews he sharply contrasts the old and new covenants, and holds that people enter into glory through the new covenant. Paul also contrasts the covenant made with Sarah—which he links to the promises to Abraham and the heavenly Jerusalem—with the Sinai covenant that pertains to the flesh and to the present time that is ending (Gal 4:21–31). Simi-

---

[235]Matt 26:28 and Mark 14:24 refer to "my blood of the covenant." The term "new" is included in some MSS, apparently as a later insertion.

[236]Some argue that Jesus did not allude to Jer 31:31–34 because the themes of the oracle are not developed (Wolff, *Jeremia*, 131–34; Grässer, *Der Alte*, 120; cf. Räisänen, *Paul*, 242–43). Yet since the expression "new covenant" is distinctive, others make the connection (Fitzmyer, *Luke*, 402; Fee, *Corinthians*, 555).

[237]Grässer argues that 2 Cor 3 does not recall Jer 31:31–34 since Paul does not develop the themes in Jeremiah's oracle (*Der Alte*, 67–68; cf. Räisänen, *Paul*, 243–45). Many do discern an echo of Jeremiah since Paul uses the distinctive expression "new covenant" and refers to the Spirit writing on human hearts (Levin, *Verheissung*, 266; Lehne, *New Covenant*, 74).

larly, Hebrews ties the first covenant to the fleshly realm and the present transient age (8:13; 9:8–9), while associating the new covenant with God's promises and the heavenly Jerusalem (9:15; 12:18–24).

3. LAW[238]

Hebrews refers to the "Law" (*nomos*, 7:5, 12, 16, 19, 28; 8:4; 9:19, 22; 10:1, 8, 28) and the "first" or Mosaic "covenant" (*diathēkē*, 8:7, 9, 13; 9:1, 15, 18, 20) with little difference in meaning. Interpreters often remark that Hebrews deals with the ritual portion of the Law, whereas Paul dealt with its ethical aspects,[239] but the distinction is not helpful. Hebrews refers not only to tithing (7:5), priests (7:28), sacrifices (8:4; 10:8), food, drink, and ablutions (9:10), but to the entire Sinaitic code (9:19), which included ethical commands that warranted punishment if broken (10:28; cf. 2:2). The Law's provisions for priesthood cannot be neatly separated from ethical matters because priests offer sacrifices for sins (5:3), and sins include transgressions of the so-called ethical commandments. Similarly, Paul deals with circumcision, keeping kosher, and observing Jewish festivals (Gal 2:11–13; 4:10; 5:2–3), which might be considered ritual matters, as well as with commandments against adultery, murder, theft, and coveting (Rom 13:8–10), which are ethical.[240] For Paul and Hebrews to speak about abrogating the Law in one respect means a change in the whole system.

The basis for both writers' reflections on the Law is the conviction that God dealt decisively with sin through the death and resurrection of Jesus. Both also assume that the Law is not terminated by human decisions concerning its validity, but by the decision of the God who instituted it. Both understand that if Christ died on behalf of others once for all (Heb 7:27; 9:12, 26; 10:10; Rom 6:10), then the Law's provisions for justification or atonement must have been inadequate (Heb 7:15–19; 8:7, 13; Gal 2:21).[241] Temporally, Hebrews says that laws concerning food, drink, and ablutions were instituted only until the "time of correction," which arrived with Christ's death and exaltation (9:9–11). God abrogated the laws concerning the Levitical priesthood by raising Jesus to serve as a priest forever after the type of Melchizedek (7:12, 18–19). Like Hebrews, Paul also argues that the Law was instituted only for a limited time (Gal 3:23–4:7). Metaphysically, Hebrews says that the Law's sphere of operation was limited to the flesh (Heb 7:16; 9:9–10), that its priests were mortal and sinful

---

[238]On the significance of the Law in Hebrews see H.-F. Weiss, *Brief*, 403–7; Grässer, *Hebräer*, 2.49–52; Attridge, *Epistle*, 204–5; H. Hübner, *EDNT* 2.477; Sowers, *Hermeneutics*, 97–105; W. Gutbrod, *TDNT* 4.1078–80; Goppelt, *Theology*, 2.256–57; Räisänen, *Paul*, 207–10; Witherington, "Influence," 146–52; von Campenhausen, *Formation*, 68–69.

[239]Attridge, *Epistle*, 204; Räisänen, *Paul*, 209; cf. Goppelt, *Theology*, 2.256; von Campenhausen, *Formation*, 68.

[240]The issue of the Law in Paul is complicated because he uses "law" (*nomos*) in various senses. Some studies focus more on legalism than on the status of Israel's Law (see the valuable discussion in Westerholm, *Israel's Law*, 105–40), which is the focus here.

[241]See E. P. Sanders, *Paul*, 442–44; Westerholm, *Israel's Law*, 220–21.

(7:23, 27), and that its sacrifices were earthly (8:4). Through Christ's death and exaltation, however, God established a priest of an order that transcends the Law's limitations. Christ was sinless (4:15; 7:26–27), he was raised to everlasting life and is not subject to death (7:24–25), and the sacrifice he offered goes beyond fleshy limitations to cleanse the conscience (9:14).

Neither Paul nor the author of Hebrews fully explains why God gave an ineffective Law in the first place. Paul sometimes says that God instituted the Law to provoke people to sin, to identify what is and is not sinful, and to make people despair (Gal 3:19, 23–24; Rom 7:4–25), yet he also says that the Law is holy, just, and good, thereby suggesting that some of these functions may have come from sin's perversion of the Law (Rom 5:20; 7:7–25; 8:3; 1 Cor 15:56). Hebrews does not suggest that sin perverted the Law, but assumes that the Law was weak from its inception (7:18): people did not keep it (8:9), it affected only the flesh (9:13), and it could not take away sins (10:4). The author of Hebrews comes close to the Pauline argument that the Law makes sin known, however, when he says that the sacrifices prescribed by Law remind people of sin, since sacrifices for sin must be offered year after year (10:3). The Law's positive role is to foreshadow the new order that Christ inaugurated (10:1).[242]

Laws pertaining to priesthood and sacrifices have been terminated, but Hebrews understands that God remains opposed to lawlessness (1:9; 10:17) and will write his laws upon human hearts (8:10; 10:16). For the author of Hebrews, the contours of Christian life are congruent with the Law, but are not derived from the Law. For example, when urging listeners to show devotion to God (12:28; 13:15), to remain faithful in marriage (13:4), and to avoid covetousness (13:5), the author could have based his appeal on the Ten Commandments (Exod 20:3, 14, 17), but he chose instead to develop his arguments on other grounds (§37 COMMENT *a–b*). Paul says that the Law is fulfilled in the command to love one's neighbor (Gal 5:14; Rom 13:8–10; cf. Lev 19:18; Matt 22:38; Mark 12:31; Luke 10:27). Hebrews urges listeners to good works and deeds of love (Heb 10:24; 13:1), which presumably express the new covenant, but the author does not explore the connection between this type of love and the Mosaic Law (Hays, *Moral*, 201–2).

D. THE SCRIPTURES[243]

Hebrews' theology emerges in large part through engagement with Israel's Scriptures, which include the promises, covenants, and Law mentioned above, as well

[242]Von Campenhausen, *Formation*, 69; Grässer, *Hebräer*, 2.51; Räisänen, *Paul*, 208; Hübner, *EDNT* 2.477.

[243]H. Anderson, "Jewish Antecedents"; Attridge, *Epistle*, 23–25; M. Barth, "Old Testament"; Burns, "Hermeneutical"; Clements, "Use"; Ellingworth, *Epistle*, 37–42; France, "Writer"; Goppelt, *Typos*; Hanson, "Hebrews"; Hofius, "Biblische Theologie"; Hübner, *Biblische Theologie*, 15–63; G. R. Hughes, *Hebrews*; Eisenbaum, *Jewish Heroes*, 89–133; Lane, *Hebrews*, 1.cxii–cxxiv; Schröger, "Das hermeneutische"; Thompson, "Hermeneutics"; H.-F. Weiss, *Brief*, 171–81. On the use of the LXX see also Bateman, *Early Jewish*, 121–47.

as other material. The author of Hebrews understood the sacred writings to include the Law, the Prophets, the Psalms, and a number of other writings. There are thirty-five passages in Hebrews that can be considered quotations, with texts coming from eleven of the books that are now included in all Jewish and Christian Bibles (Genesis, Exodus, Numbers, Deuteronomy, 2 Samuel, Psalms, Proverbs, Isaiah, Jeremiah, Habakkuk, Haggai).[244] He also used the deuterocanonical stories of the Maccabean martyrs (2 Macc 5–7; Heb 11:35–38) and perhaps the Wisdom of Solomon (Wis 7:25; Heb 1:3), as well as the tradition of Isaiah's martyrdom, which appears in later sources, but not in the canonical writings (NOTE on 11:37).

Hebrews relies on a Greek form of the OT. This is most evident in texts that conform to the LXX but differ from the MT. For example, the quotation of Ps 40:7 in Heb 10:5 reads "you fashioned a body" (LXX) rather than "ears you have dug" (MT), and the reference to Gen 47:31 in Heb 11:21 refers to "staff" rather than "bed." The idea that the son of man was made lower than the angels "for a little while" (2:7) depends on the LXX of Ps 8:5, since the MT text means "a little lower" in degree. The author connects Ps 95:11 (94:11 LXX) with Gen 2:2 on the basis of words for "rest" that appear in the Greek but not in the Hebrew version of the two passages (Heb 4:4–5). Occasionally Hebrews cites texts that differ from standard versions of the LXX. This might have resulted from several factors: the author did not feel constrained to cite texts verbatim, as can be seen in his variant renderings of Jer 31:33–34 (Heb 8:10–12; 10:16–17), he sometimes used common paraphrases (NOTES on 10:38; 13:6), and he might have known one of the variant forms of the LXX that circulated in antiquity.[245]

Quotation is one of the ways that Hebrews uses the OT. Never using an introductory formula like "as it is written," the author tells listeners that the words are what God (1:5, 7, 8, 13; 7:21; 8:8), Christ (2:12–13; 10:5), or the Holy Spirit (3:7; 10:15) "says."[246] Moreover, many of the quotations are direct speech, so that the text is not so much a record about something from the past, but a form of address, an expression of the living word of God (4:12–13). Texts address Christ as Son and priest (e.g., 1:5–6; 5:5–6), they admonish listeners not to harden their hearts (3:7–11) but to accept divine instruction (12:5–6), and they give

---

[244]The list of thirty-five quotations follows Schröger, *Verfasser*. Some count more or fewer OT quotations (Lane, *Hebrews*, 1.cxvi). The quotations are 1:5a (Ps 2:7); 1:5b (2 Sam 7:14/1 Chron 17:13); 1:6 (Deut 32:43); 1:7 (Ps 104:4); 1:8–9 (Ps 45:6–7); 1:10–12 (Ps 102:25–27); 1:13 (Ps 110:1); 2:6–8 (Ps 8:4–6); 2:12 (Ps 22:22); 2:13 (Isa 8:17–18); 3:2 (Num 12:7); 3:7–11, 15; 4:3, 7 (Ps 95:7–11); 4:4 (Gen 2:2); 5:5 (Ps 2:7); 5:6 (Ps 110:4); 6:13–14 (Gen 22:16–17); 7:17, 21 (Ps 110:4); 8:5 (Exod 25:40); 8:8–12 (Jer 31:31–34); 9:20 (Exod 24:8); 10:5–10 (Ps 40:6–8); 10:16–17 (Jer 31:33–34); 10:30 (Deut 32:35–36); 10:37–38 (Hab 2:3–4); 11:18 (Gen 21:12); 11:21 (Gen 47:31); 12:5–6 (Prov 3:11–12); 12:20 (Exod 19:13); 12:26 (Hag 2:6); 13:5 (Deut 31:6); 13:6 (Ps 118:6). In addition to quotations, note, e.g., the use of Leviticus (Heb 9:1–7), Joshua (Heb 4:8; 11:30–31), Judges (Heb 11:32), 1 Samuel (Heb 11:32), 1–2 Kings (Heb 11:35), and Daniel (Heb 11:33–34).

[245]See further McCullough, "Old Testament"; Schröger, *Verfasser*, 247–56; Ahlborn, *Septuaginta*; Howard, "Hebrews"; Combrink, "Some Thoughts." Cadwallader ("Correction") considers ways in which extant LXX MSS might have been corrected to conform to Hebrews.

[246]Sometimes words of Scripture are also said to "testify" (2:6; 7:17).

promises that listeners can apply to their own situation, like the promise of a new covenant (Jer 31:31–34; Heb 8:8–12). The author's own accounts of Melchizedek (7:1–2), the Tabernacle (9:1–7), and other OT passages help to relate episodes and institutions from the past to Christ, but the quotations address the listeners with the most forceful immediacy.[247]

Hebrews interprets Christ in light of the OT and the OT in light of Christ. Since the author understands the same God to have spoken through the prophets and through a Son (1:1–2), he understands Christ and the Scriptures in relation to each other. On the one hand, what God disclosed through the prophets is prior to Christ in time, so that the scriptural words create the context in which the meaning of Christ's work can be discerned. The author does not begin with a fully developed view of Christ that he then relates to the OT, but discerns the significance of Christ's identity and work by considering them in light of the OT. On the other hand, what God disclosed through Christ is prior to the prophets in importance, so that Christ's life, death, and resurrection provide the touchstone for understanding what had previously been said in the Scriptures.

This approach fits Hebrews' recognition that faith pertains to things that cannot be seen (11:1). Very little of what Hebrews says about Christ is available to the eye. For the author, it is a given that Jesus was crucified, but simple observation does not allow one to discern the significance of the event. Meaning emerges when Jesus' crucifixion is interpreted in light of OT sacrificial practices and the promise of a new covenant (Heb 8–10). This, rather than simple observation of Jesus' execution on the cross, is what enables the author to depict Christ's death as the definitive sacrifice for sin. Similarly, Hebrews takes for granted that Jesus rose from the dead, but he recounts the event in language reminiscent of the exodus (2:14–16; 13:20). The present situation of the ascended Christ cannot be perceived by the senses. But by linking Christ's resurrection to Ps 110:1, Hebrews can speak of the Lord being exalted to power at God's right hand (1:3, 13; 8:1; 10:12–13; 12:2).

Hebrews understands the OT to contain a shadow of what has been revealed in Christ (NOTES on 8:5; 10:1). The exalted Christ is like a person who stands in the brightness of the sun and casts a shadow upon the earth, so that those who look at the shadow can discern in it the contours of the one who made it. In a similar way, the shadows of the exalted Christ fall on the pages of the OT, allowing the reader to discern in them something of the shape of Christ himself. When the author cites some of the royal psalms and other texts in 1:5–13, he does so in a way that invites listeners to see in the OT texts a reflection of Christ reigning in glory at God's right hand (§4 COMMENT). In 7:1–10 he interprets the story of Melchizedek in Gen 14 in light of the promise concerning "a priest forever according to the type of Melchizedek" in Ps 110:4, which in turn is understood in light of Christ's resurrection (§17 COMMENT). Describing Jesus' death and exaltation in terms of the high priest's movements on the Day of Atonement (Heb 9) and identifying other OT texts as sayings of Jesus (2:12–13;

---

[247]Eisenbaum, *Jewish Heroes*, 89–133; Theobald, "Vom Text."

10:5–7) reflect the same view (pp. 106–7). Hebrews does not assume that this perspective was possible prior to Christ, but maintains that the Spirit that confirmed the message of Christ for the listeners (2:3–4) discloses the connection between the OT and Christ (9:8).

There is a similar interplay between the OT and the listeners' own situation. Interpretation of the human situation must be done from some point of view, and Hebrews' perspective is shaped by the OT. For example, the author describes the listeners' situation by comparing it to that of the wilderness generation: both groups receive the gospel and both are called to persevere in the hope of entering God's rest. The question is whether the listeners will be unfaithful like the wilderness generation or whether they will be faithful like Moses and Jesus (3:7–4:11). Conversely, the author's reading of the OT is shaped by the context of his community. Taking an interpretive key from Hab 2:4, the "righteous one will live by faith" (Heb 10:38), the author shows how the OT narrative bears this out. Along the way he introduces creative anachronisms by speaking of Abraham and his family looking for the city of God and of Moses bearing the denunciation of Christ (11:13–16, 26; pp. 69, 72).[248]

Hebrews' christological reading of the OT distinguishes it from other types of first-century Jewish biblical interpretation.[249] The author does use methods that Jewish interpreters used. Like the writers of the Dead Sea Scrolls, the author of Hebrews assumes that the meanings of biblical texts for the end times have been disclosed to him; but in contrast to them, Hebrews insists that the defining element in the end times is Jesus' death and exaltation. The result is that Hebrews has little in common with Dead Sea exegesis (p. 63). In the NOTES we will observe how Hebrews, like Philo, Josephus, and some rabbinic sources, argues from the lesser to the greater (2:1–4; 10:28–29), connects texts on the basis of a common word (4:4–5), explains the meanings of names (7:2), and considers the silences in the text (7:3). Hebrews also shares some content with them, such as the sense that the parts of the Tabernacle correspond to the parts of the universe (§22 COMMENT *a*). Despite the similarities, however, Hebrews' interpretations differ from those of Jewish writers because of the author's christological assumptions. Theology, rather than exegetical technique, is the principal factor shaping his interpretation of Scripture (cf. Rom 3:21; John 5:39).

E. Divine Action and Human Response

The interplay between Christ and the OT is evident in Hebrews' presentation of divine action and human response. The author argues that the old covenant is obsolete, but he also insists that its practices foreshadow the work of Christ that establishes the new covenant. The actions of God and Christ are construed in

---

[248]On the use of creative anachronism in the NT see Martyn, *History*, 129–30.

[249]See H.-F. Weiss, *Brief*, 177–81; cf. Schröger, *Verfasser*, 269–307; Sowers, *Hermeneutics*, 137–38. Feld (*Hebräerbrief*, 33–34) does not give adequate attention to Christology.

categories taken from the Levitical cult. *Purification* means purging away uncleanness, *sanctification* means making something fit to be brought into the presence of God, and *atonement* involves reconciling God and human beings. *Completion* is a complex idea that deals with the accomplishment of God's designs for people, culminating with everlasting life in God's presence. The human response is found in *faith*.

1. PURIFICATION, SANCTIFICATION, ATONEMENT[250]

Hebrews understands these three ideas to be part of a single process of overcoming human sin in order that people might relate rightly to God. The nuances in these concepts can be grasped by visualizing the parts of the Israelite camp, as shown in the diagram. It is unwise to press subtle distinctions in meaning too far because the terms *purification, sanctification*, and *atonement* overlap in the OT and in Hebrews. This is especially the case since Hebrews is not concerned with uncleanness that is incurred in nonsinful ways, like bodily discharge, but focuses on the impurity and defilement related to sin. For Hebrews, purifying actions are fully effective only when the conscience is cleansed, and cleansing the conscience takes place through faith.

(a) Purification. Purification of the flesh and the earthly sanctuary is associated with Levitical practices (9:13, 22–23; 10:2).[251] According to Jewish Law, people could become unclean by contact with the carcass of an unclean creature (Lev 11:5, 28, 40) or a human corpse (Num 19:11–13), by skin diseases (Lev 13:1–8, 34), rotting walls (14:43–47), and emissions from the sexual organs (15:1–33). Uncleanness could also result from sexual misconduct (18:20, 23–30), homicide (Num 35:33–34), and idolatry (Josh 22:17; Jer 2:23), and the notions of defilement and purity were extended to sin and righteousness generally (Isa 1:16; 6:5–7; Ps 18:20). Purification often meant washing and waiting for a time, but more serious defilement required sacrifice, and on the Day of Atonement, the high priest offered sacrifices for "purification of sins" (Exod 30:10 LXX).

In contrast to Levitical rites, which affect the body, Hebrews says that Christ cleanses the conscience (Heb 9:14) as he purifies people from sin (1:3). Purification is objective in that it comes from outside a person through the death of Christ, and it is subjective in that one is actually cleansed when sin is removed from the conscience. Christ's blood does not cleanse by physical contact, but through proclamation of the significance of his death. Sinful actions proceed out of a relationship with God that is marked by unbelief rather than faith (3:12–13; 6:1; 10:38; 11:24–25; 12:4). The conscience is cleansed when faith is evoked through the proclamation of Christ's death, for Christ's blood "speaks" of God's grace and mercy (12:24). Christ's blood was shed some years before Hebrews was written, yet

---

[250]See Johnsson, "Cultus"; Bénétreau, "La mort"; Dunnill, *Covenant*, 69–111; Grayston, "ἱλάσκεσθαι"; Isaacs, *Sacred*, 88–115; Lindars, *Theology*, 84–101; Peterson, *Possessed*, 33–40; Pursiful, *Cultic Motif*; Radcliffe, "Christ."

[251]Neusner, *Idea*, 7–71; D. P. Wright and H. Hübner, *ABD* 6.729–45; Milgrom, *Leviticus*, 691–1009.

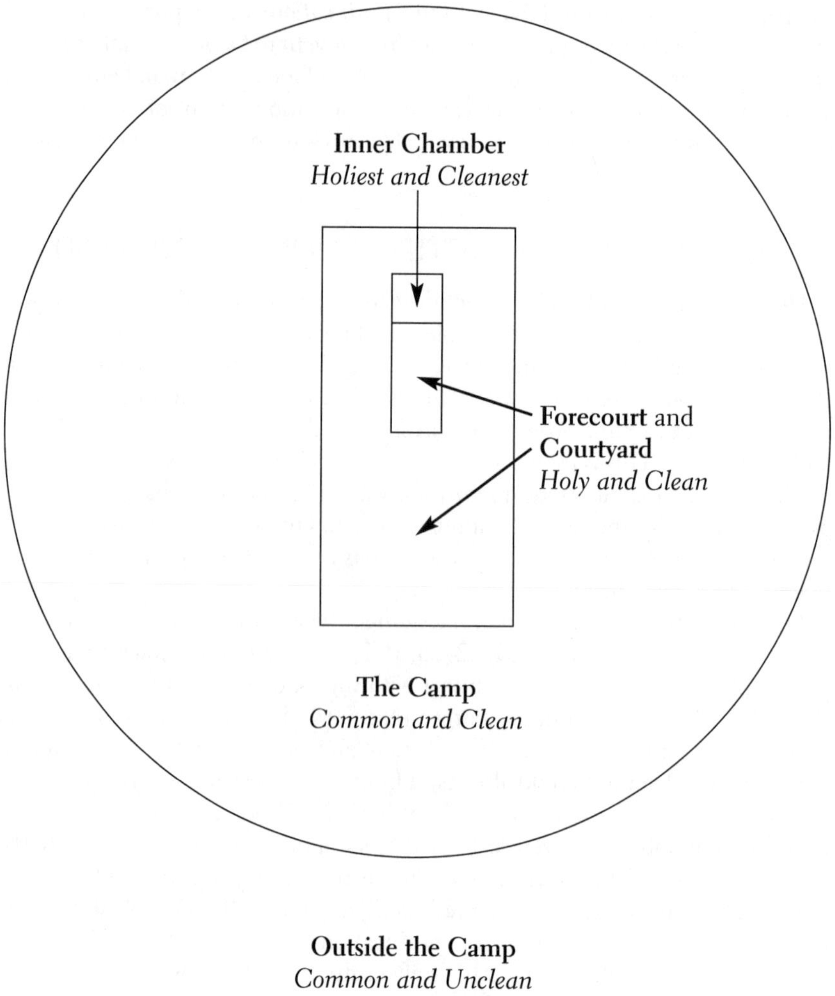

Figure 2. Clean and Unclean in the Camp of Israel.

the consciences of particular individuals living one or more generations after the event are purified when the message of Christ's self-sacrifice is announced and received through the agency of the Spirit (2:1–4; 6:4–5; 10:26). Cleansing the conscience does not mean that people become sinless, for sin remains a threat (3:12), but Christ's death is a source of cleansing that remains available to them.

(b) Sanctification. Sanctification means setting something apart *from* what is common (9:13) *for* God (13:12). In Levitical practice, a priest was set apart from the common people in order to minister in the sanctuary, which was holy. God is holy, and his holiness is a numinous power. Nothing common was to be brought into the presence of God because of the threat of his wrath breaking out (Num 3:4; 26:61). Since a sanctuary or holy place (*ta hagia*) was set apart for

God, one needed to be sanctified (*hagiazein*) or set apart before entering it. Everything holy had to be clean, but just because something was clean did not mean that it was holy (Milgrom, *Leviticus*, 732). Laypeople, for example, were normally considered clean unless they became unclean through skin disease, a discharge, or contact with something unclean. Purification would cleanse them, but would not make them holy.[252] Some forms of defilement were incurred through sins, including illicit sexual relations (Lev 18:20; Num 5:13–14), murder (Num 35:33; Isa 59:3), and idolatry (Jer 2:23; 7:30). To deal with such defilement meant dealing with sin.

Hebrews consistently links defilement with sin. Through persistent unbelief people make profane or common (*koinos*) the blood of Christ that brought them into a new covenant relationship with God through the agency of the Spirit (Heb 10:29). Immorality and contempt for God's blessings make people profane (*bebēlos*, 12:16). Sin has a contagious quality, affecting both the person who commits it and the community as a whole. When sin takes root, many become defiled (*mianesthai*, 12:15). If sin defiles, then people need to be sanctified in order to enter God's heavenly sanctuary (10:19–22). As the consummate sacrifice, Christ's blood (10:29) and death (10:10) sanctify as well as purify, setting people apart for a covenant relationship with God. Those who are sanctified by faith in what Christ has done have the hope of heavenly glory (2:10–11), for without holiness no one can see the Lord (12:14). Those whose consciences have been purified by Christ (see above) can now come before God boldly in prayer (4:14–16) together with other believers or "saints" (3:1; 6:10), and in the future they will share in God's holiness in heaven (12:10). Hebrews recognizes that people do not sanctify themselves, but are sanctified by Christ (2:11). Yet people can lose their holiness by rejecting what Christ has done and persistently embracing sin; to do so, however, brings divine wrath (10:29).

(c) Atonement. Atonement is the restoration of a relationship that has been violated by sin. It brings at-one-ment with God. The description of the atoning rites in Leviticus uses the verb *exilaskesthai* ("to atone," Lev 16:6, 11, 17, etc.) and specifies that this action took place "for the sins of the people" (Lev 16:24, 34; cf. 9:11, 15, 18). Hebrews says that Christ makes atonement (*hilaskesthai*, Heb 2:17) in a manner that is comparable to the biblical rituals for the Day of Atonement. The place of atonement (*hilastērion*, 9:5) is within the holy of holies, and God acts mercifully (*hileōs*) when he brings people into a covenant relationship in which he no longer remembers sins (8:10–12). The death of Christ is central in this process since forgiveness occurs through the effusion of blood (9:22). By stating that Christ performed his self-sacrifice in the capacity of high priest, the author suggests analogies with the Day of Atonement ritual, which was uniquely the high priest's responsibility (9:7).

Atonement has two aspects. First, expiation entails removal of the sin that caused the rift in the relationship between a person and God. The description of

---

[252]Since cleanness was a prerequisite for holiness, terms for cleansing and sanctification were sometimes used together (e.g., Lev 16:19).

the Day of Atonement ritual in Leviticus says that offerings of blood were made in order to deal with Israel's uncleanness as well as sins (Lev 16:16, 19). Moreover, after the high priest confessed the sins of the people over a goat, the goat was sent into the wilderness, so that it removed the iniquity of the people from the community (Lev 16:22). In Hebrews Christ's death is said to purify people (Heb 1:3; 9:13–14) and to set sin aside (Heb 9:26), which indicates that expiation is a primary level of meaning. The second dimension of atonement is propitiation, which has to do with averting the wrath of God. For example, when Moses learned that God was angry with Israel, he told Aaron to "make propitiation for them. For wrath has gone forth from the Lord."[253] Hebrews has a vivid sense of the threat posed by divine wrath (3:7–4:13). Since Christ's sacrifice delivers people from judgment (10:26–31; 12:29), propitiation constitutes a secondary level of meaning in Hebrews' view of atonement. Hebrews does not, however, construe Christ's death as "payment" for sin (NOTES and COMMENT on 9:12).

Atonement is an action that encompasses both purification and sanctification, because it deals with the sin that defiles people and bars them from God's presence. Where purification and sanctification prepare people to come before God, however, atonement goes further by bringing about a right relationship with God. Atonement is a singular act that was accomplished through Christ's death and exaltation and Hebrews makes clear that after Christ's exaltation no further sacrifices are needed (10:11–18). In the life of an individual, at-one-ment occurs when the message of Christ's self-offering evokes the faith that is a right relationship with God. The benefits of the atonement are appropriated on an ongoing basis by those who seek mercy from God through Christ (4:14–16; 7:25), and culminate in everlasting life in God's presence, the completion of his designs for people (see below). On atonement as victory see §8 COMMENT *c*.

2. COMPLETION OR PERFECTION[254]

The question around which Hebrews is structured concerns the future of humanity. The speech's proposition points to the apparent contradiction between the glory that God intends for people and the inglorious condition of God's people in the world. Then the author insists that in Jesus' exaltation to glory, people of faith can see the realization of God's designs (2:5–9). "Completion" is a fitting way to speak about the outcome of God's purposes, since words based on the root *tel-* have to do with reaching a goal. Hebrews identifies the *telos* with the outcome of God's work, when people of faith inherit what God has promised them (3:14; 6:11–12). The various words based on the root *tel-* encompass several di-

[253]Num 16:46 [17:11 LXX]; cf. Wis 18:20–25; Num 25:11, 13; *1 Clem.* 7:7; Herm. *Vis.* 1.2.1.

[254]See Attridge, *Epistle*, 83–87; Carlston, "Vocabulary"; deSilva, *Perseverance*, 194–204; Dey, *Intermediary*, 31–118; G. R. Hughes, *Hebrews*, 32–34; Lindars, *Theology*, 42–58; Peterson, *Hebrews*; Scholer, *Proleptic*, 185–200; Silva, "Perfection"; Walters, *Perfection*, 83–153.

mensions of God's work in the same way that several tones create a musical chord. The dominant tone concerns glory, but completion also has overtones of death and priesthood, as will be noted below.[255]

Words for completion are used both for Jesus and for other people. Jesus is made complete by his death and exaltation to heavenly glory, so that he now serves as high priest forever at God's right hand. Others are made complete when they go where Jesus has gone, following their forerunner into the presence of God. These two senses of completion frame the arguments in Hebrews. The arguments begin by declaring that God made Jesus complete in order to bring others to glory (2:10), and they culminate with the vision of the righteous being made complete in the heavenly Jerusalem (12:23). For God's purposes to be made complete, however, two barriers must be overcome: sin and death.

First, sin constitutes one barrier to the fulfillment of God's designs for people. Hebrews argues that the Law did not bring God's purposes to completion (7:11, 19). The Law established the Levitical priesthood and prescribed sacrifices that cleansed the flesh, but it did not bring the conscience to completion (9:9). Instead of removing sin from the conscience, its repetitive sacrifices actually brought sin to consciousness, reinforcing the sense of separation from God rather than bringing about a complete relationship with God (10:1–2). Hebrews will speak of completion as a present reality for those whose consciences have been cleansed by Christ's self-offering (10:14).

If purification removes sin from the conscience and if sanctification puts a person in a proper condition to approach God, then completion is the positive relationship that results from these actions. Although completion finally means everlasting life in God's presence, Hebrews can say that those who are sanctified by Christ have already been made complete in the sense of being brought into right relationship with God (10:14), and this completeness is exercised when they actually approach God in prayer (7:18–19). Such a relationship corresponds to God's new-covenant promise to write his laws on human hearts, so that people might be wholly obedient and that God might be their God and they might be his people (8:10–12).

Christ accomplishes this aspect of completion through his self-offering for sin (10:14). In order to make such an offering, God made Christ complete by appointing him to an everlasting high priesthood. When applied to Christ, the verb *make complete* is useful because it encompasses multiple dimensions of his death and exaltation. Christ's priestly service is one aspect of his being made complete and *teleoun* has some priestly overtones.[256] In 2:10–11 Christ is said

---

[255]The forms include the verb *teleioun* (2:10; 5:9; 7:19, 28; 9:9; 10:1, 14; 11:40; 12:23); the nouns *teleiotēs* (6:1), *teleiōsis* (7:11), and *teleiōtēs* (12:2); and the adjective *teleios* (5:14; 9:11).

[256]The LXX used *teleoun* in the technical expression for priestly ordination, "to fill the hands" (*teleoun tas cheiras*, Exod 29:9; Lev 4:5). In Lev 21:10 LXX, the verb alone has this sense, although it seems unlikely that the verb by itself would have been read as a technical term for ordination in Hebrews. Some argue that *teleoun* does not connote priesthood in Hebrews (Loader, *Sohn*, 40–47; Scholer, *Proleptic*, 188–94); however, the term encompasses multiple meanings, including priest-

to have been made complete through sufferings and to sanctify others, while in 2:17–18 his suffering is connected with his priestly service and atonement. Terms for being made complete and for being designated high priest are used in parallel in 5:5, 10, and Christ's appointment marks the completion of God's promise to raise up a priest after the type of Melchizedek (5:5–6). The Law appointed high priests who were subject to weakness, but God has now appointed to the priesthood a Son who has been made complete forever by his death and exaltation (7:28).

Exaltation to eternal glory is part of what it means for Christ to be made complete, but Christ's suffering is connected with his completion (2:10; 5:8–9) and priesthood (2:17–18) in a way that suggests that suffering helped prepare Christ for service (Peterson, *Hebrews*, 66–73). This idea does not suggest that Christ was previously incomplete, any more than comments about learning obedience (5:8) imply that he was formerly disobedient. Hebrews insists that Christ was without sin (4:15). The notion that Jesus was made complete through personal moral development also seems inaccurate, especially since the verbs are in the passive voice with God as the implied active subject.[257] Christ did not achieve completeness, but was made complete by God. A more viable approach is to consider the relationship of suffering to completion in vocational terms.[258] Christ is fitted to be a merciful high priest, first by suffering what human beings suffer and then by being exalted to everlasting life so that he can bring others to that same end.

A second aspect of completion has to do with overcoming death through exaltation to everlasting life in God's presence. Again, the idea has to do with the realization of God's promises. In a negative sense the heroes and heroines in Israel's past "did not receive what was promised," which is to say, they were not "made complete" (11:39–40). Instead, they persevered through disappointment, conflict, and death. In a positive sense all the righteous are "made complete" in God's celestial city, where the faithful receive everlasting life and join the company of angels in the presence of God (12:23). Completion is the consummation of humankind in an eternal relationship with God, in which people share Christ's glory (2:10), enter God's rest (4:9–10), see the Lord (12:14), and join in the festival gathering in the heavenly Jerusalem (12:22).[259]

Christ has been made complete through his exaltation in a manner that anticipates God bringing many other sons and daughters to glory (2:10). Referring to Christ being made complete is parallel to being brought to glory (2:10): it enables Christ to be a source of eternal salvation and to serve as a priest forever

---

hood as a subcategory (Vanhoye, *Old Testament*, 130–33; G. R. Hughes, *Hebrews*, 32–34; cf. Peterson, *Hebrews*, 97).

257On theories of personal development see Westcott, *Epistle*, 93–98; P. E. Hughes, *Commentary*, 187–88; Vanhoye, *Situation*, 321–23; Walters, *Perfection*, 109–29; and the critiques by Peterson, *Hebrews*, 96–103; Scholer, *Proleptic*, 187–88.

258See Peterson, *Hebrews*, 96–103; Attridge, *Epistle*, 87.

259See Peterson, *Hebrews*, 128–29. Scholer argues that completion is not synonymous with rest (*Proleptic*, 200).

(5:9–10), and it means being "exalted above the heavens" (7:26). The death that he endured did not preclude everlasting glory, but was part of the way in which he was brought to completion. Interestingly, the verb *teleoun* was sometimes used for death as well as for glorification.[260] Finally, Jesus can be called the completer of faith (12:2) because the faithful can see in his suffering and exaltation the realization of God's purposes for them.

People do not make themselves complete, but are brought to completion through the fulfillment of God's promises, and Christ's suffering is redemptive in a way that theirs is not. They can, however, persevere in faith as Christ did, trusting that God will not abandon them, but will bring them into complete and everlasting life as he promised.

3. FAITH AND THE CONFESSION[261]

The emphasis that Hebrews places on faith is evident in that Hebrews uses the noun "faith" (*pistis*) thirty-two times and the verb (*pisteuein*) twice more. The majority of these references occur in the account of Israel's ancestors, with Hab 2:4 ("my righteous one will live by faith") serving as the lens through which the OT is read. Comparison of faith in Hebrews and Paul's letters is provided in §28 COMMENT *b*. Detailed discussion of Hebrews' own view can be found in NOTES and COMMENTS on Heb 11, but some aspects of faith can be considered here.

Faith is called into being through the word of God, who spoke through the prophets and a Son (1:1–2). The principal form of the divine word is that of a promise, which points to a future fulfillment (pp. 110–112). The stories of Israel's ancestors in Heb 11 show that God's promises of life and blessing are often contradicted by experiences of death and disappointment. Accordingly, Hebrews says that the existence of faith, where there would otherwise be unbelief, demonstrates the power of God's unseen word. Like the world itself, faith is created and sustained by divine speech (11:1, 3; §30 COMMENT *a*). Faith, which has been called "a certainty of the uncertain, a seeing of the invisible," has two important dimensions of meaning[262]:

(a) Trust. Faith means hearing and receiving the gospel message (4:2–3), turning from sin to God (6:1), and drawing near to God with confidence (10:22). God's word is given in the form of a promise (see above), and one properly re-

---

260The verb *teleoun* was used for the deaths of the faithful (Philo, *Alleg. Interp.* 3.45) and especially for martyrs, "whom the faithful seal of death has made complete" (4 Macc 7:15). The term was used for the deaths by which Jesus (Luke 13:32) and Paul (Acts 20:24) would complete their ministries. The related verb *telein* is used for Jesus' last words "it is completed" in John 19:30.

261See Käsemann, *Wandering*, 37–48; Grässer, *Glaube*; Attridge, *Epistle*, 311–14; Braun, "Gewinnung"; H.-F. Weiss, *Brief*, 564–71; Hamm, "Faith"; Hurst, *Epistle*, 119–24; Dautzenberg, "Glaube"; Lane, "Standing"; Lindars, *Theology*, 108–18; Manzi, "La fede"; Rhee, "Christology"; Söding, "Zuversicht."

262Gyllenberg, "Christologie," 667. On faith's relationship to the word of promise see Käsemann, *Wandering*, 17–48.

sponds to a promise by trusting that the God who made it will keep it (10:23; 11:11) and reward those who seek him (11:6, 26). Noah built the ark trusting that it would bring salvation to his household (11:7). Abraham set out for the place that God had promised, not knowing where he was to go, but trusting that God would bring him to a homeland (11:8). He was also prepared to sacrifice Isaac because he trusted that God would raise the dead (11:19). The blessings pronounced by Abraham's descendants manifest trust that God will carry out their provisions (11:20–22).

(b) Faithfulness. Faith entails perseverance (6:12) and holding fast to the confession of the Christian community without wavering (10:23). Faithfulness is a way of life for the people of God. Faith manifests itself in steadfast assurance (NOTE on 11:1) in the face of threats, as Moses and his parents defied the king's wrath in order to do what was right (11:23, 27). The opposite of the assurance of faith is shrinking back in the face of difficulty (10:38–39) and falling away from the living God rather than holding firm until the end (3:12, 14). Thus Jesus, "the pioneer of faith," endured the cross and despised its shame (12:2). Former leaders of the Christian community provide examples of faithfulness to be imitated (13:7). To live by faith is to be faithful, as Jesus and Moses proved to be (2:17; 3:2, 5). Concepts related to faith include striving (4:11; 6:11) and boldness before God and other people (3:6; 4:16; 10:19, 35).

Faith has both individual and corporate dimensions. Many examples of faithfulness in Heb 11 involve individuals remaining steadfast in difficult circumstances. Yet Hebrews also indicates that faith does not exist in isolation but binds together the people of God (NOTE on 4:2). If faith creates community, the community engenders faith. The author of Hebrews recognizes that faith is not static and that unbelief remains a threat. Therefore, he urges members of the community to exhort one another in order to keep unbelief in check (3:12–13). The word of God accomplishes its work through the words that people address to each other in the service of faith (Käsemann, *Wandering*, 21–22).

The content of faith is summed up in the confession that believers make concerning Christ and his reign (3:1; 4:14; 10:23). By referring to "the confession," using the definite article, and urging listeners to hold fast to it, Hebrews indicates that the confession had content that could be identified and grasped.[263] Central to the confession was that Jesus is the Son of God. Hebrews explicitly links the confession with Jesus' divine sonship in 4:14. The opening lines show that divine sonship was understood to include Christ's appointment as heir of all things in a manner congruent with the Scriptures, together with his creative power, divinity, and glory (1:1–5). The author does not attempt to demonstrate these ideas, but assumes that listeners already affirm them as a part of their confession.[264]

---

[263]The confession would not have included all the teachings known to the listeners (cf. 6:1–2). Confessions briefly stated core beliefs (Dunn, *Unity*, 59; cf. Laub, *Bekenntnis*, 12). Grässer argues that faith in Hebrews does not have distinctly Christian content, but is portrayed as a virtue: constancy (*Glaube*, 63, 79). In response it should be noted that Hebrews uses the term "confession" for the content that faith affirms.

[264]See esp. Laub, *Bekenntnis*, 14–27. Confessing Jesus to be God's Son was common in Pauline

Questions about what it means to call Jesus God's Son seem to have contributed to the crisis addressed by Hebrews. The royal connotations of the title "Son of God" imply that believers have a "confession of hope" of inheriting a share in his kingdom (10:23; cf. 1:14; 6:12; 9:15; 12:28). The problem is that the implications of the confession are not borne out by the listeners' experience, which falls far short of the kingdom (10:32–34; 13:3, 13). Although some scholars have suggested that the title "high priest" was also part of the confession (3:1), this seems unlikely.[265] If the idea had been familiar, the author would not have had to demonstrate it in Heb 7–8.

Faith in its broadest sense is *theo*logical, since it has to do with God's existence (6:1; 11:6), with God's creative and life-giving power (11:3, 17–19), with God's faithfulness to his promises (11:8–9, 11, 13), and with what is pleasing to God (11:4, 6). Therefore, faith characterizes figures of the OT as well as the followers of Jesus. Within this basic theological purview, faith is also *Christ*ological, for Jesus is the "pioneer and completer of faith" (12:2). In one sense, Jesus exemplified faith by confessing his trust in God (2:13) and by faithfully enduring suffering and shame in the confidence that God would bring him to everlasting joy (12:2). Listeners are called to the same trust and faithfulness that Jesus exhibited, finding confidence by looking to Jesus, who was faithful (3:1–3; 12:2) and avoiding the unfaithfulness of the wilderness generation (3:12–19). In a deeper sense, however, Jesus makes faith possible, for his death and exaltation convey God's faithfulness to his promises, and God's faithfulness is the basis for human faith (10:23). Moreover, to say that Jesus is the completer of faith (12:2) recalls that he makes complete the human conscience by purifying it through his self-offering, establishing the new covenant by which God brings people to the end for which he created them (cf. Hamm, "Faith"; Attridge, *Epistle*, 314).[266]

F. Lord's Supper or Eucharist

Hebrews refers to Christian baptism (NOTES and COMMENT on 6:2; 10:22), but makes no clear mention of the Lord's Supper. Interpreters have debated whether he might have woven allusions to the meal into his speech, and three viewpoints have emerged. Of these, the most viable is the third, which finds no allusions to the Lord's Supper in Hebrews:

---

circles (1 Thess 1:9–10; 1 Cor 1:9; 2 Cor 1:19; cf. Acts 9:20). The way Paul emphasizes Jesus' divine sonship in Rom 1:3–4 suggests that it was important for Christians in Italy (cf. Heb 13:24). The "Son of God" title is also prominent in the gospels (e.g., Matt 14:33; 16:16; Mark 1:1; 15:39; John 1:34, 49; 11:27; 20:31; cf. 1 John 4:14). See Dunn, *Christology*, 12–64.

[265]On including "high priest" in the confession see Käsemann, *Wandering*, 167–74; Zimmermann, *Bekenntnis*, 47–52; Attridge, *Epistle*, 102–3. For critique see Laub, *Bekenntnis*, 27–41; H.-F. Weiss, *Brief*, 244. On the origins of Hebrews' priestly Christology see NOTE on 2:17.

[266]See Hamm, "Faith"; Attridge, *Epistle*, 314. For comparison of faith in Hebrews and Paul see NOTES and COMMENT on 10:38.

1. Some detect favorable allusions to the Eucharist.[267] Christians from ancient times through the Middle Ages often correlated passages from Hebrews with their own sacramental practices (see pp. 25–26, 31–32, 40). Recent discussion has focused on a number of key passages, which are summarized here and treated in more detail in NOTES on each text. Some observe that since 6:2 mentions Christian baptism, 6:4–5 might refer to the Eucharist when speaking about tasting the heavenly gift and tasting the good word of God. Others argue that calling Christ a minister *tōn hagiōn* (8:2) means that he is a minister, not "of the sanctuary," but "of holy things," including the holy bread used in earthly worship (9:2). Christ made atonement "through the greater and more perfect tent," which some identify with Christ's body, as well as through "his own blood" (9:11–12). Taken together, these are the elements in the Eucharist. The declaration that "this is the blood of the covenant" (9:20) resembles the words that Jesus spoke over the cup according to the gospels. When Hebrews invites the baptized to draw near to God through the flesh and blood of Christ (10:19–25), one might imagine that the context is a eucharistic celebration, where the faithful "eat" and receive "grace" from the "altar" (13:9–10).

2. Others propose that Hebrews takes a critical stance toward the Lord's Supper.[268] They read Hebrews' silence about the Lord's Supper more negatively, as a hesitation about the sacrament, either because the listeners evinced a misguided trust in ritual or because the meal obscured the once-for-all significance of Christ's death.[269] Hebrews depicts Christ's death as a sacrifice of atonement, and atoning sacrifices were not eaten by the priests or worshipers (13:11–12). Therefore, the author may be showing that "foods" pertain to the kind of cultic worship that Christ has made obsolete (9:10; 13:9–10). Hebrews does not suggest that the benefits of Jesus' death are mediated through a meal, but that one partakes of them directly through faith.

3. It is most plausible that Hebrews makes no allusion to the Lord's Supper.[270] Given the lack of clear reference to the meal, it seems best to interpret Hebrews without assuming that the author alludes to it in either a positive or a negative

---

[267]See esp. Swetnam, "Christology"; Andriessen, "L'eucharistie"; Vanhoye, *Old Testament*, 228–29; Feld, *Hebräerbrief*, 93–97; Thurén, *Lobopfer*, 83–89; Ruager, "Wir"; Lindars, *Theology*, 11, 138–42; Cahill, "Home"; idem, "Implications." Backhaus (*Der neue*, 228–32) does not find allusions, but presupposes common eucharistic practice.

[268]Moffatt, *Critical*, 233–34; Williamson, "Eucharist"; Dunnill, *Covenant*, 240–42; Theissen, *Untersuchungen*, 76–79; Schröger, "Gottesdienst"; Knoch, "Hält der Verfasser"; Laub, *Bekenntnis*, 270–72; cf. H.-F. Weiss, *Brief*, 726–29; Grässer, *Hebräer*, 3.379–83; Attridge, *Epistle*, 395–96.

[269]Arguments from silence are tenuous, but if the Lord's Supper had been integral to the author's argument, it is difficult to imagine him failing to connect the bread and wine offered by Melchizedek (Gen 14:18), who foreshadows Christ (Heb 7:1–3), with the bread and wine that Christ offered to his followers (pp. 25–26).

[270]See Williamson, "Eucharist"; Isaacs, "Hebrews 13:9–16," 277–80; cf. Daly, *Christian*, 262–63.

[271]Acts says that early Christians took bread, gave thanks, and broke it whether eating in the company of other believers (2:42, 46) or in ordinary meals among pagans (27:35). In Acts 20:7, breaking bread seems to be associated with worship, but in 20:11 it is an ordinary meal. Moreover, Acts never says that Christians shared the cup, as one might expect for the Lord's Supper. On the issues see Dunn, *Unity*, 161–68; H.-J. Klauck, *ABD* 4.362–72.

way. On the one hand, NOTES on specific verses show that the passages mentioned above can be read intelligibly without reference to the Eucharist and that attempts to relate them to the Eucharist are strained. On the other hand, silence about the Lord's Supper does not necessarily imply criticism about the practice, but more probably shows that it was not an essential part of every theological discussion. Paul discusses the Lord's Supper in 1 Corinthians, but is silent about it in his other letters. Luke's gospel includes Jesus' words over the bread and cup, but Acts is remarkably vague about how this tradition took shape in early Christian practice.[271] Given the lack of clear allusions to the Supper in Hebrews and the fluidity of early Christian practice, we do well not to presuppose the Lord's Supper as a background against which to interpret Hebrews.

V. TEXT OF HEBREWS

◆

Hebrews was preserved as a part of the Pauline corpus of writings. Although scholars today widely agree that Paul did not write Hebrews, the book was regularly included in MSS that included the letters ascribed to Paul. The translation in this commentary is based on the Greek text that appears in NA^{27}. The editors of NA^{27} do not follow any one ancient MS consistently, but select and compile what seem to be the best readings from many different MSS. The most important witnesses to the text of Hebrews, which are mentioned at key points in the NOTES, include the following:

Papyri. The earliest witnesses are papyri from the third and fourth centuries, many of which exist in only fragmentary form. The oldest and most complete is P^{46}, which dates from about A.D. 200 and places Hebrews in between Romans and 1 Corinthians. The Greek text in P^{46} is difficult to classify. It agrees more often with Vaticanus (B), a leading MS of the Alexandrian text type, and less often with Claromontanus (D), which is a non-Alexandrian text (Beare, "Text," 392–96; Zuntz, *Text*, 39–42). It also includes a number of distinctive readings that probably arose for a variety of reasons. Some result from misspellings (e.g., *basileis* instead of *basileias* in 11:33). There is probably an intentional alteration in 10:1, where P^{46} inserts *kai* ("and") to make "shadow" and "image" into synonyms rather than opposites (NOTE on 10:1). Referring to sin that is "easily distracting" (*euperispaston*) rather than "readily besets" (*euperistaton*) may be a transcriptional error or an attempt to clarify the text (NOTE on 12:1; see also NOTE on 9:2). Although P^{46} shows a rather free handling of the Greek text (Aland, *Text*, 69), it remains an invaluable witness when used in conjunction with other MSS.[272] Papyri preserving portions of Hebrews include:

[272]On P^{46} and Hebrews see Beare, "Text"; Zuntz, *Text*; H.-F. Weiss, *Brief*, 130–31.

P12 (3rd cent.)	1:1
P13 (3rd–4th cent.)	2:14–5:5; 10:8–22; 10:29–11:13; 11:28–12:17
P17 (4th cent.)	9:12–19
P46 (ca. A.D. 200)	1:1–9:16; 9:18–10:20, 22–30; 10:32–13:25
P79 (7th cent.)	10:10–12, 28–30
P89 (4th cent.)	6:7–9, 15–17

Uncials. Several uncial codices, which are usually identified as representatives of the Alexandrian type, are principal witnesses to the text of Hebrews. Codex Vaticanus (B), which includes Hebrews after 2 Thessalonians, breaks off after Heb 9:13, so that the MS lacks the final chapters of Hebrews as well as 1 and 2 Timothy, Titus, and Philemon. Codex Sinaiticus (א) preserves the complete text of Hebrews, although it includes numerous errors and corrections. Another important witness is Codex Alexandrinus (A), which also preserves the complete text. A Byzantine text type is reflected in Codex Mosquensis (K) and Codex Angelicus (L). Codex Claromontanus (D), which has sometimes been called a "western" text, includes a rather periphrastic Greek text along with a Latin translation. The most important uncials are:

א (01) (4th cent.)	complete
A (02) (5th cent.)	complete
B (03) (4th cent.)	1:1–9:13
C (04) (5th cent.)	2:5–7:25; 9:16–10:23; 12:16–13:25
D (06) (6th cent.)	complete
Ep or Dabsl (9th cent.)	copy of D (06)
H (015) (6th cent.)	1:3–8; 2:11–16; 3:13–18; 4:12–15; 10:1–7, 32–38; 12:10–15; 13:24–25
I (016) (5th cent.)	1:1–3, 9–12; 2:4–7, 12–14; 3:4–6, 14–16; 4:3–6, 12–14; 5:5–7; 6:1–3, 10–13; 6:20–7:2, 7–11, 18–20; 7:27–8:1, 7–9; 9:1–4, 9–11, 16–19, 25–27; 10:5–8, 16–18, 26–29, 35–38; 11:6–7, 12–15, 22–24, 31–33; 11:38–12:1, 7–9, 16–18, 25–27; 13:7–9, 16–18, 23–25
K (018) (9th cent.)	complete
L (020) (9th cent.)	1:1–13:9
P (025) (9th cent.)	complete
Ψ (044) (9th–10th cent.)	1:1–8:10; 9:20–13:25
048 (5th cent.)	11:32–38; 12:3–13:4
0121b (10th cent.)	1:1–4:3; 12:20–13:25
0122 (9th cent.)	5:8–6:10
0227 (5th cent.)	11:18–19, 29
0228 (4th cent.)	12:19–21, 23–25
0252 (5th cent.)	6:2–4, 6–7

Minuscules. Minuscule MSS of Hebrews, which date from the ninth century and later, often preserve important readings. The two most significant minuscules are 33 (9th cent.) and 1739 (10th cent.), which often lend weight to readings found in earlier MSS. Other noteworthy minuscules are 81 (A.D. 1044), 104 (A.D. 1087), 326 (10th cent.), 1881 (14th cent.), and 2464 (9th cent.).

Early Versions. By the late second century, the NT was being translated from Greek into other languages, including Latin, Syriac, and Coptic. Early versions are of some value in reconstructing the early text of Hebrews when they give clear evidence concerning the type of Greek text on which the translation was based. More importantly, however, the versions help to show how the text was understood in different contexts, since translators interpreted or paraphrased the text when rendering it into other languages (Aland, *Text*, 185–86). Interesting points at which the versions contribute in the history of the text and its interpretation include the debate over passages concerning Jesus' suffering (NOTES on 2:9; 5:7), and the Peshitta's equation of enlightenment with baptism (6:4; 10:32) and its treatment of Melchizedek (NOTE on 7:3).[273]

Significant textual problems arise at a number of points in Hebrews. Among the most interesting are those discussed in the NOTES on 1:3; 2:9; 4:2; 8:8; 9:2–3, 11; 10:1; 11:11, 37; 12:1, 3. In addition, some variants have to do with Hebrews' use of the OT. Although Hebrews commonly uses an OT text similar to the LXX, the relationship is complex, since there were various forms of the Greek OT in circulation at the time Hebrews was written, and later MSS of the LXX sometimes appear to have been corrected to conform to Hebrews (Cadwallader, "Correction"). See, for example, the NOTES on 2:7.

---

[273]On Heb 2:9 and 5:7 in the Latin tradition see von Harnack, "Zwei alte" and more generally "Studien." For the Syriac tradition see Baarda, "Syriac."

BIBLIOGRAPHY

Bibliography

◆

The bibliography includes selected works from various periods with preference given to recent contributions. In the NOTES and COMMENT commentaries are cited only by the author's last name. Other works include a short title. A footnote at the beginning of each COMMENT section lists bibliography pertinent to that section. For additional titles, especially of older works, see Feld, *Hebräerbrief*, and the commentaries by Ellingworth and Lane.

A.D. 100–600

Ephraem the Syrian (d. 373). *Epistola ad Hebraeos.* Pages 200–42 in *Commentarii in Epistolas D. Pauli nun primum ex armenio in latinum sermonem a Patribus Mechitaristis translati.* Venedig, 1893.

John Chrysostom (d. 407). *Homilies on Hebrews.* NPNF1 14.363–522 (PG 63.9–238).

Jerome (d. 420). *Saint Jerome's Hebrew Questions on Genesis.* Translated by C. T. R. Hayward. Oxford: Clarendon, 1995.

Pelagius (d. ca. 420). *Pelagius's Commentary on the Epistle to the Romans.* Edited by T. de Bruyne. Oxford: Clarendon, 1993.

Theodoret (d. 460). *Interpretatio Epistolae ad Hebraeos.* PG 82.673–786.

Severian of Gabala (ca. 400). Excerpts on pages 345–51 in K. Staab, *Pauluskommentare aus der griechischen Kirche.* Munich: Aschendorff, 1933.

Theodore of Mopsuestia (d. 428). Excerpts on pages 200–212 in K. Staab, *Pauluskommentare aus der griechischen Kirche.* Munich: Aschendorff, 1933. Also in PG 66.951–68.

______. *Les homélies catéchétiques de Théodore de Mopsueste.* Edited by R. Tonneau. Vatican City: Vatican Library, 1949.

Cyril of Alexandria (d. 444). *Explanatio in Epistolam ad Hebraeos.* PG 74.953–1004.

Gennadius of Constantinople (d. 471). Excerpts on pages 420–22 in K. Staab, *Pauluskommentare aus der griechischen Kirche.* Munich: Aschendorff, 1933.

Ps.-Oecumenius (6th cent.). *Pauli Apostoli ad Hebraeos Epistola.* PG 119.271–452. Greek fragments ascribed to him appear on pages 462–69 in K. Staab, *Pauluskommentare aus der griechischen Kirche.* Munich: Aschendorff, 1933.

A.D. 600–1500

Alcuin (d. 804). *Expositio in epistolam Pauli apostoli ad Hebraeos.* PL 100.1031–84.

Claudius of Turin (d. after 827) = Ps.-Atto. *Epistola ad Hebraeos.* PL 134.725–834.

Florus (d. ca. 860). *In epistolam ad Hebraeos.* PL 119.411–20.

Rabanus Maurus (d. 856). *Expositio in epistolam ad Hebraeos.* PL 112.711–834.

Sedulius Scotus (ca. 848–58). *In epistolas ad Corinthios usque ad Hebraeos.* Pages 718–77 in *Sedulii Scotti collectaneum in apostolum,* edited by H. J. Frede and H. Stanjek. Freiburg: Herder, 1997.

Haimo of Auxerre (d. ca. 875) = Ps.-Haimo of Halberstadt. *In epistolam ad Hebraeos.* PL 117.819–938.

Isho'dad of Merv (9th cent.). *Hebrews* in *The Commentaries of Ischo'dad of Merv Bishop of Ḥadatha.* Vol. 5, part 1 (Syriac), part 2 (English). Cambridge: At the University, 1916.

Photius of Constantinople (d. ca. 895). Excerpts on pages 637–52 in K. Staab, *Pauluskommentare aus der griechischen Kirche.* Munich: Aschendorff, 1933.

Theophylact (d. after 1125). *Epistolae divi Pauli ad Hebraeos expositio.* PG 125.185–404.

Lanfranc (d. 1089). *Epistola B. Pauli apostoli ad Hebraeos.* PL 150.375–406.

Ps.-Bruno (11th cent.). *Epistola ad Hebraeos.* PL 153.489–566.

Anselm of Laon (d. 1117). Vol. 4. *Ad Hebreos.* In *Biblia Latina cum glossa ordinaria.* Edited by K. Froehlich and M. T. Gibson. Brepols: Turnhout, 1992.

Herveus (d. ca. 1150). *In epistolam ad Hebraeos.* PL 181.1519–1692.

Ps.-Abelard (12th cent.?). *Commentarius cantabrigiensis in epistolas Pauli e schola Petri Abaelardi in epistolam ad Hebraeos.* Edited by A. Landgraf. Notre Dame, Ind.: University of Notre Dame, 1945.

Peter Lombard (d. 1160). *In epistola ad Hebraeos.* PL 192.399–519.

Ps.-Hugh of St. Victor (12th cent.). *Quaestiones in epistolas Pauli—In epistola ad Hebraeos.* PL 175.607–34.

Robert of Melun (d. 1167). *Questiones [theologice] de epistolis Pauli.* Edited by R. M. Martin. Vol. 2. Louvain: Spiclegium Sacrum Lovaniense, 1938.

Thomas Aquinas (d. 1274). *Super epistolam ad Hebraeos lectura.* Pages 335–506 in *Super epistolas S. Pauli lectura.* Edited by R. Cai. Vol. 2. Rome: Marietti, 1953.

Nicolaus of Lyra (d. 1349). *Ad Hebreos.* In *Postilla super totam bibliam.* Vol. 4. Frankfurt am Main: Minerva, 1971.

Wyclif, John (d. 1384). *Wyclif's Latin Works.* 23 vols. London: Wyclif Society, 1883–1914.

Jan Hus (d. 1415). *De Ecclesia: The Church by John Huss.* Translated by D. S. Schaff. New York: Scribner's, 1915.

A.D. 1500 TO 1750

Valla, Lorenzo (d. 1457). *Ad Hebreos.* Pages 241–50 in *Collatio Novi Testamenti,* edited by A. Perosa. Firenze: Sansoni, 1970.

______. *In Epistolam Pauli ad Hebraeos Adnotationes.* Pages 885–88 in *Opera Omnia.* Vol. 1. Torino: Bottega d'Erasmo, 1962.

Steinbach, Wendelin (d. 1519). *Commentarii in Epistolam ad Hebraeos.* In *Wendelini Steinbach opera exegetica quae supersunt omnia,* edited by H. Feld. Vols. 2–3. Wiesbaden: Steiner, 1984.

Zwingli, Ulrich (d. 1531). *The Defense of the Reformed Faith.* Vol. 1 of *Selected Writings of Huldrych Zwingli.* Allison Park, Pa.: Pickwick, 1984.

Cajetan, Thomas de Vio (d. 1534). *Epistolae Pauli, et aliorum apostolorum ad Graecam veritatem castigatae.* Paris: de Marnef Fratres, 1546.

d'Etaples, Jacques Lefèvre (Jacobus Faber Stapulensis; d. 1536). *S. Pauli epistolae XIV ex Vulgata adiecta intelligentia ex graeco, cum commentariis.* Paris, 1512. Reprint. Stuttgart: Frommann and Bad Cannstatt: Holzboog, 1978.

Erasmus, Desiderius (d. 1536). *Adnotationes in epistolam Pauli apostoli ad Hebraeos.* Pages 983–1024 in *Desiderii Erasmi Roterdami Opera Omnia,* edited by J. Leclerc. Vol. 6. Leiden, 1703–6. Reprint. London: Gregg, 1962.

______. *Paraphrase on Hebrews.* Pages 211–60 in *Collected Works of Erasmus,* edited by J. J. Bateman. Vol. 44. Toronto: University of Toronto, 1993.

Tyndale, William (d. 1536). "The Prologue to the Epistle of St. Paul to the Hebrews." Pages 345–47 in *Tyndale's New Testament.* New Haven: Yale University Press, 1989.

Luther, Martin (d. 1546). *Die Vorlesung über den Hebräerbrief*. Edited by J. Ficker. WA 57/3. Weimar: Böhlaus, 1939. Translated as *Lectures on Hebrews* by W. A. Hansen. *LuthW* 29. St. Louis: Concordia, 1968.

______. *Sermons of Martin Luther*. Translated by J. N. Lenker. Grand Rapids: Baker, 1983.

Calvin, John (d. 1564). *The Epistle of Paul the Apostle to the Hebrews and the First and Second Epistles of St Peter*. Translated by W. B. Johnston. Calvin's New Testament Commentaries 12. Grand Rapids: Eerdmans, 1963.

______. *Institutes of the Christian Religion*. LCC 20–21. Philadelphia: Westminster, 1960.

Chemnitz, Martin (d. 1586). *An Examination of the Council of Trent*. Translated by F. Kramer. St. Louis: Concordia, 1971.

Perkins, William (d. 1602). *A Commentary on Hebrews 11 (1609 Edition)*. Edited by J. Augustine. New York: Pilgrim, 1991.

Socinus, Fausto Paolo (d. 1604) et al. *Racovian Catechism*. Translated by T. Rees. Lexington, Ky.: American Theological Library Association, 1962.

Arndt, Johann (d. 1621). *True Christianity*. Philadelphia: General Council, 1906.

Lapide, Cornelius à (d. 1637). *Commentarius in epistolam ad Hebraeos*. Pages 870–1022 in *Commentarii in Scripturam Sacram*. Vol. 9. Lugundi: Mercatoria and Paris: Turnonensi, 1870.

Grotius, Hugo (d. 1645). *Ad Hebraeos*. Pages 787–896 in *Annotations in Acta Apostolorum et in epistolas catholicas*. Paris: Pele, 1646.

______. *The Truth of the Christian Religion*. Oxford: Baxter, 1815. Latin original 1622.

______. *A Defence of the Catholick Faith*. London: Parkhurst, 1692.

Gouge, William (d. 1653). *A Commentary on the Whole Epistle to the Hebrews*. Edinburgh: Nichols, 1866.

Schlichting, Jonasz (d. 1661). *Commentaria in epistolam ad Hebraeos*. Racov, 1634.

Pool, Matthew (d. 1679). *Annotations upon the Holy Bible*. London: Nisbet, 1853.

Owen, John (d. 1683). *An Exposition of the Epistle to the Hebrews with Preliminary Exercitations*. Carlisle, Pa.: Banner of Truth, 1991.

Calov, Abraham (d. 1686). *Annotata in epistolam ad Hebraeos*. Pages 1094–1388 in *Biblia Novi Testamenti Illustrata*. Vol 2. Frankfurt: Wustii, 1676.

Henry, Matthew (d. 1714). *A Commentary on the Holy Bible with Practical Remarks and Observations*. Chicago: Blessing, n.d.

Bengel, Johann Albrecht (d. 1752). *On the Epistle to the Hebrews*. Pages 333–502 in *Gnomon of the New Testament*. Vol. 4. Edinburgh: Clark, 1858. Latin original 1742.

Edwards, Jonathan (d. 1758). *Ethical Writings*. In *The Collected Works of Jonathan Edwards*. Edited by P. Ramsey. Vol 8. New Haven: Yale University Press, 1989.

______. "Notes on the Bible." *The Works of Jonathan Edwards*. Vol. 1. London: Bohn, 1865.

Carpzov, Johann Benedikt (d. 1803). *Sacrae exercitationes S. Pauli Epistolam ad Hebraeos ex Philone Alexandrino*. Helmstedt: Veygandiana, 1750.

SELECTED COMMENTARIES FROM 1750 TO THE PRESENT

Attridge, H. W. *The Epistle to the Hebrews*. Hermeneia. Philadelphia: Fortress, 1989.

Bénétreau, S. *L'Épître aux Hébreux*. Vaux-sur-Seine: Edifac, 1989–90.

Bisping, A. *Erklärung des Briefes an die Hebräer*. 2nd ed. Münster: Aschendorff, 1864.

Bleek, F. *Der Brief an die Hebräer.* 3 vols. Berlin: Dümmler, 1828–40.
Böhme, C. F. *Epistola ad Hebraeos latine vertit atque comment.* Leipzig: Barthii, 1825.
Braun, H. *An die Hebräer.* HNT 14. Tübingen: Mohr/Siebeck, 1984.
Brown, J. *An Exposition of the Epistle of the Apostle Paul to the Hebrews.* 2 vols. London: Oliphants, 1862.
Bruce, A. B. *The Epistle to the Hebrews: The First Apology for Christianity.* Edinburgh: Clark, 1899.
Bruce, F. F. *Epistle to the Hebrews.* Rev. ed. Grand Rapids: Eerdmans, 1990.
Buchanan, G. W. *To the Hebrews.* AB 36. Garden City, N.Y.: Doubleday, 1972.
Casalini, N. *Agli Ebrei: Discorso di esortazione. SBFLA* 34. Jerusalem: Franciscan, 1992.
Cockerill, G. L. *Hebrews.* Indianapolis: Wesleyan, 1999.
Craddock, F. B. "The Letter to the Hebrews." Pages 1–173 in *The New Interpreter's Bible* 12. Nashville: Abingdon, 1998.
D'Angelo, M. R. "Hebrews." Pages 455–59 in *The Women's Bible Commentary.* Edited by C. A. Newsom and S. H. Ringe. Louisville: Westminster/John Knox, 1998.
Delitzsch, F. J. *Commentary on the Epistle to the Hebrews.* 2 vols. Edinburgh: Clark, 1870.
deSilva, D. A. *Perseverance in Gratitude: A Socio-Rhetorical Commentary on the Epistle "to the Hebrews."* Grand Rapids: Eerdmans, 2000.
Ebrard, J. H. "The Epistle to the Hebrews." Pages 273–624 in *Biblical Commentary on the New Testament* 6. New York: Sheldon, 1866.
Ellingworth, P. *The Epistle to the Hebrews.* NIGTC. Grand Rapids: Eerdmans and Carlisle: Paternoster, 1993.
Grässer, E. *An die Hebräer.* 3 vols. EKK 17. Zürich: Benzinger and Neukirchen-Vluyn: Neukirchener, 1990–97.
Guthrie, D. *The Letter to the Hebrews.* TNTC 16. Leicester: InterVarsity and Grand Rapids: Eerdmans, 1983.
Guthrie, G. H. *Hebrews.* NIV Application Commentary. Grand Rapids: Zondervan, 1998.
Hagner, D. A. *Hebrews.* NIBC. Peabody, Mass.: Hendrickson, 1990.
Hegermann. H. *Der Brief an die Hebräer.* THKNT 16. Berlin: Evangelische, 1988.
Héring, J. *The Epistle to the Hebrews.* London: Epworth, 1970.
Hofmann, J. C. K. von. *Die heilige Schrift neuen Testaments.* Nördlingen: Beck, 1873.
Hughes, P. E. *A Commentary on the Epistle to the Hebrews.* Grand Rapids: Eerdmans, 1977.
Jewett, R. *Letter to Pilgrims: A Commentary on the Epistle to the Hebrews.* New York: Pilgrim, 1981.
Keil, C. F. *Commentar über den Brief an die Hebräer.* Leipzig: Dörffling, 1885.
Kistemaker, S. J. *Exposition of the Epistle to the Hebrews.* Grand Rapids: Baker, 1984.
Kittredge, C. B. "Hebrews." Pages 428–52 in *Searching the Scriptures: A Feminist Commentary* vol. 2, edited by E. Schüssler Fiorenza. New York: Crossroad, 1994.
Lane, W. L. *Hebrews.* 2 vols. WBC. Dallas: Word, 1991.
Lindsay, W. *Lectures on the Epistle to the Hebrews.* Edinburgh: Oliphants, 1867.
Long, T. G. *Hebrews.* Interpretation. Louisville: John Knox, 1997.
Lünemann, G. *Critical and Exegetical Handbook to the Epistle to the Hebrews.* New York: Funk & Wagnalls, 1885.
März, C.-P. *Hebräerbrief.* Die neue Echter Bibel. Würzburg: Echter, 1989.
Michel, O. *Der Brief an die Hebräer.* 7th ed.; KEK 13. Göttingen: Vandenhoeck & Ruprecht, 1975.

Moffatt, J. *A Critical and Exegetical Commentary on the Epistle to the Hebrews*. ICC. Edinburgh: Clark, 1924.
Moll, C. B. "Epistle to the Hebrews." Lange's Commentary 23. New York: Scribners, 1915.
Montefiore, H. *A Commentary on the Epistle to the Hebrews*. BNTC. London: Black, 1964.
Morris, L. *Hebrews*. Bible Study Commentary. Grand Rapids: Zondervan, 1983.
Pfitzner, V. C. *Hebrews*. ANTC. Nashville: Abingdon, 1997.
Rendall, F. *The Epistle to the Hebrews*. New York: Macmillan, 1888.
Riggenbach, E. *Der Brief an die Hebräer*. 2nd–3rd ed. Leipzig: Deichert, 1922.
Schulz, D. *Der Brief an die Hebräer*. Breslau: Holäufer, 1818.
Scott, E. F. *The Epistle to the Hebrews*. Edinburgh: Clark, 1922.
Seisenberger, M. *Erklärung des Briefes an die Hebräer*. Regensburg: Manz, 1909.
Seyffarth, T. A. *De epistolae quae dicitur ad Hebraeos indole maxime peculiari*. Leipzig: Reclam, 1821.
Smith, R. H. *Hebrews*. ACNT. Minneapolis: Augsburg, 1984.
Soden, H. von, "Der Brief an die Hebräer." Pages 1–108 in *Handkommentar zum Neuen Testament* 3. 2nd ed. Freiburg: Mohr, 1892.
Spicq, C. *L'Épître aux Hébreux*. 2 vols. *EBib*. Paris: Gabalda, 1952–53.
Stedman, R. C. *Hebrews*. Downers Grove, Ill.: InterVarsity, 1992.
Storr, G. C. *Pauli Brief an die Hebräer*. 2nd ed. Tübingen: Heerbrandt, 1809.
Strathmann, H. *Der Brief an die Hebräer*. NTD 9. Göttingen: Vandenhoeck & Ruprecht, 1963.
Strobel, A. *Der Brief an die Hebräer*. 4th ed. NTD 9/2. Göttingen: Vandenhoeck & Ruprecht, 1991.
Stuart, M. *A Commentary on the Epistle to the Hebrews*. London: Tegg, 1864.
Tholuck, A. *Kommentar zum Briefe an die Hebräer*. 3rd ed. Hamburg: Berthes, 1868.
Weiss, B. *Der Brief an die Hebräer*. KEK 13. Göttingen: Vandenhoeck & Ruprecht, 1888.
Weiss, H.-F. *Der Brief an die Hebräer*. KEK 13. Göttingen: Vandenhoeck & Ruprecht, 1991.
Westcott, B. F. *The Epistle to the Hebrews*. London: Macmillan, 1892. Reprinted, Grand Rapids: Eerdmans, 1980.
Wilson, R. M. *Hebrews*. NCBC. Grand Rapids: Eerdmans and Basingstoke: Marshall Morgan & Scott, 1987.
Windisch, H. *Der Hebräerbrief*. 2nd ed. HNT 14. Tübingen: Mohr/Siebeck, 1931.

OTHER BOOKS AND ARTICLES

Achtemeier, P. *1 Peter*. Hermeneia. Minneapolis: Fortress, 1996.
Aland, K. and B. *The Text of the New Testament: An Introduction to the Critical Editions and to the Practice of Modern Textual Criticism*. 2nd ed. Grand Rapids: Eerdmans, 1989.
Allen, D. L. "The Lukan Authorship of Hebrews: A Proposal." *Journal of Translation and Textlinguistics* 8 (1996): 1–22.
Allen, L. C. "Psalm 45:7–8 (6–7) in Old and New Testament Settings." Pages 220–42 in *Christ the Lord: Studies in Christology Presented to Donald Guthrie*. Edited by H. H. Rowdon, Downers Grove, Ill.: InterVarsity, 1982.
Anderson, C. P. "Hebrews among the Letters of Paul." *SR* 5 (1975–76): 258–66.
______. "Who Are the Heirs of the New Age in the Epistle to the Hebrews?" Pages

255–77 in *Apocalyptic and the New Testament: Essays in Honor of J. Louis Martyn*. Edited by J. Marcus and M. L. Soards. JSNTSup 24. Sheffield: JSOT, 1989.

Anderson, H. "The Jewish Antecedents of the Christology in Hebrews." Pages 512–35 in *The Messiah: Developments in Judaism and Christianity*. Edited by J. H. Charlesworth. Minneapolis: Fortress, 1992.

Anderson, R. D. *Ancient Rhetorical Theory and Paul*. Kampen: Kok Pharos, 1996.

Andriessen, P. "Angoisse de la mort dans l'épître aux Hébreux." *NRTh* 96 (1974): 282–92.

______. "Das grössere und vollkommenere Zelt (Hebr. 9,11)." *BZ* 15 (1971): 76–92.

______. "La communauté des 'Hébreux' était-elle tombée dans le relâchement?" *NRTh* 96 (1974): 1054–66.

______. "La teneur judéo-chrétienne de Hébr. I,6 et II,14b–III,2." *NovT* 18 (1976): 293–313.

______. "L'eucharistie dans l'épître aux Hébreux," *NRTh* 94 (1972): 269–77.

______. "Renonçant à la joie qui lui revenait . . ." *NRTh* 97 (1975): 424–38.

Andriessen, P., and A. Lenglet, "Quelques passages difficiles de l'épître aux Hébreux (5,7; 7,11; 10,20; 12,2)." *Bib* 51 (1970): 207–20.

Arowele, P. J. "The Pilgrim People of God: An African's Reflections on the Motif of Sojourn in the Epistle to the Hebrews." *Asia Journal of Theology* 4 (1990): 438–55.

Attridge, H. W. " 'Heard Because of His Reverence' (Heb. 5.7)." *JBL* 98 (1979): 90–93.

______. " 'Let Us Strive to Enter That Rest': The Logic of Hebrews 4:1–11." *HTR* 73 (1980): 279–88.

______. "New Covenant Christology in an Early Christian Homily." *QR*. 8 (1988): 89–108.

______. "Paraenesis in a Homily (λόγος παρακήσεως): The Possible Location of, and Socialization in, the 'Epistle to the Hebrews,' " *Semeia* 50 (1990): 211–26.

______. "The Uses of Antithesis in Hebrews 8–10." Pages 1–9 in *Christians among Jews and Gentiles: Essays in Honor of Krister Stendahl on His Sixty-fifth Birthday*. Edited by G. W. E. Nickelsburg and G. W. MacRae. Philadelphia: Fortress, 1986.

Auffret, P. "Essai sur la structure littéraire et l'interprétation d'Hébreux 3,1–6." *NTS* 26 (1979–80): 380–96.

______. "Note sur la structure littéraire d'Hb ii.1–4." *NTS* 25 (1978–79): 166–79.

Aulén, G. *Christus Victor: An Historical Study of the Three Main Types of the Idea of Atonement*. London: SPCK, 1970.

Aune, D. E. "Heracles and Christ: Heracles Imagery in the Christology of Early Christianity." Pages 3–19 in *Greeks, Romans, and Christians: Essays in Honor of Abraham J. Malherbe*. Edited by D. L. Balch, E. Ferguson, and W. A. Meeks. Minneapolis: Fortress, 1990.

______. *The New Testament in Its Literary Environment*. Philadelphia: Westminster, 1987.

Baarda, T. "The Syriac Versions of the New Testament." On pages 97–112 in *The Text of the New Testament in Contemporary Research: Essays on the Status Quaestionis*. Edited by B. D. Ehrman and M. W. Holmes. Grand Rapids: Eerdmans, 1995.

Bachmann, M. " '. . . gesprochen durch den Herrn' (Hebr 2,3). Erwägungen zum Reden Gottes und Jesu im Hebräerbrief." *Bib* 71 (1990): 365–94.

______. "Hohepriesterliches Leiden. Beobachtungen zu Hebr 5.1–10." ZNW 78 (1987): 244–66.

Backhaus, K. "Der Hebräerbrief und die Paulus-Schule." *BZ* 37 (1993): 183–208.

______. *Der neue Bund und das Werden der Kirche: Die Diathekedeutung des Hebräerbriefs im Rahmen der frühchristlichen Theologiegeschichte*. NTAbh 29. Münster: Aschendorff, 1996.

______. "Per Christum in Deum. Zur theozentrischen Funktion der Christologie im Hebräerbrief." On pages 258–84 in *Der lebendige Gott: Studien zur Theologie des Neuen Testaments. Festschrift für Wilhelm Thüsing zum 75. Geburtstag*. Edited by T. Söding. NTAbh 31. Münster: Aschendorff, 1996.

Bailey, J. L. "Genre Analysis." Pages 197–221 in *Hearing the New Testament: Strategies for Interpretation*. Edited by J. B. Green. Grand Rapids: Eerdmans, 1995.

Bailey, L. R. *Noah: The Person and the Story in History and Tradition*. Columbia, S.C.: University of South Carolina, 1989.

Balsdon, J. P. V. D. *Romans and Aliens*. Chapel Hill, N.C.: University of North Carolina, 1979.

Banks, R. *Paul's Idea of Community*. Rev. ed. Peabody, Mass.: Hendrickson, 1994.

Barclay, J. M. G. *Jews in the Mediterranean Diaspora*. Edinburgh: Clark, 1996.

Barr, G. K. "The Structure of Hebrews and of 1st and 2nd Peter." *IBS* 19 (1997): 17–31.

Barrett, C. K. " 'The Eschatology of the Epistle to the Hebrews." Pages 363–93 in *The Background of the New Testament and Its Eschatology*. Edited by W. D. Davies and D. Daube. Cambridge: Cambridge University, 1956.

Barth, K. *Church Dogmatics*. Edinburgh: Clark and New York: Scribners, 1936–69.

Barth, M. "The Old Testament in Hebrews: An Essay in Biblical Hermeneutics." Pages 53–78 in *Current Issues in New Testament Interpretation*. Edited by W. Klassen and G. Snyder. New York: Harper, 1962.

Bateman, H. W. *Early Jewish Hermeneutics and Hebrews 1:5–13*. New York: Lang, 1997.

______. "Two First-Century Messianic Uses of the OT: Heb 1:5–13 and 4Qflor 1.1–19." *JETS* 38 (1995): 11–27.

Battifol, P. "De l'attribution de l'Épître aux Hébreux a saint Barnabé." *RB* 8 (1899): 278–83.

Baur, F. C. *The Church History of the First Three Centuries*. 2 vols. 3rd ed. London: Williams and Norgate, 1878.

Beare, F. W. "The Text of the Epistle to the Hebrews in P[46]." *JBL* 63 (1944): 379–96.

Bénétreau, S. "La foi d'Abel: Hébreux 11/4." *ETR* 54 (1979): 623–30.

______. "La mort du Christ selon l'épître aux Hébreux." *Hokk* 39 (1988): 25–47.

Benko, S. "Pagan Criticism of Christianity during the First Two Centuries." *ANRW* II.23.2 (1980): 1055–1118.

Berényi, G. "La portée de διὰ τοῦτο en Hé 9,15." *Bib* 69 (1988): 108–12.

Berger, J. "Der Brief an die Hebräer, eine Homilie." *Göttingen theologisher Bibliotek* 3 (1797): 449–59.

Berger, K. "Hellenistischen Gattungen im Neuen Testament." *ANRW* II.25.2 (1984): 1031–1432.

Betz, O. "Firmness in Faith: Hebrews 11:1 and Isaiah 28:16." Pages 92–113 in *Scripture: Meaning and Method*. Edited by B. P. Thompson. Hull: Hull University, 1987.

Beyschlag, W. *New Testament Theology*. Edinburgh: Clark, 1896.

Bickerman, E. J. "En marge de l'écriture." *RB* 88 (1981): 19–41.

Black, C. C., II. "The Rhetorical Form of the Hellenistic Jewish and Early Christian Sermon: A Response to Lawrence Wills." *HTR* 81 (1988): 1–18.

Black, D. A. "Hebrews 1:1–4. A Study in Discourse Analysis." *WTJ* 49 (1987): 175–94.

______. "A Note on the Structure of Hebrews 12,1–2." *Bib* 68 (1987): 543–51.

______. "On the Pauline Authorship of Hebrews." *Faith and Mission* 16 (1999): 32–51, 78–86.

______. "The Problem of the Literary Structure of Hebrews: An Evaluation and a Proposal." *GTJ* 7 (1986): 163–77.

Black, M. *The Book of Enoch or 1 Enoch*. Leiden: Brill, 1985.

Bonnard, P.-E. "La traduction de Hébreux 12,2: 'C'est en vue de la joie que Jésus endura la croix,' " *NRTh* 97 (1975): 415–23.

Bonnardière, A. M. la, "L'épître aux Hébreux dans l'œuvre de saint Augustin." *REAug* 3 (1957): 137–62.

Bornkamm, G. "Das Bekenntnis im Hebräerbrief." *TBl* 21 (1942): 56–66.

______. "Sohnschaft und Leiden: Hebräer 12,5–11." Pages 214–24 in *Geschichte und Glaube* 2. *Gesammelte Aufsätze* 4. BET 53. Munich: Chr. Kaiser, 1971.

Bowker, J. W. *The Targums and Rabbinic Literature.* London: Cambridge University, 1969.

Brandenburger, E. "Text und Vorlagen von Hebr V.7–10. Ein Beitrag zur Christologie des Hebräerbriefes." *NovT* 11 (1969): 190–224.

Branick, V. P. *The House Church in the Writings of Paul.* Wilmington, Del.: Glazier, 1989.

Braun, H. "Das himmlische Vaterland bei Philo und im Hebräerbrief." Pages 319–27 in *Verborum Veritas: Festschrift fur Gustav Stählin zum 70. Geburtstag.* Edited by O. Böcher and K. Haacker. Wuppertal: Brockhaus, 1970.

______. "Die Gewinnung der Gewissheit im Hebräerbrief." *TLZ* 96 (1971): 321–30.

Brawley, R. L. "Discoursive Structure and the Unseen in Hebrews 2:8 and 11:1: A Neglected Aspect of the Context." *CBQ* 55 (1993): 81–98.

Bright, P. "The Epistle to the Hebrews in Origen's Christology." Pages 559–65 in *Origeniana sexta.* Edited by G. Dorival and A. Le Boulluec. BETL 118. Leuven: Leuven University/Peeters, 1995.

Brock, S. P. "Hebrews 2:9b in Syriac Tradition." *NovT* 27 (1983): 236–44.

Brooks, W. E. "The Perpetuity of Christ's Sacrifice in the Epistle to the Hebrews." *JBL* 89 (1970): 205–14.

Brown, P. *Augustine of Hippo.* Berkeley: University of California, 1967.

Brown, R. E. *The Birth of the Messiah: A Commentary on the Infancy Narratives in Matthew and Luke.* Garden City, N.Y.: Doubleday, 1979.

______. *The Churches the Apostles Left Behind.* New York: Paulist, 1984.

______. *The Death of the Messiah: A Commentary on the Passion Narratives in the Four Gospels.* 2 vols. New York: Doubleday, 1994.

______. *The Epistles of John.* AB 30. Garden City, N.Y.: Doubleday, 1982.

Brown, R. E., and J. P. Meier, *Antioch and Rome: New Testament Cradles of Catholic Christianity.* New York: Paulist, 1984.

Brownlee, W. H. *The Midrash Pesher of Habakkuk.* SBLMS 24. Missoula, Mont.: Scholars, 1979.

Bruce, F. F. " 'A Shadow of Good Things' (Hebrews 10:1)." Pages 77–94 in *The Time Is Fulfilled.* Grand Rapids: Eerdmans, 1978.

______. " 'To the Hebrews': A Document of Roman Christianity?" *ANRW* II.25.4 (1987): 3496–3521.

Bruyne, D. de, "Étude sur les origenes de notre texte latin de Saint Paul." *RB* 12 (1915): 358–92.

Buchanan, G. W. "The Present State of Scholarship on Hebrews." Pages 299–330 in *Christianity, Judaism and Other Greco-Roman Cults: I Festschrift Morton Smith.* Edited by J. Neusner. Leiden: Brill, 1975.

Bulley, A. D. "Death and Rhetoric in the Hebrews 'Hymn to Faith.' " *SR* 25 (1996): 409–23.

Burkert, W. *Greek Religion.* Cambridge, Mass.: Harvard University, 1985.

Burns, L. "Hermeneutical Issues and Principles in Hebrews As Exemplified in the Second Chapter." *JETS* 39 (1996): 587–607.
Cadwallader, A. H. "The Correction of the Text of Hebrews towards the LXX." *NovT* 34 (1992): 257–92.
Cahill, M. "A Home for the Homily: An Approach to Hebrews." *ITQ* 60 (1994): 141–48.
______. "The Implications of *episynagōgē* in Hebrews 10,25: The First Eucharistic Homily?" *Questions liturgiques et paroissiales* 74 (1993): 198–207.
Caird, G. B. "Son by Appointment." Pages 73–81 in *The New Testament Age: Essays in Honor of Bo Reicke*. Edited by W. C. Weinrich. Vol. 1. Macon, Ga.: Mercer University, 1984.
Camacho, H. S. "The Altar of Incense in Hebrews 9:3–4." *AUSS* 24 (1986): 5–12.
Campbell, K. M. "Covenant or Testament? Heb. 9.16f. Reconsidered." *EvQ* 44 (1972): 107–11.
Campenhausen, H. von, *The Formation of the Christian Bible*. Philadelphia: Fortress, 1972.
Cantalamessa, R. "Il papiro Chester Beatty III (P^{46}) e la tradizione indiretta di Hebr. x,l." *Aegyptus* 45 (1965): 194–251.
Caragounis, C. *The Son of Man: Vision and Interpretation*. WUNT 38. Tübingen: Mohr/Siebeck, 1986.
Carlston, C. [E.] "Commentaries on Hebrews: A Review Article." *Andover Newton Review* 1 (1990): 27–45.
______. "Eschatology and Repentance in the Epistle to the Hebrews." *JBL* 78 (1959): 296–302.
______. "The Vocabulary of Perfection in Philo and Hebrews." Pages 133–60 in *Unity and Diversity in New Testament Theology*. Edited by R. A. Guelich. Grand Rapids: Eerdmans, 1978.
Casalini, N. *Dal simbolo alla realtà: L'espiazione dall' Antica alla Nuova Alleanza secondo Ebr 9, 1–14. Una proposta esegetica*. SBFLA 26. Jerusalem: Franciscan, 1989.
______. "Ebr 7.1–10: Melchisedek prototipo di Cristo." *SBFLA* 24 (1984): 149–90.
______. "Ebr 9,11: la tenda più grande e più perfetta." *SBFLA* 36 (1986): 111–70.
______. "I sacrifici dell' antica alleanza nel piano salvifico di Dio secundo la Lettera agli Ebrei." *RivistB* 35 (1987): 443–64.
______. "Una *Vorlage* extra-biblica in Ebr 7,1–3?" *SBFLA* 24 (1984): 109–48.
Casey, J. M. "Christian Assembly in Hebrews: A Fantasy Island?" *TD* 30 (1982): 323–35.
Casson, L. *Travel in the Ancient World*. Baltimore: Johns Hopkins University, 1994.
Chapman, J. "Aristion, Author of the Epistle to the Hebrews." *RBén* 22 (1905): 50–64.
Charles, D. J. "The Angels, Sonship, and Birthright in the Letter to the Hebrews." *JETS* 33 (1990): 171–78.
Cheney, C. R., and W. H. Semple. *Selected Letters of Pope Innocent III concerning England (1198–1216)*. London: Thomas Nelson, 1953.
Chester, A. N. "Hebrews: The Final Sacrifice." Pages 57–72 in *Sacrifice and Redemption: Durham Essays in Theology*. Edited by S. W. Sykes. Cambridge: Cambridge University, 1991.
Clark, F. *Eucharistic Sacrifice and the Reformation* (Westminster, Md.: Newman, 1960.
Clements, R. E. "The Use of the Old Testament in Hebrews." *SwJT* 28 (1985): 36–45.
Cockerill, G. L. "Heb 1:1–14, *1 Clem.* 36:1–6, and the High Priest Title." *JBL* 97 (1978): 437–40.
______. "Melchizedek or 'King of Righteousness.' " *EvQ* 63 (1991): 305–12.

Cody, A. *Heavenly Sanctuary and Liturgy in the Epistle to the Hebrews.* St. Meinrad, Ind.: Grail, 1960.
Colijn, B. " 'Let Us Approach': Soteriology in the Epistle to the Hebrews." *JETS* 39 (1996): 571–86.
Colish, M. L. *Peter Lombard.* Leiden: Brill, 1994.
Collins, J. J. *The Scepter and the Star: The Messiahs of the Dead Sea Scrolls and Other Literature.* New York: Doubleday, 1995.
Combrink, H. J. B. "Some Thoughts on the Old Testament Citations in the Epistle to the Hebrews." *Neot* 5 (1971): 21–36.
Cosby, M. R. *The Rhetorical Composition and Function of Hebrews 11, in Light of Example Lists in Antiquity.* Macon, Ga.: Mercer University, 1988.
______. "The Rhetorical Composition of Hebrews 11." *JBL* 107 (1988): 257–73.
Coste, J. "Notion grecque et notion biblique de la 'souffrance éducatrice.' A propos de Héb. 5.7–8." *RSR* 43 (1955): 481–523.
Courthial, P. "La portée de diathècè en Hébreux 9:16–17." *Études évangeliques* 36 (1976): 36–43.
Crenshaw, J. L. *Education in Ancient Israel: Across the Deadening Silence.* New York: Doubleday, 1998.
Croy, N. C. *Endurance in Suffering: Hebrews 12:1–3 in Its Rhetorical Religious and Philosophical Context.* SNTSMS 98. Cambridge: Cambridge University, 1998.
______. "A Note on Hebrews 12:2." *JBL* 114 (1995): 117–19.
Cuming, G. J. "Service-Endings in the Epistles." *NTS* 22 (1975–76): 110–13.
D'Angelo, M. R. *Moses in the Letter to the Hebrews.* SBLDS 42. Missoula, Mont.: Scholars, 1979.
Dahms, J. V. "The First Readers of Hebrews." *JETS* 20 (1977): 365–75.
Daly, R. J. *Christian Sacrifice: The Judaeo-Christian Background before Origen.* Washington, D.C.: Catholic University of America, 1978.
Daniel, J. L. "Anti-Semitism in the Hellenistic-Roman Period." *JBL* 98 (1979): 45–65.
Danker, F. W. *Benefactor: Epigraphic Study of a Graeco-Roman Semantic Field.* St. Louis: Clayton, 1982.
Dautzenberg, G. "Der Glaube im Hebräerbrief." *BZ* 17 (1973): 161–177.
Davies, W. D. *The Setting of the Sermon on the Mount.* Cambridge: Cambridge University, 1964.
De Jonge, H. J. "Traditie en exegese: de hogepriester-christologie en Melchizedek in Hebreën." *NedTT* 37 (1983): 1–19.
De Jonge, M. *Jewish Eschatology, Early Christian Christology, and the Testaments of the Twelve Patriarchs.* NovTSup 63. Leiden: Brill, 1991.
______. *Studies on the Testaments of the Twelve Patriarchs.* Edited by M. De Jonge. Leiden: Brill, 1975.
De Kruijf, T. "The Priest-King Melchizedek: The Reception of Genesis 14:18–20 in Hebrews Mediated by Psalm 110." *Bijdragen* 54 (1993): 393–406.
Deichgräber, R. *Gotteshymnus und Christushymnus in der frühen Christenheit.* SUNT 5. Göttingen: Vandenhoeck & Ruprecht, 1967.
Deissmann, A. *Bible Studies.* Edinburgh: Clark, 1909.
______. *Light from the Ancient East.* London: Hodder & Stoughton, 1910.
Delcor, M. "Melchizedek from Genesis to the Qumran Texts and the Epistle to the Hebrews." *JSJ* 2 (1971): 115–35.
Delville, J.-P. "L'Épître aux Hébreux à la lumière du prosélytisme juif." *RCT* 10 (1985): 323–68.

Demarest, B. "Hebrews 7:3: A *Crux Interpretum* Historically Considered." *EvQ* 49 (1977): 141–62.

______. *A History of the Interpretation of Hebrews 7, 1–10 from the Reformation to the Present Day.* Tübingen: Mohr/Siebeck, 1976.

deSilva, D. A. "Despising Shame: A Cultural-Anthropological Investigation of the Epistle to the Hebrews." *JBL* 113 (1994): 439–61.

______. *Despising Shame: Honor Discourse and Community Maintenance in the Epistle to the Hebrews.* SBLDS 152. Atlanta: Scholars, 1995.

______. "The Epistle to the Hebrews in Social-Scientific Perspective." *ResQ* 36 (1994): 1–21.

______. "Exchanging Favor for Wrath: Apostasy in Hebrews and Patron-Client Relationships." *JBL* 115 (1996): 91–116.

Dey, L. K. K. *The Intermediary World and Patterns of Perfection in Philo and Hebrews* SBLDS 25. Missoula, Mont.: Scholars, 1975.

Dibelius, M. *Botschaft und Geschichte: Gesammelte Aufsätze.* 2 vols. Tübingen: Mohr/ Siebeck, 1953–56.

Dillon, J. M. *The Middle Platonists: A Study of Platonism 80 B.C. to A.D. 220.* Ithaca, N.Y.: Cornell University, 1977.

Dolfe, K.-G. "Hebrews 2,16 under the magnifying glass." *ZNW* 84 (1993): 289–94.

Dörrie, H. "Ὑπόστασις. Wort- und Bedeutungsgeschichte." *NAWG* 3 (1955): 35–92.

Dubarle, A. M. "Rédacteur et destinataires de l'épître aux Hébreux." *RB* 48 (1939): 506–29.

Dumbrell, W. J. "The Spirits of Just Men Made Perfect." *EvQ* 48 (1976): 154–59.

Dunn, J. D. G. *Christology in the Making: A New Testament Inquiry into the Origins of the Doctrine of the Incarnation.* 2nd ed. Grand Rapids: Eerdmans, 1989.

______. *Romans.* 2 vols. WBC 38. Dallas: Word, 1988.

______. *The Partings of the Ways: Between Christianity and Judaism and their Signifiaance for the Character of Christianity.* London: SCM and Philadelphia: Trinity, 1991.

______. *The Theology of Paul the Apostle.* Grand Rapids: Eerdmans, 1998.

______. *Unity and Diversity in the New Testament: An Inquiry into the Character of Earliest Christianity.* 2nd ed. London: SCM and Philadelphia: Trinity, 1990.

Dunnill, J. *Covenant and Sacrifice in the Letter to the Hebrews.* SNTSMS 75. Cambridge: Cambridge University, 1992.

Dussaut, L. *Synopse structurelle de l'épître aux Hébreux.* Paris: Cerf, 1981.

Ebert, D. J. "The Chiastic Structure of the Prologue of Hebrews." *TJ* 13 (1992): 163–79.

Eccles, R. S. "The Purpose of the Hellenistic Patterns in the Epistle to the Hebrews." Pages 207–26 in *Religions in Antiquity.* Edited by J. Neusner. Leiden: Brill, 1968.

Ego, B. *Im Himmel wie auf Erden: Studien zum verhältnis von himmlischer und irdischer Welt im rabbinischen Judentum.* WUNT 34. Tübingen: Mohr/Siebeck, 1989.

Ehrman, B. D. *The Orthodox Corruption of Scripture: The Effect of Early Christological Controversies on the Text of the New Testament.* New York: Oxford, 1993.

Eisbenbaum, P. M. "Heroes and History in Hebrews 11." Pages 380–96 in *Early Christian Interpretation of the Scriptures of Israel: Investigations and Proposals.* Edited by C. Evans and J. A. Sanders. JSNTSup 148. Sheffield: Sheffield Academic, 1997.

______. *The Jewish Heroes of Christian History: Hebrews 11 in Literary Context.* SBLDS 156. Atlanta: Scholars, 1997.

Ellingworth, P. "Hebrews and 1 Clement: Literary Dependence or Common Tradition?" *BZ* 23 (1979): 262–69.

______. "Jesus and the Universe in Hebrews." *EvQ* 58 (1986): 337–50.

______. " 'Like the Son of God': Form and Content in Hebrews 7:1–10." *Bib* 64 (1983): 252–62.

______. "New Testament Text and Old Testament Context in Heb. 12.3." Pages 89–95 in *Studia Biblica 1978*. JSNTSup 3. Sheffield: JSOT, 1980.

______. "The Unshakable Priesthood: Hebrews 7.24." *JSNT* 23 (1985): 125–26.

Elliott, J. H. *A Home for the Homeless: A Social-Scientific Criticism of I Peter, Its Situation and Strategy*. Minneapolis: Fortress, 1990.

Elliott, J. K. *The Apocryphal New Testament*. Oxford: Clarendon, 1993.

______. "Is Post-baptismal Sin Forgivable?" *BT* 28 (1977): 330–332.

______. "When Jesus Was Apart from God: An Examination of Heb. 2:9." *ExpTim* 83 (1972): 339–41.

Enns, P. E. "Creation and Re-Creation: Psalm 95 and Its Interpretation in Hebrews 3:1–4:13." *WTJ* 55 (1993): 255–80.

______. "The Interpretation of Psalm 95 in Hebrews 3.1–4.13." Pages 352–63 in *Early Christian Interpretation of the Scriptures of Israel: Investigations and Proposals*. Edited by C. Evans and J. A. Sanders. JSNTSup 148. Sheffield: Sheffield Academic, 1997.

Erlemann, K. "Alt und neu bei Paulus und im Hebräerbrief: Frühchristliche Standortbestimmung im Vergleich." *TZ* 54 (1998): 345–67.

Ernst, J. "Die griechische Polis—das himmlische Jerusalem—die christliche Stadt." *TGl* 67 (1977): 240–58.

Esbroeck, M. van, "Héb. XI,33–38 dans l'ancienne version géorgienne." *Bib* 53 (1972): 43–64.

Fabry, H.-F. "Die Wirkungsgeschichte des Psalms 22." In *Beiträge zur Psalmenforschung, Psalm 2 und 22*. Edited by J. Schreiner. Würzburg: Echter, 1988.

Fee, G. D. *The First Epistle to the Corinthians*. NICNT. Grand Rapids: Eerdmans, 1987.

Feld, H. *Der Hebräerbrief*. ErFor 228. Darmstadt: Wissenschaftliche, 1985.

______. "Der Hebräerbrief: Literarische Form, religionsgeschichtlicher Hintergrund, theologische Fragen." *ANRW* II.25.4 (1987): 3522–3601.

______. "Der Humanisten-Streit um Hebräer 2,7 (Psalm 8,6)." *ARG* 61 (1970): 5–35.

______. "Die theologischen Hauptthemen der Hebräerbrief-Vorlesung Wendelin Steinbachs." *Aug* 37 (1987): 187–252.

______. *Martin Luthers und Wendelin Steinbachs Vorlesungen über den Hebäerbrief*. Wiesbaden: Steiner, 1971.

Feldmeier, R. *Die Christen als Fremde: Die Metaphor der Fremde in der Antiken Welt, im Urchristentum und im 1. Petrusbrief*. WUNT 64. Tübingen: Mohr/Siebeck, 1992.

______. "The 'Nation' of Strangers: Social Contempt and Its Theological Interpretation in Ancient Judaism and Early Christianity." Pages 241–70 in *Ethnicity and the Bible*. Edited by M. G. Brett. Leiden: Brill, 1996.

Fensham, F. C. "Hebrews and Qumran." *Neot* 5 (1971): 9–21.

Fenton, J. C. "The Argument in Hebrews." *SE* 7 (1982): 175–81.

Ferguson, E. "Spiritual Sacrifice in Early Christianity and Its Environment." *ANRW* II.23.2 (1980): 1151–89.

Fernández, V. M. "La vida sacerdotal de los christianos degun la carta a los Hebreos." *RevistB* 52 (1990): 145–52.

Feuillet, A. "Le 'commencement' de l'économie chrétienne d'après He ii.3–4; Mc i.1 et Ac i.1–2." *NTS* 24 (1977–78): 163–74.

______. "L'Évocation de l'agonie de Gethsémani dans l'épître aux Hébreux." *Esprit et Vie* 86 (1976): 49–53.

______. "Une triple préparation du sacerdoce du Christ dans l'Ancien Testament: Introduction à la doctrine sacerdotale de l'épître aux Hébreux." *Divinitas* 28 (1984): 103–36.

Filson, F. V. *Yesterday: A Study of Hebrews in the Light of Chapter 13*. London: SCM, 1967.
Fischer, J. "Covenant, Fulfillment, and Judaism in Hebrews." *ERT* 13 (1989): 175–87.
Fitzmyer, J. A. *The Acts of the Apostles*. AB 31. New York: Doubleday, 1998.
______. *Essays on the Semitic Background of the New Testament*. London: Chapman, 1971.
______. *The Gospel According to Luke*. AB 28–28A. Garden City, N.Y.: Doubleday, 1981–85.
______. "Habakkuk 2:3–4 and the New Testament." On pages 236–46 in *To Advance the Gospel: New Testament Studies*. New York: Crossroad, 1981.
______. "Melchizedek in the MT, LXX, and the NT." *Bib* 81 (2000): 63–69.
Flusser, D. " 'Today If You Will Listen to His Voice': Creative Jewish Exegesis in Hebrews 3–4." Pages 55–62 in *Creative Biblical Exegesis*. Edited by B. Uffenheimer and H. G. Reventlow. JSOTSup 59. Sheffield: Sheffield Academic, 1988.
Ford, J. M. "The Mother of Jesus and the Authorship of the Epistle to the Hebrews." *TBT* 82 (1976): 683–94.
Fox, R. L. *Pagans and Christians*. San Francisco: Harper & Row, 1988.
France, R. T. "The Writer of Hebrews As a Biblical Expositor." *TynBul* 47 (1996): 245–76.
Franco Martínez, C. A. *Jesucristo, su persona y su obra, en la carta a los Hebreos*. Madrid: Ciudad Nueva, 1992.
Frankowski, J. "Early Christian Hymns Recorded in the New Testament: A Reconsideration of the Question in the Light of Heb 1,3." *BZ* 27 (1987): 183–94.
Franzmann, M. *Jesus in the Nag Hammadi Writings*. Edinburgh: T. & T. Clark, 1996.
Frey, J. "Die alte und die neue διαθήκη nach dem Hebräerbrief." Pages 263–310 in *Bund und Tora*. Edited by F. Avemarie and H. Lichtenberger. WUNT 92. Tübingen: Mohr/Siebeck, 1996.
Friedrich, G. "Das Lied vom Hohenpriester im Zusammenhang von Hebr 4,14–5,10." *TZ* 18 (1962): 95–115.
Fritsch, C. T. "ΤΟ 'ΑΝΤΙΤΥΠΟΝ." Pages 100–107 in *Studia Biblica et Semitica*. Edited by W. C. van Unnik and A. S. van der Woude. Wageningen: Veenman, 1966.
Frost, S. "Who Were the Heroes? An Exercise in Bi-testamentary Exegesis with Christological Implications." Pages 165–72 in *The Glory of Christ in the New Testament: Studies in Christology in Memory of George Bradford Caird*. Edited by L. D. Hurst and N. T. Wright. Oxford: Clarendon, 1987.
Fyfe, W. H. *Aristotle: The Poetics*. LCL. Cambridge, Mass.: Harvard University, 1965.
García Martínez, F. "Las tradiciones sobre Melquisedec en los manuscritos de Qumrán." *Bib* 81 (2000): 70–80.
Gardiner, E. N. *Athletics of the Ancient World*. Oxford: Clarendon, 1930.
______. *Greek Athletic Sports and Festivals*. London: Macmillan, 1910.
Garnet, P. "Hebrews 2:9: *chariti* or *chōris*?" in *Studia Patristica* 18/1 (1985): 321–25.
Garuti, P. "Alcune stutture argomentative nella Lettera agli Ebrei." *DivThom* 98 (1995): 197–224.
______. *Alle origini dell'omiletica christiana: La lettera agli ebrei*. *SBFLA* 38. Jerusalem: Franciscan, 1995.
______. "Ebrei 7,1–28: Un problema giridico." *DivThom* 97 (1994): 9–105.
______. "Il prologo della lettera agli Ebrei (Eb 1,1–4)." *SacDoc* 34 (1989): 533–56.
Gianotto, C. *Melchisedek e la sua tipologia: Tradizioni giudaiche, cristiane e gnostiche (sec. II a. C.-sec. III d. C.)*. RivBSup 12. Brescia: Paideia, 1984.

Gieschen, C. A. *Angelomorphic Christology: Antecedents and Early Evidence*. Leiden: Brill, 1998.

______. "The Different Functions of a Similar Melchizedek Tradition in *2 Enoch* and the Epistle to the Hebrews." Pages 364–79 in *Early Christian Interpretation of the Scriptures of Israel: Investigations and Proposals*. Edited by C. Evans and J. A. Sanders. JSNTSup 148. Sheffield: Sheffield Academic, 1997.

Glasson, T. F. " 'Plurality of Divine Persons' and the Quotations in Hebrews i.6ff." *NTS* 12 (1965–66): 270–72.

Gleason, R. C. "The Old Testament Background of Rest in Hebrews 3:7–4:11." *BSac* 157 (2000): 281–303.

______. "The Old Testament Background of the Warning in Hebrews 6:4–8." *BSac* 155 (1998): 62–91.

Glenn, D. R. "Psalm 8 and Hebrews 2: A Case Study in Biblical Hermeneutics and Biblical Theology." Pages 39–51 in *Walvoord: A Tribute*. Edited by D. K. Campbell. Chicago: Moody, 1982.

Glombitza, O. "Erwägungen zum kunstvollen Ansatz der Paraenese im Brief an die Hebräer X.19–25." *NovT* 9 (1967): 132–50.

Goldhahn-Müller, I. *Die Grenze der Gemeinde: Studien zum Problem der Zweiten Busse in Neuen Testament unter Berücksichtigung der Entwicklung im 2. Jh. bis Tertullian.* Göttingen: Vandenhoeck & Ruprecht, 1989.

Goldstein, J. A. "Creatio ex nihilo: Recantations and Restatements." *JJS* 38 (1987): 187–94.

Gollwitzer, H. "Zur Frage der 'Sundlosigkeit Jesus,' " *EvT* 31 (1971): 496–506.

Gonnet, D. "L'utilisation christologique de l'Epître aux Hébreux dans les orationes contra Arianos d'Athanase d'Alexandrie." *Studia Patristica* 32 (1997): 19–24.

Goppelt, L. A *Commentary on 1 Peter.* Grand Rapids: Eerdmans, 1993.

______. *Theology of the New Testament.* Grand Rapids: Eerdmans, 1981.

______. *Typos: The Typological Interpretation of the Old Testament in the New.* Grand Rapids: Eerdmans, 1982.

Gordon, R. P. "Better Promises: Two Passages in Hebrews against the Background of the Old Testament Cultus." Pages 434–49 in *Templum Amicitiae: Essays on the Second Temple, Presented to Ernst Bammel.* Edited by W. Horbury. JSOTSup 48. Sheffield: Sheffield Academic, 1991.

Gourgues, M. *À la droite de Dieu: Résurrection de Jésus et actualisation du Psaume 110:1 dans le Nouveau Testament.* Paris: Gabalda, 1978.

______. "Remarques sur la 'structure centrale' de l'épître aux Hébreux. A l'occasion d'une réédition." *RB* 84 (1977): 26–37.

Grant, F. C. *Hellenistic Religions.* Indianapolis: Bobbs-Merrill, 1953.

Grant, M. *Nero.* London: Weidenfeld and Nicolson, 1970.

Grässer, E. *Aufbruch und Verheissung: Gesammelte Aufsätze zum Hebräerbrief.* BZNW 65. Berlin: de Gruyter, 1992.

______. *Der Alte Bund im Neuen: Exegetische Studien zur Israelfrage im Neuen Testament.* WUNT 35. Tübingen: Mohr/Siebeck, 1985.

______. *Der Glaube im Hebräerbrief.* MTS 2. Marburg: Elwert, 1965.

Grayston, K. "ἱλάσκεσθαι and Related Words in the Septuagint." *NTS* 27 (1980–81): 640–56.

______. "Salvation Proclaimed. III. Hebrews 9:11–14." *ExpTim* 93 (1982): 164–68.

Greenlee, J. H. "By Faith Sarah Received Ability." *AsTJ* 59 (2000): 67–72.

______. "Hebrews 11:11: Sarah's Faith or Abraham's?" *Notes* 4 (1990): 37–42.

Greenspahn, F. E. "Why Prophecy Ceased." *JBL* 108 (1989): 37–49.

Greer, R. A. *The Captain of Our Salvation: A Study in the Patristic Exegesis of Hebrews.* Tübingen: Mohr/Siebeck, 1973.

Grudem, W. "Perseverance of the Saints: A Case Study from Hebrews 6:4–6 and the Other Warning Passages in Hebrews." Pages 133–82 in *The Grace of God, the Bondage of the Will.* Edited by T. R. Schreiner and B. A. Ware. Grand Rapids: Eerdmans, 1995.

Gunton, C. *The Actuality of Atonement: A Study of Metaphor, Rationality, and the Christian Tradition.* Edinburgh: Clark, 1989.

Guthrie, D. *New Testament Introduction.* 4th ed. Leicester and Downers Grove: Inter-Varsity, 1990.

Guthrie, G. H. *The Structure of Hebrews: A Textlinguistic Analysis.* NovTSup 73. Leiden: Brill, 1994.

Gyllenberg, R. "Die Christologie des Hebräerbriefes." *ZST* 11 (1934): 662–90.

Haacker, K. "Creatio ex auditu: Zum Verständnis von Hbr. 11:3." *ZNW* 60 (1969): 279–81.

______. "Der Glaube im Hebräerbrief und die hermeneutische Bedeutung des Holocaust." *TZ* 39 (1983): 152–65.

Haarhoff, T. J. *The Stranger at the Gate.* Oxford: Basil Blackwell, 1948.

Habermann, J. *Präexistenzaussagen im Neuen Testament.* Frankfurt: Peter Lang, 1990.

Hagen, K. *Hebrews Commenting from Erasmus to Bèze, 1516–1598.* Tübingen: Mohr/Siebeck, 1981.

______. *A Theology of Testament in the Young Luther: The Lectures on Hebrews.* Leiden: Brill, 1974.

Hagner, D. A. "Interpreting the Epistle to the Hebrews." Pages 217–42 in *The Literature and Meaning of Scripture.* Edited by M. A. Inch and C. H. Bullock. Grand Rapids: Baker, 1981.

______. *The Use of the Old and New Testaments in Clement of Rome.* NovTSup 34. Leiden: Brill, 1973.

Hamm, D. "Faith in the Epistle to the Hebrews: The Jesus Factor." *CBQ* 52 (1990): 270–91.

Hanson, A. T. "Hebrews." Pages 292–302 in *It Is Written: Scripture Citing Scripture. Essays in Honour of Barnabas Lindars S.S.F.* Edited by D. A. Carson and H. G. M. Williamson. Cambridge: Cambridge University, 1988.

______. "The Reproach of the Messiah in the Epistle to the Hebrews." *SE* 7 (1982): 231–40.

Hardy, E. G. *Christianity and the Roman Government: A Study in Imperial Administration.* London: Longmans, 1894. Reprint, New York: Franklin, 1971.

Hare, D. R. A. *The Son of Man Tradition.* Minneapolis: Fortress, 1990.

Harnack, A. von. "Probabilia über die Adresse und den Verfasser des Hebräerbriefes." ZNW 1 (1900): 16–41. Translated as "Probabilty about the Address and Author of the Epistle to the Hebrews" on pages 392–415 in L. A. Starr, *The Bible Status of Women.* New York: Revell, 1926.

______. "Studien zur Vulgata des Hebräerbriefs." Pages 191–234 in *Studien zur Geschichte des neuen Testaments und der alten Kirche.* Berlin: deGruyter, 1931.

______. *What Is Christianity.* London: Williams and Norgate, 1901.

______. "Zwei alte dogmatische Korrekturen im Hebräerbrief." Pages 235–52 in *Studien zur Geschichte des neuen Testaments und der alten Kirche*. Berlin: de Gruyter, 1931.

Harris, M. J. "The Translation and Significance of ὁ Θέος in Hebrews 1:8–9." *TynBul* 36 (1985): 129–62.

Hartman, L. *"Into the Name of the Lord Jesus": Baptism in the Early Church*. Edinburgh: Clark, 1997.

Harvey, G. *True Israel: Uses of the Names Jew, Hebrew, and Israel in Ancient Jewish and Early Christian Literature*. Leiden: Brill, 1996.

Hatch, W. H. P. "The Position of Hebrews in the Canon of the New Testament." *HTR* 29 (1936): 133–51.

Hay, D. M. *Glory at the Right Hand: Psalm 110 in Early Christianity*. SBLMS 18. Nashville: Abingdon, 1973.

Hays, R. B. *The Moral Vision of the New Testament*. San Francisco: HarperSanFrancisco, 1996.

Hayward, R. "Shem, Melchizedek, and Concern with Christianity in the Pentateuchal Targumim." Pages 67–80 in *Targumic and Cognate Studies. Essays in Honour of Martin McNamara*. Edited by K. J. Cathcart and M. Maher. JSOTSup 230. Sheffield: Sheffield Academic, 1996.

Hegermann, H. "Christologie im Hebräerbrief." Pages 337–51 in *Anfänge der Christologie. Festschrift für Ferdinand Hahn zum 65. Geburtstag*. Göttingen: Vandenhoeck & Ruprecht, 1991.

______. "Das Wort Gottes als aufdekende macht: Zur Theologie des Wortes Gottes im Hebräerbrief." Pages 83–92 in *Das lebendige Wort: Beiträge zur kirchlichen Verkündigung. Festgabe für Gottfried Voigt zum 65. Geburtstag*. Edited by H. Seidl and K.-H. Bieritz. Berlin: Evangelische, 1982.

Heininger, B. "Hebr. 11.7 und das Henochorakel am Ende der Welt." *NTS* 44 (1998): 115–32.

______. "Sündenreinigung (Hebr 1,3). Christologische Anmerkungen zum Exordium des Hebräerbriefs." *BZ* 41 (1997): 54–68.

Helderman, J. "Melchizedeks Wirkung: Eine traditionsgeschichtliche Untersuchung eines Makrokomplexes in NHC XI, 1, 1–27, 10 (Melchizedek)." Pages 335–62 in *The New Testament in Early Christianity*. Edited by J.-M. Sevrin. BETL 86. Leuven: Leuven University, 1989.

Helyer, L. R. "The *Prōtotokos* Title in Hebrews." *Studia Biblica et Theologica* 6 (1976): 3–28.

Hengel, M. *Crucifixion*. Philadelphia: Fortess, 1977.

______. *Studies in Early Christology*. Edinburgh: Clark, 1995.

Heschel, A. *The Prophets*. New York: Harper & Row, 1962.

Hickling, C. J. A. "John and Hebrews: The Background of Hebrews 2.10–18." *NTS* 29 (1983): 112–16.

Hill, D. *Greek Words and Hebrew Meanings*. Cambridge: Cambridge University, 1967.

Hock, R. F. and E. N. O'Neill, eds. *The Chreia in Ancient Rhetoric*. Vol. 1. Atlanta: Scholars, 1986.

Hofius, O. "Biblische Theologie im Lichte des Hebräerbriefes." Pages 108–25 in *New Directions in Biblical Theology*. Edited by S. Pedersen. NovTSup 76. Leiden: Brill, 1994.

______. "Das 'erste' und das 'zweite' Zelt: Ein Beitrag zur Auslegung von Hbr 9:1–10." ZNW 61 (1970): 271–77.

______. *Der Vorhang vor dem Thron Gottes: Eine exegetisch-religionsgeschichtliche Untersuchung zu Hebräer 6,19 f. und 10,19 f.* WUNT 14. Tübingen: Mohr/Siebeck, 1972.

______. "Die Unabänderlichkeit des göttlichen Heilsratschlusses." *ZNW* 64 (1973): 135–45.

______. "Inkarnation und Opfertod Jesu nach Hebr 10,19f." Pages 132–41 in *Der Ruf Jesu und die Antwort der Gemeinde. Festschrift Jeremias*. Edited by E. Lohse. Göttingen: Vandenhoeck & Ruprecht, 1970.

______. *Katapausis: Die Vorstellung vom endzeitlichen Ruheort im Hebräerbrief.* WUNT 11. Tübingen: Mohr/Siebeck, 1970.
______. "Στόματα μαχαίρης. Hebr 11.34." ZNW 62 (1971): 129–30.
Holladay, W. L. *Jeremiah* 2. Hermeneia: Minneapolis: Fortress, 1989.
Hollander, H. W. "Hebrews 7.11 and 8.6: A Suggestion for the Translation of *nenomothetetai epi.*" *BT* 30 (1979): 244–47.
Hoppin, R. *Priscilla, Author of the Epistle to the Hebrews and Other Essays.* New York: Exposition, 1969.
Horbury, W. "The Aaronic Priesthood in the Epistle to the Hebrews." *JSNT* 19 (1983): 43–71.
Horning, E. B. "Chiasmus, Creedal Structure, and Christology in Hebrews 12.1–2." *BR* 23 (1978): 37–48.
Horst, P. W. van der. "Sarah's Seminal Emission: Hebrews 11:11 in the Light of Ancient Embryology." Pages 287–302 in *Greeks, Romans, and Christians: Essays in Honor of Abraham J. Malherbe.* Edited by D. L. Balch, E. Ferguson, W. A. Meeks. Minneapolis: Fortress, 1990.
Horton, F. L. Jr. *The Melchizedek Tradition: Through the First Five Centuries of the Christian Era and in the Epistle to the Hebrews.* SNTSMS 30. Cambridge: Cambridge University, 1976.
Howard, G. "Hebrews and the Old Testament Quotations." *NovT* 10 (1968): 208–16.
Hübner, H. *Biblische Theologie des Neuen Testaments.* Göttingen: Vandenhoeck & Ruprecht, 1995.
Hughes, G. R. *Hebrews and Hermeneutics: The Epistle to the Hebrews as a New Testament Example of Biblical Interpretation.* SNTSMS 36. Cambridge: Cambridge University, 1979.
Hughes, J. J. "Hebrews ix.15ff. and Galatians iii.15ff.: A Study in Covenant Practice and Procedure." *NovT* 21 (1979): 27–96.
Hughes, P. E. "The Epistle to the Hebrews." Pages 351–70 in *The New Testament and Its Modern Interpreters.* Edited by E. J. Epp and G. W. MacRae. Philadelphia: Fortress and Atlanta: Scholars, 1989.
______. "Hebrews 6:4–6 and the Peril of Apostasy." *WTJ* 35 (1972–73): 137–55.
Hunt, A. S., and C. C. Edgar. *Select Papyri.* Vols. 1–2. LCC. Cambridge, Mass.: Harvard University and London: Heinemann, 1932–34.
Hurst, L. D. "The Christology of Hebrews 1 and 2." Pages 151–64 in *The Glory of Christ in the New Testament.* Edited by L. D. Hurst and N. T. Wright. Oxford: Clarendon, 1987.
______. *The Epistle to the Hebrews: Its Background of Thought.* SNTSMS 65. Cambridge: Cambridge University, 1990.
______. "How 'Platonic' Are Heb. viii.5 and ix.23f?" *JTS* 34 (1983): 156–168.
Irwin, J. "The Use of Hebrews 11:11 as Embryological Proof-Text." *HTR* 71 (1978): 312–16.
Isaacs, M. E. "Hebrews." Pages 145–59 in *Early Christian Thought in Its Jewish Context.* Edited by J. Barclay and J. Sweet. Cambridge: Cambridge University, 1996.
______. "Hebrews 13:9–16 Revisited." *NTS* 43 (1997): 268–84.
______. *Sacred Space: An Approach to the Theology of the Epistle to the Hebrews.* JSNTSup 73. Sheffield: Sheffield Academic, 1992.
Jeremias, J. "Hebräer 10:20: τοῦτ' ἔστιν τῆς σαρκὸς αὐτοῦ." ZNW 62 (1971): 131.
______. *Jerusalem in the Time of Jesus.* Philadelphia: Fortress, 1969.
Jewett, R. "The Form and Function of the Homiletical Benediction." *AThR* 51 (1969): 18–34.

Jobes, K. H. "The Function of Paronomasia in Hebrews 10:5–7." *TJ* 13 (1992): 181–91.

______. "Rhetorical Achievement in the Hebrews 10 'Misquote' of Psalm 40." *Bib* 72 (1991): 387–96.

Johnsson, W. G. "The Cultus of Hebrews in Twentieth-Century Scholarship." *ExpTim* 89 (1978): 104–8.

______. *Defilement and Purgation in the Book of Hebrews.* Ann Arbor, Mich.: University Microfilms, 1973.

______. "The Pilgrimage Motif in the Book of Hebrews." *JBL* 97 (1978): 239–51.

Johnston, G. "Christ as Archegos." *NTS* 27 (1980–81): 381–85.

Jones, P. R. "The Figure of Moses as a Heuristic Device for Understanding the Pastoral Intent of Hebrews." *RevExp* 76 (1979): 95–107.

Juel, D. *Messianic Exegesis: Christological Interpretation of the Old Testament in Early Christianity.* Philadelphia: Fortress, 1988.

Jungmann, A. *The Mass of the Roman Rite.* New York: Benzinger, 1951–55.

Kaiser, W. C. "The Abolition of the Old Order and the Establishment of the New: A Study of Psalm 40:6–8 and Hebrews 10:5–10." Pages 19–37 in *Tradition and Testament.* Edited by J. S. Feinberg. Chicago: Moody, 1981.

______. "The Promise Theme and the Theology of Rest." *BSac* 130 (1973): 135–50.

Käsemann, E. *Jesus Means Freedom.* Philadelphia: Fortress, 1970.

______. *The Wandering People of God: An Investigation of the Letter to the Hebrews.* Minneapolis: Augsburg, 1984. German original, 1939.

Kawamura, A. "ἀδύνατον in Heb 6,4." *AJBI* 10 (1984): 91–100.

Kee, H. C. *Miracle in the Early Christian World: A Study in Sociohistorical Method.* New Haven: Yale University, 1983.

Kennedy, G. A. *The Art of Rhetoric in the Roman World.* Princeton: Princeton University, 1972.

______. *New Testament Interpretation through Rhetorical Criticism.* Chapel Hill: University of North Carolina, 1984.

Keresztes, P. "The Imperial Roman Government and the Christian Church I: From Nero to the Severi." *ANRW* II.23.2 (1980): 247–315.

Kiley, M. "A Note on Hebrews 5.14." *CBQ* 42 (1980): 501–3.

Kilpatrick, G. D. "Διαθήκη in Hebrews." ZNW 68 (1977): 263–65.

______. *The Principles and Practice of New Testament Textual Criticism.* BETL 96. Leuven: Leuven University and Peeters, 1990.

Kirby, V. T. "The Authorship of the Epistle to the Hebrews." *ExpTim* 35 (1923–24): 375–77.

Kistemaker, S. *The Psalm Citations in the Epistle to the Hebrews.* Amsterdam: van Soest, 1961.

Klappert, B. "Die Eschatologie des Hebräerbriefes." *Theologische Existenz Heute* 156 (1969): 7–61.

Klassen, W. "To the Hebrews or against the Hebrews? Anti-Judaism in the Epistle to the Hebrews." Pages 1–16 in *Anti-Judaism and Early Christianity.* Edited by S. G. Wilson. Waterloo: Wilfrid Laurier University, 1986.

Klauck, H.-J. *Hausgemeinde und Hauskirche im frühen Christentum.* Stuttgart: Katholisches Bibelwerk, 1981.

______. "*Thysiastērion* in Hebr 13,10 und bei Ignatius von Antiochien." Pages 359–72 in *Gemeinde, Amt, Sakrament: Neutestamentliche Perspektiven.* Würzburg: Echter, 1989.

Klinzing, G. *Die Umdeutung des Kultus in der Qumrangemeinde und im Neuen Testament.* SUNT 7. Göttingen: Vandenhoeck & Ruprecht, 1971.

Knoch, O. "Hält der Verfasser des Hebräerbriefs die Fier eucharistischer Gottesdienste für theologisch unangemessen? Überlegungen zu einer umstritten Frage." *LJ* 42 (1992): 166–87.

Kobelski, P. J. *Melchizedek and Melchireša': The Heavenly Prince of Light and the Prince of Darkness in Qumran Literature*. CBQMS 10. Washington, D.C.: Catholic Biblical Association, 1981.

Koch, D.-A. "Der Text von Heb. 2.4b in der Septuaginta und im Neuen Testament." ZNW 76 (1985): 68–85.

Koester, C. R. *Symbolism in the Fourth Gospel: Meaning, Mystery, Community*. Minneapolis: Fortress, 1995.

______. *The Dwelling of God: The Tabernacle in the Old Testament, Intertestamental Jewish Literature, and the New Testament*. CBQMS 22. Washington, D.C.: Catholic Biblical Association, 1989.

______. "The Epistle to the Hebrews in Recent Study." *CurBS* 2 (1994): 123–45.

Koester, H. "Die Auslegung der Abraham-Verheissung in Hebr 6." Pages 95–109 in *Studien zur Theologie der alttestamentlichen Überlieferungen*. Edited by R. Rendtorff and K. Koch. Neukirchen: Neukirchener, 1961.

______. *Introduction to the New Testament*. 2nd ed. 2 vols. New York: de Gruyter. 1995–2000.

______. " 'Outside the Camp': Hebrews 13:9–14." *HTR* 55 (1963): 299–315.

Kögel, J. *Der Sohn und die Söhne: Eine exegetische Studie zu Hebr 2:5–18*. Gütersloh: Bertelsmann, 1904.

Kosmala, H. *Hebräer, Essener, Christen: Studien zur Vorgeschichte der frühchristlichen verkündigung*. Leiden: Brill, 1959.

Kugel, J. L. *In Potiphar's House: The Interpretive Life of Biblical Texts*. San Francisco: HarperSanFrancisco, 1990.

Kuhn, H. W. "Die Kreuzesstrafe während der frühen Kaiserzeit: Ihre Wirklichkeit und Wertung in der Umwelt des Urchristentums." *ANRW* II.25.1 (1982): 648–793.

Kümmel, W. G. *The New Testament: The History of the Investigation of Its Problems*. Nashville: Abingdon, 1972.

Laansma, J. *"I Will Give You Rest": The Rest Motif in the New Testament with Special Reference to Mt 11 and Heb 3–4*. WUNT 98. Tübingen: Mohr/Siebeck, 1997.

Lampe, P. *Die stadtrömischen Christen in den ersten beiden Jahrhunderten: Untersuchungen zur Sozialgeschichte*. 2nd ed. WUNT 18. Tübingen: Mohr/Siebeck, 1989.

Lampe, P. and U. Luz. "Nachpaulinisches Christentum und pagane Gesellschaft." Pages 185–216 in *Die Anfänge des Christentums: Alte Welt und neue Hoffnung*. Edited by J. Becker. Stuttgart: Kohlhammer, 1987.

Landgraf, A. "Der Paulinenkommentar des Hervaeus von Bourg-Dieu." *Bib* 21 (1940): 113–32.

Lane, W. L. *Call to Commitment: Responding to the Message of Hebrews*. Nashville: Nelson, 1985.

______. "Hebrews: A Sermon in Search of a Setting." *SwJT* 28 (1985): 13–18.

______. "Social Perspectives on Roman Christianity during the Formative Years from Nero to Nerva: Romans, Hebrews, 1 Clement." Pages 196–244 in *Judaism and Christianity in First-Century Rome*. Edited by K. P. Donfried and P. Richardson. Grand Rapids: Eerdmans, 1998.

______. "Standing Before the Moral Claim of God: Discipleship in Hebrews." Pages 203–24 in *Patterns of Discipleship in the New Testament*. Edited by R. Longenecker. Grand Rapids: Eerdmans, 1996.

———. "Unexpected Light on Hebrews 13:1–6 from a Second Century Source." *PRSt* 9 (1982): 267–74.

Larsson, E. "How Mighty Was the Mighty Minority?" Pages 93–105 in *Mighty Minorities: Minorities in Early Christianity—Positions and Strategies*. Edited by D. Hellholm, H. Moxnes, and T. K. Seim. Oslo: Scandanavian University, 1995.

Laub, F. *Bekenntnis und Auslegung: Die paränetische Funktion der Christologie im Hebräerbrief*. BU 15. Regensburg: Pustet, 1980.

———. " 'Ein für allemal hineingegangen in das Allerheiligste' (Hebr 9,12). Zum Verständnis des Kreuzestodes im Hebräerbrief." *BZ* 35 (1991): 65–85.

———. "Glaubenskrise und neu auszulegendes Bekenntnis. Zur Intention der Hohepriestertheologie des hebräerbriefes." Pages 377–96 in *Theologie im Werden*. Edited by J. Hainz. Paderborn: Schönigh, 1992.

———. "Verkündigung und Gemeindeamt: Die Autorität der ἡγούμενοι Hebr 13,7.17.24." SNTSU 6–7 (1981–82): 169–90.

Lausberg, H. *Handbook of Literary Rhetoric: A Foundation for Literary Study*. Leiden: Brill, 1998.

Layton, S. C. "Christ over His House (Hebrews 3:6) and Hebrew אשר על־הבית." *NTS* 37 (1991): 473–77.

Lee, J. A. L. "Hebrews 5:14 and Ἕξις: A History of Misunderstanding." *NovT* 39 (1997): 151–76.

Legg, J. D. "Our Brother Timothy. A suggested solution to the problem of the authorship of the Epistle to the Hebrews." *EvQ* 40 (1968): 220–23.

Lehne, S. *The New Covenant in Hebrews*. JSNTSup 44. Sheffield: JSOT, 1990.

Leipoldt, J. *Geschichte des neutestamentlichen Kanons*. Leipzig: Hinrichs, 1907–8.

Leithart, P. J. "Womb of the World: Baptism and the Priesthood of the New Covenant in Hebrews 10.19–22." *JSNT* 78 (2000): 49–65.

Leonard, W. *The Authorship of the Epistle to the Hebrews*. Rome: Vatican Polyglot, 1939.

Leschert, D. F. *The Hermeneutical Foundations of Hebrews*. Lewiston, N.Y.: Mellen, 1994.

Lescow, T. "Jesus in Gethsemane bei Lukas und im Hebräerbrief." *ZNW* 58 (1967): 215–39.

Levenson, J. D. *Sinai and Zion*. Minneapolis: Winston, 1985.

Levin, C. *Die Verheissung des neuen Bundes in ihrem theologiegeschichtliche Zusammenhang ausgelegt*. FRLANT 137. Göttingen: Vandenhoeck & Ruprecht, 1985.

Levoratti, A. J. " 'Tú no has querido sacrificio ni oblación.' Salmo 40,7. Hebreos 10,5." *RevistB* 48 (1986): 1–30, 65–87, 141–52, 193–237.

Lewis, J. P. *A Study of the Interpretation of Noah and the Flood in Jewish and Christian Literature*. Leiden: Brill, 1968.

Lewis, T. W. " 'And If He Shrinks Back. . .' (Heb. 10.38b)." *NTS* 22 (1975–76): 88–94.

Lieberman, S. *Hellenism in Jewish Palestine*. New York: Jewish Theological Seminary, 1950.

Lightfoot, N. R. "The Saving of the Savior, Heb. 5.7ff." *ResQ* 16 (1973): 166–73.

Lincoln, A. T. "Sabbath, Rest, and Eschatology in the New Testament." Pages 197–220 in *From Sabbath to Lord's Day: A Biblical, Historical, and Theological Investigation*. Edited by D. A. Carson. Grand Rapids: Zondervan, 1982.

Lindars, B. "Hebrews and the Second Temple." Pages 410–33 in *Templum Amicitiae: Essays on the Second Temple Presented to Ernst Bammel*. Edited by W. Horbury. JSOTSup 48. Sheffield: Sheffield Academic, 1991.

———. "The Rhetorical Structure of Hebrews." *NTS* 35 (1989): 382–406.

______. *The Theology of the Letter to the Hebrews.* Cambridge: Cambridge University, 1991.

Llewelyn, S. R. *New Documents Illustrating Early Christianity.* Vol. 6. New South Wales: Ancient History Document Research Centre, Macquarie University, 1992.

Loader, W. R. G. "Christ at the Right Hand: Ps cx.1 in the New Testament." *NTS* 24 (1977–78): 199–217.

______. *Sohn und Hoherpriester: Eine traditionsgeschichtliche Untersuchung zur Christologie des Hebräerbriefes.* WMANT 53. Neukirchen-Vluyn: Neukirchener, 1981.

Lohmann, T. "Zur Heilsgeschichte des Hebräerbriefes." *OLZ* 79 (1984): 117–26.

Löhr, H. "Anthropologie und Eschatologie im Hebräerbrief: Bemerkungen zum theologischen Interesse einer frühchristlichen Schrift." Pages 169–99 in *Eschatologie und Schöpfung: Festschrift für Erich Grässer zum siebzigsten Geburtstag.* Edited by M. Evang, H. Merklein, and M. Wolter. BZNW 89. Berlin and New York: de Gruyter, 1997.

______. " 'Heute, wenn ihr seine Stimme hört . . . ' Zur Kunst der Schriftanwendung im Hebräerbrief und in 1 Kor 10." Pages 226–48 in *Schriftauslegung im antiken Judentum und im Urchristentum.* Edited by M. Hengel and H. Löhr. WUNT 73. Tübingen: Mohr/Siebeck, 1994.

______. "Thronversammlung und preisender Temple: Beobachtungen am himmlischen Heiligtum im Hebräerbrief und in den Sabbatopferliedern aus Qumran." Pages 185–205 in *Königsherrschaft Gottes und himmlischer Kult im Judentum, Urchristentum und in der hellenistischen Welt.* Edited by M. Hengel and A. M. Schwemer. WUNT 55. Tübingen: Mohr/Siebeck, 1991.

______. *Umkehr und Sünde im Hebräerbrief.* BZNW 73. Berlin and New York: de Gruyter, 1994.

______. " 'Umriss und Schatten.' Bemerkungen zur Zitierung von Exodus 25,40 in Hebr 8." *ZNW* 84 (1993): 218–32.

Lombard, H. A. "Katapausis in the Letter to the Hebrews." *Neot* 5 (1971): 60–71.

Longenecker, R. N. "The Melchizedek Argument of Hebrews." Pages 161–85 in *Unity and Diversity in New Testament Theology.* Edited by R. A. Guelich. Grand Rapids: Eerdmans, 1978.

Lorenzmeier, T. "Wider das Dogma von der Sündlosigkeit Jesu." *EvT* 31 (1971): 452–71.

Lubac, H. de. *Medieval Exegesis.* Grand Rapids: Eerdmans, 1998–.

Luck, U. "Himmlisches und irdisches Geschenen im Hebräerbrief." *NovT* 6 (1963): 192–206.

Lührmann, D. "Der Hohepriester ausserhalb des Lagers (Hebr 13:12)." *ZNW* 69 (1978): 178–86.

Luz, U. "Der alte und der neue Bund bei Paulus und im Hebräerbrief." *EvT* 27 (1967): 318–36.

Lyonnet, S. and L. Sabourin, *Sin, Redemption, and Sacrifice: A Biblical and Patristic Study.* AnBib 48. Rome: Biblical Institute, 1970.

Mack, B. L. *Rhetoric and the New Testament.* Minneapolis: Fortress, 1990.

MacLeod, D. J. "The Cleansing of the True Tabernacle." *BSac* 152 (1995): 60–71.

______. "The Doctrinal Center of the Book of Hebrews." *BSac* 146 (1989): 291–300.

______. "The Literary Structure of the Book of Hebrews." *BSac* 146 (1989): 185–97.

______. "The Present Work of Christ in Hebrews." *BSac* 148 (1991): 184–200.

Macmullen, R. *Paganism in the Roman Empire.* New Haven: Yale University, 1981.

MacRae, G. W. "Heavenly Temple and Eschatology in the Letter to the Hebrews." *Semeia* 12 (1978): 179–99.

______. " 'A Kingdom That Cannot Be Shaken': The Heavenly Jerusalem in the Letter to the Hebrews." *Tantur Yearbook* (1979–80): 27–40.

Malherbe, A. *Moral Exhortation: A Greco-Roman Sourcebook*. Philadelphia: Westminster, 1986.

Malina, B. M. and J. H. Neyrey. "Honor and Shame in Luke–Acts: Pivotal Values of the Mediterranean World." Pages 25–65 in *The Social World of Luke–Acts: Models for Interpretation*. Peabody, Mass.: Hendrickson, 1991.

Mangey, J. *Philo Judaeus. Opera omnia*. Vol. 2. London: Bowyer, 1742.

Manson, W. *The Epistle to the Hebrews: An Historical and Theological Reconsideration*. London: Hodder and Stoughton, 1951.

Manzi, F. "Fil 2,6–11 ed Eb 5,5–10: due schemi cristologici a confronto." *RivB* 44 (1996): 31–64.

______. "La fede degli uomini e la singolare relazione filiale di Gesù con Dio nell'Epistola agli Ebrei." *Bib* 81 (2000): 32–62.

______. *Melchisedek e l'angelolica nell'Epistola agli Ebrei e a Qumran*. AnBib 136. Rome: Pontifical Biblical Institute, 1997.

Marrou, H. I. *A History of Education in Antiquity*. New York: Shedd and Ward, 1956.

Marrow, S. B. "Parrhesia and the New Testament." *CBQ* 44 (1982): 431–46.

Marshall, J. L. "Melchizedek in Hebrews, Philo and Justin Martyr." *SE* 7 (1982): 339–42.

Martyn, J. L. *Galatians*. AB 33A. New York: Doubleday, 1997.

______. *History and Theology in the Fourth Gospel*. Rev. ed. Nashville: Abingdon, 1979.

März, C. P. " ' . . . nur für kurze Zeit unter die Engel gestellt' (Hebr 2,7): Anthropologie und Christologie in Hebr 2,5–9." Pages 29–42 in *Von Gott Reden in säkularer Gesellschaft Festschrift für Konrad Feiereis zum 65. Geburtstag*. Edited by E. Coreth. Leipzig: Benno, 1996.

Matera, F. J. "Moral Exhortation: The Relation between Moral Exhortation and Doctrinal Exposition in the Letter to the Hebrews." *TJT* 10 (1994): 169–82.

______. *New Testament Christology*. Louisville: Westminster/John Knox, 1999.

Mathewson, D. "Reading Heb 6:4–6 in Light of the Old Testament." *WTJ* 61 (1999): 209–25.

Maurer, C. " 'Erhört wegen der Gottesfurcht', Hebr 5,7." Pages 275–84 in *Neues Testament und Geschichte Historisches Geschehen und Deutung im Neuen Testament. Oscar Cullmann zum 70. Geburtstag*. Edited by H. Baltensweiler and B. Reicke. Zürich: Theologischer and Tübingen: Mohr/Siebeck, 1972.

Mayser, E. *Grammatik der griechischen Papyri aus der Ptolemäerzeit*. Leipzig and Berlin: de Gruyter, 1906–36.

McCown, W. G. "Holiness in Hebrews." *Wesleyan Theological Journal* 16 (1981): 58–78.

McCullough, J. C. "Hebrews in Recent Scholarship." *IBS* 16 (1994): 66–86, 108–20.

______. "The Impossibility of a Second Repentance in Hebrews." *BTB* 24 (1974): 1–7.

______. "The Old Testament Quotations in Hebrews." *NTS* 26 (1979–80): 363–79.

McKane, W. "Old and New Covenant (Testament): A Terminological Enquiry." Pages 227–35 in *Understanding Poets and Prophets: Essays in Honour of George Wishart Anderson*. Edited by A. G. Auld. Sheffield: JSOT, 1993.

McKelvey, J. *The New Temple: The Church in the New Testament*. London: Oxford University, 1969.

McKnight, S. "The Warning Passages of Hebrews: A Formal Analysis and Theological Conclusions." *TJ* 13 (1992): 21–59.

McNamara, M. "Melchizedek: Gen 14,17–20 in the Targums, in Rabbinic and Early Christian Literature." *Bib* 81 (2000): 1–31.

______. *Targum Neofiti 1: Genesis*. ArBib 1A. Collegeville, Minn.: Michael Glazier, 1992.
Meeks, W. A. *The First Urban Christians: The Social World of Paul the Apostle*. New Haven: Yale University, 1983.
Mees, M. "Die Hohepriester-Theologie des Hebräerbriefes im Vergleich mit dem Ersten Clemensbrief." *BZ* 22 (1978): 115–24.
Meier, J. P. "Structure and Theology in Heb 1,1–14." *Bib* 66 (1985): 168–89.
______. "Symmetry and Theology in the Old Testament Citations of Heb 1,5–14." *Bib* 66 (1985): 504–33.
Mejîa, J. "La problématique de l'ancienne et de la nouvelle alliance dans Jéremie XXXI 31–34 et quelques autres textes." Pages 263–77 in *Congress Volume: Vienna 1980*. Edited by J. A. Emerton. VTSup 32. Leiden: Brill, 1981.
Melbourne, B. L. "An Examination of the Historical-Jesus Motif in the Epistle to the Hebrews." *AUSS* 26 (1988): 281–97.
Mende, T. " 'Wen der Herr liebhat, den züchtigt er' (Hebr 12,6). Der alttestamentliche Hintergrund von Hebr 12,1–11; 1,1–4; 2,6–10." *TTZ* 100 (1991): 23–38.
Mendels, D. *The Rise and Fall of Jewish Nationalism*. New York: Doubleday, 1992.
Ménégoz, E. *La Theologie de l'épître aux Hébreux*. Paris: Fischbacher, 1894.
Mengelle, E. "La estructura de Hebreos 11,1." *Bib* 78 (1997): 534–42.
Mercado, L. F. "The Language of Sojourning in the Abraham Midrash in Heb. XI,8–10: Its Old Testament Basis, Exegetical Traditions and Function in the Epistle to the Hebrews." *HTR* 59 (1967): 494–95.
Metzger, B. M. *The Canon of the New Testament*. Oxford: Clarendon, 1987.
Meyer, W. D. "Obedience and Church Authority: The Problem of the Book of Hebrews." *ATJ* 28 (1996): 9–28.
Michaud, J. P. "Le passage de l'ancien au nouveau, selon L'Épître aux Hébreux." *ScEs* 35 (1983): 33–52.
______. " 'Parabolê' dans l'Epitre aux Hébreux et typologie." *Semiotique et Bible* 46 (1987): 19–34.
Milgrom, J. *Leviticus 1–16*. AB 3. New York: Doubleday, 1991.
Millar, F. *The Emperor in the Roman World*. Ithaca, N.Y.: Cornell, 1977.
Miller, M. R. "What Is the Literary Form of Hebrews 11?" *JETS* 29 (1986): 411–17.
Milligan, G. *The Theology of the Epistle to the Hebrews*. Edinburgh: Clark, 1899.
Minear, P. S. "An Early Christian Theopoetic?" *Semeia* 12 (1978): 201–14.
Mitchell, A. C. "Holding On to Confidence: ΠΑΡΡΗΣΙΑ in Hebrews." Pages 203–26 in *Friendship, Flattery, and Frankness of Speech*. Edited by J. T. Fitzgerald. NovTSup 82. Leiden: Brill, 1996.
______. "The Use of πρέπειν and Rhetorical Propriety in Hebrews 2:10." *CBQ* 54 (1992): 681–701.
Moxnes, H. *Theology in Conflict: Studies in Paul's Understanding of God in Romans*. NovTSup 53. Leiden: Brill, 1980.
Mugridge, A. "Warnings in the Epistle to the Hebrews." *RTR* 46 (1987): 74–82.
Müller, P.-G. "Die Funktion der Psalmzitate im Hebräerbrief." Pages 223–42 in *Freude an der Weisung des Herrn. Beiträge zur Theologie der Psalmen. Festschrift Heinrich Gross*. Edited by E. Haag and F.-L. Hossfeld. Stuttgart: Katholisches Bibelwerk, 1986.
______. *ΧΡΙΣΤΟΣ ΑΡΧΗΓΟΣ: Der religionsgeschichtliche und theologische Hintergrund einer neutestamentlichen Christusprädikation*. Bern and Frankfurt: Lang, 1973.
Mullins, T. Y. "Greeting as a New Testament Form." *JBL* 87 (1968): 418–26.
Muntingh, L. M. " 'The City Which Has Foundations.' Heb. 11:8–10 in the Light of the

Mari Texts." Pages 108–20 in *De fructo oris sui: Essays in honour of Andrianus von Selms*. Edited by I. H. Eybergs. Leiden: Brill, 1971.

Murray, R. "Jews, Hebrews, and Christians: Some Needed Distinctions." *NovT* 24 (1982): 194–208.

Mynster, J. P. "Untersuchung über den Verfasser des Briefes an die Hebräer." *Kleine theologische Schriften*. Copenhagen: Gyldendal, 1825.

Nadeau, R. " 'Hermogenes' On Stases: A Translation with an Introduction and Notes." *Speech Monographs* 31 (1964): 361–424.

Nairne, A. *The Epistle of Priesthood*. Edinburgh: Clark, 1915.

Nardoni, E. "Partakers in Christ (Hebrews 3:14)." *NTS* 37 (1991): 456–72.

Nash, R. H. "The Notion of Mediator in Alexandrian Judaism and the Epistle to the Hebrews." *WTJ* 40 (1978): 89–115.

Nauck, W. "Zum Aufbau des Hebräerbriefes." Pages 199–206 in *Judentum – Urchristentum – Kirche. Festschrift J. Jeremias*. Edited by W. Eltester. BZNW 26. Berlin: Töpelmann, 1960.

Neander, A. *History of the Planting and Training of the Christian Church by the Apostles*. London: Bohn, 1851.

Neeley, L. L. *A Discourse Analysis of Hebrews*. *OPTT* 3–4 (1987): 1–146.

Neuner, J., and J. Dupuis, eds. *The Christian Faith: Christian Faith in the Doctrinal Documents of the Catholic Church*. New York: Alba, 1982.

Neusner, J. *The Idea of Purity in Ancient Judaism*. SJLA 1. Leiden: Brill, 1973.

Newsom, C. A. *Songs of the Sabbath Sacrifice: A Critical Edition*. HSS 27. Atlanta: Scholars, 1985.

Neyrey, J. H. " 'Without Beginning of Days or End of Life' (Hebrews 7:3): Topos for a True Deity." *CBQ* 53 (1991): 439–55.

Nickelsburg, G. W. E. *Jewish Literature between the Bible and the Mishnah*. Philadelphia: Fortress, 1981.

Nicole, R. "Some Comments on Hebrews 6:4–6 and the Doctrine of the Perseverance of God with the Saints." Pages 355–64 in *Current Issues in Biblical and Patristic Interpretation*. Edited by G. E. Hawthorne. Grand Rapids: Eerdmans, 1975.

Niederwimmer, K. "Vom Glauben der Pilger: Erwägungen zu Hebr 11,8–10 und 13–16." Pages 121–31 in *Zur Aktualität des Alten Testaments. Festschrift für Georg Sauer zum 65. Geburtstag*. Edited by S. Kreuzer and K. Lüthi. Frankfurt: Lang, 1992.

Nissilä, K. *Das Hohepriestermotiv im Hebräerbrief: Eine exegetische Untersuchung*. Schriften der Finnischen Exegetischen Gesellschaft 33. Helsinki: Oy Liiton Kirjapaino, 1979.

Oberholtzer, T. K. "The Warning Passages in Hebrews." *BSac* 145 (1988): 83–97, 185–196, 319–328, 410–19; 146 (1989): 67–75.

Olbricht, T. H. "Hebrews as Amplification." Pages 375–87 in *Rhetoric in the New Testament*. Edited by S. E. Porter and T. H. Olbricht. JSNTSup 90. Sheffield: JSOT, 1993.

Ollenburger, B. C. *Zion, The City of the Great King: A Theological Symbol of the Jerusalem Cult*. JSOTSup 41. Sheffield: JSOT, 1987.

O'Neill, J. C. " 'Who Is Comparable to Me in Glory?' 4Q491 Fragment 11 (4Q491C) and the New Testament." *NovT* 42 (2000): 24–38.

Osiek, C. *Shepherd of Hermas*. Hermeneia. Minneapolis: Fortress, 1999.

Osiek, C. and D. L. Balch. *Families in the New Testament World: Households and House Churches*. Louisville: Westminster John Knox, 1997.

Owen, E. C. E. "'Ἀποτυμπανίζω -σμός (τυμπανισμός), τυμπανίζω, τύμπανον (τύπανον)." *JTS* 30 (1929): 259–66.

Owen, H. P. "The 'stages of ascent' in Heb. 5.11–6.3." *NTS* 3 (1956–57): 243–53.
Pagels, E. *The Gnostic Paul: Gnostic Exegesis of the Pauline Letters.* Philadelphia: Fortress, 1975.
Pannenberg, W. *Jesus, God and Man.* Philadelphia: Westminster, 1977.
Parker, H. M. "Domitian and the Epistle to the Hebrews." *Iliff Review* 36 (1979): 31–43.
Parsons, M. C. "Son and High Priest: A Study in the Christology of Hebrews." *EvQ* 60 (1988): 195–215.
Paul, M. J. "The Order of Melchizedek (Ps 110:4 and Heb 7:3)." *WTJ* 49 (1987): 195–211.
Pearson, B. *Gnosticism, Judaism, and Egyptian Christianity.* Minneapolis: Fortress, 1990.
Pelikan, J. *The Christian Tradition.* Chicago and London: University of Chicago, 1971–89.
Pelser, G. M. M. "The Concept Archegos in the Letter to the Hebrews." *HvTSt* 28 (1972): 86–96.
______. "A Translation Problem. Heb. 10:19–25." *Neot* 8 (1974): 43–53.
Penna, R. "Appunti sul come e perché il Nuovo Testamento si rapporta all'Antico." *Bib* 81 (2000): 95–104.
Peterson, D. *Hebrews and Perfection: An Examination of the Concept of Perfection in the Epistle to the Hebrews.* SNTSMS 47. Cambridge: Cambridge University, 1982.
______. *Possessed by God: A New Testament Theology of Sanctification and Holiness.* Grand Rapids: Eerdmans, 1995.
______. "The Prophecy of the New Covenant in the Argument of Hebrews." *RTR* 38 (1979): 74–81.
______. "The Situation of the 'Hebrews' (5:11–6:12)." *RTR* 35 (1976): 14–21.
Petuchowski, J. J. "The Controversial Figure of Melchizedek." *HUCA* 28 (1957): 127–36.
Pfitzner, V. C. *Paul and the Agon Motif: Traditional Athletic Imagery in the Pauline Literature.* NovTSup 16. Leiden: Brill, 1967.
Pfleiderer, O. *Primitive Christianity: Its Writings and Teaching in their Historical Connections.* 2 vols. London: Williams & Norgate and New York: Putnam's, 1906–11.
Piana, G. la. "Foreign Groups in Rome during the First Centuries of the Empire." *HTR* 20 (1927): 183–403.
Pilhofer, P. "**ΚΡΕΙΤΤΟΝΟΣ ΔΙΑΘΗΚΗΣ ΕΓΓΥΟΣ**: Die Bedeutung der Präexistenzchristologie für die Theologie des Hebräerbriefs." *TLZ* 121 (1996): 319–28.
Pohlenz, M. "τὸ πρέπον." Pages 100–139 in *Kleine Schriften.* Edited by H. Dörrie. Hildesheim: Olms, 1965.
Porter, S. E. "The Date of the Composition of Hebrews and the Use of the Present Tense-Form." Pages 295–313 in *Crossing the Boundaries: Essays in Biblical Interpretation in Honour of Michael D. Goulder.* Edited by S. E. Porter, P. Joyce, J. E. Orton. Leiden: Brill, 1995.
Poschmann, B. *Paenitentia secunda: Die kirchliche Busse im ältesten Christentum bis Cyprian und Origenes.* Bonn: Hanstein, 1940.
Powell, D. L. "Christ as High Priest in the Epistle to the Hebrews." *SE* 7 (1982): 387–99.
Powell, J. M. ed. *Innocent III: Vicar of Christ or Lord of the World?* 2nd ed. Washington, D.C.: Catholic University of America, 1994.
Pretorius, E. A. C. "**ΔΙΑΘΗΚΗ** in the Epistle to the Hebrews." *Neot* 5 (1971): 37–50.
Preus, J. S. *From Shadow to Promise: Old Testament Interpretation from Augustine to the Young Luther.* Cambridge, Mass.: Harvard University, 1969.
Proulx, P., and L. Alonso Schökel. "Heb 4,12–13: Componentes y estructura." *Bib* 54 (1973): 331–39.

______. "Heb 6,4–6: Eis metanoian anastaurountas." *Bib* 56 (1975): 193–209.

Pryor, J. W. "Hebrews and Incarnational Christology." *RTR* 40 (1981): 440–50.

Puech, E. "Notes sur manuscrit de 11Qmelchisédeq." *RevQ* 12 (1987): 483–513.

Punt, J. "Hebrews, Thought Patterns and Context: Aspects of the Background of Hebrews." *Neot* 31 (1997): 119–58.

Pursiful, D. J. *The Cultic Motif in the Spirituality of the Book of Hebrews.* Lewiston, N.Y.: Mellen, 1993.

Quinot, B. "L'influence de l'Épître aux Hébreux dans la notion augustinienne du vrai sacrifice." *REAug* 8 (1962): 129–68.

Rad, G. von. "There Remains Still a Rest for the People of God: An Investigation of a Biblical Conception." Pages 94–102 in *The Problem of the Hexateuch and Other Essays.* Edinburgh and London: Oliver & Boyd, 1965.

Radcliffe, T. "Christ in Hebrews: Cultic Irony." *NBf* 68 (1987): 494–504.

Rahner, H. *Church and State in Early Christianity.* San Francisco: Ignatius, 1992.

Räisänen, H. *Paul and the Law.* Philadelphia: Fortress, 1983.

Ramsay, W. M. *Luke the Physician and Other Studies in the History of Religion.* London: Hodder & Stoughton, 1908.

Rapske, B. *The Book of Acts and Paul in Roman Custody.* Grand Rapids: Eerdmans, 1994.

Raurell, F. "Certain Affinities between Ez-LXX and the Epistle to the Hebrews with Regard to the 'Doxa' and the Cherubins." *Estudios Franciscanos* 86 (1985): 209–32.

Reiser, M. *Jesus and Judgment: The Eschatological Proclamation in Its Jewish Context.* Minneapolis: Fortress, 1997.

Rhee, V. (S.-Y.). "Chiasm and the Concept of Faith in Hebrews 11." *BSac* 155 (1998): 327–45.

______. "Christology and the Concept of Faith in Hebrews 1:1–2:4." *BSac* 157 (2000): 174–89.

______. "Christology and the Concept of Faith in Hebrews 5:11–6:20." *JETS* 43 (2000): 83–96.

Rice, G. E. "Apostasy as a Motif and Its Effect on the Structure of Hebrews." *AUSS* 23 (1985): 29–35.

______. "Hebrews 6:19: Analysis of Some Assumptions Concerning *katapetasma*." *AUSS* 25 (1987): 65–71.

Riché, P., and G. Lobrichon, eds. *Le Moyen Age et la Bible.* Paris: Beauchesne, 1984.

Riehm, E. K. A. *Der Lehrbegriff des Hebräerbriefes.* Basel and Ludwigsburg: Balmer and Riehm, 1867.

Riggenbach, E. *Die ältesten lateinischen Kommentare zum Hebräerbrief. Ein Beitrag zur Geschichte und Exegese und zur Literaturgeschichte des Mittelalters.* Vol. 1 in *Historische Studien zum Hebräerbrief.* Forschungen zur Geschichte des neutestamentlichen Kanons. Edited by T. Zahn. Leipzig: Deichert, 1907.

Rissi, M. *Die Theologie des Hebräerbriefes.* WUNT 41. Tübingen: Mohr/Siebeck, 1987.

Ritschl, A. *The Christian Doctrine of Justification and Reconciliation.* Edinburgh: Clark, 1902.

______. *Die Entstehung der altkatholischen Kirche.* 2nd ed. Bonn: Marcus, 1857.

Roloff, J. "Der mitleidende Hohepriester: Zur Frage nach der Bedeutung des irdischen Jesus für die Christologie des Hebräerbriefes." Pages 143–66 in *Jesus Christus in Historie und Theologie. Festschrift für H. Conzelmann.* Edited by G. Strecker. Tübingen: Mohr/Siebek, 1975.

Rooke, D. W. "Jesus as Royal Priest: Reflections on the Interpretation of the Melchizedek Tradition in Heb 7." *Bib* 81 (2000): 81–94.

Rose, C. *Die Wolke der Zeugen: Eine exegetisch-traditionsgeschichtliche Untersuchung zu Hebräer 10,32–12,3*. WUNT 60. Tübingen: Mohr/Siebeck, 1994.

______. "Verheissung und Erfüllung: Zum Verständnis von ἐπαγγελία im Hebräerbrief." *BZ* 33 (1989): 60–80, 178–91.

Rosenau, H. "Die Erzählung von Abrahams Opfer (Gen 22) und ihre Deutung bei Kant, Kirkegaard und Schelling, *NZSTh* 27 (1985): 251–61.

Rostovtzeff, M. *Rome*. London: Oxford University, 1960.

Röth, E. M. *Epistolam vulgo "ad Hebraeos" inscriptam non ad Hebreos, id est christianos genere judaeos*. Frankfurt: Schmerberi, 1836.

Rottmanner, O. "Saint Augustin sur l'auteur de l'épître aux Hébreux." *RBén* 18 (1901): 257–61.

Ruager, S. "Wir haben einen Altar (Hebr 13,10). Einige Überlegungen zum Thema: Gottesdienst/Abendmahl im Hebräerbrief." *KD* 36 (1990): 72–77.

Ruina, D. T. *Philo in Early Christian Literature*. Assen: van Gorcum and Minneapolis: Fortress, 1993.

Sabourin, L. " 'Crucifying Afresh for One's Repentance' (Heb 6:4–6)." *BTB* 6 (1976): 264–71.

______. " 'Liturge du Sanctuaire et de la Tente Visible' (Héb. viii.2)." *NTS* 18 (1971–72): 87–90.

Sahlin, H. "Emendationsvorschläge zum griechischen Text des NT, III." *NovT* 25 (1983): 73–88.

Saller, R. P. *Personal Patronage under the Early Empire*. Cambridge: Cambridge University, 1982.

Sanders, E. P. *Paul and Palestinian Judaism: A Comparison of Patterns of Religion*. Philadelphia: Fortress, 1977.

Sanders, J. T. *The New Testament Christological Hymns: Their Historical Religious Background*. SNTSMS 15. Cambridge: Cambridge University, 1971.

Sandmel, S. *Philo of Alexandria: An Introduction*. New York and Oxford: Oxford University, 1979.

Saucy, M. "Exaltation Christology in Hebrews: What Kind of Reign?" *TJ* 14 (1993): 41–62.

Schäfer, J. R. "The Relationship between Priestly and Servant Messianism in the Epistle to the Hebrews." *CBQ* 30 (1968): 359–85.

Schäfer, K. T. "ΚΕΦΑΛΙΣ ΒΙΒΛΙΟΥ." Pages 1–10 in *Weg zur Buchwissenschaft*. Edited by O. Wenig. Bonn: Bouvier, 1966.

Schaff, P. *The Creeds of Christendom*. 3 vols. 6th ed. New York: Harper, 1919.

Schenck, K. "Keeping His Appointment: Creation and Enthronement in Hebrews." *JSNT* 66 (1997): 91–117.

Schenk, W. "Die Paränese Hebr 13,16 im Kontext des Hebräerbriefes: Einer Fallstudie semiotisch-orientierter Textinterpretation und Sachkritik." *ST* 39 (1985): 73–106.

______. "Hebräerbrief iv.14–16: Textlinguistik als Kommentierungsprinzip." *NTS* 26 (1979–80): 242–51.

Schenke, H.-M. "Die jüdische Melchizedek-Gestalt als Thema der Gnosis." Pages 111–36 in *Altes Testament — Frühjudentum — Gnosis*. Edited by K. W. Tröger. Gütersloh: Mohn, 1980.

______. "Erwägungen zum Rätsel des Hebräerbriefes." Pages 421–37 in *Neues Testament und Christliche Existenz*. Edited by H. D. Betz and L. Schottroff. Tübingen: Mohr/Siebeck, 1973.

Schenker, A. "Der nie aufgehobene Bund: Exegetische Beobachtungen zu Jer 31,31–34."

Pages 85–112 in *Der neue Bund im alten: Studien zur Bundestheologie der beiden Testamente*. Edited by E. Zenger. Freiburg: Herder, 1993.

Schierse, F. J. *Verheissung und Heilsvollendung: Zur theologische Grundfrage des Hebräerbriefes*. Munich: Zink, 1955.

Schlosser, J. "La médiation du Christ d'après l'épître aux Hébreux." *RSR* 63 (1989): 169–81.

Schmidt, T. E. "Moral Lethargy and the Epistle to the Hebrews." *WTJ* 54 (1992): 167–73.

Schmithals, W. "Der Hebräerbrief als Paulusbrief: Beobachtungen zur Kanonbildung." Pages 319–37 in *Die Weltlichkeit des Glaubens: Feschrift für Ulrich Wickert zum siebzigsten Geburtstag*. Edited by D. Wyrwa. BZNW 85. Berlin and New York: de Gruyter, 1997.

______. "Über Empfänger und Anlass des Hebräerbriefs." Pages 321–42 in *Eschatologie und Schöpfung: Festschrift für Erich Grässer zum siebzigsten Geburtstag*. Edited by M. Evang, H. Merklein, and M. Wolter. BZNW 89. Berlin and New York: de Gruyter, 1997.

Scholer, J. M. *Proleptic Priests: Priesthood in the Epistle to the Hebrews*. JSNTSup 49. Sheffield: Sheffield Academic, 1991.

Schoonhoven, C. R. "The 'Analogy of Faith' and the Intent of Hebrews." Pages 92–110 in *Scripture, Tradition, and Interpretation*. Edited by W. W. Gasque and W. S. LaSor. Grand Rapids: Eerdmans, 1978.

Schröger, F. "Das hermeneutische Instrumentarium des Hebräerbriefverfassers." *TGl* 60 (1970): 344–59.

______. "Der Gottesdienst der Hebräerbriefgemeinde." *MTZ* 19 (1968): 161–81.

______. "Der Hebräerbrief–paulinisch?" Pages 211–22 in *Kontinuität und Einheit: Festschrift für Franz Mussner*. Edited by P.-G. Müller and W. Stenger. Freiburg: Herder, 1981.

______. *Der Verfasser des Hebräerbriefes als Schriftausleger*. BU 4. Regensburg: Pustet, 1968.

Schulz, F. "Roman Registers of Births and Birth Certificates." *JRS* 32 (1942): 78–91; 33 (1943): 55–64.

Schumpp, M. M. "Der Glaubensbegriff des Hebräerbriefes und seine Deutung durch den hl. Thomas von Aquin." *DivThom* 11 (1933): 397–410.

Schürer, E., et al. *The History of the Jewish People in the Age of Jesus Christ*. Rev. ed. Edinburgh: Clark, 1973–87.

Schüssler Fiorenza, E. "Der Anführer und Vollender unseres Glaubens: Zum theologischen Verständnis des Hebräerbriefes." Pages 262–81 in *Gestalt und Anspruch des Neuen Testaments*. Edited by J. Schreiner. Würzburg: Echter, 1969.

Scott, J. J. "*Archegos* in the Salvation History of the Epistle to the Hebrews." *JETS* 29 (1986): 47–54.

Seeberg, R. *Text-Book of the History of Doctrines*. Grand Rapids: Baker, 1954.

Seid, T. W. "The Rhetorical Form of the Melchizedek/Christ Comparison in Hebrews 7." Ph.D. diss., Brown University, 1996.

Selb, W. "Διαθήκη im Neuen Testament: Randbemerkungen eines Juristen zu einem Theologenstreit." *JJS* 25 (1974): 183–96.

Selby, G. S. "The Meaning and Function of Συνείδησις in Hebrews 9 and 10." *ResQ* 28 (1986): 145–54.

Semler, J. S. "Beiträge zu genauerer Einsicht des Briefs an die Hebräer." In J. Baumgarten, *Erklärung des Briefes St. Pauli an die Hebräer*. Halle: Gebauer, 1763.

Sen, F. "Se recupera la verdadera lectura de un texto muy citado, cuyo sentido cambia substancialmente (Hb X,l)." *CB* 24 (1967): 165–68.

Sherwin-White, A. N. *The Letters of Pliny: A Historical and Social Commentary*. Oxford: Clarendon, 1966.
Siegert, F. *Drei hellenistisch-jüdische Predigten*. WUNT 61. Tübingen: Mohr/Siebeck, 1992.
Siker, J. *Disinheriting the Jews: Abrahamn in Early Christian Controversy*. Louisville: Westminster/John Knox, 1991.
Silberman, L. H. "Prophets/Angels: LXX and Qumran Psalm 151 and the Epistle to the Hebrews." Pages 91–101 in *Standing before God: Studies on Prayer in Scriptures and in Tradition with Essays*. Edited by A. Finkel and L. Frizzell. New York: Ktav, 1981.
Silva, M. "Perfection and Eschatology in Hebrews." *WTJ* 39 (1976): 60–71.
Smyth, H. W. *Greek Grammar*. Cambridge, Mass.: Harvard University, 1956.
Soden, H. von. "Der Hebräerbrief." *Jahrbücher für protestantische Theologie* 10 (1884): 435–93, 627–56.
Söding, T. "Die Antwort des Glaubens. Die Vorbild Abrahams nach Hebr 11." *Internationale Katholische Zeitschrift/Communio* 24 (1995): 394–409.
______. "Zuversicht und Geduld im Schauen auf Jesus: Zum Glaubensbegriff des Hebräerbriefes." ZNW 82 (1991): 214–41.
Solin, H. "Juden und Syrer im westlichen Teil der römischen Welt." *ANRW* II.29.2 (1983): 587–789.
Souter, A. *Pelagius's Expositions of Thirteen Epistles of St. Paul*. TS 9. Cambridge: Cambridge University, 1922.
Sowers, S. G. *The Hermeneutics of Philo and Hebrews*. Richmond: John Knox, 1965.
Spicq, C. "L'Épître aux Hébreux, Apollos, Jean-Baptiste, les Hellénistes et Qumran." *RevQ* 1 (1959): 365–90.
______. "L'Épître aux Hébreux et Philon: Un cas d'insertion de la littérature sacrée dans la culture profane du 1er siècle (Hébr. V,11–VI,20 et le 'De sacrificiis Abelis et Caini' de Philon)." *ANRW* II.25.4 (1987): 3602–18.
______. "Le vocabulaire de l'esclavage dans le Nouveau Testament." *RB* 85 (1978): 201–26.
______. "L'exégèse de Hb 11,1 par S. Thomas d'Aquin." *RSPT* 31 (1947): 229–36.
Sproule, J. A. "Parapesontas in Hebrews 6:6." *GTJ* 2 (1981): 327–32.
Stanley, S. "Hebrews 9:6–10: The 'Parable' of the Tabernacle." *NovT* 37 (1995): 385–99.
______. "The Structure of Hebrews from Three Perspectives." *TynBul* 45 (1994): 245–71.
Stegner, W. R. "The Ancient Jewish Synagogue Homily." On pages 51–69 of *Greco-Roman Literature and the New Testament: Selected Forms and Genres*. Edited by D. E. Aune. SBLSBS 21. Atlanta: Scholars, 1988.
Stewart, R. A. "Creation and Matter in the Epistle to the Hebrews." *NTS* 12 (1965–66): 284–93.
______. "The Sinless High-Priest." *NTS* 14 (1967–68): 126–35.
Stowers, S. K. *The Diatribe and Paul's Letter to the Romans*. SBLDS 57. Chico, Calif.: Scholars, 1981.
______. *Letter Writing in Greco-Roman Antiquity*. Philadelphia: Westminster, 1986.
Strack, H., and G. Stemberger. *Introduction to the Talmud and Midrash*. Minneapolis: Fortress, 1992.
Stranahan, B. P. "Bunyan and the Epistle to the Hebrews: His Source for the Idea of Pilgrimage in *The Pilgrim's Progress*." *Studies in Philology* 79 (1982): 279–96.
______. "Bunyan's Special Talent: Biblical Texts as 'Events' in *Grace Abounding* and *The Pilgrim's Progress*." *English Literary Renaissance* 11 (1981): 329–43.
Strobel, A. "Die Psalmengrundlage der Gethsemane-Parallele Hebr. 5,7ff." ZNW 45 (1954): 252–66.

______. *Untersuchungen zum eschatologischen Verzögerungsproblem, auf Grund der spätjüdisch-urchristlichen Geschichte von Habakuk 2,2ff.* NovTSup 2. Leiden: Brill, 1961.
Stuckenbruck, L. T. *Angel Veneration and Christology: A Study in Early Judaism and the Christology of the Apocalypse of John.* WUNT 70. Tübingen: Mohr/Siebeck, 1995.
Stylianopoulos, T. G. "Shadow and Reality: Reflections on Hebrews 10:1–18." *GOTR* 17 (1972): 215–30.
Swetnam, J. "Christology and the Eucharist in the Epistle to the Hebrews." *Bib* 70 (1989): 74–95.
______. "Form and Content in Hebrews 1–6." *Bib* 53 (1972): 368–85.
______. "Form and Content in Hebrews 7–13." *Bib* 55 (1974): 333–48.
______. " 'The Greater and More Perfect Tent'. A Contribution to the Discussion of Heb. 9:11." *Bib* 47 (1966): 91–106.
______. "Hebrews 9,2 and the Uses of Consistency." *CBQ* 32 (1970): 205–21.
______. "Hebrews 10,30–31: A Suggestion." *Bib* 75 (1994): 388–94.
______. "Hebrews 11: An Interpretation." *MelT* 41 (1990): 97–114.
______. "Hebrews 11,1–13,24: A Suggested Structure." *MelT* 47 (1996): 27–40.
______. *Jesus and Isaac: A Study of the Epistle to the Hebrews in the Light of the Aqedah.* AnBib 94. Rome: Biblical Institute, 1981.
______. "Jesus as λόγος in Hebrews 4:12–13." *Bib* 62 (1981): 214–24.
______. "On the Imagery and Significance of Heb. 9:9–10." *CBQ* 28 (1966): 155–73.
______. "On the Literary Genre of the 'Epistle' to the Hebrews." *NovT* 11 (1969): 261–69.
______. "A Possible Structure of Hebrews 3,7–10,39." *MelT* 45 (1994): 127–41.
______. "Sacrifice and Revelation in the Epistle to the Hebrews. Observations and Surmises on Hebrews 9,26." *CBQ* 30 (1968): 227–34.
______. "The Structure of Hebrews 1,1–3,6." *MelT* 43 (1992): 58–66.
______. "A Suggested Interpretation of Hebrews 9,15–18." *CBQ* 27 (1965): 373–90.
______. "Why Was Jeremiah's New Covenant New?" Pages 111–15 in *Studies on Prophecy* .VTSup 26, 1974.
Talbert, C. H. *Learning through Suffering: The Educational Value of Suffering in the New Testament and Its Milieu.* Collegeville, Minn.: Liturgical, 1991.
Tanner, N. P. *Decrees of the Ecumenical Councils.* London: Sheed & Ward and Washington, D.C.: Georgetown University, 1990.
Taubenschlag, R. *The Law of Greco-Roman Egypt in the Light of the Papyri.* 2nd ed. Warsaw: Panstwowe Wydawnictwo Naukowe, 1955.
Tcherikover, V. *Hellenistic Civilization and the Jews.* New York: Atheneum, 1982.
Theissen, G. *Untersuchungen zum Hebräerbrief.* SNT 2. Gütersloh: Mohn, 1969.
Theobald, M. "Vom Text zum 'lebendigen Wort' (Hebr 4,14)." Pages 751–90 in *Jesus Christus als die Mitte der Schrift: Studien zur Hermeneutik des Evangeliums.* Edited by C. Landmesser, H.-J. Eckstein, and H. Lichtenberger. BZNW 86. Berlin and New York: de Gruyter, 1997.
______. " 'Wir haben hier keine bleibende Stadt, sondern suchen eine zukünftige' (Hebr 13,14). Die Stadt als Ort der frühen christlichen Gemeinde." *TGl* 78 (1988): 16–40.
______. "Zwei Bünde und ein Gottesvolk: Die Bundestheologie des Hebräerbriefs im Horizont des christlich-jüdischen Gesprächs." *TQ* 176 (1996): 309–25.
Theron, D. *Evidence of Tradition.* Grand Rapids: Baker, 1958.
Thomas, J. " 'Comme s'il voyait l'invisible' (Épître aux Hébreux 11,27)." *Christus* 31 (1984): 261–71.
Thomas, K. J. "The Old Testament Citations in the Epistle to the Hebrews." *NTS* 11 (1964–65): 303–25.

Thompson, J. W. "The Hermeneutics of the Epistle to the Hebrews." *ResQ* 38 (1996): 229–37.

______. *The Beginnings of Christian Philosophy: The Epistle to the Hebrews.* CBQMS 13. Washington, D.C.: Catholic Biblical Association, 1982.

Thornton, T. C. G. "The Meaning of αἱματεχυσία in Heb IX.22." *JTS* 15 (1964): 63–65.

Thurén, J. *Das Lobopfer der Hebräer: Studien zum Aufbau und Anliegen vom Hebräerbrief* 13. Åbo: Akademi, 1973.

______. "Gebet und Gehorsam des Emiedrigten (Hebr. V.7–10 noch einmal)." *NovT* 13 (1971): 136–46.

Thurston, R. W. "Midrash and 'Magnet' Words in the New Testament. *EvQ 51* (1979): 22–39.

______. "Philo and the Epistle to the Hebrews." *EvQ* 58 (1986): 133–43.

Thüsing, W. "Das Opfer der Christen nach dem Neuen Testament." *BibLeb* 6 (1965): 37–50.

______. " 'Lasst uns hinzutreten . . .' (Hebr 10,22). Zur Frage nach dem Sinn der Kulttheologie im Hebräerbrief." *BZ* 9 (1965): 1–17.

______. " 'Milch' und 'feste Speise.' " *TTZ* 76 (1967): 233–46, 261–80.

Thyen, H. *Der Stil der jüdisch-hellenistischen Homilie.* FRLANT 47. Göttingen: Vandenhoeck & Ruprecht, 1955.

Toussaint, S. D. "The Eschatology of the Warning Passages in the Book of Hebrews." *GTJ* 3 (1982): 67–80.

Trilling, W. " 'Jesus der Urbeher und Vollender des Glaubens' (Hebr XII,2)." Pages 3–23 in *Das Evangelium auf dem Weg zum Menschen. Festschrift H. Kahlefeld.* Frankfurt: Knecht, 1973.

Trompf, G. W. "The Conception of God in Hebr. 4:12–13." *ST* 25 (1971): 123–32.

Trotter, A. H. *Interpreting the Epistle to the Hebrews.* Grand Rapids: Baker, 1997.

Trudinger, L. P. " 'ΚΑΙ ΓΑΡ ΔΙΑ ΒΡΑΧΕΩΝ ΕΠΕΣΤΕΙΛΑ ΥΜΙΝ:' A Note on Hebrews XIII.22." *JTS* 23 (1972): 128–30.

______. "The Gospel Meaning of the Secular: Reflections on Hebrews 13:10–13." *EvQ* 54 (1982): 235–37.

Übelacker, W. G. *Der Hebräerbrief als Appel: Untersuchungen zur Exordium, Narratio und Postscriptum (Hebr 1–2 und 13,22–25).* ConB 21. Stockholm: Almquist & Wiksell, 1989.

Ulrichsen, J. H. "Διαφορώτερον ὄνομα in Hebr. 1.4: Christus als Träger des Gottesnamens." *ST* 38 (1984): 65–75.

Vaganay, L. "Le plan de l'épître aux Hébreux." Pages 269–77 in *Mémorial Lagrange.* Paris: Gabalda, 1940.

VanderKam, J. C. *Enoch: A Man for All Generations.* Columbia, S.C.: University of South Carolina, 1995.

Vanhoye, A. "Anamnèse historique et créativité théologique dans l'épître aux Hébreux." Pages 219–31 in *Le mémoire et le temps: mélanges offerts à Pierre Bonnard.* Edited by D. Maguerat and J. Zumstein. Geneva: Labor et Fides, 1991.

______. "Esprit éternel et feu du sacrifice en Hé 9,14." *Bib* 64 (1983): 263–74.

______. "Heb 6:7–8 et le mashal rabbinique." Pages 527–32 in *The New Testament Age: Essays in Honor of Bo Reicke.* Edited by W. C. Weinrich. Vol. 2. Macon, Ga.: Mercer University, 1984.

______. "La question littéraire de Hébreux xiii. 1–6." *NTS* 23 (1976–77): 121–39.

______. *La structure littéraire de l'épître aux Hébreux.* 2nd ed. Paris: Desclée de Brouwer, 1976.

______. "La 'teleiosis' du Christ: Point capital de la Christologie sacerdotale d'Hébreux." *NTS* 42 (1996): 321–38.

______. "Le Christ, grand-prêtre selon Hébreux 2.17–18." *NRTh* 91 (1969): 449–74.

______. "Le Dieu de la Nouvelle Alliance dans l'épître aux Hébreux." Pages 315–30 in *La notion biblique de Dieu*. Edited by J. Coppens. BETL 41. Gembloux: Duculot, 1976.

______. "L'Épître aux Ephésiens et l'épître aux Hébreux." *Bib* 59 (1978): 198–230.

______. "L'οἰκουμένη dans l'épître aux Hébreux." *Bib* 45 (1964): 248–53.

______. "L'ombre et l'image: discussions sur He 10,1." Pages 267–82 in *Ouvrir les Ecritures: Mélanges offerts à Paul Beauchamp à l'occasion de ses soixant-six ans*. Edited by P. Beauchamp, P. Bovati, and M. Roland. Paris: Cerf, 1995.

______. "Longue marche ou accès tout proche? Le contexte biblique de Hébreux 3,7–4,11." *Bib* 49 (1968): 9–26.

______. "L'oracle de Natan dans l'Épître aux Hébreux." Pages 146–52 in *Gesù Apostolo e sommo Sacerdote: Studi biblici in memoria de Teodorico Ballarini*. Edited by L. Provera. Casale Monferrato: Marietti, 1984.

______. *Old Testament Priests and the New Priest According to the New Testament*. Petersham, Mass.: St. Bede's, 1986.

______. *Our Priest is Christ: The Doctrine of the Epistle to the Hebrews*. Rome: Biblical Institute, 1977.

______. " 'Par la tente plus grande et plus parfaite . . . ' (He 9,11)." *Bib* 46 (1965): 1–28.

______. *Situation du Christ: Hébreux 1–2*. Paris: Cerf, 1969.

______. "Situation et signification de Hébreux V.1–10." *NTS* 23 (1976–77): 445–56.

______. *Structure and Message of the Epistle to the Hebrews*. Rome: Biblical Institute, 1989.

Vaux, R. de. *Ancient Israel*. New York: McGraw-Hill, 1965.

Verbrugge, V. D. "Towards a New Interpretation of Hebrews 6:4–6." *CTJ* 15 (1980): 61–73.

Verme, M. del. "La 'prima decima' giudaica nella pericope di *Ebrei* 7,1–10." *Hen* 8 (1986): 339–63.

Vincent Cernuda, A. V. "La introducción del Primogénito, segun Hebr. 1,6." *EstBib* 39 (1981): 107–53.

Vögtle, A. "Das Neue Testament und die Zukunft des Kosmos. Hebr. 12,26f. und das Endschicksal des Kosmos." *BibLeb* 10 (1969): 239–54.

Vorster, W. S. "The Meaning of ΠΑΡΡΗΣΙΑ in the Epistle to the Hebrews." *Neot* 5 (1971): 51–59.

Walker, P. W. L. "Jerusalem in Hebrews 13:9–14 and the Dating of the Epistle." *TynBul* 45 (1994): 39–71.

______. *Jesus and the Holy City: New Testament Perspectives*. Grand Rapids: Eerdmans, 1996.

Wall, R. W., and W. L. Lane. "Polemic in Hebrews and the Catholic Epistles." Pages 166–98 in *Anti-Semitism and Early Christianity*. Edited by C. A. Evans and D. A. Hagner. Minneapolis: Fortress, 1993.

Wallis, I. G. *The Faith of Jesus Christ in Early Christian Traditions*. SNTSMS 84. Cambridge: Cambridge University, 1995.

Walter, N. "Christologie und irdischer Jesus im Hebräerbrief." Pages 64–82 in *Das lebendige Word: Beiträge zur kirchlichen Verkundigung. Festgabe für Gottfried Voigt zum 65. Geburtstag*. Edited by H. Seidl and K. Bieritz. Berlin: Evangelische, 1982.

Walters, J. R. *Perfection in New Testament Theology*. Lewiston, N.Y.: Mellen, 1994.

______. "The Rhetorical Arrangement of Hebrews." *AsTJ* 51 (1996): 59–70.
Wansink, C. S. *Chained in Christ: The Experience and Rhetoric of Paul's Imprisonments.* JSNTSup 130. Sheffield: Academic, 1996.
Watson, D. F. "Rhetorical Criticism of Hebrews and the Catholic Epistles Since 1978." *CurBS* 5 (1997): 175–207.
Weeks, N. "Admonition and Error in Hebrews." *WTJ* 39 (1976): 72–80.
Weinfeld, M. "Jeremiah and the Spiritual Metamorphosis of Israel." *ZAW* 88 (1976): 17–56.
Weiss, H. "*Sabbatismos* in the Epistle to the Hebrews." *CBQ* 58 (1996): 674–89.
Weiss, W. *"Zeichen und Wunder: Eine Studie zu der Sprachtradition und ihrer Verwendung im Neuen Testament."* WMANT 67. Neukirchen-Vluyn: Neukirchener, 1995.
Welch, A. *The Authorship of the Epistle to the Hebrews.* Edinburgh: Anderson & Ferrier, 1898.
Wengst, K. *Christologische Formeln und Lieder des Urchristentums.* SUNT 7. Gütersloh: Mohn, 1972.
______. *Pax Romana and the Peace of Jesus Christ.* Philadelphia: Fortress, 1987.
Wenschkewitz, H. *Die Spiritualisierung der Kultusbegriffe Tempel, Priester und Opfer im Neuen Testament.* Angelos Beiheft 4. Leipzig: Pfeiffer, 1932.
Westerholm, S. *Israel's Law and the Church's Faith: Paul and his Recent Interpreters.* Grand Rapids: Eerdmans, 1988.
Westermann, C. *Genesis.* 3 vols. Minneapolis: Augsburg, 1984–86.
Wettstein, J. *Novum Testamentum Graecum.* Amsterdam: Dommeriana, 1751–52.
White, J. L. *Light from Ancient Letters.* Philadelphia: Fortress, 1986.
Wider, D. *Theozentrik und Bekenntnis: Untersuchungen zur Theologie des Redens Gottes im Hebräerbrief.* BZNW 87. Berlin: de Gruyter, 1997.
Wiid, J. S. "The Testamental Significance of διαθήκη in Hebrews 9:15–22." *Neot* 26 (1992): 149–56.
Wilcox, M. " 'According to the Pattern (TBNYT) . . . ': Exodus 25,40 in the New Testament and Early Jewish Thought." *RevQ* 13 (1988): 647–56.
______. "The Bones of Joseph: Hebrews 11.22." Pages 114–30 in *Scripture: Meaning and Method.* Edited by B. P. Thompson. Hull: Hull University, 1987.
Wiles, G. P. *Paul's Intercessory Prayers: The Significance of the Intercessory Prayer Passages in the Letters of Paul.* SNTSMS 24. Cambridge: Cambridge University, 1974.
Willi, T. "Melchizedek: Der alte und der neue Bund im Hebräerbrief im Lichte der rabbinischen Tradition über Melchizedek." *Jud* 42 (1986): 158–70.
Williamson, R. "The Background of the Epistle to the Hebrews." *ExpTim* 87 (1975–76): 232–37.
______. "The Eucharist and the Epistle to the Hebrews." *NTS* 21 (1974–75): 300–312.
______. "Hebrews 4:15 and the Sinlessness of Jesus." *ExpTim* 86 (1974–75): 4–8.
______. "The Incarnation of the Logos in Hebrews." *ExpTim* 95 (1983): 4–8.
______. *Philo and the Epistle to the Hebrews.* Leiden: Brill, 1970.
Willis, T. M. " 'Obey Your Leaders': Hebrews 13 and Leadership in the Church." *ResQ* 36 (1994): 316–26.
Wills, L. "The Form of the Sermon in Hellenistic Judaism and Early Christianity." *HTR* 77 (1984): 277–99.
Winston, D. "Creation Ex Nihilo Revisited: A Reply to Jonathan Goldstein." *JJS* 37 (1986): 88–91.
Winter, J. G. *Life and Letters in the Papyri.* Ann Arbor: University of Michigan, 1933.
Witherington, B., III. "The Influence of Galatians on Hebrews." *NTS* 37 (1991): 146–52.

———. *The Jesus Quest: The Third Search for the Jew of Nazareth.* Downers Grove: InterVarsity, 1995.

———. *Jesus the Sage: The Pilgrimage of Wisdom.* Minneapolis: Fortress, 1994.

Wolff, C. *Jeremia im Frühjudentum und Urchristentum.* TU 118. Berlin: Akademie, 1976.

Wolmarans, J. L. P. "The Text and Translation of Hebrews 8.8." ZNW 75 (1984): 139–44.

Worley, D. R. "Fleeing to Two Immutable Things, God's Oath-Taking and Oath-Witnessing: The Use of Litigant Oath in Hebrews 6:12–20." *ResQ* 36 (1994): 223–36.

Wray, J. H. *Rest as a Theological Metaphor in the Epistle to the Hebrews and the Gospel of Truth.* SBLDS 166. Atlanta: Scholars, 1998.

Wrede, W. *Das literarische Rätsel des Hebräerbriefes.* FRLANT 8. Göttingen: Vandenhoeck & Ruprecht, 1906.

Wrege, H. T. "Jesusgeschichte und Jüngergeschick nach Joh 12,20–23 und Hebr 5,7–10." Pages 259–88 in *Der Ruf Jesu und die Antwort der Gemeinde: Festschrift Joachim Jeremias.* Edited by E. Lohse. Göttingen: Vandenhoeck & Ruprecht, 1970.

Wright, N. T. *Jesus and the Victory of God.* Minneapolis: Fortress, 1996.

Yadin, Y. "The Dead Sea Scrolls and the Epistle to the Hebrews." *ScrHier* 4 (1958): 36–55.

Yeo, K.-K. "The Meaning and Usage of the Theology of 'Rest' (σαββατισμός and κατάπαυσις in Hebrews 3:7–4:13)." *AJT* 5 (1991): 2–33.

Young, F. M. "Christological Ideas in the Greek Commentaries on the Epistle to the Hebrews." *JTS* 20 (1969): 150–63.

———. *The Use of Sacrificial Ideas in Greek Christian Writers from the New Testament to John Chrysostom.* Patristic Monograph Series 5. Cambridge, Mass.: Philadelphia Patristic Foundation, 1979.

Young, N. H. "Αἱματεχησία: A Comment." *ExpTim* 90 (1979): 180.

———. "The Gospel according to Hebrews 9." *NTS* 27 (1980–81): 198–210.

———. "Is Hebrews 6.1–8 Pastoral Nonsense?" *Colloq* 15 (1982): 52–57.

———. "τοῦτ' ἔστιν τῆς σαρκὸς αὐτοῦ (Heb. x.20): Apposition, Dependent or Explicative?" *NTS* 20 (1973–74): 100–14.

Zerwick, M. *Biblical Greek.* Rome: Biblical Institute, 1963.

Zesati Estrada, C. *Hebreos 5,7–8. Estudio histórico-exegético.* AnBib 113. Rome: Biblical Institute, 1990.

Zimmermann, H. *Das Bekenntnis der Hoffnung: Tradition und Redaktion im Hebräerbrief.* BBB 47. Köln: Hanstein, 1977.

———. *Die Hohepriester-Christologie des Hebräerbriefes.* Paderborn: Schöningh, 1964.

Zuntz, G. *The Text of the Epistles: A Disquisition upon the Corpus Paulinum.* London: Oxford University, 1953.

Translation, Notes, and Comments

1. The Title

NOTES

To the Hebrews. The superscription *pros Ebraious* appears on P^{46} (ca. A.D. 200) and later MSS (א A B etc.). By the late second and early third centuries, similar titles were used by Greek writers like Pantaenus, Clement of Alexandria, and Irenaeus (Eusebius, *Eccl. Hist.* 5.26.1; 6.14.4; 6.25.11) as well as by Latin-speaking Christians (Tertullian, *On Modesty* 20). Some MSS place the title after 13:25.

COMMENT

The title "To the Hebrews" regularly appears as a preface to the text, subtly shaping the reader's expectations about what will follow. In the early church the title both reflected and reinforced a way of understanding the circumstances in which Hebrews was composed. Alexandrian scholars taught that Hebrews was written by Paul in the Hebrew language and later translated into Greek (Eusebius, *Eccl. Hist.* 6.13.2–4). The book's presentation of Christ in light of the institutions of Israel suggested that it addressed readers of Jewish descent. Nevertheless, the title was almost certainly not part of the earliest text of Hebrews, since letter writers often identified their intended audience in salutations, whereas superscriptions were added later when a number of writings were put into a single collection.[1]

The form of the title "To the Hebrews" (*pros Ebraious*) corresponds to those on the Pauline letters (e.g., "To the Romans," *pros Romaious*), which identify the letters according to their intended recipients. This form strengthened the traditional connection between Hebrews and the Pauline corpus. Nevertheless, the titles on the Pauline letters regularly paraphrase information found in the salutations (Rom 1:7; 1 Cor 1:2, etc.),[2] but Hebrews has no salutation and the term "Hebrews" never appears in the body of the work. Some have proposed that the salutation was lost or omitted,[3] but as early as the second century, interpreters observed that Hebrews lacked the usual identification of the author, and there is no MS evidence that Hebrews ever had a salutation (Eusebius, *Eccl. Hist.* 6.13.3–4).

The word "Hebrews" in the title has been taken both ethnically and symbolically:

(**a**) Ethnic Interpretation. Many have thought that "Hebrews" referred to people of Jewish ancestry who believed in Jesus.[4] The MT, the LXX, and non-Jewish authors use "Hebrew" as an ethnic designation that is virtually synonymous

---

[1]Westcott, *Epistle*, xxvii; cf. Thyen, *Stil*, 16; Grässer, *Hebräer*, 1.41–45; F. F. Bruce, *Epistle*, 4; Bickerman, "En marge," 32.

[2]The one exception is Ephesians where the comment that the addressees were located "in Ephesus" (Eph 1:1) is missing in many significant MSS.

[3]That the salutation was lost or omitted by a scribe was suggested by Jacques Lefèvre d'Etaples (Hagen, *Theology*, 23; cf. Ellingworth, *Epistle*, 61–62). An alternative suggestion is that a salutation was not written but conveyed orally through the person who carried the letter (B. Weiss, *Brief*, 28).

[4]Since Chrysostom, most have recognized that the intended recipients are Christians. An exception is Kosmala, who considers them to be unconverted Essenes (*Hebräer*, 44–75).

with "Jew."[5] By the first century A.D. the term had acquired an archaic quality since the OT uses "Hebrews" almost exclusively for the early history of Israel (Gen 14:13; 37:1–50:26; Exod 1:1–10:29; 1 Sam 1–31).[6] Entitling a work "To the Hebrews" seems to emphasize the connection between the intended readers and Israel's early ancestors.

The addressees have sometimes been envisioned as people in Palestine who spoke Hebrew or Aramaic. Inscriptions from Rome and Corinth, however, mention a "synagogue of the Hebrews" in each place. Their members may have come from Palestine or perhaps spoke Hebrew,[7] but in either case the inscriptions show that "Hebrews" lived outside of Palestine. Some have proposed that the author of Hebrews belonged to the Hellenist Christian circle associated with Stephen and that he called the more traditional "Hebrew" wing of the Jerusalem church to move beyond the Levitical system of religious life (Acts 6:1).[8] This seems unlikely however, since Hebrews was written in Greek using a Greek form of the OT, which does not seem fitting for an audience of Hebrew-speaking Christians based in Jerusalem.[9] Moreover, Paul referred to himself and to other Christians of Jewish background as Hebrews even though they spoke Greek and worked outside of Palestine (2 Cor 11:22; Phil 3:5).

(b) Symbolic Interpretation. Some suggest that "Hebrews" identifies the audience symbolically as pilgrims passing through this world, like Abraham, who was a transient on earth (Heb 11:13–16). Linguistically, the Hebrew words "Hebrew" (*'ibri*) and "pass through" (*'abar*) are based on the root letters *'br*. Although the LXX translator took "Hebrew" in Gen 14:13 to mean "sojourner" (*peratēs*; cf. Philo, *Migration* 20; Jerome, *On Jeremiah* 1.14),[10] Hebrews does not include the usual Greek equivalent for "Hebrew" (*peratēs*) or otherwise allude to the Hebrew *'br*. It is unlikely that early readers would have caught the wordplay.

The title "To the Hebrews" reflects the view, common in the late second and early third centuries, that Hebrews was written by Paul in the Hebrew language for Jewish Christians. Whoever first affixed the title may have used the term "Hebrews" because its archaic quality and connections with sojourning suited the

---

[5]On ethnic usage see Gen 39:14, 17; Exod 1:19; 2:11; 1 Sam 4:6; Jdt 10:12; 2 Macc 15:37. See further *GLAJJ* 2.161; Bickerman, "En marge," 32–33.

[6]See K. G. Kuhn, *TDNT* 3.367–68. On "Hebrew" as an ethnic designation see also N. P. Lemche, "Hebrew," *ABD* 3.95. The only occurrences of "Hebrew" outside the Pentateuch and 1 Samuel are in Jer 34:9, 14—which recall Exod 21:2 and Deut 15:12—and in Jonah 1:9.

[7]See Schürer, *History*, 3.97; Deissmann, *Light*, 16–17 n. 7; Solin, "Juden," 647–51.

[8]Possible connections between the book of Hebrews and the group mentioned in Acts 6:1 were noted by Theodore Beza (d. 1605). See Hagen, *Hebrews*, 91. The connection was more fully developed by Manson, *Epistle*, 44; cf. Murray, "Jews," 194–208.

[9]On possible connections between the author and the Hellenists see p. 57. Early tradition assumed that the addressees spoke the Hebrew language (Eusebius, *Eccl. Hist.* 6.13.2; 6.25.11–13). Nevertheless, the author explains the meaning of the Hebrew name Melchizedek (7:2) and formulates some arguments that are possible only on the basis of the Greek rather than the Hebrew OT (p. 116).

[10]Johannes Oecolampadius, noted in Hagen, *Hebrews*, 33; cf. Windisch, *Hebräerbrief*, 6–7; Käsemann, *Wandering*, 240 n. 182; Spicq, *L'Épître*, 1.243–46; idem, "Apollos," 372–73. Jewett entitled his commentary *Letter to Pilgrims*.

biblical motifs used in the piece, but there is little to suggest that the title was based on any knowledge of the circumstances of composition that was available independent of the text. The title appears to be an inference made by later generations based on the book's contents, and it can best be treated as an early "commentary" on the book. We cannot base historical reconstructions about the circumstances of composition on it, nor should it be a dominant feature in the shaping of interpretation (Grässer, *Hebräer,* 1.45).

I. Exordium

◆

2. The Exordium (1:1–2:4)

COMMENT

Hebrews begins with what can be called an exordium according to the canons of classical rhetoric.[11] The exordium was an introduction that was designed to make the audience receptive to the rest of what the speaker had to say. Interpreters often identify the exordium as the first sentence (1:1–4) because the style shifts from elevated poetry in 1:1–4 to a series of biblical quotations in 1:5–13, and the content changes from God's revelation in the Son in 1:1–4 to the Son's superiority to the angels in 1:5–13.[12] There are, however, reasons to think that the exordium encompasses 1:1–2:4.[13] In style, the introduction begins and ends with complex sentences known as periods (1:1–4; 2:2–4), which often introduced and concluded sections of an argument by drawing together the speaker's main points.[14] In content, the periods frame the exordium by dealing with God's mode of speaking (*lalein*, 1:1–2; 2:2–4).

Structurally, the exordium has three sections. The first (1:1–4) deals with the way God spoke through the prophets and through a Son. The second (1:5–14) consists of biblical passages that offer biblical support for the portrayal of the Son that was given in 1:1–4. The third (2:1–4) pulls together what has been said into an appeal for attention. The major shift in subject matter comes after 2:4, where the author begins considering Jesus' suffering, the topic that will be developed in the remainder of the speech. Thus, the exordium introduces the main topic of the speech indirectly (Quintilian, *Inst.* 4.1.30). The depiction of the Son of God enthroned in heaven has an important *preparatory* function: it provides a perspective from which the meaning of Jesus' death can be comprehended by reminding listeners that exaltation followed his crucifixion.

Comparison with other speeches suggests that an exordium extending from 1:1 to 2:4 would have been appropriate for Hebrews. The length of an exordium depended on the issue being addressed; a few sentences might be sufficient for

---

[11]Theodoret called Heb 1 the *prooemium* (PG 82.675A), and Augustine called it the *exordium*, perhaps in a nontechnical sense (PL 44.137). See also Calvin on Heb 1:1.

[12]Interpreters have identified the exordium as 1:1–3 (Ebrard, *Biblical Commentary*, 279; Delitzsch, *Commentary*, 1.39) and 1:1–4:13 (von Soden, *Brief*, 17). Recent commentators commonly use "exordium" for 1:1–4 (Attridge; Lane; H.-F. Weiss; Bénétreau; Übelacker, *Hebräerbrief*, 106; Backhaus, *Der neue*, 58–59).

[13]Interpreters who have identified 1:1–2:4 as a unit without calling it an "exordium" include Bengel, Stuart, Riggenbach, Hegermann. Cf. Wills, "Form," 281.

[14]On the form and rhetorical function of periods see BDF §464; *Rhet. ad Her.* 4.19.27; Quintilian, *Inst.* 9.4.128; Lausberg, *Handbook* §947.

simple matters, while longer introductions were used for more complex issues (Quintilian, *Inst.* 9.4.125). An exordium might be as brief as Heb 1:1–4 (e.g., Demosthenes, *Exordia* 3; 51), but speakers typically allowed themselves at least two to three hundred words of introduction—several minutes in delivery time—and they frequently went longer. Hebrews is a speech that would have taken about forty-five or fifty minutes to deliver, and an exordium lasting for three to four minutes—about three hundred and twenty words (1:1–2:4)—would have been appropriate for a speech of this scope and complexity.[15]

An exordium was to make listeners attentive and ready to receive instruction (*Rhet. ad Her.* 1.4.6; Quintilian, *Inst.* 4.1.5). Hebrews achieves this, in part, through masterful use of rhetorical conventions. The elevated style of the first sentence is reminiscent of the oratory of Isocrates,[16] and words beginning with the letter *p* catch the listener's ear: *polymerōs kai polytropōs palai ho theos lalēsas tois patrasin en tois prophētais* ("God, having spoken on many occasions and in many forms to the fathers of old by the prophets," Heb 1:1). A speaker could gain attention by announcing that he would address matters that were new or unusual, or that pertained to the listeners or to God, and this is what the author of Hebrews does in 1:1–2, where God's recent word "to us" is the focus. Attention could also be secured through an appeal to listen carefully, which is what the author does in 2:1–4.[17]

The author also altered conventions to suit the content of his speech. Writers often began by referring to the "many" (*poly-*) things that people had said previously about a subject. For example, Demosthenes began, "Many speeches are delivered, men of Athens, at almost every meeting of the Assembly."[18] Hebrews, however, shifts the level of discourse from human speech to divine speech (Calvin, *Epistle*, 5):

GOD

having spoken	has spoken
of old	in these final days
by the prophets	by a Son
to the fathers	to us

Presenting God as speaker was unconventional rhetorically and significant theologically. Some speeches opened with an appeal that God might help the speaker,[19] but Heb 1:1–4 centers on God himself as the speaker. The scriptural quo-

[15]Cf. Walters, "Rhetorical," 64; Cockerill, *Hebrews*, 31. Compare the opening of Romans (Rom 1:1–15), which begins with a period (1:1–6). The thesis follows the introduction in Rom 1:16–17 as in Heb 2:5–9.

[16]*Rhet. ad Her.* 3.12.21; Moffatt, *Critical*, lvi–lix; MHT 4.106–13.

[17]On gaining attention in the exordium, see *Rhet. ad Her.* 1.4.7; Lausberg, *Handbook* §270. For rhetorical questions in exordia, see Demosthenes, *Exordia* 35.4; 51; Dio Chrysostom, *Disc.* 1.10.

[18]*Third Philippic* 1; cf. *Exordia* 6.1; Dionysus of Halicarnassus, *First Letter to Ammaeus* 1; Luke 1:1–4; preface to Sirach.

[19]Philo, *Eternity* 1; cf. Plato, *Timaeus* 27b–c; Demosthenes, *On the Crown* 1.1; *Letters* 1.1.

tations in 1:5–13 maintain the focus on God as speaker since the quotations are not prefaced with the formula "as it is written," but declare what God himself "said" or "says" (1:5, 6, 7, 13). Another distinctive element is the positive value given to what God has said in the present, since speakers commonly considered contemporary speech to be inferior to that of the past: People "of the present day, apart from a small fraction of them, do not resemble those of former times in their aims and actions," for language "that was once healthy and robust they have turned into a jargon hopelessly depraved."[20] By emphasizing the superiority of what was said "in these final days," the author reverses a widespread perception of decline. Many may have thought that human speech was degenerating, but God was not captive to the trend.

The exordium presented an opportunity for the speaker to make listeners well-disposed towards himself (pp. 91–92). Establishing a speaker's integrity was important, since what was said was more persuasive when listeners were confident that the speaker was reliable (Quintilian, *Inst.* 4.1.7). The author assumes that listeners will grant the integrity of God—the chief speaker (cf. Heb 6:13)—which is important for a speech that has to do with God's faithfulness to his promises (pp. 87–89). The author depicts himself first as a listener rather than a speaker (1:2; 2:3), but the exordium does help to establish his credibility indirectly. The exordium includes what is, in effect, a confession of faith concerning the exalted Christ so that when the author later asks listeners to hold fast to their confession (4:14; 10:23) and boldness (3:6; 4:16; 10:19), his appeal has integrity, for he does not ask them to do anything that he has not done already.

3. God Spoke by a Son (1:1–4)

1 [1]God, having spoken on many occasions and in many forms to the forebears
of old by the prophets, [2]has in these final days spoken to us by a Son, whom he
made heir of all things, through whom he also created the universe; [3]who, after
having made purification for sins, sat down at the right hand of the Majesty on
high as the radiance of his glory and the impress of his substance, bearing all
things by his word of power, [4]having become as superior to the angels as the
name he has inherited is more excellent than they.

NOTES

1:1. *God, having spoken on many occasions.* The witness of the prophets came on "many occasions" (*polymerōs*) over many generations. Some suggest that the prophetic witness was fragmentary or "partial" (NAB[2]; Attridge). Nevertheless, if no one prophetic message was complete, together they constituted a manifold corpus.

[20]Philo, *Planting* 156–57. See Kennedy, *Art*, 446–64.

and in many forms. The word *polytropōs* has to do with the various forms in which divine speech was given, although here it is virtually synonymous with "many occasions" (Clement of Alexandria, *Stromata* 1.4.27.1). In a positive sense, both words could point to the "manifold" qualities of divine wisdom (Wis 7:22) and nature (Philo, *Moses* 1.117), so that Heb 1:1 can emphasize the scope and variety of the prophetic witness (Williamson, *Philo*, 70–74). In a negative sense, variety often connoted instability (Josephus, *Ant.* 1.8; 15.179; Philo, *Joseph* 32; cf. Homer, *Odyssey* 1.1–4), and God's "varied and manifold" nature meant that he was capable of judgment as well as blessing (Josephus, *Ant.* 10.142). The mixed connotations of the words in Heb 1:1 allow Hebrews to make positive use of the prophetic writings (e.g., 1:5–13), while insisting upon the superior word spoken through God's Son (cf. 7:23–24; 9:25–26; 10:11–12).

to the forebears of old. Hebrews uses "forebears" especially for Moses' generation (Heb 3:9 = Ps 95:9; Heb 8:9 = Jer 31:32), but "the forebears" presumably included all to whom the prophets came. The days "of old" contrast with the "final days" (1:2). Created things grow old and perish (1:11), and the Mosaic covenant, which has become old, is about to disappear (8:13). For many in the first century, prophecy was a phenomenon "of old," since some said that the succession of prophets ended four centuries earlier (Josephus, Ag. *Ap.* 1.41; *m. 'Abot* 1:1).

by the prophets. Hebrews quotes prophetic oracles ascribed to Moses (Heb 8:5), Nathan (Heb 1:5b), Isaiah (Heb 2:13), Jeremiah (Heb 8:8–12; 10:16–17), Habakkuk (Heb 10:37–38), and Haggai (Heb 12:26). The Psalms are attributed to David who is understood to have a prophetic role (Heb 4:7; cf. 2 Sam 23:2; Acts 2:30). Other figures in Hebrews who could be called prophets include Abraham (Gen 20:7), Aaron (Exod 7:1), and Joshua (Sir 46:1). In Heb 11:32 "the prophets" lived after the time of David (cf. Jer 7:25; Josephus, Ag. *Ap.* 1.40; *m. 'Abot* 1:1). The preposition *en* has an instrumental sense: God spoke "by [*en*] the prophets" and "by [*en*] a Son" (1:1–2a) just as messages were given at Sinai "through angels" and in later times "through the Lord" (2:2–3).

1:2. *has in these final days.* This expression for the future (Deut 4:30; Isa 2:2; Mic 4:1; Dan 10:14; Sir 48:24–25) came to have an eschatological sense. It introduced passages that came to be read messianically (Gen 49:1, 10; Num 24:14, 17; Hos 3:5). See also 1QpHab II, 5; 1QSa I, 1; 4QFlor I, 12; Acts 2:17; 2 Tim 3:1; cf. 1 Pet 1:5, 20. On eschatology see pp. 100–4.

spoken to us by a Son. In 1:1 the author used the participial form "speaking," but here the verb is indicative to show that the Son is God's definitive mode of communication. The absence of a definite article does not suggest that God's Son was merely "a son" among others; instead, it highlights the singularity of God's Son (cf. 3:6; 5:8; 7:28) in contrast to the multitude of prophets (cf. BDF §254; Isa 7:14; 9:6). When used christologically, "Son" is a synonym for "Son of God" (Heb 4:14; 6:6; 7:3; 10:29).

whom he made heir of all things. In human terms an heir is the one who can legitimately possess the testator's estate. A person would be designated as an heir while the testator was still alive, but would ordinarily not take possession of the estate until the testator died (cf. 9:16–17). A ruler would designate the son as his heir so that when the ruler died his son would govern the kingdom. The peculiarity here is that God—the testator—does not die; instead, the Son enters into his inheritance and kingly power through his own death and exaltation (Spicq; Vanhoye, *Situation*, 62–64). The Son's inheritance of "all things" through his resurrection and exaltation points to the fulfillment of God's promise that the heir of David's throne would receive the nations as his "inheritance" (Ps 2:8; cf. 89:27; Rom 4:13).

through whom he also created the universe. The term "universe" is the plural form of *aiōn*, which can be used temporally for "ages" and spatially for "worlds." Temporally (1:8; 6:20; 9:26) Hebrews distinguishes two ages: "the present time" (9:9) and the "age to come" (6:5). Some detect only the spatial sense of higher and lower "worlds" in 1:2 (Spicq; Attridge; Ellingworth), but the interplay between the temporal and spatial aspects elsewhere in Hebrews suggests that both should be included (Vanhoye, *Situation*, 65–66; Isaacs, *Sacred*, 193).

1:3. Two general questions should be considered before we turn to individual words and phrases.

(a) Syntax. *(i)* Most translations render the clauses in 1:3 in the order in which they appear in the Greek text. Meier ("Structure," 176–89) suggests that the sequence moves from the Son's exaltation (1:2b) to his preexistence (1:2c), his eternal relation to God the Father (1:3abc), and then his death and exaltation (1:3de). Lane (*Hebrews*, 1.5) takes the participles in a concessive sense: "This Son, although the radiance of God's glory . . . and although sustaining the universe . . . yet made purification for sins." *(ii)* An alternative is to show the time relationships suggested by the tenses of the participles and indicative verbs. Grammatically, aorist participles commonly indicated actions performed prior to the main verb: God spoke (aorist participle) by the prophets before he spoke (aorist indicative) by the Son (1:1–2a), and Jesus made purification (aorist participle) for sins through his death before he sat down (aorist indicative) at God's right hand (1:3; cf. Rom 1:3–5; 8:34). Present participles were used for actions contemporaneous with the main verb (Mayser, *Grammatik*, 2/1.175–76; MHT 3.79). For example, the aorist indicative "validated" and the present participle "corroborated the testimony" are concurrent (Heb 2:3c–4a; cf. 1 Thess 1:10; 1 Tim 6:16). Therefore, since "radiance of his glory" is introduced with the present participle *ōn*, which can indicate time contemporary with the main verb "he sat down" (Heb 1:3), glory is most directly related to the Son's exaltation. This sequencing does not exclude the idea of the Son's preexistence (pp. 104–5), but it focuses on the Son's present situation.

(b) Proposed Hymnic Sources. Some argue that 1:3 was a hymn to Christ that was used within the author's community. They detect a break between 1:2 and 1:3, where the subject shifts from God to Christ and the style becomes more elevated. The description of the Son in 1:3 is presented in balanced clauses and is introduced with the relative pronoun "who," which is typical of hymnic passages (cf. Phil 2:6; Col 1:15; 1 Tim 3:16). Using unusual vocabulary like "radiance," "impress," "purification," "substance," and "bearing" might suggest that the author was quoting from a source. The expression "at the right hand" is in the genitive case in Ps 110:1 LXX and in the quotation in Heb 1:13, but in 1:3 and elsewhere (8:1; 10:12; 12:2) it is in the dative case, which might mean that the author relied on a hymn rather than on the LXX. Finally, the passage traces the course of the Son from his preexistence to his existence in the flesh and exaltation, as do similar hymnic passages (Bornkamm, "Bekenntnis," 197–200; Deichgräber, *Gotteshymnus*, 137–40; J. T. Sanders, *New Testament*, 19–20; Zimmermann, *Bekenntnis*, 52–60; Loader, *Sohn*, 64–71; Übelacker, *Hebräerbrief*, 87).

There are, however, good reasons to think that this passage stems from the author. There is not a sharp break before 1:3, since the Son was already mentioned in 1:2b. Some of the vocabulary is distinctive, but none of it appears in other NT hymnic texts, making it less evident that the author was quoting a source. The variant forms of "at the right hand" may reflect the author's own idiom, because other NT authors freely paraphrase Ps 110:1 (Matt 26:64; Mark 14:62; Acts 7:55–56; Rom 8:34; Col 3:1; Eph 1:20; 1 Pet 3:22). Since the author uses Ps 110:1 flexibly, he presumably could have paraphrased a hymn. The most that can be said is that Heb 1:3 includes traditional elements (Frankowski, "Early"; Meier, "Symmetry," 524–28; Ellingworth, *Epistle*, 97–98; Bénétreau, *L'Épître*, 1.62).

who, after having made purification for sins. On purification see pp. 119–20. The participle is in the aorist tense, which is appropriate for the singular act of atonement Christ performed through his death. Some MSS (א[2] D[1] H 33 1881; cf. KJV) specify that purification was made for "our" sins, since Christ himself was sinless (4:15). Although the best MSS lack "our," this gloss is consistent with the argument of Hebrews. The translation follows the MSS (א A B 33 81 etc.) in which the reference to "word of power" is followed by "his," indicating that the word is the Son's. Other MSS (P^{46} 0121 424[c] 1739) say that Christ made purification "through himself." Zuntz (*Text*, 43–45) considers this to be the original reading, and Ehrman (*Orthodox*, 150–51) argues that the text was altered to counter the idea that Jesus accomplished purification on his own, without God. Those who prefer the shorter reading suggest that "through himself" attempts to bring out the middle voice of the verb *poiēsamenos* and that the additional words may have been inserted to stress that purification is made only through Jesus' self-offering (Braun; cf. *TCGNT*, 662).

sat down at the right hand. The language is from Ps 110:1 (NOTE on Heb 1:13). The seated position connoted authority; those who approached the throne normally stood while the ruler remained seated (Pliny the Younger, *Panegyricus* 64.2–3).

of the Majesty on high. Here and in 8:1 "Majesty" is a periphrasis for God. The term was not used in exactly this way in the LXX, but ascriptions of majesty frequently accompany references to God (e.g., Deut 32:3; Pss 79:11 [78:11 LXX]; 145:3, 6 [144:3, 6]; Jude 25; *1 Enoch* 5:4; 12:3; 14:16 [Greek]). God is also the one who dwells "on high" (Pss 93:4 [92:4]; 113:5 [112:5]).

as the radiance. This metaphor is based on the image of light. Many have asked how it depicts the Son's relationship to God. The noun *apaugasma* begins with *ap'*, which could mean that the Son actively radiates divine glory "out from"

God or that he more passively reflects "back" divine glory, like a mirror. If *apaugasma* is synonymous with "impress," which is usually understood passively, then the Son is the "reflection" of God's glory (Moffatt; Spicq; Héring), but if the terms are antithetical, then the Son is the "radiance" of divine glory (F. F. Bruce; P. E. Hughes). The same ambiguity appears in Wis 7:25–26, where *apaugasma* is used alongside "emanation" (*aporroia*) and "mirror." Many rightly acknowledge that in Heb 1:3 the word may show either radiance or reflection (Attridge; Bénétreau; Grässer). More important is that the text does not deal primarily with God's relationship *to* the Son, but with the way God communicates *through* the Son. The Son is the one through whom God's power and presence are brought into the realm of human experience (COMMENT *b*).

of his glory. Glory has to do with what God reveals of himself to human beings (Lev 9:23; Num 14:21–22; Isa 40:5). The OT ascribes to glory a luminous quality consistent with the idea of "radiance" (cf. Exod 24:16–17; 40:34–35; 1 Kgs 8:11). References to glory that "shines" around people is consonant with this revelatory quality (Isa 60:1–2; 2 Cor 4:6).

and the impress. This suggestive term (*charactēr*) functions as a metaphor parallel to "radiance." The term was often used for the image on a coin (LSJ 1977) or the impression left by a seal (Philo, *Drunkenness* 133). Two aspects should be noted: **(a)** Congruence. Calling the Son an impress emphasizes that God and the Son are congruent without explaining *how* they are alike. A statue was an impress that bore the characteristics of the person after whom it was patterned (MM, 683), and a child had the impress or *charactēr* of the parent (4 Macc 15:4). Jesus had a physical body whereas God does not. God was "without *charactēr*" in a physical sense (Philo, *Unchangeable* 55; cf. Exod 20:4; Isa 44:9–20). **(b)** Perceptibility. An impress was used for that which created an impression (Philo, *Planter* 18–20) and for the traits that enabled people to distinguish one person from another (*Posterity* 110; *Special Laws* 4.110). The word is similar to "image" (*eikōn*), which can be used for the way that Christ makes God known (2 Cor 4:4–6; Col 1:15). Jesus is God's "impress" because he reveals God's power, presence, and faithfulness.

of his substance. Translation of the Greek *hypostasis* is difficult because of its range of meanings and varied nuances in Hebrews (1:3; 3:14; 11:1; *TLNT* 3.421–23; H. Koester, *TDNT* 8.572–89). Moreover, the term functions in different ways in Trinitarian formulations. The Nicene Creed of A.D. 325 used *hypostasis* synonymously with *ousia* ("being"), insisting that the Father and the Son are of the same "being." By the Second Council of Chalcedon in A.D. 553, however, the two terms were distinguished, so there was one *ousia* ("being") in three *hypostases* or "persons" (cf. Origen, PG 11.1533; Eusebius, PG 24.908C; Greer, *Captain*, 72, 102). Translating *hypostasis* as "person" (KJV) fits the Chalcedonian formulation, while translating it "being" (NIV; NRSV; NAB2) recalls the earlier Nicene expression. "Substance" comes from the Latin *substantia*. Like *hypostasis* it is based on roots meaning to "stand under." The term "substance," which sounds peculiar in English, is useful here because *hypostasis* may have seemed unusual to the earliest readers of Hebrews. Philo used the verbal form *hyphistēmi* for God (*Worse* 160), but there is little evidence that people in the first century A.D. commonly referred to God's being as his *hypostasis*. In Wis 16:21, for example, God's *hypostasis* is the sustenance he provided for Israel in the wilderness. Hebrews may have used an unconventional word to stimulate interest.

Hypostasis and "substance" combine multiple aspects of meaning, like the tones in a musical chord: (**a**) Essential reality. Philosophical sources used "substance" for that which stands beneath appearances (Ps.-Aristotle, *On the Cosmos* 4 [395a]; Philo, *Dreams* 1.188) or as the reality that gives rise to appearance (*Eternity* 88, 92). Hebrews will address the contradiction between the glory promised to human beings and the inglorious conditions of life in the world by arguing that in Jesus the hidden reality of God is brought within the realm of human experience (2:8–9). (**b**) Steadfastness. The term sometimes points to the resolve behind acts of courage. Soldiers that are unwavering when facing the enemy are said to exhibit their "substance" (Polybius, *Histories* 4.50.10; 6.55.2; Josephus, *Ant.* 18.24). In Hebrews God is said to be unwavering in his purposes (Heb 6:17–18), and his faithfulness is the basis for human fidelity (3:14; 11:1). God's substance encompasses his being and faithfulness. Cf. NOTE on 11:1.

bearing all things. "Bearing" has several aspects of meaning: (**a**) Sustaining. God's wisdom or word is the power that sustains the universe (Wis 7:24; 8:1; Philo, *Dreams* 1.241). Similarly, Col 1:17 says that in the Son "all things hold together." Cf. Ps.-Aristotle *On the Cosmos* 6 (397b). In Heb 12:20 and 13:13 "bearing" means "enduring." (**b**) Guiding and governing. Those who "bear" something move it in a given direction. God was said to govern all things (Philo, *Heir* 7) by his word, which he "grasps as a rudder to guide all things" (Philo, *Migration* 6). Here the word of God's Son bears or directs all things. (**c**) Bringing into being. God "bears" and "generates all things" (Philo, *Heir* 36; cf. *Names* 192, 256; Williamson, *Philo*, 95–103). Although this is not the primary sense here, it fits what was said in 1:2 about God creating the universe through the Son.

by his word of power. In 1:2 the Son was the means by which God spoke to people. In 1:3 the Son is the one who speaks the word.

1:4. *having become as superior to the angels.* The term "superior" (*kreittōn*), which appears thirteen times in Hebrews, can be used for social status (7:7), access to God (7:19), an abiding covenant (7:22; 8:6), complete cleansing (9:23; 12:24), a heavenly inheritance (10:34; 11:16), salvation (6:9), and resurrection (11:35; cf. 11:40). The emphasis on superiority does not deny all value to the figures with whom Jesus is compared, such as the angels and Moses, but it does indicate that confidence is misplaced if it rests on something other than Christ. Although many have taken Jesus' superiority to be the dominant theme of Hebrews (e.g., Hagen, *Theology*, 31–55), it can better be understood as a method of argument (cf. Phil 2:9–10; Col 1:15–18; Eph 1:21; 1 Pet 3:22; Watson, "Rhetorical," 184–87). On angels see NOTE on Heb 1:5.

as the name. Two aspects of "name" can be distinguished: (**a**) Specific name. Although Ulrichsen ("Διαφορώτερον") argues that the name is "Lord" (cf. 1:8–10; Phil 2:9–11; Rev 19:12) and Vanhoye (*Old Testament*, 85–86) proposes that it is "high priest" (cf. Heb 2:17; 3:1), the prominence of "Son" in the context favors taking "Son" as "the name." Moreover, sonship encompasses lordship and priesthood. (**b**) Reputation. A name conveyed a reputation. To receive a "great name" was to receive honor and renown (Gen 12:2; 2 Sam 7:9; Sir 37:26; cf. 44:7–8). It was considered a blessing when sons reflected the honor accruing to a father's name (Sir 46:12; 1 Macc 2:51). Theologically, one who bears the name of God's "Son" in a singular sense is worthy of God's own glory (Heb 1:3).

he has inherited is more excellent than they. A person commonly received an inheritance *from* someone's "name" (*P.Oxy*. ##247.30–31; 249.8–9), and in the OT an estate was passed down according to the name of the father (Num 26:55; 27:4). Hebrews, however, speaks of inheriting the name itself. According to Roman practice, someone who was adopted as a son and heir took on his father's full name (*OCD* 1025). In imperial practice Augustus inherited the name Caesar, and his successors inherited both names: "Caesar" and "Augustus" (*RomCiv*, 1.644–45; 2.631–33).

COMMENT[21]

The elegant opening lines of Hebrews constitute an exordium, in which the speaker prepares the listeners to be attentive and receptive to his speech (§2 COMMENT). The author seems to assume that what is said in 1:1–4 would be familiar to the listeners. Rhetorically, it was good practice to establish common ground with an audience by reinforcing what they already knew to be true.[22] The author refers to "the fathers" and "the prophets" of Israel in 1:1, just as he later quotes prophetic texts and mentions figures from Israel's history in a manner that presumes that listeners will be familiar with them. In 1:2 he speaks about God's "Son" but he does not name Jesus until 2:9, assuming that readers already know the Son's identity. In 1:3 he speaks of the exaltation of the Son, a point that is never argued but one that underlies the entire speech. Moreover, much of 1:1–4 reflects early Christian tradition, which connected divine sonship with inheritance (Rom 8:17; Gal 4:7) and declared that God brought the world into being through the Son (1 Cor 8:6; Col 1:15–16; John 1:3), that Christ is the image of God (2 Cor 4:4; Col 1:15; cf. Phil 2:6), that God dealt with human sin through Christ's death (1 Cor 15:3; Col 1:20; John 1:29), and that Christ is now seated at God's right hand (Rom 8:34; Eph 1:20; Col 3:1), where he has inherited a great name (Phil 2:9).[23]

Despite these elements, 1:1–4 stands in some tension with the perspective of the intended audience (*Rhet. ad Her.* 1.4.7). If the exordium declares that the

---

[21]On 1:1–4 see D. A. Black, "Hebrews 1:1–4"; Dunn, *Christology*, 206–9; Elbert, "Chiastic"; Frankowski, "Early"; Garuti, "Il prologo"; Heininger, "Sündenreinigung"; Hurst, "Christology"; Laub, *Bekenntnis*, 14–27; Loader, *Sohn*, 62–73; Meier, "Structure"; O'Neill, "Who Is"; Parsons, "Son"; Schenck, "Keeping"; Übelacker, *Hebräerbrief*, 66–138; Ulrichsen, "Διαφορώτερον"; Vanhoye, *Situation*, 51–117; Wider, *Theozentrik*, 11–55; Witherington, *Jesus the Sage*, 275–82.

[22]See Lindars, *Theology*, 29; Isaacs, *Sacred*, 187; Übelacker, *Hebräerbrief*, 74.

[23]See Laub, *Bekenntnis*, 23–24; Lindars, *Theology*, 33–34.

Son of God is the "heir of all things" (1:2) and that he is "bearing all things by his word of power" (1:3), the proposition recognizes that "we do not yet *see* all things subjected to him" as God had promised (2:8). The lordship of Christ appears to be contradicted by the listeners' conflicted experience of life in the world. Nevertheless, in declaring that God has spoken by a Son, who is heir of all things, the author establishes a position from which he will later challenge those who are tempted to drift away from their Christian confession. Structurally, the initial section of the exordium consists of a single complex sentence (1:1–4). For convenience it can be divided into two parts, since God is the subject of the first half of the sentence (1:1–2) and the Son is the subject of the second half (1:3–4).[24]

a. God Has Spoken (1:1–2)

The first sentence of Hebrews presents listeners with God (1:1a), whose living presence is both threatening and attractive. As the speech unfolds, the author warns that "it is terrifying to fall into the hands of the living God," for God is a "consuming fire" whose judgments fall upon sinners and whose wrath condemns the disobedient (10:31; 12:29; 13:4; 3:11, 17). At the same time, the author assumes that listeners can be attracted to God and will want to draw near to him (7:19, 25).[25] God is known because he has spoken. Divine self-disclosure comes from divine speech.[26] It is fitting for Hebrews to begin with God's speaking, because human faith itself begins with God's address. People embark on a pilgrimage of faith because God has "called" them (Heb 3:1; 11:8); they persevere because God has uttered promises (6:12, 17), and they dare not shrink back because the word of God probes the heart (4:12). To reinvigorate the listeners, the author seeks to bring them into a renewed encounter with God's word.

God spoke "on many occasions and in many forms" (1:1b), an intriguing statement given the religious environment in which the author wrote. In antiquity there were many claims that various gods had spoken through oracles at shrines located throughout the Mediterranean world,[27] but Hebrews refers to the various ways in which one particular God had spoken. The manifold revelation mentioned in 1:1 finds its unity in one God, "the God,"[28] who is connected with a particular group: the forebears of Israel (Gen 26:24; 28:13; Exod 3:6). Israel's dis-

---

[24]On the style see D. A. Black, "Hebrews 1:1–4." Some discern chiastic structures within the text (P. E. Hughes, *Commentary*, 49; Lane, *Hebrews*, 1.6–7), while Meier finds numerical symmetry, with seven designations for Christ in 1:2b–4 corresponding to the seven OT citations in 1:5–14 ("Structure").

[25]The awe-inspiring aspects of God are essential for Hebrews' view of Christ as a mediator, since a mediator is important for those who are aware of the immensity and terrifying quality of God. Cf. Dunnill, *Covenant*, 72, 107, 159, 177, 194–95.

[26]See Grässer, *Hebräer*, 1.50; Vanhoye, *Situation*, 53–54; Übelacker, *Hebräerbrief*, 102.

[27]For example, Apuleius, *Metamorphoses* 11.4. On the oracles at Delphi, Didyma, Claros, and other places see Fox, *Pagans*, 168–261.

[28]Grässer (*Hebräer*, 1.49–50) points to the singularity of God assumed here, as in Deut 6:4; cf. Vanhoye, *Situation*, 52–53.

tinctive tradition sometimes created friction with non-Jews who asked, "Why, then, if they are citizens, do they not worship the same gods" as others do? (Josephus, *Ag. Ap.* 2.66; cf. Philo, *Rewards* 162). Jewish distinctiveness was generally tolerated, however, because it was understood to be a part of their ancestral religion.[29] The opening lines of Hebrews connect Christ with Israel's peculiar tradition so that the message that follows will be understood as a development of that tradition.

God's manner of speaking is further defined in that it took place "by the prophets" sent to Israel (Heb 1:1). The Scriptures recount the various ways in which God spoke to the prophets: God spoke with Moses face to face (Exod 33:11; Num 12:8; Deut 34:10), while others experienced visions (Isa 1:1; Ezek 1:1; Hos 12:10) and dreams (Num 12:6; Deut 13:1).[30] The emphasis in Heb 1:1, however, is not on the way God spoke *to* the prophets, but on the way God spoke *by* the prophets to other people. The prophets spoke on "many occasions," from Moses at Sinai (Exod 24:3; Heb 9:19) to Haggai after the exile (Ezra 5:1; Heb 12:26), and their proclamations took many forms. Nathan used a parable (2 Sam 12:1–6), Isaiah used a song (Isa 5:1–7), Jeremiah performed symbolic actions (Jer 19:1–15), and Ezekiel recounted visions (Ezek 1:1). The forms of speech vary, but it is the same God who speaks.

For many in the first century, prophecy was a phenomenon "of old" (1:1). Prophetic figures appeared from time to time, but their claims proved false,[31] and some lamented that the age of prophecy seemed to have passed: "there is no longer any prophet, and there is no one among us who knows how long" (Ps 74:9; cf. 1 Macc 9:27; cf. 2 *Bar.* 81:1, 3; 85:3; Pr Azar 15). Hebrews, however, says that God has not fallen silent, but has spoken "to us" (Heb 1:2). The word spoken through the prophets included both warning and promise. Through Moses God warned people not to approach Mount Sinai (Heb 12:18–21), and through Haggai he warned that earth and heaven would be shaken (12:26). Yet through Jeremiah God also promised mercy under a new covenant (Heb 8:8–12; 10:16–17). The warnings and the promises served the same end: that Israel remain faithful to God. As the author of Hebrews weaves OT texts into his speech, he maintains the interplay between the warnings designed to disturb those who are lethargic (Ps 95:7–11; Heb 3:7–11) and the promises designed to encourage those who are faltering (Jer 31:33–34; Heb 10:16–17) in order that his own listeners might persevere in faith (Hab 2:3–4; Heb 10:37–38; cf. Übelacker, *Hebräerbrief*, 115–18).

What is new is that God addressed the author and his contemporaries, not by prophets, but "by a Son" (1:2). This is a forceful way of describing what the lis-

---

[29]On accepting Jewish distinctiveness because of antiquity, see Tacitus, *History* 5.5. Jews were given certain rights that allowed them to observe their ancestral customs. See Josephus, *Ant.* 14.216–63. See also pp. 69–70.

[30]Medieval scholars identified dreams, open speech, and interior inspiration as the means by which prophets received revelations (Anselm of Laon, *Glossa ordinaria* on 1:1; Erasmus, *Paraphrase* of 1:1; cf. Philo, *Moses* 2.188–91).

[31]Josephus, *Ant.* 20.97–98, 169–70. See also Greenspahn, "Prophecy."

teners experienced, since they had not actually heard Jesus of Nazareth, but received the message from early Christian evangelists (2:3). The author could have said, "God spoke to the people of old by the prophets and now has spoken to us through the followers of Jesus," but there is no movement from multiple messengers in the past to multiple messengers in the present. Multiplicity gives way to the singularity of God's communication in the Son (NOTE on 1:1; cf. 7:23–24; 9:25–26; 10:11–12). The content of what God said may have included the message that Jesus preached (NOTES and COMMENT on 2:3 and pp. 65–66), but that is not the point here. If the prophets conveyed God's word by what they said, the Son conveyed God's word by who he was and what he did. God "speaks" by sending his Son to share in human blood, flesh, and death (2:14–18; 10:5; 13:12), and by exalting the Son to glory so that he might be a source of salvation for others (5:8–9; 7:25; Grässer, *Aufbruch*, 105, 126–28).

The author of Hebrews wrote during "these final days," which was a complex period (1:2a; pp. 100–4). A decisive shift occurred with the death of Christ at "the consummation of the ages" (9:26), when the order established by the Mosaic statutes in the present time was superseded (9:9) and the listeners experienced the powers of "the age to come" through God's Spirit (6:4–5; cf. 2:3–4). Nevertheless, the return of Christ (9:28), "the Day" of judgment (10:25), and the transformation of the world (12:26) have not yet occurred. Instead, Jesus' followers are subject to external threats like reproach, loss of property, imprisonment, as well as the internal threat posed by sin (10:32–34; 13:1–6).

Within this conflicted situation, the author declares that the Son of God has been "made heir of all things" (1:2b). Such a claim stands in tension with claims made by others. Many people considered the emperor to be heir of all things. Julius Caesar adopted Augustus to be his son and heir, and since Augustus, "son of the deified," had no children, he in turn adopted Tiberius—the "son of the divine Augustus"—to inherit the throne (*RomCiv*, 1.633–38; 2.2–7). Tiberius and his successors continued the practice so that the empire was, "so to speak, the inheritance of a single family."[32] Hebrews, however, calls Jesus the Son of God and "heir of all things" (1:2b). This claim, which tacitly resists competing claims, echoes OT texts that decreed that God's anointed "son" would receive "the nations" for his inheritance and "the ends of the earth" for his possession (Ps 2:7–8; cf. Ps 89:27). The opening lines of Hebrews depict the exalted Christ as the heir of the universal rule that God promised to his Son in the Scriptures (Heb 1:5).

The author expands this by saying that the Son was the means by which God "created the universe" (1:2). This claim receives biblical warrant in the next part of the exordium (1:8–12; cf. §4 COMMENT *b*), but its underlying logic involves bringing together two tenets of faith. The first is that God spoke in these final days by a Son (1:2a), who not only transmitted divine speech verbally in the manner of a prophet (1:1) but who was himself divine speech. The second tenet was that God created the universe by his word (Gen 1:3, 6; Ps 33:6,

[32]Tacitus, *History* 1.16. On imperial succession see Rostovtzeff, *Rome*, 194–95; *RomCiv*, 1.633–38; 2.2–7.

9; Heb 11:3).[33] The author assumed that there was consistency in God's manner of speech, so that the way he spoke at the consummation of time corresponds to the way he spoke at the beginning of time. Accordingly, since God's word "in these final days" is identified with his Son, his initial word is also identified with the Son. Jewish tradition provided language for making this connection by identifying God's creative speech with his wisdom, which could be portrayed in personified form as the worker who was with God at the time of creation (Prov 3:19; 8:22–31; cf. Sir 24:3; Wis 7:22; 8:1; 9:1–2). The exalted Christ bears the traits of God's preexistent wisdom (COMMENT *b*).

Hebrews' thought moves from the end of time (1:2ab) to the beginning of time (1:2c), not the reverse. The direction is important because the exaltation of Jesus discloses purposes of God that would otherwise be hidden. The proposition of the speech says that God created human beings to be in a position of glory over all things (2:5–9), but those for whom Hebrews was composed did not find this to be the case. Their faith made them "foreigners" in their society (11:13–14; 13:13–14). Confidence that God's purposes would be realized is not based on observation of the current world order, but on what had been revealed through the Son, who suffered death on earth before being exalted to glory.

At the same time, God's purposes for people and for creation cannot be separated. All things were created by God (3:4) and exist for God (2:10), and the end of all things is revealed in the Son through whom God made the universe. The community of faith and the whole created order face the prospect of being "shaken" in the future (12:25–27), but the "rest" that the faithful anticipate at the end of time is the Sabbath rest that God ordained at the dawn of time (4:3, 10). God's purposes for humankind are carried out within the scope of his purposes for the world he created through the Son.

b. The Exalted Son (1:3–4)

Statements alluding to Christ's exaltation frame what is said about the Son: in these final days the Son has been appointed heir of all things (1:2b) and has become superior to angels (1:4). Statements about the Son being appointed to a position of power stand in tension with the idea that God created the universe through the Son (1:2c), implying here as elsewhere (1:10; 7:3; 9:26) that the Son existed in power from the dawn of time. Some statements imply eternal sonship while others suggest that a change occurred with Jesus' death and exaltation,[34] and Hebrews does not reconcile these tensions. Rather than speculating about

[33]Isaacs rightly notes that 11:3 does not personify the word of God or identify that word with God's Son (*Sacred*, 193). Nevertheless, connecting 1:2 to 11:3 shows how the author of Hebrews thought of creation in terms of God's word or speech.

[34]Interpreters from antiquity through the Middle Ages ascribed the statements implying timelessness to Jesus' divinity and applied those implying change to his humanity (see p. 24). Historical critics discern a fusion of Jewish apocalyptic traditions, which emphasize change, and philosophical paradigms like those used by Plato and Philo, which are more concerned with eternal realities (e.g., Dunn, *Christology*, 52–55).

who the Son *was*, Hebrews focuses on who the Son *is*, since the exalted Christ is the one whom the listeners are called to trust (pp. 104–5).[35]

It required "boldness" (3:6; 4:16; 10:19, 35) for early Christians to confess Jesus' divine sonship in contexts where there were competing claims. Hellenistic kings often held priestly offices and the emperor regularly served as high priest (*pontifex maximus* in Latin, *archiereus* in Greek),[36] but in Hebrews Christ is the high priest who makes purification for sins. The image of a figure seated upon a throne with a staff in one hand was used for emperors,[37] but in Hebrews Christ is the one seated at the right hand of Majesty. Rulers sometimes adorned themselves in a manner designed to reflect divine radiance. Agrippa I (d. A.D. 44) wore silver robes that reflected the sun's rays, and people acclaimed him as a god, while Nero was portrayed as Apollo on statuary and on the coins that bore his "impress," with beams emanating from his head.[38] Hebrews, however, calls Christ the "radiance" of God's glory and the "impress" of his substance. The emperor's word was commonly understood to be the final authority: "all the world quietly obeys" him. "Everything is carried out by a command or nod, and it is simpler than touching a string."[39] Yet Hebrews says that Christ bears all things by his powerful word. Finally, the emperors inherited the names Caesar and Augustus, as well as titles like "father of his country," "guardian of the Roman Empire," and "protector of the whole world" (*RomCiv*, 1.636), yet in 1:4 Christ has inherited the name above all others.

Like other early Christian writers, the author of Hebrews drew some of the elevated language for Christ from Israel's wisdom traditions.[40] Wisdom was sometimes said to have lived on earth (Bar 3:37), to have been exalted to heaven (*1 Enoch* 42:1–2), to be seated beside God's throne (Wis 9:4), and to be the radiance of eternal light (Wis 7:25–26). Philo utilized these traditions when he spoke of the *logos* or "word" as the power by which God fashioned the world, sometimes calling the *logos* God's "firstborn," "high priest" (*Dreams* 1.215), and "image" or *eikōn* (*Creation* 25; *Alleg. Interp.* 396). The *logos* could function as God's seal by making the imprint of the divine upon the human soul (*Planter* 18), and it was the helmsman guiding all things on their course (*Migration* 6).[41]

---

[35]On Christ's exaltation establishing the frame of reference for Hebrews, see NOTE on 1:3; Zimmermann, *Bekenntnis*, 56; Dunn, *Christology*, 208.

[36]Note the regular use of *pontifex maximus* on imperial coinage (*RomCiv*, 2.631–33). On the use of the Greek *archiereus* for the emperor's high priesthood see Josephus, *Ant.* 14.190, 192. See further Millar, *Emperor*, 359–61.

[37]A good example of imperial symbols and titles is the denarius of Tiberius, which bears the titles "son of the divine Augustus" and "high priest," and includes a seated figure with upright staff. See *ISBE* 3.409; *IDB* 3.433 #29; 3.431 ##6, 8 for older examples.

[38]On Agrippa see Josephus, *Ant.* 19.344–45. On Nero see M. Grant, *Nero*, 218.

[39]Aelius Aristides, *To Rome* §§30–31 in *RomCiv*, 2.24. The younger Pliny called the emperor "the man whose word or gesture of command could rule land and sea" (*Panegyricus* 4.4).

[40]For example, Col 1:15–20; John 1:1–14. See C. R. Koester, *Dwelling*, 108–12; Dunn, *Christology*, 163–212; Lane, "Detecting"; Witherington, *Jesus the Sage*, 275–82.

[41]Affinities between Heb 1:3–4 and traditions about wisdom and Philo's *logos* have often been noted. The sources cited here almost certainly did not understand wisdom to be a divine being

What Hebrews says of Christ transforms as well as appropriates wisdom traditions. Some Jewish writings identified the Law as the principal locus of wisdom (Sir 24:23; cf. Bar 4:1; Wis 6:18; 9:9).[42] Hebrews acknowledges that God spoke through prophets like Moses (Heb 1:1), but ascribes the traits of wisdom to the Son of God, who "alone so embodies God's wisdom, that is, God's creative, revelatory and redemptive action, that what can be said of Wisdom can be said of Christ without remainder" (Dunn, *Christology*, 209). Neither wisdom nor Philo's *logos* were said to have taken on flesh and blood (Heb 2:14), and neither was said to have been crucified in order to atone for human sin (9:12; 12:2). Jesus' death and resurrection are the fundamental moments of revelation for the author of Hebrews, and the language of divine wisdom was one way that he conveyed the significance of these events.

The death of Jesus is presupposed by the statement that God's Son "made purification for sins" (1:3). Purification treats sin as a source of defilement from which people need to be purged. The Jewish Law considered defilement or uncleanness to be a kind of infection. Since those who became unclean through sin had the potential to contaminate both people and places, they were barred from community life and from the sanctuary until they were cleansed. According to Hebrews, Christ makes purification by his blood. The purification was physical in that Jesus shed his blood (9:12), and repentance was accompanied by washing with water (6:1–2; 10:22). But the cleansing accomplished by Christ was more than physical in that it purifies the conscience (9:14; 10:2), thereby allowing people to come before God with confidence (4:14–16; 10:19–22) and to participate fully in the community (10:25; pp. 119–22).

After the Son made purification for sins, he sat down at the right hand of Majesty on high (1:3). This recalls Ps 110:1, which has several aspects of meaning. Royal connotations are prominent in 1:3, where taking the seat at the right hand of Majesty is connected with being appointed Son of God and heir of all things. Priestly implications are developed in 10:11–14, where Christ's seated posture points to the finality of his sacrifice. Victory is connoted in 12:1–2, where Christ has endured the race and assumed his seat as victor. If rulers in antiquity depicted themselves as kings, high priests, and victors, Hebrews insists that it is Jesus who encompasses all these traits.

One of the metaphors used to describe the exalted Son is that of "radiance" (1:3).[43] The dominant interpretive approach from the fourth century through

---

independent of God, but personified wisdom to speak of God's involvement with the world without compromising divine transcendence (Dunn, *Christology*, 176; cf. Isaacs, *Sacred*, 190–92; Williamson, *Philo*, 409–34).

[42]Similarly, Philo indicated that people who wanted to live in harmony with the world that God created through the *logos* should do so by following the Law of Moses (*Creation* 3). See Sandmel, *Philo*, 53–57.

[43]The role of metaphor in speech has been widely discussed. See Aristotle, *Poetics* 21.7–15 1457b; *Rhetoric* 3.2.8–15 1405ab. See C. R. Koester, *Symbolism*, 4–7. Calvin noted that when the term "radiance" was used, "things perceptible by our senses are applied to God, so that we may know what is to be found in Christ." This manner of speech, however, means that we "must allow that there is a

the Middle Ages was to ask what the imagery says about the Father's relationship to the Son within the Godhead. Athanasius asked, "Who does not see that the radiance cannot be separated from the light, but is by nature proper to it and coexistent with it?"[44] Similarly, Ambrose said that since "we cannot have a light without radiance nor radiance without light," the Son is "the radiance of the Father's glory . . . inseparable by unity of brightness."[45] Interpretations like these informed the Nicene Creed ("God from God, light from light"), and the creed in turn shaped many of the commentaries written on Heb 1:3.[46]

An alternative approach is to ask questions of revelation rather than ontology, since the opening lines of Hebrews deal primarily with the way God *spoke* to people through the Son. The text does not "discuss the nature of Christ Himself, but His nature as He reveals it to us." Therefore, when "you hear that the Son is the glory of the Father's glory, bear in mind that the glory of the Father is invisible to you until it shines forth in Christ" (Calvin, *Epistle*, 8). "Glory" often refers to the way that God's power enters the realm of human experience. Therefore, to say that the Son is "the radiance" of God's glory is to say that he reveals God's power and presence. Hebrews does not suggest that glory characterized Jesus' work on earth—earth was where Jesus suffered. Instead, divine glory is manifested through his exaltation (2:8–9; Loader, *Sohn*, 73). Christ's glory cannot be perceived empirically. "Seeing" begins with the proclamation of Christ that engenders faith (2:3–4), and it is faith that enables people to apprehend "things not seen" (11:1).

The Son is also called the "impress" of God's "substance" (1:3). This metaphor, like radiance, was important in the ancient Trinitarian controversies (NOTE on 1:3). If we ask what this passage says about the Son's relationship to God, the word "impress" points to the congruence between God and the Son in terms of their "substance" or being. This fits the next part of the exordium, where the author cites OT texts to show the creative powers and endless existence of God's Son (1:8–12; cf. 7:3; 13:8).

Another dimension emerges when we ask what the metaphor conveys about God's way of *addressing* people through the Son. "Impress" suggests that the Son is God's identifying mark, and "substance" suggests not only being but the inner resolve that undergirds one's actions (NOTES on 1:3). If the Son is the impress of God's substance, then he is the one in whom God's inner resolve or faithfulness is displayed. God promised to make a new covenant, and he inaugurated it through Christ's death (Jer 31:31–34; Heb 8:8–12; 9:15); God promised that one he called "lord" would sit at his right hand to serve as a priest forever, and he accomplished this through Jesus' exaltation (Ps 110:1, 4; Heb 1:13; 7:15–17). Because of the substance or faithfulness that God reveals through Christ, listeners can exhibit "substance" in their faith (3:14; 11:1).

---

measure of impropriety in what is taken from earthly things and applied to the hidden majesty of God" (*Epistle*, 7).

[44]Athanasius, "*Ep. Aeg. Lib.*" 2.4 (A.D. 356); quoted by P. E. Hughes, *Commentary*, 42.

[45]Ambrose, *De fide* 4.9; P. E. Hughes, *Commentary*, 42–43.

[46]For example, Chrysostom, *Homilies* 2; Alcuin, PL 100.1033D; Peter Lombard, PL 192.402D–405C; Erasmus, *Paraphase* of 1:3.

The universe came into being through the word that God spoke through the Son (1:2), and it continues to be supported and directed by the Son's word (1:3). Those addressed by Hebrews did not see all things subjected to the will of God and his people (2:8–9), and their experience of the world made it difficult to believe that God's purposes were being carried out. Yet if listeners grant that all things exist because they are supported and directed by the divine word, then the implication is that their faith too must be supported and directed by the word. Here the word of the Son is cosmic, but later it becomes personal, when Jesus calls people his brothers and sisters (2:11–13), speaks of obedience to God (10:5–7), and makes intercession for others (7:25; cf. 12:24). The word of Christ that bears all things also bears the listeners in their pilgrimage of faith.

The declaration that the Son has been exalted above the angels (1:4) anticipates the way the author will address the situation of the listeners. By interweaving OT texts in the next part of the exordium (1:5–14), the author allows the listeners to glimpse the majesty of the risen Christ, who is enthroned in heaven. Then in the proposition, he will quote Ps 8:4–6, which speaks of "man" and the "son of man" being crowned with glory and honor after being made lower than the angels for a time. Although the psalm spoke about the glory for which God created people, the author did not expect the listeners to find glory reflected in their situation (cf. 10:32–34; 13:13–14). But if they believed that Christ had been exalted above the angels, as 1:2–14 said he was, then the glory mentioned in the psalm could be applied to Christ. Christ did not escape suffering, but was exalted through what he suffered when he was lower than the angels. Christ's suffering did not mark God's failure to carry out his purposes but were the means by which God accomplished his purposes, including bringing others who suffer to the glory for which God created them (2:10, 18).

4. God's Word to the Son (1:5–14)

5For to which of the angels did he ever say, *You are my Son, I have begotten you today*? And again, *I will be his Father and he will be my Son*? 6And when, again, he brings the firstborn into the world, he says, *And let all the angels of God bow down before him.* 7And to the angels he says, *He is the one who makes his angels spirits and his ministers a flame of fire.* 8But to the Son, *Your throne, O God, is forever and ever, and the upright staff is the staff of your kingdom.* 9*You have loved righteousness and hated lawlessness; therefore, O God, your God has anointed you with oil of gladness beyond your companions.* 10And, *You, O Lord, founded the earth at the beginning, and the heavens are the works of your hands.* 11*They will perish, but you remain; they will all become old like a garment,* 12*and you will roll them up like a cloak; as a garment, indeed, they will be changed, but you are the same, and your years will never cease.* 13But to which of the angels has he ever said, *Sit at my right hand until I make your enemies a footstool for your feet*? 14Are they not all ministering spirits, sent for service for the sake of those who are to inherit salvation?

NOTES

1:5. *For to which of the angels.* This paragraph begins and ends with nearly identical rhetorical questions (1:5, 13). Both expect listeners to supply a negative response: God at no time called any one of the angels his "son." The MT and LXX occasionally call heavenly beings "sons of God" (Gen 6:2, 4; Ps 28:1 [29:1]; 88:7 [89:7]), but the LXX sometimes rendered "sons of God" as "angels of God" (e.g., Job 1:6; 2:1; 38:7; Dan 3:25; cf. Philo, *Giants* 6–7; *Unchangeable* 1–2; Josephus, *Ant.* 1.73). Moreover, "sons of God" is only used for angels collectively; in the Scriptures no one angel is called God's "son" in a singular sense (Luther, WA 57,3.6). Philo could call the *logos* both God's angel (*Names* 87) and son (*Confusion* 63; Braun), but the idea is not attested in other sources, and the question posed in Heb 1:5 assumes that the listeners are not familiar with it.

did he ever say. On citations of the OT as divine speech, see pp. 116–17.

You are my Son. The quotation of Ps 2:7 (LXX) offers biblical support for calling Jesus God's "Son" (Heb 1:2). The context of the quotation speaks of God's son inheriting the nations (Ps 2:8), just as Heb 1:2 said that God's Son was heir of all things. Israel's kings never attained the universal reign envisioned by Ps 2:7–8, so the text retained an ideal quality that lent itself to messianic interpretations (*Pss. Sol.* 17:23; 4QFlor I, 18–19; Acts 4:25–26; 13:33; Rev 12:5; 19:15). Hebrews assumes that messianic implications are familiar to the listeners (Vanhoye, *Situation*, 134–35).

I have begotten you today. The author does not specify when the divine "begetting" occurred. Some related it to the Son's eternal generation (Augustine, NPNF1 8.3; Aquinas, *Ad Heb.* §49) or to the incarnation (Chrysostom; Spicq; cf. Luke 1:35). The Synoptic gospels echo the psalm at Jesus' baptism (Mark 1:11 par.) and the transfiguration (Mark 9:7 par.). Nevertheless most interpreters connect this text with Christ's resurrection and exaltation, since the quotation supports the exaltation of the Son mentioned in 1:2b (§3 COMMENT *b*) and since in 5:5 (cf. 7:28) it refers to the eternal high priest in heaven (Attridge; Bénétreau; F. F. Bruce; Lane; H.-F. Weiss; Meier, "Symmetry," 304–5; Vanhoye, *Situation*, 141–42). Similarly, Acts 13:15–41 relates Ps 2:7 to Jesus' resurrection (Acts 13:33), Acts 4:25–28 relates other parts of Ps 2 to Jesus' passion, and in Rom 1:4 Paul said that Jesus is "declared to be Son of God . . . by resurrection from the dead."

And again. "Again" (*palin*) is a common way for Hebrews to introduce biblical citations in a series (2:13; 4:5; 10:30; cf. 1:6; 4:7). Similar usage appears in other sources (Philo, *Alleg. Interp.* 3.4; *Sobriety* 8; *Heir* 22; *Dreams* 1.166; 2.19; John 12:39; 19:37; Rom 15:10–12; 1 Cor 3:20; *1 Clem.* 10:4, 6; 14:5; 15:3–5; *Barn.* 6:2, 4).

I will be his Father and he will be my Son. The quotation is from 2 Sam 7:14 (LXX), the oracle in which Nathan told David that God would establish a Davidic dynasty. The parallel passage in 1 Chron 17:13 does not mention the possibility of God disciplining the king as in 2 Sam 7, but emphasizes God's abiding promise to him and his enduring reign (Vanhoye, *Situation*, 138). Although the promise was fulfilled to some extent with the birth of David's son Solomon (p. 30), later writers related the promise to a fulfillment beyond Solomon's reign. A messianic interpretation of 2 Sam 7:14 appears in 4QFlor I, 10–11, where it is linked with Ps 2. A messianic interpretation of the Davidic "seed" of 2 Sam 7:12 is apparently presupposed elsewhere in the NT (John 7:42; Acts 13:23; cf. Luke 1:32–33). Other NT passages apply 2 Sam 7:14 to the sonship of believers (2 Cor 6:18; Rev 21:7) and their inheritance (cf. Juel, *Messianic*, 59–88). The manner of citation in Heb 1:5 assumes that its messianic implications would be apparent.

1:6. This verse has been correlated with several points in Christ's career, of which the first is most plausible: (**a**) Exaltation. The exordium is structured so that the OT citations in 1:5–14 support what was said in 1:1–4. Since the description of the Son began with his exaltation as heir (1:2b) and connected his superiority to angels with his exaltation (1:4), it is most natural to connect 1:6 with the exaltation (Bénétreau; F. F. Bruce; Grässer; Lane; H.-F. Weiss; Vanhoye, *Situation*, 154–57; Andriessen, "La teneur," 293–304; Helyer, "*Prōtotokos*," 3–12). In 2:5 the author explains that the "world" is the world to come. (**b**) Second coming. Proponents of this view take "again" adverbially and "world" as the present visible world, so that the verse reads, "when he brings the firstborn into the world again" (Gregory of Nyssa, PG 45.634; Käsemann, *Wandering*, 101, 112; Braun; Loader, *Sohn*, 24–25). Objections are that this takes "again" in a sense different from 1:5 and that there is no reference to the second coming elsewhere in this section. (**c**) Incarnation. Some argue that "again" introduces another OT quotation as in 1:5. They take "bring into" to mean birth (Epictetus, *Disc.* 4.1.104) and "world" (*oikoumenē*) to be the present world (Chrysostom; Theodoret; Attridge). Bateman (*Early Jewish*, 222) links the text to Jesus' baptism. The problem is that according to Heb 2:5–9—in contrast to Luke 2:8–14—Christ's life upon earth was not marked by angelic adoration, but by humiliation.

And when, again. "Again" occasionally modifies a verb in other contexts (Heb 5:12; 6:1), but the use of "again" to introduce a biblical quotation in the previous verse makes it likely that here too it introduces a biblical quotation rather than making a statement about Christ's second advent.

he brings. This introduces the idea of moving to a place of heavenly rest. Although "bring into" (*eisagein*) does not appear again in Hebrews, "enter into" (*eiserchesthai*) is used for entering rest (3:11, 18, 19; 4:1, 3, 5, 6, 10, 11) and the future heavenly sanctuary (6:19–20; 9:12, 24–25). In the one instance where the verb refers to entering this world, a different word for "world" is used (*kosmos*, 10:5). In 13:20 *anagein* is used for Jesus' resurrection, just as *eisagein* is used for exaltation here.

the firstborn. This develops the idea of divine begetting (1:5) associated with Christ's exaltation. In matters of inheritance the firstborn traditionally had special prerogatives (Deut 21:17; cf. Heb 12:16), and as firstborn from the dead, Jesus is uniquely the heir of all things. The term also had messianic connotations. The firstborn son received the kingdom (2 Chron 21:3), and Ps 89:27 says of the Davidic king, "I will make him the firstborn, the highest of the kings of the earth." Other NT writings connect being firstborn with resurrection (Col 1:18; Rom 8:29; Rev 1:5; cf. 1 Cor 15:20; Acts 26:23). Jesus is Son of God in a singular sense, but his followers are sons of God in an extended sense (Heb 2:10). He is firstborn but others who are raised from the dead are also among the firstborn (12:23). Cf. Exod 4:22; Jer 31:9 (38:9 LXX) where "firstborn" is used for Israel.

into the world. The "world" is a heavenly one. *Oikoumenē* commonly referred to the inhabited world, and in many cases it meant the Roman Empire (BAGD, 561). It was a term well suited for the sphere of the Son's reign. In 2:5 the author explains that he is speaking about the "world to come." When he speaks of the present world, he uses a different word (*kosmos*, 4:3; 9:26; 10:5; 11:7, 38). In Exod 16:35 the *oikoumenē* is the promised land, which in Heb 4:1–11 signifies the future world. Christ's entrance into the world in his incarnation entailed the humiliation of being made "lower than the angels" (2:7, 9), but his entrance into the heavenly world (1:6) meant exaltation above the angels (Lane).

he says, And let all the angels of God bow down before him. One possible source of the quotation is Ps 97:7 (96:7 LXX), which said, "all God's angels worship him" (MT says, "all gods bow down before him."). Closer in many ways is Deut 32:43 (LXX), which is longer than the MT, although it may have been based on an alternative form of the Hebrew text (4QDeut). The first half reads,

> Rejoice, O heavens, along with him, and let all the sons of God bow down before him.
> Rejoice, O nations, with his people, and let all the angels of God ascribe strength to him.

The quotation in Hebrews corresponds exactly to the last part of line one, except that it has "angels of God" instead of "sons of God." The author may have used a text of Deut 32:43 that read "angels of God," or he may have relied on the text as it appears in Ode 2, an excerpt of Deuteronomy that appears after the psalter in LXX^{A} and in printed editions of the LXX (cf. Justin, *Dialogue* 130.1). It is also possible that he changed "sons of God" to read "angels of God," which better suits his argument. In any case the author apparently did not expect that listeners would consider his quotation a significant departure from the Scriptures. See also Phil 2:10, where the angels are said to worship the exalted Christ (cf. *Mart. Ascen. Isa.* 11:21–23).

1:7. *And to the angels he says.* The *pros men* in 1:7 corresponds to the *pros de* in 1:8, contrasting the angels with the Son. The word *pros* is sometimes translated "of" or "concerning," but is better rendered "to," a meaning it clearly has in 1:13, where it is accompanied by direct address. It also has this sense in 1:8 (see NOTE below).

He is the one who makes his angels spirits and his ministers a flame of fire. Most render *pneumata* as "winds" since wind, like fire, is a natural force and since the passage contrasts the abiding position of the Son with the changeable elements in nature. Translating it "spirits" follows the meaning it has later in the exordium. In 1:14 the author asks if angels are not "ministering spirits" (*pneumata*), assuming that listeners will agree that they are. Translating *pneumata* as "spirits" in both 1:7 and 1:14 shows the connection (cf. Vanhoye, *Situation*, 220). The citation is from Ps 104:4 (103:4 LXX). The standard LXX text reads "flaming fire," while Hebrews has "flame of fire." According to the MT, God made natural elements like wind and fire into servants (cf. Ps 148:8; 1QH I, 10–11). In the LXX, which Hebrews follows, the movement is the reverse: God or Christ can reduce angels into unstable natural elements like wind and fire (Heb 12:18; cf. Philo, *Alleg. Interp.* 160, 224, 235; *Migration* 100; *Moses* 1.70; *Decalogue* 49, 173). Before God "the hosts of angels stand trembling" and at his word "they are changed into wind and fire" (*4 Ezra* 8:21–22; cf. Judg 13:20).

1:8. *But to the Son.* The word *pros* is formally similar to the *pros* in 1:7a and is followed by direct address in the second person, so that it is best translated "to" (NJB) rather than "of" (NASB; REB; NAB²; NRSV; cf. NIV). The author does not so much speak about the Son as allow listeners to overhear what is spoken to the Son.

Your throne, O God, is forever and ever. The quotation is from Ps 45:6–7 (44:7–8 LXX) with only minor variations. "God" is in the nominative case. Some take it as a predicate nominative, reading the text, "Your throne [is a throne of] God forever and ever" (Westcott). Most, however, prefer to take the nominative as a vocative (BDF §147.3; Harris, "Translation," 138–49). The passage originally was addressed to God, but now God is the speaker who addresses the Son as "God" (cf. Rom 9:5; John 20:28; Tit 2:13; 2 Pet 1:1).

and the upright staff is the staff of your kingdom. A rod or staff symbolized power. The short scepter was an ornamented form of a club (*ISBE* 4.206, 350). A longer version, about five feet in length, was a form of a staff (*ISBE* 2.333, 452). Both are mentioned in Gen 49:10: "The scepter shall not depart from Judah, nor the ruler's staff from between his feet." First century depictions of seated rulers often show the longer staff (*ISBE* 3.409). Some MSS refer to the staff of "his" kingdom (P^{46} ℵ B; cf. REB; NJB; NASB), which may be the more difficult reading since it differs from the LXX and from the "your" earlier in this verse. Proponents suggest that the reading "your" arose to make the text conform to the LXX. Other MSS read "your" kingdom (A D Ψ etc.; cf. NIV; NAB²; NRSV). This allows 1:8–9 to be read consistently as direct address to the Son. Proponents suggest that the alternative "his" arose either because of a failure to take the text as direct address or because of a transcriptional error (*TCGNT*, 662–63; Harris, "Translation," 136–38).

1:9. *You have loved righteousness and hated lawlessness.* Righteousness and lawlessness are opposites (cf. Isa 5:7; 2 Cor 6:14; Rom 6:19; Xenophon, *Memorabilia* 1.2.24). In the OT "righteousness" described those who followed the will of God (Deut 6:25; Pss 23:3 [22:3 LXX] 118:19–20 [117:19–20 LXX]) and was an especially important trait for rulers (Isa 9:7; 11:5). In the Greco-Roman world righteousness was said to encompass the virtues needed in society (Aristotle, *Nic. Ethics* 5.3 1129b; 5.5 1130b). Therefore, it was an essential virtue for rulers (Wis 1:1; Dionysius of Halicarnassus, *Roman Antiquities* 2.18.1–2; cf. *RomCiv*, 2.25; *TLNT* 1.326–28). A king who loved righteousness would serve the cause of what was right and oppose those who violated the law. He would also refrain from acting lawlessly himself, since that was characteristic of tyrants (Dio Chrysostom, *Disc.* 1.13, 43, 82). See *TLNT* 1.326–28; Schrenk, *TDNT* 2.178–201.

therefore, O God, your God. The double use of "God" can be taken in two different ways. It may be that the first occurrence of "God" is the subject of the verb and that the second one is an appositive: "God, [namely] your God, has anointed you" (KJV; Kistemaker, *Psalm*, 26; Harris, "Translation," 149–51). The translation proposed here takes the first occurrence as a vocative (BDF §147), as in 1:8, and understands the second occurrence to be the subject of the verb (REB; Attridge; Ellingworth; Leschert, *Hermeneutical*, 23–78).

has anointed you with oil of gladness. Anointing was a form of personal adornment, and the "oil of gladness" connotes celebration (Isa 61:3). Anointing was also the way that kings took office. Kings were said to be anointed by God (1 Sam 10:1; 15:17; 2 Sam 12:7; 2 Kgs 9:3; Ps 89:20), ideally within a context of joy and gladness (1 Kgs 1:39–40). Here the Son is anointed upon his exaltation to heaven.

beyond your companions. The preposition "beyond" (*para*) first means that anointing gives the Son a status that is superior to others in quality. Second, it suggests that the anointing was given ahead of others in time, which offers Jesus' followers reason to hope that they too will share in gladness and in the kingdom in the future. Although some have thought that the Son's "companions" are angels (Bénétreau; Moffatt), it is better to think of them as his followers (3:14), who share a heavenly calling (3:1), the Spirit (6:4), and divine instruction (12:8). The Son came to share (*metechein* in 2:14) human flesh and blood in order that humans might become companions (*metochoi*) in his glorious condition (1:9; cf. 12:22; Vanhoye, *Situation*, 193).

1:10. *And, You, O Lord, founded the earth at the beginning.* This text, like the previous one, was originally addressed to God, but here it is addressed to the Son (NOTE on 1:8). "Lord" refers to Christ (e.g., 2:3), who is an agent of creation (1:2c; §3 COMMENT *a*).

and the heavens are the works of your hands. Elsewhere, the similar expression "made with hands" refers to things made with human hands, which are transient (9:11, 24). Here the heavens are made by God's hands. The author does not develop a consistent contrast between the material world of earth and the eternal world of heaven. Heaven is included along with the earth in the created order that is contrasted with the eternal existence of Christ.

1:11. *They will perish, but you remain.* In 1:12 the author speaks of the world ending not by perishing in a natural way, but through a divine act that brings it to an end. Christ perished by crucifixion, yet through the resurrection he "remains" forever. He "remains" not by escaping death, but by overcoming it.

they will all become old like a garment. "Garment" could indicate various types of clothing, but the parallel use of "cloak" suggests that it is the outer robe. "Old" applies here to the world and in 8:13 to the first covenant (cf. Isa 50:9; 51:6). The language was used for clothing that wore out (Deut 8:4; Neh 9:21; Josh 9:4–5) and for human frailty: "All flesh becomes old like a garment, for the covenant from of old is 'You must die' " (Sir 14:17 LXX).

1:12. *and you will roll them up like a cloak.* The outer cloak would have been the first and easiest layer of clothing to remove. The LXX uses the verb "change" (*allassein*), which appears in the next line of Hebrews, rather than "roll up" (*helissein*), which is found here. The verb "roll up" is reminiscent of Isa 34:4 LXX, which says that "heaven will be rolled up like a scroll." It is not clear whether the author of Hebrews used an alternative form of the OT text or made the change himself. The heavens were also sometimes likened to a tent stretched over the earth (Ps 104:2; Isa 40:22), making it easier to think of them being rolled up.

as a garment, indeed, they will be changed. The LXX does not include the word "garment" here, although it was used in Heb 1:11b. Repeating the word makes the imagery more vivid. Here "change" points to an end rather than a simple alteration. Later the author warns that what has been created will be subjected to *metathesis*, which connotes "removal" (NOTE on 12:27).

but you are the same, and your years will never cease. On Christ's constancy see pp. 104–5.

1:13. *But to which of the angels has he ever said.* This essentially repeats 1:5. There is an implicit contrast between the many angels and the singular Son, just as the Son is contrasted with the multitude of prophets and priests (1:1–2; 7:23–24).

Sit at my right hand. This begins a quotation of Ps 110:1 (109:1 LXX), the text to which the author alluded in Heb 1:3. To be seated at someone's right hand was a position of favor (Sir 12:12) and a place from which to make intercession (1 Kgs 2:19). God's "right hand" was powerful (Exod 15:6; Ps 118:15–16) and protective (Ps 80:17). In judgment scenes the right was associated with acquittal (*Apoc. Ab.* 22:3–5; Matt 25:33–34, 41) and reward (*T. Job* 33:3; *T. Benj.* 10:6; Herm. *Vis.* 3.1.9–3.2).

until I make your enemies a footstool for your feet. Placing a foot upon a defeated enemy was a gesture of dominance (Josh 10:24; cf. Bar 4:25). David battled his enemies "until the Lord put them under the soles of his feet" (1 Kgs 5:3). Babylonian and Assyrian reliefs depict their leaders placing a foot upon subjugated adversaries (*ISBE* 2.332, 453; cf. Isa 51:23). Pictures of rulers sometimes show them seated upright with the soles of their feet placed squarely on a low platform or footstool (*ISBE* 2.333). The footstool suggests complete subjugation to the sovereign. In Ps 110:1 the ruler does not engage in the battle, but expects God to subdue his adversaries.

1:14. *Are they not all ministering spirits.* The question expects a positive answer. The author has already called the angels "ministers" and "spirits" in 1:7. The expression "ministering angels" occurs in other sources, suggesting that the idea might have been familiar (Philo, *Virtues* 74; *Mek.* "Beshallaḥ" 3.98, 105 [Lauterbach, 1.211–12]; cf. Str-B 3.680–81). In *T. Levi* 3:5 the angels offer bloodless sacrifices on behalf of the righteous. *Jub* 2:2 refers to the angels of fire, winds, and other natural phenomena.

sent for service. In Heb 8:2, 6; 9:21 the various terms for "ministry" (*leitourg-*) have to do with service in the sanctuary. Although the OT pictures God accompanied by heavenly beings (Isa 6:1–2; 1 Kgs 22:19; Tob 12:15), here the angels do not attend in the heavenly court but are sent to carry out "service" for God's people. The kind of service is not specified; in ordinary usage the term often had to do with attending to the day-to-day needs of people (cf. 6:10). In the NT angels are said to help prisoners (Acts 5:19; 12:6–11) and give directives (Acts 8:26; 10:3, 22; 27:23).

for the sake of those who are to inherit salvation. In 1:6 the angels worshiped the Son upon his throne, but here they minister to his followers on earth. Earlier the Son was said to have inherited all things and a great name; here his followers are the heirs of salvation. The present situation of the Son discloses something of the glory awaiting the faithful. "Are to" (*mellein*) often has to do with the age to come (2:5; 6:5; 9:11; 10:1, 27; 13:14). On "salvation" see NOTE on 2:3.

COMMENT[47]

The declaration that "God has spoken to us by a Son" (1:2a) is followed by an elevated description of the Son's identity and activity (1:2b–4). The catena of OT citations in 1:5–14 is well suited to the context. Having declared that God has spoken (1:1), the author cites a series of OT texts virtually without comment, so that instead of relating indirectly what God has said, the text has God function as the speaker. The seven quotations, which are taken from each of the major categories of OT writings, reflect some of the "many occasions" and "many forms" in which God spoke in the past (1:1). The author cites a text from the Law of Moses (Deut 32:43/Heb 1:6), an oracle of the prophet Nathan (2 Sam 7:14/Heb 1:5b), and lines from the Psalms (Pss 2; 45; 102; 104; 110). The twist is that these texts are no longer addressed to the fathers of Israel, but to the exalted Son of God and his heavenly entourage.

In content the sequence of OT passages generally follows the sequence of traits ascribed to God's Son in the opening sentence. Heb 1:2 refers to God's Son, and the first quotations give biblical warrant for using the title "Son" for Christ (1:5). At the end of 1:3 the author said that God's Son "sat down at the right hand of the Majesty on high," and the quotation of Ps 110:1 at the end of the catena (Heb 1:13) shows the OT basis for the claim. The texts in the middle (1:7–12) take up the Son's creative power and deity, although the quotations do not strictly follow the sequence of traits given in 1:2c–3 and no OT quotation pertains to the Son making "purification for sins" (1:3). There is a general correspondence between the traits in 1:1–4 and the passages quoted in 1:5–14, but one-to-one connections are not possible.[48]

---

[47]L. C. Allen, "Psalm 45:7–8"; Andriessen, "La teneur"; Bateman, "Two First-Century"; idem, *Early Jewish*; Charles, "Angels"; Glasson, "Plurality"; Harris, "Translation"; Hay, *Glory*; Helyer, "*Prōtotokos*"; Isaacs, *Sacred*, 164–78; Laub, *Bekenntnis*, 52–61; Leschert, *Hermeneutical*, 23–78; Loader, *Sohn*, 7–29; Meier, "Symmetry"; Müller, "Funktion der Psalmzitate"; Oberholtzer, "Warning," 83–97; O'Neill, "Who Is"; Saucy, "Exaltation"; Schröger, *Verfasser*, 35–79; Silberman, "Prophets/Angels"; Thompson, *Beginnings*, 128–40; Vanhoye, *Situation*, 119–226; Vincent Cernuda, "La introducción."

[48]Meier ("Structure") finds seven attributes of the Son in 1:2b–4 that he correlates with the seven OT quotations. Lane finds four corresponding categories, although the middle categories do not work as well as the first and last.

The Son as Royal Heir	1:2ab	1:5–6
The Son's Power and Deity	1:2c–3c	1:7–12
The Son's Exaltation to God's Right Hand	1:3d	1:13–14

Some scholars maintain that the quotations in 1:5–13 were taken from a collection of "testimonies."[49] They point out that passages are cited without attention to their original context, that no sources are given, and that some of the quotations differ from the standard LXX text. There is also evidence that at least Ps 2:7 and 2 Sam 7:14 were connected before Hebrews was composed (4QFlor I, 10–11). An alternative view is that the author drew on an early Christian liturgy. Several of the texts cited here (Pss 2:7–8; 104:4; 110:1) are cited in *1 Clem.* 36, and some have suggested that Hebrews and *1 Clem.* relied on a common collection of texts that was used in Christian worship. Nevertheless, it seems more likely that *1 Clement* drew its material from Hebrews than that both drew upon a common liturgical source, since *1 Clement* 36 follows the wording of Hebrews even when Hebrews differs from the LXX and from *1 Clement*'s own style and since it includes elements that seem to have been taken from other parts of Hebrews. Moreover, the similarities in thought and sequence between Heb 1:1–4 and 1:5–13 make it likely that the author of Hebrews compiled these texts for use in their present context.[50]

The author presupposes that Jesus' death and exaltation are the means by which God has spoken (1:2), and he now "exegetes" that action in light of what God said of old in the Scriptures (1:1; see pp. 117–18). Reading Heb 1 is something like looking at a mosaic that depicts the image of a person. The artist creates the mosaic by selecting various types of stones and arranging them in a way that conveys the subject's likeness. Those who look at the mosaic generally do not ask where the individual pieces came from or how each piece functioned elsewhere, but whether the arrangement of the stones conveys a genuine likeness of the person being portrayed. Similarly, to read Heb 1 on the author's own terms is to ask whether the mosaic of OT quotations is a faithful presentation of the exalted Christ.

Creating this mosaic of texts means that the author of Hebrews worked with a critical tension: the OT cannot be adequately comprehended apart from the crucified and exalted Christ, yet the crucified and exalted Christ cannot be adequately comprehended apart from the OT. The author interprets the OT in light of Christ because he understands Christ's crucifixion and exaltation to be God's definitive means of communication, and the OT as the shadow cast by that reality. At the same time, the author does not have unmediated access to the heav-

---

[49]Attridge (*Epistle*, 50) notes that catenae of biblical passages have been found among the Dead Sea Scrolls (4QTest; 4QFlor), and Grässer (*Hebräer*, 1.72) considers it formally similar to certain types of rabbinic midrash.

[50]For detailed arguments that *1 Clement* was dependent upon Hebrews see Hagner, *Use*, 179–95; Ellingworth, "Hebrews"; Cockerill, "Heb 1:1–14"; Attridge, *Epistle*, 6–7. A comparison of Heb 1 and *1 Clem.* 36 is provided on pp. 22–23. The most important point is that Hebrews must argue for the validity of calling Jesus "high priest," whereas *1 Clement* presupposes Jesus' high priesthood.

enly throne room and cannot gaze directly upon the exalted Christ. So he seeks to discern the contours of the risen Christ by examining the shadows that Christ's enthronement casts back into the Scriptures (pp. 117–18).

The author weaves the texts together in an interlocking fashion. Speakers understood that it was good practice to place the strongest arguments at the beginning and end of a section, and in the middle to use arguments that were strong when conjoined with the others even though they might not have been persuasive if taken separately.[51] This section begins with quotations of Ps 2:7 and 2 Sam 7:14, which were already interpreted messianically in various Jewish and early Christian writings, and it concludes with Ps 110:1, which was widely used in the early church as a testimony to Christ's resurrection and exaltation. The listeners would almost certainly have agreed that these texts could be used for Jesus (NOTES on Heb 1:5, 13 and COMMENT *c*). There is little to suggest, however, that the quotations in the middle part of the catena (1:5–12) had been understood in a messianic sense prior to the writing of Hebrews. The author discloses their christological significance by relating this new understanding of these texts to other established texts so that the claims about the Son's divinity could be seen as an extension of his messiahship.

The first step is to ascribe to Jesus the divine sonship promised in Ps 2:7 and 2 Sam 7:14, and then to show that sonship makes Jesus superior to the angels who bow before him (Heb 1:5–7). Second, the OT texts quoted in 1:5 assigned divine sonship to the anointed one who would inherit David's everlasting throne (cf. 2 Sam 7:12–16; Ps 2:2, 6–7). If Jesus is the Son of God, then the author finds it appropriate to apply to him Ps 45:6–7, which speaks of the everlasting throne of the one whom God anointed (Heb 1:8–9). Third, the psalm quoted in 1:8–9 indicates that God's anointed one can be called "God." If Jesus is the anointed one, or the Christ, this text gives the warrant for calling him "God,"[52] and if he can be called "God," then it is appropriate to ascribe to him the traits of deity, which according to Ps 102:25–27 include creative power and endless existence (Heb 1:10–12). Finally, the author completes the circle by seeking to show that such power and endless existence can be predicated of Christ because he is seated in the position of authority in the presence of God, as shown by Ps 110:1.

a. The Son as Royal Heir (1:5–6)

The first section of Hebrews concluded by declaring that the Son of God has become superior to the angels (1:4). The second section presses the point by asking "To what angel did God ever say, 'You are my Son'?" (1:5). The question expects listeners to respond that at no time did God say to any one of the angels, "You are my Son." The anticipated response would have been plausible on bib-

---

[51]See *Rhet. ad Her.* 3.10 §18; Quintilian, *Inst.* 5.12.14.

[52]It may be that the author of Hebrews would connect the title "God" with the divine begetting mentioned in Ps 2:7. Although traditional Jewish exegesis understood begetting and divine sonship in an adoptive sense, Christians took the idea in a more ontological sense, inferring that one who was begotten by God would bear the traits of God, his Father.

lical grounds since a few OT texts called the angels "sons of God" (NOTE on 1:5) in a collective sense, but no one angel was called God's "Son" in a unique sense. Repeating the question in 1:13 reinforces the point.

Interpreters have often asked why angels play such a prominent role in the first chapter of Hebrews. Some relate it to the contrast between the old and new covenants. The angels (1:4–14), Moses (3:1–6), and the Levitical priesthood (5:1–10:18) were all associated with the Sinai covenant. Therefore, if the author wanted to prevent listeners from reverting to Jewish practices, he needed to show that Christ and his new covenant were superior to the old covenant and those who inaugurated it. A variation is that those who had been reverting to the old covenant found it expedient to regard Christ as an angel in order to avoid ascribing deity to him.[53] Others have argued that the listeners found it difficult to distinguish Christ from other heavenly figures or that they were attracted to the teachings of the Dead Sea sect, which thought that the priestly and royal messiahs would be subordinate to the archangel Michael. Still others propose that Alexandrian Judaism identified angels and prophets as the intermediaries between God and people, which obscured Christ's unique role[54] or that the author was seeking to counter a tendency to engage in worship of angels (Col 2:18).[55] The problem with these proposals is that there is no explicit polemic against angels or an angelic Christology in the remainder of the speech (Attridge, *Epistle*, 51–52; Grässer, *Hebräer*, 1.72).

A more promising approach is to note that an exordium often leads *indirectly* to the main issue of the speech (Quintilian, *Inst.* 4.1.30). Hebrews' exordium does not speak directly to the issues confronting the listeners, but establishes a perspective from which these questions could be addressed. The question of the Son's superiority to angels functions in several ways with respect to Hebrews as a whole:

(a) Relationship to the rest of the exordium (1:1–2:4). The Son's superiority to angels, which is introduced in 1:4 and developed in 1:5–14, becomes the basis for the appeal for attention in 2:1–4. Angels are important because they were associated with the giving of the Law (NOTE on 2:2). The author assumes that the listeners will agree that the Torah, which was delivered by angels, needed to be taken seriously, but he insists that the gospel message needs to be taken even more seriously, since it was proclaimed by the Lord, who has been exalted above the angels. The Scriptures are important because they bear witness to Christ, and the angels are important because their worship of the Son of God directs the listeners' attention to the Son.

---

[53]On reading Hebrews in terms of the superiority of Christ to the angels, prophets, and priests, see Aquinas, *Ad Heb.* §2; Hagen, *Theology*, 33, 43, 45, 49; Westcott, *Epistle*, xlviii–xlix; Milligan, *Theology*, 88–95. For the idea that some may have sought to avoid ascribing deity to Christ by calling him an angel see Hagner, *Hebrews*, 30; cf. Harris, "Translation," 130–31.

[54]On this idea in relation to the Dead Sea Scrolls see Yadin, "Dead Sea," 39–49; P. E. Hughes, *Commentary*, 52–53. Those who argue on the basis of Alexandrian sources include Dey, *Intermediary*, 127–54; Nash, "Notion," 109–12; cf. Montefiore, *Commentary*, 39–42.

[55]Windisch, *Hebräerbrief*, 17; Moffatt, *Critical*, 7; Jewett, *Letter*, 5–13; Stuckenbruck, *Angel*, 119–39; Gieschen, *Angelmorphic*, 294–314.

(b) Relationship to the proposition (2:5–9). The proposition quotes Ps 8, which says that the son of man was made lower than the angels but is now crowned with glory and honor. Hebrews interprets this in light of Jesus' death and resurrection. The texts in Heb 1:5–14 establish this perspective by bringing listeners to see that Jesus, whom they know to have been crucified, is now crowned with glory above the angels. Christ's exaltation gives beleaguered listeners hope that they too may experience a glorious future with Christ and the angels in a world that transcends what can be seen with the eye.

(c) Relationship to the conclusion of the speech (12:22–24; see pp. 84–86). The body of the speech concludes with the announcement that the listeners have "approached Mount Zion and the city of the living God, heavenly Jerusalem, and myriads of angels in festival gathering" (12:22). The gathering of angels is not only for Jesus, who is God's firstborn in a singular sense (1:6), but for all the "firstborn" children of God (12:23). The festive opening section of the speech anticipates its depiction of the final celebration in the city of God, which is the destiny of the faithful.

The movement of thought in 1:5–14 brings listeners into the drama of Christ's enthronement by allowing them to overhear what God declares to the Son and to the angels.[56] The first step is the public declaration of adoption, where God says to Christ, "You are my Son, I have begotten you today" (1:5a). In the next quotation God turns to the others who are listening, announcing "I will be his Father and he will be my Son" (1:5b). Then, as the Son is introduced to the world, God commands the hosts in attendance, "Let all the angels of God bow down before him" (1:6). The next statement (1:7) continues the address to the angels by offering a rationale for their worship of the Son: It is the Son "who makes his angels spirits and his ministers a flame of fire." This affirmation directs the angels and the readers alike to the Son of God.

This glimpse into the unseen world of God stands in contrast to the ordinary world in which the listeners live. When the emperor designated a successor by adopting him as a son, he did so at a public event that took place in Rome at a temple on the Capitol. The younger Pliny recalled that for Trajan's adoption the emperor stood "before the gathered assembly of gods and men" and "chose you as his son" (*Panegyricus* 8.3; cf. 47.5; 94.5). Proclamation of adoption, which was made throughout the empire, was greeted with public displays of loyalty.[57] In the east those who approached a sovereign bowed down as the angels do in this scene, and this practice became common in the west in the mid-first century A.D. (Dio Cassius, *Roman History* 59.24.3–4; 62.2). The portrayal of Christ's enthronement encourages those who are subject to public reproach because of their faith to remain loyal to Christ (10:32–34; 13:13–14). At the same time, this experience may be unsettling to those who are adrift (2:1), since they find them-

---

[56]See M. Barth, "Old Testament," 62. The elements of an enthronement ritual have been noted by Käsemann, *Wandering*, 99; Michel; Laub, *Bekenntnis*, 56; Grässer.

[57]On the public proclamation of accession and displays of loyalty see *RomCiv* 2.7–11; cf. 1.635–38 on public attention given to the emperor's sons upon their coming of age or their death.

selves called to give attention to the one whom God has invested with divine authority (cf. 10:29).

b. The Son's Power and Deity (1:7–12)

The content of God's address to the Son in 1:7–12 is taken from the OT, but its form can be called "epideictic" in the categories of classical rhetoric. Epideictic rhetoric had to do with praise or blame and was designed to appeal to the imagination and to inspire the listeners (Kennedy, *New Testament*, 73–75). Epideictic passages were included in various kinds of speeches, often at the beginning or the end. A common setting for epideictic speaking was a public gathering, and a typical subject was the virtue of the ruler. In this festive gathering Hebrews accents the Son's righteous rule, his opposition to lawlessness, and his upright character (1:8–9).

The quotation of Ps 45:6–7 declares that the "upright staff" symbolizes Christ's love of righteousness (Heb 1:8–9; cf. 7:2), which is crucial for the listeners' perseverance. The last part of the speech tells how the righteous, who lived by faith in adverse circumstances (10:38; 11:4), will become heirs of righteousness (11:7) in the heavenly Jerusalem (12:22). The implication is that if Christ loves righteousness, he will not abandon the faithful or allow lawlessness to triumph in the end—although the lawless may sometimes appear to have the upper hand (10:32–34). The author will argue that Christ brought a change in the Law without promoting lawlessness, for he inaugurated a new covenant that ends lawlessness by bringing people into a right relationship with God (10:17). His obedience to God (5:8; 10:7)[58] makes him the supreme exemplar of the righteousness that the people of God are called upon to exhibit (10:38; cf. 11:26; 12:1–3; 13:12–13) and makes him the source of salvation for all who obey him (5:9).

In this section Christ is twice addressed as "God" (1:8a, 9b). The way that "God" is used for Christ reflects the peculiar position of Christians in first-century society. On the one hand, the dominant Greco-Roman ethos assumed that there were many gods and that human beings could be deified. Many emperors refused to be called gods during their lifetimes, yet were named gods after their deaths.[59] The term "god" was also used for living rulers, like Agrippa (Acts 12:21–22; Josephus, *Ant.* 19.345) and Nero (Tacitus, *Annals* 14.15). On the other hand, the Jewish tradition centered on faith in one God (Deut 6:4), who was not to be portrayed in human form or to be identified with a human being (Exod 20:4; Deut 5:8; 2 Macc 9:12; cf. John 5:18; 10:33). Hebrews uses the title

---

[58]Cf. Braun, *Hebräer*, 40. The gospels recall that Jesus was charged with lawless behavior since he healed on the Sabbath and did not adhere to the teachings of the Pharisees in matters of purity (e.g., Mark 2:23–3:6; 7:1–13; John 5:16; 9:16). Yet the gospels also seek to show that Jesus did not reject the Law, but acted consistently with the Law in its deepest sense (Matt 5:17–20; John 5:39–47; 7:19–24). Jesus' opponents were remembered as the lawless ones (Acts 2:23).

[59]Various "divine honors are bestowed after their death upon such emperors as have ruled uprightly, and in fact shrines are even built to them" (Dio Cassius, *Roman History* 51.20.8).

"God" not in defiance of Israel's tradition, but on the basis of Israel's tradition, using the words of Ps 45:6–7, which ascribe deity to the king that God has anointed, who here is identified as the exalted Christ.

The final portion of the address to the Son elaborates what it means to call him "God" by identifying him as the one through whom all things were brought into being and who stands above the cycles of decay (1:10–12). The idea that the Son is the means by which God created all things was introduced in 1:2 (§3 COMMENT *a*), and it is reinforced by the quotation in 1:10 that ascribes to the Lord—understood to be Christ—the creative power through which God founded the earth and made the heavens. The psalm observes that mortality is inherent in the created order (1:11–12), yet when it says, "You will roll them up like a cloak," the text indicates that heaven and earth will be brought to an end by the Lord. The world has no independent existence, but depends upon the power of the Son of God, who will remain when heaven and earth perish. The implication is that if faith is based on the empirical world, it is captive to the cycles of decay and death, and is therefore doomed to perish. For faith to endure it must be placed in the Son of God, who endures.

c. The Son's Exaltation to God's Right Hand (1:13–14)

The capstone to the catena of OT quotations is Ps 110:1, which provides an important undergirding for the argument of Hebrews[60]:

(**a**) Relationship to what has preceded (1:1–4). The first sentence of the exordium declared that after making purification for sins, the Son of God "sat down at the right hand of the Majesty on high" (1:3). Psalm 110:1 was widely used by early Christians and almost certainly would have been familiar to the listeners. According to the gospels, Jesus quoted Ps 110:1 as a messianic text that identified David's son as "lord" (Matt 22:41–46; Mark 12:35–37; Luke 20:41–44). Later, Jesus told his captors that they would see "the Son of Man seated at the right hand of Power and coming on the clouds of heaven," using the language from Ps 110:1 and Dan 7:13 (Matt 26:64; Mark 14:62).[61] The psalm was widely used as testimony to Christ's resurrection and exaltation (Acts 2:32–36; 5:29–32; 7:55–56, 59; Rom 8:34; 1 Cor 15:25; cf. Eph 1:20; Col 3:1; 1 Pet 3:22; Rev 3:21). Hebrews draws on the familiar use of Ps 110:1 as a testimony to Jesus' exaltation while giving a fresh interpretation of the psalm in terms not only of Christ's royal power but also of the definitive quality of his priestly work (10:12) and his victory over suffering and death in the contest of faith (12:1–2).

(**b**) Relation to the proposition (2:5–9). The quotation of Ps 110:1 in the exordium anticipates the issue raised in the proposition, which is that God will

---

[60]On Ps 110 see Hay, *Glory*; Gourgues, *À la droite*; Hengel, *Studies*, 119–225; Loader, "Christ." Buchanan (*To the Hebrews*, xx–xxi) stresses the importance of Ps 110 for Hebrews, but it is an overstatement to call Hebrews a homiletical midrash on the psalm. Hebrews is not a sustained explication of the psalm, but an interpretation of Christ's identity and work that draws on the psalm.

[61]The parallel in Luke 22:69 says only that "from now on" the Son of Man will be seated at God's right hand of power. No mention is made of his return on the clouds.

place all things under the feet of the son of man, as indicated in Ps 8:6 (8:7 LXX). Other early Christian writings also connected Pss 8 and 110, apparently because of similarities in language.

Ps 110:1b	*Ps 8:6b (8:7b LXX)*
I make your enemies	all things you subjected
a footstool for your feet	under his feet
thō tous echthrous sou	*panta hypetaxas*
hypopodion tōn podōn sou	*hypokatō tōn podōn autou*

Matthew 22:44 and Mark 12:36 seem to conflate these texts by saying, "Sit at my right hand until I put your enemies *under your feet*." They use the expression "under" (*hypokatō*) the feet, which corresponds to Ps 8:6, rather than referring to the "footstool" (*hypopodion*) that is mentioned in Ps 110:1 (Hay, *Glory*, 35). Paul connects the two psalms in 1 Cor 15:25, where he paraphrases the reference to subjection of enemies from Ps 110:1, then quotes Ps 8:6, which speaks of all things being placed in subjection under his feet. Similarly, Eph 1:20–22 connects Christ's exaltation to God's right hand (Ps 110:1) with a dominion that includes having "all things under his feet" (Ps 8:7). The movement from Ps 110:1 in Heb 1:13 to a proposition based on Ps 8 in Heb 2:5–9 may reflect a common connection between these texts, providing a basis from which to argue that God's design for humankind finds its realization in the crucified and risen Christ.

(c) Relation to the remainder of the speech. Applying Ps 110:1 to the exalted Christ allows the author to make the simple argument that Christ is a priest, for Ps 110:1 calls the one seated at God's right hand "lord" and 110:4 calls him "a priest forever according to the type of Melchizedek." If the listeners agree that the royal imagery in 110:1 applies to Jesus, then they will presumably agree that the priestly imagery in 110:4 also applies to him, thus preparing for the extended discussion of Jesus' priesthood and sacrifice in Heb 5–10. The author cites Ps 110:1 in Heb 10:12 to make the point that because priests always stand while conducting sacrificial ministry, Christ the priest's being seated at God's right hand indicates that his offering has been completed once and for all. The language of Ps 110:1 reappears in Heb 12:1–2, where Christ is portrayed as the victorious athlete who has run the race, who endured the cross and shame, and who is now seated at the right hand of God. Thus royal, priestly, and heroic aspects of Jesus' identity and work are all developed on the basis of the psalm.

The idea that Christ's enemies are now being placed under his feet is not as fully developed. The principal battle described in Hebrews took place when Christ entered the world to liberate people from bondage to the fear of death (2:10–18). Nevertheless, the listeners would have understood that opposition to Christ continued after his resurrection in the form of opposition to Christ's people, who suffered denunciation, arrest, and loss of property (10:32–34; 13:13–14). The author does not vilify those who showed animosity toward the community, but neither does he assume that God will allow such opposition to continue indefinitely. The promises of God will be fully realized when all things—including all enemies—are subjected to the will of God (2:5–9).

Finally, the author asks whether angels are not ministering spirits sent for the sake of those about to inherit salvation (1:14). Listeners who provide a positive answer place themselves in a position where they must conceive of their own situation in a new way. Their circumstances were dispiriting (pp. 71–72), yet if they could say that angels are sent "for the sake of those who are to inherit salvation," it would be but a small step to say that angels are sent "for our sake." The author does not pursue the theme, but having moved the listeners to consider the help that angels might offer, he directs them to consider the kind of help that Christ himself has offered (2:1–4).

5. The Message Spoken by the Lord (2:1–4)

2 1Therefore, we must keep holding fast to what we have heard so that we do
not drift away. 2For if the word spoken through angels was valid and every transgression and act of disobedience received a just reward, 3how will we escape if
we neglect such a great salvation, which was first spoken through the Lord and
validated for us by those who heard, 4while God corroborated the testimony by
signs and wonders and various powerful deeds and distributions of the Holy Spirit according to his will?

NOTES

2:1. *Therefore, we must keep holding fast.* The verb *prosechein* was sometimes used for holding a ship on course toward port (LSJ, 1512), and the contrast with "drift away" (2:1b) suggests that the author is developing a nautical metaphor. The term also meant paying attention to a speaker (Acts 8:6, 10). Cognitively, people "hold fast" what they hear by keeping it in mind. Morally, they "hold fast" to it by living in accordance with it (Deut 32:46 LXX; cf. 4:9).

drift away. The Greek word *pararrein* could refer to the flow of a river (Herodotus, *Histories*, 2.150; 6.20; Strabo, *Geography*, 9.2.31) or slipping away from one's course (LSJ, sup., 115), which suggests that it continues the nautical metaphor (cf. 6:19; Luther WA.DB 7.349; Lane; H.-F. Weiss). Some prefer to take it in a general sense as in Prov 3:21 (LXX), "Son, do not drift away, but keep my counsel and insight" (Spicq; Ellingworth).

2:2. *For if the word spoken through angels.* There was a tradition that angels acted as God's intermediaries at Sinai. Biblical warrant is from Deut 33:2 (LXX): "The Lord came from Sinai . . . his angels with him." Paul appeals to this tradition to show that the Law was inferior to the promise (Gal 3:19), but most sources refer to the angelic mediation of the Law in order to stress the Law's exalted status (Acts 7:38, 53; *Jub.* 1:27, 29; 2:1; Josephus, *Ant.* 15.136). Hebrews argues that if angelic mediation shows how great the Law is, then the message proclaimed by the Son of God must be even greater, since he is greater than the angels.

was valid. Hebrews uses legal terminology within 2:1–4 (cf. 6:16; 9:17). The adjective "valid" (*bebaios*) and the related verb "validate" (*bebaioun*, 2:3) could indicate that something was legally binding. When a seller made a "valid" sale, he gave assurances that the item belonged to the purchaser and so guaranteed the transaction against anyone who contested it (Deissmann, *Bible*, 104–9; MM, 107–8). Jewish sources viewed the Mosaic Law as a firmly established and "valid" basis for judgment (cf. Philo, *Moses* 2.14). Hebrews assumes familiarity with this idea.

and every transgression and act of disobedience. Strictly construed, "transgression" meant overstepping the bounds established by law (Rom 2:23; Philo, *Dreams* 2.123), while "act of disobedience" meant refusing to heed someone (cf. Matt 18:17). Virtually synonymous, they can be used for various types of sin.

received a just reward. Ordinarily "reward" is used in a positive sense (10:35; 11:26; cf. 11:6). Here the author speaks in an ironic sense, using "reward" to mean punishment. The term *misthapodosia* may be a new coinage (p. 96) based on the expression "to give payment" (*misthon apodidonai*; Deut 24:15; Tob 2:12; Wis 10:17).

2:3. *how will we escape.* Listeners already knew about God's judgment and the coming Day of the Lord (6:1–2; cf. 10:25). The author returns to the impossibility of "escape" in 12:25, where he warns that the universe will be shaken by God (Luke 21:36; Rom 2:5; 1 Thess 5:3). Knowledge that God would surely punish the wicked and reward the righteous gave the martyrs incentive to remain faithful in times of persecution (2 Macc 6:26; 7:35; 4 Macc 9:32).

if we neglect. Like "drift away" in 2:1, "neglect" suggests a gradual, unthinking movement away from the faith. In common practice, those who were guilty of neglect could face serious penalties, such as reproof (*P. Fay.* #112.9), being relieved of one's duties (*P. Oxy.* #1070.50), and losing tenancy or property (*P. Oxy.* ##707.31; 1223.12; 1409.21). Cf. *TLNT* 1.87–89. Here neglect is tantamount to rejection of God's purposes (Jer 4:17; Wis 3:10; 2 Macc 4:14; Matt 22:5). Heedlessness is a trait of those who are overtaken by divine judgment (Matt 24:37–39; 25:1–12).

such a great salvation. Salvation is what listeners hope to inherit at the time of Christ's return (1:14; 9:28). The noun "salvation" and the verb "save" can be used for deliverance from threats to one's life (5:7; 11:7), but here the author refers to the "eternal salvation" (5:9; cf. 7:25) that people are granted by a final favorable judgment from God (6:10), which leads to glory (2:10). On the situation from which people are saved see COMMENT *b*.

which was first spoken through the Lord. The Greek is awkward (literally "taking the beginning of speaking"), but similar expressions appear in other Hellenistic texts (Philo, *Moses* 1.81; Diogenes Laertius, *Lives* proem 3.4). Although "the Lord" could refer to God (Bachmann, ". . . gesprochen"), most interpreters take the Lord to be Christ, as in Heb 1:10.

and validated for us. See NOTE on "valid" in 2:2.

by those who heard. This translation does not specify what people heard since the text itself does not do so (NASB; NAB2). Some translations do identify the implied object: **(a)** The author could refer to Jesus and "those who heard *him*" preach (NIV; NRSV; REB; NJB; Lane; Ellingworth). The implication is that the group addressed by Hebrews was founded by eyewitnesses, although it does not necessarily mean that the community was founded by one or more of the twelve disciples, since many heard Jesus preach. **(b)** The author may refer to the message of salvation and "those who heard *it*" (Attridge; Hegermann; cf. Grässer). The message is the subject of 2:2–4, and many listeners may have understood that the message was what was heard. In any case, early Christian writers did not always make a clear distinction between eyewitnesses and Christians of later generations (cf. Pol. *Phil.* 9:1; Irenaeus, *Against Heresies* 5.1.1).

2:4. *while God corroborated the testimony.* The unusual term *synepimartyrein* (literally "bear witness together with") was sometimes used to show agreement (*Ep. Arist.* 191), but Hebrews seems to evoke the more technical legal aspects of the term. The nearly identical term *synmartyrein* could introduce legally binding testimony: "I corroborate and subscribe" (MM, 610). Paul used *synmartyrein* for the conscience that acts as a law (Rom 2:15; cf. 8:16; 9:1), and *epimartyrein* is used in 1 Pet 5:12 to testify to the truth. The language underscores the listeners' accountability in the face of such testimony.

by signs and wonders and various powerful deeds. These terms are synonyms for miracles (e.g., Deut 4:34; 6:22; Ps 135:9; Matt 24:24; John 4:48; Acts 2:22, 43; 1 Cor 12:10, 28, 29; Gal 3:5; 2 Thess 2:9). Working miracles was a feature of the ministry of Jesus and his followers (Acts 2:43; 5:12; 6:8; 8:13; Rom 15:19; 2 Cor 12:12). The miracles were often healings and exorcisms (Acts 3:1–10; 5:16; 9:32–42; 14:8–18; 16:16–18; 19:11–12; 28:8–9). Paul also listed ecstatic speech as a "sign" (1 Cor 14:22). For medieval commentators the "signs" were minor miracles, like the healings done by physicians; "wonders" were major miracles, like raising the dead; and "powerful deeds" were spiritual virtues like humility or charity (Lombard; Herveus; Aquinas, *Ad Heb.* §99). Such distinctions do not follow Greek usage, however (P. E. Hughes).

and distributions of the Holy Spirit according to his will. The Spirit of God is mentioned seven times in Hebrews (2:4; 3:7; 6:4; 9:8, 14; 10:15, 29). One passage connects the Spirit to Christ's self-offering (NOTE on 9:14). Other passages connect the work of the Spirit to enlightenment or conversion (NOTES on 6:4–5; 10:29). The Spirit is also understood to speak through the OT (Heb 3:7; 10:15). The biblical description of the Levitical cultus is taken to be the Spirit's way of foreshadowing the work of Christ (9:8).

The term "distributions" was used for various things, including inheritance (*P. Oxy.* #493.8; *P. Ryl.* #65.5). The theme of inheritance was introduced in 1:2, 4, when the author spoke of Jesus being made heir of all things, and it recurred in 1:14 where others, presumably including the listeners, are identified as those who are about to inherit salvation. The distributions of the Spirit can be understood as a kind of preliminary apportionment of future inheritance (Eph 1:14; cf. 2 Cor 1:22; 5:5).

COMMENT[62]

In 1:5–14 the listeners were privileged to hear God address his Son amid the company of angels in heaven. Now, in contrast to the grandeur of this heavenly scene, the author depicts the situation of the listeners on earth as one of potential drift and neglect. The angels may have been attentive to God's Son and to the needs of his people, but the people are in danger of becoming inattentive to the message Christ brought. Therefore, the author seeks to capture the listeners' attention for what will follow (cf. §2 COMMENT *b*). The exordium began by recalling that God spoke to the people of old by the prophets (1:1) and by stressing that now God has spoken "to us" by the Son (1:2). It ends in a similar way by recalling what was formerly spoken by angels (2:2) and by emphasizing what had now been "spoken through the Lord" and validated "for us" (2:3). The first person plural gives directness and urgency to the address, as the author places himself and his listeners before the word of God by saying that "*we* must keep holding fast to what we have heard" (2:1).

a. Present Drift from the Word (2:1–3a)

The author's goal is that the listeners keep holding fast to what they have heard (2:1), just as he will later urge them to "hold fast to our boldness and the pride of our hope" (3:6), to "hold fast the assurance that was ours at first" (3:14), and to "hold fast the confession of our hope without wavering" (10:23). He warns that they are in danger of "drift" (2:1), a term that might be used for a boat that is gradually slipping away from its moorings: the movement may be subtle and even undetected by those who are on board. Similarly, "neglect" points to the kind of inattention to one's responsibilities that could lead to a deterioration in one's situation and to censure from one's superiors (NOTES on 2:1, 3; cf. 5:11; 6:12; 10:25). Reasons for the decline are never delineated and may not have been fully apparent to either the author or the listeners.[63] Therefore, without pursuing the causes, the author defines the situation in a manner that the listeners would find plausible yet disturbing in order to make them receptive to the exhortation to hold fast to the message.

The argument is based on the assumption that "the word spoken through angels was valid" (2:2a). The "word" was the Mosaic Law, which was the basis for how Jews conducted affairs within their communities in Palestine and the Diaspora.[64] The Law's status in the early church was complex. Christians agreed that

---

[62]Auffret, "Note"; Bachmann, ". . . gesprochen"; Feuillet, "Le 'commencement' "; Grässer, *Aufbruch*, 129–42; Laub, *Bekenntnis*, 46–50; Löhr, *Umkehr*, 79–84; Oberholtzer, "Warning," 83–97; Toussaint, "Eschatology," 68–70; Übelacker, *Hebräerbrief*, 150–62; Vanhoye, *Situation*, 228–54; W. Weiss, *Zeichen*, 120–76; Wider, *Theozentrik*, 119–37.

[63]Attridge, *Epistle*, 12–13. For a fuller discussion of the situation of the listeners see pp. 64–72.

[64]Josephus reproduces a number of Roman decrees allowing Jews to observe their ancestral laws (*Ant.* 14.213–67). Jews remained subject to non-Jewish rulers and often made use of non-Jewish institutions, but Tcherikover notes that living according to the ancestral laws involved maintaining Jewish synagogues, courts, and schools (*Hellenistic*, 296–302).

they were to love God and neighbor and to refrain from murder, adultery, and other sins (Mark 12:28–34; Rom 13:8–10), but they debated the extent to which statutes pertaining to circumcision, food, and other matters remained binding, especially upon Christians of Gentile background (Acts 15:1–21; Gal 2:1–10). Hebrews does not rehearse the debates over the Law that appear in Paul's letters and Acts, but argues that Christ's self-sacrifice abrogated Levitical practice (7:12, 18) and made regulations pertaining to food and drink obsolete (9:10). Whatever the status of the Law within the first-century church, the author assumes that it had been valid during its own time (see pp. 114–15).[65]

The listeners are also expected to know that under the Law "every transgression" received a "just reward" (2:2b). On one level this concerned the human administration of justice. For major offenses the Law prescribed the death penalty, while for lesser offenses restitution was to be made. This applied to actions resulting from neglect (Exod 21:29, 33–34) and ignorance (Num 15:27) as well as those committed intentionally (de Vaux, *Ancient*, 1.158–60). On another level the idea of just punishment was often understood to mean that God himself would punish the sinful during their lifetimes.[66] Nevertheless, since the wicked sometimes seemed to escape unscathed, other sources warned that they would be subject to divine justice after death (Dan 12:2; *4 Ezra* 7:17–44) or by being left in Hades instead of sharing in the resurrection.[67]

The author insists that the consequences for disregarding the message of Christ will be even greater than those for disregarding the Law.[68] One might imagine that if the punishment is to fit the offense, then God might neglect those who "neglect" his word (2:3). This was what happened when Moses' generation refused to remain in the covenant and God "neglected" them by allowing them to die in the wilderness (8:9; cf. 3:12–19). The impossibility of "escape" (2:3a), however, suggests that listeners must reckon not only with divine indifference but also with divine judgment. Listeners had already been instructed about this (6:2; 9:27), and the author strikes this theme in the digressions at the end of each series of arguments (p. 84). He warns that judgment will be like the burning of a field (6:4–8), that it will fall relentlessly on the impenitent (10:26–31), and that no one will escape when God shakes the universe (12:25–27). Warnings are not designed to rob people of hope, but to steer them away from danger in order to preserve them so that they might persevere and inherit what has been promised (cf. 6:12; 10:39).

---

[65]Jewish writers considered the Law to be permanent (Josephus, *Ag. Ap.* 2.277; Philo, *QE* 2.53) rather than temporary as Paul and the author of Hebrews viewed it (Gal 3:19–26; Heb 7:12, 18; 9:10). See pp. 114–15.

[66]Lev 26:14–39; Deut 28:15–68; Philo, *Rewards* 127–61. See Nickelsburg, *Jewish*, 63–64.

[67]2 Macc 7:14; *Pss. Sol.* 2:31; 3:11; 13:11; 14:9. See also Schürer, *History*, 2.464–67; E.P. Sanders, *Paul*, 125–28.

[68]This mode of argument (*qal weḥōmār*) was common in Jewish circles (Strack and Stemberger, *Introduction*, 21; Schürer, *History*, 2.344; cf. Matt 6:30; 12:11–12; Luke 11:13). Rhetorically, the passage follows a pattern of logical deduction or enthymeme (pp. 93–94).

b. Past Reception of the Word (2:3b–4)

The message of salvation was "first spoken through the Lord and validated for us by those who heard" (2:3b). This suggests that the preaching received by the early community was understood to continue Jesus' own preaching. In NT accounts of Jesus' preaching there are several dimensions to salvation: (**a**) Salvation from God's judgment. When Jesus announced, "The time is fulfilled, and the kingdom of God has come near," the appropriate response was to "repent, and believe in the good news" (Mark 1:15). This message assumes that human beings are sinners in danger of condemnation and that God himself poses the threat. In calling people, Jesus offered the hope that those who repented would find mercy rather than judgment (Matt 11:21–22; Luke 1:77; 19:9–10). (**b**) Salvation from the powers of evil. This aspect of salvation perceives that human beings are oppressed by the devil and in need of liberation. Here the forces of evil constitute the threat. According to the gospels, exorcisms were signs of the coming defeat of Satan (Matt 12:25–29; Luke 10:18; 13:16).[69] (**c**) Salvation for life in God's kingdom. The word of salvation also included the hope of sharing in the blessings of divine rule (Luke 13:23–30; cf. 23:39, 42). The announcement that the kingdom of God "has come near" points to the imminence of salvation, although the gospel accounts of Jesus' preaching retain the idea that salvation will be consummated only in the future.[70]

The message of salvation presupposed by Hebrews has contours similar to those outlined above: (**a**) Salvation from God's judgment. The Christian teachings that the listeners already received included the need for repentance and faith in God, the hope of the resurrection of the dead, the coming final judgment, and other matters (Heb 6:1–2; cf. 9:27; 10:27). The hope of salvation is the hope of being delivered from judgment (6:8–9). (**b**) Salvation from the powers of evil. The author understood that Christ delivered those who had been oppressed by the devil (2:14–15), although he connects this deliverance with Christ's death rather than his preaching or miracles. (**c**) Salvation for life in God's kingdom. The future of God's people is understood to include the inheritance of salvation (1:14), which is associated with glory and everlasting life (2:10; 5:9). Salvation is a present possibility for those who draw near to God through Christ (7:25), but its consummation remains future (1:14; 9:28).[71]

The author says that the salvation that Jesus preached was validated "for us by those who heard" (2:3c), which implies that neither the author nor his audience

---

[69]On the preaching of Jesus see Dunn, *Unity*, 13–16; Goppelt, *Theology*, 1.43–138. Vanhoye (*Situation*, 242–43) notes that Hebrews may be referring to the preaching that Christ did after the resurrection rather than during his public ministry. The Synoptic Gospels emphasize the element of repentance in Jesus' preaching both before his passion and after his resurrection (Luke 24:45–48; Acts 26:15–18, 23; cf. Matt 28:18–20).

[70]On "salvation" see *TLNT* 3.349–50; W. Foerster, *TDNT* 7.990–98.

[71]There is a clear connection between salvation and preaching, yet defining that connection is difficult. To speak of "salvation *as* word" (Grässer, *Aufbruch*, 129–42) or to say that "salvation is present in the word" (Laub, "Verkündigung," 175) does not give adequate emphasis to the future dimension of God's work (Toussaint, "Eschatology," 68–70).

were eyewitnesses, but received Jesus' message from other Christians.[72] The passage's stylized manner depicts the process of transmission in three stages: (1) the message originates with Jesus; (2) is heard and preached by Christian evangelists; and (3) is received by those to whom Hebrews is addressed. There is no clear distinction in the second stage between evangelists who personally heard Jesus preach and evangelists who had received the message from his earliest followers (NOTE on 2:3. On these evangelists see pp. 65–66). The concern in Heb 2:3–4 is to connect the message the listeners had received with Jesus himself.

The performance of "signs and wonders and various powerful deeds" served the proclamation of the message (NOTE on 2:4). Miracles were important because they disclosed the power of God in a perceptible manner. Just as Jesus' power to heal was a visible sign that he had the power to forgive sins (Mark 2:1–12 par.), Peter's healing of a lame man was a visible sign that Jesus had risen (Acts 3:1–26). Miraculous demonstrations would have been valuable confirmation for a message of salvation, since those who were convinced that God could save people from palpable illnesses would also trust that God could save them from a judgment that was still hidden in the future. Jews were sometimes reputed to demand miracles in order to demonstrate someone's legitimacy (1 Cor 1:22; John 2:18), and in the Greco-Roman world stories were told about the miracles from Asclepius and other gods.[73] Signs and wonders performed by early Christian evangelists would have been seen by many as divine confirmation of the message they preached (Heb 2:4). The problem was that if the miracles truly pointed to the saving power of God, why did the faithful soon experience denunciation, dispossession, and imprisonment (Heb 10:32–34; 13:13–14), and why was their community in a state of decline (10:25)?[74]

The experience of the Holy Spirit compounded the problem. The author assumes that God had given them "distributions of the Holy Spirit" (2:4b), apparently in connection with repentance and faith, baptism and the laying on of hands (6:1–4; pp. 65–66). For those to whom Hebrews was written, the message of salvation, which was attested by the ecstatic experience of the Spirit and miracles, seemed to be contradicted by their ongoing conflict with society and by a despondency among the community's members. The author did not seek to replicate the earlier ecstatic experience, since the basis of faith was not the miracles, but the message that was confirmed by the miracles. The community's life

---

[72]The debates about 2:3 and its implications for Pauline authorship became intense in the sixteenth century. See Luther (*LuthW* 35.394), Cajetan (Hagen, *Hebrews*, 24), and Calvin (*Epistle*, 1).

[73]On miracles in the OT see Exod 4:1–9; 7:3; Deut 34:11–12; 1 Kgs 17:8–24; 18:36–40; 2 Kgs 4:1–8:6. Later, the Jewish figures Honi the Circle Maker and Hanina ben Dosa gained reputations for working wonders (*m. Ta'an.* 3:8; *b. Ber.* 34b; *b. Yebam.* 121b; *b. Ta'an.* 25a). Stories of healing in the Greco-Roman world are found in many sources (e.g., Suetonius, *Vespasian* 7; Philostratus, *Life of Apollonius* 3.39; Tacitus, *History* 4.81; cf. Kee, *Miracle*, 78–145).

[74]It is not clear whether the author assumed that miracles were still being done in his own time (Hegermann, *Brief*, 64–65) or whether the time of miracles had ceased (Grässer, *Hebräer*, 1.108 n.76). The author emphasizes perseverance rather than hope for miracles. Cf. Bénétreau, *L'Épître*, 1.102–3.

began when the message of salvation was met with effective listening, and the author's aim is to evoke the kind of listening that can issue into a renewed confession of faith.[75]

[75]Cf. Grässer, *Hebräer,* 1.106; idem, *Aufbruch,* 129–42; H.-F. Weiss, *Brief,* 189; Bénétreau, *L'Épître,* 1.106; Laub, *Bekenntnis,* 49; idem, "Verkündigung," 176–77; P. E. Hughes, *Commentary,* 79.

II. PROPOSITION

◆

6. BUT WE SEE JESUS (2:5–9)

2 [5]Now, it was not to angels that he subjected the world to come, about which we are speaking, [6]but there is a passage that testifies: *What is man that you remember him, or son of man that you watch over him?* [7]*You made him for a little while lower than the angels, you crowned him with glory and honor,* [8]*you placed all things in subjection under his feet.*

Now in *placing all things in subjection* he left nothing that is not subject to him. At present we do not yet see *all things subjected to him;* [9]but we do see that Jesus, who was *for a little while made lower than the angels,* is *crowned with glory and honor* because of the suffering of death, in order that by the grace of God he might taste death for everyone.

NOTES

2:5. *Now, it was not to angels that he subjected.* The term "now" (*gar*) introduces a new section as in 7:1 (cf. 4:12; 10:1). It was sometimes thought that God entrusted the administration of the present world to angels, perhaps because Deut 32:8 (LXX) said that God "established the boundaries of the nations according to the number of the angels of God." Angels were associated with powers and principalities (Dan 12:1; Rom 8:38) and were said to watch things in this world. Hebrews 2:5, however, focuses not on the present world but on the future world.

the world to come. This identifies the "world" that the Son entered (cf. NOTE on 1:6). Like "universe" in 1:2, "world" has both spatial and temporal connotations. In 1:6 "the world" was the heavenly abode of angels, and in 2:5 it is a future reality. That which is "to come" is not, strictly speaking, future since through Christ and the Spirit believers experience the powers of the age "to come" (6:4–5; 9:11; 10:1). Yet there remains a future consummation in "the city that is to come" (13:14). The "world" is the place of divine rule in the Psalms: "The Lord has begun to reign . . . indeed he established the world, which shall not be shaken" (Ps 93:1 [92:1 LXX]; 96:10 [95:10 LXX]); cf. Vanhoye, "L'οἰκουμένη"). According to Hebrews, God will shake the present order (Heb 12:26), yet the faithful can hope to partake of God's reign in a future world (12:28).

2:6. *but there is a passage that testifies.* The verbatim rendering "someone has testified somewhere" (NRSV; NAB2) suggests that the author cannot identify the speaker in the passage or its location in Scripture. Yet when he says that "somewhere" (*pou*) the Scriptures refer to God's rest on the seventh day, he clearly understood that the text was taken from the opening chapters of Genesis (see Heb 4:3–4). Similarly, Philo used this expression in contexts where he knew the identity of the speaker (*Unchangeable* 74; *Planter* 90; *Drunkenness* 61). Introducing OT quotations without identifying their location may reflect the idea that the OT is the word of God, for if God or the Spirit is its true source (cf. 3:7; 5:5–6; 8:8; 10:15), there is little need to cite particular biblical authors (Moffatt, *Critical*, 22; Schröger, *Verfasser*, 254; Williamson, *Philo*, 516–18; Grässer, *Hebräer*, 1.115). The verb "testify" suits a solemn statement given publicly (Acts 20:21; 23:11; 28:23; cf. 1 Tim 5:21; 2 Tim 4:1). Its legal connotations fit with the terms used for divine speech at the end of the exordium ("valid," 2:2; "validate," 2:3; "corroborate testimony," 2:4).

2:6b–8a. The text is a quotation of Ps 8:4–6 (8:5–7 LXX). One principal difference between the MT and the LXX is that the MT speaks of one who is lower than *'elōhîm*, which could mean either "lower than God" or "lower than gods," with "gods" understood to be other heavenly beings. The LXX dealt with the problem by rendering it "lower than the angels." Hebrews closely follows the LXX except for omitting the line concerning the son of man being placed over the works of God's hands (P46 B). Some MSS do include the line (ℵ A C D*), probably to make the text correspond to the LXX (Cadwallader, "Correction," 280). Some have suggested that the line was omitted because it deals with dominion over the present world rather than the world to come (Zuntz, *Text*, 172), but the same logic would also apply to the expression "all things," which is retained in the next line. It seems unlikely that the difference from the LXX reflects theological concerns (F. F. Bruce). The omission may have been accidental, or the author may have abbreviated the text to focus on what was most important for interpretation.

Hebrews	*LXX*	*MT*
What is man that	What is man that	What is man that
you remember him,	you remember him	you remember him
or son of man that	or son of man that	or son of man that
you watch over him?	you watch over him?	you watch over him?
You made him	You made him	You made him
for *a little while*	for *a little while*	*a little*
lower than *the angels*,	lower than *the angels*,	lower than *God/gods*,
you crowned him	you crowned him	you crowned him
with glory and honor,	with glory and honor,	with glory and honor,
	and you established him	you established him
	over the works of	over the works of
	your hands,	your hands,
you placed all things	you placed all things	you placed all things
in subjection	in subjection	in subjection
under his feet.	under his feet.	under his feet.

Psalm 8 celebrates the exalted position of human beings in the created order (cf. Gen 1:26–28). Jewish sources seem to have understood Ps 8 this way, although some late texts use the question "What is man?" to show that human beings are of little account (*3 Enoch* 5:10; *Pesiq. Rab.* 34a). There is little evidence that Jewish sources understood the psalm messianically (Str-B 3.681–82). Early Christians connected Ps 8:7 with Ps 110:1, since these texts refer to God placing "all things" or "enemies" under someone's feet (cf. 1 Cor 15:25–27; Phil 3:21; Eph 1:22; NOTE on Heb 1:13). The use of language from Ps 8 for Jesus (e.g., Matt 21:16) does not suggest that the psalm had come to have an exclusively messianic sense by the time Hebrews was written, and Hebrews uses the psalm both for humanity and for Jesus.

What is man. The context of Ps 8 suggests that "man" (*anthrōpos*) is a collective noun referring to humankind, but since the noun is singular, it can be applied to the man Jesus, in whom God's design for humankind is realized. Cf. NOTE on "son of man" below.

that you remember him. To remember those who neglect divine salvation (2:1–4) would mean calling their failings to mind (Pss 25:7; 79:8; Neh 13:29), but the context suggests that God "remembered" people for their good (cf. Gen 8:1; 30:22; Exod 2:24; Heb 13:3).

or son of man. This expression has two levels of meaning, referring both to human beings and to Christ:

(a) OT and Jewish tradition. In the OT the singular (e.g., Ezek 2:1, 3, 6; Ps 144:3) and plural (e.g., Pss 4:2; 31:19; 33:13) of "son of man" commonly means "a human being." A possible exception is Dan 7:13, where one "like a son of man" comes on the clouds to rule a kingdom without end. Although the son of man could be a symbol for the saints who receive power and dominion (Dan 7:27), the cosmic dimensions of the figure suggest that he is more than a symbol. In *1 Enoch* the "son of man" is a messianic figure (46:3; 48:2; 69:27–29; 70:1; 71:14, 17). Other Jewish sources use similar imagery, but they do not use "son of man" for an eschatological figure, making it difficult to claim that it was a common messianic title in the first century.

(b) Early Christian sources. Paul's letters do not use "son of man" for Jesus. In the Synoptic gospels, Jesus seems to use "son of man" as a circumlocution meaning "I" (e.g., Matt 8:20). Other passages, echoing Dan 7:13, speak of the "son of man" coming on the clouds of heaven (Matt 26:64; Mark 13:26; Luke 21:27). Some insist that the title is consistently used in a nonmessianic sense in the NT (e.g., Hare, *Son*), and others emphasize its apocalyptic quality and connection with the coming rule of God in Jesus (e.g., Caragounis, *Son*). In John's gospel, the expression is more clearly connected with Jesus' messianic identity (John 12:34) and divine status (1:51; 3:14). It remains unclear, however, whether "son of man" had generally come to connote Jesus' messianic rule or role as eschatological judge at the time Hebrews was written.

(c) Hebrews. "Son of man" is parallel to "man" in 2:6, so that both terms most naturally mean "human being." The expression "son of man" has no definite article, whereas NT passages in which it may be a christological title regularly do include the article—John 5:27 is the exception. Hebrews does not refer to Jesus as "son of man" outside this quotation, even though one might expect it to if it were a christological designation. Hebrews does not use "son of man" as a technical term for Christ, but applies it first to human beings and secondly to Jesus, in whom God's designs for people are realized.

that you watch over him. "Watch over" could refer to God's vigilance against sin (Exod 32:34), but the emphasis here is on God's saving help (Exod 13:19; Jer 15:15; cf. Gen 21:1; 1 Sam 2:21).

2:7. *You made him for a little while lower.* In the MT the *m'ṭ* can only be taken quantitatively to mean "a little" lower in status, while the LXX's *brachy* can also be understood temporally as "a little while," which is how the author of Hebrews takes it. The context of the psalm indicates that those who were somewhat lower still occupied a prestigious position. The term for "lower" in the MT is *ḥāsēr*, which often meant "to lack" something, and the Greek *elattoun* could mean "to suffer loss" (1 Sam 2:5; Sir 31:4, 30). This allows Hebrews to connect it with Christ's suffering and death. In the psalm, being made lower than the angels and being crowned with glory and honor seem synonymous; in Hebrews they are opposites.

2:8. *you placed all things in subjection under his feet.* On the christological level, subjecting all things to the Son of God can be correlated with his role in sustaining and guiding all things (NOTE on 1:3) and with his love of righteousness and opposition to lawlessness (NOTES on 1:8–9). On another level, the text refers to the eventual subjection of all things to the people of God in the unshakable kingdom (12:28). Cf. NOTE on 1:13.

Now in placing all things in subjection. Most MSS (א A C D Ψ etc.) include "to him" (*autē*) at this point, but there is strong reason to follow the MSS that omit it (P^{46} B) since "subjecting all things" is the author's paraphrase of the portion of the psalm quoted in Heb 2:8a and that quotation lacks the pronoun. The added pronoun repeats the *autē* found at the end of the verse (Attridge). On the pattern of quoting then paraphrasing a biblical text in the same passage see 3:2, 5.

he left nothing that is not subject. The aorist "he left," which corresponds to the aorist "he subjected" in 2:8a, gives a sense of finality to God's action. The verb tense heightens the apparent contradiction between the message of Ps 8 and ordinary human perception that does not see its fulfillment. Some ease the tension by taking *anypotaktos* to mean that there is nothing that is "not subjectable" (Vanhoye, *Situation*, 277; Attridge). Yet "not subject" corresponds to common usage, in which the adjective refers to those who either are not under the authority of another or who refuse to recognize the authority of a king or master (Josephus, *Ant.* 11.217; cf. Philo, *Heir* 4; Epictetus, *Disc.* 2.10.1; cf. COMMENT *b*).

to him. The text creates tension because the author has not yet explained to whom the word "him" refers: (**a**) Humankind. The author could mean that listeners do not see all things in subjection "to humanity" since the glorious picture of humanity in Ps 8 was not realized in the experience of those who had themselves been subjected to abuse (10:32–34; 13:13–14). (**b**) Christ. Hebrews 1 depicted the Son of God enthroned in heaven, yet the earthly circumstances of Christ's people called into question the idea that all things were under his control. Both aspects of meaning are possible and press for resolution in what follows.

2:9. *but we do see that Jesus.* "Seeing" is related metaphorically to faith. The object of the seeing is Jesus, who is crowned with glory and honor, who is inaccessible to physical sight, and whose exaltation seems to be contradicted by experience. The idea that faith depends on a reality that is unseen is stated in Heb 11:1, while in 12:2 the author calls listeners to look to the exalted Jesus as they run the race of faith. On participles and verbs of perception in indirect discourse ("we see that . . . ") see MHT, 3.161; Vanhoye, *Situation*, 285.

who was for a little while made lower than the angels. The author correlates this element of the psalm with Christ's suffering and death. Later, he refers to Christ's cries and tears (5:7), the shame of his crucifixion (12:2), and his suffering outside the gate (13:12). Chrysostom connected this passage to Christ's descent into hell. Erasmus and Luther emphasized that Christ was not only a little lower than the angels but the most abject of men. Aquinas and Luther understood the passage to mean being forsaken by God (Isa 54:7–8). See Hagen, *Theology*, 93–95.

is crowned with glory and honor. Kings were crowned when they assumed the throne, Israel's high priest wore "a gold crown upon his turban" (Sir 45:12), and an athlete received a crown to mark the glory and honor of victory (1 Cor 9:25; 2 Tim 2:5). Here the royal aspect of the crown is dominant, since the one who bears the crown is said to have all things subjected to him. Yet Hebrews also ascribes to Jesus the honor of high priesthood (5:4–5) and victory in the race of faith (12:1–2). Chrysostom and Alcuin identified Jesus' glory with the crucifixion, which is appropriate for John's gospel (John 12:23; 13:30–31), but not for Hebrews, where the humiliation of the crucifixion precedes and leads to Jesus' glorification.

because of the suffering of death. The rule of an ordinary king ended with death, but Jesus' reign began with exaltation after death (1:1–14). The idea that Jesus was crowned "because" he suffered death helps to establish a pattern in which suffering, faithfully endured, does not negate glorification, but is the way to glorification.

by the grace of God. The translation is based on the most commonly accepted Greek text, which reads *chariti* ("by grace"): **(a)** A number of scholars favor the variant that says that Jesus died "apart from" (*chōris*) God. They note that although only a few late MSS read "apart from," one apparently reflects a textual tradition of the third or possibly late second century (1739*). More important, Origen suggests that the variant was common reading in the MSS available to him (FC 80.86; cf. Ambrose, PL 16.573A, 670B [NPNF2 10.231, 297]; Jerome, PL 26.384B; Theodore of Mopsuestia, PG 66.956D–957A; Garnet, "Hebrews"). Stylistically, "apart from" would be consistent with the rest of Hebrews, since this word appears frequently in Hebrews and is regularly followed by an anarthrous noun, as in this variant. The variant is the more difficult reading. It is easy to imagine a scribe changing the peculiar assertion that Jesus died "apart from God" to say that Jesus died "by the grace of God" (cf. 1 Cor 15:10; 2 Cor 1:12).

There are two types of theological interpretation for the variant: *(i)* Jesus died for all "apart from" or "with the exception of" God. Patristic writers took this to mean that Jesus suffered in his humanity, but not in his divinity (Ambrose, NPNF2 10.231, 297; Theodore of Mopsuestia; cf. Theodoret). Others held that Jesus died for all "apart from" or "except for" God, who needed no redemption

(Bengel; Ebrard; cf. 1 Cor 15:27, where all things "except for" God are to be made subject to Jesus). *(ii)* Jesus died "apart from" or "separated from" God (Mark 15:34; B. Weiss; von Harnack, "Zwei"; Zuntz, *Text*, 34; J. K. Elliott, "When Jesus"; Braun; Rissi, *Theologie*, 77–78; Ehrman, *Orthodox*, 146–50; Dunnill, *Covenant*, 224). Although emphasis on Jesus' suffering fits Hebrews (5:7–8; 12:2; 13:12–13), the reading "apart from God" may have come into disfavor because it could be taken to support Gnostic claims that the divine element left Jesus prior to his death. Later writers charged that the reading was a Nestorian fabrication (Ps.-Oecumenius; Theophylact).

(b) Most MSS (P^{46} A B C D 33 81 330 614 it vg co *al*) read "by grace" (*chariti*). According to this reading, God gave Jesus up to die for others out of divine favor. "Grace" suits Hebrews' style and emphasis (4:16; 12:28; 13:9; cf. 10:29; 12:15) and fits the immediate context, since the next verse (2:10) indicates that God was not absent, but involved in the suffering and death of Jesus in order to bring many people to glory. The variant may have emerged in order to explain that God was not among those for whom Christ died. This in turn fits biblical usage, since "apart from" commonly identifies those not included in the group just mentioned (e.g., Gen 46:26; Num 16:49; Judg 20:15, 17; 1 Kgs 5:16; Matt 14:21). See *TCGNT*, 664; Vanhoye, *Situation*, 295–99; P. E. Hughes, *Commentary*, 94–97.

he might taste death. Earlier scholars proposed that Jesus "tasted death" for a short time as a physician might taste bitter medicine in order to convince those who are sick to taste it (Chrysostom; Alcuin; Aquinas; Luther, *Lectures* 131; cf. Calvin). The expression, however, means that Jesus experienced death fully (Mark 9:1 par.; John 8:52). Cf. "the bitterness of death" (1 Sam 15:32; Sir 41:1) and "seeing death" (Heb 11:5). See J. Behm, *TDNT* 1.675–77.

for everyone. Most read *hyper pantos* as a masculine singular, "for everyone," but some read it as a neuter singular, "for everything," envisioning redemption of the whole creation (cf. Rom 8:21; Ambrose, $NPNF^2$ 10.297; Theodoret; Theophylact). Although the text can best be rendered "for everyone" and understood in terms of human salvation (cf. 1:14), the patristic view calls attention to the cosmic scope of God's redemptive work. The one who brings "many sons [and daughters] to glory" (2:10b) is the one "for whom and through whom all things exist" (2:10a), and the one who made purification for human sins also bears all things by his word (1:3).

COMMENT[76]

Reminders of the wonders that accompanied the listeners' initial reception of the gospel and of the ominous consequences of neglecting the message of salvation concluded the exordium in a manner designed to awaken a sense of expectancy

[76]On 2:5–9 see Brawley, "Discoursive"; Brock, "Hebrews 2:9b"; Dunn, *Christology*, 108–11; Franco Martínez, *Jesucristo*, 65–101; Glenn, "Psalm 8"; Grässer, *Aufbruch*, 155–65; Hurst, "Christology"; Kögel, *Sohn*, 6–48; Laub, *Bekenntnis*, 61–66; Leschert, *Hermeneutical*, 79–121; März, ". . . nur für kurze Zeit"; Peterson, *Hebrews*, 49–55; Schröger, *Verfasser*, 79–87; Swetnam, *Jesus*, 137–53; Übelacker, *Hebräerbrief*, 163–82; Vanhoye, *Situation*, 255–305.

(2:1–4). The next section (2:5–9), which identifies the principal issue to be addressed, can be called the *propositio* or "proposition."[77] A proposition was effective to the extent that it framed a question in a way that would contribute to its solution.

The main theme of Hebrews has been variously identified. Some stress the importance of 2:17–18, where Jesus is introduced as a merciful and faithful high priest, since the ensuing sections take up these qualities in reverse order: Jesus' faithfulness in 3:1–6, his mercy in 5:1–10, and his high priesthood in 7:1–10:25.[78] The problem is that priesthood is one theme, but not *the* theme of Hebrews. In 2:10–18 Jesus' death includes heroic as well as priestly elements, and 3:1 refers to Jesus as an "apostle" as well as a "high priest." Jesus' priestly ministry is prominent in the central part of Hebrews, but it is absent from 3:7–4:13, it receives little attention in the transitions that precede and follow the central section (5:11–6:20; 10:26–39),[79] it is almost entirely missing from the last part of the speech (11:1–12:24), and it is mentioned only briefly in the conclusion (13:10–12).

A promising alternative is to consider the pivotal role of 2:5–9.[80] The author acknowledges that God's design is that people be given glory and honor, but he recognizes that the listeners do not find this promise fulfilled in their own experience, and so he directs their attention to the suffering of Jesus that preceded his own exaltation to glory. He also introduces two aspects of Jesus' death that will be developed in subsequent sections. One is that Jesus was "crowned with glory and honor because of the suffering of death" (2:9c), preparing for others to follow the same course. This point is developed in the first series of arguments, which are framed by statements about Christ's suffering and exaltation (2:10; 5:8–10), and deal with questions of glory and honor (2:10; 3:3; 5:4–5). The other aspect is that Jesus' death is sacrificial: he suffered that "by the grace of God he might taste death for everyone" (2:9d). The sacrificial quality of Jesus' death is most fully explored in the second series of arguments concerning Jesus' priesthood and self-offering (7:1–10:18). The final series of arguments (11:1–12:24) returns to the conflict between the hope of life in God's kingdom and the experi-

---

[77]On the proposition in rhetoric see *Rhet. ad Her.* 1.10 §17; Cicero, *De inventione rhetorica* 1.22 §31; Quintilian, *Inst.* 4.4.1–9. Many speeches included a *narratio* or statement of the facts before the proposition. Übelacker (*Hebräerbrief*, 185–96) identifies 1:5–2:16 as the *narratio* and 2:17–18 as the *propositio*. A *narratio* was generally appropriate in speeches in court, but it was not essential (Quintilian, *Inst.* 4.2.4–5; 5.preface.5) and Hebrews omits it.

[78]See especially Vanhoye, *La structure*, 81–85. Others who consider 2:17–18 to state the main theme include Grässer, *Hebräer*, 1.151; idem, *Aufbruch*, 184, 195; Loader, *Sohn*, 201; Laub, *Bekenntnis*, 97–98; Übelacker, *Hebräerbrief*, 193–96.

[79]References to the priestly theme appear only at the very end of the first transitional section (6:19–20) and the beginning of the second one (10:26–31), where they form bridges between the treatment of Jesus' priesthood in 7:1–10:25 and the adjacent material.

[80]This was suggested in the eighteenth century by Bengel (*Epistle*, 335, 359) who said that Hebrews' "proposition and sum" was first stated through the quotation and interpretation of Ps 8 in Heb 2:5–9 and then developed in 2:10. More recent works that point to the pivotal role of 2:5–9 include Hurst, "Christology"; Brawley, "Discoursive."

ence of life in the world. Christians may not yet "see" all things subjected as God has designed (2:8c), but faith is bound to what is unseen (11:1). Since listeners do "see" that Jesus, who suffered and died, is now crowned with glory and honor (2:9), they can keep looking to him (12:1–2) as they journey toward the heavenly city that is the consummation of their hope (12:22–24). This approach allows the priestly work of Christ to be interpreted within the wider question of God's purposes for people (see pp. 87–89; §7 COMMENT).

The proposition is a discrete section, consisting of a quotation of Ps 8:4–6 and a brief exposition of the text.[81] It is positioned between two other defined sections of the speech. The section that precedes it (i.e., the exordium) is framed by sentences comparing the way God formerly spoke through prophets and angels with the way he spoke through the Son, who has been exalted above the angels (1:1–4; 2:1–4). The section that follows the proposition (i.e., the first series of arguments) is framed by statements about the Son of God becoming complete through suffering so that others might receive salvation through him (2:10; 5:8–10). Thus situated at the juncture where attention turns from the glory of the exalted Christ to the significance of his suffering, the proposition sets a course for what is to come.

This way of framing the issue suited the context in which Hebrews was composed. The author was addressing a Christian community in decline due to factors that may not have been apparent even to the members of the community themselves. Outbursts of violence had occurred in the past (10:32–34), but these had apparently given way to ongoing social stigmatization (13:13–14) and internal malaise (5:11–14; 10:25). Hebrews does not address these problems singly, but identifies an issue that undergirds the whole: the contrast between the glorious destiny promised to Christ's followers and the inglorious reality of Christian life in the world. The author also proposes a response, which is that Jesus' death and exaltation reveal that suffering does not negate God's saving purposes, but is the means by which his purposes are carried out.

a. God's Design for Humanity (2:5–8a)

The proposition is introduced with a statement designed to pique the listeners' interest. Declaring that "it was *not* to angels that [God] subjected the world to come," the author refrained from saying who *would* be given dominion over the future world. Some might infer that he was speaking about the dominion that was given to the Son of God (1:4–13), while others might assume that he was referring to the people of God (1:14). The ambiguity demands that people listen carefully for clarification (Vanhoye, *Situation*, 261).

---

[81]Many include 2:5–9 with 2:10–18 (e.g., Vanhoye, *Situation*, 255–387; H.-F. Weiss; Grässer; Ellingworth; Bénétreau; Übelacker, *Hebräerbrief*, 163–84). The arguments that begin in 2:10 are closely related to 2:5–9. Nevertheless, identifying 2:5–18 as a unit tends to separate 2:10–18 too sharply from what follows in 3:1–6 (§8 COMMENT).

The basis for the argument is established through the quotation of Ps 8:4–6, a text that speaks of the glory God intends for human beings. First, the quotation provides a common ground with listeners whom the author assumes will regard the psalm as a sacred text. Second, the psalm allows the author to address their situation in a complex fashion. A tension in the psalm enables it to bear two different lines of interpretation, both of which will be utilized by the author. The psalm asks about God's will for "man," which can be understood as a question about humankind generally so that Hebrews can deal with God's design for people (1:14; 2:3; 2:10). The psalm can also be taken as a statement about Jesus, who is God's Son and heir of all things. Psalm 110:1 (Heb 1:13) said that God told the Son that he would make his enemies a footstool for his feet. Since Ps 8:7 used very similar language to declare that God had placed all things "under the feet" of the "son of man," listeners might well assume that both texts referred to Jesus. Hebrews will develop both senses so that listeners can see in Jesus the fulfillment of God's purposes in a manner that anticipates and brings about the salvation of others.

b. Realization in Christ (2:8b–9)

The ambiguity created by the remark in 2:5 and the different interpretive possibilities for Ps 8 provide an opportunity to define the crux of the issue confronting listeners. When defining an issue, speakers tried to distinguish the points of agreement from those that were disputed. The formulation of this crux or *stasis* was most widely developed in juridical cases, but it was a feature of other kinds of oratory as well.[82] Hebrews formulates the issue in three steps:

(1) Inference. Psalm 8 said that "[God] placed all things in subjection under his feet" (Heb 2:8a). The author paraphrases the text and infers that "in placing all things in subjection," God "left nothing that is not subject to him" (2:8b). This intensifies the statement by saying that God's design includes "all things" without exception. Given what the psalmist said, listeners would presumably grant the validity of the inference, yet emphasizing the scope and decisiveness of what God has done—placing *all things* in subjection—heightens the contradiction between the biblical message and experience of the listeners, thereby preparing for the objection.

(2) Objection. The author next raises an objection that, once stated, would be readily apparent to his listeners. Experience does not conform to what is stated in the psalm, since at present "we do not yet *see* all things" in subjection as God intends (2:8c). Past experiences of persecution, continuing reproach, and internal malaise sharply call into question the idea that God has placed all things in subjection to either Christ or his followers (10:32–34; 13:1–3, 13).

(3) Response. The author responds to the objection by interpreting the psalm: **(a)** The end of the quotation is read in light of its middle. The quotation ended

---

[82]On the *stasis* of a speech see Quintilian, *Inst.* 3.6.1–104; Nadeau, "Hermogenes"; Lausberg, *Handbook* §§79–254.

with a reference to the glory, honor, and dominion that had been given to the son of man (Heb 2:7b–8a), but the middle of the passage said that the one crowned with glory had been made "lower than the angels" for a time (2:7a). In the context of Ps 8, the statements about being made "lower than the angels" and being "crowned with glory and honor" are parallel and could be understood synonymously; but Hebrews takes them to be opposites. Final glory must be considered in light of the lower status that precedes it. (**b**) The movement from lowliness to glory is interpreted in terms of Jesus' death and exaltation, which were already integral to the listeners' faith. The reference to the son of man being made lower than the angels for a time is correlated with Jesus' death, and the mention of glory and honor is identified with his exaltation. (**c**) When applied to Christ, the psalm describes his present situation (2:10); when applied to the people of God, the psalm promises future glory (1:14; 2:10).[83]

Tension remains between the completed and the continuing work of Christ. To say on the basis of Ps 8:7 that God "left nothing that is not subject to him" (Heb 2:8b) means that Christ is in full possession of the kingdom. But to say on the basis of Ps 110:1 that he sits at God's right hand until all his enemies have been put under his feet (Heb 1:13) recognizes ongoing opposition to his reign and the need for God's continuing action. Christ has set free those who were held captive to the fear of death (2:14–15), yet people still face the prospect of dying (9:27); Christ offered a sacrifice for sin that is valid for all time (9:26; 10:10), yet sin remains a threat with which people must contend (12:4). But because Christ has already gained dominion over death (7:23–25) and sin (4:15; 7:26), his followers can hope to share in this triumph.[84]

Christ's death is both exemplary and salvific. Being "crowned with glory and honor because of the suffering of death" (2:9b) is exemplary in that "glory" and "honor" are connected to faithfulness in hardship and to the humility of one who did not consider it shameful to identify with humankind (2:11). Jesus' example is demanding in that those who follow him are to lay sin aside and persevere (12:1–2), enduring the reproach that Christ endured (13:12–13; cf. 11:26). Yet Christ's example is also reassuring. Since Christ suffered and was exalted to God's right hand (1:3), the followers of Christ who suffer can hope for a place in an unshakable kingdom (12:28). The glory given to the Son anticipates the glory of all God's sons and daughters (2:10).[85]

The salvific aspect of Christ's death is grounded in "the grace of God" and achieves its effect in that Jesus tasted death "for everyone" (2:9d). The central

---

[83]See also §3 COMMENT *a* on the way Hebrews views the creation from the perspective of its consummation. On the idea that the destiny of humanity is realized in Christ see Kögel, *Sohn*; P. E. Hughes; Lane; Ellingworth; Grässer; Swetnam, *Jesus*, 137–41.

[84]Cf. Grässer, *Hebräer*, 1.120. Hegermann (*Brief*, 67–68) stresses the ongoing action of God and Christ in bringing all enemies into submission (cf. 1 Cor 15:25–26; Calvin, *Epistle*, 24).

[85]The author does not develop a typology between Adam and Christ as Paul does (Rom 5:12–21; 1 Cor 15:45–49), although he does indicate that God's design for humanity is realized in Christ. The "blessing of God has no application to us until what we have lost in Adam has been restored to us through Christ" (Calvin, *Epistle*, 21; cf. Dunn, *Christology*, 109–11; Vanhoye, *Situation*, 302).

portion of the speech (7:1–10:25) shows that it was a sacrifice for human sin, resembling the offerings made on the Day of Atonement, but surpassing Levitical offerings in that Christ's sacrifice is performed only once and cleanses the conscience, not just the body (9:11–14; cf. 2:17). Jesus' death also inaugurates the new-covenant relationship between God and people, bringing about the forgiveness of sins promised in Jer 31:31–34 (Heb 9:15–22; 10:15–18). Hebrews repeatedly states that Jesus died on behalf of (*hyper*) others (2:9; 6:20; 7:25; 9:24) without guaranteeing that everyone will enter into the presence of God and have a place in his kingdom. The warning that some may be lost (10:39) does not negate the idea that Jesus died for all, since according to Hebrews, the prospect of condemnation comes from human sin and unbelief, not from a lack of divine grace (cf. 4:2; 6:4–8).[86]

[86]In medieval controversies over predestination, 5:9 played a role. Some argued that Christ did not die for those whom God had not elected to salvation. Others insisted that Christ died for all people, but some forfeited salvation through their own unbelief. See p. 31.

III. ARGUMENTS

◆

A. First Series: Jesus Received Glory through Faithful Suffering—A Way that Others are Called to Follow

7. ARGUMENTS OF FIRST SERIES (2:10–6:20)

COMMENT

This section of Hebrews weaves themes and images into a complex tapestry of thought. One common approach has been to take 3:1 as the beginning of a new section that shows Christ's superiority to the institutions of the old covenant, including the angels who attended the giving of the Law (Heb 1–2), Moses who delivered the Law (Heb 3–4), and Aaron, the founder of the priesthood established by the Law (Heb 5).[87] A variation is to take 3:1 as the beginning of a section on Christ's high priesthood,[88] since the author introduces Jesus as "a merciful and faithful high priest" in 2:17–18 and discusses Christ's faithfulness in 3:1–6 and his mercy in 4:14–5:10. There are, however, good reasons to think that the comparison of Jesus and Moses in 3:1–6 does not begin a new section. The author begins his comparison with *hothen* ("because of this"), which shows that he is in the middle of an argument rather than at the beginning of a section (NOTE on 3:1). Repetition of key words and ideas strengthens connections between 2:10–18 and 3:1–6: God is the Creator of all things (2:10; 3:4), Jesus' followers are the brothers and sisters who belong to God's household (2:11–12; 3:1, 6), and they can be called "holy" (3:1) because Christ sanctifies them (2:11). The portrayal of Christ as the one sent to deliver people (2:14–16) and as the priest who makes atonement (2:17–18) continues in 3:1, where he is called "apostle" and "high priest." The similarities between Jesus and Moses that are implicit in 2:10–18 become explicit in 3:1–6 (§9 COMMENT *a*).

---

[87]The topical approach is reflected in the traditional chapter divisions, which begin with the comparison of Jesus and Moses in 3:1 and Jesus and Aaron in 5:1. Cf. P. E. Hughes, *Commentary*, 2–7; Loader, *Sohn*, 76–77, 258–59. Some suggest that the author discusses Moses after the angels because some Jewish traditions said that Moses ranked higher than the ministering angels (*Sifre Num.* §103; D'Angelo, *Moses*, 122–25; Williamson, *Philo*, 467; Lane, *Hebrews*, 1.cxxviii, 1.73). Others, who take the central concern of the speech to be the listeners' desire for unmediated access to God, argue that Moses and Aaron are discussed after the angels because they exemplify those who have attained such access (Dey, *Intermediary*, 179–83; Nash, "Notion," 112–13).

[88]Vaganay, "Le plan"; Vanhoye, *La structure*, 38–42; Attridge, *Epistle*, 17–19; Lane, *Hebrews*, 1.54; Ellingworth, *Epistle*, 193; cf. Spicq, *L'Épître*, 2.62–63.

A second approach has been to identify 1:1–4:13 as a section that is framed by references to the word of God in 1:1–2 and 4:12–13.[89] Many observe that after 4:13 the subject changes to the priesthood of Christ, which is considered at length in the central part of the speech. Within the section, the first half deals with the identity of the Son through whom God spoke (1:1–2:18), and the second half gives an appeal to the listeners to "hear his voice," unlike the wilderness generation who rebelled (3:1–4:13). The problem with this approach is that the most noticeable break does not occur after 4:13, but after 5:10, when the author digresses to address the listeners' dull hearing.

The approach in this commentary takes 2:10–5:10 to be the first section in the body of the speech and 5:11–6:20 to be a transitional digression between the first and second sections: **(a)** The beginning of this section is marked by a shift from the exalted view of Christ presented in the exordium (1:1–2:4) to an emphasis on Christ's suffering and death at the end of the proposition (2:5–9). What follows in 2:10–5:10 explores the meaning of Christ's suffering. **(b)** The end of the section is marked by the transitional digression (5:11–6:20), which can be distinguished from what precedes it by the shift in tone and content. This digression, like the one in 10:26–39, makes the transition from one major part of the speech to the next. See §13 COMMENT. **(c)** Arguments in between the proposition and the digression are framed by references to Christ being made complete through suffering, and to his role as pioneer or source of salvation (2:10; 5:8–10), as well as to matters of glory and honor (2:10; 3:3; 5:4–5).

Paragraphs within this section are connected like links on a chain. The first paragraph (2:10–18) announces that God brings people to glory through the work of the heroic "Pioneer of their Salvation," who liberates them from the fear of death, and through the merciful and faithful high priest, who makes atonement on their behalf. The second paragraph (3:1–6) connects Jesus' glory with his faithfulness, which poses a dramatic contrast to the unfaithfulness of the wilderness generation that is portrayed in subsequent paragraphs (3:7–11, 12–19; 4:1–10, 11–13). The final part shows that Jesus received the glory and honor of high priesthood, not by being exempted from suffering but through suffering (4:14–5:10). The thread that binds these ideas together is that Jesus' suffering led to his glory and made him the source of salvation for others. Listeners can therefore trust that as they follow Jesus, God will bring them to glory as well. On 5:11–6:20 see §13 COMMENT.

8. Perfection through Suffering (2:10–18)

2 [10]Now it was fitting for him, for whom all things and through whom all things exist, in bringing many sons [and daughters] to glory, to make the pio-

[89]A version of this view was developed in the sixteenth century by Bullinger (Hagen, *Hebrews*, 24–28). For more recent forms see von Soden, *Brief*, vi; Riggenbach, *Brief*, xxvi–xxvii; Michel, *Brief*, 6; Nauck, "Aufbau"; H.-F. Weiss, *Brief*, 8.

neer of their salvation complete through sufferings; [11]for the one who sanctifies and those who are sanctified are all of one. This is the reason he is not ashamed to call them brethren, [12]saying *I will declare your name to my brethren, in the middle of the assembly I will praise you.* [13]And again, *I will trust in him*, and again, *Here am I, and the children whom God gave me.* [14]Since, therefore, the children share in blood and flesh, he also shared in the same way with them, in order that through death he might destroy the one who has the power of death, that is, the devil, [15]and deliver those who, in fear of death, were subject to a lifetime of slavery. [16]Now [in doing this] he surely does not take hold of the angels but takes hold of the descendants of Abraham. [17]Moreover, this is why he had to become like his brethren in all things, that he might become a merciful and faithful high priest in matters pertaining to God, to make atonement for the sins of the people. [18]Because he suffered when he was tested, he is able to help those who are being tested.

NOTES

2:10. *Now it was fitting.* What is "fitting" (*prepein*) conveys a range of meanings. In the OT it is fitting for righteous people to praise God (Pss 33:1 [32:1 LXX]; 65:1 [64:1]), and holiness is fitting for God's house (Ps 93:5 [92:5]). Although the LXX does not use the term "fitting" for God's actions, some actions are appropriate given God's character, e.g., "Shall not the Judge of all the earth do what is just?" (Gen 18:25). Later sources apply what is "fitting" to God's relationship to the created order. Philo considered it fitting for God to plant virtues in the soul and to swear by himself (*Alleg. Interp.* 1.48; 3.203), to include lesser powers in the creative process (*Confusion* 175), and to grant immortal gifts (*Names* 79; cf. *Planter* 130; *Decalogue* 48). Similarly, Josephus held that it was fitting to teach that God was uncreated and immutable (*Ag. Ap.* 2.168). Philosophers considered it fitting for the gods to preserve and direct the universe (Plato, *Laws* 10 [899d–903a]; Ps.-Aristotle, *On the Cosmos* 6 [397B–398B]). Although many who understood that God had power over all things would have considered it incongruous for him to choose suffering for his course of action, Hebrews contends that it was fitting for God to carry out his purposes precisely through the suffering of his emissary (Williamson, *Philo*, 88–93).

The NT does not discuss what was "fitting" for God to do, although Matt 3:15 says that it was "fitting" for Jesus to be baptized. When asking why God allowed Jesus to suffer, NT writings more commonly state that "it was necessary" (*dei*) for Christ to suffer to fulfill the Scriptures (Matt 16:21; 26:54; Mark 8:31; Luke 24:7, 26, 44; John 3:14; cf. Acts 3:18). Hebrews' argument that Jesus' passion was morally congruent ("fitting") with God's character and aims is distinctive within the NT, although later theologians argue along similar lines (e.g., Athanasius, NPNF2 4.43; Augustine, NPNF1 3.174; see P. E. Hughes, *Commentary*, 98–99; Spicq, *L'Épître*, 2.36–37).

for him, for whom all things and through whom all things exist. The preposition *dia* is used in two different ways. When followed by the accusative case, it means "for whom" (1:14; 6:7), and when followed by the genitive case, it indicates agency: "through whom." In 1:2 the Son was the agent "through whom" (*di' hou*) God made the universe, whereas God himself is the agent in 2:10. This language had broad currency in antiquity. Stoics spoke of deified nature as the source from which life comes and to which life returns (Marcus Aurelius, *Meditations* 4.23; Philo, *Special Laws* 1.208; Diogenes Laertius, *Lives* 1.3); Ps.-Aristotle wrote that all things are from God and established by God (*On the Cosmos* 6 [397b]; cf. Aristides, *Oration* 45.14). Philo agreed that God was the cause of all things, though he insisted that the Word was the agent of creation (Philo, *Cherubim* 125–28; cf. Aristobulus [*OTP* 2.838, 840]). Early Christians used comparable expressions (Rom 11:36; cf. 1 Cor 8:6; Col 1:16). Stoics used the expression in a pantheistic framework, but Hebrews locates it within a theology that distinguishes the Creator from the creation. God is not equated with "all things" (*panta*), but is the one with the power to place "all things" in subjection (Heb 2:8).

in bringing. The participle *agagonta* is in the accusative case and its subject has been disputed. Some connect it with Christ, since "pioneer" (*archēgos*) is also in the accusative case. Thus God perfects Christ the pioneer, who "brings many sons to glory" (Erasmus, *Paraphrase;* Delling, *TDNT* 1.488; Käsemann, *Wandering*, 143 n. 156; Jewett, *Letter*, 41, 45; Buchanan; see P. E. Hughes, *Commentary*, 101–2). Most interpreters connect the participle with God, since God is the implied subject of the infinitive "to complete." Accordingly, God, "in bringing many sons [and daughters] to glory," made Jesus the pioneer "complete" (cf. 13:20; Braun; Attridge; Lane; H.-F. Weiss). The aorist tense suggests ingressive action, since God will still bring many to glory (Vanhoye, *Situation*, 309–10).

many sons [*and daughters*]. Previously "son" was used in the singular for Jesus; here it is used in the plural for Jesus' followers. "Many" could suggest a limitation, implying that not "all" will receive what is promised (4:1, 6; 6:4–8; 10:26–31, 39; 12:17; cf. Grässer, *Hebräer*, 1.129), but the emphasis here is on the expansive scope of God's action: God intends glory for many, not only for a few. The word *huioi* can be rendered as "sons and daughters" (Attridge) or "children" (NRSV; NAB2) to emphasize that salvation is for both men and women. Using "son" for Jesus and his followers does not negate the differences—Jesus sanctifies while his followers are sanctified (2:11)—but its use does suggest commonalities:

(a) Origin. Both the Son and the sons and daughters exist because of God. The *mode* of their relationship to God differs, however, since the Son is God's agent of creation (1:2) and the sons and daughters are God's creatures. Hebrews does not suggest that the "many sons" of God were preexistent in the sense that Christ was (NOTE on "all of one" in 2:11). People become God's children and heirs of salvation (1:14) when the God who created them encounters them with the message of salvation and awakens in them the faith to receive it (2:3–4). These are the children whom God has "given" to Jesus (2:13).

(b) Inheritance. People normally bequeathed their property to their children; in cases of childlessness they would adopt someone as "son" in order to have an heir (E. Schweizer, *TDNT* 8.398). Theologically, God's children become heirs of God's kingdom (Gal 3:29; Rom 8:16–17). Jesus the Son is already "heir of all things" (Heb 1:2) and God's many other sons and daughters look forward to "inheriting salvation" (1:14; cf. 6:12, 17; 9:15). Jesus is already "crowned with glory and honor" (2:9), and others anticipate being brought "to glory" by grace (2:10).

(c) Suffering. Jesus the Son was made complete and learned obedience by suffering (2:10; 5:8), and Jesus' followers must therefore recognize that their afflictions may be a way in which God instructs them as "sons" in order that they might share in life and holiness (12:5–11). Cf. Bornkamm, "Sohnschaft," 188–98; Vanhoye, *Situation*, 313; H.-F. Weiss, *Brief*, 212–13.

to glory. Glory is the consummation of the salvation promised in 1:14 and 2:3. According to 2:9, Jesus already possessed the glory for which God created people; here the hope of glory extends to all the children of God. Glory has two important aspects:

(a) Honor. Glory is frequently related to honor, which is the positive value that people receive from others (2:7, 9; 3:3; 5:4–5; NOTE on 2:11b). Ancient writers often distinguished the glory given by the masses from the glory that comes from God or virtue (Isocrates, *Panathenaicus* 260–61; Seneca, *Ep.* 113.32). For Jewish and Christian writers, knowing that God was the source of genuine honor gave people the courage to act faithfully even when this meant being publicly dishonored or killed (Wis 5:4–5, 16; Bar 5:1–4; 4 Macc 17:20; deSilva, *Despising*, 80–144).

(b) Divine Presence. "Glory" was used in the LXX and Jewish and Christian writings for divine power and presence (NOTE on 1:3). Those who entered into glory entered the sphere where God's presence was manifest, which was sometimes envisioned as life in a restored Jerusalem or in God's kingdom (Isa 60:19; Tob 13:14–17; Bar 5:7–9). Entering glory would mean life everlasting in the presence of God (Rom 2:7; 5:2; 1 Cor 15:42–43; Eph 1:18; 1 Pet 1:21; 5:10). Hebrews depicts the destiny of the faithful as divine rest (Heb 4:10), entering the sanctuary (10:19), and arriving at Mt. Zion (12:22).

the pioneer. The Greek term used here and in 12:2 (*archēgos*) is formed from roots meaning "first" (*archē*) and "to lead" (*agein*). The most common uses were for a leader and a founder. The translation "pioneer" plays on both aspects of meaning:

(a) Leadership. The initial part of *archēgos* is *archē* ("first"), which could refer to primacy. For example, Exod 6:14 uses it for the heads of Israel's tribes. In Hebrews, Jesus is both the *arch-ēgos* ("chief") and *arch-iereus* ("chief priest," Heb 2:17), giving him unique and superior status. The second part of *archēgos* is based on the verb "to lead" (*agein*). By combining it with the participial form of the verb (*agagonta*) the author draws out the sense of leadership. The term was used for those who led the tribes in the wilderness (Num 10:4; 13:2–3) and in battle (Judg 5:15; 9:44; 11:6, 11; 1 Chron 5:24; 8:28; 26:26; 2 Chron 23:14; Neh 2:9; Jdt 14:2). Jesus leads God's people forward as the pioneer (cf. "apostle" in Heb 3:1) who delivers them from bondage to enter divine rest and as the high priest who leads the way into the sanctuary. In 12:2 Jesus the pioneer has completed the race that his followers are now running, just as in 6:20 he is the "forerunner" who has gone before the people into the sanctuary. We could translate that God, "in leading many sons [and daughters] to glory, made the leader of our salvation perfect through suffering" (cf. Acts 5:31).

(b) Founder or originator. This fits the use of *archē* for what is "first." Heracles was sometimes called the founder or *archēgos* of a city (Dio Chrysostom, *Disc.* 33.47). Acts 3:15 calls Jesus the originator or "author" of life, which is similar to calling him the "source of salvation" (Heb 5:9). Hebrews plays on this sense by juxtaposing *archēgos* with words for *telos* or goal ("completion"). Thus 2:10 suggests that God "brought the originator of our salvation to completion through suffering." In 12:2 the author identifies Jesus as "the founder and finisher of faith."

salvation. See NOTE on 2:3.

make . . . complete. The various forms of "complete" (*tel-*) have to do with the realization of God's promises (see pp. 122–25).

2:11. *for the one who sanctifies.* Like the OT, Hebrews distinguishes what is holy (*hagios*) from what is common (*koinos*; 9:13). To sanctify something or to make it holy is to set it apart for divine use. See pp. 120–21. God himself sanctifies people (Exod 31:13; Lev 20:8; 21:15; 22:9, 16; Ezek 20:12; 37:28; 2 Macc 1:24–26), but has sometimes done so through other agents, like Moses (Exod 19:14; 29:1; Lev 8:11–12). Here, Christ is the one who sanctifies.

and those who are sanctified. On sanctification see pp. 120–21.

are all of one. This expression (*ex henos*) is ambiguous and has been subject to two general lines of interpretation of which the first is preferable:

(a) Theological. The unity between Christ and human beings has God's action as its source. This takes "one" (*henos*) to be masculine, referring to God (Chrysostom; Theophylact; Luther, WA 57,3.13; Attridge; Lane; Laub, *Bekenntnis*, 77; cf. Deut 6:4; Rom 3:30; 1 Cor 8:6; Gal 3:20; 1 Tim 2:5). Hebrews 2:10 stated that "all things" (*ta panta*) exist for God and came into being through God; therefore, to say that sanctifier and sanctified are "all [*pantes*] of one" means that they share a common origin in God. Christ was uniquely the Son of God (1:2, 5), but others are sons of God in an extended sense (2:10). Christ can call them his "brethren" (2:11b) because of this common parentage (NASB; NRSV).

(b) Anthropological. Christ shares with others a common humanity. Some maintain that the "one" is neuter, referring to a common bloodline (cf. Acts 17:26) since Heb 2:14 refers to the "blood and flesh" Jesus shared with others (Calvin; P. E. Hughes; Vanhoye, *Situation*, 334). The text might be translated "of one stock" (NJB; REB) or "of the same family" (NIV). Others suggest that the term is masculine, referring to Adam, the "one" ancestor of all humanity (Rom 5:12–21; Ps.-Athanasius, PG 26.1224; Sedulius Scotus, PL 103.255B; Héring), although this is unlikely since Adam is not mentioned in Hebrews. More promising is that the "one" is Abraham, since Heb 2:16 speaks of Abraham's descendants and 11:12 refers to those who are born "from one," namely Abraham, the "one" progenitor of Israel (Isa 51:2; Ezek 33:24). See John of Damascus, PG 82.940B; Buchanan, *Hebrews*, 32; Swetnam, *Jesus*, 132–34; Rissi, *Theologie*, 60, 120; Ellingworth, *Epistle*, 165; Dunnill, *Covenant*, 209–13. On Gnostic sources see pp. 60–61.

"All of one" is best understood in the theological sense, since the context stresses that Christ redeems the sons or children of *God* (2:10, 13), whereas the descendants of Abraham are not mentioned until 2:16. It was fitting for God to bring many to glory because they belonged to him (see COMMENT *a*).

This is the reason. Although the NA[27] includes all of 2:11 in the same sentence, it is preferable to begin a new sentence here since the subject matter changes from sanctification to brotherhood (cf. NIV; NAB[2]; NRSV). It is not uncommon for this expression (*di' hēn aitian*) to stand at the beginning of a sentence (Philo, *Creation* 100; 2 Tim 1:6; Tit 1:13; cf. BAGD, 26 [1]). Although some suggest that "the reason" Jesus calls others his brethren is that their preexistent souls were related (Grässer, *Aufbruch*, 184–85; see COMMENT *a*), this is implausible. Brotherhood exists not because of preexistence, but because God has "given" people to Jesus (2:13; H.-F. Weiss).

he is not ashamed. The desire to gain honor (cf. 2:8–9) and to avoid shame for oneself and one's family was an important factor in shaping behavior (Sir 3:10–11; 41:6–7; 47:20). Honor and shame could be ascribed to a person by society or by God, and many recognized that public opinion was an unreliable measure of a person's worth. Therefore, Jewish and philosophical sources exhorted people not to be ashamed of doing justice and speaking the truth even if society regarded these as disgraceful (Sir 4:21; 41:16; 42:1–8; 51:29–30; Seneca, *Ep.* 113.32; 102.17). Those addressed by Hebrews were viewed with contempt by society (Heb 10:32–34; 13:13–14), but Christ was not ashamed to identify with them, just as God was not ashamed to identify with Abraham and his family, who spent their lives as foreigners (11:16). Cf. deSilva, "Despising," 457–58.

to call them brethren. The term "brother" was used not only for members of one's family but for the people of Israel (Exod 2:11; Deut 18:15; 1 Macc 5:32), friends (2 Sam 1:26; Ps 35:14; Juvenal, *Satires* 5.135), and others in a religious group (MM, 8–9; K. H. Schelke, *RAC* 2.631–40). To call someone a brother implied generosity and help (Prov 17:17; Sir 29:10; 40:24). People often reserved the term "brother" for persons of comparable social status, and when someone called another person a brother, social distinctions gave way to a sense of unity. Early Christians called members of their communities "brethren" (Heb 3:1, 12; 10:19; 13:22; cf. 1 Cor 8:11, 13; Phlm 16; Jas 2:15; 1 Pet 5:12; 1 John 2:9) and exhibited "care for the brethren" (Heb 13:1).

2:12. *saying, I will declare your name to my brethren.* The quotation is from Ps 22:22 (21:23 LXX). The one difference is that Hebrews says "I will declare" (*apangelō*), whereas the LXX says "I will recount" (*diēgēsomai*). Jewish interpreters apparently did not interpret Ps 22 messianically (Fabry, "Wirkungsgeschichte"), but Christians associated it with Jesus' death (Ps 22:1=Matt 27:46; Mark 15:34; Ps 22:18=John 19:24; cf. Matt 27:35; Mark 15:24; Luke 23:34).

in the middle of the assembly I will praise you. The word "assembly" (*ekklēsia*) was used for Israelite gatherings (Deut 31:30; Judg 20:2) and civic gatherings in Greco-Roman cities (Acts 19:39). It identified local Christian congregations (Rom 16:5; 1 Cor 16:19) and the church as a whole (Matt 16:18; Acts 9:31). Hebrews speaks of the assembly in heaven (NOTES on Heb 12:22–23), but uses *episynagōgē* for the local Christian "gathering" (10:25).

2:13. *I will trust in him.* The most probable source of the quotation is Isa 8:17, since Isa 8:18 is quoted in Heb 2:13b. Similar expressions appear in Isa 12:2 and 2 Sam 22:3. In Isaiah, the prophet is the speaker; in Hebrews, Christ is the speaker. The trust that Christ exhibits is related to the faith that is fitting for every child of God (Heb 11).

Here am I, and the children whom God gave me. The quotation is from Isa 8:18 LXX, where the prophet speaks about the children that his wife bore. These children, who were given symbolic names (Isa 8:1–4), were "signs and portents," which could suggest that the text had significance beyond its immediate context. Isaiah 8:14 is used of Christ in Rom 9:33 and 1 Pet 2:8, but Isa 8:17–18 is not interpreted messianically elsewhere in the NT.

2:14. *Since, therefore, the children share in blood and flesh, he also shared.* "Flesh" connotes limitation: Jesus spent the days of his flesh on earth (5:7), regulations of the flesh are temporary (9:10, 13), and fathers of flesh instruct children for a while (12:9). Similarly, shedding "blood" involves injury or death (12:4). Like others, Jesus shares blood and flesh, but unlike them, his flesh (10:20) and blood secure atonement (9:12, 14; 10:19; 13:12).

through death. Jesus entered the realm of death by crucifixion, but did not remain in its clutches, for through resurrection and exaltation he passed "through death," making a way to everlasting life for God's people to follow.

he might destroy. The verb *katargein* can mean depriving something of its power (Rom 3:31; Eph 2:15) or destroying it (1 Cor 6:13). Since Hebrews assumes that evil and death remain (Heb 3:12; 9:27), the sense is that the destruction of death and the devil has begun but is not yet complete. The gospels associate Jesus' conflict with the devil with exorcisms (Mark 3:26; cf. Matt 12:26; Luke 10:18; 11:18), but Hebrews stresses the conflict that took place in Jesus' death and resurrection (cf. John 12:31–32; 14:30–31; 1 John 3:8). Other NT writings look for the destruction of the devil and death at the end of time (Rev 12:7–8; 20:1–3, 10; 1 Cor 5:5; 15:24–26; 2 Tim 1:10; cf. *T. Mos.* 10:1; *T. Levi* 18:12).

the devil. The term *diabolos* was used by the LXX for the Hebrew *sātan*, which means "accuser" or "slanderer." The devil, as a personification of evil, is rare in the OT but more common in later Jewish writings (W. Foerster and G. von Rad, *TDNT* 2.72–81). Two aspects of the devil's work should be noted: **(a)** Agent of death. The serpent that lured Adam and Eve into sin and separation from the tree of life was later identified with Satan (Wis 2:23–24; cf. Rev 12:9; John 8:44; 13:2, 27). Hebrews does not speculate on the origins of death, but focuses on the devil's power to intimidate people with it. **(b)** Tempter. The devil may "test" people by inflicting suffering upon them, as in the case of Job and others (Job 1–2; Wis 2:17–20, 24; 1 Pet 5:8; Rev 2:10). The devil may also "tempt" people by making sin seem attractive (Matt 4:1; Mark 1:13; Luke 4:2, 13; 1 Cor 7:5); therefore, he could be called "the tempter" (Matt 4:3; 1 Thess 3:5; cf. 2:18; 1 Cor 7:5). When people sin, they fall prey to the devil's wiles (Eph 4:27; 1 Tim 3:7; 2 Tim 2:26; 1 John 3:8).

2:15. *deliver.* Christ's death, resurrection, and exaltation bring destruction for the devil, but deliverance for human beings. The term "deliver" (*apallassein*) could be used for the legal process of manumission (Philo, *Special Laws* 1.77) or for freeing people from slavery through conflict (Josephus, *Ant.* 13.363), which is the sense here.

in fear of death, were subject to a lifetime of slavery The idea that fear of death is a form of slavery appears elsewhere: "Are you a slave and afraid of death, which might set you free from suffering?" (Euripides, *Orestes* 1522), or "Who can be a slave if he gives no heed to death?" (Plutarch, *Mor.* 34B; 106D; Cicero, *Letters to Atticus* 9.2a). These writers argue that one overcomes the fear of death by recognizing that death brings release from suffering (Musonius Rufus, frgs. 3, 8, 17; Epictetus, *Disc.* 1.17.25; 1.27.7–10; 2.18.30; 4.7.15–17; Cicero, *Tusculan Disputations* 1; Dio Chrysostom, *Disc.* 6.42; Plutarch, *Mor.* 476B; cf. Lucretius, *Nature of Things* 1.107–111). In Hebrews, however, death is an instrument of the devil, so that it is not to be welcomed, but overcome.

2:16. *take hold.* The basic meaning of *epilambanesthai* is to lay hold of something or to hold fast to it. When the verb is read with what precedes, it suggests that Christ takes hold of people to rescue them (2:15). When read with what follows, it suggests that Christ takes hold of or offers help to those who are being tested (2:18). Formerly, many thought that the verb meant that Christ "took on" human nature by his incarnation (Chrysostom; Theodoret; Theophylact; Ambrose, NPNF2 10.255; Anselm of Laon; *Glossa ordinaria*; Aquinas, *Ad Heb.* §148; Erasmus, *Paraphrase;* Calvin; KJV; Spicq; P. E. Hughes), but this is unlikley. Hebrews 8:9 uses the verb to tell how God "took hold of [the Israelites'] hand to bring them out of the land of Egypt" (=Jer 31:32 [38:32 LXX]). Similar imagery is used in Isa 41:8–10 (LXX): "But you, Israel my child [*pais*], Jacob, whom I have chosen, descendants of Abraham whom I love, whom I took [*antilambanein*] from the ends of the earth and called you from its farthest corners and said to you, 'You are my child [*pais*]' . . . Do not fear [*phobou*], I am with you . . . I helped [*boēthēsa*] you." Hebrews echoes the italicized words: God's child (Heb 2:13–14), the "seed" of Abraham (2:16), is taken hold of by God (2:16) and told not to fear (2:15), but to trust in divine help (2:18; cf. Ellingworth, *Epistle*). In rescuing Israel God claims them (cf. Wis 2:18).

descendants of Abraham. Literally, the "seed of Abraham." The passage seems to echo Isa 41:8–10 (see the previous NOTE) in which this expression refers to Israel. In Hebrews the descendants of Abraham include Israel's ancestors and the Christian community (Heb 11:39–40; cf. Gal 3:29; Rom 4:13, 16). Abraham's descendants are God's "sons" (2:10) and Jesus' "brethren" (2:11). Abraham was "tested" (Gen 22:1; Heb 11:17) and his descendants will be tested also (2:18).

2:17. *he had to become like his brethren in all things.* When Christ became like others "in every respect," he fully entered the human condition (cf. Phil 2:7). Gregory of Nazianzus maintained that Christ had to become fully human, for what Christ did not assume in his incarnation, Christ did not redeem (NPNF2 7.440).

merciful and faithful high priest. There were some precedents for thinking of a priestly messiah. By the second century B.C., the high priest was a principal leader of the Jewish people (Sir 50:1–21) and the Maccabees gave the high priests royal powers (1 Macc 10:15–20; 13:42; 14:41). The reign of Simon, the king and high priest, was eulogized as a time when biblical prophecies concerning peace were fulfilled (1 Macc 14:4–15). Some Jewish authors looked for a messianic priest as well as a messianic king (1QS IX, 11; cf. CD XII, 23; XIV, 19; XIX, 10; XX, 1; *T. Levi* 18:1–14; Schürer, *History*, 2.550–54; Collins, *Scepter*, 74–101), but unlike Hebrews, they did not speak of the messianic priest's intercession (Heb 7:25) or self-sacrifice (9:12, 14, 26). Attridge (*Epistle*, 97–103) traces Hebrews' priestly Christology to traditions about angels conducting priestly services in heaven (Isa 6; *Jub.* 2:2; 31:14), where they offer bloodless sacrifices (*T. Levi* 3:4–6; 4Q400 1, I, 2–4, 16) and intercede for sinners (*1 Enoch* 15:2; 40:6; 47:2; 99:3). Nevertheless, these angelic ministers were not said to have taken on blood and flesh or to have sacrificed themselves. The view represented in Hebrews is difficult to derive from other sources. See NOTE on 3:1.

in matters pertaining to God. See NOTE on 5:1.

to make atonement for the sins of the people. Atonement encompasses the removal of divine wrath and the removal of human sin. See pp. 121–22.

2:18. *Because he suffered when he was tested.* The word *peirazein* has a double aspect: **(a)** Tempted. Temptation makes something sinful looks attractive. The devil was a tempter (NOTE on 2:14), and sin makes what is wrong appear to be good (3:13). **(b)** Tested. People could be put to the test either by the devil or by God. The first "descendant of Abraham" (cf. 2:16) was Isaac, and God tested Abraham by telling him to sacrifice Isaac (Gen 22:1–2; Heb 11:17–19). Nevertheless, God does not abandon those who fear him "even though for a brief time he may stand aside in order to test the disposition of the soul" (*T. Jos.* 2:6). See also NOTE on 3:9.

he is able to help. With respect to God, Christ offers help in the form of intercession so that people can find grace and mercy with God (4:16). With respect to threats from the world, "the Lord is my helper and I shall not fear; what can a human being do to me?" (13:6).

those who are being tested. If listeners are "tempted," it may be the work of the devil, but if they are "tested" it may be instruction from God (12:5–11). Abraham was tested by God (Gen 22:1), and the same may be true for his descendants. See NOTE on "tested" above.

COMMENT[90]

The mention of Christ's death in 2:9 marked a turning point in Hebrews, as the exordium's majestic portrait of Christ gave way to consideration of the suffering

---

[90]On 2:10–18 see Andriessen, "La teneur"; Aune, "Heracles"; Dey, *Intermediary*, 215–26; Dolfe, "Hebrews 2,16"; Dunnill, *Covenant*, 188–226; Fabry, "Wirkungsgeschichte," 279–317; Franco Martínez, *Jesucristo*, 103–30; Grässer, *Aufbruch*, 181–200; Hickling, "John and Hebrews"; Hurst, "Christology"; Johnston, "Christ as Archegos"; Käsemann, *Wandering*, 122–67; Kögel, *Sohn*, 49–141; Laub, *Bekenntnis*, 66–104; Minear, "Early Christian"; Mitchell, "Use"; Müller, ***ΧΡΙΣΤΟΣ ΑΡΧΗΓΟΣ***, 279–301; Nissilä, *Hohepriestermotiv*, 20–42; Pelser, "Concept"; Peterson, *Hebrews*, 55–73;

that preceded his exaltation. Conveying the significance of the crucifixion is like depicting a three-dimensional object on a flat surface: no single vantage point allows the artist to represent all its aspects. An artist might depict the object from several perspectives in order to give viewers a sense of the whole. In a similar way, Hebrews presents the meaning of Jesus' death from several perspectives, using different types of imagery, each with its possibilities and limitations, and it is through the interplay among these images that the significance of the event becomes apparent.[91]

Structurally, the paragraph is framed by references to what Jesus suffered (2:10, 18).[92] It begins with a thesis statement, which is then followed by three portraits of Christ.[93] The thesis statement summarizes the main elements of the preceding paragraph, while the three portraits are designed to affect listeners more by the power of their imagery than by the force of their arguments.

(a) Thesis: What is Fitting for God (2:10–11a). The thesis statement summarizes the main elements of the preceding paragraph: God, who has the power to subject all things (cf. 2:8a) and who created people to receive glory (cf. 2:7, 9), carries out his saving purposes through the sufferings of Jesus (cf. 2:9). The author also weaves new elements into the thesis statement in order to anticipate how the argument will unfold. People are called sons and daughters of God, while Christ is portrayed in heroic terms as the pioneer of salvation (2:10c) and in priestly terms as the one who sanctifies (2:11a).

(b) Portrait: Bonds of Brotherhood (2:11b–13). The opening thesis sentence called people sons and daughters of God, and now Christ, God's unique Son, calls them brethren. In this portrait, Christ is an exemplary member of the community of faith, for he praises God and suffers with family members.

(c) Portrait: Conflict and Victory (2:14–16). The next portrait recounts Jesus' death and exaltation as a dramatic conquest over the devil. Through his epic struggle, Jesus liberates the descendants of Abraham from bondage to the fear of death much as Moses liberated Israel from bondage in Egypt.

(d) Portrait: High-Priestly Atonement (2:17–18). In the final portrait, the author assures listeners that Christ's sufferings show him to be a merciful and faith-

---

Schröger, *Verfasser*, 88–95; J. J. Scott, "*Archēgos*"; Swetnam, *Jesus*, 165–77; Übelacker, *Hebräerbrief*, 163–85; Vanhoye, *Situation*, 305–87.

[91]Gustav Aulén considered views of Christ's death as sacrifice, as victory, and as example, but he preferred the conflict-and-victory model (*Christus Victor*). Gyllenberg argued that as a priest Jesus dealt with sin and as a leader he overcame death ("Christologie"). See Gunton, *Actuality*.

[92]Vanhoye and others consider the mention of angels in 2:5 and 2:16 to be an *inclusio* for 2:5–18. This is problematic since 2:17–18 fall outside the *inclusio* and must be taken as a kind of transition. Moreover, the focus of the section is not on angels, but on the suffering of Jesus. See G. H. Guthrie, *Structure*, 77–85. See further §7 COMMENT.

[93]Each supporting argument is characterized by distinctive content, and each is introduced by an expression indicating the reason an action was performed for the "brethren" or "children": *di' hēn aitian . . . adelphous* (2:11b); *epei oun ta paidia* (2:14); *hothen . . . tois adelphois* (2:17). The general structure is similar to that of the exordium, where the author made an opening statement (1:1–4) followed by OT support (1:5–14). That the christological portraits affect people more by drama than by logic was noted by Gyllenberg, "Christologie," 689.

ful high priest who has made atonement for others and who offers help to those who are being tested.

This manifold depiction of Christ is further elaborated in Heb 3–5 (§7 COMMENT).

a. What Is Fitting for God (2:10–11a)

Bold, even startling in its formulation, is the statement that it was "fitting" for the Creator of all things to bring people to glory by means of the suffering of Jesus. Crucifixion was a public form of execution, and its brutality was well known (cf. 5:7–8; 12:2; 13:12–13). Christian writers contended with the Jewish objection that the Messiah was to establish an everlasting kingdom, "but this so-called Christ of yours was dishonorable and inglorious, so much that the last curse contained in the Law of God fell on him, for he was crucified" (Justin, *Dialogue* 32.1; cf. Deut 21:22–23). Pagans protested that it was sheer madness to "put a crucified man in second place after the unchangeable and eternal God, the Creator of the world" (Justin, *Apology* 1.13.4).[94] Despite the offensive quality of the suffering and death of Jesus, however, Hebrews gives it central place, arguing that it was "fitting" (*prepon*) or morally consistent for God to carry out his purposes in this way.

Aristotle said that when asking whether an action was fitting one must consider it in relation to the one performing it, the goal of the action, and the situation in which the action is performed.[95] The actor in this passage is God, who created the universe (1:2) and has power to subject all things to the son of man (2:8). Reaffirming God's power, the thesis calls God the one "for whom all things and through whom all things exist" (2:10a). This expression recalls formulas that are not distinctly Jewish or Christian (NOTE on 2:10), and because the idea had such broad currency, the author could assume that almost any listener would grant its validity. By locating Christ's suffering within the cosmic sweep of God's activity, Hebrews does not permit it to be seen as a divine failure, but as an act of God who has power over all things.

The goal of God's action is to bring many sons and daughters to glory (2:10b). Hebrews assumes that listeners will accept this idea since Ps 8 said that God created people for glory and honor (Heb 2:7). The author acknowledges that his listeners do not experience such glory at present, but insists that when God exalted Christ—who suffered—God showed that he remained firm in his purpose to bring others who suffer into the glory for which he created them. The goal of God's redemptive work is consistent with his creative work: since he created people for glory, it is fitting that he should provide a way for them to reach this end.[96]

---

[94]On crucifixion see Hengel, *Crucifixion*; H. W. Kuhn, "Kreuzesstrafe."

[95]Aristotle, *Nic. Ethics* 4.2.2 (1122a); cf. Moffatt, *Critical*, 29. The classic study of "the fitting" is Pohlenz, "τὸ πρέπον." Mitchell proposes that the rhetorical use of the "fitting" shaped Hebrews' theological reflection ("Use").

[96]The congruence between creation and redemption is evident in the people of God seeking to enter the rest that God ordained at creation (4:4, 10). Note also the correlation between Christ's appointment as heir of all things and his role as agent of creation (1:2bc).

The situation in which God acts has several dimensions. The underlying reason that God sent Christ into the world is that people belong to him. Christ and those he came to save are "all of one," which means that they have a common origin in God (2:11a). It was fitting that God should deliver those who were his own. The occasion for God's action was, in part, that people needed "salvation" from oppressive powers (2:10c), for they were enslaved by fear of death, which was the weapon wielded by the devil (2:14–16). The other part of the situation was that people's own sins constituted a barrier to God, so that they needed sanctification (2:11a) and atonement (2:11, 17–18). If the focus on deliverance in 2:14–16 accents the way that powers beyond human control hold people captive, the focus on sanctification and atonement in 2:11, 17–18 gives greater weight to human accountability for sin.

The act that God performed in this complex situation was to make Christ "complete through suffering" (2:10c). Christ's suffering was not an end in itself, for "through" suffering he was brought to glory, so that those who follow him might look forward to sharing in the glory and honor for which God created them (2:5–9). The verb used to describe Christ's movement from suffering to exaltation is "to make complete," a word that combines connotations of death and glory, as well as entry into priestly service (pp. 122–25). Suffering was the way that the qualities of mercy and faithfulness became evident in Jesus the high priest, whose death is the atonement for human sin and whose ongoing help enables others who suffer to persevere in the assurance that God has not abandoned them (2:17–18). See COMMENT *d*.

Calling Jesus the pioneer of salvation (2:10c) further defines Christ's action and the listeners' situation. Salvation had previously been announced to the listeners' community by evangelists whose testimony was confirmed by miracles and distributions of God's Spirit (2:3–4). Despite these past manifestations of divine power, many listeners found the present reality of God's reign to be contradicted by conflict with others in society and an emerging despondency among the community's members (10:32–34; 13:13–14). By calling Jesus the *pioneer* of salvation (2:10c), the author identifies him as the one who leads people forward, like those who led Israel through the wilderness toward the promised land or through battle to victory (NOTE on 2:10). Christ brought salvation, not by avoiding conflict with hostile powers, but by overcoming them and making a way for others to move into the future that God promised them.[97] The exaltation that followed Jesus' passion gives listeners confidence that their own suffering is not the final word, but part of the way in which God is bringing them to glory.

God also made Christ complete through suffering in order that he might sanctify people, making them fit to approach God (2:11a). Entering the presence of God means encountering the One who is holy. Holiness both attracts and repels, for it brings both blessing and destruction. Therefore, worshipers come into God's presence safely only when they have been cleansed from uncleanness and

---

[97]One responds with gratitude to the priest who makes atonement, but one follows a pioneer (2:10; 12:2) and forerunner (6:20). See Gyllenberg, "Christologie," 681.

sanctified so that they can enter the holy realm (see the extended discussion on pp. 119–22). Christ's blood is at once a sacrifice of atonement and the inauguration of the new covenant that purifies people by removing their sins (10:29). Sanctification is not the same as completion, which includes entry into heavenly glory, but it is a step toward that end. The sanctifying effect of Christ's death, which is conveyed by the Holy Spirit (6:4), cleanses the conscience (NOTE on 9:14), giving people boldness to approach God in prayer in the present and to anticipate entering God's heavenly sanctuary in the future. Hebrews does not understand sanctification to be primarily a form of moral goodness, but sanctification does have consequences for behavior. Those who look forward to sharing God's holiness (12:10) are called to pursue holiness in daily life by seeking peace with other people and by guarding against immorality and godlessness (12:14–16; cf. 12:28–13:6).

b. Bonds of Brotherhood (2:11b–13)

Christ is next portrayed as the brother of human beings. The words that Christ speaks here, as elsewhere in Hebrews, are from the OT (pp. 106–7). Jewish authors of the period apparently did not read these texts messianically, and none of the other NT writers use the verses that are quoted in Heb 2:12–13.[98] Nevertheless, aspects of these OT texts might suggest that their meaning could be extended beyond the original context. The first passage says, "I will declare your name to my brethren" (Ps 22:22). Since the speaker in the psalm is an unnamed and perhaps representative person who suffered and was delivered, the words of the unnamed speaker can readily be extended to other righteous sufferers, including Jesus. The second quotation, "I will trust in him," was spoken by Isaiah (Isa 8:17), but the words were also included in a saying to be spoken on a future day of deliverance in Isa 12:2 as well as in David's song of deliverance in 2 Sam 22:3 LXX. The variety of OT settings in which this saying appeared might have suggested that it would also be appropriate in yet another setting—the ministry of Jesus. The third quotation, "Here am I, and the children whom God gave me," was spoken about Isaiah's children, but his children were considered signs and portents (Isa. 8:18) from God, which might suggest that the text could have extended significance.[99]

The basic criterion governing the author's use of the OT, however, is not a text's original context, but its relationship to what God has done in Christ. Hebrews assumes that the OT foreshadows what is revealed through Jesus' death and exaltation (pp. 117–18). To read 2:11b–13 on the author's terms is to ask whether the configuration of OT quotations is faithful to the past, present, and

[98]On the wider use of these texts see NOTES on 2:13–14. Some have suggested that the texts are interpreted within a schema of promise and fulfillment (e.g., Schröger, *Verfasser*, 88–95), although Jewish authors apparently did not discern a messianic quality in them. Less likely is that the author of Hebrews thought that the preexistent Christ spoke through the psalmist and Isaiah (Braun; Grässer; Ellingworth).

[99]On the symbolic names of Isaiah's children see Isa 7:3 and 8:1; cf. 7:14.

future work of Christ.[100] The author depicts Jesus in a manner that cannot be confined to one time period, but in a way that shows the abiding significance of the One who is "yesterday and today the same—and forever" (13:8).

The introductory statement is that Jesus is "not ashamed" to identify with human beings (2:11b). When applied to Jesus' incarnation in the past, the comment might recall how it could have been shameful for the Son of God to identify with mortals, who were slaves because of their fear of death (2:15), and "slavery is the most shameful" of states (Dio Chrysostom, *Disc.* 14.1). Moreover, human beings are sinners who need atonement (2:17c). Since sinners acted "shamefully and disgracefully" (Prov 13:5; Sir 6:1), godly people were not to identify with them (Ps 1:1; Sir 7:16; 12:4, 14). Yet Hebrews could echo traditions about Jesus, which said that during his ministry on earth he did associate with sinners, not to endorse sin, but to deliver people from sin (Mark 2:15–17; Luke 7:36–50; 15:1–7). After Jesus' earthly ministry ended, some of his followers—including those addressed by Hebrews—faced the disgrace of reproach and imprisonment (Heb 10:32–34; 13:13–14).[101] Nevertheless, Hebrews uses the present tense to insist that Jesus "*is* not ashamed" to call them his brethren. This assurance of continued fellowship with the exalted Christ offers incentive for them to remain faithful to Christ and to their own brothers and sisters in faith, even when they come under the reproach of society.

The quotation from Ps 22:22 is used to show that Jesus calls people his "brethren" (2:11b–12a). This is consistent with traditions about the way that Jesus spoke to people during his earthly ministry (Mark 3:31–35; Matt 12:46–50; Luke 8:19–21; Matt 25:40; 28:10; John 20:17). Moreover, the verb "call" is in the present tense, suggesting that the exalted Jesus continues to call others his brethren, just as members of the Christian community continued to address each other as "brother" (Heb 3:1, 12; 10:19; 13:22–23). Hebrews says that Jesus declared God's name and praised God "in the middle of the assembly" (2:12b). This fits early Christian traditions, which said that Jesus proclaimed God to his followers in synagogues and in the Temple (e.g., Matt 4:23; 13:54; Mark 1:21, 39; 3:1; 6:1–2; Luke 4:15–16, 44; 6:6; 19:47; John 18:20). The word "assembly" (*ekklēsia*) was also used for Christian congregations, where the followers of Jesus proclaimed and praised God's name (Heb 13:15). Although some were drifting away (10:25), Jesus exemplifies the kind of bold proclamation and praise that Hebrews insists should characterize all Christian assemblies. Praising God in the local assembly anticipates participating in the future heavenly assembly (12:23).

The next quotation indicates that Jesus put his trust in God (2:13a). The gospels do not speak about Jesus "trusting" God during his ministry, but an attitude of trust is reflected in his teachings (Matt 6:30, 33; Mark 10:27; 11:20–24;

---

[100]The variety of interpretations points to the difficulty in identifying these words with only one point in Jesus' career. The words in 2:11b–13 are variously assigned to the preexistent Christ (Braun; Grässer), the incarnate Christ (Loader, *Sohn*, 134; Attridge), and the exalted Christ (Vanhoye, *Situation*, 340; F. F. Bruce; cf. Lane).

[101]On "the tree of shame" see Cicero, *In Defense of Rabirius* 4 §13. On shame and prison see Cicero, *Pro Caecina* 34 §100; Seneca, *Ep.* 85.41; Epictetus, *Disc.* 2.1.35; Josephus, *J.W.* 4.628.

Luke 11:13). Hebrews might reflect such a tradition, especially since in Heb 5:7–8 Jesus is said to have cried out to God in godly fear during the days of his flesh (Matt 26:36–42; Mark 14:36; Luke 23:46). The exalted Christ does not need to trust God for his own deliverance, but his continued intercession for people reflects trust that God will hear him (Heb 7:25). Jesus exemplifies the faithfulness that characterizes people of God in every generation (2:13; 3:1–2; cf. chap. 11).

The last quotation presents the idea that Christians are God's children (2:13b). Christ may have been able to say "Here I am, and the children whom God gave me" while ministering upon earth, since he taught his followers to pray to God as their own Father (Matt 6:9; Luke 11:2). After Jesus' exaltation, Christians continued to speak of God as their Father (Rom 1:7; 8:15; 1 Cor 1:3; Gal 4:6; 1 Pet 1:17), considering themselves to be children of God through their relationship with Christ (cf. John 13:33; 21:5; G. R. Hughes, *Hebrews*, 62). The future of God's children is that of the firstborn in heaven, who gather for celebration in the new Jerusalem (12:23).

c. Conflict and Victory (2:14–16)

The scene now shifts to the battle that Jesus the pioneer waged against the forces of evil in order to deliver his brethren from bondage. This story of deliverance was told in a context where there were competing claims. Heracles, the hero who was sometimes called "pioneer" (NOTE on 2:10), was said to have descended into the netherworld (Homer, *Iliad* 5.394–400), where he overcame the "dark-robed lord of the dead" (Euripides, *Alcestis* 76, 843–44; Seneca, *Hercules furens* 889–90). His valor meant that he was deified and was now the helper to whom people turned in time of difficulty.[102] Drawing on this tradition, some claimed that Augustus "broke the chains which had shackled . . . the habitable world," ushering in a new world order.[103] Some of Augustus's successors appeared in the guise of Heracles to suggest that they too were divine deliverers (Philo, *Gaius* 78–79, 90; Dio Cassius, *Roman History* 62.20.5; Suetonius, *Nero* 53). Those addressed by Hebrews, however, did not find the prevailing social order to be liberating, and some actually lost freedom through imprisonment (10:32–34; 13:3). Therefore, in this social setting, Hebrews presents Jesus' death and exaltation as a battle for deliverance (2:14).

The great adversary is the devil, who wields death as a weapon that intimidates and enslaves people (2:14). Unlike others, Jesus did not encounter death as a

[102]On Heracles and Hebrews see Aune, "Heracles." The way the similarities are understood depends on one's interpretive framework. From the perspective of the history of religions, this passage is "an early form of the common Christian salvation myth," which is itself "based on the common redemption myth of various traditions of the Hellenistic period" (Attridge, *Epistle*, 81–82). In this approach the primary reality is the general mythic pattern, which finds particular expression in various texts. This commentary identifies as the primary reality Jesus' death and resurrection, which Hebrews explicates in various ways, including deliverance (2:14–15), atonement (2:17–18), enthronement (1:1–14), covenant (chaps. 8–9), and endurance (12:1–2). Multiple images are used to interpret the singular events of Jesus' death and resurrection.

[103]Philo, *Gaius* 144, 146; cf. *RomCiv*, 1.562.

slave, but as an assailant; he intruded into death's domain in order to overcome it. By dying and being raised, Jesus showed that death's power is not absolute, but is subject to the power of God. Therefore, instead of resigning themselves to death's triumph, listeners can respond in faith that God will bring life out of death. After this point in his speech, the author will no longer speak of the devil, but will address listeners as people who have been freed by Christ. The author recognizes that sin and death continue to threaten people, but he insists that Jesus' death and resurrection free people from the fear that would hold them captive to evil. Therefore, as free people, the listeners are accountable to God and called to manifest boldness in their confession (cf. Heb 3:6).

Like other early Christians, the author sought to comprehend and convey the significance of Jesus' death and resurrection in light of the OT.[104] In this passage the story of Israel's exodus from Egypt provides the contours of the story.[105] Like Jesus, Moses was not ashamed to consider enslaved people his brethren, but identified with them in order to deliver them (Exod 2:11; 4:18; cf. Heb 11:24–26). Like Jesus, Moses declared God's name to others (Exod 3:13–15; cf. Heb 2:12) and trusted God (Exod 14:13–14; cf. Heb 2:13). When Moses led the descendants of Abraham out of slavery, Pharaoh's army was destroyed and the people were delivered (Exod 14:21–31; cf. Heb 2:14b–15). When Jesus died and rose, he destroyed the devil's ability to wield death as a weapon, thereby delivering the "descendants of Abraham" from fear of death. Abraham's descendants include all who share in the promises, including the listeners (6:12–13), so that in telling listeners that Christ suffered for "the descendants of Abraham" (2:16), he indicates that Christ suffered "for you."

The allusion to the exodus from Egypt in 2:14–16 will be followed by reminders about Israel's journey through the wilderness to the promised land in 3:7–4:13. This imagery provides one of Hebrews' most compelling perspectives on Christian life. The wilderness generation contended with severe challenges in the desert between their liberation from slavery in Egypt and their entry into the promised land. Similarly, Christians face challenges during the time between the liberation that Christ won through his death and resurrection, and their entry as God's people into their promised heavenly inheritance. The idea that Christians have embarked on a journey that begins with deliverance and leads through a wilderness to eternal rest will give the author reason to urge his listeners to persevere so that they do not fall away in despair, but will endure in the confidence that God will bring them to their inheritance.

d. High-Priestly Atonement (2:17–18)

Shifting the focus yet again, the author now portrays Jesus as a high priest. Instead of dealing with slaves who need liberation, a priest deals with people who

---

[104]See pp. 117–18. Christ's work is depicted in terms of conflict and victory in John 12:31; 14:30 and other passages (see C. R. Koester, *Symbolism*, 206–9). On Christ's work as liberation see Gal 4:1–7.

[105]The story of Moses in 11:24–26 is told in a way that reflects early Christian experience (§32 COMMENT). On 2:14–16 and the exodus see Andriessen, "La teneur," 304–13.

need atonement for their sins. The OT remains the lens through which the work of Christ is viewed, only now the material is taken from traditions concerning Israel's high priesthood rather than from the story of the exodus. Like Levitical high priests (Lev 16), Jesus will make atonement for others (Heb 2:17). But unlike priests, who first had to be set apart from other people in order to minister (Exod 29; Lev 8; Sir 45:6), the Son who had been with God at the beginning of time (Heb 1:2) first had to become *like* people in order to minister on their behalf (2:17; Vanhoye, *Situation*, 368).

By sharing in human blood, flesh, and suffering, Jesus showed that he was "merciful and faithful" (2:17b), qualities that were descriptive of some but not all priests. God's promise to raise up "a faithful priest" was given after Eli's sons abused priestly prerogatives (1 Sam 2:12–17, 22–25, 35), and there were memories of priestly corruption during the Hasmonean period (2 Macc 4:7–14; 4 Macc 4:15–20; *T. Mos.* 6:6; 7:9–10). At the same time, there were idealized portraits of good priests (2 Macc 15:12; Sir 50:1–24; 4 Macc 7:6; 17:9). Jesus exemplifies the best in the priestly tradition. To say that he suffered to "become" a merciful and faithful high priest does not mean that he was once callous and only later learned mercy or that he was faithless and only later became faithful, but that these qualities emerged through testing in ways that would not be evident otherwise (NOTES on 4:15; 5:7–8).

Atonement was one of the priestly actions that Jesus performed (2:17c).[106] A complex view of atonement encompasses both expiation, which is the removal of sin, and propitiation, which is the averting of divine wrath. The idea of propitiation is appropriate in Hebrews, since the author assumes that divine wrath threatens his listeners, just as it threatened Moses' generation (3:7–4:13; 10:26–31; 12:29). The dominant element in Hebrews, however, is expiation, as indicated by the earlier comment that Christ "made purification for sins" (1:3). The Day of Atonement included rites for purifying both objects and people (Lev 16:15–19), as well as provisions for purging the community by transferring its sin to a goat that was sent away into the desert (Lev 16:20–22). Hebrews argues that such rituals may purify people physically, but the death of Christ purifies the conscience (NOTES on Heb 9:13–14). See the extended discussion on pp. 119–22.

A second priestly action that Jesus performs is providing ongoing help for those who are being tested (Heb 2:18b). The word "test" helps to define the situation of the listeners. Their despondency in the face of reproach from the wider society (13:13–14) could have easily given them reasons to test God, demanding that God show himself to be faithful to his promises by improving their lot. Yet in 3:7–19 the author will describe the way the wilderness generation tested God and failed to receive what was promised because they tested God in unbelief. The author of Hebrews wrote to people who faced challenging social realities.

106The idea that Jesus' self-sacrifice might effect atonement had some precedent in the stories of the Jewish martyrs, whose blood was said to provide cleansing and atonement (4 Macc 6:28–29; 17:21–22). The effect is a kind of *a fortiori*: if martyrs' deaths had an atoning effect before, how much more now does the death of Christ the high priest effect atonement.

Rather than viewing these challenges as occasions for them to test God, he implies that such situations might be ways in which God tests them. When people are tested, faithfulness is understood to be the appropriate response. Awareness of the help Christ offers by interceding with God would enable his followers to persevere (NOTES and COMMENT on 7:25).

9. Apostle and High Priest of Our Confession (3:1–6)

3 [1]Because of this, holy brethren who share a heavenly calling, consider that Jesus, the apostle and high priest of our confession, [2]was faithful to the one who appointed him as Moses was in his house. [3]For he has been deemed worthy of more glory than Moses to the extent that the builder of a house has more honor than the house. [4]For every house is built by someone, and the builder of all things is God. [5]Indeed, *Moses was faithful in his whole house* as a *servant*, to bear witness to what was to be spoken, [6]but Christ [was faithful] as a Son over his house. And we are his house, if we hold fast to our boldness and the pride of our hope.

NOTES

3:1. *Because of this.* The Greek word *hothen* indicates that the author is drawing out the implications of what has just been said. The term consistently appears in the middle of an argument rather than at the beginning of a new section (2:17; 7:25; 8:3; 9:18; 11:19). On the implications for the structure of the section see §7 COMMENT.

holy brethren. This refers to members of the Christian community (3:12; 10:19; 13:22), both men and women (cf. 1 Cor 16:19–20; 2 Tim 4:21). The term gains special force through Jesus calling people his brethren (NOTE on Heb 2:11b) and through the household imagery in 3:5–6. The author can call his brethren "holy" because they have been "sanctified" (2:11) by Christ. Elsewhere the author refers to Christians as "holy ones" or "saints" (6:10; 13:24; cf. Acts 9:13, 32, 41; Rom 1:7; 16:15; 1 Cor 1:2; Phil 1:1). On sanctification see pp. 120–21.

who share a heavenly calling. Listeners have not yet entered God's presence, but are called to it by God (cf. Isa 41:9; 42:6; Rom 11:29; 1 Cor 1:26). The response entails perseverance (Heb 3:7–4:13. On "share" see NOTE on "partners" in 3:14. On a primary level "heavenly" identifies the destination of the call: the heavenly sanctuary (8:5; 9:23; cf. 10:19) and the heavenly city (11:16; 12:22; cf. Phil 3:13–14; Eph 1:18; 4:4; Philo, *Planter* 26–27; *Alleg. Interp.* 3.101–3; *QE* 2.46; Dey, *Intermediary*, 161–64). On a secondary level, "heavenly" refers to the origin of the call. When the listeners were grasped by the Christian message, they received "heavenly" gifts (Heb 6:4), including the Spirit, God's word, and powers of the age to come.

consider that Jesus. Many take Jesus to be the direct object of the verb "consider" and the participle *onta* to be in the attributive position: "consider Jesus . . . who was faithful" (REB; NJB; NAB2; cf. NIV). Grammatically, however, it is preferable to render the participle by indirect discourse (NRSV; cf. Acts 8:23; 17:16; MHT, 3.161; Lane, *Hebrews*, 1.71).

the apostle. The term "apostle" (*apostolos*), which means "one who is sent," continues the idea that Jesus is the "Pioneer" (*archēgos*, 2:10). There were close connections between the noun *archēgos* and the verb "send" (*apostellein*): "Send [*aposteilon*] men to spy out the land of Canaan . . . every one a leader [*archēgos*] among them" (Num 13:2 LXX; cf. Judg 5:15; Neh 2:9 LXX). Other NT writings call Jesus the one "sent" from God (e.g., Matt 10:40; 15:24; Mark 9:37; Luke 10:16; John 3:17; 5:36; 17:3; 1 John 4:9–14). Since "apostles" had a role in church governance (Acts 15:2, 6), some suggest that Hebrews transferred the title to Jesus to counteract tendencies toward ecclesiastical hierarchy (Theissen, *Untersuchungen*, 107; Grässer, *Aufbruch*, 225; Braun). This is unlikely, however, given the positive view of church leaders in Heb 13:7, 17.

and high priest. As pioneer (2:10) and apostle (3:1), Jesus was sent to bring deliverance and to lead the way into the land of promise (3:7–4:11). As high priest (2:17–18; 3:1), he makes atonement for sin. Although the functions of an apostle and a high priest differ, they serve a common goal: enabling listeners to realize their heavenly calling (cf. Justin, *1 Apology* 63.5, 10, 14). Some propose that as apostle Christ represents God before people and as high priest he represents people before God (Luther, WA 57,3.16; Bengel). Others suggest that "apostle" applies to his earthly work and "high priest" to his heavenly work (Grässer) or vice versa (Swetnam, "Form 1–6," 371). Hebrews does not develop the ideas in this manner, however.

of our confession. Most take the "confession" to be a set body of material ("our confession," NASB; NJB; NAB2; NRSV; cf. REB), rather than the act of confessing ("whom we confess," NIV; Bénétreau), since Hebrews refers to "the confession" with the definite article, which suggests that the confession had definite content. He also urges them to "hold fast" to it, which suggests that it could be identified and grasped (cf. 4:14; 10:23). See p. 126.

3:2. *was faithful.* In Num 12:7 *pistos* seems to mean that Moses was "entrusted" with God's house. Vanhoye (*Old Testament*, 96) argues that in Heb 3:2 the word has a similar sense, identifying Jesus as the one who is worthy of the listeners' trust. Most, however, take it to mean that Jesus exhibited faithfulness, as in 2:17. Both meanings are consistent with the context, since Jesus is the object of faith as well as an exemplar of faith. Wallis (*Faith*, 145–50) argues that the present participle (*onta*) in 3:2 points to Jesus' present faithfulness in carrying out his role as priestly intercessor (cf. 2:17). It is preferable, however, to think of his faithfulness in testing (cf. 2:18; 5:8) in contrast to the unfaithfulness of Moses' generation (3:7–12). Cf. Grässer; Laub, *Bekenntnis*, 89–90. This statement echoes OT texts that deal with Moses, the heir to David's throne, and a future priest:

Num 12:7	My servant Moses is faithful in all my house.
1 Chron 17:14	I will make him faithful in my house.
1 Sam 2:35	I will raise up . . . a faithful priest . . . and I will build . . . a faithful house

The interplay among these texts allows the language to be applied to three aspects of Jesus' identity: (a) Moses and Jesus. In 3:4 the author quotes Num 12:7, which refers to the faithfulness of Moses among the people of Israel, who are called God's "house." This prepares for the comparison of Jesus and Moses in Heb 3:2b. (b) Son of God. Hebrews 1:1–14 emphasized Jesus' divine sonship, quoting the promise that God would raise up an heir for David who would be God's Son (2 Sam 7:14; 1 Chron 17:13; Heb 1:5). In raising up an heir for David, God would build up David's "house." The wording helps connect Jesus' role as Son with his faithfulness over God's own people or "house." (c) Priest. When the priest Eli's sons became corrupt, God promised to raise up a faithful priest (1 Sam 2:35). Calling Jesus a "faithful high priest" (Heb 2:17) implies that he fulfills the promises of God. On "house" see NOTE on 3:5.

to the one who appointed him. The verb *poiein* has two possible meanings in this context, of which the first is preferable: (a) Appoint. The use of *poiein* for appointment to a position of responsibility is well attested: God "appointed" Moses and Aaron (1 Sam 12:6 LXX); Jesus appointed the Twelve (Mark 3:14) and was "appointed both Lord and Christ" (Acts 2:36; Chrysostom; Theodoret; Theophylact; Erasmus, *Paraphrase*; Attridge; Lane; Ellingworth; Bénétreau). (b) Make. In the fourth century the Arians invoked this text to argue that God's Son was "made" or created by God, while Athanasius insisted that "made" referred to Christ's humanity, but not to his divinity (NPNF 2 4.348–54; Ambrose, NPNF 2 10.254–55; Alcuin; Lombard; Herveus; Aquinas). More recently, some propose that Jesus was "faithful to his Creator," since 3:4 refers to God as Creator (Dey, *Intermediary*, 173; Braun; Grässer; Hegermann). While affirming Jesus' humanity, however, Hebrews distinguishes him from other created beings (cf. 1:2b, 10–12).

as Moses was in his house. Some MSS (א A C D Ψ) read "in his whole house," but the word "whole" is not found in other MSS (P13 P46vid B). Since the word "whole" appears in the parallel statement in 3:5, it may have been omitted accidentally. It seems more probable, though, that the word was inserted later to harmonize the lines with each other and with Num 12:7 LXX. Including both a paraphrase and a more nearly verbatim citation of an OT text in the same passage is attested elsewhere in Hebrews (Ps 110:1 in Heb 1:3, 13; Ps 8:6 in Heb 2:8ab).

3:3. *deemed worthy of more glory than Moses.* It was understood that honor was to be granted in proportion to a person's merits (Aristotle, *Nic. Ethics* 4.3 [1123b]; 5.6 [1134b]; Sir 10:30–31). The verb is in the passive voice, which implies that God is the one who judged Jesus to be worthy of such glory (Heb 1:2, 9; 2:9; H.-F. Weiss; deSilva, *Despising*, 217).

the builder of a house has more honor than the house. This statement has a proverbial quality. Menander and others said that "the workman is greater than the work" (Justin, *1 Apology* 20). Philo said that "he that has gained a possession is better than the possession, and he that has made than that which he has made" (*Planter* 68; cf. *Migration* 193). Proverbial statements or maxims could be rhetorically effective since "the hearer, when he perceives that an indisputable principle drawn from practical life is being applied to a cause, must give it his tacit approval" (*Rhet. ad Her.* 4.17 §25; cf. Aristotle, *Rhetoric* 2.21.11 [1395a]; 2.21.15 [1395b]).

3:4. *For every house is built by someone.* It was a commonplace that one could infer from the design of an object that it was produced by an artificer (Epictetus, *Disc.* 1.6.7). This meant that one could infer from the cosmos that there is a Creator (Philo, *Migration* 193; *Alleg. Interp.* 3.97–100; *Cherubim* 126–27; cf. Wis 13:1–9). Hebrews, however, does not infer the characteristics of the Creator from the creation, but is aware that ordinary perceptions often contradict the promises of God. Believing that God created all things expresses faith in what cannot be seen (Heb 11:3).

and the builder of all things is God. The word *kataskeuazein* suggests both constructing something (Josephus, *J.W.* 6.191; *P. Oxy.* #892.8) and making it ready for use (MM, 332; Mark 1:2; Luke 7:27). Both senses appear in Hebrews: Noah constructed the ark to save his household (Heb 11:7) and the Tabernacle was furnished or prepared for priestly service (9:2, 6). In 3:4 the primary sense is that God "built all things" by creating the universe (cf. Isa 40:28; 45:7; Wis 9:2; 13:4; Philo, *Eternity* 39, 41), but at a secondary level the word may suggest that God "made all things ready," offering a hint of the rest, the glory, and the city that God has prepared for his people (cf. Heb 2:10; 4:4, 10; 11:16).

3:5. *Indeed, Moses was faithful.* This begins a quotation of Num 12:7 (LXX). The word order is slightly modified, and "his" replaces "my" in the next part of the quotation to accommodate its inclusion in this paragraph. The term *pistos* may mean that Moses had been "entrusted" with leadership responsibility. It can also mean that Moses was "trustworthy" (Vanhoye, *Old Testament*, 96). The sense of "faithfulness" is most prominent (Bénétreau; Swetnam, "Form 1–6," 376).

in his whole house. The "house" of God includes several senses (Chrysostom):

(a) People. God's "house" often refers to his people (Exod 16:31; Hos 8:1; Jer 12:7; Heb 8:8), the "whole house of Israel" (Lev 10:6). According to *Tg. Onq.* (cf. *Frg. Tg.*) Num 12:7 said that Moses was faithful "among my whole people." The author will pick up this sense when telling the listeners that "we are God's house" in Heb 3:6.

(b) Universe. The "house" of God is sometimes construed as the universe (Philo, *Posterity* 5; *Planting* 50; *Sobriety* 62–64; *Dreams* 1.185). In the context this is plausible since 3:4 associated God's house with the universe, and *Tg. Neof.* translates Num 12:7 cosmologically: "In the whole world I have created, [Moses] is faithful" (D'Angelo, *Moses*, 132).

(c) Sanctuary. A number of OT passages call the sanctuary or Tabernacle God's "house" (Exod 23:19; 34:26; 1 Kgs 6:1; 8:20; Ps 27:4). There may be echoes of this in Heb 3 since Moses is identified as a "servant" of God, a term sometimes used for those who served in the sanctuary, and the setting in Num 12:7 is the tent of meeting.

as a servant. Moses is called God's "servant" (*therapōn*) in Num 12:7 (cf. Exod 4:10; 14:31; Num 11:11; Deut 3:24; Josh 1:2; 8:31, 33 [9:2 LXX]; 1 Chron 16:40 [LXX]; Wis 10:16). Both the social and theological aspects of the term are important:

(a) Social Aspects. "Servant" was sometimes a synonym for "slave" (*doulos*; e.g., Jdt 9:10; Philo, *Special Laws* 2.123; Ps.-Phocylides, *Sentences* 223–26) who served in a household (Luke 12:42–45) or as someone's personal attendant (e.g., Exod 7:10; 14:5; Jdt 10:20; Josephus, *Ant.* 6.52). Faithfulness was a trait of a good servant or steward (Matt 25:21–23; Luke 12:42; 16:10–12; 19:17; 1 Cor 4:2).

(b) Theological Aspects. The term was used for those who served God (Deut 9:27; Job 1:8; 2:3; 42:7–8; Wis 10:9; 4 Macc 12:11). It could be synonymous with a "slave" of God (*doulos*; see 1 Kgs 8:53, 56; 2 Kgs 18:12 LXX; Josephus, *Ant.* 5.39; cf. Rom 1:1; Gal 1:10; Phil 1:1). Philo considered the ability to "serve" God to be the highest thing in human life (*Dreams* 1.35; *Flight* 40, 47; *Special Laws* 1.303; 4.147; *Cherubim* 107; cf. Aristotle, *Eudemian Ethics* 7.16 1249b). A "servant" was also one who ministered in the Temple or "house" of God (Tob 1:7; cf. Philo, *Flight* 42; Spicq, "Le vocabulaire"). The theological use emerges when Moses is called a servant of God, but the social connotations emerge in 3:6, where the "servant" is contrasted with the "son."

to bear witness. The noun *martyrion* is used only here, but the verb *martyrein* ("to bear witness") appears elsewhere, often for the OT's witness to what has occurred in Christ (7:8, 17; 10:15; cf. 11:2, 4, 5, 39). Identifying Moses as a "witness" allowed Christians to affirm the importance of Moses and the Law without making them the basis for faith and life. Christians considered Jesus' life, death, and resurrection to be the definitive revelation of God, and the disciples "gave their testimony [*martyrion*]" to this message (Acts 4:33; cf. 1 Cor 1:6; 2 Tim 1:8; Acts 1:8; 2:32; 3:15; 5:32). Like Jesus' disciples, Moses bore witness; the difference is that the disciples gave their testimony after Jesus' resurrection, while Moses' testimony foreshadows Christ ahead of time (Heb 10:1). The proper response to authentic witness is often said to be faith (2 Thess 1:10; cf. Isa 43:10; John 3:11). Therefore, when Moses bears witness, people are to respond with faith in that to which he testifies, which early Christians understood to be salvation in Christ (Rom 3:21; John 5:39–47).

to what was to be spoken. The passive voice of the verb assumes that God is the speaker. The comment refers to the way that Moses bore witness to what God would speak to later generations "by a Son" (1:2; cf. 11:26; Grässer; H.-F. Weiss). For example, when Moses speaks of the "blood of the covenant" (9:20), he foreshadows the new covenant that God would make through Christ.

3:6. *but Christ.* The word "Christ" means "anointed one." Anointing was the means by which someone was placed in a position of leadership (NOTE on 1:9). The LXX referred to "the anointed priest" (Lev 4:5, 16; 6:22) and to God's "anointed" king (Ps 2:2; 18:50 [17:51 LXX]; 89:20, 38 [88:21, 39]). Early Christians sometimes used the word as a title (John 7:27, 42; 10:24), but here, as in Paul's letters, it functions as a part of Jesus' name.

as a Son. According to the OT, God's anointed one was his son (2 Sam 7:14; Ps 2:6–7). Hebrews draws on both the social and theological aspects of the term "son":

(**a**) Social Aspects. The relationship of young children to their parents was like that of a slave to a master (Gal 4:1; Philo, *Decalogue* 166–67; *Special Laws* 2.226–27; Seneca, *Ep.* 94.1–3), but an adult son differed from a slave. Slaves could marry and conduct some transactions for their masters, yet the master could exploit his slaves' abilities, slaves were taxed like other property, and they could be sold or given away. Some slaves could own property, but Roman slaves could not. Sons, however, could own property, conclude valid contracts with their fathers or other parties, act as representatives for their fathers, and inherit the father's estate (Taubenschlag, *Law*, 78–96, 143–49).

(**b**) Theological Aspects. Hebrews 1:1–4 identified the Son of God as the definitive way in which God communicated to human beings, the means through which God created the world, the bearer of divine glory, and heir of all things. The simple social contrast between servant and son gives Jesus status over Moses, but the theological associations that were established in 1:1–14 go beyond social differentiation and allude to the divine aspects of Jesus' sonship.

over his house. Layton ("Christ") notes that this expression was often used for stewards who were placed in authority over someone's household (e.g., Gen 43:16; 44:1, 4; 1 Kgs 2:46 [LXX]). This suggests that the Son of God is entrusted with the care of the household of faith.

And we are his house. "His house" could be Christ's house, but it more likely is God's house, as in Num 12:7. The people of Israel were called God's "house" (Exod 16:31; Hos 8:1; Heb 8:8), and the expression was used for Jesus' followers (1 Tim 3:15). Since God's "house" could be a sanctuary (Exod 23:19; 34:26; Ps 27:4), some referred to the community of faith as a temple (1QS VIII, 5–9; 1 Cor 3:16–17; Eph 2:19–21; 1 Pet 2:4–5). Although some see that image here (Vanhoye, *Old Testament*, 104), Hebrews does not develop the idea.

if we hold fast to our boldness. "Boldness" (*parrēsia*; cf. 4:16; 10:19, 35) includes both the internal disposition of confidence (NRSV) or courage (NIV) and the external expression of clear and public speaking (John 16:25; 18:20). See Mitchell, "Holding On."

(**a**) Basis for boldness. *(i)* Freedom. Boldness was fitting for free persons rather than slaves (Euripides, *Ion* 675; *Phoenecian Maidens* 391–92; Musonius Rufus, frg. 9; Josephus, *Ant.* 11.39). Christ released people from slavery due to fear of death (Heb 2:15), making boldness possible. *(ii)* Atonement. Boldness was identified with those who could speak from a clear conscience before other people (Prov 13:5 LXX; Phil 1:20; *T. Reub.* 4:2) and God or Christ (1 John 2:28; 3:21; Josephus, *Ant.* 2.52; Philo, *Heir* 6–7; *Special Laws* 1.203). Christ's death atones for sin and cleanses the conscience (Heb 2:17; 9:14), making boldness possible.

(**b**) Context of boldness. *(i)* Boldness before God. People exhibited boldness when they spoke candidly with God in prayer (Eph 3:12; Job 22:26 LXX; Josephus, *Ant.* 5.38; Philo, *Heir* 19–20). Hebrews speaks of a bold approach to God in 4:16 and 10:19. *(ii)* Boldness before People. Socially, people exhibited "boldness" when they spoke the truth frankly to others, even when candor might evoke resistance (Acts 2:29; 4:13; 18:26; 19:8; Eph 6:19–20; 1 Thess 2:2; *P. Oxy.* #1100.15; 4 Macc 10:5; *Mart. Pol.* 10:1). Christians would exhibit boldness by confessing their faith despite public reproach (Heb 10:32–35).

and the pride. "Pride" is commonly the object of which one is proud (Rom 4:2; 1 Cor 9:16; Gal 6:4). Listeners hold fast to their pride by holding on to what God has done in Christ (cf. 1 Cor 1:31). "Pride" was also the external expression of pride. Those who are proud will boast of God with "boldness" (see previous NOTE).

of our hope. The listeners hope to receive what God promised, including glory and honor (2:5–9). Hope entails drawing near to God (7:19) and entering the heavenly sanctuary (6:19; 10:19–23). But because the realization of the promises is a hope that is as yet unseen (11:1), the listeners must exhibit faithfulness (6:11), as did Moses and Jesus.

COMMENT[107]

Comparison of Jesus with Moses reinforces the idea that faithful suffering leads to glory and honor. Favorable comparison of a person with someone of high repute was called amplification (*auxēsis*), which was "one of the forms of praise."[108] Hebrews does not depict Jesus as a new Moses, although this might have been expected since God had promised to raise up another prophet like Moses (Deut 18:15–18).[109] Instead, the author contrasts the various prophets of God with the singular Son of God (Heb 1:1–2; 3:1–6; Isaacs, *Sacred*, 133–35). Hebrews does not denigrate Moses by recalling his unfaithfulness (Num 20:12) or by contrasting Moses' fading splendor with Christ's abiding glory (cf. 2 Cor 3:7–11). The point of the comparison is not to disqualify Moses as God's servant, but to magnify Jesus' glory as God's Son.[110]

Structurally, the passage is interlaced by references to Moses, and it is framed by comments identifying the listeners in familial imagery as "brethren" (3:1a) and a "house" (3:6b). The argument unfolds through an exposition of an OT text: *Moses was faithful in his whole house as a servant* (Num 12:7). The text is paraphrased in Heb 3:2 and quoted in a more complete form in 3:5. In his argument the author takes up each part of the quotation in turn:

---

[107]On 3:1–6 see Auffret, "Essai"; D'Angelo, *Moses*, 65–199; Dey, *Intermediary*, 155–83; Grässer, *Der Alte*, 290–311; Layton, "Christ"; Marrow, "Parrhēsia"; Mitchell, "Holding On"; Nissilä, *Hohepriestermotiv*, 43–54; Schröger, *Verfasser*, 95–101; Spicq, "Le vocabulaire"; Vanhoye, "L'oracle"; idem, *Old Testament*, 95–109; Vorster, "Meaning of ΠΑΡΡΗΣΙΑ"; Wallis, *Faith*, 145–50; Wider, *Theozentrik*, 138–54; Williamson, *Philo*, 449–69.

[108]Aristotle, *Rhetoric* 1.9.39; deSilva, *Despising*, 216.

[109]For example, 4QTest 5–8; Acts 3:22–26; 7:37; cf. John 6:14; 7:40.

[110]Michel, *Brief*, 176; deSilva, *Despising*, 215. Although some think the text seeks to dissuade the listeners from trusting Moses (P. E. Hughes, *Commentary*, 133; Buchanan, *Hebrews*, 59), most interpreters rightly note the absence of polemic in this passage.

(a) *Moses was faithful.* The passage begins by pointing out that Jesus and Moses were similar in terms of faithfulness (3:1–2). Numbers says that Moses was faithful, and Hebrews points out that Jesus was faithful too.

(b) *In his whole house.* Jesus and Moses were different with respect to the kind of honor and glory due to each (3:3–4). The author recognizes that Moses was worthy of honor, but he insists that Jesus is worthy of even greater glory, using the analogy of the respective honors due to a house and its builder, and to the creation and the Creator (3:3–4).

(c) *As a servant.* The last part of the quotation allows the author to complete the contrast by showing that Moses was worthy of the honor due to a faithful servant within a household, whereas Jesus was worthy of the glory due to a faithful Son who is over the household (3:5–6).

a. Jesus and Moses Were Faithful (3:1–2)

The author defines the listeners' identity in relation to Christ. He previously said that Jesus, who is now crowned with glory, was willing to share in human blood and flesh (2:14). Now he brings out the implication: Jesus did this that others might share in his glory (3:1). Jesus suffered in order that others might be sanctified or made holy (2:11a), and the listeners are among the sanctified or "holy" ones (3:1). Jesus was not ashamed to call others his brethren (2:11b), and the author also addresses the listeners as "brethren"—those who share the hope of glory, the heavenly calling (3:1).

Jesus is identified with two titles that continue the complex Christology of 2:1–18 and anticipate the comparison with Moses. First, the author calls Jesus an "apostle," which means "one who is sent." Something similar could have been said of Moses, since God called Moses at the burning bush and "sent" him to Egypt to deliver his brothers and sisters from slavery (Exod 3:10–15). During the exodus, Pharaoh's army was destroyed and slaves were freed. Therefore, Moses was remembered as the one sent to save Israel.[111] Similarly, Jesus was sent to deliver his brothers and sisters by taking on blood and flesh, entering the realm of death to destroy the devil's power, and freeing those who had been subject to slavery (Heb 2:14–16).[112]

Second, Jesus is called "high priest," and priesthood could also be ascribed to Moses.[113] Although Moses was explicitly called a priest only once in the OT (Ps

[111]Exod 5:22; 7:16; Deut 34:11; Josh 24:5; 1 Sam 12:8; Mic 6:4; cf. Num 16:28–29.

[112]Other similarities are that like Jesus (2:11b–13), Moses left a position of power in order to identify with his suffering brothers and sisters (Exod 2:11; 4:18; cf. Heb 11:24–26), he declared God's name to his brothers and sisters (Exod 3:13–15), and he put his trust in God (14:13–14). Cf. Andriessen, "La teneur," 304–13.

[113]Milgrom, *Leviticus*, 555–58. Some have suggested that the term "apostle" compares Jesus to Moses while "high priest" anticipates the comparison of Jesus and Aaron in 5:1–10 (Calvin; Riggenbach). The comments about Jesus' priesthood in 2:17–18 do anticipate the comparison with Aaron in 5:1–10, but the dual role of "apostle" and "high priest" also allows comparison with Moses. On Moses' priesthood see Milgrom, *Leviticus*, 555–58.

99:6; cf. *Bib. Ant.* 51:6), his priestly qualities were well known. He was from the tribe of Levi (Exod 2:1–10), he sanctified Aaron and the Tabernacle (Exod 29:1; Lev 8:10–12), and he ministered at the altar (Exod 24:6). Having been appointed to a position of leadership, along with Aaron (1 Sam 12:6), Moses gained a reputation for being merciful and faithful (Sir 45:1, 4), and he made atonement for the sins of the people (Exod 32:30).[114] Similarly, Jesus was appointed to be the high priest (Heb 3:1–2) who sanctifies others (2:11a), who is merciful and faithful (2:17b), who makes atonement (2:17c), and who helps those who are being tested (2:18).

What initially distinguishes Jesus from Moses is that Jesus alone is identified with "our confession" (3:1). An appeal to "our confession" (p. 126) may have been rhetorically effective because a confession summarized the basic convictions of a group. Statements like "Jesus is the Christ" (Acts 5:42; 9:22), "Jesus is Lord" (1 Cor 12:3; 2 Cor 4:5), and "Jesus is the Son of God" (Acts 9:20; Rom 1:3–4) encapsulated the early Christian preaching that brought people to faith (cf. Heb 2:3–4). In the face of pressures that eroded solidarity within the community, confessional statements provided a point of unity. At the same time, making the confession had a public character, distinguishing those who held these beliefs from those who did not. Some who confessed their faith were subjected to the kind of ostracism that seems to have wearied the group addressed by Hebrews (10:32–34; 11:13–14; cf. Matt 10:32; Luke 12:8; John 9:22; 12:42; 1 Tim 6:12). In such circumstances it required boldness to make a confession of faith (Heb 3:6).

Hebrews seeks to embolden the listeners to remain faithful by recalling the faithfulness that Jesus showed on their behalf (3:2a). In 2:10–18 the author showed that in faithfulness Jesus was not ashamed to identify with those he was sent to save, but called them his brethren. He proclaimed God's name and trusted God, battling evil in order to free people from the fear of death with which the devil enslaved them. As high priest, Jesus faithfully made atonement and offered help to those who were tested. Much of what was said about Jesus was unique—he alone brought liberation from the devil and atonement for sin. Yet some aspects exemplify the kind of faithfulness that others are to emulate, including identifying with those who are held captive (13:3), trusting God, praising him, and declaring his name (10:39; 13:15–16).

God called Moses faithful despite opposition from other people (3:2b). After the exodus, the people complained about Moses because they lacked water and food, and wanted to return to Egypt (Num 11:4–6). Eventually, Miriam and Aaron challenged Moses' leadership (12:1–2). Against this opposition, God replied that "my servant Moses is faithful in all my house" (Num 12:7). This affirmation sets the stage for Heb 3:7–4:10, where the author will juxtapose Jesus and Moses, who were faithful, with the people of the wilderness generation, who were not (cf. 11:23–28).

---

[114]The four major facets of Moses' identity are king, lawgiver, prophet, and high priest (Philo, *Moses* 2.3). On Moses' priesthood see *Moses* 2.66–186, 292; *Heir* 182; *Rewards* 53, 56. Philo also considered Moses' "serving" (*therapeuein*) to be a kind of priestly service (*Moses* 2.67). On Moses' priesthood see Milgrom, *Leviticus*, 555–58.

b. The Builder and the House (3:3–4)

Faithfulness in testing led to honor and glory for Moses and Jesus, but each received a different kind of glory (3:3). The basis of the argument is the common view that Moses was deserving of honor. When Moses called down plagues upon the Egyptians and commanded the sea to part, God honored him (Josephus, *Ant.* 3.38) and "glorified him in the presence of kings" (Sir 45:3).[115] Philo said that God gave Moses "the whole world," so that Moses had a share in God's own possessions.[116] Another author told of a dream in which God gave Moses a crown, a scepter, and a throne. Later sources said that Moses was the one crowned with glory and honor in Ps 8 (=Heb 2:6–8).[117] Moses' glory was sometimes said to include divine honors, since God said to him, "I have made you like God to Pharaoh" (Exod 7:1).[118] Unlike his dealings with other prophets, God spoke with Moses face to face and Moses "saw the glory of the Lord" (Num 12:8) in a way that made his face radiate divine glory (Exod 34:29–30, 35; 2 Cor 3:12–18). According to Sir 45:2, God made Moses equal in glory to the holy ones, who were apparently angelic beings. The author now distinguishes Jesus' glory from Moses' glory by associating Jesus with God and Moses with the created order.

Jesus	—	Moses
builder	—	house
God	—	universe

The emphasis is on the degree of difference between the two columns: Jesus is superior to Moses to the extent that a builder is greater than a house and that the Creator is superior to the creation. Statements made in Heb 1 allow listeners to associate the items in each column: Jesus was active in creation (Heb 1:2) and is called "God" (1:8–9), while Moses has a place in God's house and in the universe (Dey, *Intermediary*, 167).

The author first distinguishes the glory appropriate for Jesus from the honor appropriate for Moses by providing a new perspective on Num 12:7, where God said that Moses was "faithful in his whole house" (Heb 3:5). In Numbers the passage shows that Moses was superior to other prophets, but Hebrews discloses new meaning by reading the text in light of the common idea that "the builder of a house has more honor than the house" (3:3b). When read in its literary context, Num 12:7 shows that Moses is worthy of more honor than others in God's house, but when read in light of a commonplace about houses and builders, it shows that the builder of the house should be given more honor than Moses.

---

[115]A biblical basis for Moses' kingship may be Deut 33:4–5 LXX, which referred to the Law "which Moses commanded us, an inheritance for the assemblies of Jacob," adding, "And he will be ruler among the beloved." Although translators generally understand God to be the ruler, it is possible on the basis of either the Greek or Hebrew text to take Moses as the ruler.

[116]Philo, *Moses* 1.155–58; *Sacrifices* 9; cf. *Rewards* 53–54.

[117]The dream is described by Ezekiel the Tragedian (*OTP* 2.811–12). Later sources connecting Moses with the glory mentioned in Ps 8 include *b. Rosh Hash.* 21b; *b. Ned.* 38a; *Midr. Ps.* 8.7.

[118]For development of the theme see Artapanus (*OTP* 2.899).

Second, the author expands his discussion to encompass God and the universe[119] by making another commonplace observation, which is that "every house is built by someone" (3:4a); few would dispute this point. The implication is that since every house has a builder, there is always someone greater than the house in terms of honor. Moreover, this leads to the point that "the builder of all things is God," which again would have been readily accepted (NOTE on 3:4). If the honor due to the builder is greater than the honor due to the house, then the glory due to God is greater than the honor due to the creation. It is fitting to respect the creation just as it is fitting to honor Moses, but this should not be confused with giving glory to the Creator and the Son, who is over all that has been made (Heb 3:6; cf. 1:10–12).

c. Servant and Son (3:5–6)

The third element in the quotation was that Moses was a "servant" in God's house. The author develops both the theological and social connotations of the term. The theological aspects predominate initially and give to Moses the dignity of being called God's servant, which meant that he was devoted to God. Nevertheless, the author shifts the listeners' perspective by reading the OT text in light of commonplace observations about the status of a servant in a household that also has a son. Socially, there were clear differences between a son and a servant. A ruler, for example, would promote the interests of his sons, whereas servants were included among the ruler's possessions (Philo, *Moses* 1.150, 152). A servant could work for the interests of the master, but the son was the heir of the estate (Matt 21:38). A servant could be respected (1 Sam 22:14), but higher honor was to be granted to a householder's son (Matt 21:37). Here Jesus is the Son, who is seated at God's right hand (Heb 1:1–14). Ascribing divine sonship to Jesus recalls that God promised to establish a "house" or dynasty for David by giving him an heir, whom God would call his own son (2 Sam 7:12–14). It would be fitting for Jesus, God's royal Son, to be over the house of God (3:6a).

In a primary sense, the house over which Jesus is positioned is the community of faith. "Moses can meaningfully be said to be 'in' that community because it extends to the faithful of old who were evangelized (4:2), who exemplified faith (chap. 11), and who are 'perfected' with members of the new covenant (11:40)" (Attridge, *Epistle*, 111), including the listeners who belong to God's house in Heb 3:6b. Yet in an extended sense, the "house" (*oikos*) over which God's Son rules encompasses the world to come, for he is heir of all things (1:2) and the one to whom the "world" (*oikoumenē*) to come is subjected (1:6; 2:5). Those who belong to God's house have hope of sharing in this future world.

Those for whom Hebrews was written are given the honor of being members of God's household through their relationship with God's Son (Heb 3:6c). This identification offers them a sense of heritage, since Israel had long been consid-

---

[119]Some treat 3:4 as an aside (Windisch; Moffatt; Spicq; Héring; P. E. Hughes), but it seems clearly to be an explication of 3:3 (Dey, *Intermediary*, 166).

ered God's house (Exod 16:31; Hos 8:1). Later the author speaks of the new covenant that will be made with the house of Israel and the house of Judah (Heb 8:8, 10). As participants in this new covenant, the listeners can be called God's house and heirs of the promises to Israel. Moreover, they are Christ's brothers and sisters (2:11; cf. 3:1), a part of the family over which the Son exercises authority.

Socially, the house or household was an important source of identity for people in antiquity. In local communities free people and slaves alike were regularly associated with someone's household. Since not all households were equally respected, belonging to one that enjoyed prestige was desirable. The house of Augustus ruled the Mediterranean world (Philo, *Flaccus* 104), and many who administered it belonged to the network known as Caesar's household (Phil 4:22). A house like that of the emperor expected to give and to receive honor (Philo, *Flaccus* 23, 35, 49; J. H. Elliott, *Home*, 170–82). In contrast, the Christians addressed by Hebrews, who probably worshiped in a house (see pp. 73–76), were denounced rather than honored (Heb 10:33; 13:13). Nevertheless, the author insists that their relationship to Christ gives them reason to be proud (3:6), since they belong to the household of God, who is worthy of the highest honor (3:3–4).

Membership in God's household is called a source of boldness (Heb 3:6). The members of a household might include people of various social strata, including family members, slaves, freedmen, hired workers, and others (Meeks, *First Urban*, 75–76). Nevertheless, the listeners can number themselves among the sons and daughters of God (2:10), the brothers and sisters of Christ (2:11–13), and the heirs of salvation (1:14). Slaves were not granted the privilege of boldness to speak, but the listeners were released from slavery by Christ (2:15). Exiles had no right to speak boldly, but were regarded as little better than slaves (Euripides, *Phoenician Maidens* 391–92). Yet the members of God's household are to speak openly, even if others consider them to be transients (Heb 11:13; 13:14). One might be an "exile, desolate, disenfranchised," yet the person of faith could claim that God is "my country . . . my boldness, my great and glorious and inalienable wealth."[120]

They also are to have pride in their hope (3:6). Early Christian congregations found themselves publicly dishonored. In the past the listeners had experienced public reproach and the loss of property, but because of their hope for an abiding possession, they were able to endure (10:32–34). In society, faith did not bring honor, yet the author insists that it is precisely such faithfulness that is honorable in the eyes of God. Holding fast to their confession and receiving the glory God has promised entails the kind of perseverance that disregards the shame associated with Jesus' cross (12:1–2). The author insists that Jesus was not ashamed of them (2:11b), but suffered and has been honored by God so that they can be proud of belonging to his household of faith. The author's question is whether the listeners will be ashamed of Jesus.

---

[120]Philo, *Heir* 26–27; cf. Mitchell, "Holding On," 222.

10. Warning of Unbelief (3:7–19)

3 7Therefore, just as the Holy Spirit says, *Today, if you hear his voice,* 8*do not harden your hearts as in the rebellion, on the day of testing in the desert,* 9*where your forebears tested and tried* [*me*], *and they saw my works* 10*for forty years. Therefore, I was angered at this generation and said, "They always go astray in their heart and they have not known my ways";* 11*so I swore in my wrath, "They shall never enter my rest."*

12Brethren, see that there is not in any one of you an evil, unbelieving heart, prone to abandon the living God, 13but exhort one another each day, as long as it is called *today*, that none of you become hardened by the deceptiveness of sin. 14For we have become partners with Christ, if we hold fast the assurance that was ours at first, firm to the end. 15When it says, *Today, if you hear his voice, do not harden your hearts as in the rebellion,* 16who then heard and rebelled? Was it not all who came out of Egypt through Moses? 17With whom was he angered for forty years? Was it not those who sinned, whose corpses fell in the desert? 18To whom did he swear that they would not enter his rest if not to those who were faithless? 19Indeed, we see that they were not able to enter because of unbelief.

NOTES

3:7. *the Holy Spirit says*. Hebrews understands the OT Scriptures to convey divine speech (pp. 117–18). According to 2 Sam 23:2, David—who was taken to be the author of the Psalms (Heb 4:7)—said, "The spirit of the Lord speaks through me" (cf. Mark 12:36; Acts 4:25; 28:25; cf. 2 Tim 3:16; 2 Pet 1:21; *1 Clem.* 13:1; 16:2; *m. Soṭah* 9:6). Inspiration was often linked to authority by Jews (*b. Meg.* 7a) and Christians. On Heb 3:7, Aquinas wrote, "The authority of the words comes from this, that they are not products of human invention, but of the Holy Spirit" (*Ad Heb.* §171; cf. pp. 45–46). The mention of the Spirit in 3:7, however, has mainly to do with the way the Spirit *continues* to speak through the text, making it a living word of God (4:12–13).

3:7b–11. The quotation is from Ps 95:7–11 (94:7–11 LXX) with some variations:

(**a**) MT and LXX. The MT begins with *'im*, which, probably indicates a wish: "If only!" The LXX uses a conditional "if" (*ean*) to create an appeal: "Today if you hear. . . ." Instead of reading that "the people" (*'am* [MT]) go astray, the LXX reads "they always" (*aei* = Hebrew *'ad*) go astray (Ps 95:10b). Instead of transliterating the place-names "Massah" and "Meribah," the LXX translates them as "rebellion" and "testing." The result of the translation of the place-names is that the text is less closely tied to what occurred at a particular place in the desert and can be more easily applied to the ongoing contentiousness of the people.

(**b**) LXX and Hebrews. Some of the differences seem to be of no significance: Hebrews reads *en dokimasia* instead of *edokomasan* in 3:9a, *eidon* instead of *eidosan* in 3:9b, *eipon* instead of *eipa* in 3:10b, and *autoi de* instead of *kai autoi* in 3:10c. The differences may reflect stylistic variations (Schröger, *Verfasser*, 102–3; Yeo, "Meaning," 4–5) or the use of a different LXX text (Attridge). Hebrews also refers to "this generation" instead of "that generation" in 3:10a, which some think applies the psalm more directly to the author's own generation (F. F. Bruce; Ellingworth; Enns, "Interpretation"; idem, "Creation"), although this is unlikely since the verbs are in past tense (McCullough, "Old Testament," 370–71). On the shift in the position of *dio* ("therefore") see NOTE on 3:10.

Today. The psalmist's emphasis on the immediacy of the word of God to the present generation is also found in Deuteronomy: "Not with our ancestors did the Lord make this covenant, but with us, who are all of us here alive today" (Deut 5:3; cf. 4:8, 39, 40; 5:1; 6:6; 7:11; 8:1; 11:2, 8, 13 and NOTES on Heb 3:13 and 4:7).

if you hear his voice. Hearing God's voice is not limited to simple audition, but it involves paying attention to and obeying what is said (Matt 11:15; 13:9). The clause that begins with "if" is parallel in form to "if we hold fast to our boldness" (Heb 3:6b) and "if we hold fast the assurance that was ours at first" (3:14). God's voice places the listeners in a position where they will respond in some way; the crucial question is whether the response will be one of faith or rejection.

3:8. *do not harden your hearts.* Hardness of heart is a metaphor for those who refuse to do God's will (Deut 10:16; 2 Kgs 17:14; Rom 2:5; cf. Zech 7:12; Jer 17:23). The metaphor often warned people not to repeat the sins of their ancestors (Neh 9:16–17, 29; 2 Chron 30:8; Jer 7:26; Acts 19:9). If Pharaoh hardened his heart before the exodus (Exod 8:15, 32; 9:34), Moses' generation did so afterward. See *TLNT* 3.258–62; K. L. and M. A. Schmidt, *TDNT* 5.1022–31.

as in the rebellion, on the day of testing in the desert. The text recalls incidents that occurred at the place that the MT calls "Massah" (from *nisāh*, "to test") and "Meribah" (from *rîb*, "to contend"), where the people of Israel were rebellious against God because of the lack of water (Exod 17:7; cf. Num 20:13). These incidents became paradigms of contentiousness (Num 20:24; 27:14; Deut 6:16; 9:22; 32:51; 33:8; Ps 81:7). Instead of transliterating the names, the LXX translates their meanings so that the connection with particular places is less clear and the passage takes on a wider significance.

3:9. *where your forebears tested and tried* [*me*]. Literally "tested by trying." The best MSS of Hebrews and the LXX do not specify who was being tested, but the clear implication is that the people tested God; some MSS make this explicit by supplying the word "me" (LXX^{A} $\aleph^{2}$ D^{2} Ψ etc.). People test God when they try to force him to give them help, as the wilderness generation did (Exod 17:1–7; Num 11:1–6; 20:2–13; Deut 9:22; Pss 78:18–20; 106:14; cf. Num 14:22; Ps 78:41). Some say that God tested the people at Massah by subjecting them to hunger (Deut 8:2, 16; cf. Ps 81:7), but most say that the people tested God, demanding to see whether he would provide them with water. Moses warned against testing God (Deut 6:16), and the refusal to test God was considered a mark of piety (Jdt 8:12–17, 26; Matt 4:7; Luke 4:12). Jesus was the consummate example of faithfulness in testing (Heb 2:18; 4:15).

and they saw my works. Elsewhere in Hebrews, God's "works" encompass the whole created order (1:10; 4:3–4), but here the works are the actions that were seen by Moses' generation: the plagues; the exodus; the miraculous gifts of water

(Exod 15:22–26; 17:1–7; Num 20:2–13), manna (Exod 16:13–36; Num 11:7–9), and quails (Exod 16:13; Num 11:31–33); and the judgments that fell upon those who rebelled (Num 16:1–50). Cf. Deut 11:1–7.

3:10. *for forty years.* Some OT texts recall the forty years as a period in which God continually provided for Israel (Deut 2:7; 8:4; 29:5; Neh 9:21; Amos 2:10), while other texts remember it as the time that God condemned the people to wander in order to humble them. A period of forty years was mandated because the spies, whose reports about the people of Canaan prompted the people to rebel, had been in the land for forty days (Num 14:33–34; cf. 32:13; Deut 8:2; Josh 5:6). Hebrews inserts *dio* ("therefore") after the "forty years," so that the "forty years" must be taken with what precedes rather than with what follows. According to traditional versification of Ps 95:9b–10a, God's anger lasted for forty years: "They saw my works. For forty years I was angry with that generation." In contrast, Heb 3:9b–10a says that Israel saw God's works for forty years: "They saw my works for forty years. Therefore, I was angered at this generation." In 3:9b–10a, the forty years is the period in which Israel saw God's gracious works, whereas in 3:17 it is the period in which God was angry with Israel.

I was angered at this generation. The word used here (*prosochthizein*) commonly meant loathing something, like manna (Num 21:5), an idol (Deut 7:26), or a wealthy liar (Sir 25:2). The psalm traces the way that God's disposition toward the wilderness generation moved from contempt (Heb 3:10a) and complaint (3:10b) to wrath (3:11a) and the oath that they would never enter his rest (3:11b; Bengel). Cf. NOTE on "wrath" in 3:11.

They always go astray in their heart. The expression "go astray" at one level means wandering or straying from the path (cf. 11:38; Ps 95:10). In Hebrews those who stray (3:10b) are those who do not recognize God's pathways (3:10c). Just as animals who stray in the desert fall prey to destruction, Hebrews warns that people who stray from God's pathways are in danger of loss. This is particularly true since "straying" also means being deceived, which according to 3:13 means being taken in by sin. See NOTES on drift and neglect in 2:1, 3.

and they have not known my ways. The "ways" of God have two aspects of meaning:

(**a**) Ways that God prescribes for people. God wanted Israel to "walk in my ways" (Ps 81:13; cf. 25:4; 119:3; Isa 2:3), and the instructions given at Mount Sinai show the ways in which he would have them go. Those who do not acknowledge God's ways "go astray" into sin (Heb 3:10; Isa 1:3; Jer 9:2–3; R. Bultmann, *TDNT* 1.698).

(**b**) The ways that God himself acts. God's ways are to support and discipline people. "The Lord is just in all his ways, and kind in all his doings" (Ps 145:17; cf. 138:5–6; Isa 55:8). Not recognizing the ways of God meant that Moses' generation did not grasp either the favor that God had shown them or the consequences of rebelling against him.

3:11. *so I swore.* The word *hōs*, which is often translated "as" (NAB2; NRSV), can best be taken in a consecutive sense here ("so"; BAGD, 898 [IV.2]; NIV; REB; NJB) since Israel's refusal to recognize God's ways in 3:10c is the reason for the oath in 3:11a. Divine oaths appear several times in Hebrews. This first oath is negative in character: God forbade the wilderness generation to enter the promised land. The negative oath is balanced by the positive oath in 6:13–20, which recalls how God swore that he would bless Abraham and his descendants. The third oath is also positive and concerns the priest "according to the type of Melchizedek" (7:21). The promises and the warnings conveyed by the oaths serve the same end: perseverance in faith. On what it means for God to swear see NOTES on 6:13, 16.

in my wrath. Wrath was often considered to be an irrational passion that needed to be controlled (Prov 15:18; 29:11; Sir 1:22; 27:30), and some were uneasy about ascribing anger to God. Philo granted that divine wrath would be a justifiable reaction to human sin (*Dreams* 2.177–79) but was hesitant to ascribe to God the anger that was characteristic of human weakness (*Unchangeable* 52; *Dreams* 1.235–36). Others, however, understood that wrath is the counterpart to God's mercy: because God is wrathful, sinners must repent; yet because he is merciful, they can repent (cf. Sir 5:4–7; 16:11–14). Divine anger could break out against the nations for their arrogance in oppressing Israel (Exod 15:7; Jer 10:25; Ezek 25:12–14) and against those within Israel who acted unjustly (Exod 22:21–24; Isa 1:23–24). God was provoked to anger when people spurned his grace. Psalm 95 first recalls how God took people to be his own (vv. 1–7a), and only later warns about the threat of wrath for putting God to the test (vv. 7b–11). Divine anger was expressed through outbreaks of fire (Num 11:1–3), plague (11:33; 12:9–10; 16:46–48), drought (Deut 11:17), or war and conquest (Isa 13:13–18; 2 Kgs 23:26–27), although the Scriptures do not assume that every disaster manifests divine wrath. Divine wrath could be associated with the coming Day of the Lord (Isa 13:9; Zeph 1:15, 18; Matt 3:7; Luke 3:7; cf. Rom 2:5, 8; Eph 5:6; Col 3:6; 1 Thess 1:10). Hebrews issues warnings to move listeners to repentance, not to make them finally despair of the grace of God.

"They shall never enter." The Greek wording is an incomplete statement that preserves the Hebrew idiom: literally, "If they enter my rest . . ." A complete oath formula includes a curse in the second half, specifying the consequences that would follow when the condition stated in the first part was met. For example, "If I have repaid my ally with harm or plundered my foe without cause, then let the enemy . . . lay my soul in the dust" (Ps 7:4–5; cf. 137:5–6). It was understood that divine agency would put the penalty for violation into effect. The oath barring Israel from entering the promised land states only the condition, not the consequences for violating it (Ps 95:11; Num 14:30; 32:11; Deut 1:35). This form is common in biblical oaths (cf. Amos 8:7). Leaving the consequence unstated may reflect uneasiness about the power of the words to inflict harm, but stating the condition allowed the threat to remain effective, while inducing listeners to imagine the results of violation (M. H. Pope, *IDB* 3.577).

"my rest." The term "rest" in the OT has several interrelated aspects of meaning:

(**a**) The land of Canaan. Moses told the wilderness generation that in Canaan God would give "rest from your enemies all around so that you live in safety"

(Deut 12:10; cf. Exod 33:14; Deut 25:19; Jos 1:13, 15; 21:44; 22:4; 23:1). The association of rest with Canaan is presupposed in Heb 3:18–19 and 4:8, although for Hebrews the promise of rest in Canaan is ultimately fulfilled in God's heavenly kingdom (12:22–24).

(**b**) The sanctuary. The ark of the covenant that the Israelites carried with them in the desert found its resting place on Mt. Zion. When the people were given rest from their enemies (1 Kgs 8:56), Solomon built the Temple in which the ark found a "resting place" (Ps 132:8, 13–14). Hebrews depicts the goal of Christian life as "rest" in 4:9–10 and as entry into the heavenly sanctuary in 10:19. The connection of the sanctuary with "rest" in the OT allows these ideas to point to the same reality.

(**c**) Sabbath day. Rest on the Sabbath was a feature of the Sinai covenant (Exod 35:2; cf. 2 Macc 15:1). Passages connected it with creation (Gen 2:2; Exod 20:11), deliverance from slavery (Deut 5:12–15), and atonement (Lev 16:31)—all of which are connected with the work of Christ in Heb 2:10–18. The rest that Christ's followers hope for will be the outcome of this work. Cf. NOTE on "rest" in 4:10.

3:12. *Brethren.* See NOTES on 2:11 and 3:1.

an evil, unbelieving heart. Israel's unfaithfulness was manifest in a persistent refusal to trust God and follow his guidance (Num 14:11; Deut 1:32; 9:23). When they refused to enter the promised land, God called them "evil" (Num 14:27, 35). Elsewhere, an "evil heart" characterized people who willfully followed their own designs rather than God's (Jer 16:12; 18:12; Bar 1:22; 2:8; *4 Ezra* 4:20–27; 4:4, 30). The "evil, unbelieving heart" is the opposite of the heart that is "true" and cleansed from an evil conscience (Heb 10:22). The explanatory comment in 3:12b shows that the unbelieving heart is not primarily one that has never come to belief, but a heart that abandons the God it has known. The author did not expect that people could eliminate the evil heart; cleansing is done by God. Yet they were to keep the effects of the evil heart in check through mutual exhortation (3:13), since exhortation is one way that the word of God accomplishes its work.

prone to abandon. The construction is an articular infinitive in the dative case and it elaborates the qualities of the unfaithful heart (MHT 3.146; cf. BDF §404 [3]). This explanatory function is enhanced by the similarity in sound between "unbelieving" (*apistia*) and "abandon" (*apostēnai*). In Num 14:9 the wilderness generation was about to "abandon" God by faulting him, together with Moses and Aaron, for bringing them out of Egypt (cf. Num 32:9; Deut 1:27). On the situation of those addressed by Hebrews see pp. 71–72.

the living God. When God vowed that none of the wilderness generation would enter the promised land, he introduced it with the formula "As I live" (Num 14:21, 28). The expression "living God" traditionally contrasted the God of Israel with lifeless idols (Jer 10:5). The "Lord is the true God; he is the living God and the everlasting King. At his wrath the earth quakes, and the nations cannot endure his indignation" (Jer 10:10; cf. 2 Cor 6:16). The living God posed a threat to human beings since God could bring them to nothing: "It is terrifying to fall into the hands of the living God" (Heb 10:31; cf. 12:29; 2 Kgs 19:4, 16; Isa

37:4, 17; 1 Sam 17:26). But since God was living, he was also capable of bestowing life and granting timely help (Josh 3:10; Dan 6:20, 26–27). The needy were said to thirst for the living God (Pss 42:2; 84:2; 1 Tim 4:10), who is long-suffering (*Jos. Asen.* 8:5; 11:10) and righteous (*Jub.* 21:4). The Messiah (Matt 16:16; 26:63) and those whom God helps can be called "sons of the living God" (Hos 1:10 = Rom 9:26; 3 Macc 6:28; *Jub.* 1:25; cf. 2 Cor 3:3; 1 Tim 3:15). True life is found by turning from sin to serve the living God (1 Thess 1:9; Acts 14:15; Heb 9:15; cf. *Herm. Vis.* 2.3.2; 3.7.2), whereas to turn from God "is to forfeit life, because in him alone is life" (Lombard, PL 192.427D). As judge, the living God is enthroned in heaven (Heb 12:22), while his "living" word scrutinizes the hearts of all upon the earth (cf. 4:12).

3:13. *but exhort one another each day.* To "exhort" (*parakalein*) and to give "exhortation" (*paraklēsis*) is integral to Hebrews. Through his "word of exhortation" (NOTE on 13:22), the author does in written form what he wants listeners to do for each other. He is concerned about individuals (i.e., "any one of you," 3:12), but gives members of the community responsibility to exhort "one another" against sin. Later, exhortation will mean "strong encouragement" (6:18) to hold fast to the promise (cf. 12:5). Exhortation to pursue virtue and to avoid vice was part of Greco-Roman philosophical tradition. Although exhortation could be sharp, its goal was to benefit the hearer (Malherbe, *Moral Exhortation*, 48). The author of Hebrews models the kind of exhortation that listeners might use with each other, coupling blunt admonitions and warnings with more comforting and encouraging words (e.g., 5:11–14; 6:4–12). The aim of such exhortation is to promote perseverance in faith and to guard against sin.

as long as it is called today. This picks up the "today" of the psalm and indicates that the force of the text was not limited to the past, but includes the time in which the author and his contemporaries live. Similarly, Paul quoted Isa 49:8, which said, "Now is the day of salvation" (2 Cor 6:2). Cf. NOTE on Heb 3:7. Hebrews intimates that "today" will not last forever. The Syriac says that "today" lasts until the Day of judgment (10:25).

hardened by the deceptiveness of sin. The psalm's reference to "hardening" the heart (Heb 3:8) and being led astray or being "deceived" in heart (3:10) is here connected with sin, which "deceives under the appearance of being good" (Luther, *LuthW* 29.154). In this context, "sin" refers primarily to unbelief and the failure to trust in the promises of God—the principal sins of the wilderness generation (NOTES on 3:12). The text does not suggest that Christians are sinless, but calls upon them to resist being hardened or made callous by sin. Chrysostom noted "As in bodies, the parts that have become callous and hard do not yield to the hands of the physicians, so also souls that are hardened do not yield to the word of God" (NPNF1 14.394). Instead of allowing sin to make them resistant to the word of God, the listeners are to allow the word of God to make them resistant to sin.

3:14. *For we have become partners.* People become Christ's partners through his saving work. The noun *metochoi* could be used in a general sense for those who "share in" something, but other connotations enrich its function:

(**a**) Commercial aspects. "Partners" (*metochoi*) were often business associates. James and John, for example, were partners in Simon Peter's fishing business (Luke 5:7). The papyri include receipts for sums paid to "Sotas and partners" (MM, 406). The term is appropriate for those who share in an inheritance. Since Christ is heir of all things (1:2), his partners can hope for an inheritance in his kingdom (1:14).

(**b**) Theological aspects. In Heb 1:9 the term was used for the companions of the Son of God, and others used it for the companions of the Messiah (2 Esd 7:28; 14:9) or the residents of heaven (*1 Enoch* 104:6; Hofius, *Katapausis*, 133, 215 n. 820). Although there is little to suggest that this was widely used as a technical term, the people addressed by Hebrews would have considered themselves to be the Messiah's companions, whose citizenship was in the heavenly city (12:22). See generally *TLNT* 2.478–82.

with Christ. The expression is in the genitive case, literally "of Christ" (*tou Christou*). It could mean that Christians partake "in Christ" himself or that they partake "with Christ" in inheritance. The second interpretation is preferable:

(**a**) "In Christ." (NIV; cf. NASB; Chrysostom, P. E. Hughes; Attridge; Nardoni, "Partakers"). Reasons for this view are that the previous word, "partners" (*metochoi*), was often used for those who share "in" something, such as a heavenly calling (3:1), the Spirit (6:4), or discipline (12:8). Similarly, the verbal form (*metechein*) indicates participating in the human condition (2:14) or a given ancestry (7:13), or partaking of milk (5:13). Theologically, this sense would be similar to the Pauline references to being "in Christ" (Rom 12:5; 2 Cor 5:17; Eph 4:15–16).

(**b**) "With Christ." (REB; NJB; cf. NRSV; NAB2; Lane). If Christ is God's Son and heir in a singular sense, the faithful are his brothers (2:11–13), who are God's sons and heirs of salvation in an extended sense (1:2, 14; 2:10). The "partners" of the Son of God are companions who share his joy (NOTE on 1:9). The idea of participation "in" Christ is Pauline, but is not apparent elsewhere in Hebrews, and in this section the hope is that of sharing in God's Sabbath rest. The closest Pauline analogy is that of being "coheirs" with Christ (Rom 8:17).

hold fast. The verb *katechein*, which means to "take" or "retain possession," was used for ownership of lands, houses, or other property (MM, 336; cf. 2 Cor 6:10). More generally it means persisting in boldness (Heb 3:6).

the assurance. This includes both objective and subjective senses (Grässer; Hegermann). See NOTE on 11:1.

that was ours at first. The expression is awkward: literally, "hold fast the beginning of the assurance." Although technically "first" (*archēn*) is a noun in the accusative case, it has an adverbial sense similar to that in 2:3 (cf. *archē* in 5:12; 6:1).

firm. The word *bebaian* is in the accusative case. When taken in an adjectival sense, the case agrees with the noun "beginning," and it may point to the abiding validity of the substance they received at first. Something that is "firm" or "guaranteed" (*bebaios*) when sold carries with it the assurance that the sale was "valid," so that the new owner can be confident of possession against any who dispute the legitimacy of his claim (NOTE on 2:2). At the same time, the accusative can be taken adverbially, and if it modifies the verb it indicates that the listeners are to hold "firmly" to what they have. The translation "firm" allows for the double meaning: God's promise is firm, which means that the listeners can remain firm.

to the end. The expression *mechri telous* anticipates 6:11–12, which calls listeners to "show the same striving for the full assurance of hope until the end [*achri telous*]" in order that they might "through faith and perseverance inherit what was promised." In practical terms the "end" could refer to the end of a person's life (cf. 9:27; 11:13; Haimo, PL 117.846C), although the dominant sense points to the end of the age that will occur at Christ's second coming (cf. 10:25, 37; Lünnemann, *Critical*, 466). In any case, the present is a time for perseverance.

3:15. *When it says.* The position of this verse in the argument is disputed. Some take the articular infinitive (*en tō legesthai*) and the quotation of Ps 95:7–8 as a summary and completion of the exhortations in 3:12–14 (NASB; NIV; NAB2; Lane; cf. 8:13). Others propose that after entreating listeners to exhort one another each day (3:13), the author digressed in 3:14, but then resumed the exhortation in 3:15 (NA27; Attridge). This commentary takes 3:15 as the introduction to 3:16–19, since the quotation reintroduces the terms "hearing" and "rebelling" that are taken up in 3:16 and because *gar* was often used to link questions to what preceded (Matt 9:5; 16:26; 23:17, 19; cf. BAGD, 152 [1f]; Smyth, *Grammar*, §2805; cf. REB; NJB; Hegermann; H.-F. Weiss; Grässer; Bénétreau; Ellingworth).

Today, if you hear his voice. The quotation is from Ps 95:7–8, which was cited in Heb 3:7–8.

3:16. *who then heard and rebelled? Was it not all who came out of Egypt through Moses?* Some MSS (K L P 0278 1739 1881; cf. KJV) took 3:16 as a statement: "For some who heard rebelled, but not all who came out of Egypt through Moses." This recalls that Caleb and Joshua did not rebel, but were allowed to enter the land (Num 14:24, 30; cf. Heb 4:2). Most now take the sentence as a question that expects a positive answer, like the other questions in 3:16–18. Listeners are to respond by affirming that "all who came out of Egypt" rebelled, which is plausible on the basis of Num 14, which says that "all" were involved in the rebellion (Num 14:2, 5, 7, 10, 22).

3:17. *With whom was he angered for forty years?* The word for "anger" is taken from the psalm (Heb 3:10). The question takes the forty years as the period of God's anger (Ps 95 MT, LXX; cf. Num 14:33–34), rather than as the people's seeing God's work for forty years as in Heb 3:9b–10a.

whose corpses fell in the desert. The people were warned that "you shall suffer for your faithlessness, until the last of your corpses lies in the desert" (Num 14:33; cf. 14:29, 32). "Corpses" (*kōla*) commonly were dead bodies that were left unburied (1 Sam 17:46; Lev 26:30), which connoted an accursed death (Gen 40:19; Deut 28:26; 1 Kgs 14:11; 21:24; 2 Kgs 9:10, 34–35; Jer 7:33; Ezek 29:5; 2 Macc 9:15). This was deemed suitable for apostates (Isa 66:24). People went to great lengths to ensure that the righteous were properly buried (Tob 1:16–19). In the Greco-Roman world, many believed that those whose bodies remained unburied would find no rest after death (Homer, *Iliad* 23.70–71; Horace, *Odes* 1.28; Virgil, *Aeneid* 6.316–83).

3:18. *To whom did he swear.* On divine oaths see NOTE on 3:11.

3:19. *they were not able to enter because of unbelief.* According to Hebrews, the failure of the wilderness generation to enter the promised land did not reflect God's faithlessness, but their own. The term "unbelief" (*apistia*, cf. 3:12) does not mean doubt, but is akin to the evil that is manifested in the hardening of one's heart (3:15), in rebellion (3:16), testing, and sin (3:17). The intensity of the term is designed to startle listeners into awareness of the need for faith, so they do not "drift" (2:1) from Christ or his community. The "ignorant and wayward" have in Christ a merciful high priest (4:14; 5:2), but Hebrews does not allow that grace eliminates the need for perseverance.

COMMENT[121]

The motif of God's people sojourning in the desert is one of the three great cycles of images in Hebrews, along with entering the sanctuary and journeying to Zion (pp. 88–89).[122] On one level, this portion of Hebrews considers the distant past by contrasting the faithfulness of Moses (3:1–6) with the faithlessness of the wilderness generation (3:7–4:13). On a second level the text has to do with Christian community. Like the wilderness generation, the Christian community lived in between the deliverance accomplished by Christ's death and resurrection (2:10–18) and entry into their eternal inheritance. They too were confronted with the issue of whether they should trust God to be faithful and to bring them into glory and rest, or whether they should trust other perceptions and give up hope. Listeners *could* follow the example of the wilderness generation and become faithless, but they need not do so. The author's aim is to awaken in them a renewed confidence in the promise of God, the realization of which they could "see" only in the exalted Christ (2:8–9).

Structurally, the portion of Hebrews that is based on Ps 95 spans Heb 3:7–4:13, but for convenience it can be divided into two sections. The first section on testing and unbelief (§10) does two things: (**a**) The author quotes Ps 95:7–11 (Heb 3:7–11) and (**b**) expounds it as a warning about the consequences of unfaithfulness (3:12–19). In these verses the author reads Ps 95 in light of Num 14, which vividly depicts Israel's refusal to trust God and God's angry re-

---

[121]On 3:7–4:13 see Attridge, "Let us strive"; Enns, "Interpretation"; idem, "Creation"; Flusser, "Today"; Gleason, "Old Testament . . . Rest"; Hegermann, "Wort Gottes"; Hofius, *Katapausis*; Isaacs, *Sacred*, 78–88; Kaiser, "Promise Theme"; Käsemann, *Wandering*, 17–66; Laansma, *I Will Give*; Laub, *Bekenntnis*, 246–53; Leschert, *Hermeneutical*, 123–97; Lincoln, "Sabbath"; Löhr, *Umkehr*, 84–107; idem, "Heute"; H. A. Lombard, "Katapausis"; Müller, "Funktion der Psalmzitate"; Nardoni, "Partakers"; Oberholtzer, "Warning," 185–96; Proulx and Schökel, "Heb 4,12–13"; von Rad, "There Remains Still"; Schröger, *Verfasser*, 101–15; Swetnam, "Jesus as Λόγος"; Thompson, *Beginnings*, 81–102; Trompf, "Conception"; Vanhoye, "Longue marche"; H. Weiss, "*Sabbatismos*"; Wider, *Theozentrik*, 72–88, 154–61; Williamson, *Philo*, 386–409, 544–57; Wray, *Rest*; Yeo, "Meaning."

[122]See Käsemann, *Wandering*, 19; Grässer, *Aufbruch*, 231–50; Arowele, "Pilgrim People."

sponse that prohibited their entry into the promised land. After having expounded Ps 95:7–11 as a warning, the author provides in the second section another reading of the text, this time as a word of promise (Heb 4:1–13), which will be taken up in §11. This second reading considers the psalm in light of the rest that God enjoyed after creation. By dealing with the psalm twice, once as warning and again as promise, the author seeks to move his listeners to a positive response to its message.[123]

a. Scriptural Summons to Listen (3:7–11)

The comparison of the faithfulness of Jesus and Moses concluded with the affirmation that the listeners are God's house and the caution that all must "hold fast to our boldness and the pride of our hope" (3:6). In order to evoke and strengthen this boldness, the author quotes Ps 95:7–11 (94:7–11 LXX), declaring that the Spirit speaks in the present tense: "as the Holy Spirit says" (*legei*, 3:7a). The text uses the second person plural, so that it encounters the listeners directly: "if *you* hear his voice, do not harden *your* hearts" as did "*your* forebears" (3:7b–9a). The "today" of the psalm is the "today" of the listeners.

Identifying the Spirit as the speaker fits Hebrews' earlier account of the community's own experience. The gifts of the Spirit that were poured out on the community when the word was first proclaimed to them validated the word that they heard (2:3–4). When they turned to God, they partook of the Holy Spirit (6:4). If Christ's death was an act of grace (2:9), it was the "Spirit of grace" that awakened in them the faith to receive it (10:29). The author does not attempt to replicate the ecstatic experience that accompanied their initial reception of the gospel because he understands the message rather than the miracles to be the basis of faith (§ 5 COMMENT *b*). The author does, however, assume that the Spirit that brought them to faith is the same Spirit that continues to speak through the Scriptures. Therefore, just as their faith was awakened when preaching became the occasion for the Spirit's work, the author seeks to reinvigorate their faith by citing a psalm through which the Spirit can address them again.

The quotation from Ps 95 fuses various moments from the wilderness period into a composite portrait of unfaithfulness. The "rebellion" (3:8) alludes to an incident that the Pentateuch recounts not once, but twice. Shortly after the exodus, the Israelites demanded something to drink, and God commanded Moses to strike a rock, from which water flowed. The place was named Massah ("test-

---

[123]Interpreters generally distinguish 3:7–19 from 4:1–13, although the subdivisions in each section vary. Most follow Vanhoye (*La structure*, 92–104), who identifies the inclusions of major paragraphs (3:12–19; 4:1–5, 6–11). G. H. Guthrie differs, finding an *inclusio* in the references to entering God's rest in 4:3, 11 (*Structure*, 67, 78–79; cf. Thompson, *Beginnings*, 96, 98). Alternatively, Hegermann (*Brief*, 92, 97, 100) proposes that 3:7–14 quotes the psalm and comments on the whole quotation; 3:15–4:2 deals with the psalmist's opening appeal not to harden one's heart; and 4:3–11 considers the psalmist's concluding comments about entering God's rest. Most interpreters conclude the section in 4:12–13. Lane (*Hebrews*, 1.96–97), however, maintains that since the "confession" is mentioned in both 3:1 and 4:14, the unit encompasses all of 3:1–4:14.

ing") and Meribah ("contentiousness") because there the people "tested the Lord, saying, 'Is the Lord among us or not?' " (Exod 17:7). A nearly identical crisis is reported later in the wilderness period (Num 20:2–13), and these incidents were widely remembered (Num 27:14; Deut 6:16; 9:22; 33:8; Ps 106:32).

The LXX enhances the incident's exemplary quality by translating rather than transliterating the place-names, so that instead of referring to the places of Massah and Meribah, the psalm refers to the "rebellion" and "testing" that characterized the whole wilderness period. The oath that prohibits the people from entering God's rest (Heb 3:11) adds to its paradigmatic quality since it is based on an entirely different incident: Israel's refusal to enter Canaan. God recalls how frequently the people demonstrated their unbelief despite the signs and wonders he had done among them, and he vowed that none that came out of Egypt would enter the land (Num 14:22–23, 30). From quarreling over the shortage of water to balking at the prospect of entering the promised land, the wilderness generation persistently manifested unbelief (cf. Num 32:6–15; Neh 9:16–17; 1 Cor 10:1–13; John 6:30–31, 41–51; Jude 5).[124]

Hebrews quotes the psalm to speak to the contradiction between what is seen with the eyes and what is perceived by faith (Heb 2:8–9). The people "saw" God's works for forty years (NOTE on 3:10a). After the plagues in Egypt and the exodus, God sustained the people with water, manna, and quails, and visibly manifested judgment on those who opposed him, yet they refused to believe in God in spite of the signs he did among them (Num 14:11, 22–23). Since seeing the works of God did not engender the obedience of faith, the implication is that faith cannot be dependent upon what is seen with the eye (Heb 11:1), but must rely on the promises of God.

The quotation ends with an oath in which God says, "I swore in my wrath, 'They shall never enter my rest' " (3:11). According to the OT, God's wrath was not a capricious or malicious outburst. God loved his people and could not be indifferent to them (Exod 34:6), but his wrath was kindled when the people he had freed from slavery and fed each day complained repeatedly against him (Num 11:1, 10) and worshiped other gods (Exod 32:10; Num 25:3). Hebrews does not introduce a text expressing divine wrath until listeners have been reminded of the grace God has shown them through the gifts of the Spirit (2:3–4) and the declaration that Christ brings atonement and freedom from the fear of death (2:10–18; cf. 6:7–8; 10:27–30). Such warnings are designed to bring about repentance rather than to make people despair of grace.[125]

b. Warning Against Unfaithfulness (3:12–19)

The first part of the exposition of the psalm is framed by references to "seeing" and "unbelief" (3:12, 19). The author identifies the problem by juxtaposing the

---

[124]In rhetorical terms using one incident of unbelief to represent a whole pattern of unbelief is synecdoche, where one part stands for the whole (Calvin, *Epistle*, 39; Enns, "Creation," 266).

[125]On the wrath of God see Heschel, *Prophets*, 2.59–78; H. Kleinknecht et al., *TDNT* 5.382–447; G. A. Herion and S. H. Travis, *ABD* 6.989–98.

situation of the listeners (3:12–14) with that of the wilderness generation (3:15–19). Moses' generation was confronted with two ways of considering the promised land. Those who placed their trust in the perceptions of the spies, who insisted that peoples of Canaan were too strong, gave up hope of entering the land. Those who remained confident that God would keep his promise were willing to continue the journey. The people addressed by Hebrews were in a similar situation. The issue for the author was whether they would remain confident of God's promises or capitulate when appearances seem to contradict those promises (2:8–9).

The author warns that an "evil, unbelieving heart" can make them fall away from God. He does not assume that listeners are immune from sin, but warns them about the consequences of being hardened by it. Similarly, he does not assume that they can eradicate evil, but urges them to control its effects through mutual exhortation. Deteriorating community life (10:25) increased the threat of apostasy, because it is through community members speaking the word to each other—as the author was doing in written form—that the community's faith is maintained.[126]

Accordingly, mutual exhortation is to continue "as long as it is still called *today*" (3:13b). This comment reflects the complexity of the author's view of the period in which he and his listeners lived (pp. 100–4). The author will argue that Christ's death established the new covenant (10:12–18), yet the ongoing need for mutual exhortation and the prospect that people might be infected by an evil heart indicates that the new covenant is not yet fully in place. The author intimates that the present will not continue forever but only "as long as it is still called *today*" (3:13b). In a positive sense this means that present conditions are not final. The faithful are reproached by society (10:32–34; 13:13–14), but they will not have to endure this forever, since there is the promise of entering divine rest (cf. 4:7). In the negative sense, the present time has a terminus, and the opportunity for repentance will not be extended indefinitely, which gives greater urgency to resisting sin in the present.

The threat posed by sin is insidious because sin is characterized by "deceptiveness" (3:13c). In some situations faith is challenged directly by public reproach, violence, and dispossession, but in other situations faith is challenged more subtly. When sin seems attractive, people are more easily seduced into it. There is not a sharp line dividing the two situations, for when faithfulness seems difficult, sin seems attractive. Sins like infidelity and greed are mentioned in Hebrews, but do not seem to have been major issues (13:4–5). The main temptation was to "drift away" (2:1) from the community and its faith in order to escape the "denunciation" that society aimed at Jesus' followers (10:32–34; 11:26; 13:13–14). The author pointedly contrasts two courses of action. One is to fall away or commit apostasy (*apostasis*), and the other is to hold fast faithfully to

---

[126]Grässer, *Hebräer*, 1.188. Käsemann said, "Only in union with Christ's companions is there life, faith, and progress on the individual's way of wandering"; isolation is associated with disobedience (*Wandering*, 21–22).

one's "assurance" (*hypostasis*). Like people on board a ship that is drifting (2:1), the listeners are depicted as being not aware of the direction in which they are moving. Therefore, by using sharply contrastive words, the author attempts to startle them into a new awareness of their situation, creating clarity where there was little clarity.

Encouragement takes the form of a metaphor with commercial and theological connotations (NOTES on 3:14). Since "partners" place themselves and their possessions at the service of each other, Christ's "partners" have the hope of sharing in the honor and dignity that he has attained through his death and exaltation (2:8–9) and of sharing in his inheritance in the world to come (1:2, 14). The listeners have assurance in the sense that they have God's promise as the "assurance" or title deed of this hope and can therefore exhibit "assurance" in their faith. God's promise is "firm," which means that no one can challenge its validity, and this firmness is the basis upon which the listeners can remain firm despite opposition. Such metaphors fit a community that endured abuse and lost material goods in the hope of an abiding possession (10:34). The author seeks to embolden them to show the same kind of confidence again.[127]

The point is driven home in a vigorous question-and-answer style.[128] The questions, which are based on Ps 95, are posed in such a way that listeners could respond in their own minds on the basis of their knowledge of Num 14. The form is designed to engage the listeners, who are described as dull (Heb 5:11), in a process of active reflection.

The first question, "Who then heard and rebelled?" (3:16a), identifies the wilderness generation as those to whom the word of God had been given. Their journey through the wilderness was undertaken because God had promised them a land (Exod 3:8, 17; 6:4; 13:5, 11) and verified the promise with signs and wonders (Exod 4:27–31). Therefore, in refusing to continue the journey they rejected the promise and the God who made it. Moreover, these people "came out of Egypt through Moses" (Heb 3:16b), which meant that they had experienced God's saving action. The unspoken implication is that Christians, who had received the word amid signs and wonders (2:3–4) and who had been delivered from the tyrant who enslaved them (2:14–16), were capable of rebellion also.

The second question is, "With whom was [God] angered for forty years?" (3:17a). The psalmist's references to divine anger are unsettling, yet the context emphasizes the validity of the anger. God was angry, not at the righteous, but at "those who sinned" (3:17b). The wilderness generation saw God's works for forty

---

[127]On the language see Lane, *Hebrews*, 1.87; deSilva, *Despising*, 239–40, 292. On the language and the listeners' experience of dispossession, see Luther, *LuthW* 29.155–57.

[128]The question-and-answer style is sometimes associated with the diatribe (Moffatt; Braun; Grässer; Bénétreau). The speaker guides listeners away from absurd conclusions through contrasts using *alla* and by expressions like "Is it not . . . ?" (*ou, ouchi*), features that appear in 3:16–19. The style had affinities with the Socratic method of teaching as reflected in Plato's dialogues. A diatribe was not merely to impart knowledge but to transform students by pointing out and curing error. Unlike Epictetus and other authors, Hebrews does not have an imaginary interlocutor who raises objections that are refuted by the author (Stowers, *Diatribe*; K. Berger, "Hellenistischen," 1124–32).

years (3:9b–10a), yet the people's resistance continued for the same period. In divine anger God let Israel's own refusal to enter the land prevail. When the people declared that it would have been better to have died in Egypt or to have died in the wilderness than to enter the land (Num 14:2), God vows that they will get what they want. God did not slay the wilderness generation, but kept them in the desert until they died there.

The third question is, "To whom did he swear that they would not enter his rest?" The answer is that it was the faithless (Heb 3:18). Rather than saying that they "did not" enter the land, Hebrews insists that they "were not able" to enter it (3:19). This was evident in Num 14:39–45, where the Israelites tried to enter the land on their own, but were defeated. Just as Esau was not able to regain his blessing after having rejected it (Heb 12:17), the wilderness generation was not able to enter the land even though they wanted to do so, for God's oath barred the way. The author will later warn that a similar impossibility confronts those who reject what God has done for them in Christ (6:4–6). The warning in this section is designed to keep listeners from repeating the sins of a previous generation, while the promise in the next section gives them encouragement to persevere in the hope of entering the rest that God has prepared for them.

11. Promise of Rest 4:1–13

4 1Therefore, let us fear that, while a promise of entering his rest remains, any
of you think to fall back. 2For the good news indeed has been spoken to us, just
as it was to them, but the word that was heard did not benefit them, since they
were not joined in faith with those who actually listened. 3For it is we who believe who are entering his rest, as he has said, *So I swore in my wrath, "They shall
never enter my rest,"* even though the works were accomplished from the foundation of the world. 4For there is a passage that has spoken about the seventh day
in this way, *And God rested on the seventh day from all his works,* 5while in our
text it says, *they shall never enter my rest.*

6Therefore, since it is still possible for some to enter it, and those to whom the
good news was spoken in former times failed to enter because of unbelief, 7he
again ordains a certain day, namely, *today,* speaking through David a long time
later, as it has been said, *Today if you hear his voice, do not harden your hearts.*
8For if Joshua had given them rest, he would not have spoken afterward of another day. 9Therefore, a Sabbath remains for the people of God. 10For the one
who has entered his rest, he indeed rests from his works just as God did from his.

11Let us strive, therefore, to enter that rest, in order that no one fall by the
same example of unbelief. 12For the word of God is living and active, more cutting than any two-edged sword, penetrating to the division of soul and spirit, of
joints and marrow, and able to scrutinize the thoughts and intentions of the
heart, 13and nothing created is concealed before him, but all are naked and defenseless before the eyes of him to whom we must render an account.

NOTES

4:1. *let us fear.* Hebrews assumes that fear has a proper place in relation to God (10:27, 31; 12:21), and previous verses depicted the grim result of the wilderness generation's unbelief (3:16–19). The author seeks to awaken fear in order to alert the listeners to the gravity of their situation and to move them to perseverance. See p. 90 on fear as a rhetorical device.

promise of entering. The word "promise" was frequently used for something good, like the promise of honor, gifts, and wealth (1 Macc 10:24; 2 Macc 7:24). In Jewish and early Christian sources the term was often used for God's promise that Abraham would become the father of a great nation and would inherit the land (Pr Azar 13; 2 Esd 3:15; Rom 4:13–25; Gal 3:16, 29), and for the return to the land after exile (2 Macc 2:18; cf. Deut 30:3). "Promise" is connected to the promises made to Abraham (Heb 6:12–17; 7:6; 11:9–17) and the promises that constitute the basis of the new covenant (8:6; 9:15). Speaking of rest as a "promise" rather than a present reality is designed to foster hope for the future (3:6), when the promise will be fulfilled. See pp. 110–12.

his rest. "Rest" (*katapausis*) can be connected with the promised land, the sanctuary, and the Sabbath (NOTE on 3:11). Discussion has focused on two ways of construing "rest":

(a) "Rest" as a place. The story of Israel in the wilderness centered on the hope of finding rest in Canaan. In Hebrews the wilderness wanderings foreshadow the situation of the later Christian community, who anticipate an inheritance in the future heavenly city of God (2:5; 11:10, 13–16; 12:22–24; 13:14). The connection between rest and God's city is evident from other sources. There was the hope that "the saints shall rest in Eden; the righteous shall rejoice in the New Jerusalem" (*T. Dan* 5:12). Similarly, "for you a paradise is opened . . . a city is built, a rest is furnished" (*4 Ezra* 8:52; cf. *Jos. Asen.* 8:9; 22:9; Rev 14:1, 13). Hebrews does not dismiss the hope of a place of rest, but relocates it in heaven (Isaacs, *Sacred*, 82).

(b) "Rest" as a condition. The term *katapausis* can be used for the rest that people enjoyed on the Sabbath regardless of their location (Exod 35:2; 2 Macc 15:1). The identification of "rest" with the Sabbath in Heb 4:9 and the comment that it entails resting in the manner that God rested in 4:10 expands the scope from a place of rest to the quality of the rest (Attridge; Grässer; H.-F. Weiss; Isaacs, *Sacred*, 82). Cf. NOTE on 4:10.

Much of the debate over "rest" stems from attempts to locate Hebrews' perspective in the history of religions (Lombard, "Katapausis"). Some interpret "rest" spatially, connecting the "rest" (*katapausis*) mentioned in Hebrews with the "rest" (*anapausis*) mentioned in Philo and in Gnostic sources (Käsemann, *Wandering*; Theissen, *Untersuchungen*, 124–29). Others interpret it temporally, linking it to Jewish apocalyptic writings (Hofius, *Katapausis*, 5–101). The terms *katapausis* and *anapausis* could be used almost interchangeably in antiquity (e.g., Exod 35:2; Philo, *Unchangeable* 12), and "rest" cannot be viewed only as a future reality or as a heavenly reality, since in Hebrews it encompasses both aspects. Comparison of Hebrews with other texts can illustrate the range of possible meanings, but the sense of the term "rest" must finally be guided by its function in Hebrews (pp. 60–61; cf. Spicq, *L'Épître,* 2.95–104; Braun, *Hebräer,* 90–93; Attridge, *Epistle,* 126–28; Bénétreau, *L'Épître,* 1.180–87).

think to fall back. The verb *dokein* can mean that no one must "seem" (NASB; NAB2; NRSV) or "be found" (NIV; REB) to have fallen short, presumably in the eyes of God. The verb can also refer to a person's own thoughts (NJB; cf. 10:29), and this seems appropriate here since the warnings have to do with attending to one's thoughts (3:12, 13; 4:1), which are exposed to God (4:12–13). The verb *hysterein* can mean "to lag behind" or "stay back" (Philo, *Joseph* 182; *Agriculture* 85). Using the synonym *hysterizein,* Philo said that as "those who are not able to proceed with firm feet, but remain back [*hysterizousan*] stumbling and worn out a long way from the goal of the way, so the soul is also hindered from completing the way leading to piety, when it hits against the impassable stretch of godlessness, because of which the reason falls short [*hysterizei*], wavering on the natural way" (Philo, Fragments [Mangey, *Philo,* 2.656]; Michel, *Brief,* 191 n. 5). "Falling back" refers to the unbelief that is the opposite of "entering" God's rest (cf. 3:12, 19; 4:11; 10:39).

4:2. *good news indeed has been spoken to us.* The verb *euangelizein* was used in the good news of God's saving acts (Pss 40:9 [39:9 LXX]; 96:2 [95:2]), for the messenger bringing news of God's rule and peace (Isa 52:7; Nah 1:15), and for salvation in Christ (Mark 1:1; Rom 1:1). Often the verb was used for what had already occurred, such as victory in battle (2 Sam 18:19, 31). In Hebrews such usage fits the announcement of Christ's enthronement (Heb 1:1–14) and his defeat of Satan (2:14–16), which was a message of "salvation" (2:3–4). The verb could also announce that deliverance (Isa 61:1–2), a birth (Luke 1:19; Josephus, *Ant.* 5.277), or a victory (*Ant.* 5.24) would occur in the future, so that "good news" could be synonymous with "promise" (cf. Acts 13:32; Philo, *Rewards* 161). In Heb 4:2 "the good news" includes the promise that the faithful will enter God's rest (4:1). See *TLNT* 2.82–92; Friedrich, *TDNT* 2.707–37.

just as it was to them. Good news came to Moses' generation as a promise that God would deliver them from slavery and bring them to Canaan (Exod 3:16–17; 4:27–31; cf. 6:1–9). In Hebrews these promises foreshadow the deliverance and rest that come through Christ—something that was not apparent to previous generations (Rose, "Verheissung," 64).

but the word that was heard. Akoē can refer to the act of listening (cf. 5:11) or to what is heard (Isa 52:7; Rom 10:16–17). In Hebrews hearing the gospel evokes faith, and faith makes the message effective (cf. 1 Thess 2:13; Gal 3:2, 5; Rom 10:14–17). Physical hearing does not automatically produce faith; Moses' generation heard the word but did not heed it.

did not benefit them. "Benefit" has to do with the effect of something. A physician might treat someone for an illness, but if the body does not respond, there is no benefit (Mark 5:26; cf. 8:36). Similarly, God promised Moses' generation a land flowing with milk and honey, yet they did not receive it because of their negative response (Num 14:4–10). To say that death in the wilderness "did not benefit them" is an understatement (Bengel).

since they were not joined in faith. The sense is that the word is beneficial when received by faith but is not beneficial when dissociated from faith (3:18–19; 4:6, 11). The verb "join" (*synkerannymi*) suggests mixing or blending. The textual issue is whether the participle is singular, referring to God's "word" mingling with faith in the listeners, or whether it is plural, referring to the Israelites' mingling with believers. The plural is preferable:

(a) Singular: "it [i.e., the word] was not joined with faith in the listeners." This reading takes "joined" (*synkekrasmenos*) as a participle in the masculine nominative singular, agreeing with *logos* ("word"). It makes excellent sense, but is weakly attested in Greek MSS (ℵ) and early versions (b d vg^{cl} sy^{p} sa^{mss}). If the singular is original, the plural may have arisen either through an error of the eye—adding an upsilon to the ending (changing *-os* to *-ous*) because the same ending appears on the adjacent word, "them" (*ekeinous*)—or through an error of the ear, since the endings would have sounded similar (Zuntz, *Text*, 16; cf. NIV; REB; Braun; F. F. Bruce; Grässer; Hegermann).

(b) Plural: "they [i.e., the Israelites] were not joined in faith with those who actually listened." This takes "join" (*synkekrasmenous*) as a masculine accusative plural, agreeing with *ekeinous* ("them"). This reading is widely attested ($P^{13vid.46}$ A B C D* Ψ etc.; cf. lat sy^{h} sa^{mss}). It is a difficult, though not unintelligible reading, indicating that some did not share in the faith of others in the comunity (NJB; NAB^2; NRSV; Attridge; Lane). If the plural is original, the singular reading may have come about by dropping the upsilon from the ending (changing *-ous* to *-os*) through an error of the eye or the ear, or it may have been altered to clarify the sense. Some MSS make the following word genitive, "the faith *of* those who heard" (D* 104 1505), or make it a neuter, "faith in the things that were heard" (1912). These variants seem to have arisen as attempts to clarify the awkward plural.

with those who actually listened. The identity of those who listened is not specified, allowing the text to encompass the faithful of both past and present: **(a)** Joshua and Caleb. These two figures were willing to enter the promised land, in contrast to those who wanted to return to Egypt (Num 14:26–30; Chrysostom; Lane). On the idea that "all" who came out of Egypt rebelled, see NOTE on 3:16. **(b)** Christians. Some propose that the wilderness generation did not share the faith of Christians of a later time. Hebrews addressed believers and said that it "is we who believe who are entering his rest" (4:3). Moreover, the faithful of previous generations only reach their goal through union with Christians (11:40; Attridge). The ambiguity serves the argument, which stresses the similarities between the situation of the listeners and that of Moses' generation.

4:3. *are entering his rest.* The verb is in the present tense, but the sense is futuristic. Some insist that the present tense means that Christians even now participate in rest (Hegermann; Lane; Lincoln, "Sabbath," 215; Yeo, "Meaning," 15). Yet to rest in the manner that God himself rested after creation (4:10) remains a future reality (H.-F. Weiss; Scholer, *Proleptic*, 202). The author does not say whether Christians enter rest immediately upon their own deaths (12:23; Loader, *Sohn*, 52) or whether this occurs at Christ's return (9:28; 10:25, 37; Hofius, *Katapausis*, 57).

So I swore in my wrath, "They shall never enter my rest." The quotation is from Ps 95:11. See NOTES on Heb 3:11.

the works were accomplished from the foundation of the world. God rested after completing his "works" of creating heaven, earth, and all living things (Gen 2:2; cf. the "works" in Heb 1:10; 2:7). Some consider an eschatological resting place to be a work that God prepared "from the foundation of the world" (Matt 25:34). In Hebrews, however, rest is not included among God's works, but follows upon the completion of God's works.

4:4. *For there is a passage.* On the idiom see NOTE on 2:6.

the seventh day. Writers in antiquity used expressions for "the seventh day" and the "Sabbath day" interchangeably (2 Macc 6:11; 12:38; 15:3–4). Cf. NOTE on 4:9.

And God rested on the seventh day from all his works. A quotation of Gen 2:2, except that Hebrews makes explicit that God is the subject of the verb, as is clearly implied in Genesis.

4:5. *they shall never enter my rest.* The quotation is from Ps 95:11. See NOTES on Heb 3:11.

4:6. *those to whom the good news was spoken in former times failed to enter.* On the "good news" see NOTE on 4:2. The oath in Ps 95:11 prevented Moses' generation from entering Canaan. Rabbinic interpreters debated whether the oath also barred them from the world to come. According to tradition, Rabbi Aqiba argued on the basis of Num 14 and Ps 95 that they would not have a share in the world to come, but Rabbi Eliezer argued on the basis of Ps 50:5 that they would have a share (*t. Sanh.* 13:10; *b. Sanh.* 110b; *y. Sanh.* 9.29c; cf. *'Abot R. Nat.* 36; *Lev. Rab.* 32:2; Hofius, *Katapausis*, 41–47).

4:7. *he again ordains a certain day, namely, today.* "Today" is a time for repentance, faith, and perseverance in the hope of future rest. It is not an endless span of time, since in Heb 3:13 the author exhorts listeners to listen "as long as it is still called *today*." The period apparently ends with Christ's return and "the Day" of judgment (10:25; cf. Acts 17:31).

speaking through David. David was considered to be the author of the Psalms (Luke 20:42–43; Acts 2:25–28, 34–35; Rom 4:6; 11:9–10). In the LXX, but not in the MT, Ps 95 bears David's name. The Spirit was said to have spoken through him (Heb 3:7; 2 Sam 23:2; Matt 22:43; Mark 12:36; Acts 1:16; 4:25).

a long time later. First Kings 6:1 says that David's son Solomon began building the Temple 480 years after the exodus from Egypt. Calculations based on this text would say that David lived four centuries after Joshua, although modern historians often suggest that a little over two centuries elapsed between Joshua and David. The argument of Hebrews depends, not on the number of years, but on the way the psalmist invites people of later generations—including those of the author's own time—to hear God's word.

4:8. *For if Joshua had given them rest.* The name *Iēsous* can be rendered Joshua or Jesus. The name, which means "the Lord saves," suited Joshua, through whom God brought salvation from enemy peoples (Sir 46:1; Philo, *Names* 121;

QE 2.43), and early Christians found that it suited Jesus, who saves people from sin (Matt 1:21). The role of the name in Hebrews is disputed:

(a) Joshua. Most modern translations refer to Joshua here (cf. Acts 7:45) and some MSS insert "son of Nun" to distinguish him from Jesus (81 330 440 823 syphmg). A reference to Joshua is plausible since Josh 21:44 and 22:4 say that in his time God gave Israel rest in the land; Hebrews would need to qualify such a statement.

(b) Jesus. Elsewhere in Hebrews *Iēsous* refers to Jesus and some think that 4:8 also refers to Jesus (KJV; cf. vg). Like Paul, Hebrews associates Jesus with the time of Moses (1 Cor 10:4; Heb 11:26). To say that "if Jesus had given *them* rest" emphasizes that Jesus did not fulfill God's promise in that earlier generation (cf. *Barn.* 12:8; Justin, *Dialogue* 24.2; 75.1–2). One might apply the text primarily to Joshua and secondarily to Jesus (Héring; Attridge), but allusions to Jesus are not developed in the context.

4:9. *Sabbath.* The usual Greek word for the Jewish Sabbath was *sabbaton*, but Hebrews uses *sabbatismos* (Plutarch, *Moralia* 166A; *LPGL* 1220). The noun is derived from the verb *sabbatizein*, which has to do with Sabbath observances that include both rest and celebration:

(a) Rest. The seventh day was to be a day of rest (Exod 35:2; 2 Macc 15:1; cf. NOTE on "rest" in Heb 3:11) for slaves as well as free people (Deut 5:12–15). In this rest, slaves receive "an ember or spark of freedom" that helps them "look forward to their complete liberation" (Philo, *Special Laws* 2.67).

(b) Celebration. Israel was not to do any work on the Sabbath "except to praise the Lord in the assembly of the elders" (*Bib. Ant.* 11:8; cf. Ps 107:32; *Jub.* 50:9–10). People "kept the Sabbath" by "giving great praise and thanks to the Lord, who had preserved them for that day" (2 Macc 8:27). Psalm 92 (91 LXX), which is a psalm of praise, bears a title assigning it for use on the Sabbath. Praise and celebration also have their place in Christian worship (Heb 13:15).

Some passages link Sabbath observance to future blessings (Isa 58:13–14; Jer 17:19–27), and others say that in the world to come, "from sabbath to sabbath, all flesh shall come to worship" the Lord (Isa 66:23). Later sources said that the resurrection would bring "the day that shall be all Sabbath and rest in the life everlasting" (*m. Tamid* 7:4; cf. *Gen. Rab.* 17:7), when "the righteous sit with their crowns on their heads" (*'Abot R. Nat.* 1; cf. *Adam and Eve* 51:2 [*OTP* 2.294]). In Hebrews the eternal Sabbath can be connected to the heavenly Jerusalem, where the righteous rejoice in the presence of God (Heb 12:22–24).

for the people of God. The author identifies his Christian readers as God's people or "house" (3:6). He does not speak of an old and a new Israel (Enns, "Creation," 272–77) or contrast Israel and the church (Braun), but perceives continuity in the people of God under the old and new covenants (11:39–40). Cf. H.-F. Weiss, *Brief*, 282; Isaacs, *Sacred*, 80.

4:10. *For the one who has entered his rest, he indeed rests from his works.* People are creatures, whose "works" differ from those of God, yet Hebrews say that they can hope that their works will end in a "rest" like his. "Works" can be related to several aspects of the human situation:

(a) Limits of Creation. People are subject to the decay that characterizes the created order (1:10–12), which will be shaken (12:26–28). Those who now labor will find true rest only in God's unshakable kingdom (Thompson, *Beginnings*, 83–87; Hegermann; Grässer).

(b) Conflict with Society. Those addressed by Hebrews were reproached by the wider society. Their support to fellow Christians included the "work" (6:10; 10:24; 13:21) of hospitality and serving those in prison (13:1–3). Christians will rest from these works in the city that is to come (12:22–24; 13:14).

(c) Struggle with Sin. The listeners had been graced by the Spirit, yet still contended with sin in themselves and in their community (12:4). When overcome by sin, people perform "dead works" (6:1; 9:14), and so they must strive to keep sin in check (12:15; 13:4–5) until they are made complete in God's presence (12:22–24).

just as God did from his. The works from which God rested according to Gen 2:2 were the works of creation. Jewish and Christian sources noted that God's rest did not entail complete inactivity, however, and affirmed that God continued to be active even on the Sabbath (John 5:16–18; *Exod. Rab.* 30:9; *Gen. Rab.* 11:10). Moses' generation saw God's "works" of grace and judgment for forty years (NOTE on 3:9). Philo sometimes argued that the verb *katepausen* in Gen 2:2 meant that God "caused to rest," since God "never leaves off making, but even as it is the property of fire to burn and of snow to chill, so it is the property of God to make" (*Alleg. Interp.* 5–6). Thus God's rest is "a working with absolute ease" (Philo, *Cherubim* 87, 90).

4:11. *that no one fall.* In 3:17 those who manifested unbelief "fell" in the desert, meaning that they died there. In 6:6 a compound form of the verb is used for apostasy or falling away from God. Falling into unbelief and falling under divine judgment are closely connected.

by the same example. The word *hypodeigma* is used elsewhere for the earthly counterpart to the heavenly sanctuary (8:5; 9:23). Here the sense is temporal, used for something in the past. An example may be negative, as in the case of Sodom and Gomorrah (2 Pet 2:6), or positive, as in exemplars of faith (Sir 44:16; 2 Macc 6:28; 4 Macc 17:23). Here it is negative, as in 1 Cor 10:11, which speaks of judgment falling on the wilderness generation: "These things happened to them to serve as an example, and they were written down to instruct us, on whom the ends of the ages have come."

4:12. *For the word of God.* The traits ascribed to the word here are similar to what is said in the OT about the word that accomplishes God's will (Isa 55:10–11), and about the word that is personified in Wis 18:14–16, where it carries a sharp sword. Some have taken "the word" to be a metaphor for the Son of God, thus forming an *inclusio* with Heb 1:1–2, where God spoke through a Son (Athanasius, *Orations against the Arians* 2.21 §72; Chrysostom, *Homilies* 7.2; Williamson, "Incarnation," 8; Swetnam, "Jesus as λόγος," 214–24; idem, *Jesus*, 151–52). Most find this unlikely since Hebrews does not develop a *logos* Christology like that in John 1:1–18. See also the function of *logos* as "account" (NOTE on 4:13).

is living and active. The expression has the same liminal quality as "the living God," who brings both life and judgment (NOTE on 3:12).

more cutting than any two-edged sword. The adjectives *tomōteros* ("more cutting") and *dystomon* ("two-edged") are based on the same root, *tomos* ("cutting"). The OT mentions a two-edged sword that was a cubit in length (Judg 3:16). Roman soldiers carried a sword that was "excellent for thrusting, and both of its edges cut effectually" (Polybius, *Histories*, 6.23.6–7). Metaphorically, speech is "a weapon more cutting than iron" (Ps.-Phocylides, *Sentences* 124; cf. Prov 5:4). Similarly, biblical sources liken God's speech to a sharp sword (Isa 49:2; Rev 1:16; 19:15, 21; cf. Wis 18:15–16).

penetrating to the division. The exterior of a person can mask the interior from other people, but not from God, according to Hebrews. The word divides or separates out the material and spiritual aspects of human life; it lays them bare for God's scrutiny (Westcott).

of soul and spirit, of joints and marrow. The first two elements are the immaterial forces that animate a person; the last two have to do with the material aspects. Together, they summarize human existence. The first pair may reflect a distinction between the soul (*psychē*) and the mind (*nous*), which was often identified with the human spirit (*pneuma*). According to Gen 2:7 (LXX), God breathed "spirit" (*pneuma*) into Adam, who then became a living "soul" (*psychē*). Thus "soul" and "spirit" were virtually identical (Wis 15:11; Josephus, *Ant.* 1.34; cf. Philo, *Worse* 80–86; *Heir* 55–57; *QG* 2.59). Hebrews uses the terms for the inner person (cf. Heb 6:19; 10:38; 12:3) and speaks, with little difference in meaning, of the salvation of one's "soul" (10:39) and the completion of one's "spirit" in the heavenly city of God (12:23).

and able to scrutinize the thoughts and intentions of the heart. The terms refer to the heart as the seat of thought and will. Previously the author exhorted listeners not to harden their "hearts" (3:8) and warned that the evil "heart" may move people to fall away from the living God (3:12). Here the listeners are reminded that God continues to gaze upon the heart, and he will judge it appropriately; hardening one's heart offers no protection against divine scrutiny.

4:13. *and nothing created is concealed before him.* It was understood that God "penetrates noiselessly into the recesses of the soul, sees our thoughts as though in bright sunlight," and "inspects our motives in their naked reality" (Philo, *Providence* 2.35). None of the things on earth that men do secretly is hidden from him (*Ep. Arist.* 132–33; cf. Ps 139:11–12; Sir 16:17; *Tg. Neof.*; *Frg. Tg.* Gen 3:9). "Nothing is shut off from the sight of God. He is witness of our souls and he comes into the midst of our thoughts" (Seneca, *Ep.* 83.1–2; cf. Epictetus, *Disc.* 2.14.11).

but all are naked. Human beings cannot conceal themselves before God. "Everything is naked and open before your sight, and you see everything; there is nothing that can hide itself from you" (*1 Enoch* 9:5; Philo, *Cherubim* 17; cf. *Unchangeable* 29; *Dreams* 1.90–91).

defenseless. The word *trachēlizein* literally has to do with being gripped by the neck (Diogenes Laertius, *Lives*, 6.61). A compound form was sometimes used for wrestlers who ply their opponents "with wrestling-grips of manifold turns and twists, with the throat-clutch which dislocates the neck [*ektrachēlizein*]" (Philo, *Dreams* 2.134). One "collapses like an athlete flung prostrate [*ektrachēlizein*] by a superior power" (*Rewards* 29). It carried the sense of "risking one's neck" (Josephus, *J.W.* 4.375), being subject to another person's control (Philo, *Moses* 1.297), and baring the neck of a sacrificial animal for the knife (Theophrastus, *Characters* 27.5). Sacrificial connotations may be suggested by the earlier reference to coming under the edge of the sword.

before the eyes of him. Since the sentence earlier referred to the word of God, some take this to mean that people are scrutinized by the eyes of God's word (Braun; Grässer). Most, however, think of exposure before the eyes of God himself (see the other NOTES on 4:13).

to whom we must render an account. The Greek word for "account" is *logos*, which was translated "word" in 4:12. Although the expression could mean "about whom we speak" (cf. 5:11), the language was commonly used for rendering an account for goods and services received (*P. Oxy.* ##522.26; 919.9, 11). More broadly, people might "have no way of escape from giving an account for their former and latter deeds" (Herodotus, *Histories* 8.100). Accountability is the sense in Heb 4:13 (cf. 13:17; Rom 14:12; Luke 16:2; 1 Pet 4:5). Through subtle shifts in meaning, the author suggests that God's word (*logos*) demands a human account (*logos*). A similar wordplay is "Every word [*logos*] is vain that is not completed by deed, and let every deed spring from reason [*logos*]" (*Greek Anthology* [LCL] vol. 4 #109; cf. *Rhet. ad. Her.* 4.14 §21).

COMMENT[129]

The author of Hebrews wields Ps 95:7–11, which was quoted in Heb 3:7–11, as a two-edged sword (4:12).[130] In the previous paragraph (3:12–19), the words of the psalm cut sharply as a warning when the author recalled how the wilderness generation's unbelief provoked God's wrath and how they perished as a result. Now the author allows the psalm to work in the other direction, as a word of promise that is designed to give listeners hope. When the author expounded the psalm as a warning, he emphasized the last line, in which God vowed that the faithless would not enter his rest, and the author connected the oath with Num 14, where God raged against the Israelites for their unbelief. To show how the psalm can be heard as a promise, the author emphasizes the first line of the quotation, where people are given the opportunity to respond to God's word "today" (Heb 3:7; 4:7), and he connects the psalm with Gen 2:2, which speaks of the rest that God enjoyed after completing the work of creation. The result is that listeners are pressed to see their own future in light of God's design for the creation. Hebrews affirms that the God "for whom all things and through whom all things exist" (Heb 2:10) will bring his people and his world to the end that he has designed for them.

[129]For bibliography on 3:7–4:13 see §10 COMMENT n. 1.

[130]Tertullian wrote of "the divine word of God, doubly sharpened with the two Testaments of the ancient law and the new law" (*Adversus Judaeos* 9), and Augustine wrote similarly that "Scripture says that the word of God is a doubly sharp sword, on account of the two edges, the two Testaments" (*The City of God* 20.21). See P. E. Hughes, *Commentary*, 164.

The journey to God's promised rest is one of the three major movements in Hebrews, and the theme of rest helps to connect each section[131]:

(a) The first series of arguments moves from deliverance out of slavery (2:10–18) to a sojourn in the desert (3:1–19) and entry into God's promised rest (4:1–13). This pattern recalls the Israelites' journey from slavery in Egypt to rest in the land of Canaan. Moses said that "in the land that the Lord your God is allotting to you," God will give "you rest from your enemies all around so that you live in safety" (Deut 12:10; cf. Exod 33:14; Deut 5:33 LXX; 25:19; Josh 1:13, 15; 21:44).

(b) The second series of arguments, which considers Christ's priesthood and sacrifice, culminates in an exhortation to enter the holiest part of the sanctuary (Heb 10:19–25). A permanent sanctuary was built in Jerusalem when the people had been given rest from their enemies (1 Kgs 8:56) and the ark of God came to rest in the sanctuary (1 Chron 6:31; Ps 132:8). The sanctuary and rest were connected.

(c) The third series of arguments, which recounts how Israel's ancestors journeyed toward God's own city, culminates with a vision of life in the heavenly Jerusalem (Heb 12:22–24). The earthly Jerusalem was considered to be a place of rest. The Lord "has chosen Zion; he has desired it for his habitation," saying "This is my resting place forever" (Ps 132:13–14).[132] By implication, the heavenly Jerusalem would also be a place of rest. Although rest is explicitly mentioned only in Heb 4, it conveys a reality that is consistent with that found in other parts of the speech.

The argument of Heb 4:1–13 is marked by statements that create tensions in the flow of thought, with resolution suspended until late in the section. The author does not create a linear argument but passes twice over the same points. The first part is framed by references to entering God's rest (4:1–5), and the second part is framed by mention of Israel's "unbelief" (4:6–11). Each part follows a similar progression:

	Part 1	*Part 2*
Promise of rest remains	4:1	4:6a
Good news previously received with unbelief	4:2	4:6b
Connection of Psalm 95 to present generation	4:3	4:7–8
Connection of Psalm 95 to Gen 2:2	4:4–5	4:9–11

The third and final part (4:12–13) adds an unsettling reminder about the power of the divine word and about human accountability before God.[133]

---

[131]Wray argues that rest is not developed in relation to Hebrews' Christology, as are the other metaphors in Hebrews (*Rest*, 90–94). Yet the christological framing of the section (3:1–6; 4:14–16) allows for christological connections.

[132]In Jewish tradition there was a tendency to move from focusing on the land to the city of Jerusalem and finally to the sanctuary. "Jerusalem becomes the quintessence of the land, and the Temple the quintessence of Jerusalem" (Isaacs, *Sacred*, 84).

[133]Interpreters often treat 4:12–13 as a discrete section (Vanhoye, *La structure*, 98–104; Attridge; Lane; Ellingworth; G. H. Guthrie, *Structure*, 129; Grässer; H.-F. Weiss; Hegermann; Bénétreau).

a. The Promise of Rest Remains (4:1–5)

The exhortation "let us fear" (4:1a) is fitting after the disturbing depiction of the bodies of Moses' contemporaries lying in the desert, which concluded the previous section. Yet against this stark background, the "promise of entering [God's] rest remains" (4:1b). Moses' generation persisted in unbelief and bore the brunt of divine wrath. According to the author this *could* be the fate of the listeners, but it *need not* be their fate because God continues to call them to faith in the promise of entering his rest. Those addressed by Hebrews were facing an issue that, from the author's point of view, had to do with God's faithfulness. Their faith had been evoked by the promise of an inheritance in God's kingdom (1:14; 12:28), but continued reproach from society (10:32–34; 13:13–14) was possibly leading them to think that the promise was void and that faith was unwarranted. The author insists that the opposite is true: the promise remains in force and its fulfillment will occur—but in the future. Therefore, their present stance must be one of endurance, not despair (Bénétreau, *L'Épître*, 1.170).

The alternatives available to those who have embarked on the pilgrimage of faith are put sharply: either "entering" God's rest (4:1b) or "falling back" (4:1c). Remaining motionless is not an option. Those addressed by Hebrews are compared to Moses' generation, for "the good news has been spoken to us, just as it was to them" (4:2a). Moses performed miracles when he brought the promises (Exod 3:16–17; 4:27–31), and the Christian evangelists who brought the gospel message to the listeners also performed wonders (Heb 2:3–4). In the time of Moses God freed people from their slavery by defeating Pharaoh's chariots at the sea, and in the time of Jesus God freed people from their bondage to the fear of death by overcoming Satan through Jesus' exaltation (2:10–18). The people of Moses' generation did not go directly from the exodus to their inheritance in the promised land, but embarked on a journey through a wilderness. Similarly, Jesus' exaltation does not bring Christians directly to their inheritance, but calls them to a journey that often leads through a social wilderness. Moses was faithful to God, but his contemporaries proved to be unfaithful (3:1–19). Jesus, too, was faithful to God; the question is whether the Christians addressed by Hebrews will follow him in the way of faith or prove faithless like the wilderness generation.

In the past the "word that was heard did not benefit" Moses' generation because it was not met with faith (4:2b). Their failure to benefit from God's promise is disturbing, yet Hebrews insists that God was not untrue; the people were. Only after they refused to enter the land did God command that they be allowed to die in the desert. The positive corollary to this is that God does not capri-

---

This view understands the references to "unbelief" in 4:6 and 11 to bracket that section, and the references to entering God's rest in 4:1 and 11 to frame the whole section. Similarly, the term *logos* ("word" / "account"), which begins and ends 4:12–13, is taken to delimit the final section, which focuses on the word of God rather than rest. Here, 4:11 is included with 4:12–13 (cf. NA^{27}; F. F. Bruce) because the comments about God's word in 4:12–13 support the exhortation to strive toward God's rest in 4:11. Each reference to entering God's rest is introduced with the transitional particle *oun* ("therefore"; 4:1, 6, 11) which is followed by one or more sentences beginning with *gar* ("for"; 4:2, 3, 4 / 4:8, 10 / 4:12), that comment on the urgency of entering God's rest.

ciously abandon those who persevere. Listeners "are entering" God's rest (4:3). Although they have not arrived, they are on the way and can trust that God will not forsake them (cf. 13:5).

In 4:4–5 the author creates tension in his argument by making two points without explicating them. First, he cites the divine oath prohibiting entry into the land to imply that those who believe will be brought into divine rest, but he does not explain *how* the text can be understood in this way. Second, he abruptly connects the prohibition against entering God's rest from Ps 95:11 with a quotation from Gen 2:2 that recalls how God rested after completing his work of creation. The two biblical texts are joined by a technique known as *gezērah šāwāh*, which is an inference by analogy. The idea is that when the same word appears in two biblical texts, the reader can use one text to interpret the other text.[134] Psalm 95 and Gen 2:2 both refer to God's rest (*katapausis / katapauein*), God's "works" (*erga*; cf. Heb 3:9; 4:3), and "today" or a "day" (*sēmeron / hēmera*). Despite the similarity in wording, however, the purpose in relating these texts is not obvious, and the introduction of Gen 2:2 initially complicates the argument, since Ps 95 seems to speak of God's rest in the future whereas Gen 2:2 refers to God's rest at the time of creation, which is past. Listeners must wait for further explanation.

b. God's Sabbath Rest (4:6–11)

Repeating the promise of entering God's rest (Heb 4:6a) and the warning about the wilderness generation's unbelief (4:6b), the author now shows how the oath at the end of Ps 95 can be read as a promise (Heb 4:7). He discloses an element of hope by reading the end of the psalm quotation (Ps 95:11) in light of its beginning (95:7), where the psalmist makes an appeal to hear God's voice "today." Despite the unbelief of an earlier generation, God ordained that there be another day in which people could respond favorably to his promise.

A further implication is that the rest that Joshua gave to the people was only penultimate (4:8), foreshadowing ultimate rest in the way that Melchizedek foreshadows the priesthood of Christ (7:1–10) and that Levitical practices foreshadow the atonement accomplished by Christ (9:1–14). The journey of the people through the desert culminated with the entry into rest in Canaan (Exod 33:14; Deut 12:10), but the OT shows that rest in the land was provisional at best. God was said to have given "rest on every side" at the end of Joshua's conquests (Josh 21:43–45; 22:4), but this soon gave way to war. There was rest under some kings (1 Kgs 8:56; 1 Chron 22:9; 2 Chron 15:15; 20:30), interspersed with periods of instability and conflict. Hebrews presses the point that Ps 95, which was ascribed to David, addressed the descendants of those who had entered the land, showing that God's rest must transcend these provisional gifts (von Rad, "There Remains Still").

---

[134]On *gezērah šāwāh* see Strack and Stemberger, *Introduction*, 21. On its relationship to Greco-Roman rhetoric, see Lieberman, *Hellenism*, 58–62. The proposal that Gen 2:2 was connected with Ps 95 in Jewish worship (Schröger, *Verfasser*, 109–15) is interesting, but difficult to verify given available sources.

The rest that God intends for people is called a "Sabbath" in 4:9. The Sabbath was a reminder of the way God created for six days, then rested on the seventh (Gen 1:1–2:4). Hebrews posits a symmetry in the activity of God, "for whom all things and through whom all things exist" (Heb 2:10).[135] If God's work culminated in a Sabbath rest at the dawn of time, Hebrews assumes that God's work will culminate in a Sabbath rest at the end of time. The Sabbath was a prominent feature of the Sinai covenant (Exod 20:8–11; 35:2–3; Deut 5:12–15), and it was understood to be a way in which God honored Israel: "great is the honor which the Lord gave to Israel" in giving them the Sabbath for rest (*Jub.* 50:10).[136] The first covenant's provision for a Sabbath foreshadows the final accomplishment of God's purposes under the new covenant—much as the first covenant's provisions for sacrifice foreshadow the work of Christ. The people of God look forward to receiving the glory and honor for which God created them (Ps 8:4–6; Heb 2:5–9), and "Sabbath" is a fitting way to envision the realization of this promise (NOTE on 4:9).[137]

The Sabbath envisioned by Hebrews will be a time when the faithful one "rests from his works just as God did from his" (4:10).[138] According to the OT God worked to bring the creation into being (Gen 2:1–3) and created humankind to labor by caring for the creation (Gen 2:15), but human work was made difficult by mortality, social conflict, and sin (NOTE on 4:10). This, however, is not the final reality to which God calls people. The psalmist spoke, not of people entering "their rest," but of entering "my rest," that is, God's rest (Heb 3:11). Hebrews draws out the implication that listeners who labor now can anticipate a rest that will correspond to God's own repose. God's rest cannot be fully comprehended in human terms, but a glimpse is given in Jesus, in whom listeners can "see" the realization of God's purposes (§6 COMMENT). God created people for glory and honor (Ps 8:4–6; Heb 2:5–9), and by faith the listeners can see that Jesus, who suffered, was exalted to glorious rest at God's right hand (Ps 110:1; Heb 1:3, 13). In the context of Hebrews rest does not mean inactivity, since from his position of rest, the Son sustains all things by his word (1:3) and actively intercedes on behalf of others (7:25).

---

[135]A more highly developed form of this hope appears in *Barn.* 15, which argues that since God created the world in six days, the whole of history will last six thousand years. Revelation also suggests that the end of God's work corresponds to its beginning by mentioning the tree of life in the New Jerusalem (Rev 22:2; cf. Gen 2:9).

[136]In the first century the Jewish Sabbath was protected to some extent by Roman law (Josephus, *Ant.* 14.242, 245, 258, 264; 16.163, 168; cf. 1 Macc 10:34–35). On positive Gentile attitudes toward the Sabbath see Josephus, *Ag. Ap.* 2.282; on negative attitudes see Tacitus, *Histories*, 5.4; Juvenal, *Satires* 14.105–6. See also Josephus, *Ag. Ap.* 2.20–21, 26–27; Seneca, *Ep.* 95.57; Safrai and Stern, *JPFC* 2.1150–52; E. Lohse, *TDNT* 7.17–18.

[137]Unlike the rabbis, Hebrews nowhere discusses the kinds of activities that are allowed or forbidden in Sabbath practice. Hebrews also shows no trace of the debates over Sabbath practice that are reflected in other early Christian writings (Matt 12:1–14 par.; John 5:16; 7:22–23; 9:14, 16).

[138]Philo said that when God rested he contemplated what he had made. Similarly, the Sabbath rest gives people opportunity for contemplation (*Decalogue* 97–98). Hebrews, however, looks for rest in the fulfillment of God's promises in the world to come (Heb 2:5).

Hope of entering eternal Sabbath rest means that the listeners, like the Son, will experience life that transcends the mortality of the present (cf. 1:10–12). They will be made complete in the city of God, where they will join in a festival celebration in the "unshakable kingdom" (12:22–29). Augustine observed that God declared the " 'Sabbaths to be a sign between me and them, that they might know that I am the Lord who sanctifies them' (Ezek 20:12). This knowledge shall be perfected when we shall be perfectly at rest, and shall perfectly know that He is God." The Sabbath will be "an eternal day, consecrated by the resurrection of Christ." There "we shall rest and see, see and love, love and praise. This is what shall be in the end without end."[139]

c. The Living Word of God (4:12–13)

Sabbath rest and celebration characterize the future of God's people, but Hebrews insists that striving characterizes the present (4:11). Settling into an abiding resting place while still on a journey would in effect mean falling back from the goal (4:1). Since future rest will be a gift from God, the author can speak of the present as a time of waiting for Christ's return (9:28), but here, he emphasizes the forward movement of the faithful. Neither the followers of Joshua in the past nor the followers of Jesus in the present can remain motionless, but are to strive in learning (5:11–6:3), in service (6:10; 13:1–3, 16), and in worship (10:25; 12:28; 13:15; Grässer).

The compelling depiction of the word of God (4:12a) concludes the section. In form 4:12–13 is a period that begins by announcing how God's word (*logos*) scrutinizes human hearts, and it ends by recalling that all people must render an account (*logos*) to God (p. 93). The author has focused on God's word as a spoken word, not an abstract concept. He introduced the quotation of Ps 95 by saying that the Spirit of God "speaks" to the listeners through the words (Heb 3:7), and the situation of God's people, both past and present, is defined by the word that they have heard (4:2). Of principal concern is the effect that the word has when it addresses people, whether through the biblical text or through the exhortations that Christians address to one another (13:22; cf. 3:13). The effectiveness of God's word was demonstrated by the oath that barred Moses' generation from Canaan (3:11). When the Israelites tried to enter the land in defiance of God, they fell by the sword (*machaira*, Num 14:43–45). Those addressed by Hebrews are also threatened by the word of God, which functions as a sword (*machaira*, Heb 4:12b) that can expose their thoughts, making them defenseless before God (Lane).

The impossibility of avoiding examination by God plays an important role in the rhetorical strategy of Hebrews. A person's sense of worth and decisions about conduct are shaped by the opinions of others. There are various "courts of repu-

---

[139]These lines conclude *The City of God* (22.30). The theme of rest also frames Augustine's *Confessions*. At the beginning, he confessed that the heart is restless until it rests in God (1.1). The book concludes with prayers for peace and rest in the Sabbath that is eternal life (13.34–38).

tation" in society, and the way a person is perceived differs from group to group. Since the wider society viewed the Christian community with reproach, a person who wanted to be deemed honorable would act according to the terms laid down by Greco-Roman society and avoid what was regarded as deviant, like participation in Christian gatherings (10:25). Hebrews places the listeners in an alternative court of reputation, one in which God scrutinizes them. The author shifts the context from one in which society's judgment is dominant to one in which God's judgment is dominant. God gives true glory and honor (2:5–9), and God also gives the final judgment.[140]

The force of this appeal is enhanced in two ways. First, the idea that people cannot hide from the sight of God was commonplace (NOTES on 4:12–13). Jesus, for example, reproved his opponents by saying, "You are those who justify yourselves in the sight of others; but God knows your hearts; for what is prized by human beings is an abomination in the sight of God" (Luke 16:15; cf. John 12:43). Because the idea was so common, it would be difficult for listeners to dispute its truth or exempt themselves from its scope. Second, the author connects being scrutinized by God with final judgment or rendering an account (Heb 4:13c). The imagery is vivid. Jesus depicted God as the owner of an estate who expects his servants to render an account of their actions or debts (Matt 18:23–35; 25:14–30; Luke 19:12–27; cf. 16:2). The parable uses language from the workplace to anticipate God's final judgment (Matt 12:36; John 5:28–29; Rom 14:12; 1 Pet 4:5). The author of Hebrews assumes that listeners are familiar with the idea of future judgment (6:7–8; 9:27; 10:25–27), and he brings that judgment into the present by reminding them that even now they are subject to the scrutiny of God. His words are designed to unsettle the listeners and prepare them for the words of encouragement offered in the next section.

12. THE SUFFERING HIGH PRIEST (4:14–5:10)

4 [14]Therefore, since we have a great high priest who has passed through the
heavens, Jesus the Son of God, let us hold fast the confession. [15]For we do not
have a high priest who is unable to sympathize with our weaknesses, but one who
has been tested in every respect, in these same ways, without sin. [16]Therefore, let
us with boldness approach the throne of grace, in order that we might receive
mercy and find grace for help at the right time.
5 [1]Now every high priest taken from human beings is appointed for human beings with respect to matters pertaining to God, in order to offer both gifts and sacrifices for sins. [2]He is able to curb his emotions toward the ignorant and erring

[140]DeSilva, *Despising*, 276–84. The function of the word of God in this context is similar to that of the conscience. "What good is it for you not to have a witness since you have a conscience?" We "are not 'in some theater of this world' watched by men, but . . . are being observed from above by Him who will be both judge and witness." Therefore, "let us always live as if we thought we were to render an account" (Lactantius, *Divine Institutes* 6 [FC 49.465]).

since he himself is also clothed with weakness, [3]and because of this he is obliged to make an offering for sins: as for the people, so also for himself. [4]And one does not take the honor for himself, but is called by God, just as Aaron was.

[5]So also Christ did not glorify himself so as to become high priest; rather it was he who said to him, *You are my Son, I have begotten you today*, [6]just as in another place he says, *You are a priest forever according to the type of Melchizedek.* [7][This is the one] who, in the days of his flesh, offered both prayers and supplications with loud cries and tears to the one who was able to save him from death, and he was heard because of [his] reverence. [8]Although he was a Son, he learned obedience by what he suffered, [9]and having been made complete, he became for all who obey him the source of eternal salvation, [10]having been designated by God high *priest according to the type of Melchizedek.*

NOTES

4:14. *we have.* Jesus the high priest has passed through the heavens, and listeners "have" such a high priest by faith. Therefore, they must hold fast the confession (4:14c).

a great high priest. The Jewish high priest was called by this title (1 Macc 13:42; Philo, *Dreams* 1.214, 219; 2.183) along with "great priest" (Heb 10:21; Num 35:25; Josh 20:6; Zech 6:11; Philo, *Gaius* 306) and "high priest" (Matt 26:62; Acts 4:6). Prior to A.D. 70 the high priest presided over the Sanhedrin and performed rites like the sacrifice on the Day of Atonement (Heb 9:7). The "high priests" who are mentioned along with elders, scribes, and other leaders (e.g., Matt 21:15, 23, 45; 26:59 par.) may have included those who had previously held the office of high priest, some members of the families from which the high priest was selected, or perhaps various high-ranking priests (Schürer, *History*, 2.227–36; Stern, *JPFC* 2.600–12). The title "great high priest" makes clear that Jesus holds a singular office. See NOTE on 2:17 and §8 COMMENT *d.*

who has passed through the heavens. The "heavens" are the created and transitory heavens (1:10–12; 12:26), the heavens through which Jesus passed (4:14), and the dwelling of God (9:24; Peterson, *Hebrews*, 143). The author may have thought that heaven had a number of levels (cf. 2 Cor 12:2), but he does not actually describe Jesus' celestial journey (*2 Enoch* 1–20; *Mart. Ascen. Isa.* 7–9). His interest is in the goal, which is "above the heavens" (Heb 7:26) or "in the heavens" (8:1; cf. 9:24). Jesus passes through the heavens like a priest moving through the forecourt of a sanctuary and into the holy of holies (6:19–20; 9:11; 10:19–20). See §22 COMMENT; C. R. Koester, *Dwelling*, 58–63, 160–61.

Jesus the Son of God. Divine sonship has royal connotations (2 Sam 7:14; Ps 2:7; Heb 1:5). The conviction that Jesus is the Son of God was almost certainly central to the community's confession of faith (pp. 126–27). The surprising element is that the Son of God is called a high priest. In Israel the roles of king and priest were commonly separated. Kings could be involved in worship (2 Sam 6:14–18; 1 Kgs 3:3–4), but attempts by kings to perform priestly functions could be punished severely (1 Sam 13:8–14; 2 Chron 26:16–21). The Qumran community expected two messiahs: one royal and one priestly (1QS IX, 11). The Hasmoneans altered the traditional practice by having the high priest serve as king (see COMMENT *b*). Under Roman rule the positions of king and high priest were again separated, but the high priest was in many respects the head of the Jewish people. High priests had accrued royal honors because of this history (Philo, *Special Laws* 1.142).

let us hold fast the confession. On "the confession" see pp. 126–27.

4:15. *sympathize.* The Greek word *sympathein* is formed from roots meaning "to feel" (*pathein*) something "with" (*syn*) someone. In its fullest sense sympathy is a bond similar to a mother's feeling for her children (4 Macc 14:13–14; 15:4, 7, 11) or one brother's feeling for another (4 Macc 13:23). Sympathy goes beyond "curbing the emotions" (Heb 5:2); it is a heartfelt bond that is expressed in acts of mercy toward those who suffer (Philo, *Special Laws* 2.115; 4.202; cf. 4 Macc 6:13). The listeners' community exhibited "sympathy" when attending to the needs of prisoners (Heb 10:34). Jesus sympathized with people by sharing their flesh and blood, suffering to deliver them (2:10–18), and offering help (4:16). See *TLNT* 3.319–20.

with our weaknesses. "Weaknesses" may encompass several aspects: (**a**) Physical weakness. The listeners are vulnerable to pain, death, and decay (cf. Luke 5:15; 2 Cor 12:7–10). Jesus understands this since he too had a body (Heb 2:14). (**b**) Social weakness. Like Christ, some of his followers were subjected to abuse and imprisonment (Heb 10:32–34; cf. 11:34; 2 Cor 11:21–33). (**c**) Vulnerability to sin. The weak often fall into sin (Heb 7:27–28) for they are "ignorant and erring" (5:2; cf. Rom 5:6). Since Israel's high priests shared this weakness, they had to offer sacrifices for their own sins (Heb 7:27). Unlike others, Jesus did not give in to the weakness of sin (4:15).

but one who has been tested. The word *peirazein* can mean both "test" and "tempt." The source of the testing is not identified, but it could be the devil and Jesus' opponents (Lombard, PL 192.435A; Aquinas, *Ad Heb.* §236) or God himself (NOTE on 2:18). Hebrews does not focus on Jesus being "tempted" to immoral behavior, but on his faithfulness being tested through crucifixion (Heb 5:7–8).

in every respect, in these same ways. These two phrases and the one that follows are introduced by prepositions beginning with similar sounds, which help to punctuate the speech: *kata panta, kath' homoiotēta, chōris hamartia.* According to the gospels, Jesus was tested in some ways that were unique: "If you are the Son of God," command stones to become bread, throw yourself off the temple (Matt 4:3, 6 par.), or come down from the cross (Matt 27:40 par.). Hebrews focuses on tests that were common to Jesus and his followers, including denunciation, arrest, and abuse (Matt 26:59–68; 27:26–31 par.; Heb 10:32–34; 13:13). Jesus was tested more severely than the listeners had been, since he endured a shameful death (12:2; 13:12) while they had not (12:4).

without sin. This terse expression (*chōris hamartia*) has been interpreted along two main lines, of which the first is preferable:

(**a**) Jesus was tested in every respect, "without yielding to sin." Most understand that Jesus was tested by suffering and facing death (5:7; 12:2; 13:12), yet he responded with "obedience" (5:8). Obedience is the opposite of sin; therefore, Jesus' sinlessness is his faithfulness. "Sin" is a matter of one's stance toward God—unfaith rather than faith (3:12–13; 10:26, 29)—and sin must be resisted by faith (11:24–25; 12:4; cf. 10:38). Sins (plural) are particular manifestations of this fundamental stance toward God. See Laub, *Bekenntnis*, 111–12; H.-F. Weiss, *Brief*, 297.

(**b**) Jesus was tempted in every respect, "with the exception of the temptation to sin." This view focuses on the dynamics of temptation within the human mind. Those who are tempted are swayed by sin, even if they do not succumb. Thus, to say that Jesus was sinless means not only that he did not sin but also that he was not enticed by sin (Westcott, *Epistle*, 107). Theologically, proponents of this view often held that Jesus was sinless by nature (see COMMENT *a*). Hebrews focuses, not on the psychological aspects of temptation, but on Jesus' obedience in suffering (5:7–8).

4:16. *with boldness*. Boldness (*parrēsia*) includes both an internal disposition of confidence (NIV; NAB2) and an external expression that is clear and public. See NOTE on 3:6.

approach the throne of grace. The throne could be where Christ was seated (1:3, 8, 13; 10:12), but it more probably is the throne of God (8:1; 12:2), since "approach" (*proserchesthai*) is used elsewhere with respect to God (7:25; 11:6). The expression has several aspects:

(**a**) Prayer. Hebrews locates the throne of God in heaven (8:1; cf. Isa 6:1; 66:1). The idea is not that by mystical experience we should ascend into heaven, but that by prayer we should come before God, who is in heaven (Scholer, *Proleptic*, 108). "Approach" could mean drawing near to God through prayer (Jer 7:16; cf. Sir 1:28, 30; *1 Clem*. 23:1; cf. Dio Cassius, *Roman History* 56.9.2). Some sources refer to prayers ascending to God (Sir 35:17; 3 Macc 5:9), but Hebrews speaks of the listeners themselves coming before God. Philo said that the virtuous could approach God (*Creation* 144; *Unchangeable* 8, 161; *Planter* 64; *Confusion* 55; *Names* 13), but in Hebrews those who have been cleansed by Christ have the "boldness" to approach God (see the previous NOTE).

(**b**) Priestly imagery. If God's throne is in heaven (8:1), the sanctuary was said to be the place where God or God's name dwelt on earth. God was said to be enthroned upon the cherubim (2 Kgs 19:15; Pss 80:1; 99:1), which were placed on top of the ark of the covenant in the holy of holies of the Tabernacle (Exod 25:17–22; Heb 9:5) and the first Temple (1 Kgs 8:7–8). Some translators use the expression "mercy seat" both for "the throne of grace" in 4:16 and for the top of the ark in 9:5 (Luther; Tyndale; F. F. Bruce). Worshipers could approach the outer limits of the sanctuary (Lev 9:5; cf. Heb 10:1) and ordinary priests could approach the altar (Lev 9:7–8; 21:17, 21; Num 4:19), but only the high priest could approach the mercy seat. Nevertheless, because Christ has gone before them, Hebrews says that listeners can "approach the throne of grace."

(**c**) Royal imagery. "The throne of grace" could be understood as the royal throne from which mercy was given (cf. Isa 16:5). People approached king's thrones with petitions concerning justice, disputes, civic affairs, and rewards.

One emperor said that some "have approached me" with a question about water rights, and he concluded that "they should be helped" (Paulus, *Digest* 8.3.35; cf. Dio Cassius, *Roman History* 59.6.3; Josephus, *Ant.* 18.107). Since requests commonly had to be made in person, submitting a petition meant approaching the throne, which for some was like approaching God (Millar, *Emperor*, 465–67). See generally Scholer, *Proleptic*, 91–149.

receive mercy. Mercy is associated with Christ the merciful high priest (2:17), who inaugurated the new covenant under which God is merciful toward transgressors (8:12).

and find grace for help at the right time. Grace is associated with liberation from fear of death (2:9, 15) and strength for the heart (13:9). Here "help" apparently means help for Christians during their pilgrimage on earth (5:9). Jesus offers help by interceding with God and helping Christians withstand the challenges posed by other people (NOTE on 2:18). Moreover, "success requires choosing the right moment" (Menander, *Dyskolos* 129; *TLNT* 2.118). A person in affliction will assume now is the "right time" for help to come, and if help does not arrive, God may seem absent (Ps 10:1 [9:22 LXX]). Yet since God is the one who gives the help (Ps 9:9), God also discerns the right time for the help (G. Delling, *TDNT* 3.462). Hebrews finds Jesus' experience to be instructive, since God responded to his prayer, not by exempting him from death, but by exalting him after death (Heb 5:7–10).

5:1. *Now every high priest taken from human beings.* "Take" meant setting apart the high priest (Lev 8:2) and Levites (Num 8:6) for service. Hebrews says that the high priest was taken "from human beings" (cf. Sir 45:16). In practice, however, Israel's high priests were taken from a highly select group among the descendants of Aaron.

is appointed. Appointing could mean giving responsibilities to a priest (7:28; 1 Macc 10:20; 2 Macc 14:13; Philo, *Moses* 2.109). A high priest assumed office by a process that included a purificatory bath, donning sacred vestments, and making offerings (Exod 29; Lev 8). He also was anointed with oil (Exod 28:41; 30:30; 40:12–15), although this apparently was not done in the first century A.D. (Schürer, *History*, 2.237–44; Safrai and Stern, *JPFC* 2.600–12). Hebrews focuses, not on the process of investiture, but on the source of the appointment—God's call.

matters pertaining to God. This expression is quite broad (Exod 18:19), but attention centers on sacrifice (see 2:17 and the next NOTE). Before the Temple was destroyed in A.D. 70, the high priest officiated on the Day of Atonement (Lev 16) and perhaps on Sabbaths, new moons, the pilgrim festivals (Passover, Pentecost, Tabernacles), and other gatherings (Jeremias, *Jerusalem*, 147–60).

to offer both gifts and sacrifices for sins. Some suggest that "gifts" are cereal offerings and that "sacrifices" are animal sacrifices (Westcott; Lane). In the LXX the Hebrew *minḥâ* is translated by either *dōron* ("gift") or *thysia* ("sacrifice"). The Hebrew *zebaḥ* is commonly rendered *thysia* ("sacrifice"), but *thysia* can also be used for bloodless offerings (Gen 4:3, 5; Lev 2:1–14; Num 5:15). Hebrews probably uses the terms as synonyms (Heb 8:3–4; 9:9; 11:4; cf. 5:3; Attridge; Grässer; Ellingworth; Kistemaker). On atonement see pp. 121–22.

5:2. *He is able to curb his emotions.* Curbing emotion entails finding the mean between indifference and extreme feelings, especially of anger and grief. One "should not grieve over-bitterly as at an utterly new and unheard-of misfortune, nor yet assume an indifference as though nothing painful had occurred, but choose the mean rather than the extremes and aim at moderation of feeling" (Philo, *Abraham* 257; cf. *Joseph* 26; Josephus, *Ant.* 12.128). Although Stoics sought to eliminate the passions, viewing them as unnatural movements in the soul (Philo, *Alleg. Interp.* 3.132, 134), Peripatetics wanted to moderate rather than eliminate these emotions (Diogenes Laertius, *Lives* 5.31; *Ep. Arist.* 256; Philo, *Virtues* 195; cf. Williamson, *Philo*, 24–30). According to Lev 21:10–21, the high priest was to restrain any show of grief (Lev 21:10–12). Curbing emotions, while a virtue, is of a lesser order than the active sympathy shown by Jesus (Heb 4:15).

toward the ignorant and erring. The wilderness generation was "ignorant" of God's ways and continually "strayed" or "erred" in their heart (Heb 3:10). Therefore, God swore that they would never enter his rest. This did not mean, however, that the ignorant and erring inevitably fell under such judgment. Hebrews' language recalls the OT distinction between types of sin to show that the ignorant and erring can look for mercy through the ministry of the high priest:

(a) Lesser sins. Sins of ignorance (*agnoia*, Lev 5:18; 22:4; cf. Sir 23:3; Tob 3:3; 1 Macc 13:39; Acts 3:17) occurred when a person was not aware that an act violated one of God's commands. Non-Jews also recognized that ignorance often led to sin (Acts 17:30; Epictetus, *Disc.* 1.26.6; Diogenes Laertius, *Lives* 7.93). Unintentional sins were committed when a person knew the law but violated it accidentally (Lev 4:2, 13, 22, 27; Num 15:24, 27–29; Philo, *Migration* 225; *Flight* 86). Rather than the technical term *akousios* for unintentional sins, Hebrews uses the more general *planan* ("err," "go astray"; Heb 3:10; cf. Tob 5:14; 2 Macc 6:25). Those who became aware that they had committed a sin in ignorance or unintentionally were to have the priest offer the appropriate sacrifice. See Milgrom, *Leviticus*, 228–29. Some added that people should deal with such sins through self-discipline (*Pss. Sol.* 3:6–8; 13:7; Sir 23:23).

(b) Greater sins. Those who sinned insolently, "with a high hand," were to be cut off from the people of Israel (Num 15:30–31), although some urged people to seek God's pardon for all sins (Philo, *Posterity* 48; *Special Laws* 1.234–38; 2.196). Hebrews echoes warnings about this type of sin when dealing with apostasy (NOTE on 10:26) without developing the distinction between voluntary and involuntary sins. Christ atoned for all sins, both voluntary and involuntary (Löhr, *Umkehr*, 22–68). Speaking of the high priest's moderation toward the "ignorant and erring" allows the author to stress the mercy available to penitent sinners, while warning of the rigorous judgment to be passed upon apostates (Heb 3:16–19; 6:4–8; 10:26–31).

clothed with weakness. The verb *perikeimai* could be used for the crowd that surrounds a runner (12:1), but it was often used for the clothing one wore (BAGD, 648 [2]). Many sources spoke of the glorious vestments worn by Israel's high priest in order to accent the priest's authority (Exod 28; Sir 45:6–7; Philo,

Moses 2.109–35; Josephus, *Ant.* 3.151–87), but what the priest wears according to Hebrews is "weakness" (Vanhoye, *Old Testament*, 139).

5:3. *he is obliged to make an offering for sins: as for the people, so also for himself.* Priests were required to offer sacrifices for sins they committed (Lev 4:3–12; cf. 9:7; 16:6, 15). This distinguishes ordinary priests, who sin, from Jesus, who does not (Heb 4:15).

5:4. *And one does not take the honor for himself.* Priesthood was "the highest honor" (Josephus, *J.W.* 4.149; cf. 4.164). Scripture showed that "God himself has judged Aaron worthy of this honor and has chosen him to be priest" (Josephus, *Ant.* 3.188, 190; 20.224; cf. Sir 45:23). Priests also received honor from the people (Sir 7:29, 31; 1 Macc 14:21; Philo, *Moses* 2.225; cf. Sir 50:5). The OT condemns those who acted as priests when they had no right to do so (Num 3:10; 16:40; 1 Kgs 12:31; 2 Chron 26:16–21). The word *lambanein* ("take") frames this paragraph: one does not "take" the honor of priesthood (Heb 5:4), one is "taken" for the office by God (5:1).

but is called by God, just as Aaron was. Aaron (Exod 28:1; Lev 8:1–2; Num 17:5; 18:1; Ps 105:26) and his immediate successors (Num 20:23–26; 25:10–13) were called by God. Subsequent generations, however, inherited the high priesthood from their fathers (Exod 29:29). Divine appointment connects Jesus with Israel's earliest high priests, while distinguishing him from priests in the Greco-Roman world, who obtained office by election or by outbidding their competitors (see COMMENT *b*). On ecclesiastical use of this text see pp. 25–26, 33.

5:5. *So also Christ did not glorify himself.* Like "honor," "glory" (*doxa / doxazein*) characterizes the high priesthood (2 Macc 14:7; Sir 50:5). See NOTE on 5:4. The theme of glory and honor was introduced in 2:9. Hebrews recognizes that "honor" is due to Moses (3:3) and Aaron (5:4), but the author reserves the term "glory" for Jesus. "Glory" is often synonymous with "honor," but "glory" also can entail entering the divine presence, which Christ did through his exaltation.

You are my Son, I have begotten you today. A quotation from Ps 2:7 LXX. See NOTE on Heb 1:5.

5:6. *You are a priest forever.* This quotation is from Ps 110:4 (109:4 LXX) with only a minor variation (LXX includes *ei*, "are"). Cf. Heb 6:20; 7:17, 21. The text says that the one addressed by God is a priest "forever," which the author later applies to Christ, who alone has risen from the dead and lives forever, in contrast to priests whose service ends with death (7:16, 23–24).

according to the type of Melchizedek. The unusual word *dibrâh* in the MT is rendered in the LXX by *taxis*, which is often translated "order" (NIV; NRSV; NAB2). The LXX does not use *taxis* for a particular group or "order" of priests, although it could have this meaning (7:11; Luke 1:8; MM, 625). Historically there was no organized group or "order" of priests associated with Melchizedek. A *taxis* could be a shape or pattern (2 Macc 9:18; *Ep. Arist.* 69; MM, 625). Later, the author replaces *taxis* with *homoiotēta* ("likeness," Heb 7:15), indicating that he understood that Jesus and Melchizedek had similar features (Lane; Ellingworth; Grässer). On these features see NOTES and COMMENT on 7:1–10.

Although *taxis* can be an order of being (Dey, *Intermediary*, 185–214; Thompson, *Beginnings*, 122–23), that is not the sense here.

5:7. *who, in the days of his flesh.* The term "flesh" reinforces the reality of Jesus' humanity (2:14). The "days of his flesh" encompass Jesus' entire life, but Hebrews focuses on his passion (cf. "flesh" in 10:19–20).

offered both prayers and supplications. Priests "offered" gifts and sacrifices (5:1, 3), but here attention centers on offering prayers (Josephus, *J.W.* 3.353; *T. Levi* 3:8; *T. Gad* 7:2). The expression "prayers and supplications" is not common in the OT (cf. Job 40:22 LXX), but it appears in classical sources (Isocrates, *On the Peace* 138; Polybius, *Histories* 2.6.1) and Hellenistic Jewish texts (Philo, *Cherubim* 47; *Gaius* 276). The call to "approach the throne of grace" in Heb 4:14–16 is a call to prayer, and in 5:7 Jesus is a model of fervent prayer. The text does not state what Jesus prayed for. There are two main possibilities, of which the second is preferable:

(a) Jesus prayed that God's will be done. A number of scholars propose that Jesus' prayer was truly "heard" because he prayed, not for deliverance from death, but for God's will to be done (Mark 14:36c par.; Aquinas, *Ad Heb.* §257; Spicq; Peterson, *Hebrews*, 92; Bénétreau; Zesati Estrada, *Hebreos*, 155–170) or because he made intercessions for those he came to save (Erasmus, *Paraphrase*; cf. Chrysostom; Alcuin; Kistemaker). A more radical idea is that Jesus prayed for his own death in order to bring about the salvation of others (Swetnam, *Jesus*, 182–84). The chief difficulty is that Jesus prayed to "the one who was able to save him from death," which gives the strong impression that he prayed for deliverance.

(b) Deliverance from death. This fits the context in which Jesus manifests "cries and tears" while praying to the one who could save him from death. In 5:3 priests were said to "offer both gifts and sacrifices" for themselves and others, and in 5:7 Jesus is said to "offer both prayers and supplications"; the parallel expression (*prospherein te . . . kai . . .*) suggests that he made the offering on his own behalf. This interpretation does not depend on knowledge of the Gethsemane prayer, although it is consistent with that tradition and with Jesus' cries from the cross (pp. 107–8). The main objection is that if Jesus prayed for deliverance from death, the text seems to contradict itself: he could not have been "heard" (5:7c) since he died. Yet being heard does not mean that the prayer was granted immediately. God did not deliver Jesus from crucifixion, but he did deliver him from death by raising him to life again (Attridge; Vanhoye, *Old Testament*, 126–28; Hegermann; Ellingworth).

with loud cries and tears. "Loud cries and tears" were common in prayers for deliverance (2 Macc 11:6; 3 Macc 1:16; 5:7, 25; Philo, *Worse* 92–93). Philo (*Heir* 19) indicates that crying to God manifests boldness (cf. Heb 3:6; 4:16). At the same time, tears alone do not ensure sincerity (Sir 12:16). Esau wept at the loss of his birthright, but his plea was not granted (Heb 12:17; cf. Matt 8:12; 22:13), and some bystanders at Lazarus's tomb were skeptical of Jesus' tears (John 11:35–37). Hebrews assumes that tears must be congruent with an internal turning to God (Philo, *QG* 4.233). Jesus was heard not simply because of his tears but because of his reverence (Heb 5:7c).

to the one who was able to save him from death. This is a circumlocution for God (cf. 1 Sam 2:6; Hos 13:14; Jas 4:12). "From death" does not necessarily mean being saved "from dying," since Jesus did die, but it can mean deliverance "from the power of death," since God saved him from death through resurrection and exaltation (cf. Heb 13:20).

he was heard because of [*his*] *reverence.* This difficult text has been taken in different ways depending on the interpretations given to *apo* ("from," "after," "because of") and *eulabeia* ("fear," "reverence"), as well as on the connections with Jesus' death. There are two main lines of interpretation, of which the first is preferable:

(**a**) "He was heard because of [his] reverence [for God]." According to this view, Jesus exhibited the reverence that is appropriate before God, who is the unstated object of reverence, as in 11:7; 12:28 (cf. Luke 2:25; Acts 2:5; 8:2; 22:12; cf. Pol. *Phil.* 6:3). "Reverence" is the right complement to "boldness" before God (Philo, *Heir* 22, 29; cf. Heb 4:16). According to this view, *apo* has a causal sense, "because of" (Luke 19:3; 24:41; BDF §210), showing that Jesus was heard, not simply because of his tears, but because of his reverence (cf. the previous NOTE). Hearing (*eisakouein*) is God's response to Jesus' obeying (*hypakouein*). See the Vulgate; NIV; REB; NJB; NAB2; NRSV; Chrysostom; Theophylact; Erasmus, *Paraphrase*; Luther, *Lectures*; Attridge; Lane; Ellingworth; Grässer; Hegermann; H.-F. Weiss.

(**b**) "He was heard [and delivered] from the fear [of death]." According to this view, Jesus experienced a fear whose unstated object is death. The words *eulabeia* and *eulabein* can be used this way (Epictetus, *Disc.* 2.1.14; Sir 41:3; 2 Macc 8:16) and could recall the "fear of death" mentioned in Heb 2:15. The preposition *apo* is taken to show what Jesus was delivered "from," as in 10:22 one is cleansed "from" an evil conscience. Accordingly, God did not respond to Jesus' prayers by exempting him from death but by giving him the strength to endure it (Ambrose, CSEL 64.382; Calvin; Bengel; Héring; Buchanan). The problem is that the grammar seems forced; no other texts have been produced to show that being "heard from" could mean "heard and delivered from" (Vanhoye, *Old Testament*, 127). Andriessen proposed that God heard Jesus "after" he had endured anguished fear ("Quelques," 208–12; "Angoisse"). Yet elsewhere in Hebrews forms of *eulab-* indicate reverence rather than fear.

Other interpretations have found little following. Some have altered the subject of expression so that God heard the prayer because of God's own reverence for Jesus (Ps.-Oecumenius; Luther, *Lectures*), yet this shift in subject is too abrupt for the context. Others have altered the punctuation, placing a period after "heard" and connecting "fear" with the suffering mentioned in 5:8: ". . . he was heard. Because of his fear and what he suffered, he learned obedience, although he was a Son" (Peshitta; cf. BDF §211). Still others altered the text to read, "He was [not] heard because of his fear," insisting that since Jesus died, his prayer for deliverance was not heard. They surmise that the negative particle *ouk* was quickly omitted from the text because the idea of Jesus' prayer going unanswered was theologically objectionable (von Harnack, "Zwei"; Windisch; Bultmann, *TDNT* 2.753). Detailed examinations of the syntax and the lack of MS support have shown that the emendation cannot be accepted (Lane).

5:8. *Although he was a Son.* The concessive *kaiper* is sometimes taken with what precedes, so that Jesus "was heard because of [his] reverence, although he was a Son." This reading stresses the importance of Jesus' piety over his special filial relation to God (deSilva, *Perseverance*, 192). Nevertheless, most translators think that *kaiper* begins a new sentence as in *T. Jos.* 105: "Although I was a child, I had the fear of God in my heart."

he learned obedience. The idea that Jesus, who was without sin (4:15), was obedient throughout his life is basic to Hebrews (cf. 10:5–10; Phil 2:8). Thus to "learn obedience" means coming to appreciate fully what conformity to God's will means (Attridge). To "learn" (*manthanein*), however, also meant practicing something. Other NT writers say that to learn from Jesus is to wear his yoke (Matt 11:29) and to learn piety is to practice piety (1 Tim 5:4). Learning to do good works means practicing them (Tit 3:14). Thus to say that Jesus "learned obedience" means that he practiced obedience.

by what he suffered. The text uses the common Greek play on the words "learn" and "suffer" (*mathein / pathein*): "learning comes by suffering [*pathei mathos*]" (Aeschylus, *Agamemnon* 177; cf. Sophocles, *Trachiniae* 143), and, "While sufferings are unwelcome to me, they have become my lessons" (Herodotus, *Histories* 1.207; Aesop, *Fabulae* 134.1–3; 223.2–3). Sometimes the idiom meant that people learned by their mistakes (Philo, *Flight* 138; *Dreams* 2.107; *Special Laws* 4.29); they learn "through experience, as a foolish child learns" (Philo, *Heir* 73; cf. *Moses* 2.55). In the case of the obstinate, "experience will show them what teaching has failed to show" (Philo, *Moses* 2.280). Suffering can issue into compassion: "Out of my experience of misfortune I learn to help the needy" (Virgil, *Aeneid* 1.630). In the case of Jesus, *pathein* refers not simply to experience but to the results of his suffering (Heb 2:18; 9:26; 13:12). See Coste, "Notion."

5:9. *and having been made complete.* Jesus was made complete by exaltation to glory and appointment to priesthood in fulfillment of God's promise (see pp. 122–25).

he became . . . the source of eternal salvation. A "source of salvation" brings salvation as the serpent on the pole brought healing (Philo, *Agriculture* 96) or as a general brings troops through battle to victory and safety (Josephus, *Ant.* 14.136). "Eternal salvation" goes beyond "help at the right time" (Heb 4:16) to include final deliverance from sin and death upon Christ's return (1:14; 9:28). It entails favorable judgment from God rather than condemnation (6:10) and in its fullest sense means glory in the presence of God (2:10). See NOTE on 2:3 on salvation.

for all who obey him. According to Hebrews, Jesus learned obedience by suffering. His obedience is the basis for Christian obedience. Obedience is not a prerequisite for receiving grace, but a characteristic of those on the journey of faith. Jesus "the Pioneer" brings salvation by overcoming hostile powers and making a way for others to move into the future that God promised them (2:10;

12:1–3). Salvation is a gift, but people come to possess it by following the path that Christ set.

5:10. *having been designated by God.* The verb *prosagoreuein* can mean to "designate" something, and it may therefore be roughly synonymous with being "taken" (5:1) or "called" (5:4) for priestly service. The term can also be used when one person "addresses" another, and that sense is possible here since Ps 110:4 uses direct address: "You are a priest forever" (Attridge; Lane; Bachmann, "Hohepriesterliches," 252). See further pp. 109–10.

high priest according to the type of Melchizedek. A paraphrase of Ps 110:4 (NOTES on 5:6). Here the author replaced "priest" with "high priest." On Melchizedek as "great priest" see Philo, *Abraham* 235.

COMMENT[141]

An abrupt shift in tone and imagery in this paragraph alters the situation in which listeners find themselves. The intricate interweaving of descriptive phrases in 4:12–13 brought the living word of God into the recesses of the human frame, removing any hope of escape from divine scrutiny. Now the horizon suddenly expands to the heights of heaven, where Christ the high priest has taken his place at the throne of grace (4:14–16). The author no longer speaks of divine wrath, but tells of the mercy, grace, and help that Christ offers. Instead of awakening a desire to flee from the gaze of God, the author invites listeners to approach the throne boldly because of Christ.

This section completes the first series of arguments by taking up the theme of Jesus' priesthood that was introduced in 2:17–18 and by underscoring that Jesus was made complete through suffering (2:10; 5:8–10; see §7 COMMENT).[142] The central question addressed by Hebrews is whether God will bring people to the glory for which he created them. The author responds by directing people to Jesus, who suffered but then was exalted to a glory that surpasses the honor given to great figures like Moses and Aaron (3:3; 5:4–5). By considering the way that God brought Jesus through suffering to glory, Hebrews calls Jesus' followers to be confident that God will also bring them to the glory that is promised to them, even though conditions on earth fall far short of the goal.

---

[141]On 4:14–5:10 see Andriessen, "Angoisse"; Andriessen and Lenglet, "Quelques," 208–12; Attridge, "Heard"; Bachmann, "Hohepriesterliches"; Brandenburger, "Text"; Feuillet, "L'évocation"; Franco Martínez, *Jesucristo*, 159–316; Hay, *Glory*, 21–51; Laub, *Bekenntnis*, 104–43; Lescow, "Jesus"; Lightfoot, "Saving"; Loader, *Sohn*, 97–111; Manzi, "Fil 2,6–11"; Maurer, "Erhört"; Nissilä, *Hohepriestermotiv*, 55–112; Peterson, *Hebrews*, 74–103, 188–90; Roloff, "Der mitleidende"; Schenk, "Hebr iv.14–16"; Schröger, *Verfasser*, 115–27; Strobel, "Psalmengrundlage"; Swetnam, *Jesus*, 178–84; Thurén, "Gebet"; Vanhoye, *Old Testament*, 111–45; idem, "Situation et signification"; Wrege, "Jesusgeschichte"; Zesati Estrada, *Hebreos*.

[142]Other ideas found in both 2:10–18 and 4:14–5:10 include Jesus sharing in human "flesh" (*sarx*; 2:14; 5:7), the appointment of priests "with respect to things pertaining to God" (*ta pros ton theon*; 2:17; 5:1), and Jesus being "tested" (*peirazesthai*) so that he can offer "help" (*boēthein* / *boētheia*) to others (2:18; 4:15–16).

Structurally, this passage can be divided into three paragraphs. The first and third paragraphs (4:14–16; 5:5–10) focus on Christ's high priesthood, and the middle paragraph (5:1–4) helps to show the congruence of Christ's priesthood with the tradition exemplified by Aaron. Three topics are taken up within each paragraph: the high priest's position, his qualities, and the service he offers. The topics follow the same order in the first and third paragraphs, and the inverse order in the middle paragraph, so that the sequence is ABC / CBA / ABC. The author does not merely repeat the topics, but looks at them from different perspectives. In *position*, the Son is high priest (4:14), a true priest is called by God (5:4), and the Son is called a priest (5:5–6). In *quality*, the Son sympathizes with weakness (4:15), a true priest curbs emotion and offers sacrifice for himself because of weakness (5:2–3), and the Son offers prayer for himself with cries and tears (5:7–8). In *service*, the Son provides mercy and help (4:16), a true priest provides offerings for sins (5:1), and the Son provides eternal salvation (5:9–10).[143] The significance of Christ's priesthood will be developed in the next section (7:1–10:25), but there the emphasis will be on the differences between Christ and the Levitical priests, rather than on the similarities between the priesthood of Christ and Aaron, as it is here.[144] Both the comparisons and the contrasts between the two forms of priesthood, however, support the same exhortations: "hold fast the confession" (4:14; 10:23) and "draw near" with "boldness" or "full assurance of faith" (4:16; 10:22), for "we have a great (high) priest" (4:14; 10:19, 21).

a. Approaching the Throne of Grace (4:14–16)

Declaring that "we have a great high priest" who is "Jesus the Son of God" (4:14ab) suggests ways in which the author offers the Christian community a focus for its identity that distinguishes it from the dominant Greco-Roman culture while allowing it to develop the tradition of Israel. Jewish high priesthood was established by the Mosaic Law, and the high priest was a chief representative of Jewish identity. Jewish writers sometimes censured high priests for corruption (COMMENT *b*) but respected the office itself, even after the Temple was destroyed and the high priesthood ceased to function.[145] More broadly, priesthood was a part of the dominant Greco-Roman culture. Titles on coins and

---

[143]The chiastic structure of 5:1–10 is widely recognized (Brandenburger, "Text," 219; Nissilä, *Hohepriestermotiv*, 79; Peterson, *Hebrews*, 81, 234 n. 79; Attridge; Lane; Bachmann, "Hohepriesterliches," 249–54). Some see only two main components in the sequence: the personal qualities of the priest and his divine appointment (H.-F. Weiss; Ellingworth). Grässer (*Hebräer*, 1.249) calls 5:1–4 the definition of a high priest, 5:5–8 its application to Christ, and 5:9–10 its consequences. Laub (*Bekenntnis*, 113–19) is unusual in positing a break at 5:3, beginning a new section on Christ's appointment with 5:4.

[144]The traditional chapter division at 5:1 reinforces the idea that Hebrews contrasts Jesus to the institutions of the old covenant: Heb 3:1 begins the contrast with Moses and 5:1 begins the contrast with Aaron. Yet the theme of Jesus' priesthood is taken up in 4:14–16 for the first time since 2:17–18, leading naturally into what follows in 5:1–10. Tyndale and Luther began new chapter divisions at 4:14 rather than 5:1.

[145]On the history of the high priesthood see Mendels, *Rise*, 107–59, 277–331.

inscriptions identified the emperor as "high priest" and "son of the deified" Julius or "son of the divine" Augustus.[146]

In this context Hebrews affirms the "confession" that Jesus is "the Son of God" (4:14c), a belief that the listeners already held. Confessional statements summarize the basic convictions of a group in a brief, memorable form. Although solidarity among those addressed by Hebrews was eroding in the face of friction with the wider society (10:25; 13:13), the author seeks to bolster commitments by affirming the confession that gave the group its identity. Introducing the idea that Jesus is a high priest—a new idea for listeners (pp. 126–27)—is designed to stimulate the kind of fresh thinking about the confession that might bring them out of their lethargy (5:11). At the time Hebrews was written, Christians no longer fit easily into the dominant Greco-Roman culture or into the Jewish subculture, each of which had its own high priesthood. The author offers listeners a way to maintain their identity by insisting that they do not lack a priest, but have a high priest who has passed through the heavens, the same Jesus whom they already confess to be the Son of God.

Jesus the high priest is identified by his ability to sympathize with the weak (4:15a). Speakers in antiquity understood that listeners were moved not only by logic but also by appeals to emotion and character (pp. 89–92). Therefore, before engaging in exegetical argument, the author seeks to touch the feelings of the listeners, inviting them to identify with the high priest who has identified with them.[147] Christ manifests sympathy because he has been tested as the listeners have been (4:15b). They had previously been denounced, abused, dispossessed, and imprisoned (10:32–34), and continued to experience friction with others in society (13:13). Some remained in prison (13:3). Those familiar with traditions concerning Jesus' passion would know that he too was denounced, abused, and imprisoned (Matt 26:59–68; 27:26–31 par.). He suffered what they had suffered and more, since he died by crucifixion (Heb 12:2; 13:12). Christ knows affliction "not just because as God he knows all things, but because as a human being he has endured the same things that we endure" (Lombard, PL 192.435A).

Jesus endured testing like other people, but unlike others Hebrews says that he was "without sin" (4:15). According to the NT, Jesus' opponents charged that he was a lawbreaker.[148] Later, pagans said that Christians revered "a criminal and his cross," while Jewish critics recalled that "the last curse in the Law of God fell

---

[146]Millar, *Emperor,* 355. On the titles see the inscriptions in *RomCiv,* 1.644–45; 2.631–33; *ISBE,* 3.409; *IDB,* 3.433 #29. The Greek *archiereus* was used for the emperor (Josephus, *Ant.* 14.192).

[147]Some Jewish texts referred to gentle high priests (2 Macc 15:12) and called disciples of Aaron to love peace and humankind (*m. 'Abot* 1:12). Others remembered the founders of the Levitical priesthood for relentlessly slaying idolaters (Exod 32:27, 29; Num 25:1–13; Deut 33:9; 1 Macc 23:26). Vanhoye emphasizes the contrast between Levitical zeal and Christ's sympathy (*Old Testament,* 115–16). Horbury qualifies the contrast by noting texts in which Levitical priests are depicted as lovers of peace ("Aaronic," 59–66); the result, however, is that he ascribes too much to tradition and downplays the impact of Hebrews' Christology.

[148]For example, Mark 14:64 par.; Tacitus, *Annals* 15.44; *b. Sanh.* 43a.

on" Jesus.[149] Because crucifixion seemed to show Jesus' guilt, the NT writings insist that there was no crime in him (Luke 23:4, 14, 22; John 18:38; 19:4, 6; cf. Matt 27:19), that he "committed no sin, and no deceit was found in his mouth" (1 Pet 2:22; cf. John 8:46). Sinlessness was basic to Christ's saving work. "For our sake he made him to be sin who knew no sin, so that in him we might become the righteousness of God" (2 Cor 5:21; cf. Rom 8:3–4; Matt 3:13–17; 1 John 3:5). Hebrews follows a common Christian tradition in declaring that Jesus was "without sin" (4:15), "holy, blameless, undefiled, separated from sinners" (7:26), who "offered himself without blemish to God" (9:14).

Hebrews' idea of Jesus' sinlessness was not derived in any simple way from current views of priesthood or messianic expectation, although it was compatible with such ideas. The messianic "Branch" of David was to be righteous (Jer 23:5–6; 33:15–16; Isa 9:7; 11:1–5), and the Messiah was to "be clean of sin" (*Pss. Sol.* 17:36) and to oppose sin and unrighteousness (17:22–32; cf. Heb 1:8–9). Priests were expected, not to be sinless, but to minister in a state of purity. Some anticipated an eschatological priest who would make sin to cease (CD XII, 23; *T. Levi* 18:9), and Philo spoke of the Logos as a priest, "immune from all unrighteousness."[150] None of these sources, however, portrays sinlessness as obedience in suffering, as does Hebrews.

Theologically, Jesus' sinlessness has been understood in terms of his nature.[151] Origen stressed Christ's uniqueness, granting that Christ had a human soul, but one that so loved righteousness that it was not vulnerable to change and had no "susceptibility to or possibility of sin" (*On First Principles* 2.6.5). In the fourth century the Arians argued that the Son of God was not divine. In response many theologians emphasized Christ's divinity, insisting that God's Son did not assume "sinful flesh," but only something like it. Augustine maintained that if sin is conveyed by physical conception, then Jesus alone is sinless, since he was born of a virgin (*Enchiridion* 13 §41). Other interpreters have focused on the activity of Christ rather than on his nature. They hold that Christ *could have* sinned, since he was truly human, but since he was perfectly faithful to God, he *did not* sin (NOTE on 4:15).[152]

---

[149]The comments by pagans are found in Minucius Felix, *Octavius* 9.4; 29.2. The Jewish view appears in Justin, *Dialogue* 32.1. The "curse" of the Law refers to Deut 21:22–23. See Hengel, *Crucifixion*, 1–10; H. W. Kuhn, "Kreuzesstrafe," 758–68.

[150]*Flight* 109; cf. *Special Laws* 1.230. Elsewhere Philo says that the high priest is "undefiled" (*Special Laws* 1.113) and "blameless" (*Dreams* 2.185). On the relationship of Philo's Logos to Hebrews see §3 COMMENT *b*. There is no evidence that Hebrews *derived* its high-priestly christology from any one of these sources, since the way in which Jesus' high priesthood is portrayed is distinctive in so many ways. The point is simply that the idea of sinlessness is *congruent* in certain respects with other views.

[151]On Jesus' sinlessness see Pannenberg, *Jesus*, 354–64. The language of Heb 4:15 appears in the Definition of Chalcedon (A.D. 451), which defines the two natures of Christ. Christ is "of the same being with the Father as far as his deity is concerned and the same being as we ourselves as far as his humanness is concerned; thus like us in all respects, only with the exception of sin."

[152]Erasmus, *Paraphrase*, 224. Cf. K. Barth, *Church Dogmatics* IV.2, p. 92; Michel; Héring; P. E. Hughes.

Some find the idea of Jesus' sinlessness incompatible with the conviction that he was fully human. They observe that if Jesus "learned obedience" (5:8) and was "made complete" (5:9), his sinlessness might have been "achieved after a struggle in which it is not inconceivable that he actually sinned."[153] Yet to say that Jesus "learned obedience" does not mean that he was formerly disobedient any more than saying that he "became a merciful and faithful high priest" means that he was formerly callous or faithless. Rather, his mercy and faithful obedience emerged through testing in ways that would not be evident otherwise. Authentic solidarity with sinners does not consist in becoming an accomplice in their faults, but in bringing about their redemption (Vanhoye, *Old Testament*, 113–15).

Speaking metaphorically, the author says that Jesus makes it possible for listeners to "approach the throne of grace" (4:16). A metaphor speaks of one thing in terms of another, which creates incongruity at one level, while disclosing new meaning on another level (p. 95). Here it would be incongruous to think that listeners should physically enter an earthly sanctuary to encounter the God enthroned above the cherubim over the ark of the covenant—the ark had vanished centuries before,[154] and the inner sanctuary was barred to all but the high priest (9:7). Rather, the metaphor invites listeners to encounter God through prayer in a manner as genuine as that of a priest entering a sanctuary. Christ the high priest has entered the sanctuary—not with the result that others need not do so, but with the result that they are invited to do so (Scholer, *Proleptic*, 112). Listeners do not approach the throne of an earthly ruler, but come before the Lord of heaven, there to find help for life on earth even when human magistrates offer resistance (10:32–34; 13:3; cf. §27 COMMENT *b*).

The benefits that are available through Christ include "mercy" and "grace for help" (4:16b), which together reflect Hebrews' understanding of the complexity of the human situation. On the one hand, human beings are sinners who are accountable for their wrongdoing, and a high priest is in a position to intercede with God in order to obtain pardon. On the other hand, human beings are subject to forces beyond their control, and they need help to cope with daily life. Socially, people in antiquity often sought the help of a patron, who could assist them with problems that were beyond their means. In order to gain the patron's favor, they would often go through a mediator whom the patron trusted (deSilva, *Despising*, 226–39). The implication is that if people value mediators in social affairs, how much more will they value Jesus, who is positioned to serve as

---

[153]Williamson, "Hebrews 4:15," 5; cf. Buchanan, *Hebrews*, 82, 130–31; Braun, *Hebräer*, 126; Lindars, *Theology*, 63 n. 53. For a critique see Peterson, *Hebrews*, 188–90. Lorenzmeier ("Wider") stresses that in Mark 10:18 Jesus undercuts the idea that he was sinless by saying, "Why do you call me good? No one is good but God alone." For a critique see Gollwitzer, "Zur Frage."

[154]The ark may have been destroyed in 587 B.C. when the Babylonians destroyed the Temple. There was no ark or mercy seat in the second Temple. There were, however, legends that the ark had been preserved and hidden, and that it would be made manifest again in the future (2 Macc 2:4–8; *Liv. Pro.* 2.11–19; *2 Bar.* 6:5–9; *Bib. Ant.* 26:12–15; cf. *Par. Jer.* 3:1–9; Josephus, *Ant.* 18.85–88; Rev 11:19). See C. R. Koester, *Dwelling*, 48–58.

the mediator through whom people can approach God in order to seek his help (NOTES on 4:16; 7:25).

b. The Tradition of Priesthood (5:1–4)

Standing between human beings and God, the priest is related to other people both by origin and by responsibilities: he is taken *from* human beings in order to minister *for* human beings before God (5:1). Effective service demands unique placement. "A priest acceptable to God but lacking the tie of solidarity with humanity would not be able to help them," since he would be cut off from them. "Conversely, a priest filled with compassion for his peers but not acceptable to God could not intervene effectively" (Vanhoye, *Old Testament*, 112). By focusing on the priest's relationship to human beings (*anthrōpoi*), the author speaks in a remarkably broad sense. All priests—Jewish, Greek, and Roman—were human. Jewish sources stressed that proper high priests were taken, not from humankind generally, but from one select group of people, the house of Aaron (Exod 29:9, 44; Num 18:1–7).[155] By speaking broadly, Heb 5:1 prepares for further arguments that the high priest recognized by the Christian community is not of Aaron's line (7:15–16), but one who stands before God in solidarity with people of faith.

A high priest serves in "matters pertaining to God" (5:1c). In the dominant culture, Greek and Roman priests helped people discern the will of God, offered sacrifices, presided at festivals, and carried out other duties.[156] The Roman high priest was the chief administrator and adviser for religious affairs. In Jewish subculture priests were to instruct people in the Law, determine whether people were clean or unclean, and offer sacrifices for thanksgiving, cleansing, and other purposes. Hebrews identifies offering "gifts and sacrifices for sins" (5:1d)—which was integral to the work of Israel's high priest—as central to the work of Jesus the high priest, whose own death was the final sacrifice offered for the sake of humankind (9:26; 10:12).

Hebrews says that a high priest must be able to curb his emotions when dealing with sinners (5:2a). The author assumes that God himself is provoked to wrath by sin (NOTE on 3:11), but since anger wreaks destruction, God was said to curb his anger in order to preserve people (Exod 32:12; Pss 6:1; 78:38; 85:1–7). Hebrews recognizes that priests also might be angry with sinners, but if they are to minister effectively they cannot act on the basis of anger, but in faithfulness to their vocation, which means offering sacrifices for sins.[157] Priests must curb their

---

[155]In early Israel the high priest remained in office for life, and after his death the position normally passed to his oldest surviving son, although a son could be disqualified because of a physical blemish (Lev 21:16–24). The stipulation that the high priest could only marry a virgin from among his own kin was designed to ensure pure descent (Lev 21:10–15). Later Jewish tradition sometimes elaborated Aaron's qualifications (Josephus, *Ant.* 3.192). Cf. Vanhoye, "Situation et signification."

[156]See J. A. Turner, "Greek Priesthoods," *CAM* 2.925–31, and M. Beard, "Roman Priesthoods," *CAM* 2.933–39.

[157]On Aaron's intercession for others see Num 14:5; 16:22, 47–48; Ps 106:16; F. F. Bruce, *Epistle*, 120.

emotion when dealing with sinners because they themselves are clothed with weakness (Heb 5:2b). The author of Hebrews could have supported this point by cataloging the weaknesses of priests who were guilty of extortion, immorality, and other sins (e.g., 1 Sam 2:12–17, 22), but he chooses instead to draw out the implications of the Mosaic Law, which said, "If it is the anointed priest who sins, thus bringing guilt on the people, he shall offer for the sin that he has committed a bull of the herd" (Lev 4:3). On the Day of Atonement the high priest was to present a bull "as a sin offering for himself" to "make atonement for himself" (Lev 16:11). Since priests are obliged to offer gifts for their own sins (Heb 5:3), one can infer that they have the same weakness as other people.

According to Hebrews, no one can rightly claim the office of high priest for himself, for the priest must be called by God (5:4). In Greco-Roman culture priests were given their positions by inheritance, appointment, election, allotment, and purchase.[158] In Italy (13:24) the emperor Augustus became high priest by popular election, and this office was given to his successors.[159] In Jewish tradition Israel's first high priest was said to have been chosen by God, although after that time the position passed from father to son. In the second century B.C., the Syrians violated the tradition by appointing high priests who lacked proper qualifications but who were deemed worthy of patronage or who had outbid their competitors (1 Macc 7:5–9; 10:20; 11:27; 2 Macc 4:24, 29; 14:3). After the Maccabean revolt, Simon was designated high priest by the populace (1 Macc 14:35, 41), but later, Herod and the Romans deposed and appointed high priests at will.[160] During the revolt of A.D. 66–73, the Zealots chose a high priest by lot, although others considered this to be a sacrilege (Josephus, *Ant.* 4.153)

Aaron's divine appointment to the priesthood remained Israel's ideal (Heb 5:4b). Although Aaron's capacity for sin became evident when he made the golden calf (Exod 32:1–6, 21–25), most sources passed lightly over Aaron's role in that incident.[161] Aaron was remembered for withstanding challenges to his position (Sir 45:18–19) and for saving Israel from a plague (Num 16:41–50; Wis 18:20–25; 4 Macc 7:11). Significantly, Josephus told the story of Aaron in a manner that reflects Greco-Roman disputes over the priesthood (*Ant.* 3.188–92; 4.14–34). According to Josephus, Aaron's opponent Korah sought to gain the honor of the priesthood by insisting that the high priest should be appointed by the assembly. A speech attributed to Moses defends Aaron by guarding against the usual Greco-Roman problems of corruption: Aaron had not been given the priesthood because of his wealth, noble birth, or nepotism. Rather, God chose

[158]M. Beard, "Roman Priesthoods," CAM 2.933. For documents pertaining to the sale of priestly offices see Hunt and Edgar, *Select Papyri* 2, ##353, 425; F. C. Grant, *Hellenistic Religions*, 30; cf. J. A. Turner, "Greek Priesthoods," CAM 2.933–39.

[159]On Augustus's election to the priesthood see "The Accomplishments of Augustus" 10 (*RomCiv*, 1.565). See further Millar, *Emperor*, 355–61.

[160]Josephus, *Ant.* 20.224–51; Schürer, *History*, 2.229–32. For criticisms see *T. Mos.* 6:6; 7:9–10; 1QpHab VIII, 8–9; XI, 4–8.

[161]Aaron is mentioned in connection with the golden calf in *Bib. Ant.* 12:2–3 and Acts 7:40, but other sources blame the people (Josephus, *Ant.* 3.95–98; Philo, *Moses* 2.161–73, 270–74; *Drunkenness* 95–96).

Aaron to serve as priest, making Aaron's rod bud (4.4.2 §66). For many first-century readers, Aaron represented the ideal.

c. Jesus the Suffering High Priest (5:5–10)

Just as Aaron received the position of high priest because God called him, "so also" with Christ (5:5a). Comparing someone favorably with a person of high repute was called amplification (*auxēsis*). Amplification was "one of the forms of praise," since it shows superiority, "and superiority is one of the things that are noble."[162] Jesus was like Aaron in that both were called by God, although Aaron and other priests served for a limited time on earth, whereas Jesus serves forever in heaven (7:23–28).

Hebrews says that when becoming high priest, Jesus "did not glorify himself" (5:5a). Strictly speaking, no one can glorify himself, because "glory" (*doxa*) has to do with what others "think" (*dokein*) of the person. One might seek glory by heroism, athletic prowess, or public service, but glory must finally be bestowed by others. Hebrews says that Jesus received priestly glory legitimately because the office was given to him by God, who raised him from the dead and exalted him to the right hand of the Majesty on high. Jesus' opponents may have sought to disgrace him (12:2), but God honored him with the post of high priest.[163] Since "glory" also refers to God's power and presence, Hebrews also implies that Jesus received priestly glory by being exalted into the presence of God (NOTE on 1:3).

The Scriptures, read in light of Christ's exaltation, supply the evidence that God called Jesus to the high priesthood (5:5b–6). The author might have cited Ps 110:1, "The Lord says to my lord, 'Sit at my right hand until I make your enemies a footstool for your feet' " (Heb 1:13). He could have observed that if Ps 110:1 refers to the exalted Jesus, then Ps 110:4 also applies to him: "You are a priest forever according to the type of Melchizedek" (5:6). Instead, he couples Ps 110:4 with Ps 2:7, "You are my Son, I have begotten you today." The assumption is that Pss 110:1 and 2:7 both apply to Jesus. A section of the exordium was framed by these texts (Ps 2:7 = Heb 1:5; Ps 110:1 = Heb 1:13), and the tradition of messianic interpretation makes it possible for the author to use these texts interchangeably (NOTES and COMMENTS on 1:5 and 1:13).

As a high priest, Jesus made an offering (5:7) that was both similar to and different from those of other priests. If priests were to offer both gifts and sacrifices because of their weakness (5:3), Jesus made an offering with loud cries and tears, which shows that he understands what it means to be weak. The difference is Jesus' weakness is not due to sin, but to his vulnerability to death, and instead of offering sacrifices for his own sins, he offers prayers and supplications for deliv-

---

[162]Aristotle, *Rhetoric* 1.9.39; deSilva, *Despising*, 216.

[163]Writers in antiquity distinguished true glory from the acclaim that comes from the masses. See Isocrates, *Panathenaicus* 260–61; Seneca, *Ep.* 113.32. Jewish sources insist that true glory ultimately comes from God. See Esth 13:12–14 LXX; Sir 1:11, 19; 4:13; 10:22; John 7:18; 8:50. See deSilva, *Despising*, 80–144.

erance.[164] Jesus' prayer was heard, but not in the sense usually found in the Psalms and other texts, since he was delivered after death, not before it. The favorable answer to his prayer for deliverance occurred despite his suffering, and it did not entail exemption from suffering. (On Gethsemane traditions see pp. 106–8.)

Jesus' suffering was exemplary in that "he learned obedience by what he suffered" (5:8). The idea that people learned by suffering was commonplace (NOTE on 5:8). Using common ideas enhances the argument rhetorically, since a hearer, "when he perceives an indisputable principle drawn from practical life is being applied to a cause, must give his tacit approval" (*Rhet. ad Her.* 4.17 §25; cf. NOTE on Heb 3:4). The fact that Jesus learned by suffering—even though he was a Son—shapes the way that the listeners see their own situation. They are among the "sons" and daughters that God is bringing to glory (2:10), and like Jesus the Son, they are being tested. Recognizing that God brought Jesus out of suffering to glory assures them that God will also bring to glory his other sons and daughters who persevere. The comment that Jesus "learned obedience" (5:8) is difficult theologically, since 4:15 indicates that he was consistently sinless. A way to approach the issue is to note that authentic obedience is practiced in particular situations (NOTE on 5:8). Although Jesus was never disobedient to God, he could not demonstrate obedience until he was placed in situations where the will of God was challenged and obedience was required. There was constancy in Jesus' unfailing obedience to God's will, yet as Jesus encountered new situations, his faithfulness to God was challenged, and his obedience was shaped accordingly.

Having learned obedience, Jesus was "made complete" (5:9a) through exaltation to glory and appointment to high priesthood. This prepares for the next section, where the author will show that placing Christ in this position is the way that God makes others complete by cleansing their consciences and opening the way to a place in his heavenly city (pp. 119–25). Here he calls Jesus the "source of eternal salvation" (5:9b), which includes eternal redemption from sin (9:12) and an eternal inheritance in the heavenly Jerusalem (9:15; 13:14). The listeners had previously received the message of salvation (2:3–4), but this message was called into question because of the ongoing experience of friction with the wider society (10:32–34; 13:13) and internal malaise (5:11; 6:12; 10:25). Here the author reminds listeners that the source of salvation is the Christ who suffered. Suffering does not negate salvation, but is the way that God brings about salvation.

The final comment about the priest after the type of Melchizedek (5:10) anticipates the second series of arguments, which will commence after the transitional digression (5:11–6:20). Since Melchizedek was a rather obscure figure, the idea that Jesus resembled him might help to pique curiosity about what is to come (*Rhet. ad Her.* 3.22 §§35–36). Awakening curiosity is valuable rhetorically, since it helps to hold the attention of those who are sluggish in their hearing (5:11).

---

[164]On the priestly connotations of Jesus' "offering" see Nissilä, *Hohepriestermotiv*, 92; Hegermann, *Brief*, 120–21; Ellingworth, *Epistle*, 288; Roloff, "Der mitleidende," 156; Zesati Estrada, *Hebreos*, 128–42. Attridge (*Epistle*, 149) disagrees.

13. Reproof concerning Maturity in Faith (5:11–6:3)

5 [11]We have much to say about this, and it is difficult to explain since you have
become sluggish in listening. [12]For though by this time you ought to be teachers, you again need someone to teach you the most elementary matters of the oracles of God and have come to need milk rather than solid food. [13]Now everyone who partakes of milk is not proficient in reasoning about righteousness since
he is a child. [14]But solid food is for the complete, who, because of this state, have
their faculties trained to discern both good and evil. 6 [1]Therefore, granting the
basic message of Christ, let us go on to completeness, not again laying a foundation of repentance from dead works and of faith in God, [2]of instruction about
baptisms and laying on of hands, of resurrection of the dead and eternal judgment. [3]And this we will do, God willing.

NOTES

5:11. *We have much to say about this.* This showed that an author was aware of the breadth of a subject, while allowing him the freedom to take up either all or only part of the topic (Philo, *Heir* 133, 221; Dionysius of Halicarnassus, *Roman Antiquities* 1.23.1; *First Letter to Ammaeus* 3). The pronoun *hou* ("this") is sometimes taken as a masculine ("him" or "whom"), referring to Melchizedek, who was mentioned in 5:10 (Peshitta; NASB; REB; Calvin; F. F. Bruce; Ellingworth). Most, however, take it as a neuter ("this" or "which"), referring to Christ's priesthood, the subject of 5:5–10 and Heb 7–10 (NIV; NJB; NRSV; Attridge; Lane).

difficult to explain. Difficulty is gauged by the nature of the subject material in relation to the audience. The adjective *dysermēneutos* often referred to subjects that were hard to put into words, such as dreams (Artemidorus Daldianus, *Onirocritica* 3.66), transcendent realities (Philo, *Dreams* 1.188), the world's creation, and divine rest (Origen, *Against Celsus* 5.59). Hebrews, however, locates the difficulty in the listeners' dullness rather than in the subject matter.

since. The preposition *epei* is causal, indicating that the listeners have become sluggish. There is some tension with 6:12, which might suggest that the listeners have not yet "become sluggish" since they do good works (6:10). The internal tension is eased when 6:12 is translated "so that you may not *be* sluggish" rather than "become sluggish" (Ellingworth, *Epistle*, 300–301).

you have become sluggish in listening. When *nōthros* is used for those who were physically sound it means that they are sluggish, lazy, (Sir 4:29), negligent, dullwitted, or timid (Polybius, *Histories* 3.63.7; 4.8.5; 4.60.2). Philosophers chided the sluggish who refused to discipline themselves in the use of reason (Musonius Rufus, frg. 44.1; Epictetus, *Disc.* 1.7.30). Speakers found that "many who come to hear a discourse have not come with their minds, but wander abroad rehearsing inwardly numberless thoughts" on "families, on outsiders, on things private and things public." The result is that speakers address "an audience not of human beings, but of lifeless statues who have ears, but no hearing in those ears" (Philo, *Heir* 12–13). See *TLNT* 2.552–54; Preisker, *TDNT* 4.1126. Listening is more than simple audition; unresponsive hearing means not heeding what is being said (Isa 6:10; Matt 13:15).

5:12. *For though by this time you ought.* Hebrews addressed a community that had existed for some time (pp. 64–72). There was a common recognition that as people advance in years they should assume greater responsibility. The rhetorical sting in these remarks would be similar to Epictetus's comment: If you "find it now your duty to lay hand to the work of a man, do you yearn for nurses" and "never get over being an infant?" (*Disc.* 3.24.53).

to be teachers. Some NT texts use "teacher" for some but not all members of the community (Rom 12:7; 1 Cor 12:28–29; Eph 4:11; cf. 1 Tim 1:6). Hebrews, however, draws on the common idea that those who learned should be able to teach. The sage Apollonius said, "I asked questions when I was a lad," but now I "teach people what I have discovered" (Philostratus, *Life of Apollonius* 1.17; cf. Plato, *Symposium* 189D; Xenophon, *Cyropaedia* 3.3.35). To those who dared not practice what they studied, Seneca said, "How long will you be a learner? From now on be a teacher as well!" (*Ep.* 33.8–9; cf. Epictetus, *Ench.* 51.1).

you again need someone to teach you. Socially, those who taught were classed with parents and others in authority, which was an honor (Philo, *Special Laws* 2.226–27; Matt 10:24; Luke 6:40; John 13:13, 16; Rom 2:20; Epictetus, *Disc.* 2.21.10; cf. Sir 37:23–26; 38:8–11; 44:4, 7). Putting the listeners in the position of those who needed instruction set them lower on the social scale, a situation they would presumably want to change (see COMMENT *a*). Theologically, Jeremiah promised that under the new covenant people would no longer need to teach each other to know God (Heb 8:11; cf. 1 Thess 4:9; 1 John 2:20). The fact that the listeners still needed instruction shows that the new covenant has not been fully realized. See §21 COMMENT *b*.

the most elementary matters. Literally "the elements of the beginning." Elsewhere "beginning" (*archē*) is used for the initial proclamation of the saving message (2:3), for its reception by the listeners (3:14), and for the "message of Christ" (6:1). The "elements" (*stoicheia*) could be parts of a word, the alphabet (Diogenes Laertius, *Lives* 7.56), elementary subjects (Xenophon, *Memorabilia* 2.1.1; cf. Quintilian, *Inst.* 1.1.1), or fundamental ideas in a field of study (Plutarch, *Mor.* 12c; Philo, *Preliminary Studies* 149–50). Here the term applies to basic Christian teachings. See Delling, *TDNT* 7.670–87; Williamson, *Philo*, 277–308.

of the oracles of God. "Oracles" (*logioi*) were prophetic utterances, including the sayings of God found in Scripture (Philo, *Posterity* 28; *Unchangeable* 50). The plural commonly referred to the Law (Deut 33:9–10; Acts 7:38; Philo, *Moses* 2.56; *Decalogue* 36; cf. Ps 119:10–11, 102–3, 162–63) or Jewish Scriptures (*Moses* 2.188; *Ep. Arist.* 176–77; Rom 3:2; *1 Clem.* 53:1; 62:3). The term "oracles" is appropriate because Hebrews takes the Scriptures to be divine speech and interprets them in light of Christ (pp. 117–18). The basic elements of God's oracles (Heb 5:12) and the basic word of Christ (6:1) are not identical, but neither can be taken without the other.

and have come to need milk rather than solid food. "Milk" and "solid food" were often used as metaphors for levels of instruction. Seeing "that for babes milk is food, but for grown men wheaten bread, there must also be soul nourishment, such as is milk-like, suited to the time of childhood, in the shape of the preliminary stages of school learning and, such as adapted to grown men in the shape of instructions leading the way through wisdom and temperance and all virtue" (Philo, *Husbandry* 9; *Good Person* 160; *Migration* 29; *Preliminary Studies* 19; *Dreams* 2.9; Epictetus, *Disc.* 2.16.39). Paul told the Corinthians that when he first preached, "I fed you with milk . . . for you were not ready for solid food" (1 Cor 3:1–4).

5:13. *Now everyone who partakes of milk.* The words "partake" and "partaker" are used for present participation in future or heavenly realities (3:1, 14; 6:4) and for instruction (12:8).

is not proficient. People gained proficiency through training and experience, as do soldiers or athletes. The term "not proficient" (*apeiros*) could be used for those at the very beginning of the educational process in contrast to those who were making progress and to those who had attained complete virtue (Philo, *Husbandry* 160; cf. *Creation* 171; *Good Person* 51–52).

in reasoning about righteousness. The expression *logos dikaiosynēs* is difficult to interpret. Since Hebrews commonly uses *logos* for a word or message (e.g., 2:2; 4:2), it is often translated "word" (NASB; NRSV; NAB[2]), "doctrine" (NJB), or "teaching" (NIV) of righteousness (cf. Pol. *Phil.* 8.1–9.1). Yet the author refers to proficiency in *logos*, which suggests that *logos* is an activity. The *logos* could mean "speaking" about righteousness (Attridge). Yet in 5:13–14 it has more to do with discernment or reasoning about good and evil than it has to do with speech (Ellingworth):

a. one partaking of milk	*a.* one partaking of solid food
b. one who is not proficient in word of righteousness	*b.* one who has faculties trained to discern both good and evil
c. one who is a child	*c.* one who is complete or mature

In Greco-Roman culture instruction in righteousness meant being "trained to discern both good and evil" (Heb 5:14b; cf. Xenophon, *Cyropaedia* 1.6.30–31). Right reasoning meant reasoning rightly about love of neighbors, truthfulness, modesty, and respect for oneself—all of which were basic to virtue (Marcus Aurelius, *Meditations* 11.1, 10; 12.1). Every Sabbath, Jews were said to gather in "schools" where righteousness and the "duties to God and men are discerned and rightly performed" (Philo, *Moses* 2.216; cf. *Special Laws* 2.62; *Embassy* 312; Spicq, "Hébraux et Philon," 3611 n. 47). Cf. NOTE on discerning good and evil in 5:14.

since he is a child. The term "child" (*nēpios*) could apply to very young children (Matt 21:16) and those who had not attained legal age (Gal 4:1; Rom 2:20). Calling adults *nēpioi* meant that they were childish (1 Cor 3:1; 13:11; Wis 12:24) and lacking in discernment (Homer, *Iliad* 17.32; Plato, *Symposium* 222B). Being compared to children would have been humiliating, goading listeners to greater zeal for understanding. See G. Bertram, *TDNT* 4.912–23.

5:14. *But solid food is for the complete.* The word *teleios* is related to other forms of the word "complete" in this context (*teleioun*, 5:9; *teleiotēs*, 6:1). Often translated "mature" (NIV; NRSV; NAB2), the word was used for those who had completed the course of education and were qualified to be teachers (Philo, *Special Laws* 4.140; *Names*, 270).

who, because of this state. The sense is that those who have reached "this state" of completeness have trained their faculties to discern both good and evil. The expression *dia hexis* is sometimes rendered "by practice" (NAB2; NRSV; NASB; NJB) or "by constant use" (NIV; REB) on the assumption that *hexis* is synonymous with "training." Yet *hexis* was used, not for the process, but for the result of training. Through training people reached a "state" in which they could serve as public speakers (Quintilian, *Inst.* 10.1.1; 10.5.1) and interpreters of Jewish tradition (prologue to Sirach). Uneducated children might happen to say things that a rational person would, but the Law enables them to act on the basis of a fixed state (*hexis*) rather than a passing mood (*Alleg. Interp.* 3.210; cf. Albinus, *Didaskalikos* §26; Kiley, "Note"; Lee, "Hebrews 5:14").

have their faculties trained to discern both good and evil. Correctly distinguishing good from evil was a mark of maturity (Deut 1:39; Isa 7:16; cf. *Rhet. ad Her.* 3.2.3). "Faculties," including the physical senses and the mind, are the means by which people apprehend things (Delling, *TDNT* 1.187–88). Physical senses can move people to assume that pleasure is good and that labor is evil even though this is not always true, since pleasure can have negative consequences and unpleasant experiences can yield great benefit (Heb 12:11; cf. Philo, *Names* 81–82). Therefore, people need to "train" themselves to assert the mind over the senses (Epictetus, *Disc.* 2.18.24–27; Musonius Rufus, frg. 6; Philo, *Names* 81–82; 4 Macc 2:22). Training did not cease when one attained proficiency but was part of continued discipline (Philo, *Husbandry* 160). According to Hebrews, Christians who were marginalized by society (Heb 10:32–34; 13:13) could remain faithful only by acting on the basis of a faith in Christ—who could not be seen empirically (2:8–9)—rather than on the basis of sense perception. Such "training" yields "righteousness," which is truly "beneficial" (12:10–11).

6:1. *Therefore, granting.* "Grant" (*aphiēmi*) is used in its common rhetorical sense of leaving one topic in order to take up another (Epictetus, *Disc.* 1.16.9; 4.1.15; Plutarch, *Mor.* 423C; 793A). It does not mean that listeners are to leave the basics behind, since repentance, faith, and other teachings (Heb 6:1b–2) are presupposed rather than abandoned.

the basic message of Christ. Literally, "the word of the beginning of Christ." In form the author contrasts the beginning (*arch-*) or basic message with the end (*tel-*) or "completeness" (next NOTE; cf. 2:10; 3:14; 12:2). Scholars sometimes contrast what Jesus said with what his followers said about him, but like other early Christian writings, Hebrews assumes continuity in the message (2:3). Many of the teachings in 6:1–2 appear in the sermons of Jesus and his followers: repentance and faith (Mark 1:15 par.; Acts 2:38; 20:21), resurrection and judgment

(Mark 12:18–27 par.; Matt 10:15; 12:36; Acts 17:31; Rom 2:16; 1 John 4:17). Early Christians practiced baptism (Acts 2:41; 9:18; Rom 6:3–4; Gal 3:27; 1 Pet 3:21) and the laying on of hands (Acts 8:17–18; 19:6), although the connections with Jesus' practice are not entirely clear. Jesus laid hands on people to bless or heal them (Mark 5:23; 6:5; 10:13) and was himself baptized (Mark 1:9 par.), but he apparently did not administer baptism (John 4:2; cf. 3:22). Christians connected baptism with Jesus' ministry, death, and resurrection (Acts 10:37, 47; Rom 6:4; cf. Matt 28:19).

let us go on to completeness. In common practice, training in grammar prepared for learning the liberal arts, and the liberal arts directed people toward virtue, but the process was complete only when people acquired virtue itself (Seneca, *Ep.* 88.20). By analogy, Hebrews urges listeners not to stop with an elementary education in faith, but to persevere in the hope of acquiring all that God has promised them as God brings his work to completion (see pp. 122–25).

not again laying a foundation. The teachings in 6:1b–2 are part of the foundation of Christian teaching. The author reinforces them in 6:4–8, where he speaks of repentance and judgment, but he wants to move beyond the basics. He wants to build on the foundation rather than relaying it, and to stop reviewing the alphabet to proceed to the study of literary composition.

of repentance from dead works. Repentance in a basic sense was a "turning": "Repent, you who err, turn back from the bottom of your heart" (Isa 46:8 LXX; cf. Acts 3:19). It could indicate an ongoing turning from sin (2 Cor 7:9), but here it points to a fundamental shift in orientation, a turning from sin to God (Luke 5:32). Together, repentance from dead works and gaining faith in God constitute conversion (cf. Mark 1:4, 15; 6:12; Luke 24:47; Acts 2:38; 17:30; 20:21; 26:20). See *TLNT* 2.471–77; Behm, *TDNT* 4.989–1006. On restoring apostates to repentance see §14 COMMENT *a* and NOTE on 12:17. "Dead works" have been understood in several ways, of which the first is preferable:

(**a**) Sinful works. "Dead works" that defile the conscience are "sins" (9:14; 10:3–4), and those who lack repentance are called "immoral" and "profane" (12:16–17). Sins are "dead works" because death is the consequence of sin (cf. Rom 5:12; 6:23). Sin may lead to death when people are allowed to suffer sin's consequences (Prov 11:19; 13:14; Wis 1:12) or when God brings judgment upon sin (*Pss. Sol.* 15:10, 13). Sin is the way of death, while obedience is the way of life (Deut 30:15; Jer 21:8; Prov 12:28; Eph 2:5; Col 2:13; *Did.* 1:1–5:2; F. F. Bruce; Attridge; Ellingworth; Bénétreau; Löhr, *Umkehr*, 150–51).

(**b**) Works of the Jewish Law. Levitical sacrifices purify the body, but Christ's sacrifice purifies the "conscience from dead works" (9:14). Some take "dead works" to be the regulations associated with the Levitical priesthood (9:10; Lane; cf. Westcott; Héring; Jewett). This interpretation is unlikely, though, for the author of Hebrews argues that Levitical sacrifices are ineffective (10:3–4), but he does not suggest that they bring death.

(**c**) Idolatry. Since idols are dead (Ps 106:28; Wis 13:10, 18; *Jos. Asen.* 8:5; 12:5; 13:11; cf. Isa 44:9–20; Jer 10:5; Dan 5:23), works performed for idols are "dead works." Conversion from paganism meant turning from dead idols to "the living

God" (Acts 14:15; 1 Thess 1:9; 2 Cor 6:16; Bel 5–6, 24–25), to whom Hebrews bears witness (Heb 3:12; 9:14; 10:31; 12:22; Braun; Grässer; H.-F. Weiss). This assumes that Hebrews addressed Gentile converts, which is not clear (see pp. 46–48). In Hebrews "dead works" can include idolatry, but they cannot be confined to idolatry and may encompass various sins (9:14; 10:3–4).

and of faith in God. If repentance means turning away *from* dead works, faith means turning *to* the living God (Wis 11:23; 12:2; Acts 14:15; 20:21; 26:20; 1 Thess 1:9). This faith has been understood in two ways, of which the first is preferable (see also pp. 125–27):

(a) Conversion of people from Jewish or Gentile background to Christian faith. "Faith in God" is the counterpart to "dead works," which include various types of sins (see the previous NOTE). Repentance means turning to God (6:1), which is enlightenment (6:4). Other sources say that both Jews and Gentiles are to "repent and turn to God" (Acts 26:20) and that the proclamation of Christ brings light to both Jews and Gentiles (Acts 26:23; Attridge; Bénétreau).

(b) Conversion from paganism. Hebrews speaks, not of faith "in Christ," but of belief that God "exists and rewards those who seek him" (11:6). Since Jews would already have believed this, some argue that coming to "faith in God" applies only to Gentile converts (cf. Jonah 3:5; Jdt 14:10; Braun; H.-F. Weiss; Grässer; cf. Löhr, *Umkehr*, 151–52). Nevertheless, the examples of unbelief in Hebrews are from Israel, not from the Gentile world (Heb 3:7–4:2). Turning from unbelief is not limited to Gentiles.

6:2. *of instruction about baptisms.* Instead of the usual word *baptisma,* the author uses *baptismos,* a term that was used for Jewish washings (9:10; Mark 7:4), the baptism administered by John (Josephus, *Ant.* 18.117), and Christian baptism (Col 2:12). Since Heb 6:1–3 concerns the teachings that are appropriate for new converts and connects "baptisms" with the laying on of hands (see the next NOTE), this passage probably refers to Christian baptism. The use of the plural, "baptisms," suggests that the instruction distinguished Christian baptism from washings like those mentioned in 9:10 (P. E. Hughes; Hegermann; Attridge; Lane; H.-F. Weiss; Bénétreau). Alternatively, the plural may have been used because all the members of the community were baptized, just as the plural "washed" is used in 10:22 (Theodoret). The idea that the plural is used because those being baptized were immersed three times (Braun) is less likely because we do not know how early this practice arose and because the three immersions were part of a single act.

and laying on of hands. The laying on of hands was done when blessing someone (Mark 10:13), setting someone apart for special service (Acts 6:6; 13:3; 1 Tim 4:14; 5:22; 2 Tim 1:6), and healing (Mark 5:23; 6:5; Acts 9:12, 17; 28:8). Christians laid hands on those who had been baptized, praying that they might receive the Holy Spirit (Acts 8:17–18; 19:6). Since Hebrews mentions baptism in 6:2 and receiving the Spirit in 6:4, the laying on of hands probably was part of their rite of initiation (cf. Tertullian, *Baptism,* 7–8; Cyprian, *Ep.* 73.6–7).

resurrection of the dead. The word "dead" is plural, referring to the many that have died, not just to Jesus (13:20). Hebrews' views concerning the mode of resurrection exhibit some of the tensions apparent in other sources:

(**a**) Death and resurrection. Some sources speak of death being followed by resurrection to life at a later time. In Hebrews the children raised by Elijah and Elisha (1 Kgs 17:21; 2 Kgs 4:35) foreshadow the resurrection of all the dead at the end of time (Heb 11:19, 35). The martyrs allowed their hands to be cut off in the conviction that they would be restored bodily in the future resurrection (2 Macc 7:9–10, 14, 29; Heb 11:35b). The idea that the dead are fully dead until the final resurrection (1 Thess 4:16; 1 Cor 15:52; Rev 20:12–13) conveys a sense of discontinuity, with resurrection being akin to a new creative act on God's part.

(**b**) Spiritual life after death. Some texts suggest that after death the person continues to exist in a spiritual state. Hebrews 9:27 seems to assume that a person is judged immediately after death, and 12:23 refers to the spirits of the righteous being in heaven. Other sources speak of martyrs who "lie buried" yet even "now stand before the divine throne and live the life of eternal blessedness" (4 Macc 17:9, 18; cf. Wis 3:1–9; Phil 1:23–24; Rev 6:9–11; Luke 16:22; 23:43). Hebrews does not resolve the tension between the idea of death and resurrection, which assumes temporal discontinuity between the present and future life, and the idea of ongoing life after death, which assumes considerable continuity in a person's existence.

and eternal judgment. Some assumed that only the righteous would be raised and that the wicked would remain in the realm of the dead (2 Macc 7:9, 14; *Pss. Sol.* 3:11–12), but more thought that all would be raised for judgment (Dan 12:2; Wis 4:20–5:23; Matt 25:31–46; John 5:28–29; Rom 2:6–10; Rev 20:12–13). Passages dealing with the last judgment correlate deeds with rewards and punishments, but do not eliminate God's grace.

6:3. *And this we will do, God willing.* The author hopes, if God wills, to go on to completeness (6:1). The idea that he will review the basics of the faith if God wills (Löhr, *Umkehr*, 215) seems unlikely since the author has been urging listeners to move beyond this stage. The expression "God willing" was common (Josephus, *Ant.* 20.267; Jas 4:15; 1 Cor 4:19; 16:7; Acts 18:21; Rom 1:10; Deissmann, *Bible*, 252). In Hebrews God is the one "for whom all things and through whom all things exist" (2:10), and to say "God willing" recognizes his power over human life and destiny.

COMMENT[165]

Hebrews 5:11–6:20 is a transitional digression that concludes the first series of arguments and prepares listeners for the next major section.[166] Initial arguments (2:10–5:10) dealt with the way Jesus reached completeness and "learned obedience" by what he suffered (5:8–9). Now the author departs from his main arguments to contrast Jesus with the listeners, for instead of learning they seem un-

[165]On 5:11–6:3 see Andriessen, "La communauté"; Delville, "L'Épître"; Kiley, "Note"; Loader, *Sohn*, 84–92; Löhr, *Umkehr*, 164–87; H. P. Owen, "Stages"; Peterson, "Situation"; Spicq, "Hébreux et Philon"; Thompson, *Beginnings*, 17–40; Thüsing, "Milch"; Wider, *Theozentrik*, 161–67.

[166]On digressions see Quintilian, *Inst.* 4.3.1–17; 9.1.28; cf. Cicero, *De inventione rhetorica* 1.51 §97; Lausberg, *Handbook* §§340–45.

responsive to learning, and instead of being complete they seem to be immature (5:11–14).[167] Following rhetorical convention (Cicero, *De oratore* 2.77 §§311–12; 3.53 §203), the author signals the end of the digression by taking up the reference to Jesus' priesthood "according to the type of Melchizedek" (6:20), which was introduced just prior to the digression (5:10). Jesus' priesthood will be a focus in the next section (cf. 7:1).

The rhetorical function of such digressions was to prepare the audience to give their full attention to what would follow. Speakers were aware that people typically "dismiss their minds elsewhere," since they are preoccupied with business, politics, and home life. Therefore, when it comes to the subject of the discourse, "they are deaf, and while they are present in the body are absent in mind, and might as well be images or statues" (Philo, *Preliminary Studies* 64–65). By this point the audience of Hebrews would have been listening for perhaps fifteen minutes, and the author was about to begin a lengthy treatment of Jesus' priesthood and sacrifice. This digression, which would have taken several minutes to deliver, is designed to secure their attention by addressing them with reproof, warning, and encouragement.

Intensity was considered appropriate in a digression. Speakers might express indignation and pity, and then rebuke or excuse someone; both praise and blame were common. The author of Hebrews begins his digression with a reproof (5:11–6:3), then warns of the devastating consequences of apostasy (6:4–8) before offering words of encouragement (6:9–12). Reproof and warning were to proceed out of concern for the listeners, to be aimed at the listeners' improvement, just as a physician sometimes makes a painful incision in order to free a patient of some malady. Reproofs were to be accompanied by more assuring comments, just as a physician uses ointment to soothe the incision that he has made.[168] Through both warning and promise the author seeks to create a willingness to listen carefully to what he is about to say concerning the work of Christ.

The first part of the digression, which is framed by references to those who are "sluggish" (*nōthros*, 5:11; 6:12), is comprised of several paragraphs:[169] **(a)** Reproof. The author chides listeners for their lethargy using imagery from the sphere of education (5:11–6:3). The remaining paragraphs, which are taken up in §14 include **(b)** Warning and **(c)** Encouragement. After reminding the listeners about their conversion, the author warns them about the consequences of falling away (6:4–8). Then he gives reasons for his confidence about the listeners' future and explains that he has spoken sharply to encourage them (6:9–12).

---

[167]The pattern is similar to previous sections where the faithfulness of Jesus and Moses (3:1–6) led to a section on the unfaithfulness of Moses' generation and the potential unfaithfulness among Jesus' followers (3:7–4:13).

[168]Plutarch, *Moralia* 74DE; cf. Philo, *Migration* 116; Dio Chrysostom, *Disc.* 77/78.38.

[169]Interpreters generally take 5:11–6:20 to be a unit. Some divide the digression into two halves distinguished by the change in tone at 6:9 (Spicq; Michel). This commentary follows Vanhoye, who argues that the word *nōthros* in 5:11 and 6:12 frames the section (*La structure*, 116–20). Some who generally favor this approach make a major division between 5:11–6:3 and 6:4–6 (Attridge).

a. Training One's Faculties (5:11–14)

The opening comment is designed to provoke a sluggish audience (5:11) to greater care in listening. By saying in effect that "this material is difficult because you are so inattentive," the author goads his listeners into objecting, "No, we are *not* inattentive, but are quite capable of understanding what you have to say."[170] The author does not assume that their sluggishness is permanent, since after commenting on it he moves to a new and complex section, assuming that listeners will benefit from the argument. He points out that the listeners ought to be teachers, since after their conversion they suffered at the hands of the wider society (10:32–34) and presumably had much to teach. The irony is that the listeners have not become teachers, but still need teaching themselves. Teachers were honored along with parents, rulers, and masters (NOTE on 5:12), but rather than calling them teachers, the author depicts them as pupils, who were classed with children and servants. This would have been a disgrace, giving listeners incentive to seek change in the situation.

After saying that they need someone to teach them (5:12b), the author elaborates by drawing on common patterns of education. He develops a metaphor that combines imagery from physical development, Greco-Roman educational theory, and Christian teaching (Attridge, *Epistle*, 162):

Image	*Primary Referent*	*Secondary Referent*
babes	beginning students	new Christians
milk	elementary education	basic Christian teaching
adults	advanced students	mature Christians
solid food	ethical philosophy	the author's teaching

Certain patterns of education were common to the Greek, Roman, and Jewish communities.[171] The content varied depending on the group, but the author assumes that the stages were similar.

Elementary instruction is the level at which the author places the listeners (5:12b). This stage extended from about age seven to age fourteen without formal distinctions between grade levels. Students were taught basic arithmetic and learned to read and write letters, syllables, words, and finally short continuous passages. The teacher (*grammatistēs*) dictated, while the students copied what was said onto waxed tablets, periodically reciting what they had learned. At about age fourteen, they began to study literature under a grammarian (*grammatikos*). In the dominant culture, elementary exercises were designed to inculcate moral principles: e.g., "Letters are the beginning of wisdom" and "You will live best by controlling your temper" (Winter, *Life*, 67). Literary study included Homer, Eu-

[170]Attridge, *Epistle*, 157. On the rhetorical force of the material see Calvin; Héring; Lane.

[171]On education see Marrou, *History*; C. Dewald, "Greek Education and Rhetoric," *CAM* 2.1097–1107; C. W. Wooten, "Roman Education and Rhetoric," *CAM* 2.1109–13; H. Fuchs, "Enkyklios Paideida," *RAC* 5.365–98. On Jewish education see Safrai, *JPFC* 2.945–70; Schürer, *History*, 2.415–22; Crenshaw, *Education*.

ripides, Menander, and Demosthenes for Greek students, and Virgil, Horace, Cicero, and other Latin writers for Roman children. Jewish children began with selected verses from the Torah and eventually turned to the entire Torah, prophets, and other writings.[172]

Hebrews assumes that Christians receive basic instruction from the "oracles of God," which are found in the Scriptures and interpreted in light of Jesus' death and exaltation. The author assumes that listeners will be familiar with oracles such as 2 Sam 7:14; Pss 2:7; and 110:1. Since these texts were widely used by early Christians, they may have been part of basic instruction in the faith (NOTES on Heb 1:5, 13). Hebrews contrasts the elementary students who partake of "milk," with more advanced students who eat "solid food" (5:12c). In practice, of course, children shift from milk to solid food and from lower to higher levels of education rather gradually.[173] Contrasting those at the beginning of the process with those at the end, however, presses listeners to see themselves as one or the other so that they will want to move beyond being classed with the primary students in order to be considered mature.

The immature lack proficiency in "reasoning about righteousness," an expression that echoes common ways of speaking about higher education (NOTE on 5:13). In Hebrews the expression is related to the problem faced by the listeners. Given the apparent contradiction between the promise of glory and the inglorious reality of life in the world, it took discernment to recognize that God was just rather than unjust (see pp. 65–72). The author wants listeners to train their faculties so that in the exalted Christ they can see the one whose rule is marked by righteousness (1:9; 7:2), and to recognize that the challenges they face are a form of the divine instruction that produces the peaceful fruit of righteousness (12:11).

Reasoning about righteousness means distinguishing good from evil (5:14), and the relationship of reason to sense perception is a key factor. Platonists valued arithmetic, geometry, astronomy, and music because these disciplines moved people beyond sense perception to higher realities. Philosophy completed the process by enabling people to contemplate the absolute good that is beyond the senses.[174] Stoics thought that the senses contributed to knowledge but insisted that virtue was the standard by which good and evil had to be assessed. Reason showed that "neither pain nor death nor poverty nor anything else which is free from wrong is an evil, and again that wealth, life, pleasure, or anything else which does not partake of virtue is not a good."[175]

Hebrews addressed Christians who faced a crisis of discernment. Their faith had been awakened by the message of salvation (2:3), which included the hope of an inheritance in the kingdom of God (1:14; 12:28), glory and honor (2:5–7).

---

[172]Rabbinic sources say that early education included reading selected verses from Lev 1–8 and Gen 1–9 (Safrai, *JPFC* 2.950–51). Sirach was written to accompany education based on the Torah (prologue to Sirach).

[173]See Philo, *Agriculture* 160. H. P. Owen ("Stages") finds three stages in Heb 5:11–14, but most interpreters recognize a contrast between only two classes: beginners and the mature.

[174]Plato, *Republic* 7.522–33; Philo, *Preliminary Studies*, 14–19; Justin, *Dialogue* 2.

[175]Musonius Rufus, frg. 6; cf. 1; Diogenes Laertius, *Lives* 7.54; Epictetus, *Ench.* 31; *Disc.* 3.8.1–6.

Their experience of the Spirit confirmed the message, but continued reproach from society now contradicted it (see pp. 65–72). Sense perception would lead to the conclusion that faith is evil rather than good, since those who professed Christ were subjected to abuse. Therefore, the author seeks to renew the listeners' commitment to a reality that transcends what can be seen (11:1) by speaking of the good that came from Christ's suffering and death, and of the exaltation that cannot be perceived with the eye but only by faith (2:8–9).

b. Going on to Completeness (6:1–3)

Given the preceding reproof concerning the listeners' dullness (5:11–14), one might expect the author to say, "Let us leave aside the difficult subject matter and return to the basics." Instead, the author moves in the opposite direction by urging them to go beyond the basics to maturity (6:1). Despite chiding them for needing milk, he proceeds to give them solid food. At the same time, he does not refrain from the basics altogether, and by listing the teachings he is *not* going to review (6:1b–2), he actually brings these teachings to mind.[176] Six items are arranged in pairs:[177]

(a) Repentance from dead works and faith in God (6:1b). Repentance means turning away from sin, while faith means turning to God. Together, these constitute enlightenment (6:4). The author speaks of those who have "been enlightened" using the passive voice, which presupposes that God works repentance and faith through his word and Spirit (6:5; cf. 2:3–4). Repentance does not mean that Christians are sinless, for they continue to need help and mercy (2:18; 4:16; 7:25). But repentance does entail a basic reorientation so that one lives on the basis of God's promises rather than confidence in something else (NOTES and COMMENT on 6:4–6; 12:17).

"Faith in God" means trusting that God will keep his promises (pp. 125–27). Although Hebrews often stresses the need for human faithfulness (6:12), the basis of human faith is the conviction that God will be true. Hebrews refers to "faith in God" because God made the promises of salvation (2:3; 6:13; 9:28), glory (2:10), and rest (4:1, 10). Fulfillment remained future and unseen (11:1) so that those who exhibit faith—including heroes and heroines from the OT and Jesus himself—do so in the conviction that God will keep his word (10:23; 11:11) and will not allow his people to be afflicted forever, but will bless them as he promised (10:34; 11:6, 20, 26).

---

[176]Rhetorically this is similar to *paraleipsis* or *praeteritio*, in which "we say we are passing by . . . that which precisely we are now saying" (*Rhet. ad Her.* 4.27 §37; cf. §33 COMMENT).

[177]Division into three pairs follows the punctuation in NA[27] (cf. *TCGNT*, 666) and some commentators (H.-F. Weiss; Grässer). Most MSS have "instruction" in the genitive case (*didachēs*) so that it relates primarily to "instruction concerning baptisms." Some prefer the variant that has "instruction" in the accusative case (*didachēn*, P[46] B 0150), so that everything that follows it relates to this instruction. Those who favor this alternative identify two groups: the "foundation" (*themelion*) of repentance and faith, and the "instruction" (*didachēn*) concerning baptisms, the laying on of hands, resurrection, and eternal judgment (F. F. Bruce; Attridge; Lane).

(b) Baptism and the laying on of hands (6:2a). The mention of this pair suggests that the listeners' experience was similar to that attested in Acts, where those who come to faith undergo baptism as a result.[178] Baptism was probably understood to involve cleansing from sin. Those who repented were washed with pure water in a manner that entailed purification of body and heart (10:22). This washing is mentioned along with a confession of faith and attending the assembly, and it would have marked a person's formal entry into the Christian community (10:22–25). Reception of the Holy Spirit was regularly connected to baptism in early Christianity, although the Spirit might be given before (Acts 10:44–48), after (Acts 8:12–17), or through baptism (1 Cor 12:13), or in connection with the laying on of hands that was commonly done after baptism (Acts 8:17; 19:6). Those addressed by Hebrews apparently experienced the Spirit through proclamation (Heb 2:3–4), and the precise relationship of the Spirit to baptism remains unclear.

(c) Resurrection from the dead and eternal judgment (6:2c). Hebrews assumes that listeners know that God will raise the dead, although theological tensions remain (NOTE on 6:2). By God's act of raising Jesus from the dead, people are freed from bondage due the fear of death (2:14–15; 13:20). All people face death (9:27), but the promise of resurrection gives hope that one's relationship with God will be renewed in the city of God (12:22–24; cf. 11:19). Final judgment occurs either immediately after a person's death (9:27) or on that future "Day" when all are judged (10:25–27). Even God's own people are subject to judgment (4:12–13; 10:30; 13:4), and the citizens of the New Jerusalem will meet there the God who is the judge of all (12:23). Nevertheless, listeners can remain confident that God's judgment for them will be "eternal salvation" (5:9), the reward of everlasting rest (4:9–10; 12:22–24).

The six items listed in 6:1–2 span the journey of faith from initial repentance to final judgment. Clearly, this summary does not encompass everything the listeners have been taught—Jesus is not mentioned, even though the message they first received was connected with Christ (2:3–4)—but the list identifies items that can be presupposed, allowing the author to focus on the significance of Christ. In the first series of arguments (2:10–5:10) the author sought to show that Jesus' suffering and glorification provide assurance that God will also bring to glory those who suffer for Jesus. In the second series of arguments (7:1–10:25) he will continue the focus on Christ, seeking to show what it meant for Christ to suffer on behalf of others.

14. Warning and Encouragement (6:4–12)

6 [4]For it is impossible to restore to repentance those who have once been enlightened, who have tasted the heavenly gift and become partakers of the Holy

[178]On baptism in Hebrews see Hartman, *Into the Name*, 123–26; cf. Dunn, *Unity*, 152–61; Goppelt, *Theology*, 2.6–9.

Spirit, [5]who have tasted the good word of God and the powers of the age to
come, [6]but who then fall away, since they crucify the Son of God to themselves
and make a spectacle of him. [7]For earth, which drinks the rain that repeatedly
comes upon it and produces vegetation beneficial to those for whom it is cultivated, receives blessing from God. [8]But if it bears thorns and thistles, it is useless
and near to being cursed, so that its end is to be burned.
[9]But concerning you, beloved, we remain confident of the superior things that
belong to salvation, even though we speak this way. [10]For God is not unjust, so
that he would forget your work and the love that you showed for his name when
you served and continue to serve the saints. [11]But we want each of you to show
the same striving for the full assurance of hope until the end [12]in order that you
not be sluggish, but imitators of those who through faith and perseverance inherit what was promised.

NOTES

6:4. *For it is impossible.* The word "impossible" (*adynaton*) is connected to the infinitive "to restore" (*anakainizein*), which comes in 6:6 in the Greek. Troubled by the severity of the statement, some softened it to "it is difficult" to restore an apostate (Nicolaus of Lyra; Erasmus, *Adnotationes*), but Hebrews is unequivocal: it is impossible to restore an apostate, just as it is impossible for God to prove false (6:18), for the blood of bulls and goats to take away sins (10:4), or for people to please God without faith (11:6). There are three lines of interpretation. The third is most plausible:

(a) "Impossible for an apostate to repent." Subjectively, one might posit a point when people "are psychologically incapable of making another about-face" (*TLNT* 1.36; cf. Poschmann, *Paenitentia*, 42; Héring, *Epistle*, 46; cf. F. F. Bruce). Objectively, Christ's sacrifice is the basis upon which people are reconciled to God. Therefore, those who reject Christ's sacrifice (10:26) have repudiated "the only basis upon which repentance can be extended" (Lane, *Hebrews*, 1.142; cf. Attridge, *Epistle*, 169). Yet Hebrews does not say that it is impossible for one who has fallen away to repent, but that "it is impossible *to restore* to repentance" one who has fallen away. The question concerns the subject of the verb. Who finds it impossible to restore the apostate?

(b) "Impossible for other Christians to restore an apostate." In the early church some argued that authorities were not to restore apostates to communion with the church, but others insisted that the lapsed could be forgiven, just not rebaptized (pp. 23–25, 40). More recently some have suggested that fellow Christians (3:13) could not restore an apostate by exhortations (Windisch; Oberholtzer, "Warning," 323). Yet related passages (10:26–31; 12:16–17) speak not of the community's inability to generate repentance, but of God's judgment (Carlston, "Eschatology," 299). This brings us to the third and most plausible view.

(c) "Impossible that God should restore an apostate to repentance." Hebrews does not suggest that God lacked the power to restore an apostate to repentance, for God is the one "for whom all things and through whom all things exist" (2:10) and his word can shake earth and heaven (12:26); therefore, restoration would not be beyond his ability. Yet God might refuse to restore an apostate. To say that "it is impossible" that God should lie (6:18) does not suggest that God lacks the power to lie, but that he refuses to lie. The wilderness generation repeatedly tested God, and God finally barred them from the land (3:7–4:13). Similarly, Esau sold his birthright and was rejected despite his show of remorse (12:17; McCullough, "Impossibility"; Ellingworth).

to restore. The term *anakainizein*, which appears in Greek in 6:6a, means "restore" or "renew" and indicates conversion (*Jos. Asen.* 8:9; 15:5, 7). A related verb indicates renewal of the mind (Rom 12:2; cf. 2 Cor 4:16; Col 3:10) and was associated with the Spirit (Tit 3:5; Heb 6:4).

to repentance. In Greek the word "repentance" occurs in 6:6a. The author might have spoken about a person being restored to grace, but he speaks instead of being restored to repentance. Here repentance refers to a decisive movement from sin to faith (NOTE on 6:1).

those who have once. Quantitatively, "once" (*hapax*, 6:4; 9:7, 26, 27, 28; 10:2; 12:26, 27; *ephapax*, 7:27; 9:12; 10:10) means that something occurs a single time. Thus Jesus' self-sacrifice differs from Levitical sacrifices because it is offered only once (9:25, 28). Qualitatively, "once" also points to completeness. Jesus' death was offered only once because it provided a complete cleansing for sin (10:2). Similarly, to be enlightened "once" does not simply point to a single occurrence. Those who have "once" been enlightened or who have "once" become partakers of the Spirit have experienced the fullness of God's goodness. Thus a person who has "once" been enlightened is like land that has been watered "repeatedly" (6:7). Emphasis is on the completeness of the grace that God has given, not merely on its onetime occurrence (cf. Josephus, *J.W.* 2.158; *Ant.* 4.140; Löhr, *Umkehr*, 198, 242–49; *TLNT* 139–42).

been enlightened. "Enlightenment" (6:4; 10:32) is conversion or receiving the message of salvation (2:3–4). The verb is in the passive voice, since God's Spirit moves people from sin to faith (6:1), from ignorance to "knowledge of the truth" (10:26), and from death to life (2:14–15; 9:28). Light imagery could encompass all of these movements:

(a) From sin to God. Light was widely associated with God (Ps 27:1) and his word (Pss 19:8; 119:105, 130; *Bib. Ant.* 11:2; 19:6). Apart from God people live in the darkness of sin (Prov 2:13; 4:19; 2 *Bar.* 56:5), but "repentance puts darkness to flight" (*T. Gad* 5:7). Paul preached in order that people "may turn from darkness to light and from the power of Satan to God" (Acts 26:18; cf. 9:3; 13:47; 22:6–11; 26:23; 2 Cor 4:6; Luke 2:32; John 1:9; Eph 1:18; 1 Pet 2:9). Darkness connoted sin and evil (Rom 13:12; Luke 22:53), and enlightenment meant turning from these things to "walk in the light" by living according to God's will (John 8:12; 1 John 2:9–11; Eph 5:8–9; cf. Prov 4:18; Sir 32:16).

(b) Ignorance to knowledge. Light was associated with God's word and instruction (Pss 19:8; 119:130; Sir 45:17; *Bib. Ant.* 11:2; 1QS IV, 2; 1QH IV, 5–6). Darkness connoted ignorance, so that those who came to know the truth of God turned "from darkness to light, from error to truth, from death to life" (*Jos. Asen.* 8:9; cf. Philo, *Virtues* 179; *Sib. Or.* frg. 1.25–30). Philosophical sources said that light draws the mind upward toward ultimate reality, the true light that is the absolute good (Plato, *Republic* 7.517–18; Plutarch, *Moralia* 563F–566C; Philo, *Creation* 54–55).

(c) Death to life. Death was associated with darkness (Ps 88:6, 12; Sir 22:16; Euripides, *Alcestis* 266) and life with light (Ps 13:3; Euripides, *Alcestis* 272). Enlightenment meant life and health (Job 33:30; Bar 1:12), and the hope of everlasting life (*Pss. Sol.* 3:12; Dan 12:2; John 8:12; Col 1:12) rather than the gloom of death (Luke 1:79; Matt 8:12). Some take "enlightenment" to be baptism (Heb 6:2; cf. 10:22, 32), which was done only "once" (Braun; H.-F. Weiss; Goldhahn-Müller, *Grenze*, 88). The Peshitta translated "enlightenment" as "baptism" in Heb 6:4 and 10:32 (cf. Justin, *1 Apology* 61.12; 65.1). In Hebrews, however, "enlightenment" refers to the repentance and faith (6:1) that precede and lead to baptism (6:2). See generally *TLNT* 3.470–91; H. Conzelmann, *TDNT* 9.310–58; and C. R. Koester, *Symbolism*, 123–54.

who have tasted the heavenly gift. "Heavenly" was used in 3:1 for the Christian's calling, which comes from heaven and leads to heaven (8:5; 9:23; 11:16; 12:22). The "gift" could refer to grace (cf. Rom 5:15; 2 Cor 9:14–15; Eph 3:7; 4:7) or to the Spirit. As the agent of grace (Heb 10:29), the Spirit is a "gift" (Acts 2:38; 8:20; 10:45; 11:17; cf. John 4:10, 23; Luke 11:13). Those who receive the Spirit "drink" of it (1 Cor 12:13; John 7:37–39), just as those who taste the heavenly gift are like soil that receives rain (Heb 6:7). Some connect "tasting" with the Lord's Supper (F. F. Bruce; Héring; Kistemaker), but this seems unlikely (see pp. 127–29).

and become partakers of the Holy Spirit. "Partakers" share in a heavenly calling and in Christ (3:1, 14). Like the word "taste" in 6:4b and 6:5a, to become a "partaker" (*metochos*) means receiving God's Spirit into oneself. Cf. "partaking" of milk (*metechein*, 5:13). The principal manifestation of the Spirit is faith.

6:5. *who have tasted the good word of God.* The Spirit and the word are related because listeners received the Spirit through hearing the Christian message (2:3–4). The OT sometimes compares God's word to food (e.g., Deut 8:3; Amos 8:11), which is good to taste (Ps 19:7–10; Ezek 2:8–3:3; cf. Ps 34:8; Rev 10:9–10). On "taste" see NOTE on 6:4. In the OT God's "good words" included promises of land and rest (Josh 21:45; 23:15). Those addressed by Hebrews have received a good word concerning salvation (2:3; 4:1; 5:9; 6:12).

and the powers of the age to come. The powers of the future age include the miracles that accompanied the initial proclamation of the gospel (2:4). A problem for the listeners was that this experience did not mean that they had actually entered the "world to come" (2:5) or "the city that is to come," the New Jerusalem (12:22; 13:14). This contradiction between spiritual experience and social conflict contributed to the crisis of perception that occasioned Hebrews. See NOTES and COMMENT on 2:3–4.

6:6. The NOTES on *to restore to repentance*, which occurs in 6:6 in Greek, appear under 6:4 above.

but who then fall away. The context speaks of falling away from light, from the Spirit, from the word of God, and from the powers of the age to come. Falling away after receiving God's gifts is like ground producing thorns and thistles after it has been blessed with rain from God (6:8). Falling away from God means falling into sin.

since they crucify the Son of God. The prefix *ana-* on the compound verb *anastauroun* might suggest that apostates *re*crucify Jesus, just as the prefix on *anakainizein* means to *re*store (NIV; NRSV; NJB, NASB; NAB2; Lane; Ellingworth). Nevertheless, the compound form normally means "crucify," with the prefix *ana-* suggesting upward movement: being lifted up onto a cross (e.g., Josephus, *J.W.* 1.97; 2.75). In form "crucify" is a participle commonly taken in the causal sense: apostates cannot be restored *because* they crucify the Son of God. Some take it in a temporal sense: people cannot be restored "*while* crucifying" the Son of God, which leaves open the possibility of restoration when they desist (NIVfn; J. K. Elliott, "Post-baptismal"). This, however, reduces the statement to a truism. Others argue that the participle means that no one can be restored by attempting to *repeat* Christ's sacrifice (Proulx and Schökel, "Heb 6,4–6"; Sabourin, "Crucifying"). This resembles the idea that apostates can be restored but not rebaptized into Christ's death (see pp. 23–25), but it is difficult to imagine someone attempting to restore a person by recrucifying Christ and "making a spectacle" of him, since that would suggest contempt (Attridge).

to themselves. The pronoun is in the dative case and is often taken as a dative of disadvantage: apostates crucify Jesus "to their own loss" (NIV; REB; Lane; Ellingworth). More likely, however, is that crucifixion brings death, and death ends the relationship (Rom 7:2–3; Gal 6:14). Those who have crucified Christ "to themselves" have terminated their relationship with him (Moffatt).

make a spectacle of him. The word *paradeigmatizein* was used for public punishments that made an example out of the victim (Polybius, *Histories* 2.60.7; 29.19.5; Plutarch, *Mor.* 520b; Num 25:4; Ezek 28:17; cf. 3 Macc 7:14). Prior to crucifixion, prisoners carried their crosses to the place of execution in "a fearful example" that was designed to deter others from such actions (Chariton, *Chaereas and Callirhoe* 4.2.7; cf. Heb 12:2; Plutarch, *Mor.* 554B). Quintilian explained, "Whenever we crucify the guilty, the most crowded roads are chosen, where the most people can see and be moved by this fear. For penalties relate not so much to retribution as to their exemplary effect" (*Declamationes* 274; cf. Josephus, *J.W.* 5.289).

6:7. *For earth, which drinks the rain that repeatedly comes upon it.* Rain cannot be created by human agency; it can only be a gift from heaven (Deut 11:11–12; Isa 55:10; Zech 10:1; Joel 2:23; Matt 5:45; Acts 14:17; Jas 5:18). The idea of frequency (*pollakis*, "repeatedly") can be negative, as in repeated sacrifices (Heb 9:25–26; 10:11), but here frequency is positive, corresponding to the manifold blessings from heaven (6:4–5).

and produces vegetation beneficial to those for whom it is cultivated. Useful vegetation includes grain, fruit, and fodder, rather than weeds (Exod 9:22; 10:15; Ign. *Eph.* 10:3; cf. Matt 13:24–30). The people "for whom" land is tilled include the owners as well as the workers. The imagery suggests that the one "for whom" cultivation is done is God (Luther WA 57,3.32; Westcott).

receives blessing from God. Some said that land that produced bountifully was already blessed by God and that productive fields and herds were a blessing in themselves (Gen 26:12; 27:27–28; Deut 28:1–14; Ps 65:9–10; Prov 28:19–20). Here, however, blessing is God's favorable judgment upon land after it has produced well. The verse indicates that God will judge the faithful favorably and the faithless negatively in the future (cf. Deut 11:26–28; 30:19).

6:8. *But if it bears thorns and thistles, it is useless and near to being cursed.* Earth was said to yield thorns and thistles as a consequence of sin (Gen 3:18) and God's judgment upon it (Isa 7:23–25; 32:13; 34:13; Hos 10:8). Thorns and thistles were worthless at best (Jer 12:13; Prov 15:19) and harmful at worst (Ezek 28:24; Prov 26:9; Philo, *Alleg. Interp.* 3.253; *Dreams* 2.161). Therefore, sins were like thorns and thistles (Nah 1:10; Prov 22:5; Philo, *Alleg. Interp.* 3.248).

so that its end is to be burned. Farmers burned piles of weeds and useless growth pruned from trees and vines (Matt 3:10, 12; 13:30; John 15:6). Sometimes an entire plot of land might be burned over to destroy unwanted growth (Plutarch, *Mor.* 529B; Pliny the Elder, *Natural History* 18.8 §47; Exod 22:6; *y. Shabb.* 10a [*TLI* 11.250]; cf. Philo, *Husbandry* 17). Such fire was an image for divine judgment (Deut 32:22; 2 Sam 23:6–7; Isa 10:16–17; 33:12; Matt 13:42, 50; 1 Cor 3:12–15). See especially Heb 10:27; 12:29.

6:9. *But concerning you, beloved.* Calling listeners "beloved" after the warnings in 6:4–8 helps to show that the author speaks out of concern, not antagonism (cf. 1 Cor 4:14; 10:14; 2 Cor 7:1; Jas 1:16; 1 Pet 2:11; 4:12; 1 John 4:1, 7). After calling them "beloved" he commends the "love" they have shown (6:10).

we remain confident. Rhetorically, expressions of confidence help to ensure that the listeners will respond favorably to what the speaker asks of them (cf. Rom 15:14; 2 Cor 7:16; Gal 5:10; 2 Thess 3:4; Phlm 21). Hebrews asks them to strive in hope and faith (Heb 6:11–12).

of the superior things that belong to salvation. "Superior things" correspond to the blessings that God gives to a fruitful land (6:7). Elsewhere, "superior" is used for Christ's superiority to angels (1:4), access to God (7:19), the abiding covenant (7:22; 8:6), a complete sacrificial cleansing (9:23; 12:24), a heavenly inheritance (10:34; 11:16), and resurrection (11:35; cf. 11:40)—all of which pertain to salvation. Listeners have salvation as a promise (cf. 6:12) that will be fully realized in the heavenly Jerusalem (12:22–24). Cf. NOTE on 2:3. On "belong to" (*echein*) see BAGD, 334 (III.1).

even though we speak this way. The sharpness of the reproof in 5:11–6:3 and of the warning in 6:4–8 does not mean that the author has lost hope for the listeners. His words are designed to motivate listeners to persevere, not to drive them to despair of God.

6:10. *For God is not unjust.* Belief that God is just was basic to Israel's faith (Ps 119:137; Neh 9:33; Zeph 3:5; 2 Macc 1:24–25; 3 Macc 2:3). For God to be just, one would assume that the righteous should be blessed and the wicked punished (Ps 62:12). God's justice is questioned when the good suffer and the unrighteous prosper (Ezek 18:2, 29; Hab 1:13). Without the conviction that God is just—though merciful—there is little reason for people to pursue righteousness if it entails hardship.

so that he would forget your work. Listeners could give thanks that under the new covenant God would no longer remember their sins (8:12; 10:17), since that would be merciful. But for God to forget the service they performed would be unjust (Ps 13:1; Isa 49:14).

and the love that you showed for his name. Hebrews does not deal with love as a feeling, but as a commitment that entails good works (10:24; cf. Gal 5:6; 1 Thess 1:3). Showing love for God's name could mean showing love toward others for God's "sake" (NRSV; cf. *m. 'Abot* 2:2, 12), but "for his name" (NJB; NAB2) also means love for God himself (Pss 7:17; 9:2; Isa 12:4; 25:1).

when you served and continue to serve the saints. Some NT texts commend love for neighbors and enemies (Matt 5:43–48; 22:39 par.; Rom 13:9; Gal 5:14; Jas 2:8). Many also stress the love and service that Christians gave to one another, since community members depended on each other for support (John 13:34–35; 15:12; Acts 2:44–45; Gal 6:10; 1 Tim 5:10; 1 Pet 4:8; 1 John 3:11, 17) and having physical needs attended to (Matt 25:44; Luke 10:40; 17:8; Rom 15:24–25). Earlier, those addressed by Hebrews showed solidarity with those who suffered public abuse, loss of possessions, and imprisonment (Heb 10:32–34). Their present service is to include hospitality and attending to prisoners (NOTES on 13:2–3).

6:11. *But we want each of you to show the same striving.* "Striving" is the opposite of "sluggishness" (5:11; 6:12). Variously translated "zeal" (NRSV), "eagerness" (NAB2), "diligence" (NIV; NASB), and "enthusiasm" (NJB), *spoudē* indicates commitment and effort toward (*pros*, cf. 2 Cor 7:12) a given end. In Heb 4:11 the goal of striving was entry into God's promised rest. Here it means holding fast to the promises of God until their realization. Zeal for God's promises is "shown" by love, service, and holding fast to the Christian confession (cf. 3:6, 14).

for the full assurance of hope. The noun *plērophoria* could perhaps be used for the "fulfillment" of the Christian hope (NAB2), but here and in 10:22 it more probably means "full conviction" (cf. Col 2:2; 1 Thess 1:5) or confidence that God will keep his promises, appearances notwithstanding (Rom 4:21; cf. 14:5). Cf. "boldness" (Heb 3:6; 10:19) and "assurance" (3:14; 11:1).

until the end. The "end" for which the faithful hope involves blessing (6:7), entering God's rest (4:9–11), final salvation from sin and death (9:28), and life in the heavenly Jerusalem (12:22–24).

6:12. in order that you not be sluggish. See NOTE on 5:11.

but imitators. People learn by imitating their teachers (Xenophon, *Memorabilia* 1.6.3) and parents (Euripides, *Helen* 940–43; Philo, *Sacrifices* 68). Imitation meant not only heeding what was said but following the pattern of someone's life (Philo, *Preliminary Studies* 70). Imitating good models could bring a reward of glory (*T. Jos.* 4:1; cf. Philo, *Sacrifices* 123; *Moses* 1.158; W. Michaelis, *TDNT* 4.659–74). In Hebrews those worthy of imitation include Abraham and other biblical figures (6:13; 11:1–40), previous leaders of the congregation (13:7; cf. 1 Thess 1:6; 2:14; 1 Cor 4:16; 11:1), and Christ himself (12:1–2; cf. 1 Pet 2:21).

of those who through faith and perseverance. "Faith" and "perseverance" are virtually synonymous here. Perseverance is steadfastness despite adversity (Josephus, *J.W.* 6.37; Ign. *Eph.* 3:1; *T. Jos.* 2:7; Jas 5:10–11). See pp. 125–27 on faith.

inherit what was promised. Inheritance was commonly a gift of an estate or property that was given to a designated heir (NOTE on 6:17). Those addressed by Hebrews hoped that God would give them an inheritance in the world to come (1:14). Many translations speak of inheriting "the promises" (NJB; NASB; NRSV; NAB2), but the author refers to receiving "what was promised" (NIV; REB). The promises, which were first made to Abraham, are taken to include blessing (6:7, 13–14) and rest in God's heavenly city (4:1–11; 11:13–16). See pp. 110–12.

COMMENT[179]

This portion of the digression (§13 COMMENT) presents an uncompromising warning (6:4–8). The author said, not that it is "not fitting" or "not profitable" or "not lawful," but that it is "*not possible*" to restore those who fall away (Chrysostom, *Homilies* 9.5). A single occurrence of such severity might be dismissed as an overstatement, but similar warnings appear elsewhere: "For if we persist in sinning willfully after receiving knowledge of the truth, there no longer remains a sacrifice for sins," but "a terrifying prospect of judgment" for one who has "trampled upon the Son of God and considered profane the blood of the covenant by which he was sanctified, and was insolent toward the Spirit of grace" (10:26–29). Similarly, Esau "gave up his rights as firstborn," but later "found no opportunity for repentance, even though he sought it with tears" (12:16–17).[180]

Historically, many of the controversies surrounding Hebrews have centered on these passages. In antiquity Christians in the west read the texts in light of questions about church discipline, with Montanists and Novatians invoking the passages to argue for more rigorous church discipline and others rejecting Hebrews altogether because it seemed to deny forgiveness to the lapsed (p. 23). Reception of Hebrews into the canon was facilitated by the idea that the text did not prohibit restoring apostates to communion with the church, but only ruled out rebaptizing them (pp. 23–25, 40). In the sixteenth century the canonical status of

---

[179]On 6:4–12 see Carlston, "Eschatology"; deSilva, "Exchanging"; J. K. Elliott, "Post-baptismal"; Gleason, "Old Testament . . . Warning"; Goldhahn-Müller, *Grenze*, 75–93; Grudem, "Perseverance"; P. E. Hughes, "Hebrews 6:4–6"; Kawamura, "ἀδύνατον"; Löhr, *Umkehr*, 188–241; Mathewson, "Reading"; McCullough, "Impossibility"; Nicole, "Some Comments"; Oberholtzer, "Warning," 319–28; Proulx and Schökel, "Heb 6, 4–6"; Rice, "Apostasy"; Sabourin, "Crucifying"; Sproule, "Parapesontas"; Vanhoye, "Heb 6:7–8"; Verbrugge, "Towards"; N. H. Young, "Hebrews 6.1–8."

[180]On the warning passages see Mugridge, "Warnings"; Oberholtzer, "Warning"; Toussaint, "Eschatology."

Hebrews was challenged again, in part because of these passages (pp. 34–35). In reply some noted that Jesus' warning about the unforgivable sin[181] and the Johannine idea of a sin unto death[182] seemed equally rigorous.

Modern interpreters[183] have often tried to explain Hebrews' rigorism by showing its affinities with Jewish texts that said that "no pardon must be granted to a blasphemer" (Philo, *Flight* 84); "for apostates let there be no hope."[184] He who "leads many to sin, to him shall be given no means for repentance" (*m. 'Abot* 5:18). Among persistent sinners, "many souls have desired to repent and not been permitted by God to do so" (Philo, *Alleg. Interp.* 3.213; cf. *Worse* 149; Sir 34:30–31; 2 *Enoch* 62:3).[185] Comparison of Hebrews with these sources shows that the author was not alone in making warnings of this sort, but important theological questions remain.

First, the idea that a person can be brought to repentance only "once" (*hapax*, 6:4) has been approached in several ways:

(a) Eschatology. Some have proposed that the author shared the early Christian belief that the final judgment was imminent (10:25) and therefore thought that there would not be time to restore apostates.[186] This is unlikely. Although the author understood himself to be living in the final days (1:2; 3:13; 9:26–28; 10:37–38), he did not base his warnings concerning apostasy on this idea. Instead, he urged listeners to exhort one another "as long as it is called *today*" (3:13) and to provoke each other to love and good works as the Day of the Lord drew near (10:24–25).

---

[181]Connections between Hebrews and the unforgivable sin were made in Tyndale's *Preface to Hebrews* and Calvin's *Institutes* 3.3.21; cf. Origen, *Commentary on John* 28.124–26; *Commentary on Matthew* 114; Theognostos, *ANF* 6.156; cf. Filastrius, PL 12.1200–2; Epiphanius, GCS 31.363–66. Hebrews probably does not allude to the unforgivable sin (Matt 12:31–32; Mark 3:28–29; Luke 12:10), since these gospel passages refer to those who persistently reject Jesus, whereas Hebrews focuses on those who come to faith, but then apostatize. Hebrews has affinities with these gospel passages in that it assumes that apostasy means turning from the Holy Spirit (6:4–6; 10:29). Moreover, all of these passages indicate that a person might come under irrevocable divine judgment during his or her own lifetime rather than on the last day.

[182]First John 5:16 says that one should ask for forgiveness for those whose sin is not unto death. The sin that is unto death is probably unbelief (R. E. Brown, *Epistles*, 617–18). Those affected by this sin may be apostates (cf. 1 John 2:19) and others who do not believe. Persistent unbelief leads to death, but 1 John does foreclose the possibility of an unbeliever coming to faith.

[183]For example, Moffatt, *Critical*, 76–82; Windisch, *Hebräerbrief*, 52–56; Spicq, *L'Épître*, 1.157–59; Braun, *Hebräer*, 170–73; Attridge, *Epistle*, 168–69. Williamson (*Philo*, 245–63) acknowledges that there are similarities in tone between Hebrews and Philo, but he argues against the idea that Hebrews depended on Philo.

[184]Twelfth Benediction, *Shemoneh Esreh* (Schürer, *History*, 2.461); cf. *t. Sanh.* 13:5.

[185]Some texts spoke of expelling members from a community (1QS VII, 23–24; VIII, 21–23; Matt 18:15–17; 1 Cor 5:1–5), although these texts are not as pertinent since Hebrews does not develop its warnings into policy regarding community discipline.

[186]Some in antiquity took warnings about the impossibility of restoration to mean that it would not be possible after a certain time (p. 23). For eschatological interpretations of the warnings in Hebrews see Windisch, *Hebräerbrief*, 53; Schierse, *Verheissung*, 146, 151; Kosmala, *Hebräer*, 27, 29. See the critique by Löhr, *Umkehr*, 229–33.

(**b**) Christology. Others argue that people are brought to repentance only once because Christ was sacrificed only once (7:27; 9:12, 26, 28; 10:10).[187] Support comes from 10:26, which warns that there is no further sacrifice for those who persist in sin after coming to knowledge of the truth. Yet this approach is also problematic. Hebrews does not appeal to the fact that Christ was sacrificed only once when discussing repentance in 6:4–8 and 12:16–17. Logically, it is difficult to see why a singular act of atonement would mean that repentance must also be a singular act (Löhr, *Umkehr*, 242–49). To be sure, those who repudiate Christ's sacrifice have no other basis for repentance, but why cannot a person be restored by being brought to a renewed appreciation of Christ's sacrifice?

(**c**) Cultural Context. Others propose that Hebrews draws on the common assumption that failing to show gratitude to one's patron was a sacrilege (Seneca, *De beneficiis* 3.17.1–2). Ancient writers sometimes warned that failing to show gratitude would preclude receiving future favors (Dio Chrysostom, *Disc.* 31.38, 65). By invoking this familiar idea and transferring it from human to divine relationships, Hebrews rules out every excuse for ingratitude toward God, the consummate benefactor (Seneca, *De beneficiis* 7.16.2; deSilva, *Perseverance*, 223–44). One problem with this approach is that some ancient writers recognized that both divine and human benefactors could continue showing favor to ungrateful people (Seneca, *De beneficiis* 7.31–32). Another problem is Hebrews did not necessarily assume that God's actions would correspond to human conventions: bringing people to glory by means of Jesus' crucifixion shows how God could act in ways that ran counter to social convention (§8 COMMENT).

(**d**) Divine-human encounter. The warning in 6:4–8 can best be understood through its own logic, which pertains to the way that the author understands God's grace and human faith. The interpretation developed in COMMENT *a* attempts to follow the argument of the passage and to relate it to similar passages, especially to the portrayal of Moses' generation in 3:7–4:13.

A second major point is that speakers in antiquity understood the *effect* of their words to be as important as their meaning. The author of Hebrews shows concern about the effect of his words when immediately after issuing a warning he reaffirms confidence concerning the listeners, "even though we speak this way" (6:9). He wanted to ensure that his warning did not make listeners despair, but motivated them to persevere. Others, too, understood that texts concerning the penalties incurred by those who abandoned God were to be read "as a warning rather than as intending their perdition" so that people would seek God rather than forsake him (Philo, *Rewards* 163). Hebrews' warnings can best be read in this way (pp. 20–21, 28).

The emotions aroused by reproofs, warnings, and words of encouragement played an important role in a persuasive speech like Hebrews (see pp. 89–91). Listeners needed to know that a warning was given out of concern, and that its purpose was to prevent something harmful from happening to them. Therefore,

---

[187]Carlston, "Eschatology," 301; Attridge, *Epistle*, 169; H.-F. Weiss, *Brief*, 349; Grässer, *Hebräer*, 1.310.

the author of Hebrews addresses his listeners as "beloved" (6:9) and assures them that his purpose is that they might remain faithful and inherit what God has promised (6:12). The severity of the warning should not be minimized, since the author clearly says that "it is impossible" to restore an apostate to repentance, and the warning must not be considered to be merely rhetorical, as if the threat of divine judgment were not real. The point is that the warning is designed to motivate rather than to discourage listeners.

Paradoxically, the digression (5:11–6:20) conveys a promise that is as uncompromising as its warnings. After warning that "it is impossible" (*adynaton*, 6:4) that God should restore an apostate to repentance, the author declares that "it is impossible" (*adynaton*, 6:18) that God should prove false after having sworn to give many blessings. Both statements are issued unequivocally, and neither should be softened; instead, we should consider the kind of response appropriate to each statement. Listeners respond properly to the warning when they heed it, and they respond properly to the promise when they trust it. The warning about apostasy and the promise of God's faithfulness function differently—the warning disturbs while the promise gives assurance—but they serve the same end, which is that listeners might persevere in faith (6:12).[188]

a. Impossibility of Restoration (6:4–8)

This section includes an argument concerning the impossibility of restoring an apostate to repentance (6:4–6) and a supporting illustration in which a well-watered field that bears thorns and thistles is subjected to fire (6:7–8).

The Argument. The argument and the illustration make similar points by depicting the blessings given by God, a negative response to God, and divine judgment:

(a) The description in 6:4–5 assumes that God is the giver of manifold blessings. The verb "enlightened" is in the passive voice with God understood to be the giver of enlightenment (cf. 10:32). Since human beings cannot enter heaven on their own (Deut 30:12; Rom 10:6), an encounter with heavenly reality (Heb 6:4b) can only be a gift from God. The Spirit of which the listeners partake is God's Spirit (6:4c), whose coming was accompanied by signs of God's power (2:3–4). The message they received was the word of God (6:5a), and the powers they encountered were from the age to come (6:5b; 2:4–5), which can only be experienced when God grants it. Rather than saying that listeners have "received" something, the author says that they have "tasted" these gifts (6:4–5), which involves personal contact, just as becoming a "partaker" of the Spirit (6:4c) means receiving the Spirit into oneself. This section refers to an authentic experience of God's manifold grace (Löhr, *Umkehr*, 197–205).

---

[188]Some have taken the text to mean that it is impossible for a human being to restore an apostate to repentance, but that with God all things are possible (Matt 19:26; cf. Ambrose, *De paenitentia* 2.2 §§6–12 [NPNF[1] 10.345–46]; Bengel; Westcott). This emphasizes the digression's movement toward encouragement, but does not fully suit Hebrews, which implies that God himself will refuse to restore an apostate to repentance. On impossibility as a rhetorical topic see Aristotle, *Rhetoric* 2.19.1–27.

(**b**) People who have been blessed may "fall away" (6:6a) by turning away from God's light, from the heavenly gift and the Holy Spirit, from the good word of God and the powers of the age to come. In this passage, rejection does not stem from ignorance since the "enlightened" have, by definition, come to knowledge of the truth (10:26). It also goes beyond drift, neglect, or sluggishness (2:1, 3; 5:11; 6:12) to a repudiation of what God has done. The author offers no clear criteria by which a person can determine when this has happened, but assumes that God must discern when a person has ended a relationship with him.

The author does not explain why anyone who received gifts from God would reject them, but some things may be inferred. Listeners live in a situation in which the power of God and the power of sin are both at work. They have tasted the powers of the age to come (6:5), but have not entered the city that is to come (13:14), and until they do they will struggle with sin (12:1, 4). Like Moses' generation, the listeners have embarked on a journey of faith that began when they received God's saving message and will end when they enter God's promised rest. The way is not easy and everyone is tested (2:18; 4:15), so that people continue only if they trust in God's promises, even when appearances seem to contradict them. Those who trust appearances that deny God's promises will act in unbelief. According to Hebrews it is the unbelieving heart, hardened by sin, that moves people to turn away from God (3:12–13; see §10 COMMENT *b*).

(**c**) It is impossible that those who have fallen away should be restored to repentance (6:4a [6:6a Gk]). The NOTE on 6:4a concluded that this verse deals with God's refusal to restore a person to repentance. According to Hebrews, one reason that God will not restore apostates is that they "crucify the Son of God to themselves" (6:6b), that is, they put to death their relationship with Christ. Since God initiates relationships by bringing people to repentance, God presumably could reinstate the relationship by bringing them to repentance again if he chose to do so. Yet Hebrews assumes that what God would offer the apostates is what they rejected: the Spirit, his word, and enlightenment (6:4–5). By refusing to restore apostates, God permits their decision to stand; he allows them to terminate the relationship. This corresponds to the way that God accepted the wilderness generation's refusal to enter the land, allowing them to die in the wilderness (§10 COMMENT *b*).

A second reason for God not to restore apostates is that they "make a spectacle" of his Son (6:6c). When apostates break off their relationship with Christ, they not only show their own contempt for him (cf. 10:29) but make him contemptible in the eyes of others. When Jesus was crucified, his adversaries derided him,[189] and later opponents of Christianity mocked "that crucified sophist" (Lucian, *Peregrinus* 13). Hebrews probably does not refer to Christians making a formal act of apostasy (*Mart. Pol.* 9:3; Pliny, *Ep.* 96.5), but does suggest that falling away from the faith had a public character.[190] Just as crucifixion was de-

[189]Heb 12:2–3; 13:13; cf. Matt 26:67–68; 27:27–31, 38–44 par.

[190]deSilva, *Despising*, 261; Spicq, *L'Épître*, 1.154.

signed to deter others from crime (NOTE on 6:6), crucifixion of a person's relationship with Christ could deter others from faith and move them to show contempt for the Christ who was rejected.

Supporting Illustration. The illustration in 6:7–8 reinforces the claims made in 6:4–6. Comparing human beings to plants was done by Israel's prophets (Isa 5:1–10; Jer 2:21), by Jesus (Mark 4:1–20 par.; Luke 13:6–9), and by Greco-Roman writers (Euripides, *Hecuba* 592–99; Quintilian, *Inst.* 5.11.24). Familiar imagery added strength to the argument because ideas that were commonly accepted were difficult for listeners to reject when applied to their situation (*Rhet. ad Her.* 4.17 §25; cf. NOTE on 3:3 and §12 COMMENT *c*). The elements in the illustration can be correlated with those in the previous section:

(**a**) Those who have tasted the heavenly gift and the goodness of God's word are like cultivated land that drinks in the rain (6:7a). Rain comes from heaven, like the Spirit and the powers of the age to come. Just as barren land must wait for rain to fall upon it from the sky, people must wait for God to shower heavenly graces upon them. Comparing people to fields upon which the rain has come repeatedly indicates that they have not lacked any divine gift, but have amply received good things from God.

(**b**) Those who fall away (6:6a) in spite of the gifts they receive from God are like a well-watered field that produces thorns and thistles (6:8). The idea was used by Isaiah, who compared Israel to a vineyard whose owner "dug it and cleared it of stones, and planted it with choice vines" (Isa 5:2). He expected the field to yield grapes, but it produced "wild grapes" (MT) or "thorns" (LXX). Therefore, when the prophet asks what more the owner could do for the vineyard, the obvious answer is "nothing"; the unwanted produce is not due to the landowner's neglect, but to something within the land itself (Isa 5:5–7). The same idea is evident in Heb 6:7–8. The author assumes that if land has been cultivated and watered well, it should produce useful fruit, and if it yields the briar of apostasy, the responsibility lies with the land or person rather than with God.[191]

(**c**) Its end is to be burned (6:8b). Sending more rain upon land that is infested with thorns and thistles would not improve the situation, but make unwanted growth proliferate. A different kind of measure is needed, and a common pattern in antiquity was to burn away the unwanted growth. Hebrews applies the practice to those who have tasted God's heavenly gifts only to apostatize. The author argues that if God has given them heavenly gifts and they respond negatively, showering them with more grace would encourage sin in the way that rain helps weeds flourish. Like a farmer contending with thorn-infested ground, God can be expected to bring fiery judgment upon sinners (10:27; 12:29).

[191]The connection between Isa 5:1–10 and Heb 6:7–8 was explored by Verbrugge ("Towards"). His proposal that Hebrews refers, not to individuals, but to the community falling away has not been widely accepted. See esp. Löhr, *Umkehr*, 236–37.

b. Sure of Better Things (6:9–12)

The warning in 6:4–8 was designed to awaken fear of divine judgment, but in order to prevent fear from debilitating the listeners, the author now expresses his confidence of their salvation (6:9). Rhetorically, "confidence is the opposite of fear" (Aristotle, *Rhetoric* 2.5.16; see p. 90), and it was understood that listeners are more likely to persevere (6:12) when convinced that the speaker himself is confident. The tone reinforces the message. The "superior things that belong to salvation" recalls that in the analogy of the field, soil that produced thorns and thistles would be cursed, while soil that produced useful vegetation would be blessed. The warning of judgment pertained to the apostasy described in 6:4–6, while the blessing applies to people like the listeners (Vanhoye, "Heb 6:7–8").

The basis for the author's confidence is that God is not unjust (6:10). It was commonly understood that "justice is equity, giving to each thing what it is entitled to in proportion to its worth."[192] This means that if God punishes sinners, he should also reward the righteous (10:35; 11:6, 26). The listeners had experienced moments in which injustice seemed to gain the upper hand through outbursts against the Christian community (10:32–34) and ongoing reproach from society (13:13). For the listeners to persevere in faith they must be convinced that God is not unjust but will keep his promise of blessing (10:23).

If apostates "made a spectacle" of the Son of God (6:6), those addressed by Hebrews showed love for the name of God (6:10b). Love for God was a central element in Jewish life (Deut 6:5), and religious observance was common among Greeks and Romans. In itself love for God would not have engendered the opposition that the listeners had experienced (Heb 10:32–34). The listeners, however, had shown love for a particular God and for "his name," which set them apart from others (13:13). The God whose name they confessed in their assemblies (13:15) had exalted Jesus to his right hand (1:3). Moreover, showing love for God's name is understood to be inseparable from showing love for the saints who are called by his name (6:10c; cf. 1 John 4:20–5:1). The community previously showed solidarity with the abused (Heb 10:32–34) and were called to continue welcoming strangers and caring for those in prison (13:1–3; §37 COMMENT *a*).

Earlier the author chided those who again needed instruction in the basics of faith (5:11–14), but here he offers the practical suggestion that they imitate exemplars of faith (6:12). Imitation was understood to be a valuable form of learning, since those who imitated someone did not merely respond to the teacher's directives but actively shaped their lives according to a pattern (NOTE on 6:12). Previously, the author presented the wilderness generation as a negative example, but now he will introduce Abraham as a positive example. Like the listeners, Abraham had received promises from God, and like them, he was called to be faithful even when his experience called the promises into question.

---

[192]*Rhet. ad Her.* 3.2.3; cf. Cicero, *De inventione rhetorica* 2.53 §160; Aristotle, *Rhetoric* 1.9.7 1033b; deSilva, *Despising*, 306–7.

15. The Impossibility of God's Unfaithfulness (6:13–20)

6 [13]Now, when God made a promise to Abraham, since he had no one greater by whom to swear, he swore by himself, [14]saying, *I will surely bless you and give you many descendants.* [15]And thus, after persevering, he obtained what was promised. [16]Now, people swear by someone greater [than themselves], and the oath for validation brings all argument to an end. [17]Accordingly, when God intended to demonstrate as clearly as possible to the heirs of the promise the unchangeable nature of his intention, he guaranteed it with an oath, [18]so that through two unchangeable things, in which it is impossible that God should lie, we refugees have strong encouragement to hold fast the hope that lies ahead, [19]which we have as a sure and steadfast anchor for the soul, [a hope] that enters the inner region behind the curtain, [20]where Jesus has gone as a forerunner on our behalf, having become a high *priest forever according to the type of Melchizedek.*

NOTES

6:13. *Now, when God made a promise to Abraham.* God promised to bless Abraham, to give him land and many descendants, and to bless others through him (see pp. 110–12). Both blessing and descendants are important for Hebrews' argument (6:14; cf. 6:7; 7:1, 6).

since he had no one greater by whom to swear. Some Jewish writers considered it inappropriate for God to swear since God's integrity neither needed nor could have any outside guarantee, for God had no peers or superiors. Philo, however, considered it proper for God to swear in order to assure people (*Alleg. Interp.* 3.207; cf. *Sacrifices* 91–94; *Abraham* 273; *Num. Rab.* 44:8). A similar view is presupposed by Hebrews (6:17–18). On God's oath concerning descendants see Exod 32:13; Sir 44:21; cf. Acts 7:17; Luke 1:73; *Jub.* 1:7.

he swore by himself. This recalls Gen 22:16, where God says, "By myself I have sworn." God also swore concerning the wilderness generation (NOTE on Heb 3:11; cf. 3:18; 4:3) and the priest like Melchizedek (7:21; see COMMENT). Many understood that it would not have been fitting for God to swear by a lesser being, but that it was fitting for God to swear "by Himself, who is the best of things" (Philo, *Alleg. Interp.* 3.203; cf. Isa 45:23; 62:8; Jer 22:5; 44:26; 49:13; 51:14; Amos 4:2; 6:8; 8:7). A saying attributed to R. Eleazar (ca. A.D. 100) aptly observes, "Lord of all the world, if you had sworn to them by heaven and earth, I would say that even as heaven and earth pass away, so shall your oath pass away. But now you have sworn to them by your great name, and just as your great name endures forever and ever, so shall your oath endure forever and ever" (*b. Ber.* 32a).

6:14. *saying, I will surely bless you and give you many descendants.* Literally, "Surely blessing I will bless you and multiplying I will multiply you." The quotation is from Gen 22:17 (LXX) with minor variations (cf. Gen 12:2–3). The repetitions of "bless" and "multiply" in different forms correspond to Hebrew infinitive absolutes (BDF §422).

6:15. *And thus, after persevering.* "Thus" (*houtōs*) refers back to 6:14, where God's oath was quoted (cf. *houtōs* in 5:5; 6:9; 9:6, 23; Hegermann), and it shows that Abraham received what was promised (6:15b) because God was faithful to his oath (6:14). "Persevering" is the shape that life takes in between the giving and fulfillment of God's promise. Abraham endured many trials, and his faithfulness was an example for others (Jdt 8:25; 1 Macc 2:51–52; Rom 4:1–25). The consummate test was to sacrifice Isaac (Gen 22:1; Heb 11:17), but other challenges are mentioned in 11:8–16 (cf. *Jub.* 17:17–18; 19:8; *Bib. Ant.* 6:15–18; *m. 'Abot* 5:3).

he obtained what was promised. This has been taken in two ways. The second is preferable:

(**a**) Abraham obtained a confirmation of "the promise," but not the fulfillment of the promise (Lane; NRSV; NAB2; REB). This reflects the tension between 6:12, 15, which say that Abraham did obtain the promise, and 11:13, 39, which say that he did not receive what was promised during his own lifetime. Therefore, Hebrews might recall that Abraham received the promise in Gen 12:1–3 and a confirmation of the promise by the oath in Gen 22:15–17.

(**b**) Abraham obtained "what was promised" (NIV; NJB) through the birth and preservation of Isaac. In 6:12 "promise" almost certainly means "what was promised," and this usage informs 6:15. The context points out that God not only makes promises but keeps promises (Rose, "Verheissung," 69; Ellingworth). The difference between 6:12, 15 and 11:13, 39 reflects a typological understanding of the OT: the promise is fulfilled penultimately in the birth of Isaac and ultimately in resurrection in the world to come (Chrysostom). Note how the binding of Isaac anticipates future resurrection (11:19).

6:16. *Now, people swear by someone greater* [*than themselves*]. The Greek *oudenos . . . meizonos* could be neuter, indicating that people swear by "something greater," such as heaven, the Temple, the gold in the Temple, or the altar (Matt 23:16–22; cf. 5:34–36). Most translations take the expression as a masculine ("someone greater"), since oaths were frequently sworn with reference to God (e.g., Gen 31:53; Josh 9:19–20; 1 Sam 30:15; cf. Diodorus Siculus, *Library of History* 1.19.4), a king (1 Sam 17:55; 2 Sam 11:11), the genius of the emperor (*Mart. Pol.* 9.2; 10.1), or the emperor himself. For example, "I swear by Tiberius Caesar Novus Augustus Imperator, son of the deified Jupiter Liberator Augustus, that I know of no one in the village aforesaid from whom extortions have been made by the soldier . . . or his agents. If I swear truly, may it be well with me, but if falsely, the reverse" (*P. Oxy.* #240.3–9; cf. ##239.5; 251.18; 255.13–23; 257.38; 259.4–21; 260.5–17; 262.12–15; Hunt and Edgar, *Select Papyri,* 2, ##327–33).

and the oath for validation. Simply defined, an "oath is an appeal to God as a witness on matters in dispute" (Philo, *Decalogue* 86; *Alleg. Interp.* 3.205). Matters "that are in doubt are decided by an oath, insecure things made secure [*bebaioutai*], assurance given to that which lacked it" (Philo, *Dreams* 1.12; *Abra-*

ham 273). Terms based on *bebaio-* have connotations from the sphere of law and commerce (NOTES on 2:2; 3:14; 9:17; Deissmann, *Bible*, 107 n. 1). When selling a slave a person said, "I swear by the emperor Vespasianus Augustus that I have sold to Heliodora . . . the slave Sarapous who belongs to me . . . and I swear that she is my property and is not mortgaged, and has not been alienated to other persons in any respect, and that I have received the price, 640 silver drachmae, and will guarantee [*bebaiōsein*] the contract. If I swear truly, may it be well with me, but if falsely, the reverse" (*P. Oxy.* #263.4–17; cf. #246.18–26; Taubenschlag, *Law*, 229, 417, 509–11, 545–47).

brings all argument to an end. Oaths were used in disputed cases with the understanding that God would punish the wicked and vindicate the righteous party (1 Kgs 8:31). See Exod 22:10–11 and the Greco-Roman example in NOTE on Heb 6:16.

6:17. *Accordingly, when God intended to demonstrate as clearly as possible.* To demonstrate something is to make it convincing (Acts 18:28; MM, 237). People "have recourse to oaths to win belief when others deem them untrustworthy," but this is not the case with God, who is trustworthy (Philo, *Sacrifices* 93). Hebrews presupposes the idea that God used oaths as a way of accommodating the human need for assurance (Philo, *QG* 4.180; cf. *Sacrifices* 94; *Abraham* 273). The word "clearly" is comparative in form but superlative in force (cf. BDF §60).

to the heirs of the promise. The promise made to Abraham also extended to his descendants (e.g., Gen 22:17–18). Those addressed by Hebrews were counted among the descendants of Abraham (Heb 2:16) who hoped to "inherit salvation" (1:14) and so to receive God's blessing.

the unchangeable nature. This anticipates the citation of Ps 110:4, "The Lord has sworn and will not change his mind," in Heb 7:21. A testator normally had the right to alter a will: "So long as I survive I am to have power over my own property, to make any further provisions or new dispositions I choose and to revoke this will, and any such provisions shall be valid. But if I die with this will unaltered I leave . . . " (*P. Oxy.* #491.3–4; cf. ##489.4–5; 490.3–4; 492.4–5; 494.4–5). A man registered property that he had inherited from his father "in accordance with the will which he drew up in his lifetime . . . which will was unchanged at the time of his death." Then he added, "I swear by the emperor Caesar Nerva Trajanus Augustus Germanicus Dacicus that I have not lied" (*P. Oxy.* #482.34–42; cf. #75.15, 34–36). People could be released from some oaths (Gen 24:8; Josh 2:17), but others were irrevocable (3 Macc 5:42) or were made without conditions so that they affected subsequent generations (Gen 47:31; 50:25; 2 Sam 21:2, 7). Hebrews stresses the unchangeable quality of God's oath.

of his intention. Some sources said that people could resist God's intentions (Luke 7:30), and others insisted that God's intentions were firm and would ultimately prevail (Isa 46:10; cf. Ps 33:11; Prov 19:21; Acts 2:23; 13:36; Philo, *Unchangeable* 26). Here God's intention to give the blessing that he promised under oath is affirmed (Heb 6:14). See G. Schrenk, *TDNT* 1.633–35.

he guaranteed it. The verb *mesiteuein* can be used for a person who mediates a dispute or for the witness and guarantor of a legal matter. This latter use is in view here, emphasizing the validity of God's promises. God is the guarantor (*mesitēs*) of human oaths (Josephus, *Ant.* 4.133) and of his own commitments. Jesus is the guarantor of the new covenant (NOTE on Heb 8:6; cf. 9:15; 12:24). See A. Oepke, *TDNT* 4.599–601; *TLNT* 2.465–68.

with an oath. God's oath sometimes concerned land (Deut 7:8; 1 Chron 16:16; Ps 105:9). Here it concerns the promise of blessing and of many descendants (cf. Sir 44:21).

6:18. *so that through two unchangeable things.* The two things are God's promise and oath. The blessings that God promised to Abraham foreshadow the blessings that the listeners—his heirs—hope to receive (F. F. Bruce; Lane). The unchangeable quality of God's oaths is developed in 7:12–13, where the Levitical priesthood is said to have been changed, whereas Christ's priesthood is confirmed by God's irrevocable oath (7:21). Providing "two" forms of validation follows Jewish practice (Deut 17:6; 19:15; Grässer; Hegermann), although Hebrews does not emphasize this point (H.-F. Weiss, *Brief*, 364 n. 22).

impossible that God should lie. Human beings use oaths when other people deem them untrustworthy, but "God is not a human being, that he should lie" (Num 23:19–20; cf. 1 Sam 15:29; Ps 89:35; Tit 1:2; 1 John 1:10; 5:10; Philo, *Drunkenness* 139; *Moses* 1.283; *Sacrifices* 93; *1 Clem.* 27:2). This idea of divine trustworthiness was also found outside Israel's tradition (Plato, *Republic* 382E–383A; *Apology* 21B; Artemidorus Daldianus, *Onirocritica* 2.69). Because it was so widely accepted, it would have been difficult to dispute.

we refugees. The verb *katapheugein* may mean fleeing from persecution or other threat (NIV; NJB; cf. 11:34; Acts 14:6), but it also means seeking refuge (NRSV; NAB2) or laying claim to someone's protection (REB). Both aspects are suitable for this passage:

(a) Seeking refuge with a person. The weak, helpless, and dispossessed who submitted a petition for help were said to "seek refuge" with a ruler or a people, thereby placing themselves under another's protection (*TLNT* 2.275–77). Thus "seeking refuge" with God means asking for his help and protection (Ps 143:9; Philo, *Sacrifices* 70–71, 119; *Jos. Asen.* 12:7; 13:1–2). A person in danger might seek refuge with someone who served as "guarantor" of certain agreements (Diodorus Siculus, *Library of History* 4.54.7). Since God is the guarantor of the promises (Heb 6:17), listeners can turn to him for help (4:16).

(b) Seeking refuge in a place. In antiquity people often sought refuge in temples, from which no one had the right to expel "those who come seeking refuge" (*TLNT* 2.276 n. 7; cf. Euripides, *Iphigeneia at Aulis*, 911; Herodotus, *Histories* 2.113; 5.46; Tacitus, *Annals* 3.60). In Israel's tradition the altar was a place of safety (1 Kgs 1:50; 2:28), and "seek refuge" was used for the Levitical cities where people could find protection (Num 35:25–26; Deut 4:42; Philo, *Special Laws* 3.130). Hebrews associates security with the inner part of the sanctuary (Heb 6:19). Note that those addressed by Hebrews are resident aliens, foreigners, and transients on earth (11:9, 13). Here they are refugees.

have strong encouragement. Here *paraklēsis* is the "encouragement" that motivates people to "strive" faithfully (6:11), resist sin (3:13), perform good works

(10:24), and accept divine instruction (12:5). Hebrews itself is a word of *paraklēsis* ("exhortation," 13:22) that is designed to give those who are being tested (2:18; 4:15) "boldness" to persevere (3:6; 4:16; 10:19, 35).

to hold fast the hope that lies ahead. The objective reality of hope (cf. 3:6; Col 1:5) gives rise to the subjective act of hope. Although some emphasize either the objective (Attridge; Lane) or the subjective (Rissi, *Theologie*, 97), neither can be excluded (H.-F. Weiss). The verb "lie ahead" can point to what that awaits people in the future (Philo, *Preliminary Studies* 159; Braun), like a contest (Heb 12:1) or future joy (12:2). Yet the verb also has a spatial sense that helps listeners picture hope as entering the sanctuary and city that lie on the horizon of their expectations (6:20; 11:10, 16; 13:14). Although some translations urge listeners to "take hold" of their hope (NIV), it is preferable to translate *kratein* as "hold fast" (NRSV; NAB2) since the same word is used in exhortations to "hold fast" the confession (4:14; cf. 3:6, 14; 10:23).

6:19. *a sure and steadfast.* In the commercial sense one did well to invest "in business that was sure and steadfast" (Plutarch, *Cato the Elder* 21.5). In common practice "when we find one or two false statements in a book and they prove to be deliberate ones, it is evident that not a word written by such an author is any longer sure and steadfast" (Plutarch, *Mor.* 1061C). According to Hebrews, however, the Christian hope is sure and steadfast because God does not prove false, and he has provided two valid statements (Heb 6:17–18; cf. Wis 7:23; Philo, *Confusion* 106; *Heir* 314; *Preliminary Studies* 141; *Virtues* 216; *Rewards* 30).

anchor. Anchors were sometimes made of stone, but by the first century the iron anchor with two flukes was common (Pliny the Elder, *Natural History* 7.209). Attached to a rope or chain, they could be connected to either end of the boat (P. Stumpf, *RAC* 1.440–43). Hellenistic writers referred to the security provided by an anchor: The "firm grip of the anchor's teeth holds the ship fast" (Virgil, *Aeneid* 6.3–5; cf. Heliodorus, *Aethiopica* 8.6.9; Pindar, *Olympian Odes* 6.100; Propertius, *Elegies* 2.22.41; Herondas, *Prokuklis* 41). The anchor was a common metaphor in moral philosophy. The "strongest anchors" are "prudence, generosity, strength" (Pythagoras in Stobaeus, *Anthology* 1.29; cf. Plutarch, *Mor.* 446A, 782D). Some said that every "hope is an anchor" (Heliodorus, *Aethiopica* 7.25.4; cf. 4.19.9), but we "ought neither to fasten our ship to one small anchor nor our life to a single hope" (Epictetus, frg. 30). "Boldness" (Heb 3:6) was also "a sacred anchor heaved over in the greatest perils" (Plutarch, *Moralia* 815D). On the anchor as a Christian symbol see *DACL* 1.1999–2031.

for the soul. See NOTE on 4:12.

[*a hope*] *that enters.* In the first series of arguments the verb "enter" (*eiserchesthai*) was used for entering into God's promised rest (3:11, 18, 19; 4:1–11). In the second series it will be used for the high priest's entry into the holy of holies (9:12, 24–25), and this usage is anticipated in 6:19. The verb "approach" (*proserchesthai*) functions similarly for the believer's approach to God in prayer (4:16; 7:19; 10:1, 22; 11:6) and the arrival in the heavenly city (12:22). The images invite listeners to approach God now in anticipation of life to come (Scholer, *Proleptic*, 176–84).

the inner region behind the curtain. Israel's Tabernacle had one curtain at its entrance and a second curtain that divided the interior into two parts. The word "curtain" (cf. 9:3; 10:20) was consistently used in the LXX for the inner curtain and only occasionally for the outer curtain (e.g., Exod 37:5 [36:37]; 39:40). With only rare objections (Rice, "Hebrews 6:19"), interpreters understand Heb 6:19 to refer to the inner curtain. The "inner region behind the curtain" was the area that the high priest entered on the Day of Atonement (Lev 16:2, 12, 15 LXX; NOTES on 9:1–5). Some point out that the curtain could symbolize the boundary between the material and transcendent realms (e.g., Josephus, *Ant.* 3.123; Philo, *Heir* 221–29; *QE* 2.68–69; see C. R. Koester, *Dwelling*, 59–63), so that in passing through the curtain Jesus left the material world and entered God's unshakable kingdom (Heb 12:27–28). Some compare this to Gnostic (Braun; Grässer) and Jewish-mystic writings (Hofius, *Vorhang*), yet Hebrews depicts the area behind the curtain both spatially by identifying it with heaven (9:24) and temporally by connecting it with the age to come (9:6–10; cf. C. R. Koester, *Dwelling*, 152–83).

Jesus' passage through the curtain must be understood in a manifold way because the way Hebrews understands the human condition "outside the curtain" is complex. On the one hand human beings are oppressed by forces that hold them captive (2:14–15); on the other hand they are sinners who stand under God's judgment (2:17–18). Accordingly, when Jesus entered the region "behind the curtain" he made a way by which people may be freed from the powers of death and the devil, and he also made the consummate act of atonement for sin.

6:20. *forerunner.* The term *prodromos* was used for heralds or messengers (Herodotus, *Histories* 1.60; 7.203), an advance group of soldiers (4.121–22; 9.14; Aeschylus, *Seven* 80; Sophocles, *Antigone* 108; Josephus, *Ant.* 7.345; 12.314; 12.372; cf. Wis 12:8), or ships (Alciphron, *Letters* 1.14.1). It could also be used for a runner who breaks away from the others to win the race (Pollux, *Onomasticon* 3.30.148). A foreunner is similar to a "pioneer," who overcomes evil powers and makes a way for others (NOTES and COMMENT on Heb 2:10), and who is the first to complete the race of faith (12:2). The term is similar to "apostle" (3:1), which also indicated leadership (NOTES and COMMENT on 3:1). See Bauernfeind, *TDNT* 8.235.

having become a high priest forever according to the type of Melchizedek. A paraphrase of Ps 110:4 (NOTES on 5:6).

COMMENT[193]

Sharp reproofs and warnings made the first part of the digression a disturbing message (§13 COMMENT), but the author soon added words of commendation and encouragement. Now he concludes his digression by reminding them

[193]On 6:13–20 see Gordon, "Better Promises"; Hofius, "Unabänderlichkeit"; idem, *Vorhang*, 1–48, 84–96; H. Koester, "Auslegung"; Moxnes, *Theology*, 95–109; Rice, "Hebrews 6:19"; Rose, "Verheissung," 65–72; Schröger, *Verfasser*, 127–30; Swetnam, *Jesus*, 184–86; Williamson, *Philo*, 201–12; Worley, "Fleeing."

of God's unshakable faithfulness and by introducing the example of Abraham, who received what God promised after persevering in faith.[194] The themes of God's oath and the impossibility that God should lie create important theological tensions in the speech:

(a) The oath of judgment and the oath of blessing. The first series of arguments (2:10–5:10) dealt with God's oath of judgment on Moses' contemporaries, who persistently tested God, so that God said, "So I swore in my wrath, 'They shall never enter my rest' " (Ps 95:11; Heb 3:11, 13; 4:3). The fact that they perished in the wilderness was a haunting reminder of the efficacy of God's oaths. A second and more positive reference recalls that God promised by an oath to bless Abraham and give him many descendants (6:13–15). The OT showed that God kept this promise by making Abraham the father of a great nation, and listeners could count themselves among Abraham's many descendants (2:16). Because God is not unjust (6:10), listeners can trust that if he kept his oath concerning judgment, he will also keep his oath concerning blessing. The reminders of the negative oath and the positive oath have different functions—one is disturbing and the other is assuring—but they serve the same end, which is that listeners remain committed to Christ and the Christian community (4:1, 11; 6:12, 18).

(b) The impossibility of restoring apostates and the impossibility of God proving false. The word "impossible" (*adynaton*) occurs twice in the digression. First, Hebrews warns that it is impossible that God should restore apostates to repentance (6:4–8). God did not lack the ability to restore them and presumably could do so if he chose, but the author warns that God could refuse to do so (NOTE on 6:4). The second occurrence has to do with God's blessing. When God made an oath to bless someone, it was impossible that God should prove false (6:18). Together, the two "impossibilities" underscore the threat of judgment and the reality of hope. Neither statement negates the other, but through juxtaposition they achieve their effect. The warning concerning the impossibility of restoration is not designed to make listeners despair of grace, but to strive in hope. Conversely, the assurance that it is impossible for God to be faithless is not designed to make listeners complacent, but to persevere in faith.

Hebrews encourages listeners to identify with Abraham the faithful one in 6:13–20, and if they do so, they will be in a position to continue identifying with Abraham in 7:1–10, where Abraham's relationship to Melchizedek foreshadows a Christian's relationship to Christ. Those who recognize God's commitment to the oath he made to Abraham are well-prepared to recognize that God must be equally unfailing in his oath to raise up a priest like Melchizedek (Ps 110:4; Heb 7:21). Some might find it improbable simply to compare Jesus with Melchizedek, but the author prepares for his comparison of the two figures by setting the question on a different footing. Hebrews implies that given God's

---

[194]Several catchwords connect 6:13–20 to the previous paragraph: "promise" (6:12, 13, 15, 17), "perseverance" and "persevere" (6:12, 15), and "inherit" and "heirs" (6:12, 17). See Vanhoye, *La structure*, 120–21.

faithfulness to his oath to Abraham, it would be improbable to think that God would *fail* to keep his oath to raise up a priest like Melchizedek. If one can expect God to keep his oath, it is not so strange for Christian listeners to think that God fulfills it in Christ.

Structurally, the argument unfolds in two phases that bridge the world of the OT and the world of the listeners, as noted above:[195]

(a) The oath that God made to Abraham (6:13–15) takes the listeners to the early period of Israel's history, reminding them of God's faithfulness in the past and of the perseverance shown by their ancestor in the faith.

(b) The place of oaths in common legal practice provides a way for the author to convey God's faithfulness to heirs of the promise who live centuries after Abraham (6:16–20). By weaving images from Israel's ancestral period together with those of law courts from the listeners' own time, the author connects Abraham's story with the listeners' experience. The same pattern persists as the author links the anchor, which was familiar to those dwelling along the Mediterranean coast, with the inner part of the Tabernacle that Moses had established in the desert (6:19). Similarly, the author calls Jesus a "forerunner," using a common Greco-Roman image, while connecting it to Israel's high priest entering the holy place (6:20).

a. God's Oath and Abraham's Perseverance (6:13–15)

Abraham is cited as an example of those "who through faith and perseverance inherit what is promised" (6:12), but God is actually the focus of attention. The author "lays stress not upon the human quality" of steadfast faith "but upon the divine basis for this undaunted reliance," which is "the word of God" (Moffatt, *Critical*, 85). God gave his word in the form of "a promise" concerning the future (6:13a; see pp. 110–12), and when God made the promise he "had no one greater by whom to swear" (6:13b). God is the one "for whom all things and through whom all things exist" (2:10), and if God proves to be unfaithful, no higher power can force him to meet his obligations. Yet Hebrews emphasizes that God "swore by himself" (6:13c), and in so doing God binds himself to keep his promise. Because God's own honor is at stake, listeners can be assured that he will keep his word.[196]

The content of God's oath, which was given after the binding of Isaac (Gen 22:17),[197] was, "I will surely bless you and give you many descendants" (Heb 6:14). For Abraham, God's blessing was connected to a great name, many descendants, and prosperity (Gen 12:2–3; 17:16; 24:1), while for the listeners,

[195]Vanhoye (*La structure*, 120–23) notes that the section unfolds in two parallel parts (6:13–15 / 6:17–20) with the comment about human oaths as the connecting link (6:16). This commentary includes 6:16 with what follows, since it begins connecting the situation of Abraham with that of the listeners.

[196]On God's zeal to maintain his reputation see Exod 32:11–13; Num 14:13–16; Isa 48:11. On social factors see deSilva, *Despising*, 241.

[197]On Gen 22 in ancient literature see Swetnam, *Jesus*, 23–85; Daly, *Christian*, 175–86.

God's blessing means receiving God's favorable judgment and the good things that belong to salvation (Heb 6:7, 9). Abraham received what was promised only after persevering for a time (6:15), and the author maintains that the same will be true for the listeners. Abraham's circumstances often called God's promise into question. Sarah's age and barrenness seemed to preclude childbearing (11:11–12)—"they were nearer the grave than the conjugal bed" (Calvin)—but God affirmed his promise (Gen 15:4–5; 17:15–16) and gave them a son (Gen 21:5). God's command to sacrifice the boy contradicted the promise again (Heb 11:17), yet God preserved the boy and reaffirmed that Abraham would have many descendants (Gen 22:17). Hebrews finds this example compelling because Abraham did not act on the basis of the senses—which told him that God's promise would not be fulfilled—but on the basis of the promise itself. The question for those addressed by Hebrews was whether they would fall away like Moses' generation (3:7–4:13) or whether they would follow Abraham and remain confident of the promises, appearances notwithstanding.

b. God's Oath and the Listeners' Perseverance (6:16–20)

The scene shifts from Abraham to the ordinary world in which the listeners live, as the author makes the observation that people swear by someone greater than themselves (6:16a).[198] Those who made oaths made themselves liable to the judgment of a higher power, such as God or the emperor, if they proved false to their commitment. Thus no one "would be willing to commit perjury, as he would be afraid of punishment from the gods and discredit with men" (Ps.-Aristotle, *Rhet. ad Alex.* 17.1432a).[199] An oath could be used for validation, which commonly meant that a seller agreed to defend the validity of the sale against any who disputed the recipient's claim to the property (NOTE on 6:16). Hebrews applies this practice to inheritance, identifying the listeners as the heirs who expect to receive the blessing God promised to Abraham (6:17a; cf. 6:7; 1:14). The problem was that instead of being blessed, they had been dispossessed (10:32–34; 13:13), and this experience raised the possibility that God's promise had been invalidated.

The author insists that God's promise to bless Abraham and his heirs was unchangeable (6:17b). This distinguishes God's practice from ordinary human practice, because people who made promises to their heirs usually reserved the

[198]Objections to taking oaths are attested among early Christians (Matt 5:33–37; Jas 5:12), Pythagoreans (Diogenes Laertius, *Lives* 8.22), and the Essenes (Josephus, *J.W.* 2.135). Rash oaths sometimes had disastrous results (e.g., Judg 11:30–40; 1 Sam 14:24–30). Those who made an oath unnecessarily cast suspicion on their own trustworthiness. Therefore, one did well to ask whether something was important enough to warrant an oath and whether the person swearing was pure enough to make an oath without sacrilege (Philo, *Decalogue* 93). One who made an oath was bound to perform it (Lev 19:12; Num 30:3; Deut 23:23; Ps 50:14); therefore, people were cautioned against making frequent oaths (Eccl 5:4–6; Sir 23:9; Philo, *Decalogue* 92). On Philo's understanding of the divine oath see Williamson, *Philo*, 201–12; Moxnes, *Theology*, 141–46.

[199]"Scorn for the sanctity of an oath has its own sufficient avenger in the god" (Justinian, *Code* 4.1.2 in *RomCiv* 2.16, n. 28).

legal right to change them (NOTE on 6:17).[200] Two assumptions inform the author's word of assurance. One is that the oath made to Abraham also applies to the listeners, who could hope to share in the blessing that God promised to their forefather (2:16). The other assumption is that listeners understood the force of an oath on the basis of common experience. Since God guaranteed his promise with an oath (6:17c), they could be sure that God would not renege on his commitment.

In common practice oaths were sometimes challenged by denigrating the character of the person making the oath (Ps.-Aristotle, *Rhet. ad Alex.* 17.1432b). Yet listeners would have found it difficult to discredit God's oath since it was widely understood that "it is impossible that God should lie" (6:18). Appeal to such a common belief was valuable in persuasive speech, since speakers assumed that people could more readily understand and apply generally familiar ideas to the specific matter at hand (*Rhet. ad Her.* 4.17 §25). Moreover, claiming that God had sworn falsely would have been considered impious.[201] The author implies that those who give up the Christian hope are saying, in effect, that God has lied. Since listeners would almost certainly not want to make this claim, the passage presses them to remain faithful.

Rather than issuing another warning at this point, the author offers strong encouragement to those whom he calls "refugees" (6:18c). Although some of the listeners had houses and resources (13:1–6), they were not fully accepted by society and no earthly city was truly their home (13:14). Like Abraham, these refugees were resident aliens, foreigners, and transients (NOTES and COMMENT on 11:9, 13). Refugees usually sought a safe place to rest and live, and Hebrews declares that listeners have a hope that is "a sure and steadfast anchor for the soul" (6:19a). Travelers lower an anchor when a ship nears land (cf. Acts 27:27–29), and Hebrews' imagery suggests that the listeners' hope has already been secured at their port of destination. To be sure, they have not disembarked at God's place of rest (Heb 4:1–11) in the heavenly Jerusalem (12:22–24), but the anchor has been planted, and they are no longer at the mercy of the winds on the open sea. The trouble is that they seem to be in danger of drifting from their Christian moorings (2:1b) and must therefore hold fast (2:1a).[202]

Shifting metaphors, the author connects hope with entering "the inner region behind the curtain" (6:19b), drawing on traditions concerning Israel's desert sanctuary. In one sense the image is encouraging. Refugees often sought safety in temples, and by speaking of a hope that enters the region behind the curtain, the author offers listeners a way to envision security in God's own sanctuary (NOTE on in 6:18). Tension arises, however, because the innermost part of God's sanctuary was closed to everyone except the high priest; unauthorized

[200]On the revocation of wills see Llewelyn, *New Documents*, 6.41–47.

[201]Plato censured Homer for claiming that God had sent a "lying dream" to Agamemnon (*Republic* 382E–383A).

[202]Chrysostom compares Christians to boats that appear to be buffeted by the waves, but are actually securely anchored.

entry would result in death (Lev 16:2, 13). Passing through the Tabernacle curtain could be appealing or threatening, depending on the circumstances.

The author heightens the tension by identifying Christ with the secular title "forerunner" (6:20a), which was used for the one who came first in a military campaign or race (NOTE on 6:20). In either case, a group of soldiers or athletes would have followed behind the forerunner. The imagery is striking because neither athletes nor soldiers on active duty were permitted to enter or to provide access to the sanctuary's inner chamber. Yet together, these images convey something of the manifold significance of Jesus' death and exaltation. As high priest Jesus passed through the curtain to make atonement for others, while as forerunner he opened a way for others to follow. Rhetorically, this helps to heighten the listeners' appreciation for what Jesus has done.[203]

Jesus' priesthood is distinctive in that it resembles that of Melchizedek (6:20b). A paraphrase of Ps 110:4 first signals that the digression is ending and that the author will resume the topic that he introduced in Heb 5:10. Furnishing such a signal was good rhetorical practice (Cicero, *De oratore* 2.77 §§311–12; 3.53 §203). Second, the author will read the story of Abraham and Melchizedek (Gen 14:17–20) through the lens of this psalm, which says that the one at God's right hand (Ps 110:1) is a priest after the type of Melchizedek (110:4). The same type of biblical interpretation also occurs at the end of the next major digression, where the author introduces Hab 2:4 (Heb 10:38) as the lens through which the narrative of the OT will be read in Heb 11 (§29 COMMENT).

B. Second Series: Jesus' Suffering is the Sacrifice that Enables Others to Approach God

16. ARGUMENTS OF SECOND SERIES (7:1–10:39)

COMMENT

Declarations that Jesus is "a priest forever according to the type of Melchizedek" concluded the first series of arguments and the digression that followed (5:6, 10; 6:20). The second series of arguments develops that theme by presenting Jesus as the fulfillment of God's promise (Ps 110:4) and by contrasting Jesus' ministry with that of the Levitical order. Differences between the earthly and heavenly sanctuaries, the old and new covenants, flesh and conscience, and the repeated sacrifices of animals and Jesus' singular sacrifice enable the author to show what it means for Jesus to have suffered death "for everyone" (2:9; cf. Attridge, "Uses,"

---

[203]Speakers in antiquity often stressed deeds that the hero of the speech was the first or only one to perform. Preference was given to actions performed for the sake of others (Aristotle, *Rhetoric* 1.9.38; Quintilian, *Inst.* 3.7.16). On the multiple aspects of Jesus' work see NOTE on the curtain in 6:19b and §8 COMMENT *a–d*.

5–9). The arguments continue to show how Jesus' death and exaltation bring about the realization of God's designs for people (pp. 87–90).

The central section begins at 7:1, after the first major digression, and it continues to 10:39 at the end of the second major digression. The discussion of Christ's priestly ministry in 7:1–10:25 can be divided into two large sections. The first (7:1–28) demonstrates that Christ is the priest after the type of Melchizedek. Psalm 110:4, which was quoted at the end of Heb 6, provides the lens through which the narrative about Abraham and Melchizedek is read in Heb 7:1–10 and it gives the basis for the argument that Christ's priesthood is superior to the Levitical priesthood and Mosaic Law in 7:11–28. The second large section (8:1–10:18) argues that Christ the high priest offered a sacrifice that brings atonement and establishes a new covenant. Formally, this block is framed by references to Christ being seated at God's right hand (8:1–2; 10:11–14), and by quotations from Jeremiah's new covenant oracle (8:8–12; 10:16–17).[204] In content, this section repeatedly refers to the covenant, the sanctuary, the offering of sacrifices, and the singularity of Christ's sacrificial death.[205] The final paragraph (10:19–25) is a kind of peroration to the section, drawing together themes from previous arguments (§26 COMMENT). A digression (10:26–39) makes the transition between the second and third series of arguments.

The arguments in this section are complex,[206] but can be understood in terms of topics that alternate like footsteps along a path (cf. Gourgues, "Remarques"):

A. PART 1 (8:1–13)
   1. Jesus' ministry and Levitical ministry (8:1–6)
   2. The promise of the new covenant (8:7–13)
B. PART 2 (9:1–28)
   1. Jesus' ministry and Levitical ministry (9:1–14)
   2. The making of the new covenant (9:15–28)
C. PART 3 (10:1–18)
   1. Jesus' sacrifice and Levitical sacrifices (10:1–10)
   2. Jesus' sacrifice and the new covenant (10:11–18)

---

[204]Vanhoye identified 8:1–9:28 as a section, proposing that the references to "offering" (*prospherein*) in 8:3 and 9:28 create an *inclusio* (*La structure*, 139). This seems unlikely since the verb occurs frequently throughout the section (see the next note) and related themes continue into 10:1–18. For critiques see Gourgues, "Remarques," 26–31; Attridge, "Uses," 1–4. Others who take 7:1–10:18 as a section and 8:1–10:18 as a major subsection include Swetnam, "Form 7–13," and Grässer, *Hebräer*, 2.77–78.

[205]A "covenant" (*diathēkē*) is mentioned in 8:6, 8, 9, 10; 9:4, 15, 16, 17, 20; 10:16) and only three times elsewhere; a "tent" (*skēnē*) is mentioned in 8:2, 5; 9:2, 3, 6, 8, 11, 21) and only twice elsewhere; the "sanctuary" (*ta hagia* or *ton hagion*) is mentioned in 8:2; 9:1, 8, 12, 24, 25; cf. 9:2–3; 10:19) and only once elsewhere; "offering" (*prospherein*) is mentioned in 8:3, 4; 9:7, 9, 14, 25, 28; 10:1, 2, 8, 11, 12) and eight times elsewhere. Terms for "once" are often used for death in this section (*hapax* in 9:7, 26, 27, 28; 10:2; *ephapax* in 9:12; 10:10) and only once in this sense elsewhere (7:27).

[206]A number of scholars propose a concentric arrangement (Vanhoye, *La structure*, 139–61; cf. Ellingworth, *Epistle*, 397–98; H.-F. Weiss, *Brief*, 428–30; Casalini, *Agli*, 245–46; cf. Bénétreau, *L'Épître*, 2.51). For critiques see Gourgues, "Remarques," 26–31; Attridge, "Uses," 1–4; Lane, *Hebrews*, 1.202–4

The author develops a complex understanding of the death of Christ in terms of atonement, covenant, and sacrifice. He fuses elements from several key biblical texts: the new covenant oracle in Jer 31:31–34, the Day of Atonement ritual in Lev 16:1–22, and the covenant sacrifice in Exod 24:3–8. No one of these OT texts includes all three of the elements noted above, but the author brings them together in order to show what it means for Jesus to have suffered death on behalf of everyone:

(a) Atonement. Jeremiah's oracle concerning the new covenant promised that God would be merciful with respect to the sins of the people (Jer 31:34), but it did not identify the means by which mercy would be given. Hebrews answers this question by depicting Jesus' death and exaltation in terms of the Day of Atonement ritual, arguing that since Christ's self-offering removes sin, it provides the forgiveness promised under the new covenant (Heb 8:7–13 and 9:1–14).

(b) Covenant. Jeremiah's oracle promised that God would make a new covenant with his people, but it does not identify the means by which the covenant would be inaugurated. Hebrews posits a parallel between the making of the old and new covenants. Since Exod 24:6–8 said that the first covenant was made through a sacrifice, the author concludes that the new covenant would also be established through a sacrifice—Christ's self-sacrifice (Heb 8:7–13 and 9:15–22).

(c) Sacrifice. The Day of Atonement ritual in Lev 16 did not inaugurate a covenant, and the covenant ceremony in Exod 24 did not make atonement, but both involved sacrifice. Once Christ's death is understood to be a sacrifice, the implications of the sacrifice can be understood in a twofold manner: making atonement (9:1–14) and inaugurating a covenant (9:15–22).

Presented schematically the relationships are as follows:

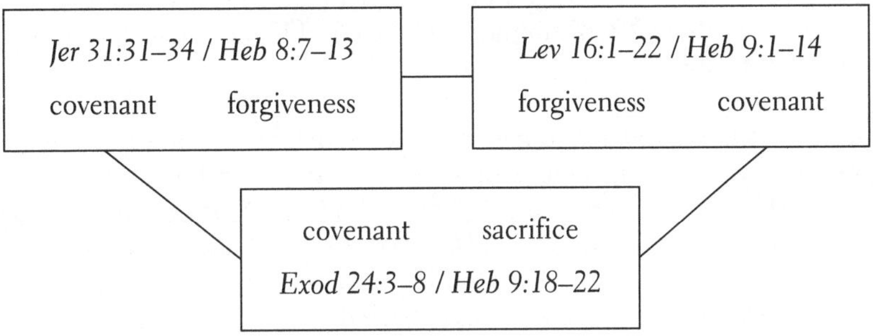

The transitional section (10:26–39) that follows these arguments digresses on the theme of the Day of the Lord that is mentioned in 10:25. As in the other digressions that make transitions between sections (2:1–4; 5:11–6:20; 12:25–27), the author calls for attention, warns about the dangers of neglecting or spurning the word of God, and encourages listeners to persevere. The mention of "faith" in the quotation of Hab 2:3–4 that concludes the digression (Heb 10:38) provides the interpretive lens through which Israel's history will be perceived in the new section that follows (11:1–12:24).

17. PRIESTHOOD OF MELCHIZEDEK (7:1–10)

7 [1]Now this *Melchizedek—king of Salem, priest of God Most High, who met
Abraham when he returned from the defeat of the kings and blessed him,* [2]*the one
to whom Abraham apportioned a tithe of everything*—is first interpreted as "king
of righteousness" and then also as king of Salem, which is "king of peace"; [3]with-
out father, without mother, without genealogy, having no beginning of days nor
end of life, but being made to resemble the Son of God, he remains a priest for
all time.

[4]See how great is *this one to whom Abraham* the patriarch *gave a tithe* of the
spoils! [5]Those of the descendants of Levi who receive the priestly office have, according to the Law, a command to receive tithes from the people, that is, from
their brethren, even though they have come from the loins of Abraham, [6]but the
one who does not have their genealogy received a tithe from Abraham and
blessed the one who had the promises. [7]Now without any dispute the lesser is
blessed by the superior; [8]indeed, in the one case people who die receive tithes,
but in the other it is someone about whom it is attested that he lives. [9]One might
even venture to say that Levi, who receives tithes, actually paid a tithe through
Abraham, [10]for he was still in the loins of his forebear when Melchizedek met
him.

NOTES

7:1–2a. The previous verse (6:20) identified Jesus as a priest after the type of Melchizedek by paraphrasing Ps 110:4. Here the author turns to Gen 14:17–20, the only other reference to Melchizedek in the OT. The author will read the Genesis story in light of Ps 110:4. Instead of quoting the biblical passage, the author summarizes the LXX version of it. The parts of Genesis that appear in Hebrews are in italics:

> Gen 14 [17]*After* [*Abram's*] *return from the defeat* of Chedorlaomer and *the kings*
> who were with him, the king of Sodom *went out to meet* him at the Valley of
> Shaveh (that is, the King's Valley). [18]And *Melchizedek king of Salem* brought
> out bread and wine; he was *priest of God Most High.* [19]*And he blessed him* and
> said, "Blessed be Abram by God Most High, maker of heaven and earth; [20]and
> blessed be God Most High, who has delivered your enemies into your hand!"
> And *Abram gave him a tithe of everything.*

Hebrews does not mention that Melchizedek "brought out bread and wine" (Gen 14:18), unlike later Christian interpreters who pointed out that Melchizedek offered bread and wine during his encounter with Abraham just as Jesus did at the Last Supper (see p. 26). The author would probably have alluded to the Lord's Supper here if it was a central aspect of his community's practice (Isaacs, *Sacred*, 151), yet its omission does not necessarily mean that the author was antisacramental (Grässer). The author may have omitted any mention of the bread and wine to avoid the impression that Melchizedek served Abraham (Williamson, *Philo*, 445; Ellingworth, "Like," 261), but the simplest explanation is that he did not mention the bread and wine because they were not germane to his argument (Lindars, *Theology*, 77; see pp. 127–29).

Now this Melchizedek. Melchizedek stands outside the mainstream of Israel's priesthood. Patristic interpreters considered him to be the harbinger of a priesthood to Gentiles, and since Melchizedek was both priest and king, popes and emperors alike cited him as precedent for expanding their authority (see p. 32). Hebrews' ascribes traits of deity to Melchizedek (NOTES on 7:3), leading to controversy about the possibility that Melchizedek was superior to Christ (see pp. 24–25). Hebrews presupposes traditions about the meanings of the names "Melchizedek" and "Salem" (NOTES on 7:2), but it is not evident that he either appropriated or rejected other views of Melchizedek, as some have suggested:

(**a**) Melchizedek as a Human Figure. Some remember Melchizedek as a human priest-king (1QapGen XXII, 12–25; Philo, *Preliminary Studies* 99; *Abraham* 235; Josephus, *Ant.* 1.179–82; Ps.-Eupolemos [*OTP* 2.880]; cf. *Jub.* 13:25, which recalls the incident but has a lacuna in the text). Josephus said that Melchizedek inaugurated temple worship in Jerusalem, thereby making Melchizedek a precursor of Levitical practice, rather than an alternative to it as in Heb 7:11–14 (*J.W.* 6.438). A rabbinic tradition says that Melchizedek turned over the priesthood to Abraham, who becomes the "priest forever" mentioned in Ps 110:4 (*b. Ned.* 32b; *Lev. Rab.* 25:6). Targums and rabbinic sources regularly identify Melchizedek with Shem the son of Noah. This could be done because Gen 11:10 says that Shem lived for five hundred years after the birth of his son, which meant that he outlived Abraham by thirty-five years (Jerome, *Hebrew Questions* 14:18–19; Horton, *Melchizedek*, 115).

Hebrews' insistence that Melchizedek has no father, mother, or genealogy (Heb 7:3) runs counter to tendencies in Jewish exegesis (Hegermann; Willi, "Melchizedek"), but it is not clear that Hebrews was written with these traditions in mind (Petuchowski, "Controversial"). Because extant sources that identify Melchizedek with Shem are later than Hebrews, interpreters more commonly propose that Jewish sources gave Melchizedek a genealogy in order to counter Christian claims (e.g., Bowker, *Targums*, 196–99). Others, however, ascribe the rabbinic identification of Shem and Melchizedek to the tendency to exalt Shem rather than to Jewish apologetics (Hayward, "Shem").

(**b**) Melchizedek as More than Human (Attridge; Pearson, *Gnosticism*, 108–23; Gieschen, "Different"). Melchizedek is connected with reason (*logos*) and virtue in Philo's writings, but he is not a heavenly figure. Philo called Melchizedek "self-learned and self-taught," which are traits associated with perfection in virtue (*Preliminary Studies* 99; cf. *Migration* 29; *Alleg. Interp.* 3.79–82; Kobelski, *Melchizedek*, 117). Yet instead of pointing to the OT's silence concerning Melchizedek's parents, which is important in Hebrews, Philo focuses on Melchizedek's gifts of bread and wine, which are not mentioned in Hebrews. Philo identifies Melchizedek with reason (*logos*), which Philo calls God's "firstborn" (*Dreams* 1.215), and some suggest that this view lies behind the high view of Melchizedek in Heb 7:3 (Thompson, *Beginnings*, 119; Dunn, *Christology*, 53–54). Yet for Philo, Melchizedek's connection with reason in no way distinguishes him from Levitical priests, since they too represent reason (*Giants* 52; *Flight* 108; *Heir* 201; *Dreams* 1.215), whereas in Hebrews the traits of Melchizedek set him apart from Levitical priests.

In the Dead Sea text 11QMelch, Melchizedek is an agent of divine judgment, and he may be identified with the "gods" (*'elōhim*) of Ps 82:1. Since the redemption he brings includes expiation for sins (11QMelch II, 8), some insist that he plays a priestly role (Puech, "Notes," 511–13; Pearson, "Figure," 112), yet 11QMelch does not actually ascribe sacral functions to Melchizedek (Kobelski, *Melchizedek*, 55, 64–65; Gianotto, *Melchisedek*, 82). Hebrews identifies Christ as the agent of eschatological deliverance from the powers of evil (Heb 2:14–15), but not in any of the passages that deal with Melchizedek. Unlike Hebrews, 11QMelch does not allude to Gen 14:17–20 or Ps 110:4, and it does not call Melchizedek a priest. There is little reason to think that Hebrews was informed by material like that found in this Dead Sea text (Kobelski, *Melchizedek*, 127–29; Horton, *Melchizedek*, 64–82, 155; Hurst, *Epistle*, 52–60).

Melchizedek is clearly a priest in *2 Enoch* 71–72. This text relates that the wife of Nir the priest, who was Noah's brother, miraculously became pregnant late in life (71:1–11). She soon died, and from her corpse was born Melchizedek, who was destined to be head of the priests in the future (71:21, 29, 37). Therefore, before the great flood Melchizedek was preserved in paradise (72:9). Given the circumstances of Melchizedek's birth, one might conclude that he had no mother or father (Heb 7:3a; Attridge, *Epistle*, 193), and given his preservation in paradise one might conclude that his life had no end (Heb 7:3c). Yet his life did have a beginning, and his genealogy from Noah was important (*2 Enoch* 71:20). This account of Melchizedek also stresses his importance in maintaining a priestly line, an idea not evident in Hebrews (Gieschen, "Different").

Despite the lack of direct connections between Hebrews and the sources noted above, some scholars argue that these texts represent a trajectory of thought that provides background for Hebrews. Gnostic sources are used to support this hypothesis. The Nag Hammadi text that identifies Melchizedek with Jesus Christ, who was raised from death after sacrificing himself, almost certainly depends on Hebrews (*Melchizedek*, NHC IX, 1 1, 4–6, 12, 15–16), but it alludes to warfare in a way that might suggest that it draws on the tradition reflected in 11QMelch. Later sources like *2 Jeu* and *Pistis Sophia* refer to a nonpriestly redeemer called Melchizedek, who may represent a late development of noncanonical traditions (Pearson, "Figure"; Attridge, *Epistle*, 191--95; cf. Dunn, *Partings*, 210–11). See pp. 24–25.

Arguments that Hebrews relied on a trajectory similar to these traditions are finally not persuasive. Neither Philo's interpretation of Melchizedek as divine Reason nor the legends concerning Melchizedek in *2 Enoch* are taken up in the other sources; they are independent treatments of the OT rather than variations of a common tradition. The Dead Sea and Nag Hammadi texts do associate a figure known as Melchizedek with the defeat of God's enemies, but otherwise have little in common. Since holy-war motifs appear in various ancient writings, they provide little evidence of a connection between these texts. The Nag Hammadi tractate's reliance on Hebrews seems clearer than its reliance on 11QMelch or something like it (Grässer, *Hebräer,* 2.19–20). Hebrews does ascribe to Melchizedek certain traits that were associated with deity in the Greco-Roman world (NOTES on 7:3), but there is not sufficient evidence to say that he did so on the basis of earlier traditions concerning Melchizedek (Gianotto, *Melchisedek,* 141–44; Manzi, *Melchisedek,* 258–71).

king of Salem. Salēm is the LXX's transliteration of the Hebrew place-name *Shālēm*, which many identified with Jerusalem (1QapGen 22:13; Josephus *J.W.* 6.438; *Ant.* 1.180; Tgs. to Gen 14:18; cf. Jerome, *Hebrew Questions* 14:18–19). The association was natural because the word Salem is included in Jeru*salem* and Abraham's meeting with Melchizedek took place at the King's Valley, which was in Jerusalem (Gen 14:17; cf. 2 Sam 18:18; Ps 76:2 MT; Josephus, *Ant.* 7.243; Stern, *GLAJJ* 3.149). Therefore, listeners would probably have associated Salem with Jerusalem rather than with Shechem (Jer 48:5 LXX [41:5 MT]; Jdt 4:4; cf. Gen 33:18 LXX; Ps.-Eupolemos [*OTP* 2.880]) or with the Salim near Aenon (John 3:23; cf. Jerome, *Ep.* 73.7).

priest of God Most High. Melchizedek is the first person to be called a "priest" in the OT. The God he served was called the "Most High" (*ho hypsistos*), which is a translation of the Hebrew *'ēl 'elyōn*. Used for various high gods (G. Bertram, *TDNT* 8.614–20; BAGD, 850), the expression was commonly used in the LXX and other Jewish and Christian sources for the God of Israel (e.g., Pss 57:2; 78:56; Sir 7:9, 15; 9:15; *Jos. Asen.* 8:9; 11:7, 9; Philo, *Flaccus* 46; Josephus, *Ant.* 16.163; Luke 1:76; Acts 7:48). When Abraham spoke of "God Most High, maker of heaven and earth" (Gen 14:22), listeners would have understood that he spoke of the God of Israel, who dwelt "on high" (Heb 1:3; 7:26; 8:1).

when he returned from the defeat of the kings. Four kings from the east invaded Canaan, seizing supplies and Abraham's nephew Lot. Abraham defeated them, recovering the goods and the captives (Gen 14:1–16). The "defeat" is called a *kopē* (Gen 14:17 LXX; Heb 7:1), which connoted being cut down (Josh 10:20; Jdt 15:7) like grass in a field (*P. Oxy.* ##280.17; 499.15).

and blessed him. Melchizedek said, "Blessed be Abram by God Most High, maker of heaven and earth" (Gen 14:19). On blessing see NOTES on Heb 6:7, 14.

7:2. *the one to whom Abraham apportioned a tithe of everything.* Genesis 14:20 reads "he gave him a tithe" without identifying the subject of the verb (Jerome, *Ep.* 73.6). Some leave the subject ambiguous (*Tgs. Neof., Onq., Ps.-J* to Gen 14:20; Jerome, *Ep.* 73.6), but Hebrews and other texts identify Abraham as the one giving the tithe (Josephus, *Ant.* 1.181; 1QapGen 22.17). On tithes see NOTES on 7:4–5.

is first interpreted. The meanings of names are frequently explained in the Old and New Testaments, including personal names (Gen 17:5; 25:26; 32:28; Matt 1:21; 16:18) and place-names (Gen 21:31; 28:17, 19; John 9:7). Both Jews and non-Jews were intrigued with names (Philo, *Preliminary Studies* 44; Cicero, *De natura deorum* 2.25–27 §§64–69; Plautus, *Persian* 4.4 §620). The author of Hebrews may not have known much Hebrew since he relied on the LXX (p. 116) and simply cited common explanations of the names in Heb 7:2.

as "king of righteousness." The first part of the name "Melchizedek" (*melchi-*) corresponds to the Hebrew word for "king" (*melek*) with the first person singular suffix. The last part (*-zedek*) corresponds to the Hebrew word for "righteous" (*ṣedeq*). The similar name Adoni-zedek (Josh 10:1) may have meant "my king is Zedek," with "Zedek" as the name of a deity, or "my king is righteous" (Kobelski, *Melchizedek*, 55). People in the first century took the two parts of the name to be in a genitive relationship: "king of righteousness" (Philo, *Alleg. Interp.* 79; Josephus, *J.W.* 6.438; *Ant.* 1.180). Righteousness had messianic associations in some OT texts (Isa 9:7; Jer 23:5; 33:15), and Hebrews depicted the exalted Christ as a righteous king (Heb 1:8–9).

"king of peace." The Hebrew word "Salem," which is transliterated in the LXX, was originally a place-name. Hebrews equated it with the Hebrew word *shālôm*, which means "peace" (cf. Philo, *Alleg. Interp.* 79; Ps 76:2 [75:3 LXX]). Peace had messianic associations in some OT texts (Isa 9:6; Zech 9:9–10).

7:3. *without father, without mother.* The series of words formed with the *a-* prefix could indicate that the parents' names simply were not recorded (Peshitta; Lane), yet the words have two markedly different types of connotations. On a human level they imply disgrace, but on another level they suggest divinity:

(**a**) Human terms. To have "no father" generally meant that the father's identity was unknown. When papyri give a person's name followed by "father unknown" (*apatōr*) and the mother's name (MM, 54–55), the implication is that the person is illegitimate (Plutarch, *Mor.* 288E), perhaps one of the "homeless, fatherless outcasts" (Sophocles, *Trachiniae* 300). To have "no mother" (*amatōr*) often meant that one's mother was of very low social status (Euripides, *Ion* 837; Herodotus, *Histories* 4.154), which would have disqualified someone from the high priesthood (Josephus, *Ant.* 13.292; cf. *T. Mos.* 5:4). A person with "no mother, no father" would be a foundling, an orphan (Euripides, *Ion* 109), or an illegitimate child (Cicero, *De oratore* 2.64 §257). Some late sources say that Melchizedek was the son of a prostitute (cf. Epiphanius, *Panarion* 55.7.1) or Canaanite (cf. Greer, *Captain*, 144).

(**b**) Divine terms. These same descriptives could be used for divine generation. The God of Israel was "without father, without mother, ungenerated" (*Apoc. Ab.* 17:10). Apollo was said to be "self-existent, taught by no one, without mother, undisturbed" (Lactantius, *Divine Institutes* 1.7.1). Motherless deities included Nike (Philo, *Creation* 100), Athena (Euripides, *Persian Maidens* 666; Philo, *Alleg. Interp.* 1.15), and Aphrodite (Plato, *Symposium* 180E). Hephaistos was fatherless (Pollux, *Onomasticon* 3.26), and Hermes had neither mother nor father (Lactantius, *Divine Institutes* 1.7.2; 4.8.5; 4.13.2–4). Philo connected Sarah with virtue, which is motherless (*Drunkenness* 61; *Heir* 62; cf. *QG* 4.68; *Heir* 170; *Decalogue* 102; *Moses* 2.210). Divine connotations are appropriate for the exalted Christ, the priest like Melchizedek. See Neyrey, "Without," 446–48; Williamson, *Philo*, 20–23; G. Schrenk, *TDNT* 5.1019–21.

without genealogy. The word *agenealogētos* may have been coined by the author (see p. 96). The expression could indicate that Melchizedek's ancestry was unrecorded (Peshitta; Lane), but other connotations are significant:

(a) Human terms. The lack of a known genealogy was a liability for Israel's priests, who were to be descendants of Levi (Num 3:10, 15–16) through proper marriages (Lev 21:7, 13–15; Ezek 44:22; Josephus, *Ag. Ap.* 1.30–36). Those who could not demonstrate their genealogy were disqualified (Ezra 2:62; Neh 7:63–65; 2 Chron 31:17–19; Josephus, *Ant.* 11.71). Some viewed the absence of genealogy more positively, as Philo did by noting that the Scriptures list Noah's virtues rather than his ancestors (Gen 6:9; *Abraham* 31). Hebrews, however, takes silence to mean that genealogy cannot be the defining trait of a priest. If the lack of genealogy did not bar Melchizedek from priesthood, then it should not disqualify Jesus.

(b) Divine terms. Greco-Roman writers said that a true deity was "unbegotten" (Plutarch, *Pelopidas* 16; *Mor.* 359C; cf. *Apoc. Ab.* 17:11) or "uncreated" (Philo, *Alleg. Interp.* 3.101; *Migration* 91; *Decalogue* 60, 64; Josephus, *Ag. Ap.* 2.167). For a figure to have "no beginning of days nor end of life" (Heb 7:3b) and no genealogy suggests that he was truly God and not merely a divinized mortal. See Neyrey, "Without."

having no beginning of days nor end of life. It could be said that Enoch (Gen 5:24; Heb 11:5) and Elijah (2 Kgs 2:11) had no "end of life" since they were taken directly to heaven, but their lives did have beginnings. Life without a beginning or ending could be predicated only of God (Ps 90:2; Plutarch, *Mor.* 393A). Jesus of Nazareth lived for a limited period of time on earth (Heb 5:7), but the Son of God existed before the creation of the world and will endure after the world's end (1:2, 10–12). See Neyrey, "Without."

but being made to resemble the Son of God. The verb "made like" indicates close relationship. Jesus "became like" (*homoioun*) other human beings in order to redeem them (2:17), and Melchizedek was "made to resemble" (*aphomoioun*) the Son of God in order to foreshadow the traits of the exalted Christ. The direction of thought is important: the Son of God is not like Melchizedek; rather, Melchizedek is like the Son of God, who is the principal reality (Bengel).

he remains a priest for all time. Hebrews values the abiding quality of the Son of God (1:11; 7:23–24) and the believer's heavenly inheritance (10:34; 13:14). "For all time" can mean that something takes place without interruption (cf. 10:1; Horton, *Melchizedek*, 162; Vanhoye, *Old Testament*, 153), but in Hebrews it means "forever" (Heb 6:20; cf. 10:12, 14).

7:4. *Abraham the patriarch.* The title "patriarch" identifies Abraham as a founder of Israel (4 Macc 7:19; 16:25; Acts 7:8–9). As the first to receive the promise of many descendants (Heb 6:14), he can represent all who descend from him (7:5, 10). Abraham's relationship to Melchizedek sets a precedent for the relationship of Abraham's descendants (2:16) to Christ.

gave a tithe of the spoils. Genesis 14:20 (Heb 7:2) says that Abraham gave Melchizedek a tithe "of everything," which Hebrews assumes means a tenth "of the spoils" (cf. Josephus, *Ant.* 1.181). The practice of giving a tenth of the spoils to a deity is attested among the Greeks (Herodotus, *Histories* 1.89; Xenophon,

Anabasis 5.3.4; *Hellenica* 4.3.21) and the Romans (Livy, *Roman History* 5.21.2). When the Israelites engaged in holy war, they were to devote all of the spoils to God, which usually meant that everything was destroyed, although valuables were sometimes placed in the sanctuary (Deut 7:5, 25; 20:16–18; Josh 6:21, 24). See de Vaux, *Ancient*, 1.260. Cf. NOTE on tithes in 7:5.

7:5. *Those of the descendants of Levi who receive the priestly office.* All of Israel's priests had Levitical ancestry, but not all Levites became priests. In some passages the Levites and priests are virtually identical (Deut 18:1–8; 21:5), but many distinguish priests from the Levites who could not come near the sacred vessels or altar (Num 3:5–10; 18:2–6). Later the Levites were temple singers and doorkeepers (1 Chron 23:3–5; Ezra 2:40–42; cf. Plutarch, *Mor.* 671E). NT sources recognize that priests and Levites are similar, but not identical (Luke 10:31–32; John 1:19).

have, according to the Law. "The Law" can be taken to govern the reception of tithes: "They have a command to receive tithes in accordance with the Law" (Grässer). In other words, tithing is not up to the individual, but is regulated by Law. Yet it is more likely that "the Law" refers to the authority upon which the command is based: "On the basis of the Law they have a command to receive tithes" (cf. NJB; NIV; REB; NRSV). See COMMENT *b*.

a command to receive tithes. A tithe was due on grain, wine, oil, and the firstlings of flocks and herds (Deut 14:22–23; cf. Lev 27:30–32), although some paid a tithe on all they owned (Matt 23:23; Luke 11:42; 18:12). Tithes were given to the Levites (Num 18:21–24; cf. Neh 10:38–40), who in turn gave a portion to the priests (Num 18:28; Philo, *Special Laws* 1.156–57; cf. Josephus, *Ant.* 4.68–69; Tob 1:6–7). Hebrews does not distinguish tithes collected by Levites from those collected by priests (cf. Jdt 11:13; *Jub.* 13:25–27; Philo, *Virtues* 95; Josephus, *Life* 80; *Ant.* 20.181, 206–7).

from the people, that is, from their brethren. Referring to "the people" as "their brethren" lessens the contrast between priests and laity (cf. NOTE on "brethren" in 2:11). The basic distinction is not between priestly and nonpriestly descendants of Abraham, but between Abraham's descendants and the priest like Melchizedek.

7:6. *but the one who does not have their genealogy.* Melchizedek not only lacks a Levitical genealogy but also has no genealogy at all (7:3). The legitimacy of a priest like Melchizedek does not depend on genealogy, but on the ability to serve "forever" (Ps 110:4; Heb 7:3, 16).

received a tithe from Abraham. On tithing see NOTES on 7:4–5.

and blessed the one who had the promises. On blessing see NOTES on 6:7, 14 and COMMENT *b*. On Abraham as recipient of God's promises (6:12–13) see §15 COMMENT *a*.

7:7. *Now, without any dispute the lesser is blessed by the superior.* Blessings were given by figures like Moses (Deut 33:1; cf. Heb 3:2), Aaron (Num 6:22–27; cf. Heb 5:4), Isaac and Jacob (Gen 27:27–29; 49:28; cf. Heb 11:20–21), and Solomon (1 Kgs 8:14). Yet it is not "without any dispute" that the lesser is always blessed by the greater, since servants or the people sometimes blessed a king (2 Sam 14:22; 1 Kgs 1:47; 8:66). In Heb 7:7 Melchizedek is not superior because he blesses Abraham, but because he receives a tithe from Abraham (Heb 7:4–6).

That is the reason Hebrews can say that Melchizedek was the superior figure when he gave the blessing (7:7). In 7:8 the author will add that Melchizedek is superior because "he lives," unlike those who die.

7:8. *indeed, in the one case people who die receive tithes.* Connecting the Levitical priesthood with death anticipates 7:23–24, where the author contrasts the many priests who have died with Jesus the high priest who remains forever.

but in the other it is someone about whom it is attested that he lives. Attestation comes either directly or indirectly from Scripture (7:17; 10:15; 11:2–5). Earlier, Hebrews noted that the OT does not record an end to Melchizedek's life (7:3), and here it states positively that Melchizedek "lives," just as the risen Christ "lives" (cf. 7:15–17, 25). See COMMENT *b*.

7:9. *One might even venture to say.* This expression can be used when speaking in general rather than exact terms (Philo, *Special Laws* 3.206) or when venturing a thought that technically goes beyond the evidence, yet is true in some sense (Philo, *Creation* 107; *Cherubim* 112; *Planter* 158; *Drunkenness* 51; Josephus *Ant.* 15.387; LSJ, 656). The author makes a point by creative suggestion rather than declaration. See Williamson, *Philo*, 103–9.

that Levi, who receives tithes, actually paid a tithe through Abraham. In relation to Abraham's other descendants, Levites have the honor of receiving tithes (NOTE on 7:5), but in relation to a priest like Melchizedek, Levites are subordinates who pay tithes, as did Abraham.

7:10. *for he was still in the loins of his forebear.* The idea that people come from the father's loins (7:5) was a common biblical notion (Gen 35:11). Yet to suggest that Levi was in the loins of his *great-grandfather* Abraham and, while there, paid a tithe may be a touch of exaggerated humor.

COMMENT[207]

Hebrews addressed Christians who already confessed Jesus to be the Son of God (4:14). The new element is that Hebrews calls Christ a high priest (pp. 126–27). In making the point the author finds Melchizedek to be invaluable as an anomaly.[208] Israel's tradition entrusted priestly office to descendants of Levi, and the

[207]On 7:1–28 see Casalini, "Una *Vorlage*"; idem, "Ebr 7.1–10"; Cockerill, "Melchizedek"; H. J. De Jonge, "Traditie"; De Kruijf, "Priest-King"; Delcor, "Melchizedek"; Demarest, *History*; idem, "Hebrews 7:3"; Dey, *Intermediary*, 185–214; Dunnill, *Covenant*, 164–68; Ellingworth, "Like"; idem, "Unshakable"; Feuillet, "Une triple"; Fitzmyer, *Essays*, 221–43; idem, "Melchizedek"; García Martínez, "Las traditiones"; Garuti, "Ebrei 7, 1–28"; Gianotto, *Melchisedek*; Hay, *Glory*, 130–53; Hayward, "Shem"; Heldermann, "Melchizedeks"; Horbury, "Aaronic"; Horton, *Melchizedek*; Isaacs, *Sacred*, 144–64; Kobelski, *Melchizedek*; Leschert, *Hermeneutical*, 199–241; Loader, *Sohn*, 142–60, 203–22; Longenecker, "Melchizedek"; McNamara, "Melchizedek"; Neyrey, "Without"; Nissilä, *Hohepriestermotiv*, 113–43; Paul, "Order"; Peterson, *Hebrews*, 104–24; Rooke, "Jesus"; Schlosser, "La médiation"; Schröger, *Verfasser*, 130–59; Thompson, *Beginnings*, 116–27; Vanhoye, *Old Testament*, 147–71; Verme, "La 'prima decima' "; Willi, "Melchizedek"; Williamson, *Philo*, 434–49.

[208]Dunnill observes that Melchizedek serves "in the paradoxical role of Priest-Stranger as a double of Christ, both like and unlike." He is "an agent of dissidence to unsettle the fixed structures of conceptions of priesthood" (*Covenant*, 167).

obvious objection to the idea that Jesus was a high priest was that he lacked the correct genealogy since he was understood to have descended from the tribe of Judah (7:14). Rather than dismissing the biblical stipulations, however, the author found within Scripture a precedent for a non-Levitical priesthood: God's promise concerning Melchizedek.[209] Moreover, Melchizedek was both priest and king. Israel's kings were commonly barred from priestly office even though they occasionally performed sacral functions.[210] Greco-Roman kings commonly did serve as priests, and the emperor was widely acclaimed as "high priest,"[211] yet the author of Hebrews does not appeal to a Greco-Roman precedent. Instead, he finds within biblical tradition a precedent for one person holding both positions: Melchizedek.

An important theological assumption undergirding Hebrews is that God raised Christ from the dead and exalted him to heaven, and the author of Hebrews explicates these events in light of the Scriptures that foreshadow them (pp. 117–18). The exalted Christ is like a person who stands before the sun and casts a shadow upon earth. Those who look at the shadow can discern in it the contours of the one who made it. Similarly, Hebrews considers Melchizedek to be an earthly shadow that the risen Christ casts back on the page of OT Scripture, and the author will speak about Melchizedek in order to bear witness to the Son of God whom he represents (7:3).

Psalm 110 is the scriptural key to what Hebrews says about Melchizedek. The author assumes that Ps 110:1 refers to the exalted Christ, when it says: "The Lord said to my lord, 'Sit at my right hand until I make your enemies a footstool for your feet' " (cf. Heb 1:13). Psalm 110:4 refers to this same exalted figure when it says: "You are a priest forever according to the type of Melchizedek" (cf. Heb 5:6, 10; 6:20; §12 COMMENT *c*). Hebrews puts the two verses together, arguing that if the royal figure in Ps 110:1 is the exalted Christ, then the priestly figure like Melchizedek in Ps 110:4 must be the exalted Christ as well. Having established a basic perspective concerning Jesus' reign and priesthood by reading Ps 110 in light of Jesus' exaltation, the author now expands his argument by reading the OT narrative concerning Melchizedek (Gen 14:17–20) in light of the psalm's declaration that the priest like Melchizedek will serve "forever." Thus, Ps 110:4 is the lens through which the author interprets the narrative about Melchizedek in Gen 14:17–20.

---

[209]When comparing Jesus to Aaron, he made no mention of genealogy, but insisted that the indispensable criterion for priesthood was that a person was called by God (5:4–5). Now he argues that Melchizedek represents a priesthood that is both different from and superior to the Levitical priesthood.

[210]Israel's kings could be involved in worship (2 Sam 6:14–18; 1 Kgs 3:3–4; 8:22, 54–55), but attempts by kings to perform priestly functions could be punished (1 Sam 13:2–10; 2 Chron 26:16–21). Psalm 110:4 is echoed in 1 Macc 14:41, and it may have been used to legitimate the combination of royal and priestly functions in the Hasmonean period (1 Macc 14:35). Under Roman rule the positions of king and high priest were again separated (cf. §12 COMMENT *b*).

[211]On Christ's priesthood in relation to Greco-Roman and Jewish priesthood see 4:14–5:10 (§12 COMMENT *a–c*). On Hebrews and traditions of Greco-Roman kingship see §3 COMMENT *a–b*; §4 COMMENT *a–b*.

Genesis 14:17–20 is connected to Ps 110:4 through a technique known as a *gezērah šāwāh*, in which a word common to two passages allowed them to be read together.[212] The key word in this section is "Melchizedek," which appears only in Ps 110:4 and Gen 14:17–20 in the OT. The author interprets Gen 14:17–20 in terms of Ps 110:4, and Ps 110:4 in terms of Christ's exaltation (Vanhoye, *Old Testament*, 151), just as he interprets the biblical narrative that is summarized in Heb 11 in light of Hab 2:4: "my righteous one will live by faith" (Heb 10:38; §30 COMMENT).[213] Some scholars argue that Hebrews relied on traditions of a heavenly Melchizedek[214] or perhaps paraphrased a hymn to Melchizedek (COMMENT *a*), but these proposals seem unlikely (NOTE on 7:1). The argument primarily explicates the eternal priesthood promised in Ps 110:4 (Heb 5:6, 10; 6:20; 7:11, 15, 17).

This section is framed by references to Melchizedek and to his "meeting" (*synantēsas / synēntēsen*) with Abraham in 7:1, 10 (Vanhoye, *La structure*, 125). The material in between can be divided into two parts: **(a)** In 7:1–3 the author summarizes Gen 14:17–20 and relates Melchizedek to the Son of God by explicating Melchizedek's name, title, and lack of genealogy. **(b)** In 7:4–10 the author argues that the priesthood of Melchizedek is different from (7:4–6) and superior to the Levitical priesthood (7:7–8). A final comment on the possibility that Levi paid tithes while in Abraham's loins reinforces the point (7:9–10).

a. Melchizedek and the Son of God (7:1–3)

Melchizedek is introduced against the backdrop of Abraham's triumph in battle. When the OT account (Gen 14:17–20) is read on its own, one might assume that attention should focus on Abraham. Melchizedek may be a "king" (Heb 7:1a), but Abraham is the conqueror of "kings" (7:1c), and Melchizedek seems to honor Abraham by coming to meet him in the manner that people came out to meet conquering heroes (7:1b).[215] Hebrews, however, reverses this to stress the greatness of Melchizedek.

First, the author explains that "Melchizedek" means "king of righteousness" and that king of "Salem" means king of "peace" (7:2b).[216] Neither explanation is unique to Hebrews, but both fit the argument. The author has acclaimed the exalted Christ as a king who loves righteousness (1:8–9). This is important for the

---

[212]In Heb 4:3–5 the author used this technique to connect Ps 95:11 with Gen 2:2 since both mentioned God's "rest." See §11 COMMENT *a*.

[213]Vanhoye, *Old Testament*, 151–52; Grässer, *Hebräer*, 2.18–20; Laub, *Bekenntnis*, 31–34; Gianotto, *Melchisedek*, 141–44; H. J. De Jonge, "Traditie"; Bénétreau, *L'Épître*, 2.21–30; Lane; Leschert, *Hermeneutical*, 199–241; Lindars, *Theology*, 72–77; Manzi, *Melchisedek*, 153–91.

[214]Braun, *Hebräer*, 136–40; Attridge, *Epistle*, 191–95; Feld, *Hebräerbrief*, 49–51; P. E. Hughes, *Commentary*, 238–39.

[215]On welcoming conquering heroes see Josephus, *J.W.* 3.459; 4.112–13; 7.70–71; 7.101–3, 119.

[216]Philo interpreted biblical names in light of philosophy, associating names with virtues and vices (*Preliminary Studies* 44). The perspective of Hebrews was shaped by the death and exaltation of Jesus, and qualities like righteousness and peace are connected with those realities (e.g., Heb 1:8–9; 13:20).

"righteous" who now endure adversity (10:38; 11:4, 7) in the hope of joining the righteous who have a place in God's heavenly city (12:23). Hebrews assures listeners that Christ, the "king of righteousness" whom Melchizedek represents, will not abandon the righteous, but ultimately will vindicate them. Melchizedek also represents the one who is "king of peace" (7:2c). The "God of peace" raised Jesus from the dead (13:20) and exalted him to reign while God puts his enemies under his feet (1:13; Ps 110:1). Peace is not envisioned as accommodation of evil, but as the result of God's triumph over oppressive powers (cf. Heb 2:14–15). Christ's followers are to pursue the peace that accords with righteousness (12:14) in the hope of joining the heavenly "festival gathering." Such festivals were times of joyous peace, making it a fitting way to envision the realization of the work of Christ (NOTE on 12:22).

Second, the author makes an argument from silence.[217] Since the Bible makes no mention of Melchizedek's parentage, the author contends that Melchizedek has no mother, no father, and no genealogy (7:3a). Remarkably, this could actually *discredit* Melchizedek, since someone "without father" would have been considered illegitimate, someone "without mother" would probably have been a foundling or a child of a woman of very low social status, and a person "without genealogy" would have been disqualified for service as a priest (NOTES on 7:3). From a human point of view, the author's claims seem to contradict the call to "see how great" Melchizedek is (7:4). The comment that Melchizedek has "no beginning of days nor end of life" (7:3b), however, makes clear that Hebrews speaks of divinity, not humanity. Deified mortals, including some emperors, were elevated to divine status after their deaths, but true gods were uncreated in the past and imperishable in the future, as Melchizedek is said to be.[218] He represents the Son of God, and the Son remains a priest for all time (7:3c) because he lives forever (1:8–9).

The claims about Melchizedek create tensions in the argument. The author says that Melchizedek has no genealogy (7:3) even though he knows that Jesus was descended from Judah (7:14) and that Melchizedek has "no beginning of days nor end of life" even though Jesus' life upon earth (5:7) began with birth and ended with crucifixion. The author is apparently not comparing Melchizedek to the earthly Jesus, but to the exalted Son of God, who existed before the world was created and who will endure after it has ended (1:2, 10–12). Melchizedek is also said to have had no mother, father, or genealogy (7:3a), yet he is compared to "the *Son* of God" (7:3c). A son must have a father, and 1:5 specifically identifies God as Christ's "Father." To make sense of this, we must assume that Hebrews speaks in strictly human terms about Christ's parentage in 7:3. As "firstborn" from the

---

[217]Note also the importance of biblical silences in 7:14b and 7:20b. Rabbinic sources argue from silence most often in *haggadic* or homiletic exegesis rather than in the *halakhic* or legal exegesis (Strack and Stemberger, *Introduction*, 260). Philo argued that the Scriptures did not mention Cain's death in order to show that the folly and impiety he embodied are deathless (*Worse* 177–78; cf. *Flight* 60–61; *Alleg. Interp.* 2.55).

[218]Neyrey, "Without," 449. He notes Diodorus Siculus, *Library of History* 6.1.2 and Plutarch, *Pelopidas* 16.

dead (1:6), Christ the Son has no genealogy since no one was raised from the dead in this same full and final way prior to Christ. Moreover, no human being bore him into everlasting life; this was God's work alone.[219]

The idea that Melchizedek had a limitless life (7:3b) was sometimes taken to mean that he was God or the Spirit (see pp. 24–25), and one might think that if Melchizedek himself served as a priest for all time (7:3c), then there would be no need for Christ to serve as a priest. Two points are important in light of such questions. First is the *nature* of the comparison. In Heb 7 Melchizedek is said to "resemble" the Son of God, which means that the two are similar, but not identical.[220] Second is the *direction* of the comparison. Hebrews does not say that the Son of God is like Melchizedek, but that Melchizedek is like the Son of God (7:3c). The author sees the traits of Christ in Melchizedek in the way that one sees the shape of a person in his shadow or in his reflection in the mirror.[221] Melchizedek died centuries before Christ and remains forever only as a foreshadowing of Christ.[222]

Some maintain that the elevated language in 7:3 comes from an earlier hymn that the author incorporated into his argument. The verse is written in a participial style with few definite articles but many adjectives, extensive alliteration based on the initial *a-* sound, and chiastic structuring (*beginning*[a], *life*[b] / *days*[b], *end*[a]). A problem is that reconstructions vary greatly, from those that include 7:1–3, 16, 26, to those that confine the hymn to parts of 7:3.[223] Moreover, stylistic criteria are unreliable since the author of Hebrews is capable of composing material with all of these features.[224] Hymnic hypotheses attempt to show that listeners would have found the author's elevated depiction of Melchizedek to be

---

[219]See Vanhoye, *Old Testament*, 156–57. Many have related this passage to the two natures of Christ. In his divinity Christ has God for his Father, but no earthly mother or genealogy, while in his humanity Christ had a mother, the virgin Mary, but no earthly father. See Greer, *Captain*, 143–44, 238, 259; Demarest, *History*, 26; Erasmus, *Paraphrase*, 230.

[220]Chrysostom, *Homilies* 12.3; cf. Epiphanius, *Panarion* 55.1.7.

[221]Some find it problematic to speak of Melchizedek and Christ in terms of shadow and reality (Dey, *Intermediary*, 186; Hurst, *Epistle*, 55). The use of the category "shadow" does not mean that the author of Hebrews thought that Melchizedek had no actual existence; clearly the author believed that the Tabernacle really existed even though it was a shadow of the heavenly one (8:5). The term "shadow" can describe Melchizedek since he is depicted in the Law, which was a shadow of the realities revealed through Christ (10:1).

[222]Haimo, PL 117.866. The Peshitta of 7:3 says that Melchizedek's "priesthood remains forever" rather than "he remains a priest forever."

[223]The most extensive reconstruction is that of Theissen (*Untersuchungen*, 20–28). The complexity is apparent since he proposes a source that consists of 7:1a, 3ab, 16b, 25ac, 26bc. Rissi (*Theologie*, 86–87) deleted the initial reference to Melchizedek. Ellingworth (*Epistle*, 351–54; cf. "Like," 260) retains the initial reference to Melchizedek, but confines the hymnic material to 7:1a, 3abd. H.-F. Weiss (*Brief*, 380) includes only the first half of 7:3 (p. 380). On earlier proposals see Zimmermann, *Bekenntnis*, 79–99.

[224]For example, frequent use of participles and adjectives (7:18; 10:19–25), chiastic structuring (4:16; 5:1–8), specifically of words based on the roots *arch-* and *tel-* (2:10; 12:2), and alliteration (1:1; 2:1–2; 7:18). In this passage the participial style serves to accent the main point: the giving of the tithe. For critical discussion see Deichgräber, *Gotteshymnus*, 176–78; Loader, *Sohn*, 208–11; Casalini, " Una *Vorlage*"; Laub, *Bekenntnis*, 31–41; Lane, *Hebrews*, 1.160; Attridge, *Epistle*, 189–90.

somewhat familiar. Rissi (*Theologie*, 89) argues that the hymn actually circulated in Christian circles as a hymn to Christ as high priest before the author applied it to Melchizedek. This is implausible, however, because the author did not assume that the listeners would be familiar with Christ's high priesthood; he had to argue the point (8:1). The alternative is that the hymn was originally about Melchizedek himself and that Hebrews used it to engage the listeners' interest (Ellingworth, "Like"). Yet it is unlikely that the author was responding to speculations about Melchizedek that were current in his own time (NOTE on 7:1).

Discussion of Melchizedek could have been intriguing to listeners precisely because so little was known about him (Hay, *Glory*, 142). Discussion of something new and astonishing could be rhetorically effective: "When we see in everyday life things that are petty, ordinary, and banal, we generally fail to remember them, because the mind is not being stirred by anything novel or marvelous. But if we see or hear something extraordinary, great, unbelievable, or laughable, that we are likely to remember a long time" (*Rhet. ad Her.* 3.22.35). The next section continues the pattern of presenting the extraordinary by concluding with hyperbolic comments (7:9–10) that suggest that the author was venturing beyond what was familiar to listeners.

b. Melchizedek, Abraham, and Levi (7:4–10)

The author urges listeners to "see how great" Melchizedek is (7:4a) by comparing him favorably with Abraham (7:4b). Rhetorically, it was helpful to show that someone was superior to a great person through amplification (*auxēsis*).[225] The "more excellent Abraham is, the higher is the dignity of Melchizedek himself" (Calvin, *Epistle*, 92). Hebrews extols Melchizedek, not for his own sake, but to convey the greatness of the Son of God, whom he prefigures (Neyrey, "Without," 455). The argument unfolds in two parallel phases (7:4–6; 7:7–8). Each begins with a comment about the greatness or superiority of Melchizedek (7:4, 7), and each advances using statements that are marked by *kai men* (7:5, 8a) and *de* (7:6, 8b) in order to contrast the Levites with Melchizedek.[226] The comment about Levi paying tithes while in Abraham's loins seems designed to appeal to the imagination rather than to add weight to the argument (7:9–10).

The first phase (7:4–6) emphasizes the differences between the Levitical priesthood and the priesthood of Melchizedek:

Descendants of Levi	One without this genealogy
Authority based on Law	________
Collect tithes from the people (their brethren)	Collects tithe from Abraham (their progenitor)
________	Blesses Abraham

---

[225]Aristotle, *Rhetoric* 1.9.39. Note the favorable comparisons of Christ to Moses (§9 COMMENT) and Aaron (§12 COMMENT *c*).

[226]A similar pattern of argument in two phases appears in 4:1–10. See §11 COMMENT.

Abraham's tithe to Melchizedek is compared to ordinary practice, in which tithes were paid to "those of the descendants of Levi who receive the priestly office" (7:5a). Descent from Levi is a major factor in Israel's priesthood, but not all of Levi's descendants become priests. Priests must "receive" their office, just as Christ was called by God (5:4–6). Appointment, rather than descent, is the determining factor. The author next reverses the traditional importance ascribed to genealogy by using the common descent of all Israelites from Abraham to level the distinction between the priests (7:5a) and the people (7:5c). Priests may be set apart from others, but at a more fundamental level all who come from Abraham are on the same level as brothers (7:5d). Abraham's relationship to Melchizedek sets the precedent for the way that all of his descendants, including priests, should relate to the Son of God, whom Melchizedek resembles (7:3).

Like Levitical priests Melchizedek received a tithe, but unlike them he "does not have their genealogy" (7:6a). The implication is that if the lack of a Levitical genealogy did not prevent Melchizedek from collecting a tithe from Abraham, it cannot disqualify Jesus from serving as priest. Levitical authority is based on the Mosaic Law (7:5b)—which the author will later argue has been abrogated (7:11–19)—whereas Melchizedek is linked to blessing and promise (7:6b). God promised Abraham a blessing (see 6:14), and Melchizedek blessed Abraham (7:6c). If the pattern holds true, then the listeners, who are the heirs of the promises (6:12, 17), can look for blessing from the exalted Son of God (6:7), whose priesthood Melchizedek foreshadows.

The second phase of the argument contrasts the lesser and superior, and mortals with the One who lives (7:7–8). The statement that "the lesser is blessed by the superior" (7:7) is not a general principle. Melchizedek's superiority is evident, not in his blessing of Abraham, but in his receiving a tithe from Abraham. Thus, the lesser figure, who paid the tithe, is blessed by the superior figure, who received the tithe (NOTE on 7:7). Support for this claim is that Levitical priests die (7:8a; cf. Num 20:28; 35:25, 28) but that the priesthood of Melchizedek is held by one who lives forever (7:8b). The Son of God is uniquely qualified for everlasting service because he alone has been exalted to everlasting life. He does not hold his position on the basis of the Mosaic Law, but on the basis of the oath made in Ps 110:4 concerning one who is a priest forever like Melchizedek (Heb 7:20–28).

Finally, the author suggests that Levi himself paid a tithe through Abraham since he was in the loins of Abraham when Melchizedek met him (7:9–10). When taken too seriously, this comment creates theological problems,[227] but

[227]Theological difficulty stemmed from the idea that if Levi paid a tithe while in Abraham's loins, then Christ would have done the same, since he was a descendant of Abraham through Judah (7:14). Often this issue developed into questions as to whether Christ inherited original sin through bodily descent. Augustine concluded that Christ was in Abraham's loins in the sense of his humanity, but not his divinity, and that Christ did not inherit the sinful nature of his forebears (*On Genesis Literally Interpreted* 10.19–21). The issue was debated in medieval commentaries on Hebrews (see p. 30). Pelagians used Heb 7:9–10 in arguments against Augustine's view of the transmission of sin (see p. 27).

the author is using hyperbole, which is "an elegant straining of the truth" that either exaggerates or minimizes something: "every hyperbole involves the incredible" (Quintilian, *Inst.* 8.6.67, 73). Speakers used hyperbole because audiences had "an innate passion for exaggeration," but hyperbole was especially useful for extraordinary subjects (ibid., 8.6.75). The priesthood of Melchizedek was an extraordinary topic, and listeners may even have found it humorous to think that Levi paid tithes while he was still in Abraham's loins. Such humor was often useful for speakers because it helped maintain rapport with the listeners and revive those who had grown weary by more weighty arguments (ibid., 6.3.1; 8.6.74).[228]

Exaggeration was a valuable way to communicate with those who have become tired of listening (*Rhet. ad Her.* 1.6 §10; Heb 5:11). By the beginning of Heb 7 the audience would have been listening to arguments and exhortations for perhaps twenty minutes, and the fanciful remark about Levi paying tithes while he was still in the loins of Abraham offers a momentary respite. The force of the argument does not depend on this remark, and in the next section the author will return to his central points, concentrating on the way that Jesus' exaltation fulfills the oath that God swore concerning someone who would serve as "a priest forever."

18. Perfection and the Levitical Priesthood (7:11–19)

7 11Now, if there had been completion through the Levitical priesthood—for
the people had been given Law about it—what need would there still be for a
different priest to be raised up *according to the type of Melchizedek* instead of
speaking about one "according to the type of Aaron"? 12For when there is a
change of the priesthood there is also, of necessity, a change of Law. 13For the
one about whom these things are spoken belongs to a different tribe, from which
no one has served at the altar. 14For it is clear that our Lord has sprung from
Judah, a tribe to which Moses said nothing about priests.

15And this is even more abundantly clear when a different priest arises in the
likeness of Melchizedek, 16who has not become [a priest] according to a Law of
fleshly command, but according to the power of an indestructible life. 17For it is
attested that *you are a priest forever according to the type of Melchizedek.* 18There
is, then, an abrogation of a previous command because of its weakness and uselessness—19for the Law made nothing complete—and the introduction of a superior hope, through which we draw near to God.

228Rhetoricians recognized that humor could have an important place in speeches (Cicero, *De oratore* 2.54 §216). Understatement and exaggeration were among the elements that contributed to humor (ibid., 2.66 §267). See Lausberg, *Handbook* §257.2a.

NOTES

7:11. *if there had been.* "If" (*ei*) introduces an unreal condition. Although unreal conditions often have *an* in the apodosis (4:8; 8:4, 7; 11:15), this is not necessary (BDF §360.1).

completion. Teleiōsis and related words point to the establishment of right relationship with God through the cleansing of the conscience and the consummation of this relationship in everlasting glory, rest, and celebration in God's heavenly city. See pp. 122–25.

through the Levitical priesthood. The adjective *leuitikos* is used in the LXX and Philo (*Alleg. Interp.* 2.105; *Planter* 26) as the title for the book of Leviticus and for the Levitical tribe (Philo, *Preliminary Studies* 98, 132; *Flight* 87, 90, 93; *Names* 2; *Moses* 2.170). The expression "Levitical priesthood" is not common outside of Hebrews.

for the people had been given Law. This parenthetical statement (BDF §465) introduces the issue of the Law. The "people" who were given the Law included those of Moses' generation and all generations of Israel (Deut 5:3; 6:20–25). The verb *nomothetein* was commonly used by Jewish writers for the Mosaic Law (Philo, *Worse* 52; *Migration* 91). The subject of the verb could be Moses (Josephus, *Ant.* 3.317) or angels (Heb 2:2), but ultimately the author of the Law was God (Exod 31:18; Philo, *Alleg. Interp.* 3.142; *Posterity* 143). Mosaic "legislation [is] in a sense a lesson on the priesthood" (Philo, *Special Laws* 2.164; cf. 1.198). See pp. 114–15.

about it. The preposition *epi* has been taken in three ways. The first is preferable:

(a) Law was given "about" the Levitical priesthood. The verb *nomothetein* is followed by *epi* and the genitive case in some MSS (P^{46} א A B etc.), and it seems to function like *peri* ("concerning"; cf. Philo, *Special Laws* 1.235; 2.35; Josephus, *Ag. Ap.* 2.276; Hollander, "Hebrews"; Lane; H.-F. Weiss).

(b) People were given the Law "on the basis of" the Levitical priesthood (NIV; NJB; NAB[2]; REB; Attridge; Ellingworth; Grässer). The idea that the Law would function on the basis of the priesthood fits the argument, but would be more likely if the object of *epi* were in the dative case, as it is in some MSS (D^2 1881 Maj) and in 8:6.

(c) People received the Law "under" or during the time of the Levitical priesthood (KJV; NRSV). Although this is a possible interpretation, the argument stresses the dependence of the Law upon the priesthood.

for a different priest to be raised up. The new priest is not "another" (*allos*) in the same line, but one of a "different" (*heteros*) sort. The verb "raise up" can be used for someone who assumes a position, such as a king (Exod 1:8; Acts 7:18) or prophet (Deut 18:15; Acts 3:22). The verb was also used for Jesus' resurrection (e.g., Mark 9:9, 31; 10:34 par.; Acts 2:24, 32; 1 Thess 4:14) to indestructible life (cf. Heb 7:15; Ellingworth). Both senses fit this context.

according to the type of Melchizedek. The language recalls Ps 110:4 (NOTE on 5:6). On Melchizedek see NOTE on 7:1.

one "according to the type of Aaron." One strain of messianic hope anticipated two messiahs: one Davidic and one Aaronic, or priestly (1QS IX, 11; 1QSa II, 12–22; 1QSb V, 20–28; cf. P. E. Hughes, *Commentary*, 256). The author of Hebrews compares Jesus to Aaron in 5:1–10 without suggesting that Jesus is an Aaronic messiah, and he contrasts Jesus with the Levites in 7:11–19, but does not seem familiar with the idea that a messianic figure might come from Levi.

7:12. *For when there is a change of the priesthood.* This runs counter to the idea that the Levitical priesthood was permanent (Exod 40:15; Num 18:19; 25:13). The high priesthood was changed from one house to another within the Levitical family (Josephus, *Ant.* 12.387), but when the Syrians changed the practice (1 Macc 7:5–9; 10:20; 11:27; 2 Macc 4:24, 29; 14:3), many Jews protested (*T. Mos.* 6:6; 7:9–10; 1QpHab VIII, 8–9; XI, 4–8; 4QpPs 37 II, 17–19). Hebrews, however, speaks not about a change within the Levitical family, but a change from the Levitical priesthood to a different type of priesthood.

there is also, of necessity, a change of Law. The necessity is logical necessity (cf. Philo, *Posterity* 4; Heb 8:3). The word "change" (*metathesis*) can imply removal, as in Enoch's removal from the earth (11:5) or the removal of transient things from the created order (12:27). The "change" is related to the "abrogation" of the Law (7:18). This runs counter to Jewish writings that said that the laws pertaining to priesthood were eternally valid (*Jub.* 13:26), but Hebrews argues that the change in the Law is consistent with God's unchangeable will (COMMENT *a*; cf. pp. 110–15).

7:13. *For the one about whom these things are spoken belongs to a different tribe.* This refers to Jesus, who descended from Judah (7:14). Melchizedek did not belong to any of the tribes of Israel (NOTE on 7:1).

from which no one has served at the altar. Serving at the altar (*thysiastērion*) was a basic duty of a priest (Num 18:5; 1 Cor 9:13). Sacrifices and offerings were made on the altar in the forecourt of the Tabernacle (Exod 27:1–8; 38:1–7) and the first (1 Kgs 8:64) and second Temples (Matt 5:23–24; 23:18–20, 35). Inside these sanctuaries was a smaller incense altar, which is probably not in view here (cf. Heb 9:4). Kings David and Solomon—who were from Judah—occasionally served at the altar (2 Sam 24:25; 1 Kgs 3:4), although neither was considered to be a priest. Some of David's sons were priests (2 Sam 8:18), but Hebrews does not deal with this tradition.

7:14. *For it is clear that our Lord.* "Lord" can refer to God (7:21; 8:8–11; 10:16, 30; 12:5–6, 14), but here it is used of Jesus (cf. 1:10; 2:3; 13:20; 1 Tim 1:14; 2 Tim 1:8; 2 Pet 3:15). In Ps 110, the priest like Melchizedek (110:4) is called "my lord" (110:1).

has sprung from Judah. Jesus' descent from Judah (Matt 1:1–3; Luke 3:23, 33; cf. Rev 5:5) is presupposed in the tradition that Jesus descended from David, who was from Judah (Matt 1:1, 6; 9:27; 15:22; Mark 10:47; Luke 1:27, 32; 2:4; 3:23, 31, 33; 18:38; Acts 2:30–31; 13:22–23; Rom 1:3; 2 Tim 2:8; Rev 5:5; 22:16). Judah was associated with kingship (Gen 49:10; 4QPBless; Rev 5:5). The verb "sprung" (*anatellein*) may recall that a star was to "spring forth from Jacob" (Num 24:17), and the related word *anatolē* was used for the messianic "branch" of David (Jer 23:5; Zech 3:8; 6:12; cf. Isa 11:1; Matt 4:16; Luke 1:78; 4QPBless 3–4; 4QFlor I, 11). Hebrews seems unfamiliar with the idea that a king from Judah would establish a new priesthood (*T. Levi* 8:14).

a tribe to which Moses said nothing about priests. Moses' blessing to Judah (Deut 33:7) said nothing about priests, whereas Moses asked God to give Levi the priestly lots (Deut 33:8–11).

7:15. *when a different priest arises.* Although "arise" refers primarily to a person coming into a position of influence (NOTE on "raised up" in 7:11), the juxtaposition of "arising" in 7:15 with "indestructible life" in 7:16 might suggest a connection with Jesus' resurrection.

in the likeness of Melchizedek. Switching from "according to the type [*taxis*] of Melchizedek" (5:6, 10; 6:20; 7:11) to "likeness" (*homoiotēta*) indicates that Hebrews takes Ps 110:4 to refer to one in the "likeness" or "type" of Melchizedek, not to an ongoing "order" of priests (cf. 2 *Enoch* 71:29).

7:16. *who has not become* [*a priest*]. On the time that Jesus became a priest see pp. 109–10.

according to a Law of fleshly command. The word "fleshly" (*sarkinos*) can mean "composed of flesh" or that which belongs to the realm of flesh (BAGD, 742; *TLNT* 3.240–41). The term refers first to the bodily descent of priests from the tribe of Levi, but it also connotes weakness and transience (cf. 7:18; 9:10, 13–14; Thompson, *Beginnings*, 122–23).

but according to the power of an indestructible life. One problem is that if Jesus was subject to death, how is his life "indestructible"? Some maintain that if Christ was a priest during his earthly life, he must have possessed an indestructible life through his divine nature (Montefiore, *Commentary*, 125–26; cf. Westcott, *Epistle*, 185). The problem is that this suggests that Christ did not die in the way that others die, even though Hebrews stresses the reality of Christ's suffering and death (2:14–15; 4:15; 5:7–8; Büchsel, *TDNT* 4.339). More viable is the idea that Christ truly died, but did not remain subject to death. He received an indestructible life through his exaltation to God's right hand (Peterson, *Hebrews*, 110–11; Lane; H.-F. Weiss).

7:17. *For it is attested that you are a priest forever.* Attestation comes from the Scriptures (Ps 110:4; Heb 5:6, 10; 6:20). On Ps 110:4 see NOTE on Heb 5:6. The psalm's reference to a priesthood that continues "forever" attests to the "indestructible life" (7:16) that Christ now enjoys after having been raised from the dead.

7:18. *There is, then, an abrogation.* "Abrogation" (*athetēsis*) was used for official annulment (MM, 12). In wills: "No one at all shall be permitted to abrogate (*athetēsin*) any of these provisions or to do anything opposed to them" (*P. Oxy.* #493.9). The one making the will, however, could abrogate it himself: "So long as I live I am to have power over my own property, to make any further provisions or new dispositions I choose and to abrogate this will, and any such provisions shall be valid" (*P. Oxy.* #492.9; cf. ##491.3; 494.4; 495.3; *b. B. Bat* 135b). It was considered sinful for someone to abrogate God's laws (Isa 24:16 LXX; cf. Ezek 22:26), and "anyone who abrogates the Law of Moses dies without pity on the basis of two or three witnesses" (Heb 10:28). Yet since God gave the Law, Hebrews assumes that he also has the right to alter it. God's annulment of the command is the opposite of his "validation" of the promise (6:16). See *TLNT*, 1.39–40.

of a previous command. This refers to the "Law of fleshly command" (7:16a) that established the Levitical priesthood (7:11). Hebrews assumes that statutes concerning the Levitical priesthood were given in Moses' time and that the oath concerning the priest like Melchizedek was given later, in the time of David (Ps 110:4; Heb 7:28).

because of its weakness and uselessness—for the Law made nothing complete. The command was weak because it appointed to the priesthood people who were liable to sin and death (7:28). Hebrews does not suggest that the Law failed only because people failed to observe it (NOTE on 8:7). Rather, the Law was fundamentally unable to complete God's design for humanity. Philo said that the Law was the way that people could be "made complete" in virtue (*Special Laws* 2.39), but Hebrews insists that it could not "make complete" God's purposes for humanity (cf. 7:11. pp. 122–25).

7:19. *and the introduction of a superior hope.* The introduction of the new actually puts the abrogation of the old (7:18) into effect (H.-F. Weiss). "Hope" seems to have the objective sense of that which is hoped for rather than the subjective act of hoping (cf. NOTE on 6:18).

through which we draw near to God. Drawing near (*engizein*) to God has several dimensions:

(**a**) Prayer and Worship. Priests drew near when they entered the sanctuary (Exod 19:22; Lev 10:3; 21:21; Ezek 40:46; 42:13; 43:19; 44:13; 45:4). All members of the community "drew near" through prayer and worship (Gen 18:23; Ps 148:14; Isa 29:13; 58:2; cf. Philo, *Unchangeable* 161; *Migration* 132). Like the invitation to "approach [*proserchesthai*] the throne of grace" (NOTE on Heb 4:16; cf. 7:25; 10:1, 22), 7:19 also encourages people to "draw near" to God in prayer.

(**b**) Faith. People "draw near" by trusting God and seeking to be faithful to him (Hos 12:6 [12:7 LXX]; Zeph 3:2; Jas 4:8). By fulfilling his promise to raise up a priest like Melchizedek, God provides a secure basis for people to trust him.

(**c**) Final Salvation. Hope (Heb 7:19a) looks for endless life in the presence of God. People are made complete in a full and final sense when they enter the heavenly city (12:22–24). People could draw near to God in prayer and faith under the Mosaic Law, but Hebrews maintains that the priestly work of Christ enables people from all times and places to come before God in this complete way (cf. 11:40).

COMMENT[51]

A number of times in previous paragraphs, Hebrews has quoted or alluded to Ps 110:4: "The Lord has sworn and will not change his mind, 'You are a priest forever according to the type of Melchizedek' " (5:6, 10; 6:20; 7:3). The author has

---

[229]For bibliography on 7:11–19 see §17 COMMENT n. 207.

also used the psalm to explicate Melchizedek's encounter with Abraham (Gen 14:17–20) and to show the similarities between Jesus and Aaron, who were both called by God (Heb 5:4–6). Now, however, he uses Ps 110:4 to contrast the limited Levitical priesthood with Jesus' eternal priesthood (Vanhoye, *Old Testament*, 148). Reasons for discussing the priesthood and Law are disputed (see pp. 114–15).

Some consider the discussion of the Law to be mainly theoretical, since Hebrews—unlike Paul (Gal 5:1–12; Phil 3:2–3)—is not contending with Judaizing opponents.[230] Hebrews refers to Jewish food laws (Heb 9:10; 13:9), but does not comment on circumcision or other issues concerning the individual Christian's adoption of Jewish practices. Attention focuses instead on laws pertaining to priesthood and sacrifice, which would not have been immediate problems for those who lived outside of Palestine or after the destruction of the Temple. Addressing weary listeners, the author could be discussing the Law in an academic manner in order to show the surpassing importance of Christ.

Others, however, assume that questions concerning the Jewish Law and priesthood must have emerged from continuing contact with Judaism.[231] Jewish people in the first century assumed that Levitical priests were entrusted with oversight of Jewish affairs and that the high priest was their chief representative.[232] Records of priestly genealogies were apparently kept by Jewish communities in Judea and the Diaspora, both before and after A.D. 70 (Josephus, *Ag. Ap.* 1.32), and people of priestly descent were recognized in synagogue life.[233] The extent to which priests actually served as teachers and administrators in local communities is unclear, but even in the early second century Josephus could *say* that priests oversaw Jewish life (*Ag. Ap.* 2.187, 194).

Given the importance of the Levitical priesthood for Jewish identity, it seems likely that Heb 7:11–19 deals with live issues. Nevertheless, two points should to be noted. First, the specific occasion for the argument remains unclear. Some Christians may have been inclined to affiliate more closely with a Jewish community in order to escape reproach from others in society (10:32–34; 13:3, 13),[234] or they might have thought that Judaism's priestly traditions would give them a stronger sense of identity since Christianity lacked the kind of priestly institutions that characterized most religious groups in the ancient world.[235]

---

[230]See Räisänen, *Paul*, 210; H.-F. Weiss, *Brief*, 403–4; Grässer, *Hebräer*, 2.51.

[231]For example, Horbury, "Aaronic"; F. F. Bruce, *Epistle*, 9, 166; Lindars, *Theology*, 10–11; Loader, *Sohn*, 258; Dunn, *Partings*, 87; P. E. Hughes, *Commentary*, 260; cf. Vanhoye, *Old Testament*, 163–69.

[232]For evidence from before the destruction see Philo, *Special Laws* 3.131; *Dreams* 2.185–87. For post–A.D. 70 evidence see Josephus, *Ag. Ap.* 2.185–87. On the high priesthood see NOTES and COMMENT on 5:1.

[233]Acts 19:14 refers to a Jewish priest in Ephesus, and an inscription from Berenice in Cyrenaica (A.D. 55) lists a priest among those who contributed to the repair of a synagogue. Cf. Horbury, "Aaronic," 49. In synagogues the "priest reads first, after him the Levite, after him the Israelite" (*m. Giṭṭ.* 5:8). Cf. Philo in Eusebius, *Preparation for the Gospel* 8.7.13.

[234]See F. F. Bruce, *Epistle*, 9; Loader, *Sohn*, 258.

[235]Lindars, *Theology*, 10; Dunn, *Partings*, 87.

Given the lack of clear information about these aspects of the situation, arguments along these lines remain speculative (pp. 71–72). Second, it is helpful to ask how the argument locates Christians in relation to Judaism *and* to the wider Greco-Roman environment since the argument's implications concern how Christians relate to the dominant Greco-Roman culture as well as to the Jewish subculture.

Structurally, this section is part of a larger argument that is framed by references to "completion" (7:11, 28). The portion that is taken up here is also framed by references to "completion" and its relation to the Law (7:11, 19). Within this section, two paragraphs explicate portions of Ps 110:4 in reverse order: (**a**) Jesus is a priest *according to the type of Melchizedek* (Ps 110:4c). This part of the psalm allows the author to show how Christ's priesthood differs from the Levitical priesthood (Heb 7:11–14). (**b**) Jesus is *a priest forever* (Ps 110:4b). This part of the psalm enables the author to show that Christ's priesthood is not only different from but superior to the Levitical priesthood, since Jesus is uniquely qualified to serve as "a priest forever" because of his resurrection from the dead. The first part of the psalm (Ps 110:4a), will be taken up in Heb 7:20–25 (§19 COMMENT).[236]

a. A Priest After the Type of Melchizedek (7:11–14)

Raising the issue of completion (7:11a), the author uses the term *teleiōsis* without defining it, allowing the term to evoke previous images for the goal of God's actions. Earlier passages have spoken about the hope of being crowned with glory and honor (2:5–10), entering God's promised rest (4:9–10), and inheriting the blessing that God promised to Abraham and his heirs (6:7, 12). Such hopes were not realized in the experience of listeners who had known reproach, abuse, dispossession, and imprisonment (10:32–34; 13:3, 13). Yet previous arguments have shown that Christ is already crowned with glory and honor (2:9), seated in a posture of rest at God's right hand (1:3, 13), and that in Christ's exaltation, the faithful catch a glimpse of the future that God has promised them. Here the author affirms that even now people can draw near to God through Christ (7:19), and he excludes the Law and Levitical priesthood as means by which God will accomplish his designs.

The initial statement places the issue at its most fundamental level: Did the Levitical priesthood ultimately accomplish God's purposes (7:11a)? The author assumes that the answer is no, and his view runs counter to the dominant tendencies in Jewish sources. Writing before the destruction of the Temple, Philo called the Levitical priesthood "that perfect priesthood by which mortality is commended to and recognized by God" (*Sacrifices* 132; *Moses* 2.5; *Special Laws* 1.80). Writing in Rome decades after the Temple's destruction, Josephus argued

---

[236]On the structure see Vanhoye, *La structure*, 128–33; cf. Attridge; Lane; Ellingworth; H.-F. Weiss; Grässer; Casalini. Bénétreau, (*L'Épître*, 2.37) identifies 7:11–22 as a section. For another example of an explication of an OT text in several steps see 3:1–6 (§9 COMMENT).

that in the Law, God established the most perfect form of community life by assigning "the administration of its highest affairs to the whole body of priests" (*Ag. Ap.* 2.184–88). Hebrews, however, contends that God did not complete his purposes through the Levitical priesthood.

Gravity is added by the comment that "the people had been given Law" concerning the Levitical priesthood (7:11b). It was understood that the Law ultimately came from God (NOTE on 7:11), so that what one said about the Law reflected what one thought about the God who gave it. Neither Jews nor early Christians divided the Law into "moral" and "ritual" components. Therefore, to speak about changing or abrogating one part of the Law meant changing an entire system (see pp. 114–15). Hebrews does not casually reject the Law, but points out that Scripture itself actually speaks about two types of priesthood (7:11d). Mosaic statutes established a priesthood that was passed down among the descendants of Levi, but Ps 110:4 spoke about a priest like Melchizedek, who was not from the tribe of Levi. There is constancy in that God provides for a priesthood and calls Jesus to the priesthood in a manner analogous to the way that he called Aaron (Heb 5:4–6). Yet there is a change in God's way of working, because the promise concerns not a Levitical priest, but one like Melchizedek.

The "change of the priesthood" (7:12a) occurred through the exaltation of Jesus. To speak of such a change contrasts with Israel's tradition, which spoke of the Levitical priesthood continuing in perpetuity (Exod 40:15; Num 18:19; 25:13; Josephus, *Ant.* 2.216; *Jub.* 32:1). Levitical priests were central to Israel's life before the destruction of the Temple in A.D. 70, and even after the destruction priests remained influential in synagogue life. In the years after 70, the sages, who reconstituted Judaism around the study of the Torah rather than the Temple, continued to accept the priesthood in principle.[237] Hebrews marks a shift from common Jewish views, but it maintains continuity with Israel's tradition over against Greco-Roman practice at a crucial point: the author assumes that there will be only one priesthood. A first-century reader might think that Ps 110:4 simply added a new Melchizedek priesthood to the old Aaronic line, but creating multiple priesthoods would mean accommodation to Greco-Roman practice. Rome had four major priestly colleges plus three more priesthoods that represented the oldest strata of Roman religion. Other priesthoods were established for certain festivals and the cults of the deified emperors. Similar practices were common throughout the Mediterranean. Some priesthoods had lifetime tenure, others were for a limited period of time, and some individuals held multiple priesthoods simultaneously.[238] In assuming that there could be but one priesthood, Hebrews develops Israel's tradition.

---

[237]On rabbinic attitudes toward the Levitical priesthood after A.D. 70 see Davies, *Setting*, 256–70.

[238]There were local priesthoods for Zeus (Herodotus, *Histories* 3.142), Dionysus (Plutarch, *Mor.* 300a), and other deities. Egypt was known for its astonishing number of priesthoods (Diodorus Siculus, *Library of History* 1.73.5; 1.88.2). When a sanctuary was established, provision needed to be made for a priesthood (Herodotus, *Histories* 3.142; Diodorus Siculus, *Library of History* 5.58.2). See Burkert, *Greek*, 95–98; J. A. Turner, "Greek Priesthoods," *CAM* 2.925–31; M. Beard, "Roman Priesthoods," *CAM* 2.933–39.

Earlier, the author said that God's purposes were unchangeable (6:18), but here he says that the Law has been changed (7:12b).[239] The author is not speaking about human alteration of God's Law, but about a change that God made by establishing the priesthood of Christ. Such a change differs from those made during the Maccabean period, for example, when some Jews altered traditional practices to conform to the norms of Gentile culture (2 Macc 11:24). According to Heb 7:12, God changes his own Law to conform to the purposes that he established by his promises. The difference between the Levitical priesthood and the priesthood of Jesus is accented by a flat acknowledgment that Jesus "belongs to a different tribe," namely "Judah" (7:13a, 14a).[240] If, on the one hand, the Law is fixed, then Jesus cannot be a priest, since Judean ancestry would have precluded it.[241] On the other hand, if Jesus can in fact be considered a priest, then the Law that requires priests to descend from Levi is not a fixed principle.

The author presses the displacement of the Law by pointing out that it does not permit those from Judah to serve at the altar (7:13b). No one "should hold God's high priesthood save him who is of Aaron's blood," and no one "of another lineage, even if he happened to be a king, should attain to the high priesthood" (Josephus, *Ant.* 20.226). Despite the lack of legal warrant, the author could have made an appeal to precedent, for David and Solomon—kings from Judah—occasionally did serve at the altar (2 Sam 24:25; 1 Kgs 3:4). But Hebrews does not make such an appeal. Instead, the author assumes that the Scriptures' silence about priests from Judah means that warrant for such priests does not exist, just as he assumed that the Scriptures' silence about Melchizedek's genealogy meant that his genealogy did not exist (7:3). If Jesus is a true priest, the legitimacy of his office must have another basis.

b. A Priest Forever (7:15–19)

Having shown that Christ's priesthood is fundamentally *different* from the Levitical priesthood, the author now argues that Christ's priesthood is *superior* to the Levitical order. The basis for the argument is that God fulfilled his promise to

---

[239]Rabbinic texts give evidence of evolving interpretations of the Law, but Hebrews is more radical, referring not to a change in interpretation, but to a change in the Law itself.

[240]On Jesus' Davidic ancestry see R. E. Brown, *Birth*, 505–12. Luke's gospel indicates that there could have been a Levitical component in Jesus' genealogy, since Mary was related to Elizabeth who was descended from Aaron (Luke 1:5, 36). Luke does not develop the idea of Jesus' priestly descent, and the idea was clearly unknown to the author of Hebrews. The ascription of Levitical ancestry to Jesus clearly emerges in the late second or early third century in the writings of Hippolytus. For texts and discussion see M. De Jonge, *Jewish*, 216–19.

[241]One text that might give evidence for Jewish expectations of a new priesthood arising from the tribe of Judah is *T. Levi* 8:14: "From Judah a king will arise and shall found a new priesthood in accord with the Gentile model and for all nations." The text seems to conflict with 8:4, which says that the priesthood is given to Levi and his posterity. The passage could allude to John Hyrcanus and the Hasmonean priest-kings (H. C. Kee, *OTP* 2.791), or it could be a Christian composition (M. De Jonge, ed., *Studies*, 222–23).

raise up a priest "in the likeness of Melchizedek" by exalting Christ to everlasting life (7:15). Several contrasts are made:

Levitical Priesthood	*Christ's Priesthood*
Law	power
fleshly	indestructible
command	life

First, Christ's priesthood is based, not on Law, but on the power by which God raised him from the dead (2:14–16). Second, Jesus' priesthood was not simply a change from one human priesthood to another, a transfer from the tribe of Levi to the tribe of Judah. The author says that human priesthoods are "fleshly," a term that connotes physical genealogy and transience, whereas Jesus' priesthood is "indestructible" and therefore permanent. Third, the Levitical priesthood was based upon God's "command," whereas Christ's priesthood was instituted by God's gift of indestructible "life." If the "command" defined what God expected the members of the tribe of Levi to do, "life" indicates what God himself has done by raising Jesus from the dead in order to fulfill his promise to raise up a priest like Melchizedek who will serve forever (7:17).

To speak of "an abrogation of a previous command" (7:18a) goes beyond the change in the Law that was mentioned in 7:12b. The idea of abrogating God's Law ran counter to the dominant strain in Jewish thinking, which held that "we who have received the Law and sinned will perish," but the Law "does not perish but survives in its glory" (*4 Ezra* 9:36–37; *2 Bar.* 77:15; Philo, *Moses* 2.14–15; Josephus, *Ag. Ap.* 2.272). Hebrews agrees that no human being can rightly abrogate a command of God (10:28), but argues that in this case it was *God* who abrogated a command. In common legal practice, someone who made a will could reserve the right to change it as long as he was alive (NOTE on 7:18). Accordingly, "the living God" (3:12; 9:14; 10:31; 12:22) presumably possesses the right to alter the covenant that he himself put in place.

Hebrews says that the Law was changed because of its weakness (7:18), but the author does not support this claim by arguing that Jewish people *felt* the Law to be ineffective—the Psalms say that "the law of the Lord is perfect, reviving the soul" (Ps 19:7) and call "blessed" those who delight in the Law (Ps 1:1–2). Instead, Hebrews bases its argument on the conviction that God brings about the completion of his purposes through Christ, which implies that all other means—including the Law—are inadequate. To say categorically that the Law made nothing "complete" (7:19a) is more provocative than explanatory. The author will argue that the Law could not purify the conscience (9:13–14) or take away sins (10:3–4), but he does not speculate as to why God gave an ineffective Law in the first place. The implication is simply that the Law foreshadowed what was to take place through Christ (10:1). See pp. 114–15 on the issue.

The superior hope that is introduced through Christ's priesthood (7:19b) corresponds in some ways to the hope of previous generations. According to Hebrews Christians have heard "good news" and seek to enter God's rest, like the people of Moses' generation (4:2). They have received promises and hope for God's blessing, like Abraham (6:11–12, 17). Hope is inseparable from the faith that characterizes all generations of God's people (11:1–2), yet Hebrews insists that the hope of fully entering God's presence (6:18–19) is not realized apart from Christ and his followers (11:13, 40). Hebrews does not deny that previous generations, in some sense, could draw near to God, but the author contrasts the limited effectiveness of the former priesthood with the absolute effectiveness of Christ's priesthood (Peterson, *Hebrews*, 112). In the present people draw near to God (7:19c) through Christ in prayer and faith (NOTE on 4:16). In the future they have hope of drawing near to God in a full and final way by entering into the company of the righteous in the heavenly city (12:22–24).

19. THE LORD WILL NOT CHANGE HIS MIND (7:20–28)

7 [20]And to the extent that it was not without swearing an oath—for they have become priests without the swearing of an oath, [21]but he through the swearing of an oath, through the one who says to him, *The Lord has sworn and will not change his mind, "You are a priest forever"*—[22]to that extent Jesus has become the surety of a superior covenant.

[23]Those who have become priests are numerous because death prevents them from continuing to serve, [24]but he holds the priesthood inviolate, because he continues forever. [25]Because of this he is indeed able to save completely those who approach God through him, since he always lives to intercede on their behalf.

[26]Now, such a high priest was indeed fitting for us: holy, blameless, undefiled, separated from sinners, exalted above the heavens, [27]who has no need, as do the high priests, to offer sacrifices each day first for their own sins and then for those of the people because he did this once for all when he offered himself. [28]For the Law establishes as high priests men who have weaknesses, but the word sworn on oath, which came after the Law, establishes a Son who has been made complete forever.

NOTES

7:20. *And to the extent that.* Hebrews 7:20–22 is a complex sentence with the *kath' hoson* ("to the extent that") in 7:20a corresponding to *kata tosouto* ("to that extent") in 7:22a. The parenthesis in 7:20b–21 explains the first half of the comparison concerning the oath. The covenant for which Jesus acts as surety is superior to the same extent that his priesthood is established by an oath. Since the oath is definitive, Jesus' superiority is definitive.

it was not without swearing an oath. "Swearing an oath" (*horkomosia*), like the related word "oath" (*horkos*), was often used for pledges made by human beings

(1 Esdr 8:90 [93]; Josephus *Ant.* 16.163). An oath called upon God or another power to hold the oath maker accountable (Ezek 17:18–19). Hebrews 7:20, however, refers to an oath made by God himself: "The Lord has sworn and will not change his mind" (Ps 110:4a; Heb 7:21b). On oaths see NOTES on 6:13, 16; cf. 3:11.

for they have become priests without the swearing of an oath. The rites by which Aaron and his sons were consecrated for priestly service included bathing, donning sacred vestments, being anointed, and offering sacrifices (Exod 29; Lev 8). God gave "commands" concerning these rites (Lev 8:4, 5, 9, 13, etc.), but the Scriptures do not say that God established them by an oath. The NRSV says that priests "took their office" without an oath, which might simply suggest that priests did not swear an oath of office. It is true that the OT makes no mention of priests taking an ordination vow, but here the point is that *God* did not swear an oath concerning Levitical priests.

7:21. *but he through the swearing of an oath.* Jesus' priesthood was established by the oath that God swore in Ps 110:4. The significance of the oath might have been especially apparent to "those from Italy" (13:24), for the emperor only admitted a priest into a college after he had taken an oath that the person was worthy (Suetonius, *Claudius* 22; Moffatt). Jesus had an oath made on his behalf, not by the emperor, but by God.

The Lord has sworn and will not change his mind. Here Hebrews quotes the initial part of Ps 110:4 (109:4 LXX). In the OT God was said to have changed his mind or relented in his anger toward Israel (Ps 106:45) and in his decision to make Saul king (1 Sam 15:35; cf. Gen 6:6). God was not capricious: "God is not a man that he should lie, or a son of man that he should repent. He has said, and will he not do it? Or has he spoken, and will he not fulfill it?" (Num 23:19). God sometimes changed his mind in order to do good (Exod 32:14; Jer 18:8; Joel 2:13–14; Amos 7:3, 6; Jon 3:9–10), although his judgments could be unrelenting (1 Sam 15:29; Jer 4:28; Zech 8:14). Paul said that God's gifts and calling were irrevocable (Rom 11:29), and Hebrews insists that God's oath is unchangeable (NOTES on Heb 6:17–18).

"You are a priest forever." Some MSS continue the quotation of Ps 110:4 by adding "according to the type of Melchizedek" ($\aleph^2$ A D Ψ Maj; cf. KJV; Heb 5:6; 6:20; 7:17). Many MSS omit the phrase (P^{46} ℵ* B C etc.), and its inclusion is almost certainly a secondary expansion.

7:22. *Jesus has become the surety.* In common practice a "surety" (*engyos*) agreed to assume responsibility for another person's debt if that person should be unable to meet the obligation (Taubenschlag, *Law*, 298–99, 411–17). A surety was often a relative or friend (Sir 29:14; cf. Plutarch, *Alcibiades* 5.4). People were to be cautious about standing surety (Prov 17:18; 22:26), since a failure to repay a debt led to lawsuits (Sir 29:19). "Being surety has ruined many who were prosperous, and has tossed them about like waves of the sea; it has driven the influential into exile" (Sir 29:18). Sureties were "liable to the same penalties as the prisoners for whom they had gone bail" (Andocides, *On the Mysteries* 44), which in extreme cases included death (Philostratus, *Gymnasticus* 24). Therefore, "do not forget the kindness of your surety, for he has given his life for you" (Sir 29:15). See *TLNT* 1.390–95. A surety is similar to an "intermediary" (NOTE on Heb 8:6). The use of "surety" in connection with a will (see the next NOTE) is unusual; the executor of a will was commonly called an *epitropos* (Michel, *Brief*, 292)

of a superior covenant. The term *diathēkē* encompasses two aspects of meaning:

(**a**) Covenant. God's relationship with Israel was identified as a *bĕrît* in Hebrew, which was translated as *diathēkē* in the LXX and as "covenant" in English. A fundamental element in the covenants is God's promise: God's covenant with Noah meant that he would not destroy the world again by water (Gen 9:9–18), and the covenant with Abraham centered on God's promise of land (Gen 15:18) and descendants (Gen 17:2–8). God's covenant at Mount Sinai was defined by the Law (Exod 24:7–8; 34:28). The term "covenant" was also used for God's promises to establish the Davidic dynasty (2 Sam 23:5; Sir 45:25) and a Levitical priesthood (Num 25:12–13; Mal 2:4–5). Hebrews refers to only two biblical "covenants": the covenant under Moses (Heb 8:9; 9:4, 15b, 20) and the new covenant. The terms "Law" and "covenant" were often synonyms (Deut 29:21; Ps 78:10; Hos 8:1; Sir 24:23; 39:8; 42:2). In the next section the author will deal at length with the new "covenant" that was promised in Jer 31:31–34 and realized in Christ (Heb 8:6, 8, 10; 9:15a; 10:16, 29; 12:24; 13:20). On Law and covenant, see pp. 112–15.

(**b**) Testament. The standard use of *diathēkē* outside the LXX is for a testament or will (e.g., *P. Oxy.* ##489.13, 23, 26; 490.4, 7; 491.4). A testament declared how property was to be distributed and debts were to be paid after a person's death (see Hunt and Edgar, *Select Papyri* 1, ##82–86; *P. Oxy.* ##489–95). This use of *diathēkē* bridges the world of ancient Israel and the Greco-Roman world of the listeners. The author will develop the idea more fully in Heb 9:16–17 (cf. Gal 3:15, 17). Interpreting the work of Christ in terms of a testament was appropriate since the listeners were the "heirs" of the promises (6:17) who hoped to "inherit" salvation (1:14; 6:12). See H. Hegermann, *EDNT* 1.299–301; G. Quell and J. Behm, *TDNT* 2.104–34.

7:23. *Those who have become priests.* The use of the perfect tense is sometimes taken to mean that Levitical priests still served in the Temple when Hebrews was written (P. E. Hughes, *Commentary*, 30–32, 268), but verb tenses are an unreliable clue to the date of composition (see p. 53).

are numerous. Many priests served in Israel's sanctuary at any given time (cf. 9:6), but here Hebrews refers to the succession of priests who served over many generations. Josephus said that there were eighty-three high priests from Aaron to Phanasus, the last high priest (*Ant.* 20.227).

because death prevents them. The death of Aaron, the first high priest, is recounted in Num 20:22–29. Eleazar, the son of Aaron, succeeded him. The Law assumed that the high priest's death would be a regular occurrence (Num 35:25, 28, 32).

from continuing to serve. The word *paramenein* can indicate continuing to serve in a given capacity, such as an apprentice, a servant (MM, 487–88), or a priest (Josephus, *Ant.* 9.273).

7:24. *but he holds the priesthood inviolate.* The word *aparabaton* ("inviolate") could be used in a prescriptive sense: a judge's decision was to "remain valid and inviolate" (*P. Ryl.* #65.18), and people were to pursue what was best, making this an inviolable law (Epictetus, *Ench.* 51.2; *Disc.* 2.15.1). The term was used descriptively for what did not deviate from the norm (Philo, *Eternity* 112; Plutarch, *Mor.* 410E), like Jews who constantly adhered to the Mosaic Law (Josephus, *Ant.* 18.266; *Ag. Ap.* 2.293). Here the term indicates that Jesus holds his priesthood in a manner unbroken by death (NASB; NIV; NRSV; REB, NJB; NAB2). The alternative is that *aparabaton* means "untransferable," since Jesus has no successor in priestly office (TEV; Chrysostom; Ps.-Oecumenius; Theodoret; Erasmus, *Paraphrase*; Moffatt; Spicq; P. E. Hughes). The problem is that this meaning is not attested in sources contemporary with Hebrews. See J. Schneider, *TDNT* 5.742–43; *TLNT* 1.143–44.

because he continues forever. Levitical priests do not "continue" (*paramenein*; 7:23), but Christ does "continue" (*menein*). Such unending duration characterizes the priesthood that is foreshadowed by Melchizedek and realized by the exalted Christ. "The absolute usage is striking. Christ is not said to remain a *priest* forever; he simply *remains*" (Attridge, *Epistle*, 209). According to some Jewish traditions, the Messiah was to continue forever (John 12:34; cf. Ps 89:36), but it was more commonly said that God continues forever (Dan 6:26 [6:27 LXX]; Pss 9:7 [9:8 LXX]; 102:12 [101:12 LXX]). Continued existence manifests the perfection of the exalted Son of God, who is not subject to death (Heb 1:10–12; 7:28).

7:25. *Because of this he is indeed able to save.* "Because of" his unending life, Jesus is uniquely positioned "to save" others. The human situation is complex: people need to be saved from divine judgment because of their sin and from the threat posed by hostile powers (see COMMENT *b*). Here, Jesus saves by interceding with God for people (NOTES below).

completely. In a temporal sense *panteles* can mean "for all time" so that it is synonymous with "forever" (7:24b), "always" (7:25b), and "to all eternity" (Dittenberger, *OGIS*, 642.2; *P.Lond.* #1164.11; Braun; NRSV; NAB2). In a qualitative sense the word can mean "completely" so that it refers to "complete salvation" (3 Macc 7:16; Philo, *Husbandry* 94, 96; *Migration* 2; cf. NIV; REB; NJB). The salvation provided by Christ is everlasting precisely because it is complete.

those who approach God through him. People approach God now through prayer (NOTE on 4:16; cf. 10:1, 22; 11:6) and in a final sense by entering the heavenly Jerusalem (12:18, 22; cf. NOTES on 4:16 and 7:19). For a person to approach God "through" Jesus means that he or she lodges a request with Jesus, trusting that he will bring it before God for a favorable response:

(**a**) Theological factors. There were precedents for asking another person to "bear messages to the Lord on their behalf" (*T. Mos.* 11:17). The hope was that a request would be favorably received if submitted by someone approved by God, such as a priest (4 Macc 4:11–13), prophet, or other godly person (Exod 8:8; 1 Sam 7:8; 12:19; 1 Kgs 13:6; Isa 37:4; Jer 37:3; 42:2; Jdt 8:31). Angels were also said to bring people's requests before God (Tob 12:12; cf. Job 16:19–22; *1 Enoch* 9:1–3; 47:1–2; 99:3). In Hebrews, Jesus is like Israel's priests and prophets in that he has favorable standing in God's eyes, but he is superior to them in that his work is heavenly and everlasting (Heb 1:1–2; 3:1–6; 5:1–10). Jesus is like the angels in that he brings requests before God in heaven, yet he is superior to angels since he understands human anguish because of his own suffering (2:10–18; 4:14–16) and since he alone is seated at God's right hand (1:1–14).

(b) Social factors. On a human level, people recognized that requests that were brought before a sovereign would be most favorably received if submitted by someone close to the throne (Pliny the Younger, *Letters* 10.5; cf. 10.6, 104, 106; cf. Sophocles, *Oedipus Tyrannus* 771–74). Members of the imperial household were especially well-positioned to provide access to the emperor (Saller, *Personal Patronage*, 59). According to Hebrews, Jesus the Son is now seated at God's right hand, which is a good place from which to make requests (NOTE on 1:13). If listeners value human intermediaries when dealing with officials, how much more should they value the Son as an intermediary when relating to God (deSilva, *Despising*, 226–42).

since he always lives to intercede on their behalf. Intercession has two aspects:

(a) Plea for assistance. Intercession often involved an appeal for assistance (1 Macc 8:32), justice (2 Macc 4:36), or permission to do something (3 Macc 6:37). The term was used when a person who had been wronged lodged a complaint with a person in authority (Acts 25:24; 1 Macc 11:25; *P. Oxy.* ##486.37; 533.25) or with God (Rom 11:2; *1 Enoch* 9:3, 10; 22:5–7). Intercession could mean asking God for deliverance from one's enemies (Philo, *Moses* 1.173; 2 Macc 15:12). Those addressed by Hebrews had suffered violence, dispossession, and imprisonment in the past as well as ongoing reproach from others (Heb 10:32–34; 13:3, 13). Christ's intercession was an ongoing source of help (2:18; 4:16). See Loader, *Sohn*, 147; Attridge; Lane.

(b) Plea for forgiveness. The word "intercede" (*entynchanein*) is not used for forgiveness in the OT, although some prayed for deliverance from divine judgment (Gen 18:22–33; Exod 32:11–14; Num 14:13–19; 1 Sam 7:5–9; 2 Macc 7:37–38; 4 Macc 6:27–29). Early Christian writings use the verb for intercessions made because of sin (*1 Clem.* 56:1; cf. Pol. *Phil.* 4:3; Herm. *Sim.* 2.6, 8). When Paul says that Christ "intercedes for us" (Rom 8:34), he could mean that Christ prays for mercy in the face of divine judgment or for deliverance from hostile powers. Forgiveness is clearly in view in 1 John 2:1. The strongest reasons for assuming that intercession in Hebrews involves petitions for forgiveness are that Heb 7:26–27 mentions human sin, that Christ's priestly work involves making atonement (2:17), and that the new covenant brings forgiveness (Heb 8:12; 10:17). The high priest was also understood to offer prayers so "that sins may be remembered no more" (Philo, *Moses* 2.134; *m. Yoma* 4:2; 6:2). Cf. Braun; Hay, *Glory*, 149–50; *TLNT* 2.6–10; O. Bauernfeind, *TDNT* 8.242–45.

7:26. *Now, such a high priest was indeed fitting for us.* On the term "fitting" see NOTE on 2:10.

holy. This word (*hosios*) is used only here in Hebrews, although it is common in the OT for faithful worshipers of God (e.g., Pss 30:4 [29:5 LXX]; 31:23 [30:24 LXX]). The NT applies this term to Jesus (Acts 2:27; 13:35). Holiness was essential for a priest since only the holy could enter the Temple (Josephus, *Ant.* 19.332).

blameless. This term could be used for the innocent (Job 2:3; 8:20), and it was virtually synonymous with "holy" (see Prov 2:21 LXX; *TLNT* 1.53–55). On Jesus' sinlessness see NOTE on 4:15.

undefiled. According to Jewish Law, people became defiled (*miainein*) in various ways (see pp. 119–21). The corresponding term "undefiled" (*amiantos*) indicated both physical and moral purity (Plutarch, *Mor.* 383B; 395E), including sexual purity (Heb 13:4; Wis 3:13) and freedom from the taint of death (1 Pet 1:4). God wants worshipers who are "pure in heart and undefiled" (*T. Jos.* 4:6; cf. Jas 1:27; *1 Clem.* 29:1). According to the Mosaic Law, the high priest was to remain undefiled by any contact with the dead (Lev 21:11; Philo, *Special Laws* 1.113, 250; cf. *Flight* 118), but Hebrews argues that Christians have a high priest who remains undefiled even though he has "tasted death on behalf of everyone" (Heb 2:9).

separated from sinners. The expression has two aspects of meaning:

(a) Qualitative separation. When read in connection with the preceding words ("holy, blameless, undefiled"), "separated" means being different from sinners. Jesus belonged to a different category (Epictetus, *Disc.* 2.9.2; 2.10.2; 4.11.1; 3 Macc 2:25). Jesus was opposed by sinners (Heb 12:3), but did not capitulate to sin (4:15; cf. Sir 13:17b; Calvin; P. E. Hughes; Bénétreau).

(b) Spatial separation. When read in connection with the following words ("exalted above the heavens"), "separated" means that by his exaltation Jesus was removed from the place of sinners. Righteous people were to maintain their distance from sinners (Ps 1:1; Sir 11:9; cf. 1 Esdr 7:13; 2 Esdr 9:1). Israel's high priest was separated from other people before the Day of Atonement in order that he might not be defiled and thereby rendered ineligible to perform his duties (*m. Yoma* 1:1). Jesus' situation varies this theme since he first became like other people by his incarnation (2:10–18) before being separated from them through his exaltation. Cf. Luther; Lane; Attridge; Braun; Ellingworth. Because of its transitional point in the sentence, neither the qualitative nor the spatial connotations can be excluded (F. F. Bruce; Grässer).

exalted above the heavens. Exaltation "above" the heavens probably does not refer to Christ's triumph over cosmic powers (Eph 4:10; 6:12; Michel; Löhr, "Thronversammlung," 188–89), an idea that is evident in Heb 2:14–15, but not in 7:26. Elsewhere Jesus is said to have entered "into" heaven (9:24) and to have taken his seat beside God "in" the heavens (8:1).

7:27. *who has no need.* The Mosaic Law said that sacrifices were to be offered when a priest sinned (Lev 4:3–12; 16:6, 11). On the basis of these statutes, Hebrews assumes that priests regularly sinned. Jesus alone was sinless (NOTE on 4:15).

as do the high priests. See NOTE on 4:14.

to offer sacrifices each day. Hebrews apparently conflates daily sacrifices and the Day of Atonement sacrifices (see the next NOTE). Priests offered "sacrifices each day," both morning and evening (Exod 29:38–42; Num 28:3–8; Sir 45:14). The Law said that daily sacrifices were to be offered by Aaron, who was high priest, and his sons so that it might be said that the high priest made daily offerings (Sir 45:14; Philo, *Special Laws* 3.131). In practice the high priest offered these daily sacrifices only if he chose to do so; otherwise ordinary priests performed the duty (Josephus, *J.W.* 5.230; *m. Tamid* 7:3).

first for their own sins and then for those of the people. On the Day of Atonement, the high priest offered sacrifice first for himself and his household (Lev 16:6–14), then for the people (Lev 16:15–16). The problem is that these sacrifices were made only once each year (Heb 9:7, 25). The author apparently fuses the Day of Atonement sacrifices with other sacrifices:

(a) "Tamid" offerings were the offerings that were made each day, both morning and evening (Exod 29:38–42). Some sources suggested that these were offered by the high priest each day (previous NOTE), but daily sacrifices were not made for the high priest's own sins. Conversely, sacrifices for a priest's sins were made on an occasional rather than a daily basis (Lev 4:3). Since daily offerings were sometimes listed together with Day of Atonement sacrifices in Scripture, Hebrews may have conflated them (Num 28:3–8; 29:7–11; Ellingworth).

(b) A "sacrifice" (*thysia*; Lev 6:20 LXX) of meal for the priests was made along with the Tamid sacrifices. Philo (*Heir* 174) closely connected the daily meal offering (Lev 6:20) with the daily offering of lambs (Exod 29:38–42). Hebrews' comments about sacrifices may reflect a conflation of these practices. The author's perspective seems to be based on the OT and tradition rather than on personal knowledge of Temple practice (Attridge).

because he did this once for all. The terms *ephapax* (7:27; 9:12; 10:10) and *hapax* (6:4; 9:7, 26–28; 10:2; 12:26–27) have the quantitative sense of singularity and the qualitative sense of completeness (cf. NOTE on 6:4). Christ's sacrifice was singular because it achieved complete cleansing for sin, whereas the multiple Levitical sacrifices did not achieve complete cleansing, and therefore had to be repeated (10:1–3; cf. Rom 6:10; 1 Pet 3:18). See *TLNT* 1.139–42.

when he offered himself. Levitical priests offered animals, but Christ offered himself, thereby making a superior sacrifice (9:13–14). Early Christians recognized that it was not only important that Christ died, but that he voluntarily "gave himself for our sins" (Gal 1:4; cf. Mark 10:45; 1 Tim 2:6; Tit 2:14; John 10:11, 18; cf. 1 John 3:16). See §24 COMMENT *b*.

7:28. *For the Law establishes as high priests.* See NOTE on 5:1.

men who have weaknesses. The weaknesses to which priests are subject include both death (7:23) and sin (7:27). Cf. NOTE on 5:2.

but the word sworn on oath, which came after the Law. Hebrews assumes that the Law was given through Moses and that the oath concerning the priest like Melchizedek (Ps 110:4) was given later, in the time of David, whom the author understands to have authored the Psalms. On oaths see NOTE on 7:20.

establishes a Son who has been made complete forever. Instead of referring to Jesus as a priest the author calls him "Son," evoking the sense of power that was established earlier (1:2, 5, 8; 3:6; 4:14; 5:5, 8; 6:6; 7:3). The idea that God's Son has been "made complete" suggests that he was brought to eternal glory and ordained to an everlasting priesthood (pp. 122–25).

COMMENT[242]

The preceding argument about the Mosaic Law and Levitical priesthood (7:11–19) raises questions about the reliability of God. The Law was the abiding basis for Jewish faith and life, yet Hebrews declared that a change had occurred in the Law (7:12) and that some of its commands had been abrogated (7:18) because the Law had failed to bring God's design for people to completion (7:19). The problem is that if God changed the Law by appointing Jesus to be a non-Levitical high priest, how can people be confident that this new arrangement will be permanent? The author responds to this question by pointing out that God's appointment of Christ to an everlasting priesthood is confirmed by an oath (7:20), and in the earlier section about God's faithfulness to Abraham, the author attempted to show that God's oaths are reliable (6:13–20). The author also addresses the issue at the end of this section, when he reaffirms that God's Son has been "made complete" (7:28), recalling how God brings his purposes to completion through the suffering and exaltation of Christ (5:8–9). In him people of faith can see the realization of God's designs.

Structurally, this section is framed by the word *horkomosia* ("swearing an oath"; 7:20, 28), and it is connected to the previous section by the theme of "completion" (7:11, 19, 28). Internally, the passage can be divided into three paragraphs: **(a)** The oath of God from Ps 110:4 is the focus of Heb 7:20–22. Previously (7:11–19), the author took up the main elements of that verse in reverse order to show that Jesus was *according to the type of Melchizedek* (Ps 110:4c), who by virtue of his resurrection serves as *a priest forever* (110:4b). Here the author takes up the first part of the psalm verse: *The Lord has sworn and will not change his mind* (110:4a; Heb 7:21b). **(b)** Jesus' superiority to those who are subject to death is emphasized in 7:22–25. The basis of the argument is the conviction that Jesus has been exalted from death to everlasting life in heaven. **(c)** Jesus' superiority to those who need sacrifices for their own sins is the focus of 7:26–28.[243]

a. "The Lord Has Sworn and Will Not Change His Mind" (7:20–22)

The oath of God (7:20a) is abruptly reintroduced in the wake of the author's comments about the Law's failure and his declaration that people now have a superior hope in Christ (cf. 7:19). The force of the comment comes first from previous associations concerning the oath. When God swore that Moses' generation would not enter the promised land, God kept the oath, and they died in the wilderness (3:11, 16–19). When God swore that he would give Abraham many descendants, God kept his oath so that the listeners could count themselves among Abraham's many children (2:16; 6:13–20). Therefore, listeners can be confident that when God makes an oath, he will be faithful to it. God's character offers listeners a second reason for confidence. It was widely acknowledged

[242]For bibliography on 7:20–28 see §17 COMMENT n. 207.

[243]On the internal structure see Vanhoye, *La structure*, 133–37; Attridge, *Epistle*, 206–7.

that God did not lie (NOTE on 6:18). A "change" may have occurred in the Law (7:12), but God does not lie under oath. His commitment is "unchangeable" (6:17), and listeners can therefore trust it.

The observation that Levitical priests assume their office without God's oath (7:20b) puts older priestly practices in a new perspective. Since the OT assigned the priesthood to the descendants of Levi for all time (Exod 40:15; Num 18:19; 25:13), Hebrews does not facilely reject the tradition, but presses a tension within the tradition. The Scriptures spoke of not one, but two types of priesthood: the Levitical priesthood established by the Law, and the priesthood after the type of Melchizedek promised in Ps 110:4. The Law included no oath of God concerning the Levitical priesthood, and the author assumes that this silence is no oversight,[244] since the Lord made it a point to swear an oath concerning the priest like Melchizedek (Ps 110:4a; Heb 7:21b). Therefore, if there can be only one priesthood—and the author assumes that this is the case (§18 COMMENT *a*)—then the permanent and superior priesthood belongs to Jesus.

A change in the priesthood means an abrogation of Law (7:12, 18), but it does not mean that God promotes "lawlessness" (1:9), for the new arrangement involves a "superior covenant" to restrain sin (7:22). Paradoxically, "lawlessness" existed despite the Mosaic Law, for people did not keep it (10:17; cf. 8:9). Therefore, in order to be true to his purposes, God inaugurates a new and superior covenant under which he will inscribe his "laws" on human hearts (8:10).[245] The new covenant is superior in that it is an "eternal covenant" (13:20) rather than a provisional one, it establishes a ministry that cleanses the conscience, not merely the flesh (9:13–14), and it provides the means by which God completes his purposes by bringing people to his heavenly city (12:22–24).

Calling Jesus the "surety" for the superior covenant (7:22a) connects the biblical idea of covenant with Greco-Roman conventions. According to common practice, people who made a legal commitment could have a second party stand surety. A surety agreed to fulfill the obligation if the party making the commitment failed to do so (NOTE on 7:22). Some have suggested that Jesus is the surety who guarantees that humanity's obligations toward God will be fulfilled,[246] yet this interpretation does not suit the context. Since God is the one who appointed Jesus to be a priest, God has established Jesus as his own surety. Jesus is the one who assures people that God will not default on his promises concerning salvation and eternal inheritance. When listeners want to take God to task for seem-

---

[244]The Bible's failure to mention an oath in connection with the Levitical priesthood is taken as seriously as its silence about Melchizedek's ancestry. See §17 COMMENT *a*.

[245]The author recognizes that the new covenant is not fully in place since sin remains a problem, even for Christians. Yet he will argue that the new covenant has its sure basis in the sacrifice of Christ. See §21 COMMENT *b*.

[246]F. F. Bruce, *Epistle*, 171 n. 70; Peterson, *Hebrews*, 247 n. 55. Philo (*Heir* 205–6) refers to the Logos as a suppliant on behalf of humanity before God and as an intermediary who ensures that created beings will adhere to the proper order of things and that God will not forget his own work (Attridge, *Epistle*, 208 n. 35). Philo's argument, however, pertains to the created order of being rather than the inauguration of a new covenant.

ing to default on his word, the author says that they can turn to Jesus and claim him as surety until the promises are kept.

b. He Holds the Priesthood Permanently (7:22–25)

In Israel's history there were "many" priests (7:23a), creating a venerable tradition. People in antiquity commonly valued ancient traditions and were suspicious of religious innovations. Jewish practices were considered eccentric by many, but non-Jews generally respected them because they belonged to Jewish ancestral religion. Christians lacked this aura of antiquity and were accused of altering custom (Acts 6:14; 16:20–21). Later, critics charged that Christians "break the laws, which require everyone to reverence ancestral custom," and that they were "meddlesome through love of innovation."[247] Appeal to another common idea, however, enables Hebrews to show the superiority of Christ's priesthood, despite its seeming novelty. People regularly agreed that life is better than death (Deut 30:15; Prov 14:27; Jer 8:3). Therefore, instead of identifying the line of Jewish priests with tradition, Hebrews associates them with mortality. The author points out that there were many priests in Jewish tradition because death prevented them from continuing in service (Heb 7:23b). Like Israel's priests, Jesus did die, yet death did not terminate his priesthood, but rather inaugurated it (cf. pp. 109–10). Jesus "offered himself" through death (7:27), yet death did not mean that he ceased to exist, for through his exaltation he continues forever.[248]

Because of his eternal priesthood, Christ is able to bring salvation (7:25a; NOTE on 2:3) and to provide a way for people to approach God (7:25b). The idea that people should draw near to God "through" a priestly mediator reflects the ambivalence that people sense when they must relate to a God who is both threatening and attractive. On the one hand, it is a fearful thing to fall into the hands of God, whose wrath falls on sinners (10:31; 12:29; 13:4; cf. 3:11, 17). On the other hand, the goal of human life is to enter God's own rest (4:10) and to rejoice in the presence of the living God (12:22). As a mediator, Christ enables people to approach God, yet he must also serve as a buffer between mortals and the consuming fire (cf. NOTE on 7:25). Christ intercedes for others from his position at God's right hand (7:25c). Insofar as people are tested and afflicted by other people or by the devil they need divine help to persevere (2:15; 13:3, 13), and insofar as they are sinful they stand under God's judgment and need forgiveness. Accordingly, Christ's intercession first means requesting help for those who are being tested, and second it involves petitions for forgiveness, which extend the benefits of Christ's once-for-all sacrifice to particular sins (NOTES on 7:25).[249]

---

[247]Eusebius, *Preparation for the Gospel* 4.1 (130C). See also *Diogn.* 1:1. On reverence for tradition see Plutarch, *Mor.* 756B; cf. 402E, 416C. On Greco-Roman acceptance of Jewish distinctiveness see p. 70.

[248]There is also an implied contrast between the many priests of the Levitical order and the singular priesthood of Jesus. This is reinforced by the instances of *hoi men . . . ho de* in 7:20–21, 23–24.

[249]Hay considers Jesus' intercession a foreign element in Hebrews since it is mentioned only once and is never developed (*Glory*, 150). Braun (*Hebräer*, 221) associates intercession with postbaptismal

Theologically, both the similarities and the differences between Christ and others are important for his intercession. On the one hand, Christ became *like* his brothers and sisters by sharing in their flesh and blood, and by suffering and dying (2:10–15). Emphasizing this aspect of Christ's work, Aquinas said that Christ's shared humanity helps move God to "take pity on us for whom the Son of God took human nature."[250] On the other hand, Christ was *different* from others in that he alone was sinless (4:15). Accenting this dimension of Christ's work, Calvin commented that Christ "turns the Father's eyes to his own righteousness to avert his gaze from our sins."[251] Having entered the heavenly sanctuary, Christ "alone bears to God the petitions of the people, who stay far off in the outer court" (Calvin, *Institutes* 3.20.20).

c. Exalted Above the Heavens (7:26–28)

The difference between Christ's exalted position and the more abject condition of humanity is further shown by the list of traits in 7:26: Christ is "holy, blameless, undefiled, separated from sinners, exalted above the heavens."[252] This kind of high priest is fitting for people (7:26a), not because they manifest these same traits, but because these traits correspond to God's designs for them. Terms like "holy," "blameless," and "undefiled" could be applied to some people (NOTES on 7:26), but when taken together and identified with exaltation above the heavens, it is clear that Christ exhibits a kind of perfection (7:28c) that goes beyond what might be said of any other human being. At the same time, he is "separat-

---

sin. It is not evident that Hebrews distinguishes sins committed before and after baptism. The idea of Christ's intercession can best be understood to be an application of Christ's once-for-all sacrifice.

[250]Thomas Aquinas, *Summa Theologia* III, ques. 57, art. 6. Gregory of Nazianzus commented that when Christ made intercession for people before God, he did so bearing his own human body—although this was no longer a body of ordinary flesh (NPNF[2] 7.315). Similarly, Gregory the Great said that for "the only-begotten Son to plead for man is to demonstrate before the eternal Father that he himself is a man" (*Mor.* 22.27.42). Interpreters did distinguish the manner of Christ's prayer upon earth from his intercession in heaven, however. Before his death he prayed with "loud cries and tears" (Heb 5:7), but the same is not said of his posture in heaven. Therefore, one should not think of Christ "prostrating himself for us before the Father, and falling down before him in slavish fashion" (Gregory of Nazianzus, NPNF[2] 7.315; cf. John Owen, *Exposition*, 5.539).

[251]Calvin, *Institutes* 2.16.16. Karl Barth said that "Jesus Christ Himself lives, His obedience pleading for our disobedience" (*Church Dogmatics*, IV/1, 315).

[252]A number of scholars maintain that the author based his depiction of Christ on an early Christian hymn. Features of the text include asyndeton, alliteration of words beginning with *a*-, parallel clauses (*hosios . . . amiantos*; *kechōrismenos . . . hamartōlōn*, *hypsēloteros . . . genomenos*), assonance (*hamartōlōn . . . ouranōn*), and chiasm (separated[a] from sinners[b] / above the heavens[b] exalted[a]). See Attridge, *Epistle*, 212. The vocabulary is unusual and depicts Christ's journey to glory (cf. Phil 2:6–11; Col 1:15–20; 1 Tim 3:13; John 1:1–18). Windisch (*Hebräerbrief*, 67) spoke of 7:26–28 as a hymn, and Theissen (*Untersuchungen*, 22–25) attempted a more elaborate reconstruction that encompassed 7:3 and 7:26 (cf. Rissi, *Theologie*, 86–87; Michel, *Brief*, 278). Zimmermann (*Bekenntnis*, 93–97) couples 7:1–3 and 7:26. Many scholars find the idea of a hymnic source implausible, recognizing that the author was fully capable of composing such elevated language (Laub, *Bekenntnis*, 33; Hegermann; Attridge; Grässer; H.-F. Weiss).

ed from sinners" (7:26), not because he rejects them, but in order that others might come to share life in God's presence (2:10).[253]

Hebrews does not criticize the Levitical order by pointing out the failings of particular priests (NOTES on 5:1–10). Instead, he points out characteristics inherent in the institution itself:

Levitical Priests	*Christ the Priest*
Daily sacrifices	Single sacrifice
For themselves	Of himself
For others	For others

Levitical priests and Christ are alike in that both minister for the sake of others, but they differ in two respects. First, Levitical priests must offer sacrifices each day, which points to their ultimate ineffectiveness (9:13–14; 10:1–4), whereas Jesus offered himself once for all (7:27c), which shows the completeness of his work. Second, Levitical priests offer sacrifices for themselves as well as for others (Lev 4:3; 16:6, 11). Christ, however, did not make an offering *for* himself but *of* himself for the sake of others (cf. NOTE on 10:11).

A final set of contrasts in 7:28 summarizes and completes the argument:

The Law establishes	*The oath establishes*
high priests	a Son
who have weaknesses	who has been made complete

Many regarded the Law as the permanent basis of Jewish life, but Hebrews argues that God's appointment of Jesus as a non-Levitical priest has altered the Law (7:12, 18). The author insists that God's oath concerning this new priest is unchangeable, however, making it a sure basis for the listeners' trust (7:20–21; cf. 6:17–18). Hebrews points out that God issued the oath after he had given the Law, and the idea that God's most recent declaration supersedes his earlier one is consistent with common legal practice. A person who made a testament (*diathēkē*) commonly said, "So long as I live I am to have power . . . to make any further provisions or new dispositions I choose and to abrogate this will, and any such provisions shall be valid" (*P. Oxy.* #492.9; NOTE on Heb 7:18). Hebrews assumes that "the living God" has the right to establish a new priesthood beyond the one based on his earlier covenant (*diathēkē*).[254]

Hebrews contrasts the multiplicity of Levitical high priests with the singular Son of God (7:28). Abruptly calling Jesus "Son" rather than high priest, the au-

[253]See Calvin, *Epistle*, 102. Braun (*Hebräer*, 224) commented that in this passage the idea that Jesus is a friend of sinners (Matt 11:19; Mark 2:16–17) seems to have been lost. The point, however, is that Jesus helps sinners, not by becoming a sinner, but by saving sinners.

[254]Paul also relativized the Law in Gal 3:15–18, but argued in the opposite direction. He insisted that God made a covenant with Abraham that was not superseded by the Law, which was instituted centuries later. On the relationship of this argument to Israel's covenant tradition and Greco-Roman legal practice see Llewelyn, *New Documents*, 6.41–47.

thor stresses Jesus' uniqueness over members of the Levitical order by reminding listeners of the majestic portrait of the Son in 1:1–14 and of the idea that the Son is in a singular position over the household of God (3:1–6). In one sense Christ's movement from suffering to completion in glory is exemplary, offering hope that since God exalted the Son who suffered, he will exalt his other sons and daughters who suffer. In another sense, Christ's completion is unique, for from his position at God's right hand he is singularly able to minister on behalf of others (see pp. 122–25). Performing a singular act on behalf of others was widely regarded as praiseworthy (Aristotle, *Rhetoric*, 1.9.38; Quintilian, *Inst.* 3.7.16).

20. Heavenly and Earthly Sanctuaries (8:1–6)

8 [1]Now, the point of what we are saying is that we have such a high priest, who sat down at the right hand of the throne of the Majesty in the heavens, [2]a minister of the sanctuary, that is, of the true tent which the Lord, not a human being, set up. [3]For every high priest is appointed to offer gifts and sacrifices; therefore this one also must have something to offer. [4]So if he were on earth he would not be a priest, because there are those who offer gifts in accordance with Law, [5]who serve in a representation and a shadow of the heavenly [sanctuary], just as Moses was divinely admonished when he was about to construct the tent; for [God] said, *See that you make everything according to the pattern that was shown to you on the mountain.* [6]But now [Jesus] has received a ministry that is superior to the same extent that he is also mediator of a superior covenant, which has been lawfully established upon superior promises.

NOTES

8:1. *Now, the point of what we are saying.* The word *kephalaion* has several uses: **(a)** Point. This is the preferred understanding in this instance. Speakers sometimes used the word for the main point of an argument (Thucydides, *Peloponesian War* 4.50.2; Plato, *Phaedo* 95b; Philo, *Names* 106; MM, 342). After a complex argument, Hebrews now identifies the main idea before introducing new material (Calvin; Attridge; Ellingworth; Hegermann; H.-F. Weiss). **(b)** Crowning affirmation. The term can indicate the point to which other points are subordinate (Philo, *Alleg. Interp.* 2.102). Some take the comment about Christ's heavenly ministry to complete the preceding argument (Williamson, *Philo*, 123–29; Lane). Although this is possible, the comment does more to lead into the next section than to complete what has already been said. **(c)** Summary (Isocrates, *Panegyricus* 149; Demosthenes, *On Organization* 36; Epictetus, *Disc.* 1.24.20; Josephus, *Ant.* 17.93). Some take Heb 8:1–2 to be a summary of the argument concerning the high priesthood of Christ (Alcuin; Lanfranc; Luther, *Lectures*; F. F. Bruce; cf. Vanhoye, *Old Testament*, 173). Yet this seems unlikely since a summary would include other items from 4:14–5:10 and 7:1–28. Christ's ministry in the heavenly sanctuary is actually a new topic.

Rhetorically "the point" could refer to "the head of the whole business" (Quintilian, *Inst.* 3.11.27), and Jesus' priesthood is sometimes taken to be the point of the whole speech (e.g., Vanhoye, *La structure*, 59; idem, "La 'teleiosis' "; Grässer, *Hebräer*, 2.103). Yet a "point" could also be one point within a wider discussion (Quintilian, *Inst.* 3.11.27; Josephus, *Ag. Ap.* 1.219; Philo, *Flight* 166). This seems appropriate here, because Christ's priesthood is a point, but not the only point in Hebrews. In Heb 1:1–2:4 there is only an allusion to priestly ministry (1:3). Priesthood was mentioned in 2:17–18 and 3:1, but was absent from 3:2–4:13. Jesus' priestly status was considered in 4:14–5:10, but not in 5:11–6:20. In 7:1–10:39 priesthood is the dominant category, but in 11:1–12:27 it receives no attention. In 12:28–13:21 it receives only a little attention (13:10–12). Hebrews 8:1 identifies the point of the section, not the point of the speech (cf. Bénétreau, *L'Épître*, 2.52).

is that we have such a high priest who sat down at the right hand. The one seated at God's right hand has both royal (Ps 110:1; Heb 1:3, 13) and priestly traits (Ps 110:4; Heb 8:1–2). According to Zech 6:13, the high priest was to stand at the right hand of the throne of the messianic king or "Branch," but in Hebrews Jesus is both Messiah and high priest. Priests did not perform their duties while seated, and 10:11–14 indicates that being seated points to the finality of Christ's sacrifice. On the "right hand" see NOTE on 1:13.

of the throne of the Majesty in the heavens. God's throne is associated with grace in 4:16 and with majesty in 8:1. "Majesty" is a circumlocution for "God" (NOTE on 1:3; cf. 12:2; *T. Adam* 1:9; 2:9). The majesty of God's throne was suggested by its gemlike quality (Ezek 1:26) and the cries of the angelic hosts that surrounded it (Isa 6:1) in the visions of the prophets.

8:2. *a minister.* The term *leitourgos* was used for God's heavenly attendants (Heb 1:7; cf. *leitourgikos* in 1:14) and for priests (Isa 61:1; Neh 10:39 [2 Esdr 20:40]; Sir 7:30; cf. Jer 33:21; Rom 15:16; Philo, *Alleg. Interp.* 3.135; *Dreams* 2.231). The noun *leitourgia* was used for service related to the sanctuary (Num 4:24, 27; 8:22, 24; Sir 50:19; cf. Heb 8:6; 9:21). See *TLNT* 2.378–84. As a minister, Christ offers intercessions (7:25) and the sacrifice of atonement (8:3, 6).

of the sanctuary. The genitive *tōn hagiōn* is a neuter plural that indicates a "sanctuary." Older interpreters sometimes took it as a masculine plural that identified Jesus as a minister "of the saints" (Theodoret; Ps.-Oecumenius; Alcuin) or as a neuter plural that identified him as a minister "of holy things" (Erasmus, *Paraphrase*; Luther, WA 57/3, 44; cf. Philo, *Alleg. Interp.* 3.135). Nevertheless, the term is used for the sanctuary elsewhere in Hebrews (9:2, 3, 12, 24, 25; 10:19; 13:11; Philo, *Flight* 93). The adjective *hagios* ("holy") was occasionally used for sanctuaries (Plutarch, *Mor.* 290B; Dittenberger, *OGIS* 56.59; cf. Moffatt, *Critical*, 105), but the most common terms for the Jerusalem Temple, and temples in the Greek-speaking world, were *hieron* and *naos*, which are not used in Hebrews.

that is. The text, which literally refers to "the sanctuary and [*kai*] the true tent," has been taken in two ways. The second is preferable:

(a) Different parts of the heavenly sanctuary. Some maintain that the *kai* distinguishes "the sanctuary" or holy of holies from "the true tent," which would be the outer court or the entire sanctuary. Such a distinction seems to be made in Heb 9:8, 11, and the biblical depiction of the Day of Atonement ritual uses *to hagion* for the holy of holies and *skēnē* for the entire tent (e.g., Lev 16:16). See Erasmus, *Paraphrase*; Attridge; Grässer; Bénétreau; Hofius, *Vorhang*, 59–60; Vanhoye, "Par le tente," 4; Rissi, *Theologie*, 37–41; Laub, *Bekenntnis*, 203–7.

(b) Synonyms for the one heavenly sanctuary. There are good reasons to think that "sanctuary" and "tent" are synonyms connected by the explanatory *kai* ("that is"). The two nouns are followed by the singular "which" (*hēn*), suggesting that only one tent is intended. The author frequently pairs synonyms like "representation" and "shadow" in 8:5 (cf. "transgression and disobedience," 2:2; "glory and honor," 2:9; "grace and mercy," 4:16; "gifts and sacrifices," 5:1; 8:3; "ignorant and erring," 5:2; "prayers and supplications," 5:7; "faith and perseverance," 6:12). Hebrews is flexible in its use of terms for the sanctuary. The expression *to hagion* designates the entire earthly sanctuary in 9:1, whereas *hagia* without the article refers to the outer court in 9:2, and *skēnē* is used for each of the Tabernacle's courts in 9:2–3. Moreover, the LXX does not use terms in a consistent manner. *To hagion* can designate the holy of holies (Lev 16:16) or the sanctuary as a whole (Num 3:38); *ta hagia* can refer to the whole sanctuary (Lev 10:4; Num 3:28) and can be virtually synonymous with *skēnē* (Exod 29:30). Cf. NOTE on "heavenly [sanctuary]" in 8:5. The main contrast in this passage is between the heavenly and earthly sanctuaries, not between the parts of the heavenly one. See Chrysostom; Braun; F. F. Bruce; Ellingworth; P. E. Hughes; Lane; Hegermann; H.-F. Weiss; Peterson, *Hebrews*, 130–31; NIV; REB; TEV.

of the true tent. The "true" is heavenly and abiding in contrast to what is earthly and transient (cf. Philo, *Worse* 160; *Special Laws* 1.66). The opposite of "true" can be "false" (Philo, *Special Laws* 1.332; *Gaius* 366; cf. 1 Thess 1:9), but in Hebrews the earthly sanctuary is not a false sanctuary, since God himself commanded that it be built (Heb 8:5). That sanctuary is the earthly and transient antitype of the true and abiding (9:24) sanctuary in heaven.

"Tent" (*skēnē*) is the Greek word used in the LXX for the Hebrew *'ōhel* ("tent") and *mishkān* ("dwelling" or "tabernacle"), which identify the sanctuary that Israel used in the wilderness (§22 COMMENT *a*). Some understood the "pattern" of the tent (Exod 25:40; Heb 8:5) to have been an actual heavenly tent (NOTE on 8:5; cf. Wis 9:8; Rev 15:5; 2 *Bar.* 4:5). Some older commentators considered the "true tent" to be the church (Aquinas, *Ad Heb.* §382) or Christ's body, "the greater and more perfect tent" (9:11) in which God's Word became flesh and "tented" among people (John 1:14; Calvin, *Epistle*, 105, 120; Bengel, *Epistle*, 411, 421), or to be a combination of the two ideas (Westcott, *Epistle*, 214, 257–58). Most now identify the tent as a sanctuary. See NOTE on 9:11.

which the Lord, not a human being, set up. God is said to have "set up" the tents of Israel (Num 24:6) and to have "set up" the heavens, which were sometimes described as a tent (Isa 42:5). The "true tent" that God "set up" was the heavenly one (see the previous NOTE). Hebrews 9:24 calls the earthly sanctuary a shrine "made with hands," which has pejorative connotations, but these connotations are not developed in 8:5. For more negative assessments see NOTE on 9:11–12.

8:3. *For every high priest is appointed to offer gifts and sacrifices.* See NOTES on 5:1.

therefore this one also must have something to offer. The present tense of "offer" is used for the ongoing action of Levitical priests (8:3a), but the aorist tense is used for Jesus (8:3b) since his death was singular and definitive (7:27; cf. the aorist tenses in 1:3; 10:12). Similarly, Christ is said to offer "something" (*ti*), in the singular, in contrast to the multiple "gifts and sacrifices" of Levitical priests. The "something" that he offered was "himself" by crucifixion (7:27).

8:4. *So if he were on earth he would not be a priest.* This is a condition contrary to fact: if he were on earth (but he is not), he would not be a priest (although in fact he is a priest). The Law defines earthly priesthood, not heavenly priesthood.

because there are those who offer gifts in accordance with Law. Some MSS specify that there are "the priests" (D^2 [Ψ] 0278 Maj; cf. KJV) who offer gifts, but other MSS lack these words (P^{46} ℵ A B D* etc.). If original, the words could have been omitted because of homoioteleuton, but it seems more likely that they were added to clarify the sentence (cf. NRSV; REB). The present tense verb "offer" could have been used whether or not the Temple was standing (see pp. 52–53).

8:5. *who serve.* The verb *latreuein* was often used for service at a sanctuary and could apply to priests (8:5; cf. *latreia* in 9:1, 6) and others (9:9; 10:2; cf. 13:10). See NOTE on 9:1. The term could also be used for a manner of life characterized by praise of God and care for other people (12:28–13:6). The term is similar in meaning to "minister" (*leitourgein*; 8:6).

in a representation. The term *hypodeigma* has been translated "copy" (NIV; NAB2), "sketch" (NRSV), "symbol" (REB), and "model" (NJB). The word was commonly used for an "example" of disobedience (Heb 4:11), repentance (Sir 44:16), noble death (2 Macc 6:28), discipleship (John 13:13), and other matters (Philo, *Confusion* 64; *Heir* 256; *Dreams* 2.3; Jas 5:10; 2 Pet 2:6). The term was also used for the perceptible shape of something, like a temple (Ezek 42:15 LXX) or creatures (Aquila's translation of Deut 4:17; Ezek 8:10; cf. Philo, *Posterity* 122; *TLNT* 3.403–5; Hurst, "Platonic"). On the question of the word's connections with Platonic philosophy see pp. 98–99.

and a shadow. This term (*skia*) can be used spatially, to distinguish heavenly reality from its earthly shadow (8:5), and temporally, to distinguish a present shadow from a future reality (10:1). Negatively, a shadow is transient (Wis 2:5; 5:9; Sir 34:2; Philo, *Posterity* 112; *Unchangeable* 177), contrasting the lower realm of the senses with the higher realm of the mind. Positively, a shadow retains the shape of the object that casts it, and it can therefore help one discern what is real (cf. Philo, *Alleg. Interp.* 3.97–99, 103; *Planting* 27; *Dreams* 1.206). Hebrews retains the ambivalence of "shadow." In a positive sense God provided Moses with the pattern of the sanctuary so that the earthly tent was the counterpart to the heavenly one, but in a negative sense the earthly tent was transient and limited in its benefits.

of the heavenly [*sanctuary*]. The plural *ta epourania* could mean "heavenly realities," but since it is the counterpart to the earthly tent, it can best be taken to modify *ta hagia* ("sanctuary").

just as Moses was divinely admonished. Chrēmatizein ("divinely admonish") has to do with receiving an oracle, like those given to Noah (11:7) and Israel (12:25; cf. 12:20). The term emphasizes that God himself gave the orders to build the Tabernacle (cf. Josephus, *Ant.* 3.212).

when he was about to construct the tent. The command was given to Moses, but the tent was built by Bezalel (Exod 31:2; 35:30; 36:1–2; 38:22).

See that you make everything . . . on the mountain. A quotation of Exod 25:40 LXX with minor variations. The author modifies the verb tense from perfect to aorist and includes the word "everything" (*panta*), as does Philo (*Alleg. Interp.* 3.102; *QE* 2.52). Both writers may have used the same variant form of the LXX, or each could have included *panta* because it appears in the similar command in Exod 25:9 (Philo does not include *panta* in *QE* 2.82, 90). See Williamson, *Philo*, 557–70; D'Angelo, *Moses*, 201–58.

according to the pattern that was shown to you. "Pattern" (*typos*) is the term the LXX uses for the Hebrew *tabnît* in Exod 25:40 (cf. Acts 7:44). Elsewhere the LXX renders *tabnît* by *paradeigma* (Exod 25:9; 1 Chron 28:11, 12, 18, 19). A *typos* is something that makes an impression, as a seal leaves its mark on wax (L. Goppelt, *TDNT* 8.246–59). Many in antiquity understood that Moses saw an actual heavenly sanctuary, which provided the model for the earthly one (Wis 9:8; cf. Ego, *Im Himmel*, 170). The design of the Tabernacle and its furnishings is given in Exod 25–30, and according to Exod 35–40, the pattern was followed exactly. Although the Tabernacle was said to have been designed by God (Exod 25:9, 39–40; 26:30; 27:8; Num 8:4), the first and second Temples only partially conformed to the pattern. Later, however, the Chronicler said that God showed David the model for the Temple (1 Chron 28:11, 19). Stephen's speech agrees that the Mosaic Tabernacle was divinely authorized, but it rejects Solomon's Temple as a purely human undertaking (Acts 7:44–50; see C. R. Koester, *Dwelling*, 79–85).

8:6. *But now.* The expression *nyni de* (P^{46c} ℵ A D^{1} etc.) or *nyn de* (P^{46*} B D^{*}) introduces the contrast between the earthly Levitical ministry (*ei men*; 8:4) and Christ's heavenly ministry. The term "now" also has a temporal quality suitable for the situation in these "final days" (1:2; cf. 9:26).

[*Jesus*] *has received a ministry that is superior.* See NOTE on "minister" in 8:2.

he is also mediator. The term *mesitēs* (cf. 9:15; 12:24) has two facets of meaning:

(**a**) Intermediary. A *mesitēs* mediates between two parties to remove a disagreement or to reach a common goal. At Sinai the people told Moses, "You speak to us, and do not let God speak to us lest we die" (Philo, *Dreams* 2.143; cf. Exod 20:19). Moses is the mediator of the first covenant (*T. Mos.* 1:14; 3:12; cf. Gal 3:19; Philo, *Moses* 2.166) and Christ is the mediator of the new covenant.

(**b**) Guarantor. A mediator could function like a "surety" (NOTE on 7:22), who would help someone in the event that agreements were violated (Diodorus

Siculus, *Library of History* 4.46.4; 4.54.7) or would prevent one party from taking further actions against another (Josephus, *Ant.* 20.62). In commerce a mediator could act as surety for a debt or ensure that a legally established contract was carried out (A. Oepke, *TDNT* 4.600; Backhaus, *Der neue*, 138–46; cf. NOTE on Heb 6:17).

of a superior covenant. See NOTE on 7:22.

lawfully established upon superior promises. God is the implied subject of the verb "lawfully established." God established the covenant at Mount Sinai, and God establishes the new covenant in Christ. The verb was used with *epi* and the genitive case in 7:11 for laws given "concerning" the priesthood, but in 8:6 *epi* is followed by the dative case to show that the covenant was established "upon" a different basis. Both the first and the second covenants are based on promises (see pp. 110–12 on their content), yet the promises of the new covenant are "superior" (COMMENT *b*).

COMMENT[255]

A depiction of a two-story universe opens Heb 8. Earlier the author said that Jesus has gone into the inner region behind the curtain as high priest (6:19–20) and that he serves as high priest above the heavens (7:26–28). Now the author takes listeners into this world that transcends sight (cf. 11:1) through the evocative power of language. References to the heavenly "throne of majesty," which recall the scene depicted in 1:5–14, are expanded to include a celestial sanctuary, where Christ ministers, and the first person plural ("we") brings listeners into the holy place. Rhetorically, "do you see, friend, how he takes you along with him . . . and turns hearing into sight? All such passages with a direct personal address put the hearer in the presence of the action itself" (Longinus, *On the Sublime* 26.2).

One question arising from Heb 8 is ecclesiological and concerns the relationship of heavenly ministry to earthly worship. Christian interpreters have generally agreed that Christ's ministry is shown to make Levitical practice obsolete (8:13) without ending earthly worship altogether. Ancient commentators thought that 8:1–6 showed the heavenly quality of Christian worship, and later interpreters said that Christ's priesthood in the heavenly tent (i.e., the church triumphant), was exercised in the earthly tent (i.e., the church militant) through the priests, who offered eucharistic sacrifice.[256] The sixteenth-century Reformers, however, read the text not only as a critique of the Levitical order but of the

[255]On 8:1–6 see Attridge, "Uses"; Cody, *Heavenly*, 9–46, 77–107; D'Angelo, *Moses*, 201–58; Horbury, "Aaronic"; Hurst, "Platonic"; Johnsson, "Cultus"; C. R. Koester, *Dwelling*, 23–75, 154–57; Löhr, "Throneversammlung"; idem, "Umriss"; MacRae, "Heavenly Temple"; Nissilä, *Hohepriestermotiv*, 148–68; Rose, "Verheissung," 72–80; Sabourin, "Liturge"; Schlosser, "La médiation"; Schröger, *Verfasser*, 159–68; Vanhoye, *Old Testament*, 173–88; idem, "La 'teleiosis' "; Wilcox, "According to the Pattern"; Williamson, *Philo*, 142–60; Wolmarans, "Text." On the new covenant see pp. 112–14.

[256]Chrysostom, NPNF[1] 14.434; Theodoret, PG 82.735BC; Sedulius Scotus, PL 103.263A; Herveus, PL 181.1595C; Ps.-Bruno (PL 153.259A).

church of their own time, which had devised rituals that God had not commanded (Calvin, *Epistle*, 107–8). In the end it is clear that Hebrews assumes that Christ's heavenly ministry (*leitourgia*; 8:2, 6) undergirds earthly Christian worship (*latreuein*; 12:28) and that his self-sacrifice gives rise to sacrifices of praise and good works among his followers (13:15–16). A place remains for leadership in the community of faith (13:7, 17), but Hebrews does not call these leaders "priests" (see pp. 75–76).

A second question is philosophical and concerns the relationship of Hebrews' two-story universe to Platonism. Some find it natural to read Heb 8:1–6 in light of Platonism, while others perceive philosophy as an intrusion into Christian thought and perhaps a step toward Gnosticism, preferring to read the text in light of apocalyptic categories (see pp. 59–63). The complex relationship of Hebrews to Platonism is considered on pp. 97–100. Here our focus is not on the origin of the spatial dichotomy, but on its function in the argument.

Disputes over the derivation of the spatial categories in Heb 8:1–6 have perhaps detracted from some of the author's presuppositions and purposes. The author presupposes that God exists (11:6), and that there is a transcendent world that can be called "true" (8:2). The author further presupposes that transcendent realities cannot be known empirically and that what can be seen with the eye often conflicts with the claims of faith (2:8b–9; 10:32–34; 11:1, 13–16, 27; §6 COMMENT *b*). Therefore, he finally presupposes that knowledge of transcendent reality must be based on divine revelation. His purpose is to declare that God spoke in a definitive way through the death, resurrection, and exaltation of Jesus (1:2), and he interprets this revelation in light of what God previously revealed through the prophets (1:1). The claims made in 8:1–2 are based on the conviction that God raised Jesus to everlasting life. They are also interpreted in light of God's promise, given in the Scriptures, that the one seated at his right hand should serve as a priest forever (Ps 110:1, 4) and is connected to God's revelation of the pattern of a heavenly tent to Moses (Exod 25:9, 40).

Structurally, this section is framed by the terms "minister" (*leitourgos*) and "ministry" (*leitourgia*) in 8:2, 6 (Vanhoye, *La structure*, 140–41; cf. G. H. Guthrie, *Structure*, 117). Internally, the passage has two main parts: **(a)** The ministry of Jesus in the heavenly sanctuary is introduced in a single complex sentence (8:1–2). **(b)** Jesus' ministry is contrasted with that of the Levitical priests in several steps (8:3–6). The author notes the correspondence between Jesus' priesthood and their priesthood in 8:3, he accents the difference between their earthly ministries in 8:4–5, and he declares the superiority of Christ's ministry and the covenant on which it is based in 8:6.[257]

---

[257]The place of 8:3 is awkward (Bleek, *Brief*, 2.2.429; Grässer, *Brief*, 2.84). Zimmermann (*Bekenntnis*, 111) ascribes the unevenness to tradition and redaction. Most scholars link 8:3 with 8:4–6 (P. E. Hughes, *Commentary*, 290; Gourgues, "Remarques"; Lane, *Hebrews*, 1.204; H.-F. Weiss, *Brief*, 433; Bénétreau, *L'Épître*, 2.54), although some connect it to 8:1–2 (Bengel, *Epistle*, 4.411; Ellingworth, *Epistle*, 399). Pointing out correspondence, difference, and superiority is a common approach to various aspects of Hebrews (Vanhoye, "Par le tente," 3–4; Grässer, *Der Alte*, 96; Lehne, *New Covenant*, 13).

a. The Heavenly Priest and Sanctuary (8:1–2)

The high priest who is seated beside God's throne (8:1) is the Son of God, who has been "made complete" forever (7:26–28; Vanhoye, "La 'teleiosis' "). To say that "we have such a high priest" means that Jesus not only is a priest but that he is *their* priest. In saying that Jesus the high priest has "sat down at the right hand of the throne of the Majesty in the heavens" (8:1b), the author uses language from Ps 110, which refers to the same figure as both king (Ps 110:1) and priest (110:4). Earlier the imagery from Ps 110 depicted Jesus as royal Son of God (Heb 1:3, 6, 8, 13), and in the central section the imagery helps to show that Jesus' priestly self-offering is complete, so that he can now sit beside God's throne (8:1–2; 10:12–18). At the end of the speech the imagery will be used for Jesus the athlete, who has endured the contest and now sits at God's right hand (12:1–2). Here, Jesus' ministry is said to take place in the heavenly sanctuary (8:2), an idea that would have been plausible to listeners on the basis of tradition. God's throne was understood to be in heaven (Ps 11:4; Isa 66:1; Matt 5:34), and his throne was associated with a sanctuary (Isa 6:1; Ezek 43:7; Jer 17:12). Later sources developed the idea of a heavenly sanctuary more fully.[258] Hebrews calls it "the true tent" (Heb 8:2) and identifies it with what Moses saw according to Exod 25:9, 40 (Heb 8:5).

Hebrews was written in the Greco-Roman world, where many sanctuaries were set up by "human beings" (8:2). Cities boasted sanctuaries that ranged from massive structures to modest shrines. Those from Italy (13:24) would have known about a plethora of temples in Rome. Augustus alone claimed to have restored eighty-two existing temples and to have built thirteen more, dedicated to figures like Apollo, Jupiter, Minerva, and the deified Julius.[259] There were many temples because many deities were worshiped, and a given deity could have shrines in more than one place. A "city without holy places," no traveler "will ever see" (Plutarch, *Mor.* 1125E). Jews, however, recognized only one God and one Temple, which was located in Jerusalem (Deut 6:4; 12:1–14).[260] The Temple was understood to be the successor to the tent that Moses built (Heb 8:5).[261] Local synagogues were for the reading of Scripture and prayer, but the Temple was the one acceptable place for sacrifices. While the Temple stood, funds were sent to Jerusalem to support it, and pilgrims made special journeys to worship

---

[258]Enoch journeys to God's throne in a heavenly house (*1 Enoch* 14:10–20); Levi sees angels performing priestly service before the throne in a heavenly sanctuary (*T. Levi* 3:1–10; 5:1). On the heavenly Temple in Jewish sources see Attridge, *Epistle*, 222–24; Cody, *Heavenly*, 9–46; McKelvey, *New Temple*, 25–41; Schierse, *Verheissung*, 13–25; Newsom, *Songs*, 39–58; MacRae, "Heavenly Temple," 179–91; Löhr, "Thronversammlung"; Ego, *Im Himmel*, 27–61, 73–110.

[259]See "The Accomplishments of Augustus" §§19–21 (*RomCiv* 1.567–68).

[260]Cf. Philo, *Special Laws* 1.67; 2.162–66; Josephus, *Ant.* 4.200; *Ag. Ap.* 2.193. There was a Jewish temple at Leontopolis in Egypt from the second century B.C. until A.D. 73, but it was viewed with ambivalence, even by Jews in Egypt. Jerusalem was considered to be the site of the one true Temple. See Schürer, *History*, 3.47–48, 145–47.

[261]The tent was said to have been made at Mount Sinai and later placed at Shiloh (Jos 18:1; 19:51) and Gibeon (1 Chron 16:39; 21:29; 2 Chron 1:3–6, 13). David placed the ark in a tent in Jerusalem (2 Sam 6:17; 7:5–7), and Solomon stored the tent in the Temple (1 Kgs 8:4). The Temple itself was later called God's "tent" (Pss 15:1; 27:4–6). See C. R. Koester, *Dwelling*, 6–22.

there.[262] When Jews prayed, they commonly turned toward Jerusalem, both before and after the Temple was destroyed.[263] (On whether the Temple was standing when Hebrews was composed see pp. 52–53.)

Hebrews stands in continuity with Israel's tradition and in contrast to Greco-Roman practice by assuming that there can be only one legitimate sanctuary: "the" sanctuary (8:2a). Hebrews also identifies this sanctuary as "the tent" that God had set up (8:2b), basing the connection on the revelation that was given to Moses in the Law (8:5). Yet for Hebrews the heavenly tent does not provide legitimation for, but an alternative to the earthly sanctuary. Jewish sources traditionally viewed the earthly sanctuary in Jerusalem as the place where God's name was present upon earth (Deut 12:5), but Hebrews directs attention to heaven itself as the place where Jesus ministers. Since Christ serves as "a priest forever" (Ps 110:4), he requires a sanctuary that will endure forever, and the only sanctuary that is eternal is the tent that God set up in heaven (cf. Exod 25:9, 40).

The vision of Christ ministering in the heavenly sanctuary offers a suggestive contrast to the situation of the listeners, who probably gathered in homes for worship (pp. 73–75). The author indicates that their modest assembly was dwindling (10:25), but Hebrews gives them a renewed focus for worship by bringing them under the canopy of Christ's heavenly ministry through the power of language. The author does not dismiss the value of a sanctuary and high priest, but points to the heavenly sanctuary where Christ ministers (Isaacs, *Sacred*, 61–66, 126). The prayer by which they approach the throne (4:14–16) is directed to a heavenly rather than an earthly sanctuary, and it is mediated by Christ (7:25). By focusing on their heavenly priest, the listeners hold fast to the center of their community life and to the basis of their own offerings of praise and service (13:15–16).

b. Earthly Priests and Sanctuary (8:3–6)

Jesus' ministry is further elaborated in relation to Levitical ministry. First, the author establishes a *correspondence* between the two ministries. The statement that "every high priest is appointed to offer gifts and sacrifices" (8:3a) summarizes priestly ministry on the basis of Israel's Scriptures. Given that Jesus is a high priest (5:1–10; 7:1–28), one can conclude that he must offer a sacrifice (8:3a). Some have wondered if the author might have thought that Jesus continued making sacrifices in heaven,[264] but the context makes clear that Jesus made his sacrifice "once for all when he offered himself" (7:27), so that his singular death on earth is the basis for his heavenly ministry. The fact that Jesus sat down (8:1)

---

[262]On pilgrimage see Philo, *Special Laws* 1.70. On the importance of the Temple for Jews in the Diaspora see Barclay, *Jews*, 418–21.

[263]On prayer toward the holy of holies in Jerusalem see 1 Kgs 8:48; Dan 6:10; *m. Ber.* 4:5–6; cf. Pss 5:7; 28:2; Ezek 8:16; 1 Esdr 4:58. Some ancient synagogues faced east, as did the Temple, while others were oriented toward Jerusalem (Schürer, *History*, 2.441–42, 449).

[264]The idea that Christ's sacrifice takes place in heaven rather than on earth was developed by the Socinians in the sixteenth century (see p. 35). Most interpreters now take 8:3 as a reference to Christ's death. See Laub, *Bekenntnis*, 204–7; Grässer, *Hebräer*, 2.85.

shows that the need for sacrifice has ended (10:11–18), although Christ's intercession on behalf of others continues.[265]

Second, the author seeks to show the *difference* between Christ's heavenly ministry and Levitical ministry on earth (8:4–5). He acknowledges that if Christ "were on earth, he would not be a priest" (8:4a), giving full weight to points that actually discredit claims about Jesus' priestly ministry when viewed from an earthly perspective. Yet by contrasting these earthly institutions with their heavenly counterparts, the author allows their limited and transient qualities to appear:

(a) Levitical priests make offerings according to the Mosaic Law (8:4b). This would have been positive for most people (*Ep. Arist.* 92–99), since failure to observe the Law would have been considered negligence at best and sin at worst. Hebrews, however, has argued that the Law was only of limited benefit, for it did not bring God's purposes to completion (Heb 7:11, 19, 28; see §18 COMMENT *a*). The Law that established Levitical ministry was altered by the unchangeable oath (Ps 110:4) that appointed Jesus to a priesthood after the type of Melchizedek (Heb 7:20–21). The Law appointed Levitical priests who were subject to sin and death, but the oath appointed Christ to be a non-Levitical priest, who is not subject to sin and who serves forever (7:23–28).

(b) The sanctuary in which Levitical priests serve is "a representation and a shadow of the heavenly" one (8:5a). Some take the comment to be pejorative, an affirmation that the earthly sanctuary is "only" a copy of the true one (NJB; REB),[266] but for most people in antiquity, the idea that the earthly sanctuary represented the heavenly one would have been reason to revere it. Jewish writers valued the Temple as a place for prayer, even though they understood that God was not confined there (1 Kgs 8:27–30; Philo, *Special Laws* 1.66, 68). Therefore, if the Temple was a copy of a heavenly design (Wis 9:8), one might assume that there could be no better sanctuary on earth. It is only through comparison with the heavenly tent (Heb 8:2) that the limitations of the earthly shrine or "shadow" can be seen (8:5).

(c) The earthly sanctuary was divinely mandated, for God commanded Moses to build it and gave him the design (8:5; cf. Exod 25:9, 40). Much of Exodus shows how the detailed plans for the sanctuary (Exod 25–30) are followed to the letter (Exod 35–40; see C. R. Koester, *Dwelling*, 7–8). A sanctuary that is based on God's own pattern and built in response to God's command is good, but a sanctuary that is built by God himself is superior. Jesus the high priest serves in a sanctuary that was not produced by human obedience, but by God's own action; it is as superior to earthly shrines as God's actions are superior to the best that human hands can fabricate.

Third, the author emphasizes the *superiority* of Jesus' ministry (8:6a). The author recognizes that the first covenant was based on God's promises. The content

---

[265]Heb 7:25. See Gourgues, *À la droite*, 114–19; Loader, *Sohn* 148–50. On Christ's heavenly ministry see pp. 109–10.

[266]Thompson, *Beginnings*, 106; Braun, *Hebräer*, 232; Grässer, *Hebräer*, 2.90; H.-F. Weiss, *Brief*, 436.

of the promises is not stated, but the Mosaic covenant was associated with the promise that Israel would be God's people (Exod 6:7; 29:45; Lev 26:12) and that God would forgive iniquities (Exod 34:7). Similarly, the promises of the new covenant (Jer 31:31–34; Heb 8:10–12) include the hope that people will belong to God (Heb 8:10) and receive mercy (8:12), yet they go beyond the old covenant in promising that God will inscribe his laws upon human hearts (8:10) and that God's people will know him so completely that no further instruction will be necessary (8:11). Hebrews interprets the text by arguing that the mercy promised in the new covenant comes through the self-sacrifice by which Jesus makes complete atonement for sins (§16 COMMENT). The "superior promises" offer the "superior hope" through which people "draw near to God" (NOTE on 7:19).[267] The old-covenant promises give way to the new-covenant promises, just as the hope of entering the land culminates in God's own eternal Sabbath rest (4:8–10).

21. The Old and New Covenants (8:7–13)

8 [7]Now, if that first [covenant] were faultless, no place would be sought for a second. [8]For finding fault with them, he says, *Behold, days are coming, says the Lord, when I will complete with the house of Israel and with the house of Judah a new covenant,* [9]*not like the covenant that I made with their forebears in the day when I took hold of their hand to bring them out of the land of Egypt, because they did not remain in my covenant, and I paid no attention to them, says the Lord.* [10]*For this is the covenant that I will establish with the house of Israel after those days, says the Lord: Putting my laws into their mind, I will even write them on their hearts, and I will be their God and they shall be my people,* [11]*and no one shall teach his fellow citizen and no one his brother, saying, "Know the Lord," because they shall all know me, from the least to the greatest of them,* [12]*for I will be merciful toward their unrighteous deeds and I will not remember their sins anymore.* [13]In speaking of a new covenant, he has made the first one obsolete. And what is becoming obsolete is also old and near obliteration.

NOTES

8:7. *Now, if that first* [*covenant*]. God made a "covenant" with Noah (Gen 6:18; 9:9–17) and another with Abraham (15:18; 17:2–14), Isaac (17:19–21), and Jacob (Exod 2:24; 6:4), which is called the "first" in Lev 26:45. Hebrews, however, refers to the "promises" made to Abraham, reserving the term "covenant" for the Mosaic and new covenants (NOTE on 7:22 and pp. 110–14).

---

[267]Rose ("Verheissung," 74–78) connects the superior promises of 8:6 with the superior hope of 7:19, but he argues that the promises are not the ones in Jer 31:31–34 (=Heb 8:8–12). He assumes that the new covenant is a present reality and therefore does not convey the hope associated with "promise." Most, however, identify the promises of 8:6 with the oracle in 8:8–12. The new covenant has been inaugurated, but not fully realized (see §21 COMMENT *b*).

were faultless. Some suggest that the problem with the covenant was that people disobeyed it (cf. 8:9; Chrysostom; Luther, WA 57,3.45; Westcott; Hegermann). Yet by replacing the first covenant with a new one, God shows that the first covenant itself was flawed and brought nothing to completion (7:11, 19; Erasmus, *Paraphrase*; Calvin; Braun; Grässer; H.-F. Weiss).

no place would be sought for a second. The passive voice of "be sought" implies that as God faulted the old covenant, God sought a new one (Ellingworth; Grässer). The term *topos* could mean "opportunity" (12:17), although the translation "place" fits the emphasis on the location of the new covenant: human minds and hearts.

8:8. *For finding fault with them, he says.* Having spoken about the faults of the first covenant in 8:7, the author turns to the faults of those who broke it. Textual evidence is divided between the accusative *autous* (א* A D* I K etc.) and the dative *autois* (P^{46} $א^{2}$ B D^{2} etc.), but many take "them" (in either case) to be the object of the participle, so that the text refers to God finding fault "with them," that is, with the people who broke the covenant. Some who favor the dative *autois* take it as the object of the verb "says," so that God finds fault (with the covenant) and "says to them" (i.e., "to the people"). See P. E. Hughes; Wolmarans, "Text"; Lane; H.-F. Weiss. This does not fit the author's style, however, since he regularly introduces biblical quotations with a form of *legein* or similar word and no indirect object (2:6, 12; 3:7, 15; 4:3, 7; 6:14; 9:20; 10:5, 15; 12:5, 26).

8b–12. A quotation of Jer 31:31–34 (38:31–34 LXX).

(**a**) The LXX and MT. For the MT "they broke my covenant" (*hēpērû 'et berîtî*) in 31:32, the LXX reads "they did not remain in my covenant." For the MT "I was their husband" (*bā'alti bām*) in 31:32, the LXX reads "I paid no attention to them." The translator may have taken the Hebrew to mean "disgusted with" (*bā'al be*; Bleek, *Brief*, 2.453). The MT has "Law" in 31:33, while the LXX has "laws," and the MT includes "says the Lord" in 31:34 but the LXX does not. See NOTES on Heb 8:9, 11.

(**b**) The LXX and Hebrews. Hebrews differs in minor ways from the Göttingen edition of the LXX (ed. J. Ziegler): Hebrews reads *legei* instead of *phēsin* in 8:8, 9, 10; *epoiēsa* instead of *diethemēn* in 8:9; *kagō* instead of *kai egō* in 8:9; *didous* instead of *didous dōs* in 8:10; *epigrapsō* instead of *grapsō* in 8:10; and *ou mē didaksōsin* instead of *ou didaksousin* in 8:11. These and the minor differences in word order are stylistic variations and may result from the use of an alternative LXX text or from the author's freedom in quoting (Schröger, *Verfasser*, 162–68; H.-F. Weiss, *Brief*, 445). On variations in the LXX see Cadwallader, "Correction," 278. On Hebrews' use of *syntelesō epi ton oikon* instead of *diathēsomai tō oikō* (LXX) see NOTE on 8:8.

Behold, days are coming, says the Lord. The "days are coming" is a common expression in Jeremiah (Jer 7:32; 9:25; 16:14; 23:5, 7), but not in other prophetic writings. In Hebrews the coming days have arrived (Heb 1:2), although final redemption remains future.

when I will complete. The word *syntelein* ("complete"), rather than *diathēsomai* ("establish") as in Jer 31:31 (38:31 LXX) and Heb 8:10, might reflect the use of a variant version of the LXX, or it may be a change made by the author, since *syntelein* is used elsewhere in Jeremiah for covenants (Jer 34:8, 15 [41:8, 15 LXX]). The verb *syntelein* echoes other words for completion (*tel-*) in Hebrews (2:10; 5:9; 7:28). The Law made nothing complete (7:11, 19), but completion of God's designs will be accomplished through Jesus' sacrifice, which inaugurates the new covenant (10:14–17). The initial *kai* has a temporal sense (BDF §442 [4]). On "completion" see pp. 122–25.

with the house of Israel and with the house of Judah a new covenant. On the new covenant see pp. 112–14.

8:9. *not like the covenant that I made with their forebears in the day when I took hold of their hand.* God's bringing Israel out of Egypt is the presupposition for the commandments in the Mosaic covenant (Exod 20:2). To say that he "took them by the hand" suggests compassion. Earlier this verb (*epilambanesthai*) was used for the descendants of Abraham—including the listeners—who have been helped by God (NOTE on 2:16). Hebrews here accents the discontinuity associated with the newness of the second covenant.

because they did not remain in my covenant. The MT says that Israel "broke" God's covenant, which occurred most memorably with the building of the golden calf, but the LXX says that Israel failed to "remain" in the covenant, which might recall their persistent contentiousness (3:7–19). Their failure to remain (*emmenein*) contrasts with God, Christ, and the heavenly world—all of which do remain (*menein*; 7:3, 24; 10:34; 12:27; 13:14) as proper objects of faith.

and I paid no attention to them. The Greek word (*amelein*) was used for people who were unresponsive (Matt 22:5; cf. Mark 4:38; Luke 10:40) or did not carry out responsibilities (2 Macc 4:14). Earlier, Hebrews used it for those who would "neglect" their salvation (NOTE on 2:3). On the use of this term for God see COMMENT *b*.

8:10. *Putting my laws into their mind.* The new covenant was "lawfully established" (8:6) just as the old one was (7:11). Its "laws" (8:10; 10:16) presumably do not include the statutes concerning the Levitical priesthood (7:12, 18), food, drink, or ablutions, all of which are obsolete (9:10). Hebrews does not list the new covenant's "laws," but like the Decalogue (Exod 20:1–20), Hebrews urges loyalty to God (Heb 10:29) and warns against adultery and avarice (13:4–5).

I will even write them on their hearts. Keeping God's laws in one's mind and heart is central to Israel's confession (Deut 6:4–6) and to Jesus' teaching (Matt 22:37; Mark 12:30; Luke 10:27). The idea that God will write his laws on human hearts has been taken in two ways:

(a) Internalization. Law that is written on the heart is internal, unlike laws that are written externally on tablets (Exod 24:12; 31:18; 34:1; Deut 4:13; 5:22; 2 Cor 3:3, 6). This might mean that the covenant "would not be enforced from without through learning and indoctrination . . . but would be implanted" (Weinfeld, "Jeremiah," 26). Yet this is only partially correct; the old covenant is faulted not because it required external enforcement, but because it failed to produce obedience.

(b) Completeness. The goal of the new covenant is to bring about complete obedience (Mejîa, "La problématique," 272–73). Jeremiah understood that the "heart is devious above all things; it is perverse" (Jer 17:9; cf. 9:8; 17:1). Having God's statutes on one's heart brings complete obedience (Ezek 11:19–20; 36:26–27; cf. 18:31; Deut 10:4–6; Prov 3:3; 7:3). Similarly, Hebrews warns about hard and evil hearts that lead people astray (Heb 3:8, 10, 12), and the new covenant is instituted in order that hearts might be true rather than evil, and faithful rather than faithless (10:22). Completeness of obedience, rather than internalization, is the concern.

and I will be their God and they shall be my people. This summarizes the covenant relationship (Exod 6:7; 29:45; Lev 26:12; Deut 26:17–18; Jer 7:23; 24:7; 30:22; Ezek 11:20; 37:27; Hos 2:23; Zech 8:8; 13:9; 2 Cor 6:16; Rev 21:3). The formula highlights the uniqueness of God's relationship to his people.

and no one shall teach. Teaching was the way that the Mosaic covenant was made effective. Moses taught the people (Deut 4:5, 14; 6:1), who in turn taught their children (Deut 4:9–10; 6:7, 9; 11:19–20). Being taught by God was a hope (Isa 54:13) that Christians associated with Christ (John 6:45) and the Spirit (John 14:26; 1 John 2:27; cf. 1 Thess 4:8–9). Since those addressed by Hebrews need teaching (Heb 5:11–14), this aspect of the new covenant remains unrealized.

8:11. *his fellow citizen.* This word (*politēs*) appears in standard texts of the LXX. The word meaning "neighbor" appears in LXX^{A} (*plēsios*), in some MSS of Heb 8:11 (P 81 104 365 etc.), and in modern translations (NIV; NJB). The reading "fellow citizen," however, has excellent textual support (P^{46} א B A D etc.). "Fellow citizens" can belong to the same ethnic group (2 Macc 9:19; 14:8; 15:30) so that it is similar to "brother" in the extended sense. Yet a *politēs* was a member of the *polis* or city (Acts 21:39). Not all residents were citizens; citizens were free persons with political rights. "Fellow citizens" could also belong to the same *politeuma* (Philo, *Creation* 143; *Special Laws* 2.45), which were sometimes ethnic groups that had some autonomy, but not full political rights, like the Jews in Alexandria. Those who belonged only to a *politeuma* often aspired to citizenship status (see Tcherikover, *Hellenistic*, 296–332). Citizens were regularly distinguished from resident aliens and foreigners (NOTES on 11:9, 13). Hebrews later refers to those who are "registered" as citizens in God's heavenly city, where they will fully participate in the civic "assembly" (12:23; cf. 11:9–10, 13–16; 13:14). Such citizenship is part of God's design for the listeners.

and no one his brother. See NOTES on 2:11; 3:1.

"Know the Lord." Knowing God encompasses two aspects of meaning:

(a) Recognition. The covenant meant knowing that it was God who brought them out of Egypt (Exod 6:7; 29:45–46). Knowing no other god (Isa 43:10) goes beyond mere belief in God's existence to include trust in and loyalty to God (Ps 9:10; Prov 3:5–6). The wilderness generation tested God because they did not know his ways (NOTE on Heb 3:10).

(b) Obedience. Evidence that the people did not know the Lord was that they sinned (Isa 1:3–4; Jer 4:22; 9:3; Hos 4:1–3). Conversely, those who know the Lord act justly, especially toward the poor and needy (Jer 22:16).

because they shall all know me. Jeremiah's oracle focuses on "all" in Israel knowing God. Others said that "the earth shall be full of the knowledge of the

Lord" (Isa 11:9; cf. Joel 2:27). Medieval interpreters applied this promise to the conversion of the Gentiles (Theophylact; Nicolaus of Lyra) and to the beatific vision (Anselm of Laon, *Glossa ordinaria*; Aquinas, *Ad Heb.* §410).

from the least to the greatest of them. Jeremiah emphasized the need for all to know God because sin affected people of every class, "from the least to the greatest of them" (Jer 6:13).

8:12. *for I will be merciful toward their unrighteous deeds.* Mercy is designed to free people from "unrighteous" deeds and to awaken the faith that characterizes the "righteous" (10:38), who have a future in the heavenly Jerusalem (12:23).

and I will not remember their sins anymore. Under the old covenant God paid "no attention" to Israel's disobedience, which meant that the people suffered the disastrous consequences of their actions (8:9). "Not remembering" does not mean that God is indifferent to sin, since he also brings about new obedience in the present by placing his laws upon the heart and mind. Here, "not remembering" means not holding past sins against people.

8:13. *In speaking of a new covenant, he has made the first one obsolete.* Legally, a person who made a covenant or testament (*diathēkē*) could alter or annul it (NOTE on 7:18). According to Hebrews, the God who made the first covenant is the God who replaces it with a new covenant. The idea that the Sinai covenant was temporary ran counter to Jewish sources that considered it to be everlasting (Sir 17:12; cf. *4 Ezra* 9:36–37; *2 Bar.* 77:15; Philo, *Moses* 2.14–15; Josephus, *Ag. Ap.* 2.272), as were God's other covenants (Gen 17:7; 1 Chron 16:15–18; Ps 105:10; Sir 44:18; 45:7, 15; 2 Esdr 3:15). Like the "first" or "former" things (Isa 43:18; Rev 21:4), however, which pass away when the new comes, the "first" covenant gives way with the advent of the new covenant.

And what is becoming obsolete is also old. To become old is to reach the end of life (Plutarch, *Mor.* 111C), to become powerless (John 21:18) and unproductive (Philo, *Eternity* 61). Like the perishable world (Heb 1:11) and the priests whose service ends with death (7:23), the Mosaic covenant itself passes away according to Hebrews.

and near obliteration. "Obliteration" meant that a law was nullified (cf. Lysias, *Against Nicomachus* 35). In the LXX the term was used for divine judgment (1 Kgs 9:7; Jer 9:11; Ezek 6:14; Joel 1:7; Mic 1:7). Ultimately, obliteration is done by God, who "abrogates" a command because of its weakness (Heb 7:18) and makes the first covenant obsolete. The first covenant is a part of the order symbolized by the "first tent," which is now giving way because the "time of correction" has arrived (9:8–10). The old order still exists, but its end is imminent.

COMMENT[268]

Hebrews previously called Jesus the surety and mediator of a new and superior covenant (7:22; 8:6),[269] but only now does the author show the force of the idea

[268]For bibliography on the old and new covenants see pp. 112–14.

[269]See generally Backhaus, *Der neue*, 157–81; Grässer, *Der Alte*, 1–134; Lehne, *New Covenant*;

through the quotation of Jer 31:31–34.[270] Negatively, the quotation critiques the old covenant. The critique is not readily apparent in the context from which Jer 31:31–34 was taken, where the new covenant is one of a chorus of promises concerning the restoration of Israel. Therefore, Hebrews accents the oracle's negative side by introducing it as a message in which God finds fault with conditions under the Mosaic covenant (Heb 8:7–8a) and by pointing out that the opposite of "new" is "old," which connotes obsolescence (8:13). Positively, the oracle gives the content of the new covenant (8:6), and 10:11–18 will conclude that the mercy provided through Christ's self-sacrifice fulfills the new covenant promise.

Rhetorically, the persuasiveness of a speech depends not only on its logic but also on the listeners' conviction that the one speaking is reliable (Quintilian, *Inst.* 4.1.7). After presenting arguments concerning the inadequacy of the Mosaic Law and Levitical priesthood, the author now recedes into the background, allowing God to be the speaker through the quotation of Jer 31:31–34. Listeners might fault the author's logic, but they will presumably find it difficult to challenge God's own promise. God's words concern "the house of Israel" and "the house of Judah," but Hebrews brings the oracle to bear on the listeners' situation, since they belong to God's "house" (Heb 3:6). Like the people whom God once took by the hand (8:9) to bring out of Egypt, they are understood to be among the descendants of Abraham of whom God has claimed (2:16). In announcing that God has promised a new covenant to "the house of Israel," the author in effect tells the listeners that God has promised a new covenant "to you."

Structurally, this section is framed by the author's comments concerning the "first" covenant (8:7, 13). The remainder consists of the extended quotation of Jeremiah's oracle, which falls into two parts: **(a)** The old covenant that Israel broke is the focus of 8:8–9, and **(b)** the qualities of the new covenant that God promised are considered in 8:10–12.

a. The First Covenant (8:7–9)

God's decision to establish a new covenant is said to reveal that the first covenant was flawed (8:7). The logic is like that of arguing that the Levitical priesthood must have been inadequate because God replaced it by raising Christ to be a priest after the type of Melchizedek (Ps 110:4; Heb 7:11, 17–18). Through God's action, the limitations of the Levitical order and the old covenant become apparent. If human disobedience had been the only problem, God might have renewed people's willingness to obey the Sinai covenant, but God promised a "new covenant," not merely a refurbishing of the existing one, which shows that he considered the covenant itself to be flawed, according to the author of Hebrews.

Levin, *Verheissung*; Luz, "Der alte"; Mejîa, "La problématic"; Michaud, "Le passage"; Schenker, "Der nie"; Wolff, *Jeremia*, 116–47.

[270]On the negative aspect of Jer 31:31–34 see Vanhoye, *La structure*, 143–44; *Old Testament*, 182–83; Peterson, *Hebrews*, 132; Lane, *Hebrews*, 1.208; Grässer, *Hebräer*, 2.99. On its positive function see Gourgues, "Remarques," 29; Attridge, *Epistle*, 226.

Questions about the reliability of God emerge from this passage. If the first covenant proved to be ineffective, one might wonder why God instituted it in the first place. The text gives no answer (cf. pp. 112–15), but focuses instead on God's faithfulness. God established a new covenant for the same reason that he established the old one with Israel: in order that he might be their God and that they might be his people (Exod 6:7; Jer 31:33; Heb 8:10). The oracle notes that Israel may have broken the first covenant, but God persistently seeks to realize his designs through a second covenant. God changes the covenant in order to overcome the problem of human sin; thus the new covenant reflects God's faithfulness in the face of human unfaithfulness.

The new arrangement[271] is like the old one in that it is called a "covenant." Both covenants are based on divine promises (8:6) and have the purpose that "I will be their God and they shall be my people" (8:10). Both were lawfully instituted (7:11; 8:6), both include laws (7:5, 16, 28; 8:10), and both provide for forgiveness of sins. Nevertheless, the new covenant is based on "superior" promises (8:6) and will be inscribed upon people's hearts and minds, ensuring obedience to God's will. The old covenant required continual instruction and exhortation (Deut 4:9–10; 6:20–25; 11:19), but under the new covenant these will not be necessary, since all will know the Lord. Given the similarities, the new covenant might be considered a "renewal" of the old covenant rather than its replacement,[272] but Hebrews argues that the covenants differ fundamentally in their ability to deal with sin. Levitical sacrifices remind people of sin (Heb 10:1–4), but Christ's self-sacrifice cleanses the conscience, fulfilling the new-covenant promise of mercy (9:14; 10:16–18). Paradoxically, the Day of Atonement ritual in the *old covenant* (Lev 16) enables Hebrews to present Christ's death as the sacrifice that fulfills the *new covenant*. In declaring the obsolescence of the old order, Hebrews uses its categories to speak of the new order.

The disobedience of the people with whom the first covenant was made (8:9b) manifests the weakness of the covenant (cf. 8:7). The account of the wilderness generation's rebellion alluded to various incidents from the wilderness wanderings, including contention over water (Exod 17:1–7; Num 20:2–13) and the refusal to believe that God would bring them into the land (Num 14:1–38; §10 COMMENT *a*). In response to their refusal to remain (*emmenein*) in the covenant, God paid them no attention (*amelein*) and allowed their unbelief to take its course. Since they refused to believe that God would give them rest in the land, declaring that they would rather die in the wilderness (Num 14:2), God let them have their way, barring Israel from the land until that generation had perished (§10 COMMENT *b*).

---

[271]On the continuity and discontinuity between the old and new covenants see Käsemann, *Wandering*, 59–60; Grässer, *Der Alte*, 113; Luz, "Der alte," 335; Lehne, *New Covenant*, 80; Michaud, "Le passage," 45–51.

[272]This may have been how it was understood in Jewish circles (Levin, *Verheissung*, 257; Schenker, "Die nie," 110). Calvin (*Epistle*, 108) thought that the superiority of the new covenant pertained more to form than to substance.

b. The New Covenant (8:10–13)

God promised a new covenant because he was not willing to let human faithlessness be the final word in his relationship with his people. Just as the Mosaic covenant was predicated upon God's saving action on behalf of Israel (Exod 20:2), the new covenant is predicated upon the death and exaltation of Christ, according to Hebrews (7:20–28; 9:15; 10:12–18; cf. Lehne, *New Covenant*, 107). The new covenant has four main elements:

(a) God will put his laws within people and write his laws on their hearts (8:10b). By inscribing his will upon human hearts, God overcomes the tendency of human hearts to be unfaithful (3:12). This new covenant not only offers forgiveness for past sins but also promises to change hearts and minds so that people no longer fall into sin. Placing his "laws" within people, God overcomes human "lawlessness" (10:17; cf. 1:9) by bringing about complete trust in and obedience to his will (NOTES on 8:10). Under the new covenant, the gap between God's command and the human will to perform it is closed by God himself (Grässer, *Hebräer*, 2.102).

Some question whether God writing his laws on human hearts would abrogate human freedom.[273] According to Jeremiah's oracle, God gave Israel freedom by bringing them out of slavery (8:9a), and without God's action there would have been no freedom. Once out of Egypt, the people broke the covenant, and God let them act freely—but the result was that they died in the desert (3:16–19). The story of Moses' generation shows that freedom apart from God is freedom to sin and that sin is destructive rather than freeing. The contrast between the freedom that occurs when God takes people by the hand (8:9a) and the negative results that occur when God allows people to go their own way (8:9b) prepares listeners for the promise that God will act again in order to prevent sin from prevailing. Under the new covenant, freedom is not abrogated by God's actions, but is created by God's actions.

(b) The promise that "I will be their God and they shall be my people" (8:10c) is at the heart of both the old and new covenants. The God who speaks in the first person ("*I* will be their God") is the God of Israel. The covenant relationship is characterized by particularity: it is made with one God and not others (cf. 1 Cor 8:5–6). The God of the covenant spoke to Israel's ancestors through the prophets (Heb 1:1) and again through Jesus his Son (1:2). The modes of communication differ, but the God remains the same (cf. §3 COMMENT *a*).[274]

God calls the people "my people" (8:10c).[275] Listeners would have understood that they were among the "people" for whom Jesus' blood effects atone-

---

[273]W. L. Holladay, *IDB*, 624; idem, *Jeremiah* 2, 198.

[274]Belief in one God (Deut 6:4) became central to Israel's faith. Others in antiquity professed to believe in one God, but this did not mean that they belonged to the covenant. The covenant bound people not just to one God, but to Israel's God (Barclay, *Jews*, 429–34).

[275]The term *laos* ("people") is sometimes connected to the Levitical order established by the old covenant (5:3; 7:5, 11, 27; 9:7, 19) and sometimes to the work of Christ (2:17; 13:12). The term encompasses previous generations and the author's own generation (94:9; 8:10; 10:30; 11:25). Cf. Lehne, *New Covenant*, 156 n. 107.

ment and sanctification (2:17; 13:12), and for whom the Sabbath rest remains (4:9). They confess God's "name" (13:15) and serve for the sake of his "name" (6:10). Socially, identifying with one particular God sometimes led to conflict, and those who abandoned the covenant often did so to accommodate the wider culture.[276] Like earlier generations, the listeners lived in tension with the wider society (10:32–34; 11:25–26; 13:13), but belonging to God's own people offers incentive to remain faithful, knowing that they have no earthly city, but are registered as citizens of God's city (12:22–23; 13:14).

(c) All God's people will know him (8:11). Hebrews recalls that the works that God performed for Moses' generation (3:9) displayed God's power, yet the people did not know God's ways (3:10). Those addressed by Hebrews had come to "knowledge of the truth" (10:26) and did "know" God (10:30) through the Spirit (2:3–4), yet they too could drift away from God (3:13). To know God is to recognize him, to trust him, and to obey his will (NOTE on 8:11). "Knowing" means not only communication from God but communion with God (Michaud, "Le passage," 40).

Full knowledge of God would mean that brothers and fellow citizens would no longer need to exhort one another to "Know the Lord" (8:11). This promise remains unfulfilled. Those addressed by Hebrews could claim to have Christ as their brother (2:11–14) and could call each other "brother" (3:1), but they needed to exhort one another (3:13), just as the author exhorted them by his speech (13:22), and they also needed teaching (5:12). They were "fellow citizens," but on earth they were regarded as foreigners (11:9, 13; 13:14). Although they presently know God to some extent, exhortation will continue until their citizenship is fully realized in the heavenly city (12:22–24).

(d) God will be merciful regarding unrighteous deeds and will remember sins no longer (8:12). Fulfillment of this promise takes place through Christ's atoning death (10:12–18) and through the exaltation that enables him to intercede on behalf of others (4:16; 7:25). The mercy provided through the new covenant does not mean that God overlooks sin, but that God overcomes sin by writing his laws on human hearts. Obedience is not a precondition for mercy, but a consequence of mercy. By giving people the will to be faithful, God will bring about a situation in which the sins of the past and the present no longer damage his relationship with people.

The shift from the old to the new covenant (8:6) has begun, but is not complete since a change has occurred, but the promises have not been fully realized. Under the new covenant, God deals decisively with sin through the death of Christ (7:27; 10:12–18), yet unbelief remains an unsettling possibility (3:7–4:10). God promised to write his will on human hearts, yet the wayward heart persists (3:12). God promised that people would no longer need instruction, yet they continue to need teaching and exhortation (3:13; 5:12; 13:22). God promised to keep for himself a people, yet some were drifting away (10:25). Listeners may not

---

[276]People abandoned the covenant when they worshiped the deities of neighboring peoples (1 Kgs 19:10, 14; Jer 22:9) and when they embraced Hellenism (1 Macc 1:15, 63).

yet "see" the realization of all of God's promises (2:8b), but Hebrews argues that the old covenant provides no assurance in the time of change. Its obsolescence means that the listeners' orientation must be toward what is yet to come.

22. Ministry in the First Tent (9:1–10)

9 [1]Now, the first [covenant] indeed had regulations for service and the earthly
sanctuary. [2]For the first tent was prepared, in which were the lampstand and the
table and the presentation of the loaves and it is called a "sanctuary." [3]Behind
the second curtain was the tent called the "holiest sanctuary," [4]containing a gold-
en incense altar and the ark of the covenant covered all over with gold, in which
were a golden jar containing the manna, the staff of Aaron that blossomed, and
the tablets of the covenant; [5]and above it were the cherubim of glory overshadowing the place of atonement—concerning these things we cannot now speak in
detail.

[6]With these things prepared in this way, the priests continually go into the first
tent to conduct their services, [7]but into the second the high priest alone goes
once a year, not without blood, which he offers for himself and for the people's
sins of ignorance. [8]By this the Holy Spirit indicates that the way into the sanctuary has not yet been manifested while the first tent still has standing, [9]and this is
a symbol for the present time, according to which gifts and sacrifices are offered
that are not able to make complete the conscience of the one who serves,
[10][since they] only concern foods and drinks and various ablutions—regulations
of the flesh imposed until a time of correction.

NOTES

9:1. *Now, the first* [*covenant*]. The particle *men* introduces the description of the earthly sanctuary and ministry. The particle *de* in 9:11 introduces its counterpart, the ministry of Jesus in the heavenly sanctuary. The word "first" (*prōtē*) is feminine, and some MSS specify that it refers to the first "tent" (*skēnē*; 6^{mg} 81 104 326 etc.), but since the feminine form of "first" referred to the covenant (*diathēkē*) in 8:13, it presumably refers to the covenant in 9:1 as well (Chrysostom).

indeed had regulations for service. The noun *latreia* and verb *latreuein* were used for priestly "service" (9:6–7; Num 16:9; 1 Chron 28:13) and general observance of God's commandments (Deut 6:13; 10:12; Exod 20:5; 23:24; 1 Macc 1:43; 2:19, 22), including those pertaining to food, drink, and ablutions (Heb 9:10). Christian "service" (9:14; 12:28) includes hospitality, attending to the afflicted, chastity, and avoiding avarice (12:28–13:6; cf. Rom 12:1).

and the earthly sanctuary. The word "sanctuary" is neuter singular (*to hagion*) in 9:1, although elsewhere the neuter plural (*ta hagia*) is used (8:2; 9:3, 8, 12, 24, 25). The LXX also alternates between the plural and singular forms with no difference in meaning (cf. Num 3:28, 38 and NOTE on Heb 8:2). The Mosaic sanctuary was "earthly" (*kosmikos*) in that it was located upon earth (8:4), within the *kosmos* (4:3; 10:5). In Hebrews "the earthly sanctuary" is the earthly tent that was contrasted with the "true" and "heavenly" one in 8:1–5. To be "earthly" is to be limited in significance (Thompson, *Beginnings*, 105; Attridge; Lane; Grässer).

9:2. *For the first tent.* On "tent" see NOTE on 8:2. The Tabernacle and the first and second Temples were bipartite structures. Each had a forecourt (*hêkal*) and an inner court (*debîr*, 1 Kgs 6:17–19). The terms "first" and "second" could be used for successive courts in a sanctuary (Josephus, *J.W.* 5.193), although the function here is more complex. See COMMENT *a*.

the lampstand. The lampstand had six branches extending from a central post, and it supported seven lamps (Exod 25:31–40; Lev 24:1–4). It was made of gold, although Hebrews does not mention this. The Tabernacle had one lampstand, Solomon's Temple had ten (1 Kgs 7:49), and the second Temple had one (Josephus, *J.W.* 5.216).

and the table. The table was made of acacia wood overlaid with gold (Exod 25:23–30), although Hebrews does not mention the gold. The table was about thirty-six inches long, eighteen inches wide, and twenty-seven inches high. It was called either "the table" or "the table of the presentation," because the loaves mentioned in the next NOTE were placed on it (Exod 39:36 [39:17 LXX]; 1 Chron 28:16; 2 Chron 29:18; 1 Macc 1:22).

and the presentation of the loaves. Twelve loaves of bread were placed upon the table and replaced with fresh ones each week (Lev 24:5–9; cf. Exod 40:23; 1 Sam 21:4; 1 Chron 9:32; 2 Chron 13:11; Matt 12:4 par.).

and it is called a "sanctuary." Most MSS have the anarthrous word *hagia*. Although many MSS lack accents (א D^1 I P), some make clear that the word is a neuter plural (*hágia*, D^2 0278 33 1739 etc.; *ta hagia*, B) as in 8:2; 9:3, 8, 12, 24, 25. A few MSS (365 629 etc.) take it to be a feminine singular adjective (*hagía*) modifying *skēnē* (tent). Some propose that it is a feminine adjective that describes the presentation (*hē prothesis*) of the loaves, which are viewed as a precursor of the sacred eucharistic bread (see pp. 28–29, 128; Swetnam, "Hebrews 9,2"; idem, "Christology," 82–84). The feminine reading is unlikely, however, given the repeated use of the neuter plural elsewhere. A few MSS read "holy of holies" (*hagia hagiōn*; P^{46} A D*), which Attridge accepts as the most difficult, but most scholars rightly consider this variant to be a mistake, since all MSS except P^{46} call the tent in 9:3 the "holy of holies" and since the compartment described in 9:3–5 is depicted as the earthly counterpart to the heavenly holy of holies.

9:3. *Behind the second curtain.* The second curtain marked the entrance to the inner chamber (Exod 26:31–35). The first curtain was a screen at the entrance to the forecourt (Exod 26:36–37). The screen and curtain were made of blue, purple, scarlet, and linen material (Exod 36:35–38). Both the first and second dividers were sometimes called "curtains" (cf. 1 Macc 4:51). On the way that Jesus opened "through the curtain" see NOTES on Heb 6:19; 10:20.

the "holiest sanctuary." This designated the inner portion of the sanctuary in both the Tabernacle and Temple. Like the Hebrew *qōdesh haqodoshîm* ("holy of holies"), it functions as a superlative: most holy place (Exod 26:33–34).

9:4. *a golden incense altar.* The LXX calls the incense altar a *thysiastērion* (Exod 30:1), but Hebrews calls it a *thymiatērion.* A *thymiatērion* was sometimes a shallow pan or censer (Ezek 8:11; 2 Chron 26:19; 4 Macc 7:11), and some take it that way in Heb 9:4 (KJV; Hegermann). Nevertheless, Hebrews uses the term for the incense altar (cf. Philo, *Heir* 226; *Moses* 2.94, 101, 105; *Special Laws* 1.231; Josephus, *Ant.* 3.147, 198; *J.W.* 5.218; Symmachus and Theodotion on Exod 30:1). This altar was about eighteen inches square and thirty-six inches high (Exod 30:1–10). It was made of wood overlaid with gold. Incense was to be offered on it morning and evening. Burnt offerings were made on the bronze altar in the outer courtyard (Exod 27:1–8), but on the Day of Atonement the high priest put blood on the horns of the incense altar (Exod 30:10).

and the ark of the covenant. The ark was the box in which the tablets inscribed with the Law or covenant were kept. OT references to the ark come from various strands of tradition (see C. L. Seow, *ABD* 1.386–93), but according to the final form of the Pentateuch, which informs Hebrews, the ark was built at Mount Sinai. The ark rested in the Tabernacle's inner chamber, and the Israelites carried it with them when they moved camp. God promised to meet with Moses from above the ark (Exod 25:22). After David made Jerusalem his capital, the ark was brought to the city and housed in a tent (2 Sam 6:1–17) until it later was placed in the inner chamber of Solomon's Temple (1 Kgs 8:4–9). The ark was apparently lost when the Babylonians conquered Jerusalem (cf. Jer 3:16), although later traditions said that it was hidden and would be restored (2 Macc 2:4–8; *Liv. Pro.* 2.11–19; *Bib. Ant.* 26:12–15; cf. 2 *Bar.* 6:5–9; *Par. Jer.* 3:1–9; *m. Shek.* 6:1–2). There was no ark in the second Temple (Josephus, *J.W.* 5.219).

covered all over with gold. The ark was made of acacia wood that was covered with gold. It was about forty-five inches long, twenty-seven inches wide, and twenty-seven inches high (Exod 25:10–16).

in which were. Most sources say that the ark contained only the tablets of the Law (1 Kgs 8:9; 2 Chron 5:10; Philo, *Moses* 2.97; Josephus, *Ant.* 3.138; 8.104). The jar of manna (Exod 16:33) and Aaron's rod (Num 17:10 [17:25 MT, LXX]) were to be placed "before" God or the ark rather than inside the ark (cf. *t. Soṭah* 13:1). Some traditions, however, refer to the ark and "the things in it" (*Liv. Pro.* 2.11; cf. *Bib. Ant.* 26:12–15), suggesting that Hebrews may have relied on a tradition concerning additional items in the ark.

a golden jar containing the manna. Manna was the food that appeared on the ground each day during Israel's sojourn in the wilderness (Exod 16:31). About two quarts of it were preserved in a jar (Exod 16:32–34). The jar was made of gold according to Exod 16:33 LXX (but not MT). It was placed "before the testimony," which probably meant "near the ark," but Hebrews says that it was inside the ark (cf. the previous NOTE). Manna was "bread from heaven" (Exod 16:4; Neh 9:15; John 6:31), and some said that manna was stored in heaven so that people might eat again of it in the end times (2 *Bar.* 29:8; Rev 2:17; cf. *Mek.* "Vayassa" 6.82 [Lauterbach ed., 2.126]).

the staff of Aaron that blossomed. This miracle occurred after Korah attempted to usurp priestly prerogatives. Aaron's staff miraculously blossomed to show that God had called him and his tribe to priestly service (Num 17:1–11 [17:16–26 LXX]), as he would later call Christ (Heb 5:4). Later Jewish tradition expected Aaron's rod to be restored in the end times (*Mek.* "Vayassa" 6.83–85 [Lauterbach ed., 2.126]).

and the tablets of the covenant. Moses was understood to have received two stone "tablets of the covenant" (Deut 9:9) on which the Law had been written by the finger of God (Deut 9:10; cf. Exod 34:27–28; 1 Kgs 8:9; 2 Chron 5:10). The tablets were put into the ark (Deut 10:1–5).

9:5. *the cherubim of glory.* These winged figures were made of gold (Exod 25:18–22). The genitive "of glory" could describe the cherubim themselves ("glorious winged creatures," NJB), but the context makes it likely that the glory is "God's glory" (REB; cf. NIV; Heb 1:3–14). God promised to meet with Moses "from between the two cherubim" (Exod 25:22; Num 7:89), and God was said to be "enthroned on the cherubim" (e.g., 1 Sam 4:4; 2 Sam 6:2; Ps 80:1). Cherubim were prominent in the inner chamber of Solomon's Temple (1 Kgs 6:23–28). See D. N. Freedman and M. P. O'Connor, *TDOT* 7.307–19. Philo said that the cherubim represented God's kingly and creative powers (*Moses* 2.99; *QE* 2.62).

overshadowing. This word (*kataskiazein*) recalls Exod 25:20 LXX (*syskiazein*). Cherubs were at each end of the ark, facing each other with their wings extended over the ark.

the place of atonement. The *hilastērion*—sometimes translated "mercy seat"—was the top of the ark (Exod 25:22; Num 7:89). On the Day of Atonement blood was sprinkled in front of the place of atonement (Lev 16:14). Paul uses the noun for Christ's death (Rom 3:25).

concerning these things we cannot now speak in detail. Like Philo (*Heir* 221), Hebrews may allude to the popular interest in the cosmic symbolism of the Tabernacle and its furnishings (see COMMENT *a*).

9:6. *the priests continually go into the first tent to conduct their services.* The LXX uses *dia pantos* ("continually") for daily incense offering (Exod 30:8), keeping loaves on the table (Exod 25:30 [25:29 LXX]), and tending lamps (Exod 27:20; Lev 24:2). Other duties included offering sacrifices each morning and evening (Exod 29:38–42). On the use of the present tense and the question of whether the Temple was still standing when Hebrews was written, see pp. 52–53.

9:7. *the high priest alone goes once a year.* The high priest was the only person allowed to enter the inner sanctuary (Philo, *Special Laws* 1.72; *Gaius* 307; Josephus, *J.W.* 5.236; Diodorus Siculus, *Library of History* 34.1.3). He did so once a year, on the Day of Atonement (Exod 30:10; Lev 16:2, 29, 34). He first sprinkled bull's blood before the place of atonement for the sins of himself and his house (Lev 16:12–13), then entered a second time with goat's blood for the sins of the people (Lev 16:15). Although the priest entered the chamber two (cf. Philo, *Gaius* 307) or more times (*m. Yoma* 5:1–7; 7:4), all was accomplished on a single day. Thus his entry "once" per year foreshadows Christ's self-sacrifice "once" for all time (Heb 7:27; 9:12, 26, 28; 10:10).

not without blood. Aaron was to enter the holy of holies "with a young bull for a sin offering and a ram for a burnt offering" (Lev 16:3). On blood see NOTES on 9:22. Like the Levitical high priest, Christ enters the holy of holies by means of blood, but unlike the Levitical high priest, the blood is his own.

which he offers for himself. The high priest first offered the blood of a bull for his own sins by sprinkling the blood seven times before the place of atonement (Lev 16:14). Levitical high priests made sacrifices for their own sins (Heb 5:3; 7:27), but Christ did not, since he was sinless (4:15).

and for the people's sins of ignorance. The high priest offered a goat for the sins of the people (Lev 16:15). The noun *agnoēma* ("sins of ignorance") is probably a synonym for "sin" (Sir 23:2; Tob 3:3; Jdt 5:20; 1 Macc 13:39). Sacrifices normally atoned for sins that were committed unintentionally or in ignorance, but not for intentional sins (NOTE on 5:2). Sacrifices on the Day of Atonement were offered "for all their sins" (Lev 16:16; cf. 16:5, 9), which Philo assumes includes voluntary and involuntary sins (*Special Laws* 2.196). Some, however, cautioned that atonement was not automatic. If one said, " 'I will sin and the Day of Atonement will effect atonement,' then the Day of Atonement effects no atonement" (*m. Yoma* 8:9; cf. *Jub.* 5:17–19). Hebrews assumes that Christ's death offers complete atonement for all sins, not just inadvertent sins, while recognizing that people can spurn the grace Christ offers (Heb 6:4–8; 10:26).

9:8. *By this the Holy Spirit indicates.* The verb "indicate" could introduce an inference based on a biblical text (12:27), but it could refer to explanations of things that were not otherwise clear (Dan 2:5–7; 7:16; Josephus, *Ant.* 3.187). Such instruction could be divinely given (Ps 51:6 [50:8 LXX]; Dan 2:28–30; 1 Pet 1:11). Hebrews refers to the biblical depiction of the Tabernacle as a "symbol" (Heb 9:9a), assuming that its temporal significance (9:9) would not have been known prior to Christ (Lane; Grässer). For the author, the Spirit that speaks through the Scriptures (3:7; 10:15) gives insight into the Scriptures.

that the way into the sanctuary. The genitive case *tōn hagiōn* can best be understood as a neuter plural: "the sanctuary." The Peshitta takes it as a masculine plural, referring to "the way of the [Christian] saints" in contrast to the way of Jewish Law (9:10). Elsewhere, however, *hagia* is neuter, referring to all or part of the sanctuary (8:2; 9:2, 3, 12, 24, 25; 10:19; 13:11). Symbolically, "the sanctuary" or "second tent" (i.e., holy of holies) is heaven and the age to come.

has not yet been manifested. The way into the inner chamber was closed to ordinary people (Josephus, *Ant.* 3.123, 181), but Hebrews says that the way was not actually known. It became manifest when Christ parted the curtain through his death and exaltation (6:20; 10:20).

while the first tent still has standing. The expression "have standing" (*stasin echein*) can be used for physical existence and social "standing" (Epictetus, *Disc.* 1.21.1; Polybius, *Histories* 10.33.6). The imagery is not purely physical, since the forecourt or "first tent" continued to stand in a physical sense as the high priest entered the inner chamber. In a symbolic sense, however, Christ's entry into the heavenly sanctuary means that the first covenant and its sanctuary no longer have normative "standing" among the people of God (cf. 7:18; 8:13; F. F. Bruce;

Attridge; Lane). On whether the Temple was standing when Hebrews was written see pp. 52–53.

9:9. *and this is a symbol.* The term *parabolē* is not used for a narrative, as in the parables of Jesus, but to indicate that the first tent was a "symbol." In rhetoric, a *parabolē* was a comparison of things where the resemblance was not obvious (Quintilian, *Inst.* 5.11.23). Hebrews uses the term for typological connections between the old and new covenants. The first tent is a symbol for "the present time," which is associated with Jewish regulations (9:9). The binding and release of Isaac is a "symbol" of resurrection (11:19). Similarly, Paul said, "whatever was written in former days was written for our instruction" (Rom 15:4; cf. 1 Cor 10:11; Michaud, "Parabolê").

for the present time. Some have taken this to mean "the time then present" (KJV; Erasmus, *Paraphrase*), that is, the past time when the Tabernacle existed. Most now take it as the author's own time, which is the way that *kairos ho enestēkōs* was usually used (Polybius, *Histories* 1.60.9; 21.3.3; Philo, *Sacrifices* 47; Josephus, *Ant.* 16.162). The imagery is complex, but yields good sense:

(a) The "present time" refers to the period when the first covenant's regulations concerning food, drink, and ablutions are in force. The time is one of unfulfillment, because the sacrifices that are offered do not bring the conscience to "completion" (9:9b). The negative connotations echo Jewish teachings concerning the two ages: the present age is dominated by sin and death, and the age to come brings redemption and resurrection (*4 Ezra* 6:7–8; 8:1; *2 Bar.* 15:7; *m. Pe'ah* 1:1; *m. 'Abot* 4:17; cf. Mark 10:30; Luke 18:30; Rom 8:18; Vanhoye, *Old Testament*, 156–57; Bénétreau).

(b) The practices of "the present time" continue "until the time of correction," when the first covenant's regulations are set aside (NOTE on 9:10). The time of correction arrived when Christ inaugurated the new covenant by his self-sacrifice, which provides complete cleansing. The way into the holiest part of the sanctuary was blocked under the first covenant, but Christ has now opened "a new and living way" into the sanctuary (10:19–20).

The "present time" does not refer to all aspects of the author's situation, but only to the practices mentioned in 9:9–10. Some take "the present time" and "the time of correction" to be synonyms (Attridge; Ellingworth; H.-F. Weiss), but it is preferable to take them as overlapping rather than identical. Listeners had already experienced "the powers of the age to come" (6:5), but had not yet received their inheritance in the world to come (1:14; 2:5). The new covenant had been inaugurated, but the old had not yet vanished (8:13). The tension is similar to that depicted by Paul, who could speak of "the present evil age" (Gal 1:4) even though "the fullness of time" had come, bringing liberation (Gal 4:4). Cf. Braun; Hegermann; Grässer.

according to which. In the best MSS (א A B D* etc.) the preposition is followed by a feminine prounoun (*kath' hēn*). The pronoun can be connected to *parabolē*: "according to which [symbol]" (Attridge; Braun). It can also be connected to *skēnē*: "according to which [tent]" (Lane; H.-F. Weiss) with little difference in meaning. Less likely is that the pronoun can be connected to "time" (*kairos*), either by adopting the variant *kath' hon* (D2 Maj) or by assuming that the pronoun is feminine by attraction: "according to the present time" (cf. NRSV).

gifts and sacrifices are offered that are not able to make complete. Making the conscience "complete" includes cleansing it from sin (9:14) and bringing about a positive relationship with God. Jeremiah said that to complete the new covenant, God would write his laws upon the human mind and heart, leading to complete obedience (8:10; cf. 10:22; cf. 9:14; 10:2; 13:18). See pp. 122–25.

the conscience. The term *syneidēsis* in a basic sense meant consciousness, but it often referred to moral consciousness. Those who have done wrong are troubled by "an evil conscience" (10:22). Even if other people are not aware of the misdeed, the wrongdoer has "consciousness of sin" (10:2). Conversely, those who are aware of their own integrity have a "good conscience" (13:18) even if others charge them with wrongdoing. Those with a good conscience do not mind the scrutiny of the crowd, but "a bad conscience, even in solitude, is disturbed and troubled. If your deeds are honorable, let everyone know them; if they are base, what does it matter that no one knows them, as long as you yourself know them?" (Seneca, *Ep.* 43.5; cf. Wis 17:10). Paul understood that the conscience was a part of the human constitution, and thus all people had accountability before God (Rom 2:15). A clear conscience is the basis for the "boldness" (Heb 3:6) needed to approach God and to maintain one's convictions before other people (Philo, *Heir* 6–7; *Special Laws* 1.203; Josephus, *Ant.* 2.52). See *TLNT* 3.332–36.

of the one who serves. Here "serving" refers not only to priests but to all worshipers.

9:10. *foods and drinks and various ablutions.* These items have two primary types of associations:

(a) Levitical sacrificial practices. Portions of some sacrifices were eaten by the worshipers, although the term "food" (*brōma*) was not commonly used for Levitical sacrifices. "Drink" may recall the drink offerings, although the term Hebrews uses (*poma*) differs from that used in the LXX (*spondē*; Num 15:5, 7, 10; 28:7–10, etc.). Ablutions were part of the preparatory rites for those engaging in priestly work (Exod 29:4; Lev 8:6; 16:4).

(b) Jewish statutes for purity. "Food" and "drink" were mentioned in statutes pertaining to clean and unclean foods (cf. *Ep. Arist.* 128, 142, 158, 162; 1 Macc 1:63; *Diogn.* 4:1; cf. Josephus, *Ant.* 4.137). Of the drinks, Jews were most wary of the wine provided by Gentiles (Dan 1:8, 12; Jdt 12:1–2; Add Esth 14:17). Ablutions were used for purification by all Jews, not only priests. Ablutions might be done before meals (Mark 7:4; Jdt 12:8–9) and after certain bodily emissions (Lev 15) or contact with a corpse (Num 19). The reference to "foods" in 13:9 is more general.

regulations of the flesh. The "regulations for service" (9:1) are now depicted pejoratively as "regulations of the flesh" (cf. 7:16).

(a) "Flesh" first connotes weakness, for fleshly life is bounded by death (2:14; 5:7). Flesh is the physical, transient (7:16) side of human existence in contrast to the conscience (9:9–10).

(**b**) "Flesh" also identifies what is common to humanity. Regulations pertaining to food, drink, and ablutions were common to many traditions. Temples in the Greco-Roman world had inscriptions "posted where strangers could not help but see the regulations they must follow" (Macmullen, *Paganism*, 11). One said, "Let no one enter who is not pure and perfect"; another directed people to "purify" themselves with water (F. C. Grant, *Hellenistic Religions*, 6–7). Meat from sacrificial victims, cereals, and wine were used in offerings to gods and meals among the worshipers (see M. H. Jameson and J. A. North in *CAM*, 2.959–86). Both Jewish and non-Jewish traditions could be identified by regulations for food, drink, and ablutions, but for Hebrews, Christ's death and exaltation are of another order.

imposed until a time of correction. The regulations were "imposed" by God, who gave the Law. "Correction" was needed when a building was in disrepair (Aristotle, *Politics* 6.5.3 1321), when an account was in arrears (Polybius, *Histories* 5.50.7), or when a law proved to be ineffective. When a law underwent correction, the existing statute was annulled and a new one put in its place (Diodorus Siculus, *Library of History* 12.17.1–5; 12.18.1–2). Josephus said that the excellence of the Jewish Law was shown in that it had needed no correction (*Ag. Ap.* 2.183), but Hebrews says the opposite, insisting that the regulations of the first covenant were changed (Heb 7:12), abrogated (7:18), and replaced by the new covenant in Christ (7:22; 8:6, 13). Cf. NOTE on "the present time" in 9:9.

COMMENT[277]

The author previously recalled that Moses had built a sanctuary on earth (8:5), and he now describes the old and earthly institution. Since God made the first covenant obsolete (8:13), the ancient Tabernacle appears in only faded splendor. After enabling listeners to picture it, the author locates them within its forecourt by telling them that this represents "the present time." Then he adds that the first covenant's regulations also belong to the forecourt. This prepares for the next section, when the author will announce that the way into the inner chamber has been opened and that the situation has been changed by Christ (9:11–14). Listeners have not fully entered the new reality, but they will be shown that the way is open (§23 COMMENT *a–b*).

The symbolism of the Tabernacle has appealed to the imagination of many (see pp. 28–29), but interpretation is difficult because the imagery is not stable. At some points, "the first tent" seems to be the *whole Mosaic Tabernacle* (9:2, 8), which is earthly and instituted for a limited time (9:1, 9). Its regulations purify only the flesh (9:10), the priests who minister in it are subject to sin and death (7:23–28), and their sacrifices are of limited benefit (cf. 10:1–4). At other points, however, the first covenant is identified with the ministry that ordinary priests perform in the *forecourt*, while the sacrifice offered by the high priest on the Day of Atonement anticipates Christ's singular self-sacrifice and entry into heaven

[277]For bibliography on 9:1–10 see §23 COMMENT n. 285.

(9:6–7). The complexity arises because the author insists that the entire Mosaic cultus has been made obsolete, yet he also affirms that a *part* of that cultus—atonement in the inner chamber—foreshadows the work of Christ.

Three aspects of the Tabernacle show its limitations, preparing for the presentation of Christ's superior ministry in 9:11–14: **(a)** Spatial. Moses set up a tent sanctuary on earth, whereas Christ is a minister of the true tent in heaven (8:2, 5). Calling the first covenant's sanctuary "earthly" in 9:1 recalls this contrast. **(b)** Temporal. The Mosaic sanctuary was based on a covenant that is old and obsolete (8:6, 13). Its regulations end with "a time of correction" (9:8–10). Superior ministry would be based on a new covenant. **(c)** Anthropological. The ministry associated with the Mosaic Tabernacle involved regulations for purifying the flesh, but these practices did not purify the conscience in a manner that enabled people to enter God's inner chamber (9:9–10). Such complete cleansing is the result of Christ's superior ministry (9:11–14).

Structurally, the section is framed by references to "regulations" (*dikaiōmata*; 9:1, 10). The two paragraphs (9:1–5, 6–10) are marked by references to "preparation" (*kataskeuazein*; 9:2, 6) and "worship" (*latreia* / *latreuein*; 9:6, 9). The topics in these paragraphs, which are stated in 9:1, include regulations for worship and an earthly sanctuary. These topics are taken up in reverse order: **(a)** the sanctuary is treated in 9:2–5, and **(b)** the regulations for worship are the focus of 9:6–10, along with a symbolic explication of the whole.

a. The Description of the Tabernacle (9:1–5)

The tentlike sanctuary prescribed by the Law (9:1) had ceased to be used centuries before Hebrews was written,[278] but the biblical statutes pertaining to the sanctuary remained important for Jewish identity. Jews were often criticized because their regulations concerning food and drink (9:10) led to separatism at meals and because they refused to recognize the religious rites of others (Barclay, *Jews*, 429–37). Apologists for Judaism argued that the biblical sanctuary reflected the structure of creation and that Jewish Law brought one into harmony with nature and its Creator.[279] The Tabernacle's two chambers were said to represent earth and heaven. The four colors on the curtain recalled the four elements, the seven branches of the lampstand symbolized the seven "planets," the twelve loaves stood for the twelve months, and the incense altar indicated thanksgiving for the elements.[280] The services of the priests were said to be of *kosmikos* or

---

[278]Hebrews 9:1–5 relies on depiction of the Tabernacle in the final form of the Pentateuch. Early traditions refer to a simple tent that stood outside the camp (Exod 33:7–11), while later elements depict a more elaborate structure in the center of the camp. See C. R. Koester, *Dwelling*, 8–11.

[279]See Philo, *Moses* 2.48; Josephus, *Ant.* 3.179–80. Principal sources for the cosmological interpretation are Philo, *QE* 2.51–106; *Moses* 2.81–108; *Heir* 221–29; Josephus, *Ant.* 3.123, 181–83; cf. *J.W.* 5.213–18. See C. R. Koester, *Dwelling*, 59–63. Some scholars find little connection between this tradition and Hebrews (Lane; H.-F. Weiss), but others find it helpful for interpretation (Attridge, *Epistle*, 223–24; Hegermann).

[280]The symbolism of the four colors was linen = earth, purple = water, blue = air, and scarlet = fire. The seven "planets" were the sun, moon, Mercury, Venus, Mars, Jupiter, and Saturn.

"universal" significance (Josephus, *J.W.* 4.324), and those who worshiped with right intent could come to share "the eternal life of the sun and moon and the whole *kosmos*" (Philo, *Moses* 2.108; cf. 2.48).

Hebrews uses similar language to argue in the opposite direction. The author does not call the first covenant's sanctuary *kosmikos* (Heb 9:1) in order to show the universal significance of Jewish worship, but to show the "earthly," and therefore limited, value of Mosaic institutions. Aspects of the description of the Tabernacle in 9:2–3 are peculiar, but serve the argument. When listeners heard the author refer to "the first tent," they almost certainly would have thought of the entire Mosaic Tabernacle in contrast to later sanctuaries (Josephus, *Ag. Ap.* 2.12). Moreover, after briefly mentioning the lampstand, table, and loaves, the author refers to this first tent as *hagia*, using a term for a "sanctuary" (NOTE on 8:2). But having called the Mosaic sanctuary to mind, he abruptly alters the picture by referring to the "second curtain" and the "tent" of surpassing holiness that stood behind it (9:3). Thus the worship that was ordinarily associated with the "first tent" or whole Tabernacle is now confined to the first compartment or forecourt, so that what listeners would have associated with the whole sanctuary is now said to be limited.

The limitations of the forecourt are disclosed by the unveiling of the inner chamber, which is of superior holiness (9:3). According to the OT, Israel's camp had concentric rings of holiness (see p. 120). Unclean people and objects had to be kept outside the camp, and anything brought into the camp had to be made clean. The outer courtyard, forecourt, and inner chamber of the Tabernacle required successively higher levels of purity and sanctity. To bring the unclean or common into the sphere of the holy would be an outrage to God (10:29). Those who want to enter the presence of God must have the most complete level of sanctity—and the author will insist that only Christ provides it.

The splendor of the inner chamber (9:4) calls attention to its superiority, allowing it to serve as a reflection of the glory of the sanctuary in which Jesus ministers (8:2; 9:11). Hebrews mentions gold only in connection with the inner court. According to Jewish traditions, the incense altar, ark, and manna were associated with worship in heaven and the end times (NOTES on 9:4). Aaron's rod marked God's call to legitimate priesthood, a pattern that Christ follows (5:4). The "cherubim of glory" invites listeners to make connections with the exordium of Hebrews, where the exalted Christ is adored by the angelic hosts (1:1–14). The cherubim overshadowed the place where atonement was made,[281] and the author has already said that the exalted Christ is the one who makes atonement (2:17) so that people can find mercy and help at God's throne (4:16).

Hebrews' description of the Tabernacle does not fully coincide with the usual reconstructions of the sanctuary based on the Pentateuch:

---

[281]The inclusion of cherubim might seem to contradict the biblical injunction against making graven images (Exod 20:4; cf. F. F. Bruce, *Epistle*, 205). During the early church's controversy about the legitimacy of using icons, this text was used to show that God did allow the use of some images in worship. See Pelikan, *Christian*, 124.

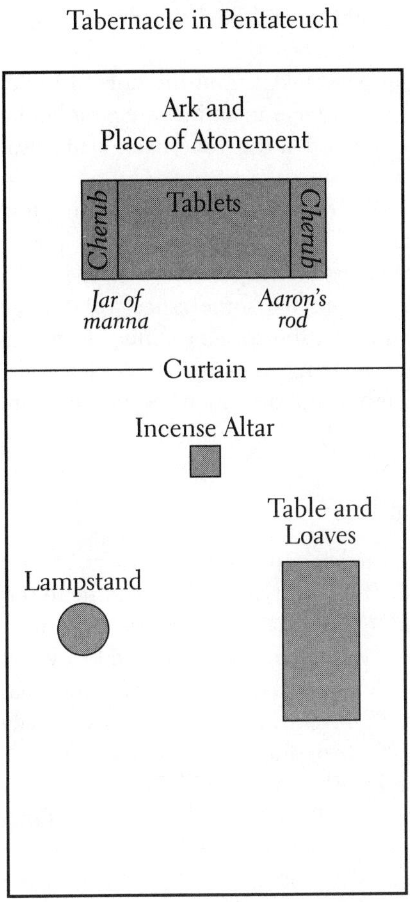

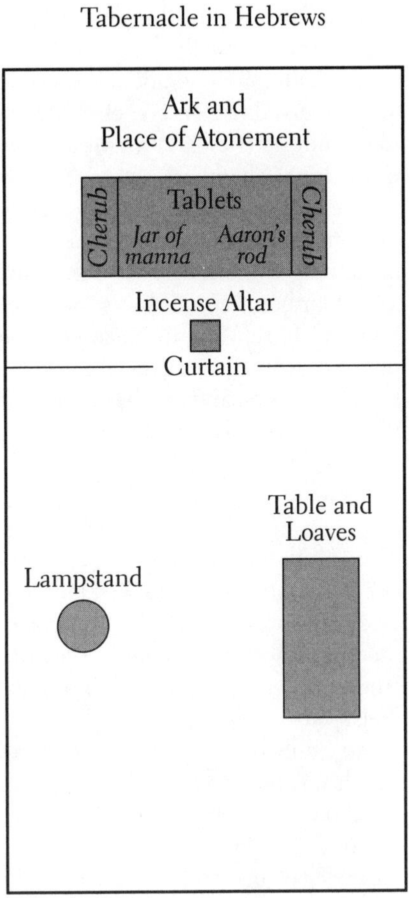

The Pentateuch seems to locate the incense altar in the forecourt, while Hebrews places it in the inner chamber.[282] At least two factors may have contributed to this:

(a) Unclarity in the OT (Attridge, *Epistle*, 234–38). The incense altar is described separately from the forecourt's other furnishings (Exod 30:1–10). Passages stating that it was to be placed "before" the ark or curtain (Exod 40:6, 26; cf. 30:6) could be taken to mean that it was inside the curtain with the ark. Since incense was burned on it both morning and evening (Exod 30:7–8), most understand that the altar was in the forecourt. The LXX of Exod 30:7, however, says that the incense was to be burned "early" rather than "daily." Since Exod 30:10 describes the altar's role in the annual Day of Atonement ritual—and incense was used on the Day of Atonement (Lev 16:12–13)—an interpreter who thought

[282]Jewish sources that located the incense altar in the forecourt include Philo, *Heir* 226; *Moses* 2.101; Josephus, *Ant.* 3.147; cf. *J.W.* 5.216; *m. Tamid* 1:4; 3:1, 6, 9; 6:1. Some MSS of Hebrews (B sa[mss]) resolve the discrepancy by including the incense altar in the description of the forecourt in Heb 9:2. The discrepancy was noted by Jerome (PL 24.98–99) and Luther (*LuthW* 29.204).

that the altar was in the inner sanctuary might have thought that incense was only burned annually.

(b) Tradition. The ark and incense altar were taken from the holy of holies and preserved (2 *Bar.* 6:7; cf. 2 Macc 2:5). References to an incense altar before God's throne (Rev 8:3) might also have implied that the Tabernacle's altar was in the inner chamber.

The author concludes his description of the furnishings by commenting that he cannot deal with these things in detail (cf. 11:32). Rhetorically, passing by something without detailed comment was called *paraleipsis* (*Rhet. ad Her.* 4.27 §37; Lausberg, *Handbook* §§882–86). By identifying some aspects of a large topic while refusing to make detailed comment, the speaker alludes to his familiarity with the subject matter, while relativizing its importance. Here, Hebrews makes clear that what is most important is not the sanctuary, but the ministry that takes place within it.

b. The Significance of the Tabernacle (9:6–10)

The "regulations for service" (9:1) are explained beginning in 9:6. Priests are said to go continually into the first tent to conduct their services. Since continual services were prescribed by the first covenant (NOTE on 9:6), those who performed them were acting obediently. A Jewish writer would have been pleased to say that "the ministering of the priests was absolutely unsurpassed in its vigor" and that their "service is unremitting" (*Ep. Arist.* 92). The limitations of this activity emerge only by contrast to the high priest's work on the Day of Atonement (9:7), which was the most significant day in the Jewish year, carefully observed even "by those who never act religiously in the rest of their life" (Philo, *Special Laws* 2.186; cf. 2.196; *Moses* 2.23). Hebrews gives no attention to the incense, the slaughter of the bull and goat, or the confession of sins over the head of the scapegoat (Lev 16), all of which were part of the Day of Atonement ritual. Instead, the author focuses on the high priest's offering of blood and his entry into the inner chamber. The result is a contrast between the ministry of ordinary priests and that of the high priest:

First Tent	*Second Tent*
Multiple priests	High priest alone
Continually	Once a year
Multiple services	Offering of blood

Details of Levitical ministry correspond in a general rather than an exact way to Jesus' ministry. Levitical high priests entered the inner chamber once each year rather than once for all time as Jesus did (9:25–26), and they offer blood for their own sins and the sins of others, while Christ made an offering only for others, since he himself was sinless (4:15).

Explicit symbolic interpretation begins in 9:8a, where "the Holy Spirit indicates" the meaning of the biblical regulations for worship. Two assumptions underlie the symbolism. First, the God who spoke by the prophets, whose words appear in Scripture, is the same God who has spoken through a Son (1:1–2). Therefore, each is interpreted in light of the other. Second, the Spirit enables what God said in Scripture to address later generations (3:7), and the Spirit is God's way of confirming the message concerning Christ (2:3–4). Thus the Spirit does not work independently of the Scriptures or of Christ, but discloses the congruence between what the Scriptures foreshadow and what Christ's death and exaltation have accomplished.

The Spirit indicates that "the way into the sanctuary has not yet been manifested while the first tent still has standing" (9:8b). In a physical sense this suggests that the forecourt or "first tent" conceals the way into the inner chamber or sanctuary that lies behind the curtain. Yet the sense is peculiar, since the forecourt remained standing in a physical sense while the high priest went into the inner chamber. The incongruity suggests that the first tent was the entire cultus established by the first covenant. The sanctuary and worship prescribed by the first covenant conceal a greater reality, which is only known when "manifested." Christ's death and exaltation disclose a reality that is not otherwise apparent (Vanhoye, *Old Testament*, 186; cf. NOTES on 8:1–2).

The symbolism of the sanctuary encompasses several dimensions:

	First Tent	*Second Tent*
temporal	transient age	eternal age
cosmological	earth	heaven
anthropological	flesh	conscience

The temporal significance of the imagery is discussed in NOTE on 9:9. The spatial sense will emerge through contrast between the earthly sanctuary (9:1) and the heavenly tent in which Jesus ministers (9:11–14). The new element is the anthropological distinction between flesh and conscience (9:9b–10). The old covenant provided means for purifying the flesh, but not the conscience (9:9). The problem is not that the cleansing was external, but that the cleansing was *incomplete*, since the conscience remained defiled. Those who have a clean body but a defiled conscience are not in a state to draw near to God. A more complete cleansing is required.

Cleansing the conscience is important because the scrutiny of God's word (4:12–13) functions like the conscience: "Why select a hiding place and remove witnesses? . . . What good is it for you not to have a witness since you have a conscience?" There is "no advantage in having a closed-up conscience; we are open to God" (Seneca, quoted in Lactantius, *Divine Institutes* 6.24). The author does not simply assume that people have troubled consciences and are looking for relief. Writing to a dull and sluggish audience (Heb 5:11; 6:12), the author has attempted to disturb the consciences of his listeners, making them uneasy before God.

The reference to "food and drinks and various ablutions" extends what was said about the Tabernacle to encompass broader patterns of Jewish life (NOTE on 9:10). People were to honor the sanctuary by honoring the laws of the covenant that were enshrined in it (9:4).[283] For Jews in the Diaspora, observance of laws pertaining to food and drink were visible forms of identifying with Jewish practice. Regulations for the Day of Atonement were especially important, since Jewish people everywhere were to abstain from food, drink, washing, and other things on that day.[284]

The specific reasons for comments about laws pertaining to food, drink, and ablutions are unclear (§18 COMMENT). Socially, some of the listeners might have wanted to affiliate more closely with a Jewish community and to distance themselves from Christian gatherings because of the animosity that Christians experienced from others in society (10:25, 32–34; 13:3, 13). They might also have thought that Jewish practices provided a way to live rightly before God as a distinctive people in an interreligious environment. When the author mentions "foods" later in the speech, he does so more for the sake of contrast with the benefits that Christ provides than to deal with Jewish teachings (NOTES on 12:16; 13:9). Here, calling these statutes "regulations of the flesh" diminishes their distinctiveness (NOTE on 9:10) in order that in the next section the author might direct listeners to Christ, in whom they see the realization of God's promises.

23. THE ATONING DEATH OF CHRIST (9:11–14)

9 11–12But Christ, having arrived as high priest of the good things that have occurred, entered once for all into the sanctuary, securing an eternal redemption through the greater and more perfect tent, which was not made by hand—that is, [it is] not of this creation—and not through the blood of goats and calves, but through his own blood. 13For if the blood of goats and bulls and the sprinkled ashes of a heifer sanctify those who have been defiled so as to purify the flesh, 14how much more will the blood of Christ, who through the eternal Spirit offered himself without blemish to God, cleanse our conscience from dead works to serve a living God.

NOTES

9:11–12. These verses consist of one complex sentence. The translation modifies the order of the clauses, which in the Greek text is as follows (Vanhoye, "Par la tente," 2; Hofius, *Vorhang*, 66):

---

[283]Sirach linked the wisdom of God with the tent and the Law (Sir 24:10, 23). Therefore, to observe the Mosaic Law is to live in accordance with the wisdom found in the Tabernacle.

[284]On the Pharisees' extension of Temple purity into the home see Schürer, *History*, 2.475. On the importance of kosher foods for Diaspora Jews see Barclay, *Jews*, 429–37. On fasting on the Day of Atonement see Philo, *Special Laws* 2.193–203; *Moses* 2.23–24; *m. Yoma* 8:1.

A But Christ, having arrived as high priest
of the good things that have occurred,
B through (*dia*) the greater and more perfect tent
C not (*ou*) fabricated by hands—that is, not of this creation—
C[1] and not (*oude*) through (*dia*) the blood of goats and calves,
B[1] but through (*dia*) his own blood,
D he entered once for all into the sanctuary
and secured an eternal redemption.

Syntactically, the participial clause in line A identifies "Christ" as the subject of the sentence, whereas the main verb, "he entered," appears in line D. To make the relationship clear, lines A and D are placed next to each other in the translation. The rest of the sentence consists of four phrases beginning with *dia* and *ou* or *oude*, which anticipate the main point. Although some understand the phrases to describe only how Christ "entered" the sanctuary (Attridge; Lane), here they are read as an explanation of all of line D, since blood is more closely associated with atonement (cf. 9:7bc) than with entry. This structure allows the sentence in 9:11–12 to end with a reference to blood, which is the topic taken up in 9:13.

But Christ, having arrived as high priest. The word "arrived" (*paragenomenos*) is a compound form of the word that was used for Christ "becoming" high priest in 6:20 (*genomenos*). Although the verb can mean "appearing" in public (1 Macc 4:46; Matt 3:1; cf. Braun; Lane), *paragenomenos* + *de* at the beginning of a sentence often indicate arrival at a destination (e.g., Luke 7:20; Acts 9:26; 14:27; 15:4). Christ the high priest "arrived" when he entered the heavenly sanctuary (Heb 8:1–2; Attridge; Ellingworth; H.-F. Weiss) rather than when he appeared on earth (Grässer). See pp. 109–10.

of the good things. These include redemption (9:12), salvation (9:28–10:1), and forgiveness (9:22).

that have occurred. MSS are divided between "have occurred" and "to come." Both fit the flow of the text: redemption "has come" in Christ, yet because it is eternal it belongs to the world "to come" (Vanhoye, *Old Testament*, 190). For translation, the first option seems preferable:

(a) "That have occurred" (*genomenōn*; [P[46]] B D* etc.; NIV; NRSV; REB; NAB[2]; Attridge; H.-F. Weiss; Lane; Grässer; Bénétreau). The MS evidence is early and diverse (*TCGNT*, 668). The variant *mellontōn* may have arisen to harmonize this passage with 10:1 and to bring out the temporal sense that was anticipated by reference to "the time of correction" in 9:10. Some render it "the real goods" (Braun; Grässer; H.-F. Weiss), since Christ's work differs from the regulations of the flesh that foreshadow redemption, but do not effect it (9:10; 10:1).

(b) "That are to come" (*mellontōn*; א A D[2] etc.; KJV; NJB; Hegermann; Casalini). This reading is well attested, and it could mean that good things were still future for the listeners (cf. *mellein* in 2:5; 13:14) or that since Christ's redemption is eternal, it belongs to the age to come even though it has already occurred (cf. *mellein* in 6:5). The alternative (*genomenōn*) could have originated as a mistake in copying, since the similar word *paragenomenos* occurs in 9:11a. Nevertheless, it would fit the author's style to include two similar words in the same sentence. For example, *apistias/apostēnai* (3:12); *parakaleite/kaleitai* (3:13; cf. Philo, *Rewards* 168; Moffatt, *Critical*, lx).

entered once for all into the sanctuary. In 9:11 some take the "tent" to be the whole heaven and "sanctuary" to be the innermost heaven, but the two expressions are virtually synonymous (cf. NOTES on 8:2 and on "the greater and more perfect tent" below). If the high priest enters the inner chamber "once" a year (9:7), Christ enters "once" for all time (cf. 7:27; 10:10; NOTE on 6:4).

securing an eternal redemption. Eternal "redemption" (*lytrōsis*), like "eternal salvation" (NOTE on 5:9), encompasses multiple aspects of meaning:

(a) Deliverance from Bondage. *Lytrōsis* and *lytron* were used for buying back property (Lev 25:24, 26, 29) or slaves that were taken into someone else's possession (Exod 21:30; Lev 25:48). The word was used for deliverance from oppressive powers (Luke 1:68; 2:38; *T. Jos.* 8:1); God redeemed Israel from slavery in Egypt (Deut 7:8; 9:26; 13:5; 15:15). According to Heb 9:9–10, those who live in "the present time" are subject to regulations that do not bring the conscience to completion. Redemption means deliverance from this situation of futility.

(b) Forgiveness of Sins. *Lytrōsis* is related to *apolytrōsis*, which refers to forgiveness (9:15). The term was not commonly used for the effects of sacrifice (cf. Philo, *Sacrifices* 128), but some said that people were "redeemed" from their iniquities (Ps 130:7–8 [129:7–8 LXX]). Jesus gave his life as a ransom (*lytron*) for many (Matt 20:28; Mark 10:45), and his death brings redemption (*apolytrōsis*) from sin (Rom 3:24; Eph 1:7; Col 1:14; Tit 2:14; 1 Pet 1:18). See *TLNT* 2.423–29; F. Büchsel, *TDNT* 4.328–56.

through. The preposition *dia* when followed by the genitive case has been taken in two ways, of which the first is preferable:

(a) Instrumental. The preposition *dia* occurs three times in 9:11–12, and the next two occurrences are instrumental. Nowhere else in Hebrews does *dia* plus the genitive have a spatial sense. Even in 13:11, where it appears alongside *eis* ("into"), *dia* is instrumental. Grammatically, the three phrases beginning with *dia* relate to the main verb in the sentence, "he entered." Yet logically, the phrases modify both "he entered" *and* the words "securing an eternal redemption." The three phrases beginning with *dia* not only explain how Jesus entered the heavenly sanctuary, but how his entry brought eternal redemption. See N. H. Young, "Gospel," 204; Lindars, *Theology*, 94; Vanhoye, "Par la tente"; Swetnam, "Greater"; cf. Casalini, *Dal simbolo*, 152.

(b) Spatial. Many scholars take *dia* to mean that Jesus moved "through" the forecourt of the heavenly sanctuary before entering the inner chamber (Lane; Ellingworth; Grässer; Bénétreau). *Dia* does appear in compound verbs for movement through a space (4:14; 11:29). Although the other occurrences of *dia* in 9:11–12 are instrumental, Hebrews can use the same preposition in different senses in the same context (e.g., *pros* in 1:7–8; *eis* in 7:25). A problem with this approach is that it concentrates too narrowly on Christ's entry into the sanctuary rather than taking "entry" and "obtaining redemption" together. Moreover, it assumes that "the greater and more perfect tent" is the forecourt of the heavenly sanctuary, which seems unlikely (see the next NOTE).

the greater and more perfect tent. The "greater" quality of the tent (cf. 6:13, 16) points to its status as "superior" (1:4; 7:19, 22; 8:6; 9:23; etc.). "More perfect" (*teleioteras*) continues the theme of "completion" that runs throughout Hebrews (pp. 122–25). The "tent" has been interpreted in several ways, of which the first is preferable:

(a) "Tent" as the whole sanctuary. The term "tent" is used for compartments of the earthly sanctuary (9:2, 3) and for the sanctuary as a whole (8:5; 9:21; 13:10). In 8:2 the author called Christ "a minister of the sanctuary, that is, of the true tent." In that passage the tent includes the whole sphere of Christ's ministry, not just one part of it (NOTE on 8:2). The tent in 9:11 is called "greater" and "more perfect" to show its superiority to the whole earthly shrine (9:1). The words are comparative in form but superlative in force (cf. BDF §§60–61). The "more perfect tent" is the "true" one (8:2). Since perfection cannot be found outside the presence of God, the "more perfect tent" must be the place where God is present (Hofius, *Vorhang*, 65–67; Löhr, "Thronversammlung," 191–92; Loader, *Sohn*, 166–67; Ellingworth; cf. Casalini, "Ebr 9, 11," 170).

(b) "Tent" as forecourt and "sanctuary" as inner chamber. Since the earthly sanctuary had a forecourt and an inner chamber (9:1–7), some infer that the heavenly sanctuary had the same two parts. Just as the Levitical high priest passed through the forecourt to enter the inner chamber, Jesus passed "through the heavens" (4:14) and "through the curtain" of the celestial forecourt (6:20; 10:19–20) to enter God's presence in the holy of holies (9:11, 24; cf. Lane; Andriessen, "Das grössere"; Grässer; cf. Attridge, *Epistle*, 223, 246–47). The problem is that "greater" and "more perfect" can scarcely describe the forecourt, since "perfection" involves coming into the presence of God (7:11, 19). Moreover, the author does not develop a consistent distinction between the parts of the sanctuary, but uses language that is unstable (§22 COMMENT).

(c) Christ's body. Some take the "tent" to be Christ's body (Chrysostom; Ps.-Oecumenius; Theophylact; Calvin), since God's Word became "flesh" and "tented" in Jesus (John 1:14), whose body was a "temple" (John 2:21). Some identify the tent with Christ's humanity (Cody, *Heavenly*, 161–65; Schierse, *Verheissung*, 57), his resurrected body (Vanhoye, *Old Testament*, 193–96), his eucharistic body (Swetnam, "Greater"), or the church as his body (Westcott). Some who take this approach note that when the passage is read as a chiasm (NOTE on Heb 9:11–12), the term "tent" parallels "his own blood" and that in 10:19–20 the "curtain" is Christ's flesh. Nevertheless, lines that are parallel in form are not necessarily parallel in content. Given the depiction of the tent in spatial (9:1–7) and temporal terms (9:8–10), it seems unlikely that the author would have shifted to an entirely different meaning without signaling this more clearly to the listeners.

not made by hand. The expression "made by hand" frequently has pejorative connotations and was used for idols (Lev 26:1, 30; Isa 2:18; 10:11; 19:1; 21:9;

31:7; 46:6; Dan 5:4, 23; Jdt 8:18; Wis 14:8; *Sib. Or.* 3.606, 618). The author understood that the Tabernacle was made by hand, since Moses had "made" it at God's command (Heb 8:5), although he did not consider the Tabernacle to be idolatrous. The Temple was "made by hand" as well and would pass away (Mark 14:58; Acts 7:48) in contrast to the heavenly tent that God set up (Heb 8:2).

not of this creation. The world was created by God (2:10; 11:3) through the Son (1:2), yet is subject to decay and death (1:10–12). It will be shaken and much will not endure (12:27).

and not through the blood of goats and calves. See NOTE on 9:7. On the Day of Atonement a goat was sacrificed for the people and a calf was sacrificed for the priest and his family. The plurals point to the repeated—and therefore ineffectual—nature of the action.

but through his own blood. On one level the imagery recalls the high priest bringing animal blood into the sanctuary on the Day of Atonement (NOTE on 9:7). On another level, Jesus would have been "covered with blood" during scourging (Josephus, *J.W.* 2.613), and during crucifixion the nails through his wrists and ankles would have brought further bloodshed. The victim let "out his life drop by drop" (Seneca, *Ep.* 101.14). Many thought that a considerable amount of blood was shed during crucifixion (Josephus, *Ant.* 19.94). According to John 19:34, blood issued from the wound in Jesus' side. The idea that Jesus' crucifixion was "essentially unbloody" (Grässer, *Hebräer,* 2.149) was not shared by early Christians, who referred to Jesus' "blood" in connection with the Lord's Supper (Matt 26:28 par.; 1 Cor 10:16; 11:25, 27) and Jesus' passion (Matt 27:4, 6, 24–25), and in references to the cleansing effect of his death (Acts 20:28; Rom 3:25; 5:9; Eph 1:7; 2:13; Col 1:14, 20; 1 Pet 1:2, 19; 1 John 1:7; Rev 1:5; 5:9; 7:14; 12:11; 19:13).

9:13. *For if the blood of goats and bulls.* The term "bull" (*tauros*), which differs from "calf" (*moschos*, 9:12), was not commonly used for sacrifice in the Pentateuch, but it does appear in later practice (Judg 6:25; Ps 50:13 [51:13 LXX]; Isa 1:11; 1 Esdr 7:7; 8:65; Philo, *Flight* 186).

and the sprinkled ashes of a heifer. The ashes of a red heifer, along with water that was "sprinkled," purified those who were defiled by contact with a corpse (Num 19:9; cf. Philo, *Special Laws* 1.262–72; Josephus, *Ant.* 4.78–81). The heifer's ashes were not used on the Day of Atonement, but people may have associated the two rites because both were performed by the high priest and because blood was sprinkled during each ceremony (Lev 16:14–15; Num 19:4).

sanctify those who have been defiled so as to purify the flesh. See pp. 119–21.

9:14. *how much more will the blood of Christ.* See NOTE on Christ's blood in 9:11–12.

who through the eternal Spirit. The expression "eternal Spirit" has been understood in several ways, of which the first is preferable:

(a) Holy Spirit. Prior to 9:14 all references to "spirit" in the singular, except 4:12, have been to the Holy Spirit. Listeners could be expected to identify "the eternal Spirit" in 9:14 with the Holy Spirit (cf. "the Spirit of grace," 10:29). Calling the Spirit "eternal" connects it to "eternal redemption" (9:12; Aquinas, *Ad*

Heb. §434; Vanhoye, "Esprit"; Lane; Ellingworth; H.-F. Weiss; Lindars, *Theology*, 58). Some MSS include "holy" in 9:14 (א[2] D* P etc.).

(b) Jesus' divine nature. Some NT passages refer to the power by which Jesus overcame death as "spirit" (Rom 1:4; 1 Tim 3:16; 1 Pet 3:18; cf. 1 Cor 15:45), and some take Heb 9:14 to refer to this power (P. E. Hughes; Braun). Hebrews says that Jesus has "the power of an indestructible life" (7:16, 24), but does not call this his "spirit."

(c) Jesus' spirit of determination. A few take "spirit" in the sense of Jesus' will to be obedient through suffering (cf. 1 Cor 4:21; Gal 6:1; Casalini; Bénétreau). Jesus' obedience is important (Heb 2:14–15; 5:7–8; 10:5–10), but there is little reason to think that listeners would have taken "spirit" in this sense in this context.

offered himself. "Offer" (*prospherein*) is used for prayers (5:7), and gifts and sacrifices (5:1, 3; 8:3, 4; 9:7, 9 etc.). The victim was first slain (*thyein* or *sphazein*; Lev 3:8), and then all or part of the victim was given to God, often by burning it (e.g., Lev 3:9–11). On the Day of Atonement the offering was completed when the victim's blood was brought into the inner chamber and sprinkled before the place of atonement. "Offering" involves the whole process (e.g., Lev 16:9; K. Weiss, *TDNT* 9.67). Christ's self-offering includes both his death and his exaltation.

without blemish. This expression connects the idea that sacrificial animals were to be physically without blemish (Deut 17:1; cf. Exod 29:1; Lev 1:3, 10; 22:18–25) with the idea that Christ was without the blemish of sin. See NOTE on Heb 4:15. The innocent and upright were said to be without blemish (Pss 15:2; 119:1; Isa 33:15; Col 1:22).

cleanse our conscience. On cleansing see pp. 119–20. On conscience see NOTE on 9:9.

from dead works. See NOTE on 6:1.

to serve a living God. Service of the living God includes brotherly love, hospitality, care for those in prison, as well as fidelity in marriage and avoiding avarice (12:28–13:9). On the "living God" see NOTE on 3:12. On "serve" see NOTE on "service" in 9:1.

COMMENT[285]

Christ's arrival as high priest in "the greater and more perfect tent" (9:11–14) marks a high point in the central part of Hebrews. The previous section sketched the first covenant's sanctuary and the priestly service that took place within it.

---

[285]On 9:1–14 see Andriessen, "Das grössere"; Camacho, "Altar"; Casalini, "Ebr 9, 11"; idem, *Dal simbolo*; idem, "I sacrifici"; Gordon, "Better Promises"; Grayston, "Salvation"; Hofius, "Das 'erste' "; idem, *Vorhang*, 60–75; Johnsson, "Cultus"; C. R. Koester, *Dwelling*, 6–75, 157–83; Laub, "Ein für allemal"; idem, *Bekenntnis*, 185–200; Loader, *Sohn* 161–202; Luck, "Himmlisches"; MacRae, "Heavenly Temple"; Michaud, "Parabolê"; Nissilä, *Hohepriestermotiv*, 169–96; Peterson, *Hebrews*, 132–44; Raurell, "Certain affinities"; Selby, "Meaning"; Stanley, "Hebrews 9:6–10"; Swetnam, "Greater"; idem, "Imagery"; idem, "Hebrews 9, 2"; Thompson, *Beginnings*, 103–15; Vanhoye, "Par la tente"; idem, *Old Testament*, 189–211; idem, "Esprit"; N. H. Young, "Gospel."

The forecourt, which is characterized by regulations that deal with the flesh but leave the conscience defiled, corresponds to the situation of those living at "the present time" (9:9). Given this situation, one might naturally ask, "How long will it continue?" And the answer is that it lasts "until a time of correction" (9:10). According to Hebrews, correction comes with Christ's arrival as high priest, for by his entry into the heavenly sanctuary he provides the definitive cleansing that can purify the conscience (9:11–14).[286]

Structurally, the description of the Tabernacle and Levitical ministry in the previous section was introduced by the Greek word *men* (9:1) and framed by references to the "regulations" of the Mosaic covenant (9:1, 10). The present section (9:11–14) is introduced by the contrastive *de* (9:11) and depicts the priestly work of Christ.[287] The passage itself consists of two lengthy sentences: **(a)** The first (9:11–12) deals with Christ's entry into the heavenly sanctuary. **(b)** The second (9:13–14) contrasts Christ's sacrifice with Levitical sacrifices.

a. Entering the Heavenly Tent (9:11–12)

Rhetorically, the declaration that Christ "arrived as high priest" (9:11) recalls that Christ did not seize priestly prerogatives, but was called by God (5:4–5) and fitted for his vocation by suffering and exaltation (4:15; 5:8). To say now that Christ "arrived" (9:11) means that Christ has arrived at his heavenly destination (7:26; 8:2), where he alone serves as a "priest forever" by virtue of his indestructible life (7:20–28). This changes the first covenant's statutes pertaining to priesthood (7:12, 18) and alters the situation of the listeners.

Christ's priesthood is known by its effects, for by it "good things" have come (9:11), according to Hebrews. This statement depends, not on sight, but on a faith that has been "trained to discern both good and evil" (NOTE on 5:14). Listeners could have affirmed that "good things" (*agatha*) occurred through the "good" (*kalos*) word of God (6:5), by which they received the gifts of the Spirit (2:3–4; 6:4–5). Yet after coming to faith, they suffered affliction, reproach, loss of possessions, and imprisonment (10:32–34; 13:3, 13), which could scarcely be considered "good things." Good things came to Christ after he suffered and was exalted to glory (1:3–4; 2:17–18; 4:14–16; 5:8–10), and Christ's exaltation, in turn, gives assurance that the faithful who now struggle will also receive the good things that God has promised them (1:14; 6:12).

The redemption that Christ brings (9:12) can best be understood as cleansing from defilement rather than as payment of a ransom.[288] To come before God

[286]Some consider 9:11–14 to be the high point of Hebrews (Grässer, *Hebräer*, 2.142; H.-F. Weiss, *Brief*, 462), yet 9:11–14 should be read as one major point rather than as the chief point.

[287]The ten verses that separate the *men* from the *de* include another *men . . . de* construction (9:6–7), but similar phenomena occur in other writers (Epictetus, *Disc.* 1.9.12–16; Philo, *Creation* 10).

[288]The word for "redemption" (*lytrōsis*) is related to the term for "ransom" (*lytron*), which some took to mean that Christ's death obtained human deliverance by a payment. Origen and Gregory of Nazianzus proposed that payment was made to the devil (see Pelikan, *Christian*, 1.148), but Hebrews says that Christ conquered the devil, not that he paid him (2:14). Against this idea, Anselm argued

with clean flesh but a defiled conscience was considered an affront to God's holiness, and people were to remain distant from God until the defilement was removed. Moreover, Hebrews also assumes that people are oppressed by forces beyond their control and need redemption from those things that hold them captive. Hebrews depicts "the present time" as one in which "regulations of the flesh" have been "imposed," even though these regulations cannot cleanse the conscience (9:9–10). The problem is not simply a failure to keep God's commands, because even those who keep the "regulations of the flesh" remain defiled in conscience, for the regulations are of only limited effectiveness (see pp. 114–15). Hebrews argues that Christ's sacrifice releases them from this situation by purifying the conscience and by opening the way to God's presence.

Although "redemption" means deliverance, some early Christians lost freedom through imprisonment (10:32–34; 13:3). Paradoxically, Christ taints listeners in the eyes of society, while cleansing them in the eyes of God, and faith in Christ can bring a loss of freedom in a social sense, while creating new freedom in relation to God (6:19–20; 10:19–20). By proclaiming that redemption has come with respect to God, the author seeks to awaken courage so that listeners do not shrink back in the face of opposition from other people (10:39; 13:14), but persevere in faith (6:12) until they enter God's promised rest (4:9–11; 12:22–24).

Redemption is obtained through "the greater and more perfect tent" in heaven (9:11), which is the goal of the listeners' pilgrimage of faith (10:19–20). The comparative adjectives "great*er*" and "*more* perfect" recognize that the Mosaic sanctuary had a degree of greatness and perfection, while insisting that the heavenly sanctuary is superior. Significantly, the author makes no mention of the second Temple—which had its critics[289]—but declares that Christ's sanctuary is greater than even the Mosaic Tabernacle, the memory of which was widely revered.[290] Hebrews' argument draws on two common ideas. One is that what God makes is superior to what human beings make. No one would dispute that the Tabernacle had been made by hand (9:11), since the Scriptures said that God commanded Moses to make it (8:5; Exod 25:40) and described its construction (Exod 35–40), yet listeners would also agree that the heavenly tent that God set up must be greater than any tent that people make (cf. NOTE on Heb 8:2). A second assumption is that heaven is superior to earth. Since the Tabernacle was "earthly" (9:1), it was therefore subject to decay (1:10–12). Only what is transcendent can be the basis of abiding faith.

---

that Christ satisfied the demands of God (see Gunton, *Actuality*, 87–93; Grässer, *Hebräer*, 2.154). Yet Hebrews defines "redemption" as cleansing (Heb 9:13–14) rather than as payment.

[289]For praise of the second Temple see Mark 13:1; *m. 'Abot* 1:2; *b. B. Bat.* 4a. Criticism commonly grew out of objections to corrupt practices (1QpHab XII, 8–9; *T. Mos.* 4:8; 5:4; 6:1; *Apoc. Ab.* 25:1–6). According to Acts 7:44–50, Stephen rejected the Jerusalem Temple as a project of merely human design, in contrast to the Tabernacle that God had prescribed (see C. R. Koester, *Dwelling*, 76–89). Some anticipate the building of a temple in the end times (*Jub.* 1:17, 27, 29; *1 Enoch* 90:29–36; 11QT[a] XIX, 8–10; *Sib. Or.* 3.703, 773; *m. Pes.* 10:6).

[290]Favorably comparing someone to something of high repute was called "amplification" (Aristotle, *Rhetoric* 1.9.39). Cf. the favorable comparison with Moses (§9 COMMENT) and Aaron (§12 COMMENT *c*). On respect for the Tabernacle see C. R. Koester, *Dwelling*, 23–75.

Hebrews' view of the sanctuary can be clarified by comparison with other sources. The prophets criticized those who thought that God was confined in the Temple (Isa 66:1) or that the Temple protected them from judgment (Jer 7:1–20). Some Jewish writers thought that the Temple had been polluted by corrupt practices, but few rejected the Temple in principle.[291] Similarly, the gospels say that Jesus denounced some Temple practices, but called the Temple his Father's house.[292] Some Greek and Latin authors criticized the expense associated with temples, and others argued that material shrines were not suitable for deities.[293] Hebrews does not dismiss the Tabernacle for its material quality, since God himself commanded Moses to build it (8:5), and Hebrews does not fault the earthly sanctuary by charging that its practices were corrupt, but by saying it was of only limited effectiveness. The earthly tent is a visible pointer to a heavenly reality (10:1), but it is not the place where complete atonement is made.

Hebrews' contrast between the offering of Christ's blood and "the blood of goats and calves" is also distinctive (9:12). Jewish and Greco-Roman authors insisted that sacrifices could not replace moral conduct, and some considered moral conduct superior to animal sacrifices (§25 COMMENT *a–b*). Hebrews can speak of prayer and service to others as "sacrifices" (13:15–16; cf. 12:28–13:9), yet these actions do not bring atonement. The author's perspective is shaped by the conviction that God dealt decisively with sin through the death of Christ (9:12).[294] If Christ's death is the way in which God deals with sin, then the author concludes that other means—including Levitical sacrifices—must be inadequate. The blood of goats and calves provides no true redemption, but foreshadows the redemption that has occurred through Christ's death and exaltation (see pp. 114–15 on the Law).

b. Cleansing the Conscience (9:13–14)

The "blood" of goats, bulls, and Christ is a central element in 9:13–14.[295] Blood functions on the boundary between the clean and unclean, the holy and pro-

[291]The fundamental objection by the Dead Sea sect seems to have been that priests had defiled the Temple (1QpHab XII, 8–9; cf. *T. Mos.* 6:1). The sect may have continued sending offerings to the Temple (Josephus, *Ant.* 18.19), while considering their own community to be a temple (4QFlor I 1–7) and hoping for a restored temple in the future (11QT[a] XXIX, 8–10). The rejection of temple worship in *Sib. Or.* 4.8, 27 is primarily aimed at pagan shrines, but it could include rejection of the Jerusalem Temple.

[292]Matt 21:13; Mark 11:17; Luke 2:49; 19:46; John 2:16.

[293]On expense see Plato, *Laws* 12 (955E). On material shrines see Plutarch, *Mor.* 1034B; Diogenes Laertius, *Lives* 7.33.

[294]Aquinas speculated that Christ's blood was reunited with his resurrected body (*Summa Theologica* IIIa, 54, 3). Bengel (*Epistle*, 476) thought that Christ's body remained bloodless after his death, but Delitzsch argued that Christ presented himself before God in a body that bore the blood that he had shed (*Commentary*, 2.84–89). On these and other theories see P. E. Hughes, *Commentary*, 329–54.

[295]On the blood of Christ in Christian piety see J. H. Rohling, "Precious Blood" III, *NCE* 11.707–8; H. Schneider, "Blut" IV/2 *TRE* 6.740–42.

fane. When lost through violent death or menstruation, blood defiles,[296] yet when offered through sacrifice, blood cleanses: "It is the blood that makes atonement" (Lev 17:11). To all appearances blood stains whatever it touches, yet Hebrews understands that blood can be used to bring cleansing, sanctification, and forgiveness (9:13–14, 22), to inaugurate covenants (9:20; 10:29), and to provide access to God (9:7, 12, 25). Hebrews agrees that there is no forgiveness without blood (9:22), but will argue that animal blood cannot remove sins (10:4) or purify the conscience (9:9, 13–14). The author couples the "blood of goats and bulls," which was offered on the Day of Atonement, with "the sprinkled ashes of a heifer," which were not used on the Day of Atonement, but for purification from defilement through contact with a corpse (NOTE on 9:13). By listing various rituals, the author suggests that a greater number of rites does not mean greater effectiveness, because all are "regulations of the flesh" (9:9–10). Something of a different order is needed.

The superior quality of Christ's sacrifice has several aspects. First, the source of the sacrifice is Christ's blood. The assumption that animal blood was of limited effectiveness is the basis for an a fortiori argument: How "much more will the blood of Christ" bring cleansing (9:14). The author did not say "how much more will the blood of a human being" or "the blood of a martyr" redeem you (4 Macc 6:29; 17:22), but emphasizes that the blood of Christ, the Son of God, is superior to any other blood, because Christ himself is superior to others.

Second, the manner of sacrifice is "through the eternal Spirit" (9:14). This expression fuses images of sacrifice with elements from the story of Jesus' death and exaltation. Sacrifices usually were made through fire. The Day of Atonement sacrifice was not a burnt offering, but the heifer (9:13) and the other "gifts and sacrifices" mentioned in Hebrews (5:1; 8:4) were offered "through perpetual fire" that burned upon the altar (1 Esdr 6:23 [24]; cf. Lev 6:9 [6:5–6 LXX]). Christ's self-sacrifice included both his death and exaltation to eternal life in God's presence. According to Christian tradition, God raised Jesus from the dead by the power of the Spirit (1 Pet 3:18; Rom 1:4; 8:11), which was associated with fire (Matt 3:11; Luke 3:16; Acts 2:3; Rev 4:5). Where Levitical sacrifices used animal blood, Christ's offering involved his own blood; where Levitical sacrifices were completed "through perpetual fire," Christ' sacrifice was accomplished "through the eternal Spirit";[297] and where the victims offered under the old covenant were to be without blemish in a physical sense, Christ was without blemish due to his sinlessness (Heb 4:15).

Third, the effect of Christ's sacrifice is to "cleanse our conscience from dead works" (9:14). Christ's blood does not cleanse by physical contact, but through proclamation. Dead works proceed from sin, and sin is a matter of one's stance toward God—unfaith rather than faith (3:12–13; 6:1; 10:38; 11:24–25; 12:4). The conscience is cleansed when faith is evoked, and faith is evoked through the

---

[296]For example, Lev 15:19, 25; Num 35:33; Ps 106:38; Isa 59:3. On the significance of blood see Johnsson, *Defilement*, 144–61, 222–50; Dunnill, *Covenant*, 91–111, 231–34.

[297]Chrysostom; Theophylact; Erasmus; H.-F. Weiss; Vanhoye, "Esprit"; Ellingworth.

proclamation of Christ's death, for Christ's blood *speaks* of God's grace and mercy (12:24). Christ's blood was shed years before Hebrews was written, yet the author can affirm that the conscience of a particular individual is cleansed when Christ's self-sacrifice is announced and received in faith through the agency of the Spirit (2:1–4; 6:4–5; 10:29). Cleansing the conscience does not mean that people become sinless, for the evil, faithless heart continues to threaten them (3:12). Nevertheless, the redemption that Christ provides is a source of salvation that is eternally valid (5:9).

Finally, the consequences of animal sacrifices differ from those of Christ's sacrifice. In 9:13–14 animal sacrifices culminate with purification, whereas Christ's sacrifice leads to worshipers serving the living God:

(a) Blood of bulls and goats and ashes of a heifer	(a) Christ's own blood offered through the Spirit
(b) Sanctify (*hagiazei*) those defiled	(b) Cleanses (*katharei*) our conscience
(c) To (*pros*) purify the flesh	(c) To (*eis*) serve a living God

Under the old covenant, the regulations for "service" (9:1) mandated that priests "conduct their service" (9:6) by making sacrifices. Christ's sacrifice is understood to be a definitive offering for sin, yet it marks not the ending, but the beginning of renewed service to God on the part of the worshipers. Those who are aware of wrongdoing will not be bold to praise God or to confess his name (13:15). The boldness needed to approach God comes from the clear conscience (NOTE on 3:6) that Christ provides. Service to God also includes serving other people by showing hospitality, and ministering to prisoners and the afflicted (6:10; 12:28–13:9). Levitical sacrifices purified those who were defiled so that they could reenter the community. Christ's sacrifice leads to service that builds up the community when it fosters committed service to the afflicted.

24. MEDIATOR OF THE NEW COVENANT (9:15–28)

9 [15]And for this reason he is mediator of a new covenant, so that after a death
took place to bring redemption from transgressions incurred on the basis of the
first covenant, those who are called might receive the promised eternal inheritance. [16]For where there is a testament, it is necessary that the death of the testator be presented. [17]For a testament becomes valid upon death, since it has no
force as long as the testator lives.

[18]Accordingly, not even the first [covenant] was dedicated without blood.
[19]For after every commandment had, in accordance with the Law, been spoken
by Moses to all the people and after he had taken calves' blood with water and
scarlet wool and hyssop, he sprinkled the book itself and all the people, [20]saying,
This is the blood of the covenant that God commanded you. [21]And the tent and
all the utensils for the service he sprinkled with blood in a similar way. [22]Indeed,
according to the Law almost everything is cleansed with blood, and without an

outpouring of blood forgiveness does not occur. 23Therefore, it is necessary that the representations of the heavenly things be cleansed by these things, but the heavenly things themselves with sacrifices superior to these.

24For Christ did not enter a sanctuary made with hands, an antitype of the true one, but into heaven itself, now to appear before the face of God on our behalf. 25And he did not do this in order to offer himself many times, as the high priest enters the sanctuary year after year with the blood of another; 26in that case he would have had to suffer many times from the foundation of the world. But now he has appeared, once, at the consummation of the ages, for the abolition of sin by his sacrifice. 27And just as it is ordained for human beings to die once, and afterward comes the judgment, 28so also Christ, having been offered once to bear the sins of many, will appear a second time, not to deal with sin, but for the salvation of those who eagerly wait for him.

NOTES

9:15. *And for this reason he is mediator.* See NOTE on 8:6.

of a new covenant. The term *diathēkē* could mean "covenant" and "testament." See NOTE on 7:22. The "new covenant" was promised in Jer 31:31–34 (Heb 8:8–12). See pp. 112–14.

to bring redemption. The term *apolytrōsis* is a compound form of the word *lytrōsis* used in 9:12. The term was often used for release from slavery or imprisonment (11:35; cf. *Ep. Arist.* 12, 33; Josephus, *Ant.* 12.27), but here it is parallel to "forgiveness" (Heb 9:22; cf. Col 1:14; Eph 1:7; Rom 3:24–25; 1 Cor 1:30). See NOTES on 9:12 and 9:22.

from transgressions incurred on the basis of the first covenant. The preposition *epi* probably identifies the first covenant as "the basis" upon which the transgressions took place (BDF §235.2). Measuring sin according to Mosaic Law does not mean that Hebrews was written solely for Jewish Christians, since similar ideas appear in texts that were written for congregations that included Gentile Christians (e.g., Rom 5:13, 20; 7:7–12). On "first covenant" see NOTE on 8:7.

those who are called might receive the promised eternal inheritance. Inheritance had especially to do with the place that God promised to Abraham (11:8), which Hebrews identifies with the heavenly city that is to come (11:13–16; 13:14). Thus the inheritance expected by the listeners would include not only mercy (Hegermann) but also those future realities that they have not received. "Promise" is in the accusative case, but it modifies "eternal inheritance," which is in the genitive case. For a similar transposition of cases see "first confidence" in 3:14.

9:16. *For where there is a testament.* Here *diathēkē* means "will" or "testament" (NOTE on 7:22). The legal sense is anticipated by the mention of "inheritance" (9:15), which was commonly governed by a testament. Some translate the word as "covenant" (Kilpatrick, "Διαθήκη"; J. J. Hughes, "Hebrews ix.15ff"). They argue that a testament did not become valid upon death, but when it was drafted, witnessed, and notarized, and that an inheritance could be distributed before a person's death. Yet this is not persuasive. A "gift" (*donatio*) could be given while someone was still alive, but a "testament" (*diathēkē*) commonly had to do with distributions that were made after the testator's death (NOTES on 9:17; Taubenschlag, *Law*, 190–200, 204–5; cf. Gal 3:15–17; Philo, *Names* 51–52).

it is necessary that the death of the testator. Jesus the "mediator" of the new covenant (7:22; 9:15) is now the testator who makes a testament. Although God promised the new covenant (8:10), Jesus is the testator who dies. On legal usage see MM, 155; J. Behm, *TDNT* 2.105.

be presented. Legally people had to present evidence that the testator had died for a will to take effect. For example, a letter addressed to the local scribe says, "My father . . . died at the said village in the month of Hathur of the present fifteenth year of the Emperor. . . . I therefore present the notice in order that his name may be enrolled in the list of the dead" (Winter, *Life*, 132; cf. Hunt and Edgar, *Select Papyri, II*, #310). Those who think that Heb 9:16–17 refers to a covenant argue that the verb refers to presenting sacrifices (cf. 9:18–20), which symbolize the death of the testator (J. J. Hughes, "Hebrews ix.15ff," 40–46; Lane). Yet there is little evidence that sacrifices represented the death of the one making the covenant. Sacrificial connotations are at most secondary.

9:17. *For a testament becomes valid upon death.* Heirs commonly have no valid way to claim inheritance until the testator dies. In this sense the testament "becomes valid" upon death. A testament had to be filed properly with a notary in the presence of witnesses while the testator was alive for it to be valid at the time of death (Taubenschlag, *Law*, 190–200). The unusual statement that a testament "becomes valid" upon death arises from the coupling of legal practice with biblical covenant traditions (see COMMENT *a*). The expression "upon death" is literally plural, "upon deaths" (*epi nekrois*), probably suggesting general practice rather than that a covenant was made "upon sacrifices" (Ps 50:5; J. J. Hughes, "Hebrews ix.15ff," 43–46; Lane).

since it has no force as long as the testator lives. Provisions of a testament commonly took effect upon the testator's death: "So long as I survive I am to have power over my own property. . . . But if I die with this will unaltered I leave. . . ." (*P. Oxy.* ##490.3–4; 491.3–4; 492.4–5; 494.4–5). On *ischyein* as legal "force" see MM, 308.

9:18. *Accordingly, not even the first* [*covenant*] *was dedicated.* The first covenant is the Mosaic covenant (NOTE on 8:7). "Dedicate" (*enkainizein*; cf. 10:20) is not the word the LXX uses for making covenants, but for putting the altar (Num 7:10, 88) and Temple (1 Kgs 8:63; 2 Chron 7:5) into service (cf. 1 Macc 4:36, 54, 57; 5:1). The author might have used this verb for the covenant because the covenant is the basis for the sanctuary (cf. NOTE on Heb 10:20).

9:19. *For after every commandment had, in accordance with the Law, been spoken by Moses to all the people.* This refers to the ceremony that formalized Israel's promise to obey God's commands (Exod 24:3, 7; *Mek.*, "Baḥodesh" 3.25 [Lauterbach ed., 2.211]). Hebrews may assume that the ceremony made atonement (*Tg. Onq.* and *Tg. Ps.-J.* of Exod 24:8) or purification (Philo, *QE* 2.33; *Heir* 185).

and after he had taken calves' blood. This follows the shortest reading, which refers only to the blood "of calves" (P^{46} $\aleph^{2}$ K L Ψ etc.). Some MSS add "and of goats" either with the article ($\aleph^{*}$ A C etc.) or without it (Maj) after the word "calves," and others mention the goats before the calves as in 9:12 (D 365). Scholars who include the extra words suggest that they were omitted accidentally, or perhaps deliberately, to harmonize with Exod 24:5 (*TCGNT*, 668; NRSV; NJB). Yet deliberate omission seems unlikely since Heb 9:19 differs at many other points from Exod 24:3–8 (see the next NOTE), and none of the other differences were altered to make Hebrews conform to the OT. It is more likely that the shorter reading was later expanded to include goats because of their mention in 9:12–13 (Zuntz, *Text*, 54–55; Attridge; Lane; NIV; REB).

with water and scarlet wool and hyssop. These details are not in the account of the covenant ceremony in Exod 24:3–8. The author seems to conflate details from various rituals. Hyssop was a plant that was used to daub blood on the doorposts at Passover (Exod 12:22) and as a flail for purification (Ps 51:7). Hyssop, scarlet material, and water were used in the cleansing of lepers (Lev 14:4–6, 49–52) and in the rite of the red heifer that purified those defiled by contact with a corpse (Num 19:1–10, 17–18; cf. Heb 9:13). Differences between Heb 9:19–20 and Exod 24:3–8 were once understood to reflect spiritual meanings (see pp. 28–29) and later led to questioning the tradition that Paul wrote Hebrews (see p. 35).

he sprinkled the book itself and all the people. Exodus and Hebrews agree that blood was spattered upon the people, but where Exod 24:6 says that blood was poured on the *altar*, Hebrews says that Moses spattered blood upon the *book*. For Hebrews, the Law and sacrifices are inseparable. "The book" presumably included the Ten Commandments (Exod 20:1–17) and the covenant code (Exod 21:1–23:33). In Heb 10:7 "the book" is probably the Law.

9:20. *saying, This is the blood of the covenant that God commanded you.* This is a quotation from Exod 24:8 that differs in minor respects from the LXX. Some discern here an echo of Jesus' words at the Last Supper: "This is my blood of the covenant," which according to Matt 26:28 was "for the forgiveness of sins." The words of Jesus and the quotation in Hebrews begin with "this" (*touto*) instead of "behold" (*idou*) as in the LXX, and both mention forgiveness (Heb 9:12, 14, 22). See Vanhoye, *Old Testament*, 202; Ellingworth; Hegermann; P. E. Hughes. Yet an echo of Jesus' words is unlikely, since Hebrews makes no mention of the Lord's Supper (see pp. 127–29) and refers only to sprinkling blood, not to consuming it as in the Lord's Supper. Moreover, Hebrews does not refer to "the Lord"—which could refer to Jesus as well as to God—but speaks of what "God" commanded, making an allusion to Christ's words less likely (Braun; Grässer; H.-F. Weiss; cf. Lane).

9:21. *And the tent and all the utensils for the service.* In 9:1–5 the author described the main furnishings, which included the table and bread, the lampstand, the incense altar, and the ark of the covenant. The utensils included the trays, snuffers, pots, shovels, basins, plates, bowls, and flagons needed to maintain the lamps and to make offerings (Exod 25:39; 27:3; 37:16).

he sprinkled with blood in a similar way. The Tabernacle (Exod 35–40) had not been built at the time the first covenant was inaugurated (Exod 24). According to Exod 40:9–10 the Tabernacle and its furnishings were consecrated with oil. For the ordination of Aaron, the altar was purified with blood (Lev 8:15), and on the Day of Atonement the high priest purified the sanctuary with blood (16:15–19). Hebrews may rely on the tradition that the Tabernacle was cleansed with blood at the time of its dedication (Josephus, *Ant.* 3.206).

9:22. *Indeed, according to the Law almost everything is cleansed with blood.* In addition to sin offerings, blood was used for cleansing from leprosy (Lev 14:6, 14) and for sanctifying priests (Exod 29:20–21). In saying that "almost" everything was cleansed with blood, Hebrews recognizes that sometimes other agents were used. Water (Lev 15:1–33; 16:26, 28; 22:6) and fire purified (Num 31:21–24; Isa 6:6), and atonement was sometimes made using flour (Lev 5:11), incense (Num 16:46), or gold (Num 31:50). The idea that blood had cleansing power was shared by Greeks and Romans (Euripides, *Iphegeneia at Tauris* 1223–24; Aeschylus, *Eumenides* 280–83; cf. Plutarch, *Mor.* 290D). Despite criticisms (§25 COMMENT *a–b*), blood sacrifice was common. See the additional NOTES below.

and without an outpouring of blood. Haimatekchysia is a compound word based on *haima* ("blood") and *ekchynnein* ("pour out"), and it may have been coined by the author (p. 96). It could refer to the slaughter of a sacrificial victim, since bloodshed frequently connoted violence and death (cf. Sir 27:15; 1 Kgs 18:28; J. Behm, *TDNT* 1.176–77; N. H. Young, "Αἱματεκχυσία"; F. F. Bruce; Grässer). It seems likely, however, that the word includes the priestly manipulation of blood, since the LXX spoke of blood being poured out at the altar (e.g., Exod 29:12; Lev 4:7, 18, 25; cf. Heb 11:28) and since bloodshed in itself did not bring forgiveness. This was accomplished when blood was brought to the altar (9:7; Thornton, "Meaning"; Johnsson, "Cultus"; Braun; H.-F. Weiss).

forgiveness does not occur. The term *aphesis* ("forgiveness") has a complex significance:

(**a**) Release. The word was often used for the release from debts, slavery, and imprisonment (Lev 25:10–13, 28–33, 40–41; Deut 15:1; Luke 4:18; Josephus, *Ant.* 12.40; 17.233; *J.W.* 1.481). Some NT texts compare sins to a debt so that forgiveness means that the creditor—in this case God—releases the debtor from the obligation to pay (Matt 18:21–35; Luke 7:41–47). In texts where sin is understood as a breach of law that brings a penalty, forgiveness means canceling the charges (Col 2:13–14; cf. Acts 13:38; Eph 1:7; Col 1:14). In the LXX the noun *aphesis* was not commonly associated with sacrifice—although it was used for the "release" of the goat bearing Israel's sins on the Day of Atonement (Lev 16:26)—but the verbal form *aphienai* had some sacral connotations: "The priest shall make atonement for them, and they shall be forgiven" (Lev 4:20; 19:22; cf. Philo, *Moses* 2.147; *Special Laws* 1.190, 215, 237).

(**b**) Purgation or cleansing. "Cleanse" in 9:22a is almost synonymous with "forgiveness" in 9:22b. Sin brings defilement, and forgiveness includes release from this contamination. In 10:18 *aphesis* is associated with the sacrifice that removes sin (10:4; cf. 1 John 1:9). The cleansing power of blood is evident in its use to purify objects like the tent and its furnishings, which do not sin, but can be defiled. See pp. 119–21; *TLNT* 1.238–44; Johnsson, "Cultus."

To say that "without blood forgiveness does not occur" summarizes much of the OT practice. Blood was used in the atonement ritual (Lev 16:14–19) and sin offerings (Lev 4:5–7, 16–18, 25, 30, 34), although God could forgive without sacrifices (e.g., Exod 32:32). According to Lev 17:11, God said, "The life of the flesh is in the blood; and I have given it to you for making atonement for your lives on the altar; for, as life, it is the blood that makes atonement." Atonement comes through blood (*b. Menaḥ.* 93b; *b. Zebaḥ.* 6a; Philo, *Special Laws* 3.150).

9:23. *Therefore, it is necessary that the representations.* On "representation" see NOTE on 8:5.

of the heavenly things be cleansed. The significance of the "heavenly things" has been approached along two main lines, of which the first is preferable:

(**a**) Heaven itself. The Tabernacle was holy, yet it needed purification. Although people were not understood to sin within the Tabernacle, the sanctuary was threatened by defilement from people's sins. In the same way, one need not envision heavenly beings committing sins to think that purification of heaven would be appropriate. Since sin affects all creation, Christ's work extends to all creation (Lane; Bénétreau, *L'Épître,* 2.92; Dunnill, *Covenant,* 232). Some refer to Satan being expelled from heaven (Luke 10:18; John 12:31; Rev 12:7–9) and to evil beings inhabiting the air (Eph 6:12; Col 1:20), so that even "the heavens are not clean in his sight" (Job 15:15; *1 Clem.* 39:5; Ign. *Smyrn.* 6:1; Grässer). This is not a primary thought in Hebrews, however.

(**b**) Human beings. Many have taken the "heavenly things" to refer to the church (Chrysostom; F. F. Bruce; Vanhoye, *Old Testament,* 205). Using the device of *hypallagē,* which occurs when speakers transfer qualities from one thing to another, the author of Hebrews might attribute human uncleanness to heaven. The "heavenly things are pure in themselves, but we needed to be purified in order that we might enjoy them" (Bengel, *Epistle,* 426). Another variation is that heaven represents the conscience (Attridge, *Epistle,* 262). Although this suits the references to conscience in 9:9, 14, the spatial quality of the imagery favors interpreting the text as heaven itself.

9:24. *For Christ did not enter a sanctuary made with hands.* The "true" heavenly sanctuary was established by God himself, so that a sanctuary made by human hands would be of a lesser order (8:2). "Made with hands" has pejorative connotations (NOTE on "not made by hand" in 9:11).

an antitype of the true one. The Tabernacle was the earthly "antitype" of the heavenly "type" (NOTE on 8:5). The term "antitype" could have negative connotations, as in something inimical or resistant (Philo, *Heir* 181), or positive connotations, as in salvation through baptism serving as the antitype of Noah's salvation through the flood (1 Pet 3:21). God commanded Moses to make the earthly tent (Heb 8:5), but the contrasts between heaven and earth, and the pejorative "made with hands" imply that it was inferior to its heavenly type (see pp. 97–100).

but into heaven itself. See NOTE on "the greater and more perfect tent" in 9:11.

now to appear before the face of God on our behalf. Jesus appears before God to intercede "on our behalf" (cf. 2:18; 4:15; 7:25). The Hebrew expression "appear before the face of God" referred to people coming to the sanctuary (Exod 23:15, 17; 34:23; Deut 16:16). In the LXX seeking God's face meant seeking help in prayer (Ps 27:8 [26:8 LXX]) and seeing God's face meant receiving favor from God (Ps 17:15 [16:15]; 42:3 [41:3]). This sense is appropriate here.

9:25. *And he did not do this in order to offer himself many times.* This text stresses the differences between multiplicity and singularity, and between animal blood and Christ's own blood.

as the high priest enters the sanctuary year after year with the blood of another. See NOTES on 9:7.

9:26. *in that case he would have had to suffer many times.* Christ's crucifixion was a singular act that breaks the parallel between Christ's death and the sacrifices of the Levitical cult. Repetition is suitable for animal sacrifices, but unthinkable for Jesus' self-sacrifice.

from the foundation of the world. The author assumes that the Son of God existed from the foundation of the world (1:2) when God's works were completed (4:3). He also assumes that sin has been in the world virtually since its founding, so that human beings have needed atonement since primeval times (cf. Rom 5:12).

But now he has appeared. This expression (*nyni de*) makes a logical contrast with the previous argument and a temporal contrast between previous periods and "the consummation of the ages." "Appeared" almost certainly refers to Christ's incarnation (cf. 1 Tim 3:16; 1 Pet 1:20; Grässer) rather than his second coming (9:28) or appearing before God in heaven (9:24; H.-F. Weiss).

once. On singularity see NOTE on 6:4.

at the consummation of the ages. The verbal echoes between *synteleia* ("consummation") and the verbs *syntelein* (8:8) and *entelein* (9:20) that were associated with the new covenant, as well as the other words for "completion" (*tel-*) in Hebrews suggest that it means that the ages have reached their goal as well as their end (cf. Matt 13:39–40, 49; 24:3; 28:20; Dan 9:27; 12:13) in a time of salvation (*T. Mos.* 12:4; *4 Ezra* 6:25; Gal 4:4: Heb 1:2).

for the abolition of sin. "Abolition" meant abrogation of a law in 7:18 (cf. *TLNT* 1.39), but here it pertains to sin. "Sin" in the singular is part of the human condition. The author recognized that sin remains a force (12:1), but its binding claim has been abolished.

by his sacrifice. See §23 COMMENT *b* and §24 COMMENT *b*.

9:27. *it is ordained for human beings to die once.* This idea was common: "Death is ordained for all mortals" (*Epigr. Graec.* 416.6; cf. 4 Macc 8:11). "Men die once" (Homer, *Odyssey* 12.22), and there is "no return from our death" (Wis 2:5). Some took comfort in the idea that one must only endure death once rather than many times (Sophocles, frgs. 67.2; Philo, *Rewards* 72; Lucian, *Dialogues of the Dead* 16.3). In Hebrews, however, death is not an escape, for it is followed by judgment.

and afterward comes the judgment. Listeners had already received instruction about the final judgment (6:2). Many sources speak of judgment at the end of time (Dan 12:2; *4 Ezra* 7:69; 14:35; *1 Enoch* 1:7; Matt 25:31–46; John 5:28–29; 1 Pet 4:5; Rev 20:12–13; cf. 2 Cor 5:10; Rom 2:5–11; Schürer, *History*, 2.539–47). Others anticipate judgment immediately after death (Luke 16:22–23; Wis 3:1–4). Traces of both views can be found in Hebrews although the emphasis falls on the end of time (cf. 4 Ezra 14:34–35) (NOTES on 6:2). Some Greeks denied that there were any punishments after death (Lucretius, *Nature of Things* 3.977–78), but others maintained that the soul would be judged (Aeschylus, *Suppliant Women* 230–31; Plato, *Republic* 10.614B–621D; Plutarch, *Mor.* 121C, 942F). Hebrews does not speculate about how soon judgment followed death, but assumes that listeners would agree that it would come.

9:28. *Christ, having been offered once to bear the sins of many.* Rather than making sacrifices "many times" Christ made one sacrifice "for many" (cf. Isa 53:12; Mark 10:45; 14:24). Some think that "for many" means "for all," since Jesus tasted death "for everyone" (Heb 2:9). Others take it to mean "for many (but not all)," since the author does not assume that everyone will be saved (10:26–27) due to their unbelief (Chrysostom; Calvin).

will appear a second time. The text combines two types of associations: **(a)** Apocalyptic. Hope for Christ's return was important in early Christian preaching (1 Thess 1:10; 1 Cor 15:23; Phil 3:20). Some texts vividly depict his return on the clouds of heaven (Matt 24:30; 26:64 par.; Rev 1:7; cf. 1 Thess 4:15–16), but others refer more simply to his future revelation or coming (1 Cor 1:7; 2 Thess 2:1; 1 Tim 6:14; 1 Pet 1:7; John 14:3; 1 John 2:28; 3:2). **(b)** Priestly. On the Day of Atonement, people gathered around the high priest as he came out of the inner sanctuary (Lev 16:18; Sir 50:5). Christ's second coming is depicted in similar terms.

not to deal with sin. The expression (literally "apart from sin"; cf. 4:15; 7:26) is a reminder that it was at his first coming that Christ dealt with sin. To say that Christ would deal with sin again would mean that his singular sacrifice was inadequate, which would counter the author's point.

but for the salvation. See NOTE on 2:3.

of those who eagerly wait for him. Eager expectation characterizes Christian life in many NT sources (Rom 8:19, 23, 25; 1 Cor 1:7; Gal 5:5; Phil 3:20).

COMMENT[298]

With broad strokes the author has led his listeners through the ancient Tabernacle (9:1–5), showing them the activity of Levitical priests (9:6–10) and the

---

[298]On 9:11–28 see Attridge, "Uses"; Berényi, "La portée"; Brooks, "Perpetuity"; Campbell, "Covenant"; Courthial, "La portée"; Dunnill, *Covenant*, 227–38; Franco Martínez, *Jesucristo*, 317–84; Fritsch, "TO ANTITYΠΟΝ"; J. J. Hughes, "Hebrews ix.15ff"; Kilpatrick, "Διαθήκη"; C. R. Koester, *Dwelling*, 6–75, 162–83; Laub, *Bekenntnis*, 206–21; idem, "Ein für allemal"; MacLeod, "Cleansing"; Nissilä, *Hohepriestermotiv*, 197–217; Pretorius, "ΔΙΑΘΗΚΗ"; Schlosser, "La médiation"; Schröger, *Verfasser*, 168–72; Selb, "Διαθήκη"; Selby, "Meaning"; Swetnam, "Suggested Interpretation"; idem, "Sacrifice"; Vanhoye, *Old Testament*, 200–11; Wiid, "Testamental." On the new covenant see pp. 112–14.

movement of Christ the high priest into the celestial sanctuary (9:11–14). Having taken his audience from earth to heaven, the author abruptly changes course and leads them into the mundane realm of law and inheritance to show the implications of Christ's death and exaltation (9:15–17). Then in almost kaleidoscopic fashion, he shifts the scene again, taking listeners to the foot of Mount Sinai, where Moses spatters the people with blood and announces the establishment of God's covenant (9:18–23).[299] Finally, he turns their gaze to the heavenly sanctuary, where Christ—now hidden from their sight—appears before God on their behalf, while they await his return for their full and final salvation (9:24–28).

Structurally, this section weaves together the motifs of atonement, old covenant, and new covenant (§16 COMMENT): **(a)** The first part (9:15–17) identifies Christ's atoning sacrifice with the establishment of the new covenant, through which forgiveness of sins is offered, according to 8:8–12. The new covenant, in turn, is identified as the testament through which inheritance will be given to God's people. **(b)** The second part (9:18–23) compares the sacrifice by which Christ inaugurated the new covenant to the sacrifice and cleansing rites by which the Mosaic covenant was put into effect. **(c)** The third part (9:24–28) relates Christ's sacrifice to his continued intercession in the heavenly sanctuary and to his expected return.

a. Covenant as Testament (9:15–17)

Identifying Jesus as "mediator of a new covenant" (9:15a) recalls the quotation of God's promise to make a new covenant under which he would forgive sins (8:8–12; Jer 31:31–34). Earlier, the author offered little comment on the quotation, but described Jesus' death and exaltation as a sacrifice of atonement (9:1–14). Now in 9:15 he brings the atonement and covenant themes together by declaring that through Christ's sacrifice the mercy promised under the new covenant is given. Not all aspects of the new covenant are in place, since the need for teaching one another has not passed (5:11–12; 8:11); but as "mediator" of the covenant, Jesus also acts as the guarantor who assures listeners that all of God's promises will be kept (NOTES on 7:22; 8:6).

A summary of previous arguments concerning the Law and Christ prefaces the discussion of the new covenant (9:15b; see §23 COMMENT *b*), but the new point is that the new covenant was made so that "those who are called might receive the promised eternal inheritance" (9:15c). The new covenant oracle (8:8–12) made no mention of inheritance, but listeners already had a hope of inheriting salvation in the world to come (1:14; 2:5), a hope that was kindled by early Christian proclamation. Listeners understood themselves to be heirs of the

[299]Many include 9:23 with what follows, but it seems preferable to include 9:23 with what precedes (Calvin; Vanhoye, *La structure*, 151–54; Nissilä, *Hohepriestermotiv*, 197–201; H.-F. Weiss) since it continues the theme of purification of items used in worship. Verses 24–28 do not deal with the purification of non-human things—although interpretations vary (see NOTES on 9:23)—but with the effect of Christ's sacrifice for human beings.

promises made to Abraham (2:16; 6:12–18; 11:8). Like Abraham, they were called by God (3:1; 11:8) and they looked forward to life in God's kingdom (11:13–16; 12:22–24, 28). The problem was that instead of inheriting glory, they experienced dispossession (10:32–34; 13:13). If listeners stand under God's scrutiny insofar as they are sinners, God stands under the listeners' scrutiny insofar as he has made promises that remain unfulfilled.

In 9:16a the author connects the new covenant promise with the hope of inheritance through a comparison[300] that plays on two different uses of the Greek word *diathēkē*.[301] In the LXX *diathēkē* was used for God's covenant with Israel, while in the Greco-Roman world the term regularly referred to a will or testament. When making a will, the testator said "I give," "I bequeath," or "I leave" stated property to others.[302] In societies where major property was passed down within the family, inheritance was of central importance for a person's future well-being. Those addressed by Hebrews are the sons and daughters (2:10) who belong to God's household (3:6). They cannot obtain for themselves what God has promised—such as a home (11:13–16) and resting place (4:1–11)—but depend on God to bequeath it to them.[303]

In common practice it was "necessary that the death of the testator be presented" by a formal statement to a local official (NOTE on 9:16). One might ask whether it was necessary for God to follow this procedure and whether God could not bestow an inheritance without a public presentation of the death of Christ. Some have attempted to demonstrate the logical necessity of Christ's death,[304] but in Hebrews Jesus' death is the presupposition rather than the conclusion of the argument. Hebrews does not assume that God is bound by secular legal practice to make death the basis for inheritance. Rather, Jesus' death is a given, and the author seeks to disclose its significance in various ways, including reference to testamentary practice.

The statement that a "testament becomes valid upon death" (9:17a) functions on two levels: human practice and divine action. In human terms a testament is valid as a promise while the testator is still alive, but its provisions become valid when they are put into effect upon the death of the testator. In divine terms God's new covenant was promised through Jeremiah, but was put into effect through Christ's death. Again, a testament "has no force as long as the testator lives" (9:17b). On a human level this means that people cannot claim their inheritance until the testator has died. On the divine level this means that people

---

[300]On a comparison or *similitudo* see Lausberg, *Handbook* §422; Grässer, *Hebräer*, 2.172.

[301]Rhetorically, the use of the same word in two senses was called *reflexio* (*Rhet. ad Her.* 4.14.21; Quintilian, *Inst.* 9.3.68; cf. Lausberg, *Handbook* §§663–64; Attridge, *Epistle*, 255). The fact that this comparison can be made only on the basis of the Greek *diathēkē*, but not the Hebrew *berît*, indicates that Hebrews was composed in Greek. See pp. 37, 39.

[302]Matt 21:38; Mark 12:7; Luke 12:13; 20:14. See the Greco-Roman wills in *P. Oxy.* ##489–94, and in Hunt and Edgar, *Select Papyri* 1, ##82–86.

[303]Luther's stress on the Lord's Supper as a promise and a gift led to his understanding of *diathēkē* as a "testament" (see p. 36).

[304]One example is Anselm's *Cur deus homo*, which seeks to show by reason alone the necessity for which God became man and by his own death restored life to the world (preface; 1.1).

could not demand that God fulfill his promise to put his laws within them (8:10) until Christ died to cleanse their consciences (9:14). The argument does not explicitly develop the connection between Christ's death and the hope of inheriting a share in the world to come, but the implication is that by dealing with sin, which is the barrier to life with God, Christ opens a new and living way into God's presence (10:19–20), where people receive their inheritance. God's bestowal of the mercy promised through the new covenant provides assurance that he will fulfill his other promises as well.

b. Covenant Blood (9:18–23)

The reminder that the Mosaic covenant was not "dedicated without blood" (9:18) turns from testamentary practice to biblical precedent. The manner of a testator's death generally did not affect the validity of the testament, and whether one died violently or peacefully, senselessly or purposefully was of no consequence. Therefore, the language of blood sacrifice allows Hebrews to accent the purposeful quality of Jesus' death. Covenants were not always established by sacrifice—the covenant with David was simply a promise on God's part (2 Sam 7:12; 23:5; Sir 45:25). The Mosaic covenant, however, was inaugurated with blood, allowing it to serve as a precedent for the new covenant established by Christ's blood.

Moses was the mediator of the Sinai covenant (9:19) just as Jesus was the mediator of the new covenant (7:22; 8:6). Moses and Jesus were alike in that they were faithful, but Moses was God's servant whereas Jesus was his Son (3:1–6). Moses saw the heavenly tent, but Jesus ministers in it (8:1–6). When making the Sinai covenant, Moses declared "every commandment . . . in accordance with the Law" (9:19a; Exod 24:3–8). Hebrews, however, has argued that the Law was inadequate, that it made nothing complete, and that its commands were set aside by Christ's priesthood (Heb 7:11–19; 9:9–10, 13; pp. 114–15). Nevertheless, the sacrifice by which Moses inaugurated the first covenant foreshadows the self-sacrifice by which Christ would inaugurate the new covenant.

The reference to "calves' blood" recalls the making of the first covenant, but the water, scarlet wool, and hyssop that are mentioned in Hebrews do not appear in the narrative of the covenant in Exod 24:3–8 (NOTES on Heb 9:19). The author of Hebrews seems to incorporate various cleansing rites prescribed by the Mosaic covenant into his account of the ceremony by which the covenant was established. Moreover, 9:21 refers to the sprinkling of the Tabernacle and its vessels, which occurred some time after the first covenant was made. Thus in Hebrews, inaugurating the covenant and dedicating the Tabernacle become a single event (D'Angelo, *Moses*, 244). The sacrifices of the first covenant may have been of limited value (9:9–10), but the way Moses sprinkled blood for cleansing under the old covenant foreshadows the way that the sprinkled blood of Christ will bring complete cleansing under the new covenant (12:24). Foreshadowing is also evident in Moses' words: "This is the blood of the covenant that God commanded you" (9:20). Moses was "to bear witness to what was to be spoken" later (3:5), and in Hebrews these words testify to the covenant that God would make later through the blood of Christ.[305]

Under the Law "almost everything is cleansed with blood, and without an outpouring of blood forgiveness does not occur" (9:22). Two assumptions underlie this point. One is that blood is a given in OT ritual. The OT does not explain *how* blood cleanses or brings atonement, but simply states *that* it does so. People were expected to recognize the value of blood without understanding how it worked.[306] Second, Hebrews assumes that Christ's death is the definitive means by which God offers forgiveness, and like other early Christians he understood Christ's death to have entailed bloodshed (NOTE on 9:12). The author understood the role of blood christologically.[307] He assumes that since forgiveness fully occurs only through the outpouring of *Christ's blood*, one can conclude that "without an outpouring of blood forgiveness does not occur."

To say "it is necessary that the representations of the heavenly things be cleansed" by such rites (9:23a) summarizes aspects of the Mosaic Law, especially the directive that the sanctuary be cleansed with goat's blood on the Day of Atonement (Lev 16:15–19). To add that the heavenly things themselves require better sacrifices (9:23b) assumes that if the lesser earthly sanctuary required goat's blood, then a superior sacrifice would be appropriate for the heavenly sanctuary. The peculiar idea that the heavenly sanctuary might need cleansing (NOTES on 9:23) reflects a view of revelation. The author understands fundamental reality to be heavenly rather than earthly. If the earthly sanctuary is a representation of the heavenly one (8:2, 5), then laws pertaining to the earthly tent presumably disclose something about the heavenly tent that it represents. One might conclude that the earthly sanctuary was cleansed because its heavenly counterpart also was to be cleansed. Christ did not purify the heavenly sanctuary because he was bound to follow the Levitical pattern; rather, the reverse is true. Levitical practice foreshadows Christ's cleansing of the heavenly tent at the turn of the ages (10:1).

c. Once For All (9:24–28)

The final paragraph shows the definitive character of Christ's work. First, the sanctuary that Christ entered was the "true one," namely, "heaven itself," rather than an "antitype" that was "made with hands" (9:24).[308] God had commanded Moses to make a sanctuary according to the heavenly type (8:5), so that people

---

305These words are sometimes thought to echo traditions concerning the Lord's Supper. See NOTE on 9:20 and more generally pp. 127–129.

306On blood see J. H. Waszink, "Blut," *RAC* 2.459–73; Grässer, *Hebräer,* 2.149–51; Braun, *Hebräer,* 256–57; Dunnill, *Covenant,* 100–3; Johnsson, *Defilement,* 227–39.

307E. P. Sanders points out that Paul begins with what God has done in Christ, not with an independent assessment of the human condition. Paul interprets the human condition in light of what he knows to be true in Christ (*Paul,* 442–43). Hebrews follows a similar movement of thought.

308The author shows no interest in accounts of Jesus' entering the outer courts of the Jerusalem Temple (Matt 21:12, 14, 23; 26:55 par.). In any case he recognized that Christ would have been barred from the Temple's inner chamber since he was not a priest of Levitical descent (Lev 7:13; 8:4).

thought of the earthly sanctuary as the divinely ordained counterpart to God's heavenly dwelling. According to tradition, the outer court represented earth and the inner chamber stood for heaven.[309] Therefore, the Levitical high priest's entry into the inner chamber symbolized movement toward heaven. In Hebrews, however, the heavenly tent is an alternative to the earthly one, and Christ's exaltation accomplishes what the high priest's action merely foreshadows (8:1–2). Unlike other groups in antiquity, Christians had no earthly sanctuary (§20 COMMENT *a*). They probably gathered in homes, and their modest assembly was dwindling (10:25). Hebrews does not dismiss the need for a sanctuary, but directs attention to the heavenly sanctuary, where Christ ministers, giving listeners a renewed focus for faith and worship.

Although Christ is visibly absent from the listeners, Hebrews says that he has gone to appear before God on our behalf (9:24b). His absence from view is not an absence of concern, but a part of his role as high priest. Christ's appearing in God's presence is an unseen reality (11:1) that takes place during the time in which the listeners live. For "Christ to have ascended profits us nothing if he ascended for his own sake. But now our glory and our joy is in this, that he went there for us and not against us" (Luther, WA 57/3.53). His intercession reflects the complexity of the human situation. Insofar as people are afflicted by others (2:15; 13:3, 13), they need help to persevere, and insofar as they are sinful, they stand under God's judgment and need the forgiveness that extends the benefits of Christ's sacrifice to particular sins (cf. NOTES and COMMENT on 7:25).[310]

Second, Christ's sacrifice is superior to Levitical offerings (9:25–26). Some points are discussed elsewhere;[311] here, the distinctive element is a *reductio ad absurdum* (Attridge). The author of Hebrews assumes that listeners understand the importance of the annual rite of atonement and the idea that the Son of God existed from the dawn of time (1:2). Now he puts these elements together by envisioning what it would mean for Christ fully to conform to the Levitical pattern: "He would have had to suffer many times from the foundation of the world" (9:26a). To imagine Christ perpetually weeping (5:7–8), being taken outside the city (13:12), and being crucified (12:2) shows the futility of repeated sacrifices. By transferring the idea of repetition from the sphere of animal sacrifice, where it is assumed, to the sphere of Christ's death, where it is absurd, the author indicates that Christ's sacrifice is superior to all others (cf. 10:1–18).

Christ appeared once, at the consummation of the ages (9:26b). "It is not that Christ happened to come at the time of fulfillment but that his coming made that time the time of fulfillment" (F. F. Bruce, *Epistle*, 231). One might have ex-

---

[309]Philo, *QE* 2.68–69; Josephus, *Ant.* 3.123, 181. See §22 COMMENT *a*; C. R. Koester, *Dwelling*, 59–63.

[310]On intercession extending the benefits of his death see K. Barth, *Church Dogmatics* IV/1, 314–15.

[311]On the contrast between Christ's singular sacrifices and repeated Levitical sacrifices see §25 COMMENT *c*. On Christ offering his own blood rather than the blood of bulls and goats see §23 COMMENT *b*. Hebrews' emphasis on the singularity of Christ's sacrifice played an important part in later Christian debates over calling the Eucharist a sacrifice. See pp. 26, 31–32.

pected the author to say that Christ appeared to abolish divine *judgment* by turning God from wrath to mercy. Instead the author spoke of "the abolition of *sin*" (9:26c). To abolish sin is to change the human condition—to write God's laws on human hearts (8:10; 10:16). The author understood that sin continued to threaten the listeners (3:12–13; 12:4). Yet he also understood that Christ's death was a complete and final sacrifice for sin—otherwise Christ's death, like the Levitical sacrifices, would be only partially effective. Sin emerges from unfaith, and for sin to be abolished means that it must be displaced by faith, which is its opposite. When the proclamation of Christ's once-for-all death awakens faith, sin is set aside, making the conscience complete (9:14; cf. §23 COMMENT *b*).

Third, the author compares Christ's death to ordinary human deaths. In stating that "it is ordained for human beings to die once" (9:27), the author was voicing a commonplace. This was valuable in persuasive speech, for the "hearer, when he perceives that an indisputable principle drawn from practical life is being applied to a cause, must give his tacit approval" (*Rhet. ad Her.* 4.17 §25). The idea that after death "comes the judgment" (Heb 9:27b) was also a commonplace and a part of the tradition that the listeners had already received (6:1–2; 10:25, 27). God's people are not exempt from judgment (10:30), and in the New Jerusalem they will meet the God who is judge of all (12:23). Nevertheless, the author can urge listeners to remain faithful in confident hope that God's judgment will bring them salvation (4:9–10; 12:22–24) rather than condemnation.

The course taken by Christ is both similar to and different from the normal pattern:

9:27	human beings die once	9:28	Christ was offered once
	afterward comes judgment		Christ saves those waiting for him

Like other people, Christ died once, but to press the analogy one would presumably have to say that Christ then faced divine judgment, was vindicated, and was brought to heavenly glory (Westcott). Nevertheless, instead of saying that Christ's death led to judgment for himself, Hebrews says that it brought salvation for others, including deliverance from divine wrath, rescue from the forces of evil, and life in God's presence (§5 COMMENT *b*). Christ's brothers and sisters were formerly held captive by the devil, and Christ came to deliver them from their fear of death (2:10–18). The people of God can therefore be confident that Christ will come again to bring final salvation from death itself.

25. The Consummate Sacrifice (10:1–18)

10 [1]Now since the Law contains a shadow of the good things to come and not
the actual manifestation of these events, it cannot make complete those who
draw near year after year with the same sacrifices, which they are constantly offering. [2]Otherwise would they not have ceased to be offered, since the worshipers who were once cleansed would have no consciousness of sin? [3]Yet in

them there is actually a reminder of sin year after year. [4]For it is impossible for the blood of bulls and goats to take away sins.

[5]Therefore, upon coming into the world he says, *Sacrifice and offering you did not want, but you fashioned a body for me;* [6]*whole burnt offerings and sin offerings you did not find pleasing.* [7]*Then I said, "Behold, I have come (it has been written about me in the book) to do your will, O God."* [8]His first point was that *sacrifices and offerings, whole burnt offerings and sin offerings are not what you wanted or what pleased you.* These are offered according to the Law. [9]His next point was, *Behold, I have come to do your will.* He abolishes the first in order to establish the second. [10]And by that *will* we have been sanctified through the offering of the *body* of Jesus Christ once and for all.

[11]Indeed, every priest has stood ministering each day and offering repeatedly the same sacrifices, which can never remove sins, [12]but this one, after offering for all time a single sacrifice for sins, sat down at the right hand of God, [13]from now on waiting until his enemies are made a footstool for his feet. [14]For by a single offering he has made complete for all time those who are sanctified.

[15]And the Holy Spirit also testifies to us, for after saying, [16]*This is the covenant that I will make with them after those days, says the Lord: Putting my laws upon their hearts, I will even write them on their mind,* [he also says,] [17]*and I will not remember their sins and their lawless deeds anymore.* [18]Where there is forgiveness of these, there is no longer any offering for sin.

NOTES

10:1. *the Law contains a shadow.* See NOTE on 8:5.

of the good things to come. The "good things" that were "to come" after the Law was given included the atonement, cleansing, and sanctification that occurred through Christ's death and exaltation (9:11–14). Some of the "good things" that will come with the return of Christ (9:28) include rest (4:1–10) and sharing in the world to come (2:5; 13:14; Casalini).

and not the actual manifestation. A "manifestation" [*eikōn*] commonly referred to what was visible, such as images on coins (Mark 12:16), statues (Dan 2:31–35), and paintings (Ezek 23:14). More broadly, Plato called the world "a moving image [*eikōn*] of eternity" (*Timaeus* 37), and Plotinus considered an *eikōn* to be a "visible manifestation" (*Enneads* 5.8). Early Christians associated *eikōn* with the "glory" that manifested God's power and presence (1 Cor 11:7; 2 Cor 3:18). Although humankind was created in God's image (Gen 1:26 LXX), Christ was uniquely identified as God's image, since God was manifest in him (2 Cor 4:4; Col 1:15). When Heb 10:1 refers to an *eikōn* of future realities, it refers to their manifestation in Christ (cf. H. Kleinknecht, *TDNT* 2.388–90; Peterson, *Hebrews*, 145; H.-F. Weiss; Spicq, *TLNT* 1.412–19).

of these events. The events (*pragmata*) are "the good things to come" (10:1a), including atonement, cleansing, and sanctification. *Pragmata* can be "things" (Plato, *Cratylus* 439a; Plutarch, *Mor.* 372A, 373AB), but often they are events, affairs, or actions (Luke 1:1; Acts 5:4; Rom 16:2; BAGD, 697). Elsewhere in Hebrews *pragmata* are God's promise, oath, and the unseen activities of the word of God (6:18; 11:1).

Hebrews is unusual in contrasting *skia* ("shadow") with *eikōn* ("image" or "manifestation"), since in philosophical writings the terms were synonyms (Plato, *Republic* 509E–510E; Philo, *Alleg. Interp.* 3.96; *Decalogue* 82; *Migration* 12; *Heir* 72; cf. Cicero, *De republica* 2.30 §52). Accordingly, one MS (P46) replaced "not" with "and" so that "shadow" and "image" become synonyms. Even though a few scholars favor this reading (Cantalamessa, "Il papiro"; Sen, "Se recupera"), it seems to have arisen to overcome the difficulties in the text (Zuntz, *Text*, 20–23; *TCGNT*, 669; Attridge; Ellingworth). Philo uses *eikōn* for incorporeal archetypes (*Dreams* 1.79; Stylianopoulos, "Shadow," 220), yet in Hebrews the *eikōn* includes the offering of the "body" of Jesus (10:10). In Hebrews the term has a revelatory sense. On Hebrews and Platonism see pp. 97–100.

it cannot make complete. On "completion" see COMMENT *a* and pp. 122–25. Some MSS say that "they" cannot (*dynantai*, א A C D1 etc.; NRSVfn), referring to priests, rather than stating that "it," (i.e., the Law), cannot (*dynatai*, P46 D*2 H K etc.). It seems likely that the plural arose accidentally because the previous verb "they offer" was plural (*TCGNT*, 669).

those who draw near. The verb *proserchesthai* was used primarily for the priests who "draw near" the altar (Lev 9:7–8; 21:17, 21; Num 4:19), but it was also used for all worshipers (Lev 9:5; Num 10:3–4). Drawing near means approaching God (NOTE on 4:16), but it falls short of being "made complete," which entails full access to the presence of God.

year after year with the same sacrifices, which they are constantly offering. Hebrews groups the annual sacrifice on the Day of Atonement (NOTE on 9:7) with other offerings (5:1; 8:3; 9:13), since all were made repeatedly rather than only once, in contrast to the singular sacrifice of Christ (9:26–28; 10:2, 10).

10:2. *Otherwise would they not have ceased to be offered.* This rhetorical question expects listeners to respond, "Yes, the sacrifices would have ceased if they had been effective" (cf. Ps.-Oecumenius; Theophylact; BDF §360.2). Some MSS omit the negative *ouk*, probably because the copyist failed to read the sentence as a question (H* 614 630 1739 etc.). Others (P46 [365] 518) take 10:2 as a statement, reading *kan* rather than *epei an* (REB; NJB). Since MS evidence strongly supports the negative, the sentence must be read as a question (Zuntz, *Text*, 45–46). Some argue that Hebrews was written when sacrifices were still being offered (F. F. Bruce; P. E. Hughes; A. Vanhoye, *TRE* 14.497), but others disagree (Attridge; Braun; Grässer; H.-F. Weiss). See pp. 52–53.

since the worshipers who were once cleansed. "Once" (*hapax*) indicates both single occurrence and definitive action (NOTE on 6:4). Hebrews argues that Levitical rites cleansed only the flesh, not the conscience (9:13–14). See pp. 118–22.

would have no consciousness of sin. The word *syneidēsis* is used for the "conscience" (NOTE on 9:9). Here it has the related sense of being "convicted by consciousness of our own acts of unrighteousness" (Philo, *Worse* 146; cf. *Special Laws* 2.49; *Virtues* 124; Diodorus Siculus, *Library of History* 4.65.7). It is comparable to the "evil conscience" (Heb 10:22).

10:3. *Yet in them there is actually a reminder of sin year after year.* The high priest recalled Israel's sins before God during the confession on the Day of Atonement (Lev 16:21), but Hebrews assumes that the sacrifices reminded people of sin. The language seems to echo Num 5:15, which spoke of offerings that recall sin. Even though these were not atoning sacrifices, the author may be generalizing the reference to include all sacrifices (cf. Philo, *Planter* 108).

10:4. *For it is impossible for the blood of bulls and goats to take away sins.* This recalls the Day of Atonement (NOTE on 9:7). Priests would "take away sins" by making atonement (Lev 10:17), and God "took away sins" out of mercy (Exod 34:7, 9; Num 14:18; Isa 6:7). Since sin is completely removed only when the conscience is purged, the partial cleansing provided by animal sacrifice is not considered a removal of sin (9:13). On atonement see pp. 121–22.

10:5. *Therefore, upon coming into the world.* "Come into the world" was a Jewish expression for birth (*m. Rosh. Hash.* 1:2; *Sifre Deut.* §312), but here it is used for the preexistent Christ coming to earth (pp. 104–5; cf. John 1:9; 6:14; 9:39; 12:46; 16:28; 18:37; cf. 1 Tim 1:15).

10:5b–7. *he says.* The comment that Christ spoke "upon coming into the world" (10:5) might suggest that the preincarnate Christ speaks (F. F. Bruce, *Epistle,* 242; cf. Ellingworth; Lane), although the words "I have come . . . to do your will" (10:7) suggest that the speaker has already entered the world (Peterson, *Hebrews,* 147). This quotation of Ps 40:6–8 (39:7–9 LXX) generally follows the most common form of the LXX:

MT	*LXX*	*Hebrews*
Sacrifice and offering	Sacrifice and offering	Sacrifice and offering
you did not want, but	you did not want, but	you did not want, but
you dug ears	*you fashioned a body*	*you fashioned a body*
for me;	for me;	for me;
whole burnt offerings	whole burnt offerings	whole burnt offerings
and sin offerings you	and sin offerings you	and sin offerings you
did not request.	*did not request.*	did not find pleasing.
Then I said,	Then I said,	Then I said,
"Behold, I have come,	"Behold, I have come,	"Behold, I have come
(it is written	(it is written	(it has been written
about me,	about me	about me
in the scroll	in the *head*	in the *head*
of the book).	of the book).	of the book)
To do your will,	To do your will,	to do your will,
O my God, *I delight.*"	O my God, *I intend.*"	O __ God _____."

(**a**) MT and LXX. (*i*) The MT of 40:6b has "ears you dug for me," which apparently means that the psalmist was given the power to listen attentively. There is evidence of a LXX tradition (La^{G} Ga) that also read "ears" (*ōtia*), but the best LXX MSS (א B A) read "body" (*sōma*). The reading "body" could have originated with Hebrews and later have been transferred to the LXX (Jobes, "Rhetorical"), although MS evidence makes this unlikely. If "ears" appeared in the earliest LXX version, "body" might have arisen as a misreading in MSS that did not separate between words, so that *ĒTHELESASŌTIA* was read as *ĒTHELESASŌMA* (Bleek). Alternatively, if "body" was the earliest LXX reading, the translator may have taken the Hebrew wording as an instance of a part standing for the whole: digging or hollowing out the ears is part of the total work of forming a human body (F. F. Bruce). Later, "body" in the LXX would have been changed to "ears" to conform to the MT in the Greek translations of Aquila, Symmachus, Theodotion, and Origen. The MS evidence favors the latter alternative. In any case Hebrews relies on a LXX text that read "body" (Schröger, *Verfasser*, 172–74). *(ii)* The MT reads "scroll of the book" (*megillot sēfer*), which is rendered in the LXX and Hebrews as "the head of the book" (*kephalis bibliou*).

(b) LXX and Hebrews. *(i)* Instead of saying that God did not ask for sacrifices, Hebrews says that God was not "pleased" with them, perhaps echoing Ps 51:16, 19 (Attridge). *(ii)* Hebrews omits the LXX's "I wish," perhaps to show that Christ did not merely "wish" to do God's will, but came "to do" it. Other textual differences (Ellingworth, *Epistle*, 500–501) are insignificant.

Sacrifice and offering you did not want. "Sacrifice" (*thysia*) often, but not always, meant animal sacrifices, while "offering" (*prosphora*) could include gifts of animals, cereals, oil, wine, and incense (Sir 38:11; 46:16; 50:13–15). Both are made for sin, according to Hebrews ("sacrifice," Heb 9:26; 10:11, 26; "offering," 10:18). Cf. NOTE on 5:1.

but you fashioned a body for me. On preexistence and incarnation see pp. 104–9.

10:6. *whole burnt offerings and sin offerings you did not find pleasing.* In whole burnt offerings the entire animal or bird was consumed by fire, so that nothing was received by the worshiper. They were used for cleansing, expiation of sin, fulfillment of vows, freewill offerings, and festival offerings (Lev 14:19–20; Num 15:3). For sin offerings, a bull, goat, doves or pigeons, or flour was used. Fat was burned, but the meat was eaten by the priests (Lev 4:1–5:13; 6:26). By listing various types of sacrifices, the speaker indicates that no such offerings were pleasing to God.

10:7. *"Behold, I have come."* Accounts of Jesus' sayings include the idea that he "has come" to do God's will (Matt 5:17; 9:13; 10:34; 11:19 par; John 10:10). Cf. Heb 10:5.

it has been written about me in the book. The "book" is literally the "head of the book," apparently referring to the knob on the top of the rod around which the scroll was wound. This is an example of *synekdochē*, where a part signifies the whole scroll (Ezek 2:9; 3:1–3; 2 Esdr 6:2). Early readers would probably have envisioned the "book" as a scroll containing a single text, like Isaiah (Luke 4:17), or perhaps several books, like the Law (1 Esdr 1:11), but not a book containing the whole OT. Medieval interpreters took "head of the book" to mean the beginning of Genesis (cf. John 1:1; Haimo; Sedulius Scotus) or the Psalms (Alcuin; Anselm of Laon, *Glossa ordinaria*), but in this context the "book" is probably the Mosaic Law, as in Heb 9:19 (K. T. Schäfer, "ΚΕΦΑΛΙΣ").

to do your will. See NOTE on 10:9.

10:8. *His first point.* This term is literally "above" (*anōteron*), which was a common way of referring to something earlier in a document (Josephus, *Ant.* 19.212; *Ag. Ap.* 2.18). Yet here it marks an antithesis in the two portions of the psalm.

sacrifices and offerings, whole burnt offerings and sin offerings. This summarizes the four types of offerings mentioned (cf. Philo, *Special Laws* 1.194; Josephus, *Ant.* 3.224–32). As in Heb 9:13, the list underscores the inadequacy of all these offerings.

These are offered according to the Law. On the Law see pp. 114–15.

10:9. *Behold, I have come to do your will.* In perfect obedience Christ was uniquely "without sin" (NOTE on 4:15). Obedience characterized Christ's life (NOTE on 5:8) and passion. That Christ died in obedience to God (Matt 26:42; Luke 22:42; John 4:34; 5:30; 6:38–40; 19:30) and not as a criminal was an important early Christian conviction.

He abolishes the first in order to establish the second. "Abolish" (*anairein*) could be used for the annulment of laws (Josephus, *J.W.* 2.4; *Ag. Ap.* 2.41; Dio Chrysostom, *Disc.* 76.2; Aristotle, *Constitution of Athens* 29.4; Aeschines, *Against Ctesiphon* 16.39) and wills (Demosthenes, *Orations* 28.5; Isaeus, *Cleonymus* 14; cf. Heb 7:18). Conversely, "establish" was used for making (Gen 6:18; 17:7; Exod 6:4) and adhering to covenants (1 Macc 2:27; Rom 3:31). In a striking reversal of usage the author speaks not of the "establishing," but the displacement of the Mosaic covenant by the new covenant.

10:10. *And by that will we have been sanctified.* The "will" is God's will, which Christ carried out (10:8–9; cf. 1 Thess 4:3; Matt 18:14; Gal 1:4; Eph 1:5, 9, 11). On sanctification see pp. 120–21.

through the offering of the body of Jesus Christ once and for all. The word *ephapax* can mean that people are sanctified once and for all, but word order suggests that Christ's body has been offered once and for all.

10:11. *Indeed, every priest has stood ministering each day.* "Ministering" was done while standing (Deut 10:8; 18:7; 1 Kgs 8:11; 13:1; 2 Chron 29:11; Josephus, *Ant.* 13.372), since it involved slaughtering animals, placing offerings on the altar, and other actions. The author alternates between the sacrifices offered each year (cf. 10:1) and those offered each day. What is similar about all these offerings is that they must be repeated, unlike Christ's singular sacrifice. The text of this verse is well attested (P$^{13.46.79\text{vid}}$ ℵ A C etc.). The variant "high priest" (A C P etc.) may reflect the wording of 5:1 and 8:3.

and offering repeatedly the same sacrifices, which can never remove sins. The verb *periairein* ("remove") is similar to *aphairein* used in 10:4 (cf. 1 Chron 21:8; Zeph 3:11, 15), and it deals with actual removal of sins. A sin offering was to "remove the guilt of the congregation" (Lev 10:17), but Hebrews argues that this did not fully happen until Christ's self-sacrifice. See *TLNT* 3.91–92.

10:12. *after offering for all time a single sacrifice.* See NOTES on 9:26–28.

sat down at the right hand of God. The language recalls Ps 110:1b (NOTE on Heb 1:13).

10:13. *from now on waiting until his enemies are made a footstool for his feet.* The language recalls Ps 110:1c (NOTE on Heb 1:13). "Waiting" suggests rest, but not inactivity, for the seated Christ intercedes for others (4:14–16; 7:25; 9:24). The "enemies" are not identified. Christ's exaltation was a victory over the devil (2:14–15), and the author may have thought of the enemies as other superhuman powers (cf. Eph 1:20–23; Isaacs, *Sacred*, 183), but the idea is not developed.

10:14. *For by a single offering he has made complete for all time.* The verb "make complete" has been used three times with reference to Christ, always in a positive sense (2:10; 5:9; 7:28), and three times for the Law and its institutions, always in a negative sense (7:19; 9:9; 10:1). Previously, Christ was "made complete," but now he makes others complete in relation to God (Vanhoye, *Old Testament*, 218). The perfect tense might have been used for this action of completion in order to emphasize the finality of Christ's sacrifice, since past tenses could indicate the certainty of present or future occurrences (Demetrius, *On Style* 214). See pp. 122–25.

those who are sanctified. See pp. 120–21.

10:15. *And the Holy Spirit also testifies to us.* See NOTE on 3:7 and pp. 116–17.

for after saying. By introducing the paraphrase of Jer 31:33–34 in this way, the author indicates that it must be read in two parts. Many understand the second part to begin with the *kai* ("also") at the beginning of 10:17, which some MSS expand to read "later he also says" (104 323 945 1739 1881 etc.; NIV; NRSV; REB; NAB^{2}) or "then he said" (1505). This is more plausible than thinking that the second part begins with "the Lord says" (10:16b; NJB; Attridge; Grässer).

10:16–17. Earlier Jer 31:31–34 was quoted in full, and detailed comments are given in NOTES on Heb 8:7–12. In 10:16–17 the oracle is paraphrased:

Heb 8:10–12	*Heb 10:16–17*
This is the covenant that	This is the covenant that
I will establish with *the house of Israel*	I will make with *them*
after those days, says the Lord:	after those days, says the Lord:
Putting my laws *into their mind,*	Putting my laws *upon their hearts,*
I will even write them	I will even write them
on their hearts	*on their minds,*
. . . *(8:10d–12a)* . . .	
and I will not remember	and I will not remember
their sins	their sins
	and their lawless deeds
anymore.	anymore.

with them. By referring generally to "them" rather than to "the house of Israel," the author allows for a connection between the new covenant and all for whom Christ's blood was shed.

their lawless deeds. Adding these words to the quotation emphasizes the scope of God's grace. Since the Son of God hates "lawlessness" (1:9), he purges it from the people of God.

I will not remember . . . anymore. See NOTES on 8:12.

10:18. *Where there is forgiveness of these.* See NOTE on 9:22.

there is no longer any offering for sin. Hebrews does not make clear whether sacrifices were still being offered (pp. 52–53). Even if they were, the author assumes that they were ineffective.

COMMENT[312]

The contrasts between Levitical offerings and Christ's singular sacrifice, which dominated Heb 9, intensify in 10:1–18 as the author declares that the sacrifices made under the Law served as a *reminder of sin* (10:1–4), whereas Jesus' sacrifice inaugurated the new covenant under which God promised *not to recall sins* anymore (10:15–18). Under the Law, obedience included sacrifices, but Hebrews argues that God wants obedience and *not* sacrifices. Hebrews does not simply argue that blood sacrifice should be replaced with the worshipers' deeds of kindness. Obedience first of all pertains to Christ, whose obedient death effected the cleansing from sin that was foreshadowed, but not accomplished, by Mosaic institutions. As the critique of Levitical sacrifice becomes more pointed, extended quotations confront listeners with the voice of God (10:15–17; Jer 31:33–34) and of Christ (Heb 10:5–7; Ps 40:6–8). The quotations shift attention from the author's opinion—which might easily be disputed—to the OT's own critique of sacrifices.[313]

Structurally, 10:1–18 is bound together by common vocabulary.[314] The Law and new covenant are treated in the first and last sections, and the superiority of Christ's sacrifice and priesthood to Levitical institutions occupies the two center sections (Lane, *Hebrews,* 2.258):

(a) Under the Law, repeated sacrifices are a reminder of sins (10:1–4).
  (b) Levitical sacrifices are repetitive and have been replaced by Christ's singular self-sacrifice in obedience to God's will (10:5–10).
  (c) Levitical priests who stand to minister have been replaced by Christ the high priest, who is seated at God's right hand (10:11–14).
(d) Under the new covenant, God does not remember sins (10:15–18).

---

[312]On 10:1–18 see Attridge, "Uses"; F. F. Bruce, "Shadow"; Caird, "Son"; Casalini, "I sacrifici"; Chester, "Hebrews"; Gourgues, *À la droite,* 110–19; Hamm, "Faith"; Hay, *Glory,* 86–91; Jobes, "Function"; idem, "Rhetorical"; Johnsson, "Cultus"; Kaiser, "Abolition"; Levoratti, "Tú no has"; Loader, "Christ"; idem, *Sohn,* 171–74; Nissilä, *Hohepriestermotiv,* 218–39; Peterson, *Hebrews,* 144–53; K. T. Schäfer, "ΚΕΦΑΛΙΣ"; Schröger, *Verfasser,* 172–79; Stylianopoulos, "Shadow"; Vanhoye, "L'ombre"; idem, *Old Testament,* 213–22. On the new covenant see pp. 112–14.

[313]See Eisenbaum, *Jewish Heroes,* 131–33. Similarly, Vanhoye observed that the "Old Testament as revelation here again signals its own end as institution" (*Old Testament,* 213)

[314]"Offering" (*prosphora,* 10:5, 8, 10, 14, 18), "sacrifice" (*thysia,* 10:1, 5, 8, 11, 12), and "sin" (*hamartia,* 10:2, 3, 4, 6, 8, 11, 12, 17, 18).

a. Shadow and Reality (10:1–4)

Saying that the Law contains a shadow of good things to come, but not their image or manifestation, gives a distinctive turn to familiar language (10:1). Cicero lamented that in civil law "we possess no substantial, lifelike image of true law"; all we have is "a shadow and a sketch" (*De officiis* 3.17 §69). Philo, however, insisted that the Mosaic Law was "the most faithful image of the constitution of the world" (*Moses* 2.51). In Hebrews the issue is not the relationship of particular laws to a transcendent Law, but the relationship of Israel's Law to the work of Christ, whose death and exaltation are the manifestation of the events foreshadowed in the Law (10:1b). A shadow glides across surfaces without altering what it touches, but the manifestation of good things includes their actual occurrence in Christ (cf. 9:11), whose death and exaltation are said to change the human situation.

Completion of those who draw near is the standard against which the Law is measured (10:1b; cf. §18 COMMENT *a*). The expression "make complete" evokes various images for the fulfillment of God's purposes, including being crowned with glory (2:5–10), entering God's rest (4:9–10), and inheriting the blessing promised to Abraham (6:7, 12). Sin defiles, and to approach God with an unclean conscience would be an outrage, even if the flesh were clean (§22 COMMENT *a*). Hebrews argues that God brings his purposes to completion through Christ. Completion involves cleansing sin from the conscience (9:14; 10:2, 22) and the positive relationship that emerges as a result of the cleansing (pp. 122–25; Peterson, *Hebrews*, 146).

Hebrews uses a rhetorical question to press the point: If the sacrifices had been effective, "would they not have ceased to be offered?" (10:2). Such questions help persuade listeners, because in answering the question, they themselves pass judgment on the matter (Quintilian, *Inst.* 9.2.7). One might argue that sacrifices were effective and that they needed to be repeated because human beings persistently failed to obey God. Hebrews, however, argues that sacrifices were ineffective and were repeated because they failed to complete God's purposes (cf. 8:7). A truly effective sacrifice would mean that "worshipers who were once cleansed would have no consciousness of sin" (10:2b). Sin involves one's stance toward God—unfaith rather than faith (3:12–13; 6:1b; 10:38; 11:24–25; 12:4). The acts of atonement that were foreshadowed in the Law were faithfully carried out by Christ (10:7, 9), according to the will of God, who remains faithful to his promises (10:10, 23). These acts of divine faithfulness, which have occurred once and for all in Christ's death and exaltation, cleanse the human consciousness when they evoke faith.

Levitical sacrifices are said to have the opposite effect—bringing sin to consciousness (10:3). Philo acknowledged that when sacrifices are offered for the sake of appearances, "it is not a remission but a reminder of past sins which they effect" (*Moses* 2.107). He therefore stressed that sacrifices should be offered with right intention (cf. *Special Laws* 1.215). Hebrews, however, says that sacrifices regularly serve as reminders of sin. Sin was most fervently remembered on the

Day of Atonement (ibid, 2.196), but Hebrews maintains that *all* sacrifices (10:8) have this effect.

The categorical judgment is that "it is impossible for the blood of bulls and goats to take away sins" (10:4). Israel's prophets (COMMENT *b*), and Greek and Roman writers sometimes criticized sacrificial practice, although most thought that sacrifice expressed piety.[315] Pythagoras "would not stain the altars with blood," but considered incense, praises, and cereal offerings to be fitting for the gods.[316] Others emphasized that moral conduct and proper intentions were more important than sacrifices. God is "not to be worshiped with immolations nor with much blood—for what pleasure is the slaughter of undeserving victims—but with pure mind, and good and upright intention." The wicked "do not escape impiety although they dye the altars with streams of blood."[317]

Similarly, Hebrews' rejection of animal sacrifices (10:4) and its emphasis on obedience (10:5–10) might be taken to mean that the author thinks that material sacrifices cannot remove moral defilement or that animal sacrifices are merely external acts, whereas God desires internal obedience.[318] The author, however, assumes that without blood there is no forgiveness (9:22). The blood of bulls and goats cannot take away sins, but *Christ's* blood does take away sins. Christ offered his body (10:10), not only his mind or will, which means that Hebrews' argument is primarily christological rather than metaphysical or moral. If other sacrifices had been adequate, there would have been no need for Christ to die. Yet Hebrews argues that Christ did die in obedience to God, and that Christ's death discloses the ineffectiveness of other sacrifices. The "sacrifices" of praise and service that are offered by his followers are a response to what Christ has done (13:15–16).

b. Sacrifice versus Obedience (10:5–10)

Hebrews' most radical point is not the rejection of sacrifice in general, but its rejection of the sacrifices prescribed by the Law. God was the giver of the Law, and to say that the Law's sacrifices could not remove sins implied that *God* prescribed sacrifices that could not remove sins. Accordingly, the argument seeks to show that it was God himself who rejected blood sacrifices. The point is made through a scriptural quotation in which Christ is the implied speaker (see pp. 106–7). This text (Ps 40:6–8 [39:7–9 LXX]) may have been selected because

---

[315]Euripides, *Hercules furens* 1345; Apollonius of Tyanna, *Ep.* 26. This idea appears in later Christian writings (e.g., *Diogn.* 3:3–5). On the value of sacrifice as an expression of piety see Epictetus, *Ench.* 31.5. On Greco-Roman attitudes toward sacrifice see Ferguson, "Spiritual Sacrifice"; Thompson, *Beginnings*, 109–15; F. M. Young, *Use*, 11–34; Wenschkewitz, *Spiritualisierung*.

[316]Philostratus, *Life of Apollonius* 1.1.

[317]The first quotation is from Seneca, *De beneficiis* 1.6.3. The second is also from Seneca, quoted in Lactantius, *Divine Institutes* 6.25. Cf. Xenophon, *Memorabilia* 1.3.3; Isocrates, *To Nicoles* 20. See also the references to Jewish sources under COMMENT *b*.

[318]See Thompson, *Beginnings*, 103–15; F. F. Bruce, *Epistle*, 238; Vanhoye, *Old Testament*, 215; Attridge, *Epistle*, 275–76.

the psalmist refers to what "has been written about me in the book" (Heb 10:7). Hebrews assumes that the Law predates the Psalms, which are understood to have come from the time of David (4:7). Since the Law was "the book" mentioned in 9:19, the author probably understood the psalmist to refer to the Law. If the Law's regulations concerning Levitical practices foreshadow what has been accomplished in Christ (10:1), then Christ is uniquely qualified to be the speaker in the psalm.

The summary of the psalm in Heb 10:8a says that God did not want any of the sacrifices that are mentioned. Some OT texts warn that sacrifice is no substitute for ethical conduct and warn that God will reject the sacrifices of the disobedient (Isa 1:10–17; 66:3–4). Others declare that obedience is actually better than sacrifice (1 Sam 15:22; Amos 5:22–24; cf. Mic 6:6–8) or treat ethical conduct and offerings of praise as sacrifices (Pss 51:18–19; 141:2).[319] Some emphasized that God is honored not "with gifts or sacrifices but with purity of heart and devout disposition."[320] Nevertheless, Jewish writers commonly assumed that making a sacrifice was a form of obedience to God.[321] Hebrews, however, contrasts the ineffective sacrifices prescribed by the Law with the effective sacrifice made by Christ, so that when Christ carries out God's will, his sacrifice displaces other sacrifices and the Law that prescribed them.

If the first part of the psalm pronounced a negative judgment upon the sacrifices offered under the Law, the declaration that "I have come to do your will" (Heb 10:9a) gives positive expression to the work of Christ. Hebrews does not contrast blood sacrifice with acts of kindness on the part of the worshipers. The principal contrast is between the lack of accomplishment of God's will under the Law and the completion of God's will by Christ. Christ came to do God's will through a blood sacrifice that had an internal dimension of obedience and an external dimension in the offering of his body through crucifixion.[322]

The Law prescribed sacrifices that could not "take away" (*aphairein*) sins (10:4); therefore, when Christ accomplished God's purpose, the Law is "abolished" (*anairein*, 10:9). The problem is that God is the giver of the Law, and to say that Christ "abolishes the first" covenant "in order to establish the second" (10:9) raises questions about God's own reliability. One might logically ask why God would want Christ to abolish the Law that God himself had instituted. A key point for Hebrews is that despite the changes, God remains constant in his

---

[319]Sir 3:3, 30; 20:28; Tob 4:10–11; 1QS IX, 4–5; *'Abot R. Nat.* 4. On Jewish attitudes toward sacrifice see Ferguson, "Spiritual Sacrifice," 1156–62; F. M. Young, *Use*, 35–70.

[320]*Ep. Arist.* 234; cf. Philo, *Special Laws* 1.201, 253, 272, 277, 290.

[321]On esteem for sacrifices in the writings mentioned above see Sir 35:1–13; *Ep. Arist.* 92–93. Philo made a pilgrimage to offer sacrifices in Jerusalem (*Providence* 64), assumed that offering sacrifice was a genuine act of piety (*Special Laws* 1.67–68), and insisted that spiritual interpretations of the Law should not lead to failure to observe its statutes, including those pertaining to the Temple (*Migration* 89–93). The Dead Sea sect considered the Jerusalem Temple to have been polluted by a corrupt priesthood, but they did not reject sacrifice in principle and offered spiritual sacrifices until true worship should be restored (1QM II, 5–6; Klinzing, *Umdeutung*, 11–20, 93–106, 143–66.

[322]On the importance of external and internal, physical and spiritual dimensions of Christ's action see Vanhoye, *Old Testament*, 218; Lindars, *Theology*, 88–91; Attridge, "Uses," 9.

purpose, which is that people be sanctified (10:10). The Law becomes void when God's intention is fulfilled by Christ, who abolishes the Law by achieving the goal of sanctification (see pp. 119–22).

To say that people "have been sanctified through the offering of the *body* of Jesus" (10:10) encapsulates the paradox of the crucifixion and its relationship to the Law. A dead human body ordinarily brought defilement, not sanctification (Num 19:11). The cross was particularly offensive. Abhorrent and shameful to Greeks and Romans, crucifixion was considered defiling under Jewish law: if someone "is executed, and you hang him on a tree, his corpse must not remain all night upon the tree; you shall bury him that same day, for anyone hung on a tree is under God's curse. You must not defile the land that the Lord your God is giving you for possession" (Deut 21:22–23). If sanctification is determined by the Law, then the cross must be rejected, but Hebrews argues that if sanctification occurs through the crucified Christ, then the Law is supplanted.

c. The Finality of Christ's Priesthood (10:11–14)

Hebrews calls up in the mind's eye how "every priest has stood ministering each day and offering repeatedly the same sacrifices" (10:11ab). Just as relief sculptures from Italy (13:24) and elsewhere fuse the dramatic moments from the entire process of sacrifice into a timeless mosaic of action—procession, slaughter, offering[323]—Hebrews similarly encapsulates centuries of Levitical practice in a single image, arguing that such perpetual offering is not a sign of vigor, but of futility, for repetitive sacrifices "can never remove sins" (10:11c). The image of the standing priest is now juxtaposed with the image of the seated Christ (10:12; cf. Ps 110:1). When compared with ordinary worshipers, who could not enter the sanctuary, priests were in a position of honor (cf. 5:4), since they stood before the Lord, but when compared with one seated at God's right hand, the seated priest has the superior honor. Moreover, a priest who is seated, unlike those who stand to offer sacrifice, can be said to have entered God's rest, for his labors have ended (4:10).

The author seeks to invigorate the hope that the listeners, too, might find rest in the presence of God by declaring that Christ "has made complete for all time those who are sanctified" (10:14). To say that people have been "made complete" (perfect tense) is appropriate insofar as Christ's death is the complete and definitive offering that precludes any further sacrifices for sins (10:18). The perfect tense is less suitable for the actual state of the listeners, since they will contend with sin until God's purposes are made complete in the heavenly Jerusalem (3:14; 12:1, 23). Although listeners will still sin and need forgiveness (4:16), they are sanctified and holy (3:1; 6:10; 13:24), not because they exhibit moral perfection, but because they have been brought into the realm of God's favor by the cleansing power of Christ (pp. 119–22).

---

[323]See J. A. North, "Sacrifice and Ritual: Rome," *CAM* 2.985–86.

d. The Finality of Christ's Sacrifice (10:15–18)

The voice that now addresses the listeners is that of the Spirit (10:15). Earlier the author recalled how the listeners received a message of salvation that was validated by gifts of the Spirit (2:3–4; 6:4–5). The author assumes that the Spirit that brought them to faith is the Spirit that continues to speak through the Scriptures. Just as their faith was awakened when Christian preaching became the occasion for the Spirit's work, the author seeks to reinvigorate their faith by citing a text in which the Spirit addresses them again. The text is the new covenant promise that was given in Jer 31:33–34 (Heb 8:8–12). The new covenant not only offers forgiveness for sins that have already been committed but also promises to transform people so that they no longer fall into sin. God overcomes lawless deeds (10:17) by inscribing his laws on human minds (10:16), thereby bringing about obedience to his will.[324] The effects of the new covenant are not fully realized, of course (§21 COMMENT *b*). The first covenant's sacrifices brought sin to mind (10:3), but under the new covenant God promises not to recall sins (10:17). God remains mindful of sin, however, insofar as sin remains a threat (4:12–13; 10:26–31). Nevertheless, by giving people a renewed will to be faithful and by promising forgiveness for offenses that have already taken place, God creates a situation in which he does not allow past or present sins to define his relationship with people.

The conclusion is that where there is complete forgiveness, "there is no longer any offering for sins" (10:18). Theologically, the assurance of forgiveness encourages listeners to turn to God with confidence, boldly passing beyond "the curtain" that barred worshipers from God (10:19–22). The singularity of Christ's sacrifice also means that there is no other source of forgiveness, so that those who spurn forgiveness in Christ welcome divine judgment (10:26–31).[325] Socially, Hebrews' insistence on the finality of Christ's sacrifice establishes a distinctive basis for Christian life in an interreligious society. With respect to Judaism, the Temple is no longer necessary for Christians who confess that Jesus' self-offering puts an end to sacrifices. The rabbis centered Jewish community life on the Law and came to consider deeds of mercy and the study of the Torah to be the equivalent of sacrifice, especially after the destruction of the Temple,[326] but Hebrews centers community life on the crucified and exalted Christ, whose sacrifice undergirds the community's offerings of praise and compassion (13:12–15). With respect to the wider Greco-Roman society, Christians resided in Greco-Roman

---

[324]On the relationship of God's action to human freedom see §21 COMMENT *b*.

[325]Chrysostom reconciled Hebrews' argument concerning the finality of Christ's sacrifice with the church's practice of calling the Mass a sacrifice by emphasizing that the Mass was done as a "remembrance" of Christ's sacrifice, not as a new or different sacrifice (NPNF[1] 14.449). Chrysostom's approach, which was widely adopted in the Middle Ages (p. 32), was criticized by the Reformers in the sixteenth century (pp. 36, 38–39) and reaffirmed by Roman Catholic theologians (p. 40). On the Lord's Supper in Hebrews see pp. 127–29.

[326]After the destruction of the Temple, R. Johanan commented that acts of loving-kindness provide atonement (*'Abot R. Nat.* 4). When "a sage sits and expounds to the congregation, Scripture accounts it to him as though he had offered up fat and blood on the altar" (ibid).

cities, but did not belong there (13:14). Those "from Italy" (13:24) would have known that animals were sacrificed before athletic contests, during festival gatherings, and on other occasions to entreat the favor of the gods.[327] Yet now the Christian community had a unique sacrifice that was central for their common life, that signaled the beginning of their contest of faith (12:1–2), and that anticipated their own festival gathering in the city to come (12:22).

26. Heavenly Sanctuary and Earthly Assembly (10:19–25)

10 19Therefore, brethren, since we have boldness for an entryway into the sanctuary by the blood of Jesus, 20a new and living way that he dedicated for us through the curtain, that is, [by means] of his flesh, 21and a great priest over the house of God, 22let us approach with a true heart, with full assurance of faith, with our hearts sprinkled clean from an evil conscience and our body washed with pure water. 23Let us hold fast the confession of hope without wavering, for he who has promised is faithful, 24and let us consider how to provoke one another to love and good works, 25not abandoning our gathering, as is the custom of some, but exhorting [one another], and this all the more as you see the Day drawing near.

NOTES

10:19. *Therefore, brethren.* This address (NOTE on 3:1) reaffirms ties between speaker and listeners.

since we have boldness. Objectively, "boldness" is authorization to enter God's presence—a contrast with the old order, which allowed only the high priest to enter the inner chamber once a year (9:6–7; Lane; Vanhoye, *Old Testament,* 222–23; Scholer, *Proleptic,* 126). Subjectively, this gives the listeners "confidence" (NIV; NRSV; NAB2). Boldness involves both internal renewal (10:22) and the external firmness that comes from it (10:24–25). See NOTE on 3:6.

for an entryway into the sanctuary. "Entryway" (*eisodon*) can be either an act of entering (1 Thess 1:9; Acts 13:24) or a means of access (2 Pet 1:11), but the connection with "way" (*hodos*) in Heb 10:20 suggests taking it in the latter sense. The entryway into the sanctuary was open to those who were clean (Philo, *Special Laws* 1.261; Josephus, *Ant.* 19.332). The "sanctuary" is the inner chamber where God is encountered (NOTE on 8:2). Entering a sanctuary (cf. 6:19–20; 9:12, 24–25) and entering God's "rest" (cf. 3:11–4:11) both point to the outcome of Christian hope.

by the blood of Jesus. See §23 COMMENT *a.*

327On Greek and Roman sacrifices see M. H. Jameson, "Sacrifice and Ritual: Greece," *CAM* 2.959–79; J. A. North, "Sacrifice and Ritual: Rome," *CAM* 2.981–86; *RomCiv* 2.515–20.

10:20. *a new and living way.* Like the covenant he inaugurated, the way that Christ opened is "new," providing unprecedented access to God (NOTE on 9:8). The imagery recalls how priests entered the Tabernacle (9:6–7). Some also detect heroic connotations, since similar imagery was used for a leader who hurled himself into thick fighting in order that "he might open up a new path to victory along the track of his own lifeblood" (Lucius Annaeus Florus, *Epitome* 1.14.3; Attridge, *Epistle*, 285 n. 26). On heroic imagery see NOTES and COMMENT on 2:14–15; 6:19–20. The spatial quality of the "way" suggests associations from the practice of making new roads. Inscriptions placed along roads would read, "The Emperor Caesar Nerva Trajan Augustus Germanicus Dacicus, son of the deified Nerva, high priest . . . paved a new road from the border of Syria to the Red Sea." Similarly, the emperor and high priest Hadrian opened "the New Hadrian Way" (*RomCiv* 2.72–75; *TLNT* 1.397). An ordinary road is not "living," but the way mentioned by Hebrews is opened by the living Christ (7:8, 25), and it leads to the living God (3:12; 9:14; 10:31; 12:22; cf. Pelser, "Translation").

that he dedicated for us. The verb *enkainizein* is used for the covenant (9:18) and for the way that Christ established. The term includes the word *kainos* ("new"), which is used for the covenant (8:8, 13; 9:15). Some associations come from Israel's sacral tradition, since the sanctuary and items for priestly service were dedicated for use (NOTE on 9:18). In Roman practice, dedicatory inscriptions along roads often honored the emperor (see the previous NOTE), who was also high priest, enabling the term "dedicate" to encompass the royal and priestly aspects of Christ's work.

through the curtain, that is, [*by means*] *of his flesh.* In Israel's sanctuaries the curtain separated the forecourt from the inner chamber (NOTES on 6:19 and 9:3). Hebrews' imagery is odd and some consider it to be a secondary gloss (Héring; Buchanan; Schenke, "Erwägungen," 426–27). For centuries it was interpreted in terms of the two natures of Christ, so that flesh was the veil of Christ's divinity (Chrysostom; Erasmus, *Paraphase*; Calvin). Some argue that "through his flesh" refers to the way, not the curtain: "the new and living way . . . the way of his flesh" (REB; Andriessen and Lenglet, "Quelques," 214; Hofius, *Vorhang*, 81; MacRae, "Heavenly Temple," 188). Nevertheless, word order and the parallel use of the genitive case indicate that "flesh" corresponds to "curtain." This fits the appositional use of "that is" in 2:14; 7:5; 9:11; 13:15.

The preposition "through" (*dia*) governs both "curtain" and "flesh," which are in the genitive case. Many take *dia* in a consistently local sense, so that Christ passed through his flesh to enter heaven (cf. 1 Cor 15:50; Braun). Alternatively, *dia* may function both locally and instrumentally (Spicq; N. H. Young, "τοῦτ'"; H.-F. Weiss). On the level of Levitical practice, the priest passes "through" the curtain, but on the level of Christ's work, Jesus secured access to God's presence "by means of" his flesh. The parallels between 10:19 and 20 are helpful (Jeremias, "τοῦτ'"):

10:19	for an entryway	10:20	a new and living way
	into the sanctuary		through the curtain, that is
	by the blood of Jesus		through his flesh

The parallel between "the blood of Jesus" and "his flesh" suggests that both should be taken instrumentally. To indicate this we can translate: "through the curtain, that is, [by means] of his flesh" (Lane; Ellingworth; Attridge; Peterson, *Hebrews*, 154). "Flesh," like "body" (10:5, 10), can be taken positively as the means by which Jesus accomplishes salvation (Laub, *Bekenntnis*, 180–85; H.-F. Weiss; Isaacs, *Sacred*, 57; Lindars, *Theology*, 103; Dunnill, *Covenant*, 234).

Some take "flesh" more negatively. Like the curtain that blocks the way into the holy of holies, they note that flesh confines one to the realm of fear, death, and impurity (2:14–15; 5:7–8; 9:10, 13) and that salvation lies beyond the curtain of flesh (6:19–20; Grässer; Braun). This view has some affinities with Gnostic sources (*Hyp. Arch.* 94.9–10; *Gos. Phil.* 84.23–85.10), but the Gnostic texts are later than Hebrews and some show dependence upon the NT (*Treat. Seth* 58.24–28). Similarities between Hebrews and these texts can better be ascribed to a shared familiarity with Jewish traditions (Josephus, *Ant.* 3.123, 181–83; Hofius, *Vorhang*, 28–48; Wilson, *Hebrews* 188–89). The most significant point is that the parallel between "blood" (Heb 10:19c) and "flesh" (10:20c) suggests that Christ's flesh is not solely negative, but that his "flesh" and "body" (10:5, 10) play a positive role in redemption (Attridge).

10:21. *and a great priest over the house of God.* On "great priest" see NOTE on 4:14. The "house of God" is the people of God, including the listeners (NOTE on 3:6).

10:22. *let us approach.* See NOTE on 4:16.

with a true heart. It is fitting that one who draws near to the "true tent" where Christ ministers (8:2; 9:24) should come with a "true heart," not an "evil, unbelieving heart" (3:12). A heart is true when it has been cleansed by God, that is, when faith emerges.

with full assurance of faith. Like "boldness" (10:19), "full assurance" includes a personal disposition and its external expression. Forms of the word connote zeal (6:11), bold preaching (1 Thess 1:5; Ign. *Magn.* 8:2; *1 Clem.* 42:3), and Abraham's confidence that God would keep his promises even when appearances contradicted them (Rom 4:21; cf. *TLNT* 3.120–23). Faith was mentioned occasionally in the first part of Hebrews (4:2; 6:1, 12) but not in 7:1–10:18. Its mention here anticipates the centrality of faith in the next series of arguments (11:1–12:27).

with our hearts sprinkled clean from an evil conscience. The new covenant was to change human hearts (8:10; 10:16), which included the conscience (NOTE on 9:9). Sprinkling involved only the flesh under the old covenant (Exod 24:8; Heb 9:13, 19). But sin manifests unfaithfulness (3:12), and under the new covenant the conscience is "sprinkled" clean when faith is evoked (NOTE on 9:14). A clean heart is what God desires (Ps 51:10; 1 Tim 1:5, 19).

and our body washed with pure water. "Pure water" (Num 5:17; Philo, *Moses* 2.143; *Special Laws* 3.58) and "washing" were used for purification (Lev 16:4; cf. 14:9; 15:11 etc.). Some make a general connection between Christ's work and fulfillment of Ezek 36:25–26: "I will sprinkle clean water upon you, and you shall be clean from all your uncleannesses," and "a new heart I will give you, and a new spirit I will put within you" (Calvin; Rissi, *Theologie*, 99–100; Bénétreau; Scholer, *Proleptic*, 130–31). Most, however, link Heb 10:22 to baptism (Theodoret; Erasmus, *Paraphrase*; Attridge; F. F. Bruce; Kistemaker; Lane; H.-F. Weiss; Vanhoye, *Old Testament*, 228; Hartman, *Into the Name*, 123–26). The text refers to a physical washing (cf. Tit 3:5; Eph 5:26) and cleansing the conscience (1 Pet 3:21). Just as faith and baptism were connected in Heb 6:1–2, the "confession" and baptismal cleansing are associated in 10:22–23. See COMMENT *a* below and §13 COMMENT *b*.

10:23. *Let us hold fast the confession of hope.* See pp. 126–27.

without wavering. The adjective is in the accusative case. Most read it adverbially, so that it describes the unwavering manner in which one holds the confession (NIV; NRSV; NAB2; REB; NJB; 4 Macc 6:7; cf. 17:3; Philo, *Heir* 95; *Rewards* 30). Others propose that "unwavering" refers to the firmness of the confession itself (Attridge; Braun; Grässer; H.-F. Weiss; cf. Philo, *Special Laws* 2.2). Since "the confession" has a definite article, whereas "unwavering" does not, the adverbial sense is preferable. See Williamson, *Philo* 31–36; *TLNT* 1.59.

for he who has promised is faithful. That God is "faithful" is well-attested (Deut 7:9; 32:4; Ps 145:13; 1 Cor 1:9; 10:13; 2 Cor 1:18; 1 Thess 5:24; 2 Thess 3:3; 1 John 1:9). God shows his faithfulness in granting through Christ's sacrifice the mercy that was promised in the new covenant. Although some of God's promises are as yet unfulfilled—like the hope of entering God's rest (Heb 4:1–11)—the promises that have been fulfilled offer assurance that God will keep the other promises as well. God's faithfulness is underscored in 11:11. See pp. 110–112.

10:24. *and let us consider how to provoke one another.* To "consider" Jesus (3:1) and other people (10:24) encompasses the two major directions of Christian life. The word "provoke" could be used positively for stimulating good will (Josephus, *Ant.* 16.125; Xenophon, *Memorabilia* 3.3.13; Isocrates, *To Demonicus* 46). Often, however, the term had negative connotations, as in provoking someone to anger (Deut 29:28 [29:27 LXX]; Jer 32:37 [39:37 LXX]). Therefore, P46 says that listeners are to keep "from provoking" one another (cf. Acts 15:39). Hebrews stimulates thought by putting a word with negative connotations to positive use.

to love and good works. Love is not simply an emotion, but entails care for others (6:10), including strangers and the afflicted (13:1–3; 13:16). Love is congruent with righteousness (1:9) and can be expressed in parental instruction (12:6). Good works of love are the opposite of the "dead works" of sin (6:1; 9:14). According to Hebrews, they express the saving work of Christ in the believers' actions.

10:25. *not abandoning.* In one sense "abandoning" the Christian assembly meant no longer attending its gatherings. Yet the word "abandon" also connotes leaving something vulnerable to destructive forces such as poverty (cf. 13:5), death (Matt 27:46; Mark 15:34; Acts 2:27), or other difficulties (2 Cor 4:9; 2 Tim 4:10, 16). By identifying nonattendance as "abandonment," the author points to the urgency of the listeners' remaining steadfast in their commitment to the community.

our gathering. Some sources call a Christian assembly a *synagogē* (Jas 2:2; Ign. *Trall.* 3; Ign. *Pol.* 4:2; Herm. *Man.* 11.9, 13, 14), but the word used here (*episynagogē*) is unusual:

(**a**) Local connotations. The prefix *epi* gives the word a local sense: coming together "at" a given location (1 Cor 11:20; 14:23). The related verb *episynagein* sometimes meant gathering at a place (Mark 1:33; Luke 12:1). If the "house of God" (Heb 10:21) is the whole community, the "gathering" would be an assembly in a particular location. Early Christians generally gathered in someone's home (Acts 18:7; Rom 16:5, 23; Phlm 2), and their assemblies were probably not large (see pp. 73–74).

(**b**) Eschatological connotations. Both the noun (2 Macc 2:7; 2 Thess 2:1) and the verb (Matt 23:37; 24:31; Mark 13:27; Luke 13:34) were used for the eschatological ingathering of Israel. Since the context refers to the coming Day of the Lord and since the listeners understood that they already shared in the powers of the age to come (Heb 6:5), they may have understood their gathering to anticipate the final ingathering of God's people. The assembly is the earthly counterpart to the heavenly "congregation" (*ekklēsia*) of God's people (12:23; cf. 2:12).

(**c**) Social connotations. The word *synagogē* often designated Jewish gatherings, and calling a Christian gathering an *episynagogē* may reflect the church's continuity with Israel's heritage. The difference between the two words also suggests that Christian gatherings were distinct from gatherings of Jews who did not profess faith in Jesus. On the similarities and differences see pp. 76–77. On the term see W. Schrage, *TDNT* 7.841–43; *TLNT* 2.63–64. On synagogues see Schürer, *History*, 2.423–54. On Christian community life see pp. 73–76.

as is the custom of some. "Custom" often referred in a positive sense to "customs" that were specified by Law (Acts 6:14; 15:1; 21:21; 26:3; 28:17), such as selecting priests by lot (Luke 1:9), making a pilgrimage (Luke 2:42), and following certain burial procedures (John 19:40). Jesus had a personal "custom" of prayer (Luke 22:39). Hebrews gives "custom" a peculiar turn, so that it speaks of a pattern of unfaithfulness rather than piety. See *TLNT* 1.405–11.

but exhorting [one another], and this all the more. Listeners were to exhort each other (3:13), just as the author exhorted them (13:22). In a positive sense exhortation means encouraging people to persevere, knowing that God is faithful. In a more negative sense exhortation warns about the consequences of disobedience, especially given the coming "Day" of judgment.

as you see the Day drawing near. The "Day" or "Day of the Lord" connotes divine presence and judgment (Amos 5:20; cf. Isa 2:12; Joel 1:15; Zeph 1:14–18; Zech 14:1). Among early Christians it was called "the day" (1 Thess 5:4; 1 Cor 3:13), the day of God (2 Pet 3:12; Rev 16:14), the day of the Lord (1 Cor 1:8; 5:5; 2 Cor 1:14; 1 Thess 5:2; 2 Thess 2:2; 2 Pet 3:10), the day of judgment (2 Pet 2:9; 1 John 4:17; Jude 6), and the day of wrath (Rom 2:5).

COMMENT[328]

Bold declarations that Jesus has entered the inner region behind the curtain of the sanctuary introduced the central section of Hebrews (6:19–20).[329] Returning to this imagery at the conclusion of the section, the author invites listeners to envision a new way stretching through the curtain. His language enables listeners to see in their mind's eye what would otherwise be hidden (cf. 11:1), "turning hearing into sight" (Longinus, *On the Sublime* 26.2). Rhetorically, 10:19–25 is a *peroration* to the second cycle of arguments.[330] A peroration is a statement that concludes a section of a speech. Since perorations often were designed to affect listeners at the emotional level, the author of Hebrews now speaks encouragingly of boldness and more ominously of the Day of the Lord. Perorations could also help to refresh listeners' memories by drawing together ideas from previous arguments so that even "though the facts may have made little impression" in detail, "their cumulative effect is considerable" (Quintilian, *Inst.* 6.1.1). The author has said that previously the way into God's presence was closed (9:8) and the conscience was not cleansed (9:9), even though the first covenant was dedicated (9:18) and people sprinkled their flesh (9:13, 19). Now Christ has dedicated a new and living way (10:19–20), sprinkling not only the body but the conscience (10:22).

Stylistically, 10:19–25 is a single complex sentence or period that summarizes the ideas of the section (*Rhet. ad Her.* 4.19 §27). A period was to exhibit symmetry in thought (p. 93). Thus at the beginning of 10:19–25 the author urges listeners to draw near to God, and at the end he warns that the Day of God is drawing near to them. Subtle turns of language stimulate the imagination. For example, "custom" ordinarily meant attending to practices, often of a religious sort, but here it refers to the opposite, namely, the failure to attend community gatherings. Similarly, "provoking" was often used negatively for words and actions that were destructive to community life, but here it is used positively for stirring new life within the community.

Structurally, the paragraph can be divided into two parts: (**a**) The first part (10:19–22) directs attention to the heavenly sanctuary. Listeners are enjoined to enter it, anticipating the idea of faith as a journey in Heb 11–12. (**b**) The second part (10:23–25) centers on the counterpart to the heavenly sanctuary, namely, the earthly community, where people encourage one another and carry out love and good works. Listeners are called to hold fast to their faith commitment, a call

---

[328]On 10:19–25 see Andriessen and Lenglet, "Quelques"; Glombitza, "Erwägungen"; Hofius, "Inkarnation"; idem, *Vorhang*, 73–84; Laub, *Bekenntnis*, 179–85; Leithart, "Womb"; Pelser, "Translation"; Peterson, *Hebrews*, 153–56; Thüsing, "Lasst"; Vanhoye, *Old Testament*, 222–38; N. H. Young, "τοῦτ'."

[329]Because of similarities in language, some argue that 4:14–16 and 10:19–25 mark the beginning and ending of the central section of Hebrews (Michel; Nauck, "Aufbau"). Others propose that 4:14–16 and 10:19–25 introduce new sections with exhortations (H.-F. Weiss; cf. Grässer). However, 4:14–16 and 10:19–25 are best taken as coming near the end of major sections of argument and before the transitional digressions (5:10–6:20; 10:26–39). See §7 COMMENT and §16 COMMENT.

[330]Quintilian, *Inst.* 6.1.1, 54–55; Lausberg, *Handbook* §§431–42; H.-F. Weiss, *Brief*, 519.

that is reinforced by the memory of past perseverance in 10:32–34. Together, the exhortations to move ahead and to hold fast shape Christian life.

a. Entering the Heavenly Sanctuary (10:19–22)

Listeners have boldness (10:19a) before God because Christ's self-sacrifice purifies (9:14), sanctifies (10:10), and provides forgiveness of sins (10:18). Given all of this, one might have expected the author to invite listeners simply to give thanks for what Christ obtained through his blood (10:19c). Instead, he encourages them to do what was otherwise unthinkable by calling them to enter the sanctuary's inner chamber (10:19b). Under the old covenant, ordinary worshipers were liable to death if they entered the inner chamber (Num 4:20; 17:13), but under the new covenant they find the way into the sanctuary to be living and life-giving (Heb 10:20a). After Christ's sacrifice no more sin offerings are needed (10:18), so that the inner chamber can be put to new use.

Dedication of a new and living way is a suggestive way to speak about what Christ has done (10:20a).[331] Roadways were often laid at imperial expense, their pavement presenting a vision of smoothness and beauty (Plutarch, *Caius Gracchus* 7). New ways commonly were dedicated by inscriptions that bore the name of the emperor, who was both ruler and high priest (NOTE on 10:20).[332] Now Hebrews announces that Christ—God's royal Son and great high priest—has dedicated a new way, not for himself, but "for us." By fusing this imagery with allusions to the Tabernacle, the author depicts a way that stretches, not through Mediterranean valleys, but through the sanctuary curtain, a way whose destination is, not an earthly city, but God's heavenly dwelling.

Christ opened the way by means of his flesh. Although peculiar (NOTE on 10:20), this mention of "flesh" is an instance of metonymy that calls Jesus' suffering to mind. "Just as the high priest entered the Holy of Holies through the veil, so we, if we wish to enter the sanctuary of glory, must enter through the flesh of Christ. . . . For faith about the deity is insufficient unless there is also faith about the incarnation" (Aquinas, *Ad Heb.* §502). The Son of God shared human blood and flesh (2:14) in order to deliver human beings from the fear of death. In "the days of his flesh" (5:7) he prayed with loud cries and tears, before becoming a source of eternal salvation. Christ offered the body that God prepared for him in order that he might prepare others to enter God's presence (10:5, 10).[333]

---

[331]On fusing biblical and Greco-Roman imagery see NOTES and COMMENT on the imagery in 6:19–20, on oaths (6:13–18), covenants and testaments (9:16–17), and the inclusion of Israel's ancestors among those in a stadium who watch the race of faith (12:1–3).

[332]On Roman road building see Casson, *Travel*, 63–75; *CAM* 1.354, 2.759–61.

[333]Hofius, "Inkarnation." Hebrews does not work with the distinction between the negative use of "flesh" (*sarx*) and the positive use of "body" (*sōma*) that is evident in some of Paul's writings (e.g., "flesh" in Gal 5:13–26 and "body" in 1 Cor 6:19–20; see Dunn, *Theology*, 62–73). Some detect allusions to the Lord's Supper in Heb 10:19–20, which would complement the allusion to baptism in 10:22 (Glombitza, "Erwägungen," 138; Thüsing, "Lasst"; Vanhoye, *Old Testament*, 228–32; Swetnam, "Christology," 89–93; Pfitzner). This seems unlikely, however. On the Lord's Supper in Hebrews see pp. 127–29.

Confessing that we have a great priest (10:21) is important theologically, because "it is a fearful thing to fall into the hands of the living God" (10:31; cf. 12:29; 13:4). Instead of downplaying the terrifying aspects of God, Hebrews announces that Christ provides the atonement, cleansing, and sanctification that people need to approach God rightly (cf. 4:14–16). Socially, Jews, Greeks, and Romans had traditions concerning high priesthood. Rather than rejecting the importance of a high priest, Hebrews declares that in Christ we have a great priest (10:21), thereby giving the Christian community a distinctive focus for its identity. Hebrews presents Christ's high priesthood in terms of the OT, maintaining some continuity with Israel's tradition, while developing the tradition in a distinctive way (§12 COMMENT *a*). Identifying the community with "the house of God" (10:21) also offers listeners the dignity of belonging to God's own household in a society dominated by prestigious households (§9 COMMENT *c*).

The author invites listeners to approach God now through prayer (10:22ab), in a manner as vivid as a priest entering a sanctuary (NOTES and COMMENT on 4:16). His invitation also anticipates that listeners will ultimately approach God by coming to everlasting life in God's heavenly city, a theme that is developed in the next series of arguments, where faith is depicted as a journey to the heavenly Jerusalem (11:1–12:27). The boldness needed to approach God comes from a heart "sprinkled clean from an evil conscience" (10:22c).[334] God searches the human frame (Heb 4:12–13), and the conscience discloses to a person the sin that is already known to God (Rom 2:15; Seneca, *Ep.* 43.5). An evil conscience could turn one away from God in the hope of avoiding judgment (John 3:19–21), although this is futile (Ps 139:11–12; Sir 16:17). The alternative is to be cleansed by Christ, who purges the conscience by evoking faith (Heb 9:14).

Along with a clean conscience, the listeners have their bodies washed with pure water (10:22d) through baptism. Although Hebrews has emphasized internal cleansing, the author assumes that a physical washing is also important. Baptism is associated with repentance (6:1–2) since the conscience is not cleansed without turning from sin (10:22c). Hebrews links baptismal washing to faith (10:22b) without saying whether baptism fosters faith or whether baptism is the external expression of faith. Receiving the Spirit was probably associated with baptism, but Hebrews does not indicate whether the Spirit was understood to come before, during, or after baptism through the laying on of hands (6:1–4; see §13 COMMENT *b*). Socially, baptism—like verbal confession (10:23a)—visibly identified a person with a community whose members were called to support each other in the face of opposition and suffering (10:32–34; 13:3).

b. Firmness in the Earthly Assembly (10:23–25)

The first part of the paragraph directed attention to the heavenly sanctuary, but the second part turns to life in the earthly community, where listeners are to hold

---

[334]On the connection between boldness and a clear conscience see Philo, *Heir* 6–7; *Special Laws* 1.203; Josephus, *Ant.* 2.52.

fast to their confession (10:23a). Internally, holding fast to the confession means believing what God has promised. Although the confession probably centered on Jesus as Son of God (pp. 126–27), the mention of hope (10:23a) suggests that listeners also anticipated sharing in the inheritance that already belongs to the Son (1:2, 14). This hope was challenged by opposition from others in society (10:32–34; 13:13), but Hebrews has argued that since God brought Christ out of humiliation to glory, Christ's followers can be confident that God will also bring them to glory (2:10). Externally, holding fast to the confession means uttering it with the lips (13:15), thereby publicly identifying a person with Christ and his community. Since a confession commonly summarized a group's convictions, it served as a point of unity in the face of the pressures that were eroding solidarity (10:25).

Theologically, the contradiction between the listeners' hope and their experience of reproach meant that they could only be expected to hold on to the confession when convinced that the God who promised is faithful (10:23b).[335] Reminders that God kept his promise to raise up a priest like Melchizedek (7:20–22) and to make a new covenant (9:15) give assurance that he will be faithful to all his promises (6:13–20; 13:5). His faithfulness is the basis for human faith.

Socially, faith is expressed through love and good works (10:24). Unlike other NT writings, Hebrews does not state that love is the essence of the Law (Matt 22:36–40 par.; Rom 13:9; Gal 5:14; Jas 2:8) or develop it as the central point of Christian discipleship (John 13:34; 1 John 3:16; 4:19; Gal 2:20; Hays, *Moral*, 220). Nevertheless, "love" is an appropriate way to speak about life that is based on what one receives through Christ (Heb 4:16; 10:17–18). If Christ sacrificed himself for others, those who share what they have make a sacrifice that is pleasing to God (13:16). Identifying with the afflicted as Christ did is a form of love (2:10–18; 13:1–3). The call to show love calls for resistance to tendencies to abandon the Christian assembly in the face of reproach from outsiders (10:25a). Few people can maintain their beliefs, values, and hopes without social reinforcement, for their ties are mutual: Social bonds reinforce belief just as expressions of belief strengthen social bonds. Both personal commitment and community support are needed for people to maintain their convictions and manner of life within a larger society that does not share their views (see pp. 67–72).

At the beginning of this paragraph, the author urged listeners to draw near to God, and at its conclusion he reminds them that the Day—with its connotations of divine judgment—is drawing near to them (10:25). In a positive sense the idea that the Day of the Lord is coming means that the present time of reproach will not continue indefinitely, for Christ will bring salvation (9:28). In a more ominous sense, however, the Day brings a judgment from which not even God's

---

[335]Christians must approach with faith because they cannot see their priest, sanctuary, or altar. In earthly things one trusts the senses, but with respect to the promises one trusts the Spirit (Chrysostom; cf. Käsemann, *Wandering*, 17–37; Isaacs, *Sacred*, 219).

people are exempt (10:26–31). Listeners had already received instruction about the judgment (6:1–2) and were urged to exhort one another "as long as it is called *today*" in order that they not be hardened by sin (3:13). The following paragraph will intensify the severity of the warning (10:26–31) before giving listeners renewed encouragement to persevere in faith and hope.

27. Day of the Lord (10:26–31)

10 26For if we persist in sinning willfully after receiving knowledge of the truth,
there no longer remains a sacrifice for sins, 27but, shall we say, a terrifying
prospect of judgment and fiery zeal that is coming to consume those who stand
in opposition. 28Anyone who abrogates the Law of Moses dies without pity on the
basis of two or three witnesses. 29How much more severe a punishment do you
suppose a person deserves who trampled upon the Son of God and considered
profane the blood of the covenant by which he was sanctified, and was insolent
toward the Spirit of grace? 30For we know the one who said, *Mine is the*
vengeance, I will repay. And again, *The Lord will judge his people*. 31It is terrifying to fall into the hands of the living God.

NOTES

10:26. *For if we persist in sinning*. The present tense suggests continued violation of God's will. Here the primary sin is rejection of Christ, the covenant, and the Spirit (10:29; cf. 3:12–19).

willfully. A distinction between willful and involuntary or unwitting sins was common in Jewish (Lev 4:1–5:13; Num 15:22–31; 2 Macc 14:3; Philo, *Alleg. Interp*. 3.141; *Cherubim* 75; Josephus, *Ag. Ap*. 1.3) and Greek sources (Aristotle, *Nic. Ethics* 3.1.10 1110B; Demosthenes, *Orations* 21.42; 25.16; Plato, *Laws* 860E–861A; Ps.-Aristotle, *Rhet. ad Alex*. 1427a. 31–35). Sacrifices were offered for sins of ignorance (NOTE on Heb 5:2), but willful sin meant expulsion from the community (Num 15:30–31) and inexorable judgment (*Pss. Sol*. 13:5–12; Philo, *Posterity* 10–11; *Unchangeable* 48). Some noted that sacrifices on the Day of Atonement were for "all their sins" (Lev 16:16), both voluntary and involuntary (Philo, *Special Laws* 1.234–38; 2.196; *Posterity* 48), but others warned that persistent sinners would not benefit from the Day of Atonement (*m. Yoma* 8:9). The Dead Sea sect disciplined deliberate sinners, but did not always expel them (1QS VI, 24–VII, 25). Hebrews assumes that Christ's death provides atonement for all sins (Löhr, *Umkehr*, 22–68), but uses the language of willful sin to show the consequences of rejecting the grace he offers.

after receiving knowledge of the truth. This refers to conversion or "enlightenment" (NOTE on 6:4). The Christian message was often called "the truth" (Gal 5:7; 2 Thess 2:12; 1 Pet 1:22; Jas 3:14; 5:19; cf. Eph 1:13; 2 Tim 2:15). By speaking of reception of "knowlege" the author precludes the idea that falling away is a sin of ignorance.

there no longer remains a sacrifice for sins. If forgiveness of sins is definitively given in Christ (10:18), those who spurn Christ's offering have no other options (Calvin; Lane).

10:27. *but, shall we say, a terrifying prospect of judgment.* "Shall we say" (*tis*) suggests restraint, but it actually intensifies the warning (BAGD, 820 [2bβ]). If it requires restraint to call God's judgment "terrifying," then the judgment must be terrible indeed (cf. 10:31; 12:27).

and fiery zeal. God was zealous in that he refused to allow Israel to worship other gods (Exod 20:5; 34:14; Deut 5:9; 6:15). God is a consuming fire (Heb 12:29) and fire implies judgment (6:7–8). The image was traditional: "The Lord your God is a consuming fire, a zealous God" (Deut 4:24). "In the fire of his zealous wrath, all the earth shall be consumed" (Zeph 1:18; cf. 3:8; Ezek 38:19; Pss 11:6; 21:9; 79:5; Jer 4:4; Ezek 22:21; Matt 3:12; 1 Cor 3:13; Rev 20:9; 1QS II, 15; 1QH VI, 18–19; 1QpHab X, 6, 15).

that is coming to consume those who stand in opposition. Those opposed to God are the enemies that God is subjecting to Christ (Ps 110:1; Heb 10:13). The language recalls Isa 26:11: "Let them see your zeal for your people. . . . Let the fire for your adversaries consume them."

10:28. *Anyone who abrogates the Law of Moses.* "Abrogating" the Law means utterly disregarding it (Isa 24:16 LXX; Ezek 22:26 LXX; Mark 7:9). God "abrogated" Levitical statutes by appointing Christ to be high priest (NOTE on 7:18), yet God did not appoint Christ to promote sin, but to "abolish" sin through his sacrifice (Heb 9:26). See pp. 114–15 on the Law.

dies without pity. This penalty was prescribed for idolatry (Deut 13:8) and murder (19:13). Other offenses also had penalties that were to be given "without pity" (19:21; 25:12).

on the basis of two or three witnesses. The Law stipulated that when someone transgresses the covenant and serves other gods, "you shall stone that man or woman to death. On the evidence of two or three witnesses the death sentence shall be executed" (Deut 17:2–6; cf. 19:15; Num 35:30; Matt 18:16; 2 Cor 13:1; 1 Tim 5:19). Hebrews applies the principle to those who reject the covenant established by Christ (Heb 10:29).

10:29. *How much more severe a punishment.* The Greek word *timōria* is related to the term for honor (*timē*). "The reason for punishment exists when the dignity and prestige of the one who is sinned against must be maintained, lest the omission of the punishment bring him into contempt and diminish the esteem in which he is held" (Aulus Gellius, *Attic Nights* 7.14.2–4; deSilva, *Despising*, 263). Moses is worthy of honor, but Jesus is worthy of greater glory (3:1–6); therefore, showing contempt for the Son's honor warrants greater punishment.

do you suppose a person deserves. Posing a question can be rhetorically powerful, for the verdict is supplied by the listeners themselves (cf. Philo, *Flight* 84; *Special Laws* 2.255).

who trampled upon the Son of God. "Trample" is a vivid metaphor for showing contempt (Mic 7:10; cf. Isa 26:6; Pss 56:2–3; Dan 8:10; Matt 5:13; 7:6). God promised to put all things under Christ's feet (Ps 110:1; NOTE on Heb 1:13), but Christ's adversaries seek to put Christ under their feet in a show of contempt (NOTE and COMMENT on 6:6).

and considered profane the blood of the covenant by which he was sanctified. The "profane" is the opposite of the sacred and is not to be brought into the presence of God (pp. 119–21). The "blood of the covenant" does not refer to the Sinai covenant (Exod 24:8), but to the blood of Jesus by which the new covenant was established (NOTE on Heb 9:20).

and was insolent. Enybrizein indicates a manifestation of *hybris*, the insolence that often results in a person's demise. The emphasis is not on the Spirit becoming "outraged" (NRSV) but on the sinner's *hybris* or outrageous behavior (NIV; NAB2; NJB; REB). *Hybris* described those who asserted themselves against the divine will (1 Macc 3:20; 2 Macc 8:17; 3 Macc 6:12). The rightness of punishing such a person was widely recognized. Both Jews and Greeks understood that *hybris* would lead to the offender's own downfall (Aeschylus, *Persians* 808; cf. Thucydides, *Peloponnesian War* 3.39.4–5; Xenophon, *Anabasis* 3.1.21; Prov 16:18; cf. Isa 13:11). See G. Bertram, *TDNT* 8.295–307.

toward the Spirit of grace. Christ offered himself through the eternal Spirit (9:14), and the listeners received the Holy Spirit through the proclamation of the message of Christ (2:4; 3:7; 6:4; 9:8; 10:15). Contrasting divine grace and human insolence shows that judgment does not manifest divine harshness, but human arrogance.

10:30. *For we know the one who said.* This indirect way of speaking about God assumes that listeners know that God will exact vengeance, which undercuts any plea of ignorance, making a refusal to heed the message all the more severe.

Mine is the vengeance, I will repay. This quotation of Deut 32:35 does not correspond exactly to the MT ("Mine is the vengeance and recompense") or to the LXX ("In a day of vengeance I will repay"). This form appears in the targums and Rom 12:19, which suggests that it circulated in an alternative text type or orally as a proverbial statement. Deuteronomy speaks of God's vengeance on Israel's enemies, but Hebrews warns about God judging his own people. The idea of repayment (cf. Heb 2:2; 10:35; 11:6, 26) does not eliminate hope of divine mercy, but affirms that God's judgment is not capricious, since it falls on sinners, not the righteous.

And again, The Lord will judge his people. These words come from OT contexts (Deut 32:36; Ps 135:14 [134:14 LXX]) that speak of God providing judgment or vindication for his people against their enemies. Hebrews, however, speaks of God judging the sin of his own people—an idea that was common in the OT (e.g., Exod 34:7; Num 14:18; Ps 99:8).

10:31. *It is terrifying.* Cf. 10:27; 12:21. God is "the great, the mighty, and the terrible" (Deut 10:17); he "is terrible, a great king over all the earth" (Ps 47:2), one "to be feared above all gods" (Ps 96:4; cf. Neh 4:14; Sir 43:29). Although *phoberos* could have the more positive sense of "awesome" (Swetnam, "Hebrews 10, 30–31"), this meaning seems unlikely here.

to fall into the hands of the living God. "Falling into the hands" means coming under someone's power, often with negative consequences (Judg 15:18; Luke

10:36). It was sometimes thought better to fall into the hands of God, who was merciful, than to be at the mercy of human beings (2 Sam 24:14; Sir 2:18), but one could fall into the hands of God for judgment (Deut 32:39; 2 Macc 6:26; cf. 7:31; Acts 13:11; *TLNT* 2.1–2). Paradoxically, "the living God" poses a threat of destruction (NOTE on 3:12; cf. 12:29). His "living" word relentlessly searches every human being (NOTES on 4:12–13).

COMMENT[336]

Mention of the Day of the Lord in 10:25 concludes the second series of arguments[337] and leads into a digression on related themes.[338] The digression provides a transition between portions of the speech much as modulations in a musical composition provide a transition between sections that are written in different keys and tempos. The arguments that preceded the digression (7:1–10:25) were written in a didactic style and focused on Jesus' priesthood, sacrifice, and new covenant. The arguments that follow it (11:1–12:24) make virtually no mention of cultic matters, but are written in a more hortatory fashion, recalling examples of heroic faith and drawing on images of the stadium and pilgrimage to Mt. Zion. The digression itself (10:26–39) warns of future judgment, recalls the community's past faithfulness, and anticipates the rewarding of the faithful and destruction of the faithless that will come with the return of Christ. Its contents correspond to those of other transitional digressions (p. 84).

Faith was mentioned occasionally in the first part of Hebrews (*pistis*, 4:2; 6:1, 12; *pistos*, 2:17; 3:2, 5), but the author does not refer to it in the second series of arguments until the concluding sentence. There he calls listeners to exhibit faith (10:22) and assures them that God is faithful (10:23). Following rhetorical convention (Cicero, *De oratore* 2.77 §§311–12; 3.53 §203), the author signals a return to his main arguments by taking up the topic of faith, which was introduced just before the digression began. Using words from Hab 2:3–4, he concludes his digression by stating that the righteous "live by faith" and exhorting listeners to persevere in the kind of faith that will be the topic of the third and final series of arguments (10:38–39).

Rhetorically, a digression prepares listeners to give full attention to the arguments that follow. Speakers were aware that listeners' minds typically wandered

---

[336]On 10:26–31 see deSilva, "Exchanging"; Löhr, *Umkehr*, 110–14; McCullough, "Impossibility"; Mugridge, "Warnings"; Oberholtzer, "Warning," 410–19; Rice, "Apostasy"; Schröger, *Verfasser*, 179–81; Swetnam, "Hebrews 10,30–31"; Toussaint, "Eschatology"; Weeks, "Admonition."

[337]Many interpreters identify 10:18 as the conclusion of the previous series of arguments and treat 10:19–39 as a block of hortatory material (e.g., Vanhoye, *La structure*, 173–81; Bénétreau; Casalini; Ellingworth; Grässer; Lane; H.-F. Weiss). Hegermann (*Brief*) and Rose (*Wolke*) make a major break after 10:31. Including the exhortation to enter the sanctuary (10:19–25) with the arguments that preceded it and treating 10:26–39 as a transition (cf. Attridge) keep the author's encouragements with their relevant topics. See §16 COMMENT.

[338]On digressions see Quintilian, *Inst.* 4.3.1–17; 9.1.28; cf. Cicero, *De inventione rhetorica* 1.51 §97; Lausberg, *Handbook* §§340–45. Note how the reference to what Jesus learned by his suffering (5:8–10) leads into a digression on the listeners' lack of learning in 5:11–6:3.

(§13 COMMENT). By this point, Hebrews' audience would have been listening for perhaps thirty minutes, and the author was about to begin a new series of arguments. The preceding section presented new and complex ideas, but the digression conveys almost no new information—listeners already knew about divine judgment (6:1–2; 10:26–31) and their community's history (10:32–34). Instead, the digression seeks to awaken uneasiness before a God who deals mercilessly with those who reject his grace. God's opponents are depicted starkly: they know what is right, but willfully sin; they have been sanctified by Christ's blood, but seek to defile it; God's Spirit is gracious, yet they are insolent. Listeners would presumably grant that such behaviors warrant divine wrath. Rhetorically this is *deinōsis*, or language that gives "additional force to things unjust, cruel, or hateful," so that the speaker not only brings the listener to a negative judgment on the matter, but awakens emotions that are stronger than the case might otherwise warrant (§28 COMMENT).[339]

Structurally, the digression consists of three paragraphs. The first warns of divine judgment (10:26–31), while the second and third paragraphs recall past solidarity during persecution (10:32–34) and call for perseverance in faith (10:35–39). These latter two paragraphs are taken up in §28. The present paragraph is framed by references to the "terrifying" (*phoberos*) quality of God and his judgment (10:27, 31; cf. Vanhoye, *La structure*, 178). Within the paragraph two parts can be distinguished: **(a)** The thesis is that a sacrifice no longer remains for those who know the truth but persist in willful sin (10:26–27). **(b)** Supporting arguments compare the consequences of sin under the old covenant to those under the new covenant (10:28–29), and quote biblical texts to warn that God will judge his people (10:30–31).

a. No Other Sacrifice (10:26–27)

Those addressed by Hebrews had problems that in many ways seemed minor: some neglected to meet with the community, and others needed prodding to do deeds of love (10:24–25). Given such unexceptional concerns, the warning of God's fiery judgment seems remarkably severe. Because of its uncompromising rigor, the significance of this and other texts (6:4–8; 12:16–17) has often been disputed. The issues are summarized elsewhere.[340] Here we must note that such warnings are issued to awaken listeners to the dangers of which they might not otherwise be aware, in order to avert disaster, not to drive them to despair of the grace of God.[341]

---

[339]Quintilian, *Inst.* 6.2.24; 8.3.88; cf. Lausberg, *Handbook* §257 (3c); Nissilä, *Hohepriestermotiv*, 254; H.-F. Weiss, *Brief*, 536; Grässer, *Hebräer*, 3.33.

[340]For a summary see §14 COMMENT. The introduction discusses debates concerning these texts in antiquity (pp. 20, 23, 25) and the Reformation (pp. 34–35). The threat of falling away or willful sin is sometimes identified with turning from Christianity to Judaism (Oberholtzer, "Warning," 413), although this is far from clear (see pp. 71–72).

[341]Chrysostom commented that the author "does not take away repentance, nor the propitiation through repentance, nor does he thrust away and cast down with despair the fallen. He is not thus an enemy of our salvation" (NPNF1 14.457).

The warning is given in the first person plural to "we" who sin "after receiving knowledge of the truth" (10:26b). The author of Hebrews assumes that his listeners would agree that they had received the word of God (2:3–4) in a manner that constituted enlightenment (6:4; 10:32). This did not mean that Christians no longer needed to learn (cf. 5:11–6:3) or that they were sinless—the author has encouraged them to seek mercy from God (4:16; 7:25). Rather, by speaking of knowledge of the truth, the author precludes the idea that he is speaking of sins of ignorance (NOTE on 10:26). If a person knows what is true, but does not do it, the problem lies not in knowledge, but in will—it is a case of "willful" sinning (10:26a). The conclusion that "there no longer remains a sacrifice for sins" (10:26c) draws out the implications of the idea that Christ's self-sacrifice provides complete cleansing for sins, putting an end to other sacrifices (10:18).[342] On the one hand, this was good news, since Levitical sacrifices had left the conscience defiled (9:8–10). On the other hand, if Christ's sacrifice alone is adequate, those who reject it have no other basis upon which to relate rightly to God (NOTES and COMMENT on 6:4–8).

Mercy is given through the sacrifice of Christ, but apart from it one faces "a terrifying prospect of judgment" (10:27a); Hebrews does not allow for a neutral position. Given the reality of human sin, the only question is whether one seeks mercy through Christ or whether one refuses to do so. Divine judgment manifests divine zeal (10:27b). When God made the first covenant he declared that he was "a zealous God" (Exod 20:5) who brings people into a relationship with himself that excludes the worship of other gods. God's zeal for his people means that he will redeem them from their adversaries (2 Kings 19:31; Isa 37:32; Ezek 36:5–6; Zech 1:14–16; 8:2), but God's zeal issues into wrath when his people sin willfully (Deut 29:20; 32:16; Ezek 5:13; cf. Heb 3:11). The new covenant does not eliminate the exclusiveness of the covenant, but reinforces it, for God declared, "I will be their God and they shall be my people" (8:10b). Hebrews assumes that no one can claim the mercy offered under the new covenant while rejecting a singular relationship with the God who offers it.

The prospect that God will "consume those who stand in opposition" to him (10:27c) is appealing only to those who are sure that the judgment is intended for others, not for themselves. Yet this passage is unsettling because it warns that God's people can become God's adversaries through persistent sin. Listeners do not appear to be guilty of heinous crimes, but they are susceptible to drift (2:1) and neglect (2:2; 10:25). The author's words are designed to cut through the vagueness of the listeners' situation and bring them to a zeal for God that is a fitting response to his zeal for them.

b. The Lord Will Judge His People (10:28–31)

Listeners would presumably grant that anyone who abrogates the Law of Moses "dies without pity on the basis of two or three witnesses," since this simply states

---

[342]On the superiority of Christ's sacrifice to other sacrifices see especially 9:11–14; 10:1–18 (§23 COMMENT *a–b*; §25 COMMENT *a–b*).

a principle of biblical Law (NOTE on 10:28b; see pp. 114–15). Questions might arise concerning the relevance of this principle for Christians, since the new covenant promised mercy (8:12; 10:16–18), but the author of Hebrews argues that the consequences of rejecting the new covenant are severe, for the new covenant is greater than the old (7:22; 8:6). To make the point clear, he describes adversaries of God in terms so outrageous that virtually any listener would grant that condemnation is warranted.

First, he speaks of those who "trampled upon the Son of God" (10:29b). That Jesus was the Son of God was central to the community's confession of faith (4:14; pp. 126–27). The author assumes that listeners will agree that the Son is worthy of glory (1:1–13; 3:3) and that he suffered in order to become a source of salvation (5:8–9; 7:25, 28). God told the Son, "Sit at my right hand until I make your enemies a footstool for your feet" (1:13; 10:13). Therefore, those who trample upon the Son act counter to the will of God by seeking to put the Son under their own feet in a show of contempt. The image is ironic and designed to make listeners shrink from the idea of such an affront (6:6; §14 COMMENT *a*).

Second, the author refers to those who "considered profane the blood of the covenant" by which they were sanctified (10:29c). Nothing could rightly be brought into the presence of God without being cleansed from impurity and being sanctified or set apart for divine use (pp. 119–21). Christ's offering of blood purges sin from the conscience through the faith that it evokes, making believers fit to approach God (9:14; §23 COMMENT *b*). This establishes the new covenant in which God's will is written on human hearts and minds (8:10; 10:16). Calling the means of sanctification "profane" would be an affront worthy of condemnation. Moreover, declaring Christ's blood "profane" reinstates the defilement that separates people from God.

Third, the Spirit is the means by which God's grace comes to people (10:29d). Christ offered himself through the Spirit (9:14) and the listeners received the message of salvation through the Spirit (2:3–4; 6:4–5). Showing insolence toward the Spirit means rejecting the grace that the Spirit offers. By pronouncing a negative judgment on God's grace, the insolent invite God's negative judgment upon themselves (cf. Matt 12:31–32; Mark 3:28–30; Luke 12:10).

Appealing to what listeners already know, the author said, "We know the one who said, *Mine is the vengeance, I will repay*" (Heb 10:30a). The quotation is from Deut 32:35, and the expected response is "Yes, we know that God said this." Those who can respond in this way tacitly acknowledge their knowledge of the truth concerning God's ways (10:26). "Vengeance" means that God will vindicate those who have been wronged.[343] Similarly, the idea that God will "repay" affirms that his judgment is not capricious, since it falls upon the impenitent, not upon those who accept his mercy. The verse "The Lord will judge his people" (Deut 32:36; Ps 135:14) reinforces the idea that not even God's own people are

---

[343]When used of human action, "vengeance" can include malicious or vindictive retaliation by a person who has been wronged, but God's vengeance is commonly associated with justice. See W. T. Pitard, *ABD* 6.786–87; E. Lipinsky, *ThWAT* 5.602–12.

exempt from judgment (NOTE on 10:30; cf. 6:2; 9:27; 12:23; 13:4). The story of Moses' generation perishing in the wilderness because of their unbelief is a haunting reminder of the way in which sin and judgment work in the life of God's own people (3:7–4:10). Such warnings are given to awaken a greater urgency for persevering in faith (4:11).

Rhetorically, the reminder that God is terrifying (10:31) prepares listeners for the next section. Fear is "a painful or troubled feeling caused by the impression of an imminent evil that causes destruction or pain" (Aristotle, *Rhetoric* 2.5.1). People had cause to fear when someone's dignity had suffered an outrage (*hybrizein*, ibid 2.5.3; Heb 10:29), and when the offended party had the power to respond forcefully, as God certainly did. The threat is all the more real when something has been done irrevocably, as is the case of one who spurns God's gifts (10:29; Aristotle, *Rhetoric* 2.5.12; deSilva, *Despising*, 267). At the same time, those who abandon hope entirely can become indifferent toward the future, so that after awakening fear the speaker must extend "some hope of being saved from the cause of their distress" (Aristotle, *Rhetoric* 2.5.14). In the next section, therefore, the author will speak in a manner designed to stir up confidence, which is the opposite of fear (see p. 90).

28. Suffering and Hope (10:32–39)

10 32But remember the former days in which, after you were enlightened, you
endured a great contest with sufferings, 33in part by being made a public spectacle through denunciations and afflictions, and in part by showing solidarity with
those who were treated that way. 34For you showed compassion for the prisoners
and accepted the seizure of your possessions with joy, knowing that you yourselves have a superior and abiding possession.
35Therefore, do not cast away your boldness, which has a great reward. 36For
you need endurance, so that having done the will of God you may receive what
was promised. 37For *yet a little while and the one who is coming will arrive, and*
he will not delay. 38*But my righteous one will live by faith,* and *if he shrinks back,*
my soul will not be favorable to him. 39Now, we are not characterized by shrinking back to destruction, but by faith for the preservation of the soul.

NOTES

10:32. *But remember the former days.* Recalling the past (cf. Pss 77:5; 143:5; Jer 6:16; Deut 5:15; 15:15; 16:3, 12; 24:18, 22; 32:7) can help to rekindle a community's commitments. Cf. Heb 3:14.

after you were enlightened. See NOTE on 6:4; cf. "receiving knowledge of the truth" (10:26).

you endured a great contest with sufferings. "Contest" (*athlēsis*) and related words were used metaphorically for enduring hardships (1 Cor 9:24–27; Phil 3:13–14; cf. 2 Tim 4:6–8; Philo, *Preliminary Studies* 162; *Dreams* 1.170). Like "a sparring athlete," Job bore the loss of health, family, and possessions (*T. Job* 4:4–10), and a martyr withstood torture without giving in (4 Macc 6:10; 17:15–16; *1 Clem.* 5:2). "Endurance" meant courageously bearing hardship for a noble goal, not merely putting up with things to avoid conflict (*TLNT* 3.414–20; F. Hauck, *TDNT* 4.582). Athletic imagery will be developed in Heb 12, where Jesus "endures" the cross (12:2–3) and his followers are called to persevere in faith like runners in a race (12:1, 7).

10:33. *in part.* The community's experience was "in part" (*men*) suffering and "in part" (*de*) showing solidarity with the afflicted (BDF §290 [5]; BAGD, 597 [1bδ]). The text might also suggest that one part (*men*) of the community experienced the brunt of the conflict, while another part (*de*) showed solidarity with them (Vanhoye, *La structure*, 179; Lane; H.-F. Weiss).

by being made a public spectacle. The verb *theatrizein* is related to the word "theater" (*theatron*). Some public denunciations of Jews (Philo, *Flaccus* 74–75, 84–85, 95, 173; Josephus, *Ag. Ap.* 1.43) and Christians (Acts 19:29) took place in theaters. Although Nero staged spectacles in which Christians were pitted against wild animals or crucified (Tacitus, *Annals* 15.44; cf. Seneca *Ep.* 7.3–5), Hebrews almost certainly does not refer to this, since no deaths are mentioned. The author probably refers to public opposition in which Christians were "mocked and reviled" like "mimes at the theater" (Philo, *Gaius* 359, 368; cf. 1 Cor 4:9). Courageously enduring, however, is a "spectacle" worthy of God (Seneca, *On Providence* 2.9; Epictetus, *Disc.* 2.19.25; 3.22.58–59).

through denunciations. This word describes the past and present situation of the listeners (11:26; 13:13). See pp. 67–71. Connotations come from two spheres:

(**a**) OT. The LXX used *oneidismos* and *oneidizein* when the righteous were reviled: "I have borne denunciation" and "shame has covered my face," for "the denunciations of those who denounce [God] have fallen on me" (Ps 69:7, 9 [68:8, 10 LXX]; cf. 69:10, 19–20; 89:50–51 [88:50–51 LXX]). The terms were also used to describe the suffering of Jesus (Matt 27:44; Mark 15:32; Rom 15:3) and early Christians (Matt 5:11; Luke 6:22; 1 Pet 4:14). Describing the listeners' experience in this way connects them to a tradition of righteous suffering. See M. Lattke, *EDNT* 2.518; *TLNT* 2.585–87.

(**b**) Social experience. Public displays of verbal contempt were ways of shaming people. Moreover, communities relied on citizens to identify lawbreakers and denounce them before the authorities, who would then imprison or discipline the accused (Acts 16:16–24; 17:1–9; Rev 2:9; 3:9; Pliny, *Letters* 10.96; Eusebius, *Eccl. Hist.* 4.9.1–3). Hebrews 10:33 connects "denunciation" with imprisonment, and 1 Pet 4:14–15 compares being "denounced" for Christ to suffering penalties for various crimes. See further pp. 67–71.

and afflictions. This probably entailed the kind of physical abuse associated with imprisonment (Matt 24:9; Acts 7:10; 20:23; Rom 8:35; Phil 1:17), beatings, and deprivation (2 Cor 6:5; 8:2; Phil 4:12–14; Col 1:24; 1 Thess 1:6; cf. 2:14–15; Rev 2:9–10). Punishments could include being whipped and beaten with rods (2 Cor 11:23–24; Acts 5:40). These were sometimes administered by officials against those who had not been convicted of a crime (Acts 16:22–23) or by a mob

(Acts 18:17; cf. Heb 11:37). Affliction could also include emotional distress generated by difficult social relations (2 Cor 1:4; 2:4). See J. Kremer, *EDNT* 2.151–53.

by showing solidarity. Christ became a partner in human suffering (2:14) in order that people might become partners with him in salvation (3:14). Christians followed Christ's example by showing solidarity with afflicted brothers and sisters in the faith.

10:34. *For you showed compassion.* This was a quality of Jesus (NOTE on 4:15). "Compassion" involves not only feelings but acts of kindness, such as visiting prisoners and providing food, water, and clothing to those in need (13:3; Matt 25:35–36). Christians provided companionship and support for Paul (Phil 2:25; 4:14–18) and other prisoners (Lucian, *Peregrinus* 12–13; Ign. *Eph.* 1:2; Ign. *Magn.* 2; Ign. *Trall.* 1:1–2; Ign. *Phld.* 11:1–2; Aristides, *Apology* 15; Tertillian, *Ad martyras* 1; Cyprian, *Ep.* 76–79). On caring for prisoners (Heb 13:3) see §37 COMMENT *a*.

for the prisoners. "Prisoners" (*desmioi*) were commonly kept in "chains" (*desmoi*, Acts 16:26; 20:23; 26:29; see §37 COMMENT *a*).

and accepted the seizure of your possessions. Seizure of property could be done through legal confiscation (NIV; NAB2), unofficial plundering (NRSV), or both:

(a) Official seizure. Property of those who were convicted of major crimes or who went into voluntary exile on such charges could be confiscated (Cicero, *Tusc. Disp.* 5.37 §106; Eusebius, *Eccl. Hist.* 3.17; *RomCiv* 2.300 #36). This was true for *maiestas*, the crime of offending the authority of the emperor (*OCD*, 641). Some suggest that the property of Christians was taken through such legal action (H.-F. Weiss; Strobel; cf. Grässer; Ellingworth).

(b) Unofficial seizure. Plundering was common during outbreaks of violence (Josephus, *J.W.* 3.177; 4.168; *T. Jud.* 23.3; 4 Macc 4:10; Polybius, *Histories* 4.17.4). During pogroms against the Jews in Alexandria, the mob would pillage houses, break open shops, and deal "with other people's property as freely as if it was their own" (Philo, *Flaccus* 56). Less dramatically, the property of one Christian in the second century was carried off while he was in prison (Lucian, *Peregrinus* 14).

The evidence is ambiguous because official confiscation could be construed as plunder by the victims, and lines between legal and illegal action were not always clear. For example, the illegal seizures at Alexandria were condoned by the magistrates (Philo, *Flaccus* 54, 76–77; cf. *Gaius* 121–23; Josephus *J.W.* 2.275, 305–6; 4.335). In the second century "shameless informers and lovers of other people's property have taken advantage of the decrees [against Christians], and pillage us openly" (Eusebius, *Eccl. Hist.* 4.26.5). Since confiscation was normally done alongside other punishments and Hebrews implies that property was lost even by those who were not imprisoned, it seems likely that the seizures were not fully legal, but might well have been tolerated by the authorities (cf. deSilva, *Despising*, 161).

with joy. Joy was not occasioned by the loss of property, but by the hope of a future inheritance (cf. 12:1–2). The paradox of joy despite suffering characterizes early Christian writings (Matt 5:11–12; Acts 5:41; 2 Cor 7:4; 8:2; Jas 1:2; 1 Pet 1:6; cf. 4 Macc 10:20).

knowing that you yourselves have a superior and abiding possession. Listeners lost multiple "possessions," but have a singular "possession" that is "abiding" rather than transient, giving them incentive for "endurance" (10:36). Hebrews centers faith in the Son of God, who will abide beyond the demise of the material world (1:11; 12:27; 13:14) and whose abiding high priesthood offers ongoing help (7:3, 24). Listeners can hope for a share in his kingdom, which will abide, in contrast to their earthly situation (2:5; 12:28; 13:14; Matt 6:19–20; 19:21, 29; Rev 2:9).

10:35. *Therefore, do not cast away your boldness.* Objectively, "boldness" is the right to speak freely, and subjectively, it is confidence before God and other people (NOTES on 3:6; 10:19). To "cast away" could mean involuntarily losing the right to free speech because one used it too much for trivial ends (Dio Chrysostom, *Disc.* 34.39 [17.39]). Those addressed by Hebrews, however, are in danger of losing their boldness, not through overuse, but by abandoning it.

which has a great reward. "Reward" is related to the justice of God. Some expected that in this life the faithful would be blessed and the faithless would suffer. Experiences like that of Job and the martyrs, however, showed that this was not always the case—although *T. Job* 4:4–10 says that Job endured in the hope that God would restore his possessions. Apocalyptic sources commonly envisioned rewards being given after death (*1 Enoch* 108:10; *4 Ezra* 7:83, 98; 8:33; 13:56; *2 Bar.* 52:7; 54:16, 21; 59:2). Hebrews assumes that listeners expect a final judgment to be made after death (NOTES on 6:2, 7–8; 9:27). The author warns that "reward" can entail punishment for sin (2:2), but offers hope that the "reward" for the faithful will entail blessing (10:35). See E. Würthwein, *TDNT* 4.710–12; *TLNT* 2.502–15; W. Pesch, *EDNT* 2.432–33.

10:36. *For you need endurance.* See NOTE on 10:32.

so that having done the will of God. The aorist tense of the participle "having done" suggests that doing God's will precedes receiving what was promised. Endurance is not a precondition for God making the promise, but an expression of confidence that God will keep the promise.

you may receive what was promised. Literally "receive the promise." The expression refers not to the word of promise, which the listeners had already received, but to the substance of the promise (NOTE on 6:15), including a share in God's rest (4:10) and a place in the heavenly city (12:22–24). The heroes and heroines of the OT experienced a partial fulfillment of the promise (6:15), but complete realization comes through Christ (11:13–19, 39–40). See pp. 110–12.

10:37a. *For yet a little while.* The word "yet" (*eti*) is from Hab 2:3; the rest of the words echo Isa 26:20, where people are told to go to their rooms "for a little while" until God has judged the wicked. The text is probably the author's own paraphrase (Rose, *Wolke*, 61–63). "For" (*gar*) indicates that the quotation explains the need for the endurance mentioned in Heb 10:36. It recognizes that Christ has not returned, but is "yet" to come. Nevertheless, since Christ will return, the faithful need to endure for "a little while," but not forever (Rose, *Wolke*, 54).

10:37b–38. The remainder of the quotation is from Hab 2:3b–4, following a text similar to the LXX, which differs from the MT (see Fitzmyer, "Habakkuk"; Koch, "Text"):

MT	*LXX*	*Hebrews*
___ ___ coming	___ who is coming	the one who is coming
it will come	will arrive	will arrive,
and will not delay.	and will not delay.	and he will not delay.
		But my righteous one
		will live by ___ faith,
Behold the proud	*If he shrinks back,*	*and, if he shrinks back,*
his soul is not	*my soul will not*	*my soul will not*
upright in him.	*be favorable to him.*	*be favorable to him.*
But the righteous one	But the righteous one	
will live by *his* faith.	will live by *my* faith.	

(**a**) MT and LXX: *(i)* Where the MT says that "his soul"—the soul of the proud—is not upright, most MSS of the LXX refer to "my soul"—God's soul. This variation probably resulted from the confusion between *waw* ("his") and *yōd* ("my"). The LXX's use of "be favorable" rather than "be upright" is more difficult to account for and may suggest that the LXX was based on a Hebrew text different from the MT (Attridge, *Epistle*, 302 n. 77). *(ii)* The MT *'aphalah* is probably derived from *'aphal* meaning "swell up," perhaps referring to one who is "proud." The LXX relates it to *'alaph* ("to cover"), rendering it "shrink back." *(iii)* The MT and 8ḤevXIIgr XVII, 29–30 have "will live by *his* faith" (or by *its*, i.e., "the vision's faith" or "faithfulness"). Most MSS of the LXX have "by *my* faith" (S B Q V W*), again apparently reading the *waw* ("his") as a *yōd* ("my").

(**b**) LXX and Hebrews. *(i)* The MT has the infinitive absolute "coming it will come" (i.e., "it will surely come"), which the LXX renders by the masculine participle *erchomenos*. Hebrews adds a definite article so that the participle becomes a substantive: "the coming one." In the MT the subject of the verb "arrive" is "the vision," but in Hebrews it is Christ, "the one who is coming." *(ii)* The sequence of clauses in Hebrews differs from the LXX and MT. The subject of the verb "shrink back" is not Christ, the "one who is coming," but the "righteous one," i.e., the believer, who is warned not to shrink back. *(iii)* Most MSS of the LXX read that the righteous live by "my" faith. In some MSS of the LXX (A C) and Hebrews (P^{46} א A H* 33 1739) the word order differs to read "my righteous one" rather than "my faith." This is the reading followed here. Some MSS of Hebrews (P^{13} D^{2} H^{c} Maj; cf. KJV) and one MS of the LXX (763*) omit "my" altogether, perhaps to harmonize with Rom 1:17 and Gal 3:11 (Zuntz, *Text*, 173–74; *TCGNT*, 669–70). Other differences are inconsequential.

and the one who is coming will arrive. The words are from Hab 2:4, but "he who is coming" was an expression that early Christians used for the Messiah (Matt 3:11; 11:3; 21:9; Mark 11:9; Luke 7:19; 19:38; John 1:15, 27; 11:27). "Arrive" was used for Christ's expected return (Matt 24:50; Luke 12:46; 13:35; Rom 11:26; Rev 2:25; 3:3).

and he will not delay. "Delay" came to be associated with the questions about Christ's return (Matt 24:48; 25:5; Luke 12:25). For Hebrews the delay of Christ's return is part of a more basic issue: the fact that God's promises have not been fully realized (§6 COMMENT *b*).

10:38. *But my righteous one will live by faith.* The "righteous" are those who exemplify faith (11:4). In the present they seek to "live" faithfully and in the future they "will live" forever in God's heavenly city, which is known by faith, the place where they will be made complete through the realization of God's promises (12:23). Faith includes trust in God and fidelity to God (pp. 125–27), and it is characterized by endurance (6:12; 10:36).

and if he shrinks back. To shrink back brings divine displeasure and destruction (10:39) as the wilderness generation failed to enter God's rest because of unbelief (3:7–4:11). Related ideas are falling away from God and his grace (3:12; 6:4–6; 12:15).

my soul will not be favorable to him. The OT sometimes refers to God's "soul" when dealing with divine emotion, whether wrath or favor (e.g., Isa 1:14; 42:1; Jer 6:8; 15:1 LXX; cf. H. Seebass, *ThWAT* 5.551–52). This text refers to divine judgment (cf. 1 Cor 10:5).

10:39. *shrinking back to destruction.* "Destruction" is the "eternal judgment" (6:2) about which the listeners had been instructed: "The destruction of the sinner is forever, and he will not be remembered when God looks after the righteous" (*Pss. Sol.* 3:11; cf. 13:11; 14:9; Matt 7:13; Rom 9:22; Phil 3:19; 2 Pet 3:7; Rose, *Wolke*, 74–77).

but by faith for the preservation of the soul. Preserving one's soul often meant saving one's life from death (Isocrates, *To Philip* 7; Xenophon, *Cyropaedia* 4.4.10; Ezek 13:19), but it ultimately means life beyond death (Luke 17:33; *TLNT* 3.100–102.). The soul is the seat of courage (Heb 12:3) and hope (6:19), and it is similar to "spirit" (NOTE on 4:12), so that Hebrews speaks interchangeably of preserving one's soul (10:39) and having one's spirit made complete in the heavenly Jerusalem (12:23).

COMMENT[344]

Ominous warnings about God's fiery judgment in the previous paragraph now give way to more encouraging words. Warning and encouragement function differently—warnings unsettle and encouragement emboldens—but both serve the same end, which is perseverance in faith.[345] The violent outburst that the author

[344]On 10:32–39 see deSilva, *Despising*, 145–64; Fitzmyer, *To Advance*, 236–46; Koch, "Text"; T. W. Lewis, "And if he shrinks back"; Rose, *Wolke*, 34–77; Schröger, *Verfasser*, 182–87; Söding, "Zuversicht"; Strobel, *Untersuchungen*, 79–86.

[345]Chrysostom compared the author to a physician, who first opens a wound in order to get at the infected part of the body, then soothes the wound with a gentle remedy that eases the pain (*Homilies*, 21.1).

recalls in 10:32–34 cannot be identified with certainty (see pp. 50–52). Although the description includes elements typical of persecutions, it seems likely that Hebrews refers to a particular incident.[346] At the time Hebrews was written, the most severe violence had abated, but Christians still experienced denunciation (13:13) and some remained in prison (13:3; pp. 71–72). The author seeks to bolster the community's commitments, but rather than vilifying opponents, he considers the believer's position with respect to God.

Structurally, this section continues the digression that makes the transition between the second and third series of arguments (§27 COMMENT). Two paragraphs are included: **(a)** Remembrance of past persecution gives the listeners reason to remain faithful in the present (10:32–34). **(b)** Encouragement to hold fast is reinforced by a quotation of Hab 2:3–4, which is positioned at the end of this transitional digression, as Ps 110:4 was positioned at the end of the previous digression (6:20). Just as Ps 110:4 provided the key to the interpretation of the OT material in Heb 7:1–10:25 (§17 COMMENT), Hab 2:3–4 will provide the lens through which the stories of figures from Israel's past will be read in Heb 11:1–12:24.

a. Remembrance of Faithful Suffering (10:32–34)

Rhetorically, calling listeners to "remember the former days" (10:32a) is similar to the general who rallies his troops by declaring that the "long road we have traveled, the forests we have threaded our way through, the estuaries we have crossed—all redound to our credit and honor as long as we keep our eyes to the front. . . . I would quote the examples of other armies to encourage you," but "as things are, you need only recall your own battle honors."[347] Conversely, the contrast between the vigor of the past and the decline of the present (5:11; 6:12; 10:25) strikes at the listeners' sense of honor in order to motivate them. It is "a shameful thing when you have started well to grow tired half way," for Christ did not enlist us "that we should look for discharge after so many years," but in order that "we should continue our service to the very end" (Calvin, *Epistle*, 151).

Hostility had been directed at those who were enlightened (10:32b), that is, it was aimed at those who professed the Christian faith. This sense of enlightenment set Christians apart from others, eliciting hostility from some outside the Christian community (see pp. 67–72). The author seeks to give meaning to past suffering by calling the outburst "a great contest" (10:32c). A criminal was expected to bear up passively under blows inflicted for punishment, but an athlete remained active and resistant when receiving blows in a boxing match.[348] Accordingly, the author says that the listeners suffered, not as mere victims, but as athletes who persevered in the hope of future glory. By speaking this way the au-

---

[346]Grässer (*Hebräer*, 3.58–65) argues that it refers to typical experiences of new congregations, but others take it to refer to a specific incident (F. F. Bruce; Lane; H.-F. Weiss).

[347]Tacitus, *Agricola* 33–34, noted by deSilva, *Despising*, 202.

[348]Philo, *Cherubim* 80–81; 1 Pet 4:12–17; Thompson, *Beginnings*, 61–69.

thor uses the dominant culture's esteem for athletics to reinforce the values of the Christian minority.[349] Outsiders may have created this degrading spectacle (10:33a) to pressure the listeners and others into renouncing the Christian confession. In Heb 11–12, however, the author will provide an alternative view of the spectacle by telling of the faithful from Israel's history, who now surround the listeners as a "cloud of witnesses," encouraging them to run with perseverance in the contest of faith (12:1–2).

Denunciations (10:33b), which commonly depicted Christians as a threat to the social order (pp. 69–70), served several functions. First, denunciations rob people of the value that they receive from others, pressuring them to give up their convictions and to conform to the beliefs of the wider society. Second, reproach did not always dissuade people from their beliefs—the Christians in 10:32–34 seemed to become more tenacious when threatened—but public denunciation could prevent others from adopting their views. People who successfully denounced others also reinforced their own influence in the eyes of others.[350] Third, denunciation brought the victims to the attention of the authorities, who could imprison or discipline them.

The afflictions (10:33b) that attended denunciation and arrest probably came from rough physical handling by the crowd (Acts 17:6; 18:17). Officials might also have beaten the accused even before any had been convicted of wrongdoing (Acts 16:22–23, 37; cf. 14:5). One reason for the violence would be to use physical pain to pressure Christians into giving up their convictions and to deter others from accepting Christian beliefs. Second, physical abuse humiliates victims, which can drive them to abandon their beliefs, while preventing others from adopting them because of the threat of disgrace. Third, public displays of violence could have communicated to the authorities how the Christians were viewed by others, thereby increasing the likelihood of arrest (cf. Acts 18:17). Solidarity with those who were treated this way (10:33c) was shown, in part, by acts of compassion for prisoners (10:34a). Prison conditions were harsh, and prisoners were expected to provide much of their own food (§37 COMMENT *a*). Those who attended to prisoners had to overcome the fear of the disgrace that was associated with incarceration.

The seizure of property, whether legal or illegal (NOTE on 10:34b), inflicted manifold harm upon a community. Economically, it subjected the victims to both immediate and long-term poverty. Philo observed that pillaging not only made victims penniless but took away their means of making a living, thereby making recovery more difficult (*Flaccus* 57). Culturally, the loss of property was degrading, since the ability to provide for oneself and others gave people a sense of dignity in the eyes of others (deSilva, *Despising*, 161–62).

In response to the outburst the community accepted the seizure of their possessions with joy (10:34b). Responses to poverty vary. Ascetics might view poverty positively, recommending that people relinquish their property for the sake of

---

[349]Jewish writers used the imagery for martyrdom. See Thompson, *Beginnings*, 64.

[350]On the dynamics of honor and shame involved see Malina and Neyrey, "Honor," 29–32.

otherworldly pursuits.[351] In contrast the worldly-minded value possessions highly, so that if professing the Christian faith leads to loss, they will relinquish faith to preserve property. Those addressed by Hebrews embraced neither alternative. On the one hand, they gave up their property rather than their faith in the face of conflict (cf. 11:24–27). On the other hand, they did not embrace poverty as an ideal. They owned property until it was seized and apparently had some possessions at the time Hebrews was written. The author cautions them not to become acquisitive (13:5), but to share what they have (13:16), to extend hospitality (13:1–2), and to care for prisoners (13:3).[352]

The theological basis for this response to dispossession was the assurance of "a superior and abiding possession" (10:34c), which is a heavenly inheritance (11:10, 16; 12:28; 13:14). During the persecution, the community had shown itself able to distinguish "good from evil" (NOTES on 5:14). On the basis of appearances one would say that if Christian faith leads to loss of property and prestige, then faith is not good and it should be given up. Nevertheless, the community had retained its faith for the sake of things that could not be seen with the eye. Where a philosopher would say that true good is discerned by reason,[353] Hebrews would say that it is given through the promises of God and discerned by faith (§13 COMMENT *a*).

b. Call to Bold Perseverance (10:35–39)

The community had previously endured the loss of their possessions, but the author now speaks as if they are about to abandon what they still have: "do not cast away your boldness" (10:35a). Paradoxically, they may have found it easier "in the fire of persecution, in the fervor of religious solidarity, to set aside the opinion of outsiders. Living with their loss, however, has proven more difficult."[354] The author assures listeners that maintaining faith bears a great reward (10:35b). Theologically, the hope of reward has to do with the justice of God. The Christian community suffered because of its faith, and for God to allow suffering to be the final word would be unjust. Moreover, God swore that he would bless people (6:13–18), and proving false would violate God's own integrity.

351Some early Christian missionaries practiced voluntary poverty for the sake of spreading the gospel (Matt 10:5–11; Luke 9:1–6). Later Christians like St. Anthony elevated poverty to an ideal on the basis of the idea that one who would be perfect should sell his possessions and give the proceeds to the poor (Matt 19:21; Athanasius, *Life of Anthony* 2). Philosophers like Antisthenes, Diogenes, and Crates demonstrated their self-sufficiency by keeping only a staff and wallet (Diogenes Laertius, *Lives* 6.13, 20–23, 87). Epictetus argued that death, poverty, and reviling could all be advantageous by training a person in virtue (*Disc.* 3.20.9–19).

352Some early Christians created a community of goods with which to support members of the community (Acts 2:44–45). More common were almsgiving (e.g., Matt 6:2–4; Acts 10:2; Rom 12:8), taking up collections for the needy (Acts 11:27–30; 2 Cor 8:1–9:15), and extending hospitality (NOTES and COMMENT on Heb 13:2).

353On altering one's perspective on poverty see Epictetus, *Disc.* 3.3.17–19; 3.9.15–19; 4.6.22.

354DeSilva, *Despising*, 163. On the community's malaise see pp. 71–72.

Listeners would presumably agree that they had a "need," but the author defines it as a need for endurance that entails doing the will of God (10:36). The author does not spell out what God's will is, but assumes that listeners generally understood the shape of obedience, since he has already commended those who persistently ministered to the saints (6:10), declared that Christ obeyed God's will by sacrificing himself for others (10:7–10), and will exhort listeners to respond to Christ's sacrifice by offering the sacrifices of praise to God and of help for other people (13:15–16). Here the issue concerns the motivation to continue doing God's will. Encouragement comes from the hope of receiving what God has promised (10:36c). God's promises of rest and an unshakable kingdom are freely given, yet people come into full possession of these gifts at the end of a journey of faith, just as Israel's ancestors traveled by faith toward the promised land.

Quotation of Hab 2:3b–4 encourages listeners by declaring, "Yet a little while and the one who is coming will arrive, and he will not delay" (Heb 10:37). The author takes the passage in a messianic sense, although it is not clear that Hab 2:3 had previously been read that way.[355] He presupposes that the "coming one" is Jesus and that the text speaks of Christ's return (Heb 9:28) rather than his first coming (10:5).[356] The author does not cite Hab 2:3 to prove that Christ will return, but to articulate a belief in the second coming that his listeners already consider to be true on the basis of common Christian teaching (NOTE on 9:28).

Where Hab 2:3 was not widely used, Hab 2:4 was significant for Hebrews and Paul, both of whom quote Hab 2:4 in a similar form: "My righteous one will live by faith" (Heb 10:38).[357] Paul's relationship to the author of Hebrews is unclear (see pp. 42–45 and 54–56). Some argue that Paul linked the words "righteous" and "faith" to show that the one who becomes righteous by faith (as opposed to works) will live, whereas Hebrews linked "faith" and "will live" to show that the righteous one will live by faith. The differences, however, are overestimated. Using Hab 2:4, Paul argued that people are made righteous by faith (Gal 2:15–18; cf. 3:11) and that the righteous "live by faith" (2:19–21). Similarly, Paul cites Hab 2:4 in the thesis statement for Romans (Rom 1:17), a letter that deals with the way

---

[355]Texts like Ps 2:7; 2 Sam 7:14; and Ps 110:1 were widely understood in a messianic sense by early Christians (NOTES and COMMENT on Heb 1:5 and 1:13). Other texts seem to have been given messianic interpretations by the author of Hebrews (Isa 8:17–18 in Heb 2:13; Ps 110:4 in Heb 5:6 and 7:21; Ps 40:6–8 in Heb 10:5–7).

[356]Some maintain that the use of the participle *erchomenos* in the LXX version of Hab 2:3 meant that the translator understood "coming" in a messianic sense (F. F. Bruce; Schröger, *Verfasser*, 187). This is possible, but not certain. Hebrews makes the messianic sense clear by adding the definite article. The Dead Sea sect understood Hab 2:3 to refer to the final age (1QpHab VII, 6–14), but apparently did not read it messianically. In any case applying the text to the Messiah's return reflects a distinctly Christian viewpoint.

[357]The Dead Sea sect applied Hab 2:4 to those in the house of Judah who observe the Law, whom God will deliver because of their deeds and their loyalty to the Teacher of Righteousness (1QpHab VIII, 1–3). The Dead Sea and NT writers are alike in relating Hab 2:3–4 to the final age and one's faith attachment to a person, either the Teacher of Righteousness or Jesus. The crucial differences lie in the sect's emphasis on obedience to the Mosaic Law and Hebrews' understanding of Christ as savior rather than as a teacher (Brownlee, *Midrash*, 126–30). On Hebrews' distinctive interpretation of Hab 2:4 see Fitzmyer, *To Advance*, 236–46; Koch, "Text"; Strobel, *Untersuchungen*, 79–86.

people become "righteous" (Rom 3:21–31) and with the way that the righteous "live" (Rom 6:2).[358] The function of Hab 2:4 in Hebrews is similarly complex, since it introduces an account of Israel's history that shows how faith is the way of life on earth and the way to everlasting life in heaven (11:13–16), while insisting that apart from faith no one is truly righteous (11:4, 6).[359]

The Habakkuk quotation says finally that no one should contemplate shrinking back (10:38b). Shrinking back does not have to do with the community's withdrawal from the world,[360] but with Christians who were withdrawing from the community and its faith. Reasons for withdrawal probably included reproach from non-Christians (13:13), fatigue from the demands of caring for those associated with the community (13:1–3), and discouragement at the apparent nonfulfillment of God's promises (see pp. 67–72). The warning that God will not be favorable to those who shrink back (10:38c) recalls the judgment that God made against the wilderness generation (3:7–4:11) and the judgment that he presumably will make against those who reject the new covenant that Christ has established (6:4–8; 10:26–31).

Hebrews does not allow for a neutral space into which the listeners can retreat: either one perseveres in faith, looking to Christ for help (4:14–16; 7:26), or one shrinks back in unbelief. Shrinking back in the face of hostility from the wider society means falling into the hands of the living God (10:31). Previously, the community suffered great loss in the hope of great gain (10:34). The author therefore urges that it would be unthinkable now to shrink back hoping to save something, only to end up losing all. Rhetorically, the warning is not designed to make the listeners despair, but to drive them toward greater faith "for the preservation of the soul" (10:39b). Affirming that the listeners are persons of faith concludes the digression and leads to a new series of arguments, which will surround listeners with a company of faithful men and women to encourage them on their way (11:1–40; 12:22–24).

C. Third Series: God's People Persevere through Suffering to Glory by Faith

29. ARGUMENTS OF THIRD SERIES (11:1–12:27)

COMMENT

The third series of arguments (11:1–12:24) begins with the unseen hope of the righteous and culminates by picturing hope's realization in God's heavenly city

[358]See the summary of the debate and the helpful comments on the relation of Hab 2:4 to all of Romans in Dunn, *Romans*, 1.45–46.

[359]The heroes and heroines in Heb 11 were frequently identified as "righteous," thereby making them suitable examples of "faith" (cf. NOTES on 11:4, 7 and §30 COMMENT *b*).

[360]This proposal was made by T. W. Lewis ("And if he shrinks back"). For detailed discussion and critiques see Lane, *Hebrews*, 2.305–6; Rose, *Wolke*, 57–59.

(11:1–2; 12:22–24).[361] Initially, Abel's blood speaks, but in the end Jesus' blood speaks even more effectively than the blood of Abel (11:4; 12:24). Within the section, the righteous endure conflict, disappointment, and death, without being made complete on earth, until they are made complete in the heavenly Zion (11:39–40; 12:23). Abraham lives as a foreigner on earth in the hope of life in the city that God prepared (11:10, 16), Moses gives up wealth in Egypt for the sake of a future reward (11:26–27), and the martyrs accept death in the hope of resurrection (11:35). Describing the heavenly city shows that their faith was rightly placed in God, who proves faithful to his promises (12:22–24).

Transitional digressions precede and follow the section. The preceding digression (10:26–39) concludes with Hab 2:4—"My righteous one will live by faith" (Heb 10:38)—which provides the key to the interpretation of Israel's history in Heb 11.[362] The topic of faith was briefly mentioned in the final sentence of the second series of arguments (10:22–23) and it becomes a central topic in the third series (§27 COMMENT). A short digression (12:25–27), similar to the one that concluded the exordium (2:1–4), makes the transition between this final series of arguments and the peroration. See pp. 84, 89.

This section begins with a memorable series of examples from Israel's history. Rhetorically, an example was an action from the past that a speaker used to persuade an audience about the truth of the point he was making.[363] Examples might relate to the author's point in different ways (Quintilian, *Inst.* 5.11.9). The wilderness generation was a negative example, whose unbelief should be avoided (3:7–19), but the figures in chapter 11 are positive examples, whose faith should be imitated. Some examples make implicit arguments from the lesser to the greater: if even Rahab the prostitute exemplified faith, the listeners should certainly be able to do so (§32 COMMENT *b*). Other examples move from the greater to the lesser: if the Maccabean martyrs were faithful in great suffering, the listeners should be able to endure lesser suffering (§33 COMMENT *b*).

Using examples is appropriate since Hebrews addresses the contradiction between the promise of glory and the experience of reproach in the world. When making a point that ran counter to what people ordinarily thought, it was useful

---

[361]Many interpreters begin a major section of Hebrews at 11:1, where faith is defined and then explicated (Vanhoye, *La structure*, 183–204; Attridge; Casalini; Ellingworth; Lane). Some maintain that the section begins with the exhortations in 10:19 (F. F. Bruce; Grässer; H.-F. Weiss) or with the comments about faithfulness in 10:32–39 (Long; Pfitzner; Smith; Rose, *Wolke*). It is more helpful to take those sections as transitional rather than a part of the third main series of arguments. See pp. 83–86. Many interpreters make a major break after 12:13, where the athletic imagery ends (Vanhoye, *La structure*, 205–16; Attridge; Ellingworth; Lane). Such a break, however, disrupts the section's movement toward the heavenly city in 12:22–24.

[362]The same pattern occurred in the previous digression (5:11–6:20), which concluded with Ps 110:4—"a priest forever according to the type of Melchizedek" (Heb 6:20)—the verse that is the basis for Hebrews' treatment of priesthood in the central section.

[363]In Greek an example is called a *paradeigma*, in Latin an *exemplum*. See generally, Quintilian, *Inst.* 5.11.6; cf. Aristotle, *Rhetoric* 2.20.9; *Rhet. ad Alex.* 8 [1429A–30B]; *Rhet. ad Her.* 2.29 §46; 4.3 §5; 4.59 §62; Lausberg, *Handbook* §§410–26. For discussion see Cosby, *Rhetorical*, 93–105; Eisenbaum, *Jewish Heroes*, 59–63; Mack, *Rhetoric*, 73–75.

to produce examples of "all the cases of things that have turned out satisfactorily though seeming to have been contrary to reasonable expectation" (*Rhet. ad Alex.* 8 [1429A–B]). Experientially, those addressed by Hebrews had good reason to think that God would not be true to the promises, yet past examples show that God proved faithful even though it was unreasonable to think that people "dead" in old age could have children, that the waters of the sea would part, or that the walls of Jericho would fall (11:12, 29–30). Moreover, using examples rather than abstract arguments can make things so vivid that they may almost "be touched by the hand" (*Rhet. ad Her.* 4.49.62). The author of Hebrews understands that the object of faith is unseen (11:1), yet by telling the stories of people who lived by faith, he makes the power of faith visible by his language (see p. 92).

Rapidly listing examples impresses upon listeners the breadth of material that supports the author's point. Showing how person after person manifests faith gives the impression that many more examples could be added (§33 COMMENT; Cosby, *Rhetorical*, 19). The author assumes that listeners are familiar with the OT figures, so that citing only a few details will call a story to mind and focus attention on the relevant point. More extensive treatment is given to Abraham and his family (11:8–22) and to Moses (11:23–28), whose stories are told with creative anachronisms to reflect the listeners' situation (see pp. 69, 72).

The list of heroes and heroines of faith in Heb 11 is almost certainly the author's composition,[364] but the form includes traditional elements. Jewish and Greco-Roman writers developed example lists, sometimes using repetition of a key word, or anaphora, to identify the unifying theme, much as Hebrews repeats "by faith."[365] Hebrews 11 most closely resembles Jewish lists in that it includes a rather large number of examples, many of which come from the ancient rather than the immediate past and which depict figures worthy of imitation. By way of contrast, the examples in Greco-Roman sources tend to be fewer in number, to come from more recent history, and to include more complex characters, not all of whom are virtuous. Most important, the examples in Hebrews and many Jewish lists create a sustained account of Israel's history, whereas Greco-Roman

[364]Some scholars maintain that Heb 11 is an edited version of a preexisting source (e.g., Attridge, *Epistle*, 306–7; Rissi, *Theologie*, 105–13; H.-F. Weiss, *Brief*, 554–58). Reasons for this position are that the chapter has a distinctive style that is marked by *pistei* ("by faith"), references to Jesus are absent apart from 11:26, and no attention is given to the priestly matters that dominated previous chapters. Since 11:33 says that Israel's ancestors did receive what was promised whereas 11:13, 39 say that they did not receive what was promised, some suggest that instances of fulfillment come from a list of examples similar to those in Jewish sources and that comments about unfulfillment come from the author. Critics of this approach point out the lack of evidence that hero lists existed as independent sources. Authors constructed lists to suit the needs of larger compositions, showing considerable variety in the figures they included. The list in Hebrews shares some elements with other sources, but the presentation is distinctive (Eisenbaum, *Jewish Heroes*, 35–59, 84–87; Ellingworth, *Epistle*, 558–61; Grässer, *Hebräer*, 3.87–91; cf. Cosby, *Rhetorical*, 17–24). On theological tensions between fulfillment and unfulfillment, see NOTES on 11:13, 33, 39.

[365]For example, note how wisdom's actions are introduced with "she" (*hautē*) in Wis 10:1, 5, 6, 10, 13, 15; how Philo repeats "hope" in *Rewards* 11–14; and how "so many" (*tosoutoi*) is used in Marcus Aurelius, *Meditations* 6.47.

sources sometimes list examples in chronological order, but do not incorporate all the examples into a single narrative framework.[366] Though Hebrews generally resembles Jewish sources in the figures it lists, it differs from Jewish sources in shaping the biblical story to foreshadow the situation of later Christians, who live as strangers on earth for the sake of Christ.

Structurally, this section has three large parts: (**a**) The grand chapter on faith (11:1–40) is framed by statements about those who were "attested" through faith (11:1–2, 39–40). It is unified by the repetition of "by faith" (*pistei*) and by material that traces a story extending from the creation to the persecutions in the Maccabean period. (**b**) The next section (12:1–17) is framed by athletic images (12:1–3, 12–17) that enclose a discussion of parental instruction. In this section the author places the OT heroes and heroines from chapter 11 in a stadium where the faith that they exhibited is perfectly realized in Jesus, who has completed the race. Together, Christ and the "cloud of witnesses" from Israel's past encourage listeners to persevere in their own race of faith. (**c**) The final section (12:18–24) brings listeners to Mount Zion, where they join the festival gathering of saints and angels rather than enduring the fear that characterized Mount Sinai (12:22–24).

30. Faith in the Unseen (11:1–7)

11 [1]Now, faith is the assurance of things hoped for, the proof of things not
seen, [2]for by this the elders were attested. [3]By faith we understand that the universe was fashioned by the word of God, so that from what cannot be seen that
which is seen has come into being. [4]By faith Abel offered to God a more acceptable sacrifice than Cain did, through which it was attested that he was righteous, since God himself testified concerning the gifts, and through it he, although dead, is still speaking. [5]By faith Enoch was taken so that he did not see
death, and *he was not found because God had taken him*. For it is attested that before being taken *he had pleased God*. [6]Without faith it is impossible to please
[him], for it is necessary for one who draws near to God to believe that he exists
and rewards those who seek him. [7]By faith Noah, after being divinely warned
about things that could not yet be seen, in reverence prepared an ark for the salvation of his household, through which he condemned the world and became
an heir of the righteousness that is based on faith.

[366]See Cosby, *Rhetorical*, 107–9; Eisenbaum, *Jewish Heroes*, 73–84. Hebrews 11 resembles the historical summaries that appear in the OT in that all assume that God's relationships with Israel are part of a single narrative (Josh 24; Ezek 20; Neh 9; Pss 78; 105; 106; 135; 136). These summaries do not focus on individual heroes and heroines as Heb 11 does. More attention to individuals appears in later lists (Sir 44–50, 1 Macc 2.51–60, 4 Macc 18.11–19, Wis 10, *4 Ezra* 7.105–111, cf. Acts 7, *1 Clem.* 17–19). For extensive comparison of the figures mentioned in Jewish lists see Rose, *Wolke*, 85. For examples of Greco-Roman lists see Isocrates, *To Philip* 58–67; Musonius Rufus, frg. 9; Cicero, *De oratore* 3.32–33 §§126–29, 132–36.

NOTES

11:1. *Now, faith is.* "Faith" encompasses both trust in God and faithfulness to God (see pp. 125–27).

the assurance. The Greek word *hypostasis* is based on roots meaning "stand under" (NOTE on 1:3; cf. 3:14). The subjective side emerges when *hypostasis* is linked with "faith," which pertains to the believing person. The objective side emerges when *hypostasis* is connected to "things hoped for," since the object of hope lies outside the believer. The word "assurance" (NASB; NRSV) is useful because objectively it is a pledge or guarantee and subjectively it is a personal state of certainty (*OED*).

(a) Objective Sense: Assurance and What Is Hoped For. *Hypostasis* often referred to property, which was the material basis that undergirded daily life, and it could be used for the title deed that assured future possession of something (MM, 659–60; *TLNT* 3.423). In an objective sense "assurance" comes to people from a source beyond themselves. Hebrews 11:1 could encourage dispossessed listeners (10:32–34) to trust that faith was the "guarantee" (NJB) that they would receive an eternal inheritance (cf. Luther, *LuthW* 29.230). Although the guarantee is finally God's faithfulness rather than human faith (10:23; 11:11), God gives what is promised to people of faith (6:12; 11:6, 7; cf. Rose, *Wolke*, 104–5).

Others who favor the objective sense stress that *hypostasis* is the "reality" behind appearances (Ps.-Aristotle, *On the Cosmos* 4 [395a]; Philo, *Dreams* 1.188; *Eternity* 88, 92) or the solid footing on which one stands (Ps 69:2 [68:3 LXX]; cf. *Pss. Sol.* 15:3). The objective sense is also suggested by the parallel between *hypostasis* ("assurance") and *elenchos*, which was the "proof" of something's existence or truth (Heb 11:1b; Attridge; Hamm, "Faith," 278–79; Hegermann; H. W. Hollander, *EDNT* 3.407; Lane; Mengelle, "La estructura"; Thompson, *Beginnings*, 70–71). Some suggest that the object of one's hope finds "realization" in faith (NAB²; cf. Chrysostom), yet this is awkward since the object of faith remained unrealized for people like Abraham (11:13, 39). More plausible is that Heb 11:1 uses metonymy, which defines something by what produced it (*Rhet. ad Her.* 4.32 §43; Attridge). Thus "faith *is* the assurance" of what is hoped for because what is hoped for produces assurance.

(b) Subjective Sense: Assurance and Faith. Luther and Tyndale took *hypostasis* to mean "sure confidence," since the LXX used it for "hope" (Ruth 1:19; Ezek 19:5; Dörrie, "Ὑπόστασις," 89–91). There is little evidence that *hypostasis* referred to a state of mind ("being sure," NIV), but it could indicate steadfastness. Soldiers showed "the immovability of their steadfastness [*hypostasis*]" in the face of death (Josephus, *Ant.* 18.24). Such "steadfastness" (*hypostasis*) is the "resolute endurance that comes from hope of support" (Polybius, *Histories* 4.50.10; cf. 6.55.2; Ps 39:7 [38:8 LXX]). Hebrews has connected "endurance" with "faith" (10:36, 38) and now identifies faith (*pistis*) with the steadfast assurance (*hypostasis*) that is the opposite of "shrinking back" (*hypostolē*, 10:39) and "abandoning" (*apostasis*, 3:12). Israel's ancestors were "attested" (11:2) because of their steadfast reliance on what cannot be seen (Rose, *Wolke,* 99–117; H.-F. Weiss; Grässer; Bénétreau).

of things hoped for. The object of hope in 11:1a is the unseen reality mentioned in 11:1b. The word "things hoped for" (*elpizomenōn*) is neuter plural, referring to the world to come (2:5), everlasting Sabbath rest (4:1–11), an eternal inheritance (9:15), heavenly Jerusalem (12:22–24), and an unshakable kingdom (12:28). Faith is steadfast assurance *concerning* what is hoped for, yet the assurance of faith comes *from* what is hoped for. Faith is evoked by the promise of future things and is directed toward the fulfillment of that promise.

the proof. The noun *elenchos* was used for the "proof" or "demonstration" of something under dispute (Demosthenes, *Oration* 4.15), just as the verb *elenchein* meant convicting someone of wrongdoing (John 8:46; Jas 2:9). Commonly the noun took the objective genitive: "proof of the matter" (Antiphon, *Oration* 1.12; cf. Josephus, *J.W.* 4.337; Philo, *Rewards* 4). There is little evidence that the noun was used in the subjective sense of personal "conviction" (NRSV; cf. NIV) or that it meant "being convinced" by God (F. Büchsel, *TDNT* 2.476; Rose, *Wolke,* 124).

of things not seen. What is "not seen" (11:1b) is synonymous with what is "hoped for" (NOTE on 11:1a). The word "things" (*pragma*) could refer to objects in a transcendent world (Philo, *Heir* 63), but it more commonly referred to actions and events (NOTE on 10:1), just as what "could not yet be seen" in 11:7 is the future event of the flood. Faith in unseen "things" pertains not only to the existence of an unseen world but to God's future acts of deliverance (cf. 2 Cor 4:18; Rom 8:24–25).

11:2. *for by this the elders.* This designated Israel's ancestors in ancient (Josh 24:31; Judg 2:7; Philo, *Moses* 1.4; *m. 'Abot* 1:1) and more recent times (Josephus, *Ant.* 13.292). The term "elders" connoted respect (Philo, *Abraham* 270).

were attested. Being "attested" meant gaining approval (NRSV) and had especially to do with public witness to a person's character. Attestation often came from other people (Acts 10:22; 16:2; cf. 6:3; 22:12; 1 Tim 5:10; cf. MM, 389; Deissmann, *Bible,* 265). Inscriptions from the Hellenistic and Roman periods frequently use forms of the verb "attest" (*martyrein*) for public honors (Danker, *Benefactor,* 442–43). Here the passive voice points to God, whose attestation is conveyed through the Scriptures (Heb 7:17; cf. 7:8; 10:15; 11:4–5, 39; cf. Philo, *Abraham* 270; *Alleg. Interp.* 2.47). Those who are "attested" (*martyrein*) in Heb 11:1–40 are among the "witnesses" (*martyres*) who surround the listeners in 12:1.

11:3. *By faith we understand that the universe.* To understand something is to apprehend it with the mind, which is where the new covenant is inscribed (8:10; 10:16). The word "universe" (*aiōnes*) is plural, which could suggest multiple worlds (NOTE on 1:2), but since "universe" is equivalent to the singular "that which is seen" in 11:3b, the plural probably designates the whole universe.

was fashioned by the word of God. This belief is basic to Judaism and early Christianity (Gen 1:3, 6, 9; Ps 33:6, 9). Hebrews 1:2 identified God's speech with the Son, who was God's agent of creation, but "word" (*hrēma*) does not have christological significance here (pp. 104–5).

so that from what cannot be seen. The words "so that" point to the result of God's creative activity (BDF §402.2). The negative *mē* is sometimes taken to modify the whole infinitival clause so that it denies that the world has a visible source (Lane; Williamson, *Philo*, 377–79; P. E. Hughes). *Mē* should be taken with the participle *phainomenōn* (BDF §433.3) so that the passage affirms that the world does have an invisible source (Attridge; Ellingworth). The question is what the invisible source might be. There are three main options, of which the third is most viable:

(a) Nothingness. Some argue that the visible "has come into being" where nothing existed before. The preposition *ek* would mean that God created the visible world "out of nothingness" as he created "light out of [*ek*] darkness" (2 Cor 4:6; cf. 2 *Enoch* 24:2; 2 Macc 7:28; 2 *Bar.* 21:4; Rose, *Wolke*, 156–57). Accordingly, Heb 11:3 would mean that "God made the things which are out of things which are not" (Chrysostom, NPNF[1] 14.465; Erasmus, *Paraphrase*; Luther, WA 57/3.62; F. F. Bruce). It is not clear, however, that invisibility means nonexistence.

(b) Transcendent realm. Some maintain that Hebrews follows the Hellenistic notion that the world that can be seen is derived from the world that cannot be seen (Plato, *Phaedo* 79A; *Republic* 524C; Philo, *Creation* 16; *Confusion* 172; Seneca, *Ep.* 58.27), just as the earthly Tabernacle was modeled after a heavenly pattern (Heb 8:1–5; 9:11–14, 23–24). According to this approach, faith reaches beyond the world of phenomena to the unseen ground of true being, and from that source gains the possibility of remaining steadfast (Attridge; Braun; Grässer; Thompson, *Beginnings*, 75; Vanhoye, *La structure*, 185; H.-F. Weiss). A problem with this approach is that Hebrews does not consistently posit connections between heavenly patterns and earthly realities. For example, Heb 11 does not treat the heavenly Jerusalem as the pattern for an earthly city, unlike earlier passages where the celestial tent was the type of its earthly representation (8:1–5).

(c) The power of God's word. The elements in 11:3 are presented in a chiastic pattern in which "what cannot be seen" corresponds to "the word of God" (Ellingworth):

(1) was fashioned	(1´) came into being
(2) the universe	(2´) that which can be seen
(3) by the word of God	(3´) by what cannot be seen

Although "word" is singular and "what cannot be seen" is plural, the neuter plural could convey a singular idea (Smyth, *Grammar* §1003). The plural generalizes what was said about the word into a principle capable of broader application (Zerwick, *Biblical Greek* §7). Similar generalizing occurs in 11:5, where the author moves from Enoch to "the one who approaches God" to "those who seek him." The dative case of "word" corresponds to the *ek* that modifies "what cannot be seen," indicating cause: "by" (BAGD, 235 [3e]). Thus the creative power of God's word is an invisible force that produces visible results (P.E. Hughes, *Commentary*, 452; Rose, *Wolke*, 156–59).

11:4. *By faith Abel.* The younger son of Adam and Eve, Abel is mentioned only in Gen 4 in the OT. He was remembered as a righteous man (see NOTE below), who deserved God's blessing (*T. Zeb.* 5:4). Some considered Abel to be the first martyr, whose example encouraged others to be faithful even to death (4 Macc 18:11).

offered to God a more acceptable sacrifice. The OT does not explain why God accepted Abel's sacrifice and rejected Cain's (Gen 4:4–5 MT). Three possibilities might be considered, of which the third best fits Hebrews:

(**a**) Quality of sacrifice. Since Abel offered the fat portions of the firstborn of the flock (Gen 4:4–5), Philo speculated that Abel's sacrifice was superior to Cain's offering of crops (*Sacrifices* 88; cf. Josephus, *Ant.* 1.54).

(**b**) Manner of sacrifice. Genesis 4:7 LXX, which differs from the MT, faults Cain's method of dividing the sacrifice (cf. Gen 15:10; Lev 1:12):

MT	*LXX*
If you do well,	If you offered rightly,
will you not be accepted?	but did not divide rightly,
And if you do not do well,	
sin is crouching at the door;	did you not sin? Be still;
its desire is for you,	he shall return to you,
but you must master it.	and you shall rule over him.

Hebrews uses the LXX, but makes no mention of faulty sacrificial procedure.

(**c**) Character of the worshiper. The explicit point is that Abel offered in faith, and faith pleases God (11:6).

than Cain did. Cain was the elder son of Adam and Eve. Mentioned only in Gen 4 in the OT, later sources remember him as a murderer (1 John 3:12; *1 Enoch* 22:7; *Jub.* 4:1–5, 31; *Bib. Ant.* 2:1; 4; 59:4; 4 Macc 18:11; *L.A.E.* 23:2–5) and an agent of wickedness (Jude 11; *T. Benj.* 7:1–5; *Apoc. Ab.* 24:5; Philo, *Worse* 68; Josephus, *Ant.* 1.52, 60–61).

attested that he was righteous. Attestation comes from God and is conveyed through the Scriptures. The OT does not state that Abel was "righteous," but indicates that God looked favorably on his sacrifice (Gen 4:4). The idea that Abel was "righteous" became common in later sources (Matt 23:35; 1 John 3:12; Josephus, *Ant.* 1.53; cf. *T. Issachar* 5:4; *Tgs.* Gen 4:8, 10; *Mart. Ascen. Isa.* 9:8).

since God himself testified. The best reading (P^{13*} P^{46} ℵ^{2} D^{1} etc.) is the emphatic "God himself" (*autou tou theou*), which forms a genitive absolute with "bearing witness." The variants "he bearing witness to God" (*autou tō theō*, ℵ* A D*) and "God bearing witness to him" (*autō tou theou*, P^{13c} z^{c}) seem to have arisen as mistakes due to the similar sounds of the words (cf. *TCGNT*, 672). On "testified" see NOTE on "attested" in 11:2.

concerning the gifts. Some take *epi* to mean that God bore witness "over" Abel's gifts, perhaps by sending fire from heaven (cf. 1 Kgs 18:38; Gen 4:4 Theodotion; Chrysostom; Jerome, *Questions on Genesis* 4:4–5). "Concerning" is a better translation since the LXX said that God showed favor both concerning (*epi*) the gifts and concerning (*epi*) Abel—who was not consumed by fire.

and through it he, although dead, is still speaking. Hebrews assumes that Abel was still dead; there is no speculation about his current heavenly existence (cf. *L.A.E.* 40). Unlike "cry out," which connotes accusation (Gen 4:10) or vengeance (*Jub.* 4:3; Philo, *Worse* 48; Matt 23:35), "speaking" is a more neutral term (cf. Heb 12:24).

11:5. *By faith Enoch was taken.* The OT does not explain what it meant for God to "take" Enoch (Gen 5:24), but most took it to mean that Enoch did not die (Philo, *Change* 38; *QG* 1.86; Josephus, *Ant.* 1.85; *Jub.* 4:23), not that he was taken by death (*Tg. Onq.* Gen 5:24; *Gen. Rab.* 25:1; Rose, *Wolke*, 182). Hebrews understood Enoch in a positive way (cf. Wis 4:10).

he was not found because God had taken him. A quotation of Gen 5:24b LXX. The MT lacks "found." The verb "take" (*metatithenai*) could mean "change," so that Enoch was sometimes said to have pleased God because he repented of sin (Sir 44:16; Philo, *Abraham* 17–26; *Rewards* 15–21; *QG* 1.82–85). Here, however, the emphasis is on immortality, not repentance.

For it is attested that before being taken he had pleased God. The MT of Gen 5:22, 24 says that Enoch "walked with God." The LXX, however, says that "he pleased God" in both verses, thereby giving prominence to the theme. Enoch's faith was rarely mentioned (*3 Enoch* 6:3), but it was common to call him "righteous" (*T. Levi* 10:5; *T. Dan* 5:6; *T. Benj.* 9:1; cf. Wis 4:4, 7, 16; *1 Enoch* 1:2; 12:1; *Jub.* 10:17). In Hebrews the righteous by definition have faith (COMMENT *b*).

11:6. *Without faith it is impossible to please* [*him*]. On pleasing God see 12:28; 13:16, 21.

one who draws near to God. See NOTE on 4:16; cf. 7:25; 10:1, 22; 12:18, 22.

to believe that he exists. People from many traditions in antiquity would have agreed that one must believe in God's existence. Jewish writers affirmed God's existence over against atheism, and the oneness of God over against polytheism (cf. Philo, *Creation* 170; 4 Macc 5:24; Wis 13:1). Some in the Greco-Roman world were agnostic, but most affirmed that there "is a God, and that he provides for the universe" (Epictetus, *Disc.* 2.14.11; cf. *Ench.* 31.1; Seneca, *Ep.* 95.50). The value of making such a broad statement in Heb 11:6 is that it would be so difficult to dispute.

and rewards. That God rewards people was common in Jewish sources: "You are the God who bestows rewards on those who love you" (*Par. Jer.* 6:6). Although some expected God to reward the righteous during their lifetimes, others expected rewards and punishments to be given out after death (NOTES on Heb 2:2; 10:35; cf. 11:26).

those who seek him. This is a common biblical expression: "I sought the Lord, and he answered me, and delivered me from all my fears" (Ps 34:4 cf. 14:2; 22:26). Listeners are to approach God in prayer, relying on the intercession of Christ (NOTES on 4:16; 7:25; 10:22).

11:7. *By faith Noah.* Some sources call Noah trustworthy (*pistos*, *1 Clem.* 9:4; *Sib. Or.* 1.125–26), but more important is that Noah was "righteous" (Gen 6:9;

7:1; cf. Wis 10:4; Sir 44:17; *Jub.* 5:19; Philo, *Worse* 105; *Posterity* 48, 173–74; *Bib. Ant.* 3:4; *Sib. Or.* 1.280; Rose, *Wolke,* 193–94). Since the righteous live by faith (Hab 2:4; Heb 10:38), Hebrews can argue that Noah, the righteous one, was motivated by faith.

after being divinely warned. God's warning about the flood is given in Gen 6:13, 17. The same verb is used for God's address to Moses in Heb 8:5; cf. 12:25 (Heininger, "Hebr. 11.7"). Noah exemplifies those who respond to God's word—as the listeners are called to do.

about things that could not be seen. For Noah what was "not seen" was the coming flood. For the listeners the comparable unseen things include God's judgment on the unfaithful and his rewarding of the faithful (10:26–39; cf. Matt 24:37–38; Luke 17:26–27; 2 Pet 2:5).

in reverence. The word *eulabein* could refer to "fear" (Sir 41:3; 2 Macc 8:16). Fear of divine wrath is an element of piety (cf. Heb 4:1; 10:27, 31), and given the prospect of a flood, 11:7 could indicate that Noah was afraid (*Sib. Or.* 1.147; Ps.-Oecumenius; Theophylact; Bengel). The meaning "attentiveness" is less common (P. E. Hughes; Lane; REB; NJB). The sense that best fits this context is that fear means reverence for God (Luther, *Lectures;* Tyndale, "Prologue"; NASB; NAB2; Luke 2:25; Acts 2:5; 8:2; 22:12; Philo, *Heir* 22, 29). The same was true of Christ in Heb 5:7.

prepared an ark. The verb "prepare" was used for constructing and making ships ready for use (Diodorus Siculus, *Library of History* 1.92.2; 1 Macc 15:3). For Noah, "faith prepared him to prepare the ark" (Theodoret, PG 82.760B). On the ark see Gen 6:15–16.

for the salvation of his household. Noah was to take his "whole house" into the ark (Gen 7:1). Noah's salvation from the flood provides a way for listeners to think of the salvation of themselves (NOTE on Heb 2:3) and others in God's "house" (3:6; 10:21) from death and judgment (cf. 1 Pet 3:20–21).

through which he condemned the world. Some interpreters relate the feminine pronoun "which" (*hēs*) to the ark (Theophylact; Calvin; D. Guthrie), but most connect it with "faith" (Haimo; Attridge; Braun; Lane; cf. 11:4bc). Some connect this verse with the tradition that Noah was a "herald of righteousness," who called people to repentance (2 Pet 2:5; Josephus, *Ant.* 1.74; *Sib. Or.* 1.125–36; *Jub.* 7:20; *1 Clem.* 7:6; 9:4; Luther, *LuthW* 29.236; Rose, *Wolke,* 197–99). Others relate it to the idea that the righteous were to pronounce condemnation upon the wicked (Matt 12:41–42; Luke 11:31–32; W. Schenk, *EDNT* 2.259). Neither view seems likely since the text emphasizes Noah's actions, not his preaching. Instead, his determination to act on the basis of God's word showed his negative judgment upon the world, for the world acts on the basis of what is seen (H.-F. Weiss).

and became an heir of the righteousness that is based on faith., Noah was "righteous" before the flood (Gen 6:9; 7:1), but here "righteousness" seems to mean the blessings that manifest God's favorable judgment, which the faithful inherit (Heb 1:14; 6:12, 17; 9:15; 11:8; 12:17).

COMMENT[367]

The epic story of the role of faith in Israel's history is told in the third series of arguments (11:1–12:27; §29 COMMENT). Used sparingly earlier in the speech (4:2; 6:1, 12; 10:22), the word "faith" became prominent in the warnings and exhortations in 10:26–39. After quoting Hab 2:4, which said, "My righteous one will live by faith" (Heb 10:38), the author underscored faith by declaring that we are characterized "by faith for the preservation of the soul" (10:39). The relationship of Hab 2:4 to the list of OT heroes is twofold. On the one hand, examples from Israel's history illustrate Hab 2:4 by showing what it means to live by faith. On the other hand, Hab 2:4 is the lens that enables the author to read Israel's history in terms of faith, just as the reference to Ps 110:4 in Heb 6:20 was the lens that focused his view of the priesthood in 7:1–10:25.

Structurally, the paragraph is framed by references to what cannot be seen (11:1, 7), and it can be divided into two main parts: **(a)** The first two verses (11:1–2) introduce the idea of being attested through faith, which informs the entire chapter and is repeated in 11:39. **(b)** The remainder of the paragraph is framed by statements about the world's creation (11:3) and its destruction (11:7), both of which have to do with powers that cannot be seen. This part of the argument makes four points, each introduced with "by faith" (*pistei*). The brevity of the examples of creation, Abel, Enoch, and Noah sets them apart from the lengthy treatment of Abraham and his family that follows (Vanhoye, *La structure*, 183–85).

a. Faith Is (11:1–2)

The words "faith is" (11:1a) introduce a definition of faith. A definition "is the statement of the fact called in question in appropriate and concise language" (Quintilian, *Inst.* 7.3.2). Many definitions in ancient literature have the same structure as 11:1a: "Now __ is" (*estin de* or *estin gar*; cf. BDF §252).[368] Therefore, Augustine and others could say that faith "is defined" in Heb 11:1.[369] Similarly, when Dante arrives in Paradise and is asked, "Faith, what is it?" he quotes Heb 11:1 and explicates it along the lines developed by Thomas Aquinas.[370]

[367]On 11:1–7 see Bénétreau, "La foi"; Betz, "Firmness"; Brawley, "Discoursive"; Bulley, "Death"; Cosby, *Rhetorical*, 17–55; Dunnill, *Covenant*, 149–53; Eisenbaum, *Jewish Heroes*, 147–53; Grässer, *Glaube*; idem, *Aufbruch*, 166–80, 201–12, 303–10; Haacker, "Creatio"; Heininger, "Hebr. 11.7"; Mengelle, "La estructura"; Rhee, "Chiasm"; Rose, *Wolke*, 78–202; Wider, *Theozentrik*, 186–94; Williamson, *Philo*, 309–85. On faith see pp. 125–27.

[368]"Now examples are" and "Now tokens are" (*Rhet. ad Alex.* 8.1; 9.1; cf. 10.1; 11.1; 12.1; 13.1; 15.1; 17.1); "Now groaning is" (Philo, *Alleg. Interp.* 3.211); "A vow is" (Philo, *Unchangeable* 87); "This is eternal life" (John 17:3); Rose, *Wolke*, 93–95.

[369]Augustine, NPNF[1] 5.43; 7.342, 369; Theodoret, PG 82.757A; Ps.-Hugh of St. Victor, PL 176.35C, 43A, 327C; Peter Lombard, PL 192.806.

[370]*Divine Comedy*, "Paradiso" 24.52–78. Aquinas himself is ambivalent. In *Ad Heb.* §§551–52 he says that Heb 11:1 "describes" faith and gives "a complete but obscure definition." In his *Summa Theologiae* (IIa IIae 4.1) he says, "This verse touches on all the elements whereby faith is definable," although "it does not cast the words in definitional form." See Spicq, "L'exégèse"; Schumpp,

Some, however, question whether 11:1 does define faith.[371] Rhetorically, a good definition should state "the full meaning and character of a thing lucidly" (*Rhet. ad Her.* 4.25.35), yet scholars debate the meaning of "assurance" and find it peculiar that faith is not said to be based on proof, but to *be* a form of proof (NOTES on 11:1). Moreover, an apt definition should state the meaning "briefly," so that "to express it in more words seems superfluous and to express it in fewer is considered impossible" (*Rhet. ad Her.* 4.25.35). Yet one might wonder whether adding words to Heb 11:1 would be superfluous, since the author says virtually nothing about the content of faith and makes no mention of Christ.

A proper definition identifies what something is and relates it to the listeners' concerns. Accordingly, Heb 11:1 defines faith and 11:2 relates it to the issue of being favorably attested by God. A definition was not expected to be comprehensive, but to enhance an argument.[372] Since a familiar concept could be defined by one of its principal properties, Hebrews calls faith "assurance,"[373] which also helps to show the effects of faith in people's lives.[374] In the examples that follow, the subject is not faith, but the people who act on the basis of faith.[375] Hebrews addressed a situation in which some were tending to "drift from" (2:1), "abandon" (10:25), or "fall away" from the faith and the community (cf. 3:12; 6:6; 10:29). Rather than "shrinking back" (10:39), the author urges listeners to "hold fast the confession" (4:14) "without wavering" (10:23). Defining faith as "assurance" sets it against tendencies of drift while allying it with "perseverance" (6:12) and "endurance" (10:36), which are expressed in "boldness" before God and other people (3:6; 4:16; 10:19, 35), and which will bring blessings from God in the future.

Relating faith to "things hoped for" (11:1a) recalls that the listeners' faith had been awakened by promises of an eternal inheritance, although experiences of denunciation, dispossession, and imprisonment clearly showed that believers had not yet arrived in God's kingdom (10:32–34; 13:13–14). Earlier sections of Hebrews showed that God kept his promises to raise up a priest like Melchizedek and to inaugurate a new covenant, allowing listeners to remain confident that God will also give them the inheritance that he has promised. Therefore, hope enables the community to exhibit the assurance of faith in the face of conflict, just as hope empowers soldiers to show assurance on the field of battle (Polybius, *Histories* 4.50.10).

Proof (11:1b) was ordinarily required for faith, because to believe without proof might be mere credulity (Josephus, *J.W.* 4.337). In a provocative twist,

---

"Glaubensbegriff." Melanchthon said that 11:1 "defines" faith and offers a "sketch" of faith (LCC 19.97).

[371]Ps.-Bruno (PL 153.550C). The *Glossa ordinaria* called it a "commendation" of faith.

[372]Quintilian, *Inst.* 7.3.19, 21; *Rhet. ad Her.* 2.12 §17. On definition, or *finitio*, see generally Lausberg, *Handbook* §§104–22.

[373]On defining familiar words see Quintilian, *Inst.* 7.3.13 and on properties see 7.3.3, 15, 25.

[374]Hugh of St. Victor, PL 176.327D, 330C; Braun; Grässer.

[375]"Faith" is not used again in the nominative case. It most often appears in the dative case (*pistei*), which is translated "by faith," focusing on how one lives by faith.

however, the author says, not that faith *has* proof, but that faith *is* proof of things unseen. The author does not assume that things exist simply because people believe they exist. Human faith does not create divine reality, but divine reality creates human faith. The unseen realities of God give proof of their existence by their power to evoke faith where otherwise there would only be unbelief. The object of Christian hope can be known by its effect upon human beings.

To say that faith is directed toward "things not seen" (11:1b), however, takes seriously the present situation of the listeners. In 2:5–9 the author affirmed that God's intention for people was that they receive glory and have all things in subjection under their feet, yet he acknowledged that "we do not yet *see* all things" in subjection (2:8). What the listeners did "see" was that Jesus, who suffered, was exalted above the angels (2:9). Now the author provides further encouragement by giving examples of others whose faith was evoked by powers unseen and directed toward ends unseen (Brawley, "Discoursive").

"The elders" (11:2a), who are a positive counterpart to the negative example of the wilderness generation (3:7–4:11), were favorably attested by God (11:2b), which is something that most listeners would want for themselves. Their experience was that Christian faith did not bring favorable attestation, but denunciation from society (10:33; 13:13), which gave strong incentive to leave the Christian community and its faith (§28 COMMENT *a*). Hebrews provides incentive to remain within the Christian fold by shifting the court of opinion in which recognition is given. The elders in Heb 11 did not receive favorable attestation from society, but from God, whose judgments do not necessarily concur with those of human beings.[376] The author seeks to show that abandoning faith in order to gain prestige from human beings would be a mistake, because true honor comes from God and is given to those who persevere in faith.

b. From Creation to Noah (11:3–7)

Creation. The reference to the elders in 11:2 raises expectations that listeners will hear about previous generations, but before the author considers Abel, Enoch, and Noah, he refers to the listeners' own faith. Saying, "By faith *we* understand" (11:3a) establishes common ground with the listeners and tacitly associates them with the "righteous" (10:38) and "the elders" (11:2), whose faith was just mentioned. To say that by faith "we *understand*" affirms that they have already grasped a key idea, which helps the author maintain rapport with his listeners. The principal point, however, is that understanding occurs "*by faith*."[377] The world can be seen, but its origins cannot. One might infer from the ordering of creation that the world has an artificer (NOTE on 3:4), but Hebrews assumes one knows by trusting what the Scriptures disclose about creation (4:4) that the world was fashioned by divine speech. By pointing out how the listeners'

---

[376]See deSilva, *Despising*, 276–79; cf. 2 Sam 16:7; Isa 55:8–9; 1 Cor 1:18–25.

[377]Augustine said, "Understanding is the reward of faith. Therefore, do not seek to understand in order to believe, but believe in order that you may understand" (NPNF[1] 7.184). Cf. Anselm, *Proslogium* 2.

view of the past relies on faith, the author helps to show that their stance toward the future must also depend on faith (11:1). If listeners rely on God's word concerning the genesis of the world, they must rely on God's word when considering the goal of the world.

When the author comments, "From what cannot be seen that which is seen has come into being" (11:3cd), he suggests a congruence between the universe and faith (p. 97). What cannot be seen is the word of God (NOTE on 11:3), which is known by its effects. God's word brought into being a universe that is seen just as it calls forth the faith that is proof of things not seen (11:1b). Therefore, both the universe and faith attest to the power of the unseen word of God. Specific examples of such faith come from the lives of Israel's ancestors.

Abel. The list of OT figures begins with Abel, who "offered to God a more acceptable sacrifice than Cain did" (11:4a) because he offered it "by faith" (11:4a). The interpretive key is Hab 2:4 (Heb 10:38), which includes three elements: "My righteous one / will live / by faith."

Hab 2:4	*Gen 4:4–5, 10*
My righteous one	Abel offered acceptable sacrifice
will live	his blood cries out from the ground
by faith	___________

Tradition had taken Abel's sacrifice to show that he was righteous (NOTE on 11:4) and Hebrews takes the cry of Abel's blood to show that he lives on, despite his death. If the first two points mentioned by Habakkuk apply to Abel, Hebrews assumes that the third must be present as well, namely, that Abel acted by faith.[378]

Abel's story shows that true attestation comes from God (11:2, 4bc). The disturbing ambiguity in the Genesis account prevents readers from distinguishing between Cain and Abel on the basis of what can be seen. To all appearances both did the right thing by offering sacrifices. God, however, was in a position to "testify concerning the gifts" and those who offered them, and Cain's murderous blow against Abel showed that God's judgment was correct. Like Abel, the listeners are to offer "sacrifices" to God (13:15–16), but there is little to suggest that others in society will attest to their righteousness on the basis of their offerings of praise and compassion (10:32–34; 13:3, 13–14). If approval from non-Christian society is their goal, then listeners will probably relinquish faith, but if they are convinced that true approval is given by God—in their case as in Abel's—then they have a basis upon which to persevere in faith. Abel's story is a vivid reminder that the righteous suffer and die, yet the comment that by his faith Abel "is still

[378]Jewish traditions sometimes elaborate the faith of Abel, indicating that Abel believed in the world to come and God's just rewarding of the righteous and the wicked. Cain denied all of this. These points are affirmed by Hebrews (10:26–35). For those familiar with such a tradition, Abel would have exemplified the kind of faith that the author sought to foster in the listeners. See McNamara, *Targum*, 66–67; Rose, *Wolke*, 163–78; Dunnill, *Covenant*, 149–53. Yet the date of the targums is unclear, and Hebrews makes no clear reference to the tradition.

speaking" emphasizes that death is not the end of his story. Attention centers not on *what* Abel is saying, but on the fact *that* Abel is still speaking.[379]

Enoch. Genesis says that Enoch was the son of Jared and the father of Methusaleh (Gen 5:18–24).[380] What interests the author of Hebrews is that Enoch "pleased God" and that he "was not found because God had taken him" (Gen 5:24b LXX). Hebrews draws on the common tradition that Enoch "did not see death," but was taken directly to heaven (NOTE on Heb 11:5). The declaration that this happened by faith (11:5) again relies on Hab 2:4 for the key to the story:

Hab 2:4	*Gen 5:24b*
My righteous one	Enoch pleased God
will live	God took him
by faith	________

One can conclude that Enoch was righteous because Genesis says that he pleased God. Since God took Enoch so that he did not see death, he shows that one who is righteous "will live." Hebrews assumes that if righteousness and life are present, faith must be present as well. Thus Hab 2:4 allows the author to make explicit the faith that was only implicit in Genesis.

Support for this interpretation is given by a logical deduction or enthymeme.[381] The general principle is that without faith it is impossible to please God (11:6a). Faith's centrality is demonstrated by two points: First, one who seeks to please God or to approach God must believe that God exists (11:6c). It would be incongruous to think that God would be pleased with anyone who denied his existence or that anyone who denied God's existence would approach God. Some in antiquity questioned God's existence on theoretical grounds (cf. Philo, *Creation* 170; *Special Laws* 1.32), and others exhibited a kind of practical atheism (Pss 14:1; 53:1), but since both Jews and Greeks commonly believed in God's existence (NOTE on 11:6c), even those who were inclined to drift away from the Christian faith would probably have affirmed some belief in God (cf. H.-F. Weiss; Grässer).

Second, God rewards those who seek him (11:6d). On a basic level, no one seeks God without the hope of receiving a favorable response from him, but the broader issue concerns the justice of God. "Reward" assumes that God bestows his favor in a fair way (NOTE and COMMENT on 10:35). Conversely, to say that God blesses the wicked and condemns the righteous would be to say that God is unjust (NOTE on 6:10). If listeners affirm that God rewards those who

---

[379]Some detect an allusion to Christ's example in Hebrews' portrayal of Abel. Both men had the dual role of sacrificer and victim, and the blood of Christ, like the blood of Abel, continues to speak after his death (12:24; Dunnill, *Covenant*, 150; Grässer, *Hebräer*, 3.112). Nevertheless, the emphasis in this passage falls on Abel's faith, rather than on his possible role as a type of Christ's priesthood.

[380]On traditions concerning Enoch see VanderKam, *Enoch*.

[381]Aristotle commented that "all orators produce belief by employing as proofs either examples or enthymemes and nothing else" (*Rhetoric* 1.2.8). Both are evident in Heb 11. For other examples of this type of argument see 2:2–3; 3:3–4; 6:16; 9:16, 22. On enthymemes see pp. 93–94.

seek him—showing mercy as well as justice (4:15; 5:2)—they have reason to persevere even when faith entails hardship.

Noah. The story of Noah and the flood is briefly told. Nothing is said about the animals or the rainbow. Attention focuses on God and the human beings involved in the story.[382]

Hab 2:4	*Gen 7:1*
My righteous one	Noah is righteous
will live	enters the ark
by faith	________

Noah was commonly recognized as a righteous man (NOTE on Heb 11:7), and building the ark meant the "salvation of his household" from the flood. Genesis does not mention Noah's faith, but since righteousness and life are part of the story, the author of Hebrews discerns that Noah acted by faith on the basis of Hab 2:4.

Noah's situation was comparable to that of the listeners in that both were given a warning about "things that could not yet be seen" (11:7a): the coming flood and the coming judgment (6:2; cf. 10:27; 12:29). Just as Noah had to respond before the flood began, the listeners must act on the basis of a warning concerning a judgment that is not yet perceptible to the eye. Given that the flood manifested *God's* judgment, it is perhaps surprising that Hebrews says that *Noah* "condemned the world" by his faith (11:7c). The passage does not allude to the idea that the righteous will one day judge the wicked (NOTE on 11:7c), since other passages in Hebrews leave final judgment to God (10:27, 30; 12:23; 13:4; cf. 6:2, 8). Rather, it means that Noah showed his negative judgment upon the world by acting on the basis of the divine word rather than acting on the basis of what is seen, as the world does. The outcome of Noah's faith was that he received God's righteousness, that is, God pronounced favorable judgment on his behalf. His example encourages listeners to persevere in the hope of righteousness, which will be fulfilled in the heavenly city, where the spirits of the righteous will be made complete (12:23).

31. The Faith of Abraham and His Descendants (11:8–22)

11 [8]By faith Abraham, when he was called, obeyed and set out for a place that he was to receive for an inheritance, and he set out not knowing where he was going. [9]By faith he resided as an alien in a land of promise as if it belonged to another, dwelling in tents with Isaac and Jacob, who were joint heirs of the same promise; [10]for he awaited the city with foundations, whose builder and maker is

[382]On traditions concerning Noah see J. P. Lewis, *Study*; L. R. Bailey, *Noah*.

God. 11By faith, even though Sarah herself was barren, he received power to father children even beyond the usual time, since he considered the one who promised to be faithful. 12Therefore, from one person, indeed from one who was "dead," were begotten [descendants] as numerous as the stars of the heaven and the countless grains of sand by the shore of the sea.

13These all died in faith, without having received the things that were promised, but having seen them and greeted them from afar, and having confessed that they were foreigners and transients on the earth. 14Now those who say such things make clear that they are seeking a homeland. 15And if they had in mind that [land] from which they had gone out, they would have had opportunity to return. 16But in fact they desire a better one, that is, a heavenly one. Therefore, God is not ashamed to be called their God, for he prepared for them a city.

17By faith Abraham, when he was tested, offered Isaac; indeed, the one who was offering his only son had received the promises; 18he was the one to whom it was said, *through Isaac shall your descendants be called.* 19[He did so] since he considered that God was able to raise even from the dead, so that he received him back as a symbol. 20By faith Isaac blessed Jacob and Esau, also [speaking] about things to come. 21By faith Jacob, when he was dying, blessed each of the sons of Joseph and *bowed over the end of his staff.* 22By faith Joseph, when he was dying, remembered the exodus of the children of Israel and gave instructions concerning his bones.

NOTES

11:8. *By faith Abraham.* When God made a promise, Abraham (2:16; 6:13; 7:1–10) "believed the Lord; and the Lord reckoned it to him as righteousness" (Gen 15:6). This verse is quoted by other NT writers (Rom 4:3; Gal 3:6; Jas 2:23), but not by Hebrews. This is surprising since righteousness and faith are linked in Heb 10:38; 11:4, 7. On faith see pp. 125–27.

when he was called, obeyed and set out. God's call was "Go from your country and your kindred and your father's house to the land that I will show you" (Gen 12:1). Heeding God's call required faith, for God's words "take the form of a promise and define the time of fulfillment not as present but future" (Philo, *Migration* 43–44). Such faith is expressed in obedience (cf. Gen 22:18; 26:5; Philo, *Abraham* 60, 85, 88).

for a place. According to Gen 12:1 God commanded Abraham to go to "the land," but Heb 11:8 speaks more vaguely of "a place." Some MSS (א^{2} D^{2} 1739 1881 Maj) insert an article ("the place"), but the shorter reading (P^{46} א* A D* etc.) leaves the place unspecified, which is appropriate given Abraham's uncertainty about the destination (11:8c).

that he was to receive for an inheritance. Many understood Canaan to be Abraham's inheritance (Ps 105:11), but Hebrews maintains that Abraham receives his true inheritance in God's heavenly city (NOTES on Heb 6:12, 17; 11:13; 12:17).

and he set out not knowing where he was going. Hebrews has spoken of "entering" God's rest and sanctuary (4:11; 10:19), but now shifts to "setting out"

(11:8; 13:13). Movement away from one's earthly home and movement into God's presence are two aspects of the journey of faith. Genesis 12:1 says that God would show Abraham where to go, but Gen 12:5 indicates that he set out for Canaan. According to Gen 11:31, Abraham and his father were actually on their way to Canaan before Abraham heard God's call. Hebrews probably did not identify the place because Abraham's destination is ultimately God's heavenly city (Heb 11:10).

11:9. *By faith he resided as an alien.* The evocative word *paroikein* is based on roots meaning "to live alongside." Associations come from two forms of common usage:

(a) Social context. Forms of *paroik-* were used for Abraham and others who lived as temporary residents in Egypt (Gen 12:10; 15:13; 47:4; Deut 26:5; Acts 13:17), in Canaan (Gen 17:8; 35:27; 37:1; Exod 6:4; Ps 105:12 [104:12 LXX]), and among foreign peoples (Gen 20:1; 21:23, 34; 23:4). People left home to become resident aliens because of famine (Gen 12:10; Ruth 1:1), war (1 Esdr 5:7; *Liv. Pro.* 12:3), or the desire to escape condemnation (Exod 2:22; Acts 7:29; *Liv. Pro.* 10:2). In Greco-Roman society resident aliens could not participate in assemblies, serve in the military, or inherit from Roman citizens. Resident aliens, however, were legally better off than foreigners (Philo, *Flaccus* 53–54).

(b) Theological development. "Resident alien" generally connoted the transient and vulnerable quality of human life. Land was not to be sold in perpetuity because it belongs to God, and human beings are merely resident aliens (Lev 25:23). When asking for help, the psalmist prays, "Hear my prayer, O Lord . . . For I am a resident alien before you, and a transient like all my ancestors" (Ps 39:12 [38:12 LXX]; cf. 1 Chron 29:15). For Philo, people became resident aliens by birth in a mortal body. For Hebrews, however, people become resident aliens by responding in faith to God's call, which sets them apart from those who do not share the same convictions (cf. 1 Pet 1:17; 2:11; Pol. *Phil.* preface; *Mart. Pol.* preface; cf. J. H. Elliott, *Home*, 24–37). See generally, K. L. and M. A. Schmidt, and R. Meyer, *TDNT* 5.841–53; Feldmeier, *Christen*, 12–22.

in a land of promise. The preposition after *paroikein* is *eis* rather than *en*, which could mean that Abraham "emigrated to" a land (BAGD; Lane). Nevertheless, *eis* seems to be synonymous with *en*, meaning "in," as in Num 20:15 (LXX^{A}), where the Israelites dwell as aliens in (*eis*) Egypt (Ellingworth). On the promise theme see pp. 110–12.

as if it belonged to another. Various peoples lived in Canaan (Gen 15:19–21). Philo said that for Abraham, coming to Canaan was like coming home (*Abraham* 62), but Hebrews calls it land that "belonged to another" (*allotrian*), using an expression that fit Moses' stay in Midian (Exod 2:22; 18:3) and Israel's stay in Egypt (Acts 7:6). Cf. NOTE on "foreigners" in Heb 11:13.

dwelling in tents. The term "dwelling" (*katoikein*) was sometimes differentiated from "residing as an alien" (*paroikein*; cf. Philo, *Husbandry* 64; *Heir* 267). But often the two terms were synonymous: "Jacob dwelt in the land where his father resided as an alien" (Gen 37:1; cf. 47:4). The word "tents" suggests the temporary nature of their situation (Gen 12:8; 13:3; 18:1).

with Isaac and Jacob. Hebrews probably means only that Abraham, Isaac, and Jacob shared the same seminomadic life. Some authors, though, took this to mean that they lived at the same time, even though the OT recounts the death of Abraham (Gen 25:7–10) before the birth of Jacob (25:19–26; cf. *Jub.* 22:10–23:3; *Tg. Ps.-J.* Gen 25:29; *b. B. Bat.* 16b). However, Abraham was one hundred when Isaac was born (Gen 21:5), and about forty years later Isaac fathered Jacob (25:20). This suggests that the lifetimes of Abraham and Jacob overlapped. Abraham died at one hundred and seventy-five years of age (25:7), which was thirty-five years after Jacob's birth.

who were joint heirs of the same promise. God promised land to Abraham and his descendants (Gen 12:7; 15:18; 24:7; 28:4, 13; cf. 35:12; Deut 1:8). On the promise theme see pp. 110–12.

11:10. *For he awaited the city.* Genesis says that Abraham looked for a land, but later tradition said that God prepared a city from the beginning of time and showed it to Adam, Abraham, and Moses (2 *Bar.* 4:1–4). This was the heavenly Jerusalem (Gal 4:26; cf. Phil 3:20), which some expected to be revealed at the end time (4 *Ezra* 7:26; 8:52; 10:27; Rev 21:2, 10). Philo says that God called Abraham to dwell in "a city good and large and very prosperous" (*Alleg. Interp.* 3.83; *Confusion* 78; *Dreams* 1.46, 181). Hope would include living as a citizen (12:23) rather than a resident alien or foreigner in the city (Heb 11:9, 13). All who share in the new covenant will be deemed "fellow citizens" of God's city (8:11; cf. 12:23).

with foundations. Rhetorically, speakers praised cities by lauding the fortifications and founders, as Hebrews does here (Quintilian, *Inst.* 3.7.26–27). Foundations of buildings and city walls were best situated on solid rock (Matt 7:24–27; Vitruvius, *On Architecture* 1.5.1) and made of stone that would "bear the great mass resting on them" (Josephus, *Ant.* 8.63). The OT said that Jerusalem had secure foundations (Pss 46:4–5; 87:1) and that God would establish the foundations of Jerusalem in the future (Isa 54:11; 4 *Ezra* 10:27; Rev 21:14, 19). The foundations of God's city will endure in a kingdom that cannot be shaken (Heb 12:28; 13:14).

whose builder and maker. God's city is produced through a kind of urban planning rather than haphazard settlement. Many new cities were established in the Greco-Roman period. A "builder" (*technitēs*) was a craftsman and a "maker" (*dēmiourgos*) could be either a craftsman or a magistrate. Here the terms seem synonymous (cf. Josephus, *Ant.* 12.35). Since the architect who designed a city often performed many tasks in the construction as well, various terms could be used for the same person (Vitruvius, *On Architecture* 1.1.1; 2.preface.15; 10.preface.1; 1 Cor 3:10; Philo, *Creation* 17, 20). A city builder was to select a site, divide the land, plan streets and public buildings, and build walls (Homer, *Odyssey* 6.7–11; Vitruvius, *On Architecture* 1.4.12–1.5.1; Philo, *Creation* 17; cf. T. D. Boyd, *CAM* 3.1691–1700). City dwellers often considered their founders to have been divinely inspired (T. J. Cornell, *RAC* 12.1107–71; *OCD*, "City-Founders"). Hebrews speaks, not of a founder being inspired by God, but of a founder who is God.

is God. The term "maker" (*dēmiourgos*) was used for the Creator of the world in Jewish (Josephus, *Ant.* 1.155; cf. 1.272; Philo, *Creation* 18, 146) and Greco-Roman sources (Xenophon, *Memorabilia* 1.4.7; cf. Epictetus, *Disc.* 2.8.21; Plato, *Timeaus* 28A, 29A). The same was true of "builder" (*technitēs*, Wis 13:1; Philo, *Creation* 135; *Change* 29–31; Lucian, *Icaromenippus* 8). Where most sources use the terms for God as Creator of the present universe (e.g., Philo, *Creation* 18–20), Hebrews refers specifically to God's establishment of the heavenly city. See Williamson, *Philo*, 42–51; W. Foerster, *TDNT* 2.62.

11:11. *By faith.* When God promised that Abraham would have many descendants, Abraham "believed the Lord" (Gen 15:6). Later, however, Sarah and Abraham contrived to have a child through Hagar (Gen 16) and laughed at the promise (17:17; 18:12). Augustine argued that this laughter "is the exultation of one who rejoices, not the scornful laughter of one who mistrusts" (Augustine, *The City of God* 16.26), but Calvin recognized that Abraham and Sarah's faith was mixed with distrust, although their unbelief was not hardened or persistent.

even though Sarah herself was barren. The OT says that "Sarah was barren" (Gen 11:30 LXX; cf. 16:1–2). Many MSS of Hebrews lack "barren" (P^{13vid} ℵ A D^2 33 Maj; cf. NA^{25}; KJV; NASB; REB; NJB), but it appears in others, either alone (P^{46} D* Ψ), prefaced by a definite article (D^1 6 81 1241^s 1739 1881), or accompanied by the participle *ousa* (P 104 365 1505). The word could have been added as a gloss, but it seems more likely that some MSS omitted it through error and that that others included additional words to improve the flow of the sentence. Therefore, "barren" should be retained (NA^{27}; NIV; NRSV; NAB^2; see *TCGNT*, 673). The entire clause can best be taken as a parenthetical comment (see the next NOTE).

he received power to father children. The subject of the verb has been taken in two different ways, of which the second is preferable:

(**a**) Sarah. When Sarah is understood to be the subject, the sentence says that by faith Sarah was given the power to conceive (Chrysostom; Calvin; REB; NJB; Bénétreau; Casalini; P. E. Hughes; Swetnam, *Jesus*, 98–101; Dunnill, *Covenant*, 184–86; Greenlee, "By Faith"). MSS that use *eteken* ("gave birth," $ℵ^2$ D^2 Maj) clearly take Sarah to be the subject, but those that use *teknoun* (D* P 81 1505) leave the matter open, since *teknoun* can indicate procreation by either male or female. One obstacle to taking Sarah as the subject is that "deposit seed" was a fixed expression for the male's role in procreation: "Just as a farmer casts down the seed of corn into the earth, so a man deposits his seed into a woman's place" (*Gk. Apoc. Ezra* 5:12). Some in antiquity understood that women contributed their own fluid in the process of conception (van der Horst, "Sarah's"), and Philo did speak of Sarah "sowing" (Sowers, *Hermeneutics*, 234–35; Eisenbaum, *Jewish Heroes*, 158). Others note that "seed" can mean "offspring," (Heb 2:16; 11:18) and *katabolē* can mean "to establish" (4:3; 9:26), so that the text could simply refer to Sarah's ability to establish a line of descendants. Yet this seems unlikely given the common technical sense of "deposit seed" for the male. Moreover, Abraham is clearly the subject of the next verse (11:12), where the Greek expressions "from one" and "as good as dead" are both masculine in gender.

(b) Abraham. The expression "deposit seed" and the focus on Abraham in the context favor taking Abraham as the subject of 11:11. The problem is how to construe the reference to Sarah. One alternative is to take *autē Sarra* as dative rather than nominative, since early MSS did not include iota subscripts. Thus Abraham was given power to procreate "*with* Sarah herself, who was sterile" (Attridge; Braun; F. F. Bruce; Ellingworth; Grässer; H.-F. Weiss). The problem is that no known MS has the dative, and the expression "deposit seed" does not seem to have used the dative case for the woman's role (Rose, *Wolke*, 230). Finally, the reference to Sarah can be read as a parenthesis, as translated here (UBS[3], NIV; NAB[2]; *TCGNT*, 672–73; Lane; Rose, *Wolke*, 228–31; cf. Hagner; Wilson).

even beyond the usual time. Both Abraham and Sarah were beyond the normal ages for procreation (Gen 18:11–13; Philo, *Abraham* 111, 195). This expression could relate to Sarah (Lane; cf. Gen 18:11), but the context emphasizes that it was Abraham who was "as good as dead" (Heb 11:12).

since he considered the one who promised to be faithful. See NOTE on 10:23.

11:12. *Therefore, from one person.* The gender of "one" is masculine, referring to Abraham. As the father of a great nation, he was the "one" from whom many were born (Isa 51:2; Ezek 33:24).

indeed from one who was "dead," were begotten. Abraham was "dead" in that his advanced age made childbearing unlikely (cf. Rom 4:19). Speaking of new life coming from the "dead" implies that Isaac's birth foreshadows resurrection from death, as does his near sacrifice (Heb 11:19).

as numerous as the stars of the heaven and the countless grains of sand by the shore of the sea. This recalls Gen 22:17 (cf. Dan 3:36 [= Pr Azar 13]; Gen 15:5; 32:12; Deut 1:10; 10:22; 28:62). Many offspring was a form of blessing (Heb 6:14). Contrasting the multitude of descendants (11:12c) with the "one" who begot them (11:12a) shows the power of faith. Listeners would have included themselves among the innumerable descendants of Abraham (2:16).

11:13. *These all died in faith.* The OT tells of the deaths of Abraham (Gen 25:8), Sarah (Gen 23:1–2), Isaac (Gen 35:29), and Jacob (Gen 49:33). To say that they died "in faith" means that faith shaped the way they dealt with death. Dying as foreigners (Heb 11:13d) in a foreign land was "a pitiable fate" (2 Macc 9:28; cf. 3 Macc 6:3; *Greek Anthology* [LCL] vol. 2 #722; cf. #446). On the low status of foreigners see Matt 27:7, where their burial field is bought with blood money.

without having received the things that were promised. The idea that Abraham did not receive what was promised (11:13, 39) stands in tension with the statement that he did receive what was promised (6:15). The difference reflects a typological understanding of the OT that allows God's promise to be taken on two levels: in a penultimate sense God's promise is fulfilled in the birth of Isaac and in Abraham's sojourn in Canaan, but in an ultimate sense the promise is fulfilled in the world to come (NOTE on 6:15).

but having seen them and greeted them from afar. God's people "see" their ultimate destination by faith in his promise (11:1). "Greeting" connotes gladness.

People who endure the rigors of a voyage "are eager to see and greet their native soil" (Philo, *Abraham* 65; cf. Virgil, *Aeneid* 3.524; Attridge). Conversely, it is a pitiable fate to be sold as slaves into a foreign land, "never even to dream again of saluting the soil of their native land" (Philo, *Special Laws* 4.17).

and having confessed. Confession of one's status as a foreigner is the corollary to confessing faith in Christ (3:1, 6; 4:14–16; 10:19, 23).

that they were foreigners. People commonly distinguished relatives from foreigners, friends from enemies, and fellow citizens from foreigners (Philo, *Special Laws* 4.70). As a ruler was above a subject and a master above a slave, the citizen was above the foreigner (Philo, *Creation* 165; cf. Cicero, *Academica posterioira* 2.44 §136; Luke 15:15). No one would easily accept being demoted to the status of a foreigner and losing one's rights (Philo, *Flaccus* 54). Threatened with the prospect of being expelled as a foreigner, one man pleaded that officials not "make me a man without a country, do not cut me off from such a host of relatives, and bring me to utter ruin. Rather than abandon them . . . I will kill myself, that at least I may be buried by them in my homeland" (Demonsthenes, *Against Eubulides* 70). Foreigners usually coveted the status of a citizen. Therefore, it was good news when the Gentiles who were once "foreigners to the covenants of promise" became "fellow citizens with the saints" (Eph 2:12, 19). See generally, G. Stählin, *TDNT* 5.1–13; *TLNT* 2.555–60; J. H. Friedrich, *EDNT* 2.485–86.

and transients. Abraham confesses that he is a "resident alien and a transient" when seeking to purchase a place to bury Sarah (Gen 23:4 LXX). In the Greco-Roman world the term "transient" (*parepidēmos*) had more to do with the temporary nature of one's stay in a given location than did "resident alien" (*paroikos*, cf. Heb 11:9), which had more to do with a person's legal status. Citizens were regularly distinguished from transients and resident aliens (Josephus, *Ant.* 2.101; 14.115; *Life* 372; *Ag. Ap.* 2.257–59; Philo, *Good Person* 7; J. H. Elliott, *Home*, 25). At the same time, citizens (*politai*) and resident aliens (*katoikountoi*) were distinguished from transient foreigners (*parepidēmountes xenoi*), who had a more marginal social status (Dittenberger, *OGIS* #339.29–30; cf. #268.9; 329.28). Like Hebrews, 1 Peter uses the term for the Christian community, which lives away from its true home and in tension with a society that does not share its convictions (1 Pet 1:1; 2:11–12). See generally *TLNT* 3.41–43; H. Balz, *EDNT* 3.38; W. Grundmann, *TDNT* 2.64–65; Feldmeier, *Christen*, 8–12; idem, "Nation." Cf. "refugees" in NOTE on 6:18.

on the earth. Being a foreigner and a transient often had to do with one's place in society, but Hebrews now uses these terms for Christians on earth, whose citizenship lies in the heavenly Jerusalem (12:22–24; 13:14). Some said that human souls became foreigners when they were put into a physical body (Philo, *Dreams* 1.181; *Cherubim* 120; *Confusion* 77–79; Plutarch, *Mor.* 607D). In Hebrews, however, Abraham becomes a transient, not by birth into a physical body, but by responding in faith to God's call (11:8). Any idea that souls *return* to their heavenly abode is excluded by 11:15, which insists that Israel's ancestors did not return to their place of origin, but traveled to a place they had never been. See Williamson, *Philo*, 326–28.

11:14. *Now, those who say such things make clear that they are seeking a homeland.* One's homeland (*patris*) could be one's birthplace, hometown, or permanent place of residence. Since "nothing is sweeter than one's native land" (Homer, *Odyssey* 9.34; Dio Chrysostom, *Disc.* 44.1), a wanderer might seek to return at considerable risk (Josephus, *J.W.* 1.434). Attachment to one's homeland was so widespread that it was said to be innate (Philo, *Gaius* 277; Josephus, *Ant.* 1.317). One who gazes upon his birthplace and says, "This is really my own homeland," understands that "a lingering attachment for the place abides in my mind and heart." Indeed, Odysseus preferred a return to his homeland to the gift of immortality (Cicero, *Laws* 2.1 §3). Loyalty to the homeland ranked alongside observance of law and loyalty to one's parents and family, so that a virtuous person would willingly die for the homeland (Cicero, *De officiis* 1.17 §§54–55; 2 Macc 8:21; 13:14; Philo, *Planter* 146; *Drunkenness* 17; Josephus, *Ant.* 12.304).

Abraham and his family sought a homeland that was different from their place of origin (cf. 11:15), and in common practice people sometimes did adopt a new homeland voluntarily. Jews living outside of Palestine continued to think of Jerusalem as their mother city, but called the places where they permanently resided their "homelands" (Philo, *Flaccus* 46). Alexander the Great tried to convince his subjects to shift their loyalties from their local communities to the empire as a whole, which was their new fatherland (Plutarch, *Mor.* 329C). The Romans followed a similar practice (Cicero, *Laws* 2.2 §5; Philo, *Gaius* 285), referring to Rome as "the single homeland of all the races" (Pliny the Elder, *Natural History* 3.5.49; cf. Josephus, *Ant.* 20.11). In Hebrews, however, the homeland of the faithful is not on earth, but in the heavenly Jerusalem (Heb 12:22–24; 13:14).

11:15. *And if they had in mind that [land] from which they had gone out, they would have had opportunity to return.* Abraham and Sarah left Haran never to return (Gen 12:4). Abraham's servant returned to Haran briefly (Gen 24:4), and Jacob lived in Haran for some years (Gen 27:43), but both returned to Canaan. The family never returned to Haran on a permanent basis.

11:16. *But in fact they desire a better one, that is, a heavenly one.* According to Hebrews, the object of Abraham's hope was not Canaan, but heaven. Abraham's heirs also have a heavenly calling (3:1) and homeland (12:22–24; 13:14).

Therefore, God is not ashamed to be called their God. Under the new covenant, God promised his people that he would be "their God" (8:10). God will give honor and glory to those of whom he is not ashamed (2:5–9). In order to carry out God's intention, Jesus overcame the shame of identifying with mortals, taking on their flesh and blood (NOTE on 2:11). Jesus also despised the shame of the cross for the sake of the joy that would be his at God's right hand (12:2).

for he prepared for them a city. The city is the heavenly Jerusalem (11:10; 12:22–24).

11:17. *By faith Abraham.* Abraham's faithful obedience in binding Isaac is made explicit in *Jub.* 17:15–16; 18:16; cf. *m. 'Abot* 5:3. Cf. NOTE on Heb 11:8.

when he was tested. The Greek *peirazein* is rendered into English by both "test" and "tempt" (NOTES on 2:18; 3:9). Testing means placing someone in a difficult situation so that the person's character is made manifest. Abraham was tested by God (Gen 22:1; Josephus, *Ant.* 1.223, 233; contrast *Jub.* 17:15–16; 18:9, 12, where an evil figure is responsible). Abraham's faithfulness in testing (Heb 6:15; Sir 44:20; 1 Macc 2:52) provides a model for listeners, who are also being tested (Heb 2:18).

offered Isaac. The word *prospherein* appears twice in this verse. The second occurrence is in the imperfect tense, which indicates that Abraham intended to sacrifice Isaac without actually saying that he did the deed (11:17b; MHT, 1.129). The first occurrence is in the perfect tense, which often indicates completed action (11:17a), and some argue that Hebrews relies on traditions that Abraham did kill the boy (*Bib. Ant.* 18:5; 40:2; *Mek.*, "Pisḥa," 7.81 [Lauterbach ed., 1.57], cf. 11.95 [1.88]; Rose, *Wolke*, 239–44; Grässer). According to this view, Isaac died and was restored through resurrection (cf. 11:35; NOTE on 11:19). Nevertheless, Hebrews probably assumes that Abraham did not slay Isaac, using the perfect to refer to things written in the OT (MHT, 1.142; Attridge; Braun; Ellingworth) or to show that the event serves as an abiding example (BDF §342[5]) or to indicate that Abraham's determination to obey God was complete (Philo, *Abraham* 177; Spicq; Bénétreau; D. Guthrie; Swetnam, *Jesus*, 122).

indeed, the one who was offering his only son. According to Gen 22:2, God commanded Abraham to sacrifice "your son, your only son Isaac, whom you love." Hebrews uses *monogenēs* ("only begotten"), which is not in Gen 22:2 LXX, but is used by Aquila (Gen 22:2), Symmachus (Gen 22:12), and Josephus (*Ant.* 1.222; cf. Philo, *Unchangeable* 4; *Dreams* 1.194; *Abraham* 168, 196). Abraham fathered Ishmael and Isaac, but since Ishmael was not born through Abraham's wife, but through Hagar, a slave, Isaac was traditionally considered Abraham's "only son" in the full sense of the word. On "offering" see NOTE on 11:17a.

had received the promises. See NOTE on 6:13 and pp. 110–12.

11:18. *through Isaac shall your descendants be called.* Genesis 21:12 LXX (cf. Rom 9:7).

11:19. *since he considered that God was able to raise even from the dead.* Genesis 22 does not mention resurrection, but since Abraham had faith, Hebrews assumes that he held common beliefs about God's power to "kill" and "make alive" (Deut 32:39; 1 Sam 2:6). "For God all things are possible" (Matt 19:26; Mark 10:27; Luke 18:27). He can raise up children for Abraham from stones (Matt 3:9; Luke 3:8). Resurrection faith enabled people to endure the martyrdom of themselves and their children (2 Macc 7:9–14, 28–29). God's power to raise the dead is attested in the Pauline writings (Rom 4:17; 2 Cor 1:9; cf. John 5:21) and in the second benediction in the Jewish liturgy: "Blessed are you, O Lord, who makes the dead alive" (Schürer, *History*, 2.456; cf. *Jos. Asen.* 20:7). Hebrews presupposes such traditions.

so that. Some take *hothen* in a spatial sense: "from" the realm of the dead (Calvin; Westcott; KJV; NASB; NIV; REB). "So that" (*hothen*) takes it in a consecutive sense that shows the flow of the argument (cf. 2:17; 3:1; 7:25; 8:3; 9:18; Attridge; Braun; Lane; H.-F. Weiss).

he received him. "Received" can have two meanings. The second is preferable: (**a**) Isaac's birth. Since in Hebrews "receive" commonly means receiving what was promised (10:36; 11:39), this verse could refer to Isaac's birth. The implication is that in Isaac's birth Abraham received a symbol of future blessings (Dunnill, *Covenant*, 197). The problem is that Isaac's birth is not the focus of the passage. (**b**) Isaac's preservation from death. Abraham was told to slay Isaac, but "received" Isaac back from the threshold of death since the boy was not actually slain (cf. Philo, *Abraham* 177). It is unlikely that Hebrews recalls a tradition in which Abraham killed Isaac and received him back through resurrection (2 Macc 7:29; Josephus, *J.W.* 2.153) as Elijah and Elisha brought dead children back to life (1 Kgs 17:17–24; 2 Kgs 4:32–37; Heb 11:35; Rose, *Wolke*, 238). See NOTE on 11:17.

as a symbol. Parabolē can best be rendered "symbol," just as the first tent is a "symbol" of the present age (NOTE on 9:9; NAB2; Attridge; Bénétreau; cf. Michaud, "Parabolê"). Some render the whole expression adverbially as "figuratively speaking" (NIV; NRSV; NJB; REB), making clear that Isaac did not really die and rise, but that his escape from death was a figurative resurrection. The translation "symbol," however, emphasizes that the incident foreshadows the future resurrection of all the faithful (Theodoret; Rissi, *Theologie*, 110; H.-F. Weiss). The incident does not specifically foreshadow Jesus' resurrection (*Barn.* 7:3; Chrysostom; Augustine, *The City of God* 16.32; Isho'dad; F. F. Bruce; Hagner; Swetnam, *Jesus*, 122–23, 128), but the resurrection of God's people.

11:20. *By faith Isaac.* The OT does not explicitly mention Isaac's faith, but it does say that Isaac pleased God (Gen 48:15 LXX). According to Heb 11:6, no one can please God without faith. Since Isaac did please God, Hebrews assumes that he had faith (Rose, *Wolke*, 253).

blessed Jacob and Esau. Jacob tricked Isaac into blessing him with prosperity and dominion (Gen 27:28–29). The idea that Isaac also blessed Esau is more problematic, since his words promise Esau a life of hardship (Gen 27:39–40). Moreover, Hebrews says that Isaac was a joint heir of the promise, but does not say the same of Esau (Heb 11:9), adding later that when Esau wanted to inherit a blessing, he was given no opportunity to repent (12:17). One reason that Hebrews might have thought that Isaac blessed Esau was because Isaac was responding to Esau's request, "Bless me also, father!" (Gen 27:38). Second, Isaac does promise that Esau will "live" and eventually be free from his brother's yoke (Gen 27:40; cf. Westermann, *Genesis*, 2.443). Third, Isaac's words to Esau as well as to Jacob pertained to "things that were to come," allowing both to be considered promises. Finally, one might distinguish between giving and receiving a blessing. According to Heb 11:20, a blessing was given to Esau, yet according to 12:17, he did not receive it. The text might suggest that Esau was like the people of the wilderness generation, who refused to receive and hold fast to the good news that was given to them (Rose, *Wolke*, 257).

also [speaking] about things to come. Isaac's words about "things to come" (cf. 1:14; 2:5; 6:5; 10:1; 13:14) point to eschatological blessings (cf. 6:7) as his deliverance anticipates resurrection (11:19).

11:21. *By faith Jacob.* Jacob was sometimes said to be faithful (*Jub.* 27:17), although the OT does not specifically mention his faith. Hebrews relies on the idea that the righteous live by faith (Hab 2:4; Heb 10:38). Therefore, if Jacob was righteous (Wis 10:10; cf. *Jub.* 19:13; 22:10–11; 27:17; 35:12), his life must have expressed faith (Rose, *Wolke*, 258).

when he was dying, blessed each of the sons of Joseph. Jacob announces his imminent death in Gen 47:29; 48:21. Although Genesis emphasizes Jacob's blessing of his twelve sons (Gen 49), Hebrews focuses on his blessing of two of his grandchildren, Ephraim and Manasseh (Gen 48:8–22).

and bowed over. In Genesis Jacob's bowing does not follow the blessing of Joseph's sons, but the blessing of his own sons (Gen 47:31 LXX). Bowing often indicated worship of God (Heb 1:6 = Deut 32:43) or reverence toward a ruler. Earlier interpreters (Chrysostom; Theodoret; Ps.-Oecumenius) thought that Jacob displayed reverence toward Joseph, who dreamt that his family members would bow to him (Gen 37:5–11). The Vulgate took *proskynein epi* + the accusative to mean that Jacob "worshiped the end of his staff," which prompted christological interpretations (see the next NOTE). Nevertheless, the Greek does not indicate the object of worship, but the posture of worship. People show reverence by bowing with their faces upon (*epi*) a bed (1 Kgs 1:47), upon the roof (Zeph 1:5), or upon the ground (Gen 18:2), just as Jacob worshiped while bowed upon (*epi*) his staff. His posture seems to show reverence for God.

the end of his staff. The Hebrew consonants in Gen 47:31 are *mṭh*, which the MT took to mean *miṭṭâh* or "bed." The LXX took it to be *maṭṭeh* or "staff," the rendering used in Hebrews. Bowing over the staff suggests humility (C. Schneider, *TDNT* 6.969; H. Balz, *EDNT* 3.206; H.-F. Weiss). Some suggest that the staff signifies weakness (Bengel; Braun; cf. Bénétreau) or wandering, since Jacob fled with only a staff (Gen 32:10; Grässer; Rose, *Wolke*, 261). Some have taken the staff to be Joseph's royal scepter (cf. Heb 1:8; Pss 2:9; 45:6; 110:2), occasionally proposing that it foreshadows Joseph, the father of Christ (Theodoret; Ps.-Oecumenius; Theophylact) or prefigures Christ's reign (Haimo; Aquinas, *Ad Heb.* §608; Erasmus, *Paraphrase*). Since Jacob is the subject of the sentence, however, "his staff" is almost certainly his own staff rather than Joseph's scepter.

11:22. *By faith Joseph.* According to Hab 2:4 (Heb 10:38), the righteous live by faith. Therefore, Hebrews assumes that if Joseph was righteous (Wis 10:13; *T. Benj.* 5:5), his life must have expressed faith (Rose, *Wolke*, 263).

when he was dying, remembered the exodus. The term *exodus* described Israel's departure from Egypt in the LXX (e.g., Exod 19:1; Num 33:38; Pss 104:38; 113:1). The word "remember" is striking because the exodus had not yet occurred and could not be remembered as a past event. Although some translate it "made mention" (KJV; NASB; NJB) or "spoke about" (NIV; REB; NAB2), the idea of remembering can be given full weight when the exodus is understood as a promise (Tyndale, "Prologue") that was given long before Joseph (Gen 15:13–14; 50:24; cf. *T. Jos.* 20:1).

instructions concerning his bones. Joseph commanded that his bones be taken from Egypt when Israel departed (Gen 50:24–25), which indicates that he did not consider Egypt to be his final resting place. The Israelites took Joseph's bones with them during the exodus (Exod 13:19; *T. Jos.* 20:1– 6), and buried them at Shechem (Josh 24:32; Acts 7:16; Josephus, *Ant.* 2.200; cf. Wilcox, "Bones"; Kugel, *Potiphar's*, 125–55). Joseph's bones help to foreshadow the final rest of the faithful in the heavenly world (Heb 4:1–11; 12:22–24).

COMMENT[383]

Abel, Enoch, and Noah were treated in quick succession in 11:4–7, but the author now lingers over Abraham, whom God promised to bless with descendants and a land. Hebrews does not engage in debates over *who* the descendants of Abraham are, assuming that listeners will include themselves among Abraham's heirs (2:16; 6:12, 17).[384] The issue is *how* Abraham's heirs receive what God has promised. Earlier the author recalled how God confirmed his promise with an unalterable oath (6:17), and showed how Abraham received a limited fulfillment of the promises in a blessing from Melchizedek (7:6) and the birth of Isaac (6:15). The issue is not whether God will prove faithful, but whether Abraham's descendants will be faithful, for Abraham's heirs receive their inheritance after a time of "faith and perseverance" (6:12).

One factor that shapes the interpretation of the OT is the principle that "my righteous one will live by faith" (Hab 2:4; Heb 10:38; §29 COMMENT). In an immediate sense, faith is a way of life on earth, and in an ultimate sense, faith is the way that people obtain everlasting life (NOTE on 10:38). Abraham lives by faith when he obeys God's command, leaves his father's house, resides as an alien in the promised land, and confesses that he is a transient on the earth. Abraham also prefigures life everlasting by receiving power to father children even though he was "dead" in old age and by receiving his only son back from death as a symbol of the resurrection (11:12, 19).

A second factor is that the OT world is depicted in terms of the Greco-Roman world of the listeners (cf. §15 COMMENT). Abraham, Sarah, and their children were tent dwellers who tended their flocks centuries before Hebrews was written. Those addressed by Hebrews spoke Greek—a language unknown to Israel's early ancestors—and almost certainly lived in or near one of the cities in the Roman Empire. In the listeners' world builders expanded existing cities and founded new ones in which foreigners lived as resident aliens rather than full citizens (NOTES on 11:9, 10, 13). Hebrews brings Abraham's story into the urban world

---

[383]On 11:8–22 see Arowele, "Pilgrim People"; Braun, "Das himmlische"; Bulley, "Death"; deSilva, *Despising*, 183–90; Dunnill, *Covenant*, 172–81; Eisenbaum, *Jewish Heroes*, 154–66; Feldmeier, *Christen*, 83–93; idem, "Nation"; Frost, "Who Were"; Greenlee, "Hebrews 11:11"; van der Horst, "Sarah's"; Irwin, "Use"; Johnsson, "Pilgrim"; Mercado, "Language"; Moxnes, *Theology*, 178–90; Muntingh, "The City"; Niederwimmer, "Vom Glauben"; Rose, "Verheissung," 178–91; idem, *Wolke*, 202–67; Siker, *Disinheriting*, 87–97; Söding, "Antwort"; Swetnam, *Jesus*, 86–129; idem, "Hebrews 11"; Wider, *Theozentrik*, 195–99; Wilcox, "Bones."

[384]Matt 3:9; 8:11–12; Luke 3:8; 13:28; John 8:31–58; Rom 9:7; Gal 3:29. On the theme see Siker, *Disinheriting*, 87–97.

of the listeners while directing their gaze beyond their immediate context to the future heavenly city that God prepared for the descendants of Abraham and Sarah.

Structurally, the passage can be divided into three paragraphs: (**a**) God's promises of land (11:8–10) and descendants (11:11–12) are summarized, allowing the author to discuss each in more detail in what follows. (**b**) The promise of land (11:13–16) is taken up first, as the author explains that Abraham's destination was ultimately not Canaan, but God's heavenly city. (**c**) The promise of descendants is taken up next, as the author traces how faith was displayed in the stories of Isaac, Jacob, and Joseph (11:17–22).[385]

a. Promises of Land and Descendants (11:8–12)

God's call and the response of faith are hallmarks of the story of Abraham. Since God's call included both a command to leave his old home and the promise of a new home, Abraham's response rightly included both obedience and faith. He obeyed (Heb 11:8b) by departing from his homeland and showed faith (11:8a) by trusting that God would bring him to the land that he had promised. The same is true for listeners, whose calling from God (Heb 3:1; 9:15) evoked repentance and faith (2:3–4; 6:1, 5), and who were directed to obey the Son of God (5:9). As is common in Heb 11, "faith" is in the dative case, since it is a means of activity. Abraham could be said to have exhibited faith only when he actually set out for the destination that was hidden from his eyes. Faith is "not knowing where you are going, what you are doing, what you are suffering," but "to follow the bare voice of God and to be led and driven rather than to drive" (Luther, *Luth*W 29.238).

Strangely, Hebrews notes that Abraham departed for a place that he was to receive for an inheritance (11:8b). Inheritance was commonly handed down from parents to their children, and it was closely tied to the home and family (§24 COMMENT *a*). Abraham, however, was not told that he would inherit his father's house or lands, but that he should leave his father's house and land for a place that he had never seen in the hope of inheriting it. This corresponds to the situation of the listeners, who await an eternal inheritance from God (1:14; 9:15), a heavenly gift that they had tasted, but had not fully received (6:4). Heirs ordinarily expected to be respected (Matt 21:37; Mark 12:6; Luke 20:13), but Abraham lived as a resident alien in the land that had been promised to him (11:9a). Legally, resident aliens lacked the rights of citizens (NOTE on 11:9),

[385]Since each promise is treated twice, some have suggested that the author inserted 11:13–16 into a previously existing catalog of examples (Rissi, *Theologie*, 106, 109) or that he composed 11:13–16 as an excursus on the apparent nonfulfillment of God's promises (Rose, *Wolke*, 247). Nevertheless, summarizing OT material and then taking up particular items is typical of Hebrews. In 3:1–6 the author quotes Num 12:7, then comments on each key word in succession. In Heb 4:1–11 he refers to Ps 95:11 and Gen 2:2, and only then indicates the significance of each verse. In Heb 7:1–10 the author summarizes the story of Abraham and Melchizedek, then explicates the important elements in their encounter. See the COMMENTS on these passages.

and socially they were subject to reviling (Sir 29:23–28). Like Abraham, the listeners found themselves treated like resident aliens, without security or honor in their earthly city (pp. 71–72).

The situation of the faithful is reflected in the contrast between living in tents (11:9b) and hoping for a city with foundations (11:10a). The tents of Israel's ancestors were not the shelters that citizens used for travel or during festivals;[386] the tent was their normal habitation. There was a vast difference between "the country's finest city" and a lesser town "with its lack of space" and "its tents and huts," where marginal members of society lived (Lucian, *Herodotus* 8). Many in the first century sought opportunities in Rome, a city with ancient foundations.[387] For the crowd of newcomers "there is hardly sufficient housing accommodation; the majority of them are aliens" who have "flooded in from the country towns of Italy, in fact from all over the world. And their motives for coming? A hope to get on in the world" or similar reason. "Most of them, you will find, have left home and come to Rome, the greatest and loveliest city in the world—but not theirs" (Seneca, *Ad Helviam* 6.2–3).

Hebrews directs hope beyond earthly cities to the heavenly one, "whose builder and maker is God" (11:10b). God's city is not known by sight, but through proclamation. Hebrews assumes that listeners are familiar with the tradition of a heavenly Jerusalem (11:16), in which God's people are to be gathered together in celebration (12:22–24). Christians—even those from Italy (13:24)—will find no lasting city upon earth, but seek the city that is to come (13:14). People are brought there by grace, through the resurrection of the dead. Faith that God will keep his promise constitutes the journey.

Many descendants, along with land, were included in God's promise to Abraham (11:11; Gen 12:2), but Sarah remained barren into extreme old age. This presented them with a contradiction between the divine promise, which said that they would have children, and ordinary experience, which said they could not. In such a context trusting experience means abandoning God's promise, while trusting God's promise requires overcoming experience. The situation is like that of a drama, in which a person must choose a course of action in circumstances where the choice is not obvious and in which everyone's choice would not be the same.[388] Here, despite the seemingly insuperable evidence that God had proven false, Abraham shows faith, not in his perception of his physical condition, but in the faithfulness of God who made the promise (NOTE on 10:23).

The final sentence in this paragraph contrasts one human being—Abraham—with the multitudes that descended from him (11:12). These descendants include the generations mentioned in the OT (e.g., Exod 1:1–7) and the listeners themselves (Heb 2:16). When Hebrews says that Abraham, who was "dead," had descendants as numerous as the stars of heaven and the grains of sand by the sea,

---

[386]Diodorus Siculus, *Library of History* 14.109.1; see generally Casson, *Travel*, 90–91, 154, 198.

[387]Ovid, *Fasti* 3.72. Virgil's *Aeneid*, which describes Aeneas's journey to the site where Rome would be built, reflects the importance of the motif in antiquity.

[388]The situation can be compared to that of the wilderness generation (§10 COMMENT *b*). On the technique in drama see Aristotle, *Poetics* 6.19–24 1450b and the notes by Fyfe in *Aristotle*, 28–39.

it indicates that the Creator of the stars and the sea is able to bring forth life out of death (cf. 2:10; 11:3). Therefore, the birth of Isaac, like Isaac's deliverance from death, foreshadows the resurrection of the faithful (11:19).

b. On the Promised Land and the City of God (11:13–16)

Hebrews poignantly comments that Israel's ancestors died without having received what was promised (11:13a). Apart from Enoch (11:5), people of faith from Abel (11:4) to Jesus (12:2) experienced death, and listeners can expect the same. Hebrews affirms that death is real, but not final, for God calls people to a destination that lies beyond it. Faith empowered Abraham and his family to "see" the outcome of their journey, like travelers catching a glimpse of their distant destination (NOTE on 11:13b). Because they have not arrived, they *must* live by faith, yet because they are sure of the destination, they *can* live by faith.

To be a foreigner and transient on the earth characterizes people of faith (11:13d). Foreigners were not entitled to full participation in civic life and were liable to expulsion at the desire of those in authority.[389] If citizens are like a kernel of wheat, resident aliens are the bran, and foreigners are the chaff (Aristophanes, *Acharnians* 502–508). In the first century there were many foreigners in the cities (Acts 17:21), and in Rome they eventually comprised the bulk of the population. Some came as slaves and others migrated voluntarily. Juvenal lamented that "for years now the Syrian Orontes has poured its sewage into our native Tiber," bringing to Rome an endless stream of outlandish manners and languages (*Satire* 3.60–61). Although some foreigners prospered, they did not necessarily find acceptance.[390] Hebrews seeks to reverse the stigma of foreignness by declaring that Abraham did not merely accept foreign status, but confessed it (11:13c). Confessing oneself to be a foreigner on earth is the counterpart to confessing faith in God's promise (Feldmeier, "Nation," 256). In a cosmological sense those whose citizenship is in heaven are foreigners upon earth. In a social sense these foreigners are set apart from others who do not share these convictions (13:13–14).

An enthymeme supports the author's case.[391] His assertion that those who speak as Abraham did "make clear that they are seeking a homeland" (11:14) assumes that listeners will agree that refugees (6:18), resident aliens (11:9), foreigners and transients (11:13) want a homeland.[392] To show that Israel's ances-

[389]Demosthenes, *Against Eubilides* 44–45, 48, 70. Cf. G. Stählin, *TDNT* 5.1–16; E. Fascher, *RAC* 8.306–47.

[390]For example, Juvenal caustically mimics the immigrant who dares to say, "Oh, I know I'm foreign. . . . But my five shops bring in four hundred thousand, see? So I qualify for gentry" (*Satires* 1.102–106). On attitudes toward foreigners see la Piana, "Foreign Groups," 226–34; Haarhoff, *Stranger*; Balsdon, *Romans*.

[391]On the tightly woven arguments known as enthymemes see Aristotle, *Rhetoric* 1.2.8. For other examples in Hebrews see 3:3–4; 6:16; 9:16, 22; 11:6. See generally pp. 93–94.

[392]For example, "What is the loss of a homeland? A great ill?" Indeed, it is the greatest, and "no words can do it justice" (Euripides, *Phoenissae* 388–89; Plutarch, *Mor.* 599E; 605F; cf. Cicero, *Tusc. Disp.* 5.37 §106).

tors sought a new homeland, he points out that Abraham's family did not desire to return to the place that they left (11:15a), which was unusual, since many foreigners wanted to return to their homes.[393] Unlike exiles,[394] Abraham's family had the opportunity to return (11:15b), but chose not to, which shows that they must have been looking for a homeland that was better than the one they had left (11:16a).

To tell listeners that "God is not ashamed to be called their God" (11:16c) redefines the listeners' social situation. Like resident aliens, foreigners, and transients, who were often treated with contempt (11:9, 13; Sir 29:23, 28; Plutarch, *Mor.* 607A; cf. Dio Chrysostom, *Disc.* 13.6), the listeners were denounced because of their beliefs. Yet if many viewed the listeners with contempt, God was not ashamed of them, but promised a new covenant under which he would be their God and they would be his people (Heb 8:10).

Some in antiquity traded one earthly homeland for another, identifying home with success: "One's homeland is wherever one does well."[395] Others considered the entire world to be their homeland, so that they could move from place to place without truly leaving home (Marcus Aurelius, *Meditations* 6.44.6; Plutarch, *Mor.* 600E–601B). For Hebrews, however, the Christian's homeland is not on earth, but in heaven (Heb 11:16b).[396] The author affirms this heavenly hope as a basis for perseverance rather than complacency in earthly life. Christians need not compromise their beliefs in the hope of finding greater security in an earthly society. Since believers are citizens of God's city, they can resist conforming to the norms of an unbelieving world and can continue professing faith in God and serving others (13:13–16; cf. *Diogn.* 5:1–17). A heavenly focus could lead to quietism and withdrawal, but it did not need to do so. For Paul the assurance of citizenship in heaven motivated him to strive in his witness upon earth (Phil 3:12–21). Later, the vision of God's eternal city helped Christians endure the sack of Rome by giving them a sense of present identity and hope for the future. Augustine's great work *The City of God*, which comes from that context, is about being otherworldly in the world.[397]

c. On the Descendants of Abraham (11:17–22)

God promised Abraham both a homeland and many descendants (Heb 11:8–12). The first three generations to descend from him included Isaac, Jacob and Esau, and Joseph, who are mentioned in 11:17–22. Faith plays an important

---

[393]For example, the story was told of Odysseus, who "forever sits lamenting on the shore of the sea because he yearns for his native land," so that even the offer of immortality was "outweighed by his yearning and love for his native land" (Dio Chrysostom, *Disc.* 9.4).

[394]Under Roman law, exile was originally a form of self-banishment that allowed a person to escape criminal proceedings. See *OCD* "exile."

[395]Cicero, *Tusc. Disp.* 5.27 §108; cf. Aristophanes, *Plutus* 1151; Plutarch, *Mor.* 601E; Euripides, *Erechtheus* frg. 362.11; Haarhoff, *Stranger*, 54.

[396]On questions about the extent to which Hebrews draws on Platonic categories, see pp. 97–100.

[397]See P. Brown, *Augustine*, 313–29. On the theme in Christian history, see Feldmeier, *Christen*, 211–17.

role in their stories because death repeatedly calls God's promises into question, and fulfillment of the promises remains "unseen" (11:1).[398]

After Isaac's birth, Abraham exhibited faith when he was tested (11:17) by a command to sacrifice the boy.[399] This test is disturbing because child sacrifice is a horrific act and because God is the one who directed Abraham to carry it out.[400] Moreover, God promised Abraham many descendants, but had given Abraham and Sarah only one son, Isaac, so that in a physical sense Isaac's life was the thread upon which the fulfillment of God's promise depended. God's command to sacrifice Isaac flatly contradicted God's promise that Abraham's descendants would be called "through Isaac" (Gen 21:12; Heb 11:18). By leaving his father's house, Abraham gave up his past; by sacrificing Isaac, Abraham would give up his future (Lane). Or would he?

The basis of Abraham's obedience was his conviction that "God was able to raise even from the dead" (11:19). Although the OT says nothing about Abraham's faith in resurrection, Hebrews interprets Gen 22 in terms of the principle that God could give life to the dead: "Is anything impossible for God?" (Gen 18:14 LXX). Paul said that Abraham believed in God (Rom 4:17b) and that Abraham's God "gives life to the dead" (4:17c). Hebrews goes on to say that if Abraham believes in God and if God can raise the dead, then Abraham's faith in God implicitly includes faith that God can raise the dead.[401] Abraham's actions imply that he not only believed that God *could* raise the dead but that God *would* raise Isaac from the dead. Isaac's birth to Abraham, who was "dead" in old age, showed God's power to give life (Heb 11:12). Since death was not the last word for Abraham, he could be confident that it would not be the last word for Isaac.

Abraham received Isaac back as a symbol of resurrection from the dead (11:19b). Hebrews does not necessarily suggest that the symbol was perceived by Abraham. As in the case of the Tabernacle (NOTE on 9:9) the author is probably pointing to meanings that were not available to previous generations. The symbolism suits the listeners' context because they, like Abraham, were being tested. To be sure, they had not been commanded to sacrifice their firstborn, but their dispiriting circumstances did call God's promises into question (pp. 71–72). The author does not explain why God would allow the listeners to be so tested (2:18), emphasizing instead that testing is not God's final word, but something that issues into new life for the faithful.

A second example of faith is Isaac blessing his sons, including (surprisingly) both Jacob and Esau, shortly before his death (Gen 27:1–2; NOTE on Heb

---

[398]Interest in the final moments of the lives of Israel's ancestors led to the writing of the *Testaments of the Twelve Patriarchs* and similar texts. See the collection in *OTP* 1.773–995.

[399]On Gen 22 and its implications for NT study see Swetnam, *Jesus*, 4–22.

[400]In 1798 Immanuel Kant cited Gen 22 as an instance where God could not have actually commanded Abraham to slay Isaac because it would have violated the moral law. In 1843 Søren Kirkegaard introduced his work *Fear and Trembling* with an account of this incident that accents the importance of Abraham's obedience. See Rosenau, "Erzählung," 251–61; Westermann, *Genesis*, 2.353–54.

[401]This fusion of horizons continues in the next section, where Moses suffers denunciation for Christ in a manner that reflects the listeners' own experience (NOTE on 11:26).

11:20). Blessing is an act of faith because Isaac cannot give the recipient what is promised, but must rely on God to put the blessing into effect. Thus Isaac said, "May *God* give you the dew of heaven" (Gen 27:28). Blessing also pertains to things that are to come (Heb 11:20b), which cannot be seen with the eye, but are perceived by faith (11:1). Like the children of Isaac, the listeners have received promises of blessing and are called to be as confident as Isaac was that God will bring the blessing about (2:16; 6:7).

The third incident involves Jacob blessing his grandsons and worshiping before his death (11:21), which expresses faith that God's favor will extend into the future. Hebrews might focus on the blessing of Jacob's grandchildren because it expresses faith in God's actions: "The God before whom my ancestors Abraham and Isaac walked . . . bless the boys" (Gen 48:15–16). In contrast, many of the "blessings" given to Jacob's own twelve sons focus more on the sons' character traits than on God's actions. Moreover, blessing the grandchildren extends blessing not just to one generation, but to the generation beyond it, which could help to encourage listeners for whom the realization of God's promises seems slow in coming.

The fourth episode focuses on the way that Joseph, at the end of his life, remembered the exodus, although the event would not happen for several centuries (Heb 11:22).[402] Joseph could speak of the exodus, not because he had experienced it, but because God had promised it. Referring to it required faith because the exodus belonged to the realm of what was hoped for, but was yet unseen (11:1). Joseph was so certain of the future exodus that he based his burial plans on it, commanding that the people should take his bones with them to Canaan (11:22b; cf. Gen 50:25b). Despite his advancement in the Egyptian court, Joseph understood that he was a resident alien in Egypt, for his true home was elsewhere. For those addressed by Hebrews, Joseph's confidence of being taken to the promised land after his death reinforces the hope that the believer's final rest will be in the place that God has promised (Heb 12:22–24).

32. The Faith of Moses (11:23–31)

11 [23]By faith Moses, after his birth, was hidden for three months by his parents, since they saw the child's good character and were not afraid of the king's edict. [24]By faith Moses, when he had grown up, refused to be called a son of Pharaoh's daughter, [25]choosing to be maltreated with the people of God rather than to have the fleeting pleasure of sin, [26]since he considered the denunciation of Christ to be wealth greater than the storehouses of Egypt, for he looked ahead to his reward. [27]By faith he left Egypt without fearing the king's rage, for he persevered as if he saw the One who cannot be seen.

[28]By faith he kept the Passover and spread the blood in order that the one sent to destroy the firstborn might not touch them. [29]By faith they crossed the Red

[402]The similarity in Jacob's and Joseph's deathbed scenes is reinforced by the similar cadences of Heb 11:21–22 (Cosby, *Rhetorical*, 22).

Sea as if it were dry land, but when the Egyptians attempted it, they were drowned. [30]By faith the walls of Jericho fell after they had been encircled for seven days. [31]By faith Rahab the prostitute did not perish with the unbelievers, since she received the spies in peace.

NOTES

11:23. *By faith Moses.* Grammatically these words ascribe faith to Moses, but the remainder of the verse focuses on the faith of Moses' parents. On Moses see NOTES and COMMENT on 3:1–6.

after his birth, was hidden for three months by his parents. The Greek *pateres* here includes both father and mother. The MT of Exod 2:2 says that Moses' mother concealed him. The LXX says "*they* concealed him," implying that both parents were involved (cf. Philo, *Moses* 1.9–11; Josephus, *Ant.* 2.217–21). The OT does not explicitly mention their faith. The logic in Hebrews is that if Moses' parents pleased God by saving the child (*Bib. Ant.* 9:7) and if no one pleases God without faith (Heb 11:6), Moses' parents must have had faith (Rose, *Wolke*, 268–70).

since they saw the child's good character. The adjective *asteios* (cf. Exod 2:2 LXX) could indicate a pleasing appearance (Josephus, *Ant.* 2.231; cf. Philo, *Moses* 1.9), which showed divine favor (cf. 1 Sam 16:12; *Jos. Asen.* 6:3; 13:14). Since Hebrews argues that faith is not based on sight (11:1, 7, 27), the idea that Moses' parents depended on appearances could suggest that their faith was inadequate (Chrysostom). Many, however, contrasted good character (*asteios*) with bad character (*phaulos*, e.g., Diogenes Laertius, *Lives* 7.199; Plutarch, *Mor.* 1038B; 1046F–47A; Philo, *Alleg. Interp.* 3.190–91). Good character was pleasing to God (Acts 7:20), and it was a gift that God could bestow at birth (Philo, *Alleg. Interp.* 3.77; cf. *Heir* 42, 77–78). A person of good character has the courage to reject pleasure and wealth if these compromise the way of God (Philo, *Alleg. Interp.* 3.23; *Posterity* 101; *Good Person* 72). For Hebrews Moses' good character was a sign of God's present favor and a portent of the future, when Moses would indeed reject the wealth and pleasure of Pharaoh's household to identify with the people of God (Heb 11:24–26).

and were not afraid of the king's edict. The decree that male Hebrew children were to be killed originally applied to the Hebrew midwives but was eventually extended to all Israelites (Exod 1:16, 22). Since the midwives "feared God" (Exod 1:17, 21), Hebrews infers that all who resisted the edict acted on the same basis. Fearing God is appropriate (Heb 4:1; 10:31; 12:28), whereas fearing a king who opposes God is not. Some assumed that Moses' parents acted in fear (Josephus, *Ant.* 2.217–20), but Hebrews depicts them acting more boldly (cf. *Bib. Ant.* 9:5).

11:24. *By faith Moses.* Moses was identified as faithful in Heb 3:2 (Num 12:7; cf. Sir 45:4). Later Jewish sources identified him as righteous, which fits the idea that it is by faith that the righteous live (*t. Soṭah* 6:7; Rose, *Wolke*, 276).

when he had grown up. Moses left Pharaoh's house at the time he killed an Egyptian (Exod 2:11–15). Tradition said that he was forty (Acts 7:23) or forty-two years old (*Jub.* 47:6–7). Some MSS (D* 1827; NRSVfn) state in Heb 11:24 that Moses "killed the Egyptian" when he saw "the humiliation of his people." Some think the words are original (Kilpatrick, *Principles*, 154), but they were more likely added to explain why Moses left (D'Angelo, *Moses*, 43; cf. *TCGNT*, 674).

refused to be called a son of Pharoah's daughter. Exodus 2:10 LXX says that Moses "became a son" of Pharoah's daughter, which implied that he was adopted (Josephus, *Ant.* 2.232; Philo, *Moses* 1.19, 32–33). Like Hebrews, other sources emphasize that Moses left by his own decision (Ezek. Trag. [*OTP* 2.809]; cf. Josephus, *Ant.* 2.233–34).

11:25. *choosing to be maltreated with the people of God.* The compound verb *synkakoucheisthai* is not attested prior to Hebrews and may be a new coinage (p. 96). In a general sense, maltreatment refers to heavy forced labor and physical abuse of the Israelite slaves in Egypt (Exod 1:11–14; 2:11; 5:14). This parallels the listeners' experience, for they associated maltreatment with prisoners who identified with the Christian community (Heb 13:3; cf. 11:36).

rather than to have the fleeting pleasure. The idea that Moses rejected comfort in order to suffer with his people may have been traditional (cf. Josephus, *Ant.* 4.42). Rejecting pleasure for the sake of virtue was an ideal that was mentioned in Hellenistic (e.g., Xenophon, *Memorabilia* 2.1.21–34; Attridge) and Jewish texts. Joseph rightly rejected the transitory pleasure of an adulterous relationship in order to uphold marital fidelity (Josephus, *Ant.* 2.50–51; cf. *Jos. Asen.* 12:15). The martyrs exemplified the ideal of rejecting "transitory" safety for the sake of the devotion to God that issues into eternal life (4 Macc 15:2, 8, 23; 2 *Clem.* 10:3–4; cf. D'Angelo, *Moses*, 28).

of sin. Rather than contrasting the fleeting pleasure of sin with the abiding bliss of salvation (Heb 5:9; 9:12, 15; cf. 7:26), this text urges listeners to reject pleasure for the sake of suffering with God's people. Like sin, suffering is transitory, but unlike sin, faithful suffering leads to inheritance in God's kingdom (10:34).

11:26. *since he considered the denunciation of Christ.* Verbal denunciation is connected with affliction, ill treatment, and shame (NOTE on 10:33; cf. 11:25; 12:2; 13:13). The expression "denunciation of Christ" recalls Ps 89:50–51 (88:50–51 LXX): "Lord, remember the denunciation of your servants" with which your enemies "have denounced . . . your anointed one." The "anointed one" could be Israel, so that Moses is said to share in the suffering of the people as in Heb 11:25 (Westcott; cf. F. F. Bruce). Yet given the use of *christos* for Jesus elsewhere in Hebrews, listeners almost certainly would have applied it to Jesus. The christological sense of the text has both primary and secondary levels of meaning (cf. Chrysostom):

(a) Reproach *like* that endured by Christ is the primary sense. Christ was reviled after his arrest and again at the time of the crucifixion. Moses suffered verbal opposition from the king of Egypt (Exod 5:4; 10:10–11, 28) and some of his own people (Exod 2:14; 5:21). The listeners had borne similar denunciation in the past (Heb 10:33) and would probably do so again (13:13).

(b) Reproach *for the sake of* Christ is the secondary sense. Some have argued that Moses suffered because of his expectations or visions of the Messiah (Bengel; D'Angelo, *Moses*, 95–149; Hanson, "Reproach"; cf. John 8:56). Paul identified Christ with the rock from which the wilderness generation drank (1 Cor 10:4), and Hebrews also could have understood Christ to have played a role in Moses' time. It is more likely however, that the author is fusing the story of Moses with the experience of the listeners, who had been denounced because of their faith in Christ (Heb 10:32–34; 13:13; cf. 1 Pet 4:12–13; Phil 3:10; pp. 67–71).

to be wealth. Early Christians sometimes distinguished between material wealth and true wealth in God's kingdom (Matt 6:19–20; 1 Tim 6:17; Luke 6:20–23; 16:25). Here, however, Hebrews says, not that heavenly wealth is superior to earthly wealth or that earthly suffering leads to heavenly wealth, but that denunciation for Christ *is* a form of wealth (cf. Rev 2:9). The author does not glorify suffering in itself (1 Pet 4:14–16). The point is that suffering as a "partner with Christ" (Heb 3:14) is of incalculable value. If Greco-Roman writers said that virtue is its own reward, even when it entails suffering (Silius Italicus, *Punica* 13.663; Diogenes Laertius, *Lives* 3.78), Hebrews says that one's relationship with Christ is its own reward, even when it entails suffering.

greater than the storehouses of Egypt. The term *thēsauroi* can be used for treasures or for storehouses. Egypt was said to have many treasures (*Mek.*, "Shirata" 7; "Beshallaḥ" 2 [Lauterbach ed. 2.55; 1.200]; cf. D'Angelo, *Moses*, 47), but calling Egypt a "storehouse" is appropriate since much of its wealth came from its grain (Gen 12:10; 42:2; 43:2). In the first century Egypt was the granary of the empire (Josephus, *J.W.* 4.605), and the Romans enriched themselves at Egypt's expense. In contrast, Moses "did not treasure up gold and silver . . . did not possess houses or chattels or livestock or a staff of slaves or revenues or any other accompaniment of costly and opulent living, though he might have had all in abundance" (Philo, *Moses* 1.150–52).

for he looked ahead to his reward. See NOTE on 10:35. To persevere in faith, Christians look to Jesus (12:2; cf. *TLNT* 1.174–75).

11:27. *By faith he left Egypt without fearing the king's rage.* There are three main ways to interpret this statement, of which the third is preferable:

(a) Moses' flight to Midian (Exod 2:14–15; Attridge; Braun; F. F. Bruce). Since Heb 11:27 mentions only Moses it might refer to his individual escape. Sequentially, Moses' flight to Midian follows his departure from the royal household (11:24–26) and precedes the Passover (11:28). Egypt's king was angry at the time (cf. Exod 2:15). A problem is that Exod 2:14–15 states that Moses was afraid, which contradicts Heb 11:27. Some respond that Moses initially fled in fear, but later confronted the king without fear (Chrysostom; Theodoret; Theophylact) or that Moses only appeared to be afraid (Haimo; Lünemann). Alternatively, the author may have forgotten that Moses was afraid (B. Weiss) or may have relied on traditions that stressed his courage in venturing to Midian (e.g., Josephus, *Ant.* 2.254–257; cf. Wis 10:16; Philo, *Alleg. Interp.* 3.11–14; *Moses* 1.49–50; D'Angelo, *Moses*, 56–59; H.-F. Weiss.).

(b) The Exodus (Exod 13:17–15:21; Anselm of Laon, *Glossa ordinaria*; Nicolaus of Lyra; Erasmus, *Paraphrase*; Calvin). Moses appeared fearless at the time of the exodus (Exod 14:13). Keeping the unseen before him (Heb 11:27b) could recall God's appearance at the burning bush, where Moses was commissioned to lead the people out of Egypt. The OT does not state that the king was enraged at the time of the exodus, but his pursuit of the Israelites could suggest anger (Exod 14:5–9). Most important, the exodus finally defied the king's wishes. Problems with this view are that Heb 11:27 refers only to Moses, whereas the exodus of the whole people is mentioned in 11:29, and that the Passover (11:28) is mentioned after the exodus (11:27) rather than before it.

(c) General statement. Given the difficulty in relating this reference to one particular episode, it can perhaps best be taken as a summary of Moses' departures from Egypt (D'Angelo, *Moses*, 59–62; Grässer; Eisenbaum, *Jewish Heroes*, 170). Hebrews sometimes follows the sequence of the OT narratives, but sometimes does not (COMMENT). He combines various sacrificial practices (9:13), dedication ceremonies (9:20–22), and episodes from the lives of Israel's ancestors (11:9, 13) to underscore their common meanings. He may have done the same with Moses' departures from Egypt.

for he persevered. Most take "persevered" as the main verb with the participle "seeing" giving the circumstances of perseverance. Some argue that "persevered" points to continued "seeing": "he kept the one who is invisible continually before his eyes" (Lane; Braun). This seems unlikely, since the verb indicates steadfastness (e.g., Job 2:9 LXX) and it echoes Hebrews' emphasis on endurance and steadfastness (Heb 3:12, 14; 6:12; 10:35, 38; 12:1). Perseverance was a virtue of Moses (Philo, *Moses* 1.154; *Alleg. Interp.* 3.11; Josephus, *Ant.* 2.256–57).

as if he saw. Some render the *hōs* in a causal sense: "because he saw" (NIV). This recalls Moses' unique status as the one who spoke with God face to face (Num 12:8; Deut 34:10). A qualitative rendering is preferable: "as if seeing." This implies that Moses did not actually see God (MHT 3.320; cf. Exod 33:20). It is difficult to identify this passage with God's revelation in the burning bush (Exod 3:6; cf. D'Angelo, *Moses*, 56; F. F. Bruce; Rose, *Wolke*, 286–87), in the pillar of cloud and fire (Philo, *Moses* 1.166), or in visions (Calvin; Eisenbaum, *Jewish Heroes*, 170; cf. Ezek. Trag., *Exagōgē* 68–82 [*OTP* 2.811–12]; Philo, *Change* 7). Instead, the text underscores the nature of faith itself (Heb 11:1; Attridge; Lane; H.-F. Weiss).

the One who cannot be seen. The idea that God cannot be seen is found in the OT (Exod 33:20), and the term *aoratos* is used in this sense in the NT (Rom 1:20; Col 1:15; 1 Tim 1:17; cf. John 1:18; 5:37; 6:46; 1 John 4:12, 20; 1 Tim 6:16). On the seen and unseen realms in Hebrews see pp. 97–104.

11:28. *By faith he kept the Passover.* The expression *poiein to pascha* commonly meant keeping the Passover festival (Exod 12:48; Num 9:2; Josh 5:10; 2 Kgs 23:21; Matt 26:18). Early Christians connected the Passover to Jesus' crucifixion (1 Cor 5:7; John 1:29, 36) and the Lord's Supper (Matt 26:17–29; Mark 14:12–25; Luke 22:15–20). Although some interpreters relate Heb 11:28 to Christ's death (Chrysostom; P. E. Hughes; Strobel), Hebrews does not develop the idea. Instead, the Passover is important because when the blood was spread upon the doorposts, there was no evidence that it would be effective. "Where truth itself is not apparent, it must be looked for in faith" (Calvin, *Epistle*, 179).

and spread the blood. According to Exod 12:22, the Israelites were to spread the blood of the Passover lamb on the doorposts and lintels of their houses. Hebrews uses the peculiar term *proschysis,* which is related to *proschein,* the verb used in the LXX for "pouring" blood upon the altar (Exod 24:6; 29:16; Lev 9:12), perhaps because in Jewish practice the blood of Passover offerings was poured out at the altar (2 Chron 35:11; *Jub.* 49:20; *m. Pesaḥ.* 5:6).

in order that the one sent to destroy the firstborn might not touch them. Some OT passages identify God as the one who destroys the firstborn (Exod 11:4–5; 12:27, 29), but others indicate that an agent of God would be the destroyer (Exod 12:23; cf. Wis 18:25; 1 Cor 10:10). The destroyer was understood to be an angel (2 Sam 24:16; 1 Chron 21:12, 15; Isa 37:36).

11:29. *By faith they crossed the Red Sea as if it were dry land.* Faith is Israel's response to the promise that God would deliver them (Exod 14:13; Grässer). The MT says that Israel crossed the *yām sûph* ("sea of reeds"), but Hebrews follows the LXX, which calls it the "Red [*erythros*] Sea" (e.g., Exod 15:4, 22 LXX). God's provision of a way through the sea was remembered as his central act of deliverance in the OT (e.g., Ps 66:6; Isa 51:10; Philo, *Moses* 1.177).

but when the Egyptians attempted it, they were drowned. Cf. Exod 15:4 LXX. The expression *peiran lambanein* can mean "to experience" (cf. 11:36), but here it has the more active meaning "to attempt" (BAGD, 640 [1]; cf. *TLNT* 3.80–90). Both Egyptians and Israelites attempted to cross the sea, but the results were very different. Hebrews implies that the Egyptians' faith was oriented toward the water, which they believed would not engulf them, whereas the Israelites' faith was oriented toward the unseen God (11:27).

11:30. *By faith the walls of Jericho fell after they had been encircled for seven days.* Faith belongs to the people of Israel, who are not explicitly mentioned, rather than to the walls. The victory at Jericho manifests not only Israel's faith in God, but God's faithfulness to them (Josh 1:1–5).

11:31. *By faith Rahab.* Rahab (Josh 2:1–21; 6:22–25) is the only woman other than Sarah to be named in Heb 11 (cf. Jas 2:25; Matt 1:5). She could be considered a believer since she believed that God would give the Israelites the land as he had promised (Josh 2:8–11; cf. *1 Clem.* 12:1–8; Grässer).

the prostitute. Some omitted the reference to Rahab's profession (Josephus, *Ant.* 5.8, 30) or referred to her as the "so-called prostitute" (א* sy^h), but the epithet was traditional. Hebrews warns that God will judge immoral people (13:4), but still cites Rahab as a positive example. The reference to her profession might have played on the listeners' sense of honor: if even a prostitute acted in faith, it would be disgraceful for the listeners to prove faithless (Chrysostom).

did not perish with the unbelievers. The "unbelievers" refer to the people of Jericho, but in 3:19 the unbelievers are the Israelites who perished in the wilderness. Unbelief is not construed along ethnic lines, and it remains a threat to the listeners themselves (3:12).

since she received the spies in peace. When Joshua sent two spies into Canaan (Josh 2:1), Rahab not only housed them, but concealed them from the king's agents. Peace characterizes God (Heb 13:20–21) and Melchizedek, who foreshadows Christ (7:2). Those who live under God's rule pursue the peace (12:14) that is the fruit of righteousness (12:11).

COMMENT[403]

The previous act in the drama of faith concluded when the patriarchs blessed their children and grandchildren, and looked for future generations to be delivered from Egypt (11:20–22). When the curtain rises, the scene shifts from the death of the older generation to the birth of a new generation. It also shows that the older generation's faith in God was well placed, since Joseph was confident that God would bring Israel out of Egypt (11:22), and in the time of Moses, God did deliver them from Egypt (11:23–29). In the previous section the principal challenge to faith was that the patriarchs had to resist disappointment at not possessing an earthly inheritance. Now the challenge shifts, as Moses' generation experiences conflict with unbelievers. Recalling the various challenges faced by Israel's ancestors would have been helpful to those addressed by Hebrews, for whom both disappointment and conflict were threats (pp. 67–72).

The author interweaves the story of Moses with the story of the Christian community. The first part of each sentence in 11:23–27 recalls something distinctive from the story of Moses: his parents hid him (11:23a), he refused to be called a son of Pharoah's daughter (11:24a), and he finally left Egypt (11:27). The second part of each sentence explains the decisions behind these actions in terms that suited the listeners' own situation. Moses and his parents faced alternative paths of action in which the better choice was consistently the more difficult choice:

valuing good character	*versus*	fearing the king's edict
accepting maltreatment with God's people	*versus*	seeking fleeting pleasures of sin
enduring denunciation for Christ	*versus*	holding on to wealth
looking to the unseen One	*versus*	fearing the king's rage

Those addressed by Hebrews faced difficult choices like those listed above. Opposition to the Christian community may not have been carried out by a king's edict, but it was supported or condoned by officials who could imprison Christians (10:34; 13:3). Some Christians had to accept maltreatment (10:32–34; 13:3). Those who professed faith in Christ were liable to denunciation, and some lost wealth and property for their faith (10:33–34; 13:13–14). By coupling the distinctive elements of the exodus story with elements typical of the listeners' own story, the author seeks to embolden listeners in the face of conflict.

---

[403]On 11:23–31 see Cosby, *Rhetorical*, 41–55; D'Angelo, *Moses*, 17–64; deSilva, *Despising*, 191–95; Eisenbaum, *Jewish Heroes*, 166–73; Hanson, "Reproach"; Jones, "Figure"; Rose, *Wolke*, 267–303; Swetnam, "Hebrews 11"; J. Thomas, "Comme s'il."

[404]On the structure see Vanhoye, *La structure*, 189–91. Rose puts 11:28 in the first paragraph, since Moses is the subject, whereas 11:29 focuses on Israel (*Wolke*, 289). Nevertheless, the text does not sharply distinguish individuals from groups.

Structurally the passage has two parts:[404] (**a**) Threats against Moses and his parents are prominent in the first paragraph (11:23–27), which is framed by references to acting without fear of the king. (**b**) Salvation of believers and destruction of unbelievers characterize the second part, which covers the period from the exodus to the entry into the land (11:28–31). The first part shows how the faithful receive negative judgments from other people, and the second part shows how unbelievers receive negative judgment from God. The flow of the passage is disputed. Some maintain that it moves in a straightforward manner from Moses' birth and departure from the royal house (11:23–26) to his escape to Midian (11:27), and then to the Passover, exodus, and conquest (11:28–31). Others think that the author moves from the exodus (11:27) back to the Passover (11:28), then forward to the exodus and conquest (11:29–31). This nonlinear approach seems best. Although much of Heb 11 follows the sequence of OT narrative, the author seems free to depart from a strict sequence.[405] His account of events follows the OT order in a general rather than a precise way.

a. Faith in the Face of Adversaries (11:23–27)

Moses' story is told in the compelling manner of a Greek drama. The plot of a drama is driven by action (Aristotle, *Poetics* 6 [1450AB]). Here the plot is that Moses' parents conceal an infant from death at the hands of a tyrant. The boy grows up in the royal house, but later renounces his status in order to embrace a life of suffering. Destruction threatens, the adversaries are destroyed, and the faithful are delivered. Along with plot, however, Hebrews considers character. "Character is that which reveals moral choice," and it is disclosed by what "a person chooses or avoids in circumstances where the choice is not obvious" (ibid., 1450B).[406] At every point in Heb 11:23–27 someone is placed in a situation where the better choice is the more difficult one.

The story begins when Moses, after his birth, "was hidden for three months by his parents" (11:23a).[407] Moses' parents were confronted with two courses of action. One was set by the king's edict (11:23c), which decreed: "Every boy that is born to the Hebrews you shall throw into the Nile, but you shall let every girl live" (Exod 1:22). Had fear of the king swayed Moses' parents, they might have killed their son.[408] The other course of action was suggested by the child's good

[405]In the previous section the author introduced the two promises of land and descendants in 11:8–12, then takes up matters pertaining to land in 11:13–16 and descendants in 11:17–22. Moreover, the deaths of the patriarchs are mentioned in 11:13, yet incidents from their lives and their last acts are recounted in 11:17–22. In the next section the author will quickly list OT episodes in a sequence that corresponds in a general rather than an exact way to that of the OT (see §33 COMMENT). Cf. Rose, *Wolke*, 284–86.

[406]"The choice of death rather than dishonourable wealth reveals character; the choice of a nectarine rather than a turnip does not" (Fyfe, *Aristotle*, 28–29). See further C. R. Koester, *Symbolism*, 36–39.

[407]Summaries of Moses' life in Wis 10:15–21 and Sir 45:1–5 mention the exodus, but not his birth. His birth is included in Acts 7:17–22, however (Eisenbaum, *Jewish Heroes*, 167).

[408]Abraham acted by faith when he determined to slay his son (11:17), but Moses' parents acted by faith when they did the opposite by hiding their son to save his life (11:23).

character or virtue (NOTE on 11:23b). It was widely understood that fear of a tyrant was a poor motive for conduct and that right decisions should uphold virtue.[409] Accordingly, Moses' parents overcame the natural fear of a tyrant and acted upon their recognition of good character, which was pleasing to God.

When Moses was grown up, he "refused to be called a son of Pharaoh's daughter" (11:24). Hebrews rules out the idea that Moses lost his position through circumstances beyond his control; change occurred through his own decision. People in the first century understood that members of the king's household received honor, protection, and benefits. To be adopted as a royal son also meant inheriting a part of the king's estate. For Moses to renounce his sonship meant that he renounced honor, influence, and the hope of a princely inheritance.[410]

Moses' had to decide between two courses of action.[411] One was "to be maltreated with the people of God" (11:25a). For Moses and for the listeners, avoiding contact with the people of God was the easiest course of action (10:25). In Moses' time the people of God were slaves who worked at heavy labor under pitiless taskmasters.[412] The listeners' community had also experienced maltreatment through verbal denunciation and physical violence, as well as through the loss of possessions and imprisonment (pp. 67–71). The second course of action was to embrace "the fleeting pleasure of sin" (11:25b). Exodus says little about life in the royal court, but Hebrews assumes that listeners can imagine the sinful opulence that Moses renounced when he joined the Israelites (Philo, *Moses* 1.152).

The implication is that listeners too will either identify with the maltreated community of faith or embrace sin's transient pleasures. The passage might imply a stark contrast between the Christian community and the pleasure-seeking tendencies of society (cf. 1 Pet 4:3–4, 14–16), but the analogy might also be more subtle. Those who leave the community in order to avoid maltreatment seek a more pleasurable situation at the price of unfaithfulness to the community and its God. Hebrews responds to this by declaring that enjoyment gained from unfaithfulness is merely fleeting, since true security is found in relationship to God and his people.

Reinforcing the point, the author speaks of bearing the denunciation of Christ (11:26a). On one level this evocative expression suggests that Moses suffered reproach in a manner *like* Christ when he was denounced by his opponents (Exod 5:4, 21; 10:10–11, 28). On another level the expression establishes a parallel to the situation of the listeners, who were denounced *like* Christ and *for the sake of* Christ by others in society (pp. 69–70). The alternative to denunciation in Moses' case was to hold on to the wealth of the legendary storehouses of Egypt

[409]Epictetus, *Disc.* 1.18.17; 1.19.8; 1.29.1–15. Although the most common reason for saving one's child is the natural bond that exists between parents and children, Hebrews emphasizes virtue.

[410]On the connection between adoption and inheritance see P. W. von Martitz, *TDNT* 8.398. On the implications for Heb 11:24 see D'Angelo, *Moses*, 42; deSilva, *Despising*, 192.

[411]Hebrews is restrained in portraying Moses' early life. For legends concerning his exploits see Artapanus (*OTP* 2.898–900); Philo, *Moses* 1.20–33; Josephus, *Ant.* 2.232–53.

[412]Exod 1:11–14; 2:11; 5:14. The maltreatment is embellished by Josephus, *Ant.* 2.201–4.

(Heb 11:26b).[413] Giving up such wealth suggests a connection with the situation of the listeners and makes an implicit argument from the greater to the lesser (Quintilian, *Inst.* 5.11.9). The Christian community sacrificed some of their possessions in an outburst of violence that occurred in the past (10:32–34), but they had not experienced nearly the kind of loss that Moses endured. Therefore, if Moses renounced all the wealth of Egypt in order to be faithful, cannot the listeners endure a much smaller loss in order to do the same?

Moses endured affliction by looking forward to his reward (11:26c). Moses was the heir of the promise that God would give Abraham's descendants a land of their own (Exod 3:16–17). Confidence that God would be faithful gave Moses incentive to persevere in the face of maltreatment. Moses never entered Canaan (Deut 34:1–6), but for Hebrews this is irrelevant since the faithful receive their reward in the heavenly city that is to come (Heb 11:13–16). Like Moses, the listeners' community lost possessions in the confidence that God would give them a superior and abiding possession (10:34). Theologically, the hope of reward has to do with the justice of God. God had promised to bless his people, and for God to prove false would violate his own integrity (6:13–18; 10:23, 35–36; 11:11). For people to remain faithful in adversity they must have hope that transcends immediate circumstances.

Moses joined the ranks of his forebears, who wandered the earth without a homeland, when he left Egypt behind (11:27a; cf. 11:13). Those familiar with the story of the exodus might recall that leaving Egypt meant hardship in the wilderness (Exod 16:3; Num 11:5; 14:4). First-century listeners would also have known of the difficulty experienced by the innumerable foreigners and transients who had left their homelands behind to live as resident aliens in other places (NOTES on 11:9, 13; Cicero, *Tusc. Disp.* 5.37 §106). Considering how Moses left his country in a physical sense prepares for the exhortation that listeners must separate themselves in a social sense from their own city in order to maintain their faith (Heb 13:13–14).

One course of action available to Moses would have been to remain in Egypt out of fear of the king's rage (11:27b). Yet Moses owed his life to parents who refused to fear the king (11:23c), and he followed their example. The text implies that the listeners should in turn follow Moses' example by refusing to fear the authorities who imprisoned members of their community (10:34; 13:3).[414] Just as Moses' parents had to choose between fear of the king and the virtue of good character, Moses had to choose between fear of the king and the virtue of endurance (11:27; cf. Philo, *Alleg. Interp.* 3.10–14; Josephus, *Ant.* 2.256–57). Ironically, endurance was valued by Greco-Roman society, but here it is exhibited by one who separates himself from society—which encourages listeners to do the same (D'Angelo, *Moses*, 31–32). The basis for Moses' endurance was the paradoxical seeing of the One who cannot be seen (11:27c). In the same way, the lis-

---

[413]With access to the Mediterranean and Red Seas, Egypt was "the greatest emporium in the inhabited world" (Strabo, *Geography* 17.1.13), and its chief city, Alexandria, was "so populous, so wealthy, so vast" (Josephus, *J.W.* 2.385).

[414]See Wengst, *Pax Romana*, 141–43; H.-F. Weiss, *Brief*, 603.

teners must endure by looking to the exalted Christ, who cannot be perceived with the physical eye, but who is discerned by faith (2:8–9).

b. Faith and Deliverance vs. Unfaith and Destruction (11:28–31)

The general reference to Moses' departure from Egypt leads to a focus on the Passover, which brought the release of the whole people (11:28). Before the Passover, God warned that the firstborn in Egypt would be slain while promising that those in homes marked by lambs' blood would be saved (Exod 12:12–13). Moses' situation was like that of Noah, who constructed an ark in response to God's warning before he could see the flood approaching. Moses had blood spread on the doorposts and lintels of Israelite homes in response to God's word, with no guarantee that the destroyer would come or that if the destroyer did come, death would be averted by the bloodstains upon the walls.

If Moses spread the blood *without* evidence that deliverance would occur, the people approached the Red Sea *against* the evidence that deliverance would occur (11:29a), since the Egyptians pursued them from one direction and the sea barred their escape in the other. While recognizing that God's power was what parted the waters, Hebrews emphasizes that faith prompted the people to follow the path that God opened for them. Those addressed by Hebrews were not called to cross a sea, but they were to risk following in the way of Christ, whose death and exaltation at once open the way to God (2:10; 6:20; 10:19–22) and chart a way of worship and service that defy opposition from the world (13:13–14).

Passing by the wilderness wanderings without further comment, presumably because the period was characterized by unbelief (3:7–4:11), the author considers the capture of Jericho (11:30). The people were told that after a trumpet blast and a shout the walls would fall down and they could capture the city (Josh 6:4–5, 14–15). Like spreading blood at Passover, there was no evidence that this tactic would work, since experience would indicate that walls do not give way before human voices. The incident implicitly bears witness to God's faithfulness to his promise and to Israel's willingness to act on the basis of the promise, appearances notwithstanding.

The story of Rahab the prostitute completes the sequence (Heb 11:31) by making an implicit argument from the lesser to the greater (Quintilian, *Inst.* 5.1.9–10): if a prostitute can exhibit faith, how much more should faith be possible for the listeners. Rahab also helps to underscore two dimensions of faith. First, Hebrews has stressed that the righteous live by faith (10:38). The fact that Rahab believed that God would keep his promises to Israel (NOTE on 11:31) and did not die with the unbelievers shows that this principle is true (11:31a). At the same time, the unbelievers perished, which reinforces the warnings that God will judge the faithless (2:3; 6:4–8; 10:26–31). Second, Rahab "received the spies in peace" (11:31b), which exemplifies the corporate dimension of faith. Just as Moses identified with God's people rather than with the royal family (11:24–25), Rahab welcomed God's people peacefully despite opposition from her own people. The listeners too are to pursue peace with others (NOTE on 11:31b) and to show hospitality, which is part of the life of faith (NOTE on 13:2).

33. FAITH DURING PERSECUTION (11:32–40)

11 32And what more shall I say? For time does not allow me to tell of Gideon,
Barak, Samson, Jephthah, David and Samuel, and the prophets, 33who through
faith overcame kingdoms, worked righteousness, obtained things that were
promised, shut the mouths of lions, 34quenched the power of fire, escaped the
edges of the sword, were made powerful out of weakness, became mighty in war,
routed the camps of foreigners. 35Women received their dead back by resurrection.

But others were tortured, after refusing release, in order that they might obtain
a superior resurrection. 36And others experienced ridicule and scourging, and
even chains and imprisonment. 37They were stoned, sawn in two, murdered by
the sword; they went about in sheepskins and goatskins, deprived, afflicted, maltreated—38of whom the world was not worthy—while they wandered over
deserts and mountains and in caves and holes in the earth.

39And all these, although attested through faith, did not receive what was
promised, 40since God provided something superior for us, so that without us
they would not be made complete.

NOTES

11:32. *And what more shall I say?* This rhetorical question (cf. Josephus, *Ant.* 20.257) is one of only four occasions when the author uses the first person singular (cf. 13:19, 22, 23).

For time does not allow me to tell. This is a common rhetorical device called *paraleipsis* or *praeterito*. "But time would fail us if we should try to recount all his activities" (Isocrates, *Oration* 1.11; cf. 6.81; 8.56; Demosthenes, *Oration* 18.296; Philo, *Moses* 1.213; cf. Cosby, *Rhetorical*, 58; see COMMENT).

of Gideon. With a band of just three hundred men, Gideon was to deliver the Israelites from a Midianite invasion. Approaching by night, Gideon's men blew trumpets, smashed jars, and waved torches, which threw the Midianites into confusion and enabled Gideon to defeat them (Judg 7:1–25). The victory was remembered as an example of God's power (Isa 9:4; cf. Isa 10:26; 1 Sam 12:11; Ps 83:9; *Tg. Neof.* 49:18). Gideon's legacy was mixed, however, in that he made an object of false worship (Judg 8:24–27; cf. *Bib. Ant.* 36:1–4; *Apos. Con.* 7.37.2).

Barak. Summoned by Deborah, Barak refused to lead unless Deborah accompanied him. The Canaanites brought nine hundred chariots into the field, but a sudden downpour immobilized them, allowing Barak's forces to prevail (Judg 4–5; cf. *Bib. Ant.* 31:1–2, 9; *Apos. Con.* 7.37.2).

Samson. Samson was set apart as a Nazirite and empowered to deliver Israel from the Philistines (Judg 13:5; 14:6, 19; 15:14). A rash and bawdy man, Samson had affairs with Philistine women, one of whom betrayed him. Blind and captive, Samson prayed for strength and brought down a house, destroying himself and his adversaries. He was remembered for both his victories and shortcomings (*Bib. Ant.* 43:1–8; *Tg. Neof.* 49:18; *Apos. Con.* 7.37.2).

Jephthah. The disinherited son of a prostitute, Jephthah foolishly vowed that if God gave him victory, he would sacrifice the first living thing he met when he returned home. After defeating the Ammonites, he was met by his daughter, who agreed to be sacrificed (Judg 11:29–40). Jephthah was remembered both for his service (*Bib. Ant.* 39:1–9) and his disastrous vow (*Bib. Ant.* 39:10–11; *Apos. Con.* 7.37.2).

David. David was remembered as Israel's greatest king. God told Samuel to anoint David, who was only a young shepherd (1 Sam 16:13). When David faced Goliath in battle, he exhibited faith by telling his adversary, "You come to me with sword and spear and javelin; but I come to you in the name of the Lord of hosts" (1 Sam 17:45). David was remembered for worshiping God alone and opposing idolatry (1 Kgs 3:3, 14; 11:4; 14:8; 15:3; 2 Kgs 18:3; 22:2). He displeased God by his affair with Bathsheba (2 Sam 11:1–12:25) and his census of Israel (2 Sam 24), but when condemned, he repented. Tradition depicted him as one who "loved his Maker" (Sir 47:8; cf. 1 Macc 4:30; *1 Clem.* 18:1–17; *Apos. Con.* 7.37.2).

and Samuel. Samuel was a judge who was known to deal rightly with people (1 Sam 12:3; Sir 46:19) and who brought victory over the Philistines (1 Sam 7:9–11; Sir 46:16–18). In contrast to corrupt leaders, Samuel was faithful and trustworthy (Sir 46:15; *Apos. Con.* 7.37.2).

and the prophets. See NOTE on 1:1. Specific prophets alluded to in 11:32–38 include Daniel, who escaped the lions; Elijah and Elisha, who were able to raise the dead; and Isaiah, who was said to have been sawn in two.

11:33. *who through faith.* The OT does not explicitly mention the faith of the figures listed in 11:32, but later sources mention the faith of Samuel (Sir 46:15; cf. 46:11), and Daniel and his three companions (1 Macc 2:59; 4 Macc 16:21). Figures on the list were often considered "righteous" (NOTE on "righteousness" below), and the righteous live by faith (Hab 2:4; Heb 10:38; Rose, *Wolke*, 309). On faith see pp. 125–27.

overcame kingdoms. Among the figures mentioned in 11:32, Barak overcame the forces of the Canaanite king Jabin (Judg 4:23–24; 5:19), Gideon defeated the Midianite kings (Judg 8:3, 12, 26), Jephthah defeated the king of the Ammonites (11:12–13), and David conquered the kings of the nations around Israel (2 Sam 8:3, 11–12). Samson fought the Philistines, although their leaders are not called "kings" in the OT.

worked righteousness. David "worked justice and righteousness for his whole people" (2 Sam 8:15; 1 Chron 18:14), exemplifying the traits of a good ruler (2 Chron 9:8; Jer 23:5; Ezek 45:9). Samuel (1 Sam 12:3, 23) and Daniel (Dan 6:23) were also noted for righteousness. Righteousness is most perfectly found in the rule of Christ (Heb 1:9; cf. 7:2), but it is fitting for every person of God, or "righteous one," who lives by faith (NOTES on Heb 5:13; 10:38; 11:4, 7; 12:11).

obtained things that were promised. The term "promise" can refer to the word of promise (6:13; 7:6; 8:6) or the substance of what was promised (6:15; 9:15; 10:36; 11:13). Hebrews can speak either of a provisional realization of a promise in this world (6:15) or an ultimate realization in the age to come (4:1; 9:15). See NOTE on 6:15. In 11:33 the author refers to a provisional realization of the promises (Attridge; Ellingworth; H.-F. Weiss) rather than to receiving the words of the promises—like the promise of Davidic dynasty (Rose, *Wolke*, 308; cf. Grässer). Examples of fulfilled promises might include victories over kingdoms (11:33a; cf. Judg 4:6–9, 14; 6:16; 7:9; 2 Sam 5:19). Ultimate fulfillment is more evident in 11:35, which mentions final resurrection. See pp. 110–12 on the promise theme.

shut the mouths of lions. This recalls Daniel's deliverance from the lions' den (Dan 6:24 Theodotion; 1 Macc 2:60; 3 Macc 6:7; 4 Macc 16:3, 21; 18:13; *1 Clem.* 45:6). Others who overcame lions include Samson (Judg 14:5–6) and David (1 Sam 17:34–37; Sir 47:3).

11:34. *quenched the power of fire.* This refers to the three young men who endured the fiery furnace (Dan 3:1–30; 1 Macc 2:59; 3 Macc 6:6; 4 Macc 16:3, 21; 18:12; *1 Clem.* 45:7). The same was said of Abraham (*Bib. Ant.* 5:15–18).

escaped the edges of the sword. David escaped from Saul (1 Sam 19:10–18; 21:10) and Absalom (2 Sam 15:14). Elijah fled from Jezebel (1 Kgs 19:1–8). Elisha (2 Kgs 6:31) and Jeremiah (Jer 26:11) faced death threats. Esther saved the Jewish people from a pogrom that would have destroyed them "by the sword" (Add Esth 13:6). "Edges" (literally "mouths") is probably plural because swords had two cutting edges (Heb 4:12; Hofius, "Στόματα").

were made powerful out of weakness. Captive and blind, Samson was given strength to pull down a house (Judg 16:19–30). Gideon defeated an army with a small band (Judg 7). *1 Clement* 55:3–6 recalls how Esther and Judith were given power out of weakness to defeat Israel's adversaries (cf. Jdt 13:7). Since the context mentions persecution and conflict, it seems less likely that this refers to Israel's return from exile (Chrysostom) or Hezekiah's recovery from illness (Calvin).

became mighty in war. This recalls how some who were not mighty "became" mighty in battle. Conflict did not weaken them, but was the occasion on which they became strong—an important idea for dispirited listeners. Examples include David (1 Sam 17:49–51; Sir 47:5), Joshua (Sir 46:1), and Barak (Judg 4:14). When Judah Maccabee was asked, "How can we, few as we are, fight against so great and so strong a multitude?" he replied, "It is not on the size of the army that victory in battle depends, but strength comes from Heaven" (1 Macc 3:17, 19; cf. 4:6–11, 30–33).

routed the camps of foreigners. Gideon routed the camp of the Midianites (Judg 7:11, 14, 21; 8:11). David told Goliath that he would "give the corpses of the camp of foreigners" to the birds and beasts (1 Sam 17:46 LXX). In Isaiah's time God "struck down the camp of the Assyrians" (Sir 48:21; cf. 2 Kgs 19:35; Isa 37:36). In the days of Elisha God routed the Syrian camp (2 Kings 7). The Maccabees repeatedly battled the Seleucid "foreigners" (e.g., 1 Macc 2:7; 4:12, 26).

11:35. *Women received their dead back by resurrection.* The widow of Zarephath's son stopped breathing and was considered dead until Elijah revived him (1 Kgs 17:17–24; Sir 48:5; *Liv. Pro.* 10:5–6). When a Shunammite woman's son died, Elisha revived him (2 Kgs 4:18–37). Jesus later did the same (Luke 7:11–17; 8:40–56; John 11:1–44), although Hebrews does not allude to Jesus' ministry here. Hebrews calls these resuscitations "resurrection." The children would presumably die again, but these actions foreshadow final resurrection to eternal life (Heb 11:35), as did Isaac's deliverance (11:19).

But others were tortured. The verb *tympanizein* ("to beat") was used for severe beatings (*Liv. Pro.* 7:1–2). The compound *apotympanizein* (Plutarch, *Mor.* 60a; *Dion* 28.2) could indicate lethal beating (Aristotle, *Rhetoric* 2.6.27 1385A; 3 Macc 3:27; Josephus, *Ag. Ap.* 1.148). Bound to a *tympanon* ("drum"), the martyr Eleazar was prepared "to die under the blows" (2 Macc 6:19, 28–30). The *tympanon* might have been a rack or wheel on which the victim was stretched out (4 Macc 5:3, 32; 9:12–25; Philo, *Flaccus* 85). This would allow the torturers to beat the victim like a drum (Attridge; Lane). Alternatively, the *tympanon* might have been the post or block to which the person was fastened for beating. For Roman practice, see Tacitus, *Annals* 2.32.5; Suetonius, *Nero* 49.2; *Claudius* 34.1. Cf. E. C. E. Owen, "'Ἀποτυμπανίζω."

after refusing release. "Release" was commonly used for release from captivity (*Ep. Arist.* 12, 33). The Maccabean martyrs were expected to commit an unlawful act, like eating pork, to obtain "release from death" (2 Macc 6:22; 4 Macc 9:16).

in order that they might obtain a superior resurrection. The superior resurrection is not so much being raised to glory, instead of condemnation (Dan 12:2; John 5:28–29; Acts 24:15), as it is being raised to eternal life, instead of being resuscitated to life on earth (Heb 11:35a; cf. NOTE on 6:2). Hope for such a resurrection emboldened Jewish martyrs (2 Macc 7:9, 11, 14, 23, 29; 4 Macc 16:25; 17:18; 18:23) and early Christians to persevere in the face of death (Phil 1:21–22; 3:9–11).

11:36. *And others experienced ridicule.* Ridicule takes away a person's value in the eyes of others. People ridiculed prophets (2 Chron 36:16) like Jeremiah (Jer 20:7–8) and Isaiah (*Mart. Ascen. Isa.* 5:2). Conquerors ridiculed defeated peoples (*Pss. Sol.* 2:11; 17:12). Ridicule accompanied the abuse endured by the Jewish martyrs (2 Macc 7:7, 10) and Jesus (Matt 27:29–31, 41–42; Luke 23:11). Those addressed by Hebrews also endured verbal abuse (Heb 10:33; 13:13).

and scourging. The scourge commonly consisted of multiple lashes fastened into a wooden handle. Metal shards, lead balls, and bone fragments were inserted into the lashes. The victim was stripped, tied to a pillar, and lashed, sometimes until the inner organs or the backbone were exposed (*J.W.* 2.612; 6.304; 4 Macc 6:6). Scourging could be punishment in itself (2 Macc 6:30; Matt 10:17), a means of extracting information (Acts 22:24; 2 Macc 7:1), or a prelude to execution (Matt 20:19; 4 Macc 9:12). See R. E. Brown, *Death*, 851–53.

and even chains and imprisonment. Imprisonment was experienced by the prophets Jeremiah (Jer 37:4–21; cf. 20:1–2), Hanani (2 Chron 16:7–10), and Micaiah (1 Kgs 22:26–27), the Maccabean martyrs (4 Macc 12:2 [12:3 LXX]), and some within the listeners' own community (Heb 10:34; 13:3). On prison life see §37 COMMENT *a*.

11:37. *They were stoned.* Stoning was done officially as a form of capital punishment (e.g., Lev 20:27; Deut 22:21; John 8:3–5) and unofficially by crowds (Exod 17:4; Luke 20:6; John 8:59; Acts 5:26). Tradition said that people stoned God's messengers (Matt 23:37; Luke 13:34; *1 Clem.* 45:4), including the prophets Zechariah (2 Chron 24:21; cf. Matt 23:35; Luke 11:51) and Jeremiah (*Liv. Pro.* 2:1). Stephen died by stoning (Acts 7:58–59), whereas Paul survived it (Acts 14:19; 2 Cor 11:25).

sawn in two. According to tradition, Isaiah denounced the wicked King Manasseh, who ordered the prophet to be sawn in two. Some accounts add that Isaiah hid in a cedar tree, which was sawn through (*Liv. Pro.* 1:1; *Mart. Ascen. Isa.* 1:9; 5:11–14; Justin, *Dialogue* 120; Tertullian, *On Patience* 14; *b. Sanh.* 103b; *b. Yeb.* 49b; *y. Sanh.* 10.28c 37–39 [*TLI* 31.334]). One Jew who resisted the Romans during the siege of Jerusalem was clamped to a sawhorse and sawn in two (*Gen. Rab.* 65.22). Some Jews were "sawed in two, from the head downwards" during a conflict in Cyrene in A.D. 117 (Dio Cassius, *Roman History* 68.32.1). Some MSS add *epeirasthēsan* ("they were tested") either before (א D* L P etc.) or after (P^{13vid} A D^2 Maj; cf. KJV; $NRSV^{fn}$) *epristhēsan* ("they were sawn"). Its varying placement beside a similar word suggests that it is the result of dittography (*TCGNT*, 674–75; Attridge).

murdered by the sword. Some escaped the sword (11:34), but others did not. Those who died included the prophet Uriah (Jer 26:20–23), other prophets (1 Kgs 19:10, 14; Jer 2:30), and Christians (Acts 12:2). See generally 1 Kgs 18:13; Matt 23:31, 34, 37; Luke 13:34; Acts 7:52; 1 Thess 2:15; Josephus, *Ant.* 10.38; *Liv. Pro.* 3:2, 18; 6:2.

they went about in sheepskins and goatskins. Animal skins, undressed and with the hair on them (Num 31:20), were the most primitive dress imaginable. Poor people and philosophers wore coarse cloth. Elijah, however, wore a sheepskin (2 Kgs 1:8; cf. *Liv. Pro.* 22:5), and this attire was associated with prophets generally (cf. Zech 13:4; Matt 7:15; *1 Clem.* 17:1). Wearing animal skins suggests severe deprivation or asceticism.

11:38. *of whom the world was not worthy.* This parenthetical remark breaks the flow of the sentence to emphasize and clarify the point of the passage (cf. 7:19). The world has judged them to be unworthy, but in reality the world is unworthy of them (cf. NOTE on 11:7).

while they wandered over deserts and mountains. Wandering suggests aimless travel in harsh places where hunger and thirst were common (Ps 107:4–5). Deserts and mountains were places of hiding for persecuted prophets (*Mart. Ascen. Isa.* 2:8–12), the Maccabees (1 Macc 2:31; 2 Macc 5:27; 10:6), and others (Judg 6:2; 1 Sam 23:14; 1 Macc 2:28; *Pss. Sol.* 17:17).

and in caves and holes in the earth. These hiding places (Judg 6:2; 1 Sam 13:6; 22:1; 24:3) were used by persecuted prophets (1 Kgs 18:4, 13; 19:9), the Maccabees (2 Macc 6:11; 10:6; Josephus, *Ant.* 12.271–72), and other righteous figures (*T. Mos.* 9:6).

11:39. *And all these, although attested through faith.* "All" the heroes in Heb 11 are included, from Abel to the Maccabees. On being "attested" see NOTE on 11:2.

did not receive what was promised. See NOTES on 11:13, 33.

11:40. *since God provided something superior for us.* The verb *problepein* means both "foresee" and "make provision." Through faith (11:1) one can confess that God makes provision for things that transcend human vision (Bengel). What is "superior" includes resurrection and the blessings of the new covenant, culminating in eternal life (7:22; 8:6; 11:35b).

so that without us they would not be made complete. See pp. 122–25.

COMMENT[415]

The press of scenes from Israel's history concludes when the author says that "time does not allow me to tell" (11:32b), followed by a rapid list of people and incidents. This rhetorical device, known as *paraleipsis* or *praeteritio*, "occurs when we say that we are passing by . . . that which precisely we now are saying" (*Ad Her.* 4.27 §37).[416] Quickly listing subjects conveys the speaker's awareness of the breadth of the subject matter, while his refraining from comment on each item shows that he is concerned not to burden the listeners (Isocrates, *Archidamus* 47).

The style shifts from scenes punctuated with *pistei* ("by faith") to a series of names and accomplishments. Rapidly listing names in 11:32b creates a "comma," in which "single words are set apart by pauses in staccato speech."[417] The accomplishments cited in 11:33–34 are given in clauses of similar length and structure, a device called isocolon, which creates a "rhythmic barrage" that gives "the impression that great numbers of people crowd into the author's mind as he speaks."[418] By stating item after item without conjunctions in 11:33–37, the author implies that his list could be extended indefinitely.[419] A similar effect is achieved in 11:38 by repeating a conjunction: deserts *and* mountains *and* caves *and* holes (see Demetrius, *On Style* 63). Stringing together clauses that generally begin with aorist verbs bearing an initial *e-* sound allows the words to strike the ear like a series of blows, pressing the content into the mind.

This section engages listeners by prompting them to recall the numerous stories to which the author alludes. Many of the accomplishments listed can be associated with more than one figure, and some can be connected with figures that are not explicitly named, so that for those familiar with Israel's tradition the text

---

[415]On 11:32–40 see Cosby, *Rhetorical*, 57–73; deSilva, *Despising*, 195–202; Dunnill, *Covenant*, 181–83; Eisenbaum, *Jewish Heroes*, 173–78; van Esbroeck, "Héb. XI,33–38"; Grässer, *Aufbruch*, 201–12; Hofius, "Στόματα"; E. C. E. Owen, "'Αποτυμπανίζω"; Peterson, *Hebrews*, 156–59; Rose, *Wolke*, 303–33.

[416]Cf. Lausberg, *Handbook* §§882–86; Rose, *Wolke*, 305.

[417]*Rhet. ad Her.* 4.19.26. On the intensity of asyndeton see 4.30.§41; Quintilian, *Inst.* 9.3.54.

[418]Cosby, *Rhetorical*, 61. He discusses the rhetorical figures in Heb 11:32–40 on pp. 57–73.

[419]The device is called asyndeton (Quintilian, *Inst.* 9.3.50). "Speech is like a banquet: a few dishes may be arranged to seem many" (Demetrius, *On Style* 62). Aristotle noted that asyndeton is fitting at the end of a speech (*Rhetoric* 3.19.6), and Hebrews uses it to end a section.

evokes associations with an ever widening circle of faithful people.[420] The passage creates a collage of people and events from various periods, showing that what matters is not the time in which people live, but the faith that they exhibit.[421]

Structurally, the passage is framed by references to those who endured "through faith" (*dia pisteōs*, 11:33, 39). There are three subsections: (**a**) Triumphant heroes, who won military victories or were delivered from danger and death, are listed first (11:32–35a). (**b**) Suffering heroes appear second (11:35b–38). A verbal cue is given when the author shifts from those who (*hoi*) triumphed through faith (11:33) to others (*alloi*) who suffered in faith (11:35b). If some received their dead back by resurrection to life on earth (11:35a), others suffered death in the hope of resurrection to eternal life (11:35b). Some escaped the sword (11:34), but others were murdered by the sword (11:37). (**c**) A concluding statement in 11:39–40 binds all generations of the faithful together. Repeating the word "attested" (11:39) connects those mentioned in 11:32–38 with preceding generations (cf. 11:2). Declaring that "without us" they will not be made complete connects previous generations with the author's contemporaries (11:40).[422] Those who are "attested" (*martyrein*) become the "witnesses" (*martyres*) who fill the stadium in 12:1, and those who await the completion (11:40) of God's purposes find that Jesus makes faith complete (12:2).

a. Triumphant Heroes (11:32–35a)

The triumphs of faith begin with six named figures—Gideon, Barak, Samson, Jephthah, David, and Samuel—and the prophets as a group (11:32). Questions arise over why these figures were selected, since Barak is obscure and Jephthah's reputation is mixed at best.[423] Tradition could have magnified their virtues and masked their imperfections, as a sculptor might do when creating a statue, yet extant sources show that their flaws were not forgotten (see NOTES). Alternatively, including some characters with dubious qualities might actually enhance the passage, since hearing only of impeccable examples of faith could be dispiriting, for it would seem to put faith beyond the reach of ordinary people.[424] If faith is

---

[420]Esbroeck ("Héb. XI,33–38") notes the tendency of ancient MSS to supply additional information for Heb 11:32–38. This illustrates how the text evokes associations.

[421]The rapid listing of examples of conflict, heroism, and suffering shows that there was no rest after the entry into the land (11:30–31). True rest is of a transcendent order (4:1–11; Dunnill, *Covenant*, 143, 181).

[422]Vanhoye, *La structure*, 191–94.

[423]Hebrews' sequence differs from that in the OT narrative, which places Barak (Judg 4–5) before Gideon (Judg 6–8), Jephthah (Judg 11–12) before Samson (Jud 13–16), and Samuel (1 Sam 1–3) before David (1 Sam 16). The order in Hebrews could be conventional, since 1 Sam 12:11 mentions Jerubbaal (= Gideon), Barak, Jephthah, and Samuel (MT) or Samson (LXX) in that order (Lane). Alternatively, the names might be arranged in pairs with the most important name placed first in each pair (Ellingworth).

[424]Eisenbaum notes that figures in Jewish lists are regularly exemplars of perfection, whereas figures in Greco-Roman lists often have checkered histories (*Jewish Heroes*, 77).

possible despite Jephthah's rashness and Barak's hesitancy, then faith is also possible for the listeners, despite their own shortcomings.

The first three accomplishments of faith (11:33abc) repeat themes that were sounded earlier in the chapter, underscoring the idea that challenges and triumphs of faith span the generations. First, those listed in 11:32 overcame kingdoms (NOTE on 11:33a). Like Moses and his parents, who defied kings (11:23, 27), all who resist tyrants are examples that encourage listeners to resist the authorities who imprison members of their community (pp. 67–71). Second, those listed worked righteousness (NOTE on 11:33b), as did Abel, Noah, and others (11:4, 7). Their example provides listeners with motivation to discern and pursue the ways of righteousness (5:14; 10:38; 12:11) rather than capitulating to the ways of unrighteousness (10:32–34). Third, they obtained things that were promised (NOTE on 11:33c), showing that it is right to trust God's promises, even though fulfillment seems slow in coming, as it was for Abraham and his family (11:13). Fulfillment of lesser promises (NOTE on 11:33) increases confidence that God will fulfill his larger commitments and bring the heirs of all his promises—including the listeners—to full possession of their eternal inheritance (6:12, 17; 9:15).

The next three items recall Daniel's deliverance from the lions' den, the preservation of Daniel's three companions from death in a fiery furnace, and the escape of others from the sword (11:33d–34b). These stories run counter to what is known from experience. In the Greco-Roman period those who were thrown to the lions and wild beasts died,[425] as did the Jewish and Christian martyrs who were burned[426] or killed by the sword (Acts 12:2). Hebrews does not naively promise that the faithful will always be spared—as will be clear in 11:35b–38—but these OT examples challenge the despair that is born of difficult experience: one cannot assume that the adversary will triumph in every case, for according to the Scriptures God has delivered the righteous in surprising ways.

The next group of examples shifts from deliverance to conquest, as the author refers to the weak who were made powerful, who became mighty in war, and who prevailed over their enemies (11:34cde). In some ways, the listeners' situation was comparable: their faltering community was susceptible to weakness (11:34c; cf. 2:1; 5:11; 6:12; 10:25), and they experienced conflict with non-Christians (cf. 10:32–34; 11:13; 13:13). In other ways, these examples might seem ill suited to the listeners' situation, since they were not being summoned to military exploits. Yet using examples from contrasting situations can be valuable in exhortation (Quintilian, *Inst.* 5.11.10). The dispiriting circumstances of the listeners may lack the drama of battle, yet the faith to which they are called is like that of soldiers confronting an enemy, and the God on whom they rely in their weakness is the God who provided strength to the weak in generations past.

---

[425] Josephus, *J.W.* 7.24, 37; *Ant.* 15.274–75. Throwing Christians to the lions was notorious in later periods (Ign. *Rom.* 4.1–3; Tertullian, *Apology* 40.1–2).

[426] 2 Macc 6:11; 7:5; 4 Macc 11:26; Tacitus, *Annals* 15.44; *Mart. Pol.* 2:3; cf. K. L. Schmidt, *TDNT* 3.464–67.

The last act of deliverance concerns the women whose dead children were brought back to life (NOTE on 11:35a). The sense of triumph persists, but it is tempered by the recognition that death does strike within the community of faith. In the days of Elijah and Elisha, children died, though after a short time, the prophets raised them up again (1 Kgs 17:17–24; 2 Kgs 4:18–37). The next section will deal with others who died in the hope of a more distant resurrection to a new and superior order of life.

b. Suffering Heroes (11:35b–38)

Chrysostom commented that faith both accomplishes great things and suffers great things (*Homilies* 27.5). Having considered those who prevailed in the face of battle, lions, and fire, Hebrews now recalls those who suffered without deliverance, yet whose steadfastness is a triumph of faith. Among those who were tortured (11:35b) was the aged martyr Eleazar, who was told that he would "be released from death" if he violated the Law by eating pork (2 Macc 6:18, 22). When he refused, he was beaten to death. Seven brothers were martyred after him, each by hideous means. Voicing hope for a superior resurrection (Heb 11:35c), they declared that "the King of the universe will raise us up to an everlasting renewal of life," (2 Macc 7:9; cf. 7:23).

The experience of the prophets and martyrs who were ridiculed, scourged, and imprisoned (Heb 11:36) resembles that of the Christians who had endured denunciation, abuse, and imprisonment. Rather than abandoning their faith in order to minimize suffering, they had remained faithful in the face of suffering (10:32–34; pp. 67–71). At the time Hebrews was written, the most severe affliction had passed, but denunciation continued and some remained in prison (13:3, 13; pp. 71–72). Having exhorted listeners to resist tendencies toward drift and faithlessness (2:1, 3; 3:12; 6:6, 12; 10:25), the author offers examples of faith that resemble those from their own community's past. He does so to encourage them not to surrender their hope in order to ease tensions with society, but to keep the faith as their forebears did.

Next the author tells of afflictions that go beyond anything experienced by his listeners. Whereas the prophets and martyrs had been stoned, sawn in two, and murdered by the sword (11:37abc), the listeners had not had their blood shed (12:4). Whereas some in previous generations were reduced to wearing animal skins (11:37d) and seeking shelter in caves and holes (11:38b), the listeners have not had to deal with this level of privation. They had suffered dispossession in the past (10:34), but by the time Hebrews was written they had apparently regained the means to offer hospitality and enough possessions that they were warned not to be greedy for more (13:1–6). The severity of the examples makes an implicit argument from the greater to the lesser (Quintilian, *Inst.* 5.11.9). If figures from the past maintained their faith in the face of great suffering, Hebrews encourages listeners to maintain their faith in the face of lesser suffering.

The positive recollection of the suffering heroes of faith challenges and reverses the judgments of the unbelieving world. By subjecting the faithful to physical abuse, prison, destitution, and death, the unbelieving world seeks to degrade them (§28 COMMENT *a*), yet Hebrews denies that the world has the right to pass judgment. The world may judge the faithful to be unworthy, yet in truth the world is not worthy of the faithful (11:38a). Those who accept the judgments of the unbelieving world will abandon faith in order to gain value in the eyes of others, but those who trust God's judgments will maintain their faith, despite opposition, in the confidence of receiving true honor from God (deSilva, *Despising*, 195–202).

c. Past Heroes and Present Christians (11:39–40)

Offering a summary comment on his review of Israel's history, the author says that the figures mentioned did not receive what was promised (11:39c). This echoes what was said of Israel's early ancestors (11:13–16) as well as the martyrs (11:35b–38), but by referring to "all these" (11:39a) the author insists that none of the figures in Heb 11—including Enoch, Noah, and military victors—fully received what God promised. Nonfulfillment in no way diminishes the faith of these heroes and heroines, who were attested by God (11:39b). Instead, recounting how they endured for the sake of an unseen hope underscores their achievement.

Rather than defining what God promised (11:39c), the author suggests that it is something superior to anything experienced under the old covenant (11:40a). God's promise to Abraham included blessing, land, and descendants (6:13–15; 11:9), and hints of fulfillment came through a blessing from Melchizedek (7:1), the ancestors' temporary residence in Canaan (11:9), and the birth of Isaac (11:11). Nevertheless, none of these incidents marks the completion of God's designs. The author has connected what is superior to salvation rather than condemnation (6:9) and to the hope of drawing near to God (7:19). The superior covenant that Jesus established provides the cleansing and sanctification needed for people to approach God rightly (7:22; 8:6). On this basis people can look for the complete realization of all of God's promises in the heavenly Jerusalem (12:22–24), the city that marks the end of the journey of faith for Abraham and his heirs (11:10, 16).

When the author says that "without us" previous generations "would not be made complete" (11:40b), he links previous generations to the Christian community of his own time. Some take this to mean that previous generations of Israel are allowed to share in the salvation given to Christians (Bengel; Braun) and others understand it to mean that Christians are allowed to share in the promises given to Israel (H.-F. Weiss). Neither approach is apt, since Hebrews emphasizes the unity of God's people over the generations, with all sharing in the realization of the promises together. At the resurrection "all will come equally into the inheritance of eternal glory and will be joined at the same moment to their Head" (Erasmus, *Paraphrase*, 252). Indeed, to "be glorified all together is a great delight" (Chrysostom, NPNF[1] 14.492). Christ has already been made complete through his death and exaltation (2:10; 5:9). He now makes others complete through the cleansing of the conscience (9:9, 14; 10:1, 14) in anticipation of the resurrection when all the people of God will be made complete in everlasting life in the heavenly Zion (12:22–24).[427] See pp. 122–25.

34. Running with Perseverance (12:1–17)

12 [1]Therefore, since we indeed have such a great cloud of witnesses surrounding us, and laying aside every weight and the sin that readily besets us, let us run with endurance the contest that is set before us, [2]looking to Jesus, the pioneer and completer of faith, who for the joy that was set before him endured a cross, disdaining its shame, and is seated at the right hand of the throne of God. [3]So consider the one who has endured from sinners such opposition against himself, in order that you may not give up and grow weary in your souls. [4]You have not yet resisted to the point of bloodshed in your contest with sin.

[5]And you have forgotten the exhortation that addresses you as sons: *My son, do not neglect the instruction of the Lord, and do not give up when reproved by him,* [6]*for the Lord instructs the one whom he loves and chastises every son whom he receives.* [7]Endure for the sake of instruction; God is treating you as sons. For what son does a father not instruct? [8]But if you are without the instruction in which all have shared, then you are illegitimate children and not sons. [9]Furthermore, we had human fathers who instructed us, and we showed respect. Shall we not to a greater extent be subject to the Father of spirits, and live? [10]For they instructed for a few days as seemed good to them, but he does so on the basis of what is beneficial, in order that we might share his holiness. [11]All instruction seems grievous rather than joyful at the time, but later it yields peaceful fruit of righteousness to those who have been trained through it.

[12]Therefore, stretch out the drooping hands and weak knees, [13]and set your feet on straight paths, in order that what is lame might not be twisted, but might heal instead. [14]Pursue peace with all and the holiness without which no one will see the Lord, [15]remaining watchful so that no one falls back from the grace of God, *so that no root of bitterness puts forth a shoot and causes trouble* and that through it many become defiled; [16]so that no one becomes immoral or profane like Esau, who for a single serving of food gave up his rights as firstborn. [17]For you know that later on, when he wanted to inherit the blessing, he was rejected, for he found no opportunity for repentance, even though he sought [the blessing] with tears.

NOTES

12:1. *Therefore, since we indeed have.* Having spoken of "all these" (*kai houtoi pantes*, 11:39), the author shifts to the first person plural: "we indeed" (*kai hēmeis*). As elsewhere, he encourages listeners to pursue a future hope by identifying what they already "have" (cf. 4:14; 10:19).

---

[427]On views of death and afterlife in Hebrews see NOTES on 6:2; 9:27.

such a great cloud of witnesses surrounding us. "Cloud" (*nephos*) was a common Greco-Roman metaphor for crowds (BAGD, 537). The term "witnesses" (*martyroi*) combines several meanings like tones in a musical chord:

(a) Spectators. The faithful of the past watch the contest in which the listeners now compete. In one sense witnesses are "spectators" (Lucian, *Anacharsis* 11; Plutarch, *Mor.* 527F; 679B; Dio Chrysostom, *Disc.* 3.11; Longinus, *On the Sublime* 14.2; Wis 1:6; Josephus, *J.W.* 6.134).

(b) Witnesses. In court "witnesses" testify to the truth (Heb 10:28). Being surrounded by witnesses underscores the listeners' accountability.

(c) Approval. Those who persevered in faith were often despised by the world, but the value of these witnesses is "attested" (*martyrēthentes*) by God, who values faithfulness (NOTE on 11:2). See generally Croy, *Endurance*, 58–62.

laying aside every weight and the sin. This metaphor draws on different senses of *onkos* ("weight," "heaviness"):

(a) Physical weight. Athletes would seek to lay aside or eliminate the excess body weight that made them unfit for running (Philostratus, *Gymnasticus* 48; Appian, *Roman History* 4.7; Philo, *Special Laws* 2.91). In a physical sense the verb "lay aside" was used for removing clothing (Acts 7:58; *Mart. Pol.* 13:2), as athletes did before competing, since clothing added unnecessary "weight" (Philo, *Sacrifices* 63).

(b) Pride or pretension. Some associated "weight" with the "swollen" sense of self with which some people cloaked themselves (Plutarch, *Marcius Coriolanus* 13.4; Philo, *Preliminary Studies* 128; cf. *Creation* 1–2; *TLNT* 2.561–63). In a metaphorical sense "lay aside" could mean renouncing drunkenness, licentiousness, quarreling, and other sins (Rom 13:12; cf. Eph 4:22; Col 3:8; 1 Pet 2:1; Jas 1:21; Philo, *Posterity* 48). For exhortations to avoid such sins see Heb 12:15–16; 13:4–5.

that readily besets us. The adjective *euperistatos* may have been coined by the author (p. 96). The prefix *eu-* can mean "easy," as in *eualōtos* ("easily caught") and *euepithetos* ("easily attacked"; cf. Ellingworth). The last part of the word (*-peristatos*) is related to the verb *periistēmi* ("to place around") and to the noun *peristasis*, which means "circumstances" and especially difficult ones (2 Macc 4:16; Epictetus, *Disc.* 2.6.17; cf. *TLNT* 2.131–32). The text suggests that the witnesses encircle the listeners to encourage, but sin encircles to entangle them (Westcott) like a bulky robe impedes running. The variant "easily distracting" (*euperispaston*, P46 1739; cf. Zuntz, *Text*, 25–29; Lane; NRSVfn) is not well attested, and it may be an error or an attempt to clarify the text (*TCGNT*, 675; Attridge).

let us run with endurance. The listeners' contest has more to do with endurance than with speed. There were reports—some fanciful—concerning feats of long-distance running (Pliny the Elder, *Natural History* 2.73 §181; 7.20 §84), but races were commonly measured in stadium lengths, or *stades* (200 yards). Hebrews says that listeners are surrounded by spectators, which implies that the race is being run within the stadium. Standard races were two, seven, twelve, and twenty stades. The longest was twenty-four stades, or a little under three miles.

The marathon was not a standard race in antiquity, but "endurance" was required even for the shorter races, in which runners became exhausted (Virgil, *Aeneid* 5.327–33; cf. Philo, *Unchangeable* 13; *Preliminary Studies* 164). References to "enduring" (Heb 12:2, 3, 7) link the athletic imagery with the hardships that the listeners had endured because of their faith (10:32, 36; cf. 1 Cor 9:24; Gal 2:2; Phil 2:16).

the contest that is set before us. An *agōn* ("contest") implies struggle, as in "agonize." Athletic contests included running, jumping, throwing the discus and javelin, wrestling, boxing, and other events. Martyrdom was compared to a "contest" (4 Macc 16:16), but Heb 12:4 indicates that the listeners were contending primarily against their own sin and that their blood has not yet been shed. The strain of the contest that is "set before" the runners (Herodotus, *Histories* 9.60; Plato, *Phaedrus* 247B; Epictetus, *Disc.* 3.25.2–3) can be endured for "the joy that is set before" them (Heb 12:2b).

12:2. *looking to Jesus.* Athletes would look down the track to one who was seated in the place of honor (COMMENT *a*). The verb *aphoran* could mean relying on someone in authority (Josephus, *J.W.* 2.410; *Ant.* 12.431; 16.134) or on God. The Maccabean martyrs were "looking to God and enduring torture even to death" (4 Macc 17:10; cf. Epictetus, *Disc.* 2.19.29).

the pioneer. On the term see NOTE on 2:10. Jesus was not the first person to have shown faith in God. Those mentioned in Heb 11:4–38 were people of faith, but none of them reached the goal of faith, the realization of God's promises (11:40). Jesus is the pioneer because he takes faith to its goal, going where others have not yet gone. He is the source and model of faith for others.

and completer. The term *teleiōtēs*, like the English "completer" (*OED* 2.726), is a very rare word. Dionysius of Halicarnassus spoke of an orator who was neither the inventor of a style of rhetoric nor the "completer" of styles invented by others (*Dinarchus* 1). According to Hebrews, Jesus does not merely follow the faith of others, nor is he a prototype that will later be superseded (Croy, *Endurance*, 175–76). On completion see pp. 122–25.

of faith. Faith involves trust in God and faithfulness to God (see pp. 125–27). Jesus pioneers and completes faith in two ways:

(a) Source of faith. Jesus inaugurates a new covenant and opens a "new and living way" into the presence of God (10:19–20). Through his death and exaltation, he became a "source of eternal salvation" (5:9). He is a source of faith because the message about him evokes faith.

(b) Model of faith. Jesus pioneers and completes faith by fully trusting God and remaining faithful to God in a way that the listeners are to follow. Cf. 6:20 on the forerunner.

who for the joy that was set before him. There are two translations of *anti*, of which the first is preferable:

(a) "For the joy" (NIV; NRSV; NAB2; REB; NJB). This use of *anti* appears in 12:16, where Esau sells his birthright "for" a single meal. The idea that people endure disgrace or pain "for [*anti*] some great and noble object" (Aristotle, *Nic. Ethics* 3.1.7) fits those who persevere in the hope of a future reward (Heb 10:34;

11:24–26). Many texts refer to prizes that are "set before" those who compete in athletics (Polybius, *Histories* 3.62; Pausanias, *Description of Greece* 9.2.6), in war (Plutarch, *Mor.* 8d; Dio Cassius, *Roman History* 41.10.1), and in the quest for virtue (Philo, *Rewards* 13; Josephus, *Ant.* 8.208). Hebrews replaces the usual idea of a prize with the "joy" of being seated at God's right hand (12:2d). On joy at winning a race see Dio Chrysostom, *Disc.* 9.14. See Bonnard, "La traduction"; Croy, *Endurance*, 177–86; deSilva, *Despising*, 173–78.

(b) "Instead of the joy" that was within his grasp, Jesus endured the shame and disgrace of the cross (BAGD, 73 [1]; NRSVfn; Lane; Andriessen, "Renonçant"). Some propose that Jesus gave up the joy of his heavenly status (cf. Phil 2:6–7; 2 Cor 8:9), just as Moses left Pharaoh's court (Heb 11:24–26). Yet this sense seems unlikely here, since it was common to speak of the prize "set before" the contestant (see **(a)** above). It was said that those who have a prize set before them do not cease striving after it (Josephus, *Ant.* 8.302; Heb 4:11; 6:11; 10:35; 11:6, 26).

endured a cross. Crucifixion was often preceded by scourging (NOTE on 11:36) and other torture. During crucifixion "some have their victims with head down to the ground; some impale their private parts; others stretch out their arms on the gibbet" (Seneca, *Consolation to Marcia* 20.3). Most pounded nails through the victims' wrists and ankles so that they hung suspended on their own wounds. Torment continued until the victim died from blood loss, shock, and other factors (Hengel, *Crucifixion*, 22–32; R. E. Brown, *Death*, 1088–92).

disdaining. "Disdain" shows a negative value judgment upon something. Rather than saying that Jesus disdained suffering, as martyrs did when they bore it courageously (4 Macc 6:9; cf. 8:28; 13:1; cf. 14:11; 16:2), Hebrews says that he disdained disgrace. Christ's standard of judgment differs from that of the surrounding society.

its shame. Crucifixions were public events, and victims were subjected to the contempt of passersby (cf. Mark 15:29–32). Crucifixion was the "tree of shame" (Cicero, *In Defense of Rabirius* 4 §13) and those who hung on the "tree" were considered accursed under Jewish Law (Deut 21:22–23; Hengel, *Crucifixion*, 22–63; H. W. Kuhn, "Kreuzesstrafe," 758–75). People feel shame only in the presence of those whose opinions they value (Aristotle, *Rhetoric* 2.6.14–15). Therefore, philosophers urged people to despise the views of the masses and judge themselves only according to virtue (Seneca, *De Constantia* 13.2; Epictetus, *Ench.* 19.2; deSilva, *Despising*, 170–71). Jesus' actions were not governed by society's views of what was shameful, but by what it meant to obey God (Heb 2:10–18; 5:7–10; 10:5–10).

and is seated at the right hand of the throne of God. The few seats in a first-century stadium were reserved for nobility. Traditionally, martyrs could expect a place beside God's throne (4 Macc 17:11–18). The right side was a place of honor (NOTE on Heb 1:3). Christ is worthy of such honor and more since he is the Son of God, who sits at God's right hand in glory (NOTE on 1:13).

12:3. *So consider the one who has endured from sinners such opposition.* Listeners who knew of Jesus' public ministry might have recalled how he met with opposition from Jewish leaders concerning the Law (e.g., Mark 2:23–3:6;

7:1–13), but given the mention of the cross in Heb 12:2, the listeners more probably would have thought of opposition from the "sinners" (Matt 26:45; Mark 14:41; Luke 24:7) and "lawless men" (Acts 2:23; cf. 1 Cor 2:6, 8) who crucified Jesus (Mark 8:31; 9:31; 10:33–34 par.).

against himself. The Greek text is uncertain and many translations simply omit these words (NIV; NAB^2; NJB; REB). There is good MS support for the plural *autous* (P^{13} P^{46} $ℵ^2$ $Ψ^c$ 33 81 1739*) or *eautous* (ℵ* D*; cf. $NRSV^{fn}$). The plural suggests that Jesus' opponents injured "themselves," just as those who crucify Christ "to themselves" do so to their own hurt (6:6; Lane) and just as Korah's rebellion resulted in his own demise (Num 16:32; Ellingworth, "New Testament"). The idea that sinners injure themselves was commonplace (Prov 8:36 LXX; Marcus Aurelius, *Meditations* 9.4; cf. Aristotle, *Magna moralia* 1.33.30 1196b; Xenophon, *Hellenica* 1.7.19). Nevertheless, internal evidence favors the singular pronoun *heauton* (A P 104 326 1241^2) or *auton* (D^2 K L Ψ*). This fits a context in which Jesus endured the kind of opposition "against himself" (NRSV) that the listeners had experienced (10:32–34). See Attridge; Grässer; H.-F. Weiss; Metzger, *TCGNT*, 675.

in order that you may not give up and grow weary in your souls. This connotes moral and physical exhaustion, like that experienced by athletes or soldiers (Polybius, *Histories* 29.17.4). Cf. Heb 12:5.

12:4. *You have not yet resisted to the point of bloodshed.* The imagery suggests resisting like an athlete in a boxing match or the pancratium, an event that combined wrestling and boxing with kicking, strangling, and twisting limbs (*TLNT* 1.128–30; cf. 1 Cor 9:24, 26). "To the point of bloodshed" has two aspects of meaning:

(a) Metaphorically: "you have not done your utmost." Pancratists and boxers wrapped their fists with leather and strove "to spatter men's cheeks with blood" (Apollonius of Rhodes, *Argonautica* 2.59; Homer, *Iliad* 23.683–99; Virgil, *Aeneid*, 5.470). As a metaphor for grappling with life's challenges, "the only contestant who can confidently enter the lists is the man who has seen his own blood" (Seneca, *Ep.* 13.2). The sense is that listeners are not yet in "mortal combat" with sin.

(b) Descriptively: "you have not suffered martyrdom." Resisting "to the point of bloodshed" (cf. Herodian, *History* 2.6.14) resembles descriptions of Jesus (Phil 2:8) and the martyrs who resisted "to the point of death" (2 Macc 13:14; 4 Macc 17:10; Rev 12:11) in their "contest" of faith (cf. 4 Macc 11:20; 13:15). Some in the listeners' community had experienced physical abuse (Heb 10:32–34; 13:3), but the violence apparently did not entail martyrdom. If it had, the author almost certainly would not have denied—even in a metaphor—that their blood had been shed. Thus 12:4 helps to show that the listeners were threatened more by fatigue than by martyrdom (see pp. 71–72).

in your contest with sin. Although the author urged listeners simply to "lay aside" sin in 12:1b, here he recognizes that opposing sin means struggle. "Sin" has been taken in two ways, of which the first is preferable:

(a) Sin within the community. In 12:1b "sin" referred to sins that cling to Christians themselves (cf. 1:3; 2:17; 3:13). Hebrews specifically warns against sins of immorality, godlessness, and greed (12:14–17; 13:4–5). Apostasy is not emphasized here, although it too must be resisted (3:12–13; 6:4–6; 10:26–31).

(b) Opponents of the church. Some argue that listeners are called to resist the sin of those who oppose the church just as Jesus resisted the sinners who opposed him according to 12:3 (Braun; Lane; Croy, *Endurance*, 194). The community had been abused as Jesus was (10:32–34; 13:13), but the focus in 12:1–17 is on sin within the community.

12:5. *And you have forgotten the exhortation.* Exhortations are designed to give encouragement, to prevent injury, and to promote the well-being of others. The author exhorts his listeners (13:22), as they are to exhort others (3:13; 10:25). The Scriptures were understood to be a source of encouragement (Rom 15:4; 1 Macc 12:9), and this particular exhortation is from Prov 3:11–12.

that addresses you as sons. Proverbs 3:11 uses the singular "son," which Hebrews extends to all God's "sons" and daughters. The *hōs* is not contrary to fact ("as if"), but predicative ("as"). God addresses them as the sons that they truly are (NOTE on 2:10; Bornkamm, "Sohnschaft," 223).

12:5b–6. Hebrews quotes Prov 3:11–12 LXX, which differs from the MT. The last part reads:

LXX	*MT*
for the Lord instructs	for the Lord instructs
the one whom he loves	the one whom he loves
and chastises every son	*as a father the son*
whom he receives.	*in whom he delights.*

The difference concerns the Hebrew *k'b*. The MT took it to be *ke* ("as") plus *'āb* ("father"), but the LXX translator took it as a form of the verb *kā'ēb*, which has to do with inflicting pain.

My son, do not neglect. To neglect suggests an unthinking disregard for something of value (Josephus, *Ant.* 5.132; *Ag. Ap.* 2.172). Cf. Heb 2:1–4 on disregarding salvation.

the instruction. Forms of the Greek word "instruction" (*paideia, paideuein, paideutēs*) occur throughout 12:5–11. The word group commonly had to do with educating the young by training in various disciplines and by correcting error (G. Bertram, *TDNT* 5.596–625). Two questions help to identify the nuances of the word group in Heb 12:

(a) Is *paideia* punitive or nonpunitive? A punitive understanding assumes that God is punishing listeners for sin in order to deter them from further wrongdoing (Calvin; NJB 12:9). The nonpunitive view is that God is training and testing the listeners so that they develop a greater capacity for endurance (Chrysostom; Theophylact; Ps.-Oecumenius). The context supports the nonpunitive sense. Listeners are to resist sin (12:1, 4), but there is no suggestion that they are being punished for sin. Since "all" God's children have shared in *paideia* (12:8a), presumably including the faithful like Abel, Abraham, Moses, and the martyrs (Heb 11), it seems unlikely that the challenges they faced were punishments from

God. Moreover, Jesus "learned obedience by what he suffered" (5:8) even though he was sinless (4:15). Finally, the outcome of *paideia* is not repentance, but a greater capacity for "endurance" in faith (12:7a; cf. Croy, *Endurance*, 77).

(**b**) Is *paideia* primarily "instruction" or "correction" of error? *Paideia* includes correction, but is not limited to correction. It includes theory and practice, preparation and testing. Those who are subject to *paideia* are equipped with certain abilities, then placed in situations where their abilities are tested. God places those who have been instructed in faith (5:11–6:2) in situations where their faith is tested (2:18) in order that it might be toughened. Instruction includes training (12:11; cf. Isocrates, *Antidosis*, 181; Herodian *History* 5.7.5; Plutarch, *Mor.* 7d), and training includes the equipping that helps people meet a challenge (Heb 5:11). Proverbs, which is quoted here, often linked *paideia* to teaching and wisdom (e.g., Prov 1:2, 7, 8; 4:1 LXX). Moreover, the quotation from Proverbs does not make *paideia* synonymous with reproof (Heb 12:5c). People might respond to *paideia* by "neglecting" it, which implies a misplaced confidence that they can get along without it, whereas "reproof" can make them "lose heart" by taking away their sense of confidence (12:5). *Paideia* is not only the process of instruction but also the goal of being educated (BAGD, 603 [2]). Therefore, Hebrews calls people to endure for the sake of their education (12:7a). Finally, a human instructor (*paideutēs*) is a teacher, not simply a disciplinarian (NOTE on 12:9).

of the Lord. God provides instruction by giving promises and commandments, and by placing people in situations where they must put what they have learned into practice. God "instructed" Moses' generation by promising them a land, allowing them to feel hunger, then commanding them to gather manna in order that they might understand their dependence upon him (Deut 8:2–5). God was sometimes said to correct the disobedient by allowing calamity to fall upon them for a time in order to turn them from sin (2 Macc 6:12–16; 7:33; 10:4; *Pss. Sol.* 13:9; 18:4). In many cases, however, God's "instruction" means "testing" people by placing them in situations that challenge them (Heb 2:18; 4:15; 11:17; Sir 18:13–14; 23:1–3; Wis 3:5; 11:9; 12:22). The force of the idea in Hebrews is enhanced by the fact that it was rather widely accepted. For example, Stoics taught that God "educates quite sternly, as strict fathers do"; God tests him, hardens him, and fits him for his own service (Seneca, *On Providence* 1.6; cf. 2.5–6; Philo, *Rewards* 119).

and do not give up when reproved by him. Reproof was commonly verbal correction, not physical punishment (e.g., Matt 18:15; 1 Cor 14:24; Tit 1:9). God sends forth "into our mind his own word, that reproves and chastens," making the mind ashamed of its errors in order to heal it (Philo, *Worse* 146). On "giving up" see NOTE on 12:3c.

12:6. *for the Lord instructs the one whom he loves.* Hebrews follows the most common LXX text in reading *paideuei* (LXX^{B} reads *elenchei*, "reprove"). In human life parents who love their children instruct and correct them (Prov 13:24). Here the same is said to be true of God. The idea was not unique to the OT. Seneca said that those "whom God approves, whom he loves, he hardens, reviews, and trains" like a father (*On Providence* 4.7; cf. 1.6; 2.6).

and chastises every son whom he receives. The term *mastigoun* could refer to scourging (11:36), but here it refers broadly to physical punishment (Sir 30:1), which was done with "the rod" (Prov 13:24; 22:15; 23:13–14). God "chastises" people to deter them from continued sinning (*Pss. Sol.* 7:9; 10:1–3).

12:7. *Endure for the sake of instruction.* Some insert words like "trials" (NAB2; NRSV) or "hardship" (NIV) after "endure," yet the context actually downplays the magnitude of the listeners' suffering (12:4). The idea is that endurance is part of their training in faith (NJB).

God is treating you as sons. See NOTE on "as sons" in 12:5a.

For what son does a father not instruct. The question expects listeners to reply that a father exempts none of his sons from instruction. The educative sense is important: "Instruct a son and he will love you" (Prov 28:17a LXX; cf. 29:17; Plutarch, *Mor.* 12C; cf. Philo, *Joseph* 74.). "Do you not see how fathers show their love?" The "father orders his children to be aroused from sleep in order that they may start early upon their pursuits—even on holidays he does not permit them to be idle, and he draws from them sweat and sometimes tears" (Philo, *Special Laws* 2.232). Fathers had the right to admonish, beat, or even imprison disobedient children (ibid), yet they were advised, "Do not be harsh with your children but gentle" (Ps.-Phocylides, *Sentences* 207 [*OTP* 2.581]; cf. Aristotle, *Nic. Ethics* 1160b). Children should be taught by "encouragement and reasoning, and most certainly not by blows or ill-treatment" (Plutarch, *Mor.* 8F; Quintilian, *Inst.* 1.3.13–18). "Fathers, do not provoke your children to anger, but bring them up in the discipline and instruction of the Lord" (Eph 6:4).

12:8. *But if you are without the instruction in which all have shared.* "Partners" (*metochoi*) who share in a heavenly calling (3:1), in Christ (3:14), and in the Spirit (6:4) also "share" (*metechein*) in the instruction that challenges their faith and produces endurance (12:11). "All" of the figures mentioned in Heb 11–12 experienced "instruction" by being placed in situations that challenged their faith. Abraham contended with disappointment (11:8–12), Moses faced conflict (11:23–27), and Jesus "learned" through his passion what obedience to God entails (5:7–8; 12:2).

then you are illegitimate children and not sons. A child was considered illegitimate if the parents were not married or if one parent—commonly the mother—was a slave. Legitimate sons received an inheritance, while illegitimate sons commonly did not (Aristophanes, *Birds* 1649–50; Gen 21:10; 25:5–6; Gal 4:30). Illegitimate children did not continue the family line (Demosthenes, *Against Macartatus* 51; cf. Plutarch, *Pericles* 37.2–5; *Agesilaus* 3.1–5). Socially they were despised (Philo, *Names* 132, 147; *Unchangeable* 121; *Preliminary Studies* 6; *Moses* 1.147; Plutarch, *Mor.* 751F; John 8:41). Under Roman law, illegitimate children were not subject to the father's control (*patria potestas*), receiving neither paternal instruction nor correction (Braun, *Hebräer,* 413).

12:9. *Furthermore, we had human fathers who instructed us.* Literally "fathers of flesh." "Flesh" connotes limitation (NOTES on 2:14; 7:16) rather than antipathy toward God or estrangement from the heavenly world as some suggest (Braun; Grässer; Thompson, *Beginnings*, 123). The noun *paideutēs* was commonly used for an instructor who provided guidance and correction (Rom 2:20; 4 Macc 5:34; 9:6; see *TLNT* 3.3). An instructor did not simply "punish" (NJB).

and we showed respect. If respect is due to one's elders and to those in authority (Matt 21:37; Mark 12:6; Luke 18:2, 4; 20:13; Wis 2:10; 6:7), then God is worthy of even greater respect.

Shall we not to a greater extent be subject to the Father of spirits. The singular "Father" contrasts with the plural "fathers" (Heb 1:1; 3:9; 7:10; 8:9). God is the "Father" of Jesus in a unique sense (1:5) and of other "sons" and daughters in an extended sense (cf. 2:10). Calling God "Father" was common among early Christians (Matt 6:9; Luke 11:2; Rom 8:15–16; Gal 4:6; cf. John 20:17, 22). The expression used here recalls that God is the "God of the spirits of all flesh" (Num 16:22; 27:16; *Jub.* 10:3; *1 Clem.* 64:1; cf. Rev 22:6; Deissmann, *Light*, 414), who will be made complete in heaven (Heb 12:23). Some propose that the spirits are angelic spirits (1:14; 2 Macc 3:24; *1 Enoch* 37:2, 4, etc.; cf. M. Black, *Book*, 189–92; BAGD, 675 [4b]; H.-F. Weiss). This seems unlikely, since Hebrews insists that angels do not have a father-son relationship with God (Heb 1:5; cf. 2:5, 16). Less plausible is the idea that spirits are preexistent souls (Braun; Grässer; see pp. 60–61).

and live. Faith is the way that the righteous "live" in the present and find eternal life in the future (Hab 2:4; Heb 10:38). The "way of life is reproof and instruction" (Prov 6:23) on earth, but it leads to life everlasting (*Pss. Sol.* 13:9–10).

12:10. *For they instructed for a few days.* A "day" is a limited period of time that might actually span a number of years (1:2; 5:7; 7:3; 8:8). Parents often provided formal "instruction" that lasted until the child's early or mid-teens (§13 COMMENT *a*). Greek youths were subject to their fathers until the third year after reaching adulthood, until they married, or until publicly registered (Dionysius of Halicarnassus, *Roman Antiquities* 2.26.2). Romans could be legally subject to their fathers for life, although the extent to which this was practiced in the first century is unclear (*OCD* "patria potestas"). Ultimately, the father's discipline would end when the father lived out his "few days" and died (cf. Ps 109:8; Ps.-Oecumenius).

as seemed good to them. Things "seem" good or evil depending on one's perceptions (Acts 15:22, 25; Josephus, *Ant.* 16.163). Human perceptions are not fully reliable, since they change with time: "all instruction *seems* grievous," but later yields good fruit (Heb 12:11).

but he does so on the basis of what is beneficial. God's instruction benefits the individual who receives it and the community to which the individual belongs. Thinkers in antiquity debated whether what was "beneficial" pertained to the individual's self-interest, the good of society, or the absolute good. Stoics stressed that what is beneficial is what is morally right and they linked the benefits of training in virtue to a life that is self-sufficient and free (Cicero, *De officiis* 3.7 §34; cf. Diogenes Laertius, *Lives* 7.98; Epictetus, *Disc.* 1.2.5–6; K. Weiss, *TDNT* 9.69–78). Hebrews connects what is beneficial to faith and its outcome, which is sharing in God's holiness (H.-F. Weiss; Croy, *Endurance*, 205).

in order that we might share his holiness. The OT rarely uses the term "holiness" (*hagiotēs*), but often refers to the "holy" God, who says, "Be holy, for I am holy" (Lev 11:44–45; cf. 1 Pet 1:15–16). On holiness, see pp. 119–21. Christians now participate in holiness (*hagiasmos*) in a limited way through faith (Heb 12:14), but finally share in God's holiness by entering the holiest region of heaven, there to live in the presence of God (10:19–20).

12:11. *All instruction seems grievous rather than joyful at the time.* Instruction "seems" good to the one administering it (12:10), but it "seems" grievous to the one receiving it (12:11). Athletes undergoing instruction have to "follow a strict diet, give up sweet cakes, train under compulsion" (Epictetus, *Disc.* 3.15.3; cf. *Ench.* 29.2). Instruction in faith also has its rigors. Joy arrives when such training comes to fruition.

but later it yields peaceful fruit of righteousness. The context from which the Proverbs quotation was taken speaks of honoring God with one's firstfruits (Prov 3:9). More broadly it was said, "the root of education is bitter, but the fruit is sweet." This saying was attributed to Aristotle (Diogenes Laertius, *Lives* 5.1.18) and to Isocrates (Hock and O'Neill, *Chreia*, 176–77, 196–97, 224–29, 252–59). It was widely applied to human instruction (Mack, *Rhetoric*, 77–78). The same is true of divine instruction (Wis 3:5). Wisdom yields a harvest of righteousness, sown in peace by those who make peace (Jas 3:18). See NOTE on pursuing peace in Heb 12:14.

to those who have been trained through it. "Training" often referred to athletics (12:1–4) and philosophy. Training enables one to discern the difference between a situation that "seems" difficult at the moment and the greatness of a goal that is yet to be realized (NOTE on 5:14).

12:12. *Therefore stretch out the drooping hands and weak knees.* This metaphor uses a physical image for the listeners' morale: (**a**) Athletes preparing to run leaned forward, with their legs slightly bent and their hands outstretched in readiness. Those who were already running extended their arms and legs as they strove to reach the finish line. For listeners who become weary during the race, straightening hands and knees means greater striving (Gardiner, *Greek*, 274–83). (**b**) Drooping hands and weak knees connoted dejection (Sir 2:12; 25:23; Jer 6:24; *Pss. Sol.* 8:5). In adversity some "faint before the struggle has begun, and lose heart altogether . . . and like weary athletes drop their hands in weakness" (Philo, *Preliminary Studies* 164). Strengthening weak hands and knees shows determination (Isa 35:3; Job 4:3–4; Zeph 3:16; 1QpHab VII, 11).

12:13. *and set your feet on straight paths.* In one sense the straight path was the most direct way to the goal. Runners focused on the posts at the end of the track in order to keep from swerving into other runners (Gardiner, *Greek*, 279). In another sense, running was best done on straight or level ground rather than on rough paths, which caused stumbling (Virgil, *Aeneid* 5.331–33; cf. Isa 40:3; Mark 1:3). Metaphorically, following a straight path means adhering to the will of God (Prov 3:6; 4:11, 26–27). The emphasis is not so much on making the way smooth for others (F. F. Bruce) as on keeping oneself straight (P. E. Hughes). A few see no moral connotations in following the straight path (Grässer, *Hebräer*,

3.281; Croy, *Endurance*, 209), yet the context has to do with resisting sin (Heb 12:1, 4).

in order that what is lame might not be twisted. Physically, lameness generally referred to the legs. Spraining an ankle in a contest was not uncommon (Epictetus, *Disc.* 3.15.4). Twisting a limb would lead to more serious injury (Hippocrates, *In the Surgery* 14). The runner who has a troublesome leg must take care not to allow further damage. Metaphorically, people who turn from right theological and ethical ways damage themselves and others (Josephus, *Ant.* 6.34; 8.251; 2 Tim 4:4). In Hebrews the danger focused on is turning away from the faith and the community (Heb 3:12; 6:4–8; 10:25). Cf. *TLNT* 1.462–63.

but might heal instead. Physically, a runner with a defective leg must take care that no further damage is done, so that the limb might heal. Metaphorically, "heal" meant restoring people to faith (Isa 6:10; Matt 13:15; John 12:40; Acts 28:27) or correcting the sinful (Philo, *Special Laws* 2.23). Hebrews suggests that healing can occur even during the race, when the listeners' faith is restored. Complete "healing," the perfection of faith, occurs only when the race is complete.

12:14. *Pursue peace with all.* An athlete would ordinarily "pursue" victory over his competitors, but here peace is the goal. The exhortation was common: "Seek peace, and pursue it" (Ps 34:14; cf. Rom 12:18; 14:19; 2 Tim 2:22; *m. 'Abot* 1:12). Similarly, Prov 4:25–27, which was echoed in Heb 12:13, says that God "will make your paths straight and will lead your ways forward in peace" (4:27b LXX). The source of peace is God (Heb 13:20) and Christ (cf. 7:2).

and the holiness. Listeners are already "holy" ones (3:1; 6:10; 13:24) who have been "sanctified" (2:11; 10:10, 14, 29), but they are to pursue the sanctity or "holiness" that is needed to see God. Through the cleansing effect of Christ's death, holiness comes to expression in life (cf. Rom 6:19, 22; 1 Pet 1:2; 1 Thess 4:3; 2 Thess 2:13). See pp. 119–21.

without which no one will see the Lord. The "Lord" is God (7:21; 8:8–11; 10:16, 30; 12:5–6), whom the righteous hope to see in the sanctuary (Pss 11:7; 17:15; 42:2; 63:2). Seeing God was an eschatological hope (Matt 5:8; 1 Cor 13:12; 1 John 3:2; Rev 22:4) that Hebrews depicts as entry into the heavenly city (Heb 12:22–24) and sanctuary (10:19), where God is present. "Seeing the Lord" is not confined to seeing Christ when he returns (Matt 26:64; Mark 13:26; 1 Pet 1:7–8; Rev 1:7), since listeners can already "see" or "look" to him in faith (Heb 2:9; 12:2).

12:15. *remaining watchful so that no one falls back from the grace of God.* Although individuals are responsible for themselves, Hebrews also assumes that community members watch for the well-being of others (3:12–13; 4:1; 10:24–25). The imagery recalls how Moses' generation refused to enter the promised land and "fell back" in the wilderness (4:1; cf. BDF §180 [5]). The text does not suggest that the listeners "lack" grace—for grace is available (4:16)—but that they let go of grace (Gal 5:4) instead of holding fast to it (Acts 13:43; Rom 5:2; 1 Pet 5:12).

so that no root of bitterness puts forth a shoot and causes trouble. The quotation is from Deut 29:18 (29:17 LXX), though the textual basis is unclear. There are differences between the MT and LXX, as well as variations among LXX texts:

MT	*LXX*[OM]
so that there not be among you a root *bearing poisonous and bitter fruit.*	so that there not be among you a root *growing up in wrath and bitterness.*

Although many MSS of the LXX read "in wrath" (*en cholē*), others combine the words and reverse two letters to read "cause trouble" (*enochlē*; LXX[ABF*]). Hebrews probably followed a text in which this shift had occurred (Attridge), although it is possible that Hebrews made the change and the LXX was corrected to conform to Hebrews (H.-F. Weiss). In its original context the "root of bitterness" was idolatry, but in a broader sense it could mean sin (*Bib. Ant.* 25:5; 1QH IV, 14). Here it involves being immoral and profane (Heb 12:16a), rather than peaceful and holy (12:14).

and that through it many become defiled. On defilement see pp. 119–21.

12:16. *so that no one becomes immoral or profane like Esau.* The term *pornos* commonly meant sexual immorality (13:4). In choosing food over his rights as firstborn Esau was said to have sought immediate physical gratification rather than abiding benefit. His marriage to two Hittite women (Gen 26:34–35) came to be considered immoral (*Jub.* 25:1, 7–8; cf. 26:34; 35:13–14; Philo, QG 4.201; cf. *Virtues* 208; *Alleg. Interp.* 3.2; *Sacrifices* 81, 120, 135; *Worse* 45; *Migration* 153; Löhr, *Umkehr*, 123–29; H.-F. Weiss). Sexual immorality was associated with idolatry (1 Cor 6:9; Eph 5:5; cf. Num 25:1–2; Hos 1:2).

who for a single serving of food. The food was a lentil stew cooked by Jacob (Gen 25:29–34). The term "food" (*brōsis*) is closely related to the "foods" (*brōmata*) that are subject to Jewish dietary regulations in Heb 9:10 and 13:9. Hebrews does not suggest that Jewish Law is an issue here, but implies that a preoccupation with food binds one to the transient realm.

gave up his rights as firstborn. This recalls Gen 25:33. The eldest son traditionally assumed a leading role in the family, and when the father died, he was entitled to a double share of inheritance (Gen 43:33; Deut 21:17). For the listeners, the "firstborn" in heaven (Heb 12:23) will receive blessing and an eternal inheritance (6:7, 12; 9:15).

12:17. *For you know that later on, when he wanted to inherit the blessing.* As firstborn, Esau was entitled to a special blessing concerning prosperity and dominance over other peoples and family members, but his brother Jacob obtained the blessing by trickery (Gen 27:27–29).

he was rejected. Although some suggest that Esau was rejected by Isaac (Tholuck; Lünemann), the context implies that he was rejected by God. Of the faithless, it was said, the Lord "has rejected them" (Jer 6:30), he "has rejected and forsaken the generation that provoked his wrath" (Jer 7:29).

he found no opportunity for repentance. On the issue of the limits of repentance see NOTES and COMMENT on 6:4–8; 10:26–31. "Repentance" indicates a change of mind (NOTE on 6:1). Its function has been taken in two ways, of which the first is preferable:

(a) Esau was not given the opportunity to repent (NRSV; cf. NAB2). Elsewhere "repentance" means turning from sin (6:1, 6; BAGD, 512). The need for repentance is clear from the context, where Esau is identified as immoral and profane. This is consistent with the use of "an opportunity to repent" in other sources (Wis 12:10; *1 Clem.* 7:5; cf. *4 Ezra* 9:11–12; *2 Bar.* 85:12; Livy, *Roman History* 44.10.2; Pliny, *Ep.* 10.96.2; cf. Löhr, *Umkehr*, 156).

(b) Esau was not able to change Isaac's mind. This view takes "repentance" as "a change of mind" rather than "a turning from sin" (Lünemann; Spicq). Esau "could find no way of reversing the decision" (NJB; cf. NIV; REB; NRSVfn). Support for this reading is that Gen 27:34–40 does not focus on Esau's sin and repentance, but on Isaac's inability to change the situation. In common usage, however, the terminology has to do with changing one's own mind, not another person's mind, as noted in **(a)** above.

even though he sought [*the blessing*]. Literally "he sought it." The feminine pronoun *autēn* has sometimes been connected with the feminine noun "repentance" (*metanoia*) to read that Esau was seeking repentance. This seems unlikely, since the object of the verb would more naturally be "an opportunity [*topos*] for repentance," and *topos* is masculine. "It" most likely refers to "blessing" (*eulogia*). On the apparent contradiction between Isaac blessing Esau (11:20) and Esau not receiving the blessing (12:17) see NOTE on 11:20.

with tears. Esau wept when he learned that Isaac had given the blessing to Jacob (Gen 27:38; *Jub.* 26:33; Josephus, *Ant.* 1.275; Philo, *QG* 4.233). Weeping was associated with the recognition and confession of sin (Ezra 10:1; cf. Neh 1:4; Tob 3:1; 3 Macc 6:14; Bar 1:5; *T. Sim.* 2:13; Josephus, *Ant.* 4.195; 7.153). Cf. Löhr, *Umkehr*, 162. Tears alone do not move God to grant a blessing, however (Sir 12:16; Matt 8:12; 22:13). God responded to Jesus' "reverence," not to his tears alone (NOTE on 5:7).

COMMENT[428]

Hebrews' dramatic account of Israel's heroes and heroines of faith reaches a surprising climax as listeners find themselves on a racetrack in a Greco-Roman stadium (12:1–4). Instead of witnessing the exploits of their forebears in their mind's eye, the listeners must picture the eyes of their forebears fixed upon them. Fusing

[428]On 12:1–17 see Andriessen, "Renonçant"; Andriessen and Lenglet, "Quelques"; D. A. Black, "Note"; Bonnard, "La traduction"; Bornkamm, "Sohnschaft"; Coste, "Notion"; Croy, *Endurance*; idem, "Note"; deSilva, *Despising*, 165–78; Ellingworth, "New Testament"; Goldhahn-Müller, *Grenze*, 102–14; Gourgues, *À la droite*, 120–25; Hamm, "Faith"; Horning, "Chiasmus"; Laub, *Bekenntnis*, 154–65; Loader, "Christ"; Löhr, *Umkehr*, 116–30; McCown, "Holiness"; McCullough, "Impossibility"; McKnight, "Warning"; Mende, "Wen der Herr"; Mugridge, "Warnings"; Müller, ΧΡΙΣΤΟΣ ΑΡΧΗΓΟΣ, 302–12, 353–93; Peterson, *Hebrews*, 168–76; Rose, *Wolke*, 334–51; Schüssler Fiorenza, "Anführer"; J. J. Scott, "*Archēgos*"; Söding, "Zuversicht"; Talbert, *Learning*; Toussaint, "Eschatology"; Trilling, "Jesus"; Wallis, *Faith*, 150–61.

the world of the Scriptures with the Greco-Roman world of the listeners' experience (cf. §15 COMMENT), the author invites hearers to envision a stadium in which Abel, Enoch, and Noah crowd along the track with Abraham, Sarah, Moses, Rahab, the judges, the prophets, and the martyrs.[429] The striking imagery is designed to transform the listeners' perception of their situation from one in which they are beleaguered victims to one in which they are vigorous contestants who can hope to participate in the festival gathering in God's city (12:22–24).

Structurally, this section can be divided into three parts: **(a)** The first part (12:1–4) is framed by references to contending in a contest (*agōn*, 12:1; *antagōnizein* 12:4) and by the repeated mention of "sin" and "sinners" (12:1, 3, 4).[430] Imagery is taken from the field of athletics, including the footrace and probably boxing or the pancratium, a contest that often involved bloodshed. **(b)** The second part (12:5–11) connects athletic discipline with parental instruction. Repetition of words based on the root *paid-* ("instruction"), which appear only in 12:5–11, binds these verses together. The quotation of Prov 3:11–12 functions as direct address to the listeners,[431] with additional encouragement coming from the elaboration of the themes in terms of divine and human instruction (Heb 12:7–11). **(c)** The third part (12:12–17) resumes the athletic motif, linking it to the pursuit of peace and holiness.[432] The positive exhortation to holiness is coupled with warnings about the danger of defilement and about rejecting the promised blessing, as in the case of Esau.

a. Running With Perseverance (12:1–4)

Listeners are taken from Israel's past to the world of the stadium and athletic competition, where they find themselves running in a footrace.[433] The *stadion,*

---

[429]Earlier the author depicted hostility against the listeners as an athletic contest that required endurance (10:32–35). Developing the athletic imagry, the author speaks of endurance (12:1, 2, 3), rather than faith, as in Heb 11.

[430]On including 12:4 in the first paragraph see Spicq; P. E. Hughes; Wilson. Lane considers 12:4 to be transitional (*Hebrews*, 2.417). Others limit the first paragraph to 12:1–3, often structuring the passage in a chiastic fashion (Horning, "Chiasmus"; D. A. Black, "Note"; Rose, *Wolke*, 334–36). Proponents of a chiastic structuring do not, however, agree on the elements in the chiasm: there are almost no verbal parallels in the proposed outlines, and the parallels involve perceived conceptual similarities. The more obvious connections in 12:4 involve the use of "contest" language and the mention of "sin," which indicate that it is part of the first paragraph.

[431]Cf. 3:7–4:10, which begins with a quotation of Ps 95 followed by related comments. Beginning a paragraph with "and" (*kai*) is not unusual in Hebrews (cf. 7:20; 9:15; 10:11; 11:32).

[432]Since athletic imagery reappears in 12:12–13, many include those verses with the previous paragraph (Vanhoye, *La structure*, 196–204; Attridge; Bénétreau; Casalini; Ellingworth; Kistemaker; Lane; H.-F. Weiss). G. H. Guthrie is unusual in identifying 12:3–17 as a unit (*Structure*, 144). It seems best, however, to include 12:12–13 with the next paragraph. The *dio* in 12:12 seems to introduce a new thought (cf. 3:7; 10:5), the references to *paideia* end with 12:11, distinguishing 12:4–11 from subsequent verses, and the imagery of racing in 12:12–13 can be connected to the exhortations to "pursue" peace and holiness in 12:14–17 (cf. NA[27]; F. F. Bruce; D. Guthrie; Hagner; Hegermann; P. E. Hughes; Strobel; Wilson; Löhr, *Umkehr*, 116–17).

[433]The footrace was especially popular in the eastern Roman Empire. Greek athletes were free

or running track, was about two hundred yards long and thirty yards wide. First-century stadiums commonly had no seats; people simply sat or stood on the earthen embankment that flanked the track. The size of a cloud of witnesses (12:1a) at an athletic contest would vary: Delphi could accommodate about seven thousand people while as many as forty thousand may have come to Olympia.[434] Crowds were not passive bystanders, for the roar of their voices energized participants, while the desire to do well in the eyes of others gave athletes incentive to run well (Seneca, *Ep.* 34.2; 109.6). The witnesses surrounding the listeners include the heroes and heroines of faith from Heb 11.[435] Awareness of the perspective of previous generations is designed to heighten the listeners' sense of accountability: if previous generations persevered, the question is whether the listeners will do the same. Yet the witnesses in the stadium are also encouraging since they, like the listeners, were confronted with disappointment and conflict (§§31–33 COMMENT). If the society that visibly surrounds the Christian community reproaches them for their faith (10:32–34; 13:13–14), listeners can trust that the invisible cloud of witnesses judges according to a different standard. For them, honor goes to the faithful.

Like athletes preparing for a race, listeners are to lay aside anything that might impede them (12:1b) in order to "run with endurance the contest that is set before" them (12:1c). In athletic festivals the starting line was marked by a line of stone slabs laid in the ground. Upright pillars, spaced about four feet apart, separated the spaces in which each runner stood. Before them a track covered with sand stretched to a second set of pillars at the far end of the stadium. At "the sound of the signal they were off, leaving the starting line and tearing over the course," each runner fixing "his eyes on the point where he would finish." They sped to "the end of the race," striving "to reach home, exhausted" (Virgil, *Aeneid* 5.315–28).

As in any metaphor, some elements transfer, and others do not. Endurance is the principal point of similarity, since both running and living out one's faith press people to their limitations. Unlike a footrace, however, there is not only one victor in faith. All who persevere are honored.[436] The goal of faith is not triumph over other participants, but serving others and building community (6:10; 13:1–17). The antagonists are not other believers, but the sin that threatens to impede each runner (12:1, 4).

---

persons seeking honor. Romans favored more violent spectacles, and the participants were often from the lower classes. See Gardiner, *Athletics*, 117–27; J. H. Humphrey, *CAM* 2.1153–65.

[434]By the second century seats in stadiums were more common. Good examples are the stadiums at Delphi and Epidaurus (Gardiner, *Athletics*, plates 82, 83). On the design and capacity of stadiums see Gardiner, *Athletics*, 128–43.

[435]Hebrews does not develop a theory of afterlife in this section. See NOTE on 6:2.

[436]Greco-Roman orators and philosophers often used athletic imagery when encouraging people to pursue virtue. Their discourses, which stressed the importance of overcoming vice and hardship, assumed that any number of people could win the prize of virtue. See generally Pfitzner, *Paul*, 26–35; Croy, *Endurance*, 43–58.

Listeners are to look to Jesus, "the pioneer and completer of faith" (12:2a).[437] In an ordinary stadium an honored guest would sit on a platform at the edge of the track, about midway along its course. According to Virgil one of the pioneers of Rome, Aeneas, sat on such a platform (*Aeneid* 5.290), but in Hebrews Jesus the pioneer of faith has the place of honor. Jesus did not simply run a course that others had laid out, but was the "forerunner" who opened a new way into God's presence through his death and exaltation (6:20; 10:19–20). By taking faith to its goal, Jesus exemplifies the faithfulness that others are called to follow, while the message about his suffering and exaltation evoke in people the faith that discipleship demands.

In saying that Jesus endured a cross (12:2b) the author could assume that listeners were familiar with crucifixion, which meant "wasting away in pain, dying limb by limb" and "letting out his life drop by drop." The victim was "fastened to the accursed tree, long sickly, already deformed, swelling with ugly weals on shoulders and chest, and drawing the breath of life amid long-drawn-out agony" (Seneca, *Ep.* 101.14). To say that Jesus "endured" the cross suggests not only that he experienced it, but that he bore it faithfully rather than allowing the ordeal to turn him away from obedience (NOTE on 10:32).

Jesus also went beyond endurance by disdaining the shame that Greeks, Romans, and Jews associated with crucifixion (NOTE on 12:2d). The threat of shame creates pressure to avoid actions that a group deems unworthy, so that if Jesus had acted on the basis of what society deemed shameful, he would have sought to avoid crucifixion. On the other hand, to despise shame is to reject the views of those people who have declared that the cross is dishonorable. Hebrews argues that Jesus suffered in obedience to God (2:10–18; 5:7–10; 10:5–10), following a standard different from that of Greco-Roman society. By despising shame, Jesus teaches us "to count as nothing the opinion of human beings" (Chrysostom, *Homilies* 28.4; deSilva, *Despising*, 173).

Rather than abandoning obedience to God in order to avoid shame in the eyes of society, Jesus persevered for the sake of the joy that was set before him *by God*, namely, a place at the right hand of God (Heb 12:2b). The imagery recalls Ps 110:1, which early Christians used widely for the exalted Christ (NOTES and COMMENT on 1:13). Hope for future joy reflects confidence that God will not allow the faithful to suffer in vain (cf. 11:26). The listeners' community had previously endured dispossession in the conviction that God would grant them an everlasting possession (10:34), but the author perceived that some were tending to become weary (12:3b; cf. 12:12). Since runners commonly found strength to endure when the end was in sight (Aristotle, *Rhetoric* 3.9.2 1409A), the reminder of future joy offers encouragement to persevere. Additional motivation comes from the way that Jesus "endured from sinners such opposition against himself"

[437]"Pioneer" and "completer" are based on the roots *archē* ("beginning") and *tel-* ("end"). Words based on these roots were sometimes paired to identify God as the one who creates all things and brings them to their appointed end (NOTE on 2:10; cf. 3:14; 7:3; Rev 22:13; Aelius Aristides, *Oration* 43.41). Here Hebrews focuses on the beginning and completion of faith rather than the cosmos.

(12:3a). Spectators at contests often found themselves identifying with an athlete who valiantly contended against great odds. Similarly, the drama of Jesus confronting sinners invites listeners' to identify with him in the battle against sin.

Finally, the comment that the listeners' blood has not been shed tries to put their situation in perspective (12:4a). The author has already encouraged listeners by affirming that they have suffered a great deal (10:32–34), but here he points out that they have not suffered as much as others have, which makes their difficulties seem more manageable (Chrysostom, *Homilies* 29.1). Rhetorically, the argument moves from the greater to the lesser (Quintilian, *Inst.* 5.11.9). The martyrs (Heb 11:35–38) and Jesus remained faithful despite great suffering. The issue now is whether the listeners can remain faithful in *lesser* suffering. The author also shifts from the contest against sinners outside the community (12:3) to the contest against sin within the community (12:4b). Although non-Christians threaten the community (10:32–34; 13:3, 13–14), the greatest threat perceived by the author is the listeners' tendency toward lethargy and a neglect of the faith and the community (2:1–3; 5:11; 6:12; 10:25; 12:12–13).

b. Divine Discipline (12:5–11)

Images shift from athletic training to parental discipline as listeners are addressed as "sons" (12:5a). There is continuity between sections since instruction (*paideia*) could include training in athletics and in right modes of conduct. Both types of instruction placed people in challenging situations to develop their capacities for endurance (12:1, 7). Yet if Jesus' example encourages listeners to disdain the negative judgment of unbelievers (12:2c), the quotation from Proverbs urges them *not* to disdain the instruction of God (12:5b). The parental imagery also differs from the athletic imagery in that God was not prominent in the image of the footrace, which focused on the way in which Jesus attained a place at God's right hand after running faithfully (12:2d). Given only that image, God might seem like a mere spectator to the listeners' situation. As Father, however, God is involved in the listeners' lives through instruction, reproof, and love (12:6–7).

Quotation. The author introduces Prov 3:11–12 by calling it an exhortation (12:5a), which shapes the way the text should be heard. As an exhortation, the quotation is designed to stir listeners to greater zeal, not to offer a comprehensive explanation of human suffering. The previous verse pointed out that the listeners were not engaged in a bloody struggle, as others had been (12:4). The main problem perceived by the author is not that God is unjust, but that the listeners are despondent.[438] The quotation addresses listeners directly,[439] urging

[438]Talbert (*Learning*) and Croy (*Endurance*) provide very helpful treatments of this passage, but link it too closely to questions of suffering in general.

[439]Cf. 3:7, 15; 4:7. On Scripture as direct address in Hebrews see Eisenbaum, *Jewish Heroes*, 90–100. This portion of Prov 3:12 was frequently cited by Augustine (Bonnardière, "L'épître," 159–60) and Leo the Great (CCCM 143B.1877) as a way to affirm both the sovereignty and grace of God when dealing with questions as to why the righteous suffer.

them not to neglect the instruction of the Lord (12:5b). Instruction involved both theory and practice.[440] Listeners have been given means for distinguishing good from evil in order that their perceptions might not sway them to follow a course contrary to the will of God (NOTE and COMMENT on 5:14). As a part of their training, God places his sons and daughters in situations that challenge them to practice what they know. To neglect God's instruction would mean failing to use what they have been given (2:1, 3).

Proverbs urges listeners not to lose heart when reproved by God (12:5c). At the time Hebrews was written, the listeners were reproached by unbelievers, and some Christians were in prison (13:3, 13), but these can hardly be construed as forms of reproof for sin. In the case of Moses and the martyrs the *righteous* suffered these things (11:26, 36). God's reproof can best be understood as the verbal reproofs that occur when the Spirit admonishes listeners through OT texts (3:7, 15; 4:7) or when Christians exhort each other (3:13). The Lord also chastises every son whom he receives (12:6). The word "chastise"—which appears in the LXX, but not the MT—assumes that God *may* afflict people in order to instruct them, but it does not suggest that *all* afflictions are due to divine instruction. Affliction may come from the devil (2:14) or human sin (12:3), and may fall on the righteous as well as on the wicked (NOTES on 12:6). When explicating Prov 3:11–12, the author repeatedly mentions "instruction" (12:7ab, 8a, 9a, 10a, 11a), but he does not use "chastise" again. Hebrews is not focusing on the need to repent in the face of divine chastisement, but to endure by drawing on divine training (12:7).

Explication. The author's comments on the quotation unfold in several steps:

(a) Relationship within which instruction occurs (12:7–8). Hebrews emphasizes the *similarities* between the relationship of human fathers to their sons and the relationship of God to his people by grouping several points together in the manner of a syllogism. The conclusion, which is given first, is that the listeners' experience must be perceived in the context of their relationship with God: God is treating them as sons (12:7b). Fathers train their sons and place them in situations that challenge them to practice what they know (12:7c). Conversely, only illegitimate children are exempted from parental instruction (12:8). This reverses ordinary perceptions of the listeners' situation. Since Christians are dishonored by others in society (10:32; 11:26; 13:13), some might think to leave the community to escape reproach (10:25). Yet if God is allowing them to be challenged as a part of their training in faith, it shows that God treats them as his children, which is truly honorable. Those who experience no challenges from society are receiving no training, implying that they have the dishonorable status of illegitimate children.

(b) Outcome of instruction (12:9–10). Hebrews now commends endurance by pointing to the positive results of discipline and emphasizing the *differences* between God and human fathers:

---

[440]For example, Musonius Rufus, frgs. 5, 6 deal with theory and practice.

human fathers	Father of spirits
we were instructed by them	we are subject to him
we respected them	we will live (with him)
instructed by what seemed good to them	instructed by what is beneficial
for a few days	that we might share his holiness

Hebrews calls human fathers, "fathers of flesh." "Flesh" connotes what is earthly, limited, and mortal (2:14; 5:7; 9:10, 13), especially in contrast to the Father of spirits. If a person's relationship to a human father is one of instruction, one's relation to the Father of spirits means being subject, since God has a more complete claim upon a person's loyalty. In a surprising move the emphasis then shifts from what a father *receives from* his children (respect) to what the Father *gives to* his children (life). The gift of life—and according to the wider context, life means living eternally in God's heavenly city—is a worthy outcome for the relationship.

The standard that human fathers used was what seemed good to them (12:10a), implying that a parent's perception is fallible. In contrast, Hebrews insists that God's standard is what is truly beneficial for people (NOTE on 12:10b). The goal of instruction is holiness (12:10c), which involves a tension. The listeners have *already* become holy through the sacrifice of Christ that cleanses the conscience by evoking faith (NOTE on 9:14), but they do *not yet* share fully in God's holiness and will not do so until they enter the holiest region of God's sanctuary (10:19–20). God's instruction is designed to strengthen the faith of those who are still on the way, so that their holiness may come to completion in God's heavenly habitation (see pp. 122–25).

(c) Perception of instruction (12:11). Hebrews responds to the common perception that instruction is grievous rather than joyful by appealing to another common experience, which is that perceptions often change with time. There is an implicit argument from the lesser to the greater: if one's own past experience shows that perceptions of instruction change when the training produces fruit, how much more will one's perception of the present challenges change when the training in faith has yielded its fruit. The idea is similar to what Paul said: "For this slight momentary affliction is preparing us for an eternal weight of glory beyond all measure, because we look not at what can be seen but at what cannot be seen; for what can be seen is temporary, but what cannot be seen is eternal" (2 Cor 4:17). Given this hope, joy can exist in the present despite affliction, as has been demonstrated in the example of Jesus (Heb 12:2) and the experience of the listeners (10:34).

c. Pursuing Peace (12:12–17)

The call to "stretch out the drooping hands and weak knees" (12:12) brings listeners back from the realm of parental instruction to the world of the stadium. The training depicted in 12:5–11 is not an end in itself. One trains for the sake of the contest (12:1–4, 12–13). By depicting the listeners again as runners, the author draws a noble image from Greco-Roman culture to help listeners resist the fatigue generated by ongoing friction with that culture (10:32–34; 13:13–14). Moreover, the words that exhort the listeners come from the Scriptures, which encouraged previous generations to "strengthen the weak hands, and make firm the feeble knees. Say to those who are of a fearful heart, 'Be strong, do not fear!' " (Isa 35:3–4).

On the one hand, the call to "set your feet on straight paths" (Heb 12:13a) draws on what people in the Greco-Roman world knew about running: the straight path leads most directly to the goal. On the other hand, the exhortation echoes OT commendations of the straight path as the way of obedience to God: "Keep straight the path of your feet," and "turn your foot away from evil" (Prov 4:26–27). Tensions arise when these two perspectives come together, since the most direct way forward in a social sense would not have been the way of obedience to God. Drifting away from the Christian faith apparently seemed easier to some, since it would presumably lessen the tensions that led to Christians being marginalized (Heb 10:25; 13:13–14). Yet if the good way is determined, not by social ease, but by obedience to God, then enduring faithfully is ultimately the best course, and "neither reward nor favor nor peril nor animosity ought to lead us astray from the right path" (*Rhet. ad Her.* 3.3 §4)

Enduring is made difficult by the community's lameness (12:13b)—a problem related to sluggishness (2:1–3; 5:11; 6:12; 10:25). Significantly, lameness does not disqualify the listeners from participating in the race. Continued participation, not speed, is the crucial element. Hebrews discerns two possible effects of the lameness. One is that the runner might turn a limb, which alludes to the danger of a person turning from the faith or from the community (3:12; 4:2; 6:6; 12:15–17). The other, more hopeful prospect is that what is lame will heal, which is a metaphor for restored faith and community life, and finally life in the world to come. The appeal is enhanced by echoes of the OT promise that "the lame shall leap" (Isa 35:6).

Those who run in the race are to pursue peace with all (Heb 12:14a). In the first instance this means pursuing peace with all the saints in the Christian community (13:24), as Rahab received people in peace and showed them hospitality (11:31; cf. 13:1). Peace with all also suggests peaceful relations with non-Christians. The author does not want peace to come at the expense of the listeners' faith, for peace comes from God and the Christ whom the community confesses (13:20), and peace does not mean accommodating injustice, for peace comes from righteousness, and righteousness opposes sin (1:9; 12:11). Yet when non-Christians denounce Christians (10:32; 11:26; 13:13), the author calls those who pursue peace to respond not in kind, but in faith.[441]

Runners also pursue "the holiness without which no one will see the Lord" (12:14b), for God's presence is among things not seen (11:1). Listeners can see

---

[441]Chrysostom; Ps.-Oecumenius; Calvin; F. F. Bruce; D. Guthrie. Those who limit the passage to peace within the Christian community include Attridge; Ellingworth; Grässer; Lane; H.-F. Weiss.

and look to Jesus in faith (2:8; 12:2), but seeing God entails a new mode of relationship, in which the barriers of sin and mortality are completely removed. Hebrews has described this as entering the sanctuary (6:19–20; 10:19–20), where only those who have been sanctified can go. People are *already* made holy by the death of Christ, which cleanses the conscience when it evokes faith (9:14), but they do *not yet* participate fully in God's holiness (12:10). This happens in a final way not only when people are cleansed from sin but when sin is abolished, and when people are free not only from the fear of death (2:15) but from death itself. In Hebrews pursuing holiness means trusting in what Christ's death has accomplished and maintaining hope for everlasting life with God.

The whole community is to remain watchful for dangers that are listed in parallel statements that begin "so that no . . . " (*hina mē*). First, they must watch "so that no one falls back from the grace of God" (12:15a). The wilderness generation hardened their hearts and fell back, instead of trusting the promise and finding rest in Canaan (4:1). Like them, listeners have received grace (2:9; 10:29) and the promise of entering God's rest (4:1–11), and like them, they can reject grace and shrink back in unbelief (10:39). Since listeners require grace for the journey of faith (4:16; 13:9), they incapacitate themselves by refusing what God offers. By exhorting one another (3:13), listeners help to awaken in each other the faith through which grace is grasped, and they strengthen the belief structure through which faith is maintained (deSilva, *Despising*, 284–89).

Second, they must watch, "so that no root of bitterness puts forth a shoot" (12:15b). The social implications of unbelief are evident in the danger posed by this bitter root. The imagery recalls Deut 29:18, which warns that a person who departs from the covenant and assimilates to the religious practices of the surrounding culture is a root that can infect the community with unfaithfulness. Earlier, the author warned about the danger to an individual (10:26–31). Now he cautions that the unbelief of one member—i.e., the root of bitterness—can defile many (12:15c). To counter this threat, the community should attend to the faith needs of each individual in the group.

Third, they must take care "so that no one becomes immoral or profane like Esau" (12:16). Esau's example is designed to reinforce the community's commitments (12:16–17). Although Esau was traditionally considered immoral and profane (NOTE on 12:16a), there is little to suggest that immorality was a special problem for the listeners. Rhetorically, referring to immorality and profanity might be epideictic, since it reinforces existing values. Rather than dwelling on Esau's sinfulness, however, Hebrews considers how he gave up his rights as firstborn (12:16b). Genesis 25:29–34 tells how Esau returned famished from the fields and saw Jacob cooking some stew. When Jacob offered Esau some food in exchange for his rights as firstborn, Esau agreed, thereby purchasing permanent regret for the price of a moment's pleasure (Erasmus, *Paraphrase*).

Hebrews connects the sale of the birthright directly to Esau's failure to obtain a blessing (Heb 12:17a), although the story in Genesis offers a more complex account in which Jacob obtained the blessing by trickery. Upon learning that Isaac had given the blessing to Jacob, Esau cried out, "Bless me, me also, father!" and he "lifted up his voice and wept" (Gen 27:34–38). Isaac was disturbed by what had happened, according to Genesis, but Hebrews says that Esau's plea for the blessing was rejected (Heb 12:17a). Some concluded that he was refused the blessing because his repentance was not genuine or was wrongly motivated (Chrysostom, *Homilies* 31.3; Aquinas, *Ad Heb.* §§692–94; Theophylact, PG 125, 379), but the point is actually sharper.

This and other passages (NOTES and COMMENT on 6:4–8; 10:26–31) warn of a point where God will allow a person to reject him.[442] Moses' generation refused to trust God's promise of rest in the land, and God eventually allowed their rejection to stand so that they perished in the wilderness (3:7–19). Similarly, Esau had the promise of a birthright and a blessing, yet he sold his long-term hope for the short-term benefit of a meal. God did not take Esau's blessing from him; Esau traded it away. And God let him bear the consequences of his action. Listeners are like Esau in that they have a firstborn's right to an inheritance and blessings in the age to come (6:7, 12–14, 17; cf. 2:5; 12:23). As Esau gave up the promise in order to ease his physical discomfort, listeners might consider giving up the promise in order to ease their social discomfort (13:13). Abandoning Christian commitments might allow greater access to the benefits offered by society, but such benefits are transient when compared to the enduring blessings that God has promised. The severity of this text can be as disturbing as those found earlier in Hebrews, and attempts to soften it have not been successful. Like other warnings, however, this passage is designed to awaken people to danger, not to make them give up hope. Warning is the counterpart to promise; both pertain to the future. Warnings disturb people, while promises encourage them, but together they serve the same end, which is encouraging people to persevere in faith (§14 COMMENT).

35. Coming to Zion (12:18–27)

12 [18]For you have not approached something palpable, and a blazing fire and
darkness and gloom and a tempest, [19]and a trumpet blast and a voice with words,
whose hearers refused that any further message be given to them, [20]for they
could not bear the command: *If even an animal touches the mountain, it shall be*
stoned; [21]indeed, so fearsome was the phenomenon that Moses said, *I am terri-*
fied and trembling. [22]Instead, you have approached Mount Zion and the city of
the living God, heavenly Jerusalem, and myriads of angels in festival gathering
[23]and the assembly of the firstborn, who are registered in heaven, and a judge,
who is God of all, and the spirits of the righteous, who have been made complete, [24]and the mediator of the new covenant, Jesus, and the sprinkled blood
that speaks in a manner superior to that of Abel.

[25]See that you do not refuse the one who is speaking! For if they did not escape when they refused the one who admonished them on earth, how much less

[442]See Löhr, *Umkehr*, 162; Goldhahn-Müller, *Grenze*, 102–7. Cf. pp. 20–24, 28, 38.

will we who turn away from the one who admonishes from the heavens, [26]whose voice then shook the earth, but who now has promised, saying, *Yet once more I will shake not only the earth but also the heaven?* [27]The *once more* portends removal of the things that are shaken, as things that have been made, in order that what is not shaken might abide.

NOTES

12:18. *For you have not approached.* See NOTE on Heb 4:16.

something palpable. This recalls the "palpable" darkness in Egypt (Exod 10:21). God himself "is not palpable" (Ign. *Pol.* 3:2), for he belongs to the "unseen" (Heb 11:1). Some MSS (D Ψ 69 1739 1881 Maj; cf. KJV; NASB; NIV; REB; NRSV[fn]) add "mountain," following Deut 4:11 LXX. There is strong MS support for omitting it (P^{46} ℵ A C 048 etc.; cf. NRSV; NAB[2]). The MSS that include "mountain" place it at different points, which suggests that it originated as a clarifying comment (*TCGNT*, 675; Attridge).

and a blazing fire and darkness and gloom and a tempest. Hebrews follows Deut 4:11 LXX: "a mountain burning with fire up to the heavens, darkness, gloom, a tempest, a great voice." God's power was associated with fire (e.g., Exod 3:2; 24:17; Ezek 1:27), darkness (Exod 20:21; Deut 5:22–23; 1 Kgs 8:12) and tempest (Exod 10:22 LXX). "Fire" (Num 16:35), "darkness" (Amos 5:20), and "gloom" are foreboding (2 Peter 2:4; Jude 6, 13). God is a consuming fire (Heb 12:29).

12:19. *and a trumpet blast.* This recalls Exod 19:16, where the trumpet is a warning signal (cf. Joel 2:1; Amos 3:6; Jer 4:19; 6:1; Ezek 33:3–4; Matt 24:31; 1 Cor 15:52; 1 Thess 4:16).

and a voice with words. This expression, which could be translated "a sound of words," stresses the sensory aspect of the voice. Only in 12:26 is God identified as the source. The "words" in 12:20 warned people not to approach Sinai, and the "voice" shook the earth (12:26).

whose hearers refused that any further message be given to them. The verb *paraiteomai* can be taken as "ask" or "beg" (NRSV; NAB[2]; NIV; NJB; REB), which implies that the people are not rejecting God's word, but only asking that nothing more be said directly to them (cf. Exod 20:19; Deut 5:25). Hebrews 12:25, however, uses the verb to warn that listeners should not "refuse" the one who is speaking (cf. 1 Tim 5:11; Tit 3:10), which implies that the people at Sinai "refused" God's word (cf. Heb 3:12–19; 4:2; Braun; Grässer). The negative *mē* after "refuse" is pleonastic (BDF §429).

12:20. *for they could not bear the command: If even an animal touches the mountain, it shall be stoned.* Cf. Exod 19:12–13. Stoning allowed people to destroy the animal without touching it. The idea is that if the prohibition applies even to an animal, how much more to a human being.

12:21. *indeed, so fearsome was the phenomenon that Moses said, I am terrified and trembling.* Moses said, "I was afraid of the anger" of the Lord concerning the golden calf (Deut 9:19). He was also afraid when God spoke at the burning bush

(Exod 3:6; Acts 7:32), and later traditions said that he was afraid when the Law was given (*b. Shabb.* 88b). Hebrews seems to fuse several theophanies into a single terrifying theophany (cf. the combining of sacrifices in Heb 9:13).

12:22. *Instead, you have approached.* One might argue that the perfect tense shows that salvation is already present in faith (Grässer; H.-F. Weiss; Peterson, *Hebrews*, 160), since listeners experience the age to come through the Spirit (6:5). Nevertheless, Hebrews recognizes that listeners have not yet arrived, but hope for the city "that is to come" (13:14). On approach see NOTE on 4:16.

Mount Zion. This was the hill in Jerusalem where the sanctuary was located. David captured the stronghold of Zion (2 Sam 5:6–9) and made it his capital. The ark of the covenant was placed in a tent in Zion and later moved to a hill to the north, where the Temple was built (1 Kgs 8:1). The name Zion was extended to the site of the Temple and to Jerusalem as a whole. On earth, Zion was where Israel gathered for worship, for the Lord loved Zion (Pss 78:68; 87:1–2) and made it his dwelling place (1 Kgs 14:21; Pss 9:11; 48:1–2; 74:2; Isa 8:18). Prophets spoke of God's deliverance coming to Zion (Isa 59:20; Zech 9:9) and of Israel being preserved in Zion (e.g., Pss 69:35; 126:1; Isa 4:5; 60:14; Jer 3:14; Joel 2:32; 3:17, 21; Zeph 3:14–15; Zech 1:17; 2:10). Zion was where one hoped to see God manifest (Pss 84:7; 102:16). Apocalyptic writings spoke of a heavenly Zion (Rev 14:1; *4 Ezra* 10:44; 13:35–36). Psalm 110:1–4 says that Zion was the place where the one seated at God's right hand, the priest like Melchizedek, was to rule. Since Hebrews has argued that the royal and priestly figure in Ps 110 is Christ, the psalm's reference to Zion is a suitable climax for the journey of Christian faith. See G. Fohrer and E. Lohse, *TDNT* 7.292–338; Levenson, *Sinai and Zion*; Ollenburger, *Zion*.

and the city of the living God, heavenly Jerusalem. "Zion," "the city of God," and "Jerusalem" were often synonymous (Pss 51:18; 102:21). The OT and Jewish traditions hoped for a restoration of the earthly city, but Hebrews focuses on the heavenly one (cf. Gal 4:26; *2 Bar.* 4:2–6; *4 Ezra* 7:26). This is the city with foundations (Heb 11:10) that Israel's ancestors saw from afar (11:13, 16). On "living God" see NOTE on 3:12.

and myriads of angels. "Myriads" of angels were said to accompany God at Sinai (Deut 33:2), at his return for judgment (Dan 7:10; Jude 14), and in the heavenly throne room (Rev 5:11). God sends his angels to minister to his people (Heb 1:14), sometimes in ways that are hidden (13:2). But in the heavenly city, the angels join the celebration (cf. 1:6). See NOTES and COMMENT on 1:5–14.

in festival gathering. In the Greco-Roman world the term *panēgyris* was used for civic festivals and athletic competitions, which drew people from all parts of the empire and from all social classes. Peace was declared during festivals (Isocrates, *Panegyricus* 43), which were times of joy, when one would see people "in white robes and crowned with garlands" (Philo, *Gaius* 12). Speaking of Athens, Isocrates boasted that "our city throughout all time is a festival gathering for those who visit her" (*Panegyricus* 46). Hebrews, however, insists that the true eternal festival gathering is in heaven itself. Greco-Roman festivals had religious elements, and Jewish sources occasionally used the term for Israel's festivals (Amos 5:21; Hos 2:13; 9:5; Ezek 46:11; Josephus, *J.W.* 5.230). The principal Jewish "festival" was the Sabbath (Philo, *Moses* 2.211), and the hope of which Hebrews speaks is God's eternal Sabbath celebration (Heb 4:1–11). See *TLNT* 2.4–8; Williamson, *Philo*, 64–70. On the syntactical relationship of the festival gathering (Heb 12:22) to the assembly (12:23) see P. E. Hughes, *Commentary*, 552–55.

12:23. *and the assembly.* This word (*ekklēsia*) was used for Israelite gatherings (Deut 31:30; Judg 20:2), Christian congregations (e.g., 1 Cor 1:2; Gal 1:2; Rev 1:4), and the whole church (Matt 16:18; Acts 9:31). In classical Greece the assembly had power to make decisions for the city (*OCD*, "ekklēsia"; MM, 195). In the Greco-Roman world some decisions were made by a municipal council (*boulē*) and others by the "assembly" of adult male citizens (Acts 19:39). In Hebrews all the righteous, from Abel on, belong to the heavenly assembly (Heb 12:23c).

of the firstborn. The firstborn had special rights of inheritance and blessing, which Esau lost (NOTE on 12:16), but which the firstborn in heaven receive. The whole people of God are God's firstborn (Exod 4:22–23). Although the firstborn in Israel were spared death in Moses' time (Heb 11:28), those who belong to God's city do die (cf. 11:13, 21–22, 35–37), but are delivered through resurrection, as was Jesus, who is God's "firstborn" in a singular sense (1:6).

who are registered in heaven. "Registration" evokes associations from two spheres:

(a) Legal usage. Registration established one's identity as a citizen. Each legitimate child of a Roman citizen was to be registered within thirty days of birth. A copy of the declaration would be given to the father as proof of the child's citizenship, helping to ensure that the child would receive the benefits of citizenship, such as fair legal treatment (Acts 22:25–29) and material help (Seneca, *De beneficiis* 4.28.2). All people could be registered for taxation (cf. Luke 2:1, 3, 5), but Hebrews focuses on the registration whereby foreigners (Heb 11:13; 13:14) become naturalized citizens (Plutarch, *Mor.* 37EF; cf. Winter, *Life*, 52–55; F. Schulz, "Roman Registers").

(b) Theological usage. The OT said that the righteous were registered in a heavenly book (Exod 32:32; Ps 69:28; Dan 12:1; Luke 10:20; Phil 4:3). The saints include "everyone who has been registered for life in Jerusalem" (Isa 4:3; cf. Ps 87:5–6; Rev 3:5; 13:8; 17:8; 20:12, 15; 21:27). The passive voice is used because people are registered by God's initiative, perhaps through baptism (H.-F. Weiss), but more broadly through receiving God's promise in faith.

and a judge, who is God of all. Cities regularly had judges (*P. Oxy.* #1195; Matt 5:25; Acts 24:10), although municipal judges were not always reliable (Luke 18:2, 6). Under Roman law contending parties identified the central issue before a magistrate, who then appointed a judge. The judge was usually a private citizen, who heard the case and issued a binding verdict (*OCD*, "iudex"). Jews in Diaspora communities could judge some internal affairs, but were also subject to local courts (Josephus, *Ant.* 16.27, 45). Like earthly cities, the heavenly

Jerusalem has a judge, but the judge is God himself (Gen 18:25; Acts 10:42; cf. NOTES on Heb 6:2; 9:27).

and the spirits of the righteous, who have been made complete. "Made complete" means receiving all that God has promised (pp. 122–25). Some expected the righteous to enter heaven immediately after death (Wis 3:1) or their spirits to be specially preserved until the last judgment (*1 Enoch* 22:3–7; Rev 6:9; *4 Ezra* 7:99), but Hebrews provides no clarity about a person's state between death and final judgment (Peterson, *Hebrews*, 163–65).

12:24. *and the mediator of the new covenant, Jesus.* See NOTES on 7:22; 8:6 and pp. 112–15.

and the sprinkled blood. Priests sprinkled animal blood to purify the flesh (9:13), and Moses sprinkled blood to inaugurate the old covenant (9:19). Jesus' death is a sprinkling that inaugurates a new covenant and cleanses the conscience (10:22; NOTES and COMMENT on 9:14).

that speaks better than that of Abel. Abel's blood continued to cry out after Cain killed him, showing that death is not the end for the righteous (11:4). Jesus' blood "speaks" in a manner that not only differs from the voice at Sinai (12:19) but is superior to the cry of Abel's blood:

(a) How does Christ's blood speak in a superior way? Some assume that Abel's blood cried out for vengeance against Cain (*Jub.* 4:3; *1 Enoch* 22:7; Philo, *Worse* 48; *Frg. Tg.* and *Tg. Neof.* Gen 4:10), while Christ's blood communicates grace (Heb 4:16; cf. Braun; F. F. Bruce; Lane; H.-F. Weiss; Wilson). Others argue that Abel's blood cried out to God "from the ground" (Gen 4:10), whereas Jesus intercedes for people in heaven (Heb 7:25–26; Grässer). Finally, some observe that martyrs' blood was thought to atone for sins (4 Macc 6:28; 17:21). Therefore, Hebrews might suggest that Abel's blood brought a limited atonement, while Jesus' blood brought complete atonement (Heb 9:14; Attridge). Whatever the nuance, Christ's blood conveys something gracious.

(b) To whom does Christ's blood speak? Some proposals assume that the blood speaks to God on behalf of the listeners, but it is more likely that it "speaks" to the listeners, since the context considers how God communicates with people (12:19, 20, 25–26; P. E. Hughes; Casey, "Christian Assembly," 331). Christ's blood purifies a person's conscience when his death is proclaimed (NOTES and COMMENT on 9:14), for it "speaks" of God's grace and new covenant.

12:25. *See that you do not refuse the one who is speaking.* The God who spoke on earth at Sinai now speaks from heaven.

For if they did not escape when they refused. Moses' generation, which heard God's word at Sinai, refused to obey and died in the wilderness (3:7–4:11; cf. 2:2; 10:28).

the one who admonished them on earth. God admonished Israel "on earth" at Sinai (12:19). The verb *chrēmatizein* was used for messages from God (8:5; 11:7).

how much less will we who turn away "Turning away" from God brings dire consequences (Num 32:15; Jer 15:6; 2 Tim 4:4; Tit 1:14). Like earlier warnings

(Heb 3:12; 6:6), this passage assumes that turning away is a danger, but not an accomplished fact.

from the one who admonishes from the heavens. Hebrews does not suggest that God sends an unmediated heavenly voice (e.g., Mark 1:11; John 12:28). He speaks from heaven through the prophets and the psalms (Heb 1:5–13; 3:7–11; 5:5–6; 8:8–12; 10:37–38), which are made effective through the Spirit that comes from heaven (3:7; 6:4–5).

12:26. *whose voice then shook the earth, but who now has promised.* At Sinai, "the earth quaked . . . at the presence of God" (Ps 68:8; cf. Exod 19:18; Judg 5:4; Pss 77:18; 114:7). The word "promise" has connoted rest (Heb 4:1), a new covenant (8:6), and eternal inheritance (9:15; cf. 11:9), but now it warns of a final shaking. On promise see pp. 110–12.

12:26b. This paraphrases Hag 2:6 LXX (cf. 2:21). Hebrews inserts "not only" and "but also" to stress the magnitude of the "shaking" yet to come (Schröger, *Verfasser*, 190–94):

MT	*LXX*	*Hebrews*
Yet once,	Yet once more	Yet once more
it is a little while,		
and I will shake	I will shake	I will shake
___ the heaven	___ the heaven	*not only* the earth
and the earth.	*and* the earth	*but also* the heaven

saying, Yet once more I will shake. Shaking was associated with God conquering his enemies and with the coming Day of the Lord (Isa 13:1–22; 34:1–17; Ezek 7:1–27; 30:1–9; Joel 2:1–11; G. Bornkamm, *TDNT* 7.198). Apocalyptic scenarios envisioned the shaking of the earth in the end times (2 *Bar.* 32:1; 4 *Ezra* 6:16; 10:26; *Sib. Or.* 3.675). Haggai relates the shaking of the world order to the wealth of many nations coming to Israel. In Hebrews the shaking is cosmic.

not only the earth but also the heaven. Although some argue that Hebrews distinguishes a lower transient heaven and earth (1:10–12) from the eternal heavens, where God and Christ abide (8:1; 9:24; Grässer), this seems unlikely. The author refers to the "heavenly" Jerusalem (12:22), the firstborn "in heaven" (12:23), and the God who speaks "from the heavens" (12:25). The idea is that not even the heavenly realm of angels and saints will escape this shaking.

12:27. *The once more.* "Once" connotes definitive action (NOTE on 6:4).

portends removal of the things that are shaken, as things that have been made. The word *metathesis* indicates "removal" (NIV; NRSV; NAB[2]; REB; NJB), since it is the opposite of "abide" (12:27b). Forms of this word indicate the removal of the legal basis for the Levitical priesthood (7:12) and Enoch's removal from the earth to everlasting life (11:5). The text does not suggest that God destroys a lower realm and preserves a higher one (Grässer)—both heaven and earth are shaken (NOTE on 12:26b). Just as heaven is cleansed by the sacrifice of Christ (9:23), heaven is purged by the shaking action of God (12:26b). There is transformation as well as annihilation (Chrysostom; Aquinas, *Ad Heb.* §720; Calvin; H.-F. Weiss). Accordingly listeners belong to the created order, yet will not be destroyed, for their spirits will be saved. On "portends" see NOTE on "indicate" in 9:8.

in order that what is not shaken might abide. "Abiding" (*menein*) is the opposite of "removal." The verb is used absolutely: the author does not say that they will remain until a certain point in time. Christ himself remains forever (1:11), as does his priesthood (7:3, 24) and the listeners' heavenly inheritance (10:34). The language might echo Ps 96:9–10 (95:9–10 LXX): "Worship the Lord in his holy court, let all the earth be shaken before him. Say to the nations, 'The Lord has inaugurated his reign.' For he will complete the heavenly world, which will not be shaken" (Vanhoye, "L'οἰκουμένη," 250–51).

COMMENT[443]

The tragic picture of Esau weeping over the loss of his blessing as firstborn (12:16–17) leads into a festive portrayal of the firstborn who are blessed in Zion (12:23). Arrival in the celestial city marks a climax in Hebrews.[444] At the beginning of his speech, the author allowed listeners to overhear God's panegyric address to the Son, his firstborn, who rules in righteousness and is worshiped by the angels (1:1–14). Now listeners return to the heavenly realm, where they see all of God's children, his firstborn, who are called righteous, joining myriads of angels in a festival gathering or *panēgyris* (12:22–23).

The first series of arguments traced Israel's journey through the wilderness, where the faithless perished without entering God's rest, yet it held out hope that a Sabbath celebration remains for those who trust God's promises (2:10–5:10). Here listeners come from the gloom of Sinai in the wilderness to the heavenly celebration that marks the goal of the journey for the people of God (12:22–24).

The second series of arguments announced that Christ inaugurated a new covenant by his blood, giving the faithful the boldness to come into God's presence (7:1–10:25). Now the author places listeners in the presence of God, reminding them of the new covenant and what the blood of Christ conveys (12:24).

The third series of arguments followed the journeys of the righteous, who lived by faith and endured conflict, disappointment, and death on earth without being "made complete" through the realization of God's promises (10:38; 11:39–40). The series culminates with the spirits of the righteous being made complete in God's own city (12:23; see §29 COMMENT).

[443]On 12:18–27 see Braun, "Das himmlische"; Casey, "Christian Assembly"; Dumbrell, "Spirits"; Ernst, "Die griechische Polis"; Grässer, *Aufbruch*, 240–50; Helyer, "*Prōtotokos*"; Laub, *Bekenntnis*, 253–57; Löhr, "Thronversammlung," 197–202; idem, "Anthropologie"; MacRae, "Kingdom"; Oberholtzer, "Warning," 67–75; Peterson, *Hebrews*, 160–67; Rice, "Apostasy"; Scholer, *Proleptic*, 137–49; Thompson, *Beginnings*, 41–52; Vögtle, "Das Neue," 76–89; Wider, *Theozentrik*, 88–115.

[444]Lindars, "Rhetorical," 401–2; Ellingworth, *Epistle*, 669; Isaacs, *Sacred*, 87; Vögtle, "Das Neue," 76; Grässer, *Hebräer*, 3.302; Wider, *Theozentrik*, 88. On connecting Heb 1 and 12 see Vanhoye, *La structure*, 233–34.

Structurally, the passage has two parts: (**a**) Mount Sinai and Mount Zion (12:18–24). Hebrews contrasts the disturbing phenomena at Sinai, which the listeners have not approached (12:18) with the assuring vision of Zion, which they have approached (12:22–24). The voice at Sinai warned people not to draw near, while the voice of Christ's blood conveys a sense of grace through the new covenant, encouraging listeners to draw near. (**b**) A transitional paragraph develops the contrast between the heavenly and earthly realities by speaking of cosmic change (12:25–27). Each major section of Hebrews concludes with a transition. Those at the end of the first and second series of arguments are lengthy (5:11–6:20; 10:26–39), while those at the end of the exordium and third series of arguments are brief (2:1–4; 12:25–27). The brevity of this transitional section is appropriate, since the peroration that follows it resembles a transitional digression (12:28–13:21).[445] Like earlier transitions, this one warns about the impossibility of escape from God, compares an aspect of the Law to the situation of Christians, and calls for careful attention in listening.[446]

a. Sinai and Zion (12:18–24)

Palpable and unsettling is the author's opening description for the listeners (12:18). The location remains nameless. The author assumes that listeners familiar with Deut 4:11–12 will be able to identify the site as Mount Sinai or Horeb, where the people encountered a numinous fire, darkness, and tempest, but only gradually do the contours of the mountain emerge (Heb 12:20b). Listeners experience a whirlwind of descriptive elements as the author lists item after item, giving the impression that many more could be added.[447] Ironically, however, God remains hidden. The physical phenomena, which might seem to manifest divine power, do more to conceal God than to reveal him. Like the mountain, the numinous power behind the phenomena is not named in 12:18–21. If the Law contains a shadow of divine reality (8:5; 10:1), it was given at a place cloaked in darkness by a God who remains unseen (11:1). In contrast, the heavenly realities in 12:22–24, which are perceived by faith, will give a clearer sense of God's presence.

Audible elements heighten the sense of uneasiness (12:19). A trumpet blast suggests alarm, and the words of an anonymous voice issue a warning out of the darkness. Prohibiting even an animal from touching the mountain under penalty of death (12:20; Exod 19:12–13), the unnamed speaker leaves the people in a situation where the physical phenomena that engulf them also bar them from the mountain. The people's response is, understandably, negative: they refused

---

[445]On the similarities between transitional digressions and perorations see *Rhet. ad Her.* 2.30 §47; Quintilian, *Inst.* 6.1.54–55; Cicero, *Partitiones oratoriae* 15 §52; Lausberg, *Handbook* §§431, 441. On using digressions of different lengths see Lausberg, *Handbook* §§340–42, 345.

[446]Many identify 12:29 as the end of the section. On reasons for making a break between 12:27 and 12:28, see §36 COMMENT.

[447]Repetition of "and" (*kai*) six times in 12:18–19 gives the impression that even more could be said, magnifying the effect of the description (Demetrius, *On Style* 54, 63). On polysyndeton see p. 94.

any further message. Soon, however, the author will warn that refusing the message does not mean escaping its consequences (Heb 12:25). The phenomena at Sinai were so fearsome that even Moses was terrified (12:21). Although Moses and his parents proved fearless before earthly kings (11:23–27), here Moses shows that fear is the proper response to a warning from God. Since Moses was remembered for his faithfulness (3:1–6), his example implies an argument from the greater to the lesser (Quintilian, *Inst.* 5.11.9): if God's most faithful servant was afraid, how much more should others—including the listeners—tremble at warnings from God.

To introduce the contrasting scene, the author says, "You have approached" Mount Zion (Heb 12:22). The use of the perfect tense is rhetorical. It adds vividness "by the use of an actual past tense, since what has already happened is more forceful than what will happen or is still happening" (Demetrius, *On Style* 214). The author not only urges them to draw near to God (4:16; 10:22) but also brings them near through the power of his language.[448] This does not mean that listeners have arrived at the heavenly city in any physical sense, and conditions in their lives were far from ideal (pp. 71–72). The portrayal of a city that transcends experience gives listeners incentive to persevere in the earthly city where they live.

In contrast to the unnamed mountain in 12:18–21, a cascade of names identifies the new location as Mount Zion, the city of the living God, heavenly Jerusalem (12:22). Listeners familiar with tradition would have sensed that this is where God's promises are realized (NOTES on 12:22). Although Abraham lived as a foreigner on earth, he hoped for the city of God (11:8–10, 13–16). Similarly, Hebrews addressed those who had no abiding city on earth (13:14), even though they were the heirs of the promises made to Abraham (2:16; 6:12, 17). The vision of the heavenly city is designed to instill confidence that God will keep his commitments and bring Abraham's heirs to the city that he has prepared.

Listeners who have been running with endurance in the contest of faith (12:1, 12) now find themselves in a festival gathering of angels (12:22). Festival gatherings in Greco-Roman society included athletic events, where contestants endured for the sake of honor at the end (NOTES and COMMENT on 10:32; 12:1–4). In 12:1 the author declared that those who run in the contest of faith are surrounded by generations of the faithful who constitute a cloud of faithful witnesses. Here he gives listeners a glimpse of the outcome of their struggle, drawing them to a festival gathering that transcends any on earth and to "the noble and glorious crown, which no human festival gathering has ever bestowed" (Philo, *Alleg. Interp.* 2.108).

Cities in the classical world were governed by an assembly of those who were registered as citizens (NOTES on 12:23). Although their powers were more limited under Roman rule, local assemblies continued to function and noncitizens

---

[448]Again, note how the author repeats the same connective "and" (*kai*), which lends grandeur to the presentation and gives the impression that the author could continue indefinitely. On polysyndeton see p. 94.

continued to aspire to membership. The listeners, who belonged to the Christian assembly or gathering (2:12; 10:25), perceived themselves to be resident aliens, rather than valued citizens in their society (6:18; 11:9, 13; 13:14). Jeremiah, however, had promised a new covenant in which the people of God would address each other as fellow citizens (Heb 8:11). Mention of the assembly of the firstborn, who are registered in God's heavenly city, points to the fulfillment of that promise, for listeners are not merely brought into the presence of this assembly, but are brought into membership (F. F. Bruce). Like earthly cities, the heavenly city has a judge—the God of all (12:23b)—and listeners understood that God judges even his own people (6:2, 7–8; 9:27; 10:30; 13:4). Nevertheless, the tone of this passage is hopeful. Society had passed negative judgments on the Christian community (10:32–34; 13:3, 13), but God commends faith and he judges rightly (6:10). Since his judgment is the final one, listeners can persevere in faith rather than relinquish faith in order to obtain a favorable judgment from society (deSilva, *Despising*, 279–84).

The population of the heavenly city includes the spirits of the righteous, who have been made complete (12:23c).[449] On earth the righteous did not fully receive what God had promised (11:39–40), but were confronted with reproach, disappointment, and affliction (10:32–34; 11:13, 26, 36–38). The depiction of the heavenly Zion affirms that God will not abandon the righteous, but will make them complete by fulfilling his promises of glory, honor, inheritance, and a share in the everlasting Sabbath celebration. God's own city is the point at which all of his promises are kept fully (see pp. 122–25). God's faithfulness is underscored by the reference to the new covenant (12:24), which Jeremiah promised and Christ inaugurated (8:6–13; 9:15; 10:12–18). Although some aspects of the new covenant are not yet fully realized, the mercy that God provides through Christ offers assurance that the whole covenant will be established (§21 COMMENT *b*).

The mention of the sprinkled blood of Christ completes the depiction of the heavenly city and its festival gathering. In the epic of Rome's founding Aeneas called an assembly and hosted athletic contests to keep a vow he had made. Accompanied by a myriad of companions, he poured out libations and offerings of blood (Virgil, *Aeneid* 5.75–83). The sprinkled blood in Hebrews also has to do with keeping a vow, that is, with God keeping his vow to make a new covenant. If festivals commonly featured an orator,[450] the speaking at the festival in Hebrews is done by Jesus' sprinkled blood, which communicates the grace of God. "It is no longer the praise of Athens, as uttered by Lysias or Isocrates, but the praise of the glory of God, the expression of his will" in the new covenant that is proclaimed in the festival (*TLNT* 3.8).

---

[449]The placement of the "spirits of the righteous" (12:23c) between references to God (12:23b) and Christ (12:24) seems odd to some interpreters. Rissi proposes that it was added to a preexisting text (*Theologie*, 100–102; Scholer, *Proleptic*, 138). Listing various items without a clear sequence is not unusual for Hebrews, however (NOTES on 11:32–35a; §36 n. 9).

[450]For example, Gorgias, *Olympic Discourse*; Lysias, *Olympic*; Isocrates, *Panegyricus*.

b. Shaking Heaven and Earth (12:25–27)

The words "do not refuse the one who is speaking" (12:25) intrude into the festive scene. The speaker's identity is not stated, and the ambiguity allows the enjoinder to function in multiple ways. In an ultimate sense, the one who is speaking is God, but those addressed by Hebrews do not hear God speak in an unmediated way. Therefore, the appeal not to refuse the word of God calls for attention to the human speaker who delivers the word. Rhetorically, speakers sometimes appealed for attentiveness when their listeners became tired. Those addressed by Hebrews would have been listening for perhaps forty-five minutes, and this kind of direct appeal was a way to reengage their attention.[451]

One reason for attentiveness is that refusing God's word has severe consequences (12:25). The text compares the lesser consequences of ignoring the word at Sinai to the greater consequences of ignoring the word from heaven (Quintilian, *Inst.* 5.11.9–12). A voice spoke to Moses' generation at Sinai, but they refused any further message (12:19), and their refusal was part of a forty-year pattern of unbelief. They did not escape judgment, for God allowed them to die in the desert (12:25b; 3:7–19). Like Moses' generation, those addressed by Hebrews are admonished by God (4:2), but unlike them, the listeners are admonished "from the heavens" through the words of the prophets, which have been confirmed by Jesus' exaltation to heaven (NOTE on 12:25c). The author expects listeners to agree that those who have heard this heavenly word will not escape judgment if they refuse it (cf. 2:3; 10:29). At the same time, the text seems designed to provoke an objection. By saying "how much less will *we who turn away*" escape (12:25c), the author presses listeners to respond, "But we are *not* turning away!" When the remark elicits such a declaration, it has the effect for which it was designed.

A second reason for attentiveness looks to the future, for God has promised to shake not only the earth but also the heaven (12:26; Hag 2:6). Hebrews has argued that Israel's journey to Canaan reflects the journey of faith toward God's rest (4:1–11), that Levitical sacrifices point to Jesus' self-sacrifice (9:1–14), and that Moses' making the first covenant foreshadows Jesus' making the new covenant (9:15–22). Here, the way God shakes the earth at Sinai anticipates the way he will shake the universe in the future. When Noah was admonished about events as yet unseen, he responded in faith before the cataclysm occurred (11:7). The listeners have now been admonished about future events, and the question is whether they too will respond in faith. The future shaking will encompass heaven itself, so that not even those in the heavenly Jerusalem can escape the testing.

Contrasts between the shakable and the unshakable, between what will be removed and what will remain, present listeners with sharp alternatives (12:27). Shakable things belong to the visible world and will perish. The created order is not inherently bad, but it is limited and inadequate as an object for faith. The ex-

[451]On listeners' fatigue see *Rhet. ad Her.* 1.4 §7; Quintilian, *Inst.* 4.1.48–49. On the use of direct appeal see Lausberg, *Handbook* §§269–71, 287.

alted Christ, however, remains forever (1:10–12), and his priesthood endures for all time (7:24), so that his kingdom is a proper object for faith. The people of God repeatedly faced situations that tested whether they would rely on what is material and transient, while surrendering their eternal inheritance, or whether they would trust the promise of life in God's eternal city, even when this entailed the loss of earthly securities. Esau gave up eternal blessing for the sake of a meal (12:16), but Moses gave up transient wealth for an enduring reward (11:25–26). Previously, the listeners' community lost earthly possessions in the hope of an enduring inheritance (10:34), but in their current situation some may have been drawn to seek social and material security at the expense of faith. Therefore, the author will now urge them to retain their hope in the promise of an unshakable kingdom (12:28–13:6).[452]

---

[452]Cf. Casey, "Christian Assembly," 333. Discussion of this passage has been dominated by questions of the traditions behind the text. The basic issue is whether the framework of thought is essentially metaphysical, emphasizing the difference between the transient material world and the eternal immaterial world (Thompson, *Beginnings*, 41–52; Grässer), or whether it is apocalyptic, emphasizing the difference between the present and the future (Lane; Isaacs, *Sacred*, 86–88). A promising alternative to this debate is to shift the perspective from the traditions that might shape the text to the way the text shapes the listeners in relation to the society in which they live.

IV. The Peroration

◆

36. The Peroration (12:28–13:21)

COMMENT

"Peroration" is the term for the conclusion of a speech, according to the canons of classical rhetoric.[453] Used in various types of speeches, the peroration gave the speaker a final opportunity to influence the listeners by reviewing key arguments and appealing to the emotions. The strength of this section comes not from new arguments, but from a creative fusion of themes and images from earlier portions of the speech, together with appeals for solidarity in community life.

The peroration extends from 12:28–13:21. The chapter division between chapters 12 and 13, common since the Middle Ages, allows chapter 12 to end forcefully, with the contrasts between what can be shaken and what is unshakable. This unifies 12:25–29, but it creates a thirteenth chapter that is so different from the rest of the speech that some have argued that it was tacked on to a completed composition in order to make Hebrews conform more closely to other early Christian letters.[454] It is preferable to recognize that the medieval chapter division obscures the natural section break, as elsewhere in Hebrews.[455] Although the unshakable kingdom in 12:28 continues the idea of shaking from 12:25–27, it works well to place the reference to the unshakable kingdom at the beginning of a new section, since Hebrews regularly begins a new section with an idea cited at the end of the previous section.[456]

---

[453]The final portion of the speech was called the *peroratio* or *conclusio* in Latin and the *epilogos* in Greek. On the peroration, see Aristotle, *Rhetoric* 3.19.1–6; Cicero, *Partitiones oratoriae* 15 §§52–60; *De inventione rhetorica* 1.52 §§98–109; *Rhet. ad Her.* 2.30 §47; Quintilian, *Inst.* 6.1.1–55; Lausberg, *Handbook* §§431–42. For Übelacker (*Hebräerbrief*, 224) the peroration begins in 13:1, and for Backhaus (*Der neue*, 61–63) the peroration extends from 10:19–13:21.

[454]Some have argued that Heb 13 was added by someone other than the author (Buchanan, *Hebrews* 243–45, 267–68), but the more common view is that it was an epistolary appendix added by the author himself (Isaacs, *Sacred*, 212; see the listing in Thurén, *Lobopfer*, 51–53). For a review of debates concerning the relation of Heb 1–12 to Heb 13 see Lane, *Hebrews*, 2.495–98.

[455]A section on Jesus' high priesthood begins, not at 5:1, but several verses earlier in 4:14, and the next section begins, not at 6:1, but several verses earlier in 5:11. Similarly, the peroration begins, not in 13:1, but several verses earlier in 12:28.

[456]The first series of arguments ended with what Jesus learned by suffering (5:7–10) while the ensuing digression considers the listeners' lack of learning (5:11–14). At the end of the digression there are references to the Tabernacle curtain and the priest like Melchizedek (6:19–20), which are then developed at length in 7:1–10:25. The second series of arguments concludes with a reference to the Day of the Lord (10:25), and the digression that follows explores the theme of judgment (10:26–39). That digression concludes by declaring that the righteous live by faith (10:38–39), and the next cycle explores the theme of faith (11:1–12:24).

Worship or service pleasing to God is the theme of the peroration. The idea is introduced in 12:28–29 (*euarestōs*) and developed in 13:1–21 through exhortations to show care of the brethren, hospitality, and compassion, and to remain faithful in marriage and avoid avarice. The author repeats that offerings of praise and sharing one's possessions are sacrifices pleasing to God (*euaresteitai*, 13:15–16), and his benediction asks God to equip the listeners to do what is pleasing (*euareston*, 13:21). If the central part of Hebrews argued that Christ's death was a sacrifice for others, the peroration urges those who receive the benefits of Christ's sacrifice to offer their own sacrifices of praise and service as a response. When read as an explication of worship or service, these exhortations form a coherent part of the speech and a compelling conclusion to the treatment of priesthood and sacrifice.[457]

Internally, the peroration contains three movements of thought, of which the first and third are parallel:

A. Service to God 12:28–29	**C.** Sacrifice to God 13:15
Serving others 13:1–6	Serving others 13:16
Attention to leaders 13:7–9	Attention to leaders 13:17–19

B. Priestly Sacrifice 13:10–11
Christ's death for others 13:12
Christians follow Christ's lead 13:13–14

Going over the same material at the beginning (12:28–13:9) and the end of the peroration (13:15–19) emphasizes that service to God involves service to others. The middle section (13:10–14) creatively fuses themes developed earlier in Hebrews of Christ's priestly self-sacrifice and the hope of entering the city of God in order to shape and support this view of Christian discipleship. The benediction in 13:20–21 concludes the speech proper.[458] Personal greetings follow in 13:22–25 (§39 COMMENT).

One main function of a peroration was to affect the listeners' commitments by influencing their emotions. Speakers often appealed to common values, such as love for God, one's parents, and one's family, and respect for virtues that promote generosity and human community (Cicero, *Partitiones oratoriae*, 16 §56). By calling for compassion, hospitality, faithfulness, and generosity (13:1–6), Hebrews emphasizes community-building values that listeners would find hard to reject. A peroration also helped evoke sympathy for the speaker's case, and Hebrews helps to generate sympathy by remembering afflicted Christians, faithful leaders of the past, and Christ's suffering on their behalf (13:3, 7, 12). The author also requests prayers for himself, implying that his integrity has been unfairly challenged (13:18–19). Such a request can reinforce bonds with the lis-

[457]On the close connection of 13:1–21 with 12:28–29 see Thurén, *Lobopfer*; Vanhoye, "La question," 137; Lane, *Hebrews*, 2.497–98; H.-F. Weiss, *Brief*, 697.

[458]Grässer, *Hebräer*, 3.400; G. H. Guthrie, *Structure*, 134; Übelacker, *Hebräerbrief*, 197; Vanhoye, *La structure*, 217–19.

teners. Finally, a peroration might seek to evoke indignation at opponents. Hebrews is remarkable for its lack of polemic against those who threaten the community (10:32–34; 13:13), but the author does warn against "those who serve in the tent" (13:10). Although the remark does more to create a foil for the argument than to upbraid actual opponents, it helps to foster opposition to positions that differ from those of the author (NOTES and COMMENT on 13:10).

A second function of a peroration was to refresh the listeners' memory. Judicial perorations sometimes summarized the main points, but other speeches exhibited more variety (Cicero, *Partitiones oratoriae* 17 §59). Hebrews' peroration draws on the second series of arguments (7:1–10:39) when recalling how regulations about food and service in the Tabernacle failed to benefit people, whereas Christ's death was an effective sacrifice for sins (10:9–12). The author also weaves in elements from the third series of arguments (11:1–12:27) by calling listeners to endure reproach for Christ, knowing that they have no abiding city on earth, but seek the one that is to come (13:13–14). In so doing, the author provides a "refreshing of the memory of the audience, rather than a repetition of the speech" (Cicero, *De inventione rhetorica* 1.52 §100).

Stylistically, a good peroration was to be brief, and Hebrews' peroration would have taken perhaps three or four minutes to deliver. When composing a peroration, speakers were counseled to use a number of short sentences that were not linked by connectives: "I have spoken; you have heard; you know the facts; now give your decision" (Aristotle, *Rhetoric* 3.19.6; cf. Cicero, *Partitiones oratoriae* 15 §53). This style, which is evident in Heb 13:1–6 and hortatory sections of other NT writings (e.g., 1 Pet 5:6–11; Phil 4:4–7), is useful because the author is not developing new arguments, but calling for decision: "Let care for the brethren abide. . . . Remember those in prison. . . . Let marriage be held in honor" (Heb 13:1, 3, 4). Using strong metaphors was encouraged (Cicero, *Partitiones oratoriae* 15 §53), and Hebrews follows this practice by comparing Christ's death outside the city to the taking of a sacrificial victim outside the Israelite camp and by calling listeners to follow Christ outside the social setting of their own city (13:10–14).

37. ACCEPTABLE SERVICE (12:28–13:9)

12 28Therefore, since we are receiving an unshakable kingdom, let us be grateful and thereby offer pleasing service to God with reverence and awe, 29for indeed, our *God is a consuming fire.* **13** 1Let care for the brethren abide. 2Do not
neglect caring for strangers, for through this some have cared for angels without
knowing it. 3Remember the prisoners as though imprisoned with them, and
those who are mistreated as though you yourselves were in [their] body. 4Let
marriage be honored among all and let the marriage bed be undefiled, for God
will judge the immoral and adulterers. 5Let your conduct be without care for
money and be content with what you have. For he himself has said, *I will never
abandon you or forsake you*, 6so that we can take courage and say, *The Lord is my
helper and I shall not fear; what can a human being do to me?* 7Remember your

leaders, who spoke the word of God to you; consider the outcome of their conduct and imitate their faithfulness. [8]Jesus Christ is yesterday and today the same—and forever. [9]Do not be carried away by all sorts of strange teachings, for it is good for the heart to be made firm by grace and not by foods that have not benefited those who walk in them.

NOTES

12:28. *Therefore.* The word *dio* introduces a new phase of argument (cf. 3:7; 6:1; 10:5; 12:12).

since we are receiving an unshakable kingdom. The idea that the place where God rules is unshakable is an OT motif (Pss 93:1; 96:10; 125:1; Isa 33:20; Lane), which here is used for the heavenly "city with foundations" (Heb 11:10). Here, "receiving a kingdom" (cf. Dan 7:18) does not mean that people obtain kingly power (Luke 19:12; cf. Heb 11:33), but that they receive a place in God's kingdom, under the rule of God and Christ (1:8). The present tense, "are receiving," recognizes that listeners still wait for the heavenly city that is to come (13:14).

let us be grateful. Some MSS have the indicative *echomen charin,* "we are grateful" (P^{46} ℵ K P Ψ etc.), but the hortatory subjunctive *echōmen charin,* "let us be grateful" (P^{46c} A C D etc.), is preferable, since exhortations follow (cf. 6:1). Some take this as an exhortation to "have grace" (KJV; Peshitta) and therefore not to fall from grace (12:15; cf. 4:16; 13:9; Aquinas, *Ad Heb.* §723; Erasmus, *Paraphrase;* Calvin). Nevertheless, *echein charin* commonly meant showing gratitude (1 Tim 1:12; 2 Tim 1:3; BAGD, 878 [5]; *TLNT* 3.503–6).

and thereby offer pleasing service to God. Serving (*latreuein*) is the way that gratitude comes to expression. Forms of this word were used for the service of priests (8:5; 9:6; cf. 13:10) and others (9:9; 10:2) under the old covenant (NOTE on 9:1), but here it refers to the services mentioned in 13:1–6, which are performed by all who serve God through Christ.

with reverence and awe. Reverence is the godly fear that led to obedience in Jesus (5:7) and Noah (11:7). Awe is a more uneasy fear (2 Macc 3:17, 30; 15:23), which is fitting here, since God's fire of judgment threatens all (Heb 10:31; 12:29).

12:29. *for indeed, our God is a consuming fire.* This expression was used when warning Israel not to abandon the covenant and when promising that God would destroy its enemies (Deut 4:24; 9:3). Fear was a fitting response to the fire that threatens the sinful (NOTES on Heb 6:8 and 10:27).

13:1. *Let care for the brethren abide.* Often translated "brotherly love," *philadelphia* is more of a bond than a feeling, like the bond between siblings (4 Macc 13:23, 26; 14:1; Philo, *Gaius* 87). Since Christians were brothers and sisters by faith (Heb 3:1, 12), the term indicates care within the Christian community (cf. Rom 12:10; 1 Thess 4:9; 1 Pet 1:22; 2 Pet 1:7). As something that "abides," care for the brethren has a future in the kingdom that "abides" (Heb 12:27; 13:14). Using "care" rather than "love" helps to show the connections with care for strangers (13:2) and care fore money (13:5).

13:2. *Do not neglect caring for strangers.* The term *philoxenia* is based on roots meaning "love" (*phil-*) of the "foreigner" or "stranger" (*xenos*; cf. Acts 10:23; 28:7; cf. Rom 12:13; 1 Tim 3:2; Tit 1:8; 1 Pet 4:9; *Did.* 12:1–2). Many were suspicious or hostile toward strangers (NOTES and COMMENT on Heb 11:13), yet caring for strangers was also a religious duty among Jews (Gen 18:1–8; 19:1–3; Judg 19:19–21; Job 31:32; *T. Zeb.* 6:4–5) and Greeks: "This man is a castaway, poor fellow; we must take care of him. Strangers and beggars come from Zeus" (Homer, *Odyssey* 6.207–8; cf. 2 Macc 6:2; Plutarch, *Mor.* 766C). A tension remains. Christians are to welcome strangers but not strange teachings (NOTE on 13:9). Openness to foreigners expresses faith, but openness to foreign doctrines erodes faith. See *TLNT* 2.555–60; G. Stählin, *TDNT* 5.1–36.

some have cared for angels without knowing it. Abraham and Sarah provided food, water, and a place to rest for three strangers who proved to be messengers of God (Gen 18:1–8; cf. 19:1–14; Judg 6:11–18; 13:3–22; Tob 12:1–20). Encountering a divine messenger in disguise was also a Greco-Roman motif (Homer, *Odyssey* 17.485–87; Ovid, *Metamorphoses* 8.626; Acts 14:11).

13:3. *Remember the prisoners as though imprisoned with them.* Those devoted to a prisoner sometimes stayed in prison with him (Lucian, *Peregrinus* 12; *Toxaris* 32). Hebrews does not ask listeners to stay in prison, but to think of what prison is like and to act accordingly.

and those who are mistreated. Mistreatment recalls the kind of abuse suffered by the Israelites in Egypt (Heb 11:25) and the Maccabean martyrs (11:37). Since those passages connect mistreatment with bondage, 13:3 probably has to do with the maltreatment of prisoners (COMMENT *a*).

as though you yourselves were in [their] body. To motivate listeners the author urges them to imagine how they would feel if their bodies were being maltreated. It is unlikely that Hebrews alludes to the church as the "body" of Christ (Rom 12:4–5; 1 Cor 12:12–27; Erasmus, *Paraphrase*; Calvin).

13:4. *Let marriage be honored among all.* The Greek *pasi* ("among all") is usually taken to be masculine, "among all people," although it could mean "at all times" or, if neuter, "in all respects" or "in all circumstances" (Theophylact; Spicq).

and let the marriage bed be undefiled. Many understood that intercourse outside of marriage was defiling (Gen 49:4; Wis 14:24; *T. Reub.* 1:6; Josephus, *Ant.* 2.55). Jewish sources detailed unlawful relationships (Lev 18; Ps.-Phocylides, *Sentences* 175–206; Josephus, *Ag. Ap.* 2.199–203). Of conditions in Italy (cf. Heb 13:24) Horace said: "Full of sin, our age has defiled the marriage bed, then our children and our homes," by casual sexual relations (*Odes* 3.6.17–32; Juvenal, *Satires* 2.29). Christians were to maintain sexual relationships that were not defiling (Mark 7:21–22; 1 Cor 7:14).

for God will judge the immoral and adulterers. "Adulterers" are those involved in violation of a marriage relationship, while "immoral" can include any sexual activity outside of marriage (1 Cor 5:1, 9–11; 6:9; Eph 5:5; 1 Tim 1:10; Rev 21:8; 22:15). Some sources outline the procedures people were to follow when punishing those guilty of sexual sins (Lev 20:10; Deut 22:20–22; 1 Cor 5:1–13), but

Hebrews warns of God's own future judgment (1 Cor 6:9–11; Eph 5:5; see NOTE on Heb 12:16).

13:5. *Let your conduct be without care for money.* The theme was common: "The love of money is a root of all kinds of evil" (1 Tim 6:10; cf. Luke 16:14; 1 Tim 3:3; 2 Tim 3:2). Financial and sexual matters were frequently mentioned together (*T. Jud.* 18:2; cf. *T. Levi* 14:6; Philo, *Posterity* 34; Epictetus, *Ench.* 3.7.21; Lucian, *Nigrinus* 16; Lane). Here, care for money is the opposite of caring for one's brothers and sisters and caring for foreigners (Heb 13:1–2). See *TLNT* 1.245–46.

and be content with what you have. A common admonition (Ps.-Phocylides *Sentences* 6; Luke 3:14; 1 Tim 6:8; *1 Clem.* 2:1; Epictetus, *Disc.* 1.1.27; BAGD, 107 [2]). If Stoics counseled people to be content for the sake of self-sufficiency, Hebrews urges them to be content for the sake of serving others in the confidence that God will give them a future reward (Heb 10:35; 11:26).

I will never abandon you or forsake you. The speaker is God. The OT source seems to be Deut 31:6, 8. Since this form appears in Philo (*Confusion* 166), it may have been a common paraphrase (Schröger, *Verfasser,* 194–96). The promise is also made elsewhere (Gen 28:15; Josh 1:5; 1 Chron 28:20), which suggests that it applied to multiple situations, including to that of the listeners.

13:6. *The Lord is my helper and I shall not fear; what can a human being do to me?* A quotation of Ps 118:6 (117:6 LXX). On "help" see NOTES on 2:18 and 4:16.

13:7. *Remember your leaders.* The term "leaders" (*hēgoumenoi*) can be used for past leaders who are apparently dead (13:7) and for present leaders of the congregation (13:17, 24). Greco-Roman sources used the term for various administrative and military positions (BAGD, 343 [1]). Jewish sources associate "leaders" with the elders who looked after the affairs of the community without defining a leader's role (*Ep. Arist.* 309–10; Sir 33:19; cf. Schürer, *History*, 3.88, 92). Christian apostles and elders chose "leading men among the brethren" to be sent to Antioch (Acts 15:22), but the text does not indicate whether these "leading men" were among the elders. Later writings, especially those connected with Rome, used the compound *proēgoumenoi* for leaders (*1 Clem.* 1:3; 21:6; Herm. *Vis.* 2.2.6; 3.9.7). See *TLNT*, 2.166–70. On their role see pp. 75–76.

who spoke the word of God to you. This could refer to missionary proclamation (Acts 8:25; 11:19; 13:46; 14:25; 16:6; Phil 1:14; cf. Mark 2:2; 4:33) and to preaching within the Christian community (Acts 4:29, 31; 1 Pet 4:11).

consider the outcome of their conduct. "Outcome" (*ekbasis*) could be the end of a person's life (Wis 2:17, cf. 2:20) or the result of a course of action (Wis 11:14). Hebrews may recall the leaders' manner of life that led up to and included their deaths. A person's death should be "an end in keeping with his life's career" (Josephus, *J.W.* 1.271), which for these leaders meant faithfulness. "Outcome" does not necessarily mean martyrdom, however. There is no mention of martyrs in the community's past or present situations (10:32–34; 12:4). The listeners are to imitate these leaders, just as they are to imitate Abraham, who was not a martyr (6:12).

and imitate their faithfulness. See NOTE on 6:12.

13:8. *Jesus Christ is yesterday and today the same—and forever.* Forms of a formula indicating that God was, is, and will be appear in various sources (Rev 1:4, 8; 4:8; cf. Plato, *Timaeus* 37E; Plutarch, *Mor.* 354C; Pausanius, *Description of Greece* 10.12.10), so that Heb 13:8 implies Jesus' divinity. The passage also affirms Christ's constant faithfulness (pp. 104–5). Of people it was said that "no one knows about anyone whether he will remain as he is until the morrow," for people "violate the compacts made with each other" and think one thing while doing another (Dio Chrysostom, *Disc.* 74.21–22). In contrast, Christ is constant in his faithfulness to God and to God's people in every generation (deSilva, *Despising*, 272). "Yesterday he was with the fathers; today he is with you; and he will be with your posterity for evermore" (Herveus, PL 181.1683C; P. E. Hughes, *Commentary*, 570).

13:9. *Do not be carried away by all sorts of strange teachings.* Being "carried away" is the opposite of the constancy exhibited by Christ according to 13:8 (cf. Jude 12; Eph 4:14). The expression "all sorts" indicates that the author is not giving a precise description of the teachings he opposes (cf. 2 Tim 3:6; Tit 3:3). To say that they are "strange" means that they come from outside the tradition of the author and listeners. It seems unlikely that Hebrews was concerned about participation in pagan meals (1 Cor 8–10; Rev 2:14, 20; Moffatt) or ascetic practices (1 Tim 4:3; Rom 14:2, 21; Michel), since there are no clear references to such problems elsewhere in the speech. Although "strange" could have referred to Jewish practices (Josephus, *J.W.* 2.414), it seems unlikely that the author confines his remarks to Jewish meal practices (NOTE below) or deals with the Lord's Supper (NOTE on 13:10). The reference is stylized and general (K. Berger, "Hellenistischen," 1349).

for it is good for the heart to be made firm. "Firmness" connotes validating a commitment (2:2–3; 6:16; 9:17) and persevering in faith (3:6, 14). Hebrews connects a "firm" heart to the kingdom of God, which cannot be shaken (12:28) or deceived by sin (3:12). Christian hope is a firm anchor for the soul (6:19). Those who are firm in heart hold fast to the confession (3:6, 14; 10:23), approach God boldly (4:16; 10:19), and bear reproach for Christ (13:13).

by grace. On receiving grace see NOTE on 4:16. On falling from grace see NOTE on 12:15.

and not by foods that have not benefited. The word "foods" in 13:9b is parallel to "teachings" in 13:9a. It functions metaphorically, indicating that one should avoid teachings that are not beneficial. This passage contrasts the food or teaching that listeners received from their leaders (5:11–14; 13:7) with divergent teachings (cf. Ign. *Trall.* 6:1). Interpreters differ over whether the passage speaks generally or focuses on Jewish meal practices. A general reference is most likely:

(a) Jewish regulations pertaining to food (NRSV; NIV; REB). In Heb 9:10 the term "food" (*brōma*) was used for Jewish regulations pertaining to food, drink, and ablutions (cf. *brōma* and *brōsis* in 1 Macc 1:63; Col 2:16; *Diogn.* 4:1; *Barn.* 10:9). Moreover, "those who serve in the tent" could refer to those who observe

Jewish statutes (NOTE on 13:10). Some Jews understood the meals that they ate in their own homes to be patterned after meals eaten in the Temple, and Jewish meal blessings sometimes quoted Ps 104:15, which declared that God gives "bread to strengthen the human heart." If Hebrews alluded to this practice, the passage might imply that grace does not come through Jewish meal customs that were inspired by Temple practice. Since the listeners' goal is a share in the world to come, Jewish regulations about food are not beneficial, for the Law brought nothing to completion (Heb 7:11–19). The admonition not to "walk in" unprofitable foods echoes a common expression for living by Jewish Law (NOTE below). God's purposes are made complete through Christ, who is the source of grace (Thurén, *Lobopfer*, 186–204; Lane; cf. Attridge; Bénétreau; Hegermann).

(b) General reference. "All sorts of strange teachings" (13:9a) encompasses more than Jewish practices. Note that when the author spoke of food, drink, and ablutions, he generalized by calling them regulations of the flesh—and flesh is common to all humanity (NOTE on 9:10). Moreover, Esau shows how someone who focuses on "food" can fall from "grace" (12:15–17). In Esau's case food is not linked to the Law, but to gratification of immediate needs rather than long-term benefit. Therefore, teachings that make one's faith firm are beneficial, while any and all teachings that erode faith are not beneficial (Grässer; H.-F. Weiss; Wilson).

those who walk in them. This clause commonly designated those who adhered to or "walked in" the Law and Jewish tradition (Bar 1:18; 2:10; Tob 3:5; Mark 7:5; Acts 21:21). It could also be used for walking or acting in accordance with Christian faith (Eph 5:2, 8, 15; Col 2:6).

COMMENT[459]

Hebrews' peroration translates what has been said about worship or service into practical directives concerning community life (§36 COMMENT). Earlier the author discussed priestly service in the sanctuary (9:1), but here he focuses on the Christian's service in the community. Having emphasized faith in God in 11:1–12:27, he now calls for faithfulness in dealing with other people (13:1–3), in marriage and money matters (13:4–6), and in adherence to Christian teachings (13:7–9). Many of those addressed by Hebrews were involved in service (6:10), but there were signs of decline in community life (10:25), and relationships between faith and community are complex. Faith in God can lead to service in the community, and community life in turn promotes faith (3:13; 10:24; Filson, *Yesterday*, 69).

Specific directives in this section reflect values that were broadly held, which may have enhanced their importance (§36 COMMENT). Accounts of Jesus' teachings and Paul's letters instructed people to care for strangers, prisoners, and

[459]On 12:28–13:9 see Filson, *Yesterday*; Lane, "Unexpected"; Schröger, *Verfasser*, 194–97; Thurén, *Lobopfer*; Vanhoye, "La question." On leaders see pp. 75–76. On 13:9 and the Lord's Supper see pp. 127–29.

the afflicted, while warning against adultery and greed.[460] Many outside the Christian community also affirmed the value of gratitude, reverence, hospitality and loyalty, chastity, and contentment (see NOTES). Hebrews does not reduce the distinctive Christian message of chapters 1–12 to these common values, but invokes common values to build up a distinctive Christian community (13:13–14).

Structurally, this paragraph states the themes that are developed in the peroration (§36 COMMENT). Each item includes an exhortation and a rationale: e.g., people are to serve God because they are receiving an unshakable kingdom (12:28), they are to care for strangers since some have cared for angels without knowing it (13:2), marriage must be honored because God judges the immoral (13:4). The items can be treated in pairs:

(a) God and other people are treated first (12:28–13:3). Juxtaposing the call to show gratitude to God with the call to provide help to other people indicates that serving God cannot be separated from serving other people.

(b) Marriage and money are second (13:4–6). These topics consider basic personal commitments in light of God's judgment and his promises of faithfulness.

(c) Teachers and teachings are third (13:7–9). The author recalls the faith of past Christian leaders, affirms the constancy of Christ, and exhorts the listeners to be unwavering in their adherence to the tradition.

a. God and Other People (12:28–13:3)

The unshakable kingdom marks the culmination of God's promises (12:28). The proposition of Hebrews affirms that God intends people to receive glory and dominion (2:5–9), and the arguments finally bring the listeners to the heavenly city with foundations (11:10; 12:22–24), where the faithful receive their eternal inheritance (1:14; 2:5; 6:12, 17; 9:15; 11:8). Those who receive what God has promised have an obligation to show gratitude (12:28), for "what is more sacred than honor or gratitude?" (Dio Chrysostom, *Disc.* 31.37). When a great gift is given, gratitude means showing loyalty to the giver. In a conflicted situation this can mean defying popular opinion and perhaps even losing one's homeland, health, wealth, and reputation (Seneca, *Ep.* 81.27). Gratitude for an unshakable kingdom means an unshakable commitment to the giver, even when this entails the risks noted above (deSilva, *Despising*, 243–44, 273–74).

The counterparts to gratitude are reverence and awe, since God is both gracious and ominous. His grace is expressed through promises of mercy, yet the fire that threatened people at Sinai (12:18) continues to threaten those who are prone to sin (12:29). Hebrews assumes that as God draws people into relationship with himself, he opposes whatever impedes that relationship. Moses' gener-

---

[460]For example, caring for strangers (13:2) is consistent with Jesus' words, "I was hungry and you gave me food, I was thirsty and you gave me something to drink, I was a stranger and you welcomed me" (Matt 25:35). Caring for prisoners and the mistreated (Heb 13:3) is consistent with Jesus' words, "I was naked and you gave me clothing . . . I was in prison and you visited me" (Matt 25:36; cf. Ign. *Smyrn.* 6:2–3; Lane). For warnings against adultery and avarice see Mark 7:22–23. See Rom 12:1, 13; 13:9.

ation experienced God's grace when they were delivered from bondage, and they received God's wrath when they refused to trust God (3:7–19). Similarly, listeners must be aware that God is their helper (13:6) and the one who judges the sinful (13:4). Only when sin ceases to threaten God's relationships with people will the consuming fire cease to threaten sinners.

The author insists that service to God involves service to God's people. Care for one's brothers and sisters in the faith was a value that was already shared by the listeners (6:10; 13:1), but it gains special force from Hebrews' Christology. Jesus the Son of God was not ashamed of human beings, but called them his "brothers" and sisters, and identified fully with them by sharing in their blood and flesh (2:11, 14). He created a fellowship of faith by giving of himself so that others too might become members of God's household (2:10; 3:6).

The counterpart to care for one's brothers and sisters (*phil-adelphia*, 13:1) is care for strangers (*philo-xenia*, 13:2), which usually meant offering travelers lodging and something to eat and drink (Acts 10:23; 21:16; 28:7).[461] In the Greco-Roman period inns were generally considered disreputable places where theft and prostitution were common. Therefore, travelers sought accommodations in private dwellings whenever possible. Although hospitality to strangers was highly regarded by Jews and Greeks (NOTE on 13:2), householders could hesitate to provide it because some travelers, including those who purported to be Christians abused the privilege (Lucian, *Peregrinus* 11–13).[462]

Hospitality would certainly have been extended to other believers (Rom 12:13; 16:23; 1 Pet 4:9). When Christians traveled, they relied on assistance from believers in the communities that they visited (Acts 21:16; Phlm 22; Rom 16:1–2), as did itinerant evangelists (3 John 5–8). Mutual support was crucial for the solidarity and expansion of the early church. It also seems likely that care for strangers meant aiding travelers of various sorts, not only those who belonged to the faith community. Abraham cared for angels without knowing it, not because he understood that they were from God (Heb 13:2b).[463] It seems unlikely that the author would have expected his Christian listeners to be less hospitable than non-Christians, who also assisted travelers.

As a rationale, the author recalls how some cared for angels without knowing it (13:2). Abraham and Sarah welcomed three visitors, who promised that the couple would have a son (Gen 18:1–15), and Lot welcomed the angels that delivered him from the destruction of Sodom (Gen 19:1–26). Such stories raise the possibility that the strangers who come to the listeners may "prove to be true messengers of God to them, bringing a greater blessing than they receive" from their

---

[461]On hospitality see J. Koenig, *ABD* 3.299–301. On inns see Casson, *Travel*, 197–218.

[462]Later the counsel was given, "Let every apostle who comes to you be received as the Lord, but let him not stay more than one day, or if need be a second as well; but if he stays three days, he is a false prophet. And when an apostle goes forth let him accept nothing but bread till he reach his night's lodging; but if he asks for money, he is a false prophet" (*Did.* 11:4–6).

[463]Philo, *Abraham* 107; Josephus, *Ant.* 1.196. When someone commented on how Abraham had served others, the reply was given that he actually waited upon angels. "Yes, but Abraham did not know that; to him they looked like Arabs" (*b. Qidd.* 32b; F. F. Bruce, *Epistle*, 371 n.).

hosts (F. F. Bruce, *Epistle,* 371). Although Hebrews has pictured the angels in God's throne room (1:5–13) and the heavenly Jerusalem (12:22–24), the author now encourages listeners to think of help that comes in less dramatic ways, through divine messengers whose identity is hidden, but who bring in surprising ways the help that God has promised (1:14).

Remembering prisoners and those who were maltreated (13:3) indicates that imprisonment was not limited to the past (10:32–34), but was a problem at the time that Hebrews was written (NOTE on 13:23). Conditions were harsh in the jails of major cities and smaller towns.[464] Stone walls, often without windows, created a dark, suffocating enclosure. Low-security rooms were gloomy, while the inner cells and those below ground placed prisoners in total darkness. "Neglect, darkness, and stench make it hideous and fearsome to behold" (Sallust, *Bellum catilinae* 55.3; Diodorus Siculus, *Library of History* 31.9.2; cf. Isa 42:7). Prisoners lived in squalor and cramped space, with the rattle of chains making sleep difficult (Lucian, *Toxaris* 29). During the day prisoners wore a collar and a manacle on one hand, while at night they slept on the ground with their legs in stocks, so they could not stretch them out (ibid. 29–30; cf. Acts 16:24; 26:29; 28:20). Jailers were "pitiless by nature and case-hardened by practice . . . brutalized day by day . . . by violence and cruelty."[465]

Listeners were to remember and attend to these prisoners (13:3) because those in prison had to provide much of their own food. A small ration of bread and water was to be distributed once a day, but officials could withhold it as punishment. Those who relied on this ration for any length of time lost weight and weakened. Listeners might have neglected prisoners, first, because of the strain on resources. Guards and local officials could demand bribes, causing those who wished to see a prisoner to provide payment to the jailer as well as supplies for their friend.[466] Second was the strain on morale. Custody could continue for an indefinite period, and delays occurred because of inefficiency, callousness, and the backlog of court cases. The passing of time compounded discouragement. Third, attending prisoners brought the risk of shame—many mentioned prison and disgrace in the same breath—and even the possibility of incarceration. It was easier to stay away and preserve one's own safety.[467]

Ministering to others as though one is afflicted and in prison with them (13:3) resembles the Golden Rule: "Do to others as you would have them do to you" (Matt 7:12). Hebrews, however, provides christological support for this. Jesus identified with mortals whom the devil held captive, sharing their physical circumstances in order to deliver them (Heb 2:14–15). Moses renounced his royal position in order to share the mistreatment God's people, foreshadowing what it

---

[464]For sources and descriptions see Rapske, *Book of Acts*, 195–225; Wansink, *Chained*, 27–95.

[465]Philo, *Joseph* 81; cf. Lucian, *Toxaris* 29; Acts 16:23; 22:24. See Rapske, *Book of Acts*, 244–76.

[466]Lucian, *Toxaris* 31; cf. Cicero, *Verrine Orations* 2.5.45 §118; Philostratus, *Life of Apollonius* 7.36; Lucian, *Peregrinus* 12. On helping prisoners see Rapske, *Book of Acts*, 369–92.

[467]On the shame of prison see Cicero, *Pro Caecina* 34 §100; Seneca, *Ep.* 85.41; Epictetus, *Disc.* 2.1.35; Josephus, *J.W.* 4.628. On risk see Seneca, *Ep.* 9.9; Philostratus, *Life of Apollonius* 4.37; Lucian, *Toxaris* 18. Cf. Rapske, *Book of Acts*, 288–98, 317–20, 388–92.

means to be denounced for Christ (11:25–26). The listeners' own community had previously supported those who were mistreated and imprisoned during a time of crisis (10:32–34), but as the intensity of the crisis faded, the listeners' zeal also faded (see pp. 71–72). Hebrews was written to foster renewed commitment during this period of lesser conflict, when discouragement posed a greater threat than did persecution.

b. Marriage and Money (13:4–6)

The exhortation to honor marriage is probably designed to reinforce a value already held by the listeners (13:4a). Jews and Christians regarded marriage as a part of God's design for humanity (Gen 2:24) and an honorable way of life,[468] as did many Greco-Roman moralists.[469] Christian tradition urged fidelity to marriage commitments rather than seeking divorce, although some noted situations in which separation might occur (Matt 19:9; 1 Cor 7:11, 15). To urge that marriage be honored by all (Heb 13:4a) tacitly recognizes the importance of social support for marriage, since fidelity in marriage is more difficult if marriage is not valued by the community.

The admonition to keep the marriage bed undefiled presupposes that sexual relations within marriage are acceptable to God and that those outside of marriage are not (13:4b).[470] Since sexual sins have not been a focus in Hebrews, this appeal might simply reflect a common topic for moral exhortation.[471] It may have been included on the assumption that sexual desire is part of the human condition and that frequent admonitions are needed to keep immoral behavior in check. Beyond this, however, those who show hospitality bring strangers into their homes (13:2), making it important to observe rigorous standards of propriety. Imprisonment of a spouse left the other spouse without marital companionship for an indefinite period (13:3). Economic difficulties (13:5; cf. 10:34) sometimes led to the exchange of sexual favors in return for benefits. Finally, Jewish and Greco-Roman moralists may have promoted chastity, but many people were more lax in their standards. By promoting sexual fidelity, Christians set themselves apart from aspects of the wider society, while creating a climate of trust in their own community (cf. 1 Thess 4:3–5; 1 Pet 4:3).

---

[468]For Jewish commendations of marriage see Ps.-Phocylides, *Sentences* 175; Josephus, *Ag. Ap.* 2.199–203. In the NT see Matt 19:4–5; Mark 10:6–8; 1 Cor 7:2; Eph 5:22–33. See generally Hays, *Moral*, 347–78; Dunn, *Theology*, 692–98.

[469]Some philosophers thought that singleness was preferable to marriage, but others considered marriage to be the natural way of life. See Musonius Rufus, frg. 13AB; 14; Hierocles, *On Duties* (text in Malherbe, *Moral Exhortation*, 100).

[470]Some Christians tried to expand the boundary for sexual relations beyond marriage, apparently misunderstanding the nature of Christian freedom (1 Cor 5:1–2). Others apparently urged abstinence within marriage (7:1–7) or prohibited marriage altogether (1 Tim 4:3), probably as a way of suppressing the urges of the flesh. Paul granted the propriety of sexual relations within marriage, but not outside it.

[471]For example, 1 Thess 4:3–5; Gal 5:19; 1 Cor 5:9; 6:9; Col 3:5; Eph 5:3. See Malherbe, *Moral Exhortation*, 152.

The warning that God judges adulterers and the immoral (13:4c) rules out the notion that sexual infidelity is acceptable if it is not discovered. Adulterers commonly tried to conceal their affairs (Job 24:15; *Pss. Sol.* 4.5), and a common double standard allowed men latitude in sexual relations, so long as they were discreet.[472] Warning that immoral behavior is finally subject to God places listeners in a situation where they cannot count on concealment in an earthly city (Heb 13:13). Just as God judges those whose unbelief defiles the new covenant that sanctifies them (10:29–31), God judges those who defile their relationships rather than pursuing the holiness that is consistent with the new covenant (12:14).

Care for money is another common topic in moral exhortation (NOTE on 13:5), but one that has a special connection to the listeners. In previous persecution they retained their faith even though this meant losing some possessions (NOTE on 10:34). The author emphasized the importance of this attitude by recounting how Moses abandoned the wealth of Egypt in order to identify with the suffering people of God (11:26). When Hebrews was written, the most intense persecution had passed, but since confession of Christian faith led to a loss of possessions, some may have been tempted to drift away from the community in order to obtain greater material security (pp. 71–72). Care for possessions (*philargyria*) can supplant care for one's brothers and sisters in the faith (*philadelphia*, 13:1) and care for the foreigner or stranger (*philo-xenia*, 13:2).

The basis for resisting a preoccupation with money is the confidence that "the Lord is my helper and I shall not fear" (13:6b). Hebrews earlier spoke of the way Moses and others proved fearless and were vindicated by God (11:23, 27, 32–35). Yet to declare, "What can a human being do to me?" (13:6c) requires a faith that runs counter to appearances, for many of God's people *had been* afflicted by human beings: Abel was slain (11:4), the Israelites were enslaved (11:25), the righteous were tortured and killed (11:35–38), and Jesus was crucified (12:1–4). The implication is that God does not exempt his people from suffering at the hands of others, but brings them through suffering to everlasting life (2:10; 5:7–10).

c. Leaders and Teachings (13:7–9)

The exhortation to "remember your leaders, who spoke to you the word of God" (13:7a) draws on the community's own experience. On leadership see pp. 75–76. Perhaps surprisingly, the leaders are not named, and the general reference invites listeners to supply the names of various leaders from the community's history. The leaders are, however, identified by their function: speakers of the word of God. Hebrews affirms that God spoke to the community (1:2), but not in an unmediated way. Human messengers brought the divine message that engendered a community of faith (2:3–4). Therefore, in considering the leaders, one must consider their message, which is the center from which faith and community life come.

---

[472]Seneca, *Ep.* 94.26; cf. S. Treggiari, "Roman Marriage," *CAM* 3.1343–54, esp. 1351; W. A. Krenkel, "Prostitution," *CAM* 2.1291–97, esp. 1293.

The call to consider the outcome of their way of life (13:7b) implies that the leaders have died and that their deaths reflected their faith. Earlier the author told how Abraham, Sarah, and others died in faith even though they had not received what was promised (11:13; cf. 11:20–22).[473] It is not clear that the community's leaders were martyred, although they may well have endured the persecution mentioned in 10:32–34. What is important, however, is not the mode of death, but their faithfulness, which is worthy of imitation (13:7c). Imitating people means not only heeding their words but also following the faith expressed in their lives (NOTE on 6:12).

To say that "Jesus Christ is yesterday and today the same—and forever" (13:8) underscores that the faith of past leaders has continuing value. Since Jesus endures, faith in him can endure. The reference to Christ remaining the same points to his constancy or faithfulness in changing situations (p. 105) and provides a reason for listeners to heed the word spoken by past leaders (13:7) rather than to be carried away by other teachings (13:9). Whether the author composed this statement or drew it from tradition, it functions like other early Christian confessions, which summarized a basic conviction in brief, memorable form. Socially, one function of a confession was to provide a point of unity for a group. Individual members of a group might elaborate the confession somewhat differently, but all must be able to affirm the confession itself. A second function was to distinguish one group from another. Those who could not affirm the confession distinguished themselves from those who did affirm it.[474]

The counterpart to the affirmation of Christ's constancy is the warning not to be carried off by all sorts of strange teachings (13:9). The author speaks broadly, deeming "strange" whatever draws people away from their confession.[475] Some maintain that the warning about foods (13:9b) and those who serve in the tent (13:10) must mean that the author opposes specifically Jewish teachings. Although the imagery is vague, one might argue that the listeners would have understood it because they were closer to the situation (Lane). A more plausible view, however, is that the statement issues a more general warning against false teachings. Such warnings were commonplace in NT letters.[476] Earlier, the author generalized when commenting about foods (NOTE on 13:9), and here he generalizes from service in the sacred tent to life in an earthly city (13:12–14). The community for which Hebrews was written defined itself in a complex way in relation to Greco-Roman culture and the Jewish subculture (pp. 76–79). This passage provides a literary contrast rather than a clear critique of specific opponents (NOTE on 13:10), allowing listeners to apply the warning to multiple situations.

---

[473]Interest in the connection between people's lives and their deaths is evident in the many texts written about the deaths of famous people (Berger, "Hellenistischen," 1257–59).

[474]See 1 Cor 12:1–3; 1 John 4:1–3. On the functions of confessions see Dunn, *Unity*, 33–59.

[475]Christians are to welcome strangers, but not strange teachings (NOTE on 13:9). Openness to foreigners expresses faith, but openness to foreign doctrines erodes faith. On the confession see pp. 126–27.

[476]Rom 16:17–18; 1 Tim 6:20–21; Tit 3:9–11; 2 Pet 3:16. See Berger, "Hellenistischen," 1349.

Literary considerations also provide a way to consider the comment about the heart that is made firm by grace, rather than by foods that are not beneficial (13:9b). The author has spoken of two possible directions for the human heart. On the negative side, he used Ps 95 to warn about the heart becoming hardened by sin and unbelief (Heb 3:8, 12, 15; 4:7, 12) so that it strays from God (3:10). On the positive side, he reiterated the promise made in Jer 31, which said that God would make a new covenant by writing his laws upon human hearts (Heb 8:10; 10:16) so that people could draw near to him with a true heart (10:22). The grace that makes the heart firm in relation to God comes through Christ (2:9; 4:16) and the Spirit (10:29). Christ's death cleanses the conscience and heart, inaugurating the new covenant (10:22). This message is the food that nurtures and benefits listeners (5:11–14); and any teaching that impedes this message is, by definition, not beneficial.

38. Christian Sacrifice (13:10–21)

13 [10]We have an altar from which those who serve in the tent have no authority to eat. [11]For the bodies of the animals, whose blood is brought into the sanctuary by the high priest as a sacrifice for sin, are burned outside the camp. [12]So
too Jesus, in order to sanctify the people by means of his own blood, suffered outside the gate. [13]Therefore, let us go out to him outside the camp, bearing denunciation for him, [14]for we have here no abiding city, but seek the one that is
to come.

[15]Through him, therefore, let us continually offer to God a sacrifice of praise,
that is, the fruit of lips that confess his name. [16]Do not neglect acts of kindness
and fellowship, for such sacrifices are pleasing to God. [17]Heed your leaders and
yield to them, for they are keeping watch for the sake of your souls as those who
must give an account for them, so that they might do this with joy and not with
groaning, for this would be unprofitable for you. [18]Keep praying for us, for we are
persuaded that we have a good conscience, desiring to act rightly in all things.
[19]I especially urge you to do this in order that I might be restored to you sooner.

[20]And may the God of peace, who by the blood of the eternal covenant
brought up from the dead the great shepherd of the sheep, our Lord Jesus, [21]pro-
vide you with everything good that you might accomplish his will, accomplishing in us that which is pleasing in his sight through Jesus Christ, to whom be
glory forever. Amen.

NOTES

13:10. *We have an altar.* "We have" echoes earlier confessional statements (4:14; 6:19; 8:1; 10:19). Several interpretations of the "altar" have been proposed, of which the first is preferable:

(**a**) The cross or sacrificial death of Christ. Hebrews uses metonymy to transfer the term "altar" (13:10) from the sanctuary to the place where carcasses were burned "outside the camp" on the Day of Atonement (13:11) and finally to Christ's suffering "outside the gate" (13:12). The "altar" is not only Golgotha. Through synecdoche, in which the part stands for the whole, the "altar" encompasses multiple dimensions of Christ's death (Attridge; Bénétreau; F. F. Bruce; Grässer; P. E. Hughes; Lane; Lindars, "Rhetorical," 389; Isaacs, "Hebrews," 280).

(**b**) Heavenly sanctuary. Some suggest that "we have an altar" recalls that "we have a high priest" in the heavenly sanctuary (8:1). Those who serve in the earthly tent (13:10b) do not "eat" from this altar (13:10c) because "foods" (13:9b) belong to the lower, material order (9:10), while grace (13:9) comes from heaven (4:14; Filson, *Yesterday*, 48–50; Thompson, *Beginnings*, 146; Laub, *Bekenntnis*, 271–72.) A problem with this view is that Hebrews does not suggest that the heavenly sanctuary contained an altar of sacrifice. An incense altar (*thymiatērion*) is mentioned in 9:4, but 13:10 refers to an altar (*thysiastērion*) on which victims can be offered (7:13). Such an altar stood in the sanctuary's outer courtyard, not in the inner court.

(**c**) The Eucharist. Some who identify the Christian "altar" with the Eucharist interpret the text positively, relating the "altar" to "foods" that convey "grace" (13:9) in the Lord's Supper (Haimo; Theophylact; Lombard; Lapide). The Eucharist enabled Christians to taste God's word (6:5) and to participate in Christ's death, just as priests partook of the sacrifices made on the altar (1 Cor 10:18; Hegermann; Strobel; Andriessen, "L'eucharistie"; Ruager, "Wir"; Swetnam, "Christology," 74; deSilva, *Despising*, 275; Vanhoye, *Old Testament*, 228–29). Others read Heb 13:9–10 as a critique of eucharistic practice, pointing out that the victims offered on the Day of Atonement were burned, but not eaten, so that Christ's death cannot be connected with any meal, including the Eucharist (Moffatt; Braun; Dunnill, *Covenant*, 240–41). Nevertheless, there is little evidence that the term "altar" was used for the Eucharist until the second century (Klauck, "*Thysiastērion*"), and the silence about the Eucharist elsewhere in Hebrews makes it unlikely that 13:10 refers to it (see pp. 127–29).

from which those who serve in the tent. Two types of questions arise from this evocative expression:

(**a**) Jews or Christians? The expression probably refers to those who minister on the basis of the Mosaic Law. Levitical priests serve in the earthly tent (8:5) where daily service occurs in the forecourt or "first tent" (9:6). Some argue that the "tent" is the heavenly tent in which Christ ministers (8:1; 9:13), so that this expression refers to those who "serve" (12:28) on the basis of what Christ has done (8:1; Grässer; Laub, *Bekenntnis*, 271). Moreover, Christians are not yet in the heavenly sanctuary, but are called to persevere in the hope of entering it (6:19–20; 10:19–22). Christians "serve" a living God on the basis of Christ's entry into the heavenly tent (9:11–14), but their "service" takes place on earth (12:28–13:6).

(**b**) Real opponents or literary foil? The Mosaic Tabernacle ceased to function centuries before Christ, so that no one literally served in the "tent" at the time that Hebrews was composed. Some take this as a metaphor for those who follow

Jewish Law, since "serve" can apply to all worshipers (9:9; 10:2), and the regulations for service in the tent pertain to "food, drink, and various ablutions," all of which are part of Jewish practice generally (NOTE on 9:10). Thus, Hebrews might be warning against seeking security in Jewish practice at the expense of Christian identity.

Nevertheless, the text can better be taken as creating a foil (Thompson, *Beginnings*, 145). The author says little about opponents of the community. The reference to "all sorts of strange teachings" is general (NOTE on 13:9), and the clearest opponents of the community are the people—apparently non-Jews (pp. 67–72)—who reproach, dispossess, and imprison Christians (10:32–34; 13:3, 13). Echoes of the community's situation in the comments about Moses being denounced for Christ suggest that the principal threat came from governmental officials, not the Law (11:24–27). Hebrews identifies the tent not so much with the Law as with the "camp," that is, the earthly "city" in which Jesus' followers are denounced (13:13–14).

have no authority to eat. Mosaic Law authorized priests to eat from certain sacrifices (Lev 6:16; 7:6), but not to eat from the Christian altar. Some propose that the reason is that no one eats from a sacrifice of atonement. As under the old covenant, where the victims' bodies were burned (Heb 13:11; cf. Lev 6:30; 16:27), no one eats of Christ's atoning sacrifice (Lane; Braun). Nevertheless, the emphasis here is on "authority." People partake of Christ's death through faith based on the new covenant, not on the authority of the old covenant and its institutions.

13:11. *For the bodies of the animals, whose blood is brought into the sanctuary.* On the Day of Atonement see NOTES on Heb 9:7.

are burned outside the camp. The Israelite camp was arranged in concentric rings of holiness (p. 120). Unclean things were taken outside its boundaries (Exod 29:14; Lev 9:11; 16:27).

13:12. *So too Jesus, in order to sanctify the people by means of his own blood.* See pp. 119–21 and NOTE on 9:14.

suffered outside the gate. Hebrews might presuppose familiarity with traditions that recounted how Jesus was "led out" to be crucified near a road (Matt 27:31; Mark 15:20; cf. Luke 23:26) that was "near the city" of Jerusalem (John 19:20). Alternatively, the author might be stating a commonplace, since executions were usually conducted outside a city according to Jewish (Lev 24:14, 23; Num 15:35–36; 1 Kings 21:13; Acts 7:58) and Roman practice. As a convict you must "trudge out beyond the gate . . . arms outspread, with your gibbet on your shoulders" (Plautus, *Braggart Warrior* 2.4.6–7 [359–60]). Crucifixions were done publicly to deter crime (Quintilian, *Declamationes* 274; Josephus, *J.W.* 5.289, 449–51; R. E. Brown, *Death*, 2.912). See pp. 108–9.

13:13. *Therefore, let us go out to him outside the camp.* The "camp" has been interpreted in a number of ways, of which the fourth is preferable:

(a) Material securities. To leave the camp might mean relinquishing material securities for a transcendent hope (13:14). Some compare the idea to Philo, who said that when Moses pitched the tent "outside the camp," he rejected bodily passion to embrace virtue (*Alleg. Interp.* 2.54–55; 3.46; *Worse* 160; *Giants* 54; *Drunkenness* 99–101; cf. 2 *Clem.* 5:1; 6:5; Erasmus, *Paraphrase*; Thompson, *Beginnings*, 147–49; Lührmann, "Hohepriester"). Unlike Philo, however, Hebrews stresses that leaving the camp means serving others on earth, despite reproach from society (H.-F. Weiss).

(b) The realm of the sacred. If the previous view called listeners to renounce the world, this one calls them to embrace it. Since Jesus' sacrifice took place in the unclean sphere outside the camp (Lev 16:28) rather than in the clean area of the Tabernacle, listeners are to leave the security of ritual in order to serve in the world (H. Koester, "Outside"; P. E. Hughes; Trudinger, "Gospel"). The problem with this view is that Jesus' blood "sanctifies" people and sets them apart from the unclean world (Heb 13:12) so that they may pursue holiness and avoid defilement (12:10, 14).

(c) Jewish practices. Many observe that "camp" is parallel to "tent" (13:10) and that the "tent" is associated with Jewish practices pertaining to food and ablutions (9:10; 13:9). Some propose that listeners might have thought that they could escape society's reproach by blending into the Jewish community, which might account for the critique of the Law in Heb 8–10 (F. F. Bruce; P. E. Hughes; Loader, *Sohn*, 181). A weakness in this view is that Abraham "set out" from his land in the hope of the city to come (11:8–16) and Moses left the royal court to bear reproach for Christ (11:24–26)—themes that appear in 13:13–14—but Hebrews says nothing about either figure leaving behind Jewish practice.

(d) The "city." For Hebrews "outside the camp" (13:11) means "outside the gate" (13:12), that is, outside the "city" (13:14). Thinking about the "camp" as urban life, with all its complexity, allows us to combine elements from the other three proposals. First, an earthly city provides opportunities for wealth and prestige, but Moses renounced these in order to suffer with the people of God (11:24–26), and Christians must be prepared to do the same (10:32–34; 13:5–6). Second, Hebrews does not call listeners to embrace what is unclean, but it does call them to minister to strangers, the afflicted, and prisoners, who live outside the mainstream of urban life (13:1–3). Third, some listeners might have sought to avoid "reproach" for Christ by observing Jewish practices as noted under (c), but this is only one aspect of the situation, since "going out" includes the positive summons to faithfulness and service.

bearing denunciation for him. Listeners are denounced "for Christ" and "like Christ" (NOTES on 10:33; 11:26).

13:14. *for we have here no abiding city, but seek the one that is to come.* Those "from Italy" (13:24) might have heard Rome called "the eternal city" (Ovid, *Fasti* 3.72; Wengst, *Pax Romana*, 142). For Hebrews the only city that abides is the heavenly one (12:22–24).

13:15. *Through him, therefore, let us continually offer to God a sacrifice of praise.* As priests offered sacrifices to God on behalf of worshipers, Christians offer praises to God through Christ. In some passages a "sacrifice of praise" signifies an animal or grain offering (Lev 7:12, 13, 15), but other texts, like Heb

13:15, speak of sacrifices that are verbal (Pss 50:14, 23; 51:15–17; 69:30–31; cf. 107:22).

the fruit of lips that confess his name. The listeners' community offered, not the fruit of the fields, but the fruit of their lips. Used in Hos 14:2 (14:3 LXX) for a response to God's removal of sin, the "fruit of lips" is a response to the sanctifying effect of Christ's death (Heb 13:12; cf. 6:7; 12:11). Although Hebrews spoke previously of a "confession" centered on Christ (3:1; 4:14), here "his name" seems to be God's name (cf. Pss 52:9 [53:8 LXX]; 99:3 [98:3]; cf. *Pss. Sol.* 15:2–3).

13:16. *Do not neglect acts of kindness and fellowship.* The word for "acts of kindness" (*eupoiia*) is rare, but the idea is not (1 Pet 2:15, 20; 3:6, 17; 4:19; Acts 4:9). Some listeners were faithful in serving others (Heb 6:10), while others tended to neglect good works (10:24; cf. 13:1–6). "Acts of kindness" build up "fellowship," but the idea that kindness is extended only to the Christian community (Schenk, "Paränese," 78) is not warranted. See NOTES on 12:14 and 13:2.

for such sacrifices are pleasing to God. Earlier Hebrews said that God was not pleased with animal sacrifices (10:5, 8), but obedience in the form of praise and service is pleasing to him (12:28; 13:21).

13:17. *Heed your leaders and yield to them.* "Heeding" means taking directives (Rom 2:8; Jas 3:3). "Yielding" assumes that there is a difference of viewpoint in which one party must give way (cf. 4 Macc 6:35). Some take the verb in a rigorous sense for the kind of obedience that would suit a servant or child (Philo, *Moses* 1.156; *Special Laws* 2.232; 4 Macc 10:13; cf. Thurén, *Lobopfer*, 205–6), but this seems overstated. On "leaders" (Heb 13:7, 17, 24), see pp. 75–76.

for they are keeping watch for the sake of your souls. "Watching" (*agrypnein*) often indicated wakefulness or sleeplessness (BAGD). It is not a technical term for oversight of a community, in contrast to *episkopein*, but was commonly used in exhortations to watch with a view to the coming judgment (Mark 13:33; Luke 21:36; cf. Eph 6:18). On the "soul" see NOTE on 10:39.

as those who must give an account for them. Hebrews assumes that everyone must give an account to God (4:13; cf. Matt 12:36; Rom 14:12; 1 Pet 4:5), but leaders have a special responsibility to do so (cf. Herm. *Vis.* 3.9.10).

so that they might do this with joy and not with groaning. Doing "this" might mean "keeping watch" with joy (Hegermann), but it more probably means "giving an account" with joy. "Joy" comes from the hope of the blessings promised by God (10:34; 12:2; cf. Phil 4:1; 3 John 4).

for this would be unprofitable for you. This is understated, since the consequences of unfaithfulness are actually terrifying (10:31; 12:29).

13:18. *Keep praying for us.* The author sometimes uses the first person singular (11:32; 13:19, 22–23). The plural could be formulaic (Attridge), but he was writing in the company of other Christians (13:24). Requests for prayer were common at the end of NT letters (Eph 6:19; Col 4:3; 1 Thess 5:25; 2 Thess 3:1).

for we are persuaded that we have a good conscience. Insistence on one's "good conscience" often means that one's integrity is being challenged: "Keep your conscience clear, so that, when you are maligned, those who abuse you for your good conduct in Christ may be put to shame" (1 Pet 3:16; cf. Acts 23:1; 24:16; 1 Tim 1:19). On conscience see NOTES on Heb 9:9; 10:2.

desiring to act rightly in all things. The author does not claim to be without fault, but insists that his desires are for right conduct (cf. 13:7).

13:19. *I especially urge you to do this in order that I might be restored to you sooner.* The hope of being "restored" implies that the author had previously been associated with the listeners' community. Reasons for the current separation are not stated, but he may have been forcibly detained, since his insistence on a "clean conscience" (13:18) suggests that he faced opposition. Being restored would mean being released and allowed to return to the community (cf. *P. Oxy.* #38.12). The passive voice assumes that restoration will be God's response to the listeners' prayers (cf. Phlm 22). References to future visits (Rom 15:22, 24, 29; 1 Tim 3:14; 2 Tim 4:9; Tit 3:12) and to the hope of coming "quickly" were common in letters (White, *Light*, ##56.14; 57.23; 91.3). The shift from the plural in Heb 13:18 to the singular in 13:19 might be a stylistic variation (cf. 2 Cor 8:3, 4, 7, 8; Col 3:3–4), or it might reflect the fact that the author is writing in company with others (Heb 13:24).

13:20. *And may the God of peace.* This resembles Pauline benedictions (Rom 15:33; 16:20; 2 Cor 13:11; Phil 4:9; 1 Thess 5:23). "Peace" does not so much describe God's character as it points to the outcome of his work, e.g., when Paul says that the "God of peace will shortly crush Satan" (Rom 16:20), peace is the result of conflict, not the absence of conflict. Here God brings peace by bringing about those things that are pleasing in his sight (Heb 13:21), which includes peaceful relations among people (12:14; cf. 7:2; 11:31).

who by the blood of the eternal covenant. The OT used "eternal covenant" for God's covenants with Noah (Gen 9:16), Abraham (17:7, 13; 1 Chron 16:17; Ps 105:10), and David (2 Sam 23:5), and for statutes concerning the Sabbath (Exod 31:16) and the sanctuary (Lev 24:8). For Hebrews, however, the "eternal covenant" was established through Christ's death (Heb 7:22; 8:6; 9:15), while the Mosaic covenant was passing away (8:13). The OT provides some precedent for thinking of the new covenant as the eternal one, since the prophets promised that God would make an "eternal covenant" that would bring salvation (Isa 55:3; 61:8; Jer 32:40 [39:40 LXX]; 50:5; Ezek 16:60) and the "peace" of which Heb 13:20 speaks (Ezek 37:26). On covenants see pp. 112–14.

brought up from the dead. Some spoke of God raising the dead generally (Acts 26:8; *Shemoneh Esreh* 2 [Schürer et al., *History*, 2.456]), but Christian sources often spoke specifically of God raising Jesus (Rom 4:24; 8:11; 2 Cor 4:14; Gal 1:1). Here Hebrews uses the term "bring up" (*anagein*) rather than "raise" (*egeirein*, 11:19) or "resurrection" (*anastasis*, 6:2; 11:35). The LXX speaks of God bringing people up from Hades (1 Sam 2:6; Tob 13:2; Wis 16:13). Hebrews could be recalling how God "brought up from the land" Moses, "the shepherd of the sheep" (Isa 63:11 LXX; Theophylact), thereby comparing Jesus' exaltation to deliverance from Egypt (Exod 33:12; Num 14:13; 20:5; cf. §8 COMMENT *c*; Loader, *Sohn*, 49–54). On death and afterlife see NOTE on 6:2.

the great shepherd of the sheep, our Lord Jesus. "Shepherd" was metaphor for leadership (Jer 23:1–4; Ezek 34:1–6; Epictetus, *Disc.* 3.22.35) and messianic hope (Ezek 34:23; *Pss. Sol.* 17:40). Christians used the image for Jesus (1 Pet 2:25; John 10:11; Matt 26:31; Rev 7:17) and may have called Jesus the "great" shepherd to distinguish him from other leaders of God's people (cf. 1 Pet 5:4), just as he is the unique and "great" high priest (Heb 4:14; 10:21).

13:21. *provide you with everything good that you might accomplish his will.* Important MSS (P^{46} ℵ D* Ψ) include only the word "good" (*agathō*), which can be construed as neuter (NASB; NRSV; NAB2; REB). God provides the good things needed for daily life as well, but "good" refers especially to salvation (9:11; 10:1). Many MSS include the word "work" (*ergon*, C D^2 0243 etc.; cf. KJV; NJB), so that "good" refers to work that follows God's will (13:21b), as in 2 Thess 2:17. This word was probably added to clarify the text.

accomplishing in us that which is pleasing in his sight through Jesus Christ. God works *en hēmin*, which can be rendered "in us" (NASB; NIV; NJB; REB), since the new covenant affects the heart, mind, and conscience (8:10; 9:14; 10:16). The same expression can also be translated "among us" (NRSV), since community life is part of God's work (10:25; 13:1, 16). Service "pleasing" to God (12:28; 13:16) includes the activities mentioned in 12:28–13:19. The reading "in you" (*en hymin*, C P Ψ etc.; NRSVfn) probably arose as an attempt to put the text in the second person consistently (*TCGNT*, 676–77).

to whom be glory forever. Some understand that here God is given glory forever, since God is the primary actor in 13:20–21 (cf. Rom 11:36; Gal 1:5; Phil 4:20; 1 Tim 1:17; Lane; Ellingworth; H.-F. Weiss). Others think that Christ is given the glory since "Jesus Christ" is the nearest antecedent to the pronoun (Attridge; cf. 2 Tim 4:18; 2 Pet 3:18; Rev 1:6). Both views are plausible.

Amen. This Hebrew word was sometimes translated "may it be so" (*genoito*) in the LXX, but it was transliterated into Greek and widely used in the early church. It often appears at the end of doxologies (e.g., Rom 11:36; 16:27; Gal 1:5; Phil 4:20).

COMMENT[477]

A haunting reference to Christ's suffering outside the gate and a call for others to follow in the path that he set continues Hebrews' appeal for service pleasing to God (§36 COMMENT). Familiar themes are repeated: service in the tent, the high priest's offering on the Day of Atonement, the sanctifying effect of Jesus' blood, the city to come, and the blood of the covenant. Yet into this collage of

---

[477]On 13:10–21 see Daly, *Christian Sacrifice*, 281–85; Ferguson, "Spiritual Sacrifice," 1162–64; Fernández, "La vida sacerdotal"; Filson, *Yesterday*; Grässer, *Aufbruch*, 251–64, 295–302; Isaacs, "Hebrews 13:9–16"; idem, *Sacred*, 205–19; Jewett, "Form"; Klauck, "*Thysiastērion*"; H. Koester, "Outside"; Lührmann, "Hohepriester"; Schenk, "Paränese"; Theobald, "Wir haben hier"; Thompson, *Beginnings*, 141–51; Thurén, *Lobopfer*; idem, "Opfer"; Trudinger, "Gospel"; Walker, "Jerusalem"; idem, *Jesus*, 216–21. On leaders see pp. 75–76; on 13:10 and the Lord's Supper see pp. 127–29; on the earthly Jesus see pp. 106–9.

images the author brings new elements, such as the listeners' "altar," movement outside the camp, and Jesus as a shepherd. The result is a complex and allusive passage that engages listeners more by images that stimulate the imagination than by a logical argument.

Structurally, the material falls into three parts: **(a)** The community's relationship to society is the focus of part 1 (13:10–14). The comment about those who have no authority to eat from the listeners' altar in 13:10 develops the idea of foods that do not benefit people in 13:9,[478] but now the author creates a multilayered effect by declaring that as sacrificial victims were taken outside the camp and as Jesus suffered outside the gate, listeners must go outside the mainstream of their city for the sake of Christ. **(b)** Relationships within the community are the focus of part 2 (13:15–19), which repeats the themes of making offerings to God, serving others, and heeding the community's leaders, all of which appeared earlier in the peroration (12:28–13:9). **(c)** The community's relationship to God is central to part 3 (13:20–21), where the author commends the listeners into God's hands. This short prayer brings the peroration and the speech itself to its conclusion by asking God to bring about the kind of service that will please him.

a. Bearing the Denunciation of Christ (13:10–14)

Hebrews distinguishes the listeners' community from the wider society by declaring that "we have an altar" (13:10a). Jews considered the altar in Jerusalem to be the only appropriate place for sacrifice—although it is unclear whether that altar still stood when Hebrews was written (pp. 52–53)—and sacrifices were offered at many places in Italy (13:24) and elsewhere in the Greco-Roman world. Given only what the eye could see, Christians possessed no altar. But rather than declaring that altars are irrelevant, Hebrews says that Christians have an altar—though one apparent only through faith (cf. 11:1). The altar has two aspects of meaning (Aquinas, *Ad Heb.* §744). In one sense, the altar is the place where Jesus was crucified (13:12). The community meets at this altar, not by assembling at Golgotha, but by gathering for the proclamation of Christ's self-sacrifice. In a second sense, the listeners' altar (*thysiastērion*) stands wherever they offer through Christ their own sacrifices (*thysia*) of praise to God and of kindness toward others (13:15–16).

Insisting that those who serve in the tent have no authority to eat from the listeners' altar (13:10) gives the impression of indignation, which was common in perorations,[479] yet the remark has more to do with literary contrast than with the community's opponents (NOTE on 13:10). Drawing on imagery from OT depictions of the Tabernacle rather than from first-century Temple practice, He-

---

[478]Many interpreters put no break between 13:9 and 13:10, but treat 13:7–17 (or through 13:18 or 19) as a unit (Vanhoye, *La structure*, 211–15; Attridge; Bénétreau; Casalini; H.-F. Weiss; cf. F. F. Bruce; Hegermann; Kistemaker; Wilson). Others recognize 13:10–16 as a subsection of the larger unit (Thurén, *Lobopfer*, 74–104; Grässer; D. Guthrie; Hagner; Lane).

[479]See Cicero, *De inventione rhetorica* 1.52–53 §§98, 100; Lausberg, *Handbook* §438. On the warnings against opponents in various NT letters see Berger, "Hellenistische," 1349.

brews contrasts two types of serving (*latreuein*). On the one hand, Levitical priests, who serve in the tent (13:10b; cf. 8:5; 9:6), offer sacrifices that do not make the conscience complete, but that deal with food, drink, and ablutions. On the other hand, service that pleases God (12:28) involves caring for other Christians, strangers, and prisoners, remaining faithful in marriage, refraining from greed, and imitating those who taught and lived faithfully (13:1–9). The listeners serve in this way in response to Christ's self-sacrifice (9:14).

A parallel description of the Day of Atonement ritual (13:11) and Christ's passion (13:12) issues into a call for listeners to follow Christ outside the camp (13:13). The mention of the high priest bringing the blood of animals into the inner chamber of the sanctuary recalls 9:7, but the author now adds the observation that the bodies of the sacrificial victims were burned outside the Israelite camp. Christ paralleled this movement by going out of the city in the course of his self-sacrifice (13:12).[480] The movement is the opposite of earlier references to Christ, in which he entered the inner chamber of the sanctuary, but only together do the movements *into* the sanctuary and *out of* the camp capture the paradox of Christian life.[481]

Theological Movement of Faith
Hebrews 9–10

Social Movement of Faith
Hebrews 13

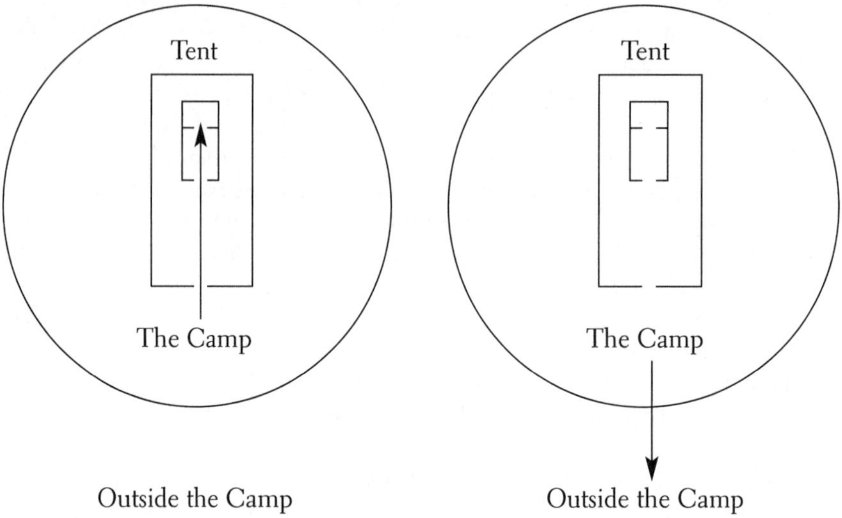

[480]The Day of Atonement sacrifice *concluded* with the victims' bodies being taken outside the camp, while Christ's sacrifice *began* with his being taken out of the city. The point of similarity is taking victims outside the camp or city.

[481]The call to follow Christ into the sanctuary frames the second major part of Hebrews (6:19–20; 10:19–22). The call to go out from one's place of residence in obedience to God is prominent in the third part of Hebrews (11:1–12:27).

People do not simply go out, but go out to Christ (13:13a). Since Christ is no longer physically accessible, going out to him is essentially a movement of faith. At the same time, going out is not defined by a location, but by a social reality: outside the camp (13:13b) is wherever one is denounced for Christ (13:13c). People denounced Christians in order to dissuade others from adopting their beliefs (§28 COMMENT *a*). According to Hebrews, people do not bear denunciation by resigning themselves to it, but by offering praises to God through Christ: serving the Christian community and caring for strangers, prisoners, and the afflicted, despite animosity from others (13:1–6).[482]

To say that the listeners have here no abiding city (13:14a) in one sense simply recognizes that their social position is tenuous. Such insecurity might make some give up their faith claims in order to conform to the norms of the wider society. Hebrews has argued, however, that no earthly city can provide true security, for earth itself will be shaken by the voice of God (12:25–27). This reverses the perception of the situation. What is truly tenuous is not the listeners' social situation, but the situation of all earthly cities. God's people are perceived to be transients (11:13–16); earth itself is transient, and what is transient cannot be the basis or the object of enduring faith.

What will abide is the city that is to come (13:14b). Abraham lived as a resident alien in the hope of a future in God's city (11:10), and Moses abandoned the royal court to suffer with God's people in the hope of a future reward (11:24–26). Jesus endured the cross for the sake of joy in the presence of God (12:2), and the listeners' community previously suffered earthly loss in the hope of an abiding possession in heaven (10:32–34). Like these exemplars of faith, the listeners are called to resist despair, persevering in the confidence that God will be true to his promises (10:23; 11:11) and will bring them to the city where the saints and angels celebrate in the presence of God (12:22–24).[483]

b. Offering Praise and Acts of Kindness (13:15–19)

The paradox of Christian life is that while being reproached by others and lacking a secure place in an earthly city (13:13–14), the faithful continue offering praises to God through the altar of Christ's death (13:10a, 15a). If under the old covenant the Levitical priests "continually" offered sacrifices in the outer court (9:6), under the new covenant believers "continually" offer praise to God and confess his name (13:15). To say that Christians make offerings through Christ (13:15a) recognizes that no one directly approaches God, the consuming fire. Intercessions and praises are brought before God by Christ, the mediator (NOTE on 7:25).

The paradox continues as the author speaks of showing acts of kindness and fellowship despite reproach from others (13:16a). Like praise and confession,

---

[482]Hebrews summons listeners "out of the assimilation which conceals the Christian confession, which promises security without danger and peaceful enjoyment of life, but which rejects solidarity with the oppressed and thus denies the abused Christ" (Wengst, *Pax Romana*, 142).

[483]On the themes of 13:14 in devotional literature see p. 29. See also Grässer, *Aufbruch*, 251–64; Theobald, "Wir haben hier."

these actions are sacrifices pleasing to God (13:16b). The author is not spiritualizing the notion of sacrifice, since the listeners are to serve fellow Christians, strangers, prisoners, and the afflicted (13:1–3) in physical ways. Moreover, the sacrifices of praise and good works that Christians offer are not simple replacements for the blood sacrifices prescribed by the Law, but are tangible responses to the physical sacrifice of Christ's blood through crucifixion (NOTES and COMMENT on 9:11–14 and 10:1–18).

Remarks about the community's leaders (13:17) assume that speaking the word of God and exemplifying faith are central to leadership (13:7). Thus heeding and yielding to the leaders mean adhering to the word of God that they speak.[484] The rationale for this appeal first concerns what the leaders do *for* the listeners: they keep watch over the souls of those who are becoming neglectful of faith and community (13:17b; cf. 2:3; 5:11; 6:12; 10:25). Watching over souls involves tending the hope that anchors the soul to heaven (6:19) and fostering the perseverance that leads to salvation (10:39). Leaders are not expected to work in isolation, for the whole community is called to watchfulness against sin and bitterness (3:12; 12:15). Rather than stressing the listeners' accountability to the leaders, the author stresses the leaders' accountability to God (13:17c). If all people render account to God concerning themselves (4:12–13), leaders also render account to God concerning others, finding joy in the well-being of those in their care and groaning when some drift away (13:17d). What is at stake is not obedience for its own sake, but what is ultimately either beneficial or unprofitable for the listeners (13:17e; pp. 75–76).

Requests for prayer and remarks about prospects for a speedy visit, which were fairly common in letters (NOTES on 13:18–19), mark a gradual shift from a rhetorical to an epistolary style (§39 COMMENT). Although the request for prayers is general, the author implies that intercessions might speed his return to the community. By basing his request on a clear conscience and a desire to act rightly, he also suggests that challenges to his integrity contributed to his delay in coming to the listeners. The details of his situation remain unclear, but earlier remarks accented two dimensions of the listeners' situation. Socially, they are denounced because of their faith (10:33; 11:26; 13:13). Theologically, faith links them to Christ, who cleanses the conscience (9:14; 10:22) and gives them boldness before God and other people (3:6; 4:14). Therefore, a clean conscience enables them to maintain their integrity in the face of conflict.

c. The Benediction (13:20–21)

Having asked listeners to pray for him (13:18–19), the author now offers his own prayer for them (13:20–21). The prayer is a benediction, rather than the kind of

[484]Hebrews assumes that the leaders' integrity is not in question. Some later interpreters argued that 13:17 meant that Christians should obey a leader whose conduct is bad, but they should not accept bad teaching or imitate bad conduct (Chrysostom; Haimo, Theophylact; Erasmus, *Paraphrase*). Others insisted that faithless leaders were not to be obeyed (Calvin).

extended doxology (Rom 16:25–27) or declaration of what God will do (Phil 4:19–20; 1 Pet 5:10) that conclude some NT letters. The benedictions that conclude sections (Rom 15:5–6, 13; 1 Thess 3:11–13; 2 Thess 2:16–17; 3:5) and entire letters (1 Thess 5:23; 2 Thess 3:16) follow a conventional form but show considerable flexibility in vocabulary and content, which suggests that writers had the freedom to compose and adapt them.[485] In this benediction references to the covenant and to doing what is pleasing to God echo themes from other parts of Hebrews, whereas expressions like "the God of peace," "the Lord Jesus," and "the great shepherd," as well as the focus on Jesus' resurrection rather than on his exaltation to heaven appear only here in Hebrews. Since these elements are found in other Christian sources, the author might have been adapting early Christian tradition (NOTES on 13:20).

The concluding prayer recognizes God's role in bringing about the service to which the listeners are called. Even though God is a consuming fire and judge (12:29; 13:4), Hebrews can speak of the God of peace (13:20a), who has made an eternal covenant that brings peace by extending forgiveness for past sins and awakening new obedience (§21 COMMENT *b* and pp. 112–14).[486] Recalling that Jesus, the mediator of the covenant, was brought up from the dead recognizes that death is real, but not final. All people face death (9:27), but Hebrews has argued that the faithful need not be intimidated by its power (2:14–16), for bringing Jesus out of the realm of the dead anticipates the way that God will bring many sons and daughters to glory (2:10).

Calling Jesus the great shepherd of the sheep shifts the focus from Jesus' sacrificial death in the past to his leadership of a living community in the present (13:20d). Members of this community are to accomplish God's will (13:21) in a manner congruent with what Christ has already done (10:5–10). First, since God provided Jesus with the means to do his will by giving him a body (10:5), the author now asks that God give listeners the means to do his will by providing them with *everything* good (13:21a). Second, after Christ was given a body, he sacrificed himself for the sake of others (10:7, 9–10). Therefore, listeners who have received good things offer their own sacrifices of praise to God and acts of kindness to other people (13:15–16). These sacrifices, rather than burnt offerings (10:5–6), truly please God (12:28; 13:21c) according to Hebrews.[487] People carry out God's will only as God works within and among them (13:21b), yet rather than making human work unnecessary, God's action makes right human action possible (cf. Eph 2:8–10; Phil 2:12–13; see §21 COMMENT *b*).

[485]The benedictions regularly begin with the particle *de* ("and") and make use of verbs in the optative mood, which had generally fallen out of use, apart from certain formulas. The wish that God might "provide" (*katartisai*, Heb 13:21) includes the only optative verb in Hebrews. See Jewett, "Form"; Wiles, *Paul's*, 22–44.

[486]Some assume that speaking of peace seeks to ease tensions within the listeners' community (Sedulius Scotus; Ps.-Oecumenius; F. F. Bruce; Lane), but community conflict does not seem to be an issue here (P. E. Hughes; Ellingworth).

[487]Some note that Hebrews places God's will, rather than the human will, at the center of the benediction—and God's will is ultimately for human good (Aquinas, *Ad Heb.*; Theophylact; Luther, *Lectures*).

V. Epistolary Postscript

◆

39. Personal Remarks and Greetings (13:22–25)

13 22I urge you, brethren, bear with my word of exhortation, for I have written
to you briefly. 23Know that our brother Timothy has been released. If he comes
soon, I shall see you with him. 24Greet all your leaders and all the saints. Those
from Italy send you greetings. 25Grace be with you all.

NOTES

13:22. *I urge you, brethren.* The verb *parakalein* ("urge") was commonly used for requests in letters (Rom 15:30; 16:17; 1 Cor 16:15; MM, 484). Issuing an appeal rather than a command implies mutuality (J. Thomas, *EDNT* 3.26). On "brethren" see NOTE on 3:1.

bear with my word of exhortation. "Exhortation" (*paraklēsis*) was a term for Christian preaching, both public (1 Thess 2:3) and in the congregation (Rom 12:8; 1 Tim 4:13). *Paraklēsis* could include both comfort (2 Cor 1:3–7) and admonition (Acts 15:31). Whether sharp or gentle, many exhortations were designed to encourage people to persevere in difficult circumstances. "Words of exhortation" were spoken to promote faithfulness and courage (1 Macc 10:24; 2 Macc 7:24; 15:11; cf. Rom 15:4). On the "word of exhortation" in worship settings see pp. 80–82.

for I have written to you briefly. Hebrews does not seem brief when compared to the Pauline letters, most of which are much shorter than Hebrews. "Brief" might better describe a short speech (Lucian, *Toxaris*, 57–61), the five chapters of 1 Peter (1 Pet 5:12) or the letters of Ignatius (Ign. *Rom.* 8:2; *Pol.* 7:3). Therefore, some propose that "briefly" applies only to Heb 13 (Buchanan; D. Guthrie; Trudinger, "KAI"). Yet the author seems to call his whole speech brief. By way of comparison, 2 Maccabees and Barnabas are considered brief, even though they are longer than Hebrews (2 Macc 2:31–32; *Barn.* 1:5).

13:23. *Know that our brother Timothy.* The name "Timothy" was not uncommon in antiquity (e.g., 1 Macc 5:6; 2 Macc 8:30; Dittenberger, *OGIS* II 584), but the Timothy who is consistently mentioned in early Christian sources was Paul's coworker (1 Thess 1:1; 2 Cor 1:1; Phil 1:1; Col 1:1; 2 Thess 1:1; Phlm 1; 1 Tim 1:2; 2 Tim 1:2). Acts relates that Timothy had a Greek father and a Jewish Christian mother and that Paul circumcised Timothy (Acts 16:1–3). Yet Paul calls Timothy "our brother" when writing to Gentile Christian congregations (1 Thess 3:2; 2 Cor 1:1; Phlm 1; cf. Rom 16:21; 1 Cor 4:17). Timothy came from

Asia Minor and accompanied Paul to Macedonia and Greece (Acts 16:1–2; 18:5; 1 Thess 3:2; 1 Cor 4:17). He returned with Paul to Troas (Acts 20:4), but nothing more is known about his travels. The Pastoral Epistles associate him with Ephesus (1 Tim 1:3).

has been released. This could mean that Timothy had simply departed from the place where he was (Acts 13:3; 15:30, 33; 28:25), but it more probably means "released" from custody (Matt 27:15, 17, 21, 26; John 18:39; 19:10; Acts 3:13; 16:35–36; 26:32; 28:18). The NT does not mention an imprisonment of Timothy. He accompanied Paul and Silas to Philippi, but was not said to have been imprisoned along with them (Acts 16:6–40; 1 Thess 2:2). The Prison Epistles mention Timothy as a cosender (Phil 1:1; Phlm 1; Col 1:1), but it is not clear whether Timothy was imprisoned or whether he simply had access to Paul.

If he comes soon, I shall see you with him. Mentioning future visits was common in ancient letters. Although such visits could be threatening, the prospect of personal contact was often encouraging (Phlm 22; Col 4:8; White, *Light*, ##56.13–14; 57.22–24; 92.12; 105.40).

13:24. *Greet all your leaders and all the saints.* A general request for recipients to greet others was common in letters of this period: "Greet all your people" (*P. Oxy.* #1061.24). "Greet all our friends, each by name" (*P. Mich.* #476.30–31). Similar requests appear in the NT (1 Thess 5:26; Phil 4:21a; cf. Rom 16:15; 2 Cor 13:12a; Col 4:15). On the leaders see pp. 75–76.

Those from Italy send you greetings. It was common to include greetings from a third party in letters of this period (e.g., *P. Oxy.* #1061.25; cf. Rom 16:21–23; 1 Cor 16:19–20; 2 Cor 13:12b; Phil 4:21b–22; Col 4:14; Phlm 23–24; 1 Pet 5:13). "From Italy" has been taken in two ways, the first of which is preferred by most scholars:

(**a**) Those who came from Italy and were living somewhere else. The preposition *apo* could identify someone's place of origin. In Acts 18:2 it is used of Aquila and Priscilla who had come "from Italy" and were living in Corinth. Expressions like Jesus "from Nazareth" (Matt 21:11), Joseph "from Arimathea" (Mark 15:43), Philip "from Bethsaida" (John 1:44), and Nathanael "from Cana" (21:2) were used to identify people outside their hometowns. Similarly, "those from Cilicia and Asia" lived in Jerusalem (Acts 6:9; cf. 21:27; 24:18).

(**b**) Those who are still in Italy. The preposition *apo* could be used for someone's place of residence. Lazarus "from Bethany" was still in Bethany in John 11:1. Believers "from Joppa" were still in Joppa (Acts 10:23; cf. 17:13; 1 Macc 11:61–62; *P. Oxy.* #81.5; Spicq, *L'Épître*, 1.261–65). The subscriptions after 13:25, which identify Italy or Rome as the place of composition, show how later scribes interpreted this passage, but provide no independent information about the location (A P 81 104 1739 etc.).

No decision can rest on grammar alone, but combined evidence best supports Italy as the destination (pp. 49–50). In any case, the reference to Italy shows that the circle in which Hebrews originated included Christians who lived outside Palestine in the Greco-Roman world.

13:25. *Grace be with you all.* Greco-Roman letters commonly conclude with a form of "farewell" (*errōso*). Early Christian letters, however, concluded with "grace" (Tit 3:15; cf. 1 Tim 6:21; 2 Tim 4:22; 1 Thess 5:28; 2 Thess 3:18; Phil 4:23; Col 4:18) or a similar theological expression. Some MSS add "Amen" (א[2] A C etc.), but other MSS lack this word (P[46] א* I[vid] 6 33). It was probably added because "Amen" was commonly used in Christian worship.

COMMENT[488]

Concluding comments about a mutual friend, plans for a visit, and the exchange of greetings may have helped to shape the earliest readers' response to Hebrews by reaffirming the author's ties with them. Many interpreters have scrutinized these remarks for clues to the genre of Hebrews (pp. 80–81), the author's identity (pp. 42–45), and the location of the intended recipients (pp. 48–50). Others, however, put little weight on these verses, arguing that they were appended to Hebrews by someone other than the author. They point out that neither the opening nor body of Hebrews has the features of a letter, but 13:22–25 adheres to conventions for letter closings. Elsewhere, the author commonly refers to speaking, not writing, and rarely uses the first person singular, but the conclusion refers to what is "written" and repeatedly uses the first person singular. Since 13:23 mentions Timothy, some propose that the postscript was added to foster a general acceptance of Hebrews' as a Pauline letter.[489]

Despite these objections, 13:22–25 seem to be closely connected to the rest of Hebrews. There is a gradual shift in style, not an abrupt transition at 13:22. Early Christian letter closings included requests for prayers, references to future visits, and benedictions like those in 13:18–21, along with the kind of personal notes and greetings that appear in 13:22–25. The author shifted to the first person singular in 13:19, so that 13:22–25 simply continues this pattern.[490] Moreover, someone intending to give the impression of Pauline authorship would almost certainly have created for Hebrews an epistolary opening similar to those of Paul's letters and would probably have mentioned Paul's name, rather than merely implying a connection by referring to Timothy.

Personal remarks reinforce relationships between the author and intended recipients. Calling the recipients "brethren" (13:22) has the familiar tone of letters between family members.[491] The request that they bear with his words might suggest that the author expected listeners to resist his message because of its length, complexity (5:11), or severity (6:4–6; 10:26–31), but the request could also be a form of self-depreciation that invites recipients to reply that listening has in fact not been burdensome. Many understood that brevity helped to make lis-

---

[488]On 13:22–25 see Cuming, "Service-Endings"; Filson, *Yesterday*; Mullins, "Greeting"; Trudinger, "KAI"; Thurén, *Lobopfer*; Übelacker, *Hebräerbrief*, 197–223.

[489]Wrede, *Das literarische*, 39; Grässer; Schmithals, "Hebräerbrief."

[490]Vanhoye, *La structure*, 219; H.-F. Weiss, *Brief*, 760–61; Übelacker, *Hebräerbrief*, 197.

[491]For example, White, *Light*, ##64.1; 65.3; cf. Stowers, *Letter*, 72.

teners more receptive to a speaker's message,[492] but brevity is relative: it means "not saying less, but not saying more than the occasion demands" (Quintilian, *Inst.* 4.2.43). In saying that he has written briefly (Heb 13:22), the author does not simply state the obvious, but seeks to shape the perceptions of his listeners. Earlier, he indicated that there was "much" to say about his subject (5:11), but he recognized the need to limit his remarks on some topics (5:11–6:2; 9:5; 11:32). The same is true for the speech as a whole: the author apparently wants them to know that he has tried to be considerate by limiting his remarks, despite the breadth of his subject.

Calling what he is sending a word of exhortation (13:22a) also seeks to shape the way in which the message will be heard. Exhortation includes both admonishment and assurance or encouragement. It goes beyond advice, which someone might accept or reject, by calling people to pursue what is truly beneficial and to avoid what is harmful. Exhortation properly served the best interests of those to whom it was given.[493] Hebrews has given assurance that through God's promise and oath there is "strong encouragement [*paraklēsis*] to hold fast the hope that lies ahead" (6:18). At the same time, the author has given listeners the exhortation (*paraklēsis*) to accept God's discipline, even when it is painful (12:5), and has urged them to exhort (*parakalein*) others to stand firm against sin (3:13) and to perform good works (10:25). Both aspects of exhortation serve the same end: perseverance in the faith by which one receives life (10:38–39).

Sharing information about "our brother Timothy" (13:23a) and mentioning the prospect of a personal visit (13:23b) also builds relationships. According to ancient epistolary theory, "the letter was regarded as a substitute for the correspondents' actual conversation. But at best, the letter remained only a substitute, and consequently we can understand how a visit became the ideal means of enhancing the correspondents' relationship with each other" (White, *Light*, 202). The expectation of a future visit also heightens the need to take the message of Hebrews seriously, since recipients will soon have personal contact with its author.

The greetings enhance relationships not only between the author and intended readers but also between communities. The request to greet *all* your leaders and *all* the saints (13:24a) implies that Hebrews addressed only some of the Christians in the recipients' locale (pp. 73–75). For them to honor the request, they would have to contact others in the community—a helpful exercise in a situation where some were drifting away (10:25). Moreover, the author not only sent greetings *to* a wider community but also brought greetings *from* a wider community: those from Italy (13:24b). Greetings from third parties were not common in official letters, but were fairly common in letters between family members and friends (White, *Light*, 196, 202). Although Rome was the domi-

---

[492]See Cicero, *De inventione rhetorica* 1.20 §28; Quintilian, *Inst.* 4.2.43–44; Lausberg, *Handbook* §§294–99.

[493]On the philosophical tradition of exhortation see Malherbe, *Moral Exhortation*, 124–29; on epistolary exhortation see Stowers, *Letter*, 92–94.

nant city of the region, the general reference to Italy suggests that some might have come from other places, such as Puteoli (Acts 28:13–14). If those "from Italy" were living outside their homeland, they would presumably have understood the social implications of living as resident aliens, foreigners, and transients on earth (Heb 11:9, 13). One might also expect Italians to know how some were denounced for Christ in their homeland during the first century (10:33; 11:26; 13:13).[494] By attaching their greetings to Hebrews, the Italian Christians give tacit support to its message of hope in the city that is to come, in order to encourage another Christian community whose situation on earth is insecure (cf. 13:14).

The parting wish, "grace be with you," is similar to those found in other early Christian letters (NOTE on 13:25). Although conventional, the expression gains depth from the earlier parts of Hebrews. Christ's death on their behalf was a gift of grace (*charis*, 2:9), allowing them to approach God's throne of grace boldly (4:16). The author has warned them not to fall away from this grace (12:15), but to respond with thanks (*charis*, 12:28) from hearts that have been made firm by grace (13:9). In light of the speech as a whole, the concluding comment extends not merely the author's own good wishes, but the grace that comes from God and shapes the listeners' lives of faith.

[494]Conflict led to the expulsion of some Jewish Christians from Rome under Claudius (Acts 18:2; see p. 51). On more general hostility toward Christians in Rome see Tacitus, *Annals* 15.44 and 1 Pet 4:1–6, which was probably written from Rome (called "Babylon" in 5:13). On the social makeup of early Roman Christianity see Lampe, *Die stadtrömischen*, 64.

SUBJECT INDEX

◆

INDEX OF COMMENTATORS AND MODERN AUTHORS

◆

THE ANCHOR BIBLE

Commentaries (C) and Reference Library (RL) volumes on the Old and New Testaments and Apocrypha

THE CONTRIBUTORS

Susan Ackerman, Dartmouth College. RL17

William F. Albright, Johns Hopkins University. C26

Francis I. Andersen, Professorial Fellow, Classics and Archaeology, University of Melbourne. C24, C24A, C24E

Markus Barth, University of Basel. C34, C34A, C34B

Adele Berlin, University of Maryland. C25A

Helmut Blanke, Doctor of Theology from the University of Basel. C34B

Joseph Blenkinsopp, University of Notre Dame. C19, RL5

Robert G. Boling, McCormick Theological Seminary. C6, C6A

Raymond E. Brown, S.S., Union Theological Seminary, New York (Emeritus). C29, C29A, C30, RL1, RL7, RL15

George W. Buchanan, Wesley Theological Seminary. C36

Edward F. Campbell, Jr., McCormick Theological Seminary. C7

James H. Charlesworth, Princeton Theological Seminary. RL4, RL13, RL14

Mordechai Cogan, Hebrew University, Jerusalem. C11

John J. Collins, University of Chicago. RL10

James L. Crenshaw, Duke Divinity School. C24C, RL16

Mitchell Dahood, S.J., The Pontifical Biblical Institute. C16, C17, C17A

Alexander A. Di Lella, O.F.M., Catholic University of America. C23, C39

David L. Dungan, University of Tennessee, Knoxville. RL18

Joseph A. Fitzmyer, S.J., Catholic University of America. C28, C28A, C31, C33, C34C

J. Massyngberde Ford, University of Notre Dame. C38

Michael V. Fox, University of Wisconsin, Madison. C18A

David Noel Freedman, University of Michigan (Emeritus) and University of California, San Diego. General Editor. C24, C24A, C24E

Victor P. Furnish, Perkins School of Theology, Southern Methodist University. C32A

Jonathan A. Goldstein, University of Iowa. C41, C41A

Moshe Greenberg, Hebrew University, Jerusalem. C22, C22A

Louis F. Hartman, C.SS.R., Catholic University of America. C23

Andrew E. Hill, Wheaton College. C25D

Delbert R. Hillers, Johns Hopkins University. C7A

Luke Timothy Johnson, Candler School of Theology, Emory University. C35A, C37A

Craig R. Koester, Luther Seminary. C36

Bentley Layton, Yale University. RL11

Baruch A. Levine, New York University. C4, C4A

Jack R. Lundbom, Clare Hall, Cambridge University. C21A

P. Kyle McCarter, Jr., Johns Hopkins University. C8, C9

John L. McKenzie, De Paul University. C20

Abraham J. Malherbe, Yale University (Emeritus). C32B

C. S. Mann, formerly Coppin State College. C26

Joel Marcus, Boston University. C27

J.Louis Martyn, Union Theological Seminary, New York. C33A

Amihai Mazar, Institute of Archaeology of Hebrew University, Jerusalem. RL2

John P. Meier, Catholic University of America. RL3, RL9

Carol L. Meyers, Duke University. C25B, C25C

Eric M. Meyers, Duke University. C25B, C25C

Jacob Milgrom, University of California, Berkeley (Emeritus). C3, C3A, C3B

Carey A. Moore, Gettysburg College. C7B, C40, C40A, C44

Jacob M. Myers, Lutheran Theological Seminary, Gettysburg. C12, C13, C14, C42

Jacob Neusner, University of South Florida at Tampa. RL8

Jerome H. Neyrey, University of Notre Dame. C37C

William F. Orr, Pittsburgh Theological Seminary. C32

Brian Peckham, Regis College, Toronto University. RL6

Marvin H. Pope, Yale University (Emeritus). C7C, C15

William H. C. Propp, University of California, San Diego. C2

Jerome D. Quinn, St. Paul Seminary. C35

Paul R. Raabe, Concordia Seminary, St. Louis. C24D

Bo Ivar Reicke, University of Basel. C37

Jack M. Sasson, University of North Carolina at Chapel Hill. C24B

Lawrence H. Schiffman, New York University. RL12

R. B. Y. Scott, Princeton University. C18

Choon-Leong Seow, Princeton Theological Seminary. C18C

Patrick W. Skehan, Catholic University of America. C39

Ephraim A. Speiser, University of Pennsylvania. C1

Hayim Tadmor, Hebrew University, Jerusalem. C11

James Arthur Walther, Pittsburgh Theological Seminary (Emeritus). C32

Moshe Weinfeld, Hebrew University, Jerusalem. C5

David Winston, Graduate Theological Union, Berkeley (Emeritus). C43

G. Ernest Wright, Semitic Museum, Harvard University. C6